W9-AVB-396

🖈 Let's Go writers travel on your budget.

"Guides that penetrate the veneer of the holiday brochures and mine the grit of real life."

—*The Economist*

"The writers seem to have experienced every rooster-packed bus and lunar-surfaced mattress about which they write."

—*The New York Times*

"All the dirt, dirt cheap."

—*People*

🖈 Great for independent travelers.

"The guides are aimed not only at young budget travelers but at the independent traveler; a sort of streetwise cookbook for traveling alone."

—*The New York Times*

"Flush with candor and irreverence, chock full of budget travel advice."
—*The Des Moines Register*

"An indispensible resource, *Let's Go*'s practical information can be used by every traveler."

—*The Chattanooga Free Press*

🖈 Let's Go is completely revised each year.

"Only *Let's Go* has the zeal to annually update every title on its list."
—*The Boston Globe*

"Unbeatable: good sightseeing advice; up-to-date info on restaurants, hotels, and inns; a commitment to money-saving travel; and a wry style that brightens nearly every page."

—*The Washington Post*

🖈 All the important information you need.

"*Let's Go* authors provide a comedic element while still providing concise information and thorough coverage of the country. Anything you need to know about budget traveling is detailed in this book."

—*The Chicago Sun-Times*

"Value-packed, unbeatable, accurate, and comprehensive."

—*Los Angeles Times*

Let's Go Publications

Let's Go: Alaska & the Pacific Northwest 2001
Let's Go: Australia 2001
Let's Go: Austria & Switzerland 2001
Let's Go: Boston 2001 **New Title!**
Let's Go: Britain & Ireland 2001
Let's Go: California 2001
Let's Go: Central America 2001
Let's Go: China 2001
Let's Go: Eastern Europe 2001
Let's Go: Europe 2001
Let's Go: France 2001
Let's Go: Germany 2001
Let's Go: Greece 2001
Let's Go: India & Nepal 2001
Let's Go: Ireland 2001
Let's Go: Israel 2001
Let's Go: Italy 2001
Let's Go: London 2001
Let's Go: Mexico 2001
Let's Go: Middle East 2001
Let's Go: New York City 2001
Let's Go: New Zealand 2001
Let's Go: Paris 2001
Let's Go: Peru, Bolivia & Ecuador 2001 **New Title!**
Let's Go: Rome 2001
Let's Go: San Francisco 2001 **New Title!**
Let's Go: South Africa 2001
Let's Go: Southeast Asia 2001
Let's Go: Spain & Portugal 2001
Let's Go: Turkey 2001
Let's Go: USA 2001
Let's Go: Washington, D.C. 2001
Let's Go: Western Europe 2001 **New Title!**

Let's Go *Map Guides*

Amsterdam	New Orleans
Berlin	New York City
Boston	Paris
Chicago	Prague
Florence	Rome
Hong Kong	San Francisco
London	Seattle
Los Angeles	Sydney
Madrid	Washington, D.C.

Coming Soon: Dublin and Venice

Let's Go

INDIA & NEPAL
2001

Paul Warham editor
Nisha S. Agarwal associate editor
Ann S. Kim associate editor
Anna Malsberger map editor

researcher-writers

John Ata Bachman   Bart Lounsbury
Allegra Churchill   Priyanka Malhotra
Jay Gardner   Li-Xing Man
Sarah Jacoby   Rebecca Reider
Christiana E. King   Gabe Struck
Honza Vihan

St. Martin's Press ☙ New York

HELPING LET'S GO If you want to share your discoveries, suggestions, or corrections, please drop us a line. We read every piece of correspondence, whether a postcard, a 10-page email, or a coconut. Please note that mail received after May 2001 may be too late for the 2002 book, but will be kept for future editions. **Address mail to:**

Let's Go: India & Nepal
67 Mount Auburn Street
Cambridge, MA 02138
USA

Visit Let's Go at **http://www.letsgo.com**, or send email to:

feedback@letsgo.com
Subject: "Let's Go: India & Nepal"

In addition to the invaluable travel advice our readers share with us, many are kind enough to offer their services as researchers or editors. Unfortunately, our charter enables us to employ only currently enrolled Harvard students.

HOW TO USE THIS BOOK

THE ORGANIZATION OF THIS BOOK

INTRODUCTORY MATERIAL. The first chapter of this book, **Discover India and Nepal**, is our attempt to squeeze a billion people and thousands of years of culture into six pages. It provides an overview of travel in India and Nepal and highlights just a few of the many things the region has to offer. The **Essentials** section that follows provides practical information to help you prepare for your trip and get the most out of things while you're there. The **India** and **Nepal** chapters provide brief accounts of the history and culture of the two countries.

INDIA. Our coverage of India is organized geographically, moving in a roughly counter-clockwise direction from **Delhi** and **Uttar Pradesh** back round to the **Northeast States**. With a few exceptions, each state gets its own chapter, with coverage radiating out from the major city in each region.

NEPAL. Coverage begins in the **Kathmandu Valley** and moves through the **Western Hills,** the lowland **Terai,** and the **Eastern Hills** before culminating in the highest point in the book. Our section on **Trekking in Nepal** includes information on planning, packing, and health concerns for trekkers. Here you will find complete coverage of Nepal's "Classic Three" treks—Annapurna, Langtang, and Everest. The **black tabs** in the margins will help you to navigate between chapters.

APPENDIX. This is where to go if you need to know how many cubic inches there are in a metric Sunday, or if you are looking for the lowdown on why the chicken crossed the road. The appendix also contains a useful **temperature chart,** a **phrasebook** of various Indian and Nepalese languages, a **glossary** of unusual terms, and a list of the biggest **festivals** taking place around the region this year.

A FEW NOTES ABOUT LET'S GO FORMAT

RANKING ESTABLISHMENTS. In each section (accommodations, food, etc.), we list establishments from best to least-good. But we only list places we think someone would want to visit, and (except in the tiniest of towns where there is not much choice), even the lowest-ranked establishments represent good value. Our researchers' favorites are marked by our funky little corporate logo, the much sought-after Let's Go Thumbs-up (🖐).

TRANSPORTATION LISTINGS. Travel in this part of the world is slow and unpredictable. We try our best to provide up-to-date, detailed transportation information, but be patient and remember, this is supposed to be a vacation. Unless otherwise noted, the prices we list for trains are for **sleeper class,** the cheapest class that can be reserved in advance.

GRAYBOXES AND WHITEBOXES. Grayboxes sometimes provide cultural background, sometimes old-fashioned crude humor. Sometimes both. Whiteboxes, on the other hand, provide important practical information, such as warnings (🖐), helpful hints and further resources (🖐), border crossing information (🖐), and advice on how to avoid being gored by rhino or trampled by an elephant.

CONTENTS

MAPS

✚ Hospital	✈ Airport	🏛 Museum	▲ Mountain			
✪ Police	🚌 Bus Station	🏨 Hotel/Hostel	▢ Park			
✉ Post Office	🚆 Train Station	⛺ Camping				
ⓘ Tourist Office	M METRO STATION	🍴 Food & Drink	▦ Beach			
$ Bank	⚓ Ferry Landing	🛍 Shopping				
⚑ Embassy/Consulate	✝ Church	♪ Arts & Entertainment	▨ Water			
▪ Site or Point of Interest	✡ Synagogue	🍸 Nightlife				
☎ Telephone Office	☪ Mosque	💻 Internet Café	The Let's Go thumb always points N O R T H.			
☕ Theater	♜ Castle	--- Pedestrian Zone				

ABOUT LET'S GO

FORTY-ONE YEARS OF WISDOM

As a new millennium arrives, *Let's Go: Europe*, now in its 41st edition and translated into seven languages, reigns as the world's bestselling international travel guide. For over four decades, travelers criss-crossing the Continent have relied on *Let's Go* for inside information on the hippest backstreet cafes, the most pristine secluded beaches, and the best routes from border to border. In the last 20 years, our rugged researchers have stretched the frontiers of backpacking and expanded our coverage into Asia, Africa, Australia, and the Americas. This year, we've introduced a new city guide series with books on San Francisco and our hometown, Boston. Now, our seven city guides feature sharp photos, more maps, and an overall more user-friendly design. We've also returned to our roots with the inaugural edition of *Let's Go: Western Europe*.

It all started in 1960 when a handful of well-traveled students at Harvard University handed out a 20-page mimeographed pamphlet offering a collection of their tips on budget travel to passengers on student charter flights to Europe. The following year, in response to the instant popularity of the first volume, students traveling to Europe researched the first full-fledged edition of *Let's Go: Europe*, a pocket-sized book featuring honest, practical advice, witty writing, and a decidedly youthful slant on the world. Throughout the 60s and 70s, our guides reflected the times. In 1969 we taught travelers how to get from Paris to Prague on "no dollars a day" by singing in the street. In the 80s and 90s, we looked beyond Europe and North America and set off to all corners of the earth. Meanwhile, we focused in on the world's most exciting urban areas to produce in-depth, fold-out map guides. Our new guides bring the total number of titles to 51, each infused with the spirit of adventure and voice of opinion that travelers around the world have come to count on. But some things never change: our guides are still researched, written, and produced entirely by students who know first-hand how to see the world on the cheap.

HOW WE DO IT

Each guide is completely revised and thoroughly updated every year by a well-traveled set of nearly 300 students. Every spring, we recruit over 200 researchers and 90 editors to overhaul every book. After several months of training, researcher-writers hit the road for seven weeks of exploration, from Anchorage to Adelaide, Estonia to El Salvador, Iceland to Indonesia. Hired for their rare combination of budget travel sense, writing ability, stamina, and courage, these adventurous travelers know that train strikes, stolen luggage, food poisoning, and marriage proposals are all part of a day's work. Back at our offices, editors work from spring to fall, massaging copy written on Himalayan bus rides into witty, informative prose. A student staff of typesetters, cartographers, publicists, and managers keeps our lively team together. In September, the collected efforts of the summer are delivered to our printer, who turns them into books in record time, so that you have the most up-to-date information available for your vacation. Even as you read this, work on next year's editions is well underway.

WHY WE DO IT

We don't think of budget travel as the last recourse of the destitute; we believe that it's the only way to travel. Living cheaply and simply brings you closer to the people and places you've been saving up to visit. Our books will ease your anxieties and answer your questions about the basics—so you can get off the beaten track and explore. Once you learn the ropes, we encourage you to put *Let's Go* down now and then to strike out on your own. You know as well as we that the best discoveries are often those you make yourself. When you find something worth sharing, please drop us a line. We're Let's Go Publications, 67 Mount Auburn St., Cambridge, MA 02138, USA (email: feedback@letsgo.com). For more info, visit our website, www.letsgo.com.

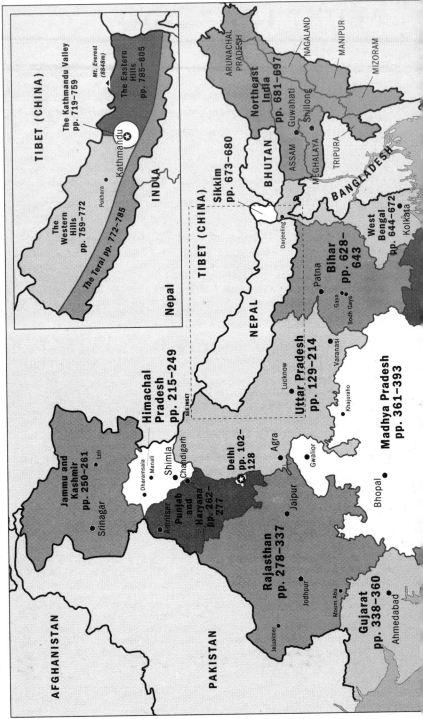

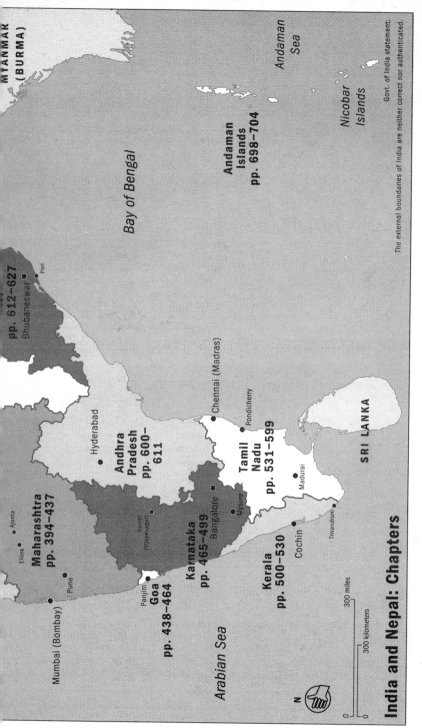

India and Nepal: Chapters

MYANMAR
(BURMA)

Bhubaneswar
Puri

Hyderabad

Chennai (Madras)
Pondicherry

Madurai

Mumbai (Bombay)
Pune
Ellora
Ajanta
Panjim
Hampi
(Vijayanagar)
Bangalore
Mysore
Cochin
Trivandrum

SRI LANKA

Arabian Sea

Bay of Bengal

Andaman
Sea

Nicobar
Islands

The external boundaries of India are neither correct nor authenticated.

Govt. of India statement:

N

0
300 kilometers
0
300 miles

XIII

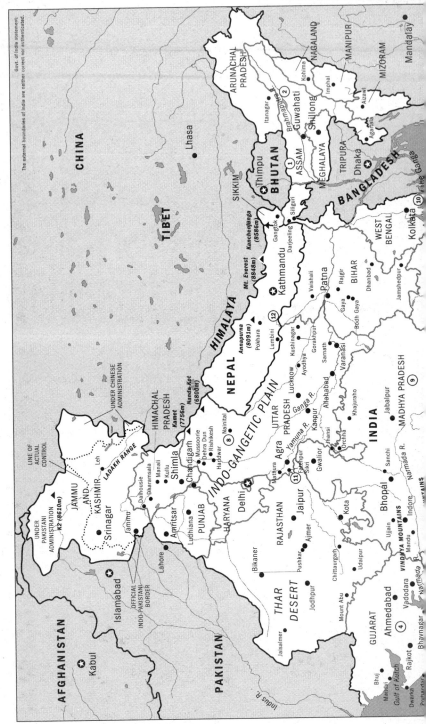

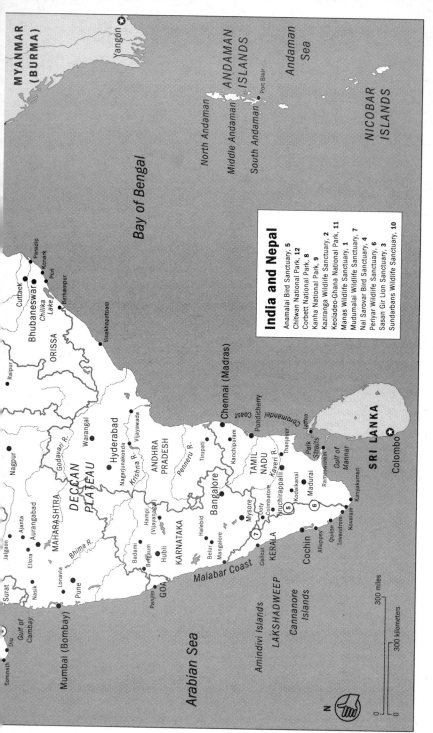

India and Nepal

Anamalai Bird Sanctuary, **5**
Chitwan National Park, **12**
Corbett National Park, **8**
Kanha National Park, **9**
Kaziranga Wildlife Sanctuary, **2**
Keoladeo-Ghana National Park, **11**
Manas Wildlife Sanctuary, **1**
Mudumalai Wildlife Sanctuary, **7**
Nal Sarovar Bird Sanctuary, **4**
Periyar Wildlife Sanctuary, **6**
Sasan Gir Lion Sanctuary, **3**
Sundarbans Wildlife Sanctuary, **10**

RESEARCHER-WRITERS

John Ata Bachman *Kathmandu Valley, Eastern Nepal*

After serving up large helpings of Turkish Delight for last year's *Let's Go: Turkey*, John took off for Kathmandu, where he revamped our coverage so thoroughly that we sometimes felt we were reading reports from an entirely new country. Certainly the drawings and doodles were out of this world. Ruthless enemy of platitudinous clap-trap wherever it could be found, and one of the few people who can claim to have eaten in every restaurant in Kathmandu, John still managed to make time for language study and tabla lessons—if you find a mistake in this book, it is our fault, not his.

Allegra Churchill *Tamil Nadu*

Old Africa-hand Allegra coasted through the tropical paradise of Tamil Nadu, charming locals and fellow travelers alike. Fascinated by the pulse of life in South India, she chatted with gurus and unearthed forgotten Gandhi museums. Though often worried about seeming too prim, Allegra still felt the need to absolve her sins in Rameswaram. It took 22 buckets of water to do the trick. We wish this Springs-teen-lovin', Indian sweetshop-addicted Aishwarya look-alike the best of luck for the future. Ending this relationship is hard for us, too.

Jay Gardner *Sikkim, Trekking in Nepal, West Bengal*

Last year's editor of *Let's Go: Central America* spent his springtime collecting an enviable set of blisters, traipsing up and down the trekking trails of the Himalayas. Keeper of the secret of the wonderful wind-hole of Sikkim and responsible for some of the most beautiful marginalia illustrations seen since the days when *Let's Go* guides were painted straight onto temple walls, Jay honed his carom skills with the monks down in the foothills before donning his best straw hat and flip-flops and disappearing into the hills. Jay completely revamped our coverage of trekking in Nepal and was an absolute pleasure to work with.

Sarah Jacoby *Goa, Kerala*

One of the funniest people ever to answer phones for a living, Sarah tooted her horn unflappably through the sunburnt back of the subcontinent, where the faded glories of Goa's churches and cathedrals took her back to her carefree days as a researcher and editor for *Let's Go: Europe*. A hit with locals despite her refusal to dress in the sequined halter top uniform of Kovalam's cosmopolitan crowds, Sarah made herself popular with us, too, sending back clippings about penguins and sex, and then coming in to type, proof, and cheer from the sidelines all summer.

Christiana E. King *Gujarat, Rajasthan*

Last year's editor was no sooner ordained as a Divinity School graduate than she was packing her bags and heading back to India again to find out first-hand all about the joys of bus timetables. Showing no mercy to "useless" facts, and exhibiting an unflinching refusal to be impressed by glossy brochures, Christiana brought a no-non-sense, no-dangling-modifiers efficiency and conciseness to our coverage of camel safari country. Christiana was last seen poring over Ramayana comic books in Oregon.

Bart Lounsbury *UP Plains, Northern Madhya Pradesh*

The only member of this year's team to count functional Wolof among his qualifi-cations, Bart followed up a stint in Senegal with a high-speed, guano-enhanced gal-livant through northern India. With little need for vacation days, Bart tackled his job with ruthless efficiency, making sense of the incomprehensible Delhi bus sys-tem and delving deeply into the mysteries of Khajuraho. Not even monkey maul-ings in Agra and crunchy crickets in his sambar could hold back this "wacky" researcher-writer, who really did love Jhansi with all his heart. After escaping into the hills to get away from all the dung, Bart ended his trip in a helicopter, airlifted to safety just in time to put the finishing touches to his final copy.

Priyanka Malhotra
UP Hills, Calcutta, Orissa

Nothing, absolutely *nothing* could bring Priyanka down. High on the air of her beloved UP hills, Priyanka retained her spunk and spirit as she wandered through the east Indian plains. She fended off lecherous *pundits* in Orissa's temples, amazed city residents by covering the whole of Calcutta on foot, and highlighted at every turn the full range of possibilities open to solo women travelers to India. Perhaps the first person ever to visit the Archaeological Survey of India headquarters, Priyanka's willingness to go the extra mile impressed us to no end; her attention to detail and exuberance are matched by only 0.0000000001% of the population.

Li-Xing Man
Karnataka, Madhya Pradesh

We worshiped Li—his thoroughness, his persistence, his brawn, his brains—even his handwriting. And everywhere he went in India, locals revered our Dalai Lama, too. Building on his extensive experience as a researcher and student in India, Li polished off Pilsners in Bangalore's pubs, trekked through the tea plantations of Ooty, and warded off numerous romantic advances with peerless skill. The women of the I&N team thank Li for Hrithik, and we all wish him the best of luck in the future as he endeavors to rid the developing world of debilitating diseases.

Rebecca Reider
Andhra Pradesh, Maharashtra

With experience as a *Let's Go* researcher-writer in Canada behind her, Rebecca set off expecting great things from the subcontinent. She was not disappointed. Overcoming the curse of the *kumkum* powder woman (and the monsoonal downpours), our rugged Rebel Reider sent back a continuous flow of her trademark copy—witty, nitty-gritty, and meticulously researched. With irrepressible enthusiasm, Rebecca scoped out the underground gay scene in Bombay, uncovered the hitherto-hidden charms of Aurangabad, and traveled vast psychological distances at the Osho Commune in Pune. And, as if being a researcher-writer were not enough, she also moonlighted as a celebrity, giving lectures on America to awestruck schoolchildren and appearing on TV travel shows. Rebecca was last seen in Auroville, studying organic potato farming. Don't break too many hearts, Rropica.

Gabe Struck
Himachal Pradesh, Jammu and Kashmir, Punjab and Haryana

As rugged as the mountains, as unstoppable as a landslide, and as dependable as a monsoonal downpour, Gabe has been aptly described as "endearingly indestructible." Gabe's appetite for adventure and love of unreliable roads took him from the Caucasus, where he proved himself a first-rate researcher last summer for *Let's Go: Eastern Europe*, to Kashmir, where he got out just before the bombing started up again. One bout of altitude sickness and several days of higher-than-Amsterdam relaxation in Manali later, Gabe was off again, arriving in HP just in time to get caught in the biggest floods in memory. Gabe marched on regardless, continuing to send back huge packets of immaculate research, even as the mud swilled around his knees and his eyeglasses sunk into the mire. Gabe made us proud, and we wish him all the best in his future travels.

Honza Vihan
Andaman Islands, Bihar, National Parks, Northeast States

Third-time *Let's Go* veteran Honza followed up last year's high-altitude exploits in the mountains of northern India with a tour that took him through the backyard of every tiger in the subcontinent and out to the octopus's gardens of the Andaman Sea. Persistent enough to squeeze a permit out of the most stubborn of office dictators and with an attention to detail that left us struggling for words, Honza's one-of-a-kind copy had us dreaming of beautiful Bihar, fantasy-trekking through jungles and hillsides, and wishing there were some way we could get him to come back and help us out yet again next year.

ACKNOWLEDGMENTS

TEAM I&N THANKS: A crore of thanks to all our peeps—Allegra, Bart, Christiana, Gabe, Honza, Jay, John, Li, Priyanka, Rebecca, and Sarah. Our legion of typists and proofers, especially Aarup, Alice, Chung, Johs, Olivia and Sarah. SEAS for making the office feel like home. China pod for being good neighbors. Special thanks to Emi for being far more qualified to write the book than any of us. We would have been lost (and so would you) without Anna the Mapper. Thanks to Anup, who took such good care of this bookteam.

PAUL THANKS: Ann and Nisha, for being such wonderful people, and such fun to work with. Thanks to Anup, for always having the answers. Thanks to Dad, for the birds; to Jane, for singing the blues down Beale St.; and to Mum, for two decades of unheeded advice. And thanks as always to Emi, skunk-spotter supreme and every hedgehog's best friend, for everything.

NISHA THANKS: Paul for his sense of humor and laid-back attitude. Ann for the long conversations and for laughing at my corny jokes. Anup for his patience and support. And Emi, our future Tamil Nadu traveler. Thanks to Peter, Dave, Jamie, Mer, and Yen for much-needed distractions and good times. To Lauren for all the dinners and that crucial "bridge housing" and to Dan for making sure I read more than just copy. Most of all, *shukriya* and lots of love to Mom, Dad, and Neil.

ANN THANKS: Thums up to Paul Indianepaul and Neesh. Thanks for your patience, humor, and special talents. Emi, agnes b. superstar. Anup whose nifty name spells Puna backwards. Tova, for taking the job. Dara, for her encouragement, and for feeding me and keepin' me laughing. George. Rachi, who is the best maker of zhen-zhu nai cha I'm ever going to meet. Mom, Dad, and Mike, for their love and understanding. And a final thanks to all those who helped me find my way to India and back.

Editor
Paul Warham
Associate Editors
Nisha S. Agarwal, Ann S. Kim
Managing Editor
Anup Kubal
Map Editor
Anna Malsberger

Publishing Director
Kaya Stone
Editor-in-Chief
Kate McCarthy
Production Manager
Melissa Rudolph
Cartography Manager
John Fiore
Editorial Managers
Alice Farmer, Ankur Ghosh, Aarup Kubal, Anup Kubal
Financial Manager
Bede Sheppard
Low-Season Manager
Melissa Gibson
Marketing & Publicity Managers
Olivia L. Cowley, Esti Iturralde
New Media Manager
Daryush Jonathan Dawid
Personnel Manager
Nicholas Grossman
Photo Editor
Dara Cho
Production Associates
Sanjay Mavinkurve, Nicholas Murphy, Rosalinda Rosalez, Matthew Daniels, Rachel Mason, Daniel Visel
Some Design
Matthew Daniels
Office Coordinators
Sarah Jacoby, Chris Russell

Director of Advertising Sales
Cindy Rodriguez
Senior Advertising Associates
Adam Grant, Rebecca Rendell
Advertising Artwork Editor
Palmer Truelson

President
Andrew M. Murphy
General Manager
Robert B. Rombauer
Assistant General Manager
Anne E. Chisholm

DISCOVER
INDIA & NEPAL

With a population that has just topped one billion, **India** bursts at the seams with dozens of different cultures and a vibrant variety to match the magnitude of its sheer numbers. Birthplace of three of the world's oldest religions—Hinduism, Buddhism, and Jainism—India today accommodates countless others and struggles to maintain its secular facade as the world's largest democracy. For the traveler swept up into this grandest of cultural confluences, India can be as challenging—and as threatening—and as rewarding and unforgettable. This is not a country that you can sit back and observe; India demands reaction. From the moment you step down from the plane, your senses will be under assault. The sublime beauty of India's natural scenery and towering temples are as likely to overwhelm as the ubiquitous smells of dirt, dust, and dung. *Paan* stains the city streets, *tilak* powder dusts the temple walls, the smell of freshly caught fish permeates the seaside air, and the traffic horns will honk you out of your senses. But the magical swirl of color and life, the mosques and the minarets, the quick and spicy meal at a roadside *dhaba*, and the early morning chime of temple bells make the subcontinent quite unlike anywhere you've ever been before. After a few weeks here, many people are only too happy to escape back to a safer world, where things move at a different pace. But nobody leaves India completely unchanged. Quite a few never leave at all.

Land-locked **Nepal** is a country shaped by its geography, which takes in some of the world's highest peaks as well as some of its greenest valleys. Ancient temple towns and palace squares help to bring true every romantic dream you ever dreamed about the Kathmandu Valley, the political and social center of the country. Soaring high above the valleys and farms, of course, are the mighty Himalayas, which offer better hiking and more spectacular scenery than you'll find anywhere else on the planet.

An open mind and a healthy dose of patience are your best inoculations against the travails of travel in the subcontinent. So, don a pair of non-leather sandals, brush up on those non-verbal communication skills, grab some anti-diarrhea medication, and get ready to roll.

INDIA	NEPAL
Population (people): 1 billion	**Population:** 23 million
Population (cows): 200 million	**Average annual ascents of Everest**
Annual mango production: 10 million tonnes	**during the 1990s:** 67.2
Spit produced per annum by paan chewers: 1.5 million tonnes.	**National Motto:** "The Motherland is worth more than the Kingdom of Heaven."
Average Income Per Capita: US$350	**Number of toes on a yeti's foot:** 4
Literacy: 66% male, 38% female	**Average Income Per Capita:** US$165
	Literacy: 41% male, 14% female

1

THINGS TO DO

From climbing the highest mountains in the world to jostling worshipers at a local temple, from partying on the beach to picnicking in the grounds of a medieval fort, you can do it all in India and Nepal. For a more detailed list of the best things to see and do, refer to the **Let's Go Picks** below and the **Highlights of the Region** box at the beginning of each chapter.

HOLY PLACES

Visit some of the subcontinent's most sacred sites and witness the rituals and traditions that have remained intact for thousands of years. Hinduism's holiest city, **Varanasi** (p. 193), is the chosen home of Lord Shiva himself, and the city where pious Hindus come to live out their last moments of earthly existence. Walk in the footsteps of the 9th-century saint, Shankara, who established India's four major *dhams* (divine abodes): **Badrinath** (p. 149) in the north, **Dwarka** (p. 343) in the west, **Rameswaram** (p. 580) in the south, and **Puri** (p. 620) in the east. Take in some of the finest Hindu temple architecture in India at **Bhubaneswar** (p. 612), or sing songs of praise to Lord Krishna in his playground, **Vrindaban** (p. 178). The holiest city for Sikhs, **Amritsar** (p. 262) houses the beautiful Golden Temple. Free yourself from worldly desire in **Bodh Gaya** (p. 636), where the Buddha attained enlightenment, or circumambulate Nepal's most important stupa in **Boudha** (p. 755). Jains head to **Mount Abu** (p. 305) and its gorgeous Dilwara temples; other religious crowd-pullers include the Sun Temple in **Konark** (p. 618), the Meenakshi Amman Temple in **Madurai** (p. 573), and the Har-ki-Pairi *ghat* in **Haridwar** (p. 137). The bloodthirsty can witness animal sacrifices to the goddess Kali at **Dakshinkali** (p. 768) in Nepal.

TREKKING AND TIGER-SPOTTING

Some of the best trekking in the world is in the Himalayas. Journey past **Mt. Everest, Annapurna,** and the **Langtang Valley** and experience head-spinning scenery as you watch the transition from Nepali villages to Tibetan hamlets (p. 800). The **Kinnaur-Spiti Road** (p. 238) in Himachal Pradesh passes through the most remote regions of India, with great hikes along the way, particularly near **Kalpa** (p. 240). Trek through **Western Sikkim** (p. 682), wander across the desert plateau of **Leh** (p. 247), or marvel at Kashmir's **Nubra Valley** (p. 254). Get up close and personal with rhinos in **Kaziranga National Park** (p. 695) or with black bears in Nepal's **Chitwan National Park** (p. 788). Elephants rumble and trumpet their way through **Jaldapara Wildlife Sanctuary** (p. 663). Tiger-hunters can enjoy the **Sariska Tiger Reserve** (p. 285) and **Corbett National Park** (p. 150), and birders will be sent into paroxysms of twitching by the world-renowned **Keoladeo Ghana National Park** (p. 287).

GOLDEN OLDIES

Delhi's **Red Fort** and **Jama Masjid** (p. 116) are an impressive introduction to the relics of India's Mughal rulers. The abandoned city of **Fatehpur Sikri** (p. 175) is an architectural time-machine that will whisk you back to Mughal times in less time than it takes you to say Shah Jahan. The erotic sculptures of **Khajuraho** (p. 369) attract visitors interested in more than just intricate stonework; the pure-of-heart get their carvings fix at the world-renowned **Ellora** and **Ajanta** caves (p. 422) in Maharashtra. Patan's **Durbar Square** (p. 761), the best of many in Nepal, is full of temples; more sacrilegious practices take place in Hampi's **Vijayanagar ruins** (p. 484), popular with homeless hippies. The **Lake Palace** in Udaipur (p. 297) encapsulates the romantic allure of Rajasthan, but it is just one of many famous forts and palaces in India, including **Gwalior Fort** (p. 381), Jaipur's **City Palace** (p. 281), the windswept **Jaisalmer Fort** (p. 318), Hyderabad's **Golconda Fort** (p. 604), and Mysore's **Maharaja's Palace** (p. 470). Oh, and then there's the **Taj Mahal** (p. 172).

BEACH BUMS

For some serious beach action, head to Goa: from the tourist-trafficked shores of **Anjuna** (p. 441) to the less-crowded beaches of **Benaulim** (p. 452) and **Palolem** (p. 453), Goa has it all. Farther north, **Dwarka's** (p. 343) shores are lapped by the waves of the Arabian Sea. Pretend you're in the south of France on the sands of **Pondicherry** (p. 554) in Tamil Nadu. The white sands of **Kovalam** (p. 503) and **Puri** (p. 620) are outdone only by the pristine shores of **Varkala** (p. 509) and temple-studded **Mahabalipuram** (p. 550). The **Andaman Islands** (p. 705), 1000km off shore in the Bay of Bengal, have been attracting larger numbers of tourists in recent years, but are still as far off the beaten track as you can get without leaving India completely.

DHARMA BUMS

Hippie hang-outs are great places to swap travel yarns, drink some tea, and make arrangements for the next leg of your journey. Among the backpacker meccas of India and Nepal are: **Manali** (p. 233) and **Dharamsala** (p. 219) in Himachal Pradesh, **Pushkar** (p. 289) in Rajasthan, **Anjuna** (p. 441) in Goa, **Kovalam** (p. 503) in Kerala, **Mahabalipuram** (p. 550) in Tamil Nadu, **Puri** (p. 620) in Orissa, **Darjeeling** (p. 665) in West Bengal, **Pokhara** (p. 775) in Nepal's Western Hills, and **Kathmandu's** Thamel district (p. 728), to name a just select few.

NO BUMS

Traveling off season is the best way to avoid the crowds, but some fascinating places see surprisingly little traffic regardless of the season: **Kausani** (p. 164) and **Ayodhya** (p. 188) in Uttar Pradesh, **Chamba** (p. 228) in Himachal Pradesh, **Bikaner** (p. 321) in Rajasthan, **Mandvi** (p. 348) and **Bhuj** (p. 345) in Gujarat, **Mandu** (p. 361) in Madhya Pradesh, **Kodaikanal** (p. 586) and **Rameswaram** (p. 580) in Tamil Nadu, and **Kirtipur** (p. 752), **Manakamana** (p. 771), and **Tansen** (p. 772) in Nepal. Other places fail to draw many travelers since they pose threats to personal safety. But if political volatility and the occasional bomb aren't enough to get you ruffled, nothing beats a night on a houseboat in **Srinagar** (p. 255) or the chance to watch the closing of the Indo-Pakistani border at **Wagah** (p. 270).

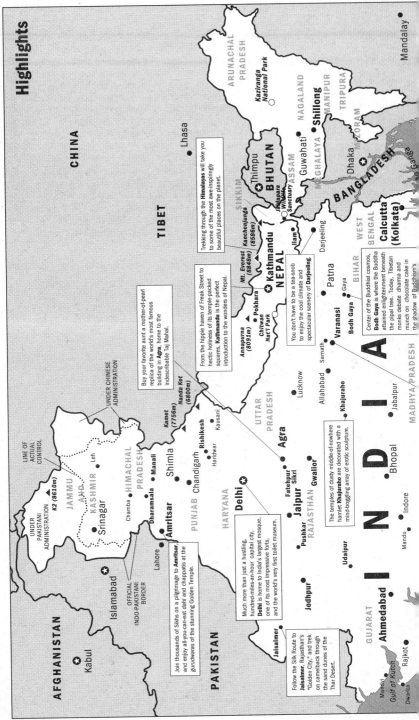

Highlights

Join thousands of Sikhs on a pilgrimage to **Amritsar**, and enjoy all-you-can-eat *dahi* and chappatis at the *gurudwaras* of the stunning Golden Temple.

Much more than just a hustling, hundred-miles-an-hour capital city, **Delhi** is home to India's largest mosque, one of its most impressive forts, and the world's very first toilet museum.

Follow the Silk Route to **Jaisalmer**, Rajasthan's "Golden City," and trek on camelback through the sand dunes of the Thar Desert.

Buy your favorite aunt a mother-of-pearl replica of the world's most famous building in **Agra**, home to the indescribable Taj Mahal.

The temples of dusty middle-of-nowhere hamlet **Khajuraho** are decorated with a mind-boggling array of erotic sculpture.

From the hippie haven of Freak Street to hectic holiness of its temple-packed squares, **Kathmandu** is the perfect introduction to the wonders of Nepal.

Trekking through the **Himalayas** will take you to some of the most awe-inspiringly beautiful places on the planet.

You don't have to be a tea-snob to enjoy the cool climate and spectacular scenery of **Darjeeling**.

Center of the Buddhist cosmos, **Bodh Gaya** is where the Buddha attained enlightenment beneath the pipal tree. Today, Tibetan monks debate dharma and munch on chocolate cake in the shadow of Buddhism's

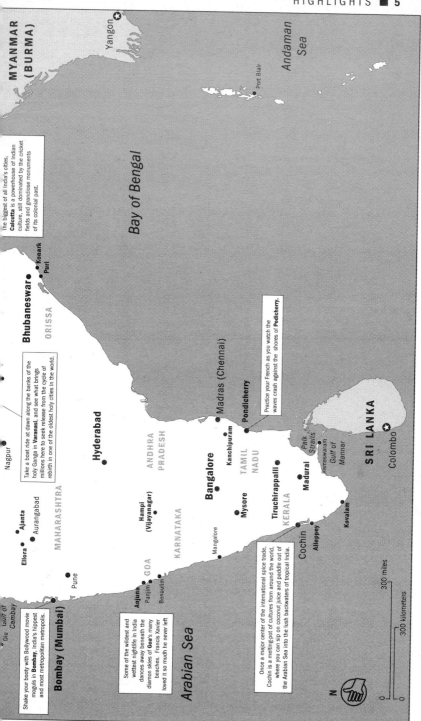

MYANMAR (BURMA)

Yangon

Andaman Sea

Port Blair

The biggest of all India's cities, **Calcutta** is a powerhouse of Indian culture, still dominated by the cricket fields and grandiose monuments of its colonial past.

Bay of Bengal

Nagpur

Take a boat ride at dawn along the banks of the holy Ganga in **Varanasi**, and see what brings millions here to seek release from the cycle of rebirth in one of the oldest holy cities in the world.

Bhubaneswar ● Konark ● Puri

ORISSA

Hyderabad

ANDHRA PRADESH

Madras (Chennai)

Pondicherry

Practice your French as you watch the waves crash against the shores of **Pondicherry.**

Kanchipuram

Bangalore

Hampi (Vijayanagar)

KARNATAKA

Mysore

TAMIL NADU

Tiruchirappalli

Madurai

Rameswaram

Palk Straits

Gulf of Mannar

SRI LANKA ✪

Colombo

Mangalore

Ellora ● ● Ajanta
● Aurangabad

MAHARASHTRA

Pune

GOA
Anjuna
Panjim ●
Benaulim

Diu
Gulf of Cambay

Shake your booty with Bollywood movie moguls in **Bombay**, India's hippest and most metropolitan metropolis.

Bombay (Mumbai)

Some of the wildest and wettest nightlife in India dances away beneath the diamond skies of **Goa's** many beaches. Francis Xavier loved it so much he never left.

Arabian Sea

Once a major center of the international spice trade, **Cochin** is a melting-pot of cultures from around the world, where you can sip on coconut juice and paddle out of the Arabian Sea into the lush backwaters of tropical India.

Cochin
Alleppey
Kovalam

KERALA

N

0 ——— 300 miles
0 ——— 300 kilometers

DISCOVER

▣ LET'S GO PICKS

BEST WAYS TO GET A BLISTER:
Wander through mind-blowing mountain-scapes and past meditative monasteries on the **Local Trek** in Sikkim (p. 685)—a 3-4 day hike that includes a visit to the holy Khechopalri Lake, where all your wishes are guaranteed to come true. Carouse through the lush **Langtang Region** (p. 808), the least crowded and least cliched of Nepal's classic trinity of treks.

BEST BENDERS: Freak out at the full-moon raves on **Anjuna beach,** Goa (p. 441), an experience sure to turn your mind inside out. Or be like the Beatles and join thousands of other body benders for the world-renowned **International Yoga Festival** along the banks of the Ganga in Rishikesh (p. 141). Twist and wind through vibrant valleys, dry, sand-stone plateaux, and breathtaking Hima-layan peaks along the **Manali-Leh Road** (p. 246), one of the highest highways in the world.

BEST PLACE TO FLAUNT YOUR MOUSTACHE: Compete for the crown of **Mr. Desert** (p. 318) in Jaisalmer if you think you're the man who best embodies Rajasthani masculinity with your full-bodied bristles.

BEST REASONS TO GET OUT OF BED IN THE MORNING: Rise at dawn to have buckets of holy water dumped over your head at the **Ramanathaswamy Temple** (p. 580), a once-in-a-lifetime experience sure to clear your head and absolve you of the sins of the night before. Keep dry and watch the sun crawl above Mt. Ever-est from the Nepalese town of **Nagarkot** (p. 766), or trace its ascent over the ancient *ghats* of **Varanasi** (p. 193), with the chime of temple bells providing the mood music.

BEST PLACES TO GET DOWN: Groove and gyrate into the wee hours at **The Ghetto** (p. 405), one of Bombay's hippest discos, and at **The Club** in Bangalore (p. 465), site of MTV's South Asia launch. Or plunge into the coral-studded depths of the Bay of Bengal—teeming with angelfish, sea anemones, silver jacks, and hammerhead sharks—at the **Mahatma Gandhi National Marine Park** (p. 710) in the Andaman Islands.

BEST PLACES FOR PACKRATS: If you've ever thought twice about tossing your elephant-shaped foot scrubbers, a visit to the **Raja Kelkar Museum** (p. 414) in Pune or the **Jai Vilas Palace** (p. 383) in Gwalior will remind you that you're not alone. Better still, slurp up the sacred spit of the thou-sands of holy rats that pack the **Karni Mata Temple** (p. 325) in Deshnok, Rajasthan.

BEST CHANCE OF GETTING BITTEN: Prowl close to endangered (though still extremely ferocious) tigers at the **Chitwan National Park** (p. 788) in Nepal or the **Periyar Tiger Reserve** (p. 512) in Kerala. If they don't get you, head to Kashmir, where *lha-ba* healers will open wide and suck evil spirits out of your soul (p. 250).

BEST HIGH: Grass and hippies grow wild in the Himachal hilltop town of **Manali** (p. 233), at the base of the Hima-layas. For a milder buzz, head to the **Happy Valley Tea Estate** (p. 665) in the hill station retreat of Darjeeling, and watch workers pluck those world-famous leaves before your eyes.

BEST KEPT SECRET: Artists and pretty people commune in the calm glow of can-dlelight at the **Villa River Cat** in the secluded beach town of Mandrem (p. 448). Find it before it gets found out.

BEST TONGUE TWISTERS: The menus might not be the most inventive, but the restaurant names are hard to beat. Try the **See Green Little Tibet Cafe Brick Oven Olive Pizza Restaurant** in Vagator (p. 444), **The Place: Touché the Sizzler** (p. 413) in Pune, or the **The Rum Doodle 40,000½-Feet Bar and Restaurant** in Kathmandu, where you can share a beer or two with the mountain-high.

BEST PARTIES IN TOWN: On Jan. 9, 2001, join 13 million of your closest friends for a dip in the holy Ganga and Yamuna Rivers in Allahabad at the **Kumbh Mela** (p. 209)—the grandest of Hindu bathing rituals, which only comes around once every 12 years. The largest event of its kind in the world, the **Interna-tional Kite Festival** kicks off that month (p. 333) in Ahmedabad. Pack it in at Pushkar in November, when 50,000 hump-backs and 200,000 humans squeeze into one square kilometer for the **Pushkar Camel Festival** (p. 289).

ESSENTIALS

WHEN TO GO

Both India and Nepal have high and low periods for tourism, which correspond to changes in the weather as well as the timing of holidays and religious festivals. The high season (roughly November to March) brings higher prices and a flood of tourists; low season (June through August—monsoon season across most of the subcontinent) means reduced services and reduced traffic at reduced prices. Some tourist towns close down altogether during this time. Peak seasons vary by location. It is worth timing your trip to coincide with one or more of the many colorful festivals that take place every year throughout India and Nepal; for more information, see **Holidays and Festivals for 2001,** p. 821. For a temperature chart, see p. 821.

INDIA

India can give you just about whatever kind of weather you are looking for. The geography of this huge country is so diverse that different regions have vastly different weather, even at the same time of year.

The mountain valleys of the Himalayan foothills have intensely cold winter nights (November-January). Fall asleep in the wrong place here, and you might find yourself chipped out of the ice and put in a museum in three thousand years' time. Daytime temperatures are comfortable all year. In northern India, some mountain roads are only accessible during the summer months (June-September), generally the best time to visit the hills. The northern reaches of Himachal Pradesh and Ladakh are in rainshadow and are not hit by the monsoonal torrents. The rest of India, however, relies heavily on the mighty **monsoon.** The two major monsoons hit the southwest and northeastern coasts in late May or early June. They advance inland over the next two months, dumping water on most of India—Tamil Nadu, southern Andhra Pradesh, and the Andaman Islands get their monsoon-lashing in mid-October. During the monsoon season it rains most days, generally in the late afternoon as the sun begins to slip. Getting caught in a monsoonal downpour is a little like taking a hot shower with all your clothes on—probably not a treat you want to be indulging in on a daily basis. Storms are generally intense and short: after thirty minutes or so of torrential rain, the sun will emerge and steam things up again—mountain views, however, remain perpetually obscured. The monsoons can be extremely destructive, causing mudslides and flooding, cutting communications and transportation lines, and causing power outages and widespread loss of temper. The mountains of Northeast India are especially hard-hit in July and August, and deadly landslides are common.

The monsoon lets up in September, when India's **cool season** begins. It takes a few months more for the Deccan plateau to dry out completely. December and January are cool, even cold, at night. Tropical ovens like Bombay and Madras go from being unbearably hot to merely uncomfortably hot, and many travelers head south to beach haunts like Goa. **Winter** (September-January) is probably the best time to visit India. By February, the heat starts to build up across the plains. April, May, and June are all very cruel months indeed, with temperatures of over 45°C (110°F). And then come the rains, and the circle repeats itself.

NEPAL

Most tourists visit Nepal in October and November, when the countryside is fresh, the temperatures mild, the air clear, and the views breathtaking. The dry, clean air makes this best time of year for trekking. March and April are also good months to visit: huge rhododendrons are in bloom on the hillsides and the days are long and warm, without being too hot. **Winter** (December-February) is probably the worst time: snow covers anything higher than 2000-3000m, and even Kathmandu gets damp and cold. The **monsoon** descends from late June to September. Most of the country is cloud-cast and beset with downpours, though western Nepal, largely in rainshadow, tends to be drier. Although the land turns noticeably greener during the monsoon, there are drawbacks: roads get washed out, flights get cancelled, and leeches become your closest companions on trekking routes.

DIPLOMATIC MISSIONS

INDIA'S CONSULAR SERVICES ABROAD

Australia: 3-5 Moonah Place, Yarralumla, **Canberra**, ACT 2600 (☎(02) 6273 3999). **Consulates:** 25 Bligh St., Level 27, **Sydney**, NSW 2000 (☎(02) 9223 9500); 195 Adelaide Terrace, Level 1, 724 Curtin Avenue East, **Eagle Farm**, Queensland 4008 (☎(07) 3260 2825); **East Perth**, WA 6004 (☎(08) 9221 1485); 15 Munro St., **Coburg**, Victoria 3058 (☎(03) 9384 0141).

Canada: 10 Springfield Rd., **Ottawa**, Ontario K1M 1C9 (☎(613) 744-3751). **Consulates:** 2 Bloor St. West, #5000, **Toronto**, Ontario M4W 3E2 (☎(416) 960-0751); 325 Howe St., 2nd fl., **Vancouver**, B.C. V6C 1Z7 (☎(604) 662-8811).

Ireland: 6 Leeson Park, **Dublin** 6 (☎(01) 497 0843).

New Zealand: 180 Molesworth St., P.O. Box 4045, **Wellington** 4045 (☎(04) 473 6390).

South Africa: 852 Schoeman St., Arcadia 0083, P.O. Box 40216, Arcadia, **Pretoria** 0007 (☎(012) 342 5392). **Consulates:** Old Station Building, 160 Pine Road, 4th fl., Durban 4001, P.O. Box 3276, **Durban** 4000 (☎(031) 304 7020); 1 Eton Road, Corner Jan Smuts Avenue, Parktown 2193, P.O. Box 6805, **Johannesburg** 2000 (☎(011) 482 8487; www.indconjoburg.co.za).

UK: India House, Aldwych, **London**, WC2 B4NA (☎(020) 7836 8484; www.hcilondon.org). **Consulates:** 20 Augusta St., Jewellery Quarter, Hockley, **Birmingham** B18 6JL (☎(0121) 212 2778); 17 Rutland Square, **Edinburgh** EH1 2BB (☎(0131) 229 2144; fax 229 2155).

US: 2536 Massachusetts Ave. NW, **Washington, D.C.** 20008 (☎(202) 939-9806; www.indianembassy.org); **Consulates:** 3 East 64th St., **New York**, NY 10021 (☎(212) 774-0600); 540 Arguello Blvd., **San Francisco**, CA 94118 (☎(415) 668-0662); 455 North Cityfront Plaza Drive, #850, **Chicago**, IL 60611 (☎(312) 595-0405); 1990 Post Oak Blvd., #600, **Houston**, TX 77056 (☎(713) 626-2148).

NEPAL'S CONSULAR SERVICES ABROAD

Tourists visas are available upon arrival in Nepal. The only advantage of arranging a visa beforehand is that it might save you a bit of time when you arrive at the airport. Travelers from Ireland should contact the embassy in London. New Zealanders are served via the Sydney office. There is no embassy in South Africa. For more information, see **Visas**, p. 10.

Australia: 48 Mitchel I St., McMahons Point, **Sydney**, NSW 2060 (☎(02) 956 8815); 18-20 Bank Place, Suite 23, **Melbourne** 300, Victoria.

Canada: Royal Bank Plaza, 200 Bay St., **Toronto**, Ontario M5R 1V9 (☎(416) 865-0110).

UK: 12a Kensington Palace Gardens, **London** W8 4QU (☎(020) 7229 1594).

US: 2131 Leroy Place NW, **Washington, D.C.** 20008 (☎(202) 667-4550; **Consulates:** 820 Second Ave., #17B, **New York**, NY 10017 (☎(212) 370-3988); 1500 Lakehorse Drive, **Chicago**, IL 60610 (☎(312) 787-9199); 909 Montgomery St., #400, **San Francisco**, CA 94133 (☎(415) 434-1111); 16250 Dallas Parkway, #110, **Dallas**, TX 75248 (☎(214) 931-1212).

CONSULAR SERVICES IN INDIA AND NEPAL

Most countries have embassies in **Delhi** (see p. 106). Many have consulates in **Bombay** (see p. 394), and a few have offices in **Madras** (see p. 538) and **Calcutta** (see p. 649). In Nepal, all foreign diplomatic missions are in **Kathmandu** (see p. 734).

> ### ENTRANCE REQUIREMENTS.
>
> **Passport:** Required for all citizens traveling to India and Nepal.
>
> **Visa** (p. 9): Required for all travelers, except citizens of India traveling to Nepal and vice versa. Visas for Nepal are issued on arrival.
>
> **Inoculations** (p. 20): Visitors who have been in Africa, South America, or Trinidad and Tobago within six days of their arrival in India must have a certificate of vaccination against yellow fever.
>
> **Work Permit** (p. 9): Required for all foreigners planning to work in India or Nepal. Hence the name.

PASSPORTS

REQUIREMENTS. Unless you are a president, king, queen, or refugee, you will not get far without a passport. India and Nepal won't let you in if your passport is due to expire in less than six months; returning home with an expired passport is illegal and may result in a fine.

PHOTOCOPIES. Photocopy the page of your passport that contains your photograph, passport number, and other identifying information, along with other important documents (visas, travel insurance policies, airplane tickets, and traveler's check serial numbers) in case you lose anything. Carry one set of copies in a safe place apart from the originals and leave another set at home.

LOST PASSPORTS. If you lose your passport, immediately notify the local police and your home country's nearest embassy or consulate. This is when you start to feel really happy about having photocopies of the passport you have just lost (see above). To expedite its replacement, you will need to know all the numbers and dates printed on your old passport, and you will also need to show identification and proof of citizenship. In some cases, a replacement will take weeks to process, and it may be valid only for a limited time. Any visas stamped in your old passport will be irretrievably lost. In an emergency, ask for immediate temporary traveling papers that will permit you to get home. You will occasionally have to surrender your passport to a foreign government official, but if you don't get it back within a reasonable length of time, then inform your embassy.

VISAS AND PERMITS

All travelers to India and Nepal (except citizens of India going to Nepal, and vice versa) need a visa to enter. Nepalese visas are issued on arrival and must be paid for in US dollars. Visas for travel to India must be arranged in advance, through your nearest embassy or consulate. Admission as a visitor doesn't include the right to work, which is authorized only by a **work permit.** Entering India or Nepal to study requires a special visa. For more information, see **Alternatives to Tourism, p. 55**.

INDIA

Tourist visas are available for six months or one year, and they normally allow for multiple entries (important for side-trips to Nepal and other countries). Other options include a one-year visa for students, journalists, or business travelers. When applying for a visa, make sure that your passport is valid six months beyond the date of intended return.

It is always faster to apply through the embassy in your home country. You'll need to fill out an application form and provide your current passport, at least two passport photos, and a visa processing fee, which varies slightly from country to country. It can take anywhere between a few hours and a few weeks to get your visa processed, depending on the country you are applying from, the volume of traffic, the time of year, and the mood and efficiency of the officials involved. **Contact your nearest embassy well in advance of your trip** for more information.

SPECIAL PERMITS

Certain areas of India require a special permit in addition to an Indian visa. Permits can be issued by Indian diplomatic missions abroad, by Foreigners' Registration Offices in various Indian cities, or by the Ministry of Home Affairs in Delhi, Lok Nayak Bhawan, Khan Market, New Delhi (open M-F 10am-5pm).

Northeast India: Many areas, such as Assam, Meghalaya, and Tripura, are now open for tourists. A permit is no longer needed for these three states, but it is still a good idea to consult your embassy about the political situation, especially in Assam, before visiting. Due to tribal insurgencies and fears of a conflict with China, the other four states of the northeast—**Arunachal Pradesh, Nagaland, Manipur,** and **Mizoram** require restricted area permits. Acquiring these often demands patience and perseverance. A minimum of 4 people are required to travel together, and the group must be sponsored by a government-approved travel agency, which generally charges Rs300-400. The permits, themselves, are free and allow 5-15 days of travel, depending on the state. **Restricted area permits are only available at the Ministry of Home Affairs in New Delhi** (see p. 106). Permits can take anywhere from 2 days to several lifetimes to process. See p. 704.

West Bengal: Some areas around Darjeeling require a 15-day permit available to individuals or tourists traveling in groups. Permits can also be obtained through the Home Department of West Bengal.

Sikkim: Sikkim borders China and is treated by the Indian government as a military buffer. Foreigners need a permit to enter. Permits allow travel as far north as Phodang and Yuksam. They can be extended at the Commissioner's Office in Gangtok in special circumstances. For North Sikkim, an inner-line permit is required. It is only issued through tour companies to groups of 4 or more. A guide must accompany the group and the minimum charge is US$30-50 per day, including guide. It takes a solid work day to procure such a permit, available only in Gangtok. See **Sikkim Permits,** p. 677.

Andaman and Nicobar Islands: All foreign visitors to the Andamans require permits (valid for 30 days). These are now issued on arrival. The Nicobar Islands are off-limits to non-Indian citizens. See **The Andaman Islands,** p. 706.

Lakshadweep: The islands of Bangaran, Suheli, and Tilkam are open only to tourists traveling on group tours. The necessary permit can be obtained through the Ministry of Foreign Affairs and the Administrator of Lakshadweep.

Bhutan: Though officially an independent country, Bhutan's foreign policy and immigration procedures are controlled by India. The number of visas to Bhutan is limited by a quota system and, though visas are granted to individuals traveling alone, those who travel in group tours are much more likely to receive one. Solo travelers are required by the government of Bhutan to spend at least US$240 per day—this fee decreases slightly with larger groups. To apply for a visa, contact the Director of Tourism, Ministry of Finance, Tachichho Dzong, Thimpu, Bhutan or the Bhutan Foreign Mission, Chandra Gupta Marg, New Delhi 110021 (☎(011) 609217).

NEPAL

Anybody with a passport and a photo can get a Nepalese visa upon arrival at the airport in Kathmandu or at any of the land border crossings from India; it's really not worth fussing over ahead of time unless you're looking for something to worry about. The fee is the same either way; **at the border it must be paid in US dollars.** Any Nepalese consulate or embassy can issue visas for up to 60 days, although this can be extended once you're in Nepal. The Department of Immigration, Tridevi Marg,

Thamel, Kathmandu (☎(01) 470650 or 494273), grants extensions for up to four months. Apply for a visa extension a day or two before you really need it. Extensions are no longer granted on a daily basis.

SURROUNDING COUNTRIES

Several of the countries surrounding India and Nepal are politically volatile; it's always a good idea to check for up-to-date information before packing your bags and catching the boat. The following info is meant merely as a starting point.

Bangladesh: Passengers arriving by air can get a visa on arrival for stays of up to 15 days. Single-entry visas are valid for 90 days. Visa rules change frequently, however. For the latest permutations contact a Bangladeshi embassy or high commission: 56 Ring Rd., Lajpat Nagar III, **Delhi** (☎(011) 683 4668); 9 Circus Ave., **Calcutta** 700012 (☎(033) 247 5208); Chakrapath, Maharajgunj, **Kathmandu** (☎(01) 414943).

Burma (Myanmar): Visas are valid for a single entry of up to 28 days. The embassy in India is at 3/50-F Nyaya Marg, Chanakyapuri, Delhi (☎(011) 317 2224) and in Nepal at Chakupat, Patan City Gate, Kathmandu, P.O. Box 2437 (☎(01) 521788 or 524788). The only border crossings into Burma are from Thailand and China.

China: To travel into Tibet from Nepal, you need a Chinese visa. These are almost impossible to get at the embassy in Kathmandu but are easy to get via the embassy in Delhi. Visas are valid for 30 days and can sometimes be extended. In Kathmandu, you need to contact one of the many agencies specializing in tours to Tibet. **Star Tours and Travel,** Thamel, Tridevi Marg (☎423742 or 423446), and **Royal Mountain Trekking,** Durbar Marg, have the greatest frequency of departures for Lhasa, as well as the lowest prices. Permits can take anywhere between a few hours and several days to process. The standard deal consists of a five-day drive to Lhasa and includes all the necessary permits, as well as four nights' dorm lodging in Nyalam, Lhatse, Gyantse, and Shigatse. US$240 might seem a lot to pay, but it's the cheapest way of getting into Tibet. Once you are in Lhasa, you are allowed to stay for a maximum for seven days. You have to reserve your return ticket when you book. A landcruiser back to Kathmandu costs about US$60. **Flying** to Lhasa is also an option, if you have US$390 you want to get rid of. **Do not attempt to enter Tibet on your own.** The Chinese Embassy in India is at 50-D Shantipath, Chanakyapuri, **Delhi** (☎(011) 6871585) and in Nepal, Baluwatar, **Kathmandu** (☎(01) 413916).

Pakistan: A visa is necessary for entry into Pakistan. These are normally valid for three months. Pakistani embassies: 2/50-G Shantipath, Chanakyapuri, **Delhi** (☎(011) 600603) and Maharajganj, **Kathmandu** (☎(01) 374012).

Sri Lanka: For stays of up to 30 days, citizens of most European countries, the US, Canada, and Australia will be granted free visas on arrival with a confirmed ticket on a flight out of the country and enough funds to support themselves during their stay.

Thailand: Citizens from most European countries and the US, Canada, and Australia need not obtain visas if they plan to be in Thailand for less than 30 days and they have a confirmed ticket as proof of departure. Visas are necessary for longer stays. In India: 56-N Nyaya Marg, Chanakyapuri, **Delhi** (☎(011) 611 8103). In Nepal: Maharajganj, **Kathmandu** (☎(01) 371408).

IDENTIFICATION

When you travel, always carry at least two forms of identification with you, including at least one photo ID; a passport combined with a driver's license is usually adequate. You will need your passport to cash traveler's checks. Never carry all your IDs together; split them up in case of theft or loss. It is useful to bring extra passport-size photos to affix to the IDs or passes you will acquire along the way.

The **International Student Identity Card (ISIC)** is the the most widely accepted form of student ID worldwide, but in India and Nepal it is of negligible usefulness, aside from the medical insurance it provides. It might be worth getting one for a discount fare on your plane ticket (many travel agencies require an ISIC for student fares). All cardholders have access to a 24-hour emergency helpline for medical, legal, and financial emergencies (US and Canada ☎ (877) 370-4742, elsewhere call US collect +1 (713) 342-4104), and US cardholders are also eligible for insurance benefits (see **Insurance**, p. 20). The card is valid for one year, costs AUS$15, UK£5, or US$22, and can be bought at travel agencies throughout the world. Applicants must be degree-seeking students of a secondary or postsecondary school. The **International Youth Travel Card** (**IYTC**; formerly the **GO 25** Card) offers many of the same benefits as the ISIC to travelers who are under 25 but are not students. The **International Teacher Identity Card (ITIC)** offers teachers the same insurance coverage, as well as similar discounts. Most organizations that sell the ISIC also sell the IYTC and ITIC for the same prices. For more info, contact the **International Student Travel Confederation (ISTC),** Herengracht 479, 1017 BS Amsterdam, Netherlands (☎+31 (20) 421 28 00; fax 421 28 10; email istcinfo@istc.org; www.istc.org).

MONEY MATTERS

Once you get there, travel in India or Nepal is extremely cheap by Western standards. Depending on the areas you visit, and your definition of comfort, you can expect to spend anywhere between $5-20 per person per day. Spending just a few dollars more on accommodations leads to huge gains in comfort. Accommodations start at about US$2-3 per night for a simple box-like room with shared bathroom and toilet. For the equivalent of US$10 you can normally find a decent-sized, clean, well-aired room, often with extra little luxuries tacked on, such as clean sheets and toilet paper. A basic sit-down meal can cost as little $1, but your chances of eating good, clean food increase dramatically if you're willing to splash out a little more. Carrying large amounts of cash with you, even in a money belt, is risky, but unavoidable; personal checks are useless, and even traveler's checks will not be accepted in more remote regions.

CURRENCY AND EXCHANGE

The charts below are based on September 2000 exchange rates. Check a newspaper or the web (finance.yahoo.com or www.bloomberg.com) for the latest rates.

THE INDIAN RUPEE
Currency is measured in rupees (Rs, IRs in the Nepal section of the book), which are divided into 100 paise (p.). Coins are issued in denominations of p.10, 25, 50, Rs1, 2, and 5. Bills come in values of Rs1, 2, 5, 10, 20, 50, 100, and 500.

INDIAN RUPEE (RS)		
US$1 = RS45.68	RS100 = US$2.18
CDN$1 = RS31.02	RS100 = CDN3.22
UK£1 = RS66.58	RS100 = UK£1.5
IR£1 = RS52.08	RS100 = IR£1.92
AUS$1 = RS26.34	RS100 = AUS$3.79
NZ$1 = RS19.59	RS100 = NZ$5.11
SAR1 = RS6.54	RS100 = SAR15.23
EUR€1 = RS41.02	RS100 = EUR€2.43
NRS1 = RS0.65	RS100 = NRS154.68

THE NEPALESE RUPEE
Currency is measured in rupees (Rs, NRs in the India section of the book), which are divided into 100 paise (p.). Money comes in the following shapes and sizes. Coins: p.1, 2, 5, 10, 25, 50, Rs1, and 2. Bills: Rs1, 2, 5, 10, 25, 50, 100, 500, and 1000. Collect the whole set, and trade them with your friends.

NEPALESE RUPEE (RS)		
US$1 = RS70.87		RS100 = US$1.41
CDN$1 = RS48.12		RS100 = CDN$2.08
UK£1 = RS103.33		RS100 = UK£0.97
IR£1 = RS80.80		RS100 = IR£1.24
AUS$1 = RS40.87		RS100 = AUS$2.45
NZ$1 = RS30.37		RS100 = NZ$3.30
SAR1 = RS10.15		RS100 = SAR9.83
EUR€1 = RS63.64		RS100 = EUR€1.57
IRS1 = RS1.55		RS100 = 64.65IRS

Neither the Indian nor the Nepalese rupee may be exported abroad. There are 24-hour branches of the national banks at most of the international airports. British pounds and US dollars are the best currencies to bring with you; others will not always be easy to exchange. Avoid changing money at luxury hotels and restaurants, which often give outrageous rates of exchange and charge shockingly high commission rates. The national **State Bank of India** and the **Nepal Bank Ltd.** are generally the best places to change money. Not all branches can change foreign currency—it is usually worth tracking down the biggest branch in town. Changing money takes a long time and requires great reserves of patience. You should aim to take part in this farce as seldom as possible. Get an **encashment certificate** as proof of the transaction whenever you change money. This is sometimes demanded when paying for plane and train tickets or large bills in rupees, and you will need it if you want to change any left-over rupees back into hard currency before you leave. Foreign banks, like ANZ Grindlays and Hong Kong Bank, are often less infuriatingly slow than their competitors. **Bank of Baroda** (in India) offers cash advances on Visa and MasterCard at most of its many locations. Banking hours are short (M-F 10am-2pm, Sa 10am-noon). ATMs are only available in major cities.

Since you lose money on each transaction, it's a good idea convert in large sums, without going overboard and changing more than you are likely to need. You should carry small denominations (the equivalent of US$50 or less) for when you are forced to exchange money at unfavorable rates. Coins and small bills are essential for maintaining sanity, as nobody ever admits to having change.

There's really not much to be gained from changing money on the **black market.** Those who are still willing to risk confiscation of their money for the small premium (and speedier service) should keep their dodgy dealings discreet.

In some places in India and Nepal, Western currency will actually be preferred to local money, but avoid using Western money when you can. Throwing the big bucks about for preferential treatment is offensive and embarrassing. It also attracts thieves like flies to dung and encourages locals to jack up prices.

TRAVELER'S CHECKS

Traveler's checks (**American Express** and **Thomas Cook** are the most widely recognized in India and Nepal) are the safest way of carrying your money about. Most banks will sell them for a small commission. Each agency provides refunds if your checks are lost or stolen, and many provide services such as toll-free refund hotlines abroad, emergency message services, and stolen credit card assistance.

While traveling, keep check receipts and a record of which checks you've cashed separate from the checks themselves. Also leave a list of check numbers with someone at home. Never countersign checks until you're ready to cash them, and always bring your passport with you to cash them. If your checks are lost or stolen, immediately contact a refund center (of the company that issued your checks) to be reimbursed; they may require a police report verifying the loss or theft.

American Express: Call ☎(800) 251 902 in Australia; in India (011) 614 5920; in New Zealand (0800) 441 068; in the UK (0800) 521 313; in the US and Canada (800) 221-7282. Elsewhere call US collect +1 (801) 964-6665; www.aexp.com. There are no offices in Nepal. *Cheques for Two* can be signed by either of 2 people traveling together.

Citicorp: In the US and Canada call ☎(800) 645-6556; in Europe, the Middle East, or Africa call the UK +44 (020) 7508 7007; elsewhere call US collect +1 (813) 623-1709. Traveler's checks available in 7 currencies at 1-2% commission. Call 24hr.

Thomas Cook MasterCard: In the US and Canada call ☎(800) 223-7373; in India (011) 335 6571; in the UK (0800) 62 21 01; elsewhere call UK collect +44 (1733) 31 89 50. There are no Thomas Cook offices in Nepal. Checks available in 13 currencies at 2% commission. Thomas Cook offices cash checks commission-free.

Visa: In the US call ☎(800) 227-6811; in the UK (0800) 89 50 78; elsewhere call the UK collect +44 (1733) 31 89 49. Call for the location of their nearest office.

FANTASTIC PLASTIC

Credit cards are gaining wider acceptance in South Asia, but they are still hardly recognized anywhere outside the big cities. And even in places like Delhi and Bombay, only the ritziest and most expensive places will accept payment by card. Cards can, however, be a useful backup to your traveler's checks, and they are invaluable in an emergency. You can use credit cards to purchase domestic airline tickets and train tickets in India.

American Express, MasterCard (a.k.a **EuroCard** or **Access in Europe**), and **Visa** (a.k.a. **Carte Bleue** or **Barclaycard**) are the cards most likely to be accepted in the subcontinent. Credit card companies get the wholesale exchange rate, which is generally 5% better than the retail rate used by banks and other currency exchange establishments. Teller machines are located only in the big cities and even then they're few and far between. **American Express** cards also work in some ATMs, as well as at AmEx offices and major airports. All such machines require a **Personal Identification Number (PIN).** Ask your credit card company for a PIN before you leave. If you already have a PIN, check with the company to make sure it will work in India or Nepal. **Credit card scams** of various sorts are common in India and Nepal. Be cautious when purchasing items with a credit card. Make sure that the card remains in view at all times to ensure that the vendor does not make extra imprints. Also, if you're planning to ship goods through a shop owner, don't believe him when he says he won't forward the credit slip for payment until you've received the goods. For more info on how to get ripped off, see p. 16.

CREDIT CARD COMPANIES. Visa (US ☎(800) 336-8472) and **MasterCard** (US ☎(800) 307-7309) are issued in cooperation with banks and other organizations. **American Express** (US ☎(800) 843-2273) has an annual fee of up to US$55. AmEx cardholders may cash personal checks at AmEx offices abroad, access an emergency medical and legal assistance hotline (24hr.; in North America call ☎(800) 554-2639, elsewhere call US collect +1 (202) 554-2639), and enjoy American Express Travel Service benefits (including plane, hotel, and car rental reservation changes; baggage loss and flight insurance; mailgram and cable services; and held mail).

CASH (ATM) CARDS

Cash cards are few and far-between in India and Nepal. Major cities such as Delhi, Bombay, Madras, and Calcutta, do have a sprinkling of ATMs, but that's about it. The two major international money networks are Cirrus (US ☎(800) 424-7787) and PLUS (US ☎(800) 843-7587). To locate ATMs around the world, consult www.visa.com/pd/atm or www.mastercard.com/atm.

HELP—I'VE RUN OUT OF MONEY!

This is not something you want to do. Having money wired to India and Nepal can be a bureaucratic fuss, subject to long delays; most travelers wisely avoid it. In an emergency, you can normally get money sent to you in a matter of two to three working days. Foreign banks such as CitiBank and ANZ Grindlays are the most reliable; be precise about the branch you want the money sent to.

AMERICAN EXPRESS. Cardholders can withdraw cash from their checking accounts at any of AmEx's major offices and many representative offices (up to US$1000 every 21 days; no service charge, no interest). Green card holders may withdraw up to US$1000 in any seven-day period (2% transaction fee; minimum US$2.50, maximum US$20). To enroll in Express Cash, cardmembers may call ☎ (800) 227-4669 in the US; elsewhere call the US collect +1 (336) 668-5041. The AmEx national number in India is ☎ (011) 614-5920.

WESTERN UNION. Travelers from the US, Canada, and the UK can wire money abroad through Western Union's international money transfer services. In Canada call ☎ (800) 235-0000; in India (011) 336 8771; in Nepal (01) 418738; in the UK (0800) 83 38 33; in the US (800) 325-6000. The rates for sending cash are generally US$10-11 cheaper than with a credit card, and the money is usually available at the place you're sending it to within an hour. To locate the nearest Western Union location, have a look at www.westernunion.com.

US STATE DEPARTMENT (US CITIZENS ONLY). In dire emergencies only, good old Uncle Sam will forward money within hours to the nearest consular office, which will then disburse it for a US$15 fee. Contact the Overseas Citizens Service, American Citizens Services, Consular Affairs, Room 4811, US Department of State, Washington, D.C. 20520 (☎ (202) 647-5225; nights, Sundays, and holidays 647-4000; http://travel.state.gov).

ECONOMICS AND ETHICS

Because of their relative wealth, foreigners are mobbed by **touts** (see p. 15), assailed by armies of **beggars** (see p. 17), accosted by slippery **con men** (see **Warning**, p. 16), and almost always charged more than locals. For budget travelers, these shenanigans can be exhausting and infuriating. After a tout has lied to you about a hotel to get you into one that would pay a commission, or after a rickshaw-*wallah* has asked you for five times the usual fare, you might find yourself arguing over small differences in money simply as a matter of "principle."

However, Western travelers trying to pinch paise should remember how much their money really means to the people they are dealing with. Foreigners are rich compared to most Indians and Nepalis—no budget travel excuses will be understood here. Even the most austere budget travelers frequently spend as much in a day as their hotel watchman or rickshaw-*wallah* earns in a month. The following sections discuss some of the issues foreign travelers in India and Nepal face when they deal with money.

TIPPING AND BAKSHEESH

The word **baksheesh** is usually translated as a "tip," but the concept really includes everything from simple gifts to outright bribes. Bribing a railway porter to find a seat on a "full" train is baksheesh; so is giving small change to beggars. **Small tips** are expected for restaurant service, "coolie" (porter) service, and unofficial tour guides. There is no need to tip taxi drivers. Tips depend on your level of satisfaction or gratitude and usually run between Rs1 and Rs20, not following any particular percentage rule. Most Indians and Nepalis expect great tips from foreigners, but don't be swayed by groans. If your first offer is met with a quick roll of the head signifying "OK," then you have done well.

TOUTS, MIDDLEMEN, AND SCAMS

Touts are the scruffy-looking men who surround travelers at bus stands and train stations or accost them in the streets of tourist ghettos, offering deals on transportation, currency exchange, drugs, or any other service rupees can buy. If you have trouble finding something, a tout will probably offer to help you for a little baksheesh, but what really distinguishes touts is their *un*helpfulness. They are pushy and will try to trap you into paying for something you don't want; they count on foreigners to be too naive or too polite to refuse. When ignored, many touts are equipped with a guilt-trip line tailored to your demographic group. "Excuse me, sir, one question: Why don't you white Americans like to talk to us Indians?" Don't let these guilt trips get to you—touts are only interested in your money.

It's hard to find a hotel without a tout getting involved; you'll usually be approached as soon as you get off the bus or train. Touts (and often taxi drivers and rickshaw-*wallahs*, as well) are paid commission by hotels to gather tourists, and this commission is usually added to your hotel bill. If the hotel isn't paying commission, touts will tell you it's full, closed, or only open to people with three heads; don't believe them. Be firm—decide on your hotel before you arrive in town and have a taxi or rickshaw-*wallah* take you there directly.

In major tourist centers you'll often meet people who want you to visit their home or their workplace or to take you on tours. Unless you have asked to go somewhere, you are under no obligation to follow them or to pay them for being taken to a place in which you have no interest. Don't give them money when they ask you for it, regardless of what they say they will do for you.

Many **travel agents** in the major tourist centers are just touts with desks and telephones. They are notorious for giving false information, charging hefty commissions, and selling bogus tickets for trains that don't exist. Most Indians buy train tickets directly from the station. It's best to do this yourself, too. **Eliminating the middleman** will give you control and save you money.

Another hassle at many monuments and temples are the unofficial **guides** who spout drivel at you, refuse to leave you alone, and then have the cheek to demand baksheesh. Be forceful with these jokers and they will usually back off—don't hesitate to push and snarl your way through. It is better to book a guide through a tourist office or other government organization than wait to be approached.

Be cautious about accepting **food or drinks** from a stranger. There have been reports of con men who drug travelers and rob or rape them while they are knocked out. Bear in mind, however, that offers of food and drink are one of the primary forms of Indian hospitality. A gracious "the doctor told me I shouldn't have that" is a good way to turn down food or drink without offending anyone.

WARNING: Travelers in the biggest tourist centers of the subcontinent (Delhi, Jaipur, Agra, Kathmandu, etc.), are frequently accosted by locals possessed by an irresistible urge to chat about tourism, education, the city, Bill Clinton's sex life, and (especially) cricket. Having thus established themselves as "friends," they offer travelers their hospitality: "You're a guest in my country. The least I can do is invite you to my place for some food." Nine times out of ten, their "place" is a jewelry, gems, or rug shop. Eventually, travelers are offered the opportunity to carry anywhere from US$500 to US$10,000 worth of jewelry abroad to be handed over to an "overseas partner." In return, these dealers offer a 100% commission. The rationale is straightforward. Export laws impose a 250% tariff on gems and jewelry, but foreigners with tourist visas are allowed to carry a certain amount of gems and jewelry out of the country. So, by having tourists do their exporting for them at 100% commission, gem dealers save a lot of money. First, however, they will insist you give them your **credit card** number for "insurance purposes," since valuables are often appropriated by corrupt customs officials. The gem dealers call it "couriering," and insist that it's done all the time. Of course, as soon as you hand over your card, they will charge hundreds of dollars to your account. **Export schemes** sound too good to be true because they are—stay away from them. If you ever feel uncomfortable in a store, just run away, even if it seems rude or awkward. (Also see **Fantastic Plastic,** p. 14.)

BARGAINING

India and Nepal are wonderful places to hone your **bargaining** skills. Vendors and drivers will automatically quote you a price that is several times too high; it's up to you to get them down to a reasonable rate. With the following tips and a bit of finesse, you might be able to impress even the most hardened of hawkers:

1. Bargaining needn't be a fierce struggle laced with barbs. Quite the opposite: good-natured wrangling with a cheerful smiling face may prove your biggest weapon.

2. Use your poker face. The less your face betrays your interest in the item the better. If you touch an item to inspect it, the vendor will be sure to "encourage" you to name a price or make a purchase. Cooing over that plastic elephant or coming back again and again to admire that marvellous mother-of-pearl Taj Mahal are good ways of ensuring that you pay a ridiculously high price. Be cool.

3. Know when to bargain. In most cases, it's quite clear when it's appropriate to bargain. Taxi and auto-rickshaw fares and things for sale in outdoor markets are all fair game. Don't bargain on prepared or pre-packaged foods on the street or in restaurants. In some stores, signs will indicate whether "fixed prices" prevail. When in doubt, ask tactfully, "Is that your lowest price?" or whether discounts are given.

4. Never underestimate the power of peer pressure. Bargaining with more than one person at a time—particularly rickshaw-*wallahs*—always leads to higher prices.

5. Know when to turn away. Feel free to refuse any vendor or rickshaw driver who bargains rudely, and don't hesitate to move on to another vendor if one will not be reasonable about the final price he offers. However, to start bargaining without an intention to buy is a major *faux pas*. Agreeing on a price and declining it is also poor form. Turn away slowly with a smile and "thank you" upon hearing a ridiculous price—the price may plummet.

6. Start low. Never feel guilty offering what seems to you a ridiculously low price.

BEGGING

Begging is impossible to ignore in India and Nepal. If you do give to beggars, remember that Rs30 is more than many Indian working people see in a week. **Carry coins and one- or two-rupee bills**—these are appropriate in almost all cases. For children, give food instead of money—a gift of biscuits is more likely to benefit the child than cash, which often goes straight into the hands of a ringleader. It is customary to give to beggars at pilgrimage sites, sadhus (wandering Hindu holy men who survive by begging), and transvestites on trains. Don't give to cute, healthy kids who approach with requests for rupees, coins, or pens. These are not beggars, but regular schoolchildren trying their luck.

SAFETY AND SECURITY

India and Nepal are generally safe; rates of crime, especially violent crime, are extremely low. The sheer mass of people in India means that you will almost always be surrounded, and most Indians and Nepalis are well-meaning, often willing to go out of their way to help a foreigner in trouble. What goes on in public is everyone's business, for better or worse.

POLITICAL INSTABILITY. Political violence is a problem in parts of India and Nepal. Punjab, which was a major site of volatility in the 1980s and early 1990s, appears to have calmed down for now, but parts of Assam have recently become unstable. Kashmir continues to be an explosively dangerous region; only that state's eastern regions of Ladakh and Zanskar are safe for tourists. Threats to foreigners are usually incidental, but in 1995 five western tourists were taken hostage by a militant group—one was beheaded. Despite the political instability, a small number of tourists opt for package tours of Srinagar in Western Kashmir. **These tours are the only remotely safe way to travel through Srinagar.** For more information, see **Srinagar**, p. 255. Even when there's not a seccessionist war going on, law and order can be sketchy in remote parts of India and Nepal, where political parties and organized thugs rule the countryside. Bihar, eastern Orissa, and some of the northeastern states are the areas that you need to be most careful about traveling through. The best place to get advice about unsafe areas is your country's embassy or high commission, and it is always advisable to read the newspapers while you are in India or Nepal to keep abreast of the latest developments.

FURTHER INFORMATION. The following government offices provide travel information and advisories by phone, fax, or the web.

Australian Department of Foreign Affairs and Trade: ☎(02) 6261 1111; fax (02) 6261 3111; www.dfat.gov.au/travel/index.html

Canadian Department of Foreign Affairs and International Trade (DFAIT): ☎(800) 267-6788, from Ottawa (613) 944-6788; fax (800) 575-2500; www.dfait-maeci.gc.ca/travelreport/menu_e.htm. Call for their free booklet, *Bon Voyage...But.*

United Kingdom Foreign and Commonwealth Office: ☎(020) 7238 4503; fax (020) 7238 4545; www.fco.gov.uk/travel.

United States Department of State: ☎(202) 647-5225, auto faxback (202) 647-3000; http://travel.state.gov. For their publication *A Safe Trip Abroad,* call (202) 512-1800.

BLENDING IN. Tourists are particularly vulnerable to crime since they carry large amounts of cash and are not as street-savvy as locals. Even if you look South Asian, most people will be able to tell (immediately) that you're a foreigner. You won't ever blend in completely, but try not to stand out too much. Follow the lead of others—you probably shouldn't be the one to start the trend. **Dress modestly,** ideally in local clothes. Don't flaunt money or extravagant jewelry in public—this will make you a prime candidate for robbery. If you are able to speak even a few words of the **local language** (see **Appendix,** p. 821) you will likely appear more confident and may gain the sympathy of someone who might not help you otherwise. For more information, see **Customs and Etiquette,** p. 51.

Try to look as if you know what you're doing (even if you don't); the gawking camera-toter is a more obvious target than the low-profile traveler. Familiarize yourself with your surroundings before setting out; if you must check a map on the street, duck into a shop or restaurant. If you are traveling alone, be sure that someone at home knows your itinerary and **never admit that you're traveling alone.**

EXPLORING. Find out about unsafe neighborhoods from tourist offices, from the manager of your hotel, or from a trustworthy local. Whenever possible, *Let's Go* warns of unsafe areas, but only your eyes can tell you for sure when you've wandered into one. Don't attempt to cross through parks or any other large, deserted areas. If you feel uncomfortable, leave as quickly as you can, but don't allow fear to close off whole worlds to you. Careful, persistent exploration will build confidence and make your travels much more rewarding. A blissful beach can become unsafe as soon as night falls. When walking at night, stick to main roads and avoid dark alleyways. Unless you are in a neighborhood that remains busy at night, it is best not to go out alone.

GETTING AROUND. Despite the occasional fatal accident, **trains** are definitely the safest way to travel in the subcontinent. Although the railways are very extensive in India, they don't run to some of the smaller towns, and they don't exist at all in Nepal. **Buses** are the only real alternative in these situations, and they can be particularly convenient for shorter trips. However, road rules are virtually nonexistent in India and Nepal, and bus accidents are quite common, particularly in hilly or mountainous regions. The sobriety of bus drivers can never be taken for granted, and this makes road travel even more hair-raising. Although **taxis** are forced to drive on the same crazy roads surrounded by the same crazy drivers, they are generally safer than buses. Not only can you insist that your driver slow down, the size of the vehicle makes it less likely to topple over the side of a mountain. When **on foot,** be very careful of the traffic, which is generally chaotic—most vehicles will not stop for pedestrians. *Let's Go* does not recommend hitchhiking, particularly for women. For more information on **Getting Around,** see p. 44.

ANIMALS. Watch out for stray animals; rabies (see p. 25) is much more prevalent in India and Nepal than in Western countries. The rhesus **monkeys** that hover in the treetops above temples are sometimes aggressive, and they will snatch food and bite. If a stray **dog** growls at you, pick up a stone and act like you're about to throw it. Even if you can't find a stone, just pretending to pick one up usually scares them away. Also be wary of **rats,** which can be a problem in some hotels. Since rats are often attracted to crumbs, keep food away from your bed. Poisonous **snakes** such as cobras also present a slight danger, even in urban areas. If you've left your shoes outdoors, it never hurts to shake them out before putting them on. Finally, India's larger wildlife, from innocuous **buffalo** to gargantuan **elephants** to Bengal **tigers** can gore, maul, and trample people. This can really ruin your holiday.

SELF DEFENSE. A good self-defense course will give you more satisfying ways to react to different types of aggression. **Impact, Prepare, and Model Mugging** can refer you to local self-defense courses in the United States (☎(800) 345-5425) and Vancouver, Canada (☎(604) 878-3838). Workshops (2-3hr.) start at US$50 and full courses run US$350-500. Both women and men are welcome.

FINANCIAL SECURITY

PROTECTING YOUR VALUABLES. To minimize disaster in the event of theft, don't keep all your valuables in one place. You should carry your **passport, traveler's checks,** and **plane ticket** on you at all times. **Photocopies** of important documents will help you to recover them if they are lost or stolen. Carry one copy separate from the documents and leave another copy at home. Never count your money in public, and carry as little as possible. **Don't put a wallet with money in your back pocket.** A **money belt** is the best way to carry cash; a nylon, zippered pouch with a belt that sits inside the waist of your pants or skirt combines convenience and security. A **neck pouch** is just as safe, but be sure to tuck it under your shirt, where it can't be snipped off and carried away. Keep a small amount of money in your pockets so that you don't need to sift through a stack of cash every time you buy a bottle of ThumsUp. If you plan to use a purse, buy a sturdy one with a secure clasp, and tote it crosswise on the side, away from the street with the clasp against you. Secure packs with small combination padlocks that slip through the two zippers. For the low-down on low-lifes, see **Touts, Middlemen, and Scams,** p. 15.

ACCOMMODATIONS. Most **hotels** have locks on the doors, but this doesn't mean you will be the only one with access to your room. Hotel staff can probably get into your room if they want to, and it's not unheard of for theft to occur in this way. Never leave valuables in your hotel room, even if it's locked. You might want to leave your luggage at a guest house while you are trekking, but don't leave your valuables there, and make sure that anything you do leave is securely locked.

TRANSPORTATION. Be particularly careful on **buses.** Carry your backpack in front of you where you can see it and don't trust anyone to "watch your bag for a second." If your bag is going on a bus roof rack, make sure it's tied down securely so that no one can jump off with it in a hurry. Thieves thrive on **trains;** professionals wait for tourists to fall asleep and then carry off whatever they can. When traveling in pairs, sleep in shifts; when alone, use a **lock** to secure your pack to the bunk. Keep important documents and other valuables on your person and try to sleep on top bunks with your luggage stored above you (if not in bed with you).

If your belongings are stolen in India or Nepal, you'll have to go to the police. There is virtually no chance you will ever see your camera again, but you can at least get an official **police report,** which you will need for an insurance claim.

DRUGS AND BOOZE

While marijuana *(ganja)* and hashish *(charas)* are grown throughout the Himalayas and are extremely cheap everywhere in India and Nepal, these **drugs are illegal** and are considered socially unacceptable by most Indians and Nepalis. An exception is made for sadhus (Hindu holy men), since *ganja* is associated with the worship of Shiva. A few ethnic groups in the Himalayas also use *ganja* and *charas* with no stigma. These indulgences do not extend to tourists, however. In fact, penalties are sometimes harsher for foreigners.

India has a 10-year minimum sentence for drug possession or trafficking, but those caught with small amounts of *ganja* are likely to get off with less. If charged with drug possession, you are likely to find yourself required to prove your innocence in an often-corrupt justice system whose rules you won't understand. Those who attempt to influence a police officer must do so discreetly and indirectly. Drug law enforcement in Nepal is more relaxed, but sentences are still stiff. If you do get into trouble with the law, contact your country's diplomatic mission. Bear in mind that if you are arrested, diplomats can visit you, provide a list of lawyers, inform your family, and lend a shoulder to cry on, but they can't get you out of jail.

In the more touristy places in India and Nepal, alcohol is easy to come by. Beer is popular, and India and Nepal also produce drinkable vodka, gin, rum, whisky, and other liquors. In India, these are classified as IMFL (Indian-Made Foreign Liquor). Beware of home-brewed concoctions, however; every year dozens of people are killed by bad batches of toddy. The Indian state of Gujarat is officially dry, and its prohibitive efforts have recently been copied by Haryana and Manipur. Although illegal, boot-legged liquor can still be found in the so-called "dry" states. Other areas, like Tamil Nadu, Bombay, and Delhi, have dry days. Liquor permits, available at embassies, consulates, and tourist offices in Delhi, Madras, Bombay, and Calcutta, are not essential but may help you get booze with less difficulty in dry areas. There is no drinking age in India or Nepal.

HEALTH

Common sense is the simplest prescription for good health when traveling. Travelers complain most often about their feet and their gut, so take precautionary measures. Drink lots of fluids to prevent dehydration and constipation, and wear sturdy, broken-in shoes. During the hot season, take extra precautions against heatstroke and sunburn. To minimize the effects of jet lag, "reset" your body's clock by adopting the time of your destination as soon as you board the plane.

BEFORE YOU GO

Preparation can help minimize the likelihood of contracting a disease and maximize the chances of receiving effective health care in the event of an emergency. For tips on packing a basic **first-aid kit** and other health essentials, see **p. 27**.

In your **passport,** write the names of any people you want to be contacted in case of a medical emergency. Also list your blood type and any allergies or medical conditions you would want doctors to know about. Matching a prescription to a foreign equivalent is not always easy, safe, or possible. Carry up-to-date, legible prescriptions, or a statement from your doctor giving the medication's trade name, manufacturer, chemical name, and dosage. When traveling, keep all medication with you in your carry-on luggage.

IMMUNIZATIONS AND PRECAUTIONS

In most cases, no inoculations are required for entry into India or Nepal, but that doesn't mean inoculations aren't recommended. Visitors who have been in Africa, South America, or Trinidad and Tobago within six days of their arrival in India must have a certificate of vaccination against **yellow fever.** Visit a doctor 4-6 weeks before your departure to allow time for the series of vaccinations.

> **INOCULATION REQUIREMENTS AND RECOMMENDATIONS.**
> The US Centers for Disease Control recommend the following inoculations for travel to the subcontinent:
>
> **Hepatitis A:** Immune globulin (IG).
> **Hepatitis B:** If you might be exposed to blood, have sexual contact, stay longer than 6 months, or undergo medical treatment. Hepatitis B vaccine is recommended for infants and for children who did not receive the series as infants.
> **Japanese encephalitis:** If you plan to be in a rural area for over 4 weeks.
> **Rabies:** If you might be exposed to wild or domestic animals.
> **Typhoid:** Vaccination is particularly important because strains in India and Nepal are resistant to multiple antibiotics.
> **Others:** As needed, booster doses for tetanus-diphtheria and measles, one-time dose of polio for adults, and haemophilus influenza B (meningitis).

USEFUL ORGANIZATIONS AND PUBLICATIONS

The US **Centers for Disease Control and Prevention** (**CDC;** ☎(877) FYI-TRIP; www.cdc.gov/travel), an excellent source of information for travelers, maintains an international fax information service. The CDC's comprehensive booklet *Health Information for International Travelers*, an annual rundown of disease, immunization, and general health advice, is free on the website or US$22 via the Government Printing Office (☎(202) 512-1800). The **US State Department** (http://travel.state.gov) compiles Consular Information Sheets on health, entry requirements, and other issues for various countries. For quick information on health and other travel warnings, call the **Overseas Citizens Services** (☎(202) 647-5225, after-hours 647-4000), contact a US passport agency or a US embassy or consulate abroad, or send a self-addressed, stamped envelope to the Overseas Citizens Services, Bureau of Consular Affairs, #4811, US Department of State, Washington, D.C. 20520. For information on medical evacuation services and travel insurance firms, see http://travel.state.gov/medical.html. The **British Foreign and Commonwealth Office,** 1 Palace St., London SW1E 5HE (☎(020) 7238 4503; www.fco.gov.uk/travel), also gives health warnings for individual countries.

For detailed information on travel health, including a country-by-country overview of diseases, try the **International Travel Health Guide,** Stuart Rose, MD (Travel Medicine, US$20; www.travmed.com). For general health information, contact the **American Red Cross** (☎(800) 564-1234).

MEDICAL ASSISTANCE ON THE ROAD

Tourist centers are full of pharmacies, and many pharmacists (called "chemists" in India) speak enough English to understand what medication you need. Most pharmacies sell prescription medicines as over-the-counter drugs. Only a few are open 24 hours. In an emergency, head to the nearest major hospital that is open all night and has an in-house pharmacy. Outside the major tourist centers, the going is a bit rougher, although every major town should have at least one pharmacy.

Both India and Nepal suffer from a lack of doctors and medical equipment. **Public hospitals** are overcrowded, short on staff and supplies, and rarely have English-speaking staff. In many places in India, "hospitals" function essentially as hospices—homes for the dying. In the case of serious medical problems, most foreign visitors to India go to more expensive **private hospitals.** These are mainly located in the big cities; elsewhere, they are usually known as nursing homes. Small private clinics, usually operated by a single physician, are also widespread and reliable. In Kathmandu, a number of tourist-oriented clinics offer care up to Western standards. For serious medical problems, however, those who can afford it have themselves evacuated to better facilities in Singapore or Europe.

You can also contact your **diplomatic mission** upon arrival and ask for their suggested **list of doctors.** Carry these names around with your other medical documents. If a **blood transfusion** is necessary, ask whether someone from your diplomatic mission can donate blood or whether family members at home can send blood by air. Also ask whether your diplomatic mission can help arrange emergency evacuation. Often, hospital syringes haven't been properly sanitized, so it's a good idea to carry a few unused syringes with you in case you need some sort of injection. Make sure you also carry a doctor's note explaining that they are for medicinal purposes, in case anyone gets the wrong idea.

Travel insurance (such as that offered with the ISIC and ITIC) is enough to cover most **medical expenses** in India or Nepal. Even for long-term stays and major surgery at top hospitals, costs are much lower than what they would be back home. Nevertheless, it's a good idea to carry a credit card for immediate payment. Unfortunately, Westerners do not have good reputations for paying their bills fairly and squarely; many hospitals are hesitant to trust them with late payments.

Two services offer access to medical support for travelers: The *MedPass* from **Global Emergency Medical Services (GEMS)**, 2001 Westside Dr., #120, Alpharetta, GA 30004, USA (☎(800) 860-1111; fax (770) 475-0058; www.globalems.com), provides 24-hour international medical assistance, support, and medical evacuation resources. The **International Association for Medical Assistance to Travelers (IAMAT;** US ☎(716) 754-4883, Canada ☎(416) 652-0137, New Zealand ☎(03) 352 2053) has free membership, lists English-speaking doctors worldwide, and offers information on immunization requirements and sanitation. If your regular insurance policy does not cover travel abroad, you should buy additional coverage (see p. 18).

Travelers with medical conditions (diabetes, allergies to antibiotics, epilepsy, heart conditions) might want to get a stainless-steel Medic Alert ID tag (first year US$35, $15 annually thereafter), which identifies the condition and gives a 24-hour collect-call number. Contact the **Medic Alert Foundation**, 2323 Colorado Ave, Turlock, CA 95382, USA (☎(800) 825-3785; www.medicalert.org). Diabetics can contact the **American Diabetes Association**, 1660 Duke St., Alexandria, VA 22314, USA (☎(800) 232-3472), for copies of the article "Travel and Diabetes" and a diabetic ID card, which carries messages in 18 languages explaining the carrier's diabetic status. If you are HIV positive, contact the CDC (see p. 21) for info regarding vaccinations and special travel risks. The Indian government screens long-term visitors for HIV.

ENVIRONMENTAL HAZARDS

Air Quality: A number of the world's most polluted cities are in the subcontinent. The exhaust fumes belched out by motor rickshaws and 1950s cars, as well as alarmingly high industrial emissions, affect big and small cities alike. This may aggravate existing respiratory problems, such as allergies and asthma, and create new problems in previously healthy travelers. If you suffer from respiratory difficulties, take inhalers and/or prescription medication with you and consult your doctor for advice before you leave.

Heat exhaustion and dehydration: Heat exhaustion, characterized by dehydration and salt deficiency, can lead to fatigue, headaches, and wooziness. Drink plenty of liquids (enough to keep your urine clear) and eat salty foods. Avoid dehydrating beverages like alcohol, coffee, tea, and caffeinated sodas. Wear a hat, sunglasses, and a lightweight long-sleeved shirt when you're out in the sun and acclimatize to the heat before exerting yourself. Continuous heat stress can eventually lead to **heatstroke,** characterized by a rising temperature, severe headache, and cessation of sweating. Victims should be cooled off with wet towels and taken to a doctor.

Sunburn: If you're prone to sunburn, bring sunscreen with you, preferably SPF15 or higher (it's often more expensive and hard to find when traveling), and apply it liberally and often to avoid burns and the risk of skin cancer. If you are planning to spend time near water, in the desert, or in the snow, you are at risk of getting burned, even through clouds. Protect your eyes with good sunglasses, since ultraviolet rays can damage the retina of the eye after too much exposure. If you get sunburned, drink more fluids than usual and apply Calamine or an aloe-based lotion.

Heat rashes: For some travelers, a visit to India and Nepal will mean an introduction to **prickly heat,** a rash that develops when sweat is trapped under the skin. Men are particularly susceptible to developing this rash in the groin area. To alleviate itch, try showering with mango *neem* soap or sprinkle talcum powder on the affected area just after bathing. Moist, hot weather can irritate the skin in other ways as well. Various **fungal infections** (athlete's foot, jock itch, etc.) can be prevented by washing often and drying thoroughly. Wear loose-fitting clothes made of absorbent fibers like cotton.

Hypothermia and frostbite: A rapid drop in body temperature is the clearest sign of over-exposure to cold. Victims may also shiver, feel exhausted, have poor coordination or slurred speech, hallucinate, or suffer amnesia. *Do not let hypothermia victims fall asleep,* or their body temperature will continue to drop and they may die. To avoid hypothermia, keep dry, wear layers, and stay out of the wind. When the temperature is below freezing, watch out for frostbite. If skin turns white, waxy, and cold, do not rub the area. Drink warm beverages, get dry, and slowly warm the area with dry fabric or steady body contact until a doctor can be found.

High altitude: Travelers to high altitudes such as the Himalayas should ascend at a gradual rate to let their bodies adjust to the lower oxygen levels in the air. High elevations can cause insomnia, headaches, nausea and **Acute Mountain Sickness** (AMS; see p. 34). At these levels, alcohol packs a more potent punch and UV rays are stronger.

PREVENTING DISEASE

INSECT-BORNE DISEASES
Many diseases are transmitted by insects—mainly mosquitoes, fleas, ticks, and lice. Be aware of insects in wet or forested areas, especially when hiking or camping. **mosquitoes** are most active from dusk to dawn. Wear long pants and long sleeves (preferably light-colored) and try tucking your pants (and your vanity) into your socks. Some travelers also bring along a mosquito net, though it can add a bit of weight to your pack. Use insect repellents containing DEET and soak or spray your gear with permethrin (licensed in the US for use on clothing). Consider natural repellents that make you smelly to insects, like vitamin B-12 or garlic pills. To stop the itch once you've been bitten, try Calamine lotion, topical cortisones (like Cortaid), or take a bath with a half-cup of baking soda or oatmeal.

Malaria: Transmitted by *Anopheles* mosquitoes that bite at night, malaria is the most serious disease that travelers to India and Nepal are likely to contract. The incubation period varies from 6-8 days to as long as months. Early symptoms include fever, chills, aches, and fatigue, followed by high fever and sweating, sometimes with vomiting and diarrhea. See a doctor for any flu-like sickness that occurs after travel in a high-risk area. Left untreated, malaria can cause anemia, kidney failure, coma, and death. It is an especially serious threat to pregnant women. To reduce the risk of contracting malaria, use mosquito repellent, particularly in the evenings and when visiting forested areas, and take oral prophylactics, like **mefloquine** (sold under the name Lariam) or **doxycycline** (ask your doctor for a prescription). Be aware that these drugs can have very serious side effects, including slowed heart rate and unforgettable nightmares.

Dengue fever: An "urban viral infection" transmitted by *Aedes* mosquitoes, which bite during the day. Dengue has flu-like symptoms and is often indicated by a rash 3-4 days after the onset of fever. Symptoms for the first 2-4 days include chills, high fever, profuse sweating, headaches, swollen lymph nodes, muscle aches, and in some instances, a pink rash on the body. And it only gets worse after that. If you experience any of these symptoms, find a doctor, drink plenty of liquids, and take fever-reducing medication such as acetaminophen (Tylenol). *Never take aspirin to treat dengue fever.*

Japanese encephalitis: Another mosquito-borne disease, most prevalent during the rainy season in rural areas near rice fields and livestock pens. Aside from delirium, most symptoms are flu-like: chills, headache, fever, vomiting, muscle fatigue. Since the disease carries a high mortality rate, it's vital to go to a hospital as soon as any symptoms appear. While the JE-VAX vaccine, usually given in 3 shots over a 30-day period, is effective for a year, it has been associated with serious side effects. According to the CDC, there is little chance of being infected if proper precautions are taken, such as using mosquito repellents containing DEET and sleeping under mosquito nets.

Other insect-borne diseases: Filariasis is a roundworm infestation transmitted by mosquitoes. Infection causes enlargement of extremities and has no vaccine. **Leishmaniasis,** a parasite transmitted by sand flies, has been found to occur in the Indian subcontinent. Common symptoms are fever, weakness, and swelling of the spleen. There is a treatment, but no vaccine. In parts of Asia the **plague** and **relapsing fever,** transmitted through fleas and ticks, still occur. Treatment is available for both, and a vaccine can keep you free of the plague.

FOOD- AND WATER-BORNE DISEASES

Food- and water-borne diseases are the biggest cause of illness among travelers to India and Nepal. Prevention is the best cure: be sure that the water you drink is clean and that everything you eat is cooked properly. **Avoid ice and drink only boiled, filtered, or otherwise purified water.** If you're a staunch purist, keep your mouth shut in the shower and don't brush your teeth with tap water or rinse your toothbrush under the faucet. To purify your own water, bring it to a rolling boil for five minutes or filter it with a portable water filter (available at camping good stores) and treat it with **iodine tablets.** An easy alternative to make-your-own clean water is buying bottled mineral water, which is sold almost everywhere in India. Beware of unsealed bottles—these have probably been refilled with tap water. **Carbonated drinks** ("cold drinks") are also safe as long as they are fizzy. **Coffee** and *chai*, which are boiled in preparation, are usually safe. As tasty as they may be, avoid *lassis* or *nimbu pani* (lemonade) except in the ritziest restaurants; these are often made with ice water. Insist on drinks without ice, even if that means desert temperatures can only be combatted with lukewarm Limca. Keep in mind that water safety is also seasonal, and that it's riskier to drink the water during the **monsoon,** when all the year's crud seeps into the water supply.

Any food that is cooked immediately before it is served is probably safe. Street vendors and juice stands are rarely sanitary, and their equipment is open to disease-carrying flies, palate pleasing as *pani puri* might be. If possible, eat in restaurants that serve local food and are popular with locals. Touristy restaurants that serve shoddy imitations of Western food are often less clean than *dhabas* that dish out *dahl bhat* to truckers all day. Everything will be much easier if you eat at regular times and eat the same sort of foods regularly every day.

The biggest risk to travelers usually comes from **fruit, vegetables,** and **dairy products.** With fruit, if you can peel it, you can eat it. Beware of watermelon, which is sometimes injected with impure water. Stick to pasteurized dairy products. Other than that, the spiciness of the food and the variation in ingredients can also put a strain on your stomach. Adjust to the food slowly. Have high-energy, non-sugary foods with you to keep your strength up; you'll need plenty of protein and carbohydrates. **Wash your hands before you eat;** bring a few packs of handi-wipes or a quick-drying purifying liquid hand cleaner since sinks and soap may not always be available. Your bowels will thank you.

Traveler's diarrhea: Results from drinking untreated water or eating uncooked foods; a temporary (and common) reaction to the bacteria in new food ingredients. Symptoms include nausea, bloating, urgency, and malaise. Try quick-energy, non-sugary foods with protein and carbohydrates to keep your strength up. Over-the-counter anti-diarrheals (e.g. Immodium) may counteract the problems but can complicate serious infections. **The most dangerous side effect is dehydration;** drink 8oz. of water with ½ tsp. of sugar or honey and a pinch of salt, try uncaffeinated soft drinks, and munch on salted crackers. If you develop a fever or your symptoms don't go away after 4-5 days, consult a doctor. Speak to a doctor for treatment of diarrhea in children and pregnant women.

Dysentery: Results from a serious intestinal infection caused by malevolent bacteria. The most common type is bacillary dysentery, also called shigellosis. Symptoms include bloody diarrhea (sometimes mixed with mucus), fever, and abdominal pain and tenderness. Bacillary dysentery generally only lasts a week, but it is highly contagious. Amoebic dysentery, which develops more slowly, is a more serious disease and can cause long-term damage if left untreated. A stool test can determine which kind you have; seek medical help immediately. Dysentery can be treated with the drugs norfloxacin or ciprofloxacin (commonly known as Cipro). If you are traveling in rural areas, consider obtaining a prescription before you leave home.

Cholera: An intestinal disease caused by bacteria that lurk in contaminated food. Symptoms include diarrhea, dehydration, vomiting, and muscle cramps. See a doctor immediately; if left untreated, it can be deadly. Antibiotics are available, but the most important treatment is rehydration. Though the CDC does not necessarily recommend cholera vaccination, you might want to consider getting a (50% effective) vaccine if you have stomach problems or will be traveling where the water is not reliable.

Hepatitis A: A viral infection of the liver acquired primarily through contaminated water. Symptoms include fatigue, fever, loss of appetite, nausea, dark urine, jaundice, vomiting, aches and pains, and light stools. The risk is highest in rural areas and the countryside, but it is also present in urban areas. Ask your doctor about the vaccine (Havrix or Vaqta) or an injection of immune globulin (IG; formerly called gamma globulin).

Parasites: Microbes, tapeworms, etc. that hide in unsafe water and food. **Giardiasis,** for example, is acquired by drinking untreated water from streams or lakes all over the world. Symptoms include swollen glands or lymph nodes, fever, rashes or itchiness, digestive problems, eye problems, and anemia. Boil water, wear shoes (always a good plan), avoid bugs, and eat only cooked food.

Schistosomiasis: Also known as bilharzia; a parasitic disease caused when the larvae of flatworm penetrate unbroken skin. Symptoms include an itchy localized rash, followed in 4-6 weeks by fever, fatigue, painful urination, diarrhea, loss of appetite, night sweats, and a hive-like rash on the body. If exposed to untreated water, rub the area vigorously with a towel and apply rubbing alcohol. Schistosomiasis can be treated with prescription drugs. In general, swimming in fresh water should be avoided.

Typhoid fever: Caused by the salmonella bacteria, typhoid is common in villages and rural areas. While mostly transmitted through contaminated food and water, it may also be acquired by direct contact with others. Early symptoms include fever, headaches, fatigue, loss of appetite, constipation, and sometimes a rash on the abdomen or chest. Antibiotics can treat typhoid, but a vaccination (70-90% effective) is recommended.

OTHER INFECTIOUS DISEASES

Hepatitis B: A viral infection of the liver transmitted via bodily fluids or needle-sharing. Symptoms may not surface until years after infection. Vaccinations are recommended for health-care workers, sexually active travelers, and anyone planning to seek medical treatment abroad. The 3-shot vaccination series must begin 6 months before traveling.

Hepatitis C: Like Hepatitis B, but with a different mode of transmission. IV drug users, those with occupational exposure to blood, hemodialysis patients, and recipients of blood transfusions are at the highest risk, but the disease can also be spread through sexual contact or sharing items such as razors and toothbrushes.

Rabies: Transmitted through the saliva of infected animals; fatal if untreated. By the time symptoms appear (thirst and muscle spasms), the disease is in its terminal stage. If you are bitten, wash the wound thoroughly, seek immediate medical care, and try to have the animal hunted down and shot. A rabies vaccine, which consists of 3 shots given over a 21-day period, is available but does not prevent rabies; it merely reduces the number of shots that are administered after a rabies infection.

AIDS, HIV, STDS

Acquired Immune Deficiency Syndrome (AIDS) is a growing problem around the world. Because of an active prostitution industry, a widespread drug subculture, and a general lack of sex education, HIV and AIDS are proliferating at a frightening rate in India and Nepal. The World Health Organization estimates that there are over four million people living with HIV/AIDS in India and over 25,000 in Nepal. If you need an injection, make sure the needle has been sterilized; to be extra safe, carry your own **syringes** with you and insist that they be used. Bring a letter from your doctor stating that the syringes are for medicinal purposes. If you get a shave from a barber, make sure he uses a new blade. The most common mode of transmission is sexual intercourse. Health professions recommend the use of latex condoms though they are by no means 100% effective. For detailed information on HIV/AIDS in India and Nepal, call the **US Centers for Disease Control's** 24-hour hotline at ☎(800) 342-2437, or contact the **Joint United Nations Programme on HIV/AIDS (UNAIDS)**, 20 av. Appia 20, CH-1211 Geneva 27, Switzerland (☎+41 (22) 791 36 66; fax 791 41 87; www.unaids.org). Council's brochure, *Travel Safe: AIDS and International Travel,* is available at all Council Travel offices and on their website (www.ciee.org/Isp/safety/travelsafe.htm). The Indian government screens for HIV all incoming travelers over 18 years of age with a visa valid for one year or more. Contact the nearest consulate of India or Nepal for up-to-date information.

Sexually transmitted diseases (STDs, not to be confused with STD phone booths), such as gonorrhea, chlamydia, genital warts, syphilis, and herpes, are easier to catch than HIV and can be just as deadly. **Hepatitis B** and **C** are also serious STDs (see **Other Infectious Diseases,** p. 25). Though condoms may protect you from some STDs, oral or even tactile contact can lead to transmission. Warning signs include swelling, sores, bumps, or blisters on sex organs, the rectum, or the mouth; burning and pain during urination and bowel movements; itching around sex organs; swelling or redness of the throat; and flu-like symptoms. If these symptoms develop, see a doctor immediately.

WOMEN'S HEALTH

Women traveling in unsanitary conditions are vulnerable to **urinary tract** and **bladder infections,** common and very uncomfortable bacterial conditions that cause a burning sensation and painful (sometimes frequent) urination. To try to avoid these infections, drink plenty of vitamin-C-rich juice and clean water, and urinate frequently, especially right after intercourse. Untreated, these infections can lead to kidney infections, sterility, and even death. If symptoms persist, see a doctor.

Vaginal yeast infections may flare up in hot and humid climates. Wearing loose-fitting trousers or a skirt and cotton underwear will help, as will over-the-counter remedies like Monostat or Gynelotrimin. Bring supplies from home if you are prone to infection, as they will be difficult to find on the road. In a pinch, some travelers use a natural alternative such as a plain yogurt and lemon juice douche. Since **tampons, pads,** and reliable **contraceptive devices** are sometimes hard to find when traveling and your preferred brand will rarely be available, you should consider bringing supplies with you.

INSURANCE

Travel insurance generally covers four basic areas: health, property loss, trip cancellation/interruption, and emergency evacuation. Although your regular insurance policies may extend to travel-related accidents, you might consider purchasing travel insurance if the cost of potential trip cancellation/interruption or emergency medical evacuation is greater than you can absorb. **Medical insurance** often covers costs incurred abroad; check with your provider. **Medicare does not cover foreign travel.** Canadians are protected by their home province's health insurance plan for up to 90 days after leaving the country; check with the provincial Ministry of Health or Health Plan Headquarters for details. **Homeowners' insurance** (or your family's coverage) often covers theft during travel and loss of travel documents (passport, plane ticket, railpass, etc.) up to US$500. **ISIC** provides basic insurance benefits, including US$100 per day of in-hospital sickness, US$3000 of accident-related medical reimbursement, and US$25,000 for emergency medical transport (see **Identification,** p. 11). Cardholders have access to a toll-free 24-hour helpline for medical, legal, and financial emergencies overseas (US and Canada ☎(800) 626-2427, elsewhere call US collect +1 (713) 267-2525). **American Express** (US ☎(800) 528-4800) grants most card-holders automatic car rental insurance (collision and theft, but not liability).

INSURANCE PROVIDERS. Council and **STA** (see p. 41) offer a range of plans that can supplement your basic coverage. Other private insurance providers in the **US and Canada** include: **Access America** (☎(800) 284-8300); **Berkely Group/Carefree Travel Insurance** (☎(800) 323-3149; www.berkely.com); **Globalcare Travel Insurance** (☎(800) 821-2488; www.globalcare-cocco.com); and **Travel Assistance International** (☎(800) 821-2828; www.worldwide-assistance.com). Providers in the **UK** include **Campus Travel** (☎(01865) 258 000) and **Columbus Travel Insurance** (☎(020) 7375 0011).

PACKING

One of Indian Railways' sternly comic admonitions sums it up: **Less Luggage, More Comfort.** As a general rule, pack only what you absolutely need, then take half of the clothes and twice the money. The less you have, the less you have to lose (or store or carry on your back).

CLOTHING. Bring lightweight clothing that you can wear in layers; avoid jeans in favor of cotton and linen pants. Women should leave the miniskirts and tank tops at home. It is considered disrespectful for women and juvenile for men to wear shorts. Even if you're in the middle of a trek, shorts are still a bad idea—you'll make yourself more vulnerable to insects and leeches. Comfortable walking shoes are essential. For heavy-duty trekking, a pair of study lace-up **hiking boots** will help out. A double pair of socks—light polypropylene inside and thick wool outside—will cushion feet and keep them dry. **Rain gear** is essential in cooler climates. A good rain jacket and backpack cover will take care of you and your stuff at a moment's notice, which is often all you'll get. If you plan to **trek,** see p. 30.

LUGGAGE. If you plan to cover most of your itinerary by foot, a sturdy **frame back-pack** is unbeatable. For the basics on buying a pack, see p. 33. Toting a **suitcase** (with wheels) is fine if you plan to stay in one or two cities and explore from there, but a bad idea if you're going to be moving around a lot. In addition to your main piece of luggage, a **daypack** (a small backpack or courier bag) is a must. **Avoid the oh-so-popular "fanny pack" (a.k.a. bum bag):** it's an invitation to thieves, even when worn in front. It also screams "I'm an inexperienced tourist, please rip me off."

TOILETRIES. Deodorant, tampons, razors, and contraceptives are difficult to find, especially in rural areas (see **AIDS, HIV, and STDs,** p. 25). Most other cosmetics are available in pharmacies and shops. Keep in mind that fragrant deodorants, shampoos, and soaps attract insects and other unwelcome creepy crawlies. Bring a small supply of **toilet paper,** enough for the day or two it takes you to find one of the many pharmacies that sell it (most Indians and Nepalis don't use toilet paper; they simply rinse with water and their left hands). Be sure to take along more than enough of any prescription drugs that you might need. **Contact lens** supplies are difficult to find; bring enough saline and cleaner for your entire trip.

SLEEPSACK. Most hotels in India and Nepal provide sheets and pillows, but it is still a good idea to bring along a sleepsack. To make your own fold a full-size sheet in half lengthwise, and then sew it closed. See your mother for further details.

FIRST-AID KIT. For a basic first-aid kit, pack bandages, aspirin or other painkiller, antibiotic cream, a thermometer, a Swiss Army knife, tweezers, moleskin, decongestant, motion-sickness remedy, diarrhea or upset-stomach medication (Pepto Bismol or Immodium), an antihistamine, sunscreen, insect repellent, burn ointment, and a syringe for emergencies (get an explanatory letter from your doctor).

WASHING CLOTHES. Many hotels in India and Nepal provide laundry service for their guests for a small, per-item fee (or can direct you to a local *dhobi,* or "launderer"). If you decide to use the sink, bring a small **bar or tube of detergent soap,** a small **rubber ball** to stop up the sink, and a **travel clothesline.**

CURRENCY ADAPTORS. In India, electricity is 220 volts AC, enough to fry any 110V North American appliance. 220V electrical appliances don't like 110V current, either. Visit a hardware store for an adapter (which changes the shape of the plug) and a converter (which changes the voltage; US$20). Don't make the mistake of using only an adapter (unless appliance instructions state otherwise). Don't count on electricity to be regular or dependable, especially in rural areas.

FILM. Photo film in India and Nepal generally costs $3-4 for a roll of 24 color exposures, and the quality is usually pretty good. Developing can cost under $1, but you might not be thrilled with the results. If you are not a serious photographer, you might want to bring a **disposable camera** or two rather than an expensive permanent one. Always pack camera and film in your carry-on luggage, since higher intensity X-rays are used on checked luggage.

OTHER USEFUL ITEMS. You should always know where your towel is. Carry your own sheets for very cheap hotels and overnight train rides. Also bring a strong **padlock** (some hotels don't have locks on room doors, and it's a good idea to lock your backpack to something on the train if you're planning on sleeping). Other useful items include: sealable plastic bags (for damp clothes, soap, food, shampoo, and other spillables), an alarm clock, waterproof matches, sun hat, needle and thread, safety pins, sunglasses, compass, flashlight, soap, earplugs (oh yes), electrical tape (for patching tears in your pack, etc.), and garbage bags.

ACCOMMODATIONS

Cheap accommodations in India and Nepal are everywhere. You can easily stay here without spending more than US$2-3 per night, as long as you don't mind life without air-conditioning. Even up-market hotels are much cheaper than at home. **Prices fluctuate wildly according to season, and seasons fluctuate wildly according to destination.** Most foreign tourists come to India during the winter months (Nov.-Feb.), so places that draw mostly foreigners have "high season" and correspondingly high prices during these months. Indian tourists head for the hills during the sweltering pre-monsoon months (May-July), causing rates to head higher too. The prices listed in this book represent our best research efforts, but often we cannot predict the frequent ups and downs of Indian and Nepali hotel prices.

BUDGET HOTELS

The main travel centers nurture **tourist districts** of shabby hotels made of bare-bones concrete cells with hard beds and a ceiling fan on overdrive. Managers are usually happy to provide any service rupees can buy. Where tourist districts have developed and most of the clientele is foreign, competition has made hotels much cheaper, cleaner, and comfortable. It is rarely necessary to make **reservations,** except at major peak times (such as festivals). However, it can be difficult to find a place to stay in big cities that see few foreign tourists—the hotels might be full of businessmen or they might lack the paperwork to accept foreigners. Budget hotels frequently have **restaurants** attached and sometimes Star TV and air-conditioning. Another attractive feature is **room service,** which usually costs no more than food in the restaurant. If you are a lazy **launderer,** you can surrender your clothes to the local *dhobi* (most hotels have their own and store-front laundries are pervasive).

One thing to look out for when choosing a hotel is the **check-out time**—many cheap hotels have a 24-hour rule, which means if you arrive in the morning after an overnight train you'll be expected to leave as early when you check out. Don't let touts or rickshaw-*wallahs* make your lodging plans. These shady characters often cart tourists off to whichever hotel offers the biggest **commission.** For more information, see **Touts, Middlemen, and Scams,** p. 15.

Many budget travelers prefer to bring their own **padlock** for budget hotels, since the locally made padlocks they provide are often suspect. You should also carry sheets, towels, soap, and **toilet paper.** Many places have **hot water** only at certain hours of the day or only in buckets. Since the power supply is erratic everywhere in India, **generators** provide a very noisy solution. **Air-cooling,** a system by which air is blown by a fan over the surface of water, is common.

Some hotels have built reputations as places for foreign travelers to hang out and share stories. Some such places have even instituted discriminatory **no-Indians policies** in order to create sanitized, foreigners-only environments for their clients.

Nepal's budget scene is the result of a very recent boom, and foreigners are its main targets. Major tourist districts, unlike anything in India, have grown up in Pokhara and Kathmandu, where fierce competition has led to rock-bottom prices and generally better hotels than in India.

HOSTELS

Youth hostels are scattered throughout India, especially in the far north and south. They are extremely cheap and popular with foreign visitors. **YMCAs** and **YWCAs** are only found in the big cities and are usually quite expensive, although the women-only policy of YWCAs makes them a safe option for women traveling alone. Hostels in India rarely exclude nonmembers or charge them extra. **Hostels in Nepal are nonexistent.** In India, the state tourism development corporations have set up large **tourist bungalows** in both popular and less-touristed areas. Combining hotel with tourist office, these places are convenient, but the slight improvement over budget hotels is seldom worth the price.

UPSCALE HOTELS

Nicer hotels offer an escape from the sometimes harsh realities of Indian and Nepalese life; sometimes such an escape is necessary to maintain your sanity. Pricier accommodations are available almost anywhere in India, offering such luxuries as air-conditioning, 24-hour hot water, and TVs. The rates will seem exorbitant when compared to those of budget hotels, but you can always wriggle out of the guilt by comparing their prices to what you'd pay at home. Many mid-range hotels are all show, however: upstairs from a spacious, carpeted lobby are rooms only marginally better than those in budget hotels. Across western and central India, many former **palaces of rajas and maharajas** have now been turned into middle-range hotels, offering travelers the decadence of a bygone era at an affordable price. Large, expensive hotels such as the Taj, Sheraton, and Oberoi chains and the ITDC's line of Ashoks are also present in the main cities and tourist centers. In Nepal, more expensive hotels are only available in Kathmandu and Pokhara. Even if a night's stay is beyond your budget, the bookstores, restaurants, and pools at these places are still great resources. Larger hotels require payment in **foreign currency;** this rule extends even farther down the price scale in Nepal.

RELIGIOUS REST HOUSES

Traditional rest houses for Hindu pilgrims known as *dharamsalas* are sometimes open to foreign guests, providing spartan accommodations free of charge, although you will be expected to give a donation. Sikh *gurudwaras* also have a tradition of hospitality. Be on your best behavior if you stay in these religious places. They are not hotels; many have curfews or other restrictions. Smoking and drinking are usually not allowed.

HOMESTAYS

Homestays with Indian families provide the paying guest with the opportunity to experience the people, country, and traditions first-hand, and the Government of India's Tourist Department is aggressively promoting the concept. The **Paying Guest Scheme** is a relatively new phenomenon in India, but it is gaining momentum in a number of states, particularly Tamil Nadu and Rajasthan. Government of India Tourist Offices publish a list of host families and information about the rooms, facilities, and meals provided. Homestays are more expensive than budget hotels, but cheaper than starred hotels. They are rare in Nepal.

TREKKING

The siren call of South Asia's mountains is being answered by ever more people. In 1986, about 25,000 people went trekking in Nepal's Annapurna region—that figure has now doubled. Serious mountaineers spend serious amounts of money here, but there are plenty of opportunities for less dedicated mountaineers to experience the mountains and life on the trail in a more low-key, low-cost, and low-impact way. Trekking is big business in Nepal and India, and mountain tourism provides jobs to guides, porters, cooks, village lodgers, and shop owners.

Trekking is neither mountaineering nor backpacking. It is simply a journey on foot through the hills that can take a day, a week, a month, or if it suits you, a lifetime. You might be walking from village to village along ancient highways or striking off into more remote areas where accommodation is sparse and a tent the only place to sleep. However you do it, you'll be living off the land, eating local food and meeting local people. Typically, a "day" involves five to six hours on the trail with frequent stops for tea and photo-taking. Most treks go through heavily populated country, but some venture over high passes and along trails previously used only by herders on their way to high-altitude pastures. Keep in mind that the Himalayas are the tallest mountains in the world, and even the foothills involve plenty of tough walking. At the end of the day, while you are putting bandages on your blisters, admire the magnificent views. A few aching muscles are a small price to pay.

WHEN TO GO

The post-monsoon reprieve (Oct.-Nov.) is the most popular season for trekking in **Nepal** (see p. 800), and the more popular routes become very crowded. March to May is Nepal's secondary trekking season when crowds thin out a little. In India, the two main trekking seasons are pre-monsoon (May-June) and post-monsoon (Sept.-Nov.) in the hill regions of **Kangra, Kullu** (see p. 230), **Shimla** (see p. 211), and **Garhwal** and **Kumaon** (see p. 124). The areas of **Upper Kinnaur** (see p. 237), **Lahaul** (see p. 244), **Spiti** (see p. 238), and **Ladakh** (see p. 247) are in the rainshadow and get none of the monsoon rains. From December to February, it is too cold for trekking at high altitudes. The temperatures rise in March and April, making trekking more feasible. The air is usually dusty and dry, but rhododendrons, magnolias, and orchids are pretty impressive compensation. In May—the hottest and least predictable of months—the monsoon is just around the corner and most trekking activities taper off, as trekkers retreat to higher regions. Few trekkers choose to endure the cloud-bound, slippery, and leech-beleaguered trail conditions of the monsoon. For the persistent and enterprising, however, trekking during the summer season has at least one benefit—the virtual absence of foreign tourists.

PLANNING A TREK

There are two ways of organizing a trek in the Himalayas. Trekking independently saves money and allows you to set the pace, choose companions, and plan rest days and side trips of personal interest. There is a downside to such freedom, however. Arranging your own trek also entails obtaining your own permits, renting equipment, buying supplies, and hiring porters and guides. If you are not blessed with the virtue of patience and the asset of time, a trekking agency can take care of the preparations for you, and their expertise might make it possible to trek through more remote backcountry. The ease and comfort come, of course, with a price tag. For more info on planning a trek in Nepal, see **Trekking in Nepal,** p. 800.

TREKKING PERMITS AND OTHER FEES

Permits are no longer required for the Everest, Langtang, and Annapurna trekking areas in Nepal. Permits for other areas can be obtained at immigration offices in Kathmandu. You can normally complete the process in one day, though long lines at the height of the season can extend the process to two or even three days. **Your permit will be checked regularly (and stamped) at police check-posts.** If your trek enters a national park, you will have to pay a fee (for more information see **Kathmandu, Practical Information: Immigration Office,** p. 735). Except in **North Sikkim** (see p. 677), trekking permits are not required in India—regular area permits give access to all trekking areas as well. Camping is not allowed in national parks.

PRACTICAL INFORMATION

NEPAL. Villages along Nepal's most popular routes have outdone themselves to accommodate passing foreigners, and they are lined with tea houses, small lodges offering food and a place to sleep. In Nepal, English signs advertise **lodging** and **food** at bargain prices (usually under NRs20), and often an English-speaking manager will greet the guests. Increasingly, private rooms are becoming available along the most popular routes in Nepal but dormitory-style accommodations still predominate in the backcountry and at high elevations. The tea house social scene can be a lively experience, and the tea houses are full of potential trekking companions—if you're looking for a good night's sleep, bring along your ear plugs.

INDIA. Trekking in India requires far more self-sufficiency than trekking in Nepal. India has nothing equivalent to Nepal's tea houses; in some areas, there might be an occasional rest house or two, but these are often out of the way, and food supplies are unreliable. Tents are essential for shelter, and the stock of supplies and equipment you will need to carry is much greater. Because of the heavier load, porters are needed more often than in Nepal—backpacks become a weighty burden on treks longer than a few days. Population tends to be a lot thinner in the Indian Himalayas than in Nepal, and trekkers often see no one for days at a time. It is important to go with someone who knows the trails.

PORTERS AND GUIDES

One variation on trekking alone is to hire your own porters and guides. You will have a knowledgeable local with you, you won't have to carry as much, and you will support the local economy. **Porters** carry most of your gear, allowing you the comfort of walking with just a small pack containing the items you will need during the day. Of course, you will have to make sure that your porter understands what you want him to do and where you want to go. There is always a small chance that your porter will disappear, leaving you with just a pair of sunglasses and a pack of playing cards. Choose your porter carefully; the expense entailed in hiring a porter through a recognized trekking agency is a sound investment.

   Guides, who usually speak English, are not necessary on the better-known routes, where it is easy to find your way. Having someone who knows English might prove helpful in negotiations and pre-trek planning, however. A guide can color your experience with his knowledge, and often, guides will take trekkers on unusual side trips to visit friends and family. Guides are generally reluctant to carry anything (that's what porters are for).

   Although the trekking service industry in the Indian Himalayas is not as developed as the one in Nepal, you can arrange your own equipment, food, and staff at most hill stations or trailheads. In general, porters and guides are easy to find, but you will want to investigate their honesty and experience. You can be almost certain to get reputable workers through a guest house or trekking agency. Ask to see letters of recommendation from previous trekkers. Guides and porters hired through companies are slightly more expensive but are usually more reliable and better qualified. In the unlikely event that your guide or porter disappears, you will at least have a company to hold responsible once you manage to find your way back down the hillside—an insurance that is worth a few extra

rupees per day. If you do hire your own guides and porters, make sure you know exactly what services are covered, where you will go, and what supplies you will need to provide along the way. Most agreements stipulate that guides and porters pay for their own food and housing. As a responsible employer, you should make sure that porters and guides are adequately clothed when trekking at high altitudes by outfitting them with good shoes, a parka, sunglasses, mittens, and a sleeping bag. Establish beforehand if you expect them to return anything. The standard salary for a porter carrying 20 kilos is about US$10 per day in Nepal, US$5 per day in India; the salary for guides is higher (US$12-20 per day in India). In addition to these fees, you are expected to tip your staff generously at the end of a trek.

ORGANIZED TREKKING

Many people do not want to spend precious vacation time planning their trek, buying equipment, and hiring porters and guides. You can book treks through a large, international adventure travel company in your home country, in which case everything is arranged before you even leave for the airport. If you wait until you arrive, you can book through a local trekking agency, which usually requires one week's notice. The agent makes reservations for hotels and transportation and provides a complete staff—guide, porters, and cooks—for the trek. You will have to commit to the prearranged itinerary, and you might also be trekking with smelly people you have never met before. Organized treks often veer off from the crowded routes into more remote areas. The group carries its own food, prepared by cooks skilled in the art of kerosene cuisine. The comforts of trekking through an agency can also include tables, chairs, dining tents, and toilet tents. All this comfort and convenience usually costs US$15 to US$150 (usually US$40-50) per person per day. Just keep in mind that almost none of this money reaches people in the trekking region; instead it pads the wallet of the middleman in the city.

PACKING AND EQUIPMENT

What you carry with you on your trek will depend greatly on where you go, the style of trekking you choose, and, if you have arranged a trek through an agency, what they provide. For the most part, outfitting yourself for a trek is significantly easier in Nepal than in India. Nepalese tea houses relieve you of the need to carry food, cooking supplies, and tents—unless you're going to high altitudes beyond the reach of tea house culture. With all its trekking stores, you could show up naked in Kathmandu and be equipped for the most arduous trek within hours, but in India it might be necessary to bring your own gear. For more information on packing see p. 27. A quick checklist of items to carry along on a trek:

CLOTHING	EQUIPMENT
boots or running shoes	sleeping bag
camp shoes or thongs	water bottle
lots of socks (polypropylene and wool)	flashlight, batteries
down jacket	insulated mat, if camping
woolen shirt	backpack and daypack
shorts/skirt	toilet paper and hand trowel
long trousers	lighter
rainwear and umbrella	sunblock and lip balm
cotton T-shirts or blouses	towel
thermal underwear	water purification system
gloves	sewing kit with safety pins
sun hat and wool hat	small knife
snow gaiters	first-aid kit (see p. 27)
snow goggles/sunglasses	zip-loc bags

IF YOU PLAN TO BUY...

Good camping equipment is both sturdy and light. Camping equipment is generally more expensive in Australia, New Zealand, and the UK than in North America.

Sleeping Bag: Sleeping bags are rated by season ("summer" means -1-5°C/30-40°F at night; "four-season" or "winter" often means below -10°C/0°F). Sleeping bags are made either of **down** (warmer and lighter, but more expensive, and miserable when wet) or of **synthetic** material (heavier, more durable, and warmer when wet). Prices range from US$80-210 for a summer synthetic to US$250-300 for a good down winter bag. **Sleeping bag pads** include foam pads (US$10-20), air mattresses (US$15-50), and self-inflating pads (US$45-80). Bring a **stuff sack** to store your bag and keep it dry.

Tent: The best tents are free-standing (with their own frames and suspension systems), set up quickly, and only require staking in high winds. Low-profile dome tents are the best all round. Good 2-person tents start at US$90, 4-person at US$300. Seal the seams of your tent with waterproofer, and make sure it has a rain fly. Other tent accessories include a **battery-operated lantern**, a **plastic groundcloth,** and a **nylon tarp.**

Backpack: Internal-frame packs mold better to your back, keep a lower center of gravity, and flex adequately to allow you to hike difficult trails. **External-frame packs** are more comfortable for long hikes over even terrain, as they keep weight higher and distribute it more evenly. Make sure your pack has a strong, padded hip-belt to transfer weight to your legs. Any serious backpacking requires a pack of at least 4000 cubic inches (16,000cc), plus 500 cubic inches for sleeping bags in internal-frame packs. Sturdy backpacks cost anywhere from US$125-420—this is one area where it doesn't pay to economize. Fill up your pack with something heavy and walk around the store with it to get a sense of how it distributes weight before buying it. Either buy a **waterproof backpack cover** or store all of your belongings in plastic bags inside your pack.

Boots: For low-altitude treks, running shoes are adequate. Boots are more comfortable in the long run over rough ground. Be sure to wear boots with good **ankle support.** They should fit snugly and comfortably over 1-2 pairs of woolen socks and thin liner socks. Break in boots over several weeks to spare yourself from debilitating blisters.

Other Necessities: Synthetic layers, like those made of polypropylene, and a **pile jacket** will keep you warm even when wet. A **"space blanket"** will help you to retain your body heat, and it doubles as a groundcloth (US$5-15). Plastic **water bottles** are virtually shatter-proof and almost never leak. Bring **water-purification tablets** for when you can't boil water. Although most campgrounds provide campfire sites, you might want to bring a small **metal grate** or **grill** of your own. For those places that don't allow fires or firewood-gathering, you'll need a **camp stove** and a **fuel bottle.** Don't forget to bring a **first-aid kit, penknife, insect repellent, calamine lotion,** and a **lighter.**

HEALTH AND SAFETY

Trekking is hard work, so don't overdo it. Go at a comfortable pace and take rest days whenever necessary. Make sure your water is safe; boiling is often impractical (and ineffective at high altitudes where water boils at a lower temperature). Some kind of chemical treatment is the best option. Either iodine solution or iodine-water purification tablets will do the job. Use Tang orange-juice powder or chewable vitamin C tablets to mask the flavor. Consider modifying your diet. If you're eating in local inns, go vegetarian and stick to fried food—a good dose of hot oil does wonders for even the most resilient of nasties, and given the rate at which calories burn as you toil uphill, the forbidden delights of the frying pan can be consumed guilt-free. The popular Nepalese trekking routes witness a lot of diarrhea and nausea-induced misery. For more information, see **Health,** p. 20.

Women should not trek alone. It is better to find a group, either on your own, through notice boards, or through a trekking agency. Some agencies now specialize in providing female porters and guides for women.

Knee and ankle strains are common trekking injuries. Knees in particular can become painfully inflamed. If you are susceptible to knee injuries, bind your knees with a cloth bandage as a preventive measure. Sprained ankles can keep you from walking for days. Good footwear with ankle support is the best prevention. A bad **blister** will ruin your trek. If you feel a "hot-spot" coming on, cover it with moleskin immediately. Keep your feet as dry as possible; take your boots and socks off at every rest stop, and change your socks regularly. Once you've got a blister, drain the fluid using a needle sterilized in a metal flame and then dress it.

Carry a first-aid kit for minor injuries (see **First-aid Kit,** p. 27). Cuts to the skin should be cleaned with water and covered with Betadine and a firm bandage. Clean and dress the wound daily. If the wound becomes infected, apply an antibiotic ointment. Although trekkers do not often need serious medical attention, trekking mishaps do happen. If urgent medical attention is needed, **emergency rescue** request messages can be sent by radio at police, army, national park, and other official offices. Helicopter rescue is very expensive (usually US$1000-2000). In Nepal, money must be deposited or guaranteed in Kathmandu before the helicopter will fly. For people on agency treks, the agency will advance the money. This process is a lot easier if you are registered with your national embassy.

ACUTE MOUNTAIN SICKNESS (AMS).
If you are trekking to altitudes above 3500m, you will probably experience mild symptoms of altitude sickness, which can worsen into Acute Mountain Sickness (AMS). AMS is the body's reaction to the low oxygen environments of high altitudes, and it can be fatal if left untreated. Since the rate of acclimatization is so variable and unpredictable, budget plenty of time for high-altitude portions of your trek. If you're trekking in Nepal, having a trekking permit valid for a week longer than you anticipate is a good idea.

Trekkers who fly directly to high altitudes are more likely to be affected by AMS than those who walk up gradually. AMS is highly unpredictable—some people have no problems acclimatizing, while others take a long time. Despite what you might have read, there are no prescriptions for avoiding AMS. The best advice is to **take it slowly** and to **sleep low, go high.** Once you're about 3000m, try to sleep no more than 300m higher than the previous night. If you have to cross a high pass, sleep at the bottom and make it a long day up and over. **Take in lots of fluids.** It's always sensible to be well hydrated, but the need for hydration is especially important at higher altitudes. Note that alcohol impedes acclimatization.

Watch for symptoms. Typically the first symptom is a mild headache, but there's a whole suite of other symptoms: dizziness, nausea, insomnia, racing heart, fatigue. If you experience any of these, do not sleep at higher altitudes. Don't ascend, and the symptoms will probably pass within 24 hours. If your condition continues to deteriorate, you **must** descend. Even a descent of just a few hundred meters can make all the difference. **Most AMS fatalities occur in groups,** since badly affected trekkers often don't want to hold up others in the group. Ensure that this does not happen by gaining altitude at a rate suited to the slowest acclimatizer. For more information on AMS and other trekking illnesses visit the **High Altitude Medicine Guide** website at www.high-altitude-medicine.com.

FROSTBITE AND HYPOTHERMIA.
Frostbite and hypothermia might seem a long way away when you're sweating in sunny valleys, but they're an ever-present danger at high altitudes. All too often people run into problems because they are determined to press on through bad conditions. If the weather turns against you, get to shelter as soon as you can, even if it means retracing your steps. For tips on preventing and combating these conditions see p. 23.

SUNBURN.
Ultraviolet light is stronger at higher altitudes, so it's necessary to protect against sunburn with sunblock and a hat. Sunburn can be particularly severe if you're on snow or ice, and because of the angle of reflected light, it can show up in the strangest places, like under your chin. You can never have too much sunblock. A good pair of sunglasses can protect you from **snow blindness,** a condition caused by the reflection of UV light off snow or ice.

LEECHES. Leeches are rampant during monsoon season. Trekkers often get them on their legs or in their boots. Carry salt with you in a small container for chemical attack on them. Carefully applying a lit cigarette is another effective way of removing them. Unlike ticks, they do not leave any part of themselves behind, so it is safe to pull them off; be careful to disinfect the bite afterwards. A leech bite isn't painful, and leeches do not transmit diseases. The effect is merely psychological.

RESPONSIBLE TREKKING

Trekking can enhance the local economy, but it can also degrade the environment. Cultivate a respectful relationship with the land you are trampling. The delicate ecological balance in the Himalayas is at risk as a result of overgrazing, pollution, and, most importantly, **deforestation.** Never cut vegetation or clear new campsites. Loss of vegetation is the beginning of an ecological spiral that leads to **erosion** and **landslides.** Whenever possible ask for kerosene or gas to be used for cooking and heating water; blazing campfire hearths are taboo where deforestation is a problem. Limit hot showers to those heated by electricity, solar energy, or back-boilers. Such industrious and innovative shower suppliers deserve encouragement.

Trekkers and their waste also contribute to litter, sanitation, and water pollution problems. The rule to follow is: **burn it, bury it, or carry it out.** Toilet paper is generally burned, biodegradables such as food wastes are buried, and non-disposables (plastics, aluminum foil, batteries, glass, cans, etc.) are packed up and carried to a suitable waste treatment site. All excrement should be buried in 40cm-deep holes in a spot far away from water sources, religious sites, village compounds, and crop fields. Use biodegradable soap and shampoo, and don't rinse directly in streams. If you can't leave the area clean, don't go. On organized treks, make sure that a person from your team is the last to leave camp; guided tour operators seldom do what they promise about garbage disposal. If you hear of a clean trek being organized, jump at the opportunity.

Trekkers can also have a profound effect on the people they encounter. If you're moved by the plight of the villagers you meet, make a donation at the end of your trip to a charity or aid program involved in education and health care.

FURTHER RESOURCES

Himalayan Rescue Association (HRA; ☎(01) 262746; email hra@aidpost.mos.com.np; www.nepalonline.net/hra), just off Jyatha, south of Thamel, in Kathmandu. A voluntary non-profit organization providing information for trekkers on where and how to trek, trekking hazards, altitude sickness, and how to protect the environment. They also have in-season clinics with volunteer Western doctors during the trekking season in Pheriche on the Everest trek and in Marang on the Annapurna Circuit. Open Su-F 10am-5pm.

Kathmandu Environmental Education Project (KEEP), P.O. Box 9178, Jyatha Thamel, Kathmandu (☎(01) 250070 or 250646; fax 411533; email tour@keep.wlink.com.np). Also off Jyatha, close to the HRA. A non-profit organization that promotes "soft trekking," which minimizes impact on the environment and culture. They offer free advice to trekkers and trekking staff. During the trekking season (Oct.-Dec. and Feb.-May) they have a free talk on eco-tourism at their office at 4pm every Friday. A good place to find trekking companies and a source of up-to-date information. Open Su-F 10am-5pm.

Annapurna Conservation Area Project (ACAP), c/o King Mahendra Trust, P.O. Box 3712, Kathmandu (☎(01) 526571; fax 526570), in the King Mahendra Trust Office, near Grindlay's bank in Jawalakhel or in the Natural History Museum on Pokhara's Prithvi Narayan campus. The most authoritative source of information on the Annapurna region of Nepal, ACAP promotes environmentally sound trekking. Open M-F 9am-5pm.

Nepal Mountaineering Association (NMA; ☎(01) 411525; fax 416278), just south of Nag Pokhari in Naxal, in Kathmandu. Issues permits for the Nepalese Himalayas.

Indian Mountaineering Foundation, 6 Benito Juarez Marg, New Delhi 110021 (☎(011) 4677935 or 4671211; fax 6883412; email indmount@del2vsnl.net.in; www.indmount.com). Information on treks above 6000m.

KEEPING IN TOUCH

MAIL

SENDING AND RECEIVING MAIL IN INDIA AND NEPAL

Airmail letters under 1 oz. take two to three weeks to get to India and Nepal. Envelopes should be marked "air mail" or "par avion" to avoid having letters sent by sea. There are several ways to get letters sent to you while you are abroad.

General Delivery: Mail can be sent to India and Nepal via **Poste Restante** to almost any city or town with a post office. Address *Poste Restante* letters to: Kate MCCARTHY, *Poste Restante*, GPO, Delhi, 110001, India. The mail will go to a special desk in the central post office. It is best to use the largest post office in the area. Mail will often be sent there regardless of what is written on the envelope. If the clerks insist that there is nothing for you, have them check under your first name as well. *Let's Go* lists post offices in the **Practical Information** section for each city and town.

American Express: AmEx's travel offices throughout the world will act as a mail service for cardholders if you contact them in advance. Under this free **Client Letter Service,** they will hold mail for up to 30 days and forward upon request. Some offices will offer these services to non-cardholders (especially those who have purchased AmEx Traveler's Checks), but call ahead to make sure. Let's Go lists AmEx locations for many large cities. A complete list is available for free (☎(800) 528-4800).

Other Options: Federal Express (US ☎(800) 247-4747; www.fedex.com) can get a letter from New York to New Delhi in 5 days for a whopping US$42. Rates among non-US locations are equally expensive; London to New Delhi, for example, costs £27.80 and up. By **US Express Mail,** a letter from New York should arrive within 4 days and cost US$21.50. **DHL** (US ☎(800) 225-5345; www.dhl.com) operates throughout South Asia; it costs about US$76 to India or Nepal. Delivery takes 3-5 business days. DHL packages sent from India or Kathmandu to the US cost US$30-40 and take 3 days.

SENDING MAIL HOME FROM INDIA AND NEPAL

Aerogrammes, printed sheets that fold into envelopes and travel via airmail, are available at post offices. Most post offices will refuse to send aerogrammes with enclosures. Allow *at least* two weeks for mail delivery from South Asia. Sending a **package** home will involve getting it cleared by customs, getting it wrapped in cloth and sealed in wax, going to the post office to fill out the customs forms, buying stamps, and finally, seeing it processed. It might take a couple of months or even a couple of years to get home by surface mail, and all packages run the risk of getting X-rayed or searched. If you need to receive a package from abroad, have it registered—this will reduce the chance that your goods will get stolen.

PLACING INTERNATIONAL CALLS. To call India or Nepal from home or to place an international call from India or Nepal dial:

1. The **international dialing prefix.** To dial out of **Australia,** dial 0011; **Canada** or the **US,** 011; the **Republic of Ireland, New Zealand,** the **UK,** 00; **South Africa,** 09; **India** or **Nepal,** 00.
2. The **country code** of the country you want to call. To call **Australia,** dial 61; **Canada** or the **US,** 1; the **Republic of Ireland,** 353; **New Zealand,** 64; **South Africa,** 27; the **UK,** 44; **India,** 91; **Nepal,** 977.
3. The **city** or **area code.** *Let's Go* lists phone codes opposite the city or town's name, alongside the following icon: ☎. If the first digit is a zero (e.g. 022 for Bombay), omit it when calling from abroad.
4. The **local number.**

TELEPHONES

Phones are almost everywhere in India and Nepal. The STD/ISD sign (Standard Trunk Dialing/International Subscriber Dialing) means that there's a phone nearby. Some STD/ISD booths are open 24 hours and offer fax services. Incoming calls are usually the cost of a local call, so it's a good idea to place your call and then have someone call you back. Discuss this with the booth operator before you try it; they may refuse to allow this since they don't make any money this way.

INDIA PHONE CODES		Jaipur	0141
Agra	0562	Khajuraho	07686
Ahmedabad	079	Leh	01982
Amritsar	0183	Madras (Chennai)	044
Bangalore	080	Manali	01902
Bhopal	0755	Patna	0612
Bhubaneswar	0674	Panjim (Panaji)	0832
Bombay (Mumbai)	022	Shimla	0177
Calcutta	033	Trivandrum	0471
Chandigarh	0172	Varanasi	0542
Delhi	011	NEPAL PHONE CODES	
Dharamsala	01892	Kathmandu	01
Guwahati	0361	Chitwan	056
Hyderabad	040	Pokhara	061

A **calling card** is another (often futile) alternative. Calls are billed either collect or to your account. Though calling cards work in the major tourist centers of India and Nepal, the STD/ISD booths in many smaller cities and villages do not have access to international operators. And even those cards that might potentially work are often disallowed by booth owners, who don't profit on these calls. **To obtain a calling card,** contact your national telecommunications service before you leave. International **collect calls** cannot be made from India or Nepal to some countries, and booth owners often won't let you try.

TIME ZONES. India is 5½ hours ahead of GMT, 4½ hours behind Australian Eastern Standard Time, and 10½ hours ahead of North American Eastern Standard Time. Summer puts the northern countries an hour closer to India. India is 15 minutes behind Nepal.

CALLING WITHIN INDIA AND NEPAL. To call within India or Nepal, dial the city code and then the number. Long-distance calls are either full price (M-Sa 8am-7pm); half-price (M-Sa 7-8am and 7-8:30pm, Su 7am-8:30pm); one-third price (daily 6-7am and 8:30-11pm); or one-quarter price (daily 11pm-6am).

EMAIL AND INTERNET

Hundreds of so-called **cybercafes** can be found all over India and Nepal, allowing Internet access from most major cities and quite a few small towns for a fixed hourly rate. The easiest way to send email from these places is via free, web-based email providers such as Hotmail (www.hotmail.com) or Yahoo (www.yahoo.com).

GETTING THERE

BY PLANE

When it comes to buying your airfare, a little effort can save you a bundle. If your plans are flexible enough to deal with the restrictions, courier fares are the cheapest. Tickets bought from consolidators and standby seating are also good deals, but last-minute specials, airfare wars, and charter flights often beat these fares. The key is to hunt around, to be flexible, and to ask persistently about discounts. Students, seniors, and anybody under 26 should never pay full price for a ticket.

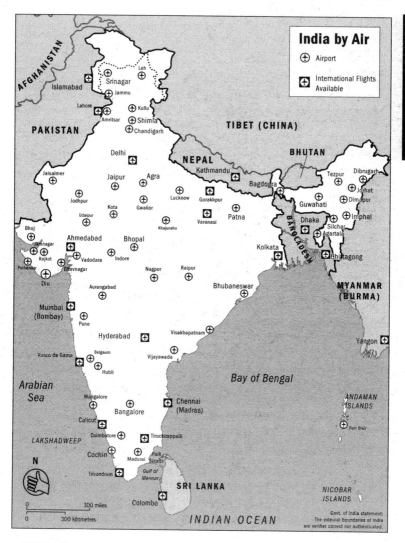

India by Air

⊕ Airport

⊞ International Flights Available

AFGHANISTAN

Islamabad

Srinagar
Leh
Jammu

Lahore
Amritsar
Kullu
Shimla
Chandigarh

PAKISTAN

TIBET (CHINA)

Delhi

NEPAL
Kathmandu

BHUTAN

Jaisalmer
Jaipur
Agra
Bagdogra
Tezpur
Dibrugarh
Jorhat

Jodhpur
Lucknow
Gorakhpur
Guwahati
Dimapur

Kota
Gwalior
Patna
Dhaka
Imphal

Udaipur
Khajuraho
Varanasi
Silchar
Agartala

Bhuj
Jamnagar
Ahmedabad
Bhopal
Kolkata
Chittagong

Rajkot
Vadodara
Indore

Porbandar
Bhavnagar
Nagpur
Raipur

Diu
Aurangabad
Bhubaneswar

MYANMAR (BURMA)

Mumbai (Bombay)
Pune

Hyderabad
Visakhapatnam

Yangon

Vasco da Gama
Belgaum
Vijayawada

Arabian Sea

Hubli

Bay of Bengal

ANDAMAN ISLANDS

Mangalore
Chennai (Madras)

Calicut
Bangalore

Port Blair

LAKSHADWEEP

Coimbatore
Tiruchirappalli

N

Cochin
Madurai
Palk Straits

Trivandrum
Gulf of Mannar

SRI LANKA

NICOBAR ISLANDS

0   300 miles
0   300 kilometers

Colombo

INDIAN OCEAN

Govt. of India statement:
The external boundaries of India
are neither correct nor authenticated.

DETAILS AND TIPS

Timing: Airfares to India and Nepal peak between mid-June and early Sept. Holidays are also expensive times to travel. Midweek (M-Th morning) round-trip flights are US$40-50 cheaper than weekend flights. Return-date flexibility is usually not an option for the budget traveler; traveling with an "open return" ticket costs more than fixing a return date when buying the ticket and paying later to change it.

Route: Round-trip flights are by far the cheapest; "open-jaw" (arriving in and departing from different cities) and round-the-world flights are pricier but reasonable alternatives. Flights between capital cities or hubs offer the most competitive fares.

Boarding: When flying internationally, pick up tickets for international flights well in advance of the departure date, and **confirm by phone within 72 hours of departure.** One carry-on item and two pieces of checked baggage is the norm for non-courier flights. Consult the airline for weight allowances.

ESSENTIALS

Fares: From **North America** round-trip fares to India range from US$900-1200 during the low season to US$1200-1700 during the summer. Many US and European carriers offer free stopovers in Europe. Flights from **London** to Delhi or Bombay run between UK£450-750 in the low season and UK£500-900 in the high season. Flights to Kathmandu are slightly more expensive. Fares to Madras and other Indian cities cost UK£40-100 more. From **Australia** and **New Zealand** peak season fare (late Nov. to late Jan.) is between AUS$2000-3000 round-trip from the east coast of Australia to Delhi, Calcutta, or Kathmandu. Low-season fares are AUS$1500-2200. Flying from Perth is usually about AUS$150 cheaper than flying from the east coast. Many agents also offer free stopovers in either Bangkok or Singapore, depending on the airline, and most tickets are valid for 3 months. A one-year ticket is usually AUS$100 extra.

✈ **FLIGHT PLANNING ON THE INTERNET.** The Web is a great place to look for travel bargains—it's fast, it's convenient, and you can spend as long as you like exploring options without driving your travel agent insane.

Many airline sites offer special last-minute deals on the Web. Other sites compile the deals for you—try www.bestfares.com, www.onetravel.com, www.lowestfare.com, and www.travelzoo.com.

STA (www.sta-travel.com) and **Council** (www.counciltravel.com) provide quotes on student tickets, while **Expedia** (www.expedia.msn.com) and **Travelocity** (www.travelocity.com) offer full travel services. **Priceline** (www.priceline.com) allows you to specify a price, and obligates you to buy any ticket that meets or beats it; be prepared for odd routes. **Skyauction** (www.skyauction.com) allows you to bid on both last-minute and advance-purchase tickets.

Just one last note—to protect yourself, make sure that the site uses a secure server before handing over any credit card details. Happy hunting!

BUDGET AND STUDENT TRAVEL AGENCIES

A travel agent specializing in flights to India and Nepal can make your life easy and help you save, too, but agents may not spend the time to find you the lowest possible fare—they get paid on commission. Students and under-26ers holding **ISIC** and **IYTC cards** (see **Identification,** p. 11) qualify for big discounts from student travel agencies. Use **Microsoft Expedia** (expedia.msn.com) or **Travelocity** (www.travelocity.com) to get an idea of the lowest published fares, then use the resources outlined here to try and beat those fares.

Air Brokers International, San Francisco, CA (☎(800) 883-3273, www.airbrokers.com; sales@airbrokers.com) will fly you from the West Coast of the US to all over India, with free stops in Southeast Asia. They also offer Round the World tickets.

Cheap Tickets (☎(800) 377-1000; www.cheaptickets.com) flies to and from the US.

Council Travel (www.counciltravel.com). US offices include: Emory Village, 1561 N. Decatur Rd., **Atlanta,** GA 30307 (☎(404) 377-9997); 273 Newbury St., **Boston,** MA 02116 (☎(617) 266-1926); 1160 N. State St., **Chicago,** IL 60610 (☎(312) 951-0585); 931 Westwood Blvd., Westwood, **Los Angeles,** CA 90024 (☎(310) 208-3551); 254 Greene St., **New York,** NY 10003 (☎(212) 254-2525); 530 Bush St., **San Francisco,** CA 94108 (☎(415) 566-6222); 424 Broadway Ave E., **Seattle,** WA 98102 (☎(206) 329-4567); 3301 M St. NW, **Washington, D.C.** 20007 (☎(202) 337-6464). **For other US cities,** call ☎(800) 2-COUNCIL (226-8624). In the UK, 28A Poland St. (Oxford Circus), **London,** W1V 3DB (☎(020) 7437 7767).

CTS Travel, 44 Goodge St., **London** W1 (☎(020) 7636 0031; fax 7637 5328; email ctsinfo@ctstravel.com.uk).

Hariworld Travel (www.hariworld.com) has offices in: **Atlanta,** GA (☎(404) 233-5005; fax 233-5020); **Chicago,** IL (☎(312) 873-2700; fax 873-2701); **San Fransisco,** CA (☎(510) 795-5000; fax 795-6183); **New York,** NY (☎(212) 997-3300; fax 997-3320); **Toronto,** Canada (☎(416) 366-2000; fax 366-6020); and **New Delhi.**

STA Travel, 6560 Scottsdale Rd., #F100, Scottsdale, AZ 85253 (☎(800) 777-0112; fax (602) 922-0793; www.sta-travel.com). A student and youth travel organization with over 150 offices worldwide. Ticket booking, travel insurance, railpasses, and more. US offices include: 297 Newbury St., **Boston,** MA 02115 (☎(617) 266-6014); 429 S. Dearborn St., **Chicago,** IL 60605 (☎(312) 786-9050); 7202 Melrose Ave., **Los Angeles,** CA 90046 (☎(323) 934-8722); 10 Downing St., **New York,** NY 10014 (☎(212) 627-3111); 4341 University Way NE, **Seattle,** WA 98105 (☎(206) 633-5000); 2401 Pennsylvania Ave., Ste. G, **Washington, D.C.** 20037 (☎(202) 887-0912); 51 Grant Ave., **San Francisco,** CA 94108 (☎(415) 391-8407). In the UK, 11 Goodge St., **London** WIP 1FE. In New Zealand, 10 High St., **Auckland** (☎(09) 309 0458). In Australia, 366 Lygon St., **Melbourne** Vic 3053 (☎(03) 9349 4344).

Trailfinders (www.trailfinders.com) offers discounted tickets to all over India and to Kathmandu, with offices in **London** at 42-50 Earls Court Rd. (☎(020) 7938 3366); 194 Kensington High St. (☎(020) 7938 3939); and 215 Kensington High St. (☎(020)7937 5400). Also, locations at 58 Deansgate, **Manchester** (☎(0161) 839 6969); 22-24 Priory Queens Way, **Birmingham** (☎(0121) 236 1234); 48 Corn St., **Bristol** (☎(0117) 929 9000); and 254-284 Sauchiehall St., **Glasgow** (☎(0141) 353 2224). Trailfinders has an office in **Dublin** at 4/5 Dawson St., Dublin 2 (☎(01) 677 7888).

Travel CUTS (Canadian Universities Travel Services Limited), 187 College St., **Toronto,** ON M5T 1P7 (☎(416) 979-2406; fax 979-8167; www.travelcuts.com). 40 offices across Canada. Also in the UK, 295-A Regent St., **London** W1R 7YA (☎(020) 7255 1944).

usit world (www.usitworld.com). Over 50 **usit campus** branches in the UK (national call center ☎(0870) 240 1010; www.usitcampus.co.uk), including 52 Grosvenor Gardens, **London** SW1W 0AG; **Manchester** (☎(0161) 273 1721); and **Edinburgh** (☎(0131) 668 3303). Nearly 20 **usit now** offices in Ireland, including 19-21 Aston Quay, O'Connell Bridge, **Dublin** 2 (☎(01) 602 1600; www.usitnow.ie), and **Belfast** (☎(02890) 327 111; www.usitnow.com). Offices also in Athens, Auckland, Brussels, Frankfurt, Johannesburg, Lisbon, Luxembourg, Madrid, Paris, Sofia, and Warsaw.

ESSENTIAL

COMMERCIAL AIRLINES

The commercial airlines' lowest regular offer is the **APEX** (Advance Purchase Excursion) fare, which provides confirmed reservations and allows "open-jaw" tickets. Generally, reservations must be made seven to 21 days ahead of departure, with seven- to 14-day minimum-stay and up to 90-day maximum-stay restrictions. These fares carry hefty cancellation and change penalties (fees rise in summer). Book peak-season APEX fares early; by May you'll have a hard time getting your desired departure date. Though APEX fares are probably not the cheapest, they will give you a sense of the average commercial price. Specials advertised in newspapers may be cheaper but have more restrictions and fewer available seats. Most major US and European airlines (Delta, United, KLM, British Airways, Lufthansa) offer flights to India and Nepal. Other popular carriers include:

Aeroflot (NY office ☎(212) 332-1050; www.aeroflot.com), with connecting service through Moscow, is usually cheapest, but their service records are close to abysmal.

Air India (NY office ☎(212) 407-1300; www.airindia.com) has direct service from London and connecting service from New York and Chicago to Bombay.

Malaysia Airlines (☎(800) 552-9264; www.malaysia-airlines.com) offers connecting service to Delhi and Madras from New York and Los Angeles.

Royal Nepal Airlines (☎(01) 220757; fax 225348; London office ☎(020) 7757 2525; www.royalnepal.com). Regular flights to Kathmandu from London, Paris, and Frankfurt.

OTHER CHEAP ALTERNATIVES

AIR COURIER FLIGHTS. Couriers help transport cargo on international flights by guaranteeing delivery of the baggage claim slips from the company to a representative overseas. Generally, couriers must travel light (carry-ons only) and deal with complex flight restrictions. Most flights also operate only out of the biggest cities, like New York. Generally, you must be over 21 (in some cases 18), have a valid passport, and procure your own visa, if necessary. Groups such as the **Air Courier Association** (☎(800) 282-1202; www.aircourier.org) and the **International Association of Air Travel Couriers**, 220 South Dixie Hwy., P.O. Box 1349, Lake Worth, FL 33460 (☎(561) 582-8320; www.courier.org) provide their members with lists of opportunities and courier brokers worldwide for an annual fee.

TICKET CONSOLIDATORS. Ticket consolidators, or "bucket shops," buy unsold tickets in bulk from commercial airlines and sell them at discounted rates. In the US, the best place to look is in the Sunday travel section of the major newspapers, where many bucket shops place tiny ads. Call quickly, as availability is typically very limited. Not all bucket shops are reliable; insist on a receipt that gives full details of restrictions, refunds, and tickets, and pay by credit card. For more information, check the website **Consolidators FAQ** (www.travel-library.com/air-travel/consolidators.html).

SPECIALTY CONSOLIDATORS. A limited number of travel agencies deal in unconventional arrangements. **Round-the-World (RTW)** and **Circle Asia** tickets string together one-way flights. These tickets are best for extended trips; most have flexible dates, good up to one year from start of travel. For itineraries more complicated than a simple round-trip, RTW and other unconventional tickets are often a better deal. Try **High Adventure Travel** (☎(800) 350-0612; fax (415) 912-5606; travel@airtreks.com; www.airtreks.com) or **Ticket Planet** (☎(800) 799-8888; www.ticketplanet.com), and leave at least a month to book and confirm tickets.

BY BOAT

For those who have travel time to spare, **Ford's Travel Guides,** 19448 Londelius St., Northridge, CA 91324 (☎(818) 701-7414; 701-7415) lists **freighter companies** that will take passengers to and from points all over the world, including ports in India. Ask for their *Freighter Travel Guide and Waterways of the World* (US$15.95, plus $2.50 postage if mailed outside the US).

BORDER CROSSINGS

India-Nepal: There are six overland border crossings between India and Nepal: Mahendranagar, Dhangadi, Nepalganj, Sunauli (see p. 784), Raxaul/Birganj (see p. 642 and p. 793), and Kakarbhitta (see p. 797). Sunauli is a 3hr. bus ride from Gorakhpur in Uttar Pradesh; from there you can catch a 10hr. bus to Pokhara or a 11hr. bus to Kathmandu. Raxaul is a 6hr. bus ride from Patna in Bihar; from Birganj, across the border, it's a 10-12hr. bus ride to Kathmandu. The Kakarbhitta crossing, at the eastern end of Nepal, is easily accessible from Siliguri, which is a transit point for Darjeeling. It is not necessary to get a Nepalese visa before you arrive at the border, but you must get your Indian visa ahead of time if you're going from Nepal to India. Visitors are also allowed to drive across the border if they possess an international *carnet.*

India-Bangladesh: Trains and buses run from Calcutta to Bangaon in West Bengal. From there it is a rickshaw ride across the border to Benapol, Bangladesh, with connections via Khulna or Jessore to Dhaka. The northern border, from Jalpaiguri to Haldibari, is only periodically open and requires an exit permit.

India-Burma: No land frontier open.

India-Bhutan: If you are lucky enough to get a Bhutanese visa, you must cross the border at Puntsholing, a 3-4hr. bus ride from Siliguri in West Bengal. Make sure you also have a "transit permit" from the Indian Ministry of External Affairs.

India-China: No land frontier open.

India-Pakistan: Only one crossing is open along the entire length of the 2000km border. A daily train runs from Amritsar in the Indian Punjab through Attari, the border town, to Lahore, in the Pakistani Punjab. There is also direct bus service between Delhi and Lahore. For more information see **Pakistan Border,** p. 270.

India-Sri Lanka: The boat service from Rameswaram in Tamil Nadu to Talaimannar in Sri Lanka has been indefinitely suspended because of the war in northern Sri Lanka. Travelers must fly to Colombo, Sri Lanka.

Nepal-China: The Arniko Rajmarg (Kathmandu-Kodari Highway) links Kathmandu with the Tibet Autonomous Region of China via the exit point of Kodari. The border is open only to travelers on organized tours. Before crossing into Tibet, check in with your embassy in Kathmandu to make sure that the border situation is stable, as there have occasionally been difficulties for tourists crossing overland into Tibet.

GETTING AROUND

BY PLANE

India and Nepal both have extensive air networks. However, air travel is a lot more expensive than surface travel, and it will not always save you much time. Waiting in airport-office queues, traveling to and from airports (often far from town), and checking-in can all slow you down. Indian and Nepalese airports love to subject passengers to purgatorial delays. Fly only to escape unbearable cross-country bus or train rides. In Nepal, where the roads are so bad—and bus rides therefore dangerous and interminable—the balance might be shifted slightly in favor of air travel. Air travel is generally safe, even though the planes are usually hand-me-downs from European or East Asian airlines and flights are often bumpy.

IN INDIA. Though government-run **Indian Airlines** (http://indian-airlines.nic.in/) still maintains the largest flight network, several private companies are challenging its former monopoly. **Jet Airways** (www.jetairways.com) is the 2nd largest domestic airline and is considered to be a mark above Indian Airlines in terms of service and quality. **Reservations** are essential on almost all flights and must be made well in advance, especially during peak season (Nov.-Mar.), as flights are almost always full. Go to one of the airline offices or use a travel agent to make a booking. If you don't get a seat, put your name on the waiting list and show up at the airport early; miracles do happen. Guard your airline ticket well—if you lose it, airlines and travel agents will accept no responsibility. Check-in time for domestic flights is one hour before departure.

✈ **AIRCRAFT SAFETY.** The airlines of third-world nations do not always meet safety standards. The *Official Airline Guide* (www.oag.com) and many travel agencies can tell you the type and age of aircraft on a particular route. This can be especially useful in the subcontinent, where less reliable equipment is often used. The **International Airline Passengers Association** (US ☎(972) 404-9980, safety office open M-F 9-11am; UK ☎(020) 8681 6555; www.iapa.com) provides region-specific safety information. The Federal Aviation Administration (www.faa.gov) reviews airlines that enter the US. Travel advisories made by the **US State Department** (☎(202) 647-5225; http://travel.state.gov/travel_warnings.html) sometimes involve foreign carriers, especially when terrorist bombings may be a threat.

Indian Airlines and Jet Airways offer **youth fares** at a 25% discount off Economy Class fares (quoted in US dollars) for passengers aged 12 to 30. Children under 12 pay 50%, and infants under 2 pay 10%. Both airlines sell package deals for foreign tourists called **"Discover India"** (Indian Airlines) and **"India Pass"** (Jet Airways) that give 21 days of unlimited air travel for US$750-800, or 15 days for US$500-550. No destinations can be visited more than once, except the first and last points (this does not apply if a city is a transfer point), and itineraries must be structured in one continuous direction (i.e. no zig-zagging across the subcontinent). Only a limited number of seats on each flight are allotted to these programs.

IN NEPAL. Air travel is essential to Nepal's economy, providing access to the mountainous regions of the north where there are no roads. Travelers should opt for air travel to avoid long, hellish bus rides. Government-operated **Royal Nepal Airlines Corporation** (RNAC; www.catmando.com/com/rnachold/rnac) operates flights to 35 airports and airstrips in Nepal, though it is suffering financially, and its planes are constantly filled to capacity. Privatization has recently given birth to three new airlines: **Everest Air, Necon Air,** and **Nepal Airways.** All airlines' prices are the same, but the new private companies are generally thought to have better service. Foreigners must pay for flights with foreign currency. Domestic flight prices range from US$50-160. On the whole, air travel in Nepal is unpredictable. Bad weather prevents take-offs and landings, so long delays at the airport are the norm. During the high trekking season it might be difficult to get tickets for popular destinations. It is best to book through travel agents.

BY TRAIN

The Indian rail network, one of the few things Indians will readily thank the British for, is incredibly extensive. For budget travelers, rail is the way to go in India. Because of its mountains and freedom from colonization, Nepal has no trains, except for one that runs across the Indian border to Janakpur.

With over 1.6 million workers on its payroll, **Indian Railways** (IR; www.indianrailway.com) is the world's largest employer, and trains are generally the best way to cover long distances at a reasonable cost. Eleven million passengers are carried daily over its vast network, which covers over 62,000km. There is a unique culture on the Indian railways—you'll meet locals eager to chat about your country and theirs as landscapes rush outside the window and *chai-wallahs* offer cups of tea for a few rupees. Indian Railways might not get you there on time, but they will get you there, Indian style.

TYPES OF TRAINS. The two main kinds of trains are **express** (or mail) and **passenger.** The express trains, preferred by most travelers, vary in duration, though they are certainly faster and a little more expensive than the passenger trains, which travel at a sluggish speed of 27.2km per hour. The extra-special **"super-fast"** types—*Shatabdi Express, Rajdhani Express,* and *Taj Express*—cover the main city lines. These cushy trains come with full air-conditioning and meals and cost at least four times as much as standard second class fares. A few hill stations, such as Darjeeling, Ooty, and Shimla, are reached by **"toy trains,"** narrow-gauge machines that run at a snail's pace but gush billowing clouds of picturesque steam.

BUREAUCRACY BLUES Nothing is ever simple in India, least of all anything logistical. Your railway journey, for example, begins not at the platform, but at the reservation booth, where your patience will be stretched to the breaking point before you get anywhere near the little piece of paper that allows you to get on a train out of town. The reservation rooms of many train stations in India are stuffy, dust-heavy rooms full of ill-tempered officials and unbreathable air. The cruel but far-from-usual punishment begins at the counter where three people are employed full-time to dole out reservation request slips. These precious pieces of paper are not given out lightly— expect a struggle, endure the wait, and treat the slip once you get it with all the respect that such a precious and irreplaceable document deserves. Once you've got your form filled in, you move next door, join the scrum that hums and heaves around the reservation counters, and start to wait. And continue to wait. In India, waiting in "line" can be a brutal and very physical full-contact sport. After 45 minutes you make it through to one of the counters, out of patience and struggling for breath. You scream your destination through the wire window, smile, and are kindly told to take your slip back outside for an official stamp. Two uniformed men sit in surly silence, keeping a stern vigil over a small made-in-Manchester metal stamp and a tired old worn-out inkpad. Smile again. With your form now "official," you tramp back inside to rejoin the line for another long wait. Next time up at the window, the cloud of smoke behind the counter kindly directs you to Counter 6, reserved for "foreign tourists, senior citizens, physically handicapped, or freedom fighters." You notice a long line of young, able-bodied Indian men already waiting in front of you, and are glad you brought a book.

CLASSES OF COMFORT. There are many, often confusing, classes of travel. In an attempt to alleviate the headache, here is a more simplified list of those likely to be useful to the budget traveler. **Second class unreserved** is cheap, but it is also crowded, uncomfortable, and risky (pickpockets have easy access to your things in such tight quarters). Ride in this class only if you want a goat in your lap and your face squashed against the window grille. Much better is the **2nd class sleeper** (requires a reservation; see "Buying a Ticket" below), featuring an active bustle of people during the day (though not even close to the crowds of 2nd class unreserved) and modest three-tiered berths for overnight trips. The lack of air conditioning is made up for by the cool breeze that streams through the open windows, though this is less of a comfort during the summer. **First class,** three to four times the price of 2nd class sleeper, is less crowded and offers a more "protected" experience, with views of the countryside through scratched, amber-tinted windows and private compartments made up of three to four berths. For air-conditioned travel, there are **chair cars** (with reclining seats) built into the "superfast" trains. **A/C 2nd class sleepers** and **A/C 1st class** round out the options at prices ranging from half to 2.5 times as much as 1st class. Women traveling on their own or with children should inquire about ladies' compartments, available on many overnight mail and express trains. Some locals advise that women should opt for the open berths in 2nd class reserved (where there are always kind but tough old ladies) rather than the private compartment cars.

BUYING A TICKET. For overnight trips, travel during the high season (Nov.-Mar.), and all reserved trains (all classes mentioned above, except 2nd class unreserved) it is necessary to make **reservations** and to purchase your ticket at least a day or two in advance of traveling. At computerized stations, you can make a reservation up to 60 days before your date of travel. It is safest to do this at the station (look for the **reservation office**), though travel agents can also get your train tickets for a commission. Expect long delays and anarchic queues (see **Bureaucracy Blues,** p. 46). At some of the biggest stations, you can pay in US dollars, pounds sterling, or in rupees (with an encashment certificate). A **tourist quota** is often set aside for travelers with foreign passports, and a few major stations even have separate lines for tourists. Some stations have ladies' queues or allow women to jump to the front of the line to avoid all the pushing and shoving.

When you arrive at the office, get a reservation slip from the window, and scribble down the train you want. Each route has a name and a number; for route information, arm yourself with a copy of the wonderful *Trains at a Glance* (Rs25), which contains **schedules** for all express and mail trains, though the timetable can be difficult to decipher and does not list every stop that each train makes. The staff at most train station **enquiry counters** are generally well-informed and normally speak English. A 21st-century alternative to the trusty old *Trains at a Glance* has recently appeared, in the shape of two excellent, all-singing, all-dancing **websites** run by the major rail companies. The official websites of India Railways (www.indianrailways.com) and Southern Railway (www.srailway.com) allow you find out more than you will ever need to know about trains in India—train names, numbers, and timetables. You can also make on-line ticket reservations.

Foreign passport holders can buy **Indrail Passes,** available for between half a day and three months in a variety of classes (paid for in US dollars or pounds sterling). They include all fares, reservation charges, and supplementary charges, but prices are very high, and it's tough to get your money's worth. Indrail Passes can save you some hassle—on super-fast trains, pass holders are exempt from reservation fees and extra charges and, on shorter journeys, don't need tickets. Reservations are still necessary for longer trips.

If you have a reservation, you'll be fine getting to the station just a few minutes before the train arrives. If you're leaving from a major station, check the computer-printed list (usually on the platform or attached to the side of each train car) for your name and seat, and listen for announcements. Don't be surprised if your train is delayed—find a waiting room and ask a coolie (porter) when he thinks your train will arrive. It's usually not difficult for foreigners to assume a place in the first class waiting room, regardless of what class they're actually traveling. Railway **retiring rooms,** usually cheaper than budget hotels, are available to anyone with a valid ticket or Indrail pass. They operate on a 24-hour basis, and most also rent for 12 hours at a stretch.

If you fail to get a reservation, you can still get on the waiting list (ask about the tourist quota) and hope. In an emergency, find the station master. He probably won't be thrilled to see you, but if anyone can find a seat on a "full" train, he's your man. As a last resort, baksheesh to porters has been known to turn up unreserved berths in the most unexpected places. If you cancel your reservation more than 24 hours before your trip, you can still get a refund, but you'll be charged Rs10-50 depending on the class; up to four hours before, you'll get 75% back, and after that (sometimes even 12 hours after the train has left), you can still get 50%.

BY BUS

Bus routes cover India and Nepal's sprawling road systems. In train-less Nepal, buses are *the* mode of long-distance transportation. In India, they finish a close second. Buses are generally as fast as, or faster than, trains. They can climb the hilly areas of India, where trains cannot go, and involve less pre-departure hassle. The main drawback is discomfort. Seats are usually narrow, with very little cushioning and no leg room. There are often more passengers than seats, and many make the trip standing up. Buses also tend to make brief but infuriating pit stops every 15 minutes. These slow down the journey, though they do give you a much-needed opportunity to stretch your legs. You will often lose your seat if you get up. But then, you might find yourself unable to stand up at all if you go a whole journey without at least one stroll. At scheduled stops, women might have a hard time finding a place to use a toilet; they should ask the conductor to wait longer for them as they search. There is also some risk involved in bus travel. Road conditions are usually bad and traffic unpredictable—expect to hear gears grinding and horns blaring, and to feel sudden lurches as the bus bumps along the way. **Never ride on the roof of a bus,** no matter how cool the breeze, how gorgeous the scenery, or how many other people are sitting on top. It is illegal and terribly dangerous.

> ⚠ **WARNING:** Poor road conditions and aggressive driving make road travel in India and Nepal dangerous, particularly in hilly or mountainous regions.

INTERCITY BUSES. Among the different of types of buses available, the **express buses** are the norm. They have (somewhat) padded seats, are jam-packed, and stop for anyone and everyone at any point along the route. **Tourist buses** or **"superdeluxe" buses,** usually only available on popular tourist routes, have cushioned seats and more space than others; although they are certainly not luxurious by Greyhound standards, they usually seat four passengers to an aisle rather than five (or six or seven). They often have fans and sometimes even air-conditioning. In Nepal, and some places in India, there are special **night buses,** which have reclining seats and a bit more leg room, though you shouldn't count on getting any sleep. They stop for *chai* endlessly (just be glad the driver is getting his caffeine). At all costs, **avoid video coaches** unless you like watching old black-and-white Hindi films for five hours (or more) at ear-splitting levels. **Luggage** on the roof rack of a bus is usually safe, but bags have been known to disappear at intermediate stops in a flurry of untraceable movement. Make sure your pack is tied down, or ask if you can put it somewhere else—in a compartment at the back, or at the front where you can keep an eye on it. If your luggage goes on the roof, it's a good idea to give baksheesh to the person who put it up there.

IN INDIA. Bus travel in India is complicated slightly by the existence of both state and private bus companies. In this guide, **bus stands** and **bus stations** are where state (and sometimes private) buses roll in and out; private buses often leave from the particular company's office. **Government buses** are often crowded, so get to the bus stand at least 30 minutes before departure. For longer trips (over 8hr.) it might be necessary to book a day ahead; do this at the bus stand rather than through an agent. Some **private bus companies** offer excellent service; others should not be licensed at all; there are so many private bus companies that it is difficult to know the quality of an operation until you're already screaming down the highway. As with train tickets, it is unwise to buy bus tickets from random travel agencies.

IN NEPAL. Bus travel is widely used in Nepal, although road conditions are poor and the hilly terrain increases travel time. Almost all buses are privately owned, but look out for the **government Sajha buses,** which are safer and much more comfortable. For these, you'll probably have to book tickets a day in advance from the bus stand. Booking bus tickets from Kathmandu or Pokhara can be a hassle because the bus stands are far from the tourist center; it might be easier to book through a travel agent. Avoid package deals for bus journeys with connections, as these often are scams. It's best to buy your second ticket once you arrive.

TOOT YOUR OWN HORN

India is a land of many gods and countless different creeds. One religious tenet, though, is followed without fail by almost everyone in India—always honk your horn!! There aren't many rules of the road here, but the few that do exist all involve the horn somehow. Try to stay on the left if it's not too much of an inconvenience, and always honk your horn. Incessantly. Honk if you are about to pass, honk if you're considering passing, being passed, or just contemplating a general theory of passing. Honk if you are approaching a blind curve, honk if you see a pedestrian, or honk just to alert the world to your existence. On a bicycle, you can ring like hell on your little tinkling bell. There are many ways to blow a horn, and the avatars of the horn itself are as are as numerous and as varied as the moods that honking gives voice to—from the majestic, almost-musical tone of the largest trucks, to the boastful bellow of the buses, the chaotic clarion call of the clanking cars, and the eruptive fart of the city scooter...It is a religion that is easy to follow and fun to obey. So join the party—rent a bike, steal a scooter, buy a truck, whatever. And when it's just you on the one lane open road, and a crowded bus, an overloaded truck, and a couple of motorcycles—don't hesitate, don't be shy—let them know you're there and just happy to be alive! Toot your own horn, sweetheart. Ain't nobody gonna do it for you.

BY CAR

Driving a car (or better yet a VW Microbus) across Asia was a classic 1960s hippie expedition. Today, it's a nightmare and certainly not for the faint of heart. Besides swerving to avoid cars, motorcycles, rickshaws, people, and cows, there is also a general disregard for anything resembling traffic regulations. Drivers are reckless and aggressive, constrained only by the general dilapidation of the roads and the vehicles they drive. Many pedestrians who have just arrived from villages lack a basic traffic sense. Not surprisingly, India and Nepal have high rates of road accidents. If you get into a traffic accident in India or Nepal, **leave the scene of the accident immediately and go to the nearest police station.** Also keep in mind that killing a cow in India and Nepal, even by accident, is punishable by law.

A car is entirely unnecessary in a large city, where buses, rickshaws, and taxis can get you anywhere cheaply. The cost of renting a four-door sedan is many times the cost of a night's stay at a guest house. Also, some rental companies do not offer insurance; a serious accident can mean spending some time in jail or the hospital and shelling out a large sum of money to cover damages. If you absolutely must have a car, keep your **international driving permit** (see below) handy, as well as a substantial amount of money. A safer alternative is to hire a car with a **driver.**

Hitchhiking is practically unheard of and unnecessary in most parts of India and Nepal, since public transportation networks are extensive and inexpensive. In mountain areas like Kumaon and Himachal Pradesh, where traffic is sparse, jeeps and cargo trucks sometimes take on passengers for a small charge.

> **! WARNING.** Let's Go strongly urges you to consider the risks before you choose to hitchhike. We do not recommend hitchhiking as a means of transportation in India or Nepal, and women should never hitchhike alone.

DRIVING PERMITS AND CAR INSURANCE

INTERNATIONAL DRIVING PERMIT (IDP). Renting a **car, motor-scooter,** or **motorcycle** while in India or Nepal usually requires an International Driving Permit (IDP). You must be over 18 and have a driver's license from your own country. Your IDP, valid for one year, must be issued in your own country before you depart. An application usually requires one or two photos, a current local license, an additional form of identification, and a fee. Contact your local automobile club or association for more information.

CAR INSURANCE. Most credit cards cover standard insurance. If you rent, lease, or borrow a car, you will need a **green card,** or **International Insurance Certificate,** to certify that you have liability insurance and that it applies abroad. Green cards can be obtained at car rental agencies, car dealers (for those leasing cars), some travel agents, and some border crossings. Rental agencies may require you to purchase theft insurance in countries that they consider to have a high risk of auto theft. Ask your rental agency about India and Nepal.

BY LOCAL TRANSPORTATION

BUSES. Getting around by **local buses** can be chaotic and confusing. Bus schedules are practically impossible to decipher, and figuring out which bus goes where takes years of patient trial and error. Smile at locals waiting at bus stops and hope they know what they're talking about. In a hurry to wedge themselves into city traffic, bus drivers roll-start, so you might want to learn the skill of leaping on and off the back stairs. Once safely in, sit or stand until the bus-*wallah*, with his little bus satchel, comes by and clicks a small metal contraption in your face. That means pay up—ask how much it is to your destination, since prices vary by distance. Women get preferential seating; men are expected to give up their seats. Women (and men) should watch out for groping hands in crowded buses.

AUTO-RICKSHAWS AND TEMPOS. To some, these podlike three-wheelers are a symbol of the South Asian experience; to others, they are diesel fume-belching beasts. Fans argue that they are cheaper than taxis, more convenient than buses, and small enough to dart through heavy traffic. Much of this, of course, depends on the driver. Detractors criticize rickshaws for the damage they do to the environment and human ears. Auto-rickshaws seat one to three adults (but often up to 10 school children). Low ceilings, minimal leg room, and narrow seats are all part of the fun. Drivers will often insist that it's "broken," but insist that they use the **meter.** Avoid pushy drivers, and always scoff at the first price demanded. If a driver won't go by the meter, aim to bring him down to at least 30-40% of his original price. **In most cities, it is illegal for rickshaw-wallahs to overcharge for local, daytime service.** A threat to report them to the police can often do wonders to squeeze out a fair fare. Depending on the town, some drivers may add a surcharge to the meter or display a government-issued "fare adjustment card," because the meters are outdated and the price of fuel has risen. **Nighttime fares** can be as much as double the standard rate. Also, **make sure your rickshaw-wallah is not drunk or stoned.**

Rickshaw-*wallahs*, who have a habit of getting in **commission** cahoots with hotels, will often inform you that the hotel you want to go to has been shut down or that its staff has been rounded up and deported to the Falkland Islands (see **Touts, Middlemen, and Scams,** p. 15). Chances are that the "insider info" is incorrect. If your driver is particularly persistent, he might just take you to an accommodation of his choice, regardless of your protests. If a driver taking you home asks if you need a ride the next day, know that if you flippantly agree he will probably sleep in his rickshaw all night waiting for you to emerge in the morning.

Tempos seat about six people, follow fixed routes, and have low fees; they are of limited use to foreigners, however, because their destinations are never marked, and they are often over-packed anyway.

CYCLE-RICKSHAWS. There are two other kinds of rickshaws in India and Nepal. Calcutta is home to India's last fleet of **hand-pulled rickshaws,** though even these are rumored to be near extinction. Far more common are **cycle-rickshaws,** where the driver pedals in front while his trusting passengers sit on a cushioned box above the rear axle. These are not always found in metropolitan areas, such as Bombay, but in the countryside wherever there are flat roads. In Nepal, rickshaws are limited to the Terai and parts of Kathmandu, where they cater mainly to tourists. The welcome breeze and open views are the main benefits of riding in a cycle-rickshaw; negative aspects include the longer traveling time and the sorrow of seeing an old man labor away (though he definitely wants your business). If he jumps out and starts pushing you up a hill that's too steep to pedal, get out and lend a hand. The worst part of a rickshaw ride is settling the **price,** which is highly negotiable. Foreigners usually pay about Rs10 per kilometer in India—more in touristy places, less in villages—but you will pay much more unless you haggle energetically.

TAXIS. you will find taxis in the larger cities of India and Nepal; in some cities, such as Bombay, only taxis (and not rickshaws or auto-rickshaws) are allowed within the metropolitan limits. India's international airports offer reliable **pre-paid taxi services**—you pay at the official office and give your receipt to a driver in the waiting queue, who takes you where you need to go. Taxis are supposed to have meters, but since these are sometimes out of date, the driver will add a percentage or wave about an official-looking "fare adjustment card" with up-to-date prices. All this varies from city to city; there are no hard-and-fast rules, but in general you should at least insist on using the meter rather than negotiating a price. Private companies rent out taxis and **drivers** for longer hours, short trips, or even days; inquire at train stations, airports, tourist offices, or travel agents. This is definitely a better alternative to driving around India or Nepal yourself; the driver looks after petrol costs and repairs, is familiar with the roads, and will take responsibility. With enough passengers to split the costs, this option is usually within reach of the budget traveler. In mountainous regions, **jeeps** (sometimes called Gypsies or Mahindras) function as taxis or mini-buses.

MOTORCYCLES, MOPEDS, AND SCOOTERS. Motorcycles can liberate you to explore rural roads not accessible by public transportation, though they can be very dangerous. While **helmets** are rarely provided, you shouldn't get onto a motorcycle or motorbike without one—**traffic fatalities on motorcycles are frighteningly high.** Rental shops are abundant near major tourist stops. An **International Driving Permit** (see p. 49) is legally required for you to rent a scooter or motorcycle, but it is rarely checked. Motorcycle and scooter engines in India and Nepal are usually 100cc and are not good for long trips. Mopeds are easy to operate, but dangerous in traffic. Scooters have a high center of gravity and small wheels, which make them very dangerous; scooters are also very difficult to operate and must be manually shifted from gear to gear. A popular alternative is to rent Kinetic-Hondas, automatic shifting scooters that are easy to operate and a bit safer on the road.

BICYCLES. Because of the over-congested streets, trying to ride a bicycle in the big Indian cities is often a dangerous exercise in futility, but on back roads through rural towns and in much of Nepal, bicycles are a great alternative to motorcycles or scooters. Most bikes don't have gears, which makes hills pretty hellish. In tourist centers like Kathmandu and Pokhara, bikes can be rented very cheaply, usually on a day-to-day basis. Clunky Indian bikes are also cheap to buy and resell.

BY BOAT

Ferries run between Bombay and Goa, and ships travel regularly from Calcutta and Madras to Port Blair in the Andamans. Ferries are the only way to cross some rivers during the monsoon. White-water rafting is the only boat travel in Nepal.

WHEN IN INDIA AND NEPAL...

CUSTOMS AND ETIQUETTE

CLOTHING. Dress modestly. In some areas, a man in shorts will be giggled at, since trouserhood is synonymous with manhood. Similarly, but for different reasons, women should try to keep legs covered, at least to the knee. Bare shoulders are another sure sign of immorality (and a quick way to get sunburned). Being well-dressed will certainly affect the way that people respond to you. In India, women will find that they are treated with more respect if they wear *salwar kameez*. Men's clothing in India is typically more "internationalized," but men might still want to buy a thin cotton *kurta pajama*. Of course, these rules vary by region. Clothing taboos are less strict in Nepal and throughout the Himalayas and in big cities like Bombay and Bangalore.

FOOD. Most Indians and Nepalis eat with their hands. While restaurants usually give cutlery to foreigners, you might have to eat with your hands if you are invited into someone's home. The most important thing is to **eat with your right hand only.** The left hand is used for cleaning after defecation and is seen as polluted. You can use your left hand to hold a fork or to pass a dish, but it should never touch food or your lips directly. Any food that comes into contact with one person's saliva is unclean for anyone else. Indians and Nepalis will not usually take bites of each other's food or drink from the same cup; watch how locals drink from water bottles, pouring the drink in without touching their lips. In Hindu houses, the family **hearth** is sacred. If food is cooked before you on a fire (as it frequently is in trekking lodges) never play with the fire or throw trash into it.

Almost all Jains and many Hindus (especially in South India) are **vegetarian,** and besides, for many non-vegetarians, meat is an expensive luxury. Because of the cow's sacred status in Hinduism, beef is scarce. Muslims do not eat pork and are supposed to shun alcohol. Only the most reckless of women drink alcohol.

HYGIENE. All **bodily secretions** and products are considered polluted. The people who come into contact with them—laundrymen, barbers, latrine cleaners—have historically formed the lowest ranks of the caste system. The **head** is the most sacred part of the body, and purity decreases all the way down to the toes. To **touch something with your feet** is a grave insult; you should never touch a person with your feet, step over a seated person's outstretched legs, or point at someone with your foot. Never put your feet on a table or any other surface. To touch somebody else's feet, conversely, is an act of veneration. If you accidentally touch someone else with your foot, touch your eyes and then their knee or foot, whichever is more accessible. The **left hand** is polluted. Always use your right hand to eat, give, take, or point.

COMMUNICATION AND BODY LANGUAGE. A quick **sideways tilt of the head,** similar to shaking one's head but more like a sideways nod, means "OK," or "I understand." Many foreigners are baffled by this gesture, thinking their hosts are answering their most innocent comments and requests with a firm "no." **Indian English,** especially when written, is full of colorful and antique-sounding phrases. You will hear people address you as "madame" or "good gentleman," and read letters asking you to "kindly do the needful" and signed "your most humble servant."

Many foreigners have trouble adjusting to the constant **stares** they get in India and Nepal. There is no taboo against staring in South Asia and no harm is intended, but be sure not to send mixed signals. Meeting someone's gaze is often tantamount to expressing a desire for further contact. At the same time, remember that it can be both acceptable and appropriate to ignore attempts at conversation.

WOMEN AND MEN. Displays of physical affection between women and men are rare. Some affection is considered completely natural and acceptable, such as that between the same sex. Everywhere men walk comfortably down the street clasping hands. Most Indian and Nepali women appear quite meek and quiet in public, and it is difficult and unusual for strange men to talk to them. Women travelers might find it hard to meet Indian and Nepali women, though women should always try to find other women to help out in emergencies (see **Women Travelers,** p. 52).

PLACES OF WORSHIP. Be especially sensitive about etiquette in places of worship. **Dress conservatively,** keeping legs and shoulders covered, and **take off your shoes** before entering any mosque, *gurudwara*, or temple. Visitors to Sikh *gurudwaras* must cover their heads as well—handkerchiefs are usually provided. At the entrance to popular temples, shoe-*wallahs* will guard your shoes for a few rupees. Ask before taking **photographs** in places of worship. Taking pictures of the deities in Hindu temples is normally not allowed. Many Hindu temples, especially those in Kerala, Nepal, and in pilgrimage sites such as Puri and Varanasi, ban non-Hindus from entering. In practice this rule excludes anyone who doesn't look sufficiently South Asian. Purity laws dictate that **menstruating women** are forbidden to enter some Hindu and Jain temples.

It is common practice in Hindu temples to partake of offerings of consecrated fruit and/or water called **prasad,** which is received with the right hand over the left (and no one takes seconds). It is protocol to leave a small donation at the entrance to the temple sanctuary, though this can cause some dilemmas when temple priests aggressively force *prasad* into your hands, expecting large amounts of cash in return. Usually a donation of one or two rupees will suffice. Hinduism and Buddhism consider the right-hand side auspicious and the left-hand side inauspicious; it is customary to walk around Hindu temples and Buddhist stupas **clockwise,** with your right side toward the shrine. In fact, any circular motion, such as the turning of Tibetan Buddhist prayer wheels, goes in a clockwise direction.

WOMEN TRAVELERS

Incidents of **sexual harassment** are very common, especially in northern India, but seldom more serious than verbal advances or groping. Too many Indian and Nepali men are under the impression that foreign women are indiscriminately promiscuous. This belief is partly due to the stereotypes from American television and movies, and partly because many foreign women do certain things that "good" Indian and Nepali women do not. The less you look like a tourist, the better off you will be. Look as if you know where you're going (even when you don't) and approach other women (or couples) if you need help or directions. **Dress conservatively, covering legs and shoulders, and always wear a bra.** Don't jump to the conclusion that since Indian women wearing saris reveal their lower backs and stomachs, it's OK to wear shorts—it's definitely not. And don't automatically assume that a T-shirt, which appears to cover the same vital areas as a sari, if not more, is appropriate. The shape of the breast should be left a mystery—most women's chests are covered by more than one layer of clothing. Consider wearing a *salwar kameez*, Indian baggy pants with a loose long-sleeved shirt. Wearing a conspicuous **wedding band** can also help to prevent unwanted overtures. Some travelers report that carrying pictures of a "husband" or "children" is extremely useful to help back up marital status. Even a brief mention of a husband waiting back at the hotel is enough in some places to counteract your potentially vulnerable, unattached appearance. Remember that **non-verbal communication** is also quite different from back home on the range—making eye contact, responding when asked a question, even smiling can be seen as a come-on by South Asian men.

Invest in secure accommodations, particularly family-run guest houses with doors that lock from the inside. Stay in central locations and avoid late-night walks. **Hitchhiking** is never safe for lone women, or even for two women traveling together. Trains often have separate **ladies' compartments** and stations may have **ladies' waiting rooms.** On buses, you should be allowed to sit near the front.

South India is safer for women than the north. Bihar and eastern Uttar Pradesh, where law and order are lax, are some of the most dangerous areas; there have even been cases of foreign women being raped. The Himalayan regions, however, from Himachal Pradesh to Nepal to Sikkim, are among the safest areas; attitudes toward women are much more liberal among many mountain ethnic groups. And in the cosmopolitan circles in major cities (especially in Bombay), women can usually feel as comfortable as they would in any other big city.

The slightest bit of resistance usually stops most harassers, who have generally encountered few foreign women before. Your best answer to harassment is no answer at all; feigned deafness, sitting motionless and staring straight ahead at nothing in particular can do a world of good. The extremely persistent can sometimes be dissuaded by a firm, loud, and very public *"Mujhe chod dho!"* ("Leave me alone!" in Hindi). If need be, **turn to an older woman** for help in an uncomfortable situation; her stern rebukes will usually embarrass even the most persistent jerk. Don't hesitate to get the attention of **passersby** if you are being harassed, as people have a strong sense of public morality, and don't hesitate to seek out a policeman. Keep in mind, however, that they, like other men, might assume that a women traveling alone is looking for sex; don't place all your trust in them, particularly in untouristed areas. Emergency numbers (uniform across India and Nepal) are listed on the inside back cover of this book, as well as in the **Practical Information** listings of cities. A **Model Mugging** self-defense course (see p. 19) will not only prepare you for a potential attack, but will also raise your awareness and confidence.

SPECIFIC CONCERNS

SENIOR CITIZENS. Senior citizens are rarely offered discounts in India or Nepal. Agencies for senior group travel are growing in enrollment and popularity. **Elderhostel,** 75 Federal St., Boston, MA 02110 (☎(617) 426-7788; www.elderhostel.org), offers programs at colleges, universities, and other learning centers in India on varied subjects lasting one to four weeks for seniors 55 and older.

GAY AND LESBIAN TRAVELERS. Homosexuality is a taboo topic in India and Nepal, and in India, male homosexual sex is illegal. Most gays and lesbians stay closeted. *Hijras* (male eunuchs) form a subculture of prostitutes in the big cites, especially Bombay and Hyderabad, but this scene is not open to foreigners (see **The Third Sex,** p. 405). While male friends may hold hands or hug in public, these gestures are not considered sexual. Most gay and lesbian organizations in India and Nepal remain underground, but in the past decade, some groups have gained recognition for their work on sex and gender issues. **Bombay Dost** (www.bombay-dost.com), a quarterly magazine by Pride Publications, was started by three gay Bombay men in 1990 and addresses issues such as sexual health and hygiene, attitudes toward sexuality, and gay activism. Bombay Dost can be purchased from select newsstands in Bombay, Delhi, Calcutta, and Hyderabad (see their web page for details), or it can be ordered directly from Pride Publications Pvt. Ltd., 105 Veena Beena Shopping Centre, Bandra Station Road, Bandra (West), Mumbai 400 050. The success of Bombay Dost inspired the founding of **The Humsafar Trust** (see **Bombay: Bi-Gay-Lesbian Organizations, p. 395**), an organization dedicated to activism, outreach, research, and advocacy for gay men in India. The following organizations offer materials addressing some specific concerns for bisexual, gay, or lesbian travelers: **Aero Travel, Inc.**, 4001 N. 9th St., #217, Arlington, VA 22203 (☎(800) 356-1109; fax (703) 807-0450; discount@aerotravel.com; www.aerotravel.com), is a travel agency specializing in travel to India and travel for gay couples. **Trikone**, P.O. Box 21354, San Jose, CA 95151 (☎(415) 789-7322; fax (408) 274-2733; email trikone-web@trikone.org; www.trikone.org), is a US-based organization for gay and lesbian South Asians. They provide a list of gay and lesbian centers in India.

DISABLED TRAVELERS. Most of South Asia is ill-equipped to deal with disabled travelers. Hospitals, even those in major cities, cannot be relied upon to replace broken braces or prostheses successfully. Public transportation is completely inaccessible and most cities have no sidewalks or ramps. Many sights also require climbing long staircases or hiking.

TRAVELERS WITH CHILDREN. If you are traveling with small children, it is particularly crucial to protect them from sunburn, excessive heat, insect bites, and diarrhea, which can cause severe dehydration and is extremely dangerous for children. Older children should carry some sort of ID in case of an emergency, and you should arrange a reunion spot in case of separation when sight-seeing. Children receive high discounts on flights within India. Finding a private place for **breast feeding** is often a problem while traveling, so pack accordingly.

> **FURTHER READING ON TRAVELING WITH CHILDREN.**
>
> *How to take Great Trips with Your Kids,* Sanford and Jane Portnoy. Harvard Common Press.
> *Have Kid, Will Travel: 101 Survival Strategies for Vacationing With Babies and Young Children,* Claire and Lucille Tristram. Andrews and McMeel.
> *Adventuring with Children: An Inspirational Guide to World Travel and the Outdoors,* Nan Jeffrey. Avalon House Publishing.
> *Trouble Free Travel with Children,* Vicki Lansky. Book Peddlers.

DIETARY CONCERNS. India and Nepal are paradise for vegetarians. The staple foods of a budget-minded connoisseur (rice and *dahl*) will meet the most stringent vegetarian standards. Vegans, however, should be warned that *ghee* (clarified butter) is widely used in Indian cooking, and that cheese often appears in otherwise vegetarian dishes. While the Muslim presence makes *halal* food a large part of the cuisine, kosher meals are next to nonexistent in India and Nepal.

ENVIRONMENTALLY RESPONSIBLE TOURISM. A visit to India or Nepal can be quite a shock for even not-so-environmentally-conscious travelers. There's a lot you can do to minimize your own environmental impact as you travel. The two biggest and often least obvious ways that tourists cause waste are the overuse of **water** and **electricity.** Most of the trash you generate will end up on the street whether you throw it there or not, so the key is to generate less garbage, period. Heavily touristed areas, whether large cities or small towns, often have water shortages. Squat toilets and bucket showers may be tough to get used to, but they consume far less water than their Western counterparts. Sending your laundry to a *dhobi* might seem like a luxury, but they use less water than you would in your hotel sink. Turn off the lights when you leave a room and make sure that doors and windows are shut while the air-conditioning is on—or don't use it at all.

In cities with good tap water, use purifying tablets and your own canteen to avoid having to throw out countless plastic water bottles. Try to reuse plastic bags, though it might be hard to convince market vendors not to give you three bags where one would suffice. One option to relieve yourself of some guilt is to volunteer for one of the many environmental organizations (see **Alternatives to Tourism,** p. 55). Should you happen to uncover great "ecotourism" operators or have other ideas of how to be a low-impact tourist, we would love to hear of them.

ALTERNATIVES TO TOURISM

What follows is a list of organized programs and resources for finding out more. A surprising number of alternatives can be arranged informally. If you're willing to work for room and board, you will find many possibilities open to you (just make sure you have the correct documentation—valid visas, work permits, etc.). We list such out-of-the-way opportunities in the specific city sections when we can, but the best advice is to look and ask around. For an extensive listing of "off-the-beaten-track" and specialty travel opportunities, try the **Specialty Travel Index,** 305 San Anselmo Ave., #313, San Anselmo, CA 94960 (☎(888) 624-4030; www.spectrav.com; US$6). **Transitions Abroad** (www.transabroad.com) publishes an on-line newsletter for work, study, and specialized travel abroad.

UNIVERSITIES AND LANGUAGE SCHOOLS

Foreign study programs vary tremendously in expense, quality, living conditions, degree of contact with local students, and exposure to local culture and languages. There are countless exchange programs for students, especially during the summer. Most undergraduates enroll in semester- or year-long programs sponsored by universities, and many colleges have offices that give advice and information on studying abroad. If you already know an Indian language, local universities can be much cheaper, though you might not be able to receive academic credit. Some schools offering study abroad programs to foreigners are listed below.

Association of Commonwealth Universities (ACU), John Foster House, 36 Gordon Sq., London WC1H OPF (☎(020) 7387 8572; email info@acu.ac.uk; www.acu.ac.uk). Administers scholarship programs such as the British Marshall scholarships and publishes information about Commonwealth universities.

College Semester Abroad, School for International Training, Admissions, Kipling Rd., P.O. Box 676, Brattleboro, VT 05302, USA (☎(800) 336-1616 or (802) 258-3267; fax 258-3500; www.sit.edu). Offers extensive semester- and year-long Study Abroad programs with homestays, intensive language classes, courses in history, politics, arts and humanities, anthropology in India and Nepal (US$10,600), and Tibetan Studies (US$11,900). Program costs include international airfare, tuition, room and board, and health insurance. Scholarships are available and federal financial aid is usually transferable from home college or university.

Friends World Program, 239 Montauk Highway, Southampton, NY 11968, USA (☎(631) 287-8474; fax 287-8463; www.southampton.liunet.edu/academic/fr_world/program.htm). Offers a semester- or year-long program in Bangalore that includes language training (in Hindi, Kannada, or Tamil) and cultural training (US$13,030 per semester, including airfare, tuition, room and board, and other costs).

International Partnership for Service Learning, 815 Second Ave., #315, New York, NY 10017, USA (☎(212) 986-0989; fax 986-5039; www.ipsl.org), offers a 3-week program in Jan. or Aug., with the option of extending each into a 9-week semester. Both combine volunteer social work (with terminal patients in Missionaries of Charity hospices and in children's rehabilitation centers) with intensive study of language (Bengali) and culture. 3-week program US$5300 (airfare included); semester-long program

US$8900 (including airfare and intercession). Study is done in Calcutta (in small hotels during 3-week program, homestays during the semester), with trips to Agra and Delhi.

Naropa Institute, 2130 Arapahoe Ave., Boulder, CO 80302, USA (☎(303) 546-3594; www.naropa.edu/studyabroad/). Runs a program in Boudha, Nepal; students take classes in art and culture, Buddhist civilization, Nepali, and meditation. Open to both undergraduate and graduate students (US$9950 for tuition, room, and board; does not include international airfare).

Peterson's Guides, P.O. Box 2123, Princeton, NJ 08543 (☎(800) 338-3282; fax (609) 243-9150; www.petersons.com). Their comprehensive Study Abroad (US$30) annual guide lists programs in countries all over the world and provides essential information on the study abroad experience in general.

Pitzer College, External Studies, 1050 N. Mills Ave., Claremont, CA 91711, USA (☎(909) 621-8104; fax 621-0518; www.pitzer.edu/academics/ilcenter/external_studies). Semester-long program (fall and spring) on Nepali language and culture. Family home-stays just outside Kathmandu, with treks in Annapurna Conservation Area and Chitwan National Park. US$15,168 includes airfare, tuition, room and board, and field trip. Financial aid usually transferable.

University of Wisconsin-Madison, 500 Lincoln Dr., 252 Bascom Hall, Madison, WI 53706, USA (☎(608) 265-6329; fax 262-6998; www.wisc.edu/studyabroad). Has college-year programs in Hyderabad, Madurai, Varanasi, and Kathmandu. The college-year programs concentrate on field work, with a year-long local language class and independently-chosen tutorial. One year of local language study is required; for an extra US$2750, the program offers a 10-week intensive language program (mid-June to mid-Aug.) Fees cover academic expenses, administrative costs, a one-way plane ticket to India from the West Coast, room, meals, and pocket expenses: US$13,500 for India and Nepal. A summer performing arts program in Kerala is also offered for US$4500 (Wisconsin residents pay only US$1400).

Visva Bharati University, Shantiniketan, West Bengal 731235 (☎(03463) 52751, ext. 362; fax 52672; email pritam@vbharat.ernet.in). Offers a one-year Foreigner Casual Course, which can be taken in any subject: painting, Indian philosophy, music, or Indian languages. Direct inquiries to Pritam Ray, advisor to foreign students.

WORK

Although it's easy to find a temporary job in India and Nepal—native speakers of English often find that their skills are in high demand—it will rarely be lucrative or glamorous, and it might not even cover your airfare. It is also very difficult to get permission to work at all (both India and Nepal are net exporters of labor, with many going to earn a living in the Middle East). Officially, you can hold a job in most countries only with a **work permit.** Your employer must obtain this document, usually by demonstrating that you have skills that locals lack—not the easiest of tasks. Students can check with their universities' foreign language departments, which may have connections to job openings abroad. Call the embassy or consulate of the country in which you wish to work to get more information about work permits (see **Diplomatic Missions, p. 8**).

Many books list work-abroad opportunities. Note especially the excellent guides put out by **Vacation Work** (www.vacationwork.co.uk). To avoid scams from fraudulent employment agencies demanding large fees and providing no results, educate yourself using publications from the following sources.

Council, Marketing Services Dept., 205 E. 42nd St., New York, NY 10017, USA (☎(888) 268-6245; fax (212) 822-2699; www.ciee.org), publishes *International and Volunteer Projects Directory* (US$20) and *Volunteer! The Comprehensive Guide to Voluntary Service in the US and Abroad* (US$12.95).

International Schools Services, Educational Staffing Program, P.O. Box 5910, Princeton, NJ 08543, USA (☎(609) 452-0990; fax 452-2690; email edustaffing@iss.edu; www.iss.edu). Recruits teachers and administrators for American and English schools in India and Nepal. All instruction in English. Applicants must have a bachelor's degree and two years of relevant experience. Nonrefundable US$150 application fee. Publishes *The ISS Directory of Overseas Schools* (US$34.95).

Office of Overseas Schools, A/OS Room 245, SA-29, Dept. of State, Washington, D.C. 20522, USA (☎(703) 875-7800; fax 875-7979; email overseas.school@state.gov; exchanges.state.gov). Keeps a list of schools abroad and agencies that arrange placement for Americans to teach abroad.

Uniworld Business Publications, Inc., 257 Central Park West, New York, NY 10024, USA (☎(212) 496-2448; fax 769-0413; www.uniworldbp.com). Check your local library for their Directory of American Firms Operating in Foreign Countries (January 1999; US$275). Now also available in a separate South Asia regional volume (US$49).

Archaeological Institute of America, 656 Beacon St., Boston, MA 02215, USA (☎(617) 353-9361; fax 353-6550; email aia@bu.edu; www.archaeological.org), puts out the *Archaeological Fieldwork Opportunities Bulletin* (US$15 for non-members), which occasionally lists field sites in India. This can be purchased from Kendall/Hunt Publishing, 4050 Westmark Dr., Dubuque, Iowa 52002, USA (☎(800) 228-0810).

VOLUNTEER

Volunteer jobs are readily available almost everywhere, and the cost of living in India and Nepal is low enough that volunteering is not a great financial setback. You might receive room and board in exchange for your labor. You can sometimes avoid the high application fees charged by the organizations that arrange placement by contacting the workcamps directly.

Dakshinayan, c/o Siddarth Sanyal A5/108, Clifton Apartments, Charmwood Village, Surajkund Road, Fariabad 121009, INDIA (from Delhi ☎525 3114; from outside Delhi (0129) 525 3114; mobile phone 98 11 19 21 33; email dakshinayan@vsnl.com; www.linkindia.com/dax). Places volunteers in short or long-term work projects in India

The Joint Assistance Center, Attn: Prof. P.L. Govil, G17/3 DLF Qutab Enclave Phase I, Gurgaon 122022, Haryana, INDIA (☎(0124) 352141), places volunteers directly in India. **Friends of JAC in the Americas,** P.O. Box 14481, Santa Rosa, CA 95402 (☎(707) 573-1740; fax 528-8917; email jacusa@juno.com), assists with placement.

New College of California, 741 Valencia St., San Francisco, CA 94110, USA (☎(800) 335-6262 ext. 406; fax (415) 776 7190). Offers volunteer programs in Nepal and India. Contact Jerry Dekker of the World Studies Project.

Peace Corps, 1111 20th St. NW, Washington, D.C. 20526, USA (☎(800) 424-8580; www.peacecorps.gov). Write for their "blue" brochure detailing application requirements. Opportunities in many fields in India and Nepal. Volunteers must be US citizens, 18 or older, willing to make a 2-year commitment. Bachelor's degree usually required.

Service Civil International Voluntary Service (SCI-IVS), 814 NE 40th St., Seattle, WA 98105, USA (☎/fax (206) 545-6585; www.sci-ivs.org). Arranges placement in workcamps in India and Nepal for those 18+. Registration fee US$65-150.

Volunteers for Peace (VFP), 1034 Tiffany Rd., Belmont, VT 05730, USA (☎(802) 259-2759; fax 259-2922; email vfp@vfp.org; www.vfp.org). A nonprofit organization that arranges speedy placement in 2-3 week workcamps in Nepal comprising 10-15 people. Their website also lists organizations that place volunteers in India. Most complete and up-to-date listings provided in the annual *International Workcamp Directory*. Registration fee US$200, not including US$20 VFP member fee. VFP will usually refund US$50 if you offer feedback on your workcamp experience. Free newsletter.

SPIRITUAL INTERESTS

The birthplace of several major world religions (Hinduism, Buddhism, Jainism, and Sikhism), South Asia remains a land of strong religious beliefs and spirituality. It is no wonder that India and Nepal attract many travelers wishing to throw off their old assumptions and try out other approaches to life's questions. Aside from the mainstream traditions in India and Nepal (see **India: Religion,** p. 76, and **Nepal: Religion,** p. 720), certain religious communities are open to initiates from abroad.

> **FURTHER READING.**
>
> *International Jobs: Where they Are, How to Get Them,* Eric Koocher. Perseus Books.
> *Work Abroad: The Complete Guide to Finding a Job Overseas,* Clayton Hubbs. Transitions Abroad.
> *International Directory of Voluntary Work,* Louise Whetter. Vacation Work Publications.
> *Teaching English Abroad,* Susan Griffin. Vacation Work.
> *Overseas Summer Jobs 2001, Work Your Way Around the World,* and *The Directory of Jobs and Careers Abroad.* Peterson's.

For **Hinduism,** these mostly take the form of ashrams (retreats), many of which are under the leadership of a modern-day guru—those who have attracted many foreign devotees are often referred to as "export gurus." Some of the most famous ashrams in India include that of the late **Sri Aurobindo** in Pondicherry (see p. 558), the **Osho Commune** in Pune (see p. 414), and **Sai Baba's** ashrams in Andhra Pradesh and Karnataka (see p. 467). **Rishikesh** is a major center for gurus and students of yoga (see p. 141). If you stay in an ashram, you will usually be required to stay clean and quiet and to avoid meat, alcohol, tobacco, *paan* (betel), and drugs.

Since the 1959 Chinese crackdown in Tibet, India and Nepal have become the most accessible places in the world to study **Tibetan Buddhism.** Dharamsala in India, the home of the Dalai Lama and the Tibetan government-in-exile, is a popular place to learn about Tibetan culture (see p. 219). In Nepal (the Buddha's birthplace), the foremost Tibetan Buddhist center is located at **Boudha** (see p. 755), just outside Kathmandu. Unlike lamas (monks), Western students of Tibetan Buddhism do not usually live in monasteries, though they are expected to live austerely. Public lectures (sometimes in English) and meditation courses are offered at the major Buddhist centers. The most thoroughly connected source for information on Tibet is the International Campaign for Tibet, based in Washington, D.C., which provides information about Tibetan organizations worldwide in the International Tibet Resources Directory (US$7). Contact the International Campaign for Tibet, 1825 K St. NW, #520, Washington, D.C. 20006, USA (☎(202) 785-1515; fax 785-4343; www.savetibet.org), or the International Campaign for Tibet-Europe, Netherlands Stichting ICT, Keizersgracht 302, 1016 EX Amsterdam, Netherlands (☎(20) 330 82 65; fax 330 82 66).

Christianity is India's third largest religion, after Hinduism and Islam. There are long traditions of faith and missionary work in the subcontinent. Many hospitals, schools, and Non-Governmental Organizations (NGOs) are run or supported by local or international Christian organizations. The **Missionaries of Charity,** founded by Mother Teresa, is the most famous of these organizations (see **p. 660**).

OTHER RESOURCES

USEFUL PUBLICATIONS

Adventurous Traveler Bookstore, 245 S. Champlain St., Burlington, VT 05401, USA (☎(800) 282-3963 or (802) 860-6776; www.adventuroustraveler.com).

Hippocrene Books, Inc., 171 Madison Ave., New York, NY 10016, USA (☎(212) 685-4371; orders (718) 454-2366; www.netcom.com/~hippocre). Free catalog. Publishes travel guides, foreign language dictionaries, and language learning guides.

Hunter Publishing, 130 Campus Dr., Edison, NJ 08818, USA (☎(800) 255-0343; www.hunterpublishing.com). Has an extensive catalog of travel books, guides, language learning tapes, and quality maps.

Specialty Travel Index, 305 San Anselmo Ave., #313, San Anselmo, CA 94960, USA (☎(415) 459-4900 or (800) 442-4922; fax. 459-4974; www.spectrav.com). Published twice yearly, this is an extensive listing of "off the beaten track" and specialty travel opportunities. One copy US$6, one-year subscription (2 copies) US$10.

Travel Books & Language Center, Inc., 4437 Wisconsin Ave. NW, Washington, D.C. 20016 (☎(800) 220-2665 or (202) 237-1322; www.bookweb.org/bookstore/ travelbks). Over 60,000 titles from around the world.

THE WORLD WIDE WEB

Information on almost every aspect of budget travel is accessible via the web. Even if you don't have Internet access at home, it is well worth seeking it out. Listed here are some budget travel sites to start off your surfing; other relevant web sites are listed throughout the book. Because website turnover is high, use search engines (such as www.yahoo.com and www.google.com) to strike out on your own.

ZEN AND THE ART OF BUDGET TRAVEL

Atevo Travel: www.atevo.com/guides/destinations. Detailed introductions, travel tips, and suggested itineraries.

Columbus Travel Guides: www.travel-guides.com/navigate/world.asp. Helpful practical information.

How to See the World: www.artoftravel.com. A compendium of great travel tips, from cheap flights to self defense to interacting with local culture.

Rec. Travel Library: www.travel-library.com. A fantastic set of links for general information and personal travelogues.

Shoestring Travel: www.stratpub.com. An e-zine focusing on budget travel.

INFORMATION ON INDIA AND NEPAL

CIA World Factbook: www.odci.gov/cia/publications/factbook/index.html. Tons of vital statistics on the geography, government, economy, and people of India and Nepal.

Geographia: www.geographia.com. Describes the highlights, culture, and people of India and Nepal.

LeisurePlanet: www.leisureplanet.com/TravelGuides. Good general background.

Indian and Nepali governments: www.indiagov.org and www.info-nepal.com. Offer collections of cultural, business, and tourism resources.

Times of India: www.timesofindia.com. The premier English-language newspaper of India.

Tour India: www.tourindia.com. A useful site on Indian tourism, providing links to the Indian airlines and tourist offices throughout the subcontinent.

Tourism India: www.tourisminindia.com. All-singing, all-dancing site with lots of groovy pictures and information on everything from heavy industry to camel safaris. Links to transport, accommodations, and cultural information.

World Wide Web Virtual Library: http://webhead.com/WWWVL/India/index.html. Hundreds of links to all things India.

AND OUR PERSONAL FAVORITE...

Let's Go: www.letsgo.com. Our recently revamped website features photos and streaming video, info about our books, a travel forum buzzing with stories and tips, and links that will help you find up-to-date info on India and Nepal.

INDIA भारत

GEOGRAPHY

India's terrain has been compared to the colors of the country's flag: green tropical jungle, white Himalayan snow, and orange-red Deccan earth. In fact, the landscape is more intricate and diverse than even this poetic description suggests. The great range of the **Himalayas** (literally, "abode of snow") crowns the country, forming a historical barrier between India and Central Asia, Tibet, and China. Highest of all the world's mountain ranges, the mighty Himalayas extend over 2000km. Here are the sources of the subcontinent's three great rivers, the **Indus,** the **Ganga,** and the **Brahmaputra.** Fed by rain and glacial melt-off, these rivers and their many tributaries nourish the vast, densely-populated **Indo-Gangetic Plain,** which stretches from Rajasthan in the west to Bengal in the east.

The **Vindhyas,** a belt of stepped hills, divide the Indo-Gangetic Plain from the **Deccan Plateau,** on which rest present-day Maharashtra, Karnataka, and Andhra Pradesh. Washed by the **Arabian Sea** to the west and the **Bay of Bengal** to the east, peninsular India narrows as it stretches south, dipping into the **Indian Ocean** at its tip, Kanyakumari. Flanking the **Malabar Coast** of Kerala, Karnataka, and Goa, the **Western Ghats** (a north-south chain of mid-sized hills) are separated from the coast by a narrow strip of richly forested coastal plain. The eastern **Coromandel Coast** is broader. The Ghats come together at the **Nilgiri Hills** of Kerala and Tamil Nadu, the southern tip of the Deccan Plateau. The **Lakshadweep Islands,** just off the Malabar coast in the Arabian Sea, and the **Andaman and Nicobar Islands** in the Bay of Bengal, are also Indian territories.

PEOPLE AND LANGUAGES

The billion or so people who live in India represent such diversity that the country sometimes feels like a dozen nations packed into one. Six major religions (see p. 76), 18 major languages, and countless racial and ethnic groups coexist in India, often harmoniously, sometimes not. Seventy-five percent of the population lives in rural areas, largely unaffected by the changes that industrialization has brought to India's huge cities. Population is densest in the valley and delta of the Ganga and in the extreme south (Tamil Nadu and Kerala). India's four largest cities, Bombay, Calcutta, Delhi, and Madras make up only 4% of the population. Population growth is a major issue in India; almost 20 million people are born each year, putting ever more pressure on the country's already depleted supply of natural resources. UN studies project that the population of India will hit 1.5 billion within the next 50 years, overtaking China as the most populous country on earth.

India's ethnic make-up reflects a mixture of the light-skinned **Aryan** peoples, who still live mostly in the north, and the darker-skinned **Dravidian** peoples of the south. Numerous smaller groups of *adivasi* **(aboriginal peoples)** are concentrated in the northeastern states of Madhya Pradesh, Orissa, and Gujarat, though they also live in other parts of the subcontinent. The *adivasi* predate the arrival of the Aryans and Dravidians in India, though many of them have been subject to exploitation and have been pushed off their ancestral lands.

The people of India speak as many as 1600 dialects, varying from state to state and village to village. North Indian languages such as **Hindi** and **Bengali** descended from Sanskrit, the language spoken by the Aryan invaders who wandered into the area around 1500 BC. These languages are part of the larger Indo-European family, and it's not unusual to find North Indian words that resemble their counterparts in English or other European languages. **Urdu,** spoken by many Muslims in India, is structurally very similar to Hindi, but borrows heavily from Persian. The major **South Indian languages,** Kannada, Telugu, Malayalam, and Tamil, all belong to the Dravidian family and are unrelated to the North Indian languages.

SCRIPTS OF INDIA Devanagari भारत is the most common script in South Asia, used for the Hindi, Marathi, Konkani, Rajasthani, and Nepali languages. Variants of the Devanagari script include **Gurmukhi ਪੰਜਾਬ,** used for Punjabi, **Gujarati** ગુજરાત, **Bengali** পশ্চিম বঙ্গ, and **Oriya** ଓଡ଼ିଶା. In the south, Dravidian languages are spoken, and the scripts used look nothing like their Sanskrit-inspired counterparts to the north. **Tamil** தமிழ் நாடு and **Malayalam** കേരളം share similar scripts, as do **Kannada** ಕರ್ನಾಟಕ and **Telugu** ఆంధ్రప్రదేశ్. **Urdu** script کشمیر, uses the Persian alphabet and is the state language of Kashmir.

The 1950s reorganization of India into new states according to linguistic boundaries recognized 18 official languages—Assamese, Bengali, Gujarati, Hindi, Kannada, Kashmiri, Konkani, Malayalam, Manipuri, Marathi, Nepali, Oriya, Punjabi, Sanskrit, Sindhi, Tamil, Telugu, and Urdu. The Indian constitution (written in English) planned for Hindi to be the national language; used by about 30% of the people, it is the most widely-spoken Indian language. Attempts to spread Hindi have met with much resentment, however; don't be surprised to find that some people in India are willing to speak anything *but* Hindi, particularly in South India. English is the first language of many upper-class Indians, and millions more learn English in school. It is easy to get around India with English, as long as you don't mind having the same simple cricket-and-culture conversation with everybody you meet. For basic Hindi, Bengali, Tamil, Marathi, Gujarati, Telugu, Kannada, Malayalam, and Nepali vocabularies, see the **Phrasebook,** p. 826.

GOVERNMENT AND POLITICS

In September and October 1999, 590 million voters in India turned out to cast their ballots for over 14,000 candidates vying for 543 parliamentary seats—the largest democratic elections anywhere in the world. The fact that India's frenzied popular politics have plodded along more or less successfully for 53 years despite persistent secessionist threats, extreme malnutrition and human suffering, and even a brief bout with totalitarian rule in the 1970s (see **Indira's India,** p. 73) has been something of a marvel to political scientists for the last half century. Somehow, the parliamentary system, inherited from Britain, has managed to adapt to the needs and peculiarities of the immense and diverse Indian state.

The country's **constitution,** adopted in 1950, is the largest in the world, with 395 articles legislating, among other things, universal suffrage and fundamental rights. The Indian constitution is distinctive in combining traditional liberal rights—freedom of press, free speech, and free association—with a series of **Directive Principles,** designed to deal with the social and economic reforms essential for a poor democracy. The framers of the constitution sought to create a **federal system** that would reflect India's diversity, but they also wanted a central government strong enough to handle poverty and religious conflict. The result has been a highly centralized form of federalism, with the national government holding the power to dismiss state governments in an emergency, an option known as **"President's Rule."**

At the head of India's government are the vice-president, a council of ministers, and the prime minister. The president, appointed for a five-year term, is essentially a figurehead. The prime minister, chosen by the majority party in the **Lok Sabha** (House of the People), the lower house, holds the real executive power. The Lok Sabha and the **Rajya Sabha** (Council of States), chosen by the state governments, together make up the Indian parliament.

Each of India's 26 states has a similar governmental structure. **Governors,** chosen by the prime minister's cabinet, act as figureheads, while the real power lies with the **chief minister.** Each state also has a legislative assembly, or **Vidhan Sabha,** whose members are elected for five years. Although the state governments depend on the national government for financial support, they have jurisdiction over education, agriculture, welfare, and the police. State governments are divided into local administrations, with the **panchayat** or village council at the lowest level. India's **Supreme Court** is remarkably independent, often asserting its right to make decisions on controversial issues that others would rather avoid.

India might be a working democracy, but its government has been dominated by one family (and their one party, the **Congress Party**) since 1947: Jawaharlal Nehru, his daughter, Indira Gandhi, and her son, Rajiv Gandhi, have all been Prime Ministers; Rajiv's brother, Sanjay, was one of the most powerful men in India, despite never being elected to any position; and in 1998 Rajiv's widow, the Italian-born Sonia Gandhi, assumed leadership of her mother-in-law's party. Despite Congress' tradition of inclusiveness, it has found it difficult to unite the conflicting interests of ideology, caste, region, and religion. As a result, politics have become highly regionalized, with parties such as the **DMK** (in Tamil Nadu), the **Communist Party of India** (in Bengal), and the **Akali Dal** (in Punjab) earning more votes in state elections than Congress. In the 1996 national elections, no single party won a majority of seats in the Lok Sabha, leading to the formation of a piecemeal left-wing coalition made up of populist, lower-caste parties such as the Janata Dal and the Communist Party of India, which ruled with the support of Congress. In the last few years, political momentum has shifted toward the **Bharatiya Janata Party (BJP),** the most prominent of a group of Hindu nationalist parties known as the *Sangh Pariwar.* Under the leadership of Atal Bihari Vajpayee, the BJP won the majority of the Lok Sabha seats in last year's elections, unnerving intellectuals and traditional Congress supporters disturbed by the manner in which India's democracy has steered the country away from the core political value of secularism.

Indian politics have been increasingly affected by **caste politics,** as lower castes have started to translate their demographic strength into political clout, particularly in northern states like Bihar and Uttar Pradesh. The widespread corruption in Indian politics is often attributed to this rise in lower-caste parties—a perceived departure from the genteel style of politics (supposedly) practiced during the heyday of Congress. Numerous state and national governments have been brought down by corruption scandals, and violence is used in some regions to intimidate voters. On the whole, though, India's democracy runs remarkably smoothly. Given the low levels of literacy, its consistently high rates of voter participation represent a major achievement.

ECONOMICS

In his famous "Tryst with Destiny" speech, delivered on the eve of Independence, Prime Minister Jawaharlal Nehru promised "the ending of poverty and ignorance and disease and inequality of opportunity" in the new state. In order to achieve these ambitious goals, Nehru, a Fabian-inspired socialist, drew from the Soviet Union and advocated a development model that emphasized heavy industrialization and state ownership of major companies. The aim of this approach, encapsulated in a series of **Five Year Plans,** was for India to attain self-sufficiency in the tradition of the *swadeshi* movement (in which India boycotted British imports). In a sense, this isolationist move worked: direct foreign investment was virtually nil throughout the 1950s and 1960s, and stringent licensing requirements, known as the **"license-permit raj,"** restricted private enterprise. The outcome was anything but self-sufficiency, however; the economy puttered along at a growth rate of 5% per annum, a figure derisively referred to as the **"Hindu rate of growth."**

In 1991, a shortfall in foreign exchange reserves resulted in a **financial crisis** that almost forced the Indian government to default on its foreign debt. Under pressure from reformers within India and from loan agencies around the world, India made dramatic changes in its economic policies, eliminating licenses, scrapping import quotas, and disbanding a handful of state-owned companies. The immediate result of these efforts was an upsurge in economic growth rates and an influx of multinational corporations, especially in the areas of communications, electricity, and computer technology. For average Indians, the impact of liberalization was more tangible, as millions were able for the first time to get their hands on popular international brands like Colgate and Pepsi, which had previously been smuggled into the country by relatives abroad.

Economic liberalization still has a long way to go. The government has delayed the sale of money-losing public sector industries for fear of massive lay-offs, and the rise to power of a Hindu nationalist government has spooked foreign investors, who fear a return to the economic isolationism of earlier eras. And the benefits of rapid economic growth have still to reach the poorer segments of Indian society. Slum communities continue to proliferate in the cities, and as much as 30% of the rural population suffers from malnutrition. Per capita income nationally is only US$440, just under half of the population remains illiterate, and life expectancy is still only 63 years.

HISTORY

PRE-HISTORY AND THE INDUS VALLEY CIVILIZATION

India gets its English name from the Indus River, and it was along the banks of this river that the first significant civilization on the subcontinent flourished around four thousand years ago. During the 1920s, the forgotten remains of what had once been huge cities were unearthed at the archaeological sites of **Harappa** and **Mohenjo-Daro** (both in modern Pakistan). This discovery added more than a thousand years to India's documented past, and historians were given their first glimpses of a civilization that was once one of the richest in the world.

The Indus valley civilization prospered for more than a thousand years. It was made up of as many as 100 cities, stretched out across an area of almost half a million square miles. The population of its metropolitan centers—like the one at Harappa—was perhaps as high as 35,000. The streets of its cities were laid out in neat grids that incorporated elaborately engineered drainage systems centered on a "Great Bath," probably used for ritual purposes. The Indus dwellers were skilled farmers and had highly developed systems of irrigation, which allowed them to harvest and keep huge stores of wheat and barley. Unearthed artifacts indicate that the Indus people traded by land and sea with the ancient civilizations that flourished along the banks of the Nile, Tigris, and Euphrates Rivers. Little else is known about the everyday life of the people who made up this culture; their script, found on numerous seals, remains indecipherable. These seals feature humans, gods, and animals, both real and imaginary, and suggest that the Indus people worshipped a mother-goddess and a deity who perhaps represents a distant precursor of the Hindu god Shiva. It was probably environmental change that brought about the eventual collapse of the Indus civilization. Tectonic plate movements around 1800 BC caused the Indus River to change its course, flooding the carefully irrigated farmland that had brought prosperity to the valley for a millennium.

THE ARYANS (1500–300 BC)

As the Indus civilization went into decline, a new group entered the subcontinent. The Aryans were a nomadic branch of the violent Indo-European tribes that had been raping and pillaging their way across the continents since being dislodged from their original home in the foothills of the Caucasus around 2000 BC. They spread out in all directions, and a group of them entered the subcontinent via the northwest frontier, establishing themselves in India by around 1500 BC.

A loose band of tribes, each ruled by a *raja* (or king), the Aryans spread out gradually from the Punjab and the Indus Valley until they occupied most of northern India. With their snorting horses and their spoke-wheeled chariots, these fight-hungry warriors brought with them a technology and a culture that permanently altered the civilizations they encountered, normally by smashing them to pieces.

The language of the Aryans was **Sanskrit** (in which *arya* means "noble one"), a member of the family of Indo-European languages that spawned Latin and Greek and which is the root of the modern North Indian languages. Their religion was characterized by a ritual worship of the forces of nature. They performed fire-sacrifices to guarantee the continued support of **Agni,** the fire god, and **Indra,** the god of war and a personification of the violent monsoon. They also sang songs to **Soma,** god of the liquor they used for making oblations to the deities they had brought with them to their new home. These rites were performed by the brahmins, sages of the priestly caste who chanted the hymns of the **Rig Veda,** a collection of Sanskrit hymns transmitted orally for several centuries until they were written down between 1200 and 400 BC (see **Vedic Literature,** p. 77).

The Aryans brought to the subcontinent not only their language and religion but also a new social order. Aryan society was divided into three classes or *varna* (colors), probably originally based on race. The social hierarchy, made up of the **brahmin** (priests), the **kshatriya** (warriors), and the **vaishya** (merchants), formed the basis for what later became the caste system (see **Caste,** p. 76). The Aryans were a wild and unruly lot. When they weren't busy fighting each other or subjugating their neighbors, their favorite pastimes seem to have been boozing, dancing, and gambling, as well as music-making and chariot-racing. As they moved deeper into new territory, the Aryans came across indigenous peoples whom they referred to as *dasa*, or slaves. The *dasa* were probably the ancestors of South India's Dravidian people, and the remaining survivors of the once-great Indus civilization, who fled south when it collapsed. Taken as slaves by the Aryans, the *dasa* were incorporated into society as a servant class, the *shudra*, who were forbidden even to hear the powerful Vedic hymns.

The environment of India did much to change the cultural practices of the Aryans. As they moved into the Doab, the fertile plain of the Ganga and Yamuna Rivers, the Aryan tribes tended to consolidate themselves into ever-larger kingdoms and began to settle down into more permanent towns and villages. By the time they reached what is now Bihar around 1000 BC, they had learned how to make tools from iron. This discovery allowed them to clear the great forests that covered the region, and they brought huge areas under cultivation for the first time.

A civilization born on the road is unlikely to do well in a more settled environment. By the end of the period depicted in the great Indian epics, the **Mahabharata** and the **Ramayana,** the Aryans were rough and rowdy nomads no longer, and many had started to grow dissatisfied with the old brahmin-run religion and its elite corps of secretive priests. Centuries of migration and assimilation had led to the development of a more elaborate, more settled culture. A re-examination of the meaning behind the sacrifice and vision of the Vedic hymns led to a revolt against the authority of the brahmin and the wisdom of their age-old ways. This reformative spirit was expressed most profoundly in the **Upanishads,** which criticized the performance of ritual as superfluous to the religious quest. During the 6th century there emerged two new faiths, Jainism and Buddhism, which both provided alternatives to that good, old-time religion (also see **Religion,** p. 76).

THE MAURYAS (300–200 BC)

By the 6th century BC, the Aryans occupied the whole of northern India, where 16 separate Aryan kingdoms struggled for supremacy. Having finished his conquest of Persia and the Mediterranean, **Alexander the Great** proceeded toward India's northwest frontier in 326 BC, ready to move into the subcontinent, plunder its lands, and add its riches to his collection. His troops had already had enough of their general's taste for empire-building, however, and they grew tired of the endless marches against unknown enemies. Alexander was forced to turn back when his troops mutinied, but the aborted Greek invasion seems to have provided both the inspiration and the instability that allowed another conqueror to bring large chunks of India under unified control before long. Shortly after Alexander's retreat, **Chandragupta Maurya,** an adventurer from eastern India, seized control of the kingdom of Magadha, the most powerful Aryan state, located in present-day Bihar. Chandragupta moved quickly to subdue the area around the Ganga valley, and he continued to consolidate his power throughout the north of India. Over the next 100 years the Mauryan Empire, ruling from its capital at Pataliputra, the site of modern Patna (see p. 628), came to control the whole of the subcontinent apart from the southern tip—the closest that anybody would come to wielding undivided power over all of India until modern times.

At the height of the empire's power, its policies of violent military expansion were abandoned after the ruthless invasion of the Kalinga Kingdom in present-day Orissa, during which more than 100,000 people were killed. The great Mauryan emperor **Ashoka** (r. 269-232 BC) was so affected by this bloody battle that he renounced violence forever and became an ardent Buddhist. With the last of his enemies now conveniently dead, Ashoka began to preach the virtues of peaceful government, and he set about propagating a policy of non-violence *(ahimsa)*. Edicts promoting the message of Buddhism to the status of official creed were inscribed on pillars and stones, and rules were passed to ensure the vast lands under Mauryan control would be governed according to the rule of "moral law." The Mauryan Empire collapsed not long after Ashoka's death, but many of his edict-inscribed pillars still stand today.

TRADE AND THE GROWTH OF BUDDHISM (200 BC-300 AD)

After the disintegration of the Mauryan Empire around 200 BC, India was politically divided once again. It would be another five hundred years before another dynasty, that of the Guptas, would exert a similar degree of unifying authority over all of northern India. In the meantime, a series of invasions from the north coincided with the growing power and assertiveness of the southern kingdoms to ensure that India remained fragmented in a number of small regional domains. Despite the lack of political unity, however, the subcontinent experienced a period of great economic prosperity and cultural ferment.

This period also witnessed the zenith of Buddhism in South Asia. **Mahayana Buddhism,** which put less emphasis on monastic seriousness and made more effort to appeal to the masses, proved attractive to many dissatisfied with the high-minded dominance of the brahmin class. Many Hindus were turning away from the old rituals, and a new devotional movement emerged, which encouraged personal worship of the gods, without the help or interference of priests and prayers. Competing with Buddhism, the **bhakti** (devotion) movement spread from the south throughout the subcontinent, and it gradually brought most of India back into the Hindu fold. (see **Hindu Practice,** p. 80).

Buddhism inspired a number of artistic and intellectual pursuits. Sculpture, in particular, reached new heights. Of particular interest is the Buddhist sculpture produced in the northwestern region of **Gandhara,** characterized by a unique fusion of Greek and Indian styles. At the same time, Indian medicine and astronomy were making rapid progress, thanks to a helping hand from the Greeks, who had settled down on the northwest frontier after Alexander's campaigns. In the fields of linguistics and mathematics, though, India was already far ahead of Greece. A scientific system for Sanskrit grammar had been developed as early as the 4th century BC, and Indian mathematicians were the first ones to make a big fuss about nothing: they invented the concept of zero, as well as the system of numerals called "Arabic" by Europeans who learned of it from Arab merchants.

GUPTAS: A GOLDEN AGE (300–500 AD)

In 319 AD another man with the name of **Chandragupta** came to power in the eastern kingdom of Magadha. No relation to the founder of the Maurya dynasty, Chandragupta II followed in the illustrious footsteps of his namesake, and launched an empire of his own. From their capital up in Pataliputra (since revamped into the ever-popular tourist town of Patna in Bihar), Chandragupta II and his successors expanded their influence up and down the Ganga Valley. At the peak of its power under **Chandragupta II** (r. 375-415), the Gupta Empire held sway over all of Northern India.

The Guptas are remembered today for the cultural refinement and religious tolerance of the period they dominated, often thought of as India's "Golden Age." They were great patrons of the arts and sciences, into which they funneled the proceeds of the overseas trade that brought such wealth to their court. This was the age of Vatsyayana's famous **Kama Sutra**, the indispensable manual that taught the young man everything he needed to know about the ins and outs of good loving. India's first stone dams and temples were built during this time, and the cave-sculptures at **Ajanta** were painstakingly carved out of a sheer cliff face (see p. 423). **Kalidasa**, perhaps India's greatest lyric poet, served at the court of Chandragupta II. Although they sponsored the activities of all religions, the Guptas themselves were Hindu, and they were especially supportive of Hindu theological studies. They donated huge sums toward the building of Hindu temples, and many of their laws were based directly on the Hindu canon.

Most of South India lay outside the borders of the Gupta Empire, but the South was an active participant in the culture of the age nonetheless. Northern traders and priests had succeeded in bringing the South into the Hindu fold by this time, and southern rulers tended to model the government of their kingdoms on Aryan political structures. Despite this Aryanization of southern politics, South Indian culture continued to be strongly independent in most other areas: distinctly southern architectural styles emerged, and Tamil poet-saints and thinkers joined the ranks of the holiest Hindus, leading the *bhakti* devotional movement that eventually overtook the north.

REGIONALISM (500–1192)

The Gupta Empire disintegrated during the 5th century when it came under attack from the Huns of Central Asia. North India broke into small kingdoms again and remained divided for 700 years—except for the years from 606 to 647, when the young conqueror and poet-king **Harsha** built an empire from his capital at **Kanauj,** just north of modern Delhi. An account of the king's life, the *Harshacarita*, is considered one of the finest examples of Sanskrit poetic style.

The strongest kingdom in India at this time was the **Chola** dynasty from Tamil Nadu, which conquered most of the southern peninsula and sent forces to the Maldives, Sri Lanka, and Malaysia. A group of warriors known as the **Rajputs** became the major force in northwest India after the 8th century. They set up several small kingdoms from their base in the **Thar Desert** in Rajasthan and developed a culture distinguished by chivalric values, a proud literary tradition, and an impressive architectural legacy. The clans were too fond of fighting one another, however, to unify as a single empire. The Rajputs would eventually have to contend with the most serious foreign challenge of the age: people from the west with big swords, new ideas, and the desire and the power to change India. The divided kingdoms were not in a good position to deal with the coming assault.

THE ARRIVAL OF ISLAM (1192–1526)

The Prophet Mohammed received his revelations from God at the beginning of the 7th century AD (see p. 82). **Islam** spread rapidly from its birthplace in Arabia, and it soon reached right up to Sindh on the western frontiers of India. Muslims traded with India by sea, and number of Muslims settled on the west coast, but Islam made little impression on the subcontinent during its first 300 years. This changed with the raids of **Mahmud of Ghazni,** the king of a Turkish dynasty in Afghanistan. Between 997 and 1030 Mahmud's armies swarmed in to loot North India on an almost annual basis. But Mahmud, content just to loot and pillage, never made any attempt at a more permanent invasion.

At the end of the 12th century, another Turko-Afghan king, **Mohammed of Ghur,** did move in on India with conquest on his mind. In 1192, he defeated a loose coalition of Rajput armies and conquered the Ganga Valley. Though Mohammed himself soon disappeared back home to Afghanistan, he left his slave-general **Qutb-ud-din Aibak** behind in Delhi to govern his newly conquered lands (see **Qutb Minar,** p. 116). When Mohammed died in 1206, Qutb-ud-din succeeded him, and he proclaimed the birth of the **Delhi Sultanate,** India's first Muslim kingdom. The Sultanate ruled most of North India for 300 years. By the early 15th century, independent Muslim kingdoms had emerged in Bengal, Gujarat, and Central India. The Delhi Sultanate's hold on power was always precarious. The palace was in constant turmoil, and the sultans' habit of financing their extravagant life at court with taxes paid by the Hindu masses caused frequent revolts and widespread unhappiness. A particularly irksome setback for India's new rulers came in 1398, when the Central Asian conqueror **Tamerlane** arrived in Delhi and burned it to ashes.

Islam won itself huge numbers of converts in India during this period. The fact that the new faith accepted members of all castes as equals worked in its favor, making the new religion particularly attractive to those at the bottom of the caste-controlled ladder of Hindu India. In some parts of the country, Hindu monarchs tried to resist the impact of the Muslim sultans. The Hindu **Vijayanagars** ruled portions of South India from 1336 to 1565, building temples wherever possible until they were defeated by a coalition of Muslim sultanates from the Deccan.

Several movements grew up at this time that attempted to mediate between the two faiths. In Punjab, **Guru Nanak** was attracting adherents to **Sikhism,** a new religion that synthesized some of the best aspects of Hinduism and Islam, with some new ideas of its own thrown in for good measure (see p. 83). Islam spread among the masses thanks to wandering Sufi mystics and saints, whose religion was similar to popular devotional movements in Hinduism. Ultimately, religious fragmentation served to undermine the centralized political authority of the **Lodis,** the last dynasty of the Delhi Sultanate. Provincial governors seceded in Bihar, Portuguese ships landed in Goa, and in central India the one-eyed, one-armed Rajput leader Rana Sanaga called for foreign intervention to vanquish the Delhi Sultanate.

THE MUGHALS (1526–1700)

Rana Sanaga's call was heeded by the Central Asian warlord **Babur** (1483-1530). Babur came from an impressive pedigree: he could count both Tamerlane and Genghis Khan among his ancestors. His career as a conqueror started early. He took Samarkand at the age of 13 and Kabul eight years later. Recalling his attack on the Delhi Sultanate, Babur later wrote, "I placed my foot in the stirrup of resolution, and my palms I placed on the reins of confidence in Allah." In the Battle of Panipat, fought outside of Delhi in the spring of 1526, Babur prevailed against numerically superior forces and crushed the Lodi dynasty. In 1530 when Babur's son **Humayun** became sick, Babur prayed that the sickness afflicting his son would be transferred to him. It worked: within weeks, Babur was dead and buried in Kabul, and Humayun had been proclaimed emperor over territories that now stretched all the way from Bihar to Kabul. The great Mughal Dynasty had begun.

Addicted to opium and dependent on the not-always-accurate predictions of his astrologers, Humayun was an unpromising leader of the ethnically diverse armies under his control, and within a decade revolt was in the air. In 1540, Humayun was deposed by the Afghan warlord Sher Shah, who had carved out a kingdom for himself in the east. Humayun was sent out to sit on the sand dunes of the Sindh desert, while Sher Shah made his position secure. But not secure enough: he was killed during a siege of a Rajput stronghold in 1545, and Humayun was quick to make his comeback. With Persian help he managed to take back Delhi, but died an ignominious death only months later, when he took a fatal tumble down the staircase that led up to his library. In 1555, his son **Akbar** (1542-1605), who had been born in the Sindh desert during Humayun's wanderings, became emperor.

Akbar was only 13 when he succeeded his father, but he quickly proved himself to be quite a leader, squashing rebellions and cementing Mughal hegemony with successful campaigns in Rajasthan, Gujarat, Orissa, Kashmir, and Bengal. As Akbar consolidated his empire through battle, he formulated policies rooted in the assumption that the Mughals' long-term future lay in the south of India, rather than in Central Asia. Akbar created a **centralized imperial bureaucracy** that gave a more permanent and more organized structure to Mughal rule. The emperor and his inner circle also drew up an efficient system of **revenue collection.** No longer would it be necessary to go out and conquer new territories every time the Emperor wanted to buy clothes for the favorite members of his harem. Akbar was wise enough to realize that if the Mughals were to maintain their dominance of South Asia, they could not rely on brute force and repression forever—the Muslim Mughals would need to earn the trust of the Hindu majority. To give the Hindu elite a stake in the success of the Mughal regime, Akbar married a Rajput princess and appointed Hindus to important government posts. In an attempt to make himself more popular with the masses, he called a halt to the destruction of Hindu temples and eliminated the *jizya*, a widely despised tax levied on non-Muslims.

In the arts, Akbar's policies and patronage made possible an unprecedented mingling of Hindu and Muslim sensibilities. North Indian music began to assimilate Persian influences, and Hindu painters began to experiment with miniature painting, a style made popular by the Mughals. The **Urdu** language, with its Persian vocabulary and Hindi grammatical structure, spread throughout the north, and Muslims began to adopt the Hindu practice of pilgrimage to the tombs of holy figures. Akbar invited Hindus, Jains, Christians, and Zoroastrians to discuss their faiths in his court, and he later attempted to found a new religion based upon ideas taken from all the major religious systems of the region.

Akbar's successors **Jehangir** (r. 1605-27) and **Shah Jahan** (r. 1628-57) continued to build on Akbar's work. Together, their reigns were a golden era for the Mughals; the populace was well-fed, and the empire's frontiers were relatively secure. This period also saw the construction of a series of stunningly beautiful buildings, including some of the most famous landmarks in the world—the marble **Taj Mahal** in Agra (p. 172) and the sandstone **Red Fort** in Delhi (p. 114). When Shah Jahan fell ill in 1657, however, his sons went to war. The bloody family feud that followed left the empire in the hands of **Aurangzeb,** who had murdered his older brother during the succession struggle and who locked Shah Jahan in the fort at Agra, in case his health should improve.

Aurangzeb ruled South Asia for 48 years. During his reign, Mughal armies conquered huge tracts of land in southern and eastern India. Fanatically pious, Aurangzeb rolled back a century of tolerant social policy and made it difficult again for Hindus to advance through the civil service bureaucracy. He banned the repair of Hindu temples and brought back the hated *jizya* tax. Aurangzeb's pagan-hating radicalism did nothing to endear him to ordinary Indians, and it caused the Hindu majority to turn against Mughal rule. By the time the Aurangzeb died, well into his eighties, the Mughal empire was already going to pieces. For the next half-century, the Mughals would continue to rule in name only. Delhi was sacked and looted by Persians in 1738 and by Afghans in 1757.

As Mughal control over northern India slipped, others stepped up to take their place; the Maratha leader **Shivaji Bhonsle** (see p. 414) posed a serious threat to the Mughals during the reign of Aurangzeb, and for much of the 18th century the **Maratha Confederacy** seemed to stand the best chance of taking over the Mughals' position of power. The Marathas were dealt a decisive defeat in 1761 by an invading Afghan army, however. The Confederacy fell to pieces, and the way was clear for another empire to play a politically dominant role in South Asia.

BRITISH INTERFERENCE (1700-57)

European ships had been sailing the seas for hundreds of years in search of the famed riches of the exotic East, but India did not see the Europeans arrive in substantial numbers until the 17th century, when ever-larger numbers of English, Portuguese, Dutch, and French began to turn up as the agents of government-chartered trading companies. The gradual decline of Portuguese sea power, together with the decision of the Dutch to concentrate their spice-collecting energies elsewhere, opened the way for the **British East India Company** to assert an almost monopolistic control over the resources of South Asia. From its posts in Calcutta and Madras, the Company ran a highly profitable trade, exchanging gold and silver for Indian finished goods, especially hand-crafted textiles.

The Company recruited small Indian armies and equipped them with European-made weapons to defend its warehouses. These mercenary armies allowed the Company to became a powerful controlling force in Bengal during the mid-18th century. It was soon to extend its influence even farther. Led by Robert Clive, the Company allied itself with a coalition of Muslims and Hindus and, after a series of battles culminating in the **Battle of Plassey** in 1757, established unrivalled authority over vast areas of Eastern India.

EAST INDIA COMPANY GOVERNMENT (1757-1857)

During the late 18th century, the Company, led first by Warren Hastings and then by Lord Cornwallis, was divided into separate political and commercial units. It soon developed a British-dominated bureaucracy to administer its Indian territories. The **Permanent Settlement** of 1793 saw land redistributed so that the Mughal *zamindars* (landowners) became owners of the lands they administered. The settlement created an elite class of moneyed Indians, who acted as a buffer between the Company and the masses.

Between the late 1820s and 1857, the Company was guided by two concerns: the elimination of practices they deemed immoral and an attempt to recast Indian society in a European mold. Railways, textile mills, and telegraphs were introduced, while other practices were outlawed, such as **sati**, the Hindu custom according to which widows were burned on their husbands' funeral pyres, and **thugi,** ritual robbery and murder practiced by devotees of the goddess Kali. In keeping with their goal of improving Indian culture by infusing it with Western ideals, British authorities changed the official language of state from Urdu to English and funded the development of secondary schools, medical colleges, and universities. In all of these, both the curriculum and language of instruction were English. India was administered by "enlightened liberals" like Lord Macaulay, who was fond of remarking that "one shelf of a good English library has more worth than native literature in its entirety."

As British imperialism undermined traditional institutions, millions of Indians grew resentful that the new rulers cared nothing about the severe and persistent poverty that continued to afflict most of India's people. British officials struggled to extend their authority in the face of seething discontent, inventing an absurd legal fiction, the **Doctrine of Lapse,** which allowed the British to annex any Indian kingdom whose ruler died without a male heir. By the 1850s, Indian discontent had grown extremely volatile, and it was not long before the situation turned violent.

MUTINY AND AFTERMATH (1857-58)

In 1857, the Company introduced a new weapon for use by its 200,000 sepoys (hired Indian soldiers). The Lee-Enfield rifle used ammunition cartridges rumored to be lubricated with a mixture of pig and cow fat. Hindus (for whom cows are sacred) and Muslims (for whom pigs are impure) were incensed when they

INDIA

learned that soldiers had to bite the tip off the cartridges with their teeth before loading them. What followed in May 1857 became known as the **Sepoy Mutiny,** in which Indian soldiers raised the Mughal flag over Delhi, indiscriminately massacring Europeans as they reclaimed the city. Lucknow also fell to forces eager to send the Brits back home. But Indian victory was short-lived. Backed by Sikh regiments, British troops retaliated four months later, recapturing Delhi and Lucknow at the cost of great numbers of Indian lives. By March of 1858, the Mutiny of 1857—or the War of Independence, as Indian nationalists prefer to call it—had been fully suppressed.

The revolt horrified the British and brought about dramatic changes in the way they governed their possessions in India. An 1858 Act of Parliament stripped the East India Company of its right to rule; within a year, the Crown was administering India directly as a full-fledged colony of the Empire. The **Raj** had begun. To ensure tight control over India, Crown authorities increased the number of British troops stationed in South Asia, banned Indians from becoming officers in the army, and staffed the upper echelons of the burgeoning Indian Civil Service with bureaucrats of British birth. Assuming an attitude marked by increasingly explicit racism, the British tended to withdraw from Indian society, setting up hill stations remote from the cities and abandoning their quest to westernize South Asia.

CROWN RULE AND INDIAN RENEWAL (1858–1915)

As British authority became more invasive, a century-long period of religious revivalism gained momentum. Hindu groups such as the mystical Ramakrishna Mission were formed. This period also saw the birth of the socio-religious **Arya Samaj** movement, which sought to reconcile traditional Hindu beliefs and practices with the growing influence of the colonialists. In order to achieve this goal, the Arya Samaj developed its own *Golden History* of India, still used today by the modern Hindu nationalist movement. Islam underwent a renewal of a different nature. Prominent leaders like **Sir Sayyid Ahmed Khan,** sharing the British contempt for Indian backwardness, worked to reverse the anti-Muslim sentiment that many of India's British rulers had felt since the events of the Mutiny. Khan sought to remedy the situation through the introduction of Western-style education. He founded a college at **Aligarh** that would grow into a center for the Muslim intellectuals later instrumental in the creation of Pakistan.

Demanding reform and more control over the way their country was governed, a group of 70 wealthy Indians met in Bombay in 1885 to form the **Indian National Congress,** a political association that would come to exert a huge influence on India's future. As it grew, Congress split into two wings: the moderates, who advocated reform but were content to remain a part of the Empire, and the extremists, who wanted to put an end to British meddling in Indian affairs once and for all. The extremist view began to win widespread support after 1905, when the British viceroy partitioned Bengal into two provinces: one with a Hindu majority, the other dominated by Muslims. President of Congress **Gopal Krishna Gokhale** articulated the anger and resentment felt by millions of Indians in 1905. "A cruel wrong has been inflicted on our Bengali brethren," Gokhale proclaimed. "The scheme of partition…will always stand as a complete illustration of the worst features of the present system of bureaucratic rule."

The terms of the debate had shifted, and from now on self-rule, or **swaraj,** was the ultimate objective. In the decade that followed the partition of Bengal, Indians from a wide variety of backgrounds did what they could to show their resistance to British rule. Millions of Indians boycotted British-made textiles, opting instead for the rougher, homespun *swadeshi* cloth, worn proudly as a symbol of national self-sufficiency. Muslims concerned about Hindu domination of Congress founded the **All-India Muslim League** in 1906.

Indian nationalist leaders cooperated with the British during the First World War, hoping that their loyalty would be rewarded with greater freedoms once the war was over. No such luck. Instead, the British introduced still more oppressive measures, suspending civil liberties and placing India under martial law. The brutality always inherent in foreign rule came to prominence in 1919, when British soldiers, led by the infamous General Dyer, opened fire on a group of unarmed Indians who had assembled in **Amritsar** to protest. Over 400 people were killed.

It was into this atmosphere of violence and unrest that **Mohandas Karamchand Gandhi** (later proclaimed the Mahatma or "Great Soul" by Bengali poet Rabindranath Tagore) returned from England in 1915. Born into a Gujarati *vaishya* family in 1869, Gandhi had gone abroad to study law. After completing his education in Britain, Gandhi spent 20 years in South Africa, where he devoted his energies to an attempt to end racial discrimination against Indians living in that country. He developed the idea of *satyagraha*, a kind of non-violent resistance he described as "soul force." For the next three decades, the ideal of *satyagraha* would lend the independence movement moral credibility in the eyes of the world.

TOWARD INDEPENDENCE (1915–47)

Gandhi enjoyed amazing popularity throughout the 1920s. His religious tolerance helped him to earn support from both Hindus and Muslims. His rejection of Western products in favor of *swadeshi* goods made him especially popular among the peasant masses. This popularity meant that the leadership of Congress was his for the taking; under Gandhi the once-elite Congress was reshaped into a mass party supported by millions of ordinary Indians.

Encouraged by Gandhi and Congress, millions of Indians participated in non-violent civil disobedience throughout the 1920s. In 1930, however, Gandhi's power appeared to have passed on to **Jawaharlal Nehru,** the young leader of the Congress party's radical wing, who had audaciously declared January 26, 1930 to be Indian Independence day. Gandhi embarked on his famous Salt March seven weeks after Nehru's declaration. Imperial authorities had declared it illegal for salt to be sold or manufactured except under the auspices of the heavily taxed official monopoly. The burden for this tax fell overwhelmingly on the very poorest of India's people. In defiance of the law, Gandhi and his supporters marched 380km from his Sabarmati Ashram in Ahmedabad all the way to the sea, attracting crowds of supporters and media coverage along the way. Staff in hand and clothing fraying, Gandhi reached the coastal town of Dandi on April 6. Wading into the water, he proceeded to make salt by taking a handful of sea-water and pouring it onto dry ground, breaking the salt law. The act meant little in itself, but its symbolic value was huge, and the British authorities responded by arresting more than 60,000 people. There was little they could do, though, to control the rising tide of nationalist sentiment. In 1932, the army granted its first commissions to Indian officers, and in 1935 the Government of India Act was passed, giving authority over provincial government to elected Indian representatives.

Meanwhile, tension continued to grow between Congress and the Muslim League. In 1940, leaders of Congress charged that the Muslim League had taken advantage of relocations of families during the war to gain power for itself. Claiming to speak for India's Muslim communities, leaders such as **Mohammed Ali Jinnah** retorted that aggressive seizure of power was the only way for Muslims to ensure that their rights would be guaranteed in the independent, Hindu-dominated India that seemed to be on its way. In 1940, the League declared the Muslims of India to be a separate nation and demanded the creation of an independent Muslim state. This state, the League declared, would be named Pakistan.

By the end of WWII it was clear that India could no longer be forced to remain a part of the Empire against the will of the majority of its people, and Britain's new Labour government agreed to grant India full independence. Vicious religious conflicts that brought bloody unrest to Calcutta, the Punjab, and the Ganga Valley in 1946 made the division of India into two sovereign states—one

Hindu, one Muslim—seem the only option. Defying geography, the new state of Pakistan was carved out of Muslim-majority areas in both the east and the west of India. Bengal and Punjab were both split in two. Independence for India arrived at the same time as **Partition,** as the vast territory that had for so long been the "the jewel in the crown" of the British Empire was divided in two. The independent nation of **Pakistan** came into existence on August 14, 1947, and India followed suit 24 hours later. The last British viceroy, Lord Mountbatten, stayed on to oversee the exchange of power, but the days of the British Raj were over. Hours before Independence, Nehru made one of the most famous speeches of the 20th century to the Constituent Assembly in New Delhi: "At the stroke of the midnight hour, when the world sleeps, India will awaken to life and freedom. A moment comes, which comes but rarely in history, when we step from the old to the new, when an age ends, and when the soul of a nation, long suppressed, finds utterance."

AFTER INDEPENDENCE (1947–64)

Midnight struck, and on August 15 a nation was born, with a host of high expectations and a mess of pressing problems before it. As countries were created, so were refugees: millions of desperate Sikhs and Hindus streamed into India, fearing for their lives, while millions of Muslims fled for Pakistan. These massive migrations, probably the largest movements of people in history, touched off stampedes and religious violence on a horrific scale, and well over 500,000 people were killed. Five months later, Mahatma Gandhi was assassinated on his way to evening prayers by **Nathuram Godse,** a Hindu extremist angered by Gandhi's attempts to behave in a civilized manner toward the Muslim League.

It was decided that India should be ruled as a federation, with power split between state and national authorities. Nehru's government passed the **States Reorganization Act** (1956), which re-drew state boundaries along linguistic lines.

On the economic front, Nehru's India faced huge difficulties. Large numbers of people in India continued to live in terrible poverty, and huge disparities of wealth existed between the urban middle classes and the village-based majority. Nehru labored heroically to make India a more prosperous nation, embarking on **five year plans** and successfully soliciting foreign aid, but sluggish economic growth could not keep up with the growing needs of an ever-larger population.

Nehru was constantly plagued by foreign policy problems. **Kashmir,** a formerly independent kingdom in the Himalayas with a Hindu maharaja and a population that was 75% Muslim, was faced at Independence with the choice of joining either India or Pakistan. Border skirmishes with Pakistan led the maharaja to accede to India, with Nehru promising fair elections soon. A brief, undeclared war between India and Pakistan ended in 1949 with a UN-brokered cease-fire. The war established a de facto—and still disputed—border between Pakistani- and Indian-controlled parts of Kashmir, but did nothing solve the more difficult problems that lay behind the conflict (see **Jammu and Kashmir,** p. 245). And the border troubles of the new nation weren't limited to disputes with Pakistan: in 1962, a boundary dispute led India to war with China.

INDIRA'S INDIA (1964–84)

When Nehru died in 1964, he was succeeded by **Lal Bahadur Shastri,** who died of a heart attack after leading India to victory in a defensive war with Pakistan. Shastri was succeeded in turn by Nehru's daughter, Indira Gandhi (see **What's in a Name?,** p. 74.). As soon as she came to power, it was clear that Mrs. Gandhi had big plans. She fought with Congress "old guard" and began to move India closer to the USSR.

In 1971, East Pakistan broke away from West Pakistan. West Pakistan promptly invaded its eastern wing. Millions of refugees fled into India to avoid persecution, inflicting a heavy burden on India's already-strained treasury. India started arming and training Bengali guerrillas, and in December, Pakistani planes attacked Indian airfields. The next day, Indira Gandhi sent the Indian Army into both East and West Pakistan. Less than two weeks later, Pakistan surrendered; the result was the creation of the independent state of **Bangladesh.** With Pakistan defeated, India became South Asia's dominant power.

The early years of Gandhi's government were promising ones for the nation's troubled agricultural sector. The so-called **Green Revolution** introduced high-yield crops, modern farm machinery, and chemical fertilizers, but none of Indira's reforms was able to solve the fundamental problem of insufficient production. Small farmers who could not afford the modern tools were unable to compete with the richer, larger-scale farmers who benefited most. In later years, Prime Minister Gandhi focused on policies designed to alleviate poverty and on introducing family-planning measures and self-sufficiency strategies. Her methods, though, became increasingly totalitarian.

The autocratic nature of Mrs. Gandhi's government (she rarely attended Parliament) meant that her rule was increasingly beset by problems. After the **oil crisis** of 1973, India was left facing runaway inflation and the threat of famine, with millions of Indians slipping toward starvation. Solving economic problems sometimes seemed to be the least important item on the agenda of a government steeped in corruption and nepotism. In 1975, Mrs. Gandhi was found guilty of election fraud. Rather than step down as the law demanded, she declared a **National Emergency,** "suspending" all civil rights. Rohinton Mistry's novel *A Fine Balance* presents a vivid fictionalized account of this period. Gandhi was ever more the tyrant, imposing sterilization on families with more than two children, aggressively censoring the press, mobilizing India's intelligence agencies as her own private police force, and locking her political opponents safely away in jail.

The state of emergency ended in January 1977, when Mrs. Gandhi believed that she would be re-elected legitimately. She wasn't. The **Janata Dal,** an anti-Indira coalition led by **Morarji Desai,** Mrs. Gandhi's former finance minister, came to power in March that year. Unable to hold his party together, however, Desai was toppled, and Mrs. Gandhi was re-elected in 1980.

Her second term was plagued by regional problems. In 1984 she ordered the dismissal of Kashmir's popular Chief Minister, Farooq Abdullah, and soon afterward gave another order to the governor of Andhra Pradesh, demanding the removal of the state's popular Chief Minister, **N.T. Rama Rao,** a former film star and the leader of an opposition party. She also confronted separatist **Sikh militants,** who had launched a terrorist campaign in **Punjab and Haryana** in an attempt to force the government to create a sovereign Sikh nation. In 1984, when armed militants seized the Golden Temple in Amritsar, the Sikhs' holiest site, Mrs. Gandhi decided to send in the troops (see p. 266). The result was a tragedy. Thousands of people died during the four-day battle that ensued. But for Mrs. Gandhi herself, the worst was yet to come. By desecrating the temple, Mrs. Gandhi had incurred the wrath of the militants, and on October 31, 1984, she was assassinated at home in New Delhi by two Sikh bodyguards. Her death sparked huge riots throughout the capital, as well as widespread massacres of Sikhs by Hindu thugs.

THE LAST 16 YEARS

A "sympathy vote" in the elections that followed Indira's assassination gave **Rajiv Gandhi's** Congress party an impressive majority. Many had high hopes that Rajiv's administration would help to bring about some of the changes that India needed so badly. But his term as prime minister began inauspiciously, when a gas leak from the Union Carbide chemical plant in December 1984 killed nearly three thousand people in **Bhopal.** Then there was the government's last-minute withdrawal from an agreement with Sikh leaders that would have given the Sikhs the city of **Chandigarh** in an attempt to improve the situation in Punjab. Rajiv's free-enterprise, trickle-down economic policies brought in the imported goods that the rich craved, but did little for the poor.

WHAT'S IN A NAME? No one in India has sparked as much controversy and as many op-ed articles as the Gandhi family. Between the charismatic Jawaharlal Nehru, his daughter Indira Gandhi, and her son Rajiv Gandhi, the Nehru-Gandhi family has dominated 40 out of 53 years of independent India's government. Rumored to have married Feroze Gandhi in order to use the Mahatma's last name (the two families were not related), Indira Gandhi was a populist tyrant—she called her rule "democracy with discipline." She was assassinated by Sikh bodyguards in 1984. Her son Sanjay, whom she had been grooming to take her place, was killed in a plane crash in 1980, so her other son Rajiv became prime minister after her death. Rajiv also met an untimely death, killed by a Tamil Tiger suicide bomber while on campaign in 1991. Sanjay's widow Maneka Gandhi is a prominent animal rights activist and environmentalist, and Rajiv's widow, the Italian-born Sonia Gandhi, was catapulted into the limelight when she became president of Congress and announced her candidacy for prime minister in the October 1999 elections.

Rajiv had mixed success with foreign policy. He improved relations with the US without moving away from the Soviet Union, but he made several ill-advised decisions in the case of **Sri Lanka,** only 35km off the south coast of India. The Tamil minority in Sri Lanka had felt increasingly alienated since 1956, as successive Sri Lankan governments instituted policies favoring the Sinhalese majority. The **Tamil Tigers,** a guerilla group fighting for an independent Tamil state on the island, had been surreptitiously armed and trained in India during Mrs. Gandhi's administration, and by the time Rajiv came power, the group had become a significant force. Rajiv sent the Indian Peace Keeping Force (IPKF) to Sri Lanka to join the fight against the Tigers, whose government was only too happy to withdraw its own troops from the fray. The Tigers routed the government forces, and by the time the IPKF withdrew, there were 100 Indian soldiers dead for every Tiger killed.

The 1989 elections transferred power to a fragile coalition of parties, including the Hindu Nationalist **Bharatiya Janata Party (BJP),** led by Prime Minister V.P. Singh of the Janata Dal. The situation in Kashmir got worse, even as Singh struggled to put an end to the crisis in Punjab. Muslim militants in Kashmir, allegedly trained and armed in Pakistan, started a campaign against Indian authority. The state capital of **Srinagar,** once a popular tourist destination, turned into a war zone. And there were other problems. A policy proposed by the Mandal Commission, formed to investigate caste affairs, required that 60% of university admissions and civil service jobs be reserved for lower castes and former Untouchables, threatening to bring about the collapse of the Singh government. Higher-caste Hindus were soon marching in the streets, and several went as far as to burn themselves to death in protest. When L.K. Advani, the leader of the BJP, was arrested, the BJP withdrew its support, and the government fell. A new government, led by Prime Minister Chandra Shekhar, lasted only a few months.

The elections of 1991 brought Congress back to power, largely thanks to another sympathy vote following the assassination of Rajiv Gandhi, who was killed by a **Tamil Tiger** suicide bomber in Tamil Nadu. The new prime minister, **P.V. Narasimha Rao,** an aging disciple of Nehru, surprised everyone with his political acumen. A 1991 financial crisis necessitated unpopular economic reforms, which included cutting government spending and opening India to foreign investment.

Late 1991 brought new life to the long-running dispute over the **Babri Masjid** in Ayodhya. In December 1992, with the BJP in power in Uttar Pradesh, Hindu nationalists called for volunteers to build a Hindu temple in place of the mosque that stood on the site supposed to mark Rama's birthplace. From all over India devotees converged on Ayodhya, bricks in hand, and proceeded to tear down the old mosque. Hindu-Muslim violence erupted across India, especially in major cities such as Bombay. Rao's government banned the Hindu nationalist parties, dismissing the governments of Uttar Pradesh and three other states ruled by the BJP.

Though weakened considerably, the Rao government managed somehow to cling to power, and continued its program of economic liberalization. By 1994 the Hindu nationalists had made a convincing comeback, winning states. In 1995 the state of **Maharashtra,** which includes the industrial powerhouse of Bombay, came under the control of a particularly fanatical nationalist party, the **Shiv Sena.** Problems continued to flare up in Kashmir as well, and the government's handling of the insurgency there brought international condemnation for alleged human rights violations.

The BJP won more seats than any other single party in the May 1996 Lok Sabha elections, but it was still in a minority, and the government it formed fell to a vote of no-confidence only two weeks later. Power passed in June to a loose coalition of low-caste, populist, and socialist parties called the United Front, which chose H.D. Deve Gowda as its candidate for prime minister.

Elections were held in Kashmir during May and September of 1996, and although there were some reports of military coercion, most people were able to vote freely. The 1996 parliamentary elections produced no obvious majority, and India stumbled from one teetering coalition government to another. The Hindu Nationalist BJP came out on top in elections in 1998. In May that year, a series of five nuclear weapons tests brought Prime Minister **Atal Behari Vajpayee** into the international spotlight and intensified the regional arms race. Later that year, Indian and Pakistani troops exchanged heavy shelling across the disputed border of Kashmir, and more than 90 soldiers and civilians were killed. In late May 1999, Indian jets attacked Muslim guerilla forces that had advanced beyond the Line of Control marking the disputed border with Pakistan. The battle that ensued killed and injured hundreds and forced thousands to flee their homes.

THIS YEAR'S NEWS

In April 1999, the government collapsed after the southern **AIADMK party** withdrew its support from the ruling coalition. The opposition, headed by Congress leader Sonia Gandhi, widow of former PM Rajiv Gandhi, was unable to form a majority in parliament, and in September the nation went to the polls for the third time in just over than three years. The **New Democratic Alliance,** dominated by Prime Minister Atal Bihari Vajpayee and his Bharatiya Janata Party (BJP), won nearly 300 of the 536 parliamentary seats up for grabs, thanks largely to the massive surge in popularity it enjoyed in the afterglow of the summer's military tussles with arch-rival Pakistan up in the Kargil region of disputed Kashmir. In October 1999, a series of monster **cyclones** ripped through the eastern state of **Orissa,** killing more than 10,000 people and causing untold damage across one of the poorest parts of the country. Kashmir's decade-long saga of violence and unrest continued to take its toll. Hopes of a settlement were raised briefly in July 2000, when breakaway militant group Hizbul Mojahedin agreed to a cease-fire, but were shattered when the bombings and massacres started up again shorty afterward. Monsoonal floods during the summer of 2000 killed hundreds of people across the north of India and made thousands homeless as whole villages were washed away in the states of Himachal Pradesh and Assam. Bill Clinton's whirlwind final year as US president brought him to India in March 2000—the first visit by an American head of state for over 20 years. Ol' Unfaithful treated himself to several Oval Offices' worth of Kashmir carpets, and had himself photographed in front of the Taj Mahal resplendent in his best *kurta pajama.* Indian Prime Minister Vajpayee returned the favor at the end of the summer, using a speech to the United Nations in New York to castigate Pakistan for its alleged interference in Kashmir, and to call for India to be given a permanent seat on the UN Security Council. The noble game of cricket had its reputation dragged through the dirt, as allegations of dodgy dealings with shady betting syndicates brought many of India's favorite heroes out of the dressing room and into court to answer charges of game-fixing and bribe-taking.

CASTE

The ancient codes of dharma divided Hindu society into four ranks, each of which was supposed to have emerged from a different part of the primordial person, **Purusha.** The brahmin, the priestly and scholarly caste, came from his mouth; the *kshatriya*, the warrior-ruler caste, from his arms; the *vaishya*, or merchants, from his thighs; and the *shudra*, or laborers, from his feet. These four *varna* (colors), form the basis of the Hindu caste system. Principles of karma and reincarnation explain a person's fortune (or lack of it) in this life, and offer the consolation that things might be better the next time around. The practical rules of conduct that have helped to preserve the caste system are concerned mostly with notions of "substance" and "purity." Social dealings lead to the mixing of different peoples' "essences," and creates "pollution" between members of different castes. Brahmin must be exceptionally pure in order to perform religious ceremonies, and they do not mix with other castes at all or even accept food cooked by non-brahmin. The group of people traditionally treated as **"Untouchables,"** now officially referred to as **"Dalits"** (the Oppressed), included those involved in occupations—usually as toilet-cleaners, leather tanners, and undertakers—so highly polluting that they were considered to be outside the caste system altogether.

In practice, however, the hierarchy of the caste system has never been as clear-cut as it sounds in theory. More socially important than the *varna* are the *jati*. These are smaller groups of people, linked by kinship and usually sharing an occupation. There are thousands of *jati* in India, some of them very small and peculiar to a few villages, others with tens of millions of members spread across huge regions. As the result of political and social upheaval, many *jati* have split and joined other groups, and people have risen or fallen in status regardless of the *varna* they belong to. Some regions of India have politically dominant *jati*, such as the *Jats* in Rajasthan and Punjab and the *Reddis* in Andhra Pradesh, whose members originally came from very low castes.

There is no sure way of guessing someone's caste, though after a while in India you'll start to recognize some common family names or styles of dress and learn to link them to caste. Occupations can be an indicator of caste, but not often a reliable one. Efforts at reform and the demands of city life have done a lot to reduce the importance of the caste system. The notion of untouchability is on the wane, and caste in general is less likely than it once was to determine a person's social position. In the cities, the so-called "Untouchables" ride the same buses and play on the same cricket teams as brahmin. But in India's villages (where 70% of the population still lives), caste continues to be important and restrictive. Even in the cities, most Hindu marriages still take place within *jati*, or at least between *jati* of equal status.

Politically, caste has been an increasingly important issue in recent years. Lower castes have managed to turn their strength-in-numbers into political clout, although the sheer size of the groups involved makes internal cohesion almost impossible. Internal squabbling has sometimes pitted Untouchables against *shudra*, or OBCs (Other Backward Castes), a group of people supposedly slightly less low-caste and therefore slightly less untouchable. Lower-caste parties have gained power in many states, but the only one with real nationwide appeal is the **Janata Party.** Affirmative action programs for lower-caste Hindus have been implemented recently, with large numbers of university places and civil service jobs reserved for the so-called "scheduled castes."

RELIGION

HINDUISM

Hinduism is one of the oldest and most versatile of the world's religions, with approximately 800 million followers in India alone. It permeates daily life in the cities and in the rural villages; street-side shrines and temples throughout the

SWASTIKAS Foreign visitors may be shocked to see swastikas painted on walls and windshields or worked into the architecture. Swastikas go a long way back in South Asia, however: the word itself is Sanskrit, and means "it is well." Used by the Greeks, Mesopotamians, Chinese, Mayans, and Navajos among others, the cross with bent arms was a widespread symbol of good luck and power in the ancient world. The ancient Indo-Aryans also used the swastika, and it remains one of the most cherished symbols of Hindus, Jains, and Buddhists. The swastika is associated with good luck and the removal of obstacles. With arms pointing clockwise, it is an auspicious symbol, since it seems to mimic the sun's path from east to south to west across the sky. The counter-clockwise swastika, however, is a symbol of night, and it is considered inauspicious. The Hindu swastika may have originated from a wheel, or from the firesticks in Vedic sacrifices, which were spread on the ground in the form of a cross.

country attract constant streams of worshipers. Heavily laden with ritual, Hinduism is a colorful blend of monotheism and polytheism that resists strict definition and easy summary. Unlike many other world religions, Hinduism is without a founding figure, a single central text, or a fixed regimen of formalized practice. It is a kaleidoscope of local and regional religions, all integrated into an ever-shifting whole that manages somehow to accommodate them all.

CENTRAL HINDU BELIEFS

Hindu belief is based on the existence of an absolute, unchanging, and omnipresent reality called **Brahman.** As the universal spirit, *Brahman* is present in every individual in the form of **atman,** the self or soul. The goal of life is to overcome the illusory separation between *Brahman* and *atman* (known as **maya**) and achieve supreme bliss. The individual is caught in a continual cycle of birth, death, and rebirth. A person is bound to the cycle of reincarnation by **karma,** the moral law of cause and effect, which teaches that present conditions are the result of past deeds. One is reborn into the world again and again, whether as an ant or a human being, until one's karmic debt has been paid. But the attainment of **moksha** (liberation) for the immortal human soul is still possible. The popular *Bhagavad Gita* describes four paths for making the first steps toward *moksha:* action, devotion, knowledge, and psychic exercises. Dying in the holy city of Varanasi will also grant *moksha.*

There are three other aims in life, in addition to *moksha.* **Dharma** has several meanings, but it most commonly refers to an individual's duty to maintain social and ultimately, cosmic order. There is also room for **kama** (sensual enjoyment) and **aartha** (wealth). Hindu thought divides life into four stages. The first 25 or so years should be devoted to the acquisition of knowledge; the second 25 to being a householder, fulfilling the duties to raise a family and to future generations; the third stage rounds out the householder's life and is preparatory to the detachment from worldly connections that marks the fourth, ascetic stage—a complete renunciation of one's life.

VEDIC LITERATURE

The written tradition of Hinduism can be traced back to the Aryans, and beyond them to the Indus Valley Civilization (see **History**, p. 63). The still-influential **Vedas** (meaning "knowledge"), are collections of poetic hymns in Sanskrit that were first transmitted orally and then transcribed between 1200 and 200 BC. The *Vedas* are regarded as unitary, eternal, and without human origin. It is only through the miraculous powers of the **rishi** (literally, "those who hear") that these timeless revelations have been made accessible to the larger community. Of these holy texts, the **Rig Veda** is the largest, containing 1028 metrical hymns dedicated to the popular deities of ancient India, such as **Indra,** the hard-drinking god of war, and **Soma,** the moon god. The word **soma** also refers to the hallucinogenic drink prepared from the plant of the same name, which brahmin priests of the Vedic period would consume while reciting passages from the *Vedas* and performing fire sacrifices *(shrauta)* and horse sacrifices *(ashvamedha).*

A HINDU WHO'S WHO

Brahma: Four-faced god, often pictured sitting on a lotus growing from Vishnu's navel. Despite his role as creator of the human world, Brahma is rarely worshiped, and only a single temple in Pushkar, Rajasthan (see p. 292) is dedicated to him.

Devi: Many Hindus worship a vast array of female deities, referred to collectively as the Devi (the Great Goddess). Goddesses embody **shakti,** an indispensable female force that drives the universe. The goddess cult probably predates worship of male gods, though specific goddesses are now incorporated into the male-dominated pantheon as consorts.

Durga: According to Hindu mythology, this beautiful heroine was created by the combined powers of male deities too weak to destroy the demon **Mahisha.** Battle Queen Durga charged forth with her trusty tiger (sometimes a lion), clutching weapons in each of her 10 hands and emerged victorious, saving the world from destruction. Celebrated especially in Calcutta, **Durga Puja** (see p. 658) marks this cosmic event with animal sacrifices and rites of fertility.

Ganesh: Beloved by many Hindus, this chubby, elephant-headed god, also known as **Ganpati,** is revered as the "remover of obstacles." He is often worshiped first in religious ceremonies, and his plump image adorns the thresholds of many homes and temples. In his four hands, he holds various weapons, as well as a bowl of *ladoo,* his favorite sweet. Why he has an elephant's head? Once, his mother Parvati asked him to guard her bathing spot. When papa Shiva returned from an extended ramp around the world and tried to approach his wife, he was stopped by a boy he no longer recognized as his son. Furious, Shiva chopped off the boy's head. After Parvati discovered what had happened, she demanded that Shiva bring Ganesh back to life. So Shiva replaced the boy's head with the head of the first creature he saw—an elephant. Ganesh's vehicle of choice is a mouse.

Hanuman: The flying monkey-god, whose celebrity derives from his role in the **Ramayana** (see p. 579) as Rama's faithful servant. This brawny god is respected for his absolute loyalty; he is often depicted tearing open his furry chest to reveal the name "Rama" etched countless times in tiny script across his heart. Hanuman is a favorite of Indian wrestlers.

Kali: Sometimes considered a consort of Shiva, Kali is an independent goddess of destruction in her own right. A force to be reckoned with, this fiery goddess is easily recognized by her terrifying appearance: long, tangled hair, dark skin, protruding red tongue, serpent bracelets, and a long necklace of freshly cut heads. She takes up residence in cremation grounds but is also often depicted on the battlefield as a combatant who gets drunk on her victims' blood.

A body of text known as the **Upanishads,** assembled toward the end of the Vedic period, did much to reform the worldview outlined in the *Vedas.* The rituals so central to religious practice were reinterpreted with an emphasis on the metaphysical. Salvation was expressed in terms of a personal philosophy of *moksha* and the doctrines of karma and rebirth that endure to this day. These texts are the first in the Hindu tradition to advocate withdrawal from society and the use of ascetic techniques in the religious quest.

Slightly later, a tradition that stressed the importance of dharma appeared in the **dharmashastras** and in the **Manusmriti,** the Laws of Manu. Dharma in this context connotes duty or fulfillment of one's proper function. Why does a river flow downhill? Because that is its role, its nature, its dharma. In the same way, it is the dharma of a *kshatriya* king to eat meat, engage in war, offer food and money to the brahmin, and rule a kingdom. Generally, there are three guidelines to follow: the adherence to cosmic dharma through religious observances; adherence to the dharma of one's caste; and adherence to one's *svadharma,* or personal moral code. Hindu epics such as the **Ramayana** (see p. 579) play on the themes of conflict between these duties, and portray the tension between adherence to dharma, with all of its worldly obligations, and the quest for *moksha.*

Krishna: Mr. Popularity among the Hindu gods, Krishna is worshipped by followers in a variety of guises corresponding to the different stages of his life. He inspires affection from his earliest days as a pudgy little blue baby who can't resist stealing butter. As a young man, Krishna is adored as the flirtatious cowherder who jams on his flute and cavorts in the Yamuna river and the forests of Vrindaban with love-struck *gopi* (milkmaids) groupies, among whom Radha is his favorite. But Krishna is not all play and no work: he is respected as the philosophical charioteer in the **Bhagavad Gita** (see p. 79).

Lakshmi: A benign, feminine goddess, Lakshmi has a reputation as a giver of luck, wealth, fertility, and general well-being. The autumn holiday of **Diwali** is an especially auspicious time of year when Hindus look to Lakshmi to bring prosperity during the new year. She is a wife of Vishnu, and is also associated with elephants.

Saraswati: Saraswati's existence can be traced back to the *Vedas,* when she was most strongly identified with the Saraswati River. Later, Saraswati's talents brought her into her current role as goddess of speech, poetry, music, culture, and learning. This pure and transcendant goddess is often seen sitting on a lotus flower holding various objects in her four hands: a book, a rosary, a water pot, and a *veena* (a stringed Indian instrument).

Shiva: He's terrifying. He's compassionate. He's a bad-ass. As the Destroyer, Shiva is portrayed as an uncouth ascetic who adorns himself with live cobras and leopard skins, smears ashes on his body, wields a trident, and rides his bull **Nandi.** From his dreadlocked head flows the mighty waters of the Ganga (see p. 149). But there is also the gentle, family-man side of Shiva who lives atop Mount Kailasha in the Himalayas with his wife **Parvati** and their two sons, **Ganesh** and the six-headed **Kartikeya.** He is most often worshipped through the **linga,** a simple, phallus-shaped stone shaft fixed in a circular base called the **yoni.** Together, they represent a symbol of divine unity between Shiva and Shakti. Shiva's other forms include: **Ardhinarishwara** (halfmale, half-female), **Rudra** (the Howler), and **Nataraja** (the King of Dance, often depicted his left leg raised, and a ring of fire surrounding him). Most sadhus (Hindu ascetics and Shiva-lookalikes), are devotees of Shiva.

Vishnu: Though sometimes spotted relaxing upon a serpent afloat on a sea of milk, Vishnu is always on call as the Preserver of the cosmos. Time and again he has stepped in to save the universe from calamity, in the form of one of his 11 avatars (manifestations), which include **Rama,** the hero the *Ramayana* (see p. 579), **Krishna,** and the **Buddha.** Vishnu, recognizable by his blue skin and four arms, travels via a man-bird named **Garuda,** and carries a discus.

A favorite of Mahatma Gandhi, the **Bhagavad Gita** (the "Song of the Lord"), makes up the sixth chapter of the great Sanskrit epic, the **Mahabharata,** and is a dialogue between **Krishna,** an avatar (incarnation) of **Vishnu,** and prince **Arjuna.** Going into battle, Arjuna is confronted with the moral dilemma of fighting against friends, teachers, and elders. Refusing to fight, he throws down his weapons and considers a path of renunciation. Arjuna's situation sheds light on the conflict between his duty as a *kshatriya* (a member of the warrior caste) and the ideal of non-violence *(ahimsa).* Krishna appears as Arjuna's chariot-driver and gives his disciple a lesson on dharma. He explains that 1) killing a person in battle does not mean death for the soul, and 2) that Arjuna should not be so attached to the fruit of his actions, but should be concerned with fulfilling his dharma and ultimately serving the Supreme Power.

GODS AND GODDESSES

From the oneness of Brahman—the impersonal, attributeless, spiritual essence—comes *atman* (see **Central Hindu Beliefs,** p. 77) and the infinite number of gods and goddesses so visible in India today. Traditional estimates have put the number of Hindu gods and goddesses at 333 million, but no one really knows how many there are. In addition to all the temples and shrines, spaces for small altars are carved out in private homes. The manifestations of the divine are visible on glossy calendar images sold by local street vendors, printed on flashy stickers stuck to the windows of rickshaws, and painted on the walls of *chai* stalls.

Shiva, Vishnu, the Devi, and their various *avatars* (incarnations) receive the most adulation, but there are countless others: local deities, those described in the Vedic hymns of the Aryans, those from long-lost prehistoric nature cults, and various syntheses of all these. From the central trinity of **Brahma** (Creator), **Vishnu** (Preserver), and **Shiva** (Destroyer) emerge the countless hundreds of other gods and goddesses, each one embodying an attribute of the eternal soul. The popularity of a god can vary from region to region, village to village, and family to family.

HINDU PRACTICE

Hindu ritual, a vital part of Hindu identity, tends to be intensely sensual, appealing to all five senses. Contrary to appearances, it is not idols that are worshiped in the temples and household prayer rooms; the images *(murti)* are merely the vessels in which the deities reside. Centering on these images is *puja* (loosely translated as "worship"), or acts of reverence to a god made through offerings such as food, flowers, and incense. These offerings are normally vegetarian-friendly, though some deities accept blood or animal sacrifices. Different kinds of ritual are offered to different deities, reflecting the unique personality of the god.

In the temple, the temple priests *(pujari)* pamper the gods by performing more elaborate *puja* services. Beginning at dawn, they bathe the image *(abhisheka)* in yogurt, milk, and *ghee*. After the bath, the deity is dressed in new clothes and adorned with fancy accessories behind a curtain (even the gods need their privacy). Finally, the climactic moment arrives when the curtain is drawn back, and devotees clamor for a glimpse of the deity. Bells ring out through the temple, and mantras are sung, as *darshan*, the auspicious eye contact between deity and worshiper, communicates divine blessing. The *pujari* waves in front of the deity an *aarti* lamp lit by small camphor flames, allows worshipers to cup their hands over the flames, and touches their eyes and faces, symbolically transferring to them the divine light and warmth. Before leaving the temple, worshipers have their foreheads marked with ash, sandalwood paste *(candana)*, or red tumeric powder *(kumkum)*. Priests also pour holy water and drop *prasad* (food blessed by the gods) into the hands of devotees.

In addition to temple rituals, ceremonies mark human rites of passage such as marriage and cremation. Festivals *(utsava)* punctuate the Hindu calendar (see **Festivals and Holidays,** p. 821). Also popular are pilgrimages *(tirtha yatra)* to the sacred points of India. Some travel to these holy places, or *tirtha* (literally "ford," a liminal space between the divine and the human), to seek the fulfillment of a wish, to spread the ashes of a relative in a holy river, to boost personal health and spiritual merit, or simply for the fun of the trip. There are seven especially sacred pilgrimage destinations: Ayodhya, Mathura, Haridwar, Varanasi, Ujjain, Dwarka, and Kanchipuram.

MODERN HINDUISM

Many people attempted to reinterpret Hinduism during the 19th century, including British and Christian missionaries, who wanted to make it more systematic and "rational." The **Brahmo Samaj**, founded by **Raja Ram Mohan Roy** in Bengal in 1828, did away with image worship and instead held Christian-style services, with readings from the *Upanishads*. A great figure in the 19th century Hindu revival was **Sri Ramakrishna** (1836-1886), whose message of religious unity left an indelible impression upon modern Hindu thought. Ramakrishna maintained that all religions provide equally valid paths to God, and held that the best religion people could follow was the one they had been brought up in. It was a disciple of Ramakrishna, **Swami Vivekananda** (1863-1902), who introduced Hinduism to the West during the World Parliament of Religions in Chicago in 1893.

Sri Aurobindo was another reformer and Indian nationalist, who was imprisoned by the British for sedition in 1908. He underwent a series of mystical experiences while practicing yoga in prison. Abandoning his political activities, he devoted his life to achieving "Supramental Consciousness" on earth, and became a prolific writer of poetry and philosophy. His work was carried on by his associate "The Mother," a French woman named Mirra Alfassa. Sri Aurobindo spent the rest of his life in seclusion in Pondicherry, where his ashram remains today (see **Pondicherry,** p. 554). Internationally controversial **Satya Sai Baba** has won a huge following as a modern miracle man with big hair who heals and conjures up jewelry out of thin air, while spreading the message of self-realization (see **The Boy Wonder,** p. 467).

ISLAM

Approximately 11% of India's population is Muslim, the fourth-largest Muslim population of any country in the world, after Indonesia, Bangladesh, and Pakistan. Islam, supported by Muslim communities in places like Hyderabad, Lucknow, Kerala, and Kashmir, has had a strong influence on Indian culture. The questions surrounding the political, religious, and cultural status of India's Muslims are some of the most emotionally charged issues facing the country today.

HISTORY

Islam was founded by the **Prophet Mohammed,** who lived in Mecca (in what is now Saudi Arabia) during the 7th century. Between 610 and 622, Mohammed received revelations from the angel Gabriel about the true nature of God. His teachings were received coolly in polytheistic Arabia, and he and his followers were driven from Mecca in 622; this **Hijra** (flight) to Medina marks the start of the Muslim calendar. The people of Medina embraced the new faith, and after building up an army, Mohammed returned in triumph to Mecca in 630, establishing himself as the temporal and spiritual leader of a new Muslim state. After Mohammed's death, the Muslims conquered Arabia and adjacent lands at an incredible rate, and by 711, less than a hundred years after its humble beginnings, Islam had extended its rule from Spain to Sindh (in eastern Pakistan).

In 661, however, not long after the Prophet's death, a dispute over leadership came to a head in the assassination of Mohammed's son-in-law, Ali. This early rivalry would deepen to become a split within Islam between the **Shi'is,** who recognized only Ali's descendants as legitimate religious leaders, and the **Sunnis,** who accepted the authority of any caliph well-versed enough in the religion to command obedience. Sunnis make up the majority of Muslims in India and in the rest of the Muslim world today, except in Iran.

Islam trickled slowly into India at first; its messengers were Arabian traders, Sufi mystics from Persia, and the armies of **Mahmud of Ghazni.** Islamic influence was much greater after 1192, however, under the **Delhi Sultanate** and then the **Mughal Empire,** as India was ruled by Muslims for more than 500 years (see **The Arrival of Islam,** p. 66). Some converted to Islam to join the new elite, and many low-caste Hindus converted to escape the caste system. Still, the majority of the population remained Hindu. Large-scale conversion took place only on the eastern and western frontiers of South Asia; these were the areas that would become Pakistan and (later) Bangladesh upon Independence, when Muslims suddenly became conscious of their minority status in a new and massively Hindu nation. Before they left in 1947, the British carved out the nation of Pakistan, a Muslim nation with one wing on the west and one wing on the east of India. Millions of people suddenly found themselves on the "wrong" side of the border at midnight on Independence day, and millions died in the violence that followed desperate migration in both directions across the border. Despite the migrations, a sizable minority of Muslims remained in India.

INDIA

BELIEFS

All Muslims believe in one supreme god, **Allah,** and worship him through the five pillars of Islam: declaration of one's faith ("there is no God but God and Mohammed is his prophet"); praying five times daily; giving alms (*zakat*) to the poor; fasting during the month of Ramadan; and making the *hajj* (pilgrimage to Mecca) at least once in a lifetime, barring physical or financial hardship. A single holy book, the **Koran,** is believed to be the direct word of God as recorded by the Prophet. Second in authority to the Koran is the **Hadith,** a painstakingly authenticated collection of the words and deeds of Mohammed.

Friday is the Muslim holy day, when special prayers are said at the mosque. The ninth month of the Muslim calendar marks the celebration of **Ramadan,** a holiday commemorating the Prophet's receipt of the holy Koran from God, during which all Muslims (with the exception of the very young and the very sick) abstain from food and drink during daylight hours. **Muharram** memorializes the death of the Prophet's grandson, and it is of particular importance to Shi'i Muslims, who observe Muharram with 12 days of singing and prayer.

ISLAM IN INDIA

Muslims and Hindus have coexisted in a tense sort of peace for most of their time together. The Mughal Emperor Akbar even tried to bridge the two faiths. Recently, however, Hindu-Muslim tensions have flared, as the ever more popular Hindu nationalists continue to claim that India is a fundamentally Hindu country. Unfriendly India-Pakistan relations have also damaged Hindu-Muslim relations within India. In recent years the Mughal legacy of temple-breaking has been flung back at Muslims. The **Babri Masjid** in Ayodhya (see p. 188) has already been destroyed by Hindu nationalists. Meanwhile the riots and massacres that began with the 1947 Partition continue to be the favorite way for both Hindus and Muslims to air their grievances.

Islam considers all people equal and strongly prohibits any discrimination on the basis of race, but Indianized Islam has succumbed to its own, less rigid version of the Hindu caste system. Many Muslim women stay secluded in their homes according to the custom of *purdah*, and after centuries of Muslim rule, this practice has spread to groups of Hindu women as well. Muslims are required by the Koran to avoid alcohol, pork, and shellfish; they do, however, eat beef, as long as the cow has been slaughtered according to religious prescription and is thus considered halal. At noon on Fridays, men gather for communal prayers at the *masjid;* women usually pray at home. Many Indian Muslims speak Urdu which, although it uses a Persian script, is linguistically similar to Hindi.

Unlike the Arab practice of Islam, often marked by doctrinal austerity, Islam in India tends to be much more devotionally and aesthetically oriented and has had a huge impact on Indian culture. While orthodox Islam frowns upon the notion of worshiping anyone but God, Indian Muslims have a tradition of *pir* (saint) worship, and both Muslims and Hindus make pilgrimages to *pir* shrines to pray for worldly things like children, good grades, and safe passage. Art and architecture flourished under the Mughals, who often ignored the Islamic injunction against painting human and animal figures. Sufi mystics were responsible for the introduction of the **qawwali,** a melancholy devotional song somewhat like the Hindu *bhajan,* and the **ghazal,** poetic songs developed by Persian Muslims in India.

SIKHISM

Guru Nanak (1469-1539), a philosopher-poet born into a *kshatriya* family in what is today Pakistan, is the venerated founder of Sikhism. After traveling to Mecca, Bengal, and many places in between, Nanak proclaimed a religious faith that brought together elements of Hinduism and Islam: he rejected image-worship just as Islam did, borrowed Hinduism's use of music in worship, and rejected Islam's reliance on a holy book. He also discarded caste distinctions, sexual discrimination, and ancestor worship. Nanak proclaimed that the one God was Sat **(Truth),** and he he asserted that liberation from samsara, the cycle of life, death, and rebirth, was possible for those who embraced God, known to people through **gurus.** Nanak taught that bathing, giving alms to charity, and meditation would help to reduce hubris and would clear the way for individuals to accept God's truth.

After Nanak's death in 1539, spiritual leadership over his *sikhs* (disciples) passed to another guru, **Angad.** Guru Angad wrote his and Guru Nanak's hymns in a new script, called **Gurumukhi** (*gurmukh* means "God"), which is still used to write the Punjabi language. The third guru, **Amar Das** (1509-74), encouraged Sikhs to worship publicly in temples called **gurudwaras;** the fifth guru, **Arjun Dev** (1563-1606), collected more than 5000 hymns into a book called the **Adi Granth** and founded the magnificent **Golden Temple** at Amritsar (see p. 268). An extended period of Mughal repression and Mughal-Sikh fighting followed the execution of Guru Arjun by the Mughal Emperor Jehangir. By the time the tenth and final guru, Gobind Singh, was assassinated in 1708, raids and skirmishes had become a sad fact of life throughout Punjab, the Siwalik Hills, and other parts of northern India where large numbers of Sikhs made their homes.

Under the leadership of the tenth guru, **Guru Gobind Singh** (1666-1708), Sikhism underwent a series of radical changes that gave the faith a more cohesive identity. These changes and the military tradition they encouraged were an attempt to defend Sikhs against the persecution they suffered at the hands of the ruling Mughals. In 1699, Gobind Singh founded the Khalsa Brotherhood. Sikh men now had to undergo a kind of "baptism," pledge not to smoke tobacco, not to eat halal meat, not to have sexual relations with Muslim women. They also had to renounce their caste names; men took the name **Singh** (Lion) and women took the name **Kaur** (Princess). The Khalsa also required its members to adopt and never go without the **five kakkars:** *kangah* (wooden comb), *kirpan* (sword), *kara* (steel bracelet), *kachch* (shorts), and *kesh* (uncut hair). Sikh men are readily identifiable by the turbans they use to wrap their long hair. Gobind Singh added new hymns to the *Adi Granth,* re-named it the **Guru Granth Sahib,** and announced that the book would stand in as the next guru. Since Gobind Singh's death, the *Guru Granth Sahib* has been the spiritual guide and holy book of the Sikhs.

Although Sikhs have a strong military tradition (the British labeled them one of the "martial races," and there are a disproportionate number of Sikhs in the Indian Army), they also have strong traditions of equality, hospitality, and community service *(seva).* There are no priests in the Sikh religion. Sikh services include *kirtan,* or hymn singing, when verses from the *Adi Granth* are sung to rhythmical clapping. Following services, Sikhs gather for a meal, where everybody sits at the same level and eats the same food cooked in the *gurudwara's* kitchen. Strong believers in hospitality and kindness, Sikhs offer shelter and food to anyone who comes to their *gurudwaras.*

Since Independence, Sikhism has also been a rallying cry for Punjabi communalism, and even a struggle for an independent Sikh homeland.

INDIA

JAINISM

Jainism began as one of a constellation of alternatives to established brahmin authority that came to the fore around 500 BC, in a remarkable hundred-year period of religious renewal and regeneration. The most important element in all these new developments was the doctrine of **samsara,** the cycle of death and rebirth. People are bound to go through this cycle, birth after birth, by their **karma,** or past actions. Release from the influence of karma by can be gained through the practice of austerities and meditation: Jainism, Buddhism, and the Upanishads each prescribe this sort of individual effort toward liberation. Of these three, Jainism has perhaps the most radical approach. It begins with the belief that all life is sacred and that every living being (human, animal, plant, or insect) possesses an immortal soul **(jiva);** an obligation of **ahimsa** (non-violence) toward all living beings is therefore fundamental to Jain belief. Jains have worked out the consequences of this obligation very carefully. First of all, they are strict vegetarians. The most orthodox Jain monks also wear a net over their mouths and nostrils to prevent the possibility of killing any insects that might fly in, and they walk with a broom, sweeping the path before them so as not to crush any crawling creatures, and they do not wear clothing. Agriculture is avoided, since pulling a plow through the soil would murder millions of tiny creatures. Their conscientiousness is an attempt to avoid the karmic consequences of taking life (even if by accident). Monks and nuns also undertake severe austerities *(tapas)*—the supreme achievement in this line of work is death by self-starvation.

Jainism was founded by the *kshatriya* prince Vardhamana, or **Mahavira** (Great Hero). At the age of 30, he renounced the world, plucked out all his hair, and began a new life as a wandering ascetic. He began to gather disciples at the death of his predecessor, the ascetic **Parshavanatha;** these were called **Jains,** meaning "followers of the *jina* (conqueror)." Mahavira is revered as the 24th and last of a line of **tirthankaras,** or "ford-makers"—those who lead the way to another side of existence. There are two sects within Jainism: the **Digambara** (Sky-Clad) and the **Shvetambara** (White-Clad). The Digambaras are distinguished from the Shvetambaras by having more austere observances; most importantly, their monks and nuns go completely unclothed.

Ornate Jain temples are found throughout India, but they are primarily seen in Western India, in Gujarat and along the west coast. The two most famous sites are at **Palitana** in Gujarat and **Sravanabelagola** in Karnataka. Today there are around four to five million Jains in India, mostly in Gujarat.

BUDDHISM

In spite of its origins in the Ganga Valley, only traces of Buddhism remain in India. **Siddhartha Gautama,** who would come to be called the Buddha (Enlightened One), was born around 560 BC in Lumbini, just within the modern borders of Nepal (see p. 785). Gautama was a *kshatriya* prince. At his birth, where he emerged from between his mother's ribs, an astrologer foretold that Siddhartha would become either a *chakravartin* (universal monarch) or a buddha. In response, his father denied him freedom and lavished him with comforts and luxuries of every description in the hope that Siddhartha would learn to appreciate life in the palace. Eventually, however, Siddhartha was able to persuade his charioteer to take him on a trip out into the world beyond the palace walls. Legend tells how he saw in turn a sick man, an old man, a dead man, and a wandering ascetic. Unsatisfied with the explanations of worldly suffering given by Hinduism and impressed by the life and attitude of the mendicant, Siddhartha fled his princely life at the age of 29, leaving behind his wife, his child, and his kingdom. He wandered the forests of India, joining a band of ascetics, starving himself, meditating, and practicing other austerities until he found himself on the brink of death. Realizing that neither abundant wealth nor punishing self-denial could offer release from suffering, he resolved to follow a middle path between the two extremes—the so-called **Third Way.** He sat and meditated under a pipal tree in Bodh Gaya, Bihar (see p. 636), achieving **nirvana,** and resisting the temptations offered to him by the demon **Mara.** He set off to preach the truth about escaping the suffering of the world by overcoming desire, and he gave his first sermon in a deer park in **Sarnath** (see p. 204).

The Buddha advocated total detachment from the world. Desire for physical and mental things, he said, brings suffering, since it causes people to believe in a self and an individual existence, both of which are impermanent and illusory. One's goals should be to end suffering by extinguishing all desire, and to attain a state of nirvana, in which the flame of the self is blown out. At some point on the path to nirvana, even the desire for nirvana must be abandoned. The Buddha outlined an **Eightfold Path** to help people to nirvana: Right Understanding, Right Thought, Right Speech, Right Action, Right Livelihood, Right Effort, Right Mindfulness, and Right Concentration. He rejected Hinduism's gods and rituals, but kept its doctrine of karma and rebirth, though not the concept of an enduring soul. The Buddha also spoke against the caste system, and, as part of the Noble Eightfold Path, Buddhists became advocates of **ahisma** (non-violence).

This path of abandoning desires and worldly life put Buddhism beyond the reach of most people, however, and the first Buddhists banded together in small monastic communities. Lay people supported and contributed to these communities, although they did not observe the central tenet of renouncing the world; their practices were more devotional and reverential so that they would gain merit in order to be reborn in a more favorable position for attaining nirvana. The Buddhist dharma, however, was responsible for the conversion of the Mauryan emperor **Ashoka** in the 3rd century BC, and his state patronage helped to make Buddhism a major religion in India and throughout Asia. Although Buddhism had more or less died out in India by the first century AD, about 7 million Buddhists are left in India, mostly at the fringes of the Hindu world in Ladakh and Sikkim, where Buddhism never let go, and in places that have experienced an influx of Tibetan refugees, like Dharamsala, the headquarters of the Tibetan leadership-in-exile (see p. 219). In 1956, the leader of the Hindu Untouchables, Dr. B.R. Ambedkar, publicly converted to Buddhism as a political protest against caste discrimination; he was followed by another 200,000 Untouchables (mainly in Maharashtra). In spite of the relative scarcity of Indian Buddhists, sites like Sarnath (see p. 204) and Bodh Gaya (see p. 636) are not only for tourists and historians: they are active pilgrimage centers, attracting millions of pilgrims every year from all over the world.

THE INFANT JESUS

He's a seven-year-old blue-eyed, blond-haired boy clad in European royal garments, brandishing an orb and scepter. He bestows blessings on all who honor him, and his name is pronounced from the pages of local newspapers and in stickers on the back of auto-rickshaws. He's the infant Jesus, the image of the savior of the world and an interesting example of the sort of religious syncretism that has typified India throughout its history. The Infant Jesus Church in southeastern Bangalore, Karnataka, is a standard Catholic compound, with a meeting-hall sanctuary and daily masses in Tamil, Kannada, and English, where priests and rectors teach the Christian gospel to the faithful and the curious.

Next door to the church, though, in the blue-domed Infant Jesus Shrine, the young savior does *darshan* with Hindu devotees, who drape garlands of flowers over the statue. They aren't praying, as a Christian would, to Christ in general—offerings and supplications are specifically to the Infant Jesus. Although the priests in charge of the church make efforts to highlight the distinction between the Catholic and Hindu views of images and idols, this difference is lost on or (more likely) ignored by the majority of the Infant Jesus' Hindu devotees.

CHRISTIANITY

Since Independence, Christianity has become increasingly visible in India, attracting followers and increasing its political relevance with a speed that would have pleased the **Apostle Thomas.** In the apocryphal *Acts of Thomas*, Thomas was chosen to spread the Gospel to India. Thomas is said to have arrived on the coast of Kerala as early as 52 AD, where he was able to attract a number of converts before being martyred near modern-day Madras.

Since Thomas, ships carrying missionaries have sailed across the Arabian Sea with some frequency, here and there seeding India's west coast with Western and Christian ideas. In the 16th century, the Portuguese sought to spread Christianity more systematically to India, and converted without compunction. Soon after the arrival of the Jesuit Saint Francis Xavier in 1542, Portuguese-ruled Goa became a major center of Catholicism. During the early years of the East India Company, Protestant Christian missionary work was actively discouraged to prevent a gospel of love and service from getting in the way of Company profit and practices. Later years of British rule were marked by an increase in missionary work, which concentrated on building schools and hospitals. Grand churches were built as well, but these were mainly meant to serve the spiritual needs of the ruling Brits.

In the post-colonial period, the diffusion of Christianity through India has been marked by the growth of local, indigenous churches rather than foreign missionary efforts. There are about 25 million Christians in India today, 50% more than there were in 1970. Most of India's Christians are Protestant; the largest denominations are the Church of South India and the Church of North India, both members of the worldwide Anglican church. There are also sizable Catholic populations in several regions of India, particularly in Goa and the South. In recent years, Christians have fallen victim to the rising tide of Hindu nationalism, and killings and forced conversions have taken place across the country.

ZOROASTRIANISM

Founded in Persia between 700 and 500 BC by Zarathustra (also known as Zoroaster), **Zoroastrianism** understands the world to be starkly divided between pure good (represented by the god **Ahura Mazda**) and pure evil (represented by the god **Angra Mainyu**). According to Zoroastrian belief, **Saoshyant,** an immaculately conceived messiah, will one day come to establish Ahura Mazda's reign of goodness on earth. Zoroastrians believe that burial and cremation pollute the earth, fire, and air, each of which is regarded as sacred for its purity; they leave their dead in specially designed Towers of Silence, where vultures have easy access to the bodies.

Zoroastrianism was brought to India in the middle of the 10th century, when Persian Zoroastrians arrived on the Gujarati coast, fleeing the advance of Islam through Iran and Central Asia. Called **Parsis** because of their ancient roots in Persia, today's dwindling numbers of Indian Zoroastrians—about 95,000 are left—are concentrated in western India, especially in Bombay. Though few in number, the Parsis are known for their great wealth. One Parsi family, the Tatas, is renowned throughout India for its manufacturing industries (including India's first steel mill, built in 1908) and for its early support of the Independence movement.

THE ARTS

VISUAL ARTS

India has an ancient artistic tradition, fed over thousands of years by contact with other civilizations. Indian artists have commonly made their works conform to some ideal, rather than show their subjects naturalistically. The idealism in Indian art comes partly from its religious function—for centuries, almost all art was used to decorate sacred buildings or to illustrate sacred stories.

ARCHITECTURE

The history of Indian architecture begins with the Indus Valley Civilization that prospered between 2500-1800 BC. Almost nothing is known about these early Indian grid-planned cities—most buildings were made of materials such as wood and brick, and little has survived. More information is available from the Maurya period (c. 324-184 BC), when builders began to use stone to erect fortified cities and monasteries. The most impressive structures to have survived from this time are the **stupas,** enormous hemispherical mounds of earth usually designed to enclose Buddhist relics. Stupas are often elaborately decorated, with the mound placed on top of a terrace, surrounded by stone railings, and capped by a stone parasol. The **Great Stupa** at Sanchi, Madhya Pradesh (built during the first century BC) is the most famous of these (see p. 356).

The centuries following the Maurya period saw the development of temple design throughout the subcontinent. Early temples were built of wood, but in western India some were carved into the rock of the Western Ghats. These Buddhist **cave temples,** or *chaityas*, were usually marked by an apse that led to a long, pillared hall, at the end of which was placed the sacred object of veneration. The cave temples of **Ajanta** in Maharashtra (see p. 423) are world-famous examples of this style of temple architecture.

The typical **Hindu temple,** encountered throughout India today, is the result of thousands of years of evolution. Temples were originally made up of little more than a small, dark, square sanctum referred to as the *garbhagriha* ("womb chamber"), which housed the deity. A tall pyramid-shaped spire, or *shikhara*, was later added to symbolize the connection between heaven and earth. As temple architecture grew increasingly elaborate, distinctive North Indian and South Indian styles began to emerge. In a typical northern temple, a series of to four rooms leads to the sanctum. Each room has its own *shikhara*, though these rarely rise above the *shikhara* of the central chamber. This row of spires resembles a mountain range and perhaps symbolizes the Himalayan peaks, inhabited by the gods. Many of the greatest North Indian temples were destroyed by Islamic anti-idol campaigns from the 12th century onward, but excellent examples remain in **Orissa** (see p. 611) and in **Khajuraho** (see p. 369). In **South India,** the sanctum was expanded, and surrounded by four rectangular entrance towers, or *gopurams*, which had *shikharas* of their own, topped by barrel-vaults. These *gopurams* eventually grew to dwarf the central *shikhara*, creating grand temple-city complexes such as those of **Madurai** (see p. 573) and **Srirangam** (see p. 572) in Tamil Nadu.

The conquest of India by Muslim forces in the 12th century brought the Islamic styles of Persia and Central Asia to India. Since Islam forbids the depiction of human and animal images, Muslim rulers were glad to put their efforts into architecture, filling India with gorgeous domes, arches, geometric patterns, and calligraphic inscriptions.

HIGHLIGHTS OF MUSLIM ARCHITECTURE IN INDIA

QUWWAT AL ISLAM MASJID AND QUTB MINAR, Delhi (see p. 116). Striking monuments from the early years of Muslim conquest, these mosques, built in 1199, use the remains of more than 20 Hindu and Jain temples.

JAMA MASJID, Ahmedabad (see p. 334). A fusion of Muslim and Hindu styles of architecture, this mosque is the best example of Mughal architecture in Gujarat.

FATEHPUR SIKRI (see p. 175). Built in the 16th century, these pink and red post-and-lintel buildings are a testament to the elegance of Muslim architecture in Uttar Pradesh.

TAJ MAHAL, Agra (see p. 172). This natty little marble ditty is named after the Indian chain of five-star hotels.

SCULPTURE

The people of the Indus Valley Civilization left behind them simple terra-cotta figurines and seals decorated with pictures of animals and marked with a script that has still not been deciphered. Little survives of Indian sculpture until the 3rd century BC, when the Mauryan emperor **Ashoka** set up stone columns all over India as a symbol of his rule (see **The Mauryas**, p. 64). These columns were often topped with elaborate animal sculptures, the greatest of which to have survived is the **Lion Capital** found at **Sarnath** in Uttar Pradesh (see p. 204). With four fierce lions sitting back-to-back on a lotus platform, this sculpture has become one of India's national emblems, and appears on all national currency. The animals of the Mauryan capitals, which show some Persian influence but also bear the marks of an emerging Indian artistic style, are muscular and naturalistic, symbolizing the strength of Ashoka's political power.

The next two centuries saw the development of two-dimensional **bas-relief sculpture,** which was often used to decorate the railings of stupas and which usually told stories from the life of the Buddha or myths about popular gods and goddesses. The beginnings of classical Indian sculpture can be traced to the 1st century AD, when artists in **Mathura** (Uttar Pradesh) began to carve three-dimensional images of the Buddha (see p. 178). Also around this time, the **Gandhara** school of art developed in areas of the Punjab. Influenced by Greek and Roman art, Gandharan artists turned out strikingly naturalistic images of the Buddha, emphasizing intricate folds of clothing and other details.

During the Gupta period (4th-6th centuries AD), sculpture in Mathura reached its peak. Spreading throughout North India, principles borrowed from Buddhist imagery were applied to depictions of Hindu gods. Distinct regional styles developed from the Mathura style, producing architectural wonders at **Sarnath** (see p. 204) and in the cave temples of **Ajanta** in Maharashtra (see p. 423).

In North India, the sensuous and voluminous style of the Mathura style of sculpture gave way to a more elegant and rhythmic look. This style reached its apex around the 10th century, when it was used to adorn the exteriors of the great North Indian temples. A distinctively **South Indian style** saw the creation of the wonderful 7th-century bas-reliefs of **Mahabalipuram** (see p. 550), and the miniature, light sculptures used to decorate temples in Tamil Nadu during the 9th century. **Bronze sculpture** in South India reached its peak during the 9th and 10th centuries; the image of Shiva as Nataraja (King of the Dance) surrounded by a ring of fire is one of South India's greatest contributions to Indian art. This image is common throughout Tamil Nadu, but the one at the **Brihadishwara Temple** in Thanjavur (see p. 567) is the most famous.

Regional traditions developed in other areas, such as Maharashtra, where large, stocky figures were produced, conforming to the properties of the material they were sculpted from; the best of these are at the **Kailasa Temple** in **Ellora** (see p. 422). Islamic laws forbidding the depiction of human and animal forms contributed to a decline in the production of sculpture from the 12th century.

PAINTING

The art of painting has ancient roots in India, since palm leaves served as the first canvases for ancient miniatures. The only ancient paintings that remain are those sheltered by rock, such as the **wall paintings at Ajanta** in Maharashtra, dating from the 2nd century BC to the 5th century AD (see p. 423). The style of Indian painting best known today began in western India during the medieval period. Colorful, cluttered scenes with figures shown in profile were made to illustrate **Jain manuscripts.** This style gradually spread throughout the country, and was used for a wide variety of religious paintings.

The Delhi sultans and Mughal emperors, who began to arrive after the 12th century, brought with them a taste for Persian art, and radically changed the course of Indian painting. **Emperor Akbar** (r. 1556-1605), a great patron of the arts, was almost single-handedly responsible for creating the Mughal school of painting. He supervised his painters closely while they produced beautiful miniature illustrations for written histories, myths, and fables. Among other works, his court artists illuminated a magnificent Persian edition of the *Mahabharata*, which is now kept in the City Palace in Jaipur. As the Mughals settled in India, many began to disregard the Islamic injunction against the representation of human forms, and during the reign of **Jehangir** (r. 1605-27), artistic emphasis shifted to portraiture.

The cool, delicate Mughal style influenced Hindu painting as well. Under the patronage of Hindu Rajput kings in the 16th and 17th centuries, the **Rajasthani School** emerged, combining the abstract forms of the western Indian style with some of the naturalism of Mughal art. Rajput paintings usually depicted religious subjects, especially myths about Krishna cavorting with his *gopis* or pining for Radha, his favorite.

Both the Mughal and Rajasthani styles had fallen into decline by the 18th and 19th centuries, when European art began to exert an overwhelming influence. The first Indian attempts to copy European styles, known collectively as the **Company School,** were mostly lifeless engravings and watercolors. In the late 19th and early 20th centuries, artists of the Calcutta-based **Bengal School,** led by Rabindranath Tagore, combined older Indian styles with modern Western art. In the 20th century, painters such as Jamini Roy and M. F. Hussain successfully combined eastern and western influences.

MUSIC

Considered a spiritual activity, classical Indian music is based on two elements: the *raga* and the *tala*. These form the melodic and rhythmical framework for any piece of music. Derived from a Sanskrit word meaning "to color," the *raga* is the foundation of all composition and improvisation. Thousands of *ragas* exist. In the Hindu tradition, each is associated with a different moment of the day or season of the year. *Ragas* differ from one another in scale and in *rasa* (mood). Unlike Western music with its fixed-pitch scales, the Indian musician places the tonic note at whatever pitch is comfortable. Once the musician has established the tone for the *raga*, he improvises within the constraints of the chosen *raga*, exploring its potential to be created anew with each performance. Opportunities for improvisation likewise exist between the fixed beats of the *tala* and its repeated rhythmical cycle. The *raga* and the *tala* interact, with intonation and inflection converging at regularly emphasized intervals.

Modern Indian classical music, often divided into northern **Hindustani** and southern **Karnatic** systems, has its origins in ancient chants. Musical form is first discussed in the *Bharata Natyashastra*, a textual source of music written between 2 BC and 4 AD by the sage Bharat. North Indian musical styles were particularly influenced by the music of Persia and Turkey, where court patronage of musicians from around the Perso-Arabic world encouraged the development of an elaborate and highly evolved musical culture. The song style of *qawwali*, popular during weddings, is a musical debate: singers form two groups, one boasting the accomplishments of the bride, the other singing the praises of the groom. In its romantic form, *qawwali* is a socially acceptable forum for flirting. The lilting *ghazals* are a kind of Indian version of the ballad.

Many Indian musicians have gained worldwide followings. **Ravi Shankar,** who introduced Hindustani music to western ears during the 1960s and attracted the attention of the Beatles, is a master of the sitar, a fretted, 20-stringed instrument with a long teak neck fixed to a seasoned gourd. **Ali Akbar Khan** has achieved acclaim around the world for the wonderful things he can do with his sarod, a fretless stringed instrument similar to a sitar. **Allah Rakha** and his son, **Zakir Hussain,** mesmerize audiences with their virtuosity on the tabla, two drums played together and capable of producing many tones. Popular Karnatic musicians include **"Mandolin" U. Srinivasan** and the legendary singer **M.S. Subbulakshmi.**

Folk music is linked closely to folk dance and varies from region to region. From Punjabi *bhangra* to Rajasthani *langa*, folk tunes remain close to the hearts of Indians, and have recently gained an even larger audience through the international releases of **Ila Arun** and *bhangra*-rap performers in the UK. A unique genre of Bengali music is *Rabindrasangit*, the poetic words of Rabindranath Tagore set to quasi-classical song, the pride of the state of Bengal.

Popular music ranges from the "filmi" love songs of **Lata Mangeshkar** to the disco-hybrid-pop of vocal diva, **Alisha**, whose album **Made in India** sold over one million copies in 1995. Played in clubs and blasted from bachelor-filled cars all over India, the subjects of **Indipop** range from the patriotic to the chaotic, and from the ecstatic to the erotic, always making for fantastic sing-alongs. Like their voiceless on-screen counterparts, back-up singers and Indipopsters are big stars in India. Popular vocalists include the playful and prolific **Kishore Kumar,** whose versatile voice has filled in the melodic blanks for more actors than anybody can remember, and Punjabi crooner **Daler Mehndi,** whose 1996 hit, "*Bolo Ta Ra Ra,*" brought *bhangra* out of the North Indian countryside and onto satellite television for "hep" young Indians and funky kids all over the world to enjoy.

DANCE

The cosmic dance of Nataraja, King of the Dance, touches every sphere of human activity in India. India's dance forms, including both classical and folk styles, evolved as acts of worship, dramatizing myths and legends. Technique and philosophy, passed down from gurus to students, have carried the "visual poetry" described in the *Natya Shastra* (dating from between the 2nd century BC and the 2nd century AD), into modern times. **Bharatnatyam,** India's most ancient dance form, originated in the temples of Tamil Nadu. It is an intricate, fluid combination of eye movements, facial expressions, hand gestures, and strong, rhythmic, ankle-bell-enhanced steps. It was originally studied as a form of worship, and performed by *devadasis,* women who lived in temples and devoted their lives to the temple's deity. **Kathak,** first performed by *nautch* (dancing courtesans) against the opulent backdrop of North India's Mughal courts, is remarkable for the dizzying speed of its characteristic footwork and hand gestures. Developed from a rigorous system of yoga, **Kathakali,** an elaborately costumed form of dance-drama unique to Kerala, presents mythological stories of heroes, lovers, gods, and battles. The dancers, all male, must study for a minimum of 15 years before they are considered ready to come out and strut their stuff. **Kuchipudi,** a decorative dramatic dance form, originated in southern Andhra Pradesh as a means of worshiping Vishnu and Krishna. The old prohibitions against female dancers have disappeared, and women are now counted among the masters of the form. **Odissi,** a devotional dance form originating in Orissa, is both lyrical and sensuous. Also popular are regional folk dances, performed at festivals and private celebrations. **Bhangra,** a Punjabi dance, is one of the most popular of all, traditionally performed by men holding large sticks and dancing in a circle while accompanied by powerful drumming.

LITERATURE

Ancient India had a distinguished religious literary record, producing such epics as the **Mahabharata** and the **Ramayana** (see p. 579). India also has an impressive secular literary history, which reached its climax in the work of **Kalidasa,** who probably lived during the 4th century AD. Kalidasa's play, *Shakuntala*, which has had a tremendous effect on Indian literature, tells the tale of a young girl who becomes the lover of **King Dushyanta.** The king, typical male that he is, forgets her when he loses the ring she gave him. At the same time, the **South** was developing its own literature, with annual **sangams**—great gatherings of bards, beginning in the 1st century BC—that eventually gave rise to anthologies of poetry. By the 6th century AD, the Tamil literary tradition had produced two epics of its own, *Silappadigaram* and *Manimegalai*.

The Muslim rulers of the 13th century patronized the popular Sufi poet **Amir Khusrau** (1253-1325), nicknamed *Tuti-i-Hindi* ("Parrot of India"). The Mughals brought Persian with them, which came to be used both as a literary medium and as a common language among the various linguistic groups of northern India. Amir Khusrau also wrote extensively in Hindi, beginning the fusion of Hindu and Muslim traditions. The broad-minded Mughal emperor **Akbar** was a great patron of literature; during his reign lived **Tulsi Das**, author of the *Ramcharitmanas*, the Hindi version of the *Ramayana*. The Urdu language (and its literature of *ghazal* poems) also emerged from the Hindu-Muslim synthesis.

The British invasion cast its greatest intellectual spell on Bengal, where the English language, used as a medium of instruction, exposed Bengalis to Western authors like Shakespeare and Milton. **Bankim Chandra Chatterjee** combined the European novelistic genre with heady Indian patriotism in *Anandamath* ("The Abbey of Bliss," 1865). The Bengali Renaissance also produced **Rabindranath Tagore**, the greatest Indian artistic figure of the 20th century, whose poems, novels, songs, paintings, and plays sent the Bengali spirit echoing around the world. Tagore's English version of his book *Gitanjali* won him a Nobel Prize in 1913, making him the first non-European to receive the honor.

British writers in India during the colonial period left a body of work that makes for some evocative, if one-sided memoirs of the Raj. The "Bard of the Empire," **Rudyard Kipling,** was born in India and returned there after completing school. He wrote many of the lasting classics of sahib literature, including *Kim* (1900), a likely tale of an orphaned boy growing up half-Indian half-European in 19th century India. **E.M. Forster** presents a slightly more nuanced view of colonialism, in his novel of cultural misunderstanding, *A Passage to India* (1924).

Prominent trends in 20th-century Indian literature have included the increased use of prose and the adoption of English as the most commonly used literary language. Among the most influential writers of the early 20th century was **Mulk Raj Anand,** whose powerful novels *Untouchable* (1935) and *Coolie* (1936) railed against the cruelty of the caste system and economic exploitation. The South Indian novelist **R.K. Narayan**, perhaps India's greatest English-language writer of the second half of the 20th century, has become well-known worldwide for such books as *The Man-Eater of Malgudi* (1961) and *The Vendor of Sweets* (1967). Proudly distinct literatures written in the various regional languages of India also thrived in the 20th century.

Indian novelists are breaking on to the international literary scene in increasing numbers. Perhaps the only thing that these wildly disparate writers have in common is the fact that most of them live outside India, and that all of them write in English. **Salman Rushdie's** great novel, *Midnight's Children* (1980) was one of the first books to spark widespread interest in this new, "post-colonial" literature among *Reader's Digest* subscribers all over the world. In recent years, Rushdie's name has been joined on the front pages of *Time* and *Newsweek* by writers such as Vikram Seth *(A Suitable Boy)*, Rohinton Mistry (two-time winner of the Commonwealth Writers' Prize for *Such a Long Journey* and *A Fine Balance*), Arundhati Roy (winner of the Booker Prize for *The God of Small Things*), Vikram Chandra, Kiran Desai, Gita Mehta, Anita Desai, and Amitav Ghosh.

FILM

When Dadasaheb Phalke produced the first Indian feature film, *Raja Harishchandra*, in 1912, it marked the beginning of the country's obsession with motion pictures. India's film industry is now the most prolific in the world. Sound first invaded the frames in 1931 with *Alam Ara*, directed by **Ardeshir Irani.** The first of the "talkies" was favorably received, but it also fragmented audiences into disparate language groups, of which Hindi and Tamil have always been the largest. When directors realized that music was the way to overcome linguistic splintering, a new Indian musical genre was born. Some films have managed to squeeze in nearly 70 songs, and you would have to look long and hard today before you found a movie

BOLLYWOOD BEAT She emerges onto the scene of a lush landscape, singing a love song as her sari-clad hips swing in time to the accompanying beat. Hearing her voice, he rushes in to hold her in a rapturous embrace, but is rudely interrupted by his evil nemesis and a band of thugs, sent by her panicky parents to tear the two lovers apart. A brief but boisterous scuffle ensues, and our hero emerges, not a hair out of place, to return to the embrace. This utopia of otherwise unattainable romance and chivalry is available to millions in the form of the ultimate kitsch, the masala movie, named for the cheap-but-effective spice mixture used in Indian cooking.

No city in the world produces more action, comedy, romance, and trash than the city of Bombay, playfully known as Bollywood. Playing to millions of people every day, churning out 800 formula flicks a year in 23 languages, and grossing more than US$850 million every year, Bollywood movie-making is a big business. Popular film tabloids such as **Stardust, Filmfare,** and **Cineblitz** (available at any newsstand) sell thousands of copies throughout India and all over the world. Over 1 million viewers in the UK tuned in for the Bollywood awards show in March 1999. Until last year, however, movie-making was not considered a legitimate industry by government authorities, and film producers were forced to seek other sources of "informal" capital (i.e. the mob) to finance their projects. Studios' connections with Bombay gangsters have seen many on-screen antics duplicated in real life: on January 21, 2000, filmstar hero and major director Rakesh Roshan was shot when he refused to capitulate to an extortion attempt by mobsters. Roshan survived the attack, and Bollywood bigwigs are now starting to form alliances with studios in Hollywood in an attempt to wriggle free of the entanglements that have come to endanger their businesses and their lives.

Frequently ridiculed for their formulaic story lines—quality typically loses out to quantity in a crushing first-round knockout—Bollywood flicks offer an easy and affordable means of escape for the average Indian, who typically wants to escape reality for a couple of hours, not to see it re-created on the silver screen. Stumble into a local theater and you're guaranteed a good three hours or so of cheap thrills such as you'll find nowhere else in the world.

without at least one happy-clappy, teary-cheery, throbbing-sobbing song and dance sequence in it somewhere. In the 1940s, the introduction of pre-recorded songs and playback singing meant that actors no longer had to be singers. The most successful playback singer was **Lata Mangeshkar,** who holds the world record for most songs ever recorded, having put out more than 25,000 songs during her career.

During the 1930s and 1940s, the **social film** served as a useful way of addressing the concerns of contemporary life. It also introduced the preference for loudness—gaudy costumes, flighty and capricious music, exciting choreography, and wink-wink, nudge-nudge sex—that has become the hallmark of Bombay film. With a sense of the epic and spectacular, **Mehboob Khan** (best known for *Mother India*) specialized in Muslim costume dramas and social tragedies. **Raj Kapoor,** the "founding father" of popular cinema, introduced a more casual attitude toward sex, against the standard backdrop of melodramatic love.

SPORTS

Cricket isn't just a game in India—it's a national obsession. Indians turn out in their thousands to watch the big games, and an informal game or two seems to be constantly underway on every street corner in the country, often by little boys wearing not much more than a pair of shorts, and using sticks for bats and bricks for wickets. Expect to be asked for the names of your favorite players at every turn, and be ready to give an opinion on the state of the national game if you don't want to be taken for an idiot. Like many other former colonies, India regularly beats England at its own game these days. One of the few occasions when India is able to forget all its internal conflicts and band together as one nation comes whenever the Indian cricket team plays against its arch-rival, Pakistan. **Test matches** are watched by millions of people across India—huge crowds gather wherever there's a game being shown on TV. Things occasionally turn nasty: the Indian team reached the semi-finals of the 1996 World Cup, only to be disqualified when fans began to throw bottles, rocks, and other missiles onto the pitch. The national side was a flop in the 1999 World Cup, held in England, and has been the focus of much unwanted attention recently, after allegations accusing players of match-fixing and bribe-taking.

India is also a consistent Olympic medal-winner at hockey. Soccer and horse racing are especially popular in the east and in urban areas. Kabbadi, a breathless game of tag, is popular throughout the north.

FOOD AND DRINK

Once upon a time, protracted Vedic prose prescribed every dash and pinch of every spice and herb, and every plate was placed to provide the therapeutic and medicinal benefits of sustenance in just the right way. Although important rules continue to govern dining in modern India, the main worry for many travelers involves moderating their exposure to the intense flavors of the subcontinent's famously uncompromising cuisine. Most people in India begin the day with a small breakfast, eat lunch between noon and 2pm, enjoy sweet tea and salty snacks in the late afternoon, and have a late dinner between 7 and 10pm. Travelers who arrive for dinner any earlier should expect to be the only people in the restaurant, the focal point of a bevy of suited waiters tripping to fill their water glasses.

Meals in India begin with the staple: usually whole wheat bread in the north, rice in the south and east. Since most Indians eat with their hands, the bread and rice replace cutlery and are used to scoop food from the plate into the mouth. In a typical North Indian meal, the bread is accompanied by one or two spicy vegetable dishes, a lentil soup called **dahl,** and sometimes by rice and curd. The most basic bread, the **chappati** (or **roti**), is thin and round like a tortilla. Though flat when served, the *chappati* fills with hot air when cooked over an open fire—the more it swells, the hungrier the person waiting for it is supposed to be. Elaborate variations on the theme include: **paratha,** a two-layered bread, sometimes stuffed with vegetables such as onions, radishes, and potatoes, and usually eaten with curds at breakfast; **naan,** a thicker, chewier kind of bread made of white flour and baked in a tandoor, or clay oven; and **puri,** a fried version of the standard *chappati* that is generally eaten with potatoes for lunch or breakfast. Common North Indian rice dishes such as **biryani** or **pulao** come mixed with vegetables and, on occasion, with meat. Non-vegetarian options normally involve either chicken or lamb, since beef is off-limits to Hindus and pork is unclean for Muslims.

DHABAS Take a bus or coach anywhere in India, and you're sure to stop off at a *dhaba*, the ubiquitous stalls set up to provide hot and filling meals to truckers and other travelers around the clock. Here the *parathas* and fried rice drip with grease, the *chai* comes with a kick, and a meal guaranteed to leave you gasping for air costs about Rs15. Not just for truckers, these dives also cater to college kids, who come in to refuel after a night at the dance clubs or for all-night cramming sessions. In the early hours of the morning, truck drivers catch a few winks on the bamboo cots that functioned earlier in the evening as *sambar*-absorbent tables. Because *dhabas* serve a steady stream of hungry diners round the clock, their food is often left to boil and simmer for hours, killing germs and generally making them safe places to eat. The *dhaba* originated in Punjab and still serve mainly Punjabi cuisine—truck drivers have taken their *dhaba*-style fast-food with them through all of South Asia.

KNEAD IT, FLIP IT, TASTE IT Just as any meal is incomplete without *chappati*, a visit to India is incomplete without learning the art of *chappati*-making. For eight tasty *chappatis*, add a dash of salt to 300g of wheat flour. Slowly add water and knead the mixture until it becomes doughy (too much water will make the mixture sticky). Divide the dough into eight little balls and roll them in extra flour until lightly coated. Grab your *belan* (*chappati* roller) and roll away to make eight, flat, circular pieces. Warm up your *tawa* (flat metal plate used for cooking) at a low heat and lather it with *ghee* (clarified butter). Cook them one at a time, continuously twisting them around to ensure even cooking. Once browned (about one minute), flip the *chappati* over. When the top starts to puff up, remove the *chappati* from heat. Don't be dismayed if your first batch of *chappatis* is sub-par: practice makes perfect.

South Indian cuisine uses rice and rice flour much more than the north, with **dosas** (thin pancakes) and **idlis** (thick steamed cakes) taking center stage. These are accompanied by vegetable broths such as **sambar** (a thick and spicy lentil soup), **rasam** (thinner, with tomatoes and tamarind), and **kozhambu** (sour), which are poured onto the rice and mixed in with it. *Dosas* are often stuffed with spiced potatoes to make *masala dosa*. Less meat is eaten in the south, though seafood is common along the coast. A standard South Indian meal comes in the form of a **thali,** a steel plate filled with *chappati*, rice, *sambar*, fresh yogurt, *dahl*, and vegetable dishes. Food in the south tends to be sweeter than in the north, thanks to the greater use of coconut.

Indians will often add further spice to their meals with condiments like **achar** (pickles) and *papadum*, a thin, crunchy, chip-like item that is roasted or fried. Popular snacks include **samosa,** a spicy, fried potato turnover served with tamarind and mint sauces, and **bhel puri,** a sweet and sour mixture of fresh sprouts, potatoes, and yogurt (see **Street Eats**, p. 398). Desserts are often made of boiled milk, fried, and are drowned in heavy cream or whole milk flavored with pounds of sugar. For a lightweight alternative, try **paan,** the after-dinner chew that is the cause of the crimson-colored spatterings that stain every street you walk down. A *paan* leaf can be filled with everything from coconut to sweetened rose petals to fennel seeds to flavored betel nut and tobacco.

Paranoia purists avoid many of India's delicious drinks because they contain ice cubes made of untreated water. **Lassi,** made with yogurt and sugar, salt, or fruit, and the widely sold sugarcane juice are good for cooling off with. Besides the famous **tea** (*chai*), coffee is also popular, especially in South India.

Drinking alcohol is an accepted practice in some parts of the country, but it is frowned upon in other regions and may be hard to find (see **Drugs and Booze,** p. 20). Popular brands of beer are **Taj Mahal** and **Kingfisher.** Be careful when ordering difficult or obscure mixed drinks—what gets called Kahlua could taste a bit like fermented Ovaltine, and is probably an example of **Indian-Made Foreign Liquor (IMFL).** Imported brands are available in big cities, and not-so-good domestic wines are available at more expensive restaurants.

OTHER SOURCES

BOOKS

GENERAL

Culture Shock! India, by Gitanjali Kolanad (1994). A guide to Indian customs and etiquette for those planning to live and work in India, with useful advice for all sorts of social situations and bureaucratic hassles.

An Introduction to South Asia, by B. H. Farmer (1993). A geography-based description of South Asia, its history, politics, and economics.

TRAVEL/DESCRIPTION

Tropical Classical, by Pico Iyer (1997). Essays and articles culled from the last 10 years of the journalist's career. Always entertaining, and the history of the Raj is solid, as are the pieces set in Bombay and Nepal.

In Light of India, by Octavio Paz (1997). Nobel laureate's perceptions of India based upon his time serving as Mexico's ambassador to the country.

Arrow of the Blue-Skinned God: Retracing the Ramayana though India, by Jonah Blank (1992). A fabulous book comparing the culture of 1990s India to the ideals of Lord Rama, hero of the epic *Ramayana.*

India: A Million Mutinies Now, by V. S. Naipaul (1990). An excellent voyage in prose, examining the subtle rebellions that characterize Indian life in the 90s.

The Great Railway Bazaar, by Paul Theroux (1975). A classic, worth reading for descriptions of what it feels like to be a Westerner jammed on a train with hundreds of others.

HISTORY

Modern South Asia: History, Culture, and Political Economy, by Sugata Bose and Ayesha Jalal (1998). A controversial volume by two of the most prominent historians of South Asia which questions the traditional dichotomy between India's "democracy" and Pakistan's "authoritarianism."

A Traveller's History of India, by Sinharaja Tammita-Delgoda (1995). A clear and readable introduction to Indian history, with references to sites that can be visited today.

India, by Stanley Wolpert (1991). An easy-to-follow sampler of Indian culture and history by a well-known historian.

The Discovery of India, by Jawaharlal Nehru (1946). Indian history as seen by the founder of modern India—a classic.

An Autobiography, or, the Story of My Experiments with Truth, by Mohandas K. Gandhi (1927). Gandhi's personal account of the development of his beliefs, with surprisingly little commentary on the political events of the time.

POLITICS AND ECONOMICS

India: Government and Politics in a Developing Nation, by Robert L. Hardgrave, Jr. and Stanley A. Kochanek (1996). The best summary of recent Indian political issues and the government of modern India.

India: Economic Development and Social Opportunity, by Jean Drèze and Amartya Sen (1995). Analyzes the economic development of India from a social perspective and with empathy for the underprivileged.

Operation Bluestar: The True Story, by Lt. Gen. K.S. Brar (1993). An in-depth (albeit slanted) account of the Golden Temple's turmoil from an Indian commando.

RELIGION

The Sikhs: Their Religious Beliefs and Practices, by W. Owen Cole and Piara Singh Sambhi (1998). A good, succinct survey of the Sikh religious tradition.

Islam: The Straight Path, by John L. Esposito (1998). An excellent introduction. Esposito traces the development of Islam from its beginnings down to the present day.

Hinduism: A Cultural Perspective, by David R. Kinsley (1993). A comprehensive, thematic introduction to Hindu beliefs, practices, and culture.

Banaras: City of Light, by Diana L. Eck (1982). An exploration of the holy city that attempts to "see Kashi through Hindu eyes." A wonderful introduction to the complexities and contradictions of Hinduism in general and a beautiful description of Varanasi.

Karma Cola, by Gita Mehta (1979). A cynical journalistic satire about Westerners' infatuation with "spiritual" India.

What The Buddha Taught, by Walpola Rahula (1959). A Sri Lankan monk's authoritative and comprehensible explanation of Theravada Buddhist philosophy.

GENDER ISSUES

Neither Man Nor Woman: The Hijras of India, by Serena Nanda (1998). A well-researched ethnography of India's transvestite *hijra* community.

May You Be the Mother of a Hundred Sons, by Elizabeth Bumiller (1990). A British journalist's exploration of *sati*, sex-selective abortion, and dowry deaths, this is a good introduction to Indian society and politics, with a great chapter on Hindi film actresses.

FICTION

The God of Small Things, by Arundhati Roy (1997). An exquisitely woven story of love, betrayal, and tragedy set against the backdrop Kerala's social and political landscape.

Such a Long Journey, by Rohinton Mistry (1992). A humanely written tale of Bombay Parsis (Zoroastrians) who inadvertently become involved in Indira Gandhi's government corruption; a great read with an introduction to Parsi culture and India in the 1970s.

Malgudi Days, by R.K. Narayan (1986). Centarian Narayan is one of the few English-language Indian writers who lives in India. No post-colonial angst here, just wry, subtle, charming stories set in a fictional village in Tamil Nadu.

Midnight's Children, by Salman Rushdie (1980). Rushdie's masterpiece tells the magical tale of children born at midnight on the eve of Independence, and how the country's life and theirs evolve together.

A Passage to India, by E.M. Forster (1924). This classic novel tells the story of a friendship between an Englishman and an Indian during the British Raj. An honest, sensitive account whose observations about culture shock still hold true today.

POETRY

Gitanjali, by Rabindranath Tagore (1913). Nobel prize-winning work of the great Bengali poet, it uses images from Indian love poetry to discuss a relationship with God.

The Meghaduta, by Kalidasa (4th century AD). The great Sanskrit poet's account of a cloud's journey across India, surveying the landscape and human activity as it carries a message between separated lovers.

PHOTOGRAPHY

River of Color: The India of Raghubir Singh, curated by David Travis (1998). A retrospective survey of Raghubir Singh's work. Captures the landscapes and people along the banks of the Ganga and in Rajasthan in amazing configurations.

A Day in the Life of India, by David Cohen (1986). A moving collection of images take by a dozen Indian photographers on one day in 1986.

FILMS

Fire, by Deepa Mehta (1996). The story of two women bound by culture and longing for love who eventually find consolation with each other. The film was banned in India for its depiction of lesbianism and is the first of an Earth, Fire, Air trilogy by Mehta.

Bandit Queen, by Shekhar Kapur (1994). The story of Phoolan Devi, a low-caste bandit-turned-politician. A horrifyingly graphic, true-life portrayal of caste oppression in UP.

Hello Photo, by Nina Davenport (1994). The next best thing to going there yourself, this stunning film shows one woman's experience of looking and being looked at in India.

Salaam Bombay, by Mira Nair (1988). A disturbing tale of Bombay's street children. This fictional story told in documentary style is somewhat exploitative, but it's a moving and well-acted film.

Pather Panchali, by Satyajit Ray (1955). The first film by the late master of Indian cinema. Produced on weekends with a borrowed camera and unpaid actors. Its visuals capture the beauty of the Bengali landscape and the isolation of the village where Apu and Durga, the hero and heroine, live. Musical accompaniment by Ravi Shankar.

DELHI दिल्ली

All of the contrasts familiar to travelers in India are in full force here in the nation's capital: rich and poor, old and new, chaos and order. Delhi maintains a dignified front as a proud metropolitan center of government and commerce, with its official-looking edifices spanning the broad green blocks that provide clean air and empty spaces to the city's south-central districts. Nobody sleeps on the lawns between the monuments, and billboards (in English, of course) exhort the city's 10 million people to join in various welfare campaigns and to help keep Delhi "clean and green." Behind this facade of order and control are Delhi's other streets, crammed with the city's legendary slow-churning traffic and threaded by careening auto-rickshaws. It is in these streets that real life is lived, where the ballyhooed cosmopolitanism of the urban elite is manufactured and displayed, and where Punjabi Sikhs, colorfully dressed Rajasthani women, dreadlocked sadhus, and down-and-out pavement-dwellers all rub shoulders, sharing space, if not conversation. And it is in these streets that North India's heat and humidity are refracted through layers of polluted air, acting as a relentless social leveler, forcing the climate-controlled few and the shelterless masses to sweat it out together—pressed together, layer upon layer, like the history of the city itself.

The history of Delhi begins in 736 AD, with the founding of Lal Kot by the Tomara clan of Rajputs. Their tumultuous and gory rule was abruptly ended in 1192 by Mohammed Gauri and his slave general Qutb-ud-din Aibak, who swept in from Central Asia and conquered great stretches of North India, introducing Islam and founding the Delhi Sultanate. For the next 300 years Delhi was wracked by political instability, especially in 1398, when the city was sacked by another Central Asian warlord, Timur. By the early 16th century the Lodi dynasty had made its share of enemies in the region. Too meek to challenge the Sultanate on their own, they requested help from Timur's great-grandson, Babur. Babur beat the Lodis into submission and launched the Mughal Empire, which would unite much of South Asia for the next two centuries. The Mughals repeatedly shifted their capital between Delhi and Agra, leaving both cities with monumental tombs, palaces, and forts. Old Delhi's grandest edifices were built during the 17th century by the Mughal emperor Shah Jahan. Mughal strength began to wane during the 18th century, however, and the British promptly moved in to fill the void. In 1911, the British capital was moved here from Calcutta, and the city began to attract the attention of Indian nationalists, who promised that the flag of an Indian republic would one day fly from the Red Fort. Marking the occasion with a speech by the Prime Minister delivered from the Red Fort and a tremendous parade in front of the city's most important British buildings, modern Delhi celebrates the vindication of the nationalists' predictions every year on August 15, Independence Day.

HIGHLIGHTS OF DELHI

Old Delhi is packed with bazaars and monuments, including the **Red Fort** (p. 114) and the **Jama Masjid** (p. 116), the largest mosque in India.

South of the city center are the emperor **Humayan's Tomb** (p. 118) and the phenomenal Mughal ruins at the **Qutb Minar** complex (p. 116).

Delhi's lotus shaped, garden-ringed **Baha'i Temple** (p. 118) is one of India's most beautiful modern structures.

The immensely intricate **Jantar Mantar** (p. 119) is an 18th-century astronomical observatory set in stone, complete with massive marble sundials.

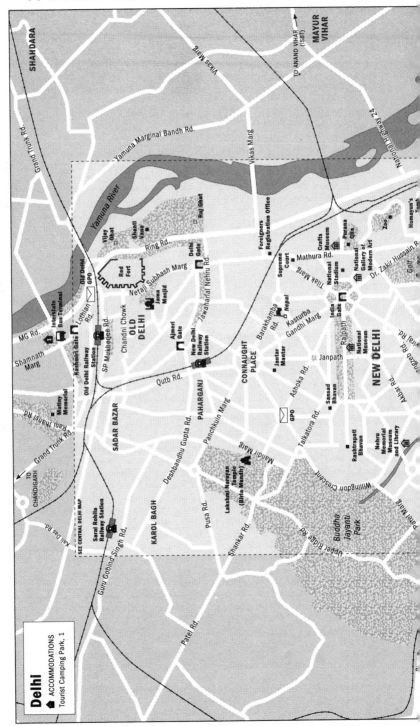

Delhi

ACCOMMODATIONS
Tourist Camping Park, 1

SHAHDARA

MAYUR VIHAR

TO ANAND VIHAR (ISBT)

Vikas Marg

National Highway 24

Yamuna Marginal Bandh Rd.

Vikas Marg

Grand Trunk Rd.

Yamuna River

Vijay Ghat

Shanti Vana

Raj Ghat

Foreigners Registration Office

Supreme Court

Crafts Museum

National Gallery of Modern Art

Purana Qila

Zoo

Humayun's Tomb

Ring Rd.

Delhi Gate

Mathura Rd.

Dr. Zakir Hussain Rd.

Golf

Interstate Bus Terminal

Old Delhi GPO

Red Fort

Netaji Subhash Marg

Jama Masjid

Chandni Chowk

OLD DELHI

Jawaharlal Nehru Rd.

Barakhamba Rd.

National Stadium

India Gate

Rajpath

MG Rd.

Kashmiri Gate

Lothian Rd.

Tilak Marg

Nepal

Kasturba Gandhi Marg

National Museum

NEW DELHI

Shamnath Marg

Old Delhi Railway Station

SP Mukherjee Rd.

Ajmeri Gate

New Delhi Railway Station

CONNAUGHT PLACE

Jantar Mantar

Janpath

Aurangzeb Rd.

Akbar Rd.

Mutiny Memorial

Rani Jhansi Rd.

Qutb Rd.

PAHARGANJ

Ashoka Rd.

Sansad Bhavan

GPO

Talkatora Rd.

Rastrapati Bhavan

Nehru Memorial Museum and Library

Patel Marg

TO CHANDIGARH

Grand Trunk Rd.

SADAR BAZAR

Deshbandhu Gupta Rd.

Panchkuin Marg

Mandir Marg

Willingdon Crescent

Kali Das Rd.

SEE CENTRAL DELHI MAP

Sarai Rohilla Railway Station

Guru Gobind Singh Rd.

KAROL BAGH

Pusa Rd.

Lakshmi Narayan Temple (Birla Mandir)

Shankar Rd.

Upper Ridge Rd.

Buddha Jayanti Park

Patel Rd.

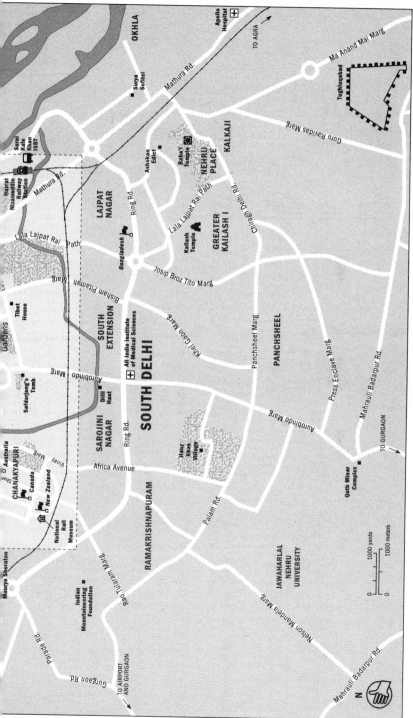

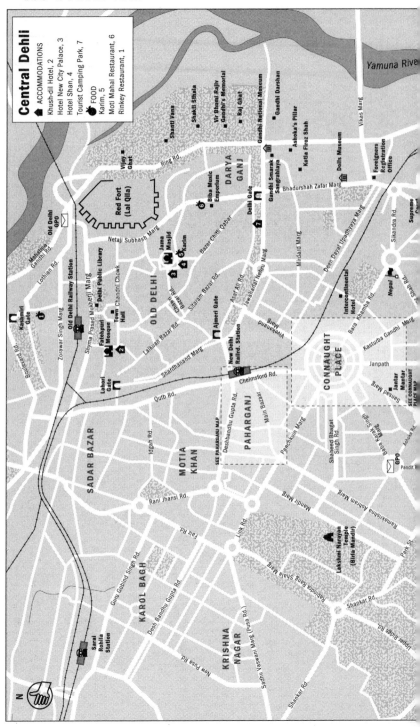

Central Dehli

🛏 ACCOMMODATIONS
Khush-dil Hotel, 2
Hotel New City Palace, 3
Hotel Shan, 4
Tourist Camping Park, 7
🍴 FOOD
Karim, 5
Moti Mahal Restaurant, 6
Rinkey Restaurant, 1

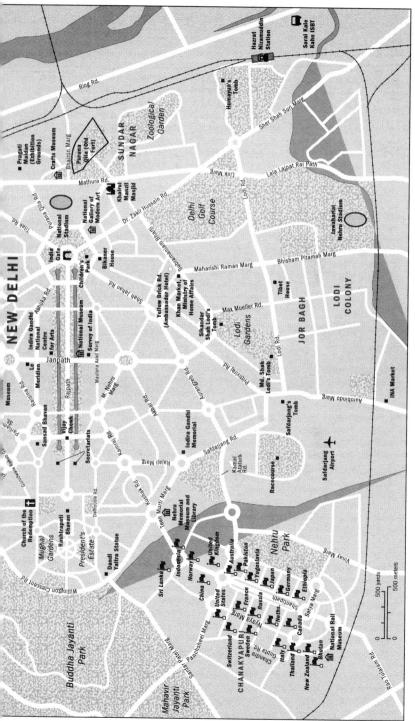

NEW DELHI

Buddha Jayanti Park

Mahavir Jayanti Park

Mughal Gardens

Church of the Redemption

Rashtrapati Bhavan

President's Estate

Dandi Yatra Statue

Willington Crescent Rd.

Sansad Bhavan

Vijay Chowk

Secretariats

Rajpath

Janpath

Le Meridien

Indira Gandhi National Centre for Arts

National Museum

Survey of India

India Gate

Children's Park

Bikaner House

National Stadium

National Gallery of Modern Art

Khairul Manzil Masjid

Purana Qila (Old Fort)

Crafts Museum

Pragati Maidan (Exhibition Grounds)

Mathura Rd.

SUNDAR NAGAR

Zoological Garden

Humayun's Tomb

Hazrat Nizamuddin Station

Saral Kale Kahn ISBT

Ring Rd.

Sher Shah Suri Marg

Lala Lajpat Rai Path

Link Rd.

Delhi Golf Course

Lodi Rd.

Maharishi Raman Marg

Bhisham Pitamah Marg

Jawaharlal Nehru Stadium

LODI COLONY

Yellow Brick Rd. (Ambassador Hotel)

Khan Market, Ministry of Home Affairs

Max Mueller Rd.

Tibet House

JOR BAGH

Sikandar Shah Lodi's Tomb

Lodi Gardens

Md. Shah Lodi's Tomb

INA Market

Aurobindo Marg

Indira Gandhi Memorial

Safdarjang's Tomb

Safdarjang Rd.

Kamal Ataturk Rd.

Racecourse

Safdarjang Airport

Vinay Marg

Nehru Memorial Museum and Library

Nehru Park

Teen Murti Marg

Sri Lanka

Indonesia

Norway

United Kingdom

Australia

Pakistan

Yugoslavia

Japan

Germany

Ethiopia

China

United States

France

Russia

Sheikhs...

Canada

Switzerland

Sweden

Italy

Thailand

New Zealand

Bhutan

National Rail Museum

CHANAKYAPURI

Chandra Gupta Rd.

Nyaya Marg

Panchsheel Marg

Sardar Patel Marg

Shantipath

Satya Marg

Rao Tularam Rd.

Tilak Rd.

Purana Qila Rd.

Bhairon Marg

Dr. Zakir Hussain Rd.

Subramaniam Bharti

Shah Jehan Rd.

Ashoka Rd.

Maulana Azad Marg

M. Nehru Marg

Akbar Rd.

Aurangzeb Rd.

Prithviraj Rd.

Kushak Rd.

Kamal Marg

Rajaji Marg

Dalhousie Rd.

Museum

Rafi Marg

Pandit St.

500 yards

500 meters

0

✈ GETTING THERE AND AWAY

INTERNATIONAL FLIGHTS

> ⚠ **WARNING.** You may be tired from your flight, but keep your wits about you, even in the airport. If you don't understand what's going on or feel pressured or herded in a particular direction, stop to collect yourself—there's really no hurry. When paying at a counter, **count out your cash as you hand it over.** Switch-the-bill schemes are common. **Never** let a cab driver convince you that the hotel you ask for is full or closed. And remember, **the more assertive someone is with offers of help, the more likely it is that there's something in it for him.** If you need help or have a question, ask someone who hasn't approached you first.

Indira Gandhi International Airport (☎565 2011 or 565 2021) serves as the main entry and departure point for international flights. There is a 24-hour **State Bank of India** office in the arrivals hall, next to the **Government of India Tourism** and the **Delhi Tourism** information desks. This is the place to pay for a **pre-paid taxi,** the most hassle-free way to get into the city (Rs200 to the city center). Once you pay, you'll receive a receipt with your destination and a taxi number written on it—make sure that the driver takes you where *you* want to go. Delhi Transport Corporation (DTC) and EATS (☎331 6530) run frequent **buses** to Connaught Pl. from the airport (Rs30 from the domestic terminal, Rs50 from the international terminal; Rs5 per bag). DTC buses also stop at New Delhi Railway Station and the Interstate Bus Terminal (ISBT) at Kashmere Gate. **Auto-rickshaws** shuttle from the airport to downtown at cheaper rates than taxis but without the security of the pre-payment system. To get to the airport (international and domestic terminals), pick up the EATS bus near Middle Circle on Janpath (4, 5:30, 7:30, 9am, 2, 3:30, 6, 7, 10, and 11:30pm).

INTERNATIONAL AIRLINES. Air France, Scindia House, Janpath (☎373 8004-7); **Air India,** Jeevan Bharati Building (☎373 6446-8); **Alitalia,** 16 Barakhamba Rd. (☎332 9551); **Biman,** World Trade Center, UGF Rd., Connaught Pl. (☎336 4401-4); **British Airways,** DLF Centre, Sansad Marg (☎91 635 9911); **Cathay Pacific,** 24 Barakhamba Rd. (☎332 3332); **Delta,** DLF Centre, Sansad Marg (☎373 0197); **El Al,** Prakash Deep Bldg., Tolstoy Marg (☎335 7965-7); **Gulf Air,** G-12, Connaught Pl. (☎332 4293); **KLM/Northwest,** Prakash Deep Bldg., Tolstoy Marg (☎335 7747); **Kuwait Airlines,** 15 Barakhamba Rd. (☎335 4373); **Lufthansa,** 56 Janpath (☎332 7268); **Qantas,** Mohan Dev Bldg., Tolstoy Marg (☎332 9027); **RNAC (Royal Nepal Airlines),** 44 Janpath (☎332 1164); **Singapore Airlines,** Ashoka Estate Bldg., Barakhamba Rd. (☎335 6283/4); **Swissair,** DLF Centre, Sansad Marg (☎332 5511); **Thai Airways,** Park Royal Hotel, American Plaza, Nehru Palace (☎623 9133); and **United Airlines,** 14 KG Marg (☎335 3377). Indian Airlines flies to **Kathmandu, Nepal** (3 per day, 2hr., US$142); for **Dhaka, Bangladesh** you must fly via Calcutta.

DOMESTIC FLIGHTS

The airport's **domestic terminal** (☎566 5125/6) is 5km from the international terminal. **Pre-paid taxis, buses,** and **rickshaws** run to and from downtown (see **Indira Gandhi International Airport,** above). Be sure to look into student fares (generally available to anyone under 30) and other discounts. Domestic airlines include: **Archana Airways** (☎684 2001); **Indian Airlines** (☎371 9168); **Jagson** (☎372 1594); **Jet Airways** (☎685 3700); **Sahara** (☎332 6851). Flights to: **Agra** (M, W, F, and Su; 40min.; US$55); **Ahmedabad** (2-3 per day, 1½hr., US$135); **Amritsar** (M, W, and F; 1½hr.; US$100); **Aurangabad** (1 per day, 3½hr., US$175); **Bagdogra** (M, W, and F; 2hr.; US$185); **Bangalore** (3 per day, 2½hr., US$255); **Bhopal** (1 per day, 2hr., US$120); **Bhubaneswar** (1 per day, 2hr., US$215); **Bombay** (10 per day, 2hr., US$175); **Calcutta** (3 per day, 2hr., US$200); **Chandigarh** (W and F, 40min., US$75); **Cochin** (1 per day, 4hr., US$330); **Goa** (1 per day, 2½hr., 235); **Guwahati** (1 per day, 3hr., US$210); **Gwalior** (M-Tu and

DELHI

Th-Sa, 45min., US$70); **Hyderabad** (2 per day, 2hr., US$205); **Jaipur** (1-2 per day, 40min., US$55); **Jammu** (1 per day, 1hr., US$105); **Khajuraho** (M, W, F and Su; 2hr.; US$100); **Leh** (M, W, F, and Su; 1½hr.; US$105); **Lucknow** (2-3 per day, 1hr., US$90); **Madras** (3 per day, 2½hr., US$260); **Nagpur** (1 per day, 1½hr., US$150); **Patna** (2 per day, 3hr., US$145); **Ranchi** (1 per day, 1½hr., US$190); **Shimla** (M, W, and F; 1hr.; US$110); **Srinagar** (1 per day, 2½hr., US$115); **Trivandrum** (1 per day, 5hr., US$360); **Udaipur** (1 per day, 2hr., US$105); and **Varanasi** (1-2 per day, 2hr., US$125).

TRAINS

> **!** **WARNING.** Delhi's **touts** (young men employed by shop-owners to bring in customers) are the best in the business; they will go to incredible lengths to get you into their employer's office. Although few are actually out to rob or hurt you, touts routinely (and elaborately) lie to tourists, using false identification and guilt trips (e.g., "Why don't you trust me? I'm trying to help you."). For more information, see **Touts, Middlemen, and Scams**, p. 15.

STATIONS. The **New Delhi Railway Station,** the main depot for trains in and out of Delhi, is north of Connaught Pl., at the east end of Paharganj Main Bazaar. It is a chaotic place, so be prepared to push your way around and beware of theft. Your best bet is to get tickets from the **International Tourist Bureau** (☎3740 5156), a large room upstairs at Platform 1. The office books reservations on tourist-quota seats and sells Indrail passes. Tickets from here must be bought in foreign currency or in rupees with encashment certificates. (Open M-Sa 8am-4:30pm.) You can also book train tickets at the usual places: at the windows in the station (for general booking) or the **Computerized Reservation Terminal,** one block south of the station on Chelmsford Rd. Book as much as a week ahead for some of the more popular trains. **Do not go to the dodgy tourist offices around the railway station.**

Delhi has three other railway stations: **Delhi Station,** in Old Delhi; **Hazrat Nizamuddin Station,** in the southeast part of the city; and **Sarai Rohilla,** in the northwest. Trains leaving from all stations can be booked at the International Tourist Bureau. Some important phone numbers are: **general enquiry** (☎131), **arrivals** and **departures** (☎1330, 1331, or 1335), and **reservations** (☎334 8686 or 334 8787).

DEPARTURES. You can make a reservation from Delhi for any train running between any two stations in India. **Timetables** for major destinations are posted in the International Tourist Bureau. The *Trains at a Glance* booklet can be bought at the enquiry counter on Platform 1 or at the book-stalls (Rs25). The air-conditioned *Shatabdi Express* and *Rajdhani Express* trains cost much more than standard 2nd-class tickets, but they get you where you're going faster, provide food and comfy seats, and feature nice India Tourism posters to make up for the fact that you won't see much out of the tinted windows. The listings that follow represent only the tiniest and fastest selection from among the many trains available from **New Delhi Railway Station.** *Shatabdi Express* trains to: **Ajmer** (#2015, 6:15am, 6½hr., Rs630) via **Jaipur** (4½hr., Rs495); **Amritsar** (#2013, 4:30pm, 6hr., Rs610); **Bhopal** (#2002, 6am, 8hr., Rs850) via **Agra** (2hr., Rs390); **Chandigarh** (#2005, 5:15pm, 3hr., Rs435); **Dehra Dun** (#2017, 7:10am, 5½hr., Rs495); **Lucknow** (#2004, 6:20am, 6½hr., Rs640) via **Kanpur** (5hr., Rs585). A/C 3-tier *Rajdhani Express* trains run to **Ahmedabad** (#2958; Tu, Th, and Sa; 2:40pm; 15hr.; Rs1190); **Allahabad** (#2306, 2424, and 2310; 5pm; 7hr.; Rs975); **Bangalore,** from H. Nizamuddin (#2430; M, Tu, and Sa; 8:50pm; 34hr.; Rs2205); **Bombay,** from H. Nizamuddin (#2952, 4pm; #2954, 4:50pm; 17hr.; Rs1485); **Calcutta** (#2302 and 2422, 5:15pm, 18hr., Rs1500); **Madras,** from H. Nizamuddin (#2434, 3:30pm, 29hr., Rs2045).

BUSES

TERMINALS. There are three **interstate bus terminals (ISBTs)** in Delhi: the new **Anand Vihar ISBT** (☎2149089), about 20km from downtown Delhi and east of the

Yamuna River; **Sarai Kale Khan ISBT** (☎469 8343), two blocks east of the Nizamuddin Railway Station; and **Kashmere Gate ISBT** (☎296 8709), north of Old Delhi Railway Station. Each ISBT serves specific cities, and there is little overlap. Make sure to go to the correct bus station for your destination. A phone call to one of the stations can prevent lots of wasted time and money. For information on ordinary and deluxe bus prices and schedules, call one of the bus companies: government-run **Delhi Transport Corporation** (☎296 8836); **Haryana Roadways** (☎296 1262); **Himachal Roadways** (☎296 6725); **Punjab Roadways** (☎296 7842); **Rajasthan Roadways** (☎296 1246 or 338 3469); or **UP Roadways** (☎296 8709 or 214 9089). Many of the private bus companies have booths or offices in the Kashmere Gate ISBT. Shop around for the best price and **steer clear of touts offering implausibly low rates.**

DEPARTURES. Where do you want to go today? Here are just a sampling of bus destinations. **Anand Vihar ISBT** runs daily buses to: **Agra, Allahabad, Almora** (11hr., Rs196), **Barielly, Bhawli, Basti, Bali, Barauni, Bageshwar, Deoria, Gorakhpur, Haldwani, Jhansi, Kanpur, Lucknow** (14hr., Rs212), **Nainital** (9hr., Rs136), **Pithoragarh, Ramnagar** (7hr., Rs107), **Rudrapur, Ranikhet, Rath, Sikandrabad, Sonauli, Sahswan, Tanakpur, Timbuktu,** and **Varanasi.**

    Kashmere Gate ISBT runs daily buses to: **Amritsar** (10hr., Rs192), **Baijnath, Chandigarh** (6hr., Rs108), **Dabawali, Dadari, Dehradun** (6½hr., Rs115), **Dharamsala** (12hr., Rs237), **Haridwar** (5½hr., Rs93), **Jammu** (14hr., Rs242), **Kullu, Manali** (17hr., Rs250), **Mussoorie** (8hr., Rs172), **Panipat, Rishikesh** (7hr., Rs107), **Shimla** (10hr., Rs180).

    Sarai Kale Khan ISBT runs daily buses to: **Agra, Ajmer, Chittor, Gwalior, Jaipur** (6hr., Rs106), **Jodhpur** (16hr., Rs222), **Mathura, Udaipur** (17hr., Rs290), and **Vrindaban.**

▐ GETTING AROUND

RICKSHAWS

Auto-rickshaw drivers have a knack for overcharging, driving around in circles, and *then* overcharging or changing the agreed fare at the end of the trip. Fluctuating petrol prices have made most meters obsolete, adding a 75% surcharge to the fare. It is usually better to set the auto-rickshaw price in advance if you don't know your way around Delhi—insisting on use of the meter can provoke the auto-*wallahs* into adding a few extra kilometers to the journey. **Pre-paid auto-rickshaws** are available at the airports, train stations, bus stations, and at the Delhi Traffic Police Booth on Janpath, near the Government of India Tourist Office. The maximum reasonable non-pre-paid fares are: Airport to Connaught Pl. or Paharganj Rs150-200; Paharganj to Connaught Pl. Rs15-20; Paharganj to Old Delhi Railway Rs40-50; Connaught Pl. to Old Delhi Rs35-50; Connaught Pl. to Chanakyapuri Rs35-40. **Cycle-rickshaws** can't go through parts of New Delhi, but in the narrow streets of Old Delhi, they are ideal. Typical fares: Old Delhi to New Delhi Station Rs30; Paharganj to Connaught Pl. Rs5.

BUSES

City buses are extremely cheap, but actually using them to get where you want to go involves a whole host of difficulties. First of all, there is the problem of overcrowding: drivers stop every five seconds to pick up passengers from the side of the road, and this tends to make trips irritatingly long and uncomfortable. And then there's the problem of figuring out which bus goes where. Not even the managers of **Delhi Transport Corp (DTC)** seem to be able work out what happens to the buses once they leave the depot. The staff at the tourist office is just as clueless when it comes to hazarding a guess about which bus goes where, from where, and how often. Some people have been stuck on the same bus for years now. Drivers sometimes post a sign on the side of the bus with a number, the origin, and destination of the bus; more often they don't. And these signs are only written in Hindi anyway. Buses run sporadically, are frustrating to ride, and cannot be relied upon. For a theoretically up-to-date city bus schedule, pick up a copy of *A Road Guide to Delhi* (Rs50). Good luck.

BICYCLES

Cycling in Delhi can be harrowing but also fun. Old Delhi is congested and slow; New Delhi fast and frantic. Exploring by bike allows you to see places tourists don't usually go and also gives you a speedy getaway option when the constant attention of touts starts to get tiresome. **Mehta Cycles** (also known as Aadya Shakti Handicrafts), 2 stores east of the Kesri Hotel on Main Bazaar, Paharganj, rents bikes (Rs40 per day, Rs6 per hr., Rs5 overnight charge; Rs600 deposit). Bell and lock are included, but the store doesn't stock helmets, claiming that they are "completely unnecessary" in Delhi. (☎354 0370. Open daily 9am-7:30pm.)

✲ ORIENTATION

Situated west of the Yamuna River, Delhi stretches 30km from north to south and 10km from east to west. The northern two-thirds of the city are circled by **Ring Rd.** Just west of the **New Delhi Railway Station** is **Paharganj,** Delhi's backpacker ghetto, crammed with budget hotels, tie-dye-clad Europeans, and shops full of plastic shoes. The area north of the station is **Old Delhi.** Built by Shah Jahan (and also called Shahjahanabad), Old Delhi is a delightfully tatty tangle of streets and bazaars. The main road in this part of town is the **Chandni Chowk,** which runs from east to west across the old city.

South of New Delhi Station, the center of **New Delhi** radiates out from **Connaught Place,** a circular hub of two-story colonnaded buildings. Connaught Pl. is the throbbing heart (and capitalist soul) of New Delhi. If you're looking for an AmEx office, a copy of last Tuesday's *USA Today,* or the Uzbekistan Airlines reservation desk, you've come to the right place. Of course, with tourists come touts and tricksters—Connaught Pl.'s hustlers are aggressive and exceptionally savvy; ignore them. Off the radial roads to the south of Connaught Pl. sprout the high-rise office buildings of India's most powerful banks, airlines, and international corporations.

Of the streets that radiate from Connaught Pl., **Sansad Marg** is the most crowded; it leads to the Raj-era parliamentary buildings, 2km west of **India Gate,** straight down **Raj Path.** One kilometer south of the parliamentary buildings is **Chanakyapuri,** home to the embassies of many western countries. **South Delhi** begins just south of Chanakyapuri. Except for Ring Rd. and **Mehrauli Badarpur Rd.,** South Delhi's major thoroughfares run north-south. In the center is **Aurobindo Marg,** which connects Safdarjang's tomb with the **Qutb Minar Complex.** In the east is **Mathura Rd.,** which slices through **Nizamuddin** and turns into **Zakir Hussain Rd.** as it proceeds southeast from India Gate.

⁊ PRACTICAL INFORMATION

TOURIST AND FINANCIAL SERVICES

WARNING. Delhi is full of "tourist offices" claiming to provide booking assistance, free maps, and other services. Several of these offices are near the railway. Their bookings are likely to be overpriced, if not fraudulent. Stick to the main government tourist office on Janpath and, for train tickets, to the tourist reservation office in the New Delhi Railway Station and government-approved private travel agencies. **Delhi is a haven of subversive activity.** Con-artists are as common as flies, particularly in Paharganj and other tourist hot-beds. If you realize that you've been cheated, contact the Government of India Tourist Office. They can at least put you in touch with the authorities and may be able to help compensate tourists who have been ripped off.

Tourist Office: Government of India Tourist Office, 88 Janpath (☎332 0005 or 332 0008), between Tolstoy Marg and Connaught Circus Rd., next to Kapoor Lamps and Delhi Photo Company. Great place to go for help getting around the city and in easing those first-arrival jitters. Open M-F 9am-6pm, Sa 9am-2pm. Two other government-sponsored agencies provide information and bookings. **India Tourism Development Corporation (ITDC),** also called India Tourism or Ashok Travels, Connaught Pl. (☎332 2336), at the corner of Middle Circle and Radial Rd. Open daily 7am-8pm. **Delhi Tourism (DTTDC),** Connaught Pl., N-block, Middle Circle (☎331 4229 or 331 5322). Open daily 7am-9pm. All 3 government agencies have branches in the international terminal at the airport. The different states of India all run offices in Delhi. The Chandralok Building, 36 Janpath, south of the Central Cottage Industries Emporium, houses the offices for **Uttar Pradesh** (☎371 1296 or 332 2251; open M-Sa 10am-5pm), **Himachal Pradesh** (☎332 5320; open daily 10am-5pm), and **Haryana** (☎332 4911; open M-F 10am-5pm). The **Indian Mountaineering Foundation,** Benito Juarez Marg, Anand Niketan (☎467 1211), has information on treks. The **Survey of India,** 124-A Janpath, (☎332 2288), provides city and trekking maps. Open M-F 9am-1pm and 1:30-5pm.

Budget Travel: Travel agencies are a dime a dozen. Many cheat unwary tourists or charge them plenty extra for what they could buy on their own. Still, there are reliable ones out there. Seek out Vini, well-travelled owner of **VINstring Holidays** (☎336 8717, mobile ☎98100 97686; fax 336 8901, in US (530) 324-8166; email vin.india@vsnl.com; www.vinstring.com), who works with "all budgets—shoestring to Sheraton and beyond" and takes care of his clientele. Open daily 8:30am-10:30pm.

Embassies: Most are in the Chanakyapuri area in south central Delhi and are open during regular business hours. **Australia,** 1/50-G Shantipath (☎688 8223; fax 688 5199). Open M-F 8:30am-1pm and 2-4:50pm. **Canada,** 7/8 Shantipath (☎687 6500; fax 687 6579). Open M-Th 8:30am-5pm, F 8:30am-1pm. **European Commission,** 65 Golf Links (☎462 9237; fax 462 9206). Open M-F 9am-5:30pm. **Ireland,** 230 Jor Bagh (☎462 6733; in dire emergencies call Mr. Francis ☎461 7435; fax 469 7053). Open M-F 9:30am-1:30pm and 2:30-5pm; visa services open M-F 10am-noon. **Israel,** 3 Aurangzeb Rd. (☎301 3238; fax 301 4298). Open M-F 9am-5pm. **Nepal,** Barakhamba Rd. (☎332 7361 or 332 9218; fax 332 6857). Open M-F 9am-1pm and 2-5pm. **New Zealand,** 50-N Nyaya Marg (☎688 3170; fax 687 2317). Open M-Th 8:30am-5pm, F 8:30am-1pm. **Pakistan,** Shantipath (☎611 0601; fax 687 2339). Open M-Tu and Th-F 8:30am-5pm. **South Africa,** B-18 Vasant Marg, Vasant Vihar (☎614 9420; fax 611 3605). Open M-F 8:30am-5pm. **Thailand,** 56-N Nyaya Marg (☎611 8103; fax 687 2029). **UK,** Shantipath (☎687 2161; fax 687 2882). Open M-F 9am-1pm and 2-5pm. **US,** Shantipath (☎419 8000 or 419 0017). Open M-F 8:30am-1pm and 2-5:30pm.

Immigration Office: Getting a visa extension is not easy, and the process brings many travelers back to Delhi again and again. For an extension (15 days max.) on a simple **tourist visa,** first head to the **Ministry of Home Affairs Foreigners Division** (☎469 3334 or 461 2543), in Lok Nayak Bhawan, behind Khan Market, off Subramaniya Bharati Marg around Lodi Estate. They're only open M-F 10am-noon, so arrive early with 4 passport photos and a letter stating your grounds for extension. If they process your application, head over to the **Foreigners Regional Registration Office** (FRRO; ☎331 9489 or 331 8179), in Hans Bhawan, near Tilak Bridge. Open M-F 9:30am-1:30pm and 2-4pm. The FRRO is also the place to get **student visas** (with a bona fide student ID issued by a recognized school/university, bank remittance certificate, and an extension application in duplicate with 4 photos and proof of stay), as well as **permits** for restricted areas of India. If you need an **exit visa,** the FRRO can process it in 20min.

Currency Exchange: American Express, A-block, Connaught Pl. (☎371 2513 or 332 4119), is probably the best place to buy (for rupees and encashment certificates) and change AmEx traveler's checks. They also cash other brands at 1% commission. There's a counter for lost and stolen cards, though the main office for 24hr. check replacement is at Bhasant Lok (☎614 2020). The A-block office issues and receives AmEx moneygrams and offers usual cardmembers' services (see p. 14). Open M-F 9:30am-6:30pm, Sa 9:30am-2:30pm. After hours, head to a legitimate money changer, such as **S.P. Securities PVT Ltd.,** M-96, Middle Circle, Connaught Pl. (☎335 7073 or 335 7070). Open M-Sa 9:30am-8pm, Su 11:30am-2pm. **Hotel Grand Regency** (☎354 0101), Main Bazaar, 300m from the New Delhi Railway Station, changes all major currencies and traveler's checks. Open 24hr. **Bank of Baroda,** Sansad Marg (☎322 1746), in the big building beyond the Outer Circle, gives cash advances on Visa and MC and cashes traveler's checks. Open M-F 9:45am-3:45pm, Sa 10am-noon. **Citibank,** in the mirror-windowed, modern high-rise before the Bank of Baroda, has a **24hr. ATM** (Cirrus compatible). **Standard Chartered Bank,** opposite the Bank of Baroda, also has a 24hr., Cirrus-compatible ATM. The **State Bank of India** branch at Chandni Chowk (☎296 0393), 200m from the east end, changes traveler's checks. Open M-F 10am-3:30pm, Sa 10am-12:30pm. The main branch, on Sansad Marg, near Connaught Pl., changes currency and traveler's checks. Open M-F 10am-4pm, Sa 10am-1pm. There is also a 24hr. branch in the international terminal of the airport. In truly desperate situations, some use the **illegal money changers** along Main Bazaar in Paharganj. Don't let them go off with your money promising to return with rupees, even if they leave a "friend" with you while you wait. **Western Union and Money Transfer,** in Sita World Travel office, F-12 Connaught Pl. (☎331 1122), charges a 5% commission to transfer money from abroad. Open M-F 9:30am-7pm, Sa 9:30am-5pm, and Su 9:30am-2pm.

LOCAL SERVICES

Luggage Storage: Many hotels store luggage at a nominal charge but only for guests. The railway stations also have luggage storage for anyone holding a valid train ticket; just be sure to lock your bags.

Bookstore: There are several well-stocked bookstores on the Inner Circle of Connaught Pl., including **Bookworm** (☎332 2260; open M-Sa 10am-7:30pm), **New Book Depot** (☎332 0020; open May-Sept. M-Sa 10:30am-7:30pm; Oct.-Apr., M-Sa 10am-7pm), and **E.D. Galgotia and Sons** (☎371 3227; open Apr.-Sept. M-Sa 10:30am-7:30pm; and Oct.-Mar. M-Sa 10am-7pm), all on B-block.

Library: The large **American Center Library,** 24 Kasturba Gandhi Marg (☎331 4251; fax 332 9499), has CD-ROM and Internet databases. Their collection includes the embassy's library. Open M-Tu and Th-Sa 10am-6pm. Admission Rs10 per day. The **British Council Library,** 17 Kasturba Gandhi Marg (☎371 1401), on the opposite side of the street. Open Tu-Sa 10am-6pm. The **Ramakrishna Mission,** at the west end of Paharganj Main Bazaar, has a library with current periodicals and newspapers; most are in Hindi, but the library's foreign magazines include Time, National Geographic, and Mad Magazine. Open Tu-Su 8-11am and 4-8pm. Entrance is free.

Bi-Lesbian-Gay Organizations: Humrahi and **Sangini,** Andrews Gunj (☎685 1970; sangini@hotmail.com). Counseling services and regular support group meetings.

Cultural Centers: The American Center and British Council (see above) have regular lectures and film screenings. **Max Mueller Bhavan,** 3 Kasturba Gandhi Marg (☎332 9506), has a library and shows films in Siddhartha Hall. Indian cultural centers include **Indian Council for Cultural Relations,** Azad Bhavan, 1P Estate (☎331 2463); **India International Centre,** 40 Lodi Estate (☎461 9431); **Indira Gandhi National Centre for the Arts,** CV Mess, Janpath (☎338 9216); and **Sangeet Natak Akademi,** Rabindra Bhavan (☎338 7246), which has information on classical music concerts.

EMERGENCY AND COMMUNICATIONS

Police: General ☎777 7229/30. Branches are all over Delhi—look for red and blue Delhi Traffic and Tourist Police kiosks with their rather ominous slogan—"Police is always with you and at your door"—at major intersections. Stations at Chandni Chowk, next to Bahrandi Mandir, and in Paharganj, just across from the railway station.

Pharmacy: The multi-story **Super Bazaar** (☎341 4176), outside the M-block of Connaught Pl., has a 24hr. pharmacy. Several pharmacies along Paharganj Main Bazaar sell tampons and toilet paper.

Hospital/Medical Services: Dr. Sharwan Kumar Gupta's **Care Clinic and Laboratory,** 1468 Sangatrashan (☎361 7841; home ☎623 3088; emergency pager ☎9632 113979). From the Paharganj Main Bazaar, take a right onto Sangatrashan before the Hotel Viveh; the clinic is 200m down on the left. English-speaking staff is used to dealing with foreign insurance companies. Recommended by IAMAT. Open M-Sa 9am-8pm, Su 9am-1pm. The **East-West Medical Clinic,** 38 Golf Links Rd., Lodi area (☎629 3701-

3), is recommended by many foreign embassies. Expensive by local standards, the clean and efficient clinic runs a 24hr. emergency room with a fully-stocked, 24hr. pharmacy. Other hospitals include **Apollo,** Mathura Rd. (☎692 5868; open 24hr.), and the **All-India Institute for Medical Services** (AIIMS; ☎686 4851).

Telephones: Most STD/ISD booths in Paharganj allow callbacks at Rs3 per min. Several hotels will permit free callbacks for guests. **Eastern Court,** on Janpath, south of the Government of India Tourist Office, has 24hr. STD/ISD, local calls, fax, and postal service.

Internet: In Paharganj, Internet service shops are everywhere and are generally much cheaper than in Connaught Pl. **Hotel Gold Regency,** Main Bazaar (☎354 0101), has an Internet cafe with full restaurant service. You might have to wait a while for a computer. Rs2 per hr. Open 24hr. **Cyber Hut,** Main Bazaar, 100m after Traveller Guest House, on the right. Rs20 per hr. Open daily 9am-9pm.

Post Office: There are branches in every part of Delhi. **New Delhi GPO** (☎336 4111), on Ashoka Rd. and Baba Kharak Singh Marg. Bring a passport to claim mail. Open M-F 10am-5pm, Sa 10am-4:30pm. To receive mail at the **Old Delhi GPO,** near the Red Fort and ISBT, use this address: GPO, Delhi, 110006. Overnight and express couriers, such as **Overnite Express** (☎336 8660; open 24hr.) and **Blue Dart** (incorporated with FedEx; ☎336 8566; open M-Sa noon-8pm) are in Kanishka Shopping Plaza on Ashok Rd., next to **Indraprastha Hotel. Belair Travel and Cargo,** 10-B Scindia House (☎331 3440), ships bulky luggage and boxes overseas. Open M-F 9:30am-6pm, Sa 9:30am-2pm. If "every second counts," head to **DHL Express,** 11 Tolstoy Marg (☎3737587). Open M-F 9:30am-8:30pm, Sa 9:30am-6pm. **Postal Code:** 110001.

ACCOMMODATIONS

Staying in Delhi can be frustratingly expensive. Prices have been driven up so much that it is hard to find anything acceptable for less than Rs100. There are three main budget hotel areas: Paharganj, Connaught Pl., and Old Delhi. **Paharganj** (Main Bazaar) is Delhi's main tourist enclave. Though it has adapted to travelers' needs, it still retains its legendary squalor and seediness and can be dangerous, especially for women traveling alone. Stories about passport scams, drugged drinks, rapes, and murders in Paharganj are plentiful. While some of these stories are true, Paharganj has also become the quintessential New Delhi urban legend. It is packed with STD/ISD booths, Kashmiri "travel agents" with the gift of gab, hash dealers, money changers, and people who cheat tourists for a living—be on your guard. If you've just arrived in India or are simply not into grime, head to **Connaught Pl.** for its own collection of nicer, though more expensive, guest houses and hotels. On the other hand, if you really want to put your nose in it, there's always **Old Delhi,** the purist's retreat (no banana pancakes here).

PAHARGANJ

Paharganj is one long, messy line of cheap hotels and restaurants. The heart of Paharganj is in the western half of **Main Bazaar** (head here if you crave the constant company of other travelers). Unless otherwise noted, check-out is at noon. Most of the better places have rooftop restaurants and generators to keep their guests alive during Delhi's all-too-frequent power outages. All of the following directions (right, left) are given as you walk west on Main Bazaar.

■ **Camran Lodge,** Main Bazaar (☎352 6053), on the right. Built into an old mosque, this creeping, crawling, crooked, low-roofed little knot of rooms has more character than you'd expect from a budget hotel. Not as sterile or modern as other places, this is a good place to dream a few Orientalist dreams before being knocked on the head by real-life Delhi in the morning. Singles with common bath Rs80; doubles Rs160-180.

■ **Hotel Rak International,** Chowk Booli (☎355 0478), down an alley to the right off Main Bazaar. Peaceful, more upscale place with fantastic views from the roof. Rooms are newly-painted, clean, and welcoming. Most have TVs. Singles with bath Rs250-500; doubles Rs350-600.

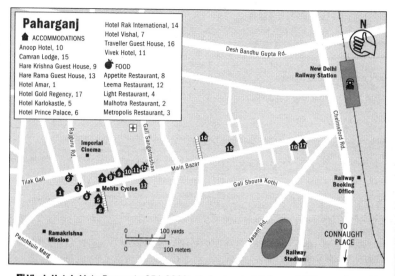

Paharganj

🏠 ACCOMMODATIONS
Anoop Hotel, 10
Camran Lodge, 15
Hare Krishna Guest House, 9
Hare Rama Guest House, 13
Hotel Amar, 1
Hotel Gold Regency, 17
Hotel Karlokastle, 5
Hotel Prince Palace, 6
Hotel Rak International, 14
Hotel Vishal, 7
Traveller Guest House, 16
Vivek Hotel, 11

🍴 FOOD
Appetite Restaurant, 8
Leema Restaurant, 12
Light Restaurant, 4
Malhotra Restaurant, 2
Metropolis Restaurant, 3

Vivek Hotel, Main Bazaar (☎ 351 2900), in the heart of Paharganj. This massive, white backpacker haven is spread over several floors—try to get a room overlooking the street. Singles with attached bath Rs200-550; doubles Rs250-600.

Hotel Prince Palace, Main Bazaar (☎ 351 8873/4), next to Hotel Karlokastle. This calm, tidy hotel has rooms with wooden furniture and lots of shelf space for all those books you've been carting around. Rooms have attached bath and color TV; some even have fridges and balconies. Singles Rs300-550; doubles Rs350-650.

Hotel Karlokastle, Main Bazaar (☎ 351 7673), down an alley opposite Hotel Vishal. Relaxed and clean with marble-lined hallways. Spacious rooms come with attached bath and TV. The rooftop restaurant looks out over the city and all the twinkling lights below. Singles Rs250; doubles Rs300.

Traveller Guest House, Main Bazaar (☎ 354 4849), to the left, not far from the railway station. Rooms are small but worth it for the TV and air-cooling. Doubles Rs240-330.

Anoop Hotel, Main Bazaar (☎ 352 1451). Popular, multi-storied backpackers' hotel with an expansive rooftop restaurant. Spacious, well-kept rooms cooled by powerful fans. Check-out 24hr. Singles Rs150-375; doubles Rs180-425.

Hotel Gold Regency, Main Bazaar (☎ 354 0101; email sushil@goldregency.com), 300m from the railway station, on the left. Not at all a budget hotel, the Gold Regency is an oasis of well-appointed rooms—all come with fridge, color TV, and a spic-and-span bathroom. Reserve at least a week ahead. 10% discount for *Let's Go* readers. Singles with breakfast Rs600-1300; doubles 700-1550.

Hare Rama Guest House, Main Bazaar (☎ 351 413). The entrance is 10m back; look for the sign for the Ajay Guest House on the left. Normally packed, often rowdy, sometimes clean. If you've been feeling the need for a somewhat seedy hotel complete with an "Art Shop" containing black-lights and psychedelic nude paintings, this is your spot. Check-out 24hr. Singles with bath Rs160-350; doubles Rs200-430.

Hotel Vishal, Main Bazaar (☎ 352 6314), west end, after the Hare Krishna Guest House. More mellow than other popular backpacker hang-outs. The bathrooms are cleaner than the bedrooms. Great rooftop for relaxation. Singles with attached bath Rs150; doubles Rs200-250.

Hotel Amar, Main Bazaar (☎ 352 4642), on the west end, past the Metropolis Hotel. Dimly lit rooms, most with TV, air-cooling, and telephone. Singles with bath Rs150-500; doubles Rs250-600.

Hare Krishna Guest House, Main Bazaar (☎ 753 3017). Quieter hotel with slightly shabby rooms. Check-out 24hr. Singles Rs180-200; doubles Rs180-230.

CONNAUGHT PLACE

The hotels in and around Connaught Pl. tend to be cleaner and quieter than those in Paharganj—they also tend to cost a lot more. The area is less chaotic, though some travelers might find it altogether *too* quiet, especially at night.

■ **H.K. Choudhary Guesthouse,** H-35/3, Middle Circle (☎332 2043). Excellent service geared toward business travelers. Rooms are exceptionally clean and nicely decorated. Follow the tree growing through the building to the rooftop terrace. Singles Rs400-500; doubles Rs550-750.

Hotel Palace Heights, Radial Rd. 6, D-block (☎332 1419), on the top floor. High above the grime and the push of the streets, this hotel's rooms are a bit drab but have plenty of furniture in case you're in the mood to sit in and write postcards. The relaxing terrace makes a welcome break from the claustrophobic stuffiness of other cheap hotels. Singles Rs300; doubles Rs375-800.

Ringo Guest House, Scindia House (☎331 0605), off Janpath, outside Outer Circle. A little hideaway above the waves of cars and people. Staggeringly popular backpackers' retreat is overcrowded and overpriced but has a pleasant garden area and a relaxed, safe, and happy atmosphere. Dorm beds Rs90; singles Rs150; doubles Rs250-400.

Sunny Guest House, Scindia House (☎331 2909), past Ringo Guest House. Standard backpacker grotto. The dorm room is just a smelly shack on the roof but is nonetheless more spacious than the one at Ringo Guest House. Dorm beds Rs90; singles Rs125-170; doubles Rs250-400.

Janpath Guest House, 82-84 Janpath (☎332 1935), near the Government of India Tourist Office. Overpriced place with the usual carpet-and-cable luxuries. Internet cafe Rs50 per hr. Singles from Rs425; doubles from Rs495.

Connaught Place

🏠 ACCOMMODATIONS
H.K. Choudhary Guesthouse, 36
Hotel Palace Heights, 6
Janpath Guest House, 20
Ringo Guest House, 19
Sunny Guest House 16

🍎 FOOD
Embassy, 5
Gaylord, 26
Kovil, 8
Mahavir Sweets, 3
Nirula's, 18
Nizam's, 2
Parikrama, 14
Rodeo, 28
Sona Rupa, 21
United Coffee House, 9
Volga, 32
Wenger & Co., 30
Zen, 33

○ SITES & SERVICES
American Express, 29
American Library & Center, 15
Belair Travel, 17
Bookworm, 34
British Council Library, 22
Central Cottage
    Industries Emporium, 24
DHL Express, 23
DLF Centre, 25
Hindustan Times, 13
Indian Airlines, 12
Jet Airways, 11
Lady Hardinge Medical College, 35
New Book Depot, 31
Odeon Conema, 4
Plaza Cinema, 1
Regal Cinema, 27
S.P. Securities, 7
Sita World Travel, 10

OLD DELHI AND TOURIST CAMP

Kiss the banana pancakes goodbye. This is the chicken-squawking, dung-covered real thing. For better and for worse, Old Delhi doesn't aspire to impress foreign tourists. While prices are cheaper and people are less likely to try to cheat you, it can be hard to find anyone who speaks English. In addition, stereotypes about foreigners—Western women in particular—are stronger here than elsewhere in the city. Many men will assume that solo female travelers are willing to give sexual favors; women should avoid dressing provocatively or going out alone after dark. Nearby, Delhi's **Tourist Camp** offers a much-better-than-it-sounds outdoors experience unlike anything in the rest of the city.

■ **Hotel New City Palace** (☎327 9540 or 325 5820), west of the Jama Masjid. Awe-inspiring views of the mosque, complete with loud prayers. Clean rooms have comfortable beds, wooden furnishings, and balconies with rooftop access. Shops below cater to late-night mechanics. Check-out 24hr. Singles with bath Rs200; doubles Rs250-650.

Hotel Shan (☎325 3027 or 326 9615), west of the Jama Masjid. The pink walls of this homey hotel are decorated with posters of New York City, totally out-of-sync with

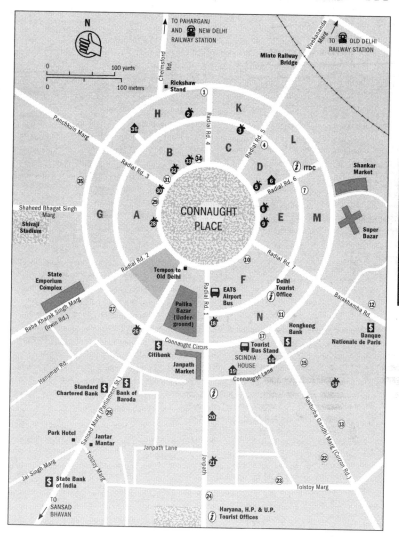

the excellent views of the Jama Masjid from the window. Check-out 24hr. Doubles Rs150-200.

Tourist Camping Park, Qudsia Garden (☎ 397 3121), across the street and to the right of the ISBT at Kashmere Gate. Great for crashing after a long bus journey. Rooms are dark and dank, and the common bathrooms do not inspire confidence, but where else does your jungle retreat come complete with its own highway? Pitch your own tent for Rs80 plus Rs10 per person. Singles Rs80-140; doubles Rs110-170.

Khush-Dil Hotel, Chandni Chowk (☎ 395 2110), at the west end, just south of the mosque on Fatehpuri Corner. Narrow beds and dank bathrooms, but enthusiastic staff and excellent views of the busy street. Check-out 24hr. Singles with common bath Rs90; doubles Rs150-200.

FOOD

It's worth shelling out a little cash for some of Delhi's fantastic meals. There are restaurants in every price range: respectable Western-style fast-food, decent Chinese and Middle Eastern cuisine, a couple of Mexican restaurants, and, of course, excellent Indian food. For a real splurge (up to Rs300-400 per entree), head to one of the 5-star hotels, such as the Maurya Sheraton or the Ashok Frontier.

PAHARGANJ

This backpackers' district has developed several hot spots for hanging out—and most of them are about five stories up. None of these places serves particularly good food (breakfasts are tolerable), but the rooftops are the place to find Paharganj's backpack-rats sipping tea and slurping curd after hours. It's best to get off the Main Bazaar for food—most of the main strip's restaurants cater to the jaded palates and fragile digestive systems of penny-pinching backpackers. Wander the streets north of Paharganj to see where the locals are eating.

Malhotra Restaurant, 1833 Chuna Mandi. Walk west along the Main Bazaar, turn right on Rajguru Rd. at the Metropolis, then take the first left. An intimate place, tucked below street level, often packed with locals. Quick, efficient service and good Indian and Chinese food. Open daily 8am-11pm.

Metropolis Restaurant, Main Bazaar, in the Metropolis Hotel. Subdued setting—both inside and on the rooftop. Large selection of Chinese, Indian, and continental dishes. "Le Poulet Sizzling" Rs175; bean sprouts and bean curd Rs60. Open daily 8am-11pm.

Leema Restaurant, Main Bazaar, in Hotel Vivek. Probably the best budget-hotel restaurant in Paharganj. A/C, fresh juices, and excellent veg. sandwiches (Rs12), though the service can be painfully slow. Open daily 7am-midnight.

Light Restaurant, Main Bazaar, at the west end. Good, authentic food at wallet-friendly prices. All-veg. *thalis* are only Rs20. Rice pudding Rs8. Open daily 9am-10:30pm.

Appetite Restaurant, Main Bazaar, on the right after the Hare Krishna Guest House. With the occasional Pink Floyd LP playing in the background, this is a good place to sit and write some postcards while munching on banana cake (Rs25). Open daily 7am-11pm.

CONNAUGHT PLACE

Catering to the elite, restaurants in Connaught Pl. serve Indian and international cuisine several times better than the muck served down the road in backpackers' paradise. Dishes are priced accordingly.

Gaylord, Outer Circle, next to the Regal Cinema. Large, spacious, chandeliered dining room. Top-notch food and excellent service. Your meal here is likely to be the most expensive you will have in India (Rs100-350 for a main course). It might also be the best. Open daily 10:30am-11pm.

Nirula's, L-block (☎332 2419). Huge multi-restaurant the size of a multi-story car park. Head to the ice cream bar for smooth mango scoops and shakes, or try Indian flavors like Zafrani Badaam Pista, 21 Love, and Delhi Delight (Rs24 per scoop). Hit the Potpourri upstairs (open daily 7:30am-midnight) for veggie burgers (Rs121), an all-you-can-eat salad bar (Rs143), and pizzas (from Rs110). Try the superb tofu noodles (Rs94) in the Orient Express-like Chinese Room (open daily 12:30-11pm), or sip drinks in one of 2 bars—the popular, pricey, **Pegasus Bar** is open 11am-midnight. Ice cream and fast-food branch near Wimpy on N-block. Pastry shop open 8am-8pm.

Rodeo, A-block, near the AmEx office. Hitch up your pony to a post on the right, hand over your pistol at the swinging doors, and sidle up to a saddle stool at the bar, where you might struggle not to giggle as waiters in Stetsons and spurs play Doc Holliday with sombreros and wide-buckle belts. Mexican food, beer, and cocktails. Nachos Rs75-125; entrees Rs175-210; "mango cowboy dessert" Rs80. Open daily noon-midnight.

Embassy Restaurant, D-block (☎332 0480). Palace-like dining hall with tasteful decor and prompt service. Good Indian food at oh-well-what-the-hell prices. Brain curry Rs106; cream of asparagus soup Rs52. Open daily 10am-11pm.

Zen Restaurant, B-block. If you took out the tables and chairs, the Zen would make a classy disco. Chinese food, a Japanese name, and American muzak—all in the middle of Delhi. Mysterious sculptures dangle from red, upholstered walls. Bring a sweater. Veg. dishes Rs80-110; non-veg. Rs115-200. Beer Rs100. Open daily 11am-10:30pm.

Sona Rupa Restaurant, Janpath, past the Government of India Tourist Office. Indian-style fast-food restaurant in marble, with piped-in Hindi muzak. Delicious veg. South Indian food (Rs40-70) and a wide range of ice cream. Buffet (Rs95) noon-4pm and 7-10pm. Open daily 11:30am-10:30pm.

Nizam's, H-block, behind Plaza Cinema. Slow service but worth the wait. The tastiest *biryani* (Rs75-80) and kebab egg-rolls (Rs45-80) in the city. Also serves delicious veg. rolls (Rs40-60). Mostly an eat-and-run place—standing room only. Open daily noon-11pm.

Wenger & Co. Pastry Shop, A-block, Inner Circle, next to the AmEx office. Take-out bakery and patisserie. Doughnuts, strudels, cakes, and tarts galore. Open daily 10am-8pm.

Parikrama, 22 Kasturba Gandhi Marg. Delhi's revolving 24th floor restaurant takes 1½hr. to go round once, and they won't let you finish in less. Good continental, Chinese, and Indian food, but with the amazing views from the window, you probably won't really care what you're eating. Open daily 12:30pm-midnight.

United Coffee House, E-block. High ceilings, ornately carved walls, and an incongruous background soundtrack of 1980s Euro-pop. A firm favorite of the chattering elite. Veg., non-veg. dishes Rs65-180. Open daily 9am-midnight. Last orders at 11:30pm.

Kovil, near United Coffee House. Popular place serving excellent South Indian veg. meals. *Thalis* Rs120. Open daily 11am-10:45pm.

Mahavir Sweets, C-block, Middle Circle. Renowned for its sugary desserts, Mahavir also serves tasty and cheap Indian dishes. *Masala dosa* Rs20; *thalis* from Rs22; sweet *ras malai* Rs15. Open M-Sa 8am-8pm.

Volga, B-block, Inner Circle. More like a fraternity sitting lounge than an eating establishment, this definitely-not-Russian restaurant rolls out the red carpet for crowds of beer-drinking men who come to smoke and shout into the cold air. Good Indian dishes Rs90-150. Open daily 1-4pm and 6:30-11pm.

OLD DELHI

Old Delhi offers every class of edible fare—from spices to squawking chickens—and a number of renowned restaurants.

Karim, in a small courtyard off Matya Mahal, about 8 shops down from the Jama Masjid (not visible from the road). One of the city's most popular and famous restaurants, Karim has been run by descendants of the cooks of Mughal royalty since 1913. Menu full of rich, meat-heavy dishes. Half dishes (at half-price) fit the bill for the budget traveler. Full chicken *biryani* Rs100; full *aloo palak* Rs45. Open daily 7am-midnight.

Moti Mahal Restaurant, Netaji Subhash Marg. Delicious tandoori cuisine served in outdoor patio and chandeliered dining rooms. Kebabs from Rs105; veg. curries Rs75. Live music every night 8pm-midnight, except Tu. Open daily 11am-midnight.

Rinkey Restaurant, Bara Bazaar. From the Kashmere Gate ISBT, turn left on Lothian Rd. and then right on Bara Bazaar. One of the few proper, sit-down restaurants within easy walking distance of the bus station. Large selection of Chinese and North and South Indian dishes. Fresh veg. pizza Rs35; onion *uttapam* Rs25. Open daily 9:30am-9:30pm.

NEW DELHI

The Yellow Brick Road, Ambassador Hotel, Sujan Singh Park, 1km south of India Gate. Old posters advertising Waterman's Pens and Potages Maggi adorn the yellow walls. The pastel chairs, tables, and floor tiles make the Yellow Brick Road feel ready for a Caribbean garden party. Listen to 80s and 90s pop music as you choose from the tabloid menu. Excellent dishes range from the mouth-tingling Bangkok vegetable curry (Rs160) to extra virgin pasta (Rs175) and sesame dumplings (Rs105). Open 24hr.

🔲 SIGHTS

Like any capital city, Delhi has a vast number of things to see. There are a whopping 1376 monuments, two of which are UNESCO World Heritage sites (Qutb Minar and Humayun's Tomb). If you're spending only a couple of days in Delhi, budget your time wisely. The must-sees are the Qutb Minar Complex and the sights of Old Delhi—Lal Qila (Red Fort), the Jama Masjid (Friday Mosque), and the bazaars. Round out your time by having a look at Rashtrapati Bhavan and Humayun's Tomb. If you need respite from the midday heat, head to the National Museum. You'll have most of these places to yourself in the early morning. As always, men (and occasionally women) will linger by the entrance to the various tourist attractions, flashing ID cards (often bogus) and offering their services as guides. While they often don't have their facts straight, some are quite knowledgeable. If you do hire a guide, be sure to negotiate a price in advance.

Several agencies offer **guided tours** of Delhi (about Rs230). These usually start in New Delhi, stopping at Jantar Mantar, the Lakshmi Narayan Temple, Humayun's Tomb, the Baha'i Temple, driving by the more notable landmarks (such as India Gate), swinging south of the city to Qutb Minar before heading north to the Red Fort and the sights of Old Delhi. Tours of Old Delhi might include the Red Fort, Raj Ghat, Shanti Vana, and a glimpse of the Jama Masjid (about Rs125). These tours are rushed, the guides are not always informed, and a full day of bus riding, even in A/C comfort, is never fun, but these tours are helpful if you've only got a short time in Delhi. Another option is to ditch the tourist bus and hire a guide and/or vehicle for four- to 12-hour stints. Standard taxis cost about Rs590 for 4hr. Book through ITDC, L-block, Connaught Pl. (☎ 332 0331; open daily 7am-8pm), or at Delhi Tourism and Transportation (☎ 331 4229; open daily 7am-9pm).

OLD DELHI

RED FORT (LAL QILA)

Enter through Lahore Gate, pass through Chatta Chowk into the palace area. Fort open daily 8am-dusk. Rs2; video camera Rs25. Museums open Sa-Th 10am-5pm. Rs2. English sound and light shows Nov.-Jan. 7:30-8:30pm; Feb.-Apr. 8:30-9:30pm; May-Aug. 9-10pm; Sept.-Oct. 8:30-9:30pm. Rs30, under 12 Rs10: To reserve tickets for the show, call ☎ 327 4580.

Shortly after moving the capital from Agra to Delhi in 1639, Mughal emperor Shah Jahan began construction of the Red Fort. Work started on April 16 and was completed nine years later to the day, at a cost of more than 10 million rupees. Soaring to a height of 33.5m, the fort's red sandstone ramparts ring a 2km perimeter and are themselves surrounded by a moat into which the Yamuna once flowed. Some of the fort's more resplendent features are now gone—the famed Peacock Throne was snatched away in 1739, the gems that adorned the palaces were removed long ago, and the canals where the Stream of Paradise once gurgled have now run dry. But the Red Fort remains what it has always been—an incredible monument to Mughal power and an architectural marvel.

LAHORE GATE AND NAUBAT KHANA. The entrance to the fort is toward the middle of its west wall, at the three-story Lahore Gate, through which the Mughal emperors would leave for the Jama Masjid. Next to the gate is the spot from which the Prime Minister addresses cheering throngs every year on Independence Day (Aug. 15). Lahore Gate leads to **Chatta Chowk,** the covered passageway filled with shops that today peddle souvenirs, but which during the Mughal era provided nobles with top-quality silks, precious jewelry, and fine velvets. Chatta Chowk opens to the rectangular, three-storied Naubat Khana (Drum House); five times a day, music was played here in tribute to the emperor and his court. The floral carvings adorning the walls of Naubat Khana were once painted with gold.

DIWAN-I-AM. Naubat Khana leads into the palace area. Across the mini-courtyard behind the simple, sturdy columns stands the Diwan-i-Am (Hall of Public Audience), where the early Mughal emperors used to sit (everyone else stood) for two hours a day, receiving visitors, chatting with nobles, deciding criminal cases, and generally having a right royal time. The throne used to sit on top of the canopied white marble platform now on display. At the back of the platform is a series of curious panels adorned with red and green flowers, birds, trees, and lions. Presiding over the entire scene is the Greek god Orpheus. Scholars speculate that the panels, returned from the British Museum in 1903, were crafted in Florence. The low marble platform in front of the emperor's platform was reserved for the prime minister, who would, within earshot of the emperor, entertain grievances.

PRIVATE PALACES. Beyond Diwan-i-Am were the private palaces of the Mughal emperor. Of the original six palaces, five remain; each was connected to its neighbor by a canal called **Nahir-i-Bihisht** (Stream of Paradise). The palaces were set in spacious formal *charbagh* gardens. The southernmost of the palaces (the one farthest to the right when coming from Diwan-i-Am), the **Mumtaz Mahal** (Palace of Jewels) originally housed the harem. These days, it houses a museum (see below). North of Mumtaz Mahal is the **Rang Mahal** (Palace of Colors), a white marble pavilion where the emperor ate his meals. During the Mughal heyday, the ceilings were decorated with silver; other parts of the ceiling are embedded with tiny mirrors that reflected the light from the emperor's candle-lit banquet tables. Just north of the Rang Mahal, the **Khas Mahal** (Private Palace) is a sumptuous display of wealth; each of the apartments was decorated in silk during back in the day. The southernmost of these is the **Baithak** (Sitting Room), with a scale of justice carved in marble upon the walls. The emperor used to sleep in the center apartment, sensibly known as the **Khwabagh** (Sleeping Chamber). Attached to the outer wall of the Khwabagh is a tower called the **Muthamman Burj** (Octagonal Tower), where the emperor would greet his subjects or watch animal fights staged below. King George V and Queen Mary sat here before thousands in 1911, when the announcement was made amidst much rejoicing that the imperial capital would be moved to Delhi from Calcutta. North of the Khwabagh is the **Tasbih Khana** (Chamber for Telling Beads), where the emperor would say his prayers.

DIWAN-I-KHAS AND MOTI MASJID. Just north of Khas-Mahal is the Diwan-i-Khas (Hall of Private Audience), constructed entirely of white marble. Here, the emperor would make crucial political decisions, consult privately with advisors, and speak with VIPs. Attempting to rekindle the old spark, Bahadur Shah II, the last Mughal emperor, held court here during the Mutiny of 1857; in retaliation, the British tried him in the Diwan-i-Am and then exiled him to Burma. To the north is the **Hammam** (Bath), whose westernmost apartment contained a rosewater fountain. West of the Hammam is the delicate Moti Masjid (Pearl Mosque), built in 1662 by Emperor Aurangzeb for his personal use. The black marble outlines on the floor were designed to help with the proper placement of *musallas* (prayer mats).

OLD DELHI BIZARRE The Jama Masjid is a good place to begin an exploration of the busy maze of shops and street vendors that make up the bazaars of Old Delhi. The streets around the Jama Masjid are cluttered with overpriced kitsch, but walk 200m north, south, or west and you'll be in a part of town rarely visited by tourists. Area vendors peddle wholesale paper, high-quality tools, used car parts, and all sorts of other goodies. To check out one of the smelliest places anywhere in the world, head south from the Jama Masjid toward the poultry markets, where chickens trussed together in cramped cages are selected by customers, then butchered on the spot, much to the delight of swarms of flies. Don't be shy about bargaining. Ducking into any of the narrow alleys between the shops on the south side of Chandni Chowk leads to another bazaar dream world; follow the labyrinthine "street" any which way and stumble upon an aromatic spice market or snag a deal on gems.

DELHI

MUSEUMS. There are three **museums** inside the Red Fort complex. Mumtaz Mahal's is the best of the three, displaying astrolabes, *hookahs*, and weapons. The museum in the Naubat Khana concentrates on military history and charts the various ways that men have killed each other over the past 200 years. The Sangrahalaya Museum traces the development of the Indian independence movement. *(Tickets for all three museums should be bought from a booth in the Naubat Khana.)*

OTHER SIGHTS

Built between 1650 and 1656 by Emperor Shah Jahan, the Jama Masjid, 1km west of the Red Fort, is the largest active mosque in India. Set on a high platform on top of a low hill, the Jama Masjid dominates the surrounding streets with the elegant mixture of red sandstone and white marble that covers its soaring minarets. The east gate was once reserved for the emperor and his family; now it is open to all worshippers on Fridays and Muslim holidays. The huge courtyard packs in nearly 25,000 worshippers during Friday prayers.

As in most South Asian mosques, a *hauz* (tank) at the center of the courtyard is used for cleansing feet and hands before prayer, and each rectangle designates the space for one worshipper. Prayers are sung from the *imam*'s platform, under the center arch at the westernmost point of the mosque; before amplification systems, other *imams* repeated prayers from the two small posts between this point and the east gate for those at the back. Just west of the mosque is the official residence of the *imam;* the Muslim priests have lived here since the time of Shah Jahan, and you can still see them before prayers. It's worth climbing up one of the minarets that rise from the courtyard for the superb views of the city from the top (Rs10). Foreigners, however, must be in groups of two or more, since the dark, claustrophobic stairwell has attracted thieves with an eye for lone tourists. Remember to dress appropriately. *(1km west of the Red Fort. Open to tourists 30min. after dawn until 12:20pm (noon on F), 1:45pm until 20min. before prayer call, and again after prayers until 20min. before sunset. Camera fee Rs20.)*

RAJ GHAT. Here, a perpetually burning flame and a simple black slab set in a grassy courtyard offer a memorial to Mahatma Gandhi, cremated at this spot after his 1948 assassination by a Hindu extremist. Gandhi's name is notably missing from the monument—the only inscription is of his last words, "Hai Ram" ("Oh God"). Hundreds of visitors come each day to cast flower petals and pray. Just south of the monument is a park full of trees and flowers planted by all kinds of dignitaries: flowers from Eisenhower, a pine from Queen Elizabeth II, and a tree planted by Nasser. *(On the west bank of the Yamuna River, 1km east of Delhi Gate and 2km southeast of the Red Fort. Open dawn-dusk. Free.)*

SHANTI VANA. North of Raj Ghat, this quiet park contains memorials to the men and women who have earned a place in India's pantheon of political heroes, including an effusive monument to slain Prime Minister Rajiv Gandhi. An adjacent memorial to his older brother Sanjay was taken down after critics reminded the government that this particular Gandhi never served in office or ever accomplished much at all. Sanjay's admirers continued to leave flowers at the barren spot, however, and eventually the monument returned. The grassy mound that marks the life and death of Jawaharlal Nehru mentions only his wish to have his ashes thrown in the Ganga. *(Open daily Apr.-Sept. 5am-7:30pm; Oct.-Mar. 5:30am-7pm.)*

SOUTH DELHI

QUTB MINAR COMPLEX

At the intersection of Aurobindo Marg and Mehrauli Badarpur Rd., 14km southwest of Connaught Pl. Open daily dawn-dusk. Rs5, free on Fridays. Video camera Rs25.

Even in a part of Delhi speckled with crumbling mosques and decaying ramparts, the ruins of the **Qutb Minar** complex are without peer. Construction on the complex began in 1199 after the Turkish ex-slave Qutb-ud-din Aibak swept into North India and knocked the Rajput empire to pieces. Qutb-ud-din Aibak installed himself at Lal Kot, the site of an old Rajput city, founding what was to become India's first Islamic kingdom here in 1206, following the murder of his general, Muhammed Ghuri. The events that led to the building of the complex were epoch-making, and the Qutb Minar serves as a 72.5m-high exclamation point.

The red sandstone Qutb Minar was designed to stand as a celebration of Qutb-ud-din Aibak's triumphs in Northern India and as a milestone marking the eastern frontier of the Muslim world. As an inscription on one of the tower notes, "the tower was erected to cast the shadow of God over both East and West." Modeled on the brick victory towers of Central Asia, the Qutb Minar also served as the minaret for the Quwwat-ul-Islam Masjid (see below). Before dying, Qutb-ud-din Aibak was able to complete only the first story of the tower. His son-in-law Iltutmish added the next three stories, and Firoz Shah Tughluq tacked on a fifth after repairing damage caused by a 1368 lightning strike. The fifth-story cupola erected by Firoz was felled by an 1803 earthquake and replaced by British major Robert Smith; Smith's Mughal-style cupola now sits in the gardens, having been removed from the Qutb Minar because it was so awkward. Visitors have been forbidden from climbing the minaret since 1981, when more than 30 panicked school children were trampled to death during a power outage. Most of the calligraphy carved on the minaret displays Arabic passages from the Koran, though a few Devanagari inscriptions prove some Indian influence in its design.

QUWWAT-UL-ISLAM MASJID. Just north of the Qutb Minar is the Quwwat-ul-Islam Masjid (Might of Islam Mosque), the oldest mosque in India aside from those in western Gujarat. Begun in 1192 and completed in 1198 (extensions were added over the next two centuries), the mosque was built from the remains of 21 Hindu and Jain temples destroyed by the fanatical Qutb-ud-din Aibak. The pillars from the razed temples support the east end of the mosque and are carved with bells, lotuses, and other Hindu and Jain icons. At the center of the courtyard is the 98% pure iron **Gupta Pillar.** According to the Sanskrit inscription, the pillar was erected in honor of Vishnu and in memory of Chandra, believed to be the Gupta emperor Chandragupta II (r. 375-415 AD). Tradition holds that Anangpal, the founder of Lal Kot, brought the pillar to the area. It is said that those who can stand with their backs against the pillar and wrap their arms around it is blessed by the gods with superhuman strength.

ALA'I DARWAZA. Just south of Qutb Minar is the domed, red sandstone Ala'i Darwaza, built in 1311 to serve as the southern entrance to the mosque. Immediately east of Ala'i Darwaza, a domed tomb with *jali* (decorative screens) holds the body of Imam Zamin, a Sufi saint who came from Central Asia in the early 16th century.

ALA'I MINAR. North of the Quwwat-ul-Islam Masjid is a massive, unfinished minaret, **Ala'i Minar,** a monument to grandiose ambitions and plans gone awry. Expansion had doubled the size of the mosque, and Ala'i Minar was designed to be twice as tall as Qutb Minar. After its first 24.5m-high story was completed around 1300, construction was stopped and the madly ambitious project was abandoned. Just south of the Ala'i Minar is the **Tomb of Iltutmish,** which the sultan himself erected in 1235, four years after building his son's tomb, 8km from Qutb Minar. Iltutmish's red sandstone tomb isn't particularly interesting from the outside, but the artfully decorated interior is well worth a look, with its mingling of Hindu and Jain themes (wheels, lotuses, and bells) and Muslim motifs (calligraphic inscriptions, geometric patterns, and alcoves facing Mecca built into the west wall). Directly south of Iltutmish's tomb are the ruins of a *madrasa*, an institution of Islamic learning. In keeping with Seljuk Turkish traditions, the tomb of the *madrasa*'s founder, Ala-ud-din Khalji, has been placed within.

OTHER SIGHTS

High up on top of a lonely, rocky outcropping is **Tughluqabad,** built as a fortified city by Ghiyas-ud-din Tughluq, who ruled the Delhi Sultanate between 1321 and 1325. These days, the abandoned fort has been conquered by weeds, monkeys, and a general air of desolation. Massive walls run along the 6.5km circumference of the fort. Thirteen separate gates lead through the walls, which are topped with stone battlements. The red sandstone and white marble **Tomb of Ghiyas-ud-din Tughluq** employs the first set of sloping walls to grace a Muslim building in India. Shortly after Ghiyas-ud-din Tughluq was murdered, Tughluqabad was abandoned, having been occupied for only five years. *(Mehrauli Badrapur Rd., 9km east of the Qutb Minar Complex and 16km southeast of Connaught Pl.)*

BAHA'I TEMPLE. Over the past three decades, members of the Baha'i faith have donated millions of dollars toward the construction of seven Baha'i Temples in locations as varied as Uganda, Samoa, and the midwestern United States. The latest addition to this series was finished in 1986 and is situated in South Delhi on a 26-acre expanse of cropped grass and elegant pools. The temple, which inevitably draws comparisons to the Sydney Opera House, is built from white marble in the shape of an opening lotus flower. Silence is requested of visitors, so there's little to do but settle comfortably onto one of the wood-backed benches, listen to the dull thudding of bare feet, and gaze up at the clean lines of the temple's splendid dome. *(4km north of Tughluqabad. Open Tu-Su Apr.-Sept. 9am-7pm; Oct.-Mar. 9:30am-5:30pm. Free.)*

CENTRAL NEW DELHI

SANSAD AND RASHTRAPATI BHAVAN. Of the scores of buildings built by the British when they moved their capital from Calcutta to Delhi in 1911, the Rashtrapati Bhavan (President's Residence) and the Sansad Bhavan (Parliament House) are the most impressive. Designed by the renowned architect Edwin Lutyens, the buildings possess a massive grandeur—a not-so-subtle display of the vast reserves of British power—intended to communicate the determination that India continue to be the jewel in the imperial crown. The effort backfired—the aesthetic anomaly of European-style buildings in the heart of an Indian city only helped to anger Indian nationalists, and the buildings became a lightning rod for criticism. In one memorable outburst, Gandhi described them as "architectural piles."

Sansad Bhavan, at the end of Sansad Marg, 1½km southwest of Connaught Pl., is a massive circular building that resembles a flying saucer. Because India's parliament, the Lok Sabha, meets here (see **Government and Politics,** p. 61), it is often difficult to get close to the building. *(To get inside, you will have to obtain a letter from your embassy.)* To reach **Rashtrapati Bhavan,** head down to Rajpath and walk between the Secretariats to the entrance; or walk due west from India Gate down Rajpath. Once the residence of the viceroy, the pink Rashtrapati Bhavan is now the home of India's president. *(To visit Rashtrapati Bhavan, you'll need to apply at the reception office at least two days in advance. Tours are offered only on M, W, and F. Don't forget to bring your passport.)* You can get a good view from Raisina Hill, the area between the Secretariat buildings. The 45m-high pillar between the gate and the residence was donated by the Maharaja of Jaipur and is known as the **Jaipur Column.** The pillar is capped with a bronze lotus and a six-pointed Star of India.

SECRETARIATS. Flanking Raisina Hill on its northern and southern sides are the symmetrical Secretariats, which now house government ministries. The buildings are adorned with a variety of slogans praising enlightened imperial rule. For some shade (and fresh air), pass under the slogans and into the **Great Hall,** a dark and airy room adorned with medallions and crowned by a baroque dome. Try to visit **Raisina Hill** on a Saturday, when troops march in front of Rashtrapati Bhavan. *(Ceremonial changing of the guard 8:30-9:15am in summer; 10:35-11am in winter.)* As you look east from the Secretariats, the arch in the distance is **India Gate,** a memorial to Indian soldiers killed in WWI and the Afghan War of 1919. A memorial beneath the arch commemorates those who were killed in the 1971 Indo-Pakistani War.

HUMAYUN'S TOMB. A poem in red sandstone and black-and-white marble, Humayun's Tomb is set amid geometrically designed gardens and rows of palm trees. Humayun was the second Mughal emperor, ruling from 1530 until he was vanquished by Sher Shah in 1540 and again from 1555 until his death one year later.

Walking down the stairs of his library in the Old Fort, Humayun heard the *azan* and quickly sat himself down on the nearest step; upon rising, the emperor tripped and slid down the stairs. The injuries incurred in his fall proved fatal—but it wasn't until 1565, nine years after his death, that the tomb was built according to his wife's orders. Later, many other prominent Mughals were buried at the site, including Dara Shikoh (Shah Jahan's favorite son) and Bahadur Shah II, the last of the Mughal emperors, who was captured here by the British during the Mutiny of 1857. Humayun's Tomb is at the center of a rectangular, quartered garden laced with channels and paths. A pioneering work of Mughal architecture, the octagonal tomb sits alone in a central hall, whose double dome rises to a height of nearly 40m and is home to hordes of squealing bats, birds, and bees. *(2½km southeast of India Gate. Open dawn-dusk. Rs5.)*

HAZRAT NIZAMUDDIN DARGAH. One of Sufism's greatest shrines, Hazrat Niza-muddin Dargah was originally built in 1325, the year its occupant, the great mystic Sheikh Nizamuddin Aulia, died. The present complex was most recently refur-bished in the 16th century by Shah Jahan, one of Nizamuddin's many devotees. Its marble verandas and delicate latticework are especially radiant at dawn and dusk. Nearby is the grave of the great Urdu poet, Mirza Ghalib. At twilight, people gather here to sing *qawwali*, Sufi songs of spiritual ecstasy. To reach the shrine, head down the street opposite **Kataria Nursery,** through the market, and into the court-yard. *(Southwest of Humayun's tomb, on the eastern end of Lodi Rd., 6km from Connaught Pl.)*

JANTAR MANTAR. This Mughal astronomical observatory looks like an M.C. Escher lithograph rendered as a red-and-white stone diorama, its rail-less stairs twisting around tight bends and soaring upward to the heavens. Charged by the Mughal emperor Mohammed Shah with the task of revising the Indian calendar in accordance with modern astronomical knowledge, Maharaja Jai Singh of Jaipur built Jantar Mantar in 1725 after studying European and Asian science and spend-ing years observing the skies above Delhi. The result is as scientifically impressive as it is visually striking: the massive sundials and instruments keep accurate time (in Delhi, London, and Japan), predict eclipses, and chart the movement of the stars. *(Sansad Marg, 750m southwest of Connaught Pl. Open daily sunrise-sunset. Free.)*

LODI GARDENS. Though the sign at the entrance is slightly worrying—"shooting," it announces, "is forbidden in the park"—the leafy glories of the Lodi Gardens are relaxing and beautifully maintained. A wide variety of trees and birds make their home here—spread around some crushed Magic Masala potato chips, and you're likely to attract hordes of fluorescent green, hyper-aggressive urban parrots. Along with splendid scenery, the gardens contain a jogging trail, a steamy green-house, and some stone benches. A few ruined buildings scattered throughout the garden rise from the closely cropped grass. Toward the center of the garden is the late 15th-century **Bara Gumbad,** a square tomb of red, gray, and black stones topped by a massive dome. Scholars have no idea who is buried here. Attached to the tomb is a mosque, built in 1494. The interior is embellished with dense floral patterns and Koranic inscriptions. The square tomb just north of Bara Gumbad is the early 16th-century **Shish Gumbad** (Glazed Dome), decorated with remnants of the blue tiles that once covered it. About 200m north of Shish Gumbad is the badly weathered **Sikandar Lodi's Tomb** (1517-18). For views of the park, climb along the walls that enclose the tomb; 75m east of Sikandar Lodi's Tomb is a 16th-century bridge with seven arches. Also in the Lodi Gardens, 200m southwest of Bara Gum-bad, is **Mohammed Shah's Tomb,** a high-domed octagonal building built in the mid-15th century. *(Gate 1, Lodi Rd. Gardens open dawn-dusk. Free.)*

SAFDARJANG'S TOMB. Built in 1753-54 for Safdarjang, prime minister to the Mughal emperor Mohammed Shah, the tomb is the last piece of great Mughal architecture in Delhi. The centerpiece of expansive *charbagh* gardens, the tall, domed edifice was constructed of marble and red sandstone stolen from another local tomb. *(West of the gardens, at the end of Lodi Rd. Open dawn-dusk. Rs2.)*

PURANA QILA. The Purana Qila (Old Fort) marks a spot that has been continuously inhabited since the Mauryan period (324-184 BC). The discovery of ceramic shards dating back to 1000 BC vindicated bearers of local tradition, who have long claimed that the fort was built on the site of Indraprastha, the capital city of the Pandava heroes of the *Mahabharata* (commemorated in a nightly sound and light show). There's never been much doubt about the 16th-century function of Purana Qila—the massive walls, finely preserved mosque, and ruined library that formed the centerpiece of Humayun's Delhi are still standing for all to see. Built in 1541 by Sher Shah, **Qila-i-Kuhna Masjid** (Mosque of the Old Fort) is an ornate tangle of calligraphic inscriptions and red sandstone. Less impressive (and less intact) is the **Sher Mandal,** which Humayun used as a library and observatory after seizing Purana Qila from Sher Shah. A small, free museum on the premises showcases some of the artifacts discovered in and around Purana Qila. The Shunga period (184-72 BC) plaques are particularly interesting. To get a good sense of the incredible height of the fort's ramparts, climb onto the top of the walls and admire the panoramic view of Delhi or walk the **exercise trail** below the walls. The trail winds pleasantly around a small lake (dry during the summer) where there are boats for rent. *(Off Mathura Rd., 1km east of India Gate. Mosque open daily dawn-dusk. Rs2. Sound and light show daily Nov.-Jan. 7:30pm; Feb.-Apr. and Sept.-Oct. 8:30pm; May-Aug. 9pm. Rs25.)*

Next to Purana Qila is the **National Zoological Park.** Check out the three much-raved-about white tigers. *(Open daily Apr. 15-Oct. 15 9am-4pm; Oct. 16-Mar. 9:30am-4pm.)*

BIRLA MANDIR. Built by the wealthy Birlas in honor of Lakshmi, the goddess of material well-being, the Lakshmi Narayan Temple is a marvel of Orissan-style temple architecture. The room of mirrors at the back of the temple allows you to see yourself together with infinite reflections of the Krishna statue in the middle. The gardens contain a brightly colored fountain in the shape of a pile of cobras, gaily painted stone sculptures of tigers and elephants that welcome riders, and a plaster cave which can be entered through the gaping mouth of a painted plastic lion. *(Mandir Marg, 2km west of Connaught Pl. Open daily 4:30am-9pm.)*

▥ MUSEUMS

NATIONAL MUSEUM. The museum's ambitious mission is to provide an overview of Indian life and culture from prehistoric times to the present. Ground-floor galleries showcase some of the museum's most popular items. Other displays trace the development of Indian scripts, iconography, and coins over the past 16 centuries. (To see the actual coins, head up to the second floor.) An air-conditioned, room-sized vault houses the museum's jewelry collection. Highlights include gaudy gilded earrings, necklaces, and bracelets dating from the first century AD. Another gallery on the ground floor houses beautiful South Asian paintings. Also on display is a collection of Neolithic stone tools (3000-1500 BC). On the second floor, the exhibit of weapons and armor includes a colorful, brass-reinforced Rajasthani vest, an 18th-century bejeweled rhino-hide shield of Maharana Sangram Singh II, and the grimy curved and serrated weapons of the Pahari. More peaceful pleasures can be found among the galleries of colorful masks and clothing associated with the peoples of the northeastern states. The top-notch collection of musical instruments in the Sharan Rani Gallery, donated in 1980 by renowned sarod player Sharan Rani, is remarkably comprehensive, displaying handcrafted Indian instruments including *sarangis* and sitars as well as a glass tabla. *(Janpath, just south of Rajpath. ☎ 301 9272. Open Tu-Su 10am-5pm. Foreigners entrance fee Rs150; camera fee Rs300. Guided tours begin at enquiry counter 10:30, 11:30am, noon, 2, and 3:30pm.)*

CRAFTS MUSEUM. Built in 1991, the Crafts Museum is one of the finest in South Asia, and not everything here is stuck in glass cases. The museum is divided into three sections. As you enter, you'll pass through an open-air demonstration area where artisans practice their craft, casting metal for sculptures, stringing jewelry, and weaving baskets from straw. Outdoors is a village complex, filled with life-sized reproductions of rural huts and houses brought to Delhi from their native regions. Highlights include the vibrantly painted Orissan Gadaha Hut and a spare construction associated with the Konyak people of Nagaland. Inside, displays showcase the diversity of traditional Indian crafts, including 18th-century wood carvings from Karnataka, dazzling storytellers' paintings, and a brightly decorated model of a Bihar wedding chamber. *(Pragati Bhawan, Bharion Marg, off Mathura Rd. ☎ 337 1887. Open Tu-Su 10am-5pm. Outdoor displays closed July 1-Sept. 15 due to monsoon.)*

NATIONAL GALLERY OF MODERN ART. Once the Delhi mansion of the Maharaja of Jaipur, this gallery houses a diverse collection of art produced in India over the last 150 years. The paintings range from European-style portraits to finger paintings of Barcelona and large green splotches on canvas. Intermingled with the paintings are a few sculptures sitting precariously in the middle of the floor. Highlights include Badrinath Arya's **Khoj,** a painting of subterranean stalactite-like staircases twisting endlessly in the back, and the paintings of the turn of the century Bengal School, which were inspired by South Asian folk art and East Asian high art. *(Jaipur House, east of India Gate. Local bus #621 and 622. ☎ 338 2835. Open Tu-Su 10am-5pm. Rs5, students Rs1.)*

NEHRU MUSEUM AND PLANETARIUM. Built inside the home of Jawaharlal Nehru, India's first prime minister, the museum has as much to say about the independence movement as a whole as it does about Nehru himself. Between voyeuristic peeks into Nehru's study, office, and bathroom, visitors are allowed to look at action shots of Nehru as a dour youth (with equally somber-looking relatives), as an ambitious student at Harrow and Cambridge, and as the humble, generous leader of India. Adjacent to the museum is the Nehru Planetarium. *(Teen Murti Bhawan, Teen Murti Rd., north of Chanakyapuri. Open Tu-Su 9am-5:15pm. Free. Planetarium exhibit open 11am-5pm. Rs1. Planetarium showings Tu-Su 11:30am, 1:30, 3, and 4pm. Rs10.)*

OTHER MUSEUMS. The **Indira Gandhi Memorial** exhibits a collection of sentimental photos and quotes from fallen leaders, all arrayed in Rajiv and Indira's former residence. If the collection bores you, the macabre exhibit of Rajiv and Indira Gandhi's last outfits will surely shock you out of complacency. *(1 Safdarjang. Open Tu-Su 9:30am-4:45pm.)* The **National Rail Museum** has indoor and outdoor exhibits on the history of Indian Railways and a miniature train for the riding. *(Chanakyapuri, near Shantipath. ☎ 688 1816 or 688 0939. Open Apr.-Sept. Tu-Su 9:30am-7:30pm; Oct.-Mar. 9:30am-5:30pm. Rs5; camera fee Rs100.)*

🎭 ENTERTAINMENT

To find out about weekly musical and cultural events, buy a copy of the *Delhi Diary* (Rs10), which comes out every Friday. **Dances of India** is a nightly performance of Indian dance and music, including *kathak* and *manipuri*. (Parsi Anjuman Hall, opposite the Ambedkar Football Stadium, Delhi Gate. ☎ 328 9464 or 642 9170. Shows 7pm.) There are many **movie theaters** in Delhi that show Hindi movies; **PVR Priya 1,** Basant Lok, Vasant Vihar (☎ 614 0048), and **PVR Anupam 4,** Saket Community Centre (☎ 689 5999), show English-language films for Rs60-130. Check daily papers for movie listings. Various cultural centers (see **Cultural Centers,** p. 107) screen foreign films and Indian "art" films not shown elsewhere.

The Red Fort's nightly **sound and light show,** focusing on the city's Mughal heritage, is unexpectedly entertaining. The silhouetted sitting halls and mosques invoke the voices of past rulers. A Pink Floyd concert it's not, but it's as good a history lesson as you're likely to get in Delhi (see **Lal Qila,** p. 114). The Old Fort also has a nightly sound and light show on the *Mahabharata* (see **Purana Qila,** p. 120).

🛍 SHOPPING

Like Delhi's hotels and restaurants, the markets and stores of the city range from the grimy and cheap to the glitzy and prohibitively expensive. The priciest of Delhi's boutiques are concentrated in the **Connaught Pl.** area, where armed guards stand in front of jewelry shops and tailors sell saris made from the finest silk. Literally under Connaught Pl. is the **Palika Bazaar,** an underground maze of stores selling anything and everything, mostly to locals. Because tourists tend not to come here, it offers better deals on clothes, fabric, and souvenirs than the stores above, provided that you have honed your bargaining skills. The quality of items here, however, is decidedly less than above-ground and the Palika Bazaar is not the place to search for a Rolex watch, or at least not a *real* one. Down Janpath from Connaught Pl., the **Central Cottage Industries Emporium,** stocks high-quality products from all over India: carved metal boxes, Mughal-style paintings, wooden elephants, oriental rugs, and the like. (☎331 2373. Open M-Sa 10am-7pm.) Opposite is the **Tibetan Market,** which sells Kashmiri crafts, mostly to tourists. The majority of Delhi residents shop outside of Connaught Pl. In Old Delhi, Chandni Chowk, which runs from the Fatepuri Masjid to the Red Fort, is one enormous bazaar—the road buzzes with people throughout the day. Most of the products sold here are household items of minimal interest to most tourists (plastic buckets and padlocks galore), but a few shops stock clothes, jewelry, and musical instruments of varying quality and price. **Netaji Subhash Marg,** which runs south from the Red Fort to Delhi Gate, has several more music stores. **Biba Music Emporium** has an extensive collection of sitars (from Rs1800), including some beautiful antique instruments, tablas (from Rs750), and harmoniums. (☎328 4558. Open M-Sa 9:30am-7:30pm.) **Bina Enterprises,** 200m closer to Delhi Gate from the Biba Music Emporium, also stocks tablas (from Rs950) and sitars (from Rs2500). (☎328 9587 Open M-Sa 9:30am-7:30pm.) Just northwest of Paharganj, Karol Bagh contains shops of all sizes and kinds. Most of the other major market centers are in the southern part of the city. These include South Extension, Greater Kailash (M block and N block), Sarojini Nagar, Lajpat Nagar, Hauz Khas Village, Dilli Haat Khan Market, and Nehru Place.

🎶 NIGHTLIFE

Despite what the shadowy and deserted streets of Connaught Pl. might imply, Delhi's nightlife is not confined to the plastic tables and chairs of Paharganj rooftops. The clubs of the capital thump and flash with the same techno and whirling lights as the best clubs anywhere. But like the luxury hotels that house them, Delhi's discos cater to the elite, and cover charges may seem forbiddingly steep to budget travelers. If you want to get down and dirty with the jet-set of India, you'll have to cough up some serious cash and dig down deep into your pack to find the necessary clothes to fit in. On the other hand, grooving 'til the morning in a classy nightclub can be a welcome change from hanging out with the tokers high up on the rooftops of some budget hotel. Most of the clubs listed below are 21 and over, require men to be accompanied (women, however, can often get in alone), and prohibit torn clothing, sneakers, and uncool insophisticates of all kinds.

Ghungroo (☎611 2233), at the Maurya Sheraton. Bronze-plated columns enclose the dance floor and a semi-circular marble bar polished like a mirror. Ghungroo welcomes a mixed crowd of locals and foreigners who strut their stuff on a translucent tiled dance floor reminiscent of Saturday Night Fever. Pulsates with everything from techno to Middle Eastern pop music. Dancers cheer whenever a Hindi film song begins. Cover Rs300 for men; women get in free. Open M-Th 10pm-2:30am; F-Sa until 3:30am.

Mirage (☎683 5070), at the Best Western Surya Sofitel. The Mirage's black-and-white decor is sparse but classy. Flashing lights hang in profusion over the dance floor and the wrought-iron railings surrounding it. The DJ sometimes takes requests and mostly spins techno, hip-hop, Hindi pop, and a bit of reggae. Cover W, Th, Su Rs300 per person; F Rs400 per couple; Sa Rs500 per couple. Open W-Su 10pm-3am.

My Kind of Place (☎ 611 0202), at Taj Palace. Nary a local in sight, MKOP is packed with Europeans and Africans. The club is one of Delhi's most popular with tourists. A thick haze of smoke hangs in the sweaty, hot air, but this doesn't stop anyone from dancing. The low ceiling pulses with inlaid fairy lights on a random fade and brighten cycle. Cover Su-Th Rs300 per couple; F-Sa Rs400 per couple. Open 9:30pm-3am.

CJ's (☎ 371 0101), at Le Meridien. From the triangular bar in the center to the dance floor on the side, everything here is in keeping with the atmosphere of the hotel: smooth and swanky. The DJ plays a mix of hip-hop, techno, filmi songs, and anything else you might want to shake your booty to. The sound-proof karaoke room near the entrance can be rented for private pleasures for 1-2hr. at Rs1100. Cover Tu, Th Rs300 per couple; all other nights Rs500 per couple. Open 10pm-2:30am; bar closes at midnight.

Annabelle's (☎ 370 9000), at the Intercontinental on Babar Rd., 200m from the intersection of Barakhamba Rd. and Tolstoy Marg. With a large central dance floor surrounded by silver railings, Annabelle's is clearly divided into a dancing section and a spacious sitting area complete with tables, chairs, and posters of foreign beers. The mostly Indian crowd grinds to the typical mix of techno and Hindi pop. Cover W, F Rs250 per couple; all other nights Rs500 per couple. Open daily 9:30pm-2am.

Some Place Else (☎ 373 3737), at the Park Hotel on Gansad Marg. Really more of a bar than a nightclub, but every Th-Sa the brick walls shake with dance music. Each night has a musical theme. M jazz night, Tu film songs, W Latino and reggae, Th hip-hop and R&B, F rock and retro, Sa techno and house, Su free-for-all. Su-W no cover charge; Th-Sa Rs400 per couple. Open Su-W 11am-midnight, Th-Sa dancing 11pm-3am.

UTTAR PRADESH
उत्तर प्रदेश

Uttar Pradesh, the "Northern State," is the true heartland of India. Its parched plains spring to life at the coming of the monsoon, and from its mountains, the Ganga descends to join her sister river Yamuna in cutting across the earth. Uttar Pradesh, which has been called "UP" for short ever since the British carved it out as the United Provinces, is India's most populous state, with nearly 150 million residents in all. The eastern half of UP is one of India's most economically depressed areas, while western UP has shared in the prosperity of neighboring Delhi. The cradle of Indian civilization from the time of the Aryan chieftains to the reign of the great Mughal emperors, UP gave India the *Ramayana*, the Hindi language, and, since Independence, eight of its 12 prime ministers. It has also been the focus of bitter communal and inter-caste violence. In 1992, the state's BJP government encouraged the destruction of the Babri Masjid in Ayodhya, leading to thousands of deaths in communal riots across India. In the spring of 2000, a bicycle bomb went off in Ayodhya, injuring more than a dozen people. The state remains a flashpoint for Hindu-Muslim tensions. Radical affirmative action politics for Dalits (former Untouchables) also have a strong base in UP. Few people visit India without visiting UP, yet there is nothing here to photograph, slap on a postcard, and declare representative of the state—not its sacred cities of Varanasi, Ayodhya, and Mathura, nor the hill stations and pilgrimage centers in the Himalayas, nor the Taj Mahal in the Mughal capital of Agra, nor the old Muslim city of Lucknow. There is no quintessential UP, because UP is quintessentially Indian.

HIGHLIGHTS OF UTTAR PRADESH

Agra (p. 166) is home to several of India's most famous and beautiful monuments, including a gem of a royal **fort** (p. 173), the abandoned Mughal capital of **Fatehpur Sikri** (p. 175), and a little marble ditty called the **Taj Mahal** (p. 172).

Hinduism's holiest city, **Varanasi** (p. 193) draws the living and the dying to its crowded streets and sacred *ghats*.

Ashram towns like **Rishikesh** (p. 141) and **Haridwar** (p. 137), pilgrimage centers like **Gangotri** (p. 148) and **Yamnotri** (p. 148), and national reserves like **Corbett** (p. 150) and the **Valley of Flowers** (p. 150) beckon lovers of the natural and the supernatural alike to northern UP's hill districts.

GARHWAL गढ़वाल AND
KUMAON कुमाऊँ

The hills of Uttar Pradesh embody the holy, the hilly, and (at times) the downright helly. The regions of Garhwal and Kumaon, with their 7000m peaks and deodar forests, frenetic hill stations, Maruti-packed roads, ashrams, and sacred rivers, encompass enough to enthrall, enlighten, amuse, and annoy any visitor.

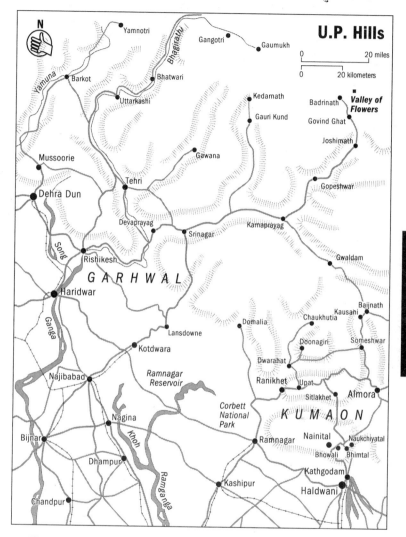

The South Indian saint Shankara came to Garhwal during the 9th century, bringing the local population into the Hindu fold and establishing several important temples. Long before that, however, parts of the *Mahabharata* and *Ramayana* had already taken place here, enveloping the hills of Uttarakhand with the religious mystique that is still in evidence today. From the source of the holy Ganga and Yamuna Rivers high up in the mountains and the abode of Lord Shiva at Mount Kailash to the eye of Sati at Nainital and the holy forests of Tapovan, these hills are a major sanctuary of Hinduism.

In the early 19th century, Garhwal and Kumaon were overrun by the Nepali commander Amar Singh Thapa. He was bumped out in 1816 by the Brits, who set up regimental headquarters here and made Garhwal and Kumaon part of the United Provinces. In 1984, there were demonstrations agitating for a separate state of Uttarakhand (Land of the North) within India, but the present BJP-led government has so far managed to resist these demands.

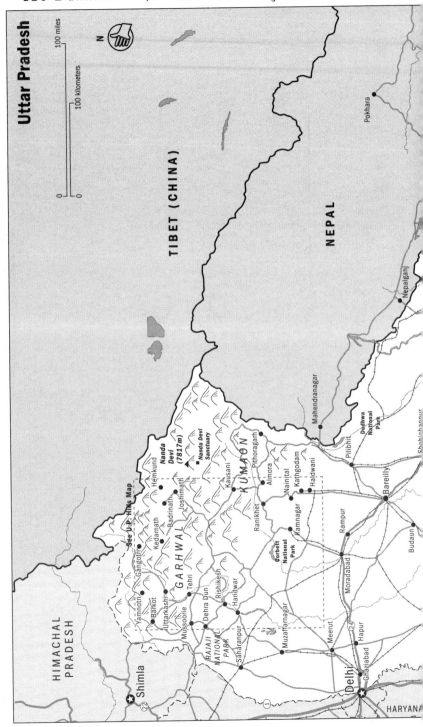

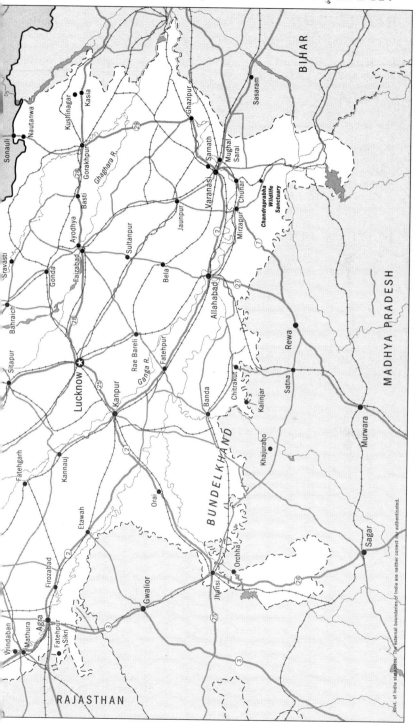

DEHRA DUN देहरादून ☎ 0135

Dehra Dun is not what you'd call a tourist town. A thriving city with most of the advantages—and many of the drawbacks—of Indian-style big-city living, Dehra Dun is the training ground for India's elite, who come here to study at the Indian Military Academy, the Doon School, and the Indian Forest Research Institute.

But there is another, more gentle side to Dehra Dun, with its heart in the laid-back, life-loving ways of the nearby mountain villages. Bus-drivers and rickshaw-*wallahs* jockey for room on the congested roadways just as they do everywhere else on the subcontinent, but at least here they do it with a smile. Residents take pride in their reputation for honesty and are fond of pointing out how kind and good-natured Dehra Dun's people are relative to the big city nasties down in Delhi. Most travelers stop in Dehra Dun for a day or two before going to the Shiwalik foothills to the north or to the hill station of Mussoorie, whose lights are visible from the city at night. There is plenty to do here—temples, parks, and sulphur springs—but in the end there's too much "city" and not enough "town" to keep visitors here for more than a couple of days.

▨ GETTING THERE AND GETTING AROUND

UTTAR PRADESH

Trains: As terminus of the **Northern Railway,** Dehra Dun sends trains all over India. The enquiry office is in the main terminal, the booking office is next door, and the computerized reservation complex is across the way. Open M-Sa 8am-1:30pm and 2:30-8pm, Su 8am-2pm. To: **Delhi** (4-5 per day, 6am-9:15pm, 7hr., Rs123); **Haridwar** (6 per day, 8am-9:30pm, 1½hr., Rs22); and **Lucknow** (2-3 per day, 6:40-8:30pm, 12hr., Rs182).

Buses: Several companies run buses from the **Delhi Bus Stand,** next to Hotel Drona. **UP Roadways** (☎ 653797) to: **Delhi** (32 per day, 5:15am-10:30pm, Rs90-140); **Haldwani** (4 per day, 9hr., Rs120); **Haridwar** (every 30min., 5am-7pm, Rs20); **Rishikesh** (14 per day, 5am-7pm, 1½hr., Rs16). **Himachal Bus Lines** (☎ 623435) to: **Shimla** (6 per day, 10hr., Rs110). **Punjab Roadways** (☎ 624410) to: **Amritsar** (5:30 and 7:30am, 14hr., Rs141). UP Roadways also leaves from the **Mussoorie Bus Stand** to: **Almora** (6am, 12hr., Rs150); **Mussoorie** (every 30min., 6am-8pm, 1½hr., Rs18); **Nainital** (8am, 11hr., Rs130); **Uttarkashi** (6, 8:30, and 10:30am; 9hr.; Rs89). **Highway Motors,** 69 Gandhi Rd. (☎ 624211), next to the railway station, serves **Hanuman Chatti** (Apr.-Aug. 6am, Sept.-Mar. 6:30am; 8½hr.; Rs78). Daily deluxe buses run to **Delhi** from Hotel Shivalik on Rajpur Rd. (11am, 6hr., Rs250). **Taxis,** opposite the bus stands, run as far as **Mussoorie** (Rs50 per person shared).

Local Transportation: Local **buses** go to nearby destinations from the City Bus Stand, north of the clock tower. **Tempos** are common and cheap and run along fixed routes from the clock tower (Rs3-4). **Auto-rickshaws** from the Delhi Bus Stand to the Botanical Gardens cost around Rs50.

✦ ORIENTATION

Understanding the three main areas in Dehra Dun—the **railway station** area, **Connaught Place,** and the **Astley Hall** area—helps greatly with orientation. The railway station is to the south; the **Mussoorie Bus Stand** is right next to the station, and the **Delhi Bus Stand** (servicing most destinations *not* in the hills) is a five-minute walk north along **Gandhi Rd.,** just past the hard-to-miss **Hotel Drona.** Following Gandhi Rd. north leads to the second main focus of the city, the area around the tall **clock tower.** The **city bus stand** and Gandhi Park are just north of the clock tower along Rajpur Rd., where many visitor services, high-end hotels, and restaurants lie. This strip is referred to as **Astley Hall** or **Dilaram Bazaar** farther north. Continuing on Gandhi Rd. from the clock tower will bring you onto Rajpur Rd. The web of streets just south of the clock tower is known as **Paltan Bazaar;** the part of the bazaar nearest to the railway station is called **Darshani Gate.**

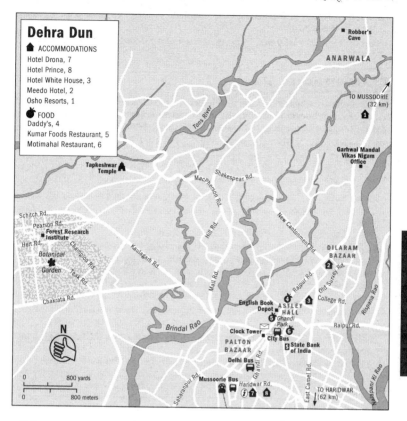

🛈 PRACTICAL INFORMATION

Tourist Office: UP Tourist Office (☎653217), on the 2nd fl. of the Hotel Drona, next to the Delhi Bus Stand. Open M-Sa 10am-5pm. For trekking tips and other information about the Garhwal region, try the government-run **GMVN Headquarters,** 71/1 Rajpur Rd. (☎746817). Open M-Sa 10am-5pm.

Trekking Agency: Private agents, such as **Garhwal Tours and Trekking** (☎654774), in Rohini Plaza near Hotel Ambassador, plan treks. Open M-Sa 9:15am-1:30pm.

Currency Exchange: The main branch of the **State Bank of India** (☎653240), 1 block east of the clock tower, changes currency and traveler's checks. Open M-F 9am-1pm and 3:30-6:30pm, Sa 10am-noon. **Punjab National Bank,** Astley Hall (☎656012), on top of Gandhi Park, changes traveler's checks. Open M-F 10am-2pm.

Bookstore: English Book Depot (☎655192), next to Kumar Restaurant. Open since 1923. Open M-Sa 10am-1:30pm and 2:30-8pm. **The Green Bookshop,** 17 Rajpur Rd. (☎653382), has maps of the Garhwal region. Open M-Sa 10am-1:30pm and 3-8pm.

Library: Mahatma Khuhiram Public Library and Reading Room, near the Delhi bus stand. Open 8-11am and 5-8pm.

Market: Paltan Bazaar, between the clock tower and railway station, has hundreds of shops, selling everything from sitars to saris. Open daily 9am-9pm.

Police: Dhara Chowki Station, Rajpur Rd. (☎653648), south of Hotel Ambassador.

Hospital: Dr. Diwan, Kacheri Rd. (☎657660), is available 9:30am-2pm and 6-8pm. **Jain Hospital** (☎627766 or 621727) is open 24hr.

Pharmacy: Fair Deal Chemists, 14 Darshani Gate (☎625252). Open M-Sa 8:30am-9pm, Su 8:30am-2pm.

Post Office: Head Post Office, by the clock tower. Open M-Sa 10am-6pm. **Postal Code:** 248001.

ACCOMMODATIONS

Hotels around the bus stands and the clock tower tend to be either bland high-end boxes or dingy budget dives, but the noise and stink are tolerable if you're only staying a night. Classier hotels line Rajpur Rd., along Astley Hall and beyond.

Hotel Prince, Gandhi Rd. (☎627070), 2 blocks south of the Delhi Bus Stand, 2 blocks east of the Mussoorie Bus Stand. A multi-story business hotel without the high prices and pretension. Great top-floor views. Basic rooms with fans, desks, and hot water (but no showers). A friendly staff adds to the value. Singles Rs200; doubles Rs300-400.

Meedo Hotel, 71 Gandhi Rd. (☎627088), 1 block from the railway station. Not to be confused with the expensive Meedo Grand out on Rajpur Rd., which shares its incongruous Art Deco architecture. Bucket showers, seat toilets, clean rooms. Attached restaurant. Check-out 24hr. Singles Rs150-265; doubles Rs265-350.

Osho Resorts, 111 Rajpur Rd. (☎749544), 1km beyond the GMVN Tourist Office. Well-kept rooms, TVs, hot water, and super-guru Osho himself (see p. 414). Read Osho books, watch Osho TV, or seek enlightenment in the lush meditation center. All rooms have a shower and seat toilet. The attached restaurant, **Heaven's Gate,** serves excellent food. Singles Rs390-490; doubles Rs490-590. Off-season rates are Rs100 less.

Hotel Drona (☎654371 or 652794), next to Delhi Bus Stand, on Gandhi Rd. Large, rooms with attached bath. A tourist office, garden, and STD booth. Doubles Rs300-550.

Hotel White House, Astley Hall (☎652765), 1 block east of Rajpur Rd. Far enough from downtown for all but those making brief stopovers. Huge rooms, pleasant gardens, and a friendly manager. Check-out noon. Singles Rs200-250; doubles Rs300-400. AmEx.

FOOD

Restaurants near Astley Hall and on Rajpur Rd. are a bit more up-market than the ones in the grime of the bus stand. The Paltan Bazaar area has good bakers and sweets vendors, plus a row of fruit stands near the clock tower. The **Venus** and **Ahuja restaurants** (opposite the explosives plant on Gandhi Rd., just east of the railway gate) are open throughout the day.

Kumar Foods Restaurant, 15B Rajpur Rd., between the post office and Motel Himshri. Magically delicious renditions of Indian specialties. The *rogan josh* (Rs55) and chicken *tikka masala* (Rs90) are superb. Great service; quiet and classy atmosphere. Open daily 11am-4pm and 7-10:30pm; closed last Tu of the month.

Motimahal Restaurant, Rajpur Rd., opposite the Hotel Ambassador, in the coolest duck-away spot in town. Quality non-veg. food from a large menu. Chicken curry Rs60; mutton *shahi korma* Rs55; *dahl makhani* Rs28. Open daily 9am-10:30pm.

Daddy's, Rajpur Rd., next to the Hotel President. A western-style burger joint with a varied menu of pizza, "thirst aids," fries (Rs35), and theme burgers (Rs50-70) that include the "Great Daddy's Twin" (Rs50). Open daily 9:30am-9:30pm.

SIGHTS

Most of the sights are outside the city. Buses and tempos will take you where you want to go from the city bus stand; taxis and auto-rickshaws charge Rs40-100 for trips to any of the sights and Rs400-500 for a full day. If you really want to take your time, pick a destination and make it a full day's excursion. The GMVN's day-long bus tour, **Doon Darshan,** covers the FRI, Tapkeshwar Temple, Malsi Deer Park, and Sahastra Dhara (Rs100). The bus stops for 45 to 90 minutes at each place (daily at 10:30am, returns at 5pm). Contact **Drona Travel,** 45 Gandhi Rd., by the Hotel Drona. (☎654371. Open daily 7am-10pm.)

FOREST RESEARCH INSTITUTE (FRI). Established under British auspices in 1906, the FRI works toward a better understanding of the many fun-filled uses and abuses of forestry, botany, and biodiversity conservation. The long building is marvellously colonial, and the lawn is reminiscent of a European palace. Even if you're not into forestry (not everybody is, believe it or not), there's still quite a bit to do here: there are six museums focusing on different aspects of forest life, from the chemicals in the leaves to the bugs in the bark. The green lawn of the institute's **Botanical Gardens** is a wonderful picnic spot. There is a canteen for afternoon tea or snacks, and at the far corner of the institute is an information desk. *(Visitors gate on Trevor Rd. Open M-F 9am-5:30pm. Museums open M-F 10am-5:30pm, Su 10am-2pm. Botanical Gardens Rs10.)*

TAPKESHWAR TEMPLE. Built into the mountain beside a running stream, this Shiva temple is the most important temple in the area. There are several shrines around the temple's entrance, and the nearby stream also serves as a popular swimming hole. Tapkeshwar Temple hosts the **Shivaratri celebration** during the last week of March and the first week of April. *(6km northwest of town. One-way auto-rickshaw Rs60; city bus or tempo from the clock tower Rs3. Open daily 5:30am-9pm.)*

ROBBER'S CAVE. Another popular picnic spot is the so-called Robber's Cave, also called **Guchu Pani,** actually a 200m long, 15m high gorge. Visitors wade through the stream at the small canyon's bottom, where the water has smoothed the rock. At the other end is an opening with large boulders for climbing and several small pools for swimming. Wear sandals, as some of the rocks in the stream can be sharp. *(8km north of town. Transport drops you off 100m from the cave's entrance.)*

MUSSOORIE मसूरी ☎ 0135

The mountain hill station of Mussoorie, a covenient access point for the tranquil forests nearby, is chintzy, overpriced, and often overcrowded. It is also refreshingly cool and because of (and *not* in spite of) its touristy, carnival atmosphere a whole lot of fun. The town certainly isn't for everyone, though—travelers looking to shun commercialism in favor of spirituality should stay in nearby Haridwar or Rishikesh, and those hoping for mountain tranquility might be better off in Kumaon. But anyone with an interest in the bizarre subculture of Indian tourism could hope for no better point of observation. A trip to Mussoorie time-warps you back to an era where big hair, clunky roller skates, and the original Nintendo ruled the entertainment scene.

A favorite destination of heat-fleeing tourists from Delhi (it's the closest hill station to the capital), the town was settled in 1827 by an Englishman, Captain Young. British officials developed Mussoorie into a Victorian home-away-from-home-away-from-home, complete with an exclusive club, several libraries, and an Anglican Church. The central promenade, The Mall, was made for afternoon strolls and crusty chit-chat, all in full view of the snow-peaked Himalayas to the northeast and the Doon Valley to the south.

Where once the British rulers ascended 11km uphill carried by porters, Indian throngs now pack their Marutis and cruise up the scenic drive from the plains. Peak season is between May and July. Mid-season extends from July to October (the foggy monsoon months) and from March to May. The off-season, November through March, is when you're more likely to find solitude and snowfall.

▐▀ GETTING THERE AND GETTING AROUND

Trains: No tracks run to Mussoorie, but computerized reservations for trains from Dehra Dun can be made at the **Northern Railways Out Agency,** on The Mall, below the post office. Open M-F 9am-1pm and 3-5pm, Sa 9-11am and noon-4pm, Su 9am-2pm.

> **WARNING.** There is an Indian Army encampment at **Chakrata**, 82km north-west of Mussoorie. No foreigners are allowed north of the east-west road between Yamuna Bridge and Kalsi without a permit from the army. Foreign tourists heading by road for Shimla or eastern Himachal Pradesh must do so via Herbertpur. Foreign tourists have been arrested for traveling north of Kalsi.

Buses: UP Roadways buses leave from **Kulri** (☎632259) or **Library Bus Stands** (☎632258), both below The Mall, and service only **Dehra Dun** (every 30min., 6am-7pm, 1½hr., Rs20). Several signs around town advertise direct Dehra Dun-Delhi deluxe service, but you have to get to Dehra Dun yourself. Try **Mussoorie Novelty Store** (☎632795), opposite the railway booking office. Non-A/C buses (11am and 10pm, Rs150) and A/C buses (8, 11am, and 10pm; Rs250) depart from the clock tower in Dehra Dun.

Taxis: Booking stands are next to both bus stands. To: **Dehra Dun** (Rs70 per seat, Rs350 per car) and **Haridwar** (Rs750 per car).

✴ ORIENTATION

Mussoorie is 15km long, stretching around the mountain overlooking Dehra Dun. The town has two centers, the **Library Bazaar** and **Kulri Bazaar** areas, connected by a 30-minute walk along The Mall, which is lined with murals and shops of all kinds. Buses from the valley stop near both bazaars. The plaza in front of the library, with a statue of the Mahatma, is called **Gandhi Chowk;** the gate by the library is **Gandhi Gate. Camel's Back Rd.** runs along the back side of the mountain and connects the two bazaars. **Landour Bazaar,** with its large clock tower, is a 10-minute walk east of Kulri. The **Tibetan Colony** is to the left of **Convent Hill** on **Kemty Falls Rd.**

🛈 PRACTICAL INFORMATION

Tourist Office: (☎632863), near the ropeway, halfway between Kulri and Library Bazaars. Open May-June daily 9am-7pm; July-Apr. M-Sa 10am-5pm.

Budget Travel: GMVN (☎631281), at the Library Bus Stand, runs tours of the northern pilgrimage sites departing from Delhi and Rishikesh. Trips range from a 4-day excursion to Badrinath (Rs2000) to 12-day trips to Yamnotri, Gangotri, Kedarnath, and Badrinath (Rs5000). Open daily May-July 9am-7pm; Aug.-Apr. 9am-5pm. For travel into the hills, **Trek Himalaya** (☎30491), on The Mall, above the ropeway, provides assistance for organized trips and drop-in consultations. Guides available. Tent rental Rs80-100 per day. Fully planned excursions US$50-70 per person for groups of 4 or more. Open daily Mar.-Oct. 10am-8:30pm.

Currency Exchange: State Bank of India, Kulri Bazaar (☎632533), changes currency and traveler's checks. Open M-F 10am-4pm, Sa 10am-2pm.

Bookstore: There are several good bookstores along The Mall in Kulri. Most open daily 8am-8pm. Also try the **Prabhu Book Depot,** near Banares House Sarees.

Market: Tibetan Market, along and below The Mall, near the library. Along **Kulri Bazaar** are many stores specializing in curios, woolens, and tourist trifles. Bazaars generally open 9am-9pm. The smaller **Five Sisters Bazaar** is on the road behind Tehri Rd., near the TV tower. **Prakash Stores,** a favorite with students at the Language School, stocks foreign food products. Open M-Su 10am-8:30pm.

Police: (☎632083), above The Mall, just west of the Hotel Mall Queen. Open 24hr.

Pharmacies: P.B. Hamers & Co. (☎632502), up from the Rialto Cinema, by President's Restaurant, has a wide selection. Open daily 10am-9pm.

Hospital/Medical Services: The **Community Hospital** (☎632541), in Landour, 1½km east of the clock tower, has 24hr. emergency care. For private treatment, try the **clinic** of Dr. Rana and Dr. Nautiyal (☎632594), on the road above the Kulri Mall. Open daily 10am-1pm and 4-7pm.

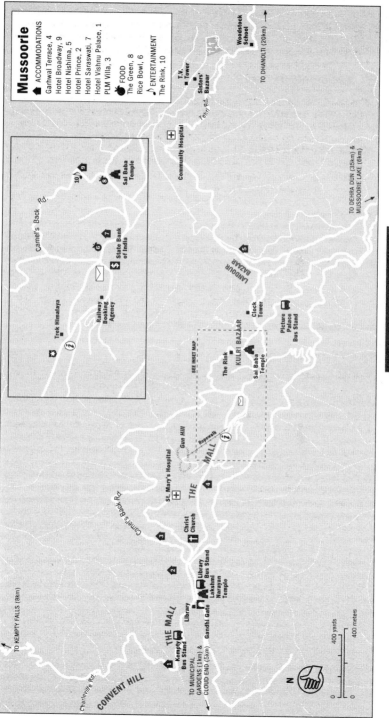

UTTAR PRADESH

Mussoorie

▲ ACCOMMODATIONS
Garhwal Terrace, 4
Hotel Broadway, 9
Hotel Nishima, 5
Hotel Prince, 2
Hotel Saraswati, 7
Hotel Vishnu Palace, 1
PLM Villa, 3

◆ FOOD
The Green, 8
Rice Bowl, 6

♪ ENTERTAINMENT
The Rink, 10

TO DHANOLTI (20km)

Woodstock School

T.V. Tower

Sisters' Bazaar

Community Hospital

Terry Rd.

Sai Baba Temple

10
9
8

Camel's Back Rd.

State Bank of India

6
7

Railway Booking Agency

Trek Himalaya

i

TO DEHRA DUN (35km) & MUSSOORIE LAKE (6km)

LANDOUR BAZAAR

5

Clock Tower

Picture Palace Bus Stand

KULRI BAZAAR

The Rink

Sai Baba Temple

SEE INSET MAP

Gun Hill

Ropeway

i

THE MALL

St. Mary's Hospital

4

Christ Church

3

Camel's Back Rd.

2

Library Bus Stand
Lakshmi Narayan Temple

Gandhi Gate

Library

THE MALL

Kempty Bus Stand

1

CONVENT HILL

Charleville Rd.

TO KEMPTY FALLS (8km)

TO MUNICIPAL GARDENS (1km) & CLOUD END (5km)

N

400 yards

400 meters

0
0

Internet: **Cyber Corner** (☎631984), right past Gandhi Gate. Rs2 per min. Open daily 8am-11pm.

Post Office: (☎632806), near State Bank of India, above The Mall in Kulri. Open M-F 9am-1pm and 1:30-5pm, Sa 9am-noon. **Postal Code:** 248179.

■ ACCOMMODATIONS

Most low-end options are in the **Kulri Bazaar** area. It's a good idea to book ahead of time in peak season (May-June), when rates are higher. Expect discounts mid-season (Mar.-May and July-Oct.) and much lower prices from November to March.

KULRI AND LANDOUR

Garhwal Terrace (☎632682 or 632683), on The Mall, between Kulri and Library Bazaars. This GMVN-run hotel has dormitories that open up to a lovely veranda with mountain views. Slightly ritzier than most government hotels. Dorm beds Rs100; rooms Rs1000. Jul. 16-Apr. 15: Rs50/Rs500. Reserve in advance during peak season.

Hotel Saraswati (☎631005), up the ramp from the more visible Hotel Amar, past Hotel Mansarovar. Because of its somewhat hidden location, it's likely to have rooms when all else is full. Immaculate rooms with mirrors, TVs, seat toilets, and hot water. The surroundings are peaceful in comparison to the activity on Mall Rd. Doubles Rs300-600. Off-season: 50% discount.

Hotel Broadway, Camel's Back Rd. (☎632243), close to the rink near Kulri Bazaar. This converted English guest house retains charm in a peaceful setting away from most of the noise. Rooms with balconies have valley views; some have seat toilets. May 1-July 15: singles Rs200; doubles Rs300-500. Off-season: 50% discount.

Hotel Nishima, Landour Bazaar (☎632227), past the clock tower. Popular among language school students, Nimisha has bright rooms and huge buckets of hot water. Rest easy on thick mattresses behind heavy metal doors. TV in the lobby. Food is available, and there are seat toilets for the lucky few. May-June: doubles Rs150-200.

LIBRARY AREA

▨ **Hotel Prince** (☎632674), off The Mall, up the ramp from the horse stand—look for the alley access 30m toward Kulri from the library. Once a British hotel, this magnificent site is high above The Mall in a century-old summer getaway. Regal halls, huge rooms, high ceilings, and high tea in the drawing room or on the patio. May 15-July 15: doubles Rs500-1500. Off-season: 50% discount.

▨ **PLM Villa** (☎631090), off Camel's Back Rd., a 5min. walk from the library. Small garden-fronted place popular with Indian families. Small rooms with spectacular views. Food 7am-10pm. Check-out noon. Doubles Rs400-900. Off-season: 50% discount.

Hotel Vishnu Palace (☎632932 or 631732), 100m toward Kempty Falls when coming from the library. Clean rooms with views and attached baths. Doubles Rs600.

OUTSIDE MUSSOORIE

Cloud End Forest Resort (☎632242; fax 625657; email cloudend@nde.vsnl.net.in), west of the library, on the road to the municipal gardens; 7km by jeep. Set in 2000 acres of forest on a ridge overlooking Mussoorie. Built in 1838, this is one of the oldest buildings in Mussoorie. The period ambience has been scrupulously preserved, with old photographs, plush armchairs, and dark wooden beds. At night, guests enjoy tea and snacks beside bonfires. The restaurant serves unusually fresh and flavorful food. The doubles are pricey, but spartan dorm bunks get you in cheaply. There are some beautiful walks from here to the George Everest House and Kempty Falls. Camping is also an option (Rs400 per person, Rs200 if you have your own tent). Reserve a day ahead to have a jeep pick you up from the library. Dorm bunks Rs400; doubles Rs1200. Off-season: 50% discount. Closed Jan. to mid-Mar. AmEx, MC, Visa.

FOOD

Roasted and boiled *masala* corn (Rs5-15) is sold along The Mall, and sweets are scooped up at **Krishna's** in Kulri. For Tibetan food, head to Convent Hill.

The Green, Kulri Bazaar, serves delicious veg. food at reasonable prices, though a long line of customers makes it impossible to take your time. For breakfast, try the buttered *paratha*, stuffed with eggs and topped with raisins and cashews (Rs18). Open daily 7am-3:30pm and 7-10pm. Off-season: 8am-3:30pm and 7:30-10:30pm.

Rice Bowl, Kulri Bazaar, opposite the President restaurant. Cubicles with street view. Chinese and Tibetan food. Garlic chicken Rs55; mutton *momos* Rs20; huge portions of noodles and rice Rs40-80. Open daily 11am-11:30pm. Off-season: 11am-9:30pm.

Chopsticks, Convent Hill, before the IAS Academy. Come early for meals, including their famous *momos*. The chow mein (Rs45) and Talumein soup (Rs35) are delicious.

Jeet Restaurant, right on Gandhi Chowk, next to the library and Jeet Hotel. The ideal place to plan your trek or your next move—the tables have maps built into them. Veg. fare Rs30-50; chicken curry Rs65; cocoa Rs20. Open daily 8am-10:30pm.

Le Chef, near the State Bank of India in Kulri. French fries (Rs15), pizza (Rs50), hot dogs (Rs35), "gravy items," and fountain drinks. A popular hang-out for roller-skating teens. Open daily 10am-11pm.

SIGHTS

GUN HILL. Directly over the town is an extinct volcano known as Gun Hill, whose name comes form a Raj-era ritual of firing guns from the top at midday—the townspeople used to set their watches by it. You can walk (40min.) or ride rented horses *(15min., Rs70)* to the top, but the best way is via Mussoorie's **ropeway** —come early or get stuck waiting for hours. *(Open daily 8am-10pm; last car up at 8pm. Off-season: 10am-7pm. Rs25 round-trip.)* The top of Gun Hill has several lookout points, food vendors, a surreal **Laugh House** *(Rs10),* and several photo stands that will capture you loud and proud in glittery local costume.

CAMEL'S BACK ROAD. Several good **walks** start from Mussoorie and pass through fragrant pine and deodar forests. Camel's Back Road, which winds behind the town (3km total), has great views of the Himalayas. Points of interest include the **cemetery** (if the main gate is closed, try the side gate), studded with interesting British tombstones; **Camel's Back Rock** itself, which is shaped like a you-know-what; and **Chatra (Umbrella) Point,** where you can buy *chai* and snacks and look through a telescope, if it isn't broken. The entire walk takes 40 minutes. On a clear day, the sunset view from the road is spectacular.

MUSSOORIE LAKE. The town's newest attraction is an artificially constructed lake 6m from town on the road to Dehra Dun. Mussoorie Lake is donut-shaped, with a fountain in the center. Catch a breeze and gaze at the hills while gliding around the lake in a paddle boat *(Rs80 per 30min.).* There's not much here apart from a few small shops, though this might be just what you're looking for.

ENTERTAINMENT

The **Basu Cinema,** in the Library area, and the **Rialto Cinema,** in Kulri, opposite the President's restaurant, show Hindi movies (4 per day). There is an abundance of **arcade games** (some date to the pre-Pac-Man era) in the parlors in Kulri (Rs3 per game). There are a few discos in the Mussoorie area. **Hotel Rockwood,** Kulri Bazaar, rocks every night, but only local men seem to go. (☎632850. Cover Rs250 per couple. Open daily 8-11pm.) Outside town, **Residency Manor,** Hotel Jaypee, has dancing on the weekends. (☎631800. Cover Rs250-375, dinner included.)

Mussoorie's true hotspot, **The Rink,** in Kulri, is India's largest roller-skating rink. It dates back 100 years when British couples experimented with what was then all the rage back home. (Open daily 8:30am-9:30pm. Admission with rental Rs40.)

STRANGE BREW Though an Englishman founded Mussoorie, it took an unruly Scot to set the tone for the revelry that has outlasted the Brits in the hill station. In the 1880s, a fellow named Mackinnon came across limestone springs near present-day Gandhi Chowk. Mackinnon thought that the waters here might be good for brewing, and he built a brewery on the land, which soon began producing Garhwal's first beer. From the beginning, Mussoorie was a fun-loving town, and the beer-brewing led to a level of bacchanalian debauchery that wrinkled more than a few official brows. Local lore has it that one English lass, well progressed in the appreciation of the Scotch-Indian brew, stood on a chair on Mall Rd. and sold kisses for Rs5. That spelled trouble for Mackinnon. Since an outright ban on Mackinnon's operation would have been illegal, the authorities shrewdly crippled him by refusing him the right to import barley on the government road. Shut down but not broken in spirit, Mackinnon would not be snubbed—especially by the English. In a daring scheme, he built his own road, 20km long, fitting it with carts to transport his barley. He even set up a watchtower and tollbooth and ran it as a private highway. Aside from barley, much of the heavy European furniture in Mussoorie was brought up on "Mr. Buckles' Bullock-Cart Train," as the venture was called. And so, Mussoorie had its beer.

To thank his consumers, Mackinnon threw a massive bash, where he cracked a huge wooden cask of new brew. The rollicking horde polished off most of the barrel, noting repeatedly that it tasted better than any beer in the history of brewing. And then came the come-down. A scream of horror suddenly broke up the festivities, and the party collapsed into pandemonium—for in the dregs of the cask lay a rotting human body. Apparently, an impatient imbiber had slipped into the cellar, helped himself to a few too many, and fallen in with the hops. The brew was through. Mackinnon's ruined brewery looms on the Lynndale Estate 3km west of Mussoorie, but his bullock-cart road now forms 20km of the present road to Rajpur.

▶ DAYTRIPS FROM MUSSOORIE

To the west of Mussoorie lie **Happy Valley** and the nearby **Municipal Garden** (3km from Mussoorie), which has a tiny pool for paddle-boats. Two kilometers from the garden are the ruins of the old Mackinnon brewery (see **Strange Brew**, p. 136). A more distant destination to the northwest of town is **Kempty Falls,** a popular "retreat" that has sadly degenerated from an idyllic spot overlooking pristine, rushing falls and peaceful pools to the same old glitz that pervades the rest of town. GMVN runs a 3-hour bus trip to Kempty falls. (Apr.-Oct. 9am, noon, and 3pm; off-season: 10am and 1pm. Rs50.) Keen hikers can spend a morning walking through the untouched forests from Cloud's End to the source of Kempty and then to the falls (12km). You can also make daytrips out to the orchards and dense deodar forest of **Dhanolti** (25km away), the artificial lake at **Jheel,** which provides boating facilities, and **Surkanda Devi** (35km from Mussoorie, Rs120). This temple, at the top of the highest mountain in the area (3300m), provides great views of snow-covered peaks. It's a strenuous 2km walk to the temple from the road head. **Cloud's End** (see p. 134), 7km away, is a fairly untouched hiking spot. A one-hour walk through apple orchards brings you to the **George Everest House,** the home of the First Surveyor General of India. Famous British-Indian author Rushkin Bond lives near the Masonic Lodge Bus Stand and always welcomes friendly visitors.

LANDOUR LANGUAGE SCHOOL. At the top of the mountain, above Landour Bazaar, is the Landour Language School. Founded in 1870 by British missionaries and grammarians, it launched the international academic study of modern Indian languages and now offers programs in tandem with the University of Chicago and UC Berkeley, among others. Classes are small, with plenty of individual instruction for the school's 80 or so students. Courses offered range from introductory to advanced-level classes. A 12-week introductory Hindi class costs Rs18,000. Private lessons are Rs75 per hour. Students usually stay in private houses (Rs5000 per month) or in one of the two guest houses near the school (Rs300 per day including food). Contact Principal Chitranjan Datt, Landour Language School, Landour, Mussoorie, UP, 248179 (☎631487; fax 631917).

HARIDWAR हरिद्वार ☎ 0133

Buried in legend, cloaked with forests, and bordered by the Ganga as it emerges from the mountains to carve its winding way across India, Haridwar (Gateway to Lord Shiva) or Hardwar (Gateway to the gods) is one of Hinduism's sacred sites. The city's spiritual pre-eminence is rooted in the belief that the Ganga flows here in its purest form at the Har-ki-Pairi (Footstep of God), the main *ghat* to the Ganga. The goddess Ganga once came down from the heavens to Haridwar to sanctify the souls of 60,000 people who were burnt to ashes when they disturbed the meditation of Rishi Kapil (see **Ganga Comes to Earth,** p. 149), and Vishnu's footprint marks a stone set in the wall of Har-ki-Pairi. Haridwar was one of the four places in India where a drop of divine nectar *(amrit kailash)* fell from the pot *(kumbh)* that the gods and demons had been fighting over for 12 days (see **The Kumbh Mela,** p. 209). At sundown, *arati* is performed at Har-ki-Pairi; pilgrims float candle-lit flower boats down the Ganga to the sound of *bhajans.* A major pilgrimage destination, Haridwar hosts the Kumbh Mela every 12 years when millions of people rush the Har-ki-Pairi *ghat* at a precisely calculated moment: 14 people were trampled to death at the last Mela held here in 1988.

UTTAR PRADESH

Haridwar

🏠 ACCOMMODATIONS
Brij Lodge, 4
Hotel Madras, 2
Rahi Motel, 1
Tourist Bungalow, 3

TO DEHRA DUN (54km)
TO TEMPLES (1km) & RISHIKESH (25km)
Swami Sukdevanand Marg
Shamshan Ghat
Hill Bypass Rd.
Ganga River
Bhimgoda Bridge
TO CHILLA
Ganga Mandir
Mansa Devi Temple
Broken Bridge
Har-ki-Pairi
Ropeway
VIP Ghat
Barrage (Lalji Wala Dam)
Pant Dweep Island
Kusha Ghat
Gau Ghat
Haridwar Tourist Office
Upper Rd.
Shatabdi Bridge
GPO
Vishnu Ghat
Laltare Bypass Rd.
Railway Station
TO DELHI (214km)
State Bank of India
New Lalita Rao Bridge
Railway Rd.
Nil Dhara
Chilla Wildlife Sanctuary (Rajaji National Park)
Regional Tourist Office
Tourist Bungalow
TO DAKSHA MAHADEV TEMPLE (1km)
TO CHANDI DEVI TEMPLE (1km)
0   600 yards
0   600 meters
N

⎗ GETTING THERE AND GETTING AROUND

Trains: Northern Railway Station, next to the bus stand on Railway Rd. Enquiries office on the right-hand side; reservation counter on the left. Tickets can be bought at the **Northern Railway Booking Office,** Railway Rd. (☎427724), north of Laltarao Bridge. To: **Bombay** (1:20pm, 48hr., Rs374/1st class Rs1334); **Dehra Dun** (6-7 per day, 5:30am-4:55pm, 2hr., Rs84); **Delhi** (3-4 per day, 7:35am-11pm, 7-8hr., Rs104/AC chair car Rs460); **Lucknow** (2-3 per day, 4:50-10:15pm, 11hr., Rs166); **Rishikesh** (3 per day, 5am-5pm, Rs80); **Varanasi** (8:30 and 10:15pm, 20hr., Rs104).

Buses: The **bus stand** is opposite the train station, at the southwest end of Railway Rd. **UP Roadways** (☎427037) runs buses to: **Agra** (6 per day, 7:30am-9:30pm, 11hr., Rs150); **Dehra Dun** (every 30min., 5:30am-10:30pm, 1½hr., Rs20); **Delhi** (every 15min., 4:30am-11:30pm, 5hr., Rs84); **Lucknow** (3 per day, noon-7:30pm, 14hr., Rs175); **Rishikesh** (every 30min., 45min., Rs18); and **Shimla** (4 per day, 6am-10pm, 12hr., Rs135).

Local Transportation: Tempos loiter on the east bank of the Shatabdi Bridge. From the station to Har-ki-Pairi Rs3-4; by **auto-rickshaw** Rs10; by **cycle-rickshaw** Rs5-10.

◀▷ ⁊ ORIENTATION AND PRACTICAL INFORMATION

Haridwar runs along the banks of the Ganga, which flows from northeast to southwest. The **bus stand** and **railway station** face each other at the southwest end of **Railway Rd.,** the town's main thoroughfare. Walking northeast on Railway Rd., you'll cross **Laltarao (Lalita Rao) Bridge** over a small stream before reaching the post office. Just south of the post office is a barricade that prohibits four-wheeled traffic from continuing up Railway Rd. North of this barricade, Railway Rd. becomes **Upper Rd.;** the **Har-ki-Pairi** is at the northeast end of Upper Rd. The main bazaar, **Moti Bazaar,** runs parallel to the river along the streets shooting out from Upper Rd. near Har-ki-Pairi. Beyond that is the **Broken Bridge.** On the other side of the river are most of the accommodations and the **taxi stand.**

Tourist Office: GMVN, Railway Rd. (☎424240), at Laltarao Bridge, provides good maps and has information on local treks. Open M-Sa 10am-5pm. **UP Tourism** (☎427370) is in Rahi Motel, opposite the railway station. Open M-Sa 10am-5pm.

Budget Travel: Ashwani Travels, Railway Rd. (☎424581), just south of Laltarao Bridge. Open daily 8am-10pm. **Shivalik Travels,** Upper Rd. (☎426855), opposite Goraksh Nath Ashram, specializes in transportation to northern pilgrimage sites. Open daily 7am-3pm and 5-10pm. Pilgrimage destinations are open May-Oct.

Currency Exchange: State Bank of India changes US currency at its branch on Sharwan Nath Nagar. Open M-F 10am-2pm, Sa 10am-noon.

Bookstore: Arjun Singh Bookseller, Bara Bazaar (☎421449). Open daily 9am-9:30pm

Market: Moti Bazaar, 2 blocks north on Railway Rd. from Laltarao Bridge.

Police: Main station (☎426200 or 425200), Laltarao Bridge.

Pharmacy: Milap Medical Hall, Railway Rd. (☎427193), south of the post office, on the opposite side of the road. Open M-Sa 8:30am-10pm. **Dr. B.C. Hasaram & Sons,** Railway Rd. (☎427860), opposite the police station, specializes in ayurvedic medicines. Open daily 8am-9pm.

Hospital/Medical Services: There are several private clinics on Railway Rd. **Dr. Kailash Pande** (☎426023, emergency ☎424343), north of Laltarao Bridge, provides **24hr. emergency care.** Open 11:30am-2:30pm and 6:30-9:30pm.

Post Office: (☎427025), on Railway Rd. north of Laltarao Bridge. Open M-Sa 10am-4pm. **Postal Code:** 249401.

ACCOMMODATIONS

Hotels near the stations are not as comfortable or in locales as pleasant as the few beyond Har-ki-Pari or across the river. Though the *dharamsalas* may look inviting, most are not open to foreigners. From November to March prices are 25-50% lower. The prices listed below are for high (pilgrimage) season.

Brij Lodge (☎426872), north of Har-ki-Pairi on the right, near the Broken Bridge (the name of the hotel is not visible from the road). Watch the nightly *arati* ritual from the expansive balcony overlooking the Ganga. All rooms have attached bath with seat toilets but no showers. Doubles Rs300. Off-season: 60-80% discount.

Hotel Alaknanda (☎426379), across the river from town, toward the railway station. Buses pass by on the way into town. Though pricey and far from most of the sights, it's the best place for peace and quiet, with a little lawn, flower garden, and a strip of riverbank on the holy Ganga. All rooms have air-cooling and attached bath with hot water and seat toilets. Restaurant open 6:30am-10:30pm. Check-out noon. Dorm beds Rs100; singles Rs555-1100; doubles Rs650-1300. Off-season: 25% discount.

Hotel Madras (☎426356), off Railway Rd., 2 blocks north of the railway station. Turn right after the Kailash Hotel. A low-end old-timer conveniently close to transport. Rooms circa 1950s with common bath. Highly attentive staff. Singles Rs50; doubles Rs80.

Rahi Motel (☎426430), opposite the railway station. Good location for the late arrival. UP Tourism Office is in the lobby. Decent-sized rooms with attached bath. Singles Rs300; doubles Rs500.

FOOD

Purity of diet follows purity of spirit in Haridwar, so alcohol and meat are not available. Most major restaurants are on Railway Rd., midway between the bus stand and Har-ki-Pairi. Some of the little places tucked into the bazaar near Har-ki-Pairi make a mean, clean *puri-aloo* for breakfast.

Ahaar Restaurant, "Asli" Railway Rd., near Laltarao Bridge. South Indian, Chinese, and Punjabi food in a dark, tranquil, subterranean wooden chamber. *Thalis* Rs35-65; *dosas* Rs18-30. Open daily 10am-11pm.

New Mysore Kwality Restaurant, on the west side of Railway Rd., two-thirds of the way to Har-ki-Pairi. Unassuming atmosphere, cool air, and great prices. *Thalis* Rs25-40; *dosas* Rs10-20. Open daily 7am-10pm, in winter 7am-9pm.

Swagat Restaurant, Railway Rd., in Hotel Mansarovar. Typical business-hotel restaurant. *Thalis* Rs55; veg. chow mein Rs28. Open daily 6am-11pm.

Chotiwala Restaurant, Upper Rd., near Har-ki-Pairi. Veg. *thalis* (Rs25-60) and a wide variety of other Indian and Chinese dishes. Open daily 8am-10pm.

SIGHTS

HAR-KI-PAIRI GHAT. The most important spot in Haridwar is the holy *ghat* of Har-ki-Pairi, site of Vishnu's footprint and the place where the sacred Ganga flows out into the plains. Hindus believe that the water from the pool here is the most sacred on the planet. Many pilgrims fill a bottle or two to take home for use in religious ceremonies. The **Ganga Mandir** marks the spot where the drop of sacred nectar fell during the mythical match-up between the demon *asuras* and the good-guy gods that is now celebrated during the Kumbh Mela. Most people bathe here at sunrise, though you'll see people here throughout the day; there are chains to keep bathers from getting swept off to Varanasi by the strong undertow. The area is constantly crowded with pilgrims, beggars, lepers, sadhus, and several uniformed men who wander the area asking for donations for various "trusts." Many of these individuals pocket their earnings—donate via the charity boxes around the area or at the office of Ganga Sabha, above the temple at the *ghat*. Every evening at sundown, the sublime and spectacular **arati** ceremony takes place. Thousands gather to pay tribute to the gods by floating *diyas* (colorful lamps made of cupped leaves filled with flower petals and a lit candle) on the river. Arrive early (around 6:45pm) in high season. The best places to watch one from are the bridge on the south end of Har-ki-Pairi and the strip by the clock tower. Check your shoes at the stand if you want to go down to the *ghat*—avoid the 8pm shoe-return stampede.

MANSA DEVI TEMPLE. Haridwar is dotted with temples, but the two most important and beautiful ones can only be reached by ropeway or trek. Just above the city, on top of Bilwa Parvat, is the **Mansa Devi Temple**, dedicated to Mansa Devi, the form of the goddess Durga who can make the wishes of faithful and holy people come true. Mansa is believed to have bathed at Har-ki-Pairi every morning. The temple houses two intricately carved statues of the goddess—one with five arms and three mouths, the other with eight arms. To get to the shrine, stand in line for one of the ropeway trolleys that whisk you up and over a garden to the hilltop where views, vendors, and the temple await. You can avoid the long wait in line by making the 30-minute hike up the hill yourself. (*Ropeway trolley Rs25 round-trip. Open daily in June 7:30am-7pm; other months 8am-6pm.*)

OTHER TEMPLES. En route to **Kankhal**, south of Haridwar, are two other temples. The **Pareshwar Mahadev Temple**, 4km down the road, is famous for a *linga* made of mercury. One kilometer farther is the **Dakseshwara Temple** (also called the Daksha Mahadev) and **Sati Kund**, where King Daksha Prajaputi, Brahma's son and Sati's father, held a public sacrifice. Sati was invited but her husband-to-be, Shiva, didn't make the guest list. Sati was so insulted that she threw herself on her father's sacrificial pyre. (For what happened next, see **Divine Dismemberment**, p. 692.)

BHARAT MATA MANDIR AND ENVIRONS. North of Haridwar on the road to Rishikesh is a group of unusual temples that are either opulent and justly grand or just chintzy and overdone. The temples can be visited by tempo (Rs200-250 for a three-hour tour), but they're all within easy walking distance of each other; it may be better to use your own two feet for transport between them. One kilometer from Har-Ki-Pairi is the **Bhimgoda Tank,** where Bhima, one of the strongest of the five Pandavas, took a bath. A little farther is the **Jai Ram Ashram,** whose bone white sculptures, depicting the battles between gods and demons, are a departure from the colorful deities that characterize most Hindu temples.

The **Pawan Dham Temple,** along Swami Sukhdevanand Rd. from Haridwar, is most representative of the local houses of worship. Its many shrines are made almost entirely of mirrors and stained glass. Shiva and Arjuna ride on mirror-covered horses while Krishna eyes his 100 lovers in 100 different directions. The road then proceeds to the **Bharat Mata Mandir,** an eight-story shrine to Mother India and its leaders that resembles a modern apartment building capped by colorful temple domes. The top story houses the Hindu gods while the floor below hosts the goddesses, including Ganga and Saraswati, goddess of knowledge. The lower floors honor the saints of India's various religions (from Guru Nanak of the Sikhs to the Buddha and Swami Vivekenanda), saintly sisters (including Gandhi's devotees Annie Besant and Sister Nivedita), and freedom fighters. The second floor has paintings highlighting characteristic features of India's states, and the ground floor has a giant relief model of the country. Near the Bharat Mata Mandir, **Maa Vaishnodevi Mandir** attempts to simulate the experience of visiting a cave in Kashmir—complete with artificial, fruit-bearing mango trees, a giant Ganga Mata with a crocodile, and a tunnel with knee-deep water through which visitors duck and wade. **Bhuma Niketan,** south of Maa Vaishnodevi Mandir, has the added bonus of automation; pay a rupee to enter a room to watch robotic representations of Hindu heroes cavort with a giant devil. Venture off to the **Sapta Rishi Ashram,** at the north end of the cluster, to pay homage to the seven saints in its seven temples. It's believed that when Ganga arrived, the seven sages were involved in deep *tapasya* (austerities). To please all seven by touching their feet, she divided herself at this spot into seven streams—distinctly visible as recently as ten years ago.

ASHRAMS

Hindu pilgrims and sadhus flock to Haridwar for spiritual enrichment and often stay at one of the numerous ashrams within or near the city. Western spiritual seekers, on the other hand, often find themselves more at home in **Rishikesh** (see p. 141), where the yoga centers and ashrams are more likely to accept foreigners. In Haridwar, if you're not Indian, you'll have to do something special to impress the gurus and gain residence in their ashrams. However, the famous **Shantikunj** (☎424309; fax 423866; email shantikunj.hardwar@sml.sprintrpg.ems.vsnl.net.in) is open to foreign types, offering 9-, 30-, and 90-day courses that use meditation, music, and chanting as means to attain higher spiritual states. The 9-day courses begin on the 1st, 11th, and 21st of every month—reserve one month in advance. Single or two-day stays are also possible. (Payment by donation.)

RISHIKESH ऋषिकेश ☎0135

Most travelers come to Rishikesh to find *something*—a cure to some deep-rooted ailment, a spiritual leader, or, most often, themselves. Something about Rishikesh has the power to transform—sages first arrived here to find a splash of holiness along the crashing Ganga before heading north through the forests to the region's pilgrimage sites. Every year, thousands turn up for the **International Yoga Week** (Feb. 2-7) on the banks of the Ganga. Even the Beatles sought a new path here in 1968 under the guidance of the Maharishi Mahesh Yogi (see **Instant Karma,** p. 144). There are fewer temples in Rishikesh than in Haridwar, but more Westerners, more ashrams, more peace, and more sadhus. Summer is yoga off-season; winter has fewer Indian tourists.

GETTING THERE AND GETTING AROUND

Trains: Railway Station, at the west end of Rishikesh on (surprise!) Railway Rd. Reservations 8am-2pm. Most connections to major destinations start in Haridwar. To: **Haridwar** (6 per day, 1½hr., Rs18); **Delhi** (6:40am, 10hr., Rs39).

Buses: Rishikesh has 2 bus stands. Smog-snorters heading for the plains leave from the **UP Roadways** bus stand, Agarwal and Bengali Rd. (☎430066), on the south side of central Rishikesh. To: **Agra** (8am and 6pm, 12hr., Rs165); **Almora** (9am, 12hr., Rs180); **Chandigarh** (9am, 6hr., Rs95); **Dehra Dun** (every 30min., 5:30am-8pm, 1hr., Rs14); **Delhi** (every hr., 4am-10:30pm, 6½hr., Rs95); **Haldwani** (9am, 10hr., Rs100); **Haridwar** (every 30min., 4am-10:30pm, Rs18); **Nainital** (8am, 12hr., Rs145). For buses to the northern pilgrimage sites, go to the **Yatra Bus Stand** (☎430344), on Dehra Dun Rd., at the northwest end of Rishikesh. A rickshaw from the UP stand to the Yatra Bus Stand costs Rs10-15. Tickets for Yamnotri, Gangotri, Kedarnath, and Badrinath can be bought one day in advance. To: **Badrinath** (3 per day, 3:30-5am, 12hr., Rs130 plus a strong shot of coffee); **Chamoli** (7hr., Rs90); **Gangotri** (5:30am, 12hr., Rs130); **Hanuman Chatti** (7am, 12hr., Rs80); **Joshimath** (6am, 10hr., Rs110); **Kedarnath** (5am, 12hr., Rs95); **Srinagar, UP** (every 30min., 4am-3pm, 4hr., Rs50); **Tehri** (every 30min., 3:15am-5:15pm, 3½hr., Rs40); **Uttarkashi** (10 per day, 3:15am-1pm, 7hr., Rs72). Tehri and Uttarkashi serve as launch points for Yamnotri and Gangotri, Srinagar for Kedarnath and Badrinath. **Shared taxis** to **Uttarkashi** (5hr., Rs1200 per cab, up to 5 seats) leave from outside the bus stand.

Local Transportation: Getting to Ramjhula and Lakshmanjhula from Rishikesh is best done via one of the **tempos** that run along Lakshmanjhula Rd. (Rs3-5). Both bridges must be traversed on foot—no cross-river traffic. Both sides of the river teem with **auto-rickshaws** and **taxis**. A seat in a taxi to Rishikesh from the Ramjhula Bridge costs Rs20; the rickshaw fare from the UP bus stand to Lakshmanjhula is Rs45.

⚡ ORIENTATION

Rishikesh is divided into three parts by the **Ganga** and the **Chandrabhaga Rivers.** Northeast of the dry bed of the Chandrabhaga River are **Ramjhula** and farther northeast, **Lakshmanjhula.** Both straddle the Ganga and are connected across it by footbridges. For better accommodations most travelers head toward the bridges. It's a 5km hike into Rishikesh if you're staying in Lakshmanjhula, but it's well worth it for the distance from the noise and clutter of the station. From the Lakshmanjhula Bridge to the road and taxi stand is a beautiful but arduous trek.

The very small business center of Rishikesh is on the triangular land mass between the Chandrabhaga and the Ganga Rivers. The river banks are lined with temples, and a grid of streets covers the rest of the land. The **railway station** and **main bus stand** are in the northwestern corner of Rishikesh. The tourist office, banks, and post office are in the small city center. **Dehradun Rd.** runs along the Chandrabhaga at the northwestern end of Rishikesh, intersecting at its eastern end with Laksmanjhula Rd. The eastern part of Ramjhula is known as **Swargashram** and its western part is called **Muni-ki-Reti** (named for the nearby hill where Lord Hanuman brought herbs to cure Lord Rama's illness). **Kailash Gate,** 1km south of Ramjhula taxi stand in the city center, is a major landmark.

ℹ PRACTICAL INFORMATION

Tourist Office: UP Tourism, Railway Rd. (☎430209), 3 blocks west of the State Bank of India, up the outdoor flight of stairs by the white statue. Open M-Sa 10am-5pm, closed second Sa. **GMVN Trekking and Mountaineering Office** (☎430799), at Kailash Gate, offers information on treks. Open daily May-June and Sept.-Oct. 10am-5pm. Off-season: closed Su. The **Yatra Tourist Office,** on Haridwar Rd., past the post office, is an authority on trips to the northern pilgrimage sites. Open M-Sa 10am-5pm.

Budget Travel: Several agencies line Lakshmanjhula Rd., north of the dry river bed, on the way to Ramjhula. **Step Himalayan Adventures** (☎432581) organizes treks and rafting trips, offers free advice for those planning their own trips, and rents equipment. **Garhwal Himalayan Explorations Pvt. Ltd.** (☎433478; fax 431654), opposite Union Bank of India, Kailash Gate, is a group of trained adventure sports buffs offering the most professional and reliable service in the area.

Currency Exchange: State Bank of India (☎430114) changes currency at its main Rishikesh office, on the north side of Railway Rd., a 5min. walk from Lakshmanjhula Rd. Open M-F 10am-4pm, Sa 10am-1pm. **Bank of Baroda,** 74 Dehradun Rd. (☎430653), changes traveler's checks in US$ and UK£. Open M-F 10am-2pm, Sa 10am-noon.

Market: Main Bazaar in Rishikesh, toward the river from the post office. There's a **didgeridoo** shop near the State Bank of India, with Hare Krishna tapes, ceramic *lingas,* and other indispensable souvenirs. Henna girls will paint you up in Lakshmanjhula. You can buy yoga books and ayurvedic herbs in Ramjhula and Swargashram.

Police: Main Rishikesh Office, Dehradun Rd. (☎430100). There's another branch (☎430228) on the south end of Lakshmanjhula. Both are open 24hr.

Pharmacy: Asha Medical Agencies (☎432696), opposite the Government General Hospital, is open 24hr.

Hospital: Government General Hospital (☎430402) and **Ladies' Hospital,** in the same building on Dehradun Rd., are clean, well-staffed, and open 24hr.

Internet: Step Himalayan Adventures (see above). Rs2 per min. **Blue Hill Travel** (☎433836), Swargashram. Rs100 per hr. Open 5am-11pm.

Post Office: Main office (☎430340), in the center of town east of Lakshmanjhula Rd., next to the big Hotel Basera. **Ramjhula branch,** Swargashram. **Lakshmanjhula branch,** a 5min. walk south from the bridge. All open M-Sa 9am-5pm. **Postal Code:** 249201.

Rishikesh

🏠 ACCOMMODATIONS

Bandari Swiss Cottage, 1
Brijwasi Palace, 11
Ganga Guest House, 13
Green Hotel, 10
High Bank Peasant's Cottage, 2
Yoga Niketan Guest House, 4

🏠 ASHRAMS

Omkarananda Ganga Sadan, 5
Vanprastha Ashram, 8
Ved Niketan, 9
Yoga Niketan, 3
Yoga Study Centre, 16

🍴 FOOD

Amrita, 12
Chotiwala & Chotiwala, 7
Ganga Durshan, 15
Ganga View Restaurant, 14
Madras Café, 6

UTTAR PRADESH

📷 ACCOMMODATIONS

Searchers for the inner light may want to stay in an ashram around Ramjhula. The less spiritually inclined will find their best options in Lakshmanjhula on the eastern bank of the Ganga. Only those needing an early getaway should stay in the loud and congested center of Rishikesh near the railway station and bus stand.

HOTELS AND GUEST HOUSES

Most hotels in Rishikesh offer yoga and music lessons upon request. Check-out time is noon unless otherwise noted.

- **High Bank Peasant's Cottage** (☎431167). From Ramjhula (west side), head toward Lakshmanjhula. Take Bypass Rd., which branches left; 50m later, turn right at the sign. Large, clean rooms with attached baths, valley views, and a lovely flower garden, perfect for a quiet retreat from the otherwise chaotic spiritual town. Doubles Rs490.

- **Brijwasi Palace** (☎435181 or 435918), behind Gita Bhavan, in Swargashram. Laundry, yoga classes (Rs100), and massages (Rs150 per hr.) to go along with clean rooms and bathrooms. Singles Rs125-225; doubles Rs250-300.

- **Green Hotel** (☎431242), 1 block from the Brijwasi Palace. Well-run place sails in seas of green. Immaculate rooms, seat toilets, hot showers, and a good attached restaurant. Yoga classes Rs45 per session (8-9:30am) in winter. Singles Rs100-150; doubles Rs200-1000. Internet access Rs2 per min.

Yoga Niketan Guest House, Muni-ki-Reti, before the taxi stand. Has a well-groomed garden and steps leading down to the Ganga. Modern, clean, spacious rooms have high-powered fans, white tile floors, seat toilets, and hot water. Convenient location near the Ramjhula bridge ensures easy access to Rishikesh proper and Swargashram. Free yoga and meditation classes at the nearby Yoga Niketan Ashram. For 3 meals at the ashram add Rs50. Singles Rs200; doubles Rs300.

Bhandari Swiss Cottage (☎ 432676), just after High Bank. Small rooms offer valley views, seclusion, and a lovely flower garden. Common bath with cold shower and squat toilets. Balconies for contemplating the long hike back to town. Singles Rs100-110; doubles Rs150-200.

ASHRAMS AND YOGA

No matter which yoga position you have managed to twist yourself into, an ashram is never far from sight in Rishikesh. Most Westerners head to Swangashram for ashram stays, which are often combined with yoga and meditation classes. Staying in an ashram is not like bunking up in a hotel—the meditative atmosphere comes with a series of rules that you have to follow. These generally include: no meat, no eggs, no smelly food, no alcohol, no tobacco, no drugs, and no noise. Most demand daily bathing (always a good plan), request that menstruating women stay out of the ashram centers, and have strict curfews. Some are set up for pilgrims and Hindu worshippers and do not allow foreigners; most ashrams in the Ramjhula and Swargashram area, however, are very welcoming.

Ved Niketan (☎ 430278), at the south end of Ramjhula's east bank. Caged deities line the entrance to this yellow and orange ashram. The main guru, now 94, still lives here, but others do the teaching. Day-long yoga (with donation) includes 7-8:30am meditation, 9-10:30am lecture (except in June), and 6:30-8:30pm yoga. Gates lock at 10pm. There are 150 rooms including singles and doubles (with bath) and for those in search of their inner selves, 108 underground "cave" rooms with only floor mattresses. STD/ISD facilities offered. Payment by donation.

Yoga Niketan (☎ 430227), in the tranquil hills over Ramjhula. 15-night min. stay includes 3 meals, 2 yoga classes, and 2 meditation classes per day. Visible security force ensures compliance with the rules at this yoga boot camp. Doubles for married

---

INSTANT KARMA When the Beatles came to Rishikesh to study Transcendental Meditation in February 1968, it was the culmination of several years of Western pop's infatuation with the Mysterious East. George Harrison-inspired sitar licks had been turning up in an increasing number of inappropriate places for several years, and the Beatles had already attended lectures by the Maharishi Mahesh Yogi during 1967. They recorded tracks for "The Inner Light," one of their most Indian-sounding songs, just before heading out for the Himalayan foothills.

In Rishikesh, George, John, Paul, and Ringo embraced the typical ashram experience—they eased off on the drugs, meditated, and mostly just hung out with other Westerners (including Mia and Prudence Farrow, the Beach Boys' Mike Love, and 60s pop anomaly, Donovan). They also wrote songs. Most of the "White Album," and much of what later became *Abbey Road* was written during the group's stay in Rishikesh. The most famous of these is "Dear Prudence," an entreaty to the latter Farrow to come out and join in the meditative fun: "The sun is up, the sky is blue/ It's beautiful and so are you/ Dear Prudence, won't you come out to play?"

Eventually, though, the blue skies clouded, and the Beatles became disillusioned with the Maharishi and his vegetarian diet. Less than a month after they left Rishikesh, John Lennon and Paul McCartney announced they'd ended their relationship with the guru. Some of the bitterness they felt come through in the thinly veiled lyrics of a John Lennon song that appears on the second disc of the White Album: "Sexy Sadie, what have you done? You made a fool of everyone...."

couples only; otherwise, buildings are single-sex. Squat toilets, no showers. Kitchen space in all rooms. Guests are expected to help with weekly cleaning. Curfew 9:30pm. Office open 8:30am-noon and 2-5pm. Rs200 per day.

Omkarananda Ganga Sadan (☎ 431473 or 430763), west side of Ramjhula, not to be mistaken for the Omarkananda Ashrani opposite the GMVN office, which takes no foreigners. Big, sterile-looking building just south of the taxi/rickshaw stand. One of the swankiest ashrams in town—clean, dazzling white rooms and bathrooms (some attached, all with squat toilets). Try for a river view. Yoga instruction Rs220 per week with one lecture/class each evening. 3-night min. stay. Breakfast (Rs20-25). Open Nov.-Mar. 4:30-6:30pm, Apr.-Oct. 8:30am-10:30pm. Rooms Rs65-110.

Yoga Study Centre (☎ 433253), at the far south end of Lakshmanjhula Rd., on the river side of the road, practically outside of town. Well-known place to learn *iyengar yoga,* though it lacks the community feeling of the ashrams. Three classes per day on alternating days. General yoga classes M-Sa 6:30-8am. Lodging can be arranged Apr.-Aug. and Oct.-Jan. Pay on a donation basis.

Vanprastha Ashram (☎ 430811; fax 433125), just before Ved Niketan. Spacious and well-lit flats surround a large and well-maintained garden. All rooms have attached bath and kitchen, sofas, and a double bed. Gas and utensils available Rs25 per day. 3-day min. stay. Open to foreigners Nov.-Mar. Book in advance from Calcutta (☎ (033) 238 6701). Singles Rs150; suites Rs500.

◖◗ FOOD

Restaurants in Rishikesh don't serve meat or booze. They do serve delicious vegetarian *thalis,* though, so just shut up and *dahl* with it.

Chotiwala and Chotiwala Restaurant (☎ 430070), in east Ramjhula near the bridge; impossible to miss, especially with the crowds that flock about the place. The two parts, side by side, were supposedly divided by two brothers. Both serve similar, standard Indian food. *Thali* Rs25-50. Open daily 7am-11pm.

Ganga View Restaurant, opposite Bombay Kshetra in Lakshmanjhula. This is where the foreign tourists staying in the Kshetra come together to enjoy good conversation, the Ganga view, and comfy rattan chairs. Peanut butter toast with honey Rs10; spaghetti Rs30; porridge with bananas, raisins, and coconut Rs20. Open daily 7am-9pm.

Ganga Darshan, next to Ganga View, closer to the bridge. Cheap *thalis* (Rs15-20), and some special dishes (like "cheese chow mein") provide respite from the spice of most Indian food. *Dosas* Rs10-18. Balcony tables are great, but the service out there is slower. Open daily 5am-8:30pm. In Winter: 5am-8pm.

Amrita, in front of Hotel Rajdeep. Outstanding fresh-baked raisin bread, jars of pure honey, cheddar cheese, lasagna with homemade noodles (Rs50), banana pancakes (Rs25), and pizza (Rs85). Great ambience inside or on the rooftop.

Madras Cafe, in the Ramjhula rickshaw stand area. Indian food, California-style—emphasis on sprouts and whole wheat. Himalayan Health *Pullao,* with sprouts, curd, and ayurvedic herbs Rs40; hot lemon-ginger-honey tea Rs15. Open daily 6:30am-10:30pm. Off-season: 8am-9pm.

◉ ♫ SIGHTS AND ENTERTAINMENT

Triveni Ghat, on the south end of Rishikesh, is believed to be the place where the Yamuna, Ganga, and Saraswati rivers meet, making it the most sacred spot in Rishikesh. The **arati** ceremony takes place here every evening at sundown. This is also a popular site at which to make river offerings at dawn. An ancient **Lakshman Temple** is on the west bank. The 13-story **Swarga Niwas** ashram and cultural center has great views from the top. Their exhibits include images and statues of all the major Hindu deities. **Boats** head across the Ganga at Ramjhula, below Sivananda Ashram (Rs10). Another way to go where everything flows is to **shoot the rapids** along the

Ganga. Companies toward the northern end of Rishikesh, such as Step Himalayan Adventures (☎432581), run 15km, 90-minute rafting trips through four "good" and two small rapids. (Sept.-May Rs500-900, depending on group size; transportation included.) Another good place is GMVN, which provides accommodations at its rafting camp in Kaudiyalaj, north of Rishikesh. (Rooms Rs350; tents Rs100. Rafting trips Sept.-May: 3-4hr., Rs400 per person; all-day trip Rs1100.)

Not content with mere meditation and vegetation, many visitors also take **music lessons. Sivananda Ramesh Music School** (left at the sign on the far side of the bridge on Lakshmanjhula Rd., just after Tehri Rd.) will teach you to make the didgeridoo drone, the tabla ring, or the sitar gently weep. Only donations are accepted. **Hindi lessons** are offered by Mr. Tilak Raj at Ramjhula, Swargashram, behind the Ganga General Store. (Enquiries daily 9-10am. 10-day advanced course Rs1000, includes 1hr. classes; 5-day beginner course Rs500.) Settle in for a **massage** at the well-advertised Baba Health and Massage Centre in Rishikesh, 100m east of Hotel Shivlok. You can enjoy an ayurvedic, Swedish, Thai, or "general" full-body massage (they even massage your ears) in a dark, cool room complete with spacey music. (☎433339. Open daily 7am-10pm. Rs150 per session.) They also teach massage in a month-long course with 4 classes a day (Rs6000, lodging included). Complete ayurvedic treatment for general physical and mental well-being is offered for a minimum of a week (Rs3000 per week, lodging included).

DAYTRIPS FROM RISHIKESH

KUNJAPURI. Wait until the sun is up and the sky is blue before heading to the temple of Kunjapuri, on top of a nearby mountain. From here you can see the whole region, including Haridwar and the snow-capped Himalayas. The temple itself is disappointingly modern and small, though the priest is friendly to visitors. To get there, take a bus headed for **Tehri** from the Yatra Bus Stand; tell the driver you want to get off at Hindolakhal (1hr., Rs15). From there, it's an hour's walk up the mountain along a paved road and up a surreal, narrow staircase at the top. Hop on a bus coming from Gangotri or Yamnotri to get back (last bus around 7 or 8pm).

NEEL KANTH MAHADEV. Another destination for a day's hike is the temple at Neel Kanth Mahadev, a place so popular with pilgrims bearing milk, *ghee*, and Ganga water that the *linga* has been eroded so that it is now just a few inches high. The jungle trail along the way, inhabited by wild elephants, is what really makes the hike worthwhile. Go early (5am) since it's a four- to five-hour climb with no stops, and the temple is more likely to be peaceful early in the day. Jeeps leave for the trailhead from the Laksmanjhula and Ramjhula taxi stands (12km; Rs40 per person, round-trip Rs70). Regular jeeps return to Rishikesh.

MANSA DEVI. About 10km from Rishikesh is the Mansa Devi, a temple that provides wall-less shelter for those seeking some distance from town. Camp for free and in relative isolation. Hindu pilgrims flood the site between the 7th and 10th of every month (especially Mar., Sept., and Oct.) for Navratri. Jeeps from the Yatra Bus Stand go to Mansa Devi (Rs25 per seat).

GLASSHOUSE ON THE GANGES. Twenty-three kilometers outside Rishikesh, on the road to Byasi, the Glasshouse on the Ganges is run by the Neemrana Hotels chain. Set in litchi orchards that were once part of the maharaja's garden, the Glasshouse overlooks the Ganga as it shoots down toward the plains. The resort is a cluster of four cottages with 12 luxurious rooms furnished in teak. The gardens and silver sand beach are home to rare birds and butterflies. (☎(011) 4616145, 4618962; fax (011) 4621112; email sales@neemrana.com; www.neemrana.com. Lunch and dinner Rs200 per person. Doubles Rs1500-Rs2500. Book in advance; order meals on arrival.)

NORTHERN PILGRIMAGES AND TREKS

Gods, sadhus, and saints have been coming to meditate among the snow-capped mountains of Garhwal and Kumaon since time immemorial. Until recently, just getting here was enough to test a person's faith—as recently as the 1960s, the northern pilgrimage sites could only be reached by foot from the plains. But new roads have made them more accessible, and a steady stream of package-tour pilgrims has made the peaceful isolation of the sites a distant memory. For true believers, the pilgrimage experience is suffused with a holiness that diesel, mud, and litter-strewn streets cannot spoil.

The temples at the pilgrimage sights are open from May to November, though it is dangerous to go during the monsoons, as frequent landslides and heavy rains often render the roads impassable. Rattling, non-A/C local buses are the only things that make the journey up the narrow roads from Rishikesh or Uttarkashi, so be ready to kiss comfort goodbye. Between pilgrimage sites and neighboring towns in the hills, you will have to either book a package tour or hire a taxi from one of the major cities (Rs2000 per day) since there is no public transport. Most *dharamsalas* do not welcome foreigners—you'd be well advised to book a rest house room at least a month in advance.

UTTARKASHI उत्तरकाशी ☎ 01374

This busy town on the banks of the Bhagirathi River is the administrative center of the Uttarkashi District, as well as the last place to stock up on supplies or catch a Hindi movie before you head out for a trek. Uttarkashi is also a major transportation hub for the pilgrimage sites to the north. The **tourist office** at the bus stand provides little help for trekking. Instead, try **Mt. Support Trekking**, BD Nautial Bhawan, Bhatwari Rd. (☎2419), about 10 minutes past the bus stand along Gangotri Rd., or the professional **Nehru Mountaineering Institute,** 5km out of town (ask anyone for directions). Mt. Support Trekking also **exchanges currency** for a hefty charge. (Open M-Sa 9am-7pm.) Buses head to: **Barkot** (for Yamnotri, in-season only, Rs45); **Bhatwari** (for treks to Sahasratal and Kedarnath, 1hr., Rs14); **Gangotri** (Rs50); **Gaurikund** (12hr., Rs97-110); **Rishikesh** (8hr., Rs65); and **Sayana Chatti** (for Dodital trek, Rs14). Morning **taxis** to Rishikesh wait at the bus stand. The 24-hour emergency **District Hospital** is midway between Gangotri Rd. and the river, near the post office. The **police roost** is on Gangotri Rd., 15 minutes from the bus station, on the right.

The **Bhandari Hotel** at the bus stand is a good place to spend the night before an early morning departure; there's a restaurant inside. (☎2203. Doubles Rs600. Off-season: Rs300.) Another option is **Meghdoot**, Main Market. (☎2278. May-June and Sept.: singles Rs100; doubles Rs180. Oct.-Apr. and July: Rs50/90). **GMVN** has clean rooms with hot water and six-bed dorms. (☎2271. Dorms Rs60; doubles Rs200-550. Off-season: Rs60/100-300; May, June, and Sept. book one month in advance.)

WHAT'S YOUR POISON? Hashish and tobacco, smoked through a *chillum*, are a big part of the daily intake of most sadhus, but the really hip holy men try something else. A krait (an extremely poisonous snake) is rolled up between two unbaked *rotis* with its tail sticking out, and then shoved into the fire. When the *rotis* are fully baked, the sadhu removes the deadly sandwich from the fire and pulls at the snake's tail, ripping off the skin and bones. Then, preparing himself, he puts a jug of water by his side, takes two to three bites of the snake, and immediately goes into a coma. Every eight to ten hours the sadhu wakes up to drink some water and take another bite, sending himself back into a poisoned stupor. The whole process lasts three to four days. **Warning: requires 30 years of practice—don't try this at home, or anywhere else!**

YAMNOTRI यमनोत्री

The source of the Yamuna River and the first stop on the Garhwal pilgrimage circuit, Yamnotri attracts 1500 pilgrims every day during the tourist season. The town essentially consists of a **temple** devoted to the goddess Yamuna and the 12 to 15 concrete buildings and numerous *dhabas* that surround it. The original temple was built by Rani Gularia of Jaipur during the 19th century but was soon worn down by heavy snowfall. The elements continue to erode away at the temple that took its place, making it essential to rebuild the structure every few years. The temple's architecture is not special—just a slapdash construction with dressed-up concrete walls and a corrugated metal roof. It is open from May to November, after which the image is carried to Kharsoli, a village opposite Janki Chatti.

Yamnotri is accessible only by a 14km trek from the town of **Hanuman Chatti** (2134m), which is well-connected by **buses** from Dehra Dun (163km) and Rishikesh (209km). The path angles gently upward for 8km to Janki Chatti (2676m), then turns steeply uphill until it reaches Yamnotri (3235m). From here, the source of the sacred river is an arduous 1km trek away, so most pilgrims pray at the temple itself. Start early in the morning—there is no shade for the first 10km out of Hanuman Chatti, and by then the higher altitudes and steep path will drain any energy you have left. **Horses** with guides can be rented for the 14km trek (Rs200-250). The path is lined with *chai* stalls and cold drink stands.

All major services, including **accommodations** are available at Janki Chatti. The closest **hospital, post office,** and **communications** system (a wireless only for emergencies) are at Janki Chatti. A seasonal **police station** is set up every year at Yamnotri. There are **GMVN lodges** at Sayana Chatti, 6km before Hanuman Chatti (Apr.-Nov.: Rs300; off-season: Rs150); Hanuman Chatti (dorm beds Rs100; rooms Rs500); and Janki Chatti (dorm beds Rs100; rooms Rs300-500). Reservations can be made through the Rishikesh GMVN office. During the pilgrimage season, many of these accommodations are fully booked for package tours operated by GMVN; you might have to stay overnight at **Barkot,** 40km south, and take early morning transport to Hanuman Chatti. There are also several private hotels in Janki Chatti.

GANGOTRI गंगोत्री

After Bhatwari, the road from Uttarkashi narrows and the surrounding mountains become more severe until the shimmering slopes of **Mt. Sudarshan** (6500m) finally come into view, towering above the small town of Gangotri. At an altitude of 3140m, Gangotri (sometimes called Bhagirathi), 98km northeast of Uttarkashi, is a major center for sadhus from all over India. It is here where the goddess Ganga made her descent from heaven (see **Ganga Comes to Earth,** p. 149) and where Raja Bhagiratha worshipped Shiva at the sacred stone Bhagiratha Shilla. The present **temple,** near Bhagiratha's stone, was built by the Gorkha commander Amar Singh Thapa in the early 18th century as a replacement for an older structure. The temple is open only from May to November because of heavy winter snowfall. Steps lead down to the *ghat,* where pilgrims bathe. In the river sits a submerged rock that is considered a *linga,* marking the place where Shiva sat while the Ganga descended and cushioned her fall with his hair. A small bridge from the bus stand arches over to Gaurikund, where the Bhagirathi (yes, the river is called Bhagirathi in these parts) gushes out of the rock into a beautiful pool. **Gaumukh** (Cow's Mouth), an easy 17km trek from Gangotri, is the spot where the Bhagirathi emerges from the Gangotri glacier; there are excellent views of the peaks along the way. **Kedartal,** a spectacular lake with the Thalaysagar peak in the background, is 18km from Gangotri. The trek is very difficult but is well worth the effort. Hire a guide from Gangotri (Rs300 per day) and carry plenty of supplies since there is nothing but views available along the way.

To get to Gangotri, take a **bus** or a **shared taxi** from Uttarkashi (see p. 147). The main bridge is next to Dev Ghat, where the Bhagirathi and the **Kedar Ganga** meet. In most accommodations, rooms are unpainted, the plaster is crumbling, and beds are dirty—bring a sleeping bag. Accommodations across the river from the temple

UTTAR PRADESH

GANGA COMES TO EARTH

Times were tough for King Bhagiratha—the world was completely dry and 60,000 of his ancestors had been burned to a crisp by a disgruntled sage. The King wanted to perform a ceremony to give their souls peace, but to do it, he needed holy water, and the parched planet presented no obvious options. A devout man, Bhagiratha took up long ascetic rituals that eventually caught the attention of Brahma, who decided to help him out. Brahma asked the goddess Ganga, who was in the heavens, to descend to earth. She was reluctant, though, since her impact upon landing would pound the earth to bits. Bhagiratha continued to practice austerities for many more years until Shiva, Lord of Ascetics (if not of Punctuality), finally arrived to soften Ganga's landing. He provided his strands of matted hair as a cushion for Ganga, who then consented to descend. A cascade of water touched the ground high up in the Himalayas and flowed down in several streams, directed by Shiva's locks (watch for the Ganga flowing through his hair in paintings). In gratitude, King Bhagiratha prayed to Ganga at Gangotri, the source of one such stream. This river is called Bhagirathi to honor the pious man who saved the world from drought and gave India her great water artery, the Ganga. Today these streams flow together as they approach the plains and emerge at Haridwar.

are quieter. **Manisha Cottage,** near the bus stand, has small doubles (Rs200-450). The **GMVN Guest House,** next to Gaurikund is spacious and clean, with a garden and a quality restaurant. (Dorm beds Rs100; rooms Rs300-600.) Most ashrams in Gangotri do not accept foreign guests, and there are few tourist services available here. A temporary **police station, post office,** and **health center** are open during the pilgrimage season.

KEDARNATH केदारनाथ

One of the 12 *jyotirlingas* in India, Kedarnath is also one of Shiva's chosen abodes. The Kedarnath **temple** was constructed thousands of years ago when the Pandavas, the heroic brothers of the *Mahabharata*, came here to serve their penance to Shiva. Viewing the Pandavas as sinners for having killed their own kin in battle, Shiva disguised himself as a bull to escape their notice. When the Pandavas discovered the ruse, Shiva turned to stone and tried to escape into the ground. But as his front half vanished, Bhima, one of the Pandavas, managed to catch Shiva's rocky rear end. Pleased with the Pandavas' diligence, Shiva appeared in his true form and forgave them. The back half of that stone form is now worshiped at Kedarnath. Shiva's front half broke off and reemerged in Nepal, where it is venerated at the **Pashupati Temple** (see p. 746). Other parts of Shiva turned up at Tungnath (arm), Rudrandath (face), Madhyamaheshwar (navel), and Kapleshwar (locks); together, they form the **Panch Kedar** (Five Fields) pilgrimage circuit.

Kedarnath remains open from May until late October and serves as the launching pad for many beautiful treks. **Buses** take pilgrims as far as Gaurikund, 216km from Rishikesh (Rs85). From there, it's a steep 14km, four- to six-hour trek. **Horses** are also available for hire (Rs250). Standard hotel rates are Rs100 for a single and Rs200 for a double in season. **GMVN** has two guest houses in Kedarnath, one immediately on your left as you approach the town (☎6210) and a second across the river and below the hillside (☎6228). Many ashrams will not accept foreigners, but the **Bharat Seva Ashram** and the **Temple Committee** cave in on occasion.

BADRINATH बद्रिनाथ ☎ 01381

The temple town of Badrinath (3133m) is the northernmost compass-point (*dham*) in India's sacred geography. Once the abode of Lord Vishnu, it is the most famous of Garhwal's Hindu pilgrimage sites, attracting the faithful from all across India during its summer season (May-Nov.). Badrinath sits alongside the Alaknanda River, 297km from Rishikesh, not far from the Tibetan border, and it serves as one of the Ganga's 12 water channels. It's accessibility by road attracts growing numbers of pilgrims and tourists every year, who forego the austerity of a walking pilgrimage (once required) in favor of a harrowing bus ride. Badrinath can be reached by **bus** from Rishikesh via Srinagar, Rudraprayag, and Joshimath (Rs90). Buses also come here directly from Kedarnath (Rs40).

The colorful Badrinath **temple** has a long main entrance gate (the Singh Dwara) that worshippers must pass through for *darshan* of the meter-high Badrivishal image inside. Probably a Buddhist temple in ancient times, the current temple is an unusual mixture of Buddhist and Hindu styles. Before visiting the temple, worshippers bathe in the **Tapt Kund** hot spring, often in preparation for a dip into the icy waters of the Alaknanda. Very basic **accommodations** are available at numerous *dharamsalas*, at the **Garhwal Hotel,** or at the GVMN hotel.

AULI औली

Skiing? In India? Whatever next? Home to 20km of seasonal (Jan.-Mar.) ski slopes, Auli has been the winter sports capital of UP since the 1970s, when the government decided that ski resorts were more fun than paramilitary training camps. **Equipment** can be rented (half-day Rs175, full-day Rs225) at the GMVN. The spectacular scenery keeps Auli open in the summer for **cable car rides** up from Joshimath (3km). There is a **GMVN lodge** in Auli. (Apr.-Nov. dorm beds Rs60; rooms Rs750-900. Nov.-Apr. Rs100/1200-1400.) Accommodation is also available at Joshimath from where you can take the ski lift to Auli.

VALLEY OF FLOWERS फूलों की घाटी

This alpine valley hidden high in the Himalayas has been attracting pilgrims and nature lovers ever since it was "discovered" by Frank Smith in 1937. Ten kilometers long, 2km wide, and enclosed by snow-capped peaks, the valley is cut in two by the Pushpawati River. Snow covers the valley floor from November to late May, when the area is inaccessible to visitors. In late May, the snow begins to melt, and the first flowers start to bloom in early June. The valley is usually opened to visitors in late June. There are over 500 species of flowers in the valley; many of them, such as the Himalayan blue poppy, are extremely rare. When the valley was first explored in the late 1930s, the plant species count was 5000. The serious ecological decline of the area has prompted the government to declare it a National Park; camping and cooking are prohibited. Visitors must trek in for the day and sleep at **Ghanghria,** 4km away, either in a government rest house or in one of the private lodges. Along the trail leading away from the valley is **Hemkund Sahib,** the Sikh *gurudwara* where Guru Gobind Singh had meditated in a previous life. Now a major Sikh pilgrimage site, the *gurudwara* has 1000 beds available for accommodation. From Rishikesh, take a **bus** to Joshimath (6am, 10hr., Rs100). Govindghat is 19km farther by road (buses leave every 30min., Rs10). From there, you have to trek or ride a mule to Ghanghria (13km). To reserve a bed in the dormitory or a room at the tourist rest house, contact the **GMVN Yatra Pilgrimage Tours and Accommodations Office** in Kailash Gate, Rishikesh (☎431783).

CORBETT NATIONAL PARK कोरबट

Corbett was India's first national park, founded in 1936 and named for James Corbett (1875-1955), a British gentleman renowned for his ability to kill tigers and other large animals with a shotgun. Corbett gave up killing tigers for kicks during the 1920s, but was still called upon to shoot tigers and leopards from time to time when they threatened human lives. He became famous for his photographs of tigers and for the books he wrote, including *The Man-Eaters of Kumaon.*

In 1973, the Indian government, with support from the World Wildlife Fund, launched "Project Tiger" (see p. 367) in an effort to save the country's dwindling population of tigers. The 1319 sq. km Corbett Tiger Reserve, comprised of the national park and the adjoining Sonandi Wildlife Sanctuary and Reserve Forest, was the first target area of this ambitious preservation project. There are currently 138 tigers in the reserve. Sightings of the Bengali beasts can come several times a day, but, even if you don't catch a glimpse of the largest cats on earth, Corbett's other wildlife will make sure you don't leave entirely disappointed. Highlights include the endangered gharial crocodile, herds of wild elephant, leopards, deer, over 500 species of birds, and more monkeys than you can shake a banana at. The park's landscape, particularly around Dhikala, is as much a treasure as its wildlife.

> **! WARNING.** The animals here have enough problems already without you throwing things at them. Don't throw burning cigarettes around, don't feed the animals, and keep noise at a minimum. For your own safety (attacks by tigers are not unheard of), never walk outside the camp perimeter, and be careful at night.

GETTING THERE AND GETTING AROUND

The various zones of the park are accessed via the town of **Ramnagar,** reachable from Delhi by **bus** (12 per day, 6am-9pm, 7hr., Rs90). Buses to **Delhi** (8:30am-8pm) and **Nainital** (2:30am and noon, 4hr.) leave from the government bus stand near the park office. If your next stop is **Ranikhet,** get off the bus at Dhangarhi and wait by the side of the road for buses headed north (last bus 2pm, 4hr., Rs40). Private buses depart from below the bazaar to **Nainital** (4 per day, 6am-1pm, 2½hr.). From Ramnagar run to: **Delhi** (9:30pm, return 11pm; 6½hr.; Rs117) and **Varanasi** (9:15pm, 21hr., Rs200). You can hire **jeeps** from in front of the Park Office for Rs4.50-6.50 per km. Most have broken mileage counters, which might make things interesting when you come to pay.

ORIENTATION AND PRACTICAL INFORMATION

Corbett has five **zones** accessible to tourists. These zones are exclusive of each other, which means that you have to exit the park and pay another hefty fee to enter another zone. **Dhikala** is the most popular, offering a range of accommodations, two restaurants, film screening facilities, and a library. The other four zones—Bijrani, Jhirna, Lohachavr, and Halduparao—offer greater solitude but fewer services. **Lohachavr** is the best place for birding; **Bijrani,** most frequented by jeeps on daytrips, contains the park's most diverse vegetation; **Jhirna** is an exceptionally beautiful area of the park; those looking for a more rugged experience and close encounters with wild elephants should head to **Halduparao.** Jhirna is accessible to visitors year-round, but the rest of the park closes during the monsoon (mid-June to mid-Nov.). The wildlife viewing is better during the summer (Mar.-June) than the winter (Nov.-Mar.).

Each zone has its own gated park entrance. **Dhangarhi Gate,** 16km north of Ramnagar, is the entrance to Dhikala. (Open 6am-6pm; in winter 7am-5pm. No entry after dark.) Here, you have to cough up the park entry fees. (Rs350 for 3 days plus Rs130 for your vehicle.) Before leaving Dhikala, all visitors must obtain a free **clearance certificate,** which should be turned in at Dhangarhi upon leaving.

Visitors must stop at the **Park Office,** opposite the Ramnagar bus stand, to secure a permit and to reserve and pay for accommodation within the park. (☎(05975) 51489. Open daily 8:30am-1pm and 3-5pm.) An all-inclusive package, including transport to and from the park and a 4-hour safari, costs around Rs1200. Show up at 8:30am at the office and wait for other visitors to share the cost. Ramnagar is your last chance to stock up on peanuts and insect repellent before trekking off into the great unknown. There is nowhere to change money here.

ACCOMMODATIONS AND FOOD

IN RAMNAGAR. Accommodations outside the park skyrocket in price and involve daily transport into the park. If you need to spend the night in Ramnagar for some reason, try the **Banbari Hotel** in Tesil Chowk (☎(05945) 51277), which has basic doubles with attached bath (Rs150) and decent meals. The **Tourist Rest House**

UTTAR PRADESH

(☎85225), next to the park office, has dorm beds (Rs60) and doubles (Rs320-420), but you'll have to put up with the noise from the gas and bus stations next door. For Indian, Chinese, and continental cuisine, head to **Govind Restaurant,** one block past the bus station from the rest house. The owner is very friendly, and the food is delicious. (Banana pancakes Rs25; fruit *lassis* Rs20. Open daily 8am-10pm.) The big package-tour oasis, **Tiger Camp,** 7km from Dhangari Gate toward Ramnagar, has two-person tents with mattresses and clean, warm blankets. (☎86088 or 87901; fax 85088. Tents Rs600.)

IN THE PARK. All lodgings within the park itself must be reserved through the Park Office in Ramnagar (see above). Log-hut dorms, **tourist "hutments"** (3 beds), and **cabins** (2 or 3 beds) are available in Dhikala. The **log hut,** just one step away from the great outdoors, has austere bunks, stacked three-high and 12 to a room, and lockers (bring your own lock). Squat toilets and showers are in a separate building. Tourist hutments and cabins have attached bathrooms. (Check-out 11am. Log hut bunk Rs100, bedding Rs25; tourist hutment Rs500; cabin Rs900.) **Rest houses** outside Dhikala tend to have nothing much to offer except for good old-fashioned peace and quiet. Old British hunting lodges, these places all come complete with fireplaces, carpets, and attached bathrooms. Cooking utensils and firewood are provided, but other essentials need to be brought from Ramnagar. (Lodges Rs300-900.) Visitors wishing to extend their stay are often told to wait until the evening to see whether space is available. This gives rise to the possibility of being stuck in Dhikala without accommodation, in which case you will have to hire a jeep out (if one is even available) before the night curfew. Calling in advance is especially important if you want to stay in the hutments or cabins. There are no reservations for the log hut, so if there is no space the first night, you are almost guaranteed a bed the next.

Dhikala has the only food available inside the park. Its two restaurants both serve all the usual items of international high cuisine for breakfast, lunch, and dinner. The government-run **KMVN Restaurant** is more expensive, with indoor seating. (Veg. *korma* Rs36. Open 7:30am-9:30pm.) At the other end of the camp, the privately-owned **canteen** serves pretty much the same menu for less; it's next to a pleasant pagoda, from which you can look down on the plains while enjoying your vegetable curry. (Open daily 5am-2pm and 4-10pm.) No alcohol is allowed, and only vegetarian food is sold inside the park. A small **kiosk** at Dhangarhi Gate sells bottled water (Rs15) and munchies. Everything is more expensive inside the park, so stock up before you get here.

MAN BITES CAT Your mahout in Dhikala may be none other than Subradar Ali, the man that one man-eater of Kumaon will remember as the one who bit back. While gathering grass for his elephant Gunti on Valentine's Day, 1984, Subradar was attacked from behind by a tiger named Sheroo. The tiger leapt nearly 6m for his target, Subradar's head. As he was being dragged away by the neck, Subradar, taking a lesson from his striped assailant, began biting back. Forcing open the jaws of the beast, he yanked on Sheroo's tongue. This put an end to the dragging, and Sheroo pinned him squarely. Another guide appeared on the scene, distracting the tiger long enough for Subradar to roll down a nearby stream bank. With bleeding gashes on his head and arm, Subradar called his elephant to come and kneel so he could crawl on top. Gunti took him the 3km to Dhikala and, not wanting to disturb his family away in Ramnagar, Subradar cleaned his wounds and changed his clothes himself. Both Rajiv and Indira Gandhi later visited him in the hospital. Rajiv asked if he wanted fame and fortune—the event has since been the subject of several movies—but Subradar preferred to return to the elephants and tigers of Corbett. In fact, he views the whole experience as having bolstered his confidence, and he admits with a smile that he is now even more excited to find the tigers than the tourists he guides. His aggressive Valentine's date, Sheroo, has not been seen for years.

🏔 THE PARK

There *are* ways to get down and dirty in Corbett without breaking any rules. By far the best option is an **elephant ride.** For Rs100, visitors get bumped, shrugged, and shouldered for two hours across the prairie and through the jungle. This is the best way to try to see a tiger or to come close to wild elephants and other animals. Sign up for a ride at the station office at least a day in advance during the high season. Tours depart at sunrise and sunset, approximately 6am and 4pm in the summer and 7am and 3pm in the winter. Both tour times have their benefits (cooler weather or more sleep, respectively) and sightings are equally likely at either time. From your elephant, marvel at what seems to delight tourists most: yes, those are 3m cannabis plants, acres and acres of them. If you do spot a tiger, your guide will expect a modest "sighting" tip.

You can also hire a **jeep**—up to eight may ride with a guide around the Dhikala Station area. You cover more ground than you would on the elephants and can get all the way out to the reservoir, where the crocodiles play. While the crocs don't normally encroach on the compound, it's best to heed the sign that warns, "NO SWIMMING: Survivors Will Be Prosecuted." Jeeps are not guaranteed from Dhikala, as they operate from Dhangari and the park office in Ramnagar—it is possible (though not likely) to get stuck in Dhikala waiting for a jeep. *(The best times for jeep tours are 5-11am and 4-7pm. Rs500 plus Rs100 for a guide.)*

The only excursion permitted **on foot** outside the camp (and only before sunset) is to the nearby **Gularghati Watchtower.** Free **films** about nature and the park are shown behind the restaurant around 7pm; check the office for schedules. To pack your brain with even more info about what you've seen and heard, visit the small **library** adjacent to the office. *(Open daily 9am-12:30pm and 5:30-8pm; in winter 9am-noon and 5:30-7:30pm.)*

There are a few places where you can experience the natural beauty and wildlife outside the park, including the area of **Sitabani,** which has some excellent bird-watching spots and a decent rest house—ask at the Ramnagar office for details. There is also a small **museum** at Dhangarhi gate, basically just one room filled with bizarre and morbid exhibits (Rs10). Beyond the scale model of the park, several stuffed mammal specimens are displayed with signs documenting how they died, along with some preserved artwork and a collection of animal embryos.

NAINITAL नैनीताल ☎ 05942

When the body of the goddess Sati broke into pieces and fell to earth after her self-immolation (see **Divine Dismemberment,** p. 692), one of her eyes landed here in the hills of what is now Uttar Pradesh, and formed the stunning emerald lake of Nainital. Many lifetimes later, a certain P. Barron of Shahjahanpur, esquire, tilted up with his yacht to found what he called a "pilgrim cottage." Barron was the first of many Brits who came here to enjoy and exploit the area's lakeland beauty. Nainital soon became a popular British hill station and the summer capital of the United Provinces. The town is still one of India's most beloved hilltop hideaways and is the favorite fresh-air bolt-hole of the beleaguered UP masses. High season (May-Jun. and Oct.) brings high prices and crowds and puts smiles on the faces of the town's residents, who make their living from tourism. The beautiful, shimmering, eye-shaped Naini Lake is the center of the town's activity, but Nainital also has outstanding views of the Himalayas in the autumn after the rains have passed.

🏞 GETTING THERE AND GETTING AROUND

Trains: The nearest station is in **Kathgodam.** From here, trains leave for **Delhi** (8:40pm) and return at 11pm.

Buses: Buses arrive at and depart from the lakefront in **Tallital.** Schedules change frequently, so check times when you arrive. To: **Almora** (7 and 8am, 3hr., Rs42); **Bareilly** (4 per day, 1:30pm-6:15pm, 4½hr., Rs66); **Bhowali** (every 30min., 6am-6:30pm, Rs8); **Dehra Dun** (5:30, 6, and 7am; deluxe 4:30 and 8pm; 10hr.; Rs150/188); **Delhi** (7 per day, 6am-7:30pm, 9hr., Rs116); **Kathgodam and Haldwani** (every 15min., 5am-6:30pm, 2hr., Rs30); **Ramnagar** (5:30 and 7pm, 5hr., Rs45); **Ranikhet** (12:30 and 2:30pm, 3hr., Rs37). Tickets to Dehra Dun and Delhi are sold at the travel agencies that line The Mall; many also run deluxe buses to Dehra Dun (Rs300) and Delhi (Rs200). **Bhowali** is the major regional transportation center, and buses leave almost every hour from here for most mountain cities. Buses leave every 30min. from Haldwani to Nainital (6am-7pm). After 7pm, jeeps and taxis are available (Rs30-40 per person).

Local Transportation: Cycle-rickshaws charge Rs4 to drive the length of The Mall. Local **jeeps** and **taxi-vans** are available to go to other places at all times. During the high season, traffic is closed to motor vehicles and cycle-rickshaws from 6-9pm.

■✴🛈 ORIENTATION AND PRACTICAL INFORMATION

The town of Nainital is split into two major parts—**Tallital** in the south and **Mallital** in the north. These are connected by **The Mall,** which runs along the east side of the lake. Buses arrive at Tallital, at the southern tip of the lake. From here, it's a 15-minute lakeside walk to Mallital. The main market is in Mallital. Most hotels and restaurants are on The Mall. The **Flats,** a common area used for football and field hockey, lies between Mallital and the northern part of the lake.

Tourist Office: (☎35337), about two-thirds of the way to Mallital along The Mall. Provides information for the town and region and arranges transport to nearby sights. Open M-Sa 10am-5pm; May-June and Oct. open daily 9am-6pm.

Budget Travel: Several travel agents along The Mall offer similar tours at similar prices. The tourist office also organizes tours. **Parvat Tours-KMVN** (☎35656), toward Mallital on The Mall, before the library, arranges day tours by taxi and bus to nearby resorts and lakes, including Bhimtal, Sat Tal, Hanumangarh (bus Rs100/taxi Rs500), and Mukteshwar (bus Rs150/taxi Rs1100). Most open daily 8am-8pm.

Currency Exchange: State Bank of India (☎35645), in Mallital, just beyond the Flats. Cashes AmEx traveler's checks. Open M-F 10am-2pm, Sa 10am-noon.

Bookstore: Modern Bookstore, on The Mall near the Flats. Open M-Sa 10:30am-9pm, Su 11am-4pm. **Consul Bookstore,** in Mallital opposite Green Restaurant. Open M-Sa 9:30am-8pm.

Market: West of the Flats in Mallital is **Bara Bazaar.** In the western part of the bazaar is a **Tibetan market,** selling fake brand-name clothes and other junk. Open M-Sa 9am-9pm.

Police: Mallital (☎35424) and Tallital (☎35525), in front of the Hotel Mansarovar at the Tallital end of The Mall.

Pharmacy: Indra Pharmacy (☎35139), by the bus stand in Tallital, is well stocked. Open M-Sa 7am-10pm, Su 7am-3pm. Another branch is in Mallital (☎35629), in Bara Bazaar. Open M-Sa 9am-10pm, Su 3-10pm.

Hospital/Medical Services: B. D. Pandey Hospital (☎35012) is near the State Bank of India in Mallital. Open daily 8am-2pm. Dr. D.P. Gangola (☎35039) is a consulting physician at **Indra Pharmacy;** he keeps hours in the Mallital branch (5-8pm) and in Tallital (9am-2pm).

Internet: Cyber Cafe, opposite the Flats, in Mallital, has one computer; connections are slow but reliable. Rs20 for 10 min. Open M-Sa 10am-8pm.

Post Office: The GPO is on the north side of Mallital, a few blocks up from The Mall's extension. There is another branch in Tallital, facing the bus stop. Open 10am-5pm. **Postal Codes:** Mallital 263002, Tallital 263001.

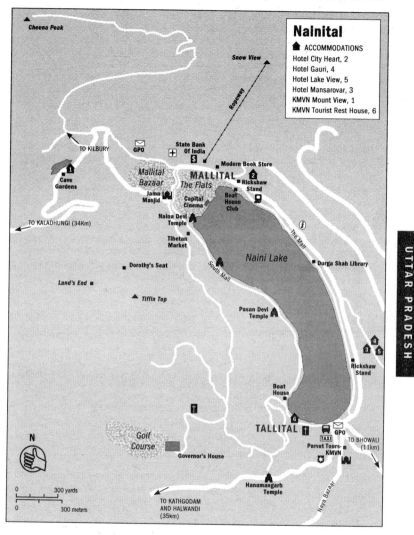

Nainital

🏠 ACCOMMODATIONS
Hotel City Heart, 2
Hotel Gauri, 4
Hotel Lake View, 5
Hotel Mansarovar, 3
KMVN Mount View, 1
KMVN Tourist Rest House, 6

UTTAR PRADESH

ACCOMMODATIONS

Hotel prices in Nainital tend to be higher and are more subject to seasonal changes than anywhere else in Kumaon. Listed prices are peak-season rates, except where noted; expect a drop of anything from 25-75% outside of May, June, and October. With over a hundred hotels to choose from, prices and services vary greatly from place to place. Most establishments along the hotel-crowded Mall are quiet and have beautiful views of the lake, though the air gets quieter and the views get better the farther up the hill you go. Most have 10am check-out, and most will charge extra for hot water if you don't bargain your way out of it.

■ **Hotel Lake View** (☎ 35632; fax 35632; email hotellakeview@hotmail.com), Tallital, behind Hotel Mansarovar. Hidden at the back of Tallital, this friendly hotel is almost per-fect. Mr. and Mrs. Shah treat all their guests like family. Spacious rooms with clean bathrooms and balconies have superb views of the lake. Room service, laundry, TV, and restaurant. Doubles Rs350-550; 4-bed, 2-room suites Rs750.

Hotel City Heart (☎35228), near Mallital, on The Mall opposite the Nainital Club. Spectacular views of the lake from every room as well as a courteous and well-informed staff. Room service, clean bedding, and spacious rooms, all with attached bath. Doubles Rs600-1000. Off-season: Rs300.

KMVN Tourist Rest House, Tallital (☎35570), 200m from the Tallital bus stand toward the far side of the lake. Above the road and away from the noise, with grand views of the lake and hills. Hot water, showers, and seat toilets. Restaurant open 7am-10:30pm. Dorm beds Rs75; suites Rs800. Off-season: Rs60/600.

Hotel Atithi (☎35080), Tallital, to the right, behind Hotel Mansarovar. Low-scale place offering rooms cheaper than most in this bracket. Restricted views of the lake from some rooms. Room service, laundry, TV, and restaurants. Doubles Rs250.

Hotel Gauri (☎36617), near Tallital, on the road parallel to The Mall, behind the Hotel Mansarovar. Cheery rooms with TVs and balconies offering views of the lake. Seat toilets and showers in some rooms. Doubles Rs300-700. Off-season: Rs200-350.

KMVN Mount View Tourist Rest House (☎35400), Mallital. A long, steep 2km walk from the Flats, this government-run rest house is cheap, clean, and uncontaminated by character of any kind. Dorm beds Rs75; doubles Rs 550. Off-season: Rs60/415.

Hotel Mansarovar (☎35581), Tallital, on The Mall. Small rooms with large clean bathrooms (squat and seat toilets). Room service, laundry, restaurant, and TV. Doubles Rs450-750; deluxe suites Rs800-1500.

🍴 FOOD

All along The Mall are countless clean and well-priced restaurants with beautiful views of the lake—restaurants at either end of town in Mallital and Tallital are generally not as clean. Most restaurants have cheap outdoor seating—a must.

Flattis Restaurant, between the library and Mallital, on The Mall. A large, dimly lit place that serves the largest variety of Indian and Western food in the area. Pizza Rs60-75; sizzlers Rs70; *dosas, thalis,* and a homesick Tuscan salad Rs30.

Ahar Vihar Restaurant, near Mallital, upstairs from the well-lit variety stores on The Mall. A popular low-end restaurant with a homey kitchen feel. Large and delicious Gujarati and Rajasthani *thalis* Rs35-40. Open daily 10am-10pm.

Sonam Tibetan Restaurant, next to the Modern Bookstore, in Mallital. Meager choices but big servings of Tibetan food. Veg. noodles in broth (Rs25). Open daily 8am-10pm.

Nanak's Restaurant, between the library and Mallital, on The Mall. A would-be Western fast-food place serving burgers (Rs25), "Jughead's trip in life" pizza, milkshakes, and mango sundaes (Rs80) in a dark room aglow with neon lights. Open daily 9am-11pm.

Green Restaurant, Bara Bazaar, in the heart of Mallital; look for the large banner. The maroon, lamp-lit interior and colorful streamers overhead make up for the uncomfortable chairs and short tables. Open daily 7:30am-11pm.

Kwality Restaurant, at lakeside on The Mall. Very crowded at lunchtime but reasonably priced. Veg. Rs40-50; Non-Veg Rs50-70.

👁 🏔 SIGHTS AND SCENERY

VIEWPOINTS. Any number of nearby hilltops and mountainside viewpoints offer views of the city. If the clouds cooperate, you can sometimes see Himalayan peaks as far away as the Tibetan border. The best way to take in the views is to rent a **horse** from one of Mallital's stables (at the mouth of Mallital before Bara Bazar) and clip-clop up to the top. Expect the ride—which runs up steep, loose-stone trails against the honking chaos of the oncoming traffic—to be difficult. *(Round-trip*

Rs125, with the guide jogging alongside your milk-white steed. Expect to pay more if you want to stop and actually enjoy the view for more than an hour.)

The easiest way to get to the top of **Snow View** is to forsake horse and foot altogether and take the **ropeway**, which leaves from a clearly marked building 30m up from The Mall in Mallital. The low-effort nature of this little excursion makes it extremely popular during high season. Getting here at opening time (8am) is your best bet for ensuring tickets and people-free views. The last cable car leaves Mallital at 7pm. The last car returns from Snow View at 6pm. *(Round-trip Rs50, with a 1hr. stop at the top. KMVN has a cottage at the top. In-season: doubles Rs500.)*

Other viewpoints around Nainital include a small spot on the road to Kilbury, an easy 4.5km walk away, and **Cheena Peak** (2611m), sometimes called China or Naina Peak. The highest thing around, Cheena Peak is 6km away, roughly one hour by horse (Rs100) or three hours by foot. At the top is a snack shop and several places to sit and muse over the view down onto the city below or, if the weather permits, the peaks of Garhwal, including Nanda Devi (7817m). You can either start from Mallital or have a taxi take you to Tonneleay on Kilbury Rd., and walk from there. **Land's End**, behind **Tiffin Peak** (immediately west of the lake), has views over the sprawling valley to the west.

NAINI LAKE. The town's pride and joy is the lake itself. If you want to get out into the middle of Parvati's emerald eye, **boats** are available for hire *(paddleboats Rs40-60 per hr.; boatman-guided rides Rs30-50)*. You can rent **yachts** from the Nainital Boat Club, though they will require membership *(yachts Rs60 per hr.; membership Rs150)*.

OTHER SIGHTS. The road heading west of Tallital leads to the colonial-era **Governor's House** and a **golf course** that is open to visitors. Three kilometers along the road to Kathgodam is a small temple, **Hanumangarh,** home to a 6-foot tall, bright orange statue of Hanuman. Just beyond the temple is an **observatory.** *(Open daily 3-5pm and 6-8pm. Admission Rs10.)* In 1880, a landslide killed 151 people and wiped out the city's largest hotel. The flattened area left behind was turned into a large, open public space. Today, the **Flats** are a favorite hang-out of snake charmers and musicians and are often busy with football and hockey games. In October, the **Autumn Festival** features sports competitions by day and cultural programs by night.

ENTERTAINMENT. On the banks of Sukhatal, by the KMVN Mallital, are the **Cave Gardens,** a newly opened underground attraction *(open daily 9am-7pm, admission Rs10)*. **Capital Cinema and Ashok Cinema,** near the Flats, run Hindi movies regularly *(tickets Rs15)*. A **stroll along The Mall** becomes more peaceful as darkness enshrouds the piles of chintz in the stores, but avoid the 6-9pm rush of tourists that arrives when the road is closed to traffic.

NEAR NAINITAL

If you're looking for lake-side solitude, there are a number of places not far from Nainital that offer not only equally lovely views, but also more peace and romantic quiet than busy Nainital.

SAT TAL. Sat Tal contains a series of seven lakes hidden deep in pine and oak forests 21km from Nainital. It is possible to stay the night here and spend a day walking to all seven lakes, which are about 1km apart from one another. You can rent boats (Rs100 per hr.) and buy snacks from stalls along the lakefront, but most of the area around the lake remains undeveloped. The only rest house at Sat Tal is run by KMVN (☎47047). Unfortunately, visitors must fork over Rs400-1000 a night in May and June (off-season: 35% discount). Most tour agencies have buses to Sat Tal and the surrounding lakes (Rs100).

BHIMTAL. A smaller and cleaner version of Nainital, Bhimtal, 22km away, has a good reputation as a center for more active aquatic pursuits like water-skiing, sailing, and boating. The tourist value of the lake has made it a commercial destination, and there's more concrete around these days than pine and blue-sky beauty. Bhimtal is home to two environmental groups: Himalayan Man and

Nature Institute (HIMANI) and the Action Group for Environment and Humanity, both situated at the Tallital end. One kilometer along the road to **Naukuchiya Tal** is a Kumaoni Folk Art Exhibition. (Open M-Sa 11am-6pm.) Tour buses don't stop here; you'll have to take a taxi. As usual, government accommodations are the cheapest. The KMVN tourist bungalow, on the opposite side of the lake of Bhimtal, is about as quiet and cheap as Bhimtal lake-side hotels get. (☎47005. Dorm beds Rs100; tidy doubles with carpets and wood cabinets Rs450.) One of the prettiest lakes, **Naukuchiyatal** offers plenty of solitude and lots of opportunities to fish and spot migrating birds. The lake is said to have nine (*nau*) Corners (*kuchiya*), and good luck is supposed to come to the person who can see all nine at once. The KMVN tourist bungalow at Naukuchiyatal has a comfortable lounge and a beautiful garden in front. (☎47138. Dorm beds Rs60; doubles Rs400).

RAMGARH. The drive to Ramgarh, 32km from Nainital, is a beautiful journey through pine and oak forests. Although the town itself has little to recommend it, the "snow viewpoint," 6km before town, commands clear views (well, sometimes) of peaks such as Nanda Devi and Nanda Kot. The best time to visit the region is during April, May, and October, when the weather has cooled, the sky is clear, and the rates have come down. The winter is also beautiful, but be sure to pack warm clothes, gloves, and boots to deal with the cold and snow.

RANIKHET रानीखेत ☎05966

At an altitude of 2000m, Ranikhet is surrounded by fields of pine and deodar forests that are inhabited by *kakar* (barking deer). Other than the loud silence of the forests and the overpowering views of Nanda Devi (7817m), the largest presence here is the military, which dates back to 1869, when British troops from UP arrived here for a bit of 19th-century R&R. The Kumaon Regiment is still stationed here today. With less traffic noise and fewer travelers than the other hill stations, Ranikhet is a prime spot for hikes and relaxation. It is a quiet town where you'll hear hardly a car horn after 8pm. The "Queen's Field" is growing fast, though, and new resorts pop up every year. A local tourist brochure points out: "How long Ranikhet can maintain its virginity is a million dollar question." Maybe that's why you now have to pay a Rs2 toll to enter.

GETTING THERE AND GETTING AROUND

Buses: UP Roadways (☎20645) runs buses to: **Almora** (5:30am, 2½ hr., Rs28); **Dehra Dun** (8:30am and 3pm, 12hr., Rs150); **Delhi** (4 per day, 3-5pm, 12hr., Rs150); **Haldwani/Kathgodam** (every 30min., 5:30am-5pm, 4hr., Rs55); **Kausani** (6am, 12:30, and 2pm; 3hr.; Rs26); **Nainital** (7am, 3½hr., Rs28); and **Ramnagar** (8:30am, 1, and 3pm; 5hr.; Rs50). **KMOU** (☎20609) has buses to: **Almora** (5 per day, 6:30am-2:30pm, 2½hr., Rs25); **Haldwani/Kathgodam** (7 per day, 7am-2:30pm, 4hr., Rs40); **Kausani** (4 per day, 6am-1:30pm, 3hr., Rs27); **Nainital** (11:30am, 3hr., Rs30); and **Ramnagar** (5 per day, 7am-3pm, 4hr., Rs40).

Local Transportation: Shared jeeps go to nearby destinations. For Chaubattia and The Mall, jeeps leave from above Alko Hotel (Rs5) or the KMOU stand (Rs5); for Dwarahat and Doonagiri, they depart near Nainital Bank (Rs30). No jeeps after 7pm to The Mall, and after 5pm to other places.

ORIENTATION AND PRACTICAL INFORMATION

Sadar Bazaar, the main road that anchors Ranikhet's meandering topography, is in the town center; most services and many of the hotels and restaurants are here. **Buses** arrive at either end of the bazaar; **UP Roadways** stops at the downhill end; **KMOU** buses arrive and depart on the west end. The Mall area, 2km above the bazaar, is a tranquil setting for some of the better hotels. To get to The Mall, keep to your left along the road next to the **Alka Hotel** (up the mountains and away from the chaos). There is a mural-sized map of Ranikhet opposite the **Rajdeep Hotel** that also gives listings of area attractions. Monday is Ranikhet's **business holiday.**

Tourist Office: (☎20227), at the east end of the bazaar, up from the UP Roadways bus stand. Open M-Su 10am-5pm. Open May-June M-Sa 8am-8pm, Su 10am-5pm.

Currency Exchange: The nearest currency exchange is in Nainital and Almora.

Markets: Sadar Bazaar has stores selling traditional Kumaoni silver and gold jewelry.

Pharmacy: Mayank Medical Hall (☎21356), at the UP Roadways end of town. Open M-Su 8am-8pm.

Medical Assistance: The **clinic** of Dr. Prakash Srivastava (☎20101) is on the bazaar, uphill from the Mayank pharmacy. Open daily 9am-5pm.

Post Office: The main branch is along The Mall, 2km from town center. Another branch is near the tourist office. Open M-F 9am-5pm, Sa 9am-noon. **Postal code:** 263648.

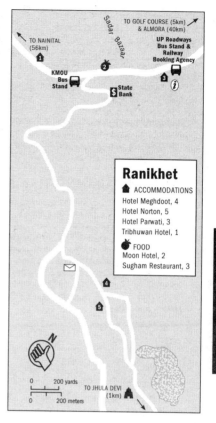

Ranikhet

🏠 ACCOMMODATIONS
Hotel Meghdoot, 4
Hotel Norton, 5
Hotel Parwati, 3
Tribhuwan Hotel, 1

🍎 FOOD
Moon Hotel, 2
Sugham Restaurant, 3

TO GOLF COURSE (5km) & ALMORA (40km)

TO NAINITAL (56km)

UP Roadways Bus Stand & Railway Booking Agency

KMOU Bus Stand

State Bank

0   200 yards
0   200 meters

TO JHULA DEVI (1km)

UTTAR PRADESH

ACCOMMODATIONS

Hotels along the bazaar are noisier and less well-kept than those tucked into the hills along The Mall. In-season (Apr.-June) prices are higher in the bazaar, and rooms harder to find. Most bazaar hotels have a 10am check-out and don't allow alcohol; those along The Mall have noon check-out and no alcohol restrictions. In-season rates are quoted. Off-season expect a 40-60% discount. Always bargain a little before accepting a room.

Hotel Meghdoot (☎20475), just past Kumaon Lodge in The Mall. Once a British officer's bungalow, with spacious, well-upholstered rooms and huge bathrooms (seat and squat toilets). A long balcony offers unobstructed views of the valley. STD/ISD service, cable TV, and restaurant. Doubles Rs400; deluxe Rs600.

Hotel Norton, just past Meghdoot. Colorful old British bungalow with the cheapest rates for standard rooms. Friendly staff. Doubles Rs300-500.

Hotel Parwati (☎20325), above UP Roadways bus stop; look for large signs. The most elevated hotel in Ranikhet, it has clean rooms and super views from its lounge, though expect to deal with blaring music throughout the day. Room service and hot water. Deluxe rooms have TVs. Singles Rs250; doubles Rs400; deluxe Rs500.

Tribhuwan Hotel (☎2524), on the west end of town, just before the KMOU bus stand. A mighty beast composed of 3 buildings. Isolated from most hotels, and a welcome change from the crowded main road. Balconies offer unobstructed views of the valley. Squat toilets and bucket showers. Carpeted rooms are larger and have small black and white TVs. Basic rooms Rs250; deluxe Rs400.

FOOD

Moon Hotel, Sadar Bazaar, opposite Hotel Rajdeep, has the nicest restaurant in town, with prices to match. The "Moon chicken Ala Numtaz" (Rs250) goes well with the dim lighting. The food is spicier than the standard regional fare. Open daily 8am-11pm.

Sugham Restaurant, in the Hotel Parwati. Although the dimly lit interior is not especially inviting, the attentive staff and good, plain food make this a safe place to eat. Chinese (Rs35-50), Indian (Rs35-50), and continental dishes (Rs40-60). Open daily 8am-9pm.

Tourist Bungalow has a restaurant that isn't worth a trek from town, but it's good if you happen to be on The Mall. Munch down "fingar chips" (Rs18) or vegetable *pakoras* (8 for Rs18) while sipping tea (Rs5) in front of the TV. Chow mein Rs45. Open daily 7-8am (tea only), 8-10am, noon-2:30pm, and 4:30-10:30pm.

SIGHTS AND ENTERTAINMENT

CHAUBATIA GARDEN. The most renowned attraction in the area, the Chaubatia Garden features large fruit and flower gardens, which are in full technicolor bloom from June to August. It is also a "Fruit Research Centre." Sneaky travelers sometimes do research of their own as they follow one of the trails along the mountainside through the forests. Apricots, apples, pears, and peaches are grown here and sold at reasonable rates at the official shop at the entrance. Indian vacationers fill the garden in the high season. *(11km away from Ranikhet. 7 buses head to Chaubatia from the UP Roadways stand 8am-6pm, 40min., Rs5. Shared taxi Rs5. Garden open daily 24hr. Shop open M-Su 10am-4:45pm.)*

OTHER SIGHTS. Closer to Ranikhet, along The Mall, is the Hindu temple of **Jhula Devi,** another name for Durga, depicted here sitting on a swing *(jhula)*. The small temple dates back to the 14th century. **Kumaon Regiment War Memorial Museum,** opposite the Nar Singh Grounds, houses ammunition from Raj days and most recent battles of any significance at all. *(Open M-Sa 10am-5pm.)* A little farther down is the **Ram Mandir.** Continuing down The Mall toward Sadar Bazaar is the impressive new (1994) **Mankameshwar Temple,** up from the phone exchange and opposite the Nainital Bank. Near the Birla Boys School is the beautiful temple of **Hare Khan.**

FESTIVALS. The **Autumn Festival** in late September is Ranikhet's largest, with sports tournaments featuring hockey, cricket, and tennis as well as a potpourri of cultural exhibits from around Kumaon. For 10 days in June, you can stop in at the Nar Singh Stadium (also called the Nar Singh Ground) for the evening **Summer Festival.** A homey country fair, it features a ring toss, magicians, kiddie rides, a mini-zoo, 10-rupee gambling, blaring music, and heartburn-inducing Chinese food.

GOLF COURSE. The **Kumaon Regiment Advanced Training Centre and Golf Course** (also known as "Upat Kalika"), is one of India's most scenic golf courses. Even if you're not keen on the game, the pine forests around the course are a pleasant place to wander. *(6km away. Shared taxis Rs5. Nine holes for Rs200; club rental Rs100; ball Rs120; tee Rs10; caddy Rs50 plus tip. Open M-Tu and F 7am-6pm, W-Th and Sa 7am-12:30pm.)*

DAYTRIPS FROM RANIKHET

After developing **Dwarahat** to be their capital, the Pandava kings moved to Dwarika instead when the river Kosi changed its course, leaving the city dry. The abandoned capital is home to a cluster of Shiva temples built by the Chaud kings during the 14th century. Traditional Kumaoni wood work and *rangoli,* intricately designed paintings adorning walls and floors, can be seen in most houses here. The region's famous **Syalde-Bikhoti Mela** is held here annually from April 13-15. *(21km from Ranikhet. Shared taxi Rs30.)* Fifteen kilometers ahead is **Doonagiri,** where there is a **Vaishno Devi Temple** and, as usual, spectacular views of the Himalayas. *(Bus Rs10, shared taxi Rs10.)*

ALMORA अलमोड़ा
☎05962

Legend has it that Almora was once the city of the gods. To commemorate the divine presence here, they left behind them an abundant source of pure water, delivered to this mile-high city from over 120 underground wells. Almora is the most mystical of Kumaon's hill stations, having drawn peace-seekers from the likes of Gandhi and Nehru (who used to meet here to talk) to Swami Vivekananda and Timothy Leary. The most central hill station in UP, Almora is also one of the few to have been developed by Indians and not by the British—it was created as the seat of the Chanda dynasty 400 years ago. A stroll through the old bazaar evokes those bygone days—the buildings are fading, but colorful facades and cobbled streets echo centuries past. But the mountains, which offer opportunities for day hikes and exploration, remain oblivious to passing decades and dynasties. Amid the frenetic activity in the air is also an unmatched tranquility. While nearby hill stations pursue the Western gods of finance and leisure, Almora is surrounded by modern and ancient Hindu temples and, off in the distance, by the magnificent natural shrines of the cloud-piercing Himalayan peaks.

⌐ GETTING THERE AND GETTING AROUND

Almora's **bus stand** is on The Mall at the center of town. **KMOU,** before the UP Roadways stand along The Mall, serves **Kausani** and **Bageswar** (11 per day, 6am-5pm, 2½hr., Rs25); **Kathgodam** and **Haldwani** (4 per day, 6am-1pm, 4½hr., Rs40); **Nainital** and **Bhowali** (5 per day, 6:30am-1pm, 3hr., Rs30); and **Ranikhet** (4 per day, 8am-3pm, 2½hr., Rs20). **UP Roadways,** down the steps, has buses to: **Bhowali** (every 30min., 5-8am and 1:30-5pm, 2½hr., Rs29); **Delhi** (4 per day, 7am-5pm, 11hr., Rs150); **Dehra Dun** (5am and 4pm, 12hr., Rs170); **Kausani** (4 per day, 7am-noon, 2½hr., Rs25); **Nainital** (8am, 3hr., Rs35); and **Ranikhet** (6:30am, 1, and 2pm; 2hr.; Rs29). The **Dharanda Bus Stand** on the road below The Mall serves **Pithoragarh** (4 per day, 7am-2pm, 5hr., Rs50).

✦? ORIENTATION AND PRACTICAL INFORMATION

The **town center** is on The Mall, the major thoroughfare for traffic and the site of most hotels and services; walking with the flow of traffic brings you to several restaurants and to the road to Kasar Devi. Most other services are southwest along The Mall. **Jauhari Bazaar,** the main bazaar, is the major parallel street up from The Mall. Sunday is Almora's **business holiday.**

Tourist Office: The **UP Tourist Office** (☎22180), by the post office, 800m southwest of the bus stand on the road veering up from The Mall, carries information about Almora and Kumaon but keeps inconsistent hours. Try M-Sa 10am-5pm. A better bet for information is one of the local **trekking companies,** including **Discover Himalaya** (☎31470), opposite the post office. The people at **High Adventure** (☎31445), on The Mall, a bit closer to town center, are also knowledgeable about the local sights.

Currency Exchange: State Bank of India (☎30048), on The Mall, near the town center. Changes AmEx checks in most currencies and grudgingly cashes Thomas Cook and Citibank checks but does not change foreign cash. Open M-F 10am-2pm, Sa 10am-noon.

Bookstore: Shree Almora Book Depot (☎30148), next to High Adventure. Open M-Sa 9:30am-8pm.

Police: (☎30323), 10m along the road veering up opposite the post office.

Pharmacy: The best-stocked pharmacy in town is the **Prakash Medical Store,** as you enter the bazaar from The Mall. Open daily 7am-10:30pm.

Hospital: Civil Hospital (☎30025, emergency 30064), up a short flight of stairs from the bazaar. Open daily 8am-2pm. Emergency open 24hr. **Base Hospital** (☎30012), 3km from town, is cleaner and less crowded. Open daily 8am-2pm.

Internet: Discover Himalaya has the only connection in town. Rs2 per min. Open M-Sa 9am-10pm.

Post Office: (☎30019), on the downside of The Mall, 600m southwest of the bus stand. Open M-Sa 10am-6pm. **Postal Code:** 263601.

ACCOMMODATIONS

Almora has a limited choice of hotels. Most are along The Mall; dingier, cheaper places are clustered around the town center. More relaxed accommodations dotting the surrounding hills are difficult to reach (see **Daytrips from Almora,** p. 163).

■ **Kailas Hotel** (☎30624), opposite the post office, 10m above The Mall. The unrivaled sweet spot for foreign budget travelers. The Kailas is run by the incomparably charming 82-year-old Mr. Shah (though the board says "run by housewives"), a marvelous source of all sorts of tales and wisdom about the Almora district and Indian history. The rooms could be cleaner, but the place has a colorful character that many find worth the price. Rooms Rs120-180. Bargaining is futile.

■ **Hotel Savoy** (☎30329), at the end of the ramp that veers upward opposite the post office. For those looking for comfort, this hotel offers nice, large rooms with large attached baths and seat toilets. Rooms on the balcony with views of the valley are more expensive; the lower ones have a lovely garden. Doubles Rs300-500.

KMVN Holiday House (☎22250), 1km southwest of the bus stand, on the descending road. Set apart from the rest of the town, this pleasant and clean government accommodation has its own garden and valley view. Combined seat/squat toilets. Dorms have bucket showers. Dorm beds Rs60; doubles Rs300. Off-season: Rs50/225.

Hotel Pawan (☎30252), opposite Trishul, closer to town center. Don't be fooled by the "Enjoy Billiards" sign; it's only for local members of the Billiards Club (don't bother asking about membership—you don't qualify). Well-kept and sufficient, with bright rooms, large mirrors, and clean bathrooms with squat toilets. Room service available. Check-out noon. Singles Rs150; doubles Rs260.

Hotel Shikhar (☎30238), at the end of The Mall. Shikhar has the most services of any of Almora's establishments—attached travel agency, general store, hair salon, restaurant, and STD/ISD. Rooms are spacious and well lit. The balcony above the restaurant has dramatic views of the valley. Singles Rs180; doubles Rs270.

FOOD

Sunrise Restaurant, past the post office, in Hotel Snow View. Enjoy creamy and heavy Punjabi and Chinese food as you contemplate the fish tank and rock sculpture decoration. *Shahi paneer* Rs35; *naan* Rs12.

Glory Restaurant, opposite Mount View, up the road to the northeast. The 2nd floor's short ceilings and red lanterns lend this veg. restaurant an unusual amount of character. Cheese butter *masala* Rs40; delicious samosas Rs10. Open daily 7am-10:30pm.

Hotel Himsagar Restaurant has decent food at cheap prices. Great views and all-veg. food. *Dahl makhani* Rs20. Open daily 8am-10:30pm.

Swagat Restaurant, on the side of the Hotel Shikhar, down the steps. An airy, homey place with a commanding view. No menus, only veg. *thalis* (Rs30) and some fried snacks (*pakora* platter Rs15). Open daily 7:30-9:30pm.

Mount View Restaurant, inside Hotel Shikhar, has a varied Indian menu. *Korma* curry Rs30; curry chicken Rs50. Open daily 6am-11:30pm. Off-season: 6am-10:30pm.

SIGHTS AND SHOPPING

KASAR DEVI TEMPLE. The main attraction near Almora is the Kasar Devi Temple, spectacularly positioned at the top of Kashyap Hill. Views from a giant, sloping mountaintop rock afford sweeping panoramas of the whole area, marred only slightly by the television antenna that shares the point. The temple is known as a center of spiritual energy—Swami Vivekananda came here to meditate, as have many soul-searching Americans and Europeans, some of whom still hang around the nearby tea stands. Follow the trail past the temple through town for the best views of the distant Nanda Devi mountain range. *(Near the hamlet of Kasar Devi, 7km from Almora. Reachable by a long hike upward past The Mall, which forks left after the Hotel Shikhar. One-way taxi Rs10 per person.)*

TRANQUILITY RETREAT. Wedged between two hills and far from everything but its own splendor and jaw-dropping views, the Tranquility Retreat is a tiny getaway paradise for the short- or long-term visitor. Now in its fourth year, Tranquility has grown to seven rooms, with an organic garden and beehive. Armelle and Kishan, French expatriate and Indian farmer, busily tend the garden, bake bread (7 loaves daily) and steaming scones served with homemade honey, and cook up a vegetarian storm—French and continental mainstays with the occasional Indian touch—while exuding a warmth and compassion that keeps their contented guests from leaving the nest. There are two paths to Tranquility Retreat from the Kasar Devi road. If you are walking toward Kasar Devi, look for a blue sign high in a tree on the left 10 minutes after the Research Institute for Yoga Therapy. When walking away from Kasar Devi, there will be a sign on your right 15 minutes down the mountain from the Kasar Devi Temple. Write for reservations. *(Tranquility Guest House c/o Kishan Joshi, ☎ 263601 Saria Pina Estate, Almora, VPM. Food is available 7am-10pm for casual visitors as well as guests. Doubles Rs1500 per month.)*

OTHER SIGHTS. A walk along the road above The Mall offers stunning views and a peaceful atmosphere. The walk is punctuated by the **Bhairav** and **Patal Devi** temples, which both offer terrific views of the sunset. Across the street is the small, government-run **G.B. Pant Museum,** which features tools and other artifacts from the Katyuri and Chanda dynasties. *(Open daily 10am-5pm daily. Free.)* Locals go to the locally important **Chitai Temple** to seek retribution if they feel they've been wronged. The King Golu Dev used to sit here as the administer of justice. Today, plaintiffs paste or hang letters in the temple, describing their situation in hopes of finding resolutions to their problems. The **Nanda Devi Temple,** which pays homage to the goddess of newlywed brides, is a pretty place that draws religious and architectural enthusiasts alike. The **Nanda Devi Fair** is held here during the last week of August or the first week of September. The **Brighton End Corner,** at the south end of town, is a popular spot for sunset watching. Katermal is home to an 800-year-old **Sun Temple.** *(12½km from Almora or 1½km by foot)*

MARKETS. Even if you don't enjoy the bustling Indian markets, stroll through Jauhari Bazaar above The Mall to catch a glimpse of the fine, intricately carved wooden architecture. Also, drop by the **jewelers** past Raja stores to buy or look at traditional Kumaoni jewelry. Almora is the center of production of *tamtas*, silver-plated copper pots, which line the lower region of the bazaar. **Anokhe Lal** sells these pots, though they are pretty heavy to carry in a backpack.

▓ DAYTRIPS FROM ALMORA

JAGESHWAR AND SANDESHWAR. Situated 38km from Almora in a valley surrounded by deodar trees is the temple complex of Jageshwar. Made up of 124 temples, the complex contains one of the 12 *jyotirlingas* of Shiva. The main temple also features two statues of Deep Chand and Pawan Chand (the third was recently stolen), two kings who were patrons of this complex. Photography is not allowed in the main temple. Two kilometers before Jageshwar is Sandeshwar, a smaller collection of temples, where Lord Shankar was exiled when he was cursed.

SURYA MANDRI KATARMAL. Built in the 8th century by the Katyuri dynasty, Surya Mandri Katarmal is the only sun temple in Kumaon. The main temple is surrounded by 44 smaller ones. *(12½km toward Kosi and a 1½hr. climb. Buses and jeeps leave frequently from Almora, Rs 5-10.)* Fifteen kilometers toward Barechhina is the historical spot of **Lakhudiyar,** featuring traditional rock paintings that mark the starting point of art in Kumaon. *(Take any bus headed for Pithoragarh or Jageshwar, Rs5.)*

BINSAR SANCTUARY AND JALNA. The Binsar Sanctuary, 30km from Almora, was the summer getaway of the Chand rulers; now, tourists come to lose themselves in the sanctuary's dense forests. Along with a handful of other hotels, there is a KMVN Tourist Rest House in the area. *(Doubles Rs300; 50% off-season discount. Make reservations at the Almora tourist office.)* The picturesque town of **Jalna**, 32km toward Lohagat from Almora, is perfect spot for a quiet afternoon. Wander about apple and apricot orchards with the snow-laden Himalayas as a background.

⚑ TREKKING

For further immersion in Kumaon's natural beauty, you might consider going on a **trek** to one of the towering glaciers up in the Himalayas. **Discover Himalaya** (see p. 161) offers trekking packages. Expect to pay Rs50-70 for advice on planning high-altitude treks. Student discounts are often available. The most popular trek in Kumaon is the one to **Pindari Glacier** (90km). Rest houses line the trail at convenient distances. Though the trek's popularity deters those seeking a true escape, there are some beautiful sights along the way (especially from Dhakusi to Phurkia). Treks to the **Milam Glacier** (200km), via stunning **Munsyari** in the Pithoragarh district, are ideal for those hoping to avoid the slow-moving glacial crowds. The **Kafni Glacier** (90km) is another good option for high-altitude trekkers. Discover Himalaya also runs a short 4-day trek through the foothills of the Himalayas (200-2500m) to the **Barahi Devi Temple** at Devidhura, the site of the weird and wonderful **Rakshabandhan Festival**, which takes place around the third week of August. Two opponents equipped with baskets as shields, throw lumps of stone and rocks at each other. Blood from the wounds is collected and offered to the virgin goddess. *(This and similar treks cost around Rs900 per person per day.)*

KAUSANI कौसानी　　　　　　　　　　　☎ 05962

If you want to touch the snow-clad Himalayas, come to Kausani. This bus stop town, nearly 2000m above sea level, offers the most awe-inspiring views of peaks anywhere in the UP Hills. Not your typical hill station, Kausani has one main road, a few restaurants, and a few more hotels. It's a perfect spot for basking in the splendor of the Himalayas, well out of range of the honking cars and busy daily life of the larger hill stations. The breathtaking sunsets have inspired many notable Indians—Hindi poet laureate Sumitra Nandan Pant was born here, and, in 1929, Mohandas Gandhi spent time in the Anashakti Ashram.

⬕ GETTING THERE AND GETTING AROUND. Buses stop in the center of Kausani, opposite the colorful Ram Krishnan and Saraswati temple. Buses leave frequently from the town center for Bageswar, Almora, Gwaldam, Ranikhet, Bhowali, and Haldwani. Inquire at the tourist office or ask locals (more than one!) about departure times.

⬔⬓ ORIENTATION AND PRACTICAL INFORMATION. The center of town is marked by the three-way intersection of the main road from Ranikhet, another road that climbs up the mountain toward the KMVN, and the road leading down to Baijnath. The **tourist office** is on the main road where the buses stop. (Open daily May-June 8am-8pm; off-season: M-Sa 10am-5pm.) The **post office** is nearby (open M-Sa 8am-4pm). There is another post office with the same hours near the KMVN. The nearest **currency exchange** is in Almora. The **Sunil Medical store** is on the road that climbs up the mountain (open daily 8am-8pm). The road continues, leading to the KMVN tourist rest house 2km away. The travel agencies and restaurants are all in this area. Most hotels have **STD/ISDs,** and there is also a booth at the bus stop. **Postal code:** 263639.

⬔⬓ ACCOMMODATIONS AND FOOD. A large number of pricey resort hotels in Kausani advertise magnificent views of the Himalayas. The good news is that these hotels do not have a monopoly on nature's beauty. The rooms at the **Hotel Uttarakhand** have unobstructed mountain views, and are far enough away from the town center to offer a modicum of peace and quiet. Follow the stairs above the bus stand. (☎45012. Doubles Rs200-300. Off-season: Rs50-150.) The attached restaurant is one of the best in town, with veg. fried rice for Rs35. (Open daily 6am-11pm.) Many of Kausani's nicer hotels are along one strip of road above the town center. Your best choice here is the **Amer Holiday Home,** which has modest-sized rooms, hot water, and a peaceful balcony. (☎45015. Open May-July and Sept.-Dec. Singles Rs150; doubles Rs300-500. Off-season: Rs100/200-350.) On the same row of hotels is the **Anashakti Ashram** (sometimes called "the Gandhi ashram"). The immaculate grounds here are one of the most calm and peaceful viewpoints around. Fees are paid on a donation basis, and the ashram is only for those interested in spiritual living. Guests are expected to help with daily cleaning, refrain from consumption of alcohol, eggs, and meat products, and attend daily prayer as often as possible. **KMVN tourist rest houses** are always a safe bet in Kumaon, and the one in Kausani, 2km from town on a road that hugs the northern face of the mountain, is no exception. Book at least one month in advance during the high season (May to June and Oct.). The attached restaurant is open 7am-10pm. (☎45006. Dorm beds Rs60; doubles Rs300-800. Off-season: 50% discount.)

Good cheap eats are much scarcer than cheap sleeps. Although you will probably end up just eating at your hotel, there are a few other options. The **Uttarkhand Restaurant** and the **Kitchen Restaurant,** next to the post office, offer reliable fare (the latter serves *thalis* Rs35). The **Ashoka restaurant,** next to the Bhatt Clinic, serves up local dishes. The lentil-based *bara* dish (Rs35), accompanied by the local chutney, is a tasty treat after weeks of *dahl* and chow mein. Kumaoni dishes take a while to cook, so order early.

🔲🏃 SIGHTS AND DAYTRIPS. As the man in the tourist office says, the main sights in Kausani are sunrise and sunset. These are also the best times to see the distant mountains, enveloped in clouds during the summer and monsoon season. Within a radius of 40km around Kausani are a number of religious and historical little towns, which can be visited in a few days. Hire a taxi (Rs1500 per day) and drive to as many as you like, making pit stops for the night at some. Most of them have only KMVN or GMVN accomodations available (Rs400-900).

If the views and treks start to get tiring after a while, you can take a daytrip to **Baijnath** (18km), the site of a group of 18 ancient temples on the banks of the Gomti River. This complex features an intricately carved black granite statue of Parvati in the main temple. The priest from the Archaeological Survey of India will describe the statue for you in excruciating detail. The temple also features a large brass *linga* where *aarti* is held daily at 8am and 7pm. *(Buses to Baijnath leave frequently from the town center. Rs8.)* Yogi's Uttarakhand Cycle Tours (☎45012), next to the Hotel Uttarakhand, rents **mountain bikes** and organizes tours for Rs375 per day.

Twenty-two kilometers from Baijnath is a beautiful drive through terraced fields and thick pine forests to **Gwaldani,** where the Himalayan peaks seem closer than ever. Twenty-three kilometers from Baijnath lies **Bageshwar,** where the rivers Gomti, Saryu (Pinder), and Bhagirathi meet. There is an ancient Shiva temple, **Bagnath Mandir,** on the banks of the Gomti and Saryu, surrounded by smaller shrines of Ganga-ma, Hanuman, Durga, and the rest of the gang.

Fifty kilometers ahead is **Chaukori,** probably one of the best places to touch the Himalayan peaks. Up at 2410m, the sun sets later, creating a fusion of all shades of yellow, orange, red, and pink against the blue and white backdrop of the sky and peaks. The clifftop KMVN has superb views. On the road to Ranikhet are **Dwarahat** and **Doonagiri,** with Shiva temples built by the Chand and Katuriya dynasties.

Forty kilometers from Chaukori is the old and relatively unknown temple of **Patal Bhubneshwar.** Naturally sculpted by underground streams and earthquakes, the cave temple is an enchanting place. The cave is said to house over 33 deities in the form of these sculpted rocks. There are also smaller caves which are said to lead to Kalyug, Kailash, and Gangalihaat, though no one (except Pandavas, the *pujari* will insist) has explored them. *(The tour lasts an hour. Wear loose comfortable clothes and go in bare foot. Expect to tip the pujari who doubles up as your guide (Rs50-100) and make a donation to the temple committee (Rs100). Photography is not permitted.)*

If you like waking up to a beautiful sunrise, then Chaukri, **Gwaldam,** and **Binsar** are ideal. Baijnath or **Jageshwar** have intricate temple architecture set against the lush green banks of mountain rivers.

THE UP PLAINS

AGRA आग्रा ☎ 0562

Over the last decade, the average tourist's stay in Agra has declined from one and a half days to barely 12 hours. Everyone seems to be mumbling the same thing: Agra is a dump. It is not difficult to see why visitors who arrive expecting some kind of exotic, oriental Shangri-la—"the immortal city of undying love," according to the official literature—might leave feeling more than just a little bit disappointed. The monuments are every bit as magnificent as they are hyped up to be; the problem is that most of the tourist literature omits any mention of the parts of the city around and between its UNESCO-sanctioned sites. The main budget hotel center, Taj Ganj, is a powerful lesson in what happens when too many over-aggressive rickshaw-*wallahs* and rug vendors try to chase too many grungy backpackers down too few overcrowded streets. There *are* parts of Agra where visitors are treated to more than just urban grime and indigestion, but they are few and far between. In the Cantonment area there are wide, clean streets, upscale stores, and a string of parks maintained by the local Sheraton, which has a multi-million dollar stake in seeing that Agra puts its best foot forward. Luckily, Agra's real draw, the incomparably grand Taj Mahal, is still no less than breath-taking to behold, despite the mess of junky establishments that has sprung up outside its gates.

Agra's monuments were all built under the Mughals, who swept in from Central Asia early in the 16th century. At the Battle of Panipat in 1526, the Mughal warrior Babur crushed the ruling Lodi dynasty; as a direct result, the Mughals won a great South Asian empire, which included Agra, the Lodi capital. For the next 150 years, the site of the Mughal capital shifted between Delhi and Agra, leaving each city with a host of beautiful landmarks. With the slow decline of Mughal power in North India, Agra fell on hard times; the British made Calcutta (and later Delhi) their capital, and Allahabad rose to surpass Agra as the local political powerhouse.

Lately, Agra has worked hard to re-invent itself, funneling some of the hard currency it earns from tourists into smoggy industrial development. It sometimes requires great reserves of patience and magnanimity to rise above the temptation to scream and shout back at the persistent crowd that will follow your every step. But despite its irritations, Agra is well worth the effort. The monuments remain serene and beautiful, and memories of the Taj at dawn will remain with you long after you have forgiven and forgotten the rickshaw driver who refused to take you anywhere but his uncle's diamond warehouse.

> **WARNING.** Agra, like all major tourist hubs in India, has a number of swindlers who'd love a chunk of that cash you're stashing. Rickshaw charges are excessive; the commissions incentive means drivers will often try to take you to the hotel or restaurant of their (and not your) choice. Be firm, be insistent, and be prepared to walk away. Also beware of crafty salesmen who persuade tourists with "parties," tea, and sweet talk to buy rugs and jewels to resell back home. Numerous schemes (credit card fraud, false identities, and even rape) can result from this, so don't get lured in. (See also **Touts, Middlemen and Scams,** p. 15.) Walk away if the price you're quoted seems too high; there is no need to bother negotiating with those who make a living out of over-charging daytripping tourists.

Agra

🔺 ACCOMMODATIONS

Agra Hotel, 2
Hotel Akbar Inn, 9
Hotel Sakura, 1
Hotel Safari, 10
Pawan Hotel, 7
Tourists Rest House, 3

🍴 FOOD

Chung Wa, 5
Dasaprakash, 4
The Park (Restaurant), 8
Priya Restaurant, 11
Zorba the Buddha, 6

UTTAR PRADESH

▣ GETTING THERE AND GETTING AROUND

Flights: Agra's **Kheria Airport** is 9km southwest of the city (enquiry ☎ 302274). To: **Delhi** (M, W, F, and Su; 4:10pm; 40min.; US$55); **Varanasi** (M, W, F, and Su; 11:35am; 2hr.; US$105) via **Khajuraho** (2hr., US$80). **Indian Airlines** office (☎ 360190), in the Hotel Clarks-Shiraz complex. Open daily 10am-1:15pm and 2-5pm. **Sita World Travel** (☎ 225038), on the north side of Sadar Bazaar, the main market. Open M-F 9:30am-1pm and 2-6pm, Sa 9:30am-2pm.

Trains: Agra has several rail stations, but most are of no use to tourists: **Agra Cantonment Railway Station** (enquiry ☎ 131), the main terminal, is southwest of the city at the west end of The Mall. A window at the computer reservation complex on the south side makes bookings for foreign tourists. To: **Bhopal** (frequent, 8:30am-12:30am, 7-10½hr., Rs 174; fastest service with *Shatabdi Exp.* 2002, 8am, 6hr., A/C chair Rs640); **Bombay** (daily; 12:50, 8:30am, and 12:35pm; additional M, Sa, 10:50pm; 22-25hr.; Rs315); **Calcutta, Howrah Station** (daily, 12:50am, 30hr., Rs326); **Delhi** (frequent, 5:30am-1:15am, 5hr., Rs84; *Shatabdi Exp.* 2001, 8:18pm, 2½hr., A/C chair Rs390); **Gwalior** (frequent, 8:40am-12:50am, 1½-2hr., Rs84); **Lucknow** (daily, 10:45pm, 4hr.; W, 7am, 6½hr.; Rs84); **Mathura** (several per day, 5:30am-3am, 1-1½hr., Rs84).

Buses: Most leave from **Idgah Bus Terminal,** northeast of Agra Cant. Railway Station. To: **Ajmer** (4 per day, 8:30am-9pm, 9hr., Rs152); **Bikaner** (11am, 12hr., Rs198); **Delhi** (every 30min., 5am-8pm, 5hr., Rs93); **Fatehpur Sikri** (every hr., 5am-10pm, 1½hr., Rs17); **Gwalior** (every hr., 6am-7:30pm, 3½hr., Rs54); **Jaipur** (every 30min., 6am-10:30pm, 7hr., Rs94) via **Bharatpur** (1½hr., Rs26); **Jhansi** (4 per day, 5am-8:30pm,

10hr., Rs74); **Khajuraho** (5:30am, 14hr., Rs119); **Mathura** (every 30min., 5am-8pm, 1½hr., Rs23); **Udaipur** (6pm, 14hr., Rs255). Buses to **Varanasi** (8:30am, 12:30, and 4:30pm; 16hr.; Rs248) leave from the **Agra Fort Bus Stand,** southwest of the fort. Deluxe buses leave from other places—contact a Taj Ganj area travel agent for details.

Local Transportation: Despite all the rip-offs, **cycle-rickshaws** are still a good way to get around. Pay no more than Rs15-20 for a cycle-rickshaw or **auto-rickshaw** going between the railway or bus stations and Taj Ganj or Agra Fort. Agra is easy to zip around on **bicycle;** there are rental shops all over town. If you have money to burn, you can hire a **car and driver** from one of the numerous places around the tourist centers: **R.R. Travels** Fatehabad Rd., Taj Ganj (☎330055), organizes a 1-day tour that lasts 8hr. and includes Fatehpur Sikri (Rs800, Rs1000 with A/C). Open daily 7am-7:30pm. UP Tourism offers a similar tour of sights (Rs700) that starts at 9:30am from the Government of India Tourist Office (see below).

✴ ORIENTATION

Agra is a large and spread-out city, most of which sprawls west from the banks of the **Yamuna River,** along which are both the Fort and the Taj Mahal, separated by 1½km, and the **Shah Jahan Park. Yamuna Kinara Rd.** runs along the river's western banks from the Taj Mahal to **Belan Ganj,** a bustling neighborhood 1km north of **Agra Fort Railway Station,** where trains from eastern Rajasthan pull in. Tourist facilities cluster south of the Taj Mahal and Agra Fort. Bargain-basement backpacker dives crowd the streets of Taj Ganj, an unremittingly ugly and irritating rabbit-warren of hotels, restaurants, and souvenir shops that surrounds, chokes, and strangles the Taj Mahal from the southern side. **Mahatma Gandhi (MG) Rd., Gwalior Rd.,** and **General Cariappa Rd.** are three major thoroughfares that cross both The Mall and **Taj Rd.** From the upscale but none-too-beautiful **Sadar Bazaar,** which is squeezed between MG and Gwalior Rd., it's 2km due west to **Agra Cantonment Railway Station;** 2km northwest along Fatehpur Sikri Rd. is the **Idgah Bus Stand.**

🔋 PRACTICAL INFORMATION

Tourist Office: Government of India Tourist Office, 191 The Mall (☎226378 or 226368), opposite the post office, is the most convenient and informative of Agra's 3 tourist offices. Open M-F 9am-5:30pm, Sa 9am-4:30pm. **UP Government Tourist Office,** 64 Taj Rd. (☎226341), near Clarks-Shiraz is less well-stocked. Open M-Sa 10am-5pm. Their **branch office** (☎368598) is at Agra Cant. Railway Station, opposite the enquiry booth. Open daily 8am-8pm.

Currency Exchange: State Bank of India, Fatehabad Rd. (☎330449), 1km from Taj Ganj; follow the blue "I" signs from the traffic circle at the Shah Jahan park entrance. Exchanges currency and traveler's checks. Open M-F 11am-2pm, Sa 11am-1pm. **LKP Merchant Financing Ltd.,** Fatehabad Rd. (☎330480), in the tourist complex area next to Pizza Hut, changes traveler's checks and major currencies. Service is much faster than at the State Bank of India, though you'll come out with about 2% less money. Open M-Sa 9:30am-7pm. Outside these hours, the black-market opportunists in Taj Ganj will be more than happy to take your dollars from you. Many of the larger luxury hotels will also change money for a fee.

Luggage Storage: Agra Cant. Railway Station. Rs7 per item per day. As always, your bags must be locked, and you must have a valid train ticket.

Bookstore: Modern Book Depot (☎22569), in Sadar Bazaar. Open W-M 10am-9pm.

Market: Taj Ganj is a high-pressure, hassle-a-minute hustlers' hang-out where you are constantly urged to buy everything from toilet paper to miniature Taj Mahals in marble and plastic. **Old Agra** is one big bazaar for buying belts, shoes, car parts, and plastic buckets. **Kinari Bazaar,** extending northwest from the fort, is especially well stocked. Shop around, and always, always bargain hard (even if a sign claims fixed prices).

Police: ☎361120; Taj Ganj branch, ☎331015.

Pharmacy: Pharmacies are everywhere around the major tourist areas and also cluster around Hospital Rd. and Garojini Naidu Hospital. Some are open 24hr.

Hospital: Sarojini Naidu Hospital (☎264428), west of Old Agra, near Bageshwarnath Temple and Kali Masjid. **Shanti Manglik,** Fatehabad Rd. (☎330488 or 330038), provides 24hr. emergency assistance and local ambulance service.

Internet: Cyberlink, Thana Chowk, Taj Ganj (☎331275), just west of the hub at the first major crossing. The best of several places in and around Taj Ganj, Cyberlink has more computers than all its rivals put together and is run by a friendly, English-speaking staff. Rs60 per hr. Fax, call-backs (Rs1 per min.), and collect calls (Rs3 per min.). Open daily 9am-11pm. **Cyber Space,** Gopi Chand Shivare Rd. (☎225032), just north of Zorba the Buddha, has several computers. Rs40 per hr. Open daily 10am-11pm.

Telephone: STD booths are throughout the city; most close around 11pm or midnight and will allow callbacks for Rs3-5 per min.

Post Office: GPO, The Mall (☎362789). Opposite the tourist office. Massive, intimidating, and notoriously inefficient. M-Sa 10am-6pm. **Postal Code:** 282001.

ACCOMMODATIONS

The area immediately south of the Taj Mahal testifies to how competition keeps prices in check. Rooms here are surprisingly cheap—except during peak times, there's no need to pay more than Rs100 for a decent double. This is where most budget travelers stay, and many cheap restaurants have sprung up to keep them watered and fed. This area also swarms with touts, con-men, and remarkably persistent rickshaw-*wallahs*. Most hotels have rooftop views of the Taj—often little more than a blurred glimpse of a marble minaret through the brown haze and electrical wires. There are, however, several good budget options outside of Taj Ganj, often closer to the real center of the city and usually a 10-minute rickshaw ride from the world's most talked-about tomb. Prices vary by season; in December, the rates listed below may inflate by as much as 200%. Most check-out times are 10am.

TAJ GANJ

The best way to orient yourself is to start with the central hub, the rickshaw-cluttered area in front of Joney's Place; Taj Ganj splits to the north (toward the Taj), east, and west. Roads also run along the sides of the Taj Mahal toward the gates.

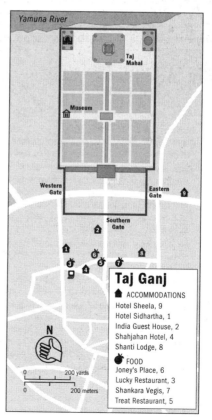

Taj Ganj

♠ ACCOMMODATIONS
Hotel Sheela, 9
Hotel Sidhartha, 1
India Guest House, 2
Shahjahan Hotel, 4
Shanti Lodge, 8

🍴 FOOD
Joney's Place, 6
Lucky Restaurant, 3
Shankara Vegis, 7
Treat Restaurant, 5

☒ **Hotel Sheela,** East Gate (☎331194 or 333074). Just far enough from the noise and the nastiness of the hub without being more than a couple of minutes' walk away from the you-know-what. Run by the Secretary of the Agra Hotel and Restaurant Association, this is strictly a no-commission, no-scams, no-rugs-or-knick-knacks zone. Pleasant rooms surround a garden patio restaurant. Singles Rs125-300; doubles Rs150-350.

Shahjahan Hotel (☎331159). One of the oldest of the Taj Ganj budget places and still one of the most popular. The cushion-equipped rooftop chill-out area has good views of the Taj and little gazebos to protect you from the sun. Two restaurants serve the standard fare; the manager is very eager to please. Singles Rs40-120; doubles Rs120-150.

Shanti Lodge (☎330900), on the left as you walk east from the hub. The tallest hotel in Taj Ganj, Shanti has a rooftop restaurant with an unobstructed view of the Taj. Less grungy than many of the bargain-basement places nearby, the second of its two buildings has better rooms with nice quilts and color TVs. First building: singles Rs80-120; doubles Rs150-200. Second building: singles Rs175; doubles Rs250-350.

India Guest House (☎330909). On the left side of the street between the hub and the Taj, within spitting distance of the gates. Run by a friendly family. Morning observances at the shrine act as an effective wake-up call. Rooms with twin beds from Rs30-45.

Hotel Sidhartha (☎331238), Western Gate. Clean, wall-papered rooms with sheets changed daily. Some have carpeting and look out on trees beyond the bustle of the street. Singles with attached bath Rs80-125; doubles Rs100-200.

CITY CENTER

▨**Tourists Rest House,** Kachahari Rd. (☎363961; fax 366910; trh@nde.vsni.com), near Meher Cinema off Gwalior Rd., northeast of the GPO. Don't confuse it with impostors that hide under similar names. Agra's best budget deal by far—spotlessly clean rooms (with soap, toilet paper, and clean towels) around a green garden courtyard. 24hr. STD/ISD, email facilities, and a multi-lingual manager, who is the long-time president of the Agra Hotel and Restaurant Association. Singles Rs100-350; doubles Rs120-350.

Agra Hotel, Field Marshal Cariappa Rd. (☎363331; fax 265830), within walking distance of the fort. Good views of the Taj from garden deck-chairs. Agra's oldest hotel still in operation (since 1926), it's beginning to show its age, but the friendly management and mellow atmosphere still make it a good deal. Attached restaurant. Singles Rs150-200; doubles Rs250-550.

Hotel Akbar Inn, 21 The Mall (☎363212), halfway between Taj Ganj and the railway station. A quiet place tucked away in the cool shade of the wide Cantonment streets, the Akbar feels a million miles away from the headaches and the hassles of the outside world. Some rooms a little small and stuffy. Singles Rs80-120; doubles Rs150-450.

Hotel Safari, Minto Rd. (☎333029), opposite Hotel Swagat and near the All India Radio station. Spotless rooms, a pleasant rooftop patio, and free bicycles for those who want to cruise to the Taj (2km). Singles Rs150-175; doubles Rs200-250.

Pawan Hotel, 3 Taj Rd., Sadar Bazaar (☎225506). The only hotel in the main Sadar strip, this sprawling and slightly run-down hotel is well-placed for restaurants, bars, and auto-rickshaw tours of the world. All rooms have air-cooling. Singles Rs240-350, with A/C Rs600; doubles Rs350-500, with A/C Rs500-600.

Hotel Sakura, 49 Old Idgah Colony (☎369793), 200m from the bus station. A fairly uninspiring place with rooms that run the gamut from luxurious to drab. The bathrooms are all very clean, however, and the hotel provides towel, soap, and toilet paper. Air-cooled singles with attached bath Rs125-450; doubles Rs175-600.

☕ FOOD

Most of Agra's foreigner-friendly restaurants are clustered around Taj Ganj, Sadar Bazaar, and other tourist centers south of the old heart of town. Most travelers tend to stick to places close to (or inside) their hotels. If you simply can't face the thought of another banana pancake or another plate of *chappati* and chow mein, the best places to go for a really good meal are the extravagant restaurants in the five-star hotels to the south of Taj Ganj.

TAJ GANJ AREA

The restaurants near the Taj Mahal are notorious for poor hygiene; most who stay more than a few days get the "Agra aches," akin to "Delhi Belly." There have even been tales of restaurants deliberately poisoning guests and pocketing a percentage of the charges levied by the dodgy doctor used to help the victim "recover." For the most part, though, you are unlikely to develop anything worse than a mild case of under-fed boredom. Most of the popular rooftop places are probably better for a sunset beer than a full-blown meal, unless you happen to have developed an addiction to greasy finger fries.

Joney's Place, at the main hub of Taj Ganj. Hardly enough room to swing a kitten in this cozy little veteran of the Taj Ganj roadside racket. Friendly, reliable, and more or less hassle-free. Renowned banana *lassis;* breakfasts (Rs15) are also good, but the Indian dishes (Rs12-35) are somewhat variable. Open daily 5am-10:30pm.

Shankara Vegis and The Door's Cafe, just east of the hub. The most popular of the roof-top gathering points. Games like Connect 4 and music from Bob Dylan to Bob Marley cover up any awkward evening silences. The food here won't win many prizes; still, you will eat far worse and survive. Happy hour daily 6-7pm and 9-10pm.

Isfahan, East Gate, past the Hotel Sheela. Heavily-curtained, heavily-cooled small dining room serves up reasonably-priced, stomach-friendly food. A definite relief from the bland cuisine and overworked ceiling fans of other restaurants. Entrees from Rs40; beer Rs75. Open daily 6am-11pm.

Lucky Restaurant, west of the hub, opposite Cyberlink. A stereo and air-cooler create a temperate, unassuming, and popular atmosphere. Delightful "Danish Farmoon," with coconut, chocolate, banana, and curd (Rs15). Other species of haute cuisine are disguised on the menu as spaghetti and veg. sandwiches. Open daily 6:30am-10pm.

Treat Restaurant, at the Taj Ganj hub, south side, opposite Joney's Place. Tiny little wooden-benched aerie with 4 different colors of light bulbs. Sit and shout abuse down at the rickshaw-*wallahs* below. Mini-breakfast (Rs15) is the best deal around. Also serves *thalis* (Rs20) and the usual stuff. Open daily 6am-midnight.

CITY CENTER

⬛ Dasaprakash, 1 Gwalior Rd., next to Meher Cinema. With branches in Delhi, Madras, Bombay, and Chicago, this is one of the best restaurants around. Excellent South Indian veg. dishes are well worth the premium you pay for tasteful interior decor, unobtrusive service, and A/C. Excellent *thalis* Rs100. Open daily 12:30-10:45pm.

Zorba the Buddha, Gopi Chand Shivare Rd. In the shopping strip north of the main part of Sadar Bazaar. Tiny, floral-theme, A/C dining room decked with photos of meditation meister Osho. No smoking, no meat, no hassles. Popular with the Euro-tourist crowd. Most dishes Rs60-120. Open daily noon-3pm and 6-9pm; closed May 1 to July 5.

The Park (Restaurant), Sadar Bazaar, before the strip mall on the left. Airy dining room with tables set far apart on the marble floor. Listen to hits from 1980s flicks while deciding between the excellent Indian food and standard variety of Chinese and continental dishes. *Haryali kofta* Rs55; spaghetti from Rs50. Open daily 9am-11pm.

Chung Wa, Gopi Chand Shivare Rd., opposite Zorba the Buddha. The interior won't win any awards from *Architectural Digest,* but for better Chinese food, you might have to head across the Himalayas. Good place to remind yourself that "Chinese food" consists of more than just soggy noodles. Open W-M noon-2:30pm and 6:30-10:30pm.

Priya Restaurant, behind Hotel Ratan Deep, off Fatehabad Rd. Cold and dark as a December cellar. Large menu of tasty Indian fare (from Rs50) and a Shah Jahan *thali* (Rs250) that could feed a camel for a month. Open daily 7am-midnight.

⬛ SIGHTS

While Agra contains several interesting monuments from the heyday of Mughal rule, most tourists come to see that marble jewel in India's crown, the Taj Mahal. Capitalizing on one of the most famous buildings in the world, the money-hungry folks at the Agra Development Authority have raised admission prices drastically over the past 12 months and have plans to raise them even higher. At the moment, admission is free on Fridays, but even this loophole might not exist for long. As a result, the Taj Mahal is a zoo on Fridays, and almost quiet during the rest of the week. The city's second-fiddle attractions are certainly worth a trip—if only as respite from the chaos of Taj Ganj. Most sights charge Rs25 for video cameras.

TAJ MAHAL

Open Tu-Su dawn-dusk. Rs505 for foreigners. Free Fridays.

Despite all the hype and hoopla, the sheer beauty of the place is so overwhelming that no amount of overexposure can diminish it. Especially at dawn and dusk, even the most jaded of globe-trotters often find themselves smiling in wonder as they behold the Taj. Emblazoned across the signs of a million-and-one restaurants, T-shirts, and biscuit tins the world over, this marble prima donna, unofficially crowned by her ardent fans as "the most beautiful building in the world," remains undeniably India's ultimate must-see.

The tale of the Taj is a sad, sweet love story. When he became Mughal emperor in 1628, Shah Jahan brought to the throne a great many virtues, among them intellect, political acumen, and a passion for fine architecture. Three years after becoming emperor, Shah Jahan received news that broke his heart: after 18 years of marriage, his favorite wife, Arjumand Banu Begum, had died giving birth to their 14th child. In his grief, Shah Jahan decided that his beloved should be buried in a tomb of timeless beauty. As the Bengali poet Rabindranath Tagore said, the Taj Mahal was designed to be a "tear [that] would hang on the cheek of time."

Work on the Taj began in 1632, one year after the death of Arjumand Banu Begum. Marble was quarried in Makrana, Rajasthan, and precious stones were brought to Agra from Yemen, Russia, China, and Central Asia. Architects were sent over from Persia, and French and Italian master craftsmen had a hand in decorating the building. In all, nearly 20,000 people worked non-stop on the construction of the Taj. By the time the tomb was completed in 1653, a great many things had changed—the Mughal capital had been moved from Agra to Delhi, the deceased Arjumand Banu Begum had become popularly known as "Mumtaz Mahal" ("Elect of the Palace"), and one of Shah Jahan's sons, Aurangzeb, had grown to manhood. In 1658, Aurangzeb staged a coup, violently surmounting the opposition of his three brothers and imprisoning his father in Agra Fort. Shah Jahan lived out his days under house arrest, staring out across the Yamuna River at the Taj Mahal. When the deposed emperor died in the winter of 1666, his body was buried next to his wife's.

The path to the Taj from the original entry arch (now the exit) is one of the most well-designed architectural approaches in the world. The tomb building and the four principal minarets rest on a large pedestal of white marble. Up close, the Taj is hardly white at all: delicately inlaid precious stones create meandering floral patterns framed by elegant Arabic script (it is said that the entire Koran is written on the walls of the Taj). While much of the tomb's interior is off-limits, visitors can enter the dimly lit, domed chamber that contains the cenotaphs of Shah Jahan and Mumtaz Mahal; the latter is inscribed with the 99 names of Allah. The tombs themselves lie directly below in a room not accessible to the public. The **mosque** is to the west, and the **Jawab** ("Answer"), its architectural mirror, is to the east. A popular local myth has it that Shah Jahan planned to construct a second Taj of black marble, to the north, on the other side of the Yamuna river. A small **museum** on the west side of the gardens showcases paintings of Shah Jahan and Mumtaz Mahal and some other curios, but few take the time to visit it. *(Open daily 10am-5pm.)*

If you prefer a serene, private audience, show up at dawn—you'll have the place practically to yourself. At other times, the monument is crawling with tourists and security guards, and you'll have a hard time getting a good photo before someone steps in your way. Changing light patterns affect the experience of viewing the Taj. On a cloudless day, the building exudes a piercingly bright white light; in the early morning and toward twilight, the Taj has a softer glow.

Agra Fort

AGRA FORT

To the east of Yamuna Kinara Rd., 1½km upriver from the Taj Mahal. Open daily dawn-dusk. Rs55 for foreigners. Entrance fee included in Rs505 ticket for the Taj Mahal.

There aren't nearly as many restaurants named after Agra's fort, but it's a close second to the Taj on most visitors' check-list itineraries. Construction began under Emperor Akbar in 1565. Its fortifications were gradually strengthened over the years—the 2½km bulky, red sandstone walls that enclose it were not completed until the time of Emperor Aurangzeb. Of the three outer gates that lead through the walls and into the fort, only the **Amar Singh Gate,** decorated with colorful glazed tiles, is accessible to the public. The gate is named for the Rajasthani maharaja who killed the royal treasurer before the emperor's eyes and then jumped from the walls here in 1644 to escape the guards.

Due north of the Amar Singh Gate is the breezy **Diwan-i-Am** (Hall of Public Audience), a low three-sided structure that served as Shah Jahan's court while Agra was the Mughal capital. At the height of Agra's Mughal fame, the Diwan-i-Am was filled with nobles, courtiers, and regal accoutrements. Shah Jahan's throne sat on the platform at the east side of the hall. The low marble platform in front of the throne was reserved for his chief minister. The tomb at the center of the courtyard is that of a British officer who was killed here during the Mutiny of 1857.

The **royal chambers** are between the eastern end of Diwan-i-Am and Agra Fort's ramparts; here the emperor's many needs were seen to in private. He also slept and prayed here from time to time. From Diwan-i-Am, the first chamber is the expansive **Macchli Bhavan** (Fish Palace), which gets its name from the stock that was dumped into its water channels so that the emperor could amuse himself with rod and reel. Unfortunately, the chamber is missing blocks of mosaic work, and huge chunks of the royal bath have been pillaged over the centuries. In the northwest corner of the Macchli Bhavan (left as you face away from Diwan-i-Am) is the **Nagina Masjid** (Gem Mosque), built by Shah Jahan for the women of his harem.

Southeast of the Macchi Bhavan is the fabulous **Diwan-i-Khas** (Hall of Private Audience), completed in 1637, where the emperor would receive visitors. The **terrace** just east of Diwan-i-Khas offers classic views over the Yamuna to the Taj Mahal. Just south of the terrace is the two-story **Musamman Burj** (Octagonal Tower), which features delicate inlay work. Legend has it that Shah Jahan spent his final hours here, as a prisoner, gazing wistfully at his Taj Mahal, which was reflected in mirrors positioned at every angle in his cell. The emperor, meanwhile, is said to have enjoyed watching as men, tigers, and elephants were pitted against one another in the cramped area between the inner and outer walls.

Heading south from the tower, it's a hop, skip, and a jump to the **Sheesh Mahal** (Palace of Mirrors), where the women of the court bathed. South of the Sheesh Mahal is a breezy enclosure that includes the **Anguri Bagh** (Vine Garden). On the east side of the garden are three buildings. The **Khas Mahal** (Private Palace) is at the center, flanked by the **Golden Pavilions.** Rendered in cool marble, the Khas Mahal is supposedly where the emperor slept. The pavilions were women's bedrooms, with walls that were discreetly packed with jewelry. Note the pavilions' roofs, which were built to resemble roofs of Bengali thatched huts. The **Jehangiri Mahal,** the large sandstone palace to the south, was designed for the Hindu queen Jodh Bai. In front of the palace is a large tub, thought to have been where Queen Nur Jahan took her rose-scented baths.

OTHER SIGHTS

JAMA MASJID. The Jama Masjid (Friday Mosque), Agra's main mosque, is 100m west of Agra Fort Railway Station. Built in 1648 by Shah Jahan, out of sandstone spliced with ornamental marble in a zig-zag pattern, the mosque complex was damaged during the Mutiny of 1857, when British forces deemed its main gate a threat to the strategically important Red Fort; the gate was promptly leveled along with some of the front cloisters of the mosque. For a while during the uprising, the Jama Masjid was, in a sense, held hostage—the mosque was planted with explosives, and the British authorities loudly proclaimed that if the Mutiny gained a large enough following in Agra, the Jama Masjid would suffer the consequences. The building remained standing, though it is in pretty bad shape today.

ITIMAD-UD-DAULAH. The so-called "Baby Taj," the Itimad-ud-Daulah, is a small but exquisite marble tomb that is always less crowded than its rival across the river. The tomb was built between 1622 and 1628 for Ghiyas Beg, a Persian diplomat who served as Emperor Jehangir's chief minister, and who was dubbed Itimad-ud-Daulah (Pillar of Government) for his loyal and exemplary service. In an intimate garden designed by Ghiyas Beg himself, the tomb was built by his daughter Nur Jahan, whom the emperor married in 1611. The semi-precious stone inlay work on white marble enhances the tomb's dazzling beauty. Several of Nur Jahan's relatives were subsequently buried in the central tomb. *(Open sunrise-sunset. Rs12.)*

CHINI-KA-RAUZA AND RAM BAGH. One kilometer north of Itimad-ud-Daulah is the **Chini-ka-Rauza** (China Tomb), the decayed burial chamber of Shah Jahan's chief minister, Afzal Khan. Glazed tiles once covered the entire construction—the few that are left are severely weathered. As you continue north, it's 2km to **Ram Bagh,** a garden said to have been designed by Babur. The scruffy-looking garden is overgrown with weeds, but there is some talk of restoring it. Besides a few foreign visitors, only peacocks roam the ruins, giving the place an atmosphere of calm and peace rare in Agra. *(Both open sunrise-sunset. Women should not visit Ram Bagh alone.)*

🎯 DAYTRIP FROM AGRA: SIKANDRA सिकान्द्रा

A small town just outside Agra, Sikandra is famous as the home of **Akbar's Tomb.** Mughal emperor from 1556 to 1605, Akbar was a great patron of the visual arts and a respectful admirer of Hinduism. The most impressive structure at the complex is the **Buland Darwaza** (Gateway of Magnificence), embellished with geometric patterns and Koranic inscriptions. The central mausoleum is sparsely adorned with colonnaded alcoves and marble domes. A narrow passageway leads down to the remarkably simple crypt itself, with its flickering candlelight and smoking sticks of incense. The dome is a wonder of acoustics, and echoes reverberate for 10 seconds or more. Mornings and evening are less crowded, while on Fridays the joint jumps with the usual mix of hawkers, hustlers, and picnickers. The untended grassy area between the northern wall of the mausoleum and the wall that encloses the entire complex is an interesting place—monkeys, deer, and peacocks enhance the architectural grandeur of the tomb. Resist the temptation to feed the animals, since they can be dangerous, especially when grabbing for food. People have been mauled by the monkeys here. Sikandra is accessible by **auto-rickshaw** (Rs80-100 round-trip from Agra) or by one of the **buses** bound for Mathura, which board at the station and along Mathura Rd. *(Open daily dawn-dusk. Rs12; free F.)*

FATEHPUR SIKRI फ़तेहपुर सीकरी   ☎ 05613

Emperor Akbar, who ruled the Mughal empire from 1556 to 1605, was a man who had almost—but not quite—everything. Neither the absolute power he enjoyed throughout his vast territory, nor his three wives, nor any of his countless consorts and courtesans could satisfy his most powerful wish and give him what he wanted above all else: a male heir to succeed him. In time, Akbar's search became desperate, and he left Agra to wander across North India in search of help. His quest brought him to the village of Sikri, where he came across a Sufi mystic named Shaykh Salim Chishti, who consoled the ruler and promised him no fewer than three sons. When, a year later, the first foretold son arrived, Akbar repaid the saint by naming his son Salim (the future emperor Jehangir) and moving the entire court close to the saint's village of Sikri. To the surprise of the population of Agra, the palace of Fatehpur Sikri became the new capital of the Mughal empire.

Palaces, mosques, and battlements were hastily constructed, and Fatehpur Sikri served as the Mughal center for 15 years before the court shifted back to Agra. Exactly what prompted the return to Agra remains uncertain. Some say that drought forced the Mughals out, while others claim that the death of Shaykh Salim prompted the move. In any case, the decision left an immaculate ghost-palace and abandoned city behind. Fatehpur Sikri often casts a haunting spell on visitors, especially at dawn and dusk, when the sunlight and shadows whirl across the deserted palace buildings.

🚍 TRANSPORTATION AND PRACTICAL INFORMATION

Vehicles drive into Fatehpur Sikri from an access to the east of the palace complex. The deserted city is on a hilltop overlooking the modern village of Sikri to the south. From the bus or train stations, it's a five-minute walk up the hill to the ruins. **Buses** head to: **Agra** (every 30min., 6am-8pm, 1hr., Rs17) and **Bharatpur** (5 per day, 1hr., Rs10). **Auto-rickshaws** also run to Bharatpur (45min., Rs70). **Trains** run daily to **Agra** (5:30, 10:35am, and 4:40pm, Rs8; express 8:20pm, Rs20). There is a bank near the bus station, but don't rely on it for **currency exchange;** ask around at the more upscale hotels.

UTTAR PRADESH

ACCOMMODATIONS AND FOOD

Everything in Fatehpur Sikri is within walking distance of the palace. In peak season (Oct.-Mar.), hotels fill up and prices may rise by 25%. Probably the best budget option in town is the recently opened **Ajay Palace Hotel,** just to the left as you come out of the bus station, which offers four spotlessly clean rooms. (☎882950. Singles with attached bath Rs75; doubles Rs120.) Down the road that heads toward Agra, on the right-hand side just before the turn-off for the railway station, the **Hotel Goverdhan Tourist Complex** has neat and shiny rooms that smell a little musty; some boast such luxuries as running hot water and TVs. (☎882643. Dorm beds Rs50; doubles Rs100-400.) East of the Goverdhan, 1km from the ruins, UP Tourism's **Gulistan Tourist Complex** has luxurious rooms at luxurious prices, as well as the standard swish-and-shiny restaurant around the standard dark-and-gloomy bar. (☎882490. Singles Rs525-775; doubles Rs575-900. Off-season discounts April-Sept.). For food, the restaurant in Ajay Palace Hotel is your best bet. Homemade cheese and mineral-water ice put this place in a different league from most roadside joints (Kashmiri *kofta* Rs40). The restaurant at the **Gulistan Tourist Complex** has large lunch and dinner buffets (Rs260). Of the several stalls by the main gate to the old city compound, try the **Kallu Restaurant,** just in front of the gate (*thalis* Rs25).

SIGHTS

Wherever tourists and their buses congregate, so do **guides** eager to offer tours of the deserted palace. Many of these "guides" falsely claim to be licensed; others insist they are students whose "duty" it is to show you around, only afterward whining for baksheesh or leading you into their handicraft shops. Ask to see proper ID. Official guides should charge around Rs40-50 for a tour of the monuments. Guides are rarely informative and the sandstone signposts can usually tell you more than they will. All sights are open daily from dawn to dusk.

The base of the **Buland Darwaza** is 13m above street level, and its gate stands 40m above that, making it the tallest doorway in Asia. The gate was added to the complex in 1595, following Akbar's triumph in Gujarat, and its style was copied in other Victory Gates around the country. As you pass through the gate, take off your shoes. The head of the **Jama Masjid** is off to the left, facing Mecca. In the middle is the pure white **mausoleum** of Shaykh Salim Chishti, the sage who prophesied the birth of Akbar's sons. The core of the tomb is made from mother-of-pearl. Visitors hoping for Shaykh Salim to intercede on *their* behalf hang threads from the marble latticework on the walls inside. Incense sticks burn inside the tomb, and musicians sometimes sit and play outside. Next to the mausoleum is a series of royal cenotaphs. The tiny white one holds the remains of the royal pigeon. From the courtyard, go through the other main gate, **Badshahi Darwaza,** cross through the parking lot, and head down the road 400m to the main entrance to the palace complex, on the eastern side of the ruins.

Coming from the east, you'll pass the **Naubat Khana** (Drum House), which was used to signal the emperor's arrival, and the ticket office for the palace complex (*Rs5, free on Fridays*). A path leads around into the **Diwan-i-Am,** the court where, from a throne between two sandstone slates, the emperor would hear the pleas and petitions of common men. To the west toward the throne is the main palace courtyard. To the right is the **Diwan-i-Khas** (Hall of Private Audience), where Akbar is thought to have met with VIPs and relatives. The hall is a massive chamber supported in the middle by one ornate column shaped like a budding flower. To the left is a meticulously carved gazebo, probably the sitting chamber of either the treasurer or royal astrologer.

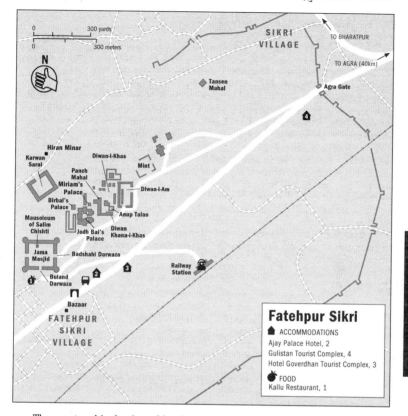

UTTAR PRADESH

Fatehpur Sikri

🏠 ACCOMMODATIONS

Ajay Palace Hotel, 2
Gulistan Tourist Complex, 4
Hotel Goverdhan Tourist Complex, 3

🍗 FOOD

Kallu Restaurant, 1

The courtyard is dominated by the five-story **Panch Mahal** tower that looms to the west of the Diwan-i-Khas. Steps to the west lead up through scores of intricately carved stone columns to the narrow fifth floor. Tourist access to the tower goes no farther than the base, however. On the south side of the courtyard is a grid tank called **Anup Talao,** the choice venue of legendary Mughal crooner Miyan Tansen (see also **Come On Baby, Fight My Fire,** p. 383). More finely carved columns and walls decorate the nearby **Turkish Sultana's Palace.** To the north of Anup Talao stands what once served as the royal **banquet hall.** To the south of the tank sits **Diwan Khana-i-Khass,** the emperor's chambers. The path from Panch Mahal leads west to **Birbal's Palace,** which was the residence of either the minister's daughters or one of Akbar's queens.

Before Panch Mahal, in the middle of the courtyard, is **Mariam's Palace,** once home to Akbar's Christian wife, where faded wall paintings are left over from the palace's glory days. From here, proceed south and cut right to the entrance of **Jodh Bai's Palace,** one of Fatehpur Sikri's largest and most evocative buildings. In the courtyard, symmetrical patterns and sandstone flowers carved into the walls surround a central fountain. This complex was probably used for the emperor's harem. Note the azure glazed tiles on the roof along the second story. To the back of Jodh Bai's palace is the *haremsara,* which once housed the palace's many servants and attendants. Leaving the palace complex and heading down past the Karwan Sarai, a path leads to the **Hiran Minar,** a 22m tower with protruding elephant tusk-shaped stones. The minaret was constructed as the memorial tomb for Akbar's favorite elephant, Hiran. The 360° view from the top makes the dark and claustrophobic climb worthwhile.

MATHURA मथुरा AND
VRINDABAN विन्दाबन
☎ **0565**

The city of Mathura teems with thousands of temples, where devotees celebrate the birthplace of Krishna. Countless Vaishnava pilgrims come here every year for Krishna Jayanti (Aug. 12, 2001), the celebration of Krishna's birth, to pay homage to the blue-skinned hero of Hindu lore. Even outside the main festival season, Mathura hums with holiness. Thousands of pilgrims and priests crowd the city, mingling saffron and incense with the dust and grime of the streets.

While Mathura draws its fair share of devotees, the main religious center of this area is the nearby pilgrimage town of Vrindaban, where Krishna performed the deeds that made him famous: lifting up **Mt. Govardhan**, jamming on his flute, and cavorting with all the *gopis* (milkmaids) he could find. Krishna's favorite *gopi* Radha is also revered here; her name is painted on walls throughout the town, and residents greet each other with a jubilant "Radhe Radhe!" Ever since the Bengali teacher Chaitanya discovered the site's importance, Vrindaban has been a huge draw for pilgrims, whose ashrams are maintained by wealthy devotees and ISKCON, the International Society for Krishna Consciousness (Hare Krishnas). Devotees show their love for Krishna during Holi (Mar. 9, 2001), the Festival of Colors, when they keep up his playful spirit by throwing colored powder and water at each other. Watch out for mischievous monkeys: they ofetn grab for food and have been known to snatch eye-glasses from peoples' faces. Mathura and Vrindaban make an easy 1-2 day stopover between Delhi and Agra.

▐ GETTING THERE AND GETTING AROUND

Trains: Buses, trains, and tempos from Mathura arrive south of the tangle of narrow streets that make up the heart of town. **Railway station,** 1½km south of the State Bank of India. To: **Agra** (frequent, 7:40am-11:45pm, 1-1½hr., Rs84); **Bombay** (10-12 per day, 20-25hr., Rs312); **Delhi** (several per day, 3hr., Rs43); **Gwalior** (at least 12 per day, 3-4hr., Rs50); **Jhansi** (3 per day, 7:40am-11:45pm, 6hr., Rs67); **Kanpur** (3 per day, 11am-7:40pm, 6½hr., Rs79).

Buses: From the **new bus stand** buses head every hr. or so (most frequent 6am-10:30pm) to: **Agra** (2hr., Rs24); **Bharatpur** (1hr., Rs18); and **Delhi** (4hr., Rs65). Buses also run to **Jaipur** (every 30min., 6am-10:30pm, 6hr., Rs87). From the **old bus stand,** UP Roadways buses head to: **Haridwar** (10pm, 8hr., Rs150); **Varanasi** (6:30, 10:30am, and 2pm; 16hr.; Rs280); **Vrindaban** (8 per day, 6:30am-7pm, 30min., Rs5).

Local Transportation: Stretch **tempos** cruise to Vrindaban (Rs5) and around town, as do **cycle-** (temple to New Bus Stand Rs10) and **auto-rickshaws** (Rs15).

✳▐ ORIENTATION AND PRACTICAL INFORMATION

At the heart of Mathura is the bazaar, stretching north from **Holi Gate,** on the eastern part of town near the Yamuna River. The **old bus stand** is 500m south of Holi Gate, and the more frequently used **new bus stand** is on Chowki Bag Bahadur Rd., about 500m northwest of the State Bank of India. The town's most important landmark is the temple **Shri Krishna Janmasthan (Janmabhoomi),** built on the site of Krishna's birth, 2km northwest of the new bus stand. Vrindaban is 15km north of Mathura on the banks of the Yamuna.

Tourist Office: UP Tourism (☎ 405351), at the north end of the old bus stand, 2nd fl. Open M-Sa 10am-5pm.

Currency Exchange: State Bank of India (☎ 407647), Bahadur and Station Rd. Changes US and UK currency and traveler's checks. Open M-F 10am-2pm.

Market: The **bazaar,** selling everything from chutneys to drums, extends just south and a long way north of Holi Gate. There is a **fruit market** next to the Jama Masjid.

Hospital: District Hospital (☎403006 or 406315), near the old bus stand. **Methodist Hospital,** Jaising Pura, Vrindaban Rd. (☎406032 or 404860).

Post Office: There is a branch in the complex next to the temple. **Postal Code:** 281001.

ACCOMMODATIONS

There are small restaurants, a few basic hotels, and tea stalls near the major temples for mid-worship munchies. The area around Holi Gate is the liveliest and noisiest part of town. Mathura has a few **ashrams,** including the **Keshvjee Gaudig,** opposite the district hospital (Rs20-50 per room).

International Rest House (☎405888), in the complex just east of the entrance to the temple. Cheap, simple rooms for pilgrims, as well as a garden where they can kick up their heels. Attached restaurant open 11am-3pm and 7-11pm for a "pious lunch and dinner." Singles Rs30-75; doubles Rs50-110.

Hotel Brij Raj (☎424172), opposite Shri Krishna temple. Large, clean but bland rooms around a courtyard within chanting range of Krishna's birthplace. Doubles Rs200-450.

Gaurav Guest House (☎406192). Walk 100m south of the Government Museum and look for the unmarked, blue and white hotel on the left; it's before the traffic circle. Dark, clean, comfortable rooms in a peaceful neighborhood. Singles Rs150; doubles Rs250-350. The more modern building next door, the **Gaurav Boarding House,** offers more luxurious rooms. Singles Rs400-750; doubles Rs500-850.

FOOD

Brij-Bhoj Restaurant, inside Hotel Mansarovar Palace. Cold enough to have numbed most of the waiters into a permanent state of frigid inactivity. *Pakora* as they're meant to be, *mutter paneer* (Rs55), and cucumber salad (Rs30). Non-veg. dishes from Rs135. Open daily 11am-11pm.

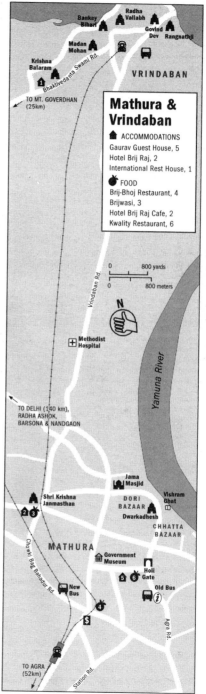

Mathura & Vrindaban

🏠 ACCOMMODATIONS
Gaurav Guest House, 5
Hotel Brij Raj, 2
International Rest House, 1

🍎 FOOD
Brij-Bhoj Restaurant, 4
Brijwasi, 3
Hotel Brij Raj Cafe, 2
Kwality Restaurant, 6

UTTAR PRADESH

Hotel Brij Raj Cafe, opposite the temple, below and next to Hotel Brij Raj. Good *thalis* (Rs20), ice-cream treats, and fresh coffee. Open daily 9am-11pm.

Kwality Restaurant, after the old bus station, on the road to Holi Gate. The Indian fast-food empire strikes back, again, this time with chandeliers and sandstone walls. Tasty Indian veg. dishes from Rs25; pineapple salad Rs30; South Indian dishes Rs20-30. Open daily 8am-10:30pm.

Brijwasi, opposite the temple, with another branch near Holi Gate. No real eats, but oodles of sweets. Open daily 7am-11pm.

SIGHTS

As rustic as the town feels in places, there's a surprising number of tourist-hungry guides knocking about (a tour should cost around Rs30-50).

MATHURA

SHRI KRISHNA JANMASTHAN TEMPLE. Most of the sights in Mathura revolve around Krishna, whose birth here has given this otherwise unremarkable town its status as one of the holiest places in India. The most important site for pilgrims is the Shri Krishna Janmasthan temple, which marks the spot of Krishna's appearance—the original temple, Kesava Deo, was destroyed by Aurangzeb and replaced with a mosque. The similar histories of the temples here and at the birthplace of Rama in Ayodhya have made the authorities particularly cautious—visitors must check all belongings (bags, cameras, etc.) at the cloakroom off to the left, pass through a metal detector, and undergo a zealous frisking. Dotted amid all the souvenir shops inside are several small temples and shrines. The main shrine, at the back of the complex to the right as you come in, is a small, dimly lit room believed to mark the exact site of the birth. The room is designed to represent the prison cell where Krishna was born while the nefarious King Kamsa held his parents captive. Barbed wire and uniformed guards with guns stand around the complex between the temple and the mosque with its green and white domes. Nearby is **Potara Kund,** where baby Krishna's diapers were supposedly washed. *(A straight, 1½km shot west from Holi Gate. Open daily 5am-9pm.)*

JAMA MASJID. The Jama Masjid, Mathura's main mosque, was built by Abo-in Nabir Khan in 1661. The mosque is unusually colorful, its teal domes brightening up the already striking bazaar and fruit market. *(A 1km walk northwest on the main road from Holi gate through the bazaar.)*

GOVERNMENT MUSEUM. Founded in 1874, the Government Museum houses a large collection of ancient Indian sculpture. Its pieces help shed light on Mathura's overall religious and cultural significance—for nearly 1200 years it was the artistic center for early Indian and visiting Hellenistic cultures. The museum contains several excellent examples of the mottled red sandstone sculpture for which the area is famous. The gems of the collection are two pristine Buddha images from the 4th and 5th centuries. *(600m west of Kwality Restaurant. Open Tu-Su, July-Apr. 10:30am-4:30pm; May-June 7:30am-12:30pm.)*

OTHER SIGHTS. Mathura's other attractions are on the east side of town. As you head north from the bazaar, the **Dwarkadheesh Temple** is on the left. Built in 1814 by local merchants, this temple is the main point of worship for local Hindus. The building itself almost seems to glow with its glossy paint and glittery shrines. *(Open daily 6:30-10:30am and 4-7pm.)* A little south on the bazaar, the street forks off to the right toward the river and the sacred **Vishram Ghat,** where Krishna came to rest after slaying the menacing King Kamsa and where many priests, guides, and beggars now congregate. From the *ghats,* **boats** take visitors on an hour-long tour of the city's shore (Rs30-50), with a prime view of the dilapidated **Sati Bur,** built in 1570 and dedicated to the *sati* of Behari Mal. Sunset boat trips offer a front-row view of the nightly *arati* ceremony, when priests bring fire to the sacred water amid the sound of gongs.

VRINDABAN

KRISHNA BALRAM TEMPLE. None of the holy places in Vrindaban draws more foreigners than the Krishna Balram Temple, the dazzling marble house of worship built by **ISKCON**, the International Society for Krishna Consciousness. The founder of the society, Srila Prabhupada, lived and worked here before embarking at the advanced age of 69 on a world tour to spread the word of "Krishna Consciousness." Next to three shrines and several murals of Krishna's exploits is a life-sized mannequin of Prabhupada, which sits over his burial site. Hare Krishnas, who come here from all over the world, are extremely eager to talk to newcomers. The temple echoes throughout the day with chants, drums, clicking beads, and donation requests, though the pervasive atmosphere of peace and serenity somehow manages to rise above all the chaos and commotion. *(Temple open daily 4:30am-8:30pm with periodic breaks for meals.)* The Hare Krishnas serve a free meal of *dahl* and rice mush in front of the temple at 10am and 5pm. There is also a **guest house** (☎442478) offering 45 clean doubles with attached baths (Rs200-500). The temple is likely to be full during August, September, and March. A **museum** dedicated to Prabhupada displays the *swami's* rooms as he kept them, including books, clothes, jars of vaseline, and other bits of holy paraphrenalia he used while still contained within his mortal body. *(Museum open daily 9:30am-1pm and 5-8:30pm. Free.)*

OTHER SIGHTS. In many of the town's temples, the original idols were removed to Jaipur when Aurangzeb attacked in 1670. Since the temples were pillaged by Muslims; some are no longer considered fit for worship. The large, intricately carved **Govind Dev Temple** is one of the oldest in Vrindaban. It lacks the characteristic *gopuram* of most temples, and the top four stories were destroyed by Aurangzeb and never replaced. *(Open daily 7am-11am and 3:30-9pm.)* One hundred meters northeast of the Govind Dev is the **Rangnathji Temple,** India's longest at over 200m. Seth Govind Das combined Rajput and South Indian designs when he built the temple in 1851. The 15m **Dhwaja Stambha,** the central column, is said to be plated in gold. Non-Hindus are not permitted inside but can catch a glimpse through either entrance. Among the other more notable temples in Vrindaban, the **Madan Mohan Temple,** on the banks of the Yamuna, near Kali Ghat, has a small shrine in the base of its 19m sandstone tower, which is colored by a good amount of vegetation. Other popular sights include the dilapidated **Radha Vallabh Temple,** dating from 1626; the more modern **glass temple,** east of the Rangnathji Temple; and **Bankey Bihari,** literally "crooked Krishna," which is probabaly the most popular of Vrindaban's many temples. *(Open daily 9am-noon and 6-9pm.)* Launch off from **Chir Ghat** for a **boat ride** on the Yamuna river. Evening cruises are especially picturesque, as the sun sets behind the glowing skyline of Vrindaban accompanied by the mellow *bhajans* echoing through its tangled streets.

LUCKNOW लखनऊ ☎ 0522

Today, cycle-rickshaws and noisy scooters screech and careen their way through modern city streets overflowing with batteries, tires, and stereo parts, but Lucknow remains a city indelibly marked by its past. The skyline is dominated by crumbling monuments to the opulence of the nawab aristocracy of centuries past. Amid the ruins stand the battered souvenirs of the British Raj, along with ten-story high cement office buildings and red-and-white cellular phone towers. The history of this city of nearly two million people, now the modern capital of UP, stretches back into legend, but things didn't really start happening here until it became the capital of Avadh in 1775. The local nawab rulers, keen to assert the authority they had recently wrested from the Mughals, embarked on a series of ambitious building projects that soon thrust Lucknow forward to challenge Delhi and Calcutta for the title of India's most sparkling city. Before long, the British reduced the nawabs to mere puppet rulers, though Lucknow continued to flourish under their patronage as a major center of Muslim poetry, music, and architecture. The British formally annexed Avadh in 1856, citing as their mandate the alleged "incompetence to rule" of the last nawab, Wajid Ali Shah, whom they accused of being a "debauched and capricious" king who squandered his wealth on courtesans. The nawab was sent into exile in Calcutta, and the ensuing British take-over was one of the sparks that ignited the Indian Mutiny the following year. The siege of the Lucknow Residency during the uprisings was to loom large in British legend until Independence.

Since Partition, when many of the city's Muslims fled to Pakistan, Lucknow's status as a major center of Muslim culture came to an end, though many traditions live on. Local products such as *chikan* embroidery and *attar* perfume (see p. 186) endure, and it is still common to see signs written in Urdu rather than Hindi. The Muslim religious presence also survives; the most important event in Lucknow's religious calendar continues to be the Shi'a Muslim commemoration of Muharram (March 26, 2001)—a mourning for the martyrdom of Imam Husain (grandson of the Prophet) and his 72 companions. During the celebration, marchers wail laments as they carry replicas of Husain's tomb to the fire-walking ceremonies that take place in the *imambaras*.

GETTING THERE AND GETTING AROUND

Flights: Amousi Airport (☎436132 or 436327), 11km from Charbagh. Hire a taxi (Rs200) in front of the main railway station. **Indian Airlines** (☎220927 or 224618) flies daily to: **Bombay** (2hr., US$250); **Calcutta** (2hr., US$155); **Delhi** (1hr., US$90); **Patna** (1hr., US$100).

Trains: Lucknow Station, Charbagh, 3km from Hazratganj. A rickshaw from the station to Hazratganj should cost around Rs30. To: **Allahabad** (5-6 per day, 6am-10:30pm, 3½-5hr., Rs89); **Ayodhya** (1-2 per day, 2:40-7:15am, 3hr., Rs62); **Delhi** (at least 12 per day, 5:30am-1:30am, 6½-9hr., A/C chair Rs675); **Faizabad** (6-8 per day, 3:20am-2pm, 3hr., Rs61); **Gorakhpur** (at least 12 per day, 24hr., 5½-6hr., Rs109); **Kanpur** (at least 12 per day, 5am-11pm, 1½-2hr., Rs44).

Buses: The **Charbagh bus station** is on Station Rd. From the railway station, walk 100m to the main road. Take a left; the station is 300m down in a lot on the right. To: **Agra** (7 per day, 12:30-9:30pm, Rs110); **Allahabad** (4 per day from 10:30am, Rs89); **Ayodhya** (every 30min., 5am-midnight, Rs60); **Delhi** (3 per day, 8-9:30pm, Rs189); **Faizabad** (every 30min., 5am-midnight, Rs60); **Gorakhpur** (every 30min., 5am-midnight, Rs110); **Kanpur** (every 30min., 5am-midnight, Rs35); **Varanasi** (5 per day, 6am-10pm, Rs120). Another bus station, in **Kaiserbagh,** services **Delhi** (every hr., Rs213).

ORIENTATION AND PRACTICAL INFORMATION

Lucknow occupies the south bank of the **Gomti River** and extends far inland. In the center of the city is **Mahatma Gandhi (MG) Rd.** (referred to by locals as **Hazratganj**), along which are several bookstores, the GPO, and the police station, as well as many restaurants and shops. Hazratganj runs through the city northwest to southeast before sweeping south and out of the city. To the northwest is **Husainabad,** where many of the monuments are located. The main bus and railway stations are in the area of **Charbagh** to the southwest of Hazratganj. The way from Charbagh to Hazratganj is a major route, going along **Motilal Nehru Marg** and then **Vidhan Sabha Marg** past the state legislature (Vidhan Sabha). **Subhash Rd.** goes almost directly from Charbagh to Husainabad, completing the Hazratganj-Husainabad-Charbagh triangle. In the middle of the triangle is **Aminabad,** an old bazaar area.

Tourist Office: UP Government Tourist Reception Centre, Charbagh (☎452533). Inside the Lucknow Railway Station. Open daily 7am-8pm. **UP Tours** (☎212659) runs daily tours of the city starting from the Hotel Gomti. There must be at least 5 people for the tour to take place (9:45am-2:15pm, Rs50).

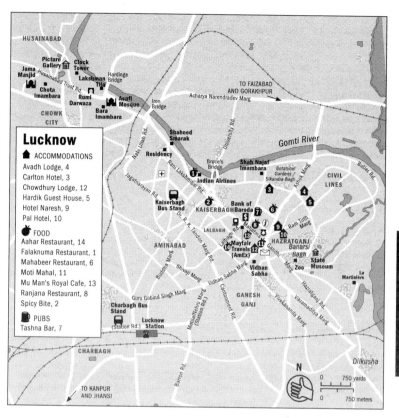

Lucknow

⌂ ACCOMMODATIONS
Avadh Lodge, 4
Carlton Hotel, 3
Chowdhury Lodge, 12
Hardik Guest House, 5
Hotel Naresh, 9
Pal Hotel, 10

🍴 FOOD
Aahar Restaurant, 14
Falaknuma Restaurant, 1
Mahabeer Restaurant, 6
Moti Mahal, 11
Mu Man's Royal Cafe, 13
Ranjana Restaurant, 8
Spicy Bite, 2

🍺 PUBS
Tashna Bar, 7

UTTAR PRADESH

Currency Exchange: Bank of Baroda, MG Rd. (☎202625), opposite the turn-off onto Lalbagh Rd. Open M-F 10:30am-2:30pm and 3-4pm, Sa 10:30am-1pm.

Bookstore: Universal Bookseller, 82 MG Rd. (☎225894), Hazratganj. Take a left onto MG Rd. from Vidhan Sabha Marg; Universal is on the right side. Open daily 10am-8pm.

Library: The **British Library** in Hazratganj, next to the Mayfair Cinema. Open Tu-Sa 10:30am-6:30pm.

Market: Main bazaars at **Aminabad, Hazratganj,** and **Chowk.** Aminabad is a short rick-shaw ride from Hazratganj. Open daily from dawn until late.

Police: Hazratganj Police Station, MG Rd. (☎222555). Turn left onto Hazratganj from Vidhan Sabha Marg. The police station is on the right side, next to the Kashmir Government Arts Emporium.

Hospital: Nishat, 3JC Base Rd., Kaiserbagh (☎219753), is a small, private hospital that has doctors of all specialities on call.

Telephones: Sahu Talk Point, 39/55 Ram Tirath Marg (☎275948). Take the right-hand fork of Ram Tirath Marg after the Hotel Naresh. Open 24hr. Callbacks Rs5 per min. Collect calls at Rs5 per min.

Internet: Fast Business Centre, Faridi Building, 2nd fl. (☎210592), Hazratganj. From MG Rd. turn down Lalbagh. FBS is the first major building on the right. Rs100 per hr. Open 24hr. Internet facilities are also available inside the GPO. Rs65 per hr.

Post Office: GPO, Vidhan Sabha Marg (☎222887). Take a right from MG Rd. onto Vidhan Sabha. The GPO is the large yellow colonial building with the clock tower. Open M-Sa 8am-7pm. **Postal Code:** 226001.

THE NAWABS OF AVADH Even 150 years after the last of their number was dispatched into well-paid exile by the British in 1856, the nawabs still seem to be everywhere in Lucknow. The fishy duo that was their motif can still be found all over town, and many of Lucknow's hotels and restaurants are named after one or another of the men who ruled from here for 100 years. Particularly popular is the portrait of the last nawab, Wajid Ali Shah, whose left nipple peeks out from between his jewelled robes on walls all over Lucknow. Ali Shah's feckless lifestyle—he was rumored to be more interested in poetry and dance than in trade treaties or politics—so scandalized the British that they annexed Avadh in 1856 in order to "save" its people from the dissolute misrule of the playboy nawab.

⌐ ACCOMMODATIONS

Most of Lucknow's budget hotels are in Hazratganj and in and around the Narhi Bazaar area along Ram Tirath Marg.

Avadh Lodge, 1 Ram Mohan Raj Marg (☎206927), a 10min. walk from Hazratganj. Walk down Ashok Marg and turn right onto Ram Tirath Marg at the fruit market. At the end of the street turn left, then take your second right; it's on the corner. This former residence of a Lucknow Raja features crumbling balconies and turrets and animal heads hanging from the walls, along with a sorry-looking stuffed crocodile. *Fawlty Towers* with an Indian accent. Spacious, clean rooms with fans and attached baths. Laundry service, massage, and cold drinks all but unavoidable. Common lounge with color TV. Check-out noon. Singles Rs200-290; doubles Rs300-390.

Hotel Naresh, Ram Tirath Marg (☎275160). From MG Rd. turn onto Ashok Marg at the big intersection. Fork right onto Ram Tirth Marg at the fruit market. The hotel is 400m down on the left hand side, through the Narhi Bazaar. Check-out 24hr. Singles Rs170-185; doubles Rs200-225.

Chowdhury Lodge, 3 Vidhan Sabha Marg (☎221911 or 273135), down an alley opposite the post office just before it intersects with MG Rd. Ideally situated in the heart of the city. Singles Rs90-200; doubles Rs170-275.

Pal Hotel, Ram Tirath Marg (☎229476), 50m down on the right. In the heart of Narhi Bazaar, this bare-bones, no-frills hotel has reasonably clean, basic rooms with common or attached bath. Check-out 24hr. Singles Rs100-120; doubles Rs120-170.

Carlton Hotel, Rana Pratap Marg (☎209497 or 222439; fax 231886). Turn left from Ashok Marg onto Rana Pratap Marg. The Carlton is 400m down on the left. Transformed palace with tastefully appointed rooms, filtered water, and TVs (upon request). Bar and restaurant downstairs look out on extensive gardens (green!). Breakfast included. Check-out noon. Singles Rs500-800; doubles Rs600-1100.

Hardik Guest House, 16 Rana Pratap Marg (☎209497 or 209597). Turn left at the end of Ram Tirath Marg and then right at the traffic circle. Cool, quiet, clean, and friendly. Room service available. Restaurant downstairs. Check-out 24hr. Air-cooled singles/doubles with TV and attached bath between Rs600-700.

◖ FOOD

Lucknow owes its reputation for rich and refined cuisine to the nawabs. For the famous Avadhi kebabs you will either have to hit one of the big hotel restaurants or sift through the small kiosks in the old city. Lucknow is also well known for its mangoes—the fruit market on Ram Tirth Marg is open every day. If you are in Lucknow during June, check around for the *Avadhi Food Festival*, a twelve-day affair celebrating the city's gastronomic heritage.

Vyanjan Vegetarian Restaurant, on Ashok Ganj, in the Vinay Palace Mall, on the right-hand side. Popular A/C restaurant serves a wide range of excellent veg. meals. Dishes Rs35-50. Open daily 9am-11pm.

Aahar Restaurant, Lalbagh. Turn left onto Lalbagh after the Mayfair Travels building on MG Rd., and walk to the traffic circle; it's on the left. Cool place with an intimate atmosphere. Excellent food with a smile. *Paneer korma* Rs35. Open daily 10am-10pm.

Moti Mahal, Hazratganj, on the left, opposite the police station. Look for the trademark golden arches. Air-conditioned restaurant upstairs serves Chinese food; 1st fl. and basement-level Mini Mahal serves breakfast, fast-food, and cakes 7:30am-11:45pm.

Falaknuma Restaurant, Clark's Avadh Hotel, 9th fl., on the MG Rd. traffic circle, after the cricket stadium. Overlooking the River Gomti on one side, this luxury restaurant serves luxury food to a luxury crowd at luxury prices. Menu includes a full range of lamb and chicken kebabs (starting at Rs180). A good place to recuperate from the outdoor dust and grime, even if it is a bit pricey (beer Rs150 a pop). *Ghazal* singing starts nightly at 8:30pm. Lunch 1-3pm, dinner 8-11:30pm.

Mu Man's Royal Cafe, Hazratganj, in front of Capoor's Hotel. Dark and hushed restaurant serves tastefully presented meals from Rs55. Excellent, gourmet-style *pakoras*, with shredded cheese, cucumber, and tomato (Rs30). Open daily 11am-11pm.

Spicy Bite, MG Rd., in the Tulsi Theatre Building near the traffic circle. A favorite with locals, Spicy Bite serves everything from fish and chips to pizza to Hong Kong style noodles. Dishes from Rs54. Open daily 11am-10:30pm.

Mahabeer Restaurant, at the intersection of Sapru Marg and Ashok Marg. Quiet, classy restaurant serves sumptuous vegetarian food. The staff is very attentive. Tasty *thalis* from Rs55. Open daily 9am-10:30pm.

Ranjana, MG Rd., opposite Capoor's Hotel. Something of a Hazratganj institution, this place has been around for years and is starting to show age. Tables and benches are set out on either side of a long, dark hall. Creaking ceiling fans keep the flies at bay. Serves Indian and Chinese food. Open daily 10am-11pm.

🎵🛍 ENTERTAINMENT AND SHOPPING

Lucknow isn't renowned for its nightlife, but if you need a drink to take the edge off a nerve-racking day, there are budget **bars** along Station Rd. and pricey drinks (Rs110-300) are available in the **Falaknuma Restaurant** (see above). The only proper bar in Hazratganj is the pine-paneled **Tashna Bar** in the Hotel Gomti. Full of chain-smoking, hard-drinking local businessmen crowded around a small TV, this small and dark, air-conditioned place serves booze and basic munchies. (Beer Rs100; liquor from Rs50. Open daily 11am-10:30pm.) A little farther from the city center, the **Simba Bar** at the Carlton Hotel has about the same stuff on offer, but the bar area is more informal, with couches and lounging chairs and psychedelic paintings of animals on the walls. (Open daily 10am-2pm and 6-11pm.) **Novelty Cinema,** on Lalbagh opposite Aahar's Restaurant, sometimes shows English-language movies. Lucknow is also home to the **Bhatkhande Music College,** one of the two major schools of **kathak dance** in India. Check newspapers for information on performances. **Aminabad,** to the south, is one of Lucknow's old bazaar areas and the best place to shop for Lucknawi crafts. Clothing with *chikan* embroidery prices range from Rs50-5000 per piece. Also sold here are tiny bottles of *attar*, alcohol-free perfumes worn by Indian Muslims.

👁 SIGHTS

Most of what remains of old Lucknow's glittering mosques and flamboyant palaces is concentrated around the **Husainabad** area to the northwest of the city, far from the din of Hazratganj.

THE RESIDENCY

Off MG Rd., northwest of Hazratganj. Open daily from sunrise to sunset. Rs2, free on Fridays.
If the British Raj still governed India, the ruins of Lucknow's Residency would be one of its proudest monuments. One of the lengthiest struggles of the great upris-

ing (the Indian "Mutiny" or "Revolt," depending on who's talking) took place when rebelling sepoys (Indians enlisted in the East India Company's army) besieged Lucknow's British community from June to November of 1857 (see also **Mutiny and Aftermath,** p. 69). The against-the-odds defense of the Residency was to leave a lasting impression on the colonial psyche. Once they had retaken the city, the British left the ruins as a monument to the stiff-lipped stubbornness and resilience of those trapped and killed inside. The battered remains of the Residency compound, still visibly scarred by the shots that pounded them 150 years ago, stand today within a shady green park near the center of the city.

The siege began when news reached Lucknow of sepoy rebellions throughout the region. The Residency, a mansion for the East India Company's agent in Avadh, was turned into a fortress for the 3000 people trapped there. After five months, the British finally succeeded in breaking the siege, and the remaining survivors—less than a third of the original population—were evacuated to Allahabad. Meanwhile, the battle to take back the rest of the city raged on, and Lucknow was not completely back under British control until March of the following year.

As you enter the complex through the Ballie Gate, there are several buildings on the right and left that were used during the siege as hospitals and armories. The Residency building itself sits amidst squirrel-infested ruins and wide lawns. One tall tower still stands on the Residency building, and the view from the top is well worth the climb. A British cemetery is near the river. There is a tatty miniature version of the complex in the **Model Gallery,** along with several old weapons, prints, and a copy of the florid, jingoistic poem Tennyson knocked off to commemorate the event. Below the Model Gallery is the basement where many of the British women and children hid.

HUSAINABAD

BARA IMAMBARA. Marking the resting place of Asaf-ud-Daula and his wives, the Bara Imambara was constructed in 1784 as part of a a food-for-work program instituted in the wake of a great famine. An *imambara* is a replica of the tomb of an *imam,* a martyred descendant of the Prophet Mohammed revered by Shi'a Muslims. Dedicated to Husain Ibn Ali, grandson of the Prophet, the Bara Imambara is the center of the Muharram festival in April, which mourns his death. Domes and arches span the ceiling of the great blue hall, one of the largest vaulted spaces in the world at the time it was built. A staircase to the side of the main building leads up to the roof and toward the entrance to the **Bhulbhalaiya,** a multi-level labyrinth designed for the entertainment of the nawab's harem. A guide is not necessary, although one might be helpful at places where dark, narrow passages turn suddenly and drop off into the sunlit courtyard 50m below.

SNIFFING THE SUBCONTINENTAL SUBLIME

Mention India and odor in the same sentence and you're likely to get a less-than-positive reaction. Indeed, for many a traveler, India is The Land of Don't-Breathe-Too-Deeply. In Lucknow, though, olfactory observation is more likely to run along the lines of *eau de toilette* than *eau de* toilet: this is a center for production of *attar,* India's finest class of perfumes. For centuries *attar* has remained the scent of choice in both the secular and religious domains of Indian culture. The *attar* oil is extracted from pre-dawn flower buds and left in a large container of water. As the sun rises, the buds secrete an oily film which is then carefully preserved. There is an *attar* for every season and time of day: for summer, rose and Indian jasmine; for winter, musk. The undisputed raja of Lucknow's perfume biz is the **Azam Ali-Alam Ali Industry,** renowned for authentic *attars* since Mughal days. Their products are sold all over India and have been worn by the likes of Empress Nuz Jahan and Princess Diana.

To the right of the Bara Imambara is the beautiful **Asafi Mosque,** built by Asaf-ud-Daula. The mosque is closed to non-Muslims. Opposite the Asafi mosque is the *bauli,* once a spiraling series of water-cooled state apartments, now home to a viscous, green pool of algae and a shit-streaked colony of chattering bats. Straddling Husainabad Trust Rd. outside the *imambara* is the **Rumi Darwaza,** another work of Asaf-ud-Daula. This gate, intended as a copy of the Sublime Port in Istanbul, is covered by a spine of trumpets. *(Open daily sunrise to 7pm. Rs10, includes entry to the bauli, the Rumi Darwaza, and the Picture Gallery.)*

OTHER SIGHTS IN THE HUSAINABAD AREA. Farther along Husainabad Trust Rd. after the Rumi Darvaza and the clock tower is the **Chota Imambara** (literally, "little *imambara*"), which was begun in 1837 by Nawab Mohammed Ali Shah. Two Taj-shaped buildings in the courtyard mark the tombs of the nawab's daughter and her husband. Ali Shah himself is buried below the main *imambara* structure. Inside are the nawab's silver-gilt throne, religious regalia used during Muharram, and dozens of dusty chandeliers. *(Open from sunrise to 7pm.)* Farther up, past the sights of Husainabad Trust Rd., is the **Jama Masjid,** Lucknow's largest mosque, and another conspicuous reminder of Ali Shah's legacy. The mosque is closed to non-Muslims. *(Down the road to the left after the Chota Imambara.)* The **Picture Gallery,** inside a summer house built by the nawab during the 19th century, has a collection of portraits of all the nawabs along with forlorn-looking busts of Dante and Aristotle. *(In Husainabad, near the clock tower. Open daily 8am-6pm.)*

SIGHTS NEAR THE HAZRATGANJ AREA

BOTANICAL GARDENS. Once the site of Nawab Wajid Ali Shah's pleasure garden, this is where the final battle for the relief of the Residency took place. Now the gardens, a big draw for early-morning walkers, contain the **National Botanical Research Institute.** *(Sikandra Bagh. Open daily 5-8am and 2-4:30pm. Free.)*

SHAH NAJAF IMAMBARA. North of the Hazratganj area and up the street from the Botanical Gardens is the Shah Najaf Imambara. The monument holds the tomb of Nawab Ghazi-ud-din Haidar (r. 1814-27) and was the base for the rebels of 1857. Its interior is decked with chandeliers; sparkling replicas of mosques cover the floor and platforms around the central, domed room. Shi'a Muslims come here to express their devotion to Shah-i Najaf, the first Shi'a *imam,* and to the spiritual successor of the Prophet, Ali Ibn Abi Talib. On the fifth day of Muharram, fire-walking takes place in the *imambara*'s complex. *(Open daily 6am-7pm.)*

ZOO AND STATE MUSEUM. Marked by a high-gated entrance, Lucknow's old and tired-looking zoo features an expanse of pleasant, green grounds and lots of suicidal animals trapped in tiny cages with piles of their own shit and whatever else the day's visitors have seen fit to throw through the bars. *(Banarsi Bagh, southeast of Hazratganj. Rs10. Open daily 8am-6pm.)* Within the same grounds is the **State Museum,** whose unremarkable collection includes an Egyptian mummy that was at least dead before it was put in its coffin. *(Open daily 10:30am-4:30pm. Rs2, with camera Rs15.)*

LA MARTINIERE. The Martiniere school is one of Lucknow's most distinctive architectural survivals. Frenchman Claude Martin, money-lender and architectural advisor to the nawab as well as military man and colonial entrepreneur *par excellence,* designed this building as his own mausoleum after deciding toward the end of his life that he would live out his days in India. Martin built and owned dozens of houses throughout India, but his final creation, built in the 1700s, is the only one to have survived intact, thanks to its conversion into a school shortly after his death. Described by one observer as a product of "the heterogeneous fancies of a diseased brain," La Martiniere is an eclectic mishmash of architectural styles and flavors. Startled-looking lions cling to colonnades, while a spritely collection of classical figurines congregates on the rooftop waving and pointing frantically at each other. A large turbaned turret completes the ensemble. Report to the principal's office first if you come during school hours. *(Off MG Rd., southeast of Hazratganj. 15min. by rickshaw. Rs5-10.)*

FAIZABAD फ़ैज़ाबाद   ☎ 05278

Once the capital of the kingdom of Avadh—until the nawab moved to Lucknow in 1775—Faizabad today serves travelers as a stop-off for daytrips to neighboring Ayodhya. Several monuments remain from the city's heyday, including the famous mausolea of Nawab Shuja-ud-Daula and his wife Bahu Begum. If you're stuck in Faizabad, these monuments prove themselves to be an excellent diversion.

⨭ GETTING THERE AND GETTING AROUND. Rickshaw rides from the bus and train stations to the Chowk area average ten minutes. **Buses** head to: **Allahabad** (every 45min., 5:30am-12:30am, Rs70); **Delhi** (every 45min., 5:30am-12:30am, Rs250); **Gorakhpur** (every 45min., 5:30am-12:30am, Rs61); **Lucknow** (every 45min., 5:30am-12:30am, Rs55); and **Varanasi** (7 per day, 5am-2pm, Rs90). Bus departures are erratic and unpredictable. **Tempos** to Ayodhya leave regularly from the Gurdi Bazaar, Chowk, and the bus station. **Trains** run to: **Delhi** (1-3 per day, 4:30-10pm, 13-15hr., Rs132); **Lucknow** (at least 6 per day, 6:45am-10:15pm, 3hr., Rs39); and **Varanasi** (at least 10 per day, 6:15am-9pm, 5hr., Rs54).

⨭⨭ ORIENTATION AND PRACTICAL INFORMATION. There are two main roads in Faizabad. **Station Rd.,** which starts at the railway station, becomes **Civil Lines** and eventually leads to the **Chowk** area, where the hotels and sights are. **National Highway (NH) 28** is the major bus route to Ayodhya and Gorakhpur. **The Regional Tourist Office** is in an alley off Civil Lines. From the bus stand look for signs to the poorly marked office, 100m before the Krishna Palace. The tourist officer speaks very little English. (☎813214. Open M-Sa 10am-5pm.) The **State Bank of India,** Civil Lines, changes AmEx traveler's checks. From the railway station, take Station Rd. to the traffic circle. Take the middle road at the traffic circle, and turn right at the end of the road. The bank is on the left. (☎20430 or 22210. Open M-F 10am-2pm, Sa 10am-noon.) Faizabad's **post office** is just off NH 28. With the bus stop behind you, turn left and walk toward the Chowk. Take the first major street to the left; the post office is on the right. (☎22301. Open M-Sa 10am-6pm.) There are several **STD/ISD booths** in the area around the bus station.

⨭⨭ ACCOMMODATIONS AND FOOD. There are several budget places in the Chowk area and a couple of cheap, clean hotels near the bus and train stations. Several of these have restaurants; otherwise, simple roadside *dhabas* are about the only place to eat. The well-appointed **Abha Hotel,** in an alley off Bazaza Rd. in Motibagh (a 15min. rickshaw ride from the train station), is probably the best of the several small hotels in this area. All rooms have baths, and several have balconies. (☎22550 or 22930. Singles Rs135; air-cooled doubles Rs175.) The air-conditioned restaurant downstairs serves decent food. (Open daily 7am-10pm.) The **Priya Hotel,** down the same alley as the Abha, you get what you pay for. (☎23783. Singles Rs75; doubles Rs100). **Shane Avadh,** Civil Lines, has spacious, institutional rooms with attached bath. (☎23586 or 27075. Singles Rs150; doubles Rs175.) The restaurant downstairs has all the usual suspects out on parade. The Krishna Palace Hotel's **Caveri Restaurant** in Civil Lines is probably the classiest in town with entrees from Rs50. A bar is soon to open in the hotel annex. (Open daily 7am-11pm.) The **Tirupati Hotel** next door has a very similar layout and offers the same amenities as its neighbor. (☎23231. Singles Rs120-195; doubles Rs150-245.)

AYODHYA अयोध्या   ☎ 05238

All over India, the sacred and the profane jockey side by side, competing chaotically for prominence. In Ayodhya, a small city dotted with dozens of temples and crowded by countless sadhus and other pilgrims, the sacred has definitely gotten the upper hand. Ayodhya has an ancient history as one of India's holiest cities. According to legend, the city was founded by the Hindu law-giver Manu and Lord Rama, hero of the Ramayana epic and the seventh incarnation of Vishnu, was born here into the ruling Surya dynasty. Many of Ayodhya's most important sites are sacred to him and his faithful servant Hanuman, the monkey god. A major pilgrimage destination for thousands of Hindus, Ayodhya sees few foreign visitors—a stay here makes a welcome break from the stresses and strains of some of India's more popular tourist destinations. Off the main road, every street and alley is home to at least one temple, and a peaceful air of religious serenity pervades most everywhere. The lack of Western tourists gives visitors a glimpse of the unspoiled (or at least un-Westernized) heart of India.

Ayodhya made international news in 1992, when Hindu-Muslim unrest broke out over the controversial Babri Masjid (see **Sights,** below). Thousands were killed in the nationwide riots that followed, and Ayodhya has since remained a flash point for communal violence. Foreigners are unlikely to encounter any difficulties, but should check the news before visiting, especially during the heady and unpredictable **Ramnaumi** festival celebrating Rama's birth.

GETTING THERE AND GETTING AROUND. There is nowhere to change money in Ayodhya. There is sporadic **train** service from Ayodhya (some stop for a minute or two on the way to or from Faizabad), but it's easier to catch trains from Faizabad. Regular **buses** to and from Gorakhpur stop briefly; catch them at the bus station on NH 28.

ORIENTATION AND PRACTICAL INFORMATION. National Highway (NH) 28 cuts through Ayodhya on its way from Faizabad to Gorakhpur. The **railway station,** tourist bungalow, and several of the major sights (including Hanuman Gardhi and Kanak Bhavan) are on either side of the highway, within walking distance of the bus station and tempo stop. Ayodhya is not a big city; it's not much more than a 20-minute walk from one side of town to the other along the main highway. The best way to see Ayodhya, though, is to escape as quickly as possible from the clamor of the built-up strip and walk north through the winding, climbing, temple-packed streets of the area between the highway and the river. The **tourist office** is inside the **Pathik Niwas Saket** (also known as the **UP Tourist Bungalow** and the **Hotel Saket**). To get there, turn right with the bus station behind you, walk down NH28 toward Faizabad, and take a left on the first road. The bungalow is at the bottom of the lane, to the left after the railway station. The cheerful attendant will fish out a set of keys and unlock his secret stash of maps and pamphlets if prompted. (Open M-Sa 10am-5pm.) **Sri Ram Hospital** (☎32840) is near the bus station. The **post office** is at Shrinagar Hat. (☎32025. Open M-Sa 10am-5pm.)

ACCOMMODATIONS AND FOOD. For lodgings, ashrams seem to be the most popular choice among the thousands of pilgrims who flock here every year. Better ashrams have single rooms (with attached bath and fan) and are concentrated near the bus station. Opposite the bus station, the **Birla Dharamsala** is centrally located in a peaceful garden compound near the main road. (☎32252. Singles with fan and attached bath Rs100; doubles Rs150. Sheets are Rs10 but remember to bring your own mosquito coil.) The small but beautiful **Birla Mandir** is just to the right of the ashram, in the same complex. Ayodhya's only "proper" hotel, the **Pathik Niwas Saket,** houses the town's only "proper" restaurant. Unfortunately, neither is particularly inspiring. The somewhat drab and institutional hotel has clean, large rooms. (☎312435. Dorm beds Rs60; singles with bath Rs175; doubles Rs200-250.) The slow but steady restaurant is nothing special but is just about the only place in town to get a sit-down meal. The vegetarian *thali* is Rs40. (Open daily 6am-10pm.) Head to Faizabad if you insist on institutional comforts.

SIGHTS. Ayodhya is a temple-lover's paradise. There really does seem to be at least one sacred site around every street corner. Sadhus and pilgrims are everywhere, and stalls selling sparkling bangles and cone-shaped piles of red and saffron *tilak* powder line the streets between temples. Many of the most important religious sites are within a 5-15 minute walk of the bus and train stations, but Ayodhya is not the kind of town that comes with a convenient checklist of must-see attractions. The whole of the town is really one huge stretching temple complex, marked by an atmosphere of holy hustle and bustle. The best way to drink in the atmosphere is to do as the sadhus do and let your footsteps lead you unhurriedly and at random from one temple to the next.

The **Babri Masjid** (known as Ram Janam Bhumi to Hindus) is the contested holy site that led to Hindu-Muslim clashes in 1992 and brought international attention to Ayodhya. The trouble began over the location of a mosque, built during the 16th-century by the Mughal Emperor Babur on a site that many Hindus hold to be the birthplace of the god Rama. The mosque became a symbol for the resentment and prejudice many Hindus felt (and still feel) toward Indian Muslims. Hindu Nationalists such as the Vishwa Hindu Parishad (VHP) used the Babri Masjid as a rallying cry, and the mosque was eventually closed due to the controversy. On December 6, 1992, religious fervor turned to violence when 200,000 VHP-led militant Hindus (most of them from outside Ayodhya) descended on the town, smashing through police barricades to destroy the Babri Masjid and erect a makeshift temple in its place. The Masjid is primarily of interest to the history buff or the student of contemporary Indian politics, for it is now a pile of rubble, and the makeshift Hindu temple erected in its place is nothing more than a tent with a glittering altar. The compound is surrounded by high fences and hundreds of armed soldiers; visitors are often searched before they are admitted. No cameras or luggage are allowed. *(Open daily 7-10am and 3-6pm.)*

The **Hanuman Garhi,** in a white fort near the bus station, is one of Ayodhya's most important temples. It is abuzz with worshippers throughout the day and into the night. Supposed to mark the spot where Hanuman the monkey god sat guard in a cave overlooking Rama's birthplace, the main shrine is at the top of a flight of 76 steps. Leave your shoes at the bottom and look out for monkey droppings. To get to the **Jain Temple** on Hanuman Rd., take a right from the railway station, and turn left at the end of the road. The temple is on the right after about 600m. Other temples include the **Kanak Bhawan** *(open daily 8am-noon and 4:30-9pm)*, off the main road farther up from the Hanuman Garhi, and the **Nageshwar Nath** temple, by the river **ghats** over on the east side of town.

GORAKHPUR गोरखपुर ☎ 0551

As the major transportation hub between India and Nepal, Gorakhpur is more often traveled through than to, and few people arrive here without definite plans to move on again as soon as possible. Buses leave regularly for the border, and the main railway station has trains to major cities in India, so getting out is easy enough—a good thing, as Gorakhpur offers little to the visitor, though residents might try to convince you otherwise. Founded around 1400 and named for the Hindu saint Gorakhnath, Gorakhpur still hosts the temple of the patron saint of the Natha Yogis, 4km from the railway station on Nepal Rd. The Vishnu Temple on Medical College Rd. houses a 12th-century stone image of Vishnu that was carted off by Raj-era art collectors and taken to London, where it stayed until a court case ordered it returned to India. Gorakhpur became an army town under the Mughals and again under the British, who used it as a base for recruiting Gurkha soldiers from Nepal; it is still a major military center today. Insect repellent is a must if you're going to be overnighting here; hungry mosquitos seem to penetrate even the most carefully netted hotel room windows.

▌ GETTING THERE AND GETTING AROUND

Trains: Railway Station, Station Rd. To: **Allahabad** (5am and 10:10pm, 10-11hr., Rs81); **Hajipur** (5:25am and 11:35am, 5½-6hr, Rs59); **Jhansi** (7 and 11:50pm, 12-14hr., Rs186); **Kanpur** (3 per day, 4:45pm-12:40am, 7-9½hr., Rs84); **Lucknow** (several per day, 4:45pm-12:30am, 5½-6hr., Rs59); **Varanasi** (3 per day, 6:30am-4:50pm, 5½ hr., Rs117).

Buses: Gorakhpur Bus Station, 400m down the road from the railway station. To: **Faizabad** (every hr., 4hr., Rs60); **Kushinagar** (every hr., 6am-9pm, 1½hr., Rs20); **Lucknow** (every hr., 6am-10pm, 8hr., Rs113); **Sunauli** (frequent, 4am-9pm, 2hr., Rs43). Frequent buses also run to the border with Nepal; make sure you are getting on a government bus. From the border, you will have to change buses and buy a new ticket. There are many **private buses** to the border operating from the same area, but they tend to charge as much as Rs250 for tickets through to **Kathmandu** or **Pokhara.** The so-called "direct" service offered on these buses is, in fact, no faster than the government bus route. Either way, you will have to spend several hours at the border arranging your visa and switching buses in Nepal. For more information, see **Sunauli,** p. 784.

✦ 🛈 ORIENTATION AND PRACTICAL INFORMATION

Most of Gorakhpur lies south of its **railway station.** Inside the station is a small tourist information booth. Budget hotels and restaurants are on **Station Rd.,** directly opposite the station; the downtown area on **Park Rd.** also contains several cheap places to eat and spend the night. The road that runs straight down from the railway station's entrance leads to the **bus stand,** 400m south, before intersecting with Park Rd., which runs parallel to Station Rd. and marks the beginning of the **Civil Lines** region. The **State Bank of India,** on Bank Rd., downtown, cashes AmEx traveler's checks and exchanges US/UK currency (☎338497; open M-F 10am-2pm, Sa 10am-noon). There is a small sub-branch of the **post office** 100m left of the main exit from the railway station (open daily 7:30am-2pm). **Postal code:** 273001.

🛏 ACCOMMODATIONS

There are several decent budget hotels directly opposite the railway station, along with several cheap restaurants and any number of young men competing to put you on a bus bound for Nepal. In the center of the city (Rs10-15 rickshaw ride from the station), are a couple of mid-range options, which are a bit quieter, if less convenient. Most places have 24hr. check-out and black-and-white TVs in the rooms.

Hotel Elora, L-block, Station Rd., opposite the railway station (☎200647), has simple, clean rooms with attached baths. Those at the back are away from most of the Station Rd. noise. Singles Rs110; doubles Rs150.

Hotel Siddhartha, Station Rd., past Hotel Elora (☎200976), is nothing to get excited about, but clean enough and enthusiastically run. Currency exchange available. Singles Rs100-150; doubles Rs150-200.

Hotel Marina, Golghar (☎337630), is in an alley off Jalkal Bhawan Rd., in the center of town. More upscale than most, its large, clean singles and attached baths are popular with families. Singles Rs170; doubles Rs245-325.

Hotel Kanishka, at the intersection of Bank and Station Rd. (☎537748), has the same amenities as the Marina, with more refinement. Singles Rs200; doubles Rs300.

🍴 FOOD

Plenty of little places serving snacks and simple meals are opposite the railway station and along the road leading down to the buses. For anything more elaborate, you'll have to make the hike into town.

Vardan Restaurant is on Station Rd., between Hotel Standard and Hotel Elora. Small and dark, this is probably the best of the many places dotted around the station area. Food ranges from omelettes to tandoori dishes (Rs70-100); wine of any kind is "strictly forbidden." Open daily 8am-11pm.

Queen's Restaurant, in the President's Hotel, next door to the Marina Hotel, is a popular place serving excellent food in a calm, quiet, and well-cooled setting. *Navratan korma* Rs40; *rogan josh* Rs45. Open daily 7am-11:30pm.

Hotel Ganges Deluxe Restaurant is on Park Rd. in Golghar. If you've just missed your train out of town and need to drown your sorrows, or if you're looking for something to guarantee a good night's sleep on an overnight express, then this rough-and-tumble, spit-and-polish hotel bar has a wide selection of beers and industrial-strength spirits might just do the trick. Basic food menu features cheap "Chinese" dishes and tandoori selections for Rs30-80. Open daily 8am-10:30pm.

KUSHINAGAR कुशीनगर ☎05563

All things must pass. Decay is inherent in all things. With words to this effect, the Buddha preached his last sermon and breathed his last breath here in Kushinagar, where he was cremated and went on to attain the ultimate happily-never-after of *parinirvana*. For centuries after the Buddha's death, Kushinagar flourished as a major religious pilgrimage destination. Foremost among the rulers who patronized the place was Ashoka, whose conversion to Buddhism helped the religion prosper and spread throughout India.

With the decline of Buddhism in India during the 12th century, however, Kushinagar faded from prominence, and its many temples and monasteries soon fell into forgotten jungle decay. It was not until the mid-19th century, when a group of archaeologists working under the auspices of the East India Company started exploring the area with spades, that Kushinagar again rose to widespread attention. The stupas and images they unearthed and the inscriptions written on them were enough to establish beyond doubt Kushinagar's holy heritage, and the tiny town was soon back on the map as a major religious center.

A lot of money has made its way west into Kushinagar since then. Today, the streets are paved, flat and smooth, with Japanese financial backing and lined with temples, stupas, and study centers built in most of the architectural styles of Buddhist East Asia. Very much a beggar-free, truck-free, cow-free zone, Kushinagar is a small village remarkable for its pervasive air of peace and prosperity. Though it is small enough to be visited on a daytrip from Gorakhpur, it is worth an overnight stay to enjoy its atmosphere of untouristed calm and quiet.

■ GETTING THERE AND GETTING AROUND. Regular buses go between Kushinagar and Gorakhpur, 1½ hours away. The **bus station** is in the neighboring town of **Kasia,** 3km from Kushinagar. Ask to be let off at the gate; otherwise, you will have to get another bus back to the gate from Kasia station (Rs5). The last bus to **Gorakhpur** leaves at 7pm.

■ ORIENTATION AND PRACTICAL INFORMATION. Fifty-one kilometers east of Gorakhpur, Kushinagar is on **National Highway (NH) 28.** All the places of worship, tourist attractions, and accommodations are on Kushinagar's main road, **Buddh Marg,** which can be entered through the **Buddha Dwar gate** off the highway. The **Regional Tourist Office** is 100m down Buddh Marg on the right, in front of the Myanmar Temple and next to the Birla Buddhist temple. (Open M-Sa 10am-5pm.) The **post office** next to the **police station,** is a small, white building opposite the Buddha Dwar on NH 28. (Open M-Sa 10am-6pm.) **Postal Code:** 274403.

■ ACCOMMODATIONS AND FOOD. The main tourist season in Kushinagar runs from October to March; many hotels and restaurants close down completely in the off-season. Those listed below are open throughout the year. The **Linh-Son Chinese Temple** (☎71019) and the **Myanmar Buddhist Temple and Guest House** (☎71035), both on Buddh Marg, opposite the tourist office, are run by temple monks for pilgrims visiting Kushinagar's Buddhist sites. These places provide clean, basic accommodations in rooms adjoining the main temple buildings. At the Linh-Son Chinese Temple, a room with three beds and attached bath is Rs300. The Myanmar Buddhist Temple operates on a donation basis (at least Rs50 is expected). **Hotel Pathik Niwas,** Buddh Marg, 300m down from the tourist office on the right-hand side, has a wide range of accommodations. A white-walled complex built around manicured gardens and lined with paintings depicting the life of the Buddha, the Pathik Niwas is run by a friendly and responsive staff. The rooms and bathrooms are clean (toilet seats "sanitized for your protection"), and sheets and towels are changed daily. (☎05563 or 71038. Singles Rs300; doubles Rs400; A/C deluxe rooms Rs700/800; small, kitchen-equipped "American huts" Rs600/700.) The restaurant does everything from cheeseburgers (Rs30) to *malai kofta* (Rs40), as well as the obligatory chow mein menu. (Open 6am-10pm.) The **Yama Kwality Cafe,** next to the Myanmar Temple, is the only other restaurant open all year. The cafe serves up healthy-sized portions of noodles and fried rice and maintains a good selection of recent newspapers and magazines—a good place to sit and relax out of the midday sun.

🔲 **SIGHTS.** Kushinagar's main attractions are the ancient stupas and images re-discovered here during the last century. These range along the kilometer or so of the main Buddh Marg stretch. Dotted between the historical remains are several modern temples and an expansive green **Meditation Park.** Next to the Myanmar Temple, set in beautiful lawns is Kushinagar's holiest site, the **Buddha Mahaparin-irvana Temple,** said to mark the spot where the Buddha was liberated from the cycle of re-birth and attained the ideal state of *parinirvana*. Extensive traces remain of the original temple, and a 6m reclining Buddha survives inside the main temple building. Behind the reclining image is a large modern stupa, built to pro-tect the age-weathered original beneath it. The original stupa is believed to con-tain a portion of the Buddha's cremated remains. Left out of the temple grounds and farther down Buddh Marg just as the road shifts left, the small **Matha Kunwar Temple** stands on the site of the Buddha's last sermon, and contains a small, golden statue of the Buddha. One kilometer farther down the road, past the Japa-nese, Korean, and Thai temples, is what remains of the **Ramambhar Stupa,** built on the sacred site of the Buddha's cremation. Pay no attention to what the Indian tourists do: climbing on the stupa will do your karma no good at all. *(Stupas open daily sunrise to sunset.)*

VARANASI वाराणसी ☎ 0542

For Hindus, Varanasi (also known as Benares) is the holiest place on earth and the chosen residence of Shiva, who abides in the city's every nook and cranny. Hindus believe that the whole of Varanasi is a sacred zone, with a power so great that it permeates the city with its divine glow—hence the city's other name, Kashi (the Luminous). Those who die in Varanasi are guaranteed *moksha*, or liberation from the cycle of death and rebirth, and everyone here knows it. This otherworldly con-fidence has made Varanasi the chosen residence of many a mere mortal, too— over 1.2 million of them, in fact. In addition, countless thousands of pilgrims come here every day to bathe in the sacred waters of the Ganga and to pay their respects at the temples that stretch all along the riverside *ghats*.

Shiva settled in Varanasi with his new bride, Parvati, and was so taken with the place that he vowed never to leave. Nowadays, the city's glory takes time and tim-ing to appreciate. At sunrise, a quiet band of several thousand descends to the riv-erside *ghats*, scorched by a godlike sun. The Old City is a maze of torturous lanes smeared with cow dung and congested with animals and people. Small boys make small fortunes guiding foreigners to the Golden Temple through little-used alleys. Dead bodies, sometimes stretched between two bicycles or tied to the roof of a jeep, are delivered to the pyre to the traditional chant, *"Ram Nam Sata Hai"* (Ram is Truth). On the main street, buses bellow madly and spew exhaust over strings of shaven-headed pilgrims, their baldness an expression of earthly loss and the small pigtail of hair a hook for the gods to grasp should they decide to snatch them up. When the power goes out in the City of Light (as it does almost every night), the unprepared visitor must navigate the slippery narrow lanes of the old city by the teasing flicker of candlelight.

Due to five centuries (1200-1700) of levelings at the hands of Muslims, no building in the city is more than 300 years old. But the attacks never really succeeded; they wiped out the city's temples and images but not the traditions that have kept Varanasi alive since at least as far back as the 6th century BC. In the early days of Aryan settlement in India, Varanasi, one of the world's oldest continuously inhabited cities, sat at the great ford where traders traversing North India would cross the Ganga. It gained fame as a glorious bazaar town and as a center of spiritual life. Teachers and ascetics came to mingle with the local deities in the ponds and rivers of Anandavana, the Forest of Bliss, that grew here before the city developed. The Buddha came to Sarnath, on the outskirts of Kashi, to preach his first sermon. Varanasi's Hindu priests were active in developing their religion through the millennia, and the city itself soon became an object of worship: a holy place inhabited by holy beings and bounded by a holy river.

Never a military or political powerhouse, Varanasi became a sanctuary for Indian culture, renowned for its silk broacades (Benares silk saris are still some of the best), its refined Sanskrit and Hindi, and its music. Especially since the foundation of Benares Hindu University, Varanasi continues to support a thriving arts culture. But piety and devotion are what bring the millions who come for brief glimpses of the city, as well as the many who come to settle and die in Varanasi.

◧ GETTING THERE AND GETTING AROUND

Flights: Babatpur Airport, 22km from Varanasi Junction Railway Station. **Indian Airlines office,** Cantonment (☎343746 or 345959). To: **Agra** (M, W, F, and Su, 1:55pm, 2hr., US$105); **Bombay** (5pm, 5hr., US$235); **Delhi** (5pm, 2½hr., US$125); **Kathmandu** (12:55pm, 1½hr., US$80); **Khajuraho** (M, W, F, and Su, 1:55pm, 45min., US$80); **Lucknow** (5pm, 45min., US$70).

Trains: Varanasi Junction Railway Station. Rs10 by cycle-rickshaw or Rs20 by auto-rickshaw from Godaulia Crossing. To: **Allahabad** (7-13 per day, 4am-11pm, 3hr., Rs84); **Bombay** (11:30am and 11:10pm, 28hr., Rs340); **Delhi** (2-5 per day, noon-11:45pm, 19 hr., Rs231; *Rajdhani Exp.* 2309, 11pm, 11hr., Rs1130); **Gorakhpur** (4-5 per day, 12:15am-4:30pm, 5½hr., Rs92); **Patna** (4-8 per day, 3:20pm-1:50am, 4-5hr., Rs84); and **Satna** (4-9 per day, 6:20am-3:35am, 6½hr., Rs97; a 4hr. bus ride takes you to **Khajuraho**).

Buses: Cantonment Bus Station, 300m to the left on Station Rd. as you exit Varanasi Junction Station. To: **Agra** (7:30, 10:30am, and 5pm; 14hr.; Rs248); **Allahabad** (every 30min., 4am-11pm, 3hr., Rs54); **Delhi** (7pm, 20hr., Rs309); **Gaya** (6am, 8hr., Rs91); **Gorakhpur** (every hr., 6hr., Rs95); **Kanpur** (9 per day, 7:30am-11pm, Rs135); **Lucknow** (every hr., 5am-9pm, Rs120); **Sonauli** (10 per day, 5am-9pm, Rs134).

Local Transportation: Auto-rickshaws from Varanasi Station to Godaulia or Cantonment area cost Rs20, shared Rs5. To **Sarnath** Rs35. Cycle-rickshaws cover most major points in the city. Don't take any nonsense from the drivers, who have grown accustomed to over-charging clueless tourists. **Tempos** run between Lanka and Ramnagar Fort (Rs7). **City buses** connect Varanasi Station and **Sarnath** (Rs6).

▨ ORIENTATION

Varanasi's city limits are marked by the **Varuna River** to the north and the **Assi River** to the south, hence the city's hybrid name. **Panch Koshi Rd.,** which circles the city's 16km radius, marks the boundary of the sacred zone of Kashi. Old Varanasi is squeezed up against the western banks of the Ganga at the point where the river begins to flow north. There is virtually nothing on the east bank; it's believed that those who die there will be reincarnated as donkeys. Uphill from the river rises a maze of narrow streets lined with temples, shrines, budget hotels, and restaurants. Finding your way through this tangle can seem impossible at times, though many of the main backpackers' hang-outs are well marked, and the *ghats* are clearly

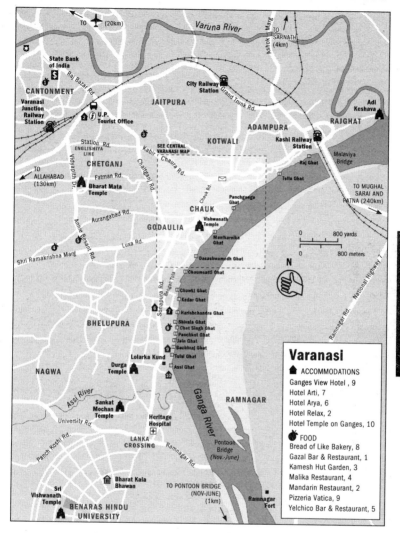

Varanasi

🏠 ACCOMMODATIONS
Ganges View Hotel , 9
Hotel Arti, 7
Hotel Arya, 6
Hotel Relax, 2
Hotel Temple on Ganges, 10

🍎 FOOD
Bread of Like Bakery, 8
Gazal Bar & Restaurant, 1
Kamesh Hut Garden, 3
Malika Restaurant, 4
Mandarin Restaurant, 2
Pizzeria Vatica, 9
Yelchico Bar & Restaurant, 5

labeled in English. Be wary of accepting random offers of help in finding your way; lost-looking foreigners are easy targets for the hundreds of touts and commission-merchants who prowl the streets. Also, be sure that the hotel you find is actually the one you're looking for. Fakes flourish—as soon as one place becomes popular, half the hotels around it change their names to something confusingly similar.

Sticking to the river is the best way to navigate Varanasi, as most points of interest are along the waterfront. The two main goalposts along the riverbank are the **Assi Ghat** at the south end and **Raj Ghat** to the far north. **Dasashwamedh Ghat,** the city's main *ghat,* is easily reached via **Dasashwamedh Rd.** from **Godaulia Crossing,** a central traffic circle. The surrounding area near the **Vishwanath Temple,** known as **Godaulia,** contains many of the budget hotels and is connected to the northern parts of Varanasi by **Chowk Rd.,** one of the few roads near the *ghats* wide enough for cars. Trains from the east cross the **Malaviya Bridge,** next to Raj Ghat; the railway stations are inland in the northern part of the city.

❓ PRACTICAL INFORMATION

Tourist Office: The **UP Regional Tourist Office** (☎345379), in the main railway station, is small but helpful and well-run. Open daily 8am-6pm. The **Tourist Bungalow**, Parade Kothi, Cantonment (☎343413), directly in front of the railway station, has detailed information on festivals and local events. Open M-Sa 10am-5pm.

Currency Exchange: State Bank of India, Cantonment (☎343410), in the Best Western (or Kashika) Hotel on The Mall (20min. by cycle-rickshaw from the *ghats*, Rs20). Open M-F 10am-2pm, Sa 10am-noon. **Bank of Baroda,** Godaulia (☎321471), on the left, between Godaulia Crossing and Dasashwamedh Ghat, is more conveniently but *only* gives advances on MC and Visa. Open M-F 11am-3pm, Sa 11am-1pm.

Luggage Storage: Varanasi Junction Station. Rs5-7 per day. Open 24hr. Locks are required on all bags.

Bookstore: Harmony: The Book Shop, Assi Ghat (☎310218), just down from Pizzeria Vaatika. Open daily 10am-8pm. **Indica Books,** Godaulia (☎321640). With your back to the river at Godaulia Crossing, turn left; Indica is 500m down on the right. Open daily 9am-8pm. **Universal Book Co.,** Godaulia (☎450042). 50m after Indica Books.

Market: A large fruit market is near the GPO at **Vishersarganj.** Hop in a rickshaw at Godaulia Crossing for the short ride north. Most of your mango and banana needs can also be met around **Dasashwamedh Ghat.**

Police: Dasashwamedh Police Station (☎353777).

Pharmacy: Heritage Hospital Pharmacy, Lanka Crossing (☎367977 or 366726). From Godaulia Crossing, take an auto-rickshaw (Rs20) toward Benares Hindu University. The hospital and its 24hr. pharmacy are on the left, just before Lanka Crossing.

Hospital: The best private hospital is **Heritage Hospital** (see above), where you can usually see an English-speaking doctor right away. The hospital at **Benares Hindu University** (☎316833 or 316801) is also reputable.

Telephones: Two 24hr. **STD/ISD** booths are inside the railway station. Callbacks Rs5 per min. Near the *ghats,* anyone with enough space to squeeze in a phone seems to be offering STD and Internet services; most open until 10pm.

Internet: Zee Services (☎391399), 200m down the alley opposite the 3-domed gate on Dasashwamedh Rd. Rs30 per hr. Open daily 6:30am-10:30pm. **Yelchiko Bar and Restaurant,** Dasashwamedh Rd. charges Rs60 per hr. Open daily noon-10pm.

Post Office: Kotwali (☎330050). A Rs10 rickshaw ride from Godaulia Crossing through Chowk. Open M-Sa 10am-6pm. **Postal Code:** 221001.

🏠 ACCOMMODATIONS

Dozens of budget hotels are packed into the winding maze of the Old City near Godaulia Crossing. Mid-range hotels can be found throughout the city, especially along Vidyapith Rd. and on the main streets in Godaulia. Luxury hotels in the cantonment area north of the railway station are far removed from the break-neck rhythm of Godaulia, and a world away from the traditional life of the city.

> **WARNING.** Rickshaw-*wallahs* in Varanasi often collect commission from hotel owners for delivering guests. Beware of anyone who offers you a "ride anywhere" for "Rs5 only;" you will have very little control over your destination. Be firm about where you want to go, and don't believe your rickshaw-*wallah* when he tells you that the hotel you asked for is "full" or "closed." If you have any concerns or doubts upon arrival, call a hotel yourself from the train station, or ask the staff at the tourist office to do so for you.

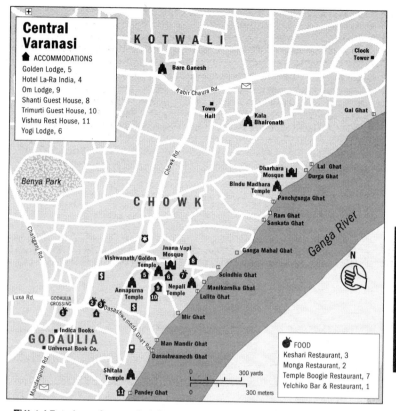

Central Varanasi

ACCOMMODATIONS
Golden Lodge, 5
Hotel La-Ra India, 4
Om Lodge, 9
Shanti Guest House, 8
Trimurti Guest House, 10
Vishnu Rest House, 11
Yogi Lodge, 6

KOTWALI

Clock Tower ■

Bare Ganesh

Kabir Chaura Rd.

Town Hall

Kala Bhaironath

Gai Ghat

Benya Park

Chowk Rd.

CHOWK

Dharhara Mosque
Lal Ghat
Durga Ghat

Bindu Madhara Temple

Panchganga Ghat

Ram Ghat
Sankata Ghat

Ganga Mahal Ghat

Ganga River

N

Chaitganj Rd.

Jnana Vapi Mosque

Vishwanath/Golden Temple

Scindhia Ghat

Annapurna Temple
Nepali Temple
Manikarnika Ghat
Lalita Ghat

Luxa Rd.
GODAULIA CROSSING

Dasashwamedh Ghat Rd.

Mir Ghat

Indica Books

GODAULIA
Universal Book Co.

Man Mandir Ghat

Dasashwamedh Ghat

Mandapura Rd.

Shitala Temple

Pandey Ghat

300 yards
300 meters

FOOD
Keshari Restaurant, 3
Monga Restaurant, 2
Temple Boogie Restaurant, 7
Yelchiko Bar & Restaurant, 1

UTTAR PRADESH

Hotel Temple on Ganges, Assi Ghat (☎312340 or 312740), a 20min. walk (or boat ride) down from the "main *ghat*." A spotlessly clean place with offerings—including evening yoga lessons—way beyond most budget places. The staff will serve the hotel restaurant's food to guests anywhere in the hotel, from bedrooms to the lounge downstairs to the rooftop terrace looking out on the river. All rooms have attached baths with hot water. ISD service. Dorm beds Rs50; singles Rs150-250; doubles Rs250-550.

Hotel Arya, Sonar Pura (☎313869), 1km from Godaulia Crossing, on the main road to Assi Ghat. Just far enough from the action to allow you to catch your breath, but still only minutes from a plunge back into the thick of things. Newly-painted rooms, some with TVs and balconies and a very pleasant little rooftop restaurant. Extremely friendly, eager-to-please manager. Bike rentals. Call ahead for a free pick-up from the railway station. Singles Rs125; doubles Rs175-300.

Yogi Lodge, Kalika Gali (☎392588 or 321427), around the corner from Golden Temple. This popular backpacker guest house feels a lot more like a home than most hotels in the area. Restaurant and sitting room at the bottom of a steep staircase serve the usual fare (8am-3pm and 5:30-9pm). Dorm beds Rs50; singles Rs80; doubles Rs100.

Ganges View Hotel, Assi Ghat (☎313218). Next to the Harmony Book Shop. Live like a maharaja in this family-run home-cum-hotel. Each room is an exquisitely decorated work of art; the main living room glitters with glass chandeliers. Hosts free lectures and concerts during the regular season. Singles from Rs350; doubles Rs400-1200.

Om Lodge, Nichi Brahmapuri (☎392728), Bansphatak area, Old City. Facing Dasashwamedh Ghat, turn left from Godaulia Crossing onto the road to Chowk. Take a right at the signs for Om Lodge, and follow these down increasingly narrow and desolate alleys.

Run by a friendly family headed by a welcoming, intelligent, Santa-turned-sadhu. Extremely basic rooms, but TV, VCR, video games, and library for guests' use in the common room make for a homey feel. Yoga classes Rs25 per hr. Tabla lessons Rs50 per hr. Dorm beds Rs25; singles Rs40-60; doubles Rs60-80.

Vishnu Rest House, Pandey Ghat (☎450206). Facing the Ganga, walk right along the shore from Dasashwamedh Ghat until you see "Pandey" written above the *ghats*. Not to be confused with the Vishnu Guest House, Old Vishnu Rest House, or any other variation on the theme. The Rest House pays no commissions, so rickshaw-*wallahs* often claim it's closed. The most popular backpacker hang-out in town, this place fills up quickly. Terrace restaurant has superb views of the Ganga. Restaurant open daily 7am-2pm and 6-9:30pm. Dorm beds Rs35; singles Rs70; doubles with bath Rs120-200.

Shanti Guest House (☎392568 or 320956), near Manikarnika Ghat. Huge high-and-wide hotel has rooms of all shapes and sizes that are crowded around a steep staircase. Rooftop restaurant, which serves as Party Central for the Old City during high season, has breathtaking views of the main burning *ghats*. Changes every currency under the sun and AmEx traveler's checks. Singles Rs30-80; doubles Rs50-125.

Trimurti Guest House, Saraswati Phatak, Old City (☎323554). From Godaulia Crossing, follow Dasashwamedh Rd. toward Dasashwamedh Ghat. Take the last left before the *ghat* (there will be signs for Trimurti and for Kashi Vishwanath "Golden" Temple); the guest house is 300m down on the right. Simple but adequate rooms—the views of the Golden Temple are as good as any you're likely to get if you're not a Hindu. Dorm beds Rs30; singles Rs50; doubles Rs80-120.

Hotel Arti, Harischandra Ghat (☎313921), 200m up the road from the second of Varanasi's burning *ghats*, offers good views of the crowds on their way to the cremations. Clean, carpeted doubles have attached bathrooms with hot water. Internet service Rs40 per hr., free for guests after 11pm. Single occupancy Rs150-200; doubles Rs200-450.

Golden Lodge, Kalika Gali (☎393832 or 328788), near the "Golden" Temple. Clean, simple, slightly shabby looking budget hotel offers "homely and comfortable staying" amidst "temple spires and holy zingling bells." Attached Fagin's Restaurant serves Indian, Western, and Israeli favorites and has A/C and satellite TV. Check-out 10:30am. Singles Rs40-100; doubles Rs80-100.

Hotel La-Ra India, Dasashwamedh Ghat Rd. (☎320323), between Godaulia Crossing and the river, provides marble-floored relief from the grunge of the Old City surrounding it. All rooms have attached bath and phone. Singles Rs225–425; doubles 275-525.

Hotel Relax, Parade Kothi, Cantonment (☎343503), is a good late-night or early-morning train-dropping place. A short walk from the station. Decent rooms Rs75-350.

◖ FOOD

Keshari Restaurant, off Dasashwamedh Rd. As you walk away from the river, it will be down a small alley on the right, opposite the La-Ra India Hotel. Cool, two-floored, and normally packed full of prosperous-looking people, the Keshari serves good *thalis* and countless other Indian dishes for Rs35-60. Open daily 10am-10:30pm.

Malika Restaurant, in Hotel Padmini, near Sigra Crossing. Classy and upscale with arctic-standard A/C, wood paneling, mirrored walls, and a miniature railway for you to sit and play silly buggers in while you wait for your food to arrive. Western breakfasts and a good range of Indian meals. Vegetable *jhal frezi* Rs70. Open daily 7am-10:30pm.

Bread of Life Bakery and Western Restaurant, B3/322, Shivala (☎313912), on the main road between Assi Ghat and Godaulia. A world apart from most of Varanasi's restaurants, this place manages (more or less) to capture the feel of a small European bistro. The cinnamon buns (Rs15) are somewhat soggy, but where else in Varanasi can you find brownies (Rs25) and garlic bread (Rs20)? Open daily 8am-9pm.

Mandarin Restaurant, next to the Hotel Relax, a short walk from the railway station. This airy, calm restaurant serves a wider selection of (you guessed it) Chinese dishes than most other places. They taste a lot better, too. Try the vegetable Manchurian, drenched in a rich tomato and onion gravy (Rs40). Open daily 6:30am-11pm.

Pizzeria Vatica, on Assi Ghat, at the top of the steps, in a hedged-off garden. A mellow outdoor restaurant perfect for munching on pizza (Rs45) or pasta (Rs30-45) to the sound of temple bells as the sun slips behind the city skyline. Open daily 7am-10pm.

Temple Boogie Restaurant and German Bakery, near Manikarnika Ghat. From the front door of the Shanti Guest House, turn right. Turn left into the next alley; the restaurant is at the next intersection. Pastries, and Italian and (wow) Mexican food, as well as backgammon and newspapers. Burritos Rs45; *muesli* from Rs25. Open daily 7am-10pm.

Kamesh Hut Garden Bar and Restaurant, Jagatganj. With your back to the Hotel Pradeep, walk right. Turn right at the first alley. Green, fresh-air urban oasis provides relief from the chaotic honking outside. Beer Rs75. Open daily 7:30am-11pm.

Monga Restuarant, Dasashwamedh Ghat Rd., just after Godaulia Crossing, on the right. The low-hanging wicker lamps and thumping Hindi pop music of this underground restaurant will make the burning sun and crowds outside seem worlds away. Huge portions. Filling veg. *thalis* Rs35-50. Open daily 10am-10pm.

Yelchico Bar and Restaurant, a chain with two branches in Varanasi. The first is near Godaulia Crossing. As you approach from the river, it's down a flight of stairs on the left. Just about the only place in the Old City where you can get your grubby hands on a glass of beer (Rs80), though it is not on the menu and comes disguised as frothy tea. Open daily noon-10pm. The second branch, at Sigra Crossing, is more of a civilized bar than a restaurant, though it does serve a range of meals. Open daily 11am-10:30pm.

Shanti Guest House Rooftop Restaurant, near Manikarnika Ghat. With superb views over Manikarnika Ghat and the mighty Ganga, this is a very popular round-the-clock backpacker hang-out. Intrepid young curfew-breakers and other explorers congregate to share tales of the day's events. The food itself is bland and unremarkable, and the service is slow. Things quiet down around 2am, when you can sit and enjoy the fine view of the Ganga. Guest house gate closes at midnight, but you can knock loudly for entry.

Gazal Bar and Restaurant, inside Hotel Vaibhav, 600m north of the main railway station, after the Hotel India. With its cold air, cold beer (Rs80), and free peanuts, this is a comfortable and spit-free alternative to the crowded railway waiting-rooms.

UTTAR PRADESH

🔆 SIGHTS

THE GHATS OF THE GANGA

A little religious imagination and some knowledge of what is going on at the city's countless sacred sites can help, but to experience the life and vibrancy of Varanasi—its crowded temples and teeming *ghats*—all you really need are your five senses and an open mind ready to be bent gently out of shape.

The holy Ganga is what draws millions of pilgrims to Varanasi, and the series of **ghats** (steps) that line the river are at the heart of city life; abuzz with crowds of people from before dawn until long after nightfall, the *ghats* are where the pounding pulse of the ancient city beats fastest. Thousands come at dawn to make offerings to the heavenly water, but the *ghats* are far from reserved for purely sacred activities. Dive-bombing teenagers crash into the river from the steps, while others bathe and wash their clothes in the waters. All along the river banks, people wander and stroll. Meditation, music-making, and cricket all have their place here. The Ganga draws all sorts of life and death as well, for in Varanasi, **cremations** are viewed as auspicious events (a reversal of traditional beliefs). They take place right on the *ghats* rather than out of town on inauspicious soil, as they do everywhere else. The bodies of those who can't afford cremation, as well as holy men and children under 12, are dumped straight into the river and can sometimes be seen floating by. Water buffalo also bathe and die in the river, and sewers dump directly into the Ganga. *Let's Go* does not recommend bathing with buffalo.

The steps themselves are huge and sometimes number more than 100 from top to bottom, though some are hidden when the water is high. The name of each *ghat* is painted on the retaining walls in large letters in both Devanagari and Roman scripts. Memorizing the location of some of the major *ghats* will make finding your way around a lot easier. A **boat ride** along the river is one of the highlights of any Varanasi itinerary. The best time to do this is at dawn, when the *ghats* are at their most crowded and the whole city shines like gold in the early-morning light. (A small boat seating four people should cost no more than Rs40 for an hour's trip from Dasashwamedh.) The *ghats* are presented here from south to north.

ASSI GHAT. The southern end of Varanasi's riverfront begins with Assi Ghat, a broad clay bank at the meeting point of the Ganga and Assi Rivers. Assi Ghat is one of the busiest and most important of all the bathing *ghats*. Its muddy banks are alive throughout the day with pilgrims crowding to pay their respects to the large Shiva *linga* that stands in the shade of a pipal tree just a few feet from the water's edge. Shops, drink-stalls, and restaurants make this a popular destination for non-religious travelers too. Assi Ghat is surrounded by temples, several of them among the most popular in the whole city (see **The Banks and Beyond,** p. 201).

TULSI GHAT. Tulsi Ghat, named for the famed poet, Tulsi Das, whose house sits at the top of the steps, is the next significant *ghat* after Assi (see **The Banks and Beyond,** p. 201). Back from the water above Tulsi Ghat is one of Varanasi's most ancient sacred spots, the **Lolarka Kund.** Sunk deep into the ground, this tank was at one time the site where early Hindus worshiped Surya, the sun god. Today, it is a major point of pilgrimage during the annual festival of Lolarka Shashthi (Aug. or Sept.), when thousands of couples come here to pray for sons.

HARISHCHANDRA GHAT. The next major *ghat* as you head north is Harishchandra Ghat, Varanasi's second most important cremation ground, distinguished by the spires of black smoke that rise throughout the day from the funeral pyres. The constant stream of mourners and attendants makes Harishchandra one of the busiest *ghats*. Though widely believed to be the oldest cremation site in Varanasi, it has not been accorded quite the same level of religious importance as Manikarnika farther north. **Photography is strictly prohibited at both cremation ghats.**

KEDAR GHAT AND CHOWKI GHAT. The *ghat* with the red-and-white stripes is **Kedar Ghat.** Kedar means "field," and this is the field in which liberation is said to grow; the Kedar Temple, one of Varanasi's oldest and most important Shiva temples, is so holy that just resolving to come here is enough to liberate a person from the accumulated sins of two whole lifetimes. The rough stone mound that marks Shiva's presence here is thought to be the oldest *linga* in the city. **Chowki Ghat** has a fierce collection of *nagas*, early aquatic snake-gods, around a central tree. From here to Dasashwamedh Ghat, a long stretch of *ghats* used principally for laundry is marked by a collage of colorful saris and *lungis* stretched out to dry.

DASASHWAMEDH GHAT. The next major bathing spot and the most crowded *ghat* in Varanasi, Dasashwamedh Ghat is often referred to as the **"Main Ghat."** Every morning, busloads of pilgrims make their way past the fruit stalls and flower sellers that line the wide road leading to the steps. Dasashwamedh is said to be the spot where the creator god, Brahma, performed 10 royal horse-sacrifices (*ashwamedhas*) with the mythical King Divodasa. Bathing here is supposed to bestow on pilgrims all the benefits of ten horse sacrifices. On the *ghat* is **Brahmeshwar,** the *linga* that Brahma established here after performing his sacrifices. Just south of Dasashwamedh Ghat, Shitala, the goddess of smallpox and other diseases, is worshipped in the **Shitala Temple.** Adorned with colorful paint and tinsel, this square, white temple is more popular than any of the *lingas* of Dasashwamedh.

MAN MANDIR GHAT TO LALITA GHAT. The next *ghat* from Dasashwamedh is **Man Mandir Ghat,** topped by one of the observatories built in the 18th century by Maharaja Jai Singh of Jaipur. Climb up on the right side of the building to see a collection of astronomical scales made of stone. Above **Mir Ghat** and **Lalita Ghat** are several important temples. The **Vishalakshi Temple** belongs to a "Wide-Eyed" local goddess, but it is also a *Shakti pitha*—the eye of the goddess Sati (or, by some accounts, her earring) is said to have landed here when she was chopped apart in the heavens (see **Divine Dismemberment,** p. 692). Nearby, a deep well, the **Dharma Kup,** marks the site where Yama, the god of death, paid homage to Shiva.

MANIKARNIKA GHAT. An axis of holiness runs between the **Vishwanath Temple** (see **The Banks and Beyond,** p. 201) and the next *ghat,* Manikarnika Ghat. This is the most sacred of all the *ghats* and the final stop on the popular *panchathirthi* pilgrimage, which leads devotees along the length of the city's riverside banks. Bathing here and worshipping at Vishwanath is a daily routine for many Benarsis and an essential part of any pilgrimage. Manikarnika Ghat takes its name from **Manikarnika Kund,** the small white tank just past the cremation grounds, which Vishnu is said to have dug out at the beginning of time and filled with his sweat. This first pool of water so delighted Shiva that he dropped his bejeweled earring *(manikarnika)* in it. Vishnu's footprints are nearby, under a circular shelter.

The area just south of Manikarnika has become the city's **primary cremation ground.** Boats full of wood are moored here, and the pyres burn throughout the day and night, consuming the corpses of those lucky enough to have been liberated here. Bodies are carried on stretchers down the winding streets to the riverside, where they are dipped in the Ganga before being burned for three hours on fires lit from an eternal flame on the *ghat.* When the burning is complete, the eldest son of the deceased throws a pot of Ganga water onto the fire, and the ashes are sprinkled in the river. Above the *ghat* are hospices where the dying come to wait their turn. Visitors can watch the cremations from boats or buildings above the *ghat,* but you are likely to offend and upset mourners and workers if you linger too long or too conspicuously on the *ghat.* **Photographing the cremations is strictly prohibited.**

SANKATA GHAT AND NORTHERN SIGHTS. Next in line is **Sankata Ghat,** above which is the baby-blue temple of **Sankata Devi,** a powerful mother-goddess. The important bathing site is **Panchganga Ghat.** Five rivers are said to converge here: the Ganga, Yamuna, and Saraswati, which flow together from Allahabad, and two old rivulets, the Dhutapapa and Kirana, which have now disappeared. Vishnu chose this place as the greatest spot in Kashi, and his creaky, painted **Bindu Madhava** temple sits above the *ghat.* During the month of Karthik (Oct.-Nov.) the temple and the *ghat* are decked with lamps at night. For the rest of the year the most prominent feature of Panchganga Ghat is the tall **Dharhara Mosque** at the top. Emperor Aurangzeb built the mosque over the ruins of an earlier Bindu Madhava temple, and it now dominates a section of the riverbank skyline. It is closed to visitors because of threats from Hindu zealots to "take it back." A statue of a sacred cow at **Gai Ghat** watches over an array of Shiva *lingas.* Close to this is **Trilochan Ghat,** with the popular temple of the "Three-Eyed" Shiva. **Varanasi Devi,** the patron-goddess of Varanasi, also inhabits this temple.

Despite being in the oldest part of the city, the *ghats* farther north are more spaced out and less crowded those in the southern part of the city. The next *ghat* of visible importance is **Raj Ghat,** the last before the Malaviya Bridge. This is the crossing-point where, since ancient times, traders have ferried across the Ganga. The temple of **Adi Keshava** (Original Vishnu) sits on a high bank to the north of the bridge and marks the northern city limits. Vishnu washed his feet here, and the image inside the temple was shaped by Vishnu himself. There is not much to see nowadays, besides some pasture land.

THE BANKS AND BEYOND

THE VISHWANATH TEMPLE (GOLDEN TEMPLE). Up Dasashwamedh Rd. from the river and right through a temple-like archway, signs lead to the center of Varanasi's religious geography: the temple of Shiva as Vishwanath (Lord of All). Nicknamed the "Golden" Temple, it contains the Vishweshwar *linga,* the first one on earth and one of India's 12 *jyotirlingas,* which are said to have shot up from the ground as shafts of light. All of Varanasi is measured in circles around Vishwanath, making it the city's most important pilgrimage site. The temple is closed to non-Hindus, but shopkeepers across the road happily charge visitors for the view from their rooftops *(Rs5)*. The temple's gilded spire soars high above the city, and bells chime at the many smaller temples that lead to it. There has been a Shiva temple on this site since ancient times, but the present building dates back only to 1777. Earlier temples here were repeatedly destroyed by waves of Muslim invasions; the last of these took place in 1669, when the temple was torn down at the command of Aurangzeb. On top of the half-demolished ruins of an earlier Vishwanath Temple was constructed the Jnana Vapi Mosque, which still stands today, surrounded by a cordon of barbed wire, iron fences, and soldiers. Hindu extremists have made repeated threats to destroy the mosque and reclaim the old holy site.

JNANA VAPI. In between the temple and the mosque is the **Jnana Vapi** itself, a "Well of Wisdom" said to have been in existence since the very beginning of the world. The waters that sprang up here when Shiva dug up the earth with his trident were the first pure waters anywhere on earth; the well's sacred waters of wisdom are ladled out daily under police supervision.

ANNAPURNA TEMPLE. The most important goddess temple in Varanasi is dedicated to Shakti, the divine embodiment of power or energy and Shiva's consort, in the form of Annapurna. Armed with spoons and saucepans, Annapurna is a provider of food; a **Mountain of Food Festival** occurs here in late October or early November. *(Opposite Vishwanath, just down the lane. Closed to non-Hindus.)*

KALA BHAIRONATH. Once an angry and sinful form of Shiva, Kala Bhaironath (also known as Bhairava) chopped off the fifth head of the god Brahma after he failed to recognize Shiva, embodied in a shimmering *linga* of light, as supreme among all the gods. As punishment, the rotting head stuck to his hand, and for years, Bhairava had to wander remorsefully around the whole of India, using the skull as a begging bowl for his food. It was not until he got to Varanasi that the head miraculously dropped from his hands, and Shiva appointed him the "chief justice" of the sacred city. He keeps an eye on Varanasi's residents, devours their sins as they are washed away by the Ganga's holy waters, and metes out instant retribution for the accumulated misdeeds of those who die here to pay their karmic debt. The temple is often crowded with supplicant sinners offering incense and garlands to the image of the holy police chief. *(Up Chowk Rd. from Godaulia, near the intersection with Kabir Chaura Rd. Open daily 5am-noon and 2-10pm.)* Not too far away, on the other side of the Chowk-Kabir Chaura Rd. crossing, is the temple of **Bare Ganesh,** the central Ganesh shrine in Varanasi.

TULSI MANAS MANDIR. Built of white marble and flanked by palm trees, this modern Vishnu temple was erected in honor of Tulsi Das, the premier poet of the Hindi language who translated the Sanskrit epic, the *Ramayana*, into Hindi in the 16th century. The complete epic is inscribed on the inside walls in the poet's Hindi version, and painted depictions of scenes from the story also line the temple walls. Toward the back of the temple, a collection of brightly painted mechanical figures acts out the timeless tale to the delight of parents and children passing through. *(Rs1 to enter.)* The great poet himself sits, book in hand, by the temple door. *(Up the road from the Assi Ghat, a short rickshaw ride from the river. Open daily 5am-noon and 4-9pm.)*

DURGA TEMPLE. The impressive red tower of this temple stretches up into the sky above the tank. It is believed that the goddess Durga rested here after saving the world from an otherwise "unassailable" demon, and she continues to be regarded as the protectress of Southern Kashi. The walls inside are inscribed with Tulsi Das's verses and adorned with paintings, the most notable of which depicts the love of Bharat, Rama's step-brother, who worshipped Rama's wooden sandals for the 14 years of Rama's exile. *(Next to the Tulsi Manas Mandir. Open 24hr.)*

SANKAT MOCHAN TEMPLE. The Sankat Mochan Temple, inland from the river and south of the Assi Ghat, is dedicated to Hanuman and is considered by locals to be one of the three most important temples in Varanasi; orange *sindur* smears attest to its popularity. *(Open daily 4:30am-10:30pm.)*

BENARES HINDU UNIVERSITY (BHU). Founded in 1916 by the reformer Madan Mohan Malaviya, the university was intended to merge modern ideas with traditional Hindu learning. For those not planning to study Indian languages or philosophy, the campus has two places suited to shorter visits. The **Sri Vishwanath Temple,** the largest temple in the city, has one large, white spire modeled on the one knocked down by Aurangzeb in 1669. *(Open daily 4am-noon and 1-9pm.)* **Bharat Kala Bhawan,** the BHU museum, has an extensive collection of miniature paintings, artifacts, and sculptures. The second floor contains the sculptures and paintings of Alice Boner, the renowned Indophile who claimed to understand India "on its own terms." There is plenty here from Varanasi, too, from 19th-century etchings of *ghats* to a great statue of Krishna lifting Mt. Govardhana. The most stunning artifacts, a collection of coins, intricately carved jewelry, and emperor's jade mugs, are kept in a safe room in the **Nidhi Gallery.** *(Across Panch Koshi Rd., at the south end of town. Museum open M-Sa 11am-4:30pm. Rs40.)*

RAMNAGAR FORT. The barren expanse of the Ganga's eastern shore does hold one point of interest: Ramnagar Fort, the castle of Varanasi's maharaja. The fort contains a **royal museum;** though most of the exhibits are rather dilapidated, there are plenty of the royal family's sedan chairs and swords to glint a hint of days gone by. *(Open daily 9am-noon and 2-6pm; Rs7.)* Ramnagar is probably not worth the trip unless it's for the **Ram Lila,** the festive Ramayana pageant, held in September and Oct. *(In the village of Ramnagar opposite BHU at the south end of the city. The river can be crossed by ferry for Rs2.)*

BHARAT MATA TEMPLE. A spirit of urbane and modernized Hinduism can be seen in the Bharat Mata Temple, on the city's western outskirts, south of the Cantonment. Mahatma Gandhi inaugurated this temple, which has a swimming-pool-sized marble relief map of Mother India in place of a deity. The upper balconies offer great views of Varanasi. *(A 15min. walk down Vidyapith Rd. from the railway station.)*

🎵 MUSIC

Varanasi is well-known as a center for Indian classical music (see p. 89), and many Westerners come here to do a George Harrison and learn how to play the sitar or tabla. The best resource is the music school at **Benares Hindu University** (☎307641), near Lanka Gate. Though the school itself only offers degree courses in Hindi and English, the faculty give **private music lessons** and can also refer students to other teachers. Another good place to learn sitar or tabla is the **Triveni Music Centre** (☎328074), on Keval Gali in Godaulia, not far from the Vishnu Rest House. Instructor Nandu and his father come highly recommended. (Lessons Rs50 per hr.) Despite the pressure, however, do not buy instruments from the Triveni Music Centre: they are not worth their inflated prices. The **International Music Centre,** near Dasashwamedh Ghat, also offers private sitar and tabla lessons (Rs60 per hr.).

Buying musical instruments can be a tricky business. There is no shortage of sitar and tabla stores in the Old City. One in particular comes recommended by the faculty at BHU; the proprietor, Mr. Nitai Chandra Nath, is a sage of string instruments and a true artisan. From Godaulia Crossing, facing Dasashwamedh, turn right, go straight, and turn on the third lane on your left (200m after Universal Book Co.); the Jangambali (Bengali Tola) Post Office will be immediately on your left, and the unmarked sitar store is several doors down. If you cannot find the shop, ask in the street for **Nitai Babu** and someone will show you the way. (Sitars Rs2000-5000.) **Imtiyaz Ali,** Siddh Giri Bagh, is a tabla shop recommended by Mr. Nath. Hop in a cycle-rickshaw and ask for the Maulavi Bagh Masjid in Siddh Giri Bagh; the store is next door to the mosque. (Brass tablas Rs1500; copper tablas Rs2000.)

🛍 SHOPPING

Varanasi is famous for its silk, and the touts will never let you forget it. There are several silk shops in Varanasi with fixed prices and government-enforced quality control. Two of these are on Vishwanath Gali in the Old City, on the same road as the Golden Temple: **Mohan Silk Stores,** 5/54 Vishwanath Gali (☎392354), and **Bhagwan Stores,** D10/32 Vishwanath Gali (☎392365), both on the right-hand side shortly after the main gate leading off from Dasashwamedh toward the Golden Temple. **J.R. Ivory Arts and Curios,** D20 Vishwanath Gali (☎321772), farther up the road on the left, used to carry silk but now stocks only beautiful wood carvings that range in price from Rs80 to Rs60,000. Two other silk shops are at Sindhu Nagar, off Aurangabad Rd., near the intersection of Aurangabad and Vidyapith: **M/S Bhagwanlila Exports,** 41 Sindhu Nagar Colony, Sigra (☎224192), and **Mahalakshmi Saree House,** 10 Chandrika Nager, Sigra (☎221319). Also notable is **Chowdhary Brothers,** Thatheri Bazaar (☎392469), opposite the police station. **Mehrotra Silk Factory,** SC21/22 Englishia Line, Cantonment (☎345289), may be small, but is probably the best of these shops. The store carries shawls (US$9-80), tapestries (US$10-20), and raw fabric (US$5 per meter). To get there, walk down Vidyapith Rd., make a right on Station Rd., and then look for signs on the left. It's a good idea to visit these shops to get a sense of the prices of top-quality silk before bargaining in the Chowk or Old City. (Shops open daily 10am-8pm.) When buying silk, also remember to insist on buying both a horizontal and vertical thread. Real silk, when burned, has the odor of burning hair. Many fabrics in the market are woven with silk in one direction and a synthetic fiber in the other. When the fake thread is burned, it will smell like paper or plastic.

SARNATH सरनाथ

In the wooded suburbs north of Varanasi lies Sarnath, a quiet and well-maintained site of ruins marking the location of Gautama Buddha's first sermon, the famous "Sermon in the Deer Park." After the Buddha attained enlightenment in Bodh Gaya, he walked the 200km to Sarnath, with lotuses blooming where his feet touched the ground. Gathering his former companions here, among the deer and peacocks, he revealed the Noble Eightfold Path. In later years, he occasionally returned to this quiet grove to meditate.

In the 3rd century BC, when the region was under the rule of the Mauryas, stupas were built to commemorate the Buddha's visits. This construction continued until the 4th century AD, when the Hindu Guptas rose to power and Buddhist influence began to wane. Sarnath had achieved fame by this time for its sandstone images of the Buddha, many fine examples of which are displayed in the excellent archaeological museum. Sarnath's prestige as a center of Buddhism came to an abrupt end during the 12th century when it was demolished by Qutb-ud-din Aibak. Sarnath's Deer Park is dotted with the remains of numerous stupas, though only one monument, the Dhamekh Stupa, remains wholly intact.

Sarnath is a pleasant place to wander. Even in the time-tired state they are in today, the monuments here provide impressive evidence of the rich Buddhist culture that once flourished here and the importance that Buddhist philosophy once held throughout much of northern India. There has been little modern development in Sarnath since its monuments were excavated and explored during the 19th century by spade-*wallah* supreme, Sir Alexander Cunningham. With a bit of selective squinting, it is still possible to imagine Sarnath as it might have been when the Buddha himself walked through its woods more than 2000 years ago.

■■ **ORIENTATION AND PRACTICAL INFORMATION.** Sarnath is contained within a triangle of road. From the south, Sarnath Rd. comes from Varanasi and splits in two by the Rangoli Garden Restaurant. The branch heading northwest is **Ashoka Rd.** and runs past the Archaeological Museum. The branch going northeast goes past the UP Tourist Bungalow. Connecting these two roads after they diverge is the main road, **Dharmapal Rd.,** which runs east-west and contains almost all of the sights. The **bus stand** is at the intersection of Dharmapal Rd. and the road that passes the UP Tourist Bungalow. Buses go to the railway station (frequent 7am-7:30pm, 40min., Rs6). **Tempos** go to many different points in Varanasi, including the railway station (Rs8). **Auto-rickshaws** putter wherever the money takes them (Rs50 to Varanasi). The **post office** (open M-Sa 8:30am-4:30pm) is near the bus stand and opposite the **UP Tourist Bungalow.** There's a small information counter in the bunga-low, which gives out maps of the sites (open M-Sa 10am-5pm). **STD/ISD** booths are along Dharmapal Rd. in front of the sights and ruins.

▟▙ ACCOMMODATIONS AND FOOD. Most tourists don't spend the night, but it's possible to stay in some of the monasteries for a small donation. The **Tourist Bungalow,** also known as the **Hotel Mrigadava,** is the standard UP government-issue, mid-range place: clean, boring, and overpriced. (☎586965. Dorm beds Rs70; sin-gles Rs250-450; doubles Rs300-550.) The large **dining room** (open daily 7am-10pm) serves breakfast and all the usual Indian and Chinese dishes (Rs50-100). The only other restaurant worth mentioning is the **Rangoli Garden Restaurant,** at the point where Sarnath Rd. splits. The food here is not the best, nor is the service the quick-est, but the place is clean and cool enough. The menu contains nothing you haven't seen a hundred times already.

▣ SIGHTS. Most of Sarnath's points of interest are recently excavated piles of rubble: this is a place with more atmosphere and history than sights to write home about. However, the first stop on the way into the archaeological enclosure is intact. The sandstone spires of the modern Buddhist temple, **Mulgandha Kuti Vihar,** beckon from the main gate, its peaceful interior decorated by the Japanese artist, Kosetsu Nosi, with paintings inspired by the *Buddhacarita* (The Acts of the Bud-dha). The pipal tree in the shrine is supposed to be a close relative of the tree under which the Buddha attained enlightenment. A small book stall inside the tem-ple sells Buddhist literature. *(Cross the intersection at the bus stand; the gate to the park is 200m down Dharmapal Rd., on the right. Open daily 4-11:30am and 1:30-8pm.)*

Looming above the temple trees to the left of the temple is the **Dhamekh Stupa,** the only ancient structure left intact by Qutb-ud-din's armies. It commemorates the spot where the Buddha delivered his first sermon. Begun sometime during the 5th or 6th century, in the twilight of Buddhist predominance in North India, it remains unfinished. The bottom is made of elaborately decorated stone, with eight niches that once held images of the Buddha; the top is made up of little more than small clay bricks. Next to the Damekh Stupa lie the remains of the **Dharmarajika Stupa;** it must have been an impressive building in its day, but today only the foun-dations remain. It was built by the Mauryan emperor Ashoka in the 3rd century BC to house the relics of the Buddha; Ashoka himself is thought to have come here to meditate in what was once a major monastic center. The structure was reduced to rubble in the 19th century by hopeful locals hunting for long-lost treasure.

Next to the stupa are the remains of the **Main Shrine,** built by Ashoka to mark a favorite meditation spot of the Buddha. At the end of the ruined structure, down a shallow well, is the bottom portion of **Ashoka's column.** The pillar is engraved with Buddhist edicts in Brahmi script that warn Buddhist monks and nuns against cre-ating rifts among the followers of the Buddha (the advice wasn't taken). The capi-tal is one of the great masterpieces of early Indian art and is the centerpiece of the Archaeological Museum's collection. A high fence runs all around **Deer Park,** adja-cent to the ancient ruins. *(Entrance to stupa and ruins park Rs2.)*

Opposite the main entrance to the Dharmarajika Stupa compound and at the intersection of Dharmapal and Ashoka Rd. is the **Archaeological Museum.** On dis-play directly in front of the museum entrance is the famous splendidly engraved capital from Ashoka's column, with its four roaring lions seated back to back. It was adopted as the emblem of the Indian republic and appears on all national cur-rency. The museum's collection includes a number of excellent pieces, including at least one certifiable work of genius: a perfectly wrought teaching Buddha from the Gupta period. *(Open Sa-Th 10am-5pm. Rs2.)* One kilometer from the museum, on Ashoka Rd. near the split, is a curious melange of Buddhist-Mughal architecture in the **Chowkhandi Stupa.** The rectangular Gupta-period foundation commemorating the site where the Buddha met his five disciples is topped by a crowning tower in the Mughal style. It was built by either Emperor Akbar or Raja Govandhan, the local ruler, to mark the site where Emperor Humayun once spent the night.

UTTAR PRADESH

ALLAHABAD इलाहाबाद ☎ 0532

The holy city of Allahabad stands at the sacred *sangam*, or confluence, of the Ganga and the Yamuna Rivers. Into these two rivers flows a third, the mystical Saraswati, river of wisdom. Lord Brahma called this spot Tirth Raj ("King of Pilgrimage Sites"), and all devout Hindus try to bathe in the waters at least once in their lives. Known for thousands of years as Prayag (Confluence), the city is nowadays more commonly known as Allahabad, the Perso-Arabic name meaning "Place of God" given to the city by the Mughal emperors.

The British decared Allahabad the capital of the United Provinces in 1901. The Indian Independence movement was strongly rooted here thanks to the work of the Nehrus, the Allahabad family that forged a political dynasty after Independence. Quieter and calmer than most large Indian cities, Allahabad is mercifully free from predatory touts. A relatively tourist-free city, Allahabad is well worth a couple of days, and it becomes the focus of national attention every 12 years when it hosts the **Maha Kumbh Mela,** the most important of all Hindu festivals in which millions of pilgrims converge at the Sangam.

▐▀ GETTING THERE AND GETTING AROUND

Trains: Allahabad Junction Railway Station, Leader Rd. To: **Agra** (4:35am, 11½hr., Rs204); **Delhi** (22-35 per day, 1am-10:55pm, 8hr., Rs210; *Rajdhani Exp.* 2301 and 2309, Tu, W, Sa, Su, 2:45am, 7hr., A/C chair Rs975); **Gorakhpur** (8:45am and 9:15pm, 9-11hr., Rs130); **Gwalior** (1-3 per day, 6:40am-6:30pm, 11-15hr., Rs149); **Kanpur** (at least 20 per day, 4:40am-1:20am, Rs107); **Lucknow** (4 per day, 6:20am-10:30pm, 3-5hr., Rs89); **Satna** (8-15 per day, 6:20am-3:35am, 3hr., Rs84, then a 4hr. bus trip to **Khajuraho**).

Buses: Civil Lines Bus Stand, MG Rd., next to the Tourist Bungalow. To: **Ayodhya** (every hr., 6am-10pm, 5hr., Rs72); **Gorakhpur** (8 every hr., 6-10am, 8hr., Rs119); **Lucknow** (frequent, 4am-8pm, 6hr., Rs86); **Varanasi** (every hr., 4am-5pm, 3hr., Rs54). **Leader Rd. Bus Stand,** opposite the main Allahabad Junction Railway Station, has buses to: **Agra** (11am, 3 and 7pm; 13hr.; Rs205); and **Delhi** (6pm and midnight, 20hr., Rs 268). **Zero Rd. Bus Stand** is north of Chowk.

Local Transportation: Cycle-rickshaws from the Allahabad Junction Railway Station to the Tourist Bungalow are Rs10. **Tempos** wait at the bus or railway stations. To reach the Sangam, take a tempo to Daraganj Railway Station and walk south from the tracks.

✳▐ ORIENTATION AND PRACTICAL INFORMATION

North of the railway tracks is the shady, British-built **Civil Lines** area, with all of its roads laid out in a grid; south is the congested and gritty **Chowk** area. The **Yamuna River** flows south of Allahabad until it reaches the sacred confluence point at the southeastern extremity of the city. The Ganga flows down along the eastern edge of the city. In Civil Lines, **Mahatma Gandhi (MG) Rd.,** with its hotels, restaurants, and ice cream stands, is the road to stick to for orientation; it is lined with tall and distinctive statues that make good landmarks. **Kamla Nehru Rd.** turns up from MG Rd. toward Allahabad University. **Leader Rd.** runs along the tracks on the Chowk side. The **Grand Trunk Rd.** streaks through the heart of Chowk. Triveni Rd. leads from the Grand Trunk Rd. to the **Sangam.**

Tourist Office: Tourist Bungalow, MG Rd. (☎601873). Just around the corner from the Civil Lines Bus Stand. Stern and serious-minded pamphlet custodians dispense maps and advice in return for patience and smiles. Open M-Sa 10am-5pm.

Currency Exchange: State Bank of India, 4 Kacheri Rd. (☎607932), near District Court. Changes major currencies and AmEx and Thomas Cook traveler's checks. Open M-F 10am-2pm, Sa 10am-noon.

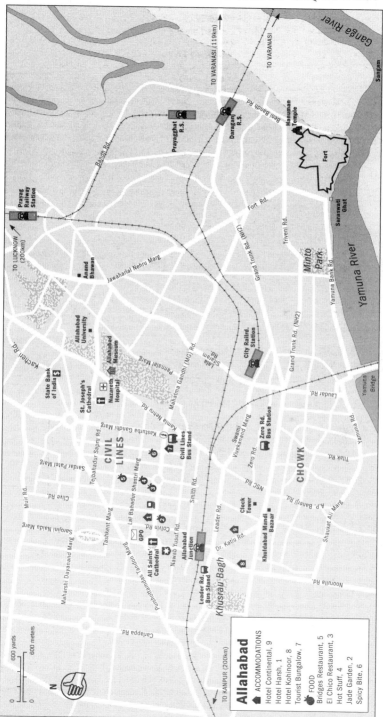

UTTAR PRADESH

Allahabad

▲ ACCOMMODATIONS
Hotel Continental, 9
Hotel Harsh, 1
Hotel Kohinoor, 8
Tourist Bungalow, 7

♦ FOOD
Bridges Restaurant, 5
El Chico Restaurant, 3
Hot Stuff, 4
Jade Garden, 2
Spicy Bite, 6

Bookstore: M/S A.H. Wheeler Book Shop, MG Rd. (☎624106), to the right of the Palace Theatre, on the left side of the road. Facing away from the Tourist Bungalow, walk 500m to the left. One of the best bookstores in UP Open M-Sa 10am-7pm.

Market: There's a large fruit market at **Khuldabad Mandi Bazaar** near the clock tower, at the intersection of Dr. Katiu and Grand Trunk Rd.

Police: (☎622592), on the main road that leads from All Saints' Cathedral to Allahabad junction railway station.

Hospital: Nazareth Hospital, 13/A Kamla Nehru Rd. (☎600430). From the intersection of MG and Kamla Nehru Rd., it's 1km to the northeast, on the left, marked by a red cross and a Hindi sign. The best private hospital in town, with a fully stocked **pharmacy.**

Internet: Pioneer, MG Marg (☎621058), opposite the Palace Theatre. Rs80 per hr. Open daily 8am-9pm.

Post Office: GPO, Queen's Rd. Go left at the Tourist Bungalow until you reach All Saints' Cathedral. Turn right and walk for 1 block. Possibly the only post office in UP with an attached "volleyball complex." Open M-Sa 10am-5pm. **Postal Code:** 211001.

ACCOMMODATIONS

Civil Lines lends luxury to the hotel scene, with quiet, mid-range hotels strung out along MG Rd. The cheapies concentrate around Leader Rd., near the bus stand.

Hotel Harsh, MG Rd. (☎622197), on the right just before All Saints' Cathedral. A colonial-era hotel once open only to *pukka sahibs,* the Harsh is today a dusty, faded relic of times gone by. A team of friendly old men sits and waits patiently under creaking fans to welcome guests to musty old rooms big enough to house a couple of royal elephants. Rooms with bath Rs200-230.

Hotel Kohinoor, 10 Noorulla Rd. (☎655501 or 656323). From the railway station, head down Noorulla Rd.; the hotel is 300m down on the left. Classy, well-kept place with tasteful rooms, some overlooking a lawn and garden. A/C restaurant. Check-out 24hr. Singles Rs225-350; doubles Rs275-450.

Tourist Bungalow (Hotel Ilawart), MG Rd. (☎601440), next to the Civil Lines Bus Stand. Clean-but-pricey place with a pleasant garden. Downstairs restaurant open daily 6am-11pm. Bar serves beer (Rs80) daily noon-11pm. Check-out noon. Dorm beds Rs100; singles from Rs300; doubles from Rs400.

Hotel Continental, Dr. Katiu Rd. (☎652058). From Allahabad Junction Railway Station, walk to Leader Rd., turn right, and then left onto Dr. Katiu Rd. An OK place to crash the night before an early train departure. Check-out 24hr. Singles with bath Rs140-450; doubles Rs200-500.

FOOD

Dining outside is the norm along MG Rd. Crowded benches surround fast-food stalls serving Indian snacks and imitation American junk food, though there are some more up-scale options if you're craving A/C and tablecloths.

El Chico Restaurant, MG Rd. Take a left from the Tourist Bungalow; it's on the right after the 4-way crossing. No enchiladas here; just a classy, unpretentious restaurant. Well-heeled crowd sips at coffee and fruit juice and calls the waiters with a hushed "excuse me, sir." Good Indian (*aloo dum kashmiri* Rs55) and continental dishes as well as some excellent veg. fried rice (Rs40). Open daily 10am-10:30pm.

Bridges Restaurant, 22 Sardar Patel Marg. From the Tourist Bungalow, take a left and then a right at the four-way crossing; it's 500m down on the left in Hotel Vilas. Dimly lit and as cold as a Siberian funeral parlor, this place claims to "bridge" the world by offering a choice of fine cuisines from around the globe. Chow mein and omelettes lead the charge. *Thalis* Rs60; *shahi korma* Rs50. Open daily 10am-10:30pm.

Jade Garden Restaurant, MG Rd., opposite Hotel Harsh. Sparsely decorated and accented with dark red window frames and paintings, this restaurant feels like a ballroom with a lowered ceiling. A wide selection of veg. and non-veg. Indian and Chinese food. Veg. spring roll Rs40; *channa masala* Rs50. Open daily 10am-11pm.

Hot Stuff, Sardar Patel Marg. From the Tourist Bungalow, take a left and then a right at the four-way crossing; it's on the left after 300m. Allahabad's coolest fast-food joint. If you've just been dying for a "Boyish Burger" (Rs30) or a "Hot Stuff Special Foot-Long" (Rs45), then search no more. No questions asked. Open daily 10am-10pm.

Spicy Bite, left out of the Tourist Bungalow, and across the street, is one of several good open air stalls on MG Rd. for late lunch and dinner. Cheap, tasty Indian and Chinese dishes and a lively atmosphere.

◉ SIGHTS

TRIVENI SANGAM. Allahabad's chief attraction for millions of Hindu pilgrims is the Triveni Sangam, the meeting point of the rivers Ganga, Yamuna, and Saraswati, and the site of the **Maha Kumbh Mela.** The Yamuna skirts the south side of Allahabad, and the Ganga rushes along the east. The Saraswati, the mythical river of wisdom, is said to flow underground. For a negotiable fee (no more than Rs20) **boats** will take visitors from the side of the fort to the meeting place of the rivers. The difference in color between the muddy brown Ganga and the pale green Yamuna is plainly visible from the shore. In the summer, the water is warm and shallow, and it is sometimes possible to walk to the Sangam over the floodplains that spread out from the city. Millions of pilgrims camp here during the Kumbh Mela. At other times, especially at dusk, the banks along the Sangam offer enjoyable views of the fort, with the rest of the city in the background. Alongside the road approaching the Sangam is the **fort** built by Emperor Akbar in 1583. The Indian Army still finds the confluence strategically important, so the fort is full of soldiers, and visitors are not allowed to enter.

HANUMAN TEMPLE. In the shadow of the fort's outer wall facing the Sangam is the Hanuman Temple, dedicated to the monkey god. The temple itself is only a shed with an army of red and gold flags out front, but it's an extremely popular shed nonetheless, not to be confused with the multi-storied affair grinning out over the trees— that's the Shankar Viman Mandapam. A constant stream of chanting worshipers snakes around the tiny temple, showering offerings of flowers on the huge image of the god that lies smeared with vermilion just below ground level. The floodwaters are said to flow over Hanuman's feet each year before they recede. *(Open daily 4am-10pm.)*

THE KUMBH MELA
The Maha (Great) Kumbh Mela at Allahabad in 1989 set the record for the world's largest human gathering. An estimated 13 million people came to the city to be present at Hinduism's greatest festival, which marks the holiest time to bathe in the Sangam. Every 12 years, at one precisely calculated moment, all the pilgrims splash into the water in a ritual act believed to undo lifetimes of sin. Columns of charging sadhus, often naked and smeared with ash, are among the most zealous bathers.

The story behind the Kumbh Mela concerns a *kumbh* (pot) that is said to have contained an immortality-bestowing nectar. The demons battled the gods for this pot in a struggle that lasted 12 days, during which time four drops of the divine nectar were spilled. One landed at **Haridwar** (see p. 137), one at **Nasik** (see p. 408), one at **Ujjain** (see p. 363), and one at **Allahabad.** The mythical 12-day fight translates into 12 human years, the length of the festival's rotation between cities. Every three years a Kumbh Mela is held in one of the four cities in January or February. The **Maha Kumbh Mela,** held at Allahabad every 12th year, is the greatest of all. Smaller *melas,* known as Magh Melas, are held in Allahabad in off-years during the month of Magh (Jan.-Feb.). In the sixth year, midway between Maha Kumbh Melas, an Ardha ("Half") Kumbh Mela is held. The next Kumbh Mela will take place Jan. 9-Feb. 21, 2001, in Allahabad.

ANAND BHAWAN. Once the mansion of the **Nehru family,** Anand Bhawan is now a museum devoted to their legacy. Independence leader Motilal Nehru, his son, Prime Minister Jawaharlal Nehru, and Jawaharlal's daughter and Prime Minister, Indira Gandhi, all lived and worked here, hosting meetings of the Independence movement. The Mahatma even had a room and working area in Anand Bhavan. The surprisingly modest Nehru showcase exhibits the family's passion for books—their bookshelves are stacked with everything from Roman Law to Tagore, and all the volumes can be peered at through glass panels. One of the most interesting, historically significant, and well-presented museums in UP, the Anand Bhawan is definitely worth a visit. (*At the northeast corner of the city, close to Allahabad University. Open Tu-Su 9:30am-5pm. Rs5.*) On the grounds, there's also a **bookstore** and a **planetarium.** (*Shows daily at 11am, noon, 2, 3, and 4pm. Rs10*). Next door is the **Swaraj Bhawan Museum,** the home of patriarch Motilal Nehru. This mansion has an excellent sound and light show in Hindi, which gives you a tour of the house while leading you through the events of the Independence movement. Apart from the show, however, there's not much else here. (*Open Tu-Su 9:30am-5pm. Show Rs5.*)

ALL SAINTS' CATHEDRAL. The boldest reminder of the British in Allahabad is All Saints' Cathedral, with its soaring Victorian gothic revival spires and its stained glass windows. It was designed by Sir William Emerson, the same architect who designed the Victoria Memorial in Calcutta. There are more weeds on the lawn than when the English last prayed from these pews for God, King, and Country and more bats screeching and squealing up in the belfry, but it is not difficult to sense the old ghosts of the empire click-clacking their heels through the reverberant hall and down the steps into the sunshine for tea and cakes with the rest of Allahabad's Sunday-best expatriate crowd. (*In Civil Lines, at the intersection of Mahatma Gandhi Rd. and Sarojini Naidu Marg.*)

KHUSRAU BAGH. If All Saints' is the most Raj-reminiscent relic in Allahabad, then Khusrau Bagh is the most impressive reminder of Mughal rule. These gardens hold the speckled tombs of Khusrau (a son of Emperor Jehangir) and his mother. Following Mughal royal family tradition, Khusrau plotted against his father and was subsequently murdered in 1615 by his brother, the future emperor Shah Jahan. The gardens, shaded by fruit trees and lined with paths, are a popular place for people to come and relax. In the evenings the place comes alive with games of cricket. (*In the Chowk area down Leader Rd., past the bus station.*)

OTHER SIGHTS. Beyond the fort, on the bank of the Yamuna, is **Saraswati Ghat,** where boats dock and evening ceremony lamps are floated down to the confluence. Follow Yamuna Bank Rd. away from the fort to reach **Minto Park** on the right, where Lord Canning proclaimed in 1858 that India would be ruled by the Queen of England. Independent India has reclaimed the historic site by renaming the park for Madan Mohan Malaviya (an Independence figure and critic of the caste system) and erecting a part-Mauryan, part-Italian monument. (*To reach the other side of the fort, take either a boat ride or detour through the fenced-off military installation behind the fort.*) The **Allahabad Museum,** Kamla Nehru Marg, has a large sculpture collection, including many terra-cotta figures from Kausambi, the ancient city and Buddhist center 60km from Allahabad. There is also a room with photographs and a few Nehru mementos. (*Open Tu-Su 10:15am-4:30pm. Rs100 for foreigners.*)

HIMACHAL PRADESH
हिमाचल प्रदेश

Travel through Himachal Pradesh ("Lap of Snow") is an experience of complete detachment from the urban world, a rare feeling for most visitors to India. You'll walk through apple orchards and paddy fields, cross rivers swollen with glacial run-off, and be left breathless by the scenery and splendor of high-altitude mountain passes. Different worlds exist alongside each other in Himachal Pradesh: cross the Rohtang Pass, and the rain-drenched forests of Manali suddenly give way to the rock, ice, and harsh winds of the Lahaul Valley or the vast emptiness and harsh heat of Spiti; travel from Shimla to Kaza, and Hindu temples are replaced by Buddhist prayer flags and *gompas*. And if you take the road from Manali to Leh in Kashmir, you'll experience an exhilaration that defies description.

With the deteriorating political situation in Kashmir, Himachal has been "discovered" by foreign tourists, and the three main towns in HP have become not only tourist-thronged backpacker retreats but gateways to the lands beyond. Dharamsala, somehow peaceful despite it all, has a strong Tibetan population and is the base for treks into the Dhauladars and the Pir Panjal. Manali and Shimla are favorite vacation spots with both Indian and foreign travelers. The less touristed rain-shadow areas—Lahaul, Spiti, and Upper Kinnaur—can be reached from Manali via the Rohtang Pass or from Shimla via Kalpa and Kaza. Road maintenance is tricky up here and routes that are theoretically open from June to September are liable to close down at any time as a result of avalanches, floods, and fallen bridges. The main tourist season in most of Himachal Pradesh runs from May to June and from September to October, but winter—when roads to Shimla, Manali, and Dharamsala and from Shimla to Chango remain open—is also an ideal time to visit.

HIGHLIGHTS OF HIMACHAL PRADESH

The Kullu Valley towns of **Manali** (p. 233), **Kullu** (p. 230), and **Naggar** (p. 231) are famous for green pastures, apple orchards, and great views of the Western Himalayas.

Dharamsala (p. 219) is where the mythic East meets and mixes with the equally mythic West, to the delight of hippies, pop stars, and Buddhist saints alike.

From its green forests to its icy mountain tops, HP has some of the most beautiful **trekking** in India, particularly in **Kinnaur** and **Spiti** (p. 238).

SHIMLA सिमला
☎ 0177

Stretching along a crescent-shaped ridge at an altitude of 2200m, Shimla casts a spell on the visitor with its cool air, magnificent views, and lingering spirit of the Raj. A stroll along the Ridge can be a strange experience, as you walk along broad streets lined with Scottish-style houses and crowded with monkeys. Down the steps from The Mall runs a maze of alleys and crushed houses where, as Rudyard Kipling once observed, you could stay hidden from the police for months at a time.

Shimla's history as a modern city began in the 19th century, when persistent Gorkha raiders ravaged with stunning efficiency what was then a small village. Local rulers appealed to the British for military aid; the British, seeing a chance to extend their power into the Sutlej River area, obliged and defeated the Gorkhas in

Himachal Pradesh

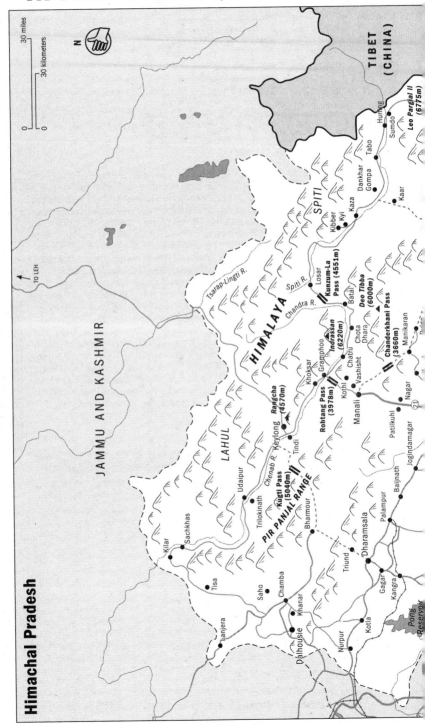

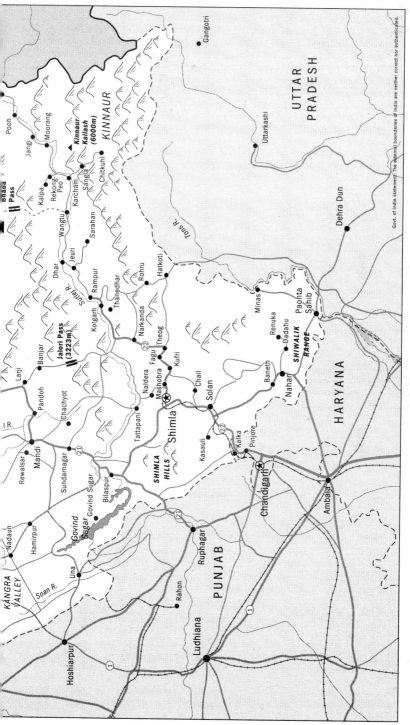

Govt. of India statement: The external boundaries of India are neither correct nor authenticated.

1815. Over the next half-century, British civil servants and injured soldiers flocked to Shimla each summer to seek rest from the rigors of ruling an empire. In 1864, imperial authorities made the summer haul to Shimla official and declared that it would serve as a seasonal capital for the Raj. Shimla became a social center, with gala balls, tailor's shops, and mad dogs and Englishmen parading along The Mall. Keep your eyes peeled and you might glimpse one of the aging, tweedy Brits who still make their homes in Shimla.

There is little to do in Shimla except enjoy the views; the city makes a good stop-over before you head to busier (or rougher) parts of the state. It is connected by road to Kullu and Lahaul in the north, Kangra and Chamba in the west, and Kinnaur and Spiti in the east. In the summer, Shimla is drenched by the monsoon, and in the winter, it's buried in the snow. During May, June, September, and October, the mountain quiet disappears, and the area is flooded with crowds of tourists who drive up hotel prices and create such a ruckus that even the monkeys hide.

▐ GETTING THERE AND GETTING AROUND

Flights: Jubbarhatti Airport, 30km from town. Flights to **Delhi** (M, W, F; 10:20am; 1hr.; US$110) via **Kullu** (30min., US$65). Book **Indian Airlines** flights and taxis to the airport at Ambassador Travels (see p. 216).

Trains: Shimla is connected to **Kalka** via the narrow-gauge railway (10:45am from Town Rail Station, 2:30 and 5:30pm from Main Rail Station; 5hr.; Rs40). From Kalka, connections can be made to: **Ambala** (7am, 5:30, and 9pm; 2hr.; Rs40); **Amritsar** (4pm, 9hr., Rs140); and **Delhi** (4:45 and 11:30pm, 8hr., Rs130).

Buses: There are 2 bus stands in Shimla. Most buses leave from the **Main Bus Stand** next to Victory tunnel. To: **Chamba** (4:30am, 5, and 6pm; 15hr; Rs210); **Chandigarh** (every 15min., 5:15am-6:40pm, 10hr., Rs70); **Delhi** (10 per day, 6am-10pm, 10hr., Rs160; deluxe 8:25am and 7:50pm, 9hr., Rs310); **Dharamsala** (10 per day, 6am-9:30pm, 8hr., Rs150; deluxe 9:30pm, 8hr., Rs227); **Haridwar** via **Dehra Dun** (5:15am-6:30pm, 10hr., Rs183); **Manali** (4 per day, 8am-7:30pm, 10hr., Rs180); **Pathankot** (6 per day, 5am-8:45pm, Rs205). The **Rivoli bus stand,** down a path that starts before the Himachal Tourist Marketing Office, deals with buses going in the direction of Lahaul, Kinnaur, and Spiti. To: **Rampur** (4:30-9:10am, 6hr., Rs75) and **Kalpa** (6:15am, 12hr., Rs150) via **Rampur, Jeuri,** and **Rekong-Peo.**

> ▌ **WARNING.** Foreigners planning to travel between Jangi and Sumdo in the eastern regions of Kinnaur must obtain an all-inclusive **inner-line permit** from the sub-divisional magistrate, as these areas are sensitive border regions. In Shimla, see the **Additional District Magistrate,** on the second floor of the left side of the green colonial building just north of The Mall, beneath the telegraph office (open M-Sa 10am-5pm). Fill out an application and have a local travel agent sign on as a sponsor. As of June 2000, the inner-line permit costs Rs1350.

✴ ⁊ ORIENTATION AND PRACTICAL INFORMATION

Shimla stretches west from Himachal Pradesh University across a ridge to the area east of **Lakkar Bazaar,** where many of the town's 5000 Tibetan refugees live. Major streets run from east to west, each at a different elevation. Trains and many buses arrive on **Cart Rd.** Above Cart Rd. is the crowded jumble of the bazaar, and above the bazaar is Shimla's main drag, **The Mall,** which is off-limits to all motorized vehicles. The easiest (and laziest) way to get up and down is to take the **tourist elevator** on Cart Rd., where the street starts to bend right (open in summer 8am-9pm, in winter 9am-8pm). For a good workout, take any path or stairway leading up. At **Scandal Corner,** directly above the main bus stand, The Mall divides into a lower section and a wide upper section known as **the Ridge,** which becomes Lakkar Bazaar as it curves left beyond **Christ Church.**

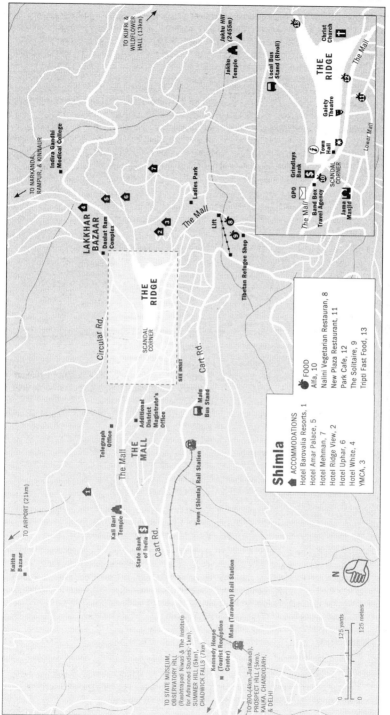

SHIMLA सिमला

TO KUFRI &
WILDFLOWER HALL (13km)

Jakhu Hill
(2455m)

Jakhu
Temple

Local Bus
Stand (Rivoli)

Christ
Church

THE
RIDGE

The Mall

Galety
Theatre

Lower Mall

Grindlays
Bank

Town
Hall

SCANDAL
CORNER

GPO

The Mall

Band Box
Travel Agency

Jama
Masjid

Indira Gandhi
■ Medical College

TO NARKANDA,
RAMPUR, & KINNAUR

Ladies Park

LAKHAR
BAZAAR

Daulat Ram
Complex

The Mall

Lift

Tibetan Refugee Shop

Circular Rd.

THE
RIDGE

SCANDAL
CORNER

SEE INSET

Cart Rd.

Main
Bus Stand

Additional
District
Magistrate's
Office

Telegraph
Office ■

THE
MALL

The Mall

Kali Bari
Temple

State Bank
of India

Cart Rd.

Town (Shimla) Rail Station

Kaithu
Bazaar

TO AIRPORT (21km)

Kennedy House
(Tourist Reception
Center)

Main (Taradevi) Rail Station

TO STATE MUSEUM,
OBSERVATORY HILL
(Rashtrapati Niwas & The Institute
for Advanced Studies, 1km),
SUMMER HILL (5km),
CHADWICK FALLS (7km)

TO ZOO (4km, Jutikandi),
PROSPECT HILL (5km),
KALKA, CHANDIGARH,
& DELHI

N

125 yards

125 meters

Shimla

🏠 ACCOMMODATIONS
Hotel Barovalia Resorts, 1
Hotel Amar Palace, 5
Hotel Mehman, 7
Hotel Ridge View, 2
Hotel Uphar, 6
Hotel White, 4
YMCA, 3

🍴 FOOD
Alfa, 10
Nalini Vegetarian Restauran, 8
New Plaza Restaurant, 11
Park Cafe, 12
The Solitaire, 9
Tripti Fast Food, 13

HIMACHAL PRADESH

Tourist Office: Himachal Tourism Marketing Office (☎252561), on the left, next to Scandal Corner. Open M-Sa 10am-6pm. Two doors down is the Road Transport Booth, which gives information on bus schedules and road conditions. Open 10am-5pm.

Budget Travel: There are travel agents on every corner of The Mall; all give transport and trekking assistance. **Ambassador Travels** (☎258014), below The Mall, near Gaiety Theatre, does airline bookings. **Band Box Heights and Valleys** (☎258157), on Scandal Corner, arranges **inner-line permits** (Rs150 commission) and 9-10 day jeep tours of Kinnaur-Spiti. Open 9am-9pm. **Transmount Adventures,** on the 2nd fl. of the Daulat Ram Complex in Lakkar Bazaar, specializes in adventure travel.

Currency Exchange: State Bank of India (open M-F 10am-2pm, Sa 10am-noon) and **ANZ Grindlays** (open M-F 9:30am-2:30pm, Sa 9:30am-12:30pm), on The Mall, change cash and traveler's checks. Grindlays gives advances on MC and Visa for a Rs100 fee.

Bookstore: Minerva Bookhouse, on The Mall opposite the Gaiety Theatre. Open M-Sa 10am-8pm. See also **Shopping,** p. 218.)

Library: Two colonial buildings shelter the HP State Library. The brown-and-white cottage next to Christ Church has a selection of scholarly books in English. The church-like building above the telegraph office has a collection of books left behind by the British. Open W-M 11am-5pm. Closed last Sa of the month.

Police: (☎212344), on The Mall, next to the town hall. For **inner-line permits,** see the Additional District Magistrate's office, just north of The Mall and below the telegraph office. Open M-Sa 10am-5pm.

Pharmacy: Several are along the lower Mall, including **Vohra's** (☎205530). Open daily 9am-8pm. There is a pharmacy inside the **Indira Gandhi Medical College** complex (☎203073), on Circular Rd. Open 24hr.

Hospital: Nehru Clinic, The Mall (☎201596), down a side alley. Open M-Sa 10am-2pm and 4-6pm. In emergencies, call **Indira Gandhi Medical College** (☎203073). **Tara Hospital** (☎203275) also has 24hr. service.

Telephones: The telegraph office has 24hr. **STD/ISD.**

Internet: The cybercafe in the telegraph office is the cheapest place in town. Rs65 per hr. **Electronica,** on Scandal Corner, next to Band Box Travels, has good connections but long waits. Rs80 per hr. Open daily 10am-7pm.

Post Office: GPO, just above Scandal Corner. Open M-Sa 10am-6pm. **Postal Code:** 171001.

▛ ACCOMMODATIONS

From May to June, September to October, and during Christmas season, vacancies are few and far between, and they come only at very inflated prices. Off-season, Shimla's near-empty hotels offer bourgeois comfort at ragamuffin prices; expect discounts of up to 50% off-season. The really cheap places near Victory Tunnel and the bus station are crowded and tend to have only common baths (in-season Rs200-250). Better hotels are up The Mall. Most levy an additional 10% tax.

YMCA (☎204085 or 252375; fax 211016), up the stairs behind Christ Church. Not just for young Christian men, this is quite possibly the last affordable, truly worthwhile place to stay in Shimla. Colonial grandeur blends seamlessly with postcolonial kitsch. Rooms are clean, and the rec. rooms have TV, billiards, and other diversions. The staff arranges treks and jeep safaris to Kinnaur, Spiti, Leh, and the Kullu Valley. Breakfast included. Hot water 7pm-9am. Prices are constant year-round. Singles Rs150; doubles Rs250-430. Rs40 membership fee valid for one week.

Hotel Uphar (☎257670). From the Ridge, walk up the path behind the clock, past the Dreamland Hotel; it's on your right. Rooms of varying quality and size have differing views and attached baths. Hanuman's temple is close by, and the windows and balconies are all barred to protect guests from the god's curious retinue. Check-out noon. Doubles Rs275-425. Off-season: 50% discount, at least. Haggling is the owner's hobby, and even the duration of the "season" is fair game for bargaining.

MURKY BREWS India is not a country known for its booze, and some states have been misguided enough to declare themselves "dry." But in the north, there are small pockets of resistance to tee-totality. In eastern Kashmir and HP, many locals are quite fond of *chung*, a powerful brew made from fermented rice or barley. The rice version tastes a bit like sake, while the barley verges on wheat beer. Both vary greatly in strength and texture. While technically illegal, *chung* can be found in any of the seedier *dhabas* or bus stands across Himachal Pradesh and Ladakh. Chug your *chung* with care, though—drink too much of this stuff, especially at high altitudes, and you'll wake up to find yourself quite *chung*-over the next morning.

Hotel Amar Palace (☎204055), right below Hotel Uphar. Good views of the valley. Rooms with color TV. Doubles Rs400-700. Off-season: 50% discount.

Hotel Mehman, Daisy Bank Estate (☎213692 or 204390). Rooms have carpets, TVs, and bathrooms with 24hr. hot water. Laundry, doctor on call, heat in the winter. Check-out noon. Doubles Rs550-1100. Off-season: 25% discount. Credit cards accepted.

Hotel Ridge View, Ridge Rd. (☎255002), behind Christ Church, up the steps past Mayur Hotel. All rooms have attached bath and 24hr. hot water. Some have TV, Ridge views, and carpeting. Room service, laundry service, and a doctor on call. Doubles Rs200-600. Off-season: Rs100-300.

Hotel Barovalia Resorts (☎252900), in the Fingask Tourist Complex. Facing the State Bank of India, turn left off The Mall and walk to the Palace Hotel; take the steps on the right and follow the narrow alley on your left for 100m. Hidden from the bustle of The Mall despite being a 5min. walk from it, Barovalia offers sunset views and luxury rooms with TVs and bathrooms with shower. Doubles Rs700-1200. Off-season: Rs350-600.

Hotel White (☎255276), Lahur Bazaar, 2min. from the Ridge. Aging but clean. Top-floor rooms have balconies. Rooms Rs450-650. Off-season: 30% discount.

FOOD

Nalini Vegetarian Restaurant, on The Mall, down past the lift. Crammed into two small rooms, Nalini is well-known among locals for serving the best Indian food in town. Steeper prices than in the lower bazaar *dhabas*, but worth it for exquisite sauces and a wide selection of South Indian cuisine. The walls are covered with a mural of Olde England. *Thalis* Rs70. Open daily 9am-10:30pm.

Park Cafe, on the slope between The Mall and the Ridge. Bamboo-decorated cafe keeps the regulars enthralled with American classic rock, the daily papers, and decent foreign standards. The wait can be long, but the pizza (Rs35) and the milkshakes (Rs20-30) are excellent. Open daily 8am-9pm.

Alfa, on The Mall, near Scandal Corner. Soft brown chairs and benches. *Masala chai* is served in tin pots, and the sweets are brought in from the bakery shop in front. The art of afternoon tea lives on. Open daily 11am-10pm.

New Plaza Restaurant, on the lower Mall, down the staircase from the Gaiety Theatre. A wide selection of Indian and not-quite-Chinese meat and veg. dishes. Chicken curry Rs60. Open daily 10am-11pm.

The Solitaire, on The Mall, past the lift and Nalini's. Part plush lounge, part posh restaurant. Window seats with splendid views of the valley below. *Malai* mushroom Rs80. Open daily noon-10pm.

Tripti Fast Food, on the right between the Ridge and Lakkar Bazaar. A wide variety of South Indian *dosas* and *uttapams*. Meals Rs25. Open daily 10am-9:30pm.

SIGHTS

HIMACHAL PRADESH STATE MUSEUM. It's a long walk to the museum, but the widely varied collection is worth it. The first floor contains the remains of 2000 year-old sculptures and even older specimens of Indo-Greek coinage unearthed in HP On the second floor are a number of incredible Kangra Pahari miniature paintings and works by contemporary artists. If you plan to hike up to the **Jakhu Temple** (see below), the precisely rendered "Hanuman Adoring Rama" is worth a special look. *(Walk west along The Mall until you reach a concrete ramp labeled "Museum," directly next to the Ambedkar Chowk sub-post office. Open Tu-Su 10am-1pm and 2-5pm.)*

VICEREGAL LODGE (RASHTRAPATI NIVAS). This neo-Tudor style lodge, which houses the learned fellows of the Indian Institute of Advanced Study, was built between 1884 and 1888 and was once the summer headquarters of the Raj. The lodge was designed to impress—it was the first government building in British India equipped with electricity. In 1945, it was the site of important (but failed) negotiations between the would-be Indian and Pakistani leaders. *(Pass the entrance to the state museum and walk 10min. west along The Mall. Open daily 10am-1pm and 2-4:30pm. Rs10 admission includes a guide.)*

HIMALAYAN AVIARY. Opened in August 1994, this small aviary houses red jungle fowl, pheasants, and some magnificent peacocks. *(Opposite the entrance to the Viceregal Lodge. Open Tu-Su 10am-5pm. Rs5.)*

JAKHU TEMPLE. This red-and-yellow temple is at the top a 2455m hill. The 20-minute walk to the top is a steep huffer and puffer, especially if you've been smoking too many *bidis*. The temple itself is fairly uninspiring, but the views of the surrounding mountains more than make up for it. Inside the temple are what some believe to be the footprints of the monkey god Hanuman. Hordes of monkeys revel in their heritage and in the snacks tourists feed them. The temple, surrounded by forests, has a canteen and a swing on its grounds. Two networks of paths lead back to town. Both cut through magnificent forests, but the sinuous paths directly to the right of the temple afford better opportunities for enjoying the scenery and taking detours. Neither set of paths is marked, but they all eventually lead down. Allow 45 minutes to an hour to reach town on the way down from Jakhu; expect to emerge from the forest near Lakkar Bazaar, 15 minutes or so from Scandal Corner. *(At the east end of the city, with the trail beginning just left of Christ Church.)*

🎵 ENTERTAINMENT

Most visitors are content just to stroll along The Mall or the Ridge, enjoying the breezes and the architecture. A number of book shops and snack stores line The Mall, also home to a fairly dismal second-story billiard hall and numerous small video arcades. Luckily, there are a few pubs. **Himani's** serves drinks at inflated prices (beer Rs60-70) until 9 or 10pm. Other options are the bar at **Rendezvous,** just next to the statue of Lalalajpatrai (beer Rs40), and **The English Wine Shop,** which sells bottled spirits from a spot on the lower Mall, a long way down from Christ Church. For **movies,** head to **Rivoli** or **Ritz.** Rivoli, down the ramp between ANZ Grindlays Bank and Rendezvous, usually shows its English-language flicks at 4:30pm. The Ritz, east of Christ Church, on the ramp leading up to the YMCA Guest House, usually screens sexy English-language films at 5:30 and 9pm. Below Rivoli is an **ice-skating rink,** which typically opens in January.

🛍 SHOPPING

Himachal Pradesh has evolved a tradition of extraordinary handicrafts: fine woodwork, leather embroidery, engraved metalwork, patterned carpets, and traditional woolen shawls. **Kashmir Craft Emporium,** 92 The Mall, has a particularly impressive collection of shawls (Rs100-5000) and silk saris (Rs250-4000). **Maria Brothers,** 78 The Mall, just below the church, specializes in bizarre and beautiful old books. Prices aren't cheap, but owner Rajiv Sud is equally friendly to browsers and buyers alike. (Open daily 10:30am-1pm and 3-8pm.)

DHARAMSALA धर्मशाला

☎ 01892

After China's occupation of Tibet began in 1959, the 14th Dalai Lama and his Buddhist government were given asylum in Dharamsala, a former British hill station and headquarters of the Kangra district. Since then, a steady stream of Tibetan exiles has relocated here, some of them walking across the winter Himalayas to escape oppression and be near the man they regard as their religious and political leader. Today, Upper Dharamsala, also called **McLeod Ganj**—named after David McLeod, a former governor of the Punjab—attracts students, tourists, hippies, and devotees of Buddhism to its monasteries, meditation centers, and Tibetan shops, giving this refugee community the feel of an energetic international crossroads.

Embraced by the craggy Dhauladar mountains, and covered with pine and deodar forests, Dharamsala commands fantastic views of Himalayan peaks and the Kangra Valley. Several easy hikes from McLeod Ganj lead to the slopes, while more serious treks head up and over the snowy passes. In the summer, unfortunately, daily fog and rain bother even the most devout, but in July and August the flowers blossom, infusing the mountain air with a sweet-smelling freshness.

⌐ GETTING THERE AND GETTING AROUND

Buses: Intercity government **buses** usually arrive at and depart from the **New Bus Stand** in Lower Dharamsala. Booking Office (☎24903). Open daily 8am-1pm and 2-7pm. To: **Amritsar** (5am, 6hr., Rs55-98); **Chamba** (5pm, 9hr., Rs130); **Chandigarh** (10:30am, 8hr., Rs125-227); **Dalhousie** (3pm, 8hr., Rs55-86); **Delhi** (8 per day, 5am-8:30pm, 13hr., Rs125-390); **Haridwar** (3pm, 12hr., Rs125-227); **Manali** (5 per day, 4:15am-8:30pm, 9hr., Rs163); **Pathankot** (9 per day, 7am-5pm, 3½hr., Rs55); **Shimla** (11 per day, 5am-9:30pm, 8hr., Rs153). From **Mcleod Ganj,** buses run to: **Delhi** (4am and 7:30pm, 14hr., Rs240); **Manali** (5pm, 10hr., Rs180); **Pathankot** (6 per day, 10am-4pm, 3½hr., Rs52). Deluxe buses depart from McLeod Ganj to: **Dehra Dun** (8pm, 12hr., Rs220); **Delhi** (every hr., 5-8pm, 12hr., Rs370-420); **Manali** (8am and 7pm, 9½hr., Rs250). Book at any of the travel agencies. Blocked roads and mudslides mean that buses to Manali and Chamba are sporadic during the monsoon and winter.

Local Transportation: Buses run between the New Bus Stand and McLeod Ganj (every 30min., 6:30am-8:30pm, Rs5). The **Shared jeeps** that run between Kotwali Bazaar and McLeod Ganj (Rs6) are cramped but faster. Both bus and jeep service are erratic, but you can easily hike along Jogibara Rd. (1hr. up, 45min. down) if you aren't carrying much. The **Taxi Union Stand** beside the bus circle has high fixed rates for most destinations (Rs70 from lower to upper Dharamsala); they're generally only worth it if you're heading up to Dharamkot or Bhagsu at night.

✵ ORIENTATION

Dharamsala is split into two sections differing by 500m in altitude; the odd geography is the result of a massive 1905 earthquake that destroyed all of the buildings and killed 900 people in the Kangra Valley. Alarmed at the destruction, the British administration established **Lower Dharamsala,** which now houses mostly offices, banks, and the Indian population. The largely Tibetan enclave of **Upper Dharamsala (McLeod Ganj)** attracts the most tourists. Seven roads branch off the **main bus circle** in McLeod Ganj. The first is **Cantonment Rd.,** the route used by buses to travel to and from Lower Dharamsala. As you go clockwise, the next road is **Taxi Stand Rd.,** which leads to the Tibetan Children's Village. Next is a steep road leading to **Dharamkot** (50min.). The fourth spoke off the bus circle is **TIPA Rd.,** which also leads to Dharamkot, passing the Tibetan Institute of Performing Arts (TIPA) on its way. Next, **Bhagsu Rd.** leads to Bhagsu (20min.) after passing many restaurants and hotels. The sixth road is **Jogibara Rd.,** full of restaurants and guest houses. Finally, **Temple Rd.** leads to the Dalai Lama's residence, Tsuglagkhang (Main Temple), and Namgyal Monastery. A steep 30-minute walk down either Jogibara or Temple Rd. lands you in Gangchen Kyishong, the Tibetan government-in-exile complex and home to the Library of Tibetan Works and Archives. From there, a 15-minute descent takes you to **Kotwali Bazaar** in the center of Lower Dharamsala.

🛈 PRACTICAL INFORMATION

Tourist Office: Himachal Tourism Marketing Office (☎/fax 24212), 50m below Kotwali Bazaar in Lower Dharamsala, before Bank of Baroda. Open daily 9am-7pm. The McLeod Ganj Office (☎21205), off Temple Rd., behind the State Bank of India, is less helpful. Open M-Sa 8am-5pm.

Budget Travel and Trekking: Most agencies in McLeod Ganj reserve bus and plane tickets; a few also organize treks. For computerized airline, train, and deluxe bus bookings, **Dhauladar Travel,** Temple Rd., accepts AmEx, Mastercard, Visa for charges above Rs500. Open daily 9am-1pm and 2-6pm. Farther up Temple Rd., **Western Travels** (☎21946) is also helpful. **Occidental Travel** (☎21938), Taxi Stand Rd., a few meters from the bus stand, arranges treks (US$10-20 per day). Trekking season in Dhauladhar runs from July-Dec.; in the wet summer months you can see eight kinds of orchids and 130 kinds of herbs in bloom. **Yetti Trekking** (☎21032), 50m above the bus circle on the road to Dharamkot. For more information on **Trekking,** see p. 30.

Currency Exchange: Bank of Punjab, Temple Rd., in McLeod Ganj, a few steps from the bus circle, changes currency and traveler's checks. Open M-F 10am-2pm, Sa 10-11am. **Western Union** money transfers are available at **Paul Merchants** (☎21418), in the **Surya Resorts Hotel,** a few houses after Bookworm bookshop. Open M-Sa 10am-7pm. **Bank of Baroda** (☎23175), Lower Dharamsala, opposite the Museum of Kangra Art, changes money and gives Visa and MC cash advances. Cash advances require 24hr. processing time. Open M-F 10am-2pm, Sa 10am-noon.

Bookstore: Bookworm, Temple Rd. At the fork, follow the sign to Hotel Bhagsu; it's 10m down on the right. Open Tu-Su 9am-7pm; in winter 10am-5pm. **Little Lhasa Bookshop,** Temple Rd. Open Tu-Su 9:30am-7pm. **Namgyal Bookshop,** Namgyal Monastery, next to the Tsuglakhang. Open M-Sa 9am-noon and 1:30-5pm. **Charitable Trust Bookshop,** Jogibara Rd., near the prayer wheels, has books on yoga and Sanskrit and Tibetan language textbooks with tapes. Open Tu-Su 9am-7pm.

Laundry: RK Laundry, Bhagsu Rd., is the cheapest in town. Open daily 8am-8pm.

Police: The main police station is in Lower Dharamsala (☎21483), below the GPO, in Forsyth Ganj, west of McLeod Ganj.

Hospital: The Tibetan **Delek Hospital,** Jogibara Rd. (☎22053, 24hr. emergency ☎23381), just before Gangchen Kyishong, has a good walk-in clinic. Open M-Sa 10am-1pm and 2-5pm. They have a branch in McLeod Ganj on Bhagsu Rd., just before the Green Cybercafe. **Dr. Yeshi Dhonden** (☎21461), off Jogibara Rd. in McLeod Ganj, practices Tibetan herbal medicine. The well-known doctor's 2-week herbal pill therapy makes you 90% immune to all stomach disorders. Open Su-F 8am-1pm.

Telephones: STD/ISD booths are on Jogibara, Temple, and Bhagsu Rd.; some stay open until 1am. You can receive callbacks everywhere, and in some places you can use AT&T and MCI calling cards. In both cases, the standard charge is Rs2-3 per min.

Internet: Every hotel and shop in McLeod Ganj seems to be hooked up to the net. The connection is fast, and the standard price is Rs60-100 per hr. The **Green Cyberspace Cafe,** Bhagsu Rd., in Green Hotel, has more than 10 computers. Rs100 per hr. Open daily 9am-10pm. **Western Travels,** Temple Rd., has fewer computers but is cheaper. Rs60 per hr. Open 10am-7pm.

Post Office: GPO, Lower Dharamsala, 1km south of Kotwali Bazaar. Another branch is along Jogibara Rd., past the State Bank. Both open M-F 9am-2pm and 3-5pm. **Postal Code:** McLeod Ganj 176219; Lower Dharamsala 176215.

🏠 ACCOMMODATIONS

Dharamsala is usually packed in spring and autumn, and even in the summer it is often hard to find a room. Most tourists stay in McLeod Ganj, and guest houses

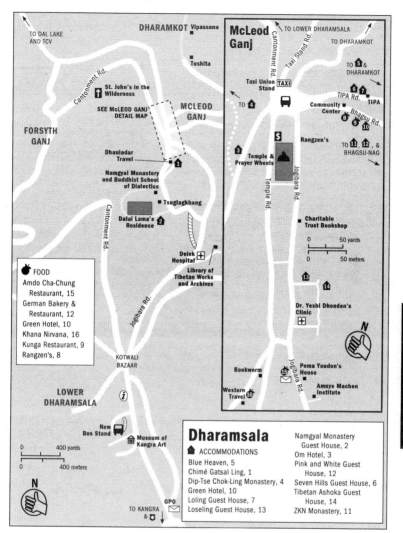

continue to spring up along the already packed tourist sections of Jogibara, Temple, and Bhagsu Rd. A local joke advises against parking here—your car might be turned into a guest house while you're gone. If spiritual interests are what bring you here, you might want to stay in one of the monasteries. These fill up quickly, but if you put yourself on a waiting list when you arrive, you should get a room in a day or two. **Bhagsu** and **Dharamkot** are a 20-minute walk from McLeod Ganj and are generally much cheaper; doubles cost as little as Rs50. These areas are choked with private houses that rent rooms (Rs50-90, Rs500-1000 per month).

MCLEOD GANJ GUEST HOUSES

■ **Loling Guesthouse** (☎21072), TIPA Rd., 100m from the bus circle, has basic rooms that share the cleanest common bath you're likely to encounter in India. Hot shower Rs10. Singles Rs50-75; doubles Rs100. Obeying the same standards of hygiene is **Loseling Guesthouse** (☎21087), Jogibara Rd., on the left, 50m from the bus circle. Doubles Rs150-250.

Tibetan Ashoka Guest House (☎21763), off Jogibara Rd., on the left, 75m from the bus circle. With over 40 rooms, this place is likely to have one for you during high-season. The common squat toilets are clean. Some rooms have valley-view balconies. Gates close at 11pm. Small, spare doubles Rs60-275.

Green Hotel, Bhagsu Rd. (☎21200), 150m from the bus circle. This open, lively place has more rooms than its neighbors but still fills up for most of the year. Gates shut at midnight. Good views in back rooms. Small singles Rs55-80; doubles Rs120-300.

Om Hotel (☎21313), just down the paved path from the bus stand, to the right of Temple Rd. Travelers flock to the balcony restaurant to sip *chai* and enjoy a sunset view. The upscale rooms are large, and the attached bathrooms have seat toilets and hot water. In-house restaurant and laundry service. 2 rooms with common toilet each Rs80. Doubles Rs200-275, depending on the view. Off-season: Rs200.

Seven Hills Guest House (☎21580), next to Loling Guest House, on the left side of TIPA Rd., 100m from the bus circle. The only place in town with a garden and beauty salon. The restaurant and Internet lab make it entirely self-sufficient. All rooms have double beds, private baths, and great views. Doubles Rs150-250. Winter prices negotiable.

Tara Guest House (☎21181), next to the Chime Gatsal Ling monastery. Rooms are sparkling new and clean, with hot showers. The rooftop balcony has the best view in McLeod Ganj of His Holiness' residence. The studios downstairs are an amazing deal if you are staying long term. Doubles Rs165-250. Studios Rs3000-3700 per month.

MONASTERIES

Dip Tse Chok Ling Monastery (☎21726), past Om Hotel; a 10min. walk down the steps on the right ridge. The isolated monastery seems far removed from the bustle on the ridge, making it the perfect spot for meditation. Join in evening prayer with the lamas. All rooms have two single beds, writing tables, and a common, blue-tiled toilet. Rooms Rs250-300. Off-season: Rs100-150.

Zilnan Kagyeling Nyingmapa (ZKN) Monastery, 15min. up Bhagsu Rd. Turn left up the driveway just past Last Chance Tibetan Restaurant. Dimly lit, spare rooms with common bath line the sides of this new monastery. Step out of your room into the transcendental, temple-style courtyard. Singles Rs50; doubles Rs80.

Chime Gatsal Ling, Temple Rd. (☎21340), 75m up the driveway opposite the School of Dialectics; the big, orange building is on the left. Part hotel, part housing for Nyingmapa-sect monks. Spotless, carpeted rooms are huge, and the roof is perfect for watching the sun set on the Dhauladars. Doubles Rs80-140.

Namgyal Monastery Guest House (☎21492), allows you to share a courtyard with His Holiness' residence and the Tsuglagkhang (Main Temple). The style of the cells matches the lavish surroundings. Doubles with bath Rs225.

BHAGSU AND DHARAMKOT

Pink and White Guest House (☎24527), up the hill from the center of Bhagsu, a 15-20min. walk from McLeod. Not cheap, but has an array of nice rooms with private bath and 24hr. hot water. Room service 6am-11pm; dishes Rs20-55. Singles Rs200; doubles 350-500. Off-season: 40% discount.

Blue Heaven (☎21005), just below Dharamkot., a 20min. walk up TIPA Rd. Turn right on the forest path. This most tranquil of places has enormous doubles with or without cushy carpet and tiled bathrooms. Doubles Rs150-200.

🌓 FOOD

The appearance of heavy, flat noodles and hunks of mutton should remind you that you're in Tibetan culinary territory. Yet the apple pie on the dessert menu leaves no doubt that Dharamsala is, at the same time, a tourist trap and a traveler's heaven—you can find just about any national cuisine represented here.

Amdo Cha-Chung Restaurant, Jogibara Rd., on the left past the post office. The owners toss up authentic *Amdo* cuisine from the northeastern region of Tibet. Try the hand-pulled noodles (*thankthuk*) and szechuan hot sauce while you keep company with *Amdo* monks and other tourists. Meals Rs20-45.

Khana Nirvana, Temple Rd., above Western Travels. Has possibly the best burritos this far east; guitars and drums flirt in the background as you sit on comfortably cushioned chairs. This happenin' joint features a "Sunday at Sunset" lecture series, Monday jam sessions, and an Interfaith Shabbat on Fridays. Inquire here for volunteer opportunities in Dharamsala. Open Su-F 10am-10pm.

Kunga Restaurant and Nick's Italian Kitchen, Bhagsu Rd., before the Green Hotel. A native New Yorker once taught his Bologna-acquired art to Tibetan chefs who have taken the skill to the requisite bodhisattva level of perfection. The pasta is home-made, and the parmesan is flown in fresh from the Apennines. Open daily until 9:30pm.

Rangzen's, Bhagsu Rd., just before Nick's Italian Kitchen. This tiny, comfortable place has great valley views and serves up Tibetan specialities. Nothing beats the *tsampa* (barley porridge), a Tibetan staple cooked here according to a *Bonpo* shaman's magic formula (see **A Bona-fide Religion,** p. 683). Open daily 8am-10pm.

Green Hotel and Restaurant, Bhagsu Rd. As much of a Western hangout as a good restaurant, this place serves carefully prepared Tibetan and Chinese dishes. A lip-smacking cappuccino makes it clear why this is a traveler's favorite. Open daily 7:30am-10pm.

Kailash Hotel and Restaurant, Temple Rd., near the bus circle. Owned by a warm Tibetan family, Kailash dishes out spicy *momos* to a mostly local crowd; wash 'em down with a cup of mild jasmine tea. Open daily 8am-9pm.

Om Restaurant, near the bus circle, has good food and even better prices. The terrace makes a delightful spot to enjoy the sunset over a cup of tea. Open daily 8am-10pm.

German Bakery and Restaurant, above the Pink and White Guest House, up the hill from central Bhagsu. This hungry hikers' haven has an array of rye breads and apple pies to complement its assortment of homemade noodle soups. Open daily until 10pm.

SIGHTS

GANGCHEN KYISHONG. The site of the administrative offices of the **Tibetan government-in-exile,** Gangchen Kyishong also houses several Non-Governmental Organizations (NGOs), including the **Tibetan Center for Human Rights and Democracy.** Stop by the Ministry of Information for an update on Tibet's political situation. The **Library of Tibetan Works and Archives,** at the far end of Gangchen Kyishong, has 10,000 volumes in English and other languages on Buddhism, Tibet, and related subjects. The books and many scholarly periodicals are available for general use in the reading room. *(Library reading membership Rs15 per month.)* Language and philosophy courses taught by renowned lamas are offered as well. You can attend a session or two for free, although the Tibetan government would, no doubt, appreciate the registration fee. Arrive on time for opening prayers and behave respectfully during class hours; remove your shoes before entering the study hall, and, for philosophy sessions, don't stand up until the lama has left. *(9-month courses in Buddhist philosophy: M-Sa 9 and 11am, except 2nd and 4th Sa; Rs100 per month, plus Rs50 registration fee. Tibetan language courses: daily 10am spring, summer, and fall; Rs200 per month. Rooms available to students enrolled in 2 or more classes simultaneously; Rs500-2000 per month.)* The **museum** has beautiful *thankas*, Tibetan coins, and several rooms rescued from the pillage of the Chinese Red Guards (Rs5). The **Nechung Monastery,** next to the library, is a peaceful spot for meditation. *(On Jogibara Rd., halfway between McLeod Ganj and Lower Dharamsala; turn left through the archway.* ☎ *22467. Open M-Sa 10am-1pm and 2-5pm, closed 2nd and 4th Sa and on Buddhist holidays. Free.)*

TSUGLAGKHANG TEMPLE. This temple, whose Tibetan name simply means "Main Temple," houses images of the Buddha, Padmasambhava, and Avalokiteshvara ("Chenresig" in Tibetan). This last image, representing the bodhisattva of

HIMACHAL PRADESH

SO YOU THINK YOU'RE RICHARD GERE...

To schedule a private audience with His Holiness the Dalai Lama, send your request four months in advance and start praying. Private audiences are rare but not unheard of, particularly if your reason is truly specific to the Dalai Lama. Much more common are public audiences of 300 people or so, held once or twice a month for foreigners and recent arrivals from Tibet. At a public audience, the crowd files slowly past His Holiness, who takes time to speak and laugh with each person (despite his aides' attempts to speed things up). You need to bring your passport a few days ahead to be cleared for the audience. You can contact the Office of His Holiness the Dalai Lama by mail, phone, or email (Thekchen Choeling, McLeod Ganj, Dharamsala, HP, 176219; ☎/fax 21813; email ohhdl@cta.unv.ernet.in). Check with the security branch office near Hotel Tibet on Bhagsu Rd. to see when the Dalai Lama will next be in town.

whom the Dalai Lama is an incarnation, was rescued from the Tokhang Temple in Lhasa and brought here during the massive destruction wrought by the Chinese Cultural Revolution. On the days of the Buddha's birth, death, and enlightenment, hundreds of monks circumambulate the temple three times on their hands and knees, giving money to the hundreds of beggars who flock to this path during the ceremony. Remember always to walk clockwise on this path, spin the prayer wheels clockwise, and remove footwear before entering the temple. Monks from the School of Dialectics come to debate—snapping, clapping, and shouting at each other—in the temple's courtyard in the afternoons. Each snap, clap, and stomp corresponds to a specific moment in the argument being advanced by the standing member of the debating pair. The debates are one of the defining features of the Gelugpa sect's teachings and are governed by an immensely complex system of logic. *(Behind the Buddhist School of Dialectics; a 10min. walk from the bus circle in McLeod Ganj. Open daily sunrise to sunset.)*

THE BHAGSU-NAG TEMPLE. This serene temple rests beside several cool *kunds* (pools) where Hindus and monks bathe. According to legend, 9000 years ago, there was a drought in the kingdom of Ajmer, in present-day Rajasthan. To save his realm, King Bhagsu headed to a 5400m-high peak nearby, where he discovered two lakes and trapped their waters in his bowl. But as the king lay down to sleep, Nag, the cobra who owned the lakes, challenged him to a fight. Mortally wounded in the ensuing struggle, the king made a dying request for the people of Ajmer to be rid of the drought. Impressed by Bhagsu's devotion to his people, Nag granted him his wish. The fruit of his efforts is today known as the Indira Gandhi Canal, which irrigates most of Rajasthan. The temple at Bhagsu-Nag marks the event and the snake-god's respect for the king. The **Bhagsu Waterfall** beyond the temple cascades for 30 spectacular feet during the monsoon season. There are small open-air cafes above and below the falls. The lower cafe has cold drinks, crackers, and a crowd of Indian bathers strutting around in their underwear (if you're lucky). The upper one, Shiva Cafe, has hot meals, chessboards, and opium-inspired paintings. Above the path to the falls there are caves, where devout monks meditate for extended periods, only leaving for meals. *(At the north end of Bhagsu; a 25min. walk from McLeod Ganj. The waterfall is 15min. beyond the temple; follow signs to the path.)*

NORBU LINGKA. To see Tibetan art at its best, head to Norbu Lingka, a compound 10km from Dharamsala. Its bamboo groves enclose a rare display of Tibetan architecture designed to resemble the symmetries of a bodhisattva. The **Norbu Lingka Institute,** dedicated to preserving Tibetan culture in both its literary and artistic forms, is here. It offers a unique opportunity to watch *thanka* masters, woodcarvers, metal-workers, and their pupils at work. The **Losel Doll Museum** exhibits costumes from every region of Tibet. *(Take a jeep or bus to Lower Dharamsala, (Rs5.) From there, take the Palampur bus, and get off at Sacred Heart High School (Rs2). From the school it's a 20min. walk up the road to the left. ☎ 22664; www.norbulingka.org. Open M-Sa 9am-6pm; arrive before 4pm to see the workshops or catch a guided tour. Doll Museum Rs25.)*

THE TIBETAN CHILDREN'S HANDICRAFT AND VOCATIONAL CENTER. The vocational center instructs refugees in the arts of *thanka* painting, carpet weaving, and good old-fashioned capitalist marketing. The **Tibetan Children's Village School (TCV),** under the patronage of the Dalai Lama, has been housing, caring for, and educating more than 2400 orphaned Tibetan children since 1960. Foreigners are welcome to visit the school. A late afternoon soccer match with the kids is topped only by a weekend visit to help them practice English. You can volunteer here for a few months or sponsor a child (US$30 per month). Donations are welcome. *(The center is a 30min. walk up the hill from the McLeod Ganj taxi stand. The TCV is a 10min. walk farther uphill, past Dal Lake on the right. School open M-F 9am-4pm.)*

OTHER SIGHTS. The **Dip-Tse-Chok-Ling Monastery** is home to a small (and largely young) community of monks, who built the monastery after the destruction of their own in Tibet. *(A 10min. walk from the bus circle down a stone path that begins just past Om Hotel. Open daily 7am-7pm.)* The original monastery once lay south of Lhasa; in recent years, it has again become functional. Some of the monks alternate between the two locations. The church of **St. John's in the Wilderness** is a functioning relic of the bygone British era. The pastor will happily converse with you about your country or his. Lord Elgin, an ex-Viceroy of India, is buried in the church cemetery, where dusk fog swirls around grave stones. *(Follow the narrow road from the Dip-Tse-Chok-Ling monastery guest house up to Cantonment Rd.; from there it's a 15min. walk downhill toward Lower Dharamsala. Open daily 9am-5pm. Sunday services in English 11:30am. Candle-light services on Christmas.)* The **Amnye Machen Institute** aims to bring Tibetan culture into the 21st century. The institute gathers contemporary writers and scholars, translates classical works into Tibetan, publishes journals on history and culture, and serves as the main cartographic center for Tibet. The institute has film festivals, lectures, and other Tibet-related events; details are on their website. *(On Jogibara Rd., just past the post office. ☎ 20173; email ami@amnyemachen.org; www.amnyemachen.org.)* The **Museum of Kangra Art,** opposite the Bank of Baroda in Lower Dharamsala, has nice exhibits of old carpets, Pahari miniatures, and archeological artifacts from the Kangra region. *(Open Tu-Su 10am-1:30pm and 2-4pm; closed for local and national holidays. Free.)* A pleasant day-hike from Dharamkot takes you to the rolling, grassy ridgetop of **Triund.** There's a small rest house here as well as a comfortable cave 50m uphill. A second basic rest house is 5km up the trail at a spot where you can see the peaks in their massive entirety. Resist the urge to climb higher unless you have detailed advice and some mountaineering experience, and be prepared for rain in the early afternoon.

🎵 ENTERTAINMENT

The market section of Jogibara Rd. is home to two hole-in-the-wall **movie houses** showing what seems like a random assortment of recent American blockbusters, cult classics, and bizarre low-grade flicks. The wooden benches are only slightly more comfortable than the seats on a bus, but the big TV screens compensate with good reception. (Check schedule outside theaters for show times; Rs10.) **McLeo's** third-floor bar, on the bus circle, with its Hawaiian decor and haphazard mix of the Beatles, techno, and reggae, is a surreal place to swill beer (Rs75) and eat good, but overpriced food. Young, unemployed Tibetans gather here to mingle with and vent to the mobs of foreigners. Occasional Godfather-infused **dance parties** last until the 95% male dance floor clears. The **Tibetan Institute of Performing Arts (TIPA)** has cultural shows, performs a Tibetan opera for the New Year, and usually has shows on other Tibetan holidays. Stop in for more details. *(A 10min. walk up TIPA Rd. toward Dharamkot. ☎ 21748 or 21033. Open M-Sa 10am-5pm, closed 2nd and 4th Sa. Call or stop by to check the schedule; if you want to see the theater, be persistent.)*

✚ VOLUNTEER OPPORTUNITIES

In its struggle for freedom, the Tibetan community has deemed the ability to speak English a priority; therefore, English teachers and simple conversationalists are eagerly welcomed. The enthusiastic monks and Tibetan students, mostly McLeod Ganj regulars, often agree to exchange regular language lessons with foreigners. Ask around at the various monasteries to see if they would be willing to take on short or long term English teachers. The **Tibetan Children's Village** (☎21528) is always interested in committed, long-term English, math, and science teachers.

The **Earthville Institute,** Temple Rd., at the Khana Nirvana Restaurant, serves as a community center, non-profit educational society, and clearing house for information about volunteer opportunities in and around Dharamsala. (☎21252; www.earthville.net; email dnm@earthville.net; or write to Mandala, Dalai Lama Temple Rd., McLeod Ganj, Dharamsala, HP 176219. Open Su-F 10am-9pm.) The official **Community Center,** near Rangzen's on Bhagsu Rd., has postings on local events. The **Green Shop,** part of the Center, employs a squad of dedicated workers who operate the recycling unit and teach volunteers how to make paper or bind books. Contact the Tibetan Welfare Office, Environmental Desk (☎21059).

Those interested in short-term or day projects should consider the **Yong Ling Creche** (☎21028), opposite the nunnery on Jogibara Rd., where anyone can stop by for a conversation with the kids in the morning or with the adult students in the evening. Yong Ling also organizes a home-stay program (Rs200 per day including meals). Growing numbers of Tibetan organizations want to put their message online; as a result, volunteers with graphic and web-designing skills are in high demand. Try the **Amnye Machen Institute** (see p. 225). Finally, there may be opportunities of a more conventional sort at the **Tibetan Centre for Human Rights and Democracy,** Gangchen Kyishong, northern building (☎23363; email dsala@tchrd.org; www.tchrd.org); the **Tibetan Youth Congress,** Bhagsu Rd., opposite the Green Shop; the **Tibetan Women's Association** (☎21527 or 21198; fax 21528; email twa@del2.vsnl.net.in); and the **Tibetan Medical Institute** (☎22618), in the Delek Hospital. All have English publications and translations that need proofreading. You can contact any of the above institutions in writing: Name of the institution, P.O. McLeod Ganj, Dharamsala, HP 176219.

MEDITATION

Everyone in Dharamsala seems to be involved in some sort of mind and body twisting activity, be it Thai massage, Reiki, Yoga, or meditation. If you're interested in joining the fun, ask people who are already involved for recommendations or check the postings around in McLeod Ganj. The **Tushita Meditation Centre** offers 10-day or shorter residential courses that provide a good introduction to Tibetan Buddhism and analytical meditation. The classes are taught by a Tibetan lama and a Western monk. Register by phone or email two months in advance. (☎21866; email tushita@ndf.vsnl.net.in. Classes Mar.-June and Sept.-Nov. Open M-Sa 10am-noon and 1-4pm; registration M-Sa 1-3pm.) The center also has a library with a good selection of books on Buddhism, which anyone can borrow after depositing a passport. (Rs10 per book per week. Open M-Sa 10am-4pm.) Another option is the **Vipassana Meditation Centre,** next door, which runs residential courses in single point meditation. Vipassana has centers all over the world so you can continue your course after leaving Dharamsala. Register by mail by sending a brief resume. Registrations are not accepted over the phone. Both meditation centers operate on expected donations. For professional **acupuncture** or **Thai massage,** head to the third floor of the Mount View Hotel, on Jogipurn Rd., past the post office. (☎/fax 21309; www.dhamma.org. Open 9am-6pm. Reserve a few days in advance.)

DALHOUSIE डलहौज़ी   ☎01899

Built along the edge of the Dhauladar mountain range, Dalhousie was named for Lord James Ramsey, Marquis of Dalhousie, who became Governor General of

India in 1848. The hill station was founded in 1854, when the British rented the land from the largely autonomous Chamba raja in order to expand vacation options for their increasingly stressed-out administrators and bureaucrats. Designed as a colonial retreat, Dalhousie also had a part to play in the drama that led to Indian Independence, when Subhas Chandra Bose came here during the 1940s to cook up anti-British strategies for the Indian National Army. Today, Dalhousie is a popular destination for Indian honeymooners and Punjabi tourists trying to escape the heat. Walk along the Ridge in the evening, and you will see droves of them, strolling and cooing and making the most of the cool air.

⊟ GETTING THERE AND GETTING AROUND. Buses depart from the main bus stand to: **Chamba** via **Ranikhet** (5 per day, 7am-4:30pm, 2hr.); **Dharamsala** (3 per day, 7am-2pm, 7hr., Rs75); **Pathankot** (10 per day, 5am-4:30pm, 3hr.); and **Shimla** (12:45pm, 12hr., Rs185). For more buses to Dharamsala and for buses to **Amritsar** and **Jammu,** change in Pathankot. Two buses (9:30 and 10:10am) go to **Khajjiar, Chamba,** and back, stopping in each place for 1½ hours (to Khajjiar only: 1hr., Rs15; roundtrip to Dalhousie: 8hr., Rs70). More frequent connections run from **Buniket,** reachable by bus (8am-5pm, 20min., Rs5) or shared jeep (Rs10).

▪️🔧 ORIENTATION AND PRACTICAL INFORMATION. In Dalhousie, everything you need is within walking distance. The narrow road that heads to the right from the **bus stand** leads to **Subhash Chowk** (a 10min. walk). The steps slightly to the left climb up to **Gandhi Chowk.** The *chowks* are connected by two horizontal roads, **Mall Rd.** on the northern side of the Ridge and **Garam Path** to the south. Most of the hotels and restaurants are on these two streets. The **Tourist Marketing Office,** two houses down from the main bus stand, has hotel information and booking. (☎42136. Open daily 10am-5pm.) **Treks 'n' Travels** (☎40277; fax 40476) does as its name claims: books hotels in all of H.P., makes ticket reservations, and organizes treks. **Punjab National Bank,** next to the Aroma 'n' Claire Hotel on the loop road off Subhash Chowk, changes traveler's checks. (☎42190. Open M-F 10am-2pm, Sa 10am-noon.) The **Civil Hospital,** near Aroma 'n' Claire, has bare-bones facilities. **St. Joseph's Clinic,** just up the road, is a little better (open daily 9am-4pm). The **police station** (☎42126) is opposite Aroma 'n' Claire. The **Post Office** is at Gandhi Chowk (open M-Sa 10am-5pm). **Postal Code:** 176304.

🏠🍴 ACCOMMODATIONS AND FOOD. There are plenty of hotels in Dalhousie, and during the low season you can get a sizeable room with a view and private bath for Rs200 (plus Rs100 for a heater). In season (Apr. 15-July 1 and Sept. 15-Nov. 15), prices are at least double. Dalhousie has a water shortage problem, and running water is often limited or unavailable. The friendly **Hotel Crags,** Garam Sarak, a five-minute walk from Subhash Chowk, has some of the best views on the Ridge. Most rooms are equipped with wood-framed beds and mirrors, cable TV, and seat toilets. (☎42124. Curfew 10:30pm. Rooms Rs400-700. Off-season: Rs150-200.) Farther along Garam Sarak is the **Hotel Fair View,** which has large rooms with immaculate bathrooms that, uniquely, have running water all day (☎42206. Rs175-330.) On Mall Rd., near Gandhi Chowk, is **Mehar's Hotel,** touted as the "Biggest Hotel in Dalhousie." The rooms have cable TVs and clean bathrooms. The attached restaurant serves decent food and a clear day's view of the Pir Panjal range. (☎42179. Doubles Rs350-840.) If you are short on cash, walk up the road opposite State Bank of India to the **Youth Hostel.** The bathroom with squat toilets is not exactly sparkling but is still bearable. Check-in from 7-10am and 5-9pm. You must be back by 10pm, and lights must be out by 11pm. (☎42189. Floor mats Rs20; dorm beds Rs40; rooms Rs100.) In Khajjiar, the six-bed dorm in **Hotel Devdar,** with its spotless beds and bathrooms, is a good deal. (☎36333. Rooms Rs75). If the dorm is full, **Parne** (☎36344) has doubles for Rs300.

At Subhash Chowk, **Punjabi Friends Dhaba** is well-known for its good food and dedicated service. At Gandhi Chowk, **Lovely Restaurant** serves the largest menu in town in a setting that matches its name.

⬛ **SIGHTS.** Most people come to Dalhousie to stroll the tree-lined streets, breathe the pine-fresh air, and enjoy the mountain views. The **Garam Sarak walk** is especially pleasant, since no cars are allowed on the road. Along the road, Tibetan refugees have painted reliefs onto the stone cliffs of Chenresig (of whom the Dalai Lama is an incarnation) and other Tibetan notables. There are two old churches at the *chowks.* Panch Pulla Rd., off Gandhi Chowk, leads to the dried-up **water spring,** notable because Ajit Singh, a supporter of Subhash Chandra Bose, died here on Independence Day. On a clear day, you can see all the major rivers of the area—the Chenab, the Beas, and the Ravi—from **Dainkunt Peak,** a beautiful 9km walk uphill from Gandhi Chowk. **Khajjiar,** a pristine meadow 22km from Dalhousie, is trumpeted by the local tourist industry as "the Switzerland of the East." The scenery is beautiful, but be prepared to share it with hundreds of yodeling tourists, who arrive by the busload for an afternoon of picnicking and picture-taking. Horse riding is available for Rs50 per hour. Dalhousie was one of the first places Tibetans came to when the Chinese invaded, and they have monopolized **market** activities in town; aim for their stands at Gandhi Chowk and at the bus station if you need a watch or a leather bag. For fruits and sweets, head to **Sadar Bazaar.**

CHAMBA चम्बा ☎ 01899

Locked in between four major mountain ranges (Shivalik, Dhauladhar, Pir Panjal, and the Greater Himalayas), the region of Chamba is often referred to as the lap of the Himalayas. At an altitude of 990m, Chamba is high enough to escape the heat that scorches Punjab, but it remains warmer and drier than Dalhousie or Dharamsala. The town itself stretches in a medieval haze of porticoed houses and hidden temples along the slopes that rise above the Sal and Ravi Rivers. The town was founded in 940 AD as the new capital of an older princely state administered from Bharmour. Mountain ridges, isolation, attitude, and wily diplomacy have kept the Chamba Valley pretty much independent ever since. The Mughals never managed to reach this far, and Chamba's temples were spared the miserable fate of so many Hindu shrines in other parts of the country. Even the Brits left little trace here—not much more than one hydro-electric plant. The result is a rich and undisturbed local culture; Chamba and the surrounding area have developed trademark styles of cooking, politics, handicrafts, religious art, and even a regional literary dialect, Chambiali. Town spirit peaks in early August, when residents throw a riotous week-long harvest festival called Minjar.

▐ GETTING THERE AND GETTING AROUND

Buses leave for: **Bharmour** (6 per day, 3½hr., Rs32); **Dalhousie** via **Kajjiar** or **Banikhet** (9 per day, 6am-6pm, 2½hr., Rs32); **Dharamsala** (6am and 9:30pm, 10hr., Rs110) via **Pathankot** (11:30am and 4pm, 10hr., Rs100) or **Gaggal** (noon, 10hr., Rs80); **Manali** via **Kullu** (11:30am, 16hr., Rs260); and **Pathankot** (9 per day, 4:30am-4pm, 5hr., Rs57). At the bus station there is a 24-hour cloak room where you can leave your bags (Rs5 per day). There are more connections from **Buniket** (10 per day, 6am-5pm, 2hr., Rs30).

▟ ▐ ORIENTATION AND PRACTICAL INFORMATION

Most of the businesses are concentrated around **Court Rd.,** which runs from the crowded **bus stand** area in the south of town along the eastern side of the **Chaugan,** Chamba's wide, grassy mall and cricket ground. Court Rd. becomes **Hospital Rd.** beyond Chaugan's shops and markets and then loops back through chicken shacks and liquor counters as **Museum Rd.** Uphill from Court Rd., past the Chaugan, is **Temple Rd.,** which leads to the **Laxmi Narayan Temple** and into alleys packed with ancient shrines. **Mami Mahesh Travels** (☎22507), next to the entrance to Laxmi Narayan Temple, is very helpful with train reservations, treks, and information on temples. Farther down, on Hospital Rd., the **Punjab National Bank** changes traveler's checks and foreign currency (open M-F 10am-2pm, Sa 10am-noon). **Pharmacies** line Hospital Rd., including **Shrikanth Chowfla and Sons,** which proudly announces that it's also "Licensed to Deal Arms and Ammunition." (☎22735. Open M-Sa 9am-8pm.) Medical facilities in Chamba are not first-rate, but there is a **District Hospital,** Hospital Rd. (☎22392), as well as a few private clinics. The **police station** is on Hospital Rd. (☎22736). On the Chaugan, 20m past Hotel Inavati, is the antediluvian **post office** (open M-F 10am-5pm). **Postal Code: 176310.**

ACCOMMODATIONS AND FOOD

Chamba's budget scene isn't spectacular. Most rooms are small, and hotels fill up fast in season (Apr. 15-July 1 and Sept. 15-Nov. 15). **Rishi Hotel and Restaurant,** up Temple Rd., on the right, crams guests into plain but clean rooms, all with attached bath. (☎24343. Singles Rs150; doubles Rs200.) The HPTDC runs **Hotel Champak,** 50m behind the Tourist Development Office, down the hill from the western side of the Chaugan. The dorm room is sparse but clean. (☎22774. Check-out noon. Dorm beds Rs80; doubles Rs220-275.) **Jimmy's Inn,** offering standard rooms with fans, is the first place you'll see after stepping off the bus. (☎24748. Check-out noon. Doubles Rs150-250.) **☑Orchard Hut** (☎22607) is a wood-and-clay guest house and restaurant high up on the slope away from the Sal River, 5km from Chamba in the Panj-La Valley. Everything you eat, from the plum preserves served with crisp *parathas*, to the fresh vegetables, is grown around the hut. Enjoy your meal amid the noise of a roaring river and a chorus of birdsong—over 50 species of birds live in the area. Call ahead or stop by Mami Mahesh Travels (see above), run by the same family. To get to the hut, take the Chamba-Sahoo bus from the Brijeshwari Temple and get off at the Chaminu stop. Walk across the river and continue 20 minutes uphill; ask in the Chaminu store for directions. The hut is the base for various treks into the hills. Cooking lessons are also available (Rs50). Accommodations range from simple tents to spacious doubles (Rs50-300).

Local cuisine can be hard to come by; your best bet is the street-side *dhabas.* The **Olive Green Restaurant,** Temple Rd., tosses up the Chamba valley specialty *madhara*, a dish of kidney beans and curd cooked in *ghee* (Rs45). Chamba is well-known for its sweet-but-fiery chili sauce, *chukh*, which the bold palate can sample on deep-fried chicken at shops along Museum Rd. Two floors above the shops, the **Park View Restaurant and Milk Bar** soothes tongues with the best sweets in town.

SIGHTS

BHURI SINGH MUSEUM. To learn about Chamba's royal and military past, head north on Museum Rd. to the Bhuri Singh Museum. Named for Raja Bhuri Singh, ruler of the Chamba district from 1904-1919, the museum displays his collection of small weaponry, giant doors, musical instruments, *rumals* (a form of silk embroidery native to the valley), and a good sized collection of *pahari* miniatures. *(Open Tu-Su 10am-5pm. Free.)*

LAXMI NARAYAN TEMPLE. Chamba's collection of temples is enough to satisfy any but the most insatiable of temple freaks. The largest complex is the Laxmi Narayan Temple, up Temple Rd., opposite the enormous Akhand Chandi Palace. The shrines in the complex date from the 9th to the 10th centuries, when Chamba's founder commissioned the main temple and the statue of Laxmi Narayan (Vishnu asleep on the cosmic ocean) inside it. The copper statue of Gauri Shankar is a marvellous example of Chamba's renowned metal work. *(Open daily 6am-9pm.)* The Hari Rai Temple, on Museum Rd., next to the red gate, was built in the Shikhara style in the 9th century and is covered on all sides with Kama Sutra carvings, for those interested.

DURGA TEMPLES. A walk along the outskirts of town will take you past several other important holy sites. From the bus stand, a short climb south and east leads to the long staircase up to **Chamunda Devi Temple.** Chamunda Devi is a form of the goddess Durga in a wrathful temper; the brass bells (meant to clear your head of worldly scheming) and stunning views ensure that you remain unruffled. At the northern edge of Chamba, above the road to Sahoo, is the ancient temple of **Vajreshwari.** Tradition has it that this is the oldest temple in Chamba, a thank-you gift from Raja Sahil Varman to the family who donated the land for the town. Although a number of stone carvings have been looted from the sides of the main shrine, finely crafted images of Durga, Undavi (the goddess of food), and other deities still grace its walls. Look for the Tibetan-style demonic faces at the back of the main shrine—their presence here remains a mystery. The stone lions out front are the gods' preferred mode of transportation (not for hire).

RANG MAHAL AND HIMACHAL EMPORIUM. When they weren't trying to keep the gods happy at the temples, Chamba's 18th-century elite retired to the Mughal-style corridors of the **Rang Mahal** ("Old Palace"). Dominating the upper center of Chamba, the palace today houses the **Himachal Emporium,** a one-room shop selling *rumals*, hand-woven shawls, candleholders, and molded brass plates. Ask the shopkeeper to see the workshop upstairs, where some of these items are made.

▶ DAYTRIPS FROM CHAMBA

BHARMOUR. The capital of the Chamba Valley from the 6th to the early 10th centuries, Bharmour is a bumpy bus ride away from Chamba town (3½hr.). Its temple square encloses 84 separate shrines, some of them dating back to the 7th century. The most famous of these is the Narsingha Temple with its half-lion, half-man statue dedicated to the incarnation of Vishnu who descended to earth to destroy an evil spirit who could not be killed by either man or animal. Once Narsingha tasted blood, however, he just kept on killing. Realizing the demonic powers within himself, he went up into the mountains where there was less to kill. The temple is supposedly built on the site where he secluded himself.

Bharmour is the trailhead for **treks** over the Dhauladhar and Pir Panjal ranges. In the summer, you're likely to meet some of the nomadic shepherds who make seasonal migrations up and down the valley. Bharmour is the starting point of the **Manimahesh Yatra,** a devotional procession that winds its way 34km up to the lake at Manimahesh, where people worship and bathe in the icy waters. The procession takes place in September, fifteen days after Janmashtami, Krishna's birthday.

SAHOO. The quiet farming village of Sahoo is in the opposite direction from Bharmour, up the Sal River valley—a one-hour bus ride from Chamba or a gorgeous 20 minute bike ride from the Orchard Hut. It has an 11th-century temple and breathtaking views of the Pir Panjal range. The **Chandra Shekhar** (moon-crowned Shiva) temple houses an ancient Shiva *linga*, apparently given to spurts of rapid and inexplicable growth—a hole had to be cut into the temple's stone ceiling to accommodate the *linga's* sky-high ambitions until a visiting priest was able to bring it back down to size. The ceiling has since been removed and now stands in front of the temple, where worshipers crawl through it for luck and strength. Opposite the *linga* is a particularly fine stone sculpture of Nandi. In earlier times, when the temple bell was struck, the ball around Nandi's neck would resonate. These days, devotees coat the image with a thick layer of *ghee*, muffling the sound.

KULLU कुल्लू ☎ 01902

Kullu is tucked between two green mountains at the southern end of the Kullu Valley. Most tourists only see Kullu from the grimy bus stand; the town has little to offer besides bus connections to the beautiful Parvati Valley and nearby Naggar and Manali. Every year in early October, however, tourists and Indians crowd Kullu for **Dussehra,** a huge festival celebrating the 360 gods of the Himachal valley.

⌷ GETTING THERE AND GETTING AROUND.

Bhuntar Airport is 10km to the south of town; local buses heading to and from Manali stop at the airport (Rs8), while taxis cost Rs100. **Ambassador Travel,** the only agent for Indian Airlines in town, has an office a short walk off the maidan on the road to Manali. **Flights** go to Delhi (M, W, and F; 11:10am; US$130). **Buses** leave for: **Amritsar** (4 and 5:30pm, 14hr., Rs220); **Delhi** (5 per day, 4am-5pm, 16hr., Rs250; semi-deluxe 7pm, 16hr., Rs290; deluxe 6:30pm, 13hr., Rs452); **Dharamsala** (5 per day, 7am-8pm, Rs110-140); **Jammu** (6pm, 14hr., Rs190); **Leh** (7:30am, 48hr., Rs355); **Manali** (every 30min., 4am-7pm, 2hr., Rs20); **Manikaran** (7 per day, 6:30am-3pm, 2½hr., Rs25); **Naggar** (every 30min., 4am-7pm, 1hr., Rs12); and **Shimla** (5 per day, 4am-8:45pm, 9hr., Rs113-152). **Deluxe buses,** booked through **HARI Travel** in the maidan, go to: **Delhi** (6:15pm, 12hr., Rs325); **Dharamsala** (9pm, 8hr., Rs250); and **Shimla** (9pm, 8hr., Rs250).

⌷ ORIENTATION AND PRACTICAL INFORMATION.

The main **bus station** is at the north end of town, next to the river. Above the bus station, across the foot-bridge and to the left, extends the **market street,** leading to the **maidan,** Kullu's main square and cricket ground. The **Tourist Office** is on the upper side of the maidan. (☎22349. Open M-Sa 10am-7pm.) The **State Bank of India,** 2km from the center of town, is the nearest place to exchange currency and traveler's checks. (Open M-F 10am-2pm, Sa 10am-noon.) Hotel Rohtang, at the far end of the maidan, has **Internet access** (Rs120 per hr.; open M-Sa 9am-7pm). **STD/ISD booths** cluster near the footbridge and in the maidan. The **post office** is a few meters to the right, off the maidan. Open M-Sa 10am-5pm. **Postal Code:** 175101.

⌷⌷ ACCOMMODATIONS AND FOOD.

Turn right at the top of the pedestrian market and walk 50m past the post office to reach **Baba Guest House,** which rents small rooms, some with eagle's nest views and access to a kitchen—budget back-packer paradise. (☎22821. Rooms Rs30-70.) To the left of the bus station and over the footbridge is the immaculate **Aaditya Guest House,** severed from the bus stand by a river, yet close enough that you can look out your window to make sure you don't miss the morning bus. (☎23511. Doubles Rs100-350.) **The Madhu Chandrika Guest House**, next door, has spacious balconies that look out over the town, the Beas River, and surrounding mountains. (☎24395. Dorm beds Rs40; doubles Rs150-300. Off season: 50% discount.) **Hotel Bijleshwar,** behind the tourist office, on the upper side of the maidan, surrounds a garden and patio restaurant. (☎22677. Doubles with bath Rs250.) Most of the food in Kullu is of the street-stall variety, taking the form of *dahl* and rice, large raw vegetables, or small deep-fried ones. Kill your hankering for road-stall samosas, *pakoras*, and "sweets" at the pedestrian market across the river from the bus stand. Hotel Bijleshwar has more standard restaurant fare, with good fish curry (Rs50), beer (Rs90), and pizza (Rs40).

⌷ DAYTRIP FROM KULLU: BIJLI MAHADEV TEMPLE.

An ideal daytrip from Kullu takes you up to the **Bijli Mahadev** ("God of Electricity") **Temple** where, legend has it, lightning strikes each year and breaks the massive *linga*, which then has to be reassembled by a priest. Take a bus from town (Rs8) to the Chan Sari stop; from there, hike 3km uphill to the temple, which commands fantastic views and affords an opportunity to observe the pilgrimage rites.

NAGGAR नाग्गर   ☎ 01902

Halfway between Kullu and Manali, on the eastern side of the Beas River, rests the hillside village of Naggar, blissfully blanketed by pine forests, apple orchards, and fields of cannabis. The regional capital until the mid-1600s, Naggar is now a serene town with slate-shingled roofs, delicate temples, and perhaps the best art gallery in the Western Himalayas. While Manali has become overrun by hash-smoking tourists and Kullu remains frantic and noisy, Naggar has a very peaceful feel, making it an excellent place to get a sense of life in the Kullu Valley as it once was.

⚡🚊 ORIENTATION AND PRACTICAL INFORMATION. Buses arrive and depart by the shops on the highway 1km below the **Castle**. To: **Kullu** (every 30min.-1hr., 1½hr., Rs12) and **Manali** (every 30min.-1hr., 1½hr., Rs15). Buses to Kullu, Manali, and other destinations such as Dharamsala and Chandigarh are more frequent at **Patilkahl,** on the other side of the river. To get to the castle from Patilkahl, walk across the bridge, and then take the shortcut path along the creek in front of you; it's a 45-minute walk up. Or, take a taxi or rickshaw (Rs50). There is a small **hospital** opposite Hotel Alliance. The tiny **post office** is on the narrow road below the Castle. Open M-Sa 10am-5pm. **Postal Code:** 175130.

▐▌▐▌ ACCOMMODATIONS AND FOOD. Hotel Alliance, up the hill toward the Rerich Gallery, is run by a Frenchman and has eyrie-like rooms. The attached restaurant offers excellent French and local cuisine. (☎47763. Rooms Rs80-150, with bath Rs200-250.) **Poonan Mountain Lodge,** 50m below the castle, blends with the traditional village architecture. The friendly owner will tell you about local traditions as you sit in the adjoining veg. restaurant. In addition to its regular rooms, Poonan also rents a fully-equipped cottage, 1km above the village. (☎47747. Doubles with tiled bath Rs150-250; cottage Rs200.) **Shertal Guest House,** next to the castle, has rooms ranging from a dark double with common bath to a spacious room with shower and magnificent views from the balcony. (☎47750. Singles Rs450; doubles Rs125.) Also near the Castle, **Ragini Hotel** has large rooms, baths with tubs, 24-hour hot water, balconies, and a rooftop garden. (☎47855. Rooms Rs350-450. Off-season: Rs250-350.) **La Purezza Hard Rock Cafe,** by the bus stop, loads you with fresh pasta (Rs50-70) and other Italian carbs before that climb up to the Castle. (Open daily 10am-10pm.) **Chanchakhami Cafe,** on the road above the Tripuri temple, has such favorites as hummus and tofu. The terrace at **Rag Cafe** terrace, before the entrance to the gallery, serves tea while you soak in the surroundings.

📷 SIGHTS. Naggar's 504-year-old castle, 1km up from the highway, houses an expensive hotel and a sacred slab of stone called **Jagti Patt.** Local legend says the valley's gods "transformed into honey bees endowed with great strength" to cut the hefty block and fly it up. On top of the hill, past the Castle Hotel, the **Tripuri Sundri Temple,** with its three-tiered pagoda roof, is the site of a local *mela* in mid-May. Farther up the pine-lined road, past the Alliance Hotel, stands the **Nikolai Rerich Art Gallery.** Earlier in the century, the Russian artist N. Rerich settled here with his wife, Yelema, and their two sons. The house displays paintings of the mountains which uniquely capture the spirit of the Himalayas. Rerich was also very respected by the Indian government: letters from the state authorities and a portrait of Indira Gandhi, done by Rerich's son, adorn the gallery. The Rerich-founded **Urusvati Institute,** 200m farther, once had a faculty of leading scholars of Himalayan culture. *Urusvati* means "Light of the Morning Star," and the institute was supposed to "radiate" the sacred knowledge revealed by the mountains. Now, it is the site of the **Himalayan Folk and Tribal Gallery,** which holds fine collections of traditional North Indian dress and metalwork. The gallery upstairs has some of Nikolai's earlier mystic paintings, a few works by his son Sviatoslav, and a number of contemporary paintings by local Kullu artists influenced by Rerich. *(Both galleries open Tu-Sa 9am-1pm and 2-5pm. Rs10 ticket covers both.)*

NEAR NAGGAR

Naggar is an ideal base for treks up the slopes of the Valley of Gods. **Himalayan Mountain Treks,** at Poonam Lodge, is one of the most reliable trekking agencies in the valley. (☎47748. Fully organized treks Rs1000 per person per day; treks with only a guide and a tent Rs500.)

A hike (1-2 days) over the Chandrakhani Pass (3660m) takes you to **Malana,** a mountain village whose inhabitants claim to be descendants of Greek soldiers brought here by Alexander the Great. Malana has never come under the patronage of the Government of India Tourism Department, and visitors are not allowed to touch the villagers or the holy stones; the fine for violating this law is

Rs1000. There is only one guest house, with mattresses on the ground (Rs150), so you're better off bringing your own tent. From here, you can continue to the **Malana glacier** or to **Manikaran**, in the Parbatti Valley. The springs in Manikaran are said to cure rheumatism (and soothe trekkers' strained muscles), but the town is less than charming. You're better off staying at the **Raja Guest House** (rooms Rs50-100) in the nearby village of **Kasol**. Manikaran is the base for treks over the Pin-Parvati Pass (see **Treks around Kaza**, p. 243). Streams in both the Kullu and Parbatti Valleys are jumping with trout; many trekking agencies offer fishing trips and rent equipment. **Buses** run from Manikaran to Kullu (6 per day, 2½hr., Rs32).

MANALI मनाली ☎ 01902

Cradled between the mountains of the lesser Himalayas, Manali has long been a favorite hang-out of hashish-seeking hippies, Indian newlyweds, and travelers looking for a place to rest up before heading out on treks. Once quiet and remote, Manali's apple orchards and pine forests are now dotted with wooden guest houses and concrete hotels as the precarious political situation in Kashmir has sent ever more tourists to Himachal Pradesh in search of a replacement paradise. The Mall and the Model Town next to it are the head-quarters of the tourist invasion, but friendly locals and choice guest houses and restaurants make Old Manali a more mellow and inviting option. The surrounding slopes offer superb hikes, and the nearby village of Vashisht, 3km away, is well worth a daytrip.

 PARANOIA, CHAPTER XX. Manali, where cannabis grows wild, has been touted as the cool place to hang out and smoke hash, but stories of local use have been greatly exaggerated. It is used by locals only in times of duress or during cold weather. A number of foreigners every year are searched and arrested for hash possession, resulting in hefty fines of Rs1000-10,000. Saying that you were feeling cold or under duress will get you nowhere. It might not look like it, but **hashish is illegal, even in Manali.** If you've got it, *don't* flaunt it.

◗ GETTING THERE AND GETTING AROUND

Flights: The nearest airport is in **Bhuntar,** 52km from Manali (see **Kullu,** p. 230). **Matkon Travel** (☎ 52838), on the intersection of Old Manali Rd. and the Mall, is the agent for Indian Airlines. To **Delhi** (daily, 10am, US$130).

Buses: The **bus stand** is right in the center of the Mall. To: **Amritsar** (2pm, 14hr., Rs267); **Chamba** (3pm, 15hr., Rs295); **Dehra Dun** (5:15pm, Rs305); **Delhi** (5 per day, 11:30am-5pm, 16hr., Rs305; deluxe 4:30 and 5pm, 14hr., Rs492); **Dharamsala** (8:10 and 9:10am, 10hr., Rs157; deluxe 7:30pm, 10hr., Rs250); **Haridwar** (10am, Rs280); **Jammu** (6 and 7pm, 16hr., Rs260); **Keylong** (every 45 min., 4:30am-6pm, 6hr., Rs72); **Kullu** (every 15min., 5am-6:30pm, 2hr., Rs24); **Leh** (noon, 2 days, Rs405); **Naggar** (every 30min., 5am-6:30pm, 1½hr., Rs15); **Shimla** (6 and 7am, 10hr., Rs160; semi-deluxe (no, we don't know what that means, either) 6pm, 9hr., Rs202). Government "deluxe" buses can be booked at the **Himachal Tourism Marketing Office** (☎ 53531), on the Mall. The deluxe bus stand is at the southern end of town, a 300m walk down along the Mall. Confirm where your bus departs from. Private deluxe buses operated by **Matkon** or **Swagatam Travel** are usually cheaper and can be booked at any travel agency around town. To: **Delhi** (4:30 and 5:30pm, 15hr., Rs400); **Dharamsala** (7:30pm, 10hr., Rs250); **Leh** (10am, 2 days, Rs800); **Shimla** (6am, 10hr., Rs135). For information on the **Manali-Leh Road,** see p. 246.

✦ ⁊ ORIENTATION AND PRACTICAL INFORMATION

Manali is built in a rough "Y" shape. **The Mall** makes up the trunk, where you'll find a **bus stand** and most of the other tourist services. Off to either side are alleys lined with gift shops, *dhabas*, and provision stores. These are particularly common just behind and north of the bus stand. The left fork at the Nehru Statue leads uphill 1km on the **Old Manali Rd.**, separating the **Model Town** on the left from the **Himalayan National Park** on the right before making a sharp descent to the bridge over the Manalsu River. Across the bridge, **Old Manali** spreads out along the uphill road to your left. Taking the right fork at the statue takes you across the **Beas River bridge.** Continue 2km upstream along the road and turn right for the steep 1km ascent that leads up to the village of **Vashisht.**

Tourist Office: Government of India Tourist Office (☎ 52175), on the Mall, next to Hotel Kunzam. Open M-Sa 10am-5pm. **HPTDC Marketing Office** (☎ 52116), on the Mall, in a white building on the right as you face away from the bus stand. Open M-Sa 8am-8pm.

Budget Travel: Plenty of travel agents offer treks (US$30 per person per day, all inclusive) and rafting trips (starting at Rs850 per day). Two reliable companies are **Dragon Tours** (☎ 52790; fax 52769), with offices opposite the bus stand and in Old Manali, and **Himalayan Journeys** (☎ 52365; fax 53065), just past the bus stand.

Currency Exchange: State Bank of India, Old Manali Rd., just past the Mall, does all the usual stuff. Poor service and miserable rates. Open M-F 10am-2pm, Sa 10am-1pm.

Bookstore: Bookworm (☎ 52920), in the New Market behind the bus stand.

Police: The police station (☎ 52326) is next to the deluxe bus stand.

Hospital: Mission Hospital (☎ 52379), down the alley from Hotel Kanzam. **Khana's Clinic,** Old Manali Rd. Open M-Sa 8am-2pm and 4-8pm, Su 10am-2pm. For holistic medicine, try **Kerala Ayurvedic Center** (☎ 54446), in Old Manali, next to Tibetan Kitchen. Open M-Sa 9am-6pm.

Internet: Valley of Gods, just off the road in Old Manali, 50m above Moondance. Plenty of computers. Open daily 8am-10pm. **Cyberia,** to the left of the bridge, is email central and the wait can be long. Rs60 per hr. Open daily 9am-10pm. **Nirvana Cybercafe,** on the road between Model Town and Old Manali, has more computers. Rs100 per hr. Open daily 10am-9pm.

Post Office: Down the alley opposite the bus stand and to the right of Monal Himalayan Travels. Open M-Sa 10am-5pm. **Postal Code:** 175131

⌐ ACCOMMODATIONS

Most travelers trek to Old Manali, where guest houses can't be told apart from village houses. The farther up the hill, the quieter the lodgings and the better the views. To avoid the crowds and enjoy a soak in some hot springs, head down to **Vashisht** (rickshaw from Manali Rs30 up, Rs20 down), where most guest houses are around the temple and hot baths. The area between the Old Manali Rd. and the Hadimba Temple, known as the **Model Town,** is an agglomeration of large hotels inundated by Indian tourists and honeymooners.

OLD MANALI

▨ **Hotel Splendour.** Head up the hill in Old Manali and look for signs on your right; 5min. down a side path takes you through apple orchards and cornfields. Each room has a hot water heater and seat toilet. Singles Rs140; doubles Rs250. Off-season: Rs100/200. Pitch your own tent Rs75; 2-person tent rental Rs200.

▨ **Monal Guest House** (☎ 53848). On the top of the hill, Monal is the last house in the village. Quiet, with beautiful views of the river and mountains. Bring a flashlight to find your way back at night. Front rooms Rs150; back Rs70.

Raj Guest House (☎ 53570), left of the path to Splendour. The older rooms share a bathroom and a porch with gorgeous views. The new rooms in the back all have tiled baths but lack the views. A little more lively than some of the places farther up the hill. Older rooms Rs60-80; newer rooms Rs150. Off-season: Rs50/130.

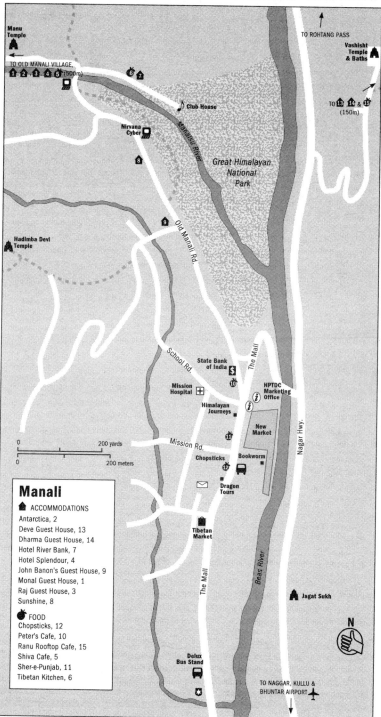

Manu
Temple

TO ROHTANG PASS

Vashisht
Temple
& Baths

TO OLD MANALI VILLAGE (500m)

TO 13 14 & 15
(150m)

6 7

♪ Club House

Nirvana
Cyber

8

Great Himalayan
National
Park

Manalsu River

9

Old Manali Rd.

Hadimba Devi
Temple

School Rd.

State Bank
of India

The Mall

HPTDC
Marketing
Office

Mission
Hospital

10

Himalayan
Journeys

i

New
Market

Nagar Hwy.

11

Mission Rd.

Chopsticks

12

Bookworm

Dragon
Tours

Tibetan
Market

200 yards

200 meters

The Mall

Beas River

Jagat Sukh

N

Manali

⌂ ACCOMMODATIONS
Antarctica, 2
Deve Guest House, 13
Dharma Guest House, 14
Hotel River Bank, 7
Hotel Splendour, 4
John Banon's Guest House, 9
Monal Guest House, 1
Raj Guest House, 3
Sunshine, 8

🍎 FOOD
Chopsticks, 12
Peter's Cafe, 10
Ranu Rooftop Cafe, 15
Shiva Cafe, 5
Sher-e-Punjab, 11
Tibetan Kitchen, 6

Delux
Bus Stand

TO NAGGAR, KULLU &
BHUNTAR AIRPORT

HIMACHAL PRADESH

Antarctica (☎53079), above the road and to the left. All rooms have attached bath. The restaurant has a balcony. Rooms with hot showers Rs150.

Hotel River Bank (☎53004 or 52968), to the right of the bridge in Old Manali. A typical concrete luxury complex. Out-of-this-country ski resort feel. Red velvet chairs on plush blue carpets. All rooms have attached seat toilets and hot water. Doubles Rs450, but bargain away. Off-season: Rs250.

VASHISHT

Dharma Guest House (☎52354), on a steep path 100m above the springs. Porch for reading and meditation. Wooden doubles share a common toilet; the new concrete annex has rooms with extra facilities. Rs80; new rooms Rs200. Off-season: Rs50/150.

Kalp Taru Guest House (☎53443). Right next to the baths. Doubles with bath Rs100. Off-season: Rs50.

MODEL TOWN

John Banon's Guest House (☎52335 or 52388; fax 52392), a 5min. walk up Old Manali Rd. from the Mall. One of the oldest hotels in Manali, with its own private apple orchard. Spacious, carpeted rooms with huge windows and working fireplaces. Doubles Rs450-550. Reservations recommended one month in advance in season.

Sunshine (☎52320), halfway between the Mall and Old Manali. Each room has a private dressing room, bathroom, and a veranda overlooking the valley. Old-style dining room with a massive wooden table and fireplace. If you get cold, the staff will supply your fireplace with wood (Rs100 per day). Rooms Rs350. Closed Dec.-Mar.

🍴 FOOD

There are numerous restaurants in Old Manali with imaginative, inventive cooks. Near the bus station, there's at least one *dhaba* down every alley. There are also plenty of falafal joints in Manali and several strudel-serving "German bakeries."

◼ **Tibetan Kitchen,** 50m to the right of the bridge in Old Manali. This place, with tablecloths and well-decorated walls, would win the prize for cleanliness and style, if there were one. Extensive Tibetan menu, as well as Japanese and Chinese food. Hong Kong chicken Rs60. Open daily 8am-midnight.

Shiva Cafe, after the bend in hill-road, has tasty Italian dishes, as well as a covered veranda and pleasant garden. Lasagna Rs45. Open daily 8am-11:30pm.

Shiv Shakti Cafe, just below Monal Guest House, has some of the best views in Manali. Serves up fresh trout (Rs100) and a variety of other tasty stuff. Open daily 9am-11pm.

Chopsticks Restaurant, across the Mall from the bus stand, tries to serve authentic Tibetan/Chinese food. Szechuan chicken Rs75. Open daily 8am-11pm.

Peter's Cafe, down a dingy lane in a small garden, near the State Bank. Psychedelic shack serves quiche (Rs20), pie (Rs25), and cheddar omelettes (Rs30). Pete will treat you to his razor-sharp wit and collection of classical records. Open daily 8am-8pm.

Sher-e-Punjab, has two branches in the middle of the Mall. Authentic Punjabi food for those sick of Italian food and *momos*. Meals Rs30-55. Open daily 9am-11pm.

Ranu Rooftop Cafe, in Vashisht, refuels hot-spring bathers with carbohydrates of both the pasta and *thukpa* variety. Open daily 8am-10pm.

👁 SIGHTS

HADIMBA DEVI TEMPLE. The four-tiered Hadimba Devi Temple, with its pagoda-shaped roof, is dedicated to the demoness-turned-goddess Hadimba, wife of Bhima. Valley residents claim that the king cut off the builder's hand to prevent the temple's duplication. Undaunted by the amputation, the builder trained his left hand and constructed an even more elaborate temple at Tritoknath. This time, he lost his head. *(Walk 5min. along Old Manali Rd., take a left, and follow the signs.)*

MANU TEMPLE. The Manu Temple, a pleasant 30-minute walk uphill from Old Manali, is supposed to be the spot where Manu first stepped onto the earth after a great flood. Manu, the first man to possess knowledge, and his wife, Shatrupa, had a series of thoughtful, philosophical children who developed the world's religions. The temple was rebuilt in 1992, with vaulted ceilings, elaborate woodwork, and marble floors. The townspeople appreciate foreigners who show respect by dressing appropriately and displaying reverence at the temple.

GREAT HIMALAYAN NATIONAL PARK. The park shows visitors what the towering pine forests might have looked like before the modern architectural invasion. *(Entrance at the Wildlife Information, Education, and Awareness Center, Old Manali Rd. Open daily 10am-5pm. Rs2; camera charge Rs5.)*

ENTERTAINMENT AND SHOPPING

The Himachal Tourism-run **Club House,** to the right of the bridge in Old Manali, offers sundry attractions, not the least of which is a fully stocked bar (beer Rs80). Try your hand at billiards (Rs100 per hr.), carom (Rs40 per hr.), badminton (Rs60 per hr.), or just kick back in the plush lounge with one of the books from the library. (☎52141. Open daily 10am-9pm. Rs5.) There are reasonably frequent **all-night raves** in Manali. Check the German Bakery and Cafe in Old Manali for notices. In addition to all the shawl shops on the Mall and Old Manali Rd., the **Tibetan Market,** at the southern end of town, provides good opportunities for good old-fashioned hard bargaining. (Open daily 8am-10pm.)

DAYTRIPS FROM MANALI

The temple in Vashisht has free **hot baths,** separated for men and women (open daily 5am-9pm). The **Mountaineering Institute** (☎52206 or 53788; fax 53509), 2km south of the bridge over the Beas River, offers courses in mountaineering, skiing, and water sports throughout the year, with fees ranging from US$190 (skiing) to US$250 (for a 4-week mountaineering course). The institute can also organize expeditions for large groups. For information, write to: Mountaineering Institute, Manali, HP 175131. Farther south is **Jagat Suk** and its glorious wood-and-stone Shiva temple. The regular bus from Manali (every 15min., 5am-6:30pm, 30min., Rs3) will drop you in Jagat Suk, where you can check out the temple and drink *chai* with the locals. The **Rohtang Pass** (3998m), open erratically between June and September, is the only motorable way into the Lahaul-Spiti area from Manali (see **Kinnaur-Spiti Road,** below). Nowadays, it's best described as a polar dump; the place is a mess of tea tents and scattered debris. Rohtang can still make for a decent trip, though, if you're looking for high-altitude scenery without the exercise. Buses, as well as HPTDC tours (Rs150), will take you here, and you can rent fabulous fur coats on the way. Check out the creative HPPWD road advice on the way up, including slogans like "Divorce speed" and "Peep, peep, don't go to sleep."

KINNAUR-SPITI किन्नौर स्पीती

One of the most incredible routes in the world, the road from Shimla cuts through mountains of solid rock and traverses Kinnaur, Spiti, and Lahaul, eventually crossing the Rohtang Pass and winding down into Manali. The ride can be harrowing— at times the river churns violently hundreds of feet below the road, and you'll see the locals sitting next to you praying that the bus doesn't do the same. The reward for accepting the risks of travel is an up-close and personal experience of some of the most awe-inspiring natural beauty in all of India. Each of the three regions that the road cuts across presents a distinct landscape. The deep Sutlej Valley connects fertile valleys inhabited by the Kimmauri, round-hut dwellers who all share the name "Nogi" and a unique blend of religious traditions. The Spiti River cuts through mountain deserts dotted by oases of barley fields and enclaves of Tibetan

culture. After crossing the Kunsum Pass, it enters the Lahaul Valley, a land of gla-ciers and moss-covered granite too rocky to sustain life apart from fields of grass and the nomadic shepherds who bring their flocks to feed.

The road was opened to outsiders in 1992, when Public Works Department (PWD) rest houses were the only accommodation options. Today, lodges, hotels, and guest houses line the route. The road is open between June and October, but it is unlikely that you will make it through without encountering at least one road-block or delay (mudslides, stone avalanches, fallen bridges, etc.). Road conditions change in minutes, and bus drivers rely on updates from passing vehicles. If it rains, especially in the drier Spiti Valley, the roads can become treacherous, and you might get stuck until the roads clear. If you're traveling by bus, you can usually get off, cross the obstacle on foot, hike to the next town, and then catch another bus from there—but make sure you can reach the next town by nightfall. Hiking in the rain is very dangerous on certain stretches of the road, as rain-softened ground tends to loosen large boulders, which come rolling down the slopes at speeds that make them difficult to dodge. If you're prone to altitude sickness, it's best to start in Shimla, where the climb is more gradual. Non-Indians traveling between Jangi and Sundo must obtain an **inner-line permit** (available from the sub-divisional mag-istrates in Shimla, Rampur, Peo, Kaza, Chamba, Kullu, Keylong, and the home office in Delhi; for more information, see **Warning**, p. 214). The **Kaza-Manali Road** is theoretically open from mid-June to mid-September, but weather makes it unreli-able as well. **There are no facilities for currency exchange along the route.**

> ❗ **WARNING.** During July 2000, huge floods hit Himachal Pradesh. Whole vil-lages were swept away, hundreds of people were killed, and hundreds of thou-sands lost their homes. The long-term implications of the floods for travel along the high-altitude roads of the state are not yet clear, but you should seek an informed second opinion before making plans to travel here. Many of the routes described below may no longer be passable; some of them might not exist at all.

THE KINNAUR-SPITI ROAD

SUTLEJ VALLEY. From Shimla, the road climbs to **Narkanda** (60km, 2½hr. by bus) and then descends steeply to **Rampur** (120km, 3½hr. by bus). From **Jeuri** (or Jeori), 23km farther on, you can reach the Kinnauri village of **Sarahan** (see p. 239), site of the Bhima-Kali Temple. The green concrete building by the road in Jeuri has sim-ple beds (Rs40)—an option if you get stranded here. Two hours up the road, a path cut into the rock takes you past a hydroelectric facility to **Wangtu**, the trailhead for treks over the Bhaba Pass. Another hour of prayers gets you to Karcham, where you can catch a bus heading up to **Sangla** in the Lower Sangla Valley (see p. 239). Beds are available in one of the shacks across the bridge over Baspa River (Rs50). From Karcham, it's an hour or so to **Rekong-Peo** (see p. 240), the district headquar-ters of Kinnaur and gateway to **Kalpa** (see p. 240), Shiva's winter residence. From Peo, the landscape grows arid, and military bases become common as you near the Tibetan border. You will need to show your permit and passport in Jangi—the bus will wait for you. At **Khab** (or Kabo), 70km from Peo (5hr. by bus), the road turns left and climbs to the plateau above. In the middle of this brown plain is the village of **Kah**. Farther down from Yang Thang, you can take a detour to see the Tibetan village of **Nako** (see p. 241), cradled in a high-altitude bowl with a green lake. Nako has the only guest houses around (a 2km uphill hike or 10km bus ride). But if you get stranded in Yang Thang, there are simple beds available (Rs50). You can stay in **Chango**, 100km (3½hr.) from Peo, where there is a 13th-century temple that was supposedly hewn out of a single stone in one day.

SPITI VALLEY. The bus then proceeds through **Shalkar,** the checkpost at **Sumdo** (the Spiti boundary), and the truck-stop of **Hurling** (beds Rs50) on its way to the thousand year-old *gompa* at **Tabo** (see p. 241). After Sumdo, the responsibility for road maintenance passes from an army organization to the Public Works Department, and the transfer in authority shows—the ride becomes very bumpy. The 47km Tabo-Kaza stretch passes the villages of **Poh** and **Shichling.** A few hundred meters after Shichling, a road branches off to **Dhankar Gompa.** One kilometer down, a bridge leads off to the **Pim Valley.** Between Hurling and Tabo and between Poh and Shichling, the road passes under mountains of mud—**do not attempt to walk this route in the rain.** From **Kaza** (see p. 242), the road gets even bumpier as it winds its way 50km up to the village of **Losar** (5hr.). Losar has two small guest houses and is the access point for the **Kanzam-La Pass** (4500m), 18km (1½hr.) away.

LAHAUL VALLEY. After the pass, the road drops steeply to the four tents that make up **Batal,** in the Lahaul Valley (see p. 244); beds are available here. An 18km hike takes you to **Chandratal Lake.** After Batal, there is a *dhaba* in **Chota Dhara** (12km) and tented accommodations in **Chatru** (16km) before the route turns back onto a main road at **Gramphoo** (17km). From here, it's a four hour ride over the polar dump of Rohtang Pass to **Manali** (64km). The Lahaul Valley gets a lot of snow in winter, and the opening date of the segment between Losar and Gramphoo is entirely dependent on how long the snow takes to melt.

SARAHAN सराहान   ☎ 01782

Eight hundred meters above the Sutlej River Valley, the Kinnauri village of Sarahan is notable for its impressive wooden **Bhima-Kali Temple** complex. The temple used to be the site of human sacrifice, until the practice was banned by the British. Inside the Durga shrine, the council of marble Buddhas, mountain deities, and Hindu gods is the most conspicuous evidence of the rich mingling of beliefs and traditions that characterizes the Kinnauri region. The views of the snowclad Shrimakand peak, endless fruit orchards, and groves of jacaranda pine make a perfect setting for walks through the surrounding area. The Himalayan pheasant farm in the forest above the village is worth a visit. Buses from Jeuri go to Sarahan (every hr., 6am-5pm, 1hr., Rs12). The **Temple Rest House** (☎ 74248), in front of the temple, has rooms for Rs150-300 and a 12-bed dorm (beds Rs50). The huge **Shrimakand Hotel** is expensive, but the eight-bed dorm is a good deal, with pleasant views and large bathrooms (beds Rs75). **Ajay Chinese Food,** next to the temple entrance, serves delicious noodles and Shanghai *momos.*

LOWER SANGLA VALLEY सांगला

After a perilous 17km bus ride on a road carved out of the mountain face, with the Baspa River dashing hundreds of feet below, the deep canyon suddenly widens, and the fertile Sangla Valley unfolds in all its splendor. For centuries, the natural barriers of the wild river and the snow-capped peaks were enough to keep this area isolated from the rest of the world, and its distinct vegetative and cultural features developed free from outside influences. The scenery between **Sangla** and the last village of **Chitkuhl** is unforgettable. The landscape and vegetation changes almost every hundred meters—the day-long hike, which takes you past villages with houses of peaked roofs, is well worth doing. The valley was not open to outsiders (including Indians) until 1992, so **be very careful about where you wander.**

From Sangla, the 2km road that turns left past the police station leads to the village of **Kamru,** former capital of the Baspa kingdom. On top of a rock overlooking the entrance into the valley are a Buddhist temple with rich Tibetan wall paintings and a Hindu shrine adorned with exquisite woodcarving. High above all of this is a temple dedicated to one of the mountain deities and guarded by a legion of lizards; ask permission before entering. From Chitkuhl it's another week farther up the valley and over a pass to the holy town of **Gangotri** (see p. 148) in UP. You must be fully self-sufficient for this trek; there are no settlements of any type on the way.

HIMACHAL PRADESH

The **bus** from Karcham (7 and 9:30am, 1hr., Rs12) drops you off in **Sangla**. Buses from Sangla go to **Peo** (7, 8am, and 2pm; 3hr.; Rs25) and **Rampur** (noon, 5hr., Rs60). In the market in Sangla, there are a few restaurants, guest houses, and a **National Travelers** branch (☎42358), which organizes treks. The **Mount Kailash Guest House,** just off the road in Sangla, has a clean, four-bed dorm (beds Rs75) and several doubles (Rs250-450). On the first floor, there is a restaurant and an **STD/ISD** telephone. **Banjara Camps,** 6km up from Sangla, has luxury tents with attached toilets (Rs1000, includes 3 meals and 2 snacks). Six kilometers along the route before you reach Rakchham village, the **Fayal Guest House** has double rooms (Rs150-300), a dorm, and a restaurant serving local specialties. Down the path past Fayal is the **Ganga Gardenview Guest House,** offering doubles (Rs250), local cuisine, and apple orchards. In Chitkul, the **Chiranjan Guest House** has doubles (Rs150-300).

REKONG-PEO (PEO) पिओ ☎017852

Halfway between Shimla and Tabo, where the landscape starts to become arid, Peo serves as the district headquarters of Kinnaur. Just off the main road, the town is a small collection of concrete military barracks, *dhabas*, and market stalls that does not merit more than a few hours' visit. **Lavi Fair,** during the first week of November, however, is not to be missed. A variety of goods, including pashmina wool, dried fruits, and horses, are traded on the grounds near the District Commissioner's office. Peo is also famous for the forests nearby (10min. walk up from the bus station, toward Kalpa). Twenty minutes uphill from Peo is the **gompa** that was the site of the *kalachakra* ceremony performed by the Dalai Lama in 1992 (see p. 242). The village of Kalpa (see below), is only 3km away from Peo. An overnight stay in Peo might be necessary if you need to catch an early-morning bus. Although **buses** also stop in the market, it is better to catch them at the bus stand (a 10min. walk away) since they are usually packed by the time they reach the market. Buses run to: **Chandigarh** (5:30, 7, and 10:30am; 15hr.; Rs190); **Kalpa** (5 per day, 7:30am-5pm, 30min., Rs5); **Kaza** (7:30am, 13hr., Rs115); **Nako** (7:30am Kaza bus and 1pm, 6hr., Rs55); **Rampur** (every hr., 4am-1:30pm, 3hr., Rs30); and **Sangla** (9:30am and 4:30pm, 2hr., Rs25). The Additional District Magistrate who issues **inner-line permits** (see p. 214) for the road between Jangi and Sundo has an office on the first floor of the administrative complex near the market (open M-F 9am-5pm), but you must go through a travel agent such as **National Travellers** (☎228830), down the steps before Fairyland Guest House. Ask for Bhagwan Singh Negi. National Travellers can also help with treks, including a seven-day trek that takes you from **Wangtu** (3hr. by bus from Peo) over the Bhaba Pass to Pim Valley and Spiti. The **police station** is in the same building. The **district hospital** is 2km up from the town, on the road to Kalpa. The **post office** is next to the bus stand (open M-Sa 9am-1pm and 2-5pm). **Postal Code:** 172107.

The **Fairyland Hotel,** above the market, has simple, clean rooms and a restaurant. (☎22477. Doubles Rs200-300.) **Mayur Guest House,** next door, is another option. (☎22771. Dorm beds Rs50; rooms Rs125.) The **Shivling View Guest House,** past the bus stand, has rooms with hot showers, TVs, and a restaurant. (☎22421. Simple bed Rs80-120; doubles Rs200-300.)

KALPA कल्पा ☎017852

The village of Kalpa, or Chini-Gaon ("Chinese Village"), is noteworthy for its proximity to **Kimmer Kailash,** where, according to Hindu mythology, Shiva himself resides. It is believed that he moves to Kalpa's temple in the winter to escape the cold. Aside from its religious distinction, Kalpa offers a glimpse into traditional Kinnauri village life. Age-old festivals synthesizing traditions of Hinduism, Buddhism, and various mountain cults dominate the calendar; among these, **Fullaich,** the festival of flowers in September, is the most famous.

At the center of Kalpa is a handful of wood and stone houses and Kinnauri shrines crammed onto an outcrop that looks out over the valley. The rest of the vil-

NAKO नाको ■ 241

lage stretches up the ridge, and getting from one place to another can be a small trek in itself. There are apricots, apples, plums, and blackberries everywhere, as well as spectacular views of the valley and mountains. To reach Kalpa, walk from the bus stand along the road to the left until you reach Shivalik View Guest House. Behind the guest house begins the 3km path that takes you through woods of pine and past village houses (see below). Buses leave from the market and the bus stand to: **Peo** (5 per day, Rs5) and **Shimla** (6am, 12hr., Rs120). More connections can be made from Rekong-Peo, farther down the hill. From the market, the stone path leads to a paved road; turn right and walk 400m to reach **Aucktong Guest House,** with bright flowers out front. (☎26019. Doubles Rs200.) The family prepares meals for their guests. The **Shivalik Guest House,** just to the left of where the stone path reaches the road, offers rooms ranging in size and quality of view. (☎26158. Singles Rs150; doubles Rs400.) For real snazz, head farther down to the left to **Kimmer Villa,** which has luxurious rooms with a terrace. (☎26079. Rs900.) Food is available in the hotels and in the **Snow White Coffee House** in the market. The **sub-post office** is next to the temple (open M-Sa 9am-5pm). **Postal Code: 172108.**

⚑ TREKS AROUND KALPA. The most popular trek within Kalpa is to **Chaka** (5-6km, a 2hr. hike one-way), a plateau above the village that makes an ideal camping or picnic spot. But Kalpa can also serve as a starting point for longer treks. The famed **Parikrama trek** begins at **Thangi** (60km from Kalpa, approachable by road) and ends 3-4 days later in Chitkul, with nights spent in a cave in the middle of the mountain. The descent to Chitkul is extremely steep, so walk in the opposite direction only if you really want to challenge your knees. There are villages and shepherd huts on the way; tents and food supplies are therefore not necessary. Sleeping bags and good shoes, however, are a must, as you reach altitudes of over 5000m. The climb can be done in August and September without any mountaineering equipment. **Timberline Tent Camps** (☎26006), in Kimmer Villa, can arrange guides for Rs500 per day. The most difficult route in this region—one that should only be attempted by seasoned trekkers—is the trail leading up **Kinnaur Kailash** (6050m). The base of the mountain is in **Powari,** 20km from Kalpa. The best time to do this trek is in July and August. Expect the trek to take two days each way.

NAKO नाको

Fringing a small green lake in a high-altitude bowl, this village of stone walls and mud-roof houses is one of the first fully Tibetan settlements along the way; the surrounding ridges are dotted by mud *gompas*, prayer flags, and piles of *mani* stones. The barren hills contrast sharply with the greenery of Kinnaur; the views of the deep Spiti canyon and the distant white mountains complete this region's distinctive landscape. A seven-hour hike takes you to an abandoned monastery near the Tibetan border where you can spend the night, provided you bring a sleeping bag and some food. A daily **bus** runs from Peo to Nako (1pm, 6hr., Rs55). You can also reach Nako by taking the Kaza- (7:15am, 6hr., Rs55) or Shalkar-bound bus and getting off at **Yang Thang.** From there it is a steep, 2km walk. A bus runs back from Nako to Peo at 6am (Rs60). To continue from Nako to Spiti, walk down and catch the one Kaza bus that passes through Yang Thang (anytime after 11am). **Loulan Guest House,** next to the bus stand, has dorm beds (Rs50) and doubles with baths (Rs200-300). It also has the only *dhaba* in town, serving *dahl*, rice, and the local barley brew (upon request). Another guest house 100m up the path to the left has rooms (Rs200) and a porch where you can snooze (Rs25) if everything else is full.

TABO ताबो ☎01906

The hamlet of Tabo is home to 350 or so intensely devout people, whose mud huts cluster around the Tabo *gompa* near the river. Tabo remained in virtual isolation until the border disputes with China during the 1950s, when the geopolitical importance of this region brought it to center stage. Today the area is home to several Indian military outposts, and **foreigners must obtain a permit before visiting.**

[E7] GETTING THERE AND PRACTICAL INFORMATION. The bus to Peo arrives any time after 10am (9hr., Rs125), and two buses go to Kaza, one after 9am and another after 4pm (2hr., Rs35). Tabo's **Primary Health Center,** at the edge of town, has treatment and medicine and operates on donations. (☎33325. Open M-Sa 9am-1pm and 3-5pm.) The closest **police** assistance is in Sumdo or Kaza. The **post office** is farther down the cow path in a barn (open M-Sa 10am-3pm). If the postmaster isn't there (most of the time he isn't), ask around; he's usually having tea in one of the nearby *dhabas.* There is one **STD/ISD** booth at the back side of the Tenzin Restaurant behind the Temple Guest House. **Postal Code:** 172113.

ACCOMMODATIONS AND FOOD. The wooden **Monastery Guest House** has a number of clean doubles and a spacious dorm. (☎33315. Dorm beds Rs50; doubles Rs150-250.) Ask the receptionist to be let into the library, where you can read up on Buddhist thought or Tibetan *thankas* (open M-Sa 1-7pm). **Ajanta Guest House,** also near the temple, has carpeted doubles with common baths. (☎33312. Rs150 first floor; Rs200 second floor.) There are two food options: the monastery restaurant and the Tenzin *dhaba* across the street. Their identical menus include Tibetan bread, *thukpas*, and *momos* (both open 5:30am-9:30pm). **Banjara Camps,** in Kurith, 4km outside Tabo, a village of 22 (including sheep and goats), has luxury tents with double beds and private baths (Rs1100, all meals included).

SIGHTS. According to an ancient inscription, the foundation of Tabo has been dated to the year 996. The **Tabo Gompa** is the largest monastic complex in Spiti, one of the largest in the Spiti valley, and one of the holiest Buddhist sites anywhere in the Himalayas. Following the massive cultural purges of Tibet by the Chinese government, Tabo assumed a role as treasury of Tibetan art. On the *gompa's* 1000th birthday, the Dalai Lama came to perform the sacred **Kalachalena** ceremony, a rite of initiation, rejuvenation, and prayer offered once every four years. The monastery consists of what are believed to be five temples from the original settlement and four shrines that were added at a later date. At the core of the complex is the Temple of the Enlightened Gods, otherwise known as the **Assembly Hall.** At the center is a statue of the four-fold Vainocana, the Divine Being regarded by Vajnayana Buddhism as one of the spiritual sons of Adibuddha, the self-creative primordial Buddha. Vainocana is depicted here turning the wheel of law. On brackets along the wall are images of the other 33 deities of the pantheon. Hidden in darkness, the sanctum immediately behind Vainocana is adorned with wall paintings depicting the life of the Buddha. In the ante-room, ask the lama to show you the **Bom-khang,** the Temple of Wrathful gods. Twice a day, a lama shielded by protective meditation performs a secret ceremony to appease the fierce deities. Daily prayers are performed in the hall every morning at 6am. To the right of the Assembly Hall is the **Maitreya Temple,** with a 6m-high statue of the Buddha of the Future. To the left is the **Mystic Mandala Temple,** where the initiation to monkhood takes place. Above the complex, on the sheer cliff face overlooking the town, is a series of **caves** that once functioned as monastic dwellings. With a flashlight, you can see dim traces of the paintings that once adorned these walls. *(To visit the temples, ask at the reception of the monastery guest house for the temple keeper, and make sure to bring your own flashlight.)*

KAZA काज़ा ☎01906

Strategically situated in the middle of the valley, Kaza has traditionally been the trading center of Spiti. Half old village and half government post, Kaza has become a major base for travelers to this long-forbidden land. The millennial Kalachara ceremony was held in the Kyi Gompa, and new hotels spring up every year.

[E] GETTING THERE AND GETTING AROUND. Bus service to **Manali** (4am, 12hr., Rs100) begins in spring in the Lahaul Valley, sometime between early June and mid-August, and continues until October. Buses also go to: **Kibber** (2pm, 1½hr., Rs12) via **Kyi; Lasar** (9am, 3½hr., Rs45); **Mikim** in the Pin Valley (8am, 2hr., Rs25);

and **Peo** (7am, 12hr., Rs120) via **Tabo** (3hr., Rs30). Bus schedules depend on the whims of weather and drivers.

⚡🚻 ORIENTATION AND PRACTICAL INFORMATION. Both **Old Kaza** and **New Kaza** lie between the main road and the river—a small, often dry stream separates the two. New Kaza can be reached by following the road that goes up above the bus stand. The **bazaar** and restaurants are all in Old Kaza; the **hospital, police station,** and government buildings are in the new town. The **bus stand** is just off the main road in Old Kaza. The **hospital** (☎22218), in a big shed, runs an ambulance service. The Sub-divisional Magistrate's office, which grants **permits** for the journey onward to Kinnaur, is in New Kaza. The **post office** is two minutes from the road (open M-F 10am-5pm). There's an **STD/ISD** booth near the market in Old Kaza (open daily 6am-10pm). Postal Code: 172114.

▌▛ ACCOMMODATIONS AND FOOD. Lodging in Kaza is available from April to November. **Mahabaudha,** at the top end of the market road in Old Kaza, has the cleanest rooms in town and a traditional Tibetan kitchen. (☎22232. Common bath with hot water. Doubles Rs150.) **Snowlion,** a few meters higher up, on the main road, has rooms with baths and pleasant views from the porch. (☎34257. Doubles Rs250-400.) **Sakya's Abode,** across the stream in New Kaza, has a beautiful garden area, and is where the tour groups stay. (☎22254. Dorm beds Rs50; singles with bath Rs150; doubles with hot shower Rs250-450.) **Milarepa,** next door, has basic rooms. (☎22234. Doubles Rs160-185.) If you need to catch an early bus, **Art Guest House,** below the bus stand, has clean rooms, all with common bath. (Doubles Rs150-250.) **Il Pomo d'Oro,** left of the market, is run by a globe-trotting Italian family, who are a fountain of local wisdom. The veg. dishes (Rs50-80) and the stuffed pasta (Rs120) reveal the touch of a master chef. Try the rum-filled *tiramisu* (Rs50), and camp out in the garden if you cannot find your way home afterward. *Dhabas* along the market serve *dahl* and noodles; the one on the second floor near the bus station is frequented by bus drivers and is the best source for road information. The **bakery** next to Snowlion has crisp samosas and tender breads.

🔼 TREKS AROUND KAZA. The most popular trek takes you through the Pin Valley National Park and over the Pin-Parvati pass to **Manikaran** (6 days), where there are soothing hot springs and bus connections to Kullu and Manali. From Kaza, take a bus to **Mikim** (8am, 2hr., Rs25), where a *jula* will transport you on a rope across the river to the trailhead at Kaar village—ask for Chine Dorge, who can arrange guides for your trek. Instead of turning west over Pin-Parvati, you can continue south over the Bhaba pass to **Wangtu** on the Shimla-Peo road (5 days).

NEAR KAZA

KYI. The largest fort monastery in Spiti, Kyi rests on the top of a cliff 12km from Kaza. The monastery, home to 1000 lamas, has a superb collection of *thankas*. The *gompa* received a major face-lift in preparation for the **Kalachakra** ceremony: a road was cut through sand and stone to connect the new monastery guest house to the village, a large assembly hall was constructed on the hill, solar panels were installed, and repairs were made to the temples. To get to Kyi, put your faith in the erratic **bus** from Kaza (2pm), or just walk and hope to hitch a ride with someone going up. If, on the way, a smiling young man in jeans whizzes past you in a Hyundai, you have just had the honor of a brush with His Holiness, the 19th incarnation of Kyi Gompa's head lama.

KIBBER. On a hilltop, in the shadow of the imposing Pasargla mountain, Kibber is a Tibetan village of white mud houses surrounded by barley fields. At an altitude of 4250m, Kibber is one of the highest villages in the world reachable by motor vehicle. Kibber and the adjoining wildlife sanctuary offer amazing day treks and a feeling of remoteness that has disappeared from most other spots in the valley. A daily **bus** leaves Kaza (2pm, 1½hr., Rs12) and loops around at Kibber. If the bus driver is having a bad day, though, you might have to hike the 18km stretch or take a taxi (Rs250). The best thing to do is to start walking and hitch a ride (Rs30-50). The **Resang Hotel,** at the village entrance, has doubles with baths and a kitchen (Rs150). Farther down the road, the **Pasargla Guest House** charges inflated prices for its rather bleak rooms (doubles Rs300-500). Many travelers report pleasant stays in village houses (Rs60-100 per night, including food); ask around. In the village, there is a huge prayer wheel, a *gompa* for curing spiritual afflictions, and a "hospital" (i.e. local healer) for bodily ones (open M-Sa 9am-1pm and 3-5pm).

DHANKAR GOMPA. Named for its precarious location (*dhankar* means "cliff"), Dhankar Gompa was one of the first fort monasteries incorporated into Spiti's defense system. The *gompa* is an 8km hike up from the road near Shichling, about 20km from Kaza. You can either take the **Peo** bus (7:30am, 1hr., Rs15) or catch a ride with anyone going that way. The views and artwork here are amazing, and the *gompa* provides beds for Rs50.

LAHAUL VALLEY लाहौल

With glaciers within arm's reach, the Chandra River canyon takes you back to the end of the ice age. The valley below is watered by fresh water springs and melted snow, its grassy pastures grazed upon by wild horses. Above, framed by majestic peaks and massive glaciers, is **Chandrathal Lake,** the jewel of the valley.

When road conditions permit, the Kullu-Kaza **bus** runs through the valley between **Gramphoo** and **Batal.** Many visitors prefer to deal with the bumpy dirt road on foot. Situated on the Manali-Keylong road, Gramphoo's two *dhabas* have beds available (Rs50). Expect shepherds or family members to join you in bed at any time. It is 17km to **Chatru,** where food and tented accommodation (Rs30) are available; bring a sleeping bag unless you want to freeze to death. Chatru is the trailhead for a trek over the Hamta Pass to Manali. The hike takes two days on the way down and three days to return, and it can get incredibly wet during the monsoon. From Chatru, another 16km takes you to **Shkota Dhara,** where there is rice and *dahl,* a campground, and accommodation in the PWD rest house for an outrageous Rs1000. Fortunately, it's only 12km to Batal, where there are cheap tents and bowls of *thukpa.* After the bridge in Batal, the road forks: the right branch scales the Kunzum-La Pass, while the left one stretches for 18km through the valley until it reaches Chandrathal Lake. There is an idyllic campground nearby. Alternatively, you can descend to Chandrathal on a narrow path that starts at the *gompa* on the Kunzum-La Pass. From Chandrathal, it is another three days of high-altitude walking to **Baralacha-La Pass** on the Manali-Leh road (p. 246). There is no accommodation available between Batal and Baralacha-La, and the closest medical assistance is in Keylong.

JAMMU जम्मू AND KASHMIR کشمیر

India's northernmost state has been called paradise on earth. For centuries travelers have been drawn to Kashmir by its stunning natural beauty. Until a decade or so ago, it was one of the most popular tourist destinations in the whole of Asia, and a Bollywood starlet was filmed frolicking aginst the backdrop of Kashmir's sunning mountainscapes. But Jammu and Kashmir is not just the most beautiful state in India, it is also the most volatile. In recent years, the western half of the state has been wracked by an armed insurgency. So far, the violence has been confined to this area, which includes the predominantly Muslim Kashmir Valley and the region of Jammu, populated by Dogra Hindus. The lake-rimmed capital, Srinagar, is still dominated by the military, and most foreign state departments advise against traveling here or anywhere else in the western part of the state. The eastern part of the state, which consists of the Tibetan Buddhist regions of Ladakh and Zanskar, remains relatively free of violence.

JAMMU & KASHMIR

Jammu and Kashmir

HIGHLIGHTS OF JAMMU AND KASHMIR

The beautiful, medieval town of **Leh** (p. 247), at 3500m, is a base for treks through the surrounding mountain ranges and to the *gompas* which dot the Indus valley.

Approached by the highest motorable pass in the world, the radiant **Nubra Valley** (p. 254) features flower-filled villages, sand dunes, wild camels, and stunning views of the Karakoram.

Kashmir's troubles began when India was partitioned along religious lines in 1947. Although the population was predominantly Muslim, the Hindu raja did not want his kingdom to become part of Pakistan *or* India—and most Kashmiri Muslim leaders agreed with him. In late 1947, however, thousands of Pathan tribesmen, supplied with arms by Pakistan, crossed the border in an attempt to force Kashmir into Pakistan. Desperate, the maharaja turned his state over to India in exchange for military help. The Indian government accepted the offer, agreeing to hold a plebiscite to determine whether the Kashmiri people, and not just the maharaja, wanted to join India. When the shooting stopped, however, Pakistan still held large chunks of Kashmir, and in 1962 China annexed the area of the state now known as Aksai Chin. India and Pakistan went to war over Kashmir again in 1965, but no territory changed hands. The 1948 cease-fire line remains the de facto India-Pakistan border. The plebiscite promised by India has never been held.

At the end of the 1980s, many Kashmiris who had fought against the Soviet presence in Afghanistan returned home with better guns and better training. This, together with widespread Kashmir fears of absorption into India, led to an outbreak of violence in 1989. The violence continues, and has claimed as many as 100,000 lives over the past ten years. In 1995, five foreign tourists were taken hostage in Kashmir; one of them was beheaded. In July 2000, a German backpacker was kidnapped and killed in the Zanskar Valley. Hundreds of people are killed in Kashmir every year, and the rise of extremist Taliban-style military groups makes peace and reconciliation seem unlikely in the short term. Elections were held in autumn 1999, amid bomb blasts, knifings, and an intrusive miliatary presence. The large-scale intrusion across the line of control in Kargil in 1999 nearly escalated into another Indo-Pakistani war. Bombings and guerilla activity continue to be a routine part of life in many areas of the state, and Kashmir's future is uncertain. Although most visitors to the area come across nothing more threatening than high-altitude hikes and breathtaking scenery, the political situation remains dangerous and hard to predict. Think long and hard about your priorities in life before you decide to travel anywhere in Jammu and Kashmir.

THE MANALI-LEH ROAD

Two routes connect Leh to the rest of the world: the Manali-Leh Road and the Srinagar-Leh Road. Each is a two-day-plus haul requiring you to cross several passes well over 5000m. These roads are supposed to be open from mid-June to mid-September, but they can be washed out for days or even weeks by rains and mudslides. Travel is often delayed by accidents, herds of goats, and military checkpoints. If you're on a tight schedule and can get a seat, you might want to fly to Leh, but you'd be missing out on a lot.

WARNING. Following the large-scale Pakistani intrusion across the Line Of Control (LOC) in spring 1999, India has cemented its position in the Dras-Kargil area, leading to increased militant activity in northern and western Kashmir. Traveling along the **Srinagar-Leh Road** can get hairy at times. Stay within the limits of the road, where a strong military presence reduces the risks.

The **Manali-Leh Road** is one of the most beautiful overland journeys on the planet, winding its bumping and grinding way through green mountains, roaring streams, and the bare, stunning, high-altitude desert of Ladakh. The second-highest motorable road in the world, the Manali-Leh road crosses the Rohtang Pass (3980m) to reach the rainshadow and then twists through the Baralacha-La (4892m) and Taglang-La (5325m) passes, before descending to Upshi and following the Indus River to Leh. **Bring warm clothes:** it can get below freezing at the high passes. And try to get a seat at the front: you'll need a crash helmet if you get stuck at the back of the bus. The landscape changes constantly—the lush, green valleys of Manali give way to rugged gorges and barren plateaus, and then to sandstone cliffs and the towering peaks of the Himalayas. The trip comes to an end in green valleys speckled with herds of goats. Local and deluxe buses leave Manali daily (10am, Rs405/800-1000), but if you can make yourself three friends then it might be worth taking a taxi (Rs4000), which will let you stop along the way and still get you into Leh much more quickly. It rarely rains along this road, but when it does, the muddy hills disintegrate and take the road with them. You might have to get off the bus and trudge through the mud past the obstruction.

Small settlements line the road from Manali to Leh, and there are places to stay all along the road. The trip can take anywhere from 30 hours to two or more days, depending on weather conditions, accidents, and the number of military checkpoints. Where you stop is determined by where you happen to be as it starts to get dark. The bus first descends into the Lahaul Valley, often with an overnight stop in Keylong, Lahaul's administrative center, leaving the next morning (4am). In Keylong, **Gyespa Hotel** has rooms with attached bath (Rs200) and hot showers (Rs250). At sunrise, the bus reaches **Darcha** (1hr.; tents Rs35), the trailhead for treks into the **Zanskar Valley.** Over the next two to three hours, the bus climbs the main Himalayan ridge, crossing it at **Baralacha-La** (4892m). The three-day trail for **Chandratal Lake** begins here (see p. 239). The first tea stop is in **Bharatpur** (tents Rs35), 3km below Baralacha-La. A gentle descent into a vast plain brings you to **Sarchu** (4hr., tents Rs150) after which the road makes 27 turns, climbing 1000m to cross the Zanskar range at **Lunga-lacha-La** (5059m). From here, it's "badlands" territory. You first hit the village of **Pang** (8hr.; tents Rs30-50), and, after crossing an unimpressive pass, the road enters the plains of **Rupshu.** At the end of the plains, below the glacier-lined **Taglang-La** (5325m) pass (12hr.), there are thousands of sheep, Pashmina-producing goats, and views of the Karakoram range and the Great Himalayas. The bus then descends into the Ladakhi village of **Rumtse** (14hr.), screeching through more villages and *gompas* before it reaches **Upshi** (16hr.). From then on, it's smooth cruising and happy tooting down the main road to **Leh** (18hr.).

LEH लेह

☎ 01982

The capital of the old kingdom of Ladakh, Leh is remarkably distinct from cities farther south in Kashmir, and often seems closer to Central Asia. Its location at the corner of a 3500m high desert plateau in the middle of the Indus valley, halfway between Punjab and Yarkand on the "southern" silk route and halfway between the Tibetan plains and Kashmir, has made it a vibrant meeting-place for Tibetan Buddhist culture from the east and Islamic influences from the west. Old Leh seems to be stuck in a time-warp—a maze of narrow lanes winding up to the ruins of the Namgyal Palace still dominates the old town, while New Leh thrives on the steady stream of visitors that trickles in during the summer. If the hawking of the Kashmiri traders or the clicking of tourists' cameras gets to be too much, you can always seek refuge in one of the many gorgeous *gompas* and deserted mountain trails just outside the city. Some of these follow the same routes used for centuries by traders hauling goods from Western Tibet over the Chang-La (5547m) and Kardung-La (5602m) and into the bustling bazaars of the ancient city.

> **WARNING.** When you make the road journey, **carry your passport with you at all times.** The routes to Leh come close to areas under Pakistani and Chinese control. When arriving by plane, remember that Leh is 3505m above sea level. **Rest for at least one day** (that means not even walking around and definitely not consuming alcohol) before undertaking anything strenuous, and **watch for any signs of Acute Mountain Sickness (AMS).** The symptoms—headaches, breathlessness and nausea—normally develop during the first 36 hours (see **Trekking: Health and Safety,** p. 34). Leh has an emergency facility for dealing with AMS (24hr. ☎52012 or 52360). Several seats are reserved on every plane out of town for people with AMS symptoms.

GETTING THERE AND GETTING AROUND

Flights: Airport (☎52255), 4km from Leh down Fort Rd. **Taxi** to town Rs80. **Tushita Travel** (☎52076) is an authorized Indian Airlines agent. Open M-Sa 10am-1pm and 2-4pm. During the summer, book several months in advance. Flights are often delayed or cancelled because of bad weather. To: **Chandigarh** (W, 7:50am, 1hr., US$70); **Delhi** (daily, 1½hr., US$105); **Jammu** (M and F, 7:30am, 1hr., US$65); **Srinagar** (Su, 7:30am, 1hr., US$60). Security is tight, especially on flights to Jammu or Srinagar.

Buses: The Tourist Information Office on Fort Rd. by the taxi stand has up-to-date schedules and prices. To: **Diskit** (Tu, Th, and Sa; 5:30am; 8hr.; Rs50); **Hemis** (9:30am, 2hr., Rs25); **Kargil** via **Lamayuru** (5am, 12hr., Rs120); **Matho** (3 per day, 8am-5pm, 1hr., Rs10); **Manali** (3:30am, 48hr., Rs400); **Panamik** (Tu, 5:30am, 8hr., Rs70); **Phyang** (3 per day, 8am-5pm, 30min., Rs10); **Shey, Tikse,** and **Spituk** (every 30min., 8am-7pm, Rs15); **Srinagar** (daily, 5:30am, 48hr., Rs200); **Stok** (3 per day, 8am-5pm, 45min., Rs10). **Minibuses** go to **Alchi, Saspul, Likir,** and **Bagso** (all 4pm).

Local Transportation: The **taxi union** is in the center of town, near the top of Fort Rd. There is a fixed rate of Rs14 per km for all destinations during the tourist season (July-Aug.), but the best way to get around town is on your own two feet.

ORIENTATION AND PRACTICAL INFORMATION

The **main bazaar** marks the western edge of the **Old City.** Running west from the center of the main bazaar is **Fort Rd.,** which has the highest density of restaurants, travel agents, and carpet shops in the city. **Zangsty Rd.** begins at the north end of the main bazaar, connects to Fort Rd. via **Library Rd.,** and then runs north, where two lanes, **Changspa** and **Karzoo,** pass several small guest houses. Buses arrive in the south on **Airport Rd.,** a 10-min. walk from the bazaar.

Tourist Office: Tourist Information Office (☎52935), in the State Bank of India compound on Fort Rd. Open M-Sa 8am-7pm. Off-season: 10am-4pm.

Trekking Agents: Fort Rd. is full of trekking agents. Not all are trustworthy: ask around before putting your life in the hands of a stranger. **RIMO Expeditions,** Zangsty Rd. (☎53348, in Delhi ☎(011) 6136568; www.atrav.com/rimo), is a reputable agency that deals mostly with package tours. Most of the agencies on Fort Rd. such as **Paradise Travels,** Fort Rd., PO Box 137 (☎52408) are better with small groups or solo travelers. Full expeditions with ponies and guide cost US$20-25.

Currency Exchange: State Bank of India has an exchange counter in the same building as the tourist office, just off Fort Rd. Open M-F 10am-2pm, Sa 10am-noon.

Bookstore: Book Worm, Library Rd., next to Pumpernickel German Bakery. Open daily 9am-8pm. **Lehling Bookshop,** in the main bazaar, sells books on Ladakhi and Buddhist art. Open daily 9am-8pm.

Library: Jek State District Library, at the end of Library Rd. Open M-Sa 10am-5pm.

Meditation Centers: Mahabodi Society, up Changspa Rd.; watch for signs on the right. Guided meditation meetings (M-F 4:30pm) and yoga classes (T-Th 3:30) run from June

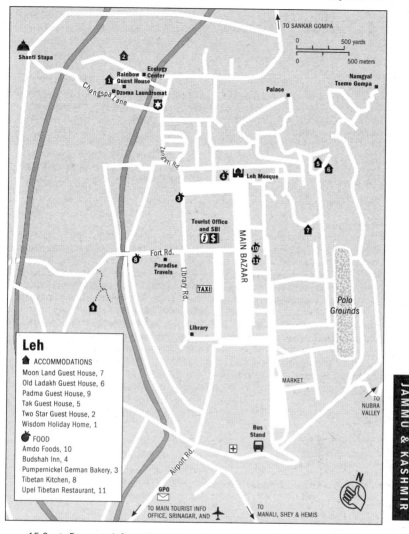

TO SANKAR GOMPA

0   500 yards
0   500 meters

Shanti Stupa

Ecology Center

Rainbow Guest House

Dzoma Laundromat

Changspa Lane

Namgyal Tsemo Gompa

Palace

Zangsti Rd.

Leh Mosque

Tourist Office and SBI

MAIN BAZAAR

Fort Rd.

Paradise Travels

Library Rd.

TAXI

Polo Grounds

Library

MARKET

TO NUBRA VALLEY

Bus Stand

Airport Rd.

GPO

TO MAIN TOURIST INFO OFFICE, SRINAGAR, AND

TO MANALI, SHEY & HEMIS

N

Leh

🏠 ACCOMMODATIONS
Moon Land Guest House, 7
Old Ladakh Guest House, 6
Padma Guest House, 9
Tak Guest House, 5
Two Star Guest House, 2
Wisdom Holiday Home, 1

🍴 FOOD
Amdo Foods, 10
Budshah Inn, 4
Pumpernickel German Bakery, 3
Tibetan Kitchen, 8
Upel Tibetan Restaurant, 11

15-Sept. For more information, or longer meditation retreats, contact **Milarepa Meditation Centre** (☎44025), in Davachan, Choglamsar, on the road to Tikse.

Laundry: Dzomsa, Zangsty Rd., tries to protect the river by dumping in a desert pit away from Leh. The service is highly recommended (Rs10-15). Open M-Sa 9am-8pm.

Police: (☎52167), halfway up Zangsty Rd., on the right after the Changspa Rd. turn off.

Pharmacy: Himalaya Medical Store, opposite SNM Hospital. Open daily 9am-6pm.

Hospital: SNM Hospital (☎52012, 24hr. emergency ☎52360), below the bus stand, is well maintained and has a special ward for tourists (most of them AMS-afflicted).

Internet: Slow and expensive. **Gypsy's World,** Fort Rd., in the White House complex between town and the Indian Airlines office, has Internet access for Rs5 per min., Rs50 per page to send emails written off-line. Open daily 9am-10pm.

Post Office: GPO, 2km from town on Airport Rd. Open M-F 10am-5pm. There is a small sub-branch in the middle of the Main Bazaar. **Postal Code:** 194101.

STRANGE MEDICINE Sniffly? Rheumatic? Plagued by vindictive demons? Ladakhi *lha-bas* can treat all of these afflictions (and more) merely by sucking the appropriate vile liquid directly through your skin! A *lha-ba* typically begins her therapeutic career by being possessed by spirits. Qualified lamas administer an initiation rite that enables her to control these spirits, channeling their influence into powers of healing. During a healing session, an *lha-ba* is first led into a trance by ritual drumbeating and singing. In that state, she is able to locate the afflicting agent, in the form of internal fluids or objects, and draw them out with her mouth without breaking the patient's skin. Reports of these nasty substances (which the *lha-ba* repeatedly spits out during the process) cover everything from "red and lumpy" or "black and tarry" to "pebble" or "small, moving, salamander thing." *Lha-bas* still practice in Ladakh; ask around, but be warned—sessions can get violent to the point of necessitating slaps on the head with a sword. *Let's Go* does not recommend this. You should see a *lha-ba* only if you have a serious, long-term problem.

ACCOMMODATIONS

Leh is full of little guest houses, most of them on the outskirts of town along Changspa Rd. and off Fort Rd.

- **Old Ladakh Guest House** (☎52951), Old Town. Facing the mosque, turn right into a narrow alley. Continue for 150m through the labyrinth. Centrally located with pleasant rooms off a small, shaded courtyard. Singles Rs80; doubles Rs120.

- **Two Star Guest House** (☎52250), in Karzoo, 20m past the path to Wisdom and Rainbow. You will be treated like family as you sit in the windowed kitchen gazing at the snow-clad Stok Kangri. Ladakhi specialties take time, so tell "mother" a few hours ahead if you want *skiw* for dinner. Dorm beds Rs80; singles Rs150; doubles with huge windows and great views Rs350.

- **Wisdom Holiday Home** (☎52427), in Karzoo. Walk up Zangsty Rd., continue along the road from the Ecology Centre, and follow the signs. In a wheat patch, with views of a bleached-white *chorten* and the rugged cliffs behind it. Doubles Rs150-350.

- **Padma Guest House** (☎52630). 10min. down Fort Rd.; watch for a sign pointing to a path on the left. 15-room complex with rooftop restaurant, sparkling new rooms, and hot showers. Old rooms Rs250-300, new rooms Rs1200. Bargain mercilessly.

- **Tak Guest House** (☎53643), opposite the Old Ladakh Guest House, Old Town. Everything here is tiny, but the friendliness of the family that runs the place turns its small size into a plus. Singles Rs80; doubles Rs150-250.

- **Moonland Guest House** (☎52175), Old Town; continue 50m down the alley from Old Ladakh toward the polo ground and watch for signs on the right. Stands out from the dinginess of the Old Town. A good chance to experience a medieval atmosphere while protected by modern comforts. Singles Rs150; doubles Rs250

FOOD

With authentic Tibetan and Indian restaurants, not-so-authentic Italian ones, and Punjabi samosa/sweets/tea stalls in the bazaar, Leh is capable of satisfying just about any craving. Bottled mineral water is hauled over the passes on diesel-chugging Tata trucks; head to Dzomsa, on Zangsty Rd., for pressure-boiled, eco-safe drinking water. Although there are more overpriced "German" bakeries in town than you can shake a strudel at, the tastiest bread is the Kashmiri *naan* sold in the bakeries behind the mosque. No restaurants serve Ladakhi food, but some guest houses will cook you *skiw* or *chutagi* if you give them enough notice.

◪ **Upel Tibetan Restaurant,** in the middle of the Main Bazaar, 3rd fl. The Darjeeling cooks seem to have mastered the culinary arts of Tibet and China. Great views of the bazaar. Dishes Rs30-80. Open daily 7:30am-9:30pm.

◪ **Budshah Inn Restaurant,** at the end of the Main Bazaar, just to the left of the mosque. One of the few places in Leh (outside of the kebab vendors of the evening bazaar) to get Kashmiri cuisine. *Rista* (Rs70) and various tandoori meats are accompanied by enough rice to feed an army. Open daily 8am-10pm.

Tibetan Kitchen, 5min. down Fort Rd., just before the White House. Clean tablecloths and artistic decor. Tibetan specialties like *shaba-gleb* (meat bread; Rs40) and Amdo bean stew (Rs45). Wash it all down with a pot of mint tea in a funny-looking lama hat teapot. Open daily 8am-3pm and 6-11pm.

Penguin Bar and Restaurant, 3 min. down Fort Rd. Serves breakfast and decent veg. food to a backpacker crowd. Dishes Rs40-80. Beer Rs60. Open daily 7am-10pm.

Pumpernickel German Bakery, between Fort Rd. and Zangsty Rd. As much an expat community center as an eatery. Board posts bulletins about taxis to Manali and ads for more trekking partners. Desserts Rs30-45; excellent yak-cheese and tomato sandwiches Rs30; huge breakfasts Rs50; and a range of breads. Open daily 7am-9pm.

Edelweiss, Fort Rd. Small and white, crisp and bright, and not a Wiener Schnitzel in sight. Good Indian and Chinese food and barbecue Rs40-80. Open daily 8am-10pm.

👁 SIGHTS

SENGGE NAMGYAL PALACE. Towering above the Old Town, this nine-story palace was built during the 1630s to emphasize Leh's ascendancy over Shey as the Ladakhi capital. It is said to have inspired the Potala Palace in Lhasa. The opening of the East Gate used to be marked by the roar of a caged lion; nowadays the gate serves as the entrance to the only well-maintained room in the palace, which houses old *thankas* and swords. Badly damaged by war, the rest of the palace is in ruins. *(Open daily 8am-5pm. Rs25.)*

SHANTI STUPA. Referred to by locals as the **Japan Stupa,** the Shanti Stupa in Changspa village is at the top of 560 steps. If you haven't passed out by the time you get to the top, feast your eyes on the legacy of Fujii Guraji, a Japanese Buddhist who moved to India in 1931. One of many Japanese-built stupas in the region, this Peace Pagoda, built in 1983, features gilt panels depicting episodes from the life of the Buddha. *(3km west of the bazaar; walk to Changspa and follow a direct line to the stupa. Open 24hr.)*

NAMGYAL TSEMO GOMPA. High above the palace, the red Namgyal Tsemo Gompa is distinguished by its *gon-khang*, which features sculptures of wrathful deities and wall-paintings of benign bodhisattvas. *(Open briefly in the morning and evening when a lama climbs up from Samkar to light the butter lamps. The lama's movements are hard to predict. The inside is dark—bring a flashlight.)*

OTHER SIGHTS. The imposing **masjid** at the end of the main bazaar was built in 1666 by the Ladakhi king Deldan Namgyal as a vassal's offering to the Mughal emperor. The mosque is built in a style more Ladakhi than Islamic. The *namaaz* prayer calls can be heard five times a day in every corner of Leh. The **polo grounds** above the Old Town see annual tournaments and occasional games between locals and soldiers, who chase the ball on sturdy ponies amid clouds of dust, parked trucks, and barking dogs. If you see a man with a mallet riding through town on horseback, follow him to the polo grounds to witness the spectacle. The **Sankar Gompa,** the official local residence of the reformist Gelug-pa ("Yellow Hat") sect, houses a hundred-headed, thousand-armed image of Avalokitesvara, the Bodhisattva of Compassion. *(Walk along the footpath across the fields from the Ecological Centre. Open daily 8-11am and 3-6pm. Rs20.)*

THE LION KING The mysterious circumstances surrounding King Sengge Namgyal's birth provide a fairy-tale accompaniment to his castle's splendor. In the early 1600s, Ladakhi king Vamyang Namgyal's army suffered ignominious defeat at the hands of the Balti king, Ali Min. Ladakh was looted, its king imprisoned, and doom was in the air. Then, inexplicably, the Balti forces withdrew. Vamyang was subsequently restored to power, and he married one of Ali Min's daughters. A few months later, she bore a son. Legend tells of a romance between the imprisoned king and the beautiful Balti princess, resulting in an illicit pregnancy. Balti sources record a dream of king Ali Min's in which he saw a lion jump out of the river and enter his daughter; at that instant, she conceived a baby, Sengge. These things happen. The greatest of Ladakhi kings, Sengge Namgyal ("Lion Victorious"), left the region with a legacy of grand castles and monasteries.

🛍 SHOPPING

There are plenty of opportunities to shop (and get swindled) in Leh. Masks, carpets, jewelry, shawls, and so-called "antiques" fill the shops along Fort Rd., but prices are often significantly higher than those in Delhi, Shimla, or Dharamsala. Many of the traders are "hello friend" Kashmiris who come to Leh only during the tourist season. The **Tibetan Children's Village Handicrafts Centre,** on the road toward Choglamsar, sells crafts made at the Tibetan Children's Village (open M-Sa 9:30am-5pm). The **Tibetan Handicraft Emporium,** in the main market, is approved by the Dalai Lama, no less (open M-Sa 9am-1pm and 2-7pm). The **Ecology Centre's** handicraft store sells local Ladakhi goods (open M-Sa 11am-5pm), and the **Co-operative store,** in the Galdan Hotel complex just off Fort Rd., sells similar items. These places support the local community and have fixed prices. **Cashmere Ladakh Arts,** on Zangsty Rd., is a private shop that prides itself on its fixed prices and no-hassle salesmanship. **Kpleasure Arts,** on Fort Rd., specializes in pashmina and in Ladakhi art. Shopping elsewhere is much like a sophisticated mugging.

🏳 VOLUNTEER OPPORTUNITIES

Travelers who would like to volunteer either with the **Leh Women's Alliance** or the **Ecology Centre,** or those wishing to arrange homestays at a Ladakhi farm (1 month min.) should contact **The International Society for Ecology and Culture (ISEC),** Apple Barn, Week, Totnes, Devon TQ9 6JP, UK—preferably a year ahead. The center has ongoing projects that need volunteers from time to time and can also refer would-be volunteers to other local organizations. (☎(44 1803) 868650; fax 868651; email isecuk@gov.apc.org; www.isec.org.uk. Open M-Sa 10am-4pm.) The **Student Educational and Cultural Movement of Ladakh** (SECMOL), at the Ridzong Labrang Complex in Old Leh (☎52421; fax 53012), between the bazaar and the polo grounds, has volunteer positions at its camp for Ladakhi youth in Choglamsar.

🏔 TREKKING AROUND LEH

Set between the world's two highest mountain ranges, Ladakh is a favorite destination for trekkers, who come both for the scenery and for the relatively reliable weather. During the trekking season (June-Oct.), the days are scorchingly hot and the nights bitterly cold. Depending on your previous experience, you may want to hire a porter or a guide, but you should not attempt treks deep in the mountains with fewer than three people. You can rent and occasionally buy equipment (tent Rs100 per day, stove Rs15 per day) in the **White House,** Fort Rd. (☎53048).

LIKIR-KHALSE TREK. Also known as the "Baby Trek," the **Likir-Khalse** (2-4 days), leads over moderate passes to more remote villages and *gompas*. One of the routes best suited to solo trekking is the one through the **Markha Valley** (7-9 days), which

> **WARNING.** Allow several days to acclimatize before setting out on a trek; altitude sickness is very common among visitors. If you pass out halfway up a mountain, you will probably die. Consult one of the many **trekking agents** in town (see p. 248). In case of accidents, the only available rescue is the military helicopter that operates at a cost of at least Rs40,000 per hour, flying out only if there is a guarantee that the cost will be met. Before setting out, whether you're alone or with an organized group, be sure to leave the following with your guest house owner in Leh: detailed itinerary; photocopies of your passport, visa, and insurance policy; three filled-out forms guaranteeing payment; acceptance certificate; and indemnity bond. All are available from any travel agent in town.

starts either in Stok or Spitak and ends in **Hemis.** There are supplies along the route and no difficult river crossings, though passing the Stok-La (4900m) on the second day is a challenge. The demanding **Lamayuru-Padum-Darcha** trek (19 days), which crosses both the Samskar range and the Himalayas, is probably the best known and most traveled trek in the Western Himalayas. Provisions are sold from tents along the way.

KARZOK-KIBBER TREK. The demanding **Karzok-Kibber trek** is one of the best in the area. It starts at **Tso-Morari Lake,** one day from Leh by car (you need a **permit** to reach Tso-Morari; see p. 254), and takes you through **Rupshu,** inhabited by the nomadic **Changpas.** On day four, you'll cross the **Ohirsta Phu River,** which usually flows from Tibet to Tso-Morari, but reverses flow seasonally. This difficult crossing requires proper equipment. From there, the trek climbs to the **Parang Pass,** where it descends to the beautiful village of **Kibber** in Spiti (see Near Kaza, p. 243).

📷 DAYTRIPS FROM LEH

Fifteen kilometers up the main road from Leh is the ancient Ladakhi capital of **Shey.** The surrounding hillsides are home to the famous giant twin images of Sakyamuni. The one of gilt copper is a part of a palace temple; the other, supposedly made in the 17th century by Nepalese craftsmen, is in a large temple 300m from the palace, past a group of *chortens* (open daily 8am-8pm. Rs20). Four kilometers farther up the road, on a craggy bluff, is **Tikse,** the most photographed *gompa* in Ladakh. A few kilometers above Tikse, you can get off the bus and cross the Indus to reach the **Stakma Gompa,** which rises dramatically on a 60m-high rock from the flat Indus Valley. The *gompa*'s three temples are small but well-maintained, and the views from their windows are superb. (Admission Rs20.)

From Stakma, you can make out the **Matho Gompa** to the southwest, set on a hill at the foot of the glacier-carved mountain. Separated from the Stakma *gompa* by 7km of meadows and barley fields, Matho, the only monastery in Ladakh that belongs to the Saskya-pa sect, is famous for the oracles delivered here. Lamas are chosen every three years and then spend several months following a strict regime of fasting and prayer until they are able to perform miraculous feats and deliver prophecies. The tiny *gon-khang* at the top of the *gompa* contains fierce images of deities armed with shining sabres. Unlike in most other *gon-khangs*, the ferocious faces here are not covered; women are not allowed to enter.

From Matho, descend to the left and follow the path at the foot of the ridge for 12km until you reach **Stok,** the current residence of the Namgyal dynasty. The queen has converted four rooms into a museum that displays *thankas* and other family heirlooms. The turquoise-inlaid crown once belonged to a Chinese princess of the Tang dynasty who married a Tibetan king. Curiously enough, this is China's oldest claim to Tibet. (Open daily 8am-6pm. Rs25.)

Four kilometers from Saspol (up the Indus Valley from Leh) and across the river is Ladakh's oldest and most precious *gompa*, **Alchi,** a village founded in the 11th century. Volumes have been written about the wall paintings inside the two low buildings. Bring a strong flashlight; the *gompa* is unlit. **Lotsava Guest House,** 50m to the left of where the taxis stop, has a quiet garden (singles Rs80; doubles Rs150).

THE NUBRA VALLEY

For centuries, caravans have trekked across Khardung-La on the road between Punjab and Yarkand. The Nubra ("green") Valley used to be a major stopover point just before (or just after) the scorching trials of the Karakoram. Surrounded by the mighty mountains of Ladakh, the Nubra Valley has a highly varied landscape, covering long stretches of barren desert as well areas of lush greenery. Recent conflicts have reduced the passage of caravans, and only a small section of the valley (between Panamik and Hunder) is now open to the latest sources of foreign exchange: tourists. A new road has made Khardung-La the highest motorable pass in the world, traveled along daily (in one direction per day, because of safety concerns) by military and tourist convoys and the occasional camel.

> ▼ **WARNING.** Four newly opened areas in Ladakh—Drok-pa, Nubra Valley, Pangong Lake, and Tso-Morari Lake—require a **special permit,** issued by the Deputy Commissioner in Leh. The 7-day permit can be obtained only through a travel agent; bring a photocopy of your passport and visa. Officially, you need five people to get the permit, though there is nothing to stop you from traveling alone once you have the permit. Most travel agencies have a ready stock of photocopies recently taken from other travelers' passports. These will be provided at a cost; expect to pay Rs100 each. The permit takes a day to arrange. You will be asked to leave a copy of your permit at every check-post; bring at least 5 photocopies with you.

DISKIT

The administrative headquarters of the Nubra Valley, the western part of Diskit is an unimpressive collection of ugly concrete buildings and the eastern half is a jumble of village houses and barley fields. There are paths on both sides of the *chortens,* but you should not use the ones on the left because the prayer-wheels should be turned only in a clockwise direction. From the prayer wheel on the main road, it's a 30-minute climb up to the *gompa* along the path to the left, over a hill covered in *chortens.* There are great views from the windows of the new *du-khang* (assembly hall). You can also visit the protective deities in the *gon-khang.* Their fierce faces are unmasked on only one day of the year; their veils, however, make it safe for women to enter (Rs20).

Buses from Leh go to Diskit (Tu, Th, and Sa; 5am; 8hr.; Rs50), and return to Leh the next day. Guest houses line the *mani* wall, and most serve good, cheap food. When coming from the *gompa* and the main road, **Sunrise Guest House** (☎20011) is on your right. (Doubles Rs150.) **D. Khangsar Guest House** (☎20014), farther down a path to the right, is probably the best place to experience village life—you'll be shacking up with the cows. Nothing but the best is good enough for the cows: the rooms are clean, carpeted, and dirt cheap. (Rooms Rs50. Breakfast Rs15, dinner Rs25.) Follow the road for 10 minutes to New Diskit, near the bus stand, where the only restaurant in town serves rice and *dahl* (Rs25).

HUNDER

At the end of New Diskit, a dirt road turns off to the right into barley fields, continuing along spectacular pastures, creeks, and sand dunes for 7km until it reaches Hunder. This easy walk is one the most picturesque in the whole valley. The furthest your permit will allow you to go is the *gompa* by the bridge along the main road, but most of the interesting sights lie outside the *gompa* itself; the paintings inside the biggest *chorten* are 50m below it; the temples are on the ridge above.

Once in Hunder, walk with the military barracks on your left until you see a sign for the **Snow Leopard Guest House** on the right. (Singles Rs60; doubles with bath Rs150.) They serve an enormous dinner (Rs40). **Moon Land (Nerchungpa) Guest House,** deeper inside the village, is kind of hard to find, but rooms (Rs75) are spacious and meals (Rs40) can be taken in the flower-filled garden. There are also **campsites** in Hunder (Rs100-150), but it gets cold at night.

SUMUR

A large village well worth exploring, Sumur is lined by *chortens* and a *mani* wall. Keeping these always on your right, walk up to **Sampan Ling Gompa.** Almost as big as Diskit Gompa, it has spectacular views and a school for young monks. A daily **bus** runs from Diskit to Sumur (evenings, 2¼hr., Rs7) and returns the next morning. There are a number of guest houses along the way. **Stakrey Guest House,** farther to the right, is the best—ask locals for directions. Doubles with semi-private, almost-clean bathrooms are Rs200, including breakfast and dinner. **Tashis Khahgsar Guest House,** next to the school, 30m off the main road, has new rooms with common baths (doubles Rs150) and a spacious, shaded garden. There are also few campsites in town, including **Sun and Sun,** off the main road (Rs100-150).

SRINAGAR سرینگر ☎ 0194

Until ten years ago, Srinagar was one of the biggest tourist destinations in India, with over half a million people visiting every year. Things have changed. Between 1989 and 1996, Srinagar was a war zone. Kidnappings, bomb blasts, and random shoot-outs conspired to make Srinagar a very dangerous place indeed. The situation in Kashmir is still dangerous and unpredictable: bring yourself up to date on recent developments before considering traveling here. Over the past couple of years, tourism has started to return to Srinagar, and though your embassy will advise you against going anywhere near western Kashmir, the risks to safety-conscious tourists these days are small enough to make a trip dangerous but doable. This is one of the most beautiful places in the world; come here now and you will be one of the lucky few to see this wonderful city before the package tours return.

> **WARNING.** Tensions in Kashmir have eased significantly since 1996, but travel to the western half of Jammu and Kashmir (including the Kashmir Valley) is still risky. **Foreign tourists have been the targets of acts of extreme violence as recently as summer 2000. People's heads have been lopped off.** Border skirmishes between India and Pakistan erupted into a crisis in Kargil in June 1999, and militant activity remains widespread throughout the state. Travelers are strongly advised to stay within the limits of Srinagar city, where the strong presence of the Indian Army somewhat mitigates the risk.

GETTING THERE. Delhi is the best access point for Srinagar. **Jet Airways** has an office near the bank and is open M-Sa 10am-5pm. Both Indian Airlines and Jet Airways have daily flights (1 per day, 1hr., US$90-115). Buses leave daily (12-15hr., Rs250). Alternatively, you can fly in from **Leh** (Sa, 1hr.) or take the bus along one of the world's highest highways (daily, 48hr., Rs200).

ORIENTATION AND PRACTICAL INFORMATION. Situated between the shores of the **Dal** and **Nagin Lakes** and flush against the **Jhelum River,** Srinagar is divided into two parts: the old town and the new. On **Residency Rd.** in new town, most tourist needs can be met. The main **bank** in town, **ANZ Grindlays,** directly on Bund Residency Rd., changes currency and traveler's checks and gives cash advances on Visa and MC. (Open M-Sa 10am-3pm.) There is slow Internet access available all over town (normally Rs50-80 per hr.). Also in this area are the **tourist registration office,** which extends visas (open M-Sa 10am-6pm), and the central **post office** (open M-Sa 10am-5pm). **Postal Code** 190001.

ACCOMMODATIONS AND FOOD. A trip to Srinagar would be incomplete without a stay on one of Dal Lake's houseboats, especially since most of the on-land hotels remain occupied by the good old Indian Army boys. Nagin is the quieter of the city's two lakes, but it is the houseboat itself and its location that really matter. Pre-booking in Delhi will save you a lot of hassle, provided you can find a travel agent who won't charge you a huge commission. Any tourist office should be able to recommend a reliable booking agent (most places tend to book only for one particular houseboat or group of houseboats). One reputable agent is **Trail Finders**, 125 Bhagat Singh Market (☎ (011) 3340967; fax 3340973; email trailfinder37@hotmail.com). If you arrive without a place to slumber, a travel agency at the airport will be happy to find a houseboat for you.

A stay on a houseboat generally costs significantly more than other lodgings elsewhere in India, but it's usually more than worth it, if only for the incredible people you will meet aboard. Prices range from around US$4 to more than US$60 per day. A good price bracket to aim for is US$10-15; you should only chose the very cheapest places if you are ready to get used to the smell of raw sewage. One reliable option is **Lily of World** on Nagin Lake. Although pricey (US$20 per night), it's worth it for excellent food and superb service. If your houseboat owner hasn't been feeding you enough curry, there are two commendable restaurants on Residency Rd. **Moghul Darbar** serves Kashmiri favorites for Rs100-150. (Open daily 10am-6pm.) **Cafe de Linz**, just a block away, has meals from Rs100.

🔲 **SIGHTS.** Many of the city's most beautiful sights are in the old town, where most of the serious fighting took place ten years ago. The streets are poorly marked, if they are marked at all, and if you are without a guide (not a good idea), it would be wise to hire a rickshaw (Rs100-150) to take you around. The **Jhomia Mosque,** Nowhatta Rd., is the largest in Srinagar, and is open to the public. Srinagar's oldest mosque is on Fatehkadal Rd. It was built entirely from wood during the 14th century by a Persian *shah*, who brought Islam to India after the Prophet appeared to him in a dream. Non-Muslims and women are not allowed inside. The tomb at **Roza bal Kangar** purportedly holds the remains of none other than Jesus, who allegedly wandered through Kashmir in his youth.

Many of Srinagar's world-renowned Mughal Gardens were closed during the worst period of violence in Kashmir, but most are open today. **Shalimar Garden** is open, but parts of its central fountains are under repair. The awe-inspiring **Nishat Garden,** however, is in full working order. *(Both open sunrise-7pm; until 6pm in winter.)*

🔼 **SCENERY AND TREKS.** Srinagar's biggest attractions are the mountains that surround the city. These offer some of the most spectacular trekking anywhere in the Himalayas. While it is simply a good idea to have someone accompany you around the city, especially at night, you **absolutely must** take a guide with you when you leave the city to trek. **It is not safe to go trekking alone,** and the police will certainly hassle you if you are found outside the city without a guide.

The best way to organize a safe trek into the hills is to do it through your houseboat or through another tourist agency in town, who will arrange a guide, food supplies, and horses (Rs40-60 per day). Popular treks include those to **Sonomarg** (80km from Srinagar), where you can ride horseback through a pass and climb a glacier, and to the **Gulmag Valley,** which has the world's highest 18-hole golf course. One of the most beautiful treks is around **Pahalgam** (97km from Srinagar), where you can go on horse to the Andranath Cave, a holy Hindu pilgrimage site.

📖 **SHOPPING.** No one escapes Srinagar without some exposure to high-intensity Kashmiri salesmanship—whether it's carpets, papier-mâché, silver, or shawls, you'll be tempted to drop some serious rupees. Prices for Kashmiri **handicrafts** are generally better here than anywhere else, and there's also less hassle; most salesmen aren't working for a commission. Family-owned or collective outfits are the most reliable sources for quality products; your houseboat owner will probably have a cousin who runs a carpet shop.

PUNJAB ਪੰਜਾਬ AND HARYANA हरियाणा

In 1947, when Partition divided the Punjab between India and Pakistan, only two of the five rivers to which the Persian *punj aab* refers were left inside India's new borders. Nineteen years later, what was left of the Indian state was divided again, this time along linguistic lines, to form the states of Punjab and Haryana. These states share a capital (Chandigarh), a fertile geography, and the pride of overcoming a long and turbulent history to become India's most prosperous region.

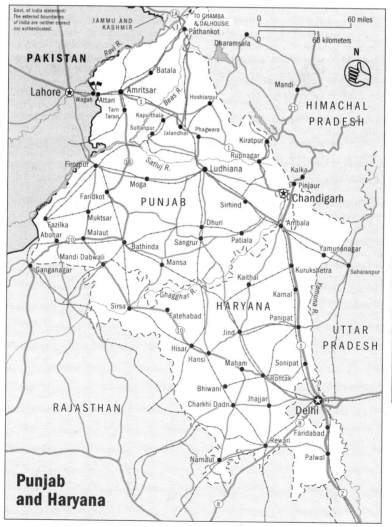

Punjab has long been the foyer through which aggressive guests have entered the subcontinent—and stayed. The arrival of the Aryans here in 1500 BC led to the writing of the *Vedas* and the *Mahabharata*. With the 1526 Battle of Panipat came the Mughals, who dominated the region until the advent of the British viceroyalty in the mid-18th century. Punjab has had a strong cultural impact on India, largely through the Sikh religion, founded during the 15th century by Guru Nanak. Although Nanak's religion spread throughout India, the majority of Sikhs—and their holy city of Amritsar—are in Punjab (see **Sikhism**, p. 83).

But prosperity and peace have not gone hand in hand in Punjab. Of the estimated 500,000 people killed in the massacres that followed Partition of 1947, more died in Punjab than anywhere else. More recently, there has been friction in Punjab between moderates and Sikh militants of the Shiromani Akali Dal party, who demand the formation of an independent Sikh nation, Khalistan ("Land of the Pure"). Things came to a head in 1983-84, with Sikh-militant massacres of Hindus and a subsequent army raid on the militants' headquarters in Amritsar's Golden Temple. The siege of the holy site led to Sikh army desertions, mutinies, and, eventually, the murder of Indira Gandhi by two of her Sikh bodyguards. Ensuing Hindu rioting, in which thousands of Sikhs were slaughtered, meant an increase in support for the Khalistan movement that has only recently begun to wane.

HIGHLIGHTS OF PUNJAB AND HARYANA

Amritsar's **Golden Temple** (p. 266), the most sacred site of the Sikh religion, is one of the most astoundingly beautiful places in the whole of India.

Weird and wonderful **Chandigarh's** (p. 258) pre-planned sectors and structures represent a dead Frenchman's dream of the future, set in pre-poured concrete.

CHANDIGARH चंडीगढ़ ਚੰਡੀਗੜ੍ਹ ☎ 0172

Chandigarh was born of the starry-eyed optimism of India's newly independent government. When Punjab (including present-day Haryana) had been partitioned, its original capital, Lahore, lay across the border in Pakistan. A new capital was needed, and the Nehru government decided on the present site of Chandigarh because of its scenic views and fertile land. Nehru employed a team of crack Western architects, transplanting their ideas for a functional, well-organized European habitat into an Indian setting. The most prominent of the architects, Le Corbusier (the artist formerly known as M. Charles Jeanneret), seized this opportunity to mobilize his plans for a revolution in urban landscape; the result was a huge grid of broad, park-filled avenues and clean-cut "sectors." Today, Le Corbusier's California dream of "sun, space, and silence" has become crowded and polluted, but it still has some tranquil and refreshing spots. Many Indians love Chandigarh for its cleanliness, orderliness, and relative lack of animals in the streets, but foreigners are often disappointed for the same reasons; this is not the India as seen on TV. But Chandigarh can be a welcome contrast to traditional India, and a stay here provides a break from the whirl and swirl of other Indian cities.

▣ GETTING THERE AND GETTING AROUND

Flights: Airport, 11km out of town (auto-rickshaw Rs80-120). **Indian Airlines** (☎ 703510) flies to: **Amritsar** (W and F, 30min., US$65); **Delhi** (W and F, 1:15pm, 40min., US$75); and **Leh** (W, 9:20am, 1hr., US$70). Book well in advance for Leh.

Trains: The **railway station** is 8km southeast of town. Local bus #37 connects the station to the bus stand (20min., Rs5). Auto-rickshaws will go the distance for Rs20-30. **Train Reservation Enquiry** (☎ 653131), on the 3rd fl. of the bus stand, open M-Sa 8am-8pm, Su 8am-2pm. To: **Delhi** (4 per day, 1am-5:30pm; *Shatabdi Exp.* 2006, 6:50am; *Shatabdi Exp.* 2012, 12:30pm; 3½hr.; A/C chair Rs450). For **Jammu** and **Rishikesh**, go to **Ambala** (several per day, 1hr., Rs45) and get your connection there. Tickets for

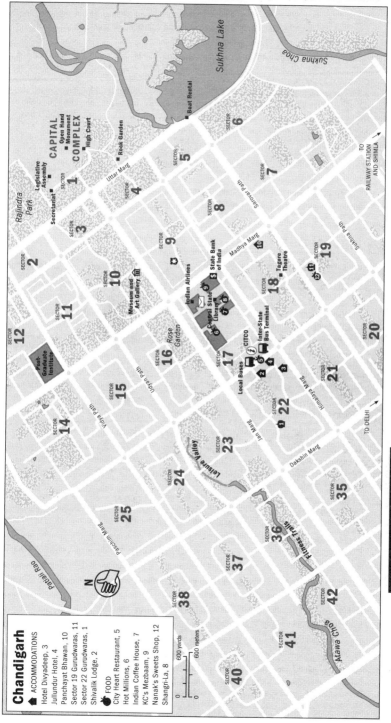

Chandigarh

⌂ ACCOMMODATIONS
Hotel Divyadeep, 3
Jullundur Hotel, 4
Panchayat Bhawan, 10
Sector 19 Gurudwaras, 11
Sector 22 Gurudwaras, 1
Shivalik Lodge, 2

🍴 FOOD
City Heart Restaurant, 5
Hot Millions, 6
Indian Coffee House, 7
KC's Mezbaan, 9
Nanak's Sweets Shop, 12
Shangri-La, 8

trains from Ambala can be bought in Chandigarh if you book a day in advance. For **Amritsar** and **Shimla**, you have to change in **Kalka** (several per day, 30min., Rs30) for the narrow-gauged rail. Tickets sold only in Kalka.

Buses: Inter-State Bus Terminal, on the southwest side of Sector 17, opposite the hotels in Sector 22. Buses depart for **Amritsar** (every 30min., 4am-11pm, 5hr., Rs92; deluxe 2:15pm, 4hr., Rs200); **Dehra Dun** (every 10min., 6:45am-8:30pm, 5½hr., Rs95; deluxe every hr., 6:45am-8:30pm, 5hr., Rs205); **Delhi** (frequent, 7am-10:30pm, 5½hr., Rs95; deluxe Rs250); **Dharamsala** (10 per day, 5am-1pm, 8hr., Rs110; deluxe 3am and 11pm, Rs220); **Jaipur** (6 per day, 4am-2:50pm, 12hr., Rs185; deluxe 8:30am, Rs380); **Jammu** (7, 10am, and 1pm; 8hr.; Rs135); **Manali** (7 per day, 5am-3:30pm, 12hr., Rs165); **Rishikesh** (10:30am and 8:30pm, 8hr., Rs108); **Shimla** (4:30am-7pm; deluxe 9:30, 11:30am, and 1pm, Rs140). **Dalhousie** or **Chamba** can be reached via **Pathankot** (8hr., Rs110). Pathankot to Dalhousie (10 per day, 6:40am-5pm, 3½hr., Rs40).

Local Transportation: Cycle-rickshaws charge Rs10 for a 2-sector trip. **Auto-rickshaws** charge about double. Local **buses** leave from the main bus station, Sector 17. Bus #13 goes to the Rock Garden (15min., Rs5), Bus #37 to the train station (20min., Rs5).

✦ ORIENTATION

No one could accuse Chandigarh of being illogical—it is a planned city plotted onto on a massive grid—but it can be confusing nonetheless, as all the roads look practically identical. The streets run northwest to southeast and northeast to southwest, dividing the town into 50 sectors. Each sector is a self-sufficient unit with its own market places and shopping centers. **Sector 1** is to the north, where the main government buildings, **Sukhna Lake,** and the **Rock Garden,** are situated. The rest are numbered from west to east, then east to west, in rows proceeding to the south. **Sector 17** is the heart of the city where most services, including the **bus station,** are located. The adjacent **Sector 9** affords a look into Chandigarh's affluent homes and suburban tranquility. **Sector 22** has its share of cheap restaurants and hotels and is home to several interesting temples.

▨ PRACTICAL INFORMATION

Tourist Office: Chandigarh Industrial and Tourism Development Corp. (CITCO), (☎704614, railway station ☎658005) has offices upstairs in the bus stand (open M-Sa 9am-5pm) and at the railway station (open during train arrivals). At the bus stand, there are also **Punjab** (☎781138), **UP** (☎707649), and **HP** (☎708569) **Tourist Information Centres.** Open M-F 9am-5pm.

Currency Exchange: Banks cluster around the "Bank Square" in Sector 17B. **Bank of Baroda** (☎709692) changes traveler's checks and gives cash advances on Visa and MC. Open M-F 10am-2pm, Sa 10am-noon.

Luggage Storage: At the bus terminal, for Rs2 per day. Open daily 9am-5pm.

Bookstore: Many in Sector 17. **The English Bookstore,** Sector 17E. **Capital Book Depot,** farther west along the row past the cinema. Both open M-Sa 10am-8pm.

Library: Central State Library, Sector 17B (☎702565). Open M-F 10am-5pm, Sa 10am-2pm; closed the last Sa of every month.

Market: Sectors 17, 22, and 23 are said to have the best markets.

Police: (☎742655) Police Headquarters, opposite Sector 9. Open M-Sa 10am-6pm.

Pharmacy: All around the medical center in Sector 17. Several late-night pharmacies in Sector 22-C, like **Anil and Co.,** Bayshop #42 (☎777565). Open daily 8am-9:30pm.

Hospital/Medical Services: Post Graduate Institute (PGI), Sector 12 (☎543823-27). The best hospital in Chandigarh and one of the most reputable in India. 24hr. emergency services. **Government Medical College and Hospital,** Sector 32, Dakshin Marg (☎665253-59, emergency ext. 1200), has an ambulance service.

Internet: Cyber Cafe, Sector 17B (☎712209), opposite KC Mezbaam's. Connections are most reliable in the morning and late evening. Rs35 per hr. Open M-Sa 9am-10pm.

Post Office: GPO, Sector 17A. Open M-Sa 10am-5pm. **DHL** and other express couriers are in Sector 17. **Postal Code:** 160017.

▟ ACCOMMODATIONS

Staying in Chandigarh is easy on the wallet and can be an experience in itself. Treat yourself to simplicity in that bastion of Sikh hospitality, the **gurudwara,** where stubborn persistence in the face of glowering, spear-wielding guardians will eventually be rewarded with a large room with floor mats open to everyone, usually for free. Unless you plan to stay in one in Amritsar, don't pass up this chance to see Sikhism from the inside. No cigarettes, alcohol, or other intoxicants are allowed inside the compound. If this isn't quite your cup of tea, trot across the street from the bus station into the hotel jungle of Sector 22 or try the government *bhawan,* which fills up quickly.

Gurudwaras. The Sikh owners of Sector 19's *gurudwara* are extremely friendly and eager to instruct you about their faith, once you persuade them to let you stay. Large communal room (free) and a maximum stay of 3 days. Sector 22 and Sector 9 *gurudwaras* have large communal rooms (free) or doubles with fan and shared bathroom (Rs50).

Hotel Divyadeep, 1090-91, Sector 22B (☎705191), on the southwest side of Sector 22, 250m from the bus station. Immaculate, spacious, wood-paneled rooms with seat toilets. Check-out 24hr. Singles Rs250-450; doubles Rs300-500.

Panchayat Bhawan, Sector 18 (☎780701), on the northeast side. Enormous rooms around a courtyard. Doubles with bath Rs200-500. Reservations recommended.

Shivalik Lodge, Sector 22B (☎774540), just behind the restaurant/hotel, opposite the bus station. Clean bathrooms with squat toilets and hot water. Check-out noon. Doubles with air-cooling and TV Rs250.

Jullundur Hotel, Sector 22 (☎706777 or 701121), opposite the bus station, next to Sunbeam. Rooms are a bit pricey but all have A/C, fan, color TV, and hot water. Singles Rs300-550; doubles Rs750. Check-out noon.

▟ FOOD

There's no shortage of restaurants in Chandigarh. Sector 17 offers a combination of somewhat pricey restaurants and American-style fast-food joints, as well as a number of cheap *dhabas.* To sample the local *thalis, samosas,* and sweets, wander through the markets of any Sector except 17 or 22.

▨ **KC's Mezbaam,** Sector 17, on the north side, behind KC Cinema. A mosaic of Muslim-influenced culinary styles—from the nawab of Avadh's favorite *gushtaba* (Kashmiri meatballs in a yogurt sauce, Rs125) to the nizam of Hyderabad's beloved *mung malai tikka* (Rs125). Flowers, fountains, and beer on tap (Rs25). Open daily 11am-11:30pm.

Shangri-La, SCO 96, Sector 17C. Nepali-run Chinese restaurant decorated with red paneling, dragon paintings, silk lanterns, and a picture of the Dalai Lama. Szechuan-style sliced lamb Rs90; jasmine tea Rs12. Open daily 11am-10pm.

Indian Coffee House, on Sector 17's main square, has the town's largest selection of *dosas* (Rs20-30), served by the best-dressed waiters in town.

Hot Millions. There are 4 branches in Sector 17. Three of them serve the usual quick and easy food from slick and greasy menus. Chicken burger Rs38; pizza Rs45-80. The fourth is a classy, 2nd floor restaurant with an amazing salad bar (9-salad combination platter Rs110). Open daily 11am-11pm.

City Heart Restaurant, Sector 22, directly opposite the bus station, is the place to refuel between bus rides. Helpings of veg. fried rice (Rs25) and *muttar paneer* (Rs20) are huge, but the prices still leave you enough for that ticket to Dharamsala.

Nanak's Sweets Shop, Sector 19D, next to the 19D *gurudwara.* Brave palates will be rewarded with a chalky, dough-based taste-sensation. Strong whiskey-and-beer aperitifs. Chocolate, coconut, and pineapple *barfi* Rs80.

SIGHTS

ROCK GARDEN. The birth of the city of Chandigarh as a government-supervised golden child gave rise to heaps of concrete waste and piles of debris. In 1985, road construction supervisor Nek Chand used one of the many government dumps as a playground for his creativity, turning it into a garden well beyond the imagination of the government and most other earthlings. Visit Nek Chand's Rock Garden, and you'll never look at Indian concrete the same way again. The former construction worker has brought this humble material and even some road trash into a state of grace, assembling an escapist wonderland that now meanders through 40 surreal acres. Highlights include stone duck armies, waterfalls, dancers, and a forthcoming glass-and-plastic fantasy. *(Sector 1, near the Capital Complex. Open daily Apr.-Sept. 9am-1pm and 3-7pm; Oct.-Mar. 9am-1pm and 2-6pm. Rs5. Appointments with Nek Chand, the garden's creator, occasionally available; inquire at the ticket window.)*

PARKS. In the north is **Sukhna Lake,** a small reservoir-turned-tourist-trap with cafeteria, pub, mini-amusement park, and paddleboats. Come at sunset, hop in one of the **swan boats,** and float over to the mangrove **alcoves** across the lake. *(2-seater Rs30 per 30 min., 4-seater Rs60 per 30 min.)* **Leisure Valley** is the term Le Corbusier used for the long parkland stretching through the heart of Chandigarh that is meant to provide "care for the body and spirit." The highlight of this public park is the Dr. Zakir Hussain **Rose Garden,** off Jan Marg in Sector 16, which is the largest rose garden in Asia and features 4000 species of roses. In February, the garden hosts the giant Rose Festival. Also worth visiting is the **Chhatbir Zoological Park,** 15km from Chandigarh, where you can meet (hopefully not face-to-face) the Royal Bengal Tigers or take a lion safari.

OTHER SIGHTS. Sector 1 contains several other notable attractions. The **Capital Complex,** with its monumental concrete buildings, was Le Corbusier's way of staging the functions of government in symbolic and geometric relation to one another and to the rest of the city (as "head" to "body"—the parks were to be the "lungs"). The **High Court** and **Open Hand Monument** are more accessible than the **Legislative Assembly** and heavily-guarded **Secretariat.**

NIGHTLIFE AND ENTERTAINMENT

Chandigarh, unlike much of India, has 25 pubs and a well-developed beer-drinking culture. The basement of **KC's Mezbaam** (see **Food,** above) caters to the beer-deprived with Thunderbolt on tap. If you need longer hours, **Pub 22,** Sector 22, directly opposite the bus station, is open until midnight. Both pubs, however, serve nothing but beer (Rs25). If you need cakes to soak up the booze, try the **Ambrozia Restaurant and Pub,** Sector 17C, opposite the library. (Small plates of tandoori and Chinese Rs35-80; Riviera wine Rs65. Open until 11:30pm.) Another popular pub is **Gymkhana Pub,** in Sector 17D, which has a small selection of beers and decently priced snacks. For some disco-boogie action, head to the **Las Vegas Den,** SCO 915, Kulka Highway, where you can get down to a curious blend of Indian and Western beats with well-dressed locals. (☎554487. Couples Rs150; single women Rs50. Single men often not allowed.) For a more refined experience, head to the **Tagore Theatre,** Sector 18 (☎774278), which stages Shakespeare in Punjabi and features dancing troupes in costumes.

AMRITSAR ਅੰਮ੍ਰਿਤਸਰ　　　　　☎0183

Named for the sacred tank or "pool of immortal nectar" at its heart, the holy city of Amritsar is the largest city in the Indian half of partitioned Punjab and the focal point of Sikhism. An awe-inspiring monument to the Sikh faith, Amritsar's Golden Temple is a must-see for all visitors. Guru Ram Das started construction of the temple in 1579, but the city did not begin to form around it until the Sikh holy book, the Guru Granth Sahib, was enshrined here by the fifth Guru, Arjun. Centuries of Mughal invasions kicked off a cycle of destruction and reconstruction, and the calamities continued into the 1980s. Early in the 20th century, Amritsar played an important role in the formation of the Indian nationalist movement. In 1919, British Brigadier General Dyer shot dead 400 unarmed Indians in the closed compound of Jallianwala Bagh, sparking waves of protest all over India. Tanks bulldozed through the city gates in 1984, as the government put down an uprising of Sikh extremists. Amritsar today is a thriving industrial center that stretches far beyond the labyrinth of narrow streets that winds between the 20 gates of the old city. The proximity to the Pakistani border is itself an attraction; every evening an elaborate military ceremony accompanies the closing of the border gates.

▐ GETTING THERE AND GETTING AROUND

Flights: Raja Sanhsi Airport, 12km northwest of town. To: **Delhi** (M and F, 9am; W and F, 2:30pm; 2hr.; US$100). Book at the **Indian Airlines** office, Court Rd. (☎ 213392), halfway between Albert and Mall Rd. Open M-Sa 10am-5pm.

Trains: The **computer reservation** complex (☎ 562811 or 562812) is in the south end of the railway station. Open M-Sa 8am-1:30pm and 2-8pm, Su 8am-2pm. To: **Agra** (5:30 and 8:15am, 11hr., Rs132); **Bombay** (3 per day, 7:55am-9:30pm, 33hr., Rs105); **Delhi** (8 per day, 5:15am-9:30pm, 5½-8hr., Rs150); **Haridwar** (7:30am and 8pm, 12hr., Rs187); **Jaipur** (W and Su 4pm, 19hr., Rs280); **Lahore, Pakistan** (*Lahore Exp.* 4607, M and Th 7am, 4hr., Rs50; no reservations—purchase ticket at the platform); **Lucknow** (2-3 per day, 5:45-9:15pm, 18hr., Rs265); **Patna** (5:30 and 6:30pm, 34hr., Rs350).

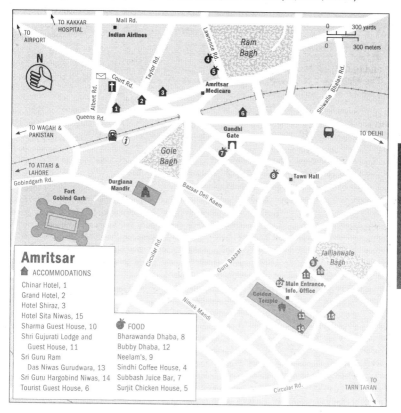

Amritsar

🏠 ACCOMMODATIONS

Chinar Hotel, 1
Grand Hotel, 2
Hotel Shiraz, 3
Hotel Sita Niwas, 15
Sharma Guest House, 10
Shri Gujurati Lodge and
  Guest House, 11
Sri Guru Ram
  Das Niwas Gurudwara, 13
Sri Guru Hargobind Niwas, 14
Tourist Guest House, 6

🍴 FOOD

Bharawanda Dhaba, 8
Bubby Dhaba, 12
Neelam's, 9
Sindhi Coffee House, 4
Subbash Juice Bar, 7
Surjit Chicken House, 5

PUNJAB & HARYANA

Buses: Enquiry Office (☎551734). Departure times change frequently. To: **Attari** (every 30min., 6:40am-5:30pm, 1hr., Rs12); **Chandigarh** (every 20min., 4:20am-4pm, 5hr., Rs100; deluxe 9am, noon, and 3pm, Rs200); **Dehra Dun** (7am, 7hr., Rs177); **Delhi** (frequent, 5:45am-9pm, 9hr., Rs180; deluxe every hr., 6:10-8:10pm, 8hr., Rs320); **Dalhousie** (9:15am, 6hr., Rs89); **Dharamsala** (11:50am, 7hr., Rs98); **Jammu** (every 30min., 5am-4:30pm, 7hr., Rs100); **Shimla** (5:30am and 7:20pm, 11hr., Rs177; or go to Chandigarh and change there). For connections at friendlier hours, go to **Pathankot** (4:30am-8pm, 3hr., Rs45).

Local Transportation: Bicycle rental is available at **Raja Cycles,** across the street north of the bus stand, next to the Janta Stores signs. Rs25 per day plus Rs1000 deposit. Open M-Sa 10am-6pm. **Cycle-rickshaws** will run anywhere in town for Rs10-20. In the "new sections," **auto-rickshaws** can speed things up; in the old parts they have to move at the snail's pace of the cycle-rickshaw-dominated narrow streets.

ORIENTATION

Amritsar's **railway tracks** divide the city into northern and southern sections. The older, livelier section of the city is beyond the gates to the south of the railway. **Bhandari Bridge** is the major vehicle conduit connecting north and south. North of the bridge is the **Ram Bagh** park and the modern parts of the city. The old town is farther south, enclosed by **Circular Rd.,** which runs where the wall once stood. The Golden Temple is at the center of the circle. Most visitors visit only the temple compound and the area immediately north of it, but the maze of alleys and bazaars south and west of the temple also capture the feel of old Amritsar. The **bus stand** is northeast of the center, on the road from Delhi to the **railway station.**

PRACTICAL INFORMATION

Tourist Office: Punjab Government Tourist Office (☎402452), in the Palace Hotel, opposite the railway station. Open M-F 9am-5pm. There is also a helpful Information Center at the Golden Temple.

Foreigner Registration Office: (☎228786), in the office of the Senior Superintendent of Police at the Court government compound, just past the intersection of Court and Mall Rd. Tourist visas can only be extended in Delhi. Open M-Sa 10am-5:30pm.

Currency Exchange: Grindlays Bank (☎224626), at the intersection of Lawrence and Mall Rd., accepts traveler's checks. Cash advances on MC and Visa. The railway area also has several offices that change **Pakistani rupees.**

Luggage Storage: At the railway station, for Rs5-6 per day. Open 24hr.

Market: The **bazaar** immediately in front of the main entrance to the Golden Temple carries a wide selection of merchandise, from Rajasthani shoes to Sikh daggers and swords. The steel bracelets (*kara*) worn by all Sikhs, symbolizing strength of will and determination, are sold here. Be discriminating—*kara* that are not made of stainless steel will erode after a few months of wear. Each narrow lane south and west of the shrine specializes in a particular product or craft.

Library: Sri Guru Ram Das Library, in the basement of Hargobind Niwas next to the Golden Temple. Open M-Sa 9:30am-5pm.

Bookstore: Booklover's Retreat (☎545666), on Hall Bazaar, south of Gandhi Gate. Open M-Sa 10am-8pm.

Police: ☎211864 or 220043.

Pharmacy: Chemists are all over town and many are clustered on Cooper Rd., around the corner from Crystal Restaurant, several blocks northeast of the railway station. Among these, **Sham Medicine** (☎228905) carries tampons and is otherwise well-stocked. Open daily 8:30am-10pm.

Hospital: Kakkar Hospital, Green Ave. (☎210964), near the intersection of Mall and Albert Rd., is the most reputable in town; enough people know the name to point the way. **24hr. emergency room** on Mahna Singh Rd., in the Golden Temple area.

Internet: Cyber City (☎210706), off Lawrence Rd., near the intersection of Queens and Lawrence Rd. Rs60 per hr. Open daily 7:30am-11pm. **Tourist Guest House** also has one computer hooked to the web. Rs90 per hr.

Post Office: Court Rd. (☎566032), northwest of the railway station. Open M-Sa 9am-5pm. The **Golden Temple Post Office** is open M-Sa 9am-5pm. **Postal Code:** 143001.

ACCOMMODATIONS

Amritsar's hotels are in three parts of the city: by the bus stand, near the railway station, and around the Golden Temple. The cheapest places are near the bus stand, but many of these are neither clean nor safe—over the years the area has become a red-light district where rooms are rented out by the hour. A number of decent hotels near the railway station are good if you're anxious to keep the heart of the city at a safe distance. Hotels near the temple are more scarce, but this is the most vibrant part of the city. The best place to stay, of course, is in the temple compound itself, although all the rules can get pretty tiresome after a few days.

INSIDE THE GOLDEN TEMPLE

Sri Guru Ram Das Niwas Gurudwara, outside the east gate of the temple, past the community kitchen. Foreign guests sleep on floor mats in an open-ceiling bunker. No smoking or drinking allowed. Prayers broadcast periodically through the courtyard, adding to the atmosphere. Foreign compound is guarded 24hr.; in-house closets provided. Donations at the charity box up front are appreciated. Maximum stay 3 days.

Sri Guru Hargobind Niwas (temple manager ☎553953, Hargobind Niwas ext. 323), 100m south of Ram Das Niwas Gurudwara. If the free digs are a bit too free for your taste, pay a token tariff for a sparkling new, marble-covered double with attached bath. The place is nearly always full, but if you are persistent, or if you keep coming back, you'll get in eventually. No drinking or smoking. Doubles with bath Rs60.

GOLDEN TEMPLE AREA

Sharma Guest House, Mahna Singh Rd. (☎551757), on the street between the main and the eastern entrances to the temple. Familial atmosphere and excellent room service. Clean doubles with seat toilets, cable TV, and phones. A few rooms look into Jallianwalla Bagh. Check-out 24hr. Doubles Rs200-350. Reservations recommended.

Hotel Sita Niwas (☎543092), near the eastern temple entrance. Signs aplenty—you can't miss it. Often noisy during the day, but with 85 rooms around a big indoor courtyard you are sure to find one to suit you. Doubles with TV, tub, and seat-toilet have great temple views. STD/ISD. Check-out 24hr. Singles Rs150; doubles Rs250-550.

Shri Gujrati Lodge and Guest House (☎557870), a block in front of the main temple entrance, next to the passage to Jallianwala Bagh. The 8-bed dormitory overlooks the memorial park; cramped doubles with tiny bathrooms open onto Amritsar's chaotic central market. The huge 3rd floor balcony is ideal for a game of cricket. Dorm beds Rs80; doubles with seat toilets Rs200-300. No reservations accepted.

RAILWAY AREA

Tourist Guest House, GT Rd. (☎553830), near Nandan Cinema, on the road from the bus stand to the railway station. Fifty years ago, a British colonel turned his mansion into this guest house; since then, tourists have flocked here for a taste of the Raj lifestyle. Rooms have high ceilings; some have TVs. Internet Rs100 per hr. Dorm beds Rs85; doubles with fans and bath Rs100-250.

Grand Hotel (☎562424), directly opposite the railway station. Well-kept rooms surround a pleasant courtyard with a garden and lawn chairs. Attached baths with seat toilets, running hot water, and color TV. Room service 7am-10pm. Check-out noon. Excellent restaurant and bar downstairs. Singles Rs375-675; doubles Rs500-775.

Hotel Shiraz (☎220886), off Queen's Rd., a 7min. walk from the station. Large rooms with color TVs, seat toilets, and hot water. Room service 7am-11pm. Check-out noon. Singles Rs275-350; doubles Rs350-425; add Rs150 for A/C.

Chinar Hotel, Railway Links Rd. (☎564655). A half-block up from the railway station. Moderately clean, with huge front-side rooms. Check-out noon. Doubles Rs150-550.

FOOD

You should try to eat at least one meal in the Golden Temple itself—the *dahl* might leave you yearning for more.

Neelam's, a few doors down from the entrance to Jallianwala Bagh. A/C and cushy booths make it the most comfortable *dhaba* in the temple area. Enormous and tasty portions. Veg. curry Rs35; excellent *masala dosa* Rs15. Open daily 10am-10pm.

Bubby Dhaba, directly in front of the main temple entrance, provides a standard menu. Relax in the A/C room in the back and watch all the action in the front of the Golden Temple, or stay up front to chat with the cooks. Open daily 6:30am-11pm.

Bharawanda Dhaba, opposite the Town Hall and next door to Punjab National Bank. Well-known, well-stocked, well-lit cafeteria with superb *thalis* (Rs30). Speedy service and foreigner-friendly. Open daily 8:30am-11:30pm.

Surjit Chicken House, right below Cyber City, off Lawrence Rd. The best grilled chicken in town (Rs65) according to locals. Open 10am-9pm.

Subhash Juice Bar, one block southwest of Gandhi Gate. Black, mirrored booths, livened up by a colorful selection of juices and shakes. Mango shake with *pista badam* Rs15. Open daily 7am-11pm.

Sindhi Coffee House, Lawrence Rd., opposite Ram Bagh Gardens. Comfy chairs and palatable coffee (Rs20). A good place to bring a date for ice cream. Open daily 9am-9pm.

SIGHTS

THE GOLDEN TEMPLE

Golden Temple Information Centre is on the northeast side of the complex. No tobacco, alcohol, or stimulants of any kind are allowed. Visitors must deposit cigarettes a block away from the temple's entrance. Shoes, socks, and umbrellas must be left at free depositories at each of the main entrances or at the Tourist Information Centre. Visitors must rinse their feet in the tanks in front of the entrances. Photography is allowed inside the temple complex, but not inside the temple itself. Head-coverings are required at all times inside the temple. They are available for free at the Information Centre and for sale (Rs10) outside the temple, but any scarf, hat, or towel will do. Information Centre open daily 8am-8pm, Sept.-Mar. 8am-7pm. ☎ 553954. Complex open daily 24hr. Free.

No matter what you choose to call it—the Golden Temple, Hari Mandir, or Darbar Sahib (as it's known in Punjabi)—Amritsar's focal monument is inspiringly beautiful and hauntingly serene, oblivious to the grind and grime just a few feet outside its walls. The Golden Temple's tranquility is especially impressive given the tumultuous history of the Sikhs and of the temple itself. Ever since it was built nearly 400 years ago, the temple has been plagued by almost incessant destruction and desecration from outsiders. All Sikhs try to make a pilgrimage here at least once in their lifetime. The best time to visit is at night when the lights sparkling in the blackened tank and the lanterns illuminating the causeway impart a soft, ethereal glow to this awe-inspiring place of worship.

Although Guru Nanak, the founder of Sikhism, once lived near the site of the modern tank, it was **Guru Ram Das** who ignited the growth of a religious center here when he began work on the pool in 1574. That project was completed under Guru Arjun 15 years later, when the area was named Amritsar. Guru Arjun built the **Hari Mandir** at the center of the tank and placed the Guru Granth Sahib, the Sikh holy book, inside it. A series of destructive Mughal invasions followed the completion of the temple in 1601. The temple alternated between Mughal and Sikh control until Ahmad Shah Abdali captured it and, taking no chances, blew it to smithereens. The Sikhs regained control of the site under the leadership of Punjab ruler Maharaja Ranjit Singh. The one-eyed maharaja rebuilt the complex, decorated parts of it with marble and copper, and coated the newly built Hari Mandir in gold leaf. The British assumed a less-than-reverent management of the temple during the 19th century, and it wasn't until the 1920s that the practice of pure Sikhism was restored within the temple's walls.

The temple has continued to be a site of frequent violence. The 1980s saw the rise of a vocal Sikh militant group that called—and, in small factions, continues to call—for the creation of an independent Sikh nation. Tensions came to a head in 1983, when the movement's leader, Sant Bhindranwale, sequestered himself in the Golden Temple and incited acts of violence against Hindus. With over 350 Hindus killed by the summer of 1984, Indira Gandhi ordered the national army to storm the temple, a plan dubbed **Operation Bluestar.** What was intended as a commando raid became a three-day siege. When the smoke had cleared, more the 750 people were dead, including Bhindranwale and 83 soldiers. Tour guides and brochures tend to be hush-hush about this latter-day violence, emphasizing bloodbaths in the distant past and the site's current state of peace.

PARIKRAMA. The main entrance to the Golden Temple is on the north side of the complex, beneath the **clock tower.** Here also is the main shoe depository and the **Tourist Information Centre,** which provides informative brochures about the temple and the Sikh religion and also conducts hourly tours in English. The clock tower leads to the Parikrama, the 12m-wide marble promenade that encircles the tank. The four entrances to the temple complex symbolize an openness to friendly visitors from all sides—both geographically and metaphorically in terms of caste and creed. Guru Arjun once exclaimed, "My faith is for people of all castes and all creeds from whichever direction they come and to whichever direction they bow." Traffic moves clockwise around the Parikrama. Here, the **68 Holy Places** represent the 68 holiest Hindu sites in India—just to walk along this northern edge, Guru Arjun declared, is to attain the holiness a Hindu takes a lifetime to acquire. Some of the holy sites have been converted into the **Central Sikh Museum,** or Gallery of Martyrs, housed in the northern part of the temple complex; the entrance is to the right of the main gate. Along the walls are portraits of renowned Sikhs, including Baba Deep Singh and Sevapanthi Bhai Mansha Singh, who swam across the tank through gunfire to keep the temple lit. The display of heavy-duty arms includes everything from spears to blunderbusses. Paintings of martyred bodies sawed to pieces at Chandni Chowk in Delhi and photographs of slain Sikh martyrs with pop-eyed, bloody faces are not for the faint of heart. *(Open daily 8am-6pm. Free.)* The small tree at the northeast corner of the tank is said to have been the site of the miraculous healing of a cripple; today the healthy, wealthy, crippled, and destitute alike seek the benefits of the tank's curative powers at the adjoining **bathing ghats.** Just next to the *ghats* is one of four booths where priests read from the Guru Granth Sahib. Ongoing readings are meant to ensure the survival of Sikh beliefs. Each priest recites for three hours, and a complete reading takes 50 hours.

On the east side of the Parikrama are the **Ramgarhia Minars,** two brick towers that were damaged when tanks rumbled through this entrance in 1984. This access leads to the Guru-ka-Langar, the communal kitchen, and the *gurudwaras.* The south side of the tank has a shrine to **Baba Deep Singh,** whose struggles made him a Sikh hero. When the Mughal Ahmad Shah Abdali blew up the Golden Temple in 1761 and filled the sacred tank with trash, Baba Deep Singh began a defense of the desecrated temple. On his way, however, his head was cut off by a Muslim soldier. Disembodied and with head in hand, the Sikh leader trudged on, eventually crossing the temple's gates and plopping his head in the water before dying. 'The west end of the tank has several notable structures. The first window is where devotees collect *prasad,* the sweet lumps of cornmeal used as an offering inside the Hari Mandir. Moving clockwise, opposite the entrance to the Hari Mandir, is the **Akal**

Takhat, the second-holiest place of the temple. Guru Hargobind, the sixth Sikh guru, built the Akal Takhat in 1609 as a decision-making center. Many weapons, fine pieces of jewelry, and other Sikh artifacts are stored here. The two towering flagstaffs next to the Akal Takhat represent the religious and political facets of Sikhism; the two are joined by the **double swords of Hargobind,** demonstrating how intertwined these aspects of Sikhism are. Illuminated at the very top, the poles are intended as beacons for pilgrims heading into Amritsar. Near the flagstaffs is the shrine to the last and most militant guru, Gobind Singh. The last noteworthy spot along the Parikrama, other than the Hari Mandir itself, is the 450-year old **jujube** tree under which the Baba Buddhaja, the temple's first priest, used to spend his time. The tree is thought to bring fertility to anyone who touches it.

HARI MANDIR. Seemingly afloat in the middle of the tank, the Hari Mandir is the holiest part of the entire complex. Photography is not allowed past the gate to the temple walkway. The architecture of the Golden Temple fuses Hindu and Muslim styles—this is particularly noticeable in the synthesis of the Hindu temple's rectangular form with the domes and minarets of the Muslim mosque. The three stories of the Hari Mandir, capped by an inverted lotus dome, are made of marble, copper, and about 100 kilograms of pure gold leaf. Inside the temple on the ground floor, the chief priest and his musicians recite *gurbani* (hymns) from the Guru Granth Sahib. People sit around the center and toss flowers and money toward the jewel-studded canopy, where the silk-enshrouded Guru Granth Sahib lies.

The **Guru Granth Sahib** (considered by the Sikhs as a living teacher, and not just a book) is brought to the temple from the Akal Takhat each day and returned at night. The morning ceremony takes place at around 3:30am, the procession at 10pm. Arrive about an hour early to observe the ceremony from the second floor of the Hari Mandir. Hymns echo through the building before the book is revealed and the priest takes over the prayers; he chants, folds the book in gold leaf and more silk, and finally places it on the golden palanquin. Head downstairs at this point, and you might end up in the line of devotees pushing each other for the privilege of bearing the holy burden. Finally, a blaring serpentine horn and communal drum signal a final prayer that puts the book to bed, near the flagstaff. The entire ceremony lasts about an hour and a half.

AROUND THE TEMPLE. Step outside to the left (north) side onto the *pradakhina*, the marble path leading around the temple. On this north side is a stairwell leading to the second floor, where flowers, animals, and hymns ornament the walls and where you can catch a good look at the procession and Adi Granth below. On the east side of this floor is a small *shish mahal* (hall of mirrors). Once occupied by the gurus, the halls now reverberate with the voices of priests engaged in the *akhand path*, the ongoing reading of the holy book. The **Har-ki-Pari** (Steps of God), on the ground floor on the temple's east (back) side, allows visitors easy access to the most sacred section of the tank's waters.

GATAKA: THE ART OF WAR

The Sikhs' success in resisting centuries of oppression is partly due to their skill as warriors. Through countless battles, they developed a martial art known as *gataka*. Today, young would-be warriors practice *gataka* on the roof of the Guru-ka-Langar (daily 8:30-11pm). They enjoy having visitors watch as they wield their *neja* (spears), swords, bamboo sticks, and other ancient weapons and practice *talwar baji* (fencing), or as it's more bluntly known, *kirpan* (the art of stabbing). The most impressive weapon is the *chakkar,* a wooden ring with stone spheres dangling from it by 4-foot strings. The warrior stands in the middle and spins the ring, the whirling balls forming a barrier around him, and then tosses it up into the air (still spinning) for someone to catch. Watching the spectacle is exciting but participating is even better, which the warriors will often let you do. To really indulge in *gataka*, they recommend heading out to Raia, 50km outside of Amritsar, where you can visit Baba Bakala, the training center for the most hard-core students.

No visit to the Golden Temple would be complete without a meal at the **Guru-ka-Langar,** the enormous community kitchen characteristic of all Sikh temples. Sikh founder Guru Nanak instituted the custom of *pangat* (dining together) to reinforce the idea of equality. *Pangat* continues in the dining hall, where basic meals are dished out daily to rows of thousands who sit together, regardless of wealth or caste. As one row eats, the next gathers, in an ongoing cycle. The meal consists of all-you-can-eat *dahl* and chappatis; simply hold out cupped hands as the chappati chappie walks by, and he'll toss you more. Afterwards, leave a donation in one of the charity boxes—these meals are largely funded by such contributions.

Just south of the Hargobind *gurudwara* is the nine-story **Tower of Baba Atal Rai,** named after the son of Guru Hargobind. According to legend, he performed a miracle at age nine, which annoyed his father to no end. In shame, the young *baba* came here and died. On the first floor are some detailed miniatures depicting episodes from Guru Nanak's life and a *nagarah* (drum). The other floors are empty, but you can climb to the top for unsurpassed views of Amritsar, the Golden Temple, and the tank of Kamalsar to the south.

OTHER SIGHTS

JALLIANWALA BAGH. About two blocks north of the temple's main entrance is Jallianwala Bagh, the site of one of the most horrific moments in the history of colonial India. On April 13, 1919, crowds filled Jallianwala Bagh to peacefully protest a law allowing the British to imprison Indians without trial. British Brigadier-General Reginald E.H. Dyer was brought in to quell the disturbance. Dyer stood behind 150 troops in front of the main alley, the only entrance and exit to the compound and ordered his men to open fire without warning on the 10,000 men, women, and children who had gathered here. The shooting continued for 15 minutes. People were shot as they perched to jump over walls; others drowned after diving into wells. Dyer's troops had fired 1650 rounds, and nearly all of them found their mark. In all, about 400 people died, and 1500 were left wounded. The massacre sparked a rallying cry for Indian insurgence. The Bengali poet Rabindranath Tagore, who had been knighted after winning the Nobel Prize for Literature in 1913, returned his knighthood after the massacre. Dyer was reprimanded and relieved of his duties but never charged with any crime. In 1997, Queen Elizabeth II visited Jallianwala Bagh. Although no official apology was made during her controversial visit, the British Monarch remarked on the regrettability of the massacre and laid a wreath at the memorial to the victims. Today, Jallianwala Bagh is a calm garden, frequented by college kids and picknicking families. The stone well is a monument to the drowned Indians who jumped to their deaths in an attempt to flee. The Martyr's Gallery features portraits of some of those involved in the massacre. *(Open daily in summer 9am-5pm, in winter 10am-1pm and 3-7pm.)*

RAM BAGH. Northeast of the railway station is Ram Bagh, the park between The Mall and Queens Rd. At the south edge of the park, the impressive Darshani Deorhi gate is all that is left of the solid ramparts and moat that once surrounded the area. At the northwest corner stands a menacing statue of Maharaja Ranjit Singh, the Sikh leader who was responsible for the early 19th-century restoration of the Golden Temple. Ram Bagh served as his summer residence between 1818 and 1837, and the central building now houses the Ranjit Singh Museum, which contains oil paintings, weapons, manuscripts, and miniatures from the maharaja's era. The tourist office's pamphlet, *Amritsar: Spiritual Centre of Punjab,* is a good guide to the museum. *(Museum open Tu-Su 10am-4:45pm. Rs5.)*

DURGIANA MANDIR. The high profile of the Golden Temple overshadows the tiny Hindu shrines tucked into the alleyways all around it, as well as the impressive Durgiana Mandir. This temple, set back from the busy street four blocks northwest of the Golden Temple, honors the goddess Durga.

INDIAN ACADEMY OF FINE ARTS. Opposite Ram Bagh on Lawrence Rd., east of the Sindhi Coffee House, the Indian Academy of Fine Arts puts on periodic exhibitions of modern Indian art. *(Open daily 9am-7pm. Free.)*

🏴 DAYTRIP FROM AMRITSAR: TARN TARAN ਤਰਨ ਤਾਰਨ

Once the Hari Mandir has whetted your appetite for shiny, golden Sikh temples, head 22km south to the town of Tarn Taran. Buses leave every 30 minutes from the main bus stand (1hr., Rs10). From the Tarn Taran bus stand, it's a 15-minute walk along the main road and through the narrow alley of the bazaar up to the local *gurudwara*. Its founder, Guru Arjun Dev, built the temple in 1768 to commemorate Guru Ram Das, who slept side-by-side with a leper to show his compassion. Though local doctors can't provide any evidence for the common belief that the water here cures leprosy, they do attest to its curative effects on several minor skin conditions. The architectural style here resembles that of the Amritsar complex; the *parikrama* encircling the still waters is actually larger than its counterpart in the Golden Temple. The *gurudwara* provides decent rooms (free) in the large yellow building just outsides the west (not the main) entrance.

🏴 PAKISTANI BORDER

> **❗ WARNING.** If you want to cross into Pakistan, **make sure you have your Pakistani visa and that your Indian visa allows multiple entries.** Crossing the line isn't easy. For more information, see **Surrounding Countries**, p. 11.

The *only* border crossing between India and Pakistan is at **Wagah**, 28km from Amritsar. Take a **bus** to **Attari** (every 15min., 7am-6pm, 1hr., Rs12), and look for the impressive Khalsa College on the right. From Attari, it is a 2km rickshaw ride to the border (Rs10-20). The border is open daily from 10am to 4pm. If you only wish to visit, wait until after 4pm, or better still, arrive at 6:30 for the 7pm ceremony (see **Border Ballet,** below). The last bus to **Amritsar** leaves Attari at 6pm. If you are here for the 7pm flag ceremony, you can take a taxi back (Rs50). If you are crossing over, pass through customs on the left and walk the remaining 200m to the actual line. Enter Pakistan by taking the **train** from Amritsar to **Lahore** (M and Th, 9am). For the trains, all checking is done in Attari. There is also a direct **bus** between Delhi and Lahore (Tu, W, F, and Sa).

At Wagah, **Punjab Tourism,** just behind the checkpoint, supplies the standard, outdated brochures and maps (open M-Sa 10am-4pm). Next door, the **State Bank of India** changes traveler's checks but not Pakistani rupees (open 11am-4pm). The money-changers, however, will. There is a **post office** for last minute send-offs. If you are stranded overnight, the **Niagara Falls Guest House** (☎382646) provides both spacious (Rs350) and cramped (Rs200) rooms.

> **BORDER BALLET** A few people go to Wagah to *cross* the border, but a crowd always shows up to *watch* the border. A half-hour before sunset, an elaborate nightly ritual accompanies the closing of the border and the lowering of the flags. Tourists clamor around the spiked gate on either side and jostle for the best views. Right on schedule, with a near-farcical dose of solemnity, the ceremony unfolds. As one officer barks an order and another follows with furious stomping and wild high-stepping, the audiences on both sides break into raucous applause. After some machismo-packed face-offs and lengthy siren-like yells, the respective flags are lowered, the lights go bright, the bugles blare, and the visitors mob the gate for a glimpse of the faces on the other side—or for a chance to toe one of the world's most famous white lines.

RAJASTHAN
राजस्थान

The northwestern desert state of Rajasthan is India's "Land of Kings," ruled for more than a millennium by the legendary Rajput warrior clans. The days of blood-shed and mass immolation are long gone now, but the vivid memories of the gory glories of Rajasthan's colorful past continue to dominate most visitors' impres-sions of one of the most romantic regions of tourist-brochure India.

Rajasthan's fiercely independent maharajas had turned the region into a mess of uncooperative kingdoms by the time the Mughals began to extend their power across northern India, and the proud kingdoms fell one after another under the control of the new empire. The Mughals allowed the Rajputs to retain many of the trappings of power within the new hierarchy, however, soon tiring of continual battles against unwavering foes for whom war was a way of life. When the British arrived and overthrew the Mughals, the maharajas collaborated with the Raj; in return, they were given license to continue their lives of decadence and indul-gence, depleting the state's resources and doing little to help its social and eco-nomic development. More than half of the population still lives in villages and works in the fields, a lifestyle that has been threatened by the severe drought of the last few years.

Rajasthan is made up of three geographical regions. The flat lands of the east are studded with rich national parks and cosmopolitan centers like Jaipur, the state's capital and the western corner of India's "Golden Triangle" of tourism. In the west-ern Marwar region, the plains yield to the vast arid emptiness of the Thar Desert and its huge hulking forts. In the south, the majestic Aravalli Mountains of the Mewar region contrast with the rest of the state's sand-duned landscape, with lush valleys and mountain-top lakes.

In recent years, the state's colorful history and the relics of the riches that once lured Mughal invaders here have helped to make Rajasthan the most visited state in India. Old palaces have been converted into "Heritage Hotels," and travelers now wander the halls of maharajas' homes. The tourist boom has brought money and a much-needed infrastructure to Rajasthan, but it has also brought about a fiercely competitive clamor for dollars, pounds, and yen. An over-abundance of tourist traffic threatens to obscure the local culture in many cities; many of today's Rajput warriors have traded their swords for cell-phones, and they now devote much of their legendary bloody-mindedness to a never-say-die fight for baksheesh. But traces of the old storybook India still survive—in the colored *bandhani* cloth of Jaipur's marketplaces, in the pastoral lifestyle of the hilly countryside and the camels of Pushkar, and in the elaborately painted *havelis* and palaces of Udaipur.

HIGHLIGHTS OF RAJASTHAN

Jaipur is Rajasthan's most popular destination. Its **City Palace** (p. 281), **Hawa Mahal** (p. 282), and **Amber Fort** (p. 283) are worth all the hype.

The **lake palace** of **Udaipur** (p. 301) has long been a draw for honeymooners and secret agents alike—one glimpse of the sunrise city and you'll see why.

Jaisalmer's (p. 314) illuminated fort sates most tourists' cravings for a taste of life in the middle ages—the rest journey into the desert on the hump of a camel.

Peaceful **Pushkar** (p. 289) is a quiet oasis, soothing weary pilgrims and travelers 361 days a year. The four-day **Pushkar Fair** (p. 292) is another story entirely.

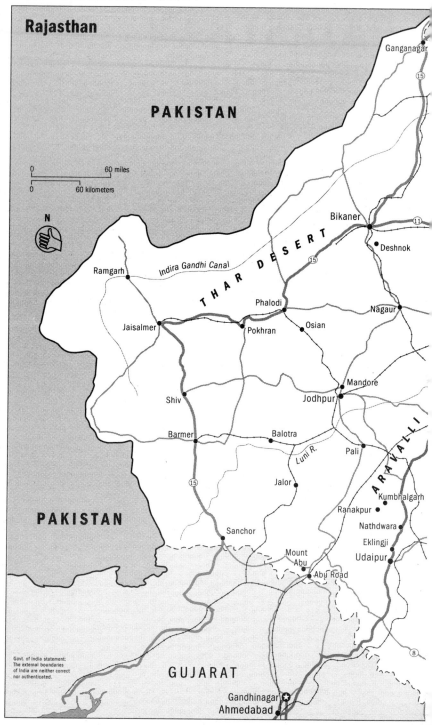

Rajasthan

PAKISTAN

PAKISTAN

GUJARAT

THAR DESERT

ARAVALLI

0   60 miles

0   60 kilometers

N

Indira Gandhi Canal

Luni R.

Ganganagar

Bikaner

Deshnok

Ramgarh

Phalodi

Nagaur

Jaisalmer

Pokhran

Osian

Shiv

Mandore

Jodhpur

Barmer

Balotra

Pali

Jalor

Kumbhalgarh

Ranakpur

Nathdwara

Sanchor

Eklingji

Udaipur

Mount
Abu

Abu Road

Gandhinagar

Ahmedabad

Govt. of India statement:
The external boundaries
of India are neither correct
nor authenticated.

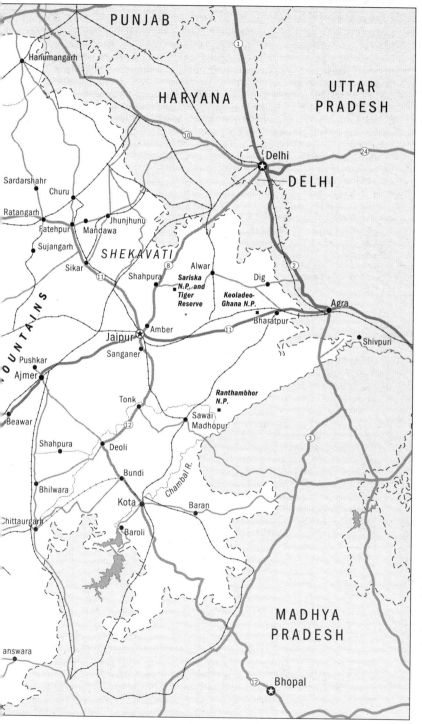

JAIPUR जयपुर ☎ 0141

Rajasthan's most popular tourist destination, Jaipur forms the southwest corner of India's "Golden Triangle," together with Delhi and Agra. Many tourists stay only long enough to have their pictures snapped in front of all the major attractions, but it's worth digging in for a longer stay; Jaipur's easy-going, cosmopolitan spirit and elegant architecture give an unmistakable regal air to the Rajasthani capital.

The city was born out of the vision and prudent urban planning of the remarkable 18th-century Rajput leader Maharaja Sawai Jai Singh II, who ruled the region from 1699 to 1744. By all accounts, he possessed a rare erudition and a ferocious scientific curiosity. During the early years of his reign, his kingdom was threatened by both the Marathas and the Mughals. But fortune favored the maharaja; his intelligence won him the respect and alliance of Mughal emperor Aurangzeb (see **History**, p. 67), and his military savvy led the Rajput forces to decisive victories against the Marathas. Having established political stability in his territories by the mid-1720s, Jai Singh decided to move the capital from its hillside fort in Amber to a new city of his own design. With help from the renowned Bengali architect Vidyadhar Chakravarti, the maharaja built the magnificent walled city of Jaipur.

Carefully laying out Jaipur according to the mathematical grid model of the ancient Hindu map of the universe, Jai Singh and Chakravarti strove to make their city beautiful as well as functional. High walls were constructed for defense, and the entrances to stores and homes were placed on side streets so that the maharaja's massive royal processions could pass without disrupting daily life. Wide pavements and streets were designed to facilitate the easy flow of pedestrian traffic, and a complex system of underground aqueducts brought drinking water into the fortified city.

The British presence during the 19th century brought about a drastic cosmetic transformation that has persisted to this day. To celebrate a visit in 1856 by Prince Albert, the city painted itself pink. Newsman Stanley Reed dubbed Jaipur the "Pink City," and the name stuck. Modern Jaipur has long since outgrown the walls of Reed's Pink City, but this old enclave continues to be the cultural and commercial center of the city, full of extraordinary museums, forts, temples, and palaces, as well as the crowded markets and congested streets that characterize India at its hectic best and worst.

▐ GETTING THERE AND GETTING AROUND

Flights: Sanganer Airport, 15km south of the city. Buses leave Ajmeri Gate for the airport (every 30min., Rs4-5). Taxis cost Rs200-250. **Air India,** Ganpati Plaza, MI Rd. (☎368569 or 368742; fax 360756). Open M-F 9:30am-1pm and 2-5:30pm, Sa 9:30am-2pm. **Jet Air Limited,** Jaipur Towers 1st fl., MI Rd. (☎375430 or 367409; fax 374242), is an agent for **Gulf Air, Royal Jordanian, Bangladesh Biman, TWA, Air Canada,** and **American Airlines. Air France,** Jaipur Towers, 2nd fl. (☎377051 or 370509; fax 369317). Open M-Sa 9:30am-1pm and 2-5:30pm. **British Airways,** Usha Plaza, MI Rd., next to Jaipur Towers (☎361065; fax 370374). Open M-F 9:30am-1pm and 2-6pm, Sa 9:30am-2pm. **KLM/Northwest Airlines,** Jaipur Towers, 2nd fl., MI Rd. (☎367772; fax 360053). Open M-Sa 9:30am-1:30pm and 2-6pm. **Lufthansa,** Saraogi Mansion, MI Rd. (☎562822; fax 562944), near New Gate. Open M-F 9:30am-6pm, Sa 9:30am-2pm. **Indian Airlines,** Nehru Place, Tonk Rd. (☎743500 or 742340; airport ☎721333 or 721519). Open daily 10am-1pm and 2-5pm. The more centrally located **Satyam Travels and Tours,** Jaipur Towers, ground floor (☎378794; fax 375426), is an authorized agent for Jet Airways and Indian Airlines. Books and delivers tickets at no extra fee. Open M-Sa 9:30am-7:30pm. **Jet Airways,** MI Rd. (☎360763 or 370594; fax 374242; airport ☎551729 or 551733), is in the same office as Jet Air Limited. Open daily 9:30am-5:30pm. To: **Ahmedabad** (M, W, F, 5:50pm, US$105); **Bombay** (4-5 per day, 1½-3½hr., US$140-155); **Calcutta** (M, W, F, 5:50pm; T, Th, Sa, 7:30pm, 2½-3½hr., US$220); **Delhi** (3-4 per day, 40min., US$55); **Jaisalmer** (T, Th, Sa, 11:10am, 2hr., US$125); **Jodhpur** (M, 12:50pm; T, Th, Sa, 11:10am, 50min., US$80); and **Udaipur** (2-3 per day, 45min., US$70-80).

Trains: Jaipur Railway Station (☎131). **Advance Reservation Office** (☎135), to the left of the station. Open M-Sa 8am-8pm, Su 8am-2pm. To: **Agra** (3pm, 7hr., Rs77); **Ahmedabad** (7 per day, 2:55am-10:35pm, 13hr., Rs187); **Ajmer** for **Pushkar** (6 per day, 4:30am-10:50pm, 2-4hr., Rs40); **Bikaner** (3:20pm and 9pm, 7-10hr., Rs113); **Bombay** (1:40pm, 18hr., 24hr., sleeper Rs349); **Delhi** (10 per day, 5-7hr., Rs77); **Jodhpur** (6 per day, 5:30pm-4am, 5-6hr., Rs132); **Madras** (Su-M and W-F, 4:15pm, 43hr., sleeper Rs430); and **Udaipur** (4:30am and 9:30 pm, 13-16hr., Rs96).

Buses: Sindhi Camp Central Bus Stand, Station Rd. (☎205790 or 205621). Information listed is for deluxe buses. To: **Agra** (10 per day, 6am-midnight, 5hr., Rs114); **Ajmer** for **Pushkar** (10 per day, 5am-10:45pm, 4hr., Rs65); **Chittaurgarh** (4 per day, 10am-midnight, 8hr., Rs140); **Delhi** (every 30min., 5:30am-1am, 5½hr., Rs200); **Jaisalmer** (9:45pm, 13hr., Rs177); **Jodhpur** (7 per day, 5am-11:30pm, 7hr., Rs160); **Mt. Abu** (8pm, 12hr., Rs246); and **Udaipur** (6 per day, 9:15am-midnight, 9hr., Rs200). **Private buses** depart from the same stand. Private bus companies line Station Rd. and Motilal Atal Rd., off MI Rd.; most hotels can make reservations.

Local Transportation: Unmetered **auto-rickshaws** and **cycle-rickshaws** are the best way to get around; prepare for heavy haggling (Rs15-30 by auto-rickshaw between places in the old city). **Local buses** leave from the Central Bus Stand, from all the sights, and at most major intersections every 5min. within the old city and every 10-15min. in other areas (Rs4-10). **Cars** (with driver) can be hired from the RTDC at the Tourist Hotel on MI Rd. (Rs160 per hr., Rs785 per day) and from some private companies. **Bicycles** are convenient for exploration, and many budget hotels will arrange rentals. Near Ajmeri Gate in **Kishanpol Bazaar,** you can rent bicycles for Rs35-50 per day. Open daily 8am-10pm. **Mohan Cycle Works,** MI Rd. (☎372335), opposite the Indian Coffee House, charges Rs25 per day (10 day min.). Open M-Sa 10:30am-8pm.

✳ ORIENTATION

Jaipur's wide, straight roads make getting around town a piece of cake. The walled **Pink City**, encompassing most of the sights, is in the northeast; the **new city** sprawls south and west. From **Jaipur Railway Station**, on the western edge of town, **Station Rd.** leads past the **Central Bus Stand** on its way to **Chand Pol**, the western gate into the Pink City. **Mirza Ismail (MI) Rd.,** the new city's main thoroughfare, forks off Station Rd. to run along the southern edge of the walled city past several restaurants and shopping centers before it turns into **Agra Marg** and heads out of town. Just south of New Gate and beyond the Ram Niwas Gardens, **Jawaharlal Nehru Marg** runs south past several hospitals and the Birla Mandir.

From Chand Pol, the Pink City's main thoroughfare changes names four times—**Chandpol, Tripolia, Ramganj,** and **Surajpol Bazaars**—before exiting the walled city under **Suraj Pol,** the eastern gate. The **City Palace Complex** is just north of Tripolia Bazaar, and **Johari Bazaar** leads south past most of the old city's tourist services.

❷ PRACTICAL INFORMATION

TOURIST AND FINANCIAL SERVICES

Tourist Office: Despite the inexhaustible supply of tourist offices, the **Government of India Tourist Office,** in Hotel Khasi Kothi (☎1363 or 372200), south of the MI Rd. and Station Rd. intersection, is just about the only helpful place for information. Open M-F 9am-6pm, Sa 9am-4:30pm. The **Tourist Information Bureau** (☎315714), platform 1 of the railway station, houses an RTDC as well as a Dept. of Tourism office. Open daily 7am-6pm. The monthly publication, *Jaipur Vision,* available at most bookstores for Rs20, also has lots of useful tourist information.

Tours: RTDC runs full-day and evening **city tours,** which jam the Pink City into a compact, unimaginative, and uncomfortable drive-by (half-day Rs85; full-day Rs125; does not include entrance fees). Both the RTDC and the Government of India Tourist Office can arrange government-approved private **guides** (half-day Rs230 for up to 4 people).

Jaipur

⌂ ACCOMMODATIONS
Aangan Guest House, 8
Anurag Guest House, 2
Atithi Guest House, 7
Evergreen Guest House, 14
Hotel Arya Niwas, 12
Hotel Diggi Palace, 18
Hotel Kailash, 22
Jaipur Inn, 3
Karni Niwas, 9
Tirupati Guest House, 1

🍴 FOOD
Green Tandoori Dhaba, 13
Hanuman Dhaba, 20
LMB, 21
Milky Way, 17
Niro's, 16
Shri Shanker Bhojnalya, 4
Surya Mahal, 15
Swaad, 10

♪ NIGHTLIFE
Polo Bar, 19
Rana Sanga Roof Top Bar, 11
Sheesh Mahal, 6
Talab Bar, 5

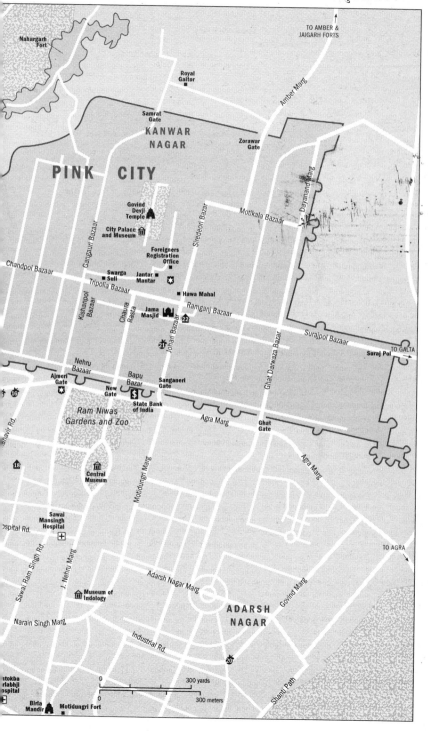

TO AMBER &
JAIGARH FORTS

Nahargarh
Fort

Royal
Gaitor ■

Samrat
Gate

KANWAR
NAGAR

Zorawar
Gate

PINK   CITY

Govind
Devji
Temple ▲

City Palace
and Museum 🏛

Foreigners
Registration
Office

Gangauri Bazaar

Sredeori Bazaar

Motikala Bazaar

Dayanand Marg

Amber Marg

Chandpol Bazaar

Swarga
■ Suli

Jantar
Mantar ✠

Tripolia Bazaar

Kishanpol
Bazaar

Chaura
Rasta

■ Hawa Mahal

Ramganj Bazaar

Jama
Masjid 🕌
22

Johari Bazaar

Surajpol Bazaar

TO GALTA

Suraj Pol

Ghat Darwaza Bazaar

Nehru
Bazaar

Bapu
Bazar

Sanganeri
Gate

Ajmeri
Gate ✠

New
Gate

State Bank
of India $

16

Ram Niwas
Gardens and Zoo

Agra Marg

Ghat
Gate

anavir Rd.

18

Central
Museum 🏛

Motidungri Marg

Agra Marg

Sawai
Mansingh
Hospital ✚

ospital Rd.

Sawai Ram Singh Rd.

J. Nehru Marg

TO AGRA

Adarsh Nagar Marg

ADARSH
NAGAR

Govind Marg

Museum of
Indology 🏛

Narain Singh Marg

Industrial Rd.

20

Shanti Path

0   300 yards

0   300 meters

ntokba
riabhji
ospital
✚

Birla
Mandir ▲

Motidungri Fort

Budget Travel: Rajasthan Tours, Rambagh Palace Hotel (☎381668; fax 381784). Open daily 7:30am-6pm. **Tourist Guide Service,** MI Rd., near Panch Batti (☎367735; fax 376251). Open daily 9am-6pm.

Immigration Office: Foreigners Registration Office (☎669391), behind Rajasthan Police Headquarters, near Jantar Mantar. Contact at least 1 week before visa expiration date. Open M-Sa 10am-5pm. Closed 2nd Sa of each month.

Currency Exchange: State Bank of India (☎561163), off MI Rd., near Sanganeri Gate. Currency exchange and traveler's checks. Open M-F 10am-5pm, Sa 10am-1pm. **Andhra Bank,** MI Rd. (☎374529), near Panch Batti. Cash advances on Visa, MC. 1% service charge per transaction. Open M-F 10am-2pm, Sa 10am-noon. **Thomas Cook,** Jaipur Towers, 1st fl. (☎360940). Currency exchange, traveler's checks, and money wiring. Open M-Sa 9:30am-6pm. **ATM** at HDFC Bank, near Evergreen Guest House.

LOCAL SERVICES

Luggage Storage: Jaipur Railway Station, Rs8-10 per item per day. Open 24hr.

Bookstore: Ganpati Books, Ganpati Plaza, MI Rd. (☎366323). Open M-Sa 10:30am-9pm. **Books Corner,** MI Rd. (☎366323), next to Niro's. Open daily 10am-11pm.

Library: Radhakrishnan Public Library, Jawaharlal Nehru Marg (☎516694). Open W-M 7am-7pm.

Market: Food and vegetable stalls are all over the old city—most near Chand Pol and Tripolia Bazaar. Most open dawn-dusk, closed Su; Bapu Bazaar open Su, closed M.

EMERGENCY AND COMMUNICATIONS

Police: Rajasthan Police Headquarters (☎607735 or 606657), inside the City Palace complex, behind Hawa Mahal. **Police Control Room** (☎565630), in King Edward Memorial Bldg., near Ajmeri Gate.

Hospital/Medical Services: Sawai Mansingh Hospital, Sawai Ram Singh Rd. (☎560291). Government-run, large, and efficient. Of the many private hospitals, the best are **Santokba Durlabhji Memorial Hospital,** Bhawani Singh Marg (☎566251), and **Soni Hospital, Kahota Bagh** (☎562028), off Jawaharlal Nehru Marg.

Pharmacy: Pharmacies line Station Rd. and surround the hospitals. There is also one in Shiv Marg, opposite Jaipur Inn. Most open daily 8am-10pm. The pharmacy in front of Santokba Durlabhji Memorial Hospital (☎571301) is open 24hr.

Telephones: The **Central Telegraph Office,** MI Rd. (☎367001), next to the GPO, has 24hr. STD/ISD service.

Internet: Communicator, G-4/5 Jaipur Towers ground floor (☎368061 or 204100). 8 terminals. Rs1 per min. Open M-Sa 9am-9pm, Su 11am-4pm. **Universal Courier and Communications,** MI Rd. (☎367901 or 367903), opposite the Indian Coffee House. Rs1 per min. Open M-Sa 9am-9pm, Su 9am-noon. Atithi Guest House, Aangan Guest House, Karni Niwas, and Evergreen Guest House has Internet access for Rs1.50 per min.

Post Office: GPO, MI Rd. (☎368740). Open M-Sa 8am-7pm, Su 10am-6pm. Branch near the Govt. of India Tourist Office and at the Central Bus Stand. Open M-Sa 9am-5pm. **Postal Code:** 302001.

◤ ACCOMMODATIONS

The budget hotel scene in Jaipur is frustratingly competitive. As soon as you arrive, you will be mobbed by rickshaw drivers prodding or pushing you to a particular hotel. It's a win-win-win situation for them: if you choose their hotel, they get a 50% commission, which will show up on your hotel bill; if you insist on another budget hotel, they simply charge you triple fare (or refuse to take you); and if you opt for a higher-end hotel, they quadruple their fare since you're "rich." Your cheapest bet is to shell out the triple fare and go where you want to go. Or just walk down a block and find slightly less ruthless local transportation.

Hotels around MI Rd., near the bus and railway stations, offer easy access to the services of the new city. Those in the residential area of Bani Park provide a more peaceful environment. There are very few hotels are within the Pink City itself. Home-stays can be arranged through the tourist office at the railway station (Rs150-800 per night).

Atithi Guest House, 1 Park House Scheme (☎378679; fax 379496), MI Rd. A home-away-from-home with bright, airy, rooms with marble floors, attached baths, and phones. Garden and plant-filled rooftop terrace provide a getaway from the bustle and noise. Great veg. cooking. 24hr. hot water. STD/ISD, fax, email, and Internet. Check-out noon. Singles Rs300-600; doubles Rs350-650. Reservations recommended.

Jaipur Inn, Shiv Marg (☎/fax 201121), Bani Park. From Sawai Jai Singh Highway, go right onto Shiv Marg 5min. down the circle, and into the large pink building. Clean, well-lit, plant-filled corridors surround a wide range of accommodations from tiny, log-cabin inspired rooms with common bath to more expensive options with air-cooling, balconies and great views. Roof-top restaurant with panoramic views of the city. Facilities include ping-pong table, washing machine (Rs100 per load), and store. Check-out 10am. Camping in the front garden Rs50 per person; dorm beds Rs80-100; singles Rs100-300; doubles Rs150-700. Reservations recommended.

Hotel Diggi Palace, Sawai Ram Singh Marg (☎373091; fax 370359), about 1km south of Ajmeri Gate. A spacious, 200-year-old converted palace in a mellow location. All food in the terrace restaurant is organically grown by the owner, and the cooking fuel is produced from the manure of his cows and polo horses. Surrounded by a beautiful garden, all the rooms look in on courtyards with outdoor sitting areas. Unreliable but friendly service. Check-out noon. Singles Rs100-250; doubles Rs100-950.

Evergreen Guest House (☎363446 or 362415; fax 204234; email evergreen34@hotmail.com), off MI Rd. Head past the GPO on the left and take the next right. Clubhouse atmosphere: palm trees, bench swings, swimming pool, and restaurant. Rooms (all with attached bath) are rather bare. STD/ISD service, email, Internet, and luggage storage. 24hr. hot water. Check-out 10am. Singles Rs100-400; doubles Rs200-450. Reservations recommended Oct.-Mar.

Anurag Guest House, D-249 Devi Marg (☎201679 or 205016), Bani Park. Spacious rooms and a lovely lawn area are the highlights of this small guest house. All rooms have attached baths with hot water. Check-out 24hr. Singles Rs200; doubles Rs250.

Karni Niwas, Moti Lal Atal Rd. (☎365433 or 216947; fax 375034; email karniniwas@hotmail.com), behind Hotel Neelam. Clean rooms lead to a number of tiny terraces. Restaurant, laundry service, STD/ISD, Internet, 24hr. hot water, and free pick-up at the train or bus station. Check-out noon. Singles 250-700; doubles Rs275-750.

Hotel Kailash, Johari Bazaar (☎565372). Look for the narrow door between stores. One of the few in the heart of the Pink City. Sure, it's noisy, but it's where the action is. Tiny stairways and corridors lead to adequate rooms, with central air-cooling, telephones, black-and-white TV, and hot water until 10am (free buckets after 10am). Check-out 24hr. Singles Rs130-315; doubles Rs140-365. Reservations recommended.

Tirupati Guest House, D-152 Durga Marg (☎201801), Bani Park. Large, bright rooms marked by ashram-style austerity. All have attached bath. Check-out 24hr. Dorm beds Rs75; rooms Rs200-300.

Aangan Guest House, 4 Park House Scheme (☎373449 or 214588; fax 364596; email aangan25@hotmail.com), off MI Rd., near All India Radio. A friendly place with a range of rooms and a garden. STD/ISD, fax, phones, Internet, and car hire. Check-out 24hr. Singles Rs125-500; doubles Rs175-700.

Hotel Arya Niwas, Sansar Chandra Rd. (☎372456 or 371773; fax 364376; email arya-hotel@jp1.dot.net.in). A simple, well-run hotel in a renovated *haveli*. Natural light and cross-ventilation keep the place bright and cool. STD/ISD, email, Internet, currency exchange, and small shop. All rooms have attached bath and air-cooling. Check-out noon. Singles Rs300-600; doubles Rs400-750. Reservations essential Oct.-Mar.

RAJASTHAN

🔆 FOOD

For cheap quickies, the *bhojnalyas* (diners) on Station Rd. are where the locals go. For those with a sweet tooth, the *mishri*, *mawas*, and *ghevars* of Jaipur are the best in the state. **Domino's Pizza, Pizza Hut,** and **Baskin Robbins** are all in Ganpati Plaza if you're yearning for international haute cuisine.

Swaad, Ganpati Plaza (☎360749), MI Rd. Sit back in the comfy chairs while the classical Indian music and delicious food lull you to sleep. The *naan* is *swaad*, indeed. Most dishes Rs50-100. Live music W-M 8pm. Open daily 11am-11pm.

Niro's, MI Rd., near Panch Batti. Their card justly claims "quiet grandeur, warm hearted courtesy, personalized service." All your old Indian, Chinese and continental friends are here, alive and well, and yours for Rs80-150. Open daily 10am-11pm.

Shri Shanker Bhojnalya, Station Rd., west of the bus stand. One of the most popular *bhojnalyas* in town. Cheap, quality food: excellent *thalis* (Rs30) and tandoori. Open daily 9am-11:30pm.

Surya Mahal, MI Rd. (☎369840), next to Niro's. Popular among local businessmen, families, teens, and tourists alike. Specializes in South Indian, Chinese, and pizza. A/C sweet shop in the back. Most dishes under Rs65. Open daily 8am-11pm.

LMB, Johari Bazaar. Incredible veg. food in a quirky A/C environment. Try not to fill up first at the sweet shop in front. Open daily 8am-11:30pm.

Green Tandoori Dhaba (☎362791), off MI Rd., near Indian Panch Batti. Locals come here for quality non-veg. food at great prices. Tandoori oven heats up the street along with delicious *rotis* and kebabs (Rs50-70). Those with adventurous tastebuds can munch on *magaj* (goat brain) for a mere Rs30. Open daily 11am-11pm.

Fun and Food Garden Restaurant, Meel Bhawan (☎331034), opposite Jyoti petrol pump, 8km from town. The garden, complete with live geese, provides the "fun" (not the "food") in this all-veg. restaurant. Dishes Rs30-55. Open daily 9am-11pm.

Hanuman Dhaba, Rd. 1, Raja Park (☎620582), near where Govind Marg turns into Industrial Rd. Locals come here for quality veg. food at cheap prices (Rs20-45). Streetside seating with views of the busy kitchen. Open daily 9:30am-11pm.

Milky Way, off Bhagwandas Marg. Midway between MI Rd. and Statue Circle, on a side street to the left. Best ice cream in town. Thick shakes Rs25; fountain sodas Rs10; sundaes Rs30. "Herbonic Shake" Rs30. Open daily 9am-midnight.

📺 🎵 NIGHTLIFE AND ENTERTAINMENT

BARS AND NIGHTCLUBS. Due to a strange prohibition law that's been in effect for years, only hotels can legally serve anything stronger than beer. For classy, air-conditioned boozing, try the popular **Polo Bar** in Rambagh Palace, off Bhawani Singh Rd. (☎381919. Open daily 11am-11:30pm), **Rana Sanga Roof Top Bar,** in Mansingh Palace off Sansar Chandra Rd. (☎378771, ext. 2677; open daily noon-3pm and 6:30-11pm), or the **Sheesh Mahal,** in the Rajputana Palace Sheraton near the railway station (☎360011, ext. 1713; open daily 11am to 11pm). Getting sloshed at cheaper prices with locals and budget tourists is better accomplished at the **Talab Bar,** in Swagatam Tourist Bungalow. (☎200595. Open noon-3pm and 6-11pm.) Other cheap bars include **Amrapali Bar,** in Chandragupt Hotel, opposite the bus stand (☎206300; open daily 7am-11pm), and **Dubki Bar,** Moti Lal Alal Rd., in Hotel Sangam near Ganpati Plaza (open daily 10am-11:30pm).

FESTIVALS. The **Gangaur Fair,** dedicated to the goddess Gauri, celebrates women, and lasts for 18 days after Holi (beginning Mar. 28-29, 2001; Apr. 15-16, 2002). The festival features singing, dancing, and parades with incredible costumes and decorations. The **Elephant Festival** features elephant polo and a tug-of-war that pits man against beast (March 9, 2001; March 28, 2002). The **Teej Fair** (Festival of Swings) celebrates the monsoon (July 23-24, 2001; Aug. 11-12, 2002). Decorated swings are hung from trees, and the city goes wild.

THE ARTS. Most regularly scheduled performances take place only during the high season. For authentic Rajasthani dance and music, the **Panghat Theater** (☎381919), in Rambagh Palace, off Bhawani Singh Rd., has in-season nightly performances in high-class surroundings for Rs300 per person. Shows are generally 7-9pm. Call in advance. **Ravindra Manch** (☎669061), in Ram Nivas Gardens, offers evening performances of Rajasthani dance, music, and plays, usually for Rs20 or less. Occasional films and fashion shows can be more expensive. The Modern Art Gallery upstairs is free (☎668531; open daily 10am to 5pm). **Jawahar Kala Kendra,** Jawaharlal Nehru Marg (☎510501), shows regular in-season performances of Rajasthani dance and music, as well as plays in Hindi and Rajasthani. Performances in the indoor theater are Rs5; shows in the open-air theater are free. There is also an arts library, and a modern art gallery. The **Surbhai Restaurant** (☎376060), inside the Tourist Hotel opposite the GPO, runs daily cultural programs.

OTHER DIVERSIONS. Jaipur's 16 **cinemas** are packed with people at every showing. Regardless of your interest in or comprehension of Hindi films, the plush, luxurious, world-renowned **Raj Mandir Cinema** (☎374694), just south of Panch Batti, is an experience in itself. The four daily showings are *always* sold out; arrive at *least* 1 hour in advance to get tickets. Look for the tourist/student queue. (Rs20-50.) The Evergreen Guest House (☎363446), off MI Rd., lets outsiders use its **swimming pool** (Rs75). Mansingh Palace (☎378771), off Sansar Chandra Rd., charges Rs200 for the use of their pool (daily 7am-8pm). For a glimpse of "authentic" village life, **Chowki Dhani,** 20km south of the city, promises a night of wild entertainment. Camel and ox rides, parrot astrology, palmistry, snake charming, *mehendi* hand-art, puppet shows, acrobatics, and music, all in traditional style, are available in this exhibition of village living. The highlight of the evening is the over-spiced dinner, served on leaf plates in a large mud hut. (Dinner Rs150. Open daily 6-11pm. Auto-rickshaw Rs250 round-trip.)

🔘 SIGHTS

THE PINK CITY

THE CITY PALACE. Built between 1729 and 1732 by Jai Singh II, founder of Jaipur, the City Palace encompasses nearly 15% of the Pink City's total area. Early maharajas filled the palace with scientific and artistic treasures. Others concentrated on public affairs. Those more interested in pleasure than in business cultivated a lively palace harem, which reputedly held over 1000 women into the 20th century. In recent decades, the palace has taken on a new public role in the life of the city. It opened to tourists in the 1950s, and scenes from over 400 films—including *North by Northwest* and the Errol Flynn version of Rudyard Kipling's *Kim*—have been shot within its walls. As the home of the current maharaja, Sawai Bhawani Singh, much of the palace is off-limits, but what you can see is delightful.

Upon entering, you'll find yourself in a large courtyard at the center of which is an attractive building adorned with carved patterns, marble pillars, and arched balconies. This once served as a secretariat, containing the offices used by the maharaja for state business. Today, the ground floor is occupied by the offices of the director of the palace, a museum complex, and a library that is accessible only with the permission of the director. The second floor of the building houses a **Textile Museum,** with collections of cloth and costumes, including the massive robes of the notorious "Fat Maharaja," Sawai Madho Singh I, who was 2.15m tall and reportedly weighed over 250kg.

Up the stairs in the northwest corner of the courtyard is the **Arms and Weapons Museum.** Just to the right of the entrance is one of the best displays, the exhibit of daggers, with elaborately crafted hilts concealing secret chambers and gunpowder holders made of seashells. The ceilings are expertly decorated with mirrors, paintings, and dense floral patterns.

> # MEETING THE MAHARAJA
> The current maharaja of Jaipur, Sawai Bhawani Singh, is a man of refinement and verve. Paying him a visit is about the coolest thing you can do in Jaipur. An old military man, the maharaja is an avid polo player who enjoys driving fancy cars and talks with excitement about computers and ham radio. The maharaja typically grants **private audiences** to visitors on weekdays. To make an appointment, ask at the main entrance of the City Palace for the ADC (Aide de Camp) Office. Be persistent in confirming the date and time of the appointment. There you can speak with the PPS (Principal Private Secretary), who organizes the maharaja's schedule. It's best to give the PPS a couple of days' advance notice. Throughout the process, modest, respectful clothing and behavior are expected.

Exiting the courtyard, you'll pass through an elaborate gate with massive brass doors flanked by two marble elephants and several red-turbaned soldiers. In the next courtyard is the **Diwan-i-Khas,** or Hall of Private Audience, where two *ganga-jalis*, silver urns built to contain incredible quantities of Ganga water, are on display. A sign notes that each urn holds 9000 liters of water and weighs 345kg, giving them the Guinness-certified distinction as the largest pieces of silver in the world. In the corner of the courtyard is the **Diwan-i-Am**, Hall of Public Audience, housing the **Art Museum,** which displays a hodgepodge of objects collected by the maharajas over the centuries. A large collection of manuscripts demonstrates the maharajas' traditional patronage of learning, and the collection of works on astronomy includes a 16th-century edition of Aristotle. One of the museum's highlights is its outstanding collection of miniature paintings. Particularly interesting is the **Wall of Mercury,** a painting of a beautiful woman in front of flowing water. The work has caused some controversy among scholars; while traditionally it has been understood as an illustration of a Hindu myth, some argue that it is a coded visual explanation of how to extract mercury from the earth. Exit the courtyard, and you'll find yourself in a smaller one, surrounded by four gates, each representing a different season. Lording over the courtyard is the **Chandra Mahal,** the maharaja's residence. Parts of the first floor are open to the public. (*In the center of the Pink City, flanked by Gangauri Bazaar to the west and Siredeori Bazaar to the east. Open daily 9:30am-4:45pm. ☎ 608055. Rs130; video fee Rs150. No photography in the galleries. Government-authorized guides Rs150.*)

HAWA MAHAL (PALACE OF WINDS). Jaipur's most recognizable landmark, the Hawa Mahal's five-story pink sandstone edifice was built in 1799. Maharaja Sawai Pratap Singh built the palace as a comfortable retreat, a place where he could go to compose his devotional songs to Krishna, some of which are still sung in the Govind Devji Temple, behind the palace. Designed to catch the breeze, the Hawa Mahal was named for the many brass wind vanes that adorned it until the 1960s. Underground tunnels connected the palace to the harem. (*On the eastern edge of the City Palace Complex. The facade faces Siredeori Bazaar. The entrance to the palace, is just off Tripolia Bazaar. ☎ 668862. Open Sa, Th 9am-4:30pm. Rs3; camera fee Rs30; video Rs70.*)

JANTAR MANTAR. The largest stone observatory in the world, Jantar Mantar is one of the Maharaja Jai Singh's most conspicuous contributions to the Jaipur cityscape. Before building it, Jai Singh sent emissaries east and west; they returned with cutting-edge technical manuals, including a copy of La Hire's "Tables," which the maharaja had coveted. Ironically, after building the Jantar Mantar, Jai Singh found that it produced readings 20 seconds more accurate than those reported by La Hire. The observatory features 18 instruments, including a 30m sundial—impressive, but incomprehensible without a guide or a solid knowledge of astronomy. (*South of the City Palace. ☎ 660494. Open Sa-Th 9am-4:30pm. Rs4, free M; camera fee Rs50; video Rs100. Guides Rs80.*)

GOVIND DEVJI TEMPLE. Perhaps the most popular Hindu house of worship, the temple contains an image of Lord Krishna as Govind Devji, the patron deity of the royal family, that was installed by Jai Singh himself. Seated to Govind Devji's left is his mate, Radha. The temple was constructed so the maharaja could easily view the deities from the comfort of his own palace across the street. *(North of the City Palace, off Siredeori Bazaar. Summer darshan: 4:45, 7:45, 10, 11:30am, 6:45, and 8:45pm. Winter darshan: 5:15, 8:15, 10:30am, noon, 6:30, and 8pm. ☎ 660494. Rs4, free M; camera fee Rs50; video Rs100. Guides Rs80.)*

SWARGA SULI. This towering minaret lies southwest of the City Palace and is the highest structure within the walls of the Pink City. The maharaja would sometimes bring criminals to the top of the tower and throw them to their deaths below.

NORTH OF THE PINK CITY

AMBER FORT. Standing guard over the Pink City, the three Garland Forts dominate the northern horizon. Foremost among these is the Amber Fort. Amber today is a reflection of the legendary Kachhwaha dynasty, a Rajput clan that dominated the area from the 12th to 18th centuries. Built in 1592 by Raja Man Singh, Amber is a blend of Hindu and Islamic architecture. While Jaigarh Fort was built primarily for defensive purposes, Amber was intended mainly as a residential fort, and its elaborate and extensive palace complex features decorative artwork and many other creature comforts.

Half the fun is getting up to the fort from the main road. A 15-minute walk up the steep, curvy road affords beautiful views of the surrounding valleys. Other means of access include jeep (Rs100) or elephant rides (a whopping Rs400 for up to 4 people; watch out for elephant sneezes!); rates include round-trip fare and an hour-long wait at the fort. To the side of the courtyard is the **Shri Sila Devi Temple**, dedicated to the goddess of strength. Entry through the majestic silver doors leads to a black marble idol of the deity. *(Closed daily noon-4pm.)* From the main courtyard, a flight of stairs leads to **Diwan-i-Am** (Hall of Public Audience). Opposite is the magnificently frescoed, mosaic-tiled **Ganesh Pol**, the main gate into the palace. The three windows above the gates were intended for the Maharani and the two Ranis that followed her; they sat up here and threw flowers and colorful powder on the maharaja as he passed through the gate. Just inside are the maharaja's former apartments, with their labyrinthine corridors, balconies, terraces, and rooms. Built for the maharaja, his 12 wives, and his 350 little bits on the side, the apartments were designed in such a way as to allow nighttime visits from the maharaja without any of the other women finding out. Parts are in poor repair but some, like the famous **Jai Mandir** (Hall of Victory), are in better condition, exhibiting blinding mirror work and beautiful, well-preserved coloring. Other attractions include the **Sheesh Mahal,** the original private chambers of the maharaja, whose walls and ceilings are completely covered with colored glass and mirrors, and the **Sukh Mahal** (Pleasure Palace). The government-approved **guides** (Rs200 for up to 4 people) are extremely well-informed, and are armed with stories that make the palace come alive. *(11km north of Jaipur. Bus leaves from the front of the Hawa Mahal every 15min., Rs5. Open daily 9am-4:30pm. Rs4; camera fee Rs50; video fee Rs100.)*

JAIGARH FORT. From the Amber Fort balconies, you can see this stocky fort, the second in the Garland trio, on top of a nearby hilltop. Its chambers and courtyards are hardly as elaborate as Amber's, but it does possess the gigantic **Jaivana**, the largest wheeled cannon in the world. It was once capable of firing a shot 35km. The main courtyard contains three enormous underground water tanks: one originally used by prisoners for bathing; one that held the jewels that financed Jaipur's foundation; and one, the largest, that contained nothing at all when the Indian government ransacked it in 1976 in a futile attempt to locate legendary treasure. Jaigarh's museum contains a rather bland selection of relics. The real attraction is the breathtaking view of Amber Fort and Jaipur from the ramparts. *(The fort can be reached by jeep or a 20min. climb from Amber Fort. ☎ 630848. Open daily 9am-4:30pm. Rs15, free with City Palace ticket stub; camera fee Rs50; video Rs100.)*

RAJASTHAN

NAHARGARH FORT. The third Garland Fort, the Nahargarh, is also known as the Tiger Fort. Painted floral patterns brighten the walls of the many chambers, which are strung together in a maze-like floorplan to add to the romantic atmosphere. The views of the nearby valleys are stunning. A shaded, open cafeteria next door serves overpriced food and drink. Because of Nahargarh's isolated locale, tourists have been warned against bringing valuables or traveling here alone. *(A shadeless 20min. walk uphill from the road leading from Amber to Jaigarh. Open daily 10am-4:30pm. Rs4; camera fee Rs30; video Rs100; guides Rs100.)*

ROYAL GAITOR. Just north of the old city, set against a backdrop of hills are the cenotaphs of the maharajas of Jaipur. The older ones are toward the back of the complex, including the beautifully carved cenotaph of Jai Singh. On the hill to the left, you can see Nahargarh Fort; to the right, steps lead uphill (20min.) to a **Ganesh temple.** *(North of Samrat Gate. Open daily 9am-4:30pm. Free. Camera Rs10; video Rs20.)*

SOUTH OF THE PINK CITY

BIRLA MANDIR. Officially called the Lakshmi Narayan Mandir, this blindingly white temple is rapidly becoming one of Jaipur's most beloved buildings. Built by the wealthy Birla family, a dynasty of Indian industrialists, the temple was styled with the family's multi-denominational approach to religion in mind: the three domes have each been styled according to a different type of religious architecture. The theme of pluralism is further evident in the artwork of the *parikarima*—done by a Muslim—and the pillars flanking the temple, which include carvings of Hindu deities as well as depictions of Moses, Jesus, Zarathustra, and Socrates. Close to the entrance of Birla Mandir are a variety of small temples, including one dedicated to Ganesh where devotees line up to bring items to be blessed. On the hill overlooking the Birla Mandir are the crumbling remains of **Motidungri Fort,** owned but not maintained by the maharaja. The fort complex contains a **Shiva temple** that is open to the public only once a year on Shivaratri, during the first week of March. *(Jawaharlal Nehru Marg, where it intersects with Bhawani Sing Marg. Open daily Nov.-Feb., 6:30am-noon and 3-9:30pm. Mar.-Oct. 6am-noon and 3-10pm.)*

GALTA (MONKEY TEMPLE). This series of temples and pavilions within a rocky valley surrounds a sacred pool. Worshippers can be seen bathing, washing, swimming, and diving from the cliffs, while monkeys scamper around the washing wells. The best time to visit is before noon, when the tide of worshippers is at its fullest. Galta can be reached by road from Agra Marg (rickshaw Rs100-200 roundtrip) or via a 30min. climb from just outside Suraj Pol. This route takes you past the **Surya Mandir,** with exquisite views, before leading you down into the gorge.

CENTRAL MUSEUM. Ram Niwas Gardens shelters Jaipur's Central Museum, often called **Albert Hall.** The building itself, a mixture of pillars, arches, and courtyards adorned with murals, is more interesting than the museum, which showcases various facets of Rajasthani culture and history. The ground floor contains exhibits on traditional Rajasthani dance and music, including a creative display of musical instruments. The halls upstairs showcase an extensive collection of miniature paintings and various other odds and ends. *(In the Ram Niwas Gardens, south of the old city. ☎ 560796. Open Sa-Th 10am-4:30pm. Rs30, M free. Photography prohibited inside.)*

MUSEUM OF INDOLOGY. The eccentric, encyclopedic, privately funded Museum of Indology features the trashy treasure troves of Vyakul (poet, painter, and super-nice guy who has been collecting stuff since he was 13 and can't bear to part with any of it): knick-knacks, curio pieces, and some real treasures. The museum holds a collection of textiles, designs, architectural drawings, and 20,000 buttons. In one room, the marriage contract of the last Mughal emperor vies for attention with a grain of rice with a full-color map of India drawn on it. *(About 500m south of the Central Museum, just off Nehru Marg. Open daily 9am-6pm. ☎ 607455. Admission with guide Rs40, though a tip may be expected.)*

🛍 SHOPPING

Jaipur is essentially a series of interconnected bazaars. Shopping here means heavy bargaining and constant harassment—it can be draining, but the effort is well worth it. You'll find a huge assortment of handicrafts, clothing, textiles, jewelry, and perfumes. Rajasthan is known for its colorful tie-dyed fabrics called *bandhani* (the tie-dye technique was invented in this state). Though tie-dyed items are available in other parts of India, they probably won't match the selection you'll find in the Pink City. Other unique local specialties include *meenakari* (enamel work on silver and gold) and blue pottery. The jewelry and gem work of Jaipur is world-famous and remarkably inexpensive, but be on the lookout for scams. In the Pink City, **Johari Bazaar** and two lanes off it—**Gopal ka Rasta** and **Haldiyon ka Rasta**—are the prime spots for jewelry and gem stores and gold and silver smiths. Connecting the Ajmeri, New, and Sanganeri Gates are **Nehru Bazaar** and **Bapu Bazaar.** These specialize in textiles, perfumes, camel-skin shoes, and *mojiris* (a type of sandal). **Tripolia Bazaar** and **Charra Rasta** have a variety of stores selling lace work, ironwork, miscellaneous wooden and ivory pieces, and local trinkets. Watch master carpet-makers at work in **Siredeori Bazaar,** and find exquisite marble sculpture and carvings in **Chandpol Bazaar.** (Most stores open M-Sa 10am-8pm.)

🔼 SARISKA TIGER RESERVE AND NATIONAL PARK

The dry, temple-studded Aravalli Mountains, 108km northeast of Jaipur and 200km west of Delhi, is home to the 866 sq. km Sariska Tiger Reserve and National Park (☎ (0144) 41333), whose rich wildlife population includes *nilgai* (blue bulls), *sambar* (large deer), spotted deer, wild boar, monkeys, leopards, hyenas, and wild dogs. A protected reserve under the Indian government's "Project Tiger" (see p. 367), the park is popular these days with tourists who come here hoping for a shot of the elusive tigers against the backdrop of their native environment. The park is also famous as the site of the **Hanuman Mandir,** which marks the spot where the monkey god fought against the hero Bhima in the *Mahabharata.*

The park and temple can be visited on a three-hour jeep tour that starts from the Sariska Park Office on the Alwar-Jaipur road. *(Office open 6:30am-4:30pm; in winter 7am-4pm. Entrance Rs100 per person.)* Jeeps wait in front of the office. The best times to see the wildlife are early in the morning and late in the afternoon. Vehicles charge Rs500 plus the Rs125 vehicle entrance fee and Rs100 for your (compulsory) guide. Chances are that you will meet other visitors willing to share the cost.

Sariska can be reached by bus from **Alwar** (every 30min., 5am-8pm, 1hr., Rs10) and from **Jaipur** (7 per day, 2½hr., Rs50). Buses going the other way can be flagged down in front of the park office. From Alwar, connections are available to **Bharatpur** (3½hr., Rs65). The only real place to stay is the **Hotel Tiger Den** next to the park entrance; it's clean but overpriced. (☎ 41342. Dorm beds Rs50; doubles Rs600-800.) This is also the only place to get a meal without going out and shooting something; you are better off bringing your own provisions. **Hotel Sariska Palace,** across the road, is the former maharaja's hunting lodge, and it continues to provide regal luxury at prices even the maharaja himself couldn't afford these days.

BHARATPUR भरतपुर   ☎ 05644

A convenient stop on the popular tourist route between Agra (56km) and Jaipur (172km), Bharatpur's spectacular Keoladeo Ghana National Park, one of the biggest and best bird sanctuaries in the world, is well worth a visit. The beautifully maintained park draws thousands of migrating birds every winter, and the crowds of twitchers are never far behind. Founded by Badan Singh in 1733 as a princely state, Bharatpur soon became known for the fierce armies of Suraj Mal, who plundered Delhi in 1753 and occupied Agra from 1761 to 1774. The state of Bharatpur was recognized as autonomous by the Mughals and successfully resisted two attacks by the British before it was finally captured by Lord Combermere in 1826. After Independence, it became a part of Rajasthan.

GETTING THERE AND GETTING AROUND. The **train station** is in the northern section of town. To: **Bombay** (10:50am and 7:50pm, 20hr., Rs304); **Delhi** via **Mathura** (3 per day, 6:30am-3:45pm, 5hr., Rs52). **Buses** from Jaipur drop off passengers on the west side of town. Buses leave from the state transport bus stand to: **Alwar** (every 1½hr., 7:30am-5:30pm, 3½hr., Rs40); **Bikaner** (12:30pm, 12hr., Rs150); **Delhi** (every hr., 4:30am-midnight, 5hr., Rs72); **Jaipur** (every 30 min., 5:30am-1am, 2hr., Rs52); and **Udaipur** (3 per day, 7:45am-7:45pm, 11hr., Rs210). Buses to **Agra** via **Fatehpur Sikri** (every 30min., 5:30am-1am, 2hr., Rs24) can be flagged down in front of Hotel Saras near the park area. **Rickshaws** (Rs15-20) make the journey to the hotel area. Shared **tempos** (Rs4) run between the train and bus terminals. You can rent **bicycles** at several hotels near the sanctuary (Rs30-50 per day).

ORIENTATION AND PRACTICAL INFORMATION. The bird sanctuary and the hotels are a few kilometers south of the center of town, along the road to Agra and Fatehpur Sikri. The chaotic town itself sprawls around the ruins of an ancient fort and is best avoided unless you need to change money or mail a postcard. The **RTDC Tourist Reception Centre,** adjacent to the Hotel Saras, has basic information booklets on the area and maps of Keoladeo and the city for Rs2. (☎22542. Open M-F 10am-5pm.) The **State Bank,** near Binarayan Gate, northwest of Birdland, changes currency and traveler's checks, but has a US$100 limit. (☎22441. Open M-F 10am-5pm, Sa 10am-2pm.) Other services include: 24-hour **luggage storage,** on platform #1 of the train station (Rs5-7 per day); **Lokesh Medicos,** 3km from the railway station (☎26879; open 24 hours); and the **General Hospital,** Station Rd. (☎23633, emergency 22451). Collect calling and callbacks are available at **Shree Prabhu,** between Hotel Pratap Palace and Hotel Sunbird, on the road leading to the sanctuary. (☎25446. Open 24 hours.) **Police:** ☎22526. The **post office** is opposite Jama Masjid to the east. (☎23586. Open M-Sa 6am-6pm.) **Postal Code:** 321001.

ACCOMMODATIONS AND FOOD. All the hotels below are out of town, just a short trip from the park entrance. Most establishments rent bicycles, binoculars, and field guides. Discounts of 50% can be negotiated April-August. Prices listed are for the winter. Reservations are recommended September-December. The ▨ **Jungle Lodge,** at the end of the hotel-filled alley behind Hotel Saras, is set in a peaceful garden and run by a couple who will wow you and charm you with their excellent cooking and encyclopedic knowledge of local birdlife. (☎25622. Doubles with attached bath Rs200-300. Rich *thalis* Rs55.) **Kinam Guest House** (☎23845) is another family-run place mercifully removed from the honking trucks of Agra Rd. From Hotel Saras, take the road toward Bharatpur, and then take the first left. Kinam is 100m down, on the right. Rooms here are spotlessly clean, with immaculate attached baths. Good home-style dinners are served in the hotel courtyard. **Hotel Pelican** is the most popular of the places on the main road. Several small cells are fitted with large beds, so that you can stick your feet out of the window and let them air overnight for Rs80. (☎24221. Doubles with attached bath Rs200-250.) Next door, **Sumbind** is the choice of many real-life bird-addicts and professional photo snappers. (☎25701. Doubles Rs250-650.) Farther down the road, the huge **Hotel Eagle's Nest** should be able to help you out in the event of a sudden room shortage. (☎25144. Singles Rs250; doubles Rs300-600.) **Spoonbill Guest House** (☎23571) behind the Hotel Saras, has just a few cramped rooms, but has a wide range of services, from an on-site goodies shop to laundry service and Rajasthani home-cooking. All of these places have attached restaurants that can prepare packed lunches for out-all-day birders. A five-minute bike ride from Saras toward Bharatpur, next to the Old Powerhouse Chowk, is the **Jeet Restaurant,** a local favorite serving rich Punjabi food. After a sizzling pot of mutton *do pyaza* (Rs45) and a burning *masala channa* (Rs25), the ice-cold Kingfisher might just be the best bird you have seen all day.

☒ SIGHTS. The main reason foreigners flock to Bharatpur is to go cuckoo over the hordes of birds at the Keoladeo Ghana National Park (see below). If you're in town and are sick of binoculars, you could check out the 18th-century **Lohagarh Fort,** near Nehru Park, north of the center of town. Built by Maharaja Suraj Mal, the fort has a reputation of being notoriously resistant to attack; British armaments are said to have bounced off the walls. The **museum** here features three large galleries of ancient Jain sculpture and fort artifacts. *(Open Sa-Th 10am-4:30pm. Rs3.)*

☒ KEOLADEO GHANA NATIONAL PARK. Created in the late 19th century by the maharaja of Bharatpur, and now one of the best birdwatching spots in the world, the Keoladeo Ghana National Park started out as a 29 square km anything-goes play zone for the maharaja and his buddies to indulge their passion for hunting and shooting. A sandstone plaque in the park bears testimony to a bag of 4276 duck and geese shot down in one long record-breaking day. Renowned in birding circles as the finest wetland reserve in northern India, the park has plenty to offer, even if your interest in birds doesn't normally go much beyond an occasional trip to Kentucky Fried Chicken. The best time to visit is after the monsoon, when the waterways are occupied by thousands of nesting waterbirds. More than 300 species of birds have been recorded here.

Motor vehicles are not allowed past Keoladeo's only entrance. To explore the grounds, you will have to rent a **bicycle** at the **main office** at the gate. *(Bicycles Rs20; binoculars Rs50; deposit your passport or Rs1000.)* Many local hotels also rent bikes for Rs30-50. Alternatively, you can hire one of the **tongas** *(Rs60 per hr.)* or **cycle-rickshaws** *(Rs30 per hr.)* that depart from the gate. Guides can also be hired at the gate for Rs35 per hour. The best way to see the birds is to take an early-morning boat trip, which allows you float right up to hundreds of nesting herons, egrets, cranes, storks, and spoonbills. You can hire a **boat** in season for up to four people *(1hr., Rs80),* or inquire at the office in front of the park about suggested **walking tours.**

Inside the office, a small visitors' center features nests, eggs, and stuffed specimens, as well as a color map of the park. A bookstore at the check-post 1km past the entrance gate sells bird-books and postcards. *(Open 8:30am-sunset.)* Within the park, the only sustenance available is tea and biscuits from a stall next to the Shiva temple. If tea and biscuits isn't going to be enough, make sure to bring your own provisions. *(☎ 22777. Open daily sunrise to sunset; 6am-6pm during the monsoon. Rs100 for foreigners; with cycle additional Rs3; with video camera additional Rs200.)*

AJMER अजमेर
☎ 0145

The bustling town of Ajmer, 132km west of Jaipur in the heart of the Aravalli Mountains, is important to tourists more for its proximity to Pushkar than for any sights of its own. For many, however, Ajmer is significant as the final resting place of Khwaja Muin-ud-din Chishti, founder of India's most important Sufi order. Hundreds of thousands of Muslims and Hindus make a pilgrimage to Ajmer during the annual Urs Ajmer Sharif, which takes place in September and October, when the town bursts with people and festivities. The rest of the year, Ajmer's streets and bazaars offer plenty of opportunities for good people-watching and bargaining.

☒ GETTING THERE AND GETTING AROUND. The **railway station** is in the western part of town. The reservation office is on the second floor above the main entrance. (Enquiries ☎ 131, reservations ☎ 431965. Open M-Sa 8am-8pm, Su 8am-2pm.) Trains head to **Delhi** (3-5 per day, 2:15am-12:45am, 7-9 hr., Rs99); **Jaipur** (5-7 per day, 5:30am-7:45pm, 2-3hr., Rs41); and **Udaipur** (1:50am and 8.45am, 9-10hr., Rs73). Buses run from the **Main Bus Stand** (☎ 429398) to: **Ahmedabad** (5 per day, 5:45am-8:45pm, 13½ hr., Rs200); **Abu Road** (3 per day, 5:45am-8:15pm, 9hr., Rs142); **Bikaner** (11 per day, 6:15am-11:45pm, 7hr., Rs108); **Chittaurgarh** (every hr., 5am-1am, 5½ hr., Rs75); **Jaipur** (every 15min., 3hr., Rs55; deluxe 9 per day, 7:45am-10:30pm, 3hr., Rs66); **Jodhpur** (15 per day, 5hr., Rs87); **Udaipur** (12 per day, 7hr., Rs118, deluxe Rs140). The **Pushkar Bus Stand,** near the Station-Kutchery Rd.

junction, sends buses to Pushkar (hence the name) every 15 minutes (5am-midnight, 30min., Rs5). **Private bus** companies line Kutchery Rd. and send deluxe buses to most destinations. Most will pick up in Pushkar if needed; check in advance. For Rs10-25, cycle- and auto-**rickshaws** will get you anywhere. Crowded **tempos** charge Rs3-5.

⚑🛈 ORIENTATION AND PRACTICAL INFORMATION. Ajmer is a small town, only about 3km long, and once you have spent some time roaming about, its geography should become clear. **Station Rd.** runs east from the station, intersecting the southeast-bound **Kutchery Rd.,** which leads to the **Main Bus Stand.** The **Bank of Baroda,** Station Rd., near the GPO, changes foreign currency and traveler's checks and does cash advances on Visa, MC, AmEx. (☎432124. Open M-F 10am-2pm, Sa 10am-noon.) Dr. Yadava's **Pratap Memorial Hospital,** Kutchery Rd. (☎626406), the best private hospital, has a 24-hour **pharmacy** in front. The **police** (☎425080) are opposite the railway station. The main **tourist office** is on the east side of town, not far from the bus stand, inside the Hotel Khadim. (☎627426. Open M-Sa 8am-noon and 3-6pm.) Also inside Hotel Khadim is **Surya Tours and Travels** (☎878110). The **GPO** is near the Station-Kutchery Rd. intersection. (☎432145. Open M-Sa 10am-6pm.) **Postal Code:** 305001.

🍴🛏 ACCOMMODATIONS AND FOOD. Ajmer has a disappointing selection of hotels. Most tourists head to Pushkar for a wider range of accommodations and visit Ajmer as a daytrip. Opposite the railway station is a group of dirt-cheap, no-frills hotels. Prithviraj Marg and Kutchery Rd. have more of the same. Hotels are booked heavily, so call in advance. Prices go nuts during the Urs Ajmer Sharif and the Pushkar Mela (see p. 292). The **City View Paying Guest House,** Nalla Bazaar, a 5 minute walk from the railway station, is a tiny, family-run hotel on a narrow, winding street in the old city. The rooms are big but very basic, and the rooftop has spectacular views. (☎431243. Singles Rs50-150; doubles Rs100-200.) The best of the cheapies is **Bhola Hotel,** Agra Gate, which has well-decorated rooms with tiled bathrooms and a tiny terrace overlooking the vegetable market. (☎432844. Singles Rs125; doubles Rs200.) The **Hotel Nagpal,** Station Rd., features clean rooms with phones and attached baths (☎429503. Check-out 24hr. Singles Rs175-650; doubles Rs300-1000).

There aren't many **restaurants** in Ajmer, but the few that you will find are decent enough. For a quick bite, try the snack, juice, and egg stalls around Delhi Gate. The **Bhola Hotel** has an excellent and inexpensive restaurant that serves up a delicious *aloo paneer* for Rs25. (Open daily 9am-11pm.) **Rasna,** Prithviraj Marg, has pure veg. food (Rs24-45) served in underground A/C bliss. (Open daily 8am-11pm.) The **Honeydew Restaurant,** Station Rd., serves continental, Chinese, and Indian cuisines in a clean, calm environment and has two pool tables in the front room. (☎622498. Most dishes Rs35-60. Pool Rs60 per hr. Open daily 8am-11pm.)

📷 SIGHTS. When thousands of people flock to Ajmer during the Urs Ajmer Sharif, **Dargah** is what they come to see. On the north side of town, in the old city, the tomb of the Sufi saint **Khwaja Muin-ud-din Chishti** looms high above the surrounding bazaars. Originally a simple brick cenotaph, Dargah has been expanded and improved upon as rich rulers have paid tribute; today it is an elaborate marble complex. A tall, elaborate gateway leads to the first courtyard, where two massive cauldrons called *degs* are filled with rice that is then sold to devotees as *tabarukh,* a sanctified food. Akbar's mosque is to the right and Shah Jahan's grand mosque is farther inside. The tomb of the saint himself is in a central marble mosque, encircled by silver railings. The tomb draws huge crowds, often making it difficult to see for extended periods of time. Guides will almost certainly offer their services, but they are not really necessary. A head scarf is required to enter certain parts of the complex; if you don't have one, pick one up from the bazaar that leads up to the tomb. Be sure to keep a close eye on your personal belongings when you enter. Respectful behavior and a small donation are expected.

Continuing on the road past Dargah for about 500m brings you to the **Adhai-din-Ka-jhonpra** (Mosque of Two-and-a-Half Days), named for the remarkably short time the legendary Muhammad of Ghur took to build it in 1193. The towering facade consists of seven arches elaborately carved with Persian calligraphy. It's best to view the mosque late in the day when the setting sun gives it a warm glow. The magnificently red **Nasiyan Temple,** in the bazaars near Agra Gate, houses a museum, where the Jain conception of the universe is illustrated with golden models. A local Jain family used over 1000kg of gold to construct the exhibit in 1865, and the project took 20 artisans 40 years to complete. The colored glass that decorates the walls and columns may or may not conceal enormous diamonds. *Let's Go* does not recommend trying to find out. (Open daily 8:30am-5:30pm. Rs3.)

On the northeast side of town, the 11th-century **Ana Sagar Lake** is a nice spot for a stroll or picnic. The **Dault Bagh** gardens along the banks of the lake contain marble pavilions built by Shah Jahan. Boats can be rented from Subash Bagh. (Pedal boats Rs30 per 30min.)

PUSHKAR पुष्कर ☎ 0145

Legend has it that at the beginning of time Lord Brahma dropped a *pushkara*, or lotus flower, into the desert. A holy lake sprang up where the flower fell and became a place where pilgrims could be cleansed of all their sins. This lake is now the central attraction of the calm town of Pushkar, the site of the only Brahma temple in India. For many Hindu pilgrims, Pushkar represents the final stop on a tour of India's sacred sites, and a dip in the waters completes the circuit of redemption. Besides spiritual enlightenment, Pushkar offers respite from many of the hassles of bigger cities: the noisy auto-rickshaws that plague other towns are delightfully absent from Pushkar. However, the town is transformed into a swarming beehive of activity every November for the annual **Pushkar Mela.**

> **WARNING.** Pushkar is a purely vegetarian town (no eggs allowed), and drugs and booze are strict verboten. There is also an explicit rule against public displays of affection—prevalent signs admonish that there is "no public kissing or hand-holding" allowed in this sacred town.

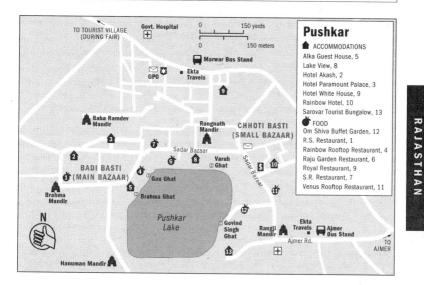

Pushkar

🔺 ACCOMMODATIONS
Alka Guest House, 5
Lake View, 8
Hotel Akash, 2
Hotel Paramount Palace, 3
Hotel White House, 9
Rainbow Hotel, 10
Sarovar Tourist Bungalow, 13

🍴 FOOD
Om Shiva Buffet Garden, 12
R.S. Restaurant, 1
Rainbow Rooftop Restaurant, 4
Raju Garden Restaurant, 6
Royal Restaurant, 9
S.R. Restaurant, 11
Venus Rooftop Restaurant, 11

RAJASTHAN

▮ GETTING THERE AND GETTING AROUND

Buses: Ajmer Bus Stand, Ajmer Rd. To: **Ajmer** (every 15min., 5:30am-9pm, 30min., Rs5). The **Marwar Bus Stand** serves: **Jaipur** (6 per day, 8am-6:30pm, 3½hr., Rs50); **Jodhpur** (3 per day, 10am-11:30pm, 5hr., Rs68). All other destinations can be reached via the **Main Bus Stand** (☎429398) in Ajmer. **Private bus** companies line Sadar Bazaar and the area around Marwar Bus Stand. Most private buses depart from Ajmer, though free transport from Pushkar to Ajmer is included. **Ekta Travels** (see below), the only government-recognized agency in Pushkar, has daily buses from Pushkar to major cities in Rajasthan.

Local Transportation: Most visitors travel everywhere on foot, but **bicycles** can be rented from several shops near the Ajmer Bus Stand (Rs5 per hr., Rs25 per day).

▮ ORIENTATION AND PRACTICAL INFORMATION

Pushkar is a small town, and getting lost is hardly an issue. Most travelers arrive at the **Ajmer Bus Stand,** on Ajmer Rd., in the southeast of town. As it winds into town, Ajmer Rd. becomes **Sadar Bazaar,** the main thoroughfare, which follows the northern shore of **Pushkar Lake** and ends on the west side of town, near the **Brahma Mandir.** Roughly speaking, the eastern half of the town is referred to as **Choti Basti (Small Bazaar),** while the west half is known as **Badi Basti (Main Bazaar).** A right turn on any one of the twisting side streets off Sadar Bazaar leads to the road that marks the northern boundary of the town, where you'll find the GPO, the **Marwar Bus Stand,** and the government hospital.

Tourist Office: There is no official tourist office in Pushkar, though Ekta Travels (see below) can provide maps and brochures. Ajmer's **Tourist Information Bureau** (☎52426) has information about Pushkar. Open M-Sa 10am-1:30pm and 2-5pm. During the Pushkar Fair, the RTDC-run **Tourist Village** (☎72074) provides information.

Budget Travel: Ekta Travels (☎72131), near the Marwar Bus Stand. Another branch near the Ajmer Bus Stand (☎72931). Authorized agents for Indian Airlines (they issue tickets), Indian Railways, and Srinath Buses. Both open daily 7am-10pm.

Currency Exchange: State Bank of Bikaner and Jaipur (☎72006), at the end of Sadar Bazaar, changes currency and traveler's checks. Open M-F 10am-2pm, Sa 10am-noon.

Bookstore: There are several bookstores in the eastern half of Sadar Bazaar near the post office. **Vijay Book House** is open daily 9am-10pm.

Police: Main Police Station (☎72046), opposite the Government Hospital. Tourist-friendly and English-speaking. Open 24hr.

Pharmacy: Most pharmacies line the northern side of town near the hospital and Marwar Bus Stand, but there are several in Sadar Bazaar as well. Most open daily 8am-8pm.

Hospital/Medical Services: Dr. Sanjay Gupta (☎72672 or 72928), next to Sarovar Tourist Bungalow, runs an excellent clinic specializing in medical assistance to travelers. Open daily 9:30am-9pm; on call after-hours. **Government Community Hospital** (☎72029), near Marwar Bus Stand. English-speaking staff. Open 24hr. for emergencies.

Telephones: Mahesh Pal Communication, Ghumar Niwas (☎72486 or 72596), opposite the Government Hospital has free callbacks. Open 24hr.

Internet: Internet facilities are abundant in and around Sadar Bazaar for Rs2 per min. **Goyal Internet** (☎72315), near Venus Rooftop Restaurant, seems to have the fastest connections in town. **Shree Internet** (☎72399), near the center of Sadar Bazaar. Both open daily 7am-11pm.

Post Office: GPO (☎720222), on the north side of town, next to the police station. There is a branch in Sadar Bazaar. Open M-Sa 9am-5pm. **Postal Code:** 305022.

ACCOMMODATIONS

Amenities get better every year, but most of Pushkar's budget hotels are still very basic—small rooms, hard beds, and common baths. There is no shortage of hotels right on the lake, but the places just off the main bazaar tend to be quieter. Hotels have different policies regarding drinking, smoking, and curfews—check in advance before you plan your party. Pushkar is so small that you can safely check out many hotels one by one, even with a big pack sticking to your back. During the Pushkar Fair, when prices can be more than 10 times as high, it is cheaper to stay in Ajmer and commute to Pushkar.

Hotel Akash (☎ 72498), near Brahma Mandir. This hotel's owners promise a very "Shanti, Shanti" stay, with no techno music allowed. The charming building has good vibes, basic-but-homey rooms around a shaded central courtyard, and a very pleasant rooftop restaurant complete with hammocks. Great facilities include 24hr. water, bike rental, kitchen, and a free pick-up from Ajmer. Check-out 10am. Rooms (some with common bath, some attached) are rented on a pay-what-you-can basis—roughly Rs30-120 depending on the type of room and the size of your budget.

Hotel White House (☎ 72147 or 72885), near the Marwar Bus Stand. Spacious, spotless rooms around an airy, open courtyard. Rooftop restaurant overlooking the surrounding gardens. Tons of facilities. Morning yoga instruction on the roof. Check-out 10am. Singles Rs60-80, with bath Rs100-250; doubles Rs100-350.

Rainbow Hotel (☎ 72167 or 73309), near the State Bank of Bikaner and Jaipur. Rooms are small but bright and clean in this modern (for Pushkar) hotel. 24hr. room service, washing machine, and rooftop restaurant with beautiful views across town to the lake. Check-out noon. Singles Rs60-150; doubles Rs100-250.

Alka Guest House, Sadar Bazaar (☎ 72738), near Rainbow Rooftop Restaurant. Spacious, clean rooms overlooking the lake; run by a friendly family. Common baths. The rooftop has beautiful views of the lake and the desert. Terrace restaurant offers a huge selection of food and Indian music. Luggage storage. Check-out noon. Singles Rs70; doubles Rs100; deluxe room with view of lake Rs150.

Sarovar Tourist Bungalow, Ajmer Rd. (☎ 72040), 100m west of the Ajmer Bus Stand. Wow—a government building with character. RTDC-run establishment has nice, cool rooms and a pool with mountain views. Check-out noon. Dorm beds Rs50; singles Rs125-375; doubles Rs200-500.

Hotel Paramount Palace (☎ 72428 or72747), near Rainbow Rooftop Restaurant. Pleasant rooms in a tranquil location. Terrific scenery from the rooftop restaurant. Check-out noon. Rooms Rs100–300, with balcony Rs350-600.

Lake View (☎ 72106), in the center of Sadar Bazaar. The lake views can't be beat, but there's not much else going for this pack-em-in hotel. Tiny, more or less clean rooms. Check-out 11am. Singles (common bath) Rs50-80; doubles Rs100-250.

FOOD

Pushkar has its share of good Indian cuisine, but, as usual, most travelers indulge in the local interpretations of Western food. Imposters are everywhere—don't be fooled by restaurants bearing remarkably similar names to more popular places.

S.R. Restaurant, Sadar Bazaar. Don't be deterred by the food-stall set-up. This open-air restaurant whips up delicious food in enormous helpings at great prices. Massive special *thali* Rs45. Open daily 8:30am-10:30pm.

Om Shiva Buffet Garden Restaurant, near Hotel Pushkar Palace, on the eastern end of off Sadar Bazaar. Fresh, healthy food you can trust. Breakfast (7am-12:30pm), lunch (1-4pm), and dinner (5-10pm) buffet Rs45.

Rainbow Rooftop Restaurant, near Brahma Mandir. Well-prepared Indian and Western dishes from a menu almost as stunning as the rooftop view. Homemade peanut butter

Rs15; falafal Rs40-90; real cappuccino Rs15; homemade pasta Rs30-70; mouth-watering chocolate truffles Rs10. The best lemon soda (Rs15) in town. Open 8am-11pm.

R.S. Restaurant, opposite Brahma Mandir. Popular among locals. Great Indian dishes (Rs20-28), as well as spaghetti and macaroni (Rs30-40). Garden and terrace seating. Fresh juice (Rs10-15). Open daily 7am-10:30pm.

Raju Garden Restaurant, Badi Basti. Small selection of international cuisine "all cooked with love by Raju." Lakeside view. Indian dishes Rs20-50. Open daily 8:30am-11pm.

Venus Rooftop Restaurant, Chhoti Basti. Another multi-cuisine restaurant, but with particularly tasty Indian dishes (Rs15-40), fresh juice (Rs10-12), and a rooftop view of the street below. Limited *thalis* Rs25. Open daily 7am-11pm.

Royal Restaurant, inside Hotel White House. Fresh cooked vegetables from the garden below and a pool table "coming soon." Open daily 8am-10pm.

◉ SIGHTS

TEMPLES. Most of Pushkar's 540 temples were rebuilt after pillaging raids by the Mughal emperor Aurangzeb in the 17th century. Several are open only to Hindus. The most popular is the **Brahma Mandir,** the only temple in India dedicated to Brahma, the Hindu creator-god. Expect to be mobbed by eager guides, though their services are hardly necessary to view the temple. Other temples of interest include the **Rangji Mandir,** with its white stone facade, the **Hanuman Mandir,** a colorful tower depicting Hanuman's exploits, the turquoise-green **Baba Ramdev Mandir,** and the 800 year-old **Ragnath Mandir.** Two major hillside temples in Pushkar command superb views over the town and valley, especially at sunset and sunrise. Named for two of Brahma's wives, **Savithri Mandir** and **Gayatri Mandir** crown hills on the east and west side of town. (*Each a 1½hr. climb.*)

GHATS. Surrounding Pushkar Lake are the broad ghats that connect the temples and the holy waters. Of Pushkar's 52 *ghats*, the most important are the **Gau Ghat,** where an assortment of politicians, ministers, and VIPs have paid their respects, **Brahma Ghat,** which Brahma himself is said to have used, and the central **Varah Ghat,** where Vishnu once appeared in the form of a boar. Signs in hotels instruct visitors to remove their shoes and to refrain from smoking and taking photographs. Pilgrims and tourists at the *ghats* are frequently accosted by local priests (some carry a small "certified Brahmin" photo ID card) to perform a Pushkar *puja*, a ceremony of scripture-reading and flower-scattering. Do not feel pressured into donating the exorbitant amounts that the priests insist are "standard." After the *puja*, your patronage is officially recognized with a red wrist-band—the "Pushkar Passport"—theoretically giving you the freedom to visit *ghats* and stroll around town without priestly harassment.

CAMELS. Camel safaris into the desert are becoming increasingly popular in Pushkar, along with camel treks across the desert to Jaisalmer, Jodhpur, or Bikaner. Most hotels and travel agents can arrange these for you; expect to pay around Rs350 per day for a good camel safari. If you don't have enough time for a safari or trek but want get close to a dromedary, go for a camel ride—loops around the city cost Rs40-50 per hour.

✿ FESTIVALS

The annual **Pushkar Mela,** or **Pushkar Fair** (Nov. 27-30, 2001; Nov. 16-19, 2002), is an event that involves colossal numbers, crowding 200,000 people from all over the world into one square kilometer. Thousands of pilgrims bathe in the lake's holy waters to seek redemption for their sins. Beyond the lake, the dry desert landscape teems with more than 50,000 camels (*oont* in Hindi), who excite the masses in races, auctions, contests, parades and safaris. Check out the hair-cuts on them camels! Stalls selling handicrafts from all over India fill the streets, while street performers jump and juggle on every corner. Lending a more modern edge to the festival are the carnival rides set up next to the camel campgrounds. It wouldn't be a fair without food—specialty cuisines are everywhere. Make hotel reservations well in advance and expect to pay dearly for your square inch of space.

CHITTAURGARH चित्तौड़गढ़   ☎ 01427

Rajasthan has many wind-swept cities with impressive forts, but few of them have anything to rival Chittaurgarh's air of tragic nostalgia. Enjoying a prime location on a rocky plateau 115km northeast of Udaipur, the Chittaurgarh Fort has a long past overshadowed by misfortune. In 1303, the Delhi Sultan Ala-ud-din Khilji besieged the fort in an attempt to capture the beautiful Padmini, wife of Maharaja Ratan Singh. When Padmini fell into the sultan's hands, Rajput women were outraged by the loss of their queen. In an act of bitter sacrifice, 13,000 of them declared *jauhar* (self-immolation) and jumped onto a burning funeral pyre, infuriating the Sultan and prompting him to ravage the city. Two centuries later, in 1535, the Sultan Bahadur Shah attacked the city by surprise, annihilating another generation of Rajput warriors, even as their wives burned themselves alive. In 1568, the Mughal emperor Akbar laid siege to the city, killing over 30,000 inhabitants; again, the women wasted no time in leaping into the flames. The fort today, the largest in Asia, is a 5km stretch of ruined palaces and temples, the last vestiges of the city's past glory. Chittaurgarh is a lot quieter today than it once was; the only invaders these days are a small handful of tourists pursuing their photographic plunder.

▐ GETTING THERE AND GETTING AROUND

Trains: Railway Station, Station Rd. (☎ 40131). Reservation office open daily 10am-5pm. To: **Ahmedabad** (daily, 1:55pm, 14½ hr., Rs93); **Jaipur** (5:30am, 2, and 10pm; Rs79) via **Ajmer** (5hr., Rs53); **Udaipur** (6:50am and 1:55pm, 3½-7hr., Rs35).

Buses: Roadways Bus Stand (☎ 41177). To: **Abu Road** (7am, 10hr., Rs125); **Ahmedabad** (7:30am, 10hr., Rs138); **Bundi** (8:45 and 11:15am, 5½hr., Rs68); **Jaipur** (frequent, 5am-midnight, 8hr., Rs114) via **Ajmer** (5hr., Rs75); **Jodhpur** (3 per day, 7:30-11:30am, 8hr., Rs135); **Kota** (7 per day, 6:30am-4:30pm, 5½hr., Rs51-82); **Udaipur** (every hr, 7:30am-8pm, 2½hr., Rs45). **Private buses** on Station Rd. go to most places.

Local Transportation: Shared **auto-rickshaws** are the most common modes of transport. An auto-rickshaw ride within town costs Rs3-5, to the fort Rs15-20; a round-trip up to the fort and all the sights should cost Rs100, Rs70 off-season. **Bicycles** can be rented (Rs25 per day) from shops near the railway station.

✳ ⁊ ORIENTATION AND PRACTICAL INFORMATION

Chittaurgarh (or "Chittor") is too spread out to get around on foot. The **railway station** is on the southwest side of town. **Station Rd.** heads north, becoming **Ajmer Rd.** on its way to **Collectorate Circle,** which houses the State Banks of Bikaner and Jaipur and the General Hospital. From here, **City Rd.** heads east, passing the **Roadways Bus Stand** before crossing the **Gambheri River** and proceeding to the base of the Fort, where it becomes **Fort Rd.** The main commercial area and the **new city** are here. Fort Rd. zig-zags steeply up to the **Fort,** which sprawls 5km across the plateau. One main road loops inside the Fort and leads to Chittor's major sights.

Tourist Office: The **Tourist Reception Centre,** Station Rd. (☎ 41089). Open M-Sa 10am-1:30pm and 2-5pm. Mr. Sudhir Sukhwal runs the travel counter at **Hotel Pratap Palace** (☎ 40099). He leads tours of Chittor's sights and arranges cultural programs in the neighboring villages.

Currency Exchange: Because of recent problems with phony traveler's checks, no banks in Chittor will exchange money at the moment. The **State Bank of Bikaner and Jaipur,** Collectorate Circle (☎ 40933), is likely to resume currency exchange services soon.

Market: Food, provisions, and craft markets are on Fort Rd., across the river from Roadways Bus Stand. Most stalls open daily 9am-8pm.

Police: Main Police Station (☎41060), opposite the bus stand. Open 24hr.

Pharmacy: Chittaurgarh Cooperative (☎41276), in the General Hospital compound, is the only 24hr. pharmacy.

Hospital: General Hospital, Station Rd. (☎41102). English-speaking, large, and efficient. Consultations daily 9am-2pm. Open 24hr.

Post Office: GPO, Station Rd. (☎41159), near the railroad crossing. Open M-Sa 7-10:30am and 2:30-6pm. **Postal Code:** 312001.

ACCOMMODATIONS

Hotels are concentrated near the railway station along City Rd. and on Fort Rd., where it passes the bus stand and crosses the river into the old city. Budget hotels in Chittaurgarh tend to be basic and not very well maintained. So what else is new?

Hotel Pratap Palace, Station Rd. (☎40099 or 43563), north of the railway station, opposite the GPO. Beautiful lobby and clean, well-furnished rooms with phones and TVs. 24hr. hot water. Laundry service. Singles Rs250-550; doubles Rs300-625.

Hotel Bhagwati, Fort Rd. (☎46226 or 42275), across the bridge from the Roadways Bus Stand, near the old city. Large, dimly lit rooms with attached baths around a tiled courtyard. 24hr. room service. Check-out 24hr. Singles Rs80-125; doubles Rs150-200.

Hotel Ruchika (☎40419), near the railway station; follow signs to Hotel Meera. Basic rooms are surprisingly quiet, given their proximity to the railway station. Singles Rs75-150; doubles Rs100-200.

Hotel Gaurav Palace (☎43107), off Fort Rd., on the first big side street to the right as you move away from the City Rd. intersection. Modern hotel—all rooms have attached baths with hot water. Check-out noon. Singles Rs200-325; doubles Rs270-425.

FOOD

For cheap eats in Chittaurgarh, your best bet is to head toward the Roadways Bus Stand, where roadside *bhojnalyas* serve steaming *thalis* (Rs25-30).

Maheshwari Restaurant, off Fort Rd., on the second big street to the right after the river crossing, behind Kazi Chal Phir Shah Mosque. No menus or cold drinks, but they do have boiled drinking water and substantial veg. *thalis* (with a mango) for Rs25. Open daily 10am-3pm and 6:30-10:30pm.

Ritu-Raj Vatika Restaurant, opposite the bus stand. A small but popular place specializing in snacks, tandoori, and South Indian dishes, all under Rs45. Delicious *lassis* Rs10; fresh juices Rs10. Open daily 7am-11pm.

Shakti Restaurant, Hotel Pratap Palace. Quiet, comfortable, garden dining with a range of cuisines. Most dishes Rs25-50; excellent continental breakfast Rs80; full tandoori chicken Rs120; and lip-smacking buffet dinner Rs240. Open daily 7am-10:30pm.

Hotel Padmini Restaurant, Chanderiya Rd., about 3km from the Station and City Rd. intersection. Garden dining in a beautiful resort, far removed from the noise and pollution of the city. Meals Rs35-50. Open daily 7am-11:30pm.

SIGHTS: THE FORT

Jutting out abruptly from the plateau below, the Chittaurgarh Fort is perhaps the single most impressive structure in all of Rajasthan. Believed to have been constructed by the Pandava brother Bhima, of *Mahabharata* fame, the fort contains 113 temples in varying stages of collapse as well as 84 tanks.

Padan Pol is the first gate *(pol)* in a series of seven that leads a kilometer from the east side of town to the fort entrance. The climb to the top is grueling; even the

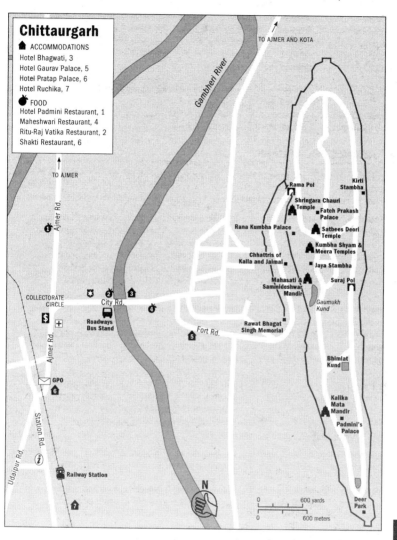

Chittaurgarh

ACCOMMODATIONS
Hotel Bhagwati, 3
Hotel Gaurav Palace, 5
Hotel Pratap Palace, 6
Hotel Ruchika, 7

FOOD
Hotel Padmini Restaurant, 1
Maheshwari Restaurant, 4
Ritu-Raj Vatika Restaurant, 2
Shakti Restaurant, 6

auto-rickshaws struggle. Near the second *pol* are the **chattris** (cenotaphs) of heroic martyrs Kalla and Jaimal, who died in the third sacking of Chittaurgarh in 1568. The final gate, **Rama Pol,** is the entrance to the fort proper. All the sights in Chittaurgarh are inside the fort, and the view from the ramparts on all sides is spectacular. Rickshaw-*wallahs* offer rides around the fort, but it's worth it to take the time to walk the narrow, tree-studded streets from sight to sight. *(Free.)*

THE SHINGARA CHAURI MANDIR. This 15th-century Jain temple shows Hindu influences in its elaborate decoration. The stone wall that extends to the right and left was hastily constructed by Banvir Singh, cousin of Udai Singh. Legend has it that when the young Udai Singh's father died in battle and his mother immolated herself, Banvir Singh devised a plan to kill the prince and seize the throne for himself. The prince's nurse, Pannadhai, uncovered Banvir Singh's plan and sacrificed her own son, switching him with the prince, whom she whisked away to safety.

When Banvir Singh learned of the young prince's survival, he started to partition the fort in the hope of sharing power with Udai Singh. He conveniently constructed the wall so that his section of the fort included the treasury and the tax-paying residential area. *(From the main road, the temple is just inside the fort to the left.)*

THE RANA KUMBHA PALACE. The half-ruined Rana Kumbha Palace is believed to be where Chittaurgarh's third *jauhar* took place in an underground tunnel leading to Gaumukh Kund. All that remained after the siege of the city were stables (including a stable said to house Genda Hathi, a sword-wielding military elephant) and a Shiva temple. To the back is the nurse's palace, where Pannadhai's son was slain in the place of the young prince. Also nearby are the elegant **Meera Mandir,** which honors the Jodhpuri mystic poet Mirabai (see **Mirabai,** p. 304) and the towering **Kumbha Shyam Mandir.** *(To the right, off the main road.)*

THE JAYA STAMBHA. On the cover of every Chittaurgarh brochure and postcard, the Jaya Stambha (Tower of Victory) is an imposing sandstone tower whose 37m-high exterior walls illustrate the story of the city's gory past. The tower's construction began in 1458 to commemorate an important military victory, and it took 10 years to complete. You can climb eight of its nine stories; the view from the top is breathtaking. *(Open daily 8am-5:30pm. Rs2, free F.)* The **Sammidheshwar Mandir** is just down the hill from the Jaya Stambha. Also nearby is **Mahasti,** which is marked by the handprints of thousands of *sati,* or women who immolated themselves on the funeral pyres of their husbands. *(Follow the shady Fort Rd. south. Rs3, free on F; video fee Rs25.)* The **Gaumukh Kund** (Cow's Mouth Tank), farther south, features a carved cow who fills the tank with water.

PADMINI'S PALACE. This run-down palace is set in a shallow pool. According to legend, Ala-ud-din-Khilji saw beautiful Padmini's reflection in a palace mirror, and setting his sight on her (and his army on Chittaurgarh), he staged the first siege of the city. The **Kalika Mata Mandir,** directly opposite, was dedicated during the 8th century to the sun god Surya, but now pays tribute to the goddess Kali.

BHIMLAT KUND. The road loops south past the often-empty **Deer Park** to the quiet Bhimlat Kund. This legendary tank was created by the Pandava brother Bhima to satiate his mother's thirst. The giant Bhima, who was said to have the strength of 1000 elephants, stomped his foot down in this spot, and the lake was formed by the imprint it left. The road then turns north again past **Suraj Pol,** the eastern gate of the fort, originally the main entrance.

OTHER SIGHTS. Built by a Jain merchant, the **Kirti Stambha** (Tower of Fame) contains images of the Jain pantheon, particularly that of Adinath, the first *tirthankara,* to whom the tower is dedicated. The tower is not open to visitors. Back toward Rama Pol, the white **Fateh Prakash Palace** houses a small museum of archaeological finds from Chittaurgargh and surrounding areas. *(Open Sa-Th, 10am-4pm, Rs3).* Just south of this lies the 11th-century Jain **Satbees Deori Temple.**

NEAR CHITTAURGARH

In the villages surrounding Chittaurgargh are a pair of Heritage Hotels (government jargon for a hotel in a building older than 100 years old), which offer lavish accommodations in a peaceful environment.

BIJAIPUR. Forty kilometers south of Chittaurgarh is the town of Bijaipur, a less-than-spectacular village with a spectacular 200-year-old palace that has been converted into the **Hotel Castle Bijaipur.** This palace hotel has fancy rooms, excellent dinners (Rs300), and blissful solitude, along with jungle trekking and safaris of the horse-and-village variety. (☎76222. Check-out noon. Singles Rs1350; doubles Rs1500.) Reserve ahead at Hotel Pratap Palace (☎(01472) 40099) in Chittaurgarh. Buses run from Chittaurgarh to Bijaipur (5 per day, 1½hr., Rs12).

BASSI. A small town 25km east of Chittaurgarh, Bassi is famous for its wooden crafts and is home to the recently renovated **Bassi Fort Palace** (☎(01472) 79248.

Singles Rs800; doubles Rs1000; suites Rs1190), overlooking the nearby Bassi Wild-life Sanctuary. The town bursts with activity during the **Teejaji Fair** (late Aug. and early Sept.). Buses to Bundi or Kota from Chittaurgarh stop in Bassi.

UDAIPUR उदयपुर ☎ 0294

Udaipur, City of Sunrise, epitomizes the romantic allure of Rajasthan; countless visitors who plan three-day tours end up staying for weeks in this oasis in the Thar Desert. The old city overlooks the green Lake Pichhola, whose postcard perfection is a world away from the ugly industrial mess farther out. Rooftop restaurants offer pristine views and lazy-day release from the craft and jewelry stores below. The modern world has done little to improve this ancient city of cobblestone streets—logging barons have left the once fertile valleys barren, and crowds and chaos fill the new urban center outside the old city walls. Udaipur's architectural marvels are surpassed only by Jaipur's. Its lakeside languor is second to none.

Maharaja Udai Singh II founded Udaipur when he fled after the final siege of Chittaurgarh in 1568. Four years later, Udai Singh's son and his troops successfully defended Udaipur against an invasion led by the Mughal emperor Akbar. The next 150 years were peaceful for the thriving city; miniature painting became a specialty, and architects built majestic palaces. In 1736 the city was crippled by the mighty Marathas, but it bounced back again with British aid, somehow managing to remain firmly independent. Since then, the city's arts have continued to flourish, James Bond films notwithstanding (yes, *Octopussy* was filmed here). The **Mewar Festival** (March 28-29, 2001; April 15-16, 2002) brings colorful dances, music, fireworks, and a scintillating lake parade.

▐▀ GETTING THERE AND GETTING AROUND

Flights: Dabok Airport (☎ 655453), 25km east of Udaipur (taxi Rs200). **Indian Airlines,** Delhi Pol (☎ 410999). Open daily 10am-1:15pm and 2-5pm. To: **Bombay** (daily 8:30am, 1hr., US$125); **Delhi** (daily 9:50am, 2hr., US$110); **Jaipur** (M, W, F 6:10pm; 40min.; US$80); **Jodhpur** (T, Th, Sa, Su 6:10pm; 40min.; US$80). **Jet Airways,** Blue Circle Business Centre (☎ 561105), near the GPO. To: **Bombay** (daily 9:25pm, Su-F 7:15pm; 1½hr.; US$125); **Delhi** (daily, 8:10am, 2½hr., US$110) via **Jaipur** (1hr., US$80). **Gangaur Tour 'n' Travels,** 28 Gangaur Ghat (☎ 411476), sells Indian Airlines tickets and reconfirms international flights. Open daily 9am-9pm.

Trains: Udaipur City Railway Station (☎ 131). Reservations office open M-Sa 8am-2pm. To: **Ahmedabad** (daily, 7pm, 9½hr., Rs73); **Ajmer** (8am and 6pm, 8-12hr., Rs77-130), both via **Chittaurgarh** (4-6hr., Rs36); **Delhi** (8am and 6pm, 20hr., Rs144) via **Jaipur** (12hr., Rs99).

Buses: Main Bus Stand (☎ 484191). To: **Ahmedabad** (14 per day, 5am-11pm, 7hr., Rs95; deluxe 3:15, 7, 10am, and 11pm, 6hr., Rs117-135); **Bikaner** (4:30pm, 15hr., Rs190); **Chittaurgarh** (16 per day, 6am-11:30pm, 3hr., Rs38; deluxe 8:30, 10:15am, 12:30pm, Rs54); **Delhi** (5 per day, 6am-7:30pm, 15hr., Rs245; deluxe 3:45pm, Rs398); **Jaipur** (frequent, 5am-midnight, 10hr., Rs135-200) via **Ajmer** (7hr., Rs98-144); **Jodhpur** (8 per day, 5:30am-11:30pm, 7hr., Rs102-130); **Mt. Abu** (8 per day, 5am-4:30pm, 6hr., Rs67; deluxe 8:15pm, Rs125) via **Ranakpur** (deluxe 4 per day, 5:30am-11:30pm, 2½ hr., Rs31). Many companies have **private buses** to major cities (see **Budget Travel,** below).

Local Transportation: The best way to get around is by **bicycle. Vijay Cycles,** BC, next to Raj Palace Hotel, rents bikes for Rs20 per day. Scooters Rs150 per day or Rs25 per hr. Open daily 9am-8pm. **Heera Cycle Store,** Gangaur Marg, opposite the road to Lal Ghat. Bikes Rs25 per day; scooters Rs100-200 per day; motorcycles Rs250 per day. Open daily 7:30am-9pm. **Auto-rickshaws** are unmetered but not exorbitant. Rs15 from railway or bus station to Jagdish Mandir. **Tempos** will get you anywhere for Rs1-4. **Taxis** can be hired through travel agents.

✴ ORIENTATION

Udaipur rests in the shadows of the Aravalli mountains, 113km southwest of Chittaurgarh and 270km south of Ajmer. The **Old City** curves along the northeastern bank of Lake Pichhola; the **New City** expands to the north, east, and south. The **Udaipur City Railway Station** is to the southeast of town, along **City Station Rd.** The **bus stand** is 2km north of the station, opposite **Udai Pol,** one of the four main entrances to the Old City. The main road leads to **Suraj Pol,** another city entrance that opens onto the two main shopping streets, **Bapu Bazaar** and **Bara Bazaar,** and also leads north to **Delhi Pol.** From Delhi Pol, the road left leads west down Ashwani Rd. and **Hathi Pol,** on the north end of the Old City. Right from the gate is **Chetak Circle,** where you'll find the Tourist Bungalow, the GPO, and the General Hospital. Hathi Pol affords the easiest access to the **City Palace** and **Jagdish Mandir** by way of the **clock tower.** The right fork uphill leads southwest toward the Mandir. The road to **Gangaur Ghat** extends to the north from Jagdish Mandir; **Lal Ghat** extends behind the temple to the lake. From Jagdish Mandir, **Bhatiyani Chohotta (BC)** leads south, becoming **Lake Palace Rd.** before dead-ending in Bapu Bazaar. Heading north on BC takes you past the palaces and the *ghats* to **Chand Pol,** and west and north over bridges to the beautiful **Fateh Sagar Lake.**

❼ PRACTICAL INFORMATION

Tourist Office: Tourist Reception Centre, Suraj Pol (☎ 411535 or 411364), has current maps and brochures and arranges home stays (see **Accommodations,** below). Open M-Sa 10am-5pm. Closed 2nd Sa. **Tourist Information Bureau,** at the railway station, has less information. Open M-Sa 8-11am and 4-7pm. Closed 2nd Sa. A small **information counter** at Dabok Airport (☎ 655433) is open when flights arrive and depart. The bimonthly publication *Out & About* contains a wealth of tourist information and can be found at many bookstores, hotels, and travel agencies.

Budget Travel: Agents line City Station Rd. and the Jagdish Mandir area, with more around Delhi Pol and Chetak Circle. Most hotels double as travel agencies and can book train, bus, and plane tickets; city tours by car (Rs350-450); airport taxis (Rs200); camel, horse, and elephant safaris (from Rs400 per day); and bus tours. Competition keeps prices virtually equal. **Namaskar Tours and Travels,** Lal Ghat (☎ 520043), is open daily 9:30am-11pm. **Shrinath Travels,** Udai Pol (☎ 422201; fax 422206), is near the bus stand. Open daily 8:30am-11pm. **Rajasthan Tours,** Lake Palace Rd. (☎ 525777; fax 414283), near Gulab Bagh. Open daily 7am-7pm.

Currency Exchange: There are many licensed money changers around Jagdish Mandir, including **One Stop Shop,** Lal Ghat (☎ 419810). Open daily 9am-11pm. **Vijay Bank** (☎ 411381), inside the City Palace complex, gives cash advances on Visa and MC for a 1% commission. Open M-F 10am-2pm, Sa 10am-noon. **State Bank of India,** Hospital Rd. (☎ 528857), exchanges foreign currency. Open M-F 10am-4pm, Sa 10am-1pm.

Bookstore: Mayur Book Paradise, 60 BC (☎ 410316), opp. Hotel Shakti Palace. Open daily 10:30am-8pm. **English Book Shop,** Lal Ghat (☎ 418924), sells and exchanges books. Open daily 10am-10pm. **Sun Book Point,** 117 BC. Open daily 10am-9pm.

Market: In addition to **Bara Bazaar** and **Bapu Bazaar,** market areas, food stores, and food stalls are around **Jagdish Mandir,** the **clock tower, Chetak Circle,** and all of the gates. Most open daily 8am-10pm.

Police: A major police station is at every gate. The biggest are at **Delhi Pol** and **Udai Pol.** There is a branch at the clock tower (☎ 411942). Superintendent (☎ 413949).

Pharmacy: Hospital Rd. and Udai Pol have several pharmacies. Most open daily 7am-9:30pm. **Udaipur Hospital** (☎ 421900) has a well-stocked 24hr. pharmacy.

Hospital: RNT General Hospital, Hospital Rd. (☎ 528811 to 528817). Government-run. **Udaipur Hospital,** Gulab Bagh Rd. (☎ 420322), near Udai Pol, has excellent facilities. Both English-speaking and open 24hr.

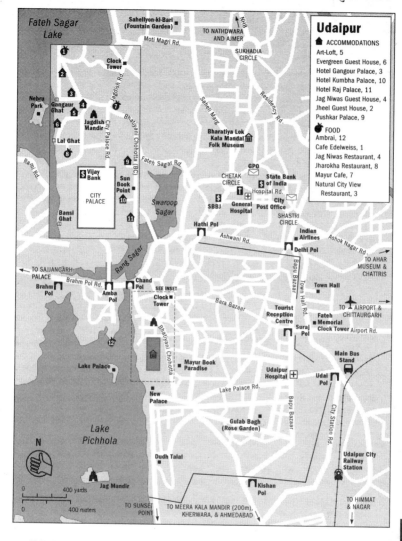

Udaipur

⌂ ACCOMMODATIONS
Art-Loft, 5
Evergreen Guest House, 6
Hotel Gangour Palace, 3
Hotel Kumbha Palace, 10
Hotel Raj Palace, 11
Jag Niwas Guest House, 4
Jheel Guest House, 2
Pushkar Palace, 9

🍴 FOOD
Ambrai, 12
Cafe Edelweiss, 1
Jag Niwas Restaurant, 4
Jharokha Restaurant, 8
Mayur Cafe, 7
Natural City View
    Restaurant, 3

Telephones: One Stop Shop, 25 Lal Ghat (☎419810) allows credit card/calling card calls (Rs3 per min.), collect calls, and callbacks (Rs2 per min). Open daily 9am–11pm.

Internet: One Stop Shop (Mewar International) and **Mayur Cafe** (☎415287), opposite Jagdish Mandir, both have Internet access for Rs80 per hr.

Post Office: GPO, Chetak Circle (☎528622). Open M-Sa 10am–7pm, Su 10am–3pm. **Postal Code:** 313001.

▌ ACCOMMODATIONS

Most of Udaipur's 200-plus hotels pay auto-rickshaw drivers to deposit lost-looking wayfarers at their doorstep. You can ask to be dropped off at one hotel area and easily check out the others nearby. The hotels on the beautiful **east bank** of Lake Pichhola are far better than any others in the city. Next best are those along

Lake Palace Rd. and **BC.** Hotels in the **new city** are cheap and noisy. **Homestay** accommodation is an alternative, with more than 80 families participating. The Tourist Reception Centre (p. 298) makes arrangements (Rs50-500 per night). Most hotels listed below have laundry, travel agencies, 24hr. room service, and 24hr. hot water.

▨ **Hotel Gangour Palace,** Gangaur Ghat (☎422303; fax 561121), in the 250-year-old Ashoka Haveli, has spacious, clean rooms surrounding a central courtyard. Soft mattresses, long beds, and large, tiled bathrooms. Equally excellent attached restaurant (see below). Doubles Rs100–500.

▨ **Art-Loft,** Lal Ghat (☎420304 or 420163). Beautiful rooms with marble floors and modern amenities. Run by a wonderful family of chefs and artists, this guest house features art and cookery lessons and serves excellent food. Check-out noon. Singles Rs300-400; doubles Rs400-500.

Jheel Guest House and **Paying Guest House,** 56/52 Gangaur Ghat (☎421352; fax 520008), on the edge of the lake. Spacious, well-kept, breezy rooms. Some baths have hot water. Check-out 10am. Singles Rs50-200; doubles Rs80-350. Deluxe rooms with balconies overlooking the lake Rs600-700.

Hotel Raj Palace, 103 BC (☎410364 or 527092; fax 410395). Great location, service, and food. The rooms have stained-glass windows, spotless bathrooms, and garden views. 24hr. hot water. Check-out 10am. Singles Rs300; doubles Rs500-1200.

Jag Niwas Guest House, 21 Gangaur Marg (☎416022), near Jagdish Mandir. No longer owned by the Maharaja, but still has style. Well-maintained rooms with attached baths and air-cooling. Check-out noon. Singles Rs120; doubles Rs150-300.

Hotel Kumbha Palace, 104 BC (☎422702). Distinctive rooms have colorful stained-glass windows and Jaisalmeri desert decorations, as well as attached baths and air-coolers. Lovely garden area borders the walls of the City Palace. Check-out 10am. Singles Rs50-50; doubles with bath Rs150-200.

Pushkar Palace, 93 BC (☎417685), near Asha Pala Temple. Family-run "palace" with huge, well-kept rooms around beautiful courtyards. Great common baths and funky bedspreads. Check-out 10am. Singles Rs50-80; doubles Rs80-120.

Evergreen Guest House, 32 Lal Ghat (☎421585). Small, delightful guest house with a garden courtyard in the center and a popular roof-top restaurant above. Check-out 10am. Singles Rs100-200; doubles Rs150-250.

◖ FOOD

Udaipur has a fairly good range of restaurants to choose from, many of which are spoilt only by their round-the-clock screenings of *Octopussy*.

▨ **Jharokha Restaurant,** inside the Jagat Niwas Pvt. Ltd. Hotel, Lal Ghat. Affordable, lake-view dining luxury inside a gorgeous renovated *haveli*. The rooms are expensive, but dinner is not. Veg. dishes Rs35-50; non-veg. Rs45-70; beer Rs70. Have a romantic meal for two in the center alcove on the balcony. Attentive service. Open daily 7:30am-11pm.

▨ **Natural City View Restaurant,** inside Hotel Gangour Palace. 3-tier rooftop restaurant prepares incredible food at reasonable prices. Veg. dishes Rs25-40. Evening entertainment consists of two TV sets (only one of which shows *Octopussy*) and an unobstructed view of the sunset over the mountains. Open daily 8am-10:30pm.

▨ **Ambrai,** Panch Devri Marg, in Amet-ki Haveli, outside Chand Pol, clinches the romantic dining cliche with its underneath-the-mango-tree lakeside setting. You couldn't get any closer to the Lake Palace without getting wet. Wonderfully prepared veg. and non-veg. Indian dishes Rs35-100. Open daily 9am-10:30pm.

Natraj Hotel, New Bapu Bazaar, behind Ashoka Cinema. Far from the main tourist hub. Mouth-watering Gujarati *thalis* Rs35. Open daily 8am-3pm and 6:30-10:30pm.

Cafe Edelweiss, 36 Gadiya Devra, Chandpol Rd. Favorite Udaipur hang-out of the von Trapp family. If an apple strudel is what you're looking for, this new German bakery has the best breads, cakes, and pastries in town. Open daily 8am-11pm.

Jag Niwas Restaurant, inside Jag Niwas Guest House. What it lacks in lake view, Jag Niwas more than makes up for in delicious food and a relaxed, intimate ambience. Open daily 8am-11pm.

Mayur Cafe, Jagdish Mandir. Quality food, quick service, and an A/C dining hall make the Mayur a popular local haunt. Leafy garden dining in back. Especially popular are the Indian dishes (Rs30-60) and the east-meets-west entrees, including Rajasthani pizza (Rs40). Open daily 8:30am-10:30pm.

🔍 SIGHTS

CITY PALACE. The toast of Udaipur is its grand palace, begun in 1559 by **Udai Singh,** the proud Mewar migrant who founded the city. An amalgamation of the architectural efforts of more than 20 kings, the City Palace is part museum, part royal residence, and part luxury hotel. Before entering the museum, note the two large paved stone indentions—they were once elephant beds. The museum opens into the **Raja Angan Chowk,** surrounded by rooms of Udaipuri miniature paintings, one of which appears in three dimensions when viewed at a distance. The palace is filled with tributes to Rana Pratap, Udai Singh's legendary son; among them are an eerie, larger-than-life marble bust and a 400-year-old suit of armor worn by his equally brave Arabian steed, Chetak (see **A Helluva Horse,** p. 302). The palace is best known for the **Mor Chowk,** with its blue-and-green inlaid glass peacocks and convex mirrors. **Krishna Vilas,** a small room with walls completely covered by miniature paintings, is dedicated to Krishna Kumari, a 16-year-old princess who was betrothed to two princes and chose to commit suicide to prevent a war for her hand. The **Zenana Mahal,** the women's quarters, is ill-maintained and houses little more than Maharaja Bhopal Singh's 1922 Rolls-Royce. *(Open daily 9:30am-4:30pm. Rs35; camera fee Rs75; video fee Rs300. Tours for up to 5 people Rs95 per hr.)*

JAGDISH MANDIR. Built by Maharaja Jagat Singh this 17th-century temple is at the very heart of the old city. It is dedicated to Vishnu's avatar Jagannath, whose black marble image resides in the sanctum. The outer structure is a pyramid-like *shikhara* of worn stone decorated with rows of elephants and *apsaras* as well as figures from Mewari mythology. The entrance is guarded by a large bronze Garuda, Vishnu's mount. The cornerstone at the left base of the stairs brings good luck to anyone who rubs it seven times. The central dome teems with mythological figures, and a huge silver bed meant for the gods rests in front of the sanctuary entrance. *(Down the steep hill from the City Palace. Open daily 5am-2pm and 4-10:30pm; Oct.-Feb. 5:30am-2pm and 4-10pm.)*

LAKE PICHHOLA. Once the royal summer palace, the **Jag Niwas (Lake Palace)** seems to float gently on the waters of Lake Pichhola. The palace grounds and open-air courtyard cafes, with marble inlay and corner towers and turrets, are stunning. The Lake Palace, now a luxury hotel and popular honeymoon destination, is worth a trip for the buffet dinner for Rs750 (☎527961, reserve ahead) that comes with short boat rides from Bansi Ghat. *(Cruises depart daily 10am-5pm. Rs75 per 30min.; Rs150 per 1hr., including jaunt to Jag Mandir).* Not far from the Lake Palace, on another island, is **Jag Mandir,** a domed pavilion famous for the safety it provided to the exiled Shah Jahan, when he led a revolt against his father Jehangir, and later to British women and children during the Mutiny of 1857.

SHILPIGRAM. A self-ordained "rural arts and crafts complex," Shilpigram has wide paths that lead to model homes representing the rural and indigenous communities of Rajasthan, Gujarat, Maharashtra, and Goa. Styles range from the circular, white stone, clay-roofed homes of the Meghwal Bahni to the thatched-roofed, square home of a Kohlapuri shoe maker. The village supports itself by selling the work of potters and cloth-makers and with lively performances by musicians and dancers from various rural communities. Shilpigram is most exciting in December during the 15-day Shilpigram Festival. *(West of Udaipur, off Lake Fateh Sagar. Rickshaws around Rs70-100 round trip. ☎431304. Open daily noon-8pm; Oct.-Feb. 11am-7pm. Rs10.)*

MUSEUMS. A large complex intended as a center for the preservation and promotion of indigenous arts, the **Bharatiya Lok Kala Mandal Folk Museum** has several rooms, each containing a variety of items ranging from colorfully painted masks to clay figure dioramas of local festivals. The museum's highlight is its collection of traditional Rajasthani **puppets** called *kathpurli*—wide-eyed wooden string puppets dressed in bright, traditional costumes. A minimalist **puppet show** is staged in the puppet theater; music accompanies the shimmying hips of wooden dancing girls. The puppets are expertly (and a trifle obscenely) manipulated. *(Saheli Marg, just past Chetak Circle. ☎529296. Museum open daily 9am-5:30pm. Rs10; camera fee Rs10; video fee Rs20. Puppet shows noon and 6pm.)* The Ahar Museum, northeast of the city, houses the relics of the Ahar civilization, which date back over 4000 years. *(Open M-Sa 10am-4:30pm. Rs2, M and F free.)* The **Bangore-ki Haveli** was built by the prime minister of Mewar in the 18th century. Restorations on the mansion began in 1986; its many balconies and courtyards, adorned with fresco paintings and glass inlay work, can be viewed by the public. *(Gangour Ghat. Open M-Sa 10am-5pm. Rs10).*

CHATTRIS. More than 200 cenotaphs of Mewari maharajas and their families stand in an enclosed plot northeast of the city. These were completely overgrown and inaccessible to the public until a recent renovation project unearthed them. Most are simple in detail and design (that of Sangram Singh is a notable exception), but their sheer number and their isolation from the city make this a wonderful addition to Udaipur's list of must-see sights. *(Open 24hr. Free.)*

GARDENS. Udaipur's famous gardens are extremely well-maintained but also quite tourist-trampled. **Nehru Park,** by Fateh Sagar Lake, was built in part as a public works project to create jobs during a famine. It is spread over open, fountain-sprinkled grounds, with beige-domed cupolas, swaying palm trees, and bright bushes of bougainvillea. Small, crowded boats leave the banks of Fateh Sagar for the island park. *(Every 20min.)* It is also possible to take a 30-minute tour around the lake. *(Open daily 8am-7pm; winter 8am-6pm. Rs5. Boats Rs40 for up to 4 people.)* The 18th-century **Saheliyon-ki-Bari** (Garden of the Maids of Honor), built by Maharana Sangram Singh for the maharani and her friends and servants, lies 2km to the north of town. The garden, with its palm-lined walks and lotus pool, is more of a tourist sight these days than the refuge it was originally meant to be. The pool is spectacular during the monsoon rains. *(Open daily 9am-6pm. Rs5.)* **Sajjan Niwas Park** contains the **Gulab Bagh** (Rose Garden). Wide paths are lined with local flora, including giant umbrella neem trees. *(Open daily 5am-8pm. Free.)*

VIEWPOINTS. Although you can't go inside, head to **Sajjangarh (Monsoon) Palace** for a mind-blowing view of the city and valley. *(On a steep hill 5km west of Udaipur. Auto-rickshaws Rs100-150 round-trip. Entrance fee Rs40, vehicle fee Rs15.)* **Dudh Talal** and **Sunset Point** offer more solitary, serene views of the lake. *(Off Lake Palace Rd.)*

A HELLUVA HORSE The cow might be a more common object of worship for Hindus, but the Rajputs of Rajasthan have a special place in their hearts for a certain white stallion named Chetak. Indeed, his name lives on in Udaipur's main circle and is emblazoned across the carriages of Rajasthan's main express trains. Chetak, whose statues are a common sight in Udaipur, was the loyal battle companion of Rana Pratap. At the famous bloodbath of Haldighati in 1532, Chetak's leg was cut by an enemy elephant wielding a machete in its trunk; Pratap was also wounded. Though hobbled, Chetak carried his master from the battlefield through a narrow passage, leaping a 3m crevice before coming to rest under a tree 6km away. Having saved his master's life, poor Chetak breathed his last. Many tours of the Udaipur area stop at Haldighati to pay respects at Chetak's tomb and hear the tale of his valiant death.

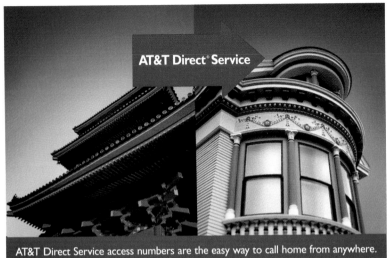

The best way to keep in touch when you're traveling overseas is with **AT&T Direct**® Service. It's the easy way to call your loved ones back home from just about anywhere in the world. Just cut out the wallet guide below and use it wherever your travels take you.

For a list of AT&T Access Numbers, tear out the attached wallet guide.

AT&T

Macao 0800-111	Reunion Isl.....0800-99-0011
Malaysia ●▲..1-800-80-0011	**Saipan ● 1-800-2255-288**
Marshall Isl....1800-225-5288	Singapore 800-0111-111
Micronesia 288	Solomon Islands 0811
Nepal ●▲ 0800-77-001	**Spain 900-99-00-11**
Netherlands ●...0800-022-9111	Sri Lanka 430-430
New Zealand ● 000-911	**Switzerland ●..0800-89-0011**
Pakistan ▲ 00-800-01001	**Taiwan..........0080-10288-0**
Palau 02288	Thailand ❮....001-999-111-11
Papua New Guinea...0507-12880	**U.K. 0800-89-0011**
Philippines ● 105-11	Vietnam ❤ 1-201-0288

FOR EASY CALLING WORLDWIDE

1. Just dial the AT&T Access Number for the country you are calling from.
2. Dial the phone number you're calling.   *3.* Dial your card number.

For access numbers not listed ask any operator for **AT&T Direct**® Service.
In the U.S. call 1-800-331-1140 for a wallet guide listing all worldwide AT&T Access Numbers.

Visit our Web site at: **www.att.com/traveler**

Bold-faced countries permit country-to-country calling outside the U.S.

  ● Public phones require coin or card deposit to place call.
  ▲ May not be available from every phone/payphone.
  ✔ Use U.K. access number in N. Ireland.
  ✚ Available from payphones in Phnom Penh and Siem Riep only.
  ❤ Available in select hotels in Ho Chi Minh City, calling centers in Hanoi, post offices in Da Nang, Ho Chi Minh City and Quang Ninh.
  ❮ When calling from public phones, use phones marked "Lenso."

When placing an international call *from* the U.S., dial 1 800 CALL ATT.

Macao 0800-111	Reunion Isl.....0800-99-0011
Malaysia ●▲..1-800-80-0011	**Saipan ● 1-800-2255-288**
Marshall Isl....1800-225-5288	Singapore 800-0111-111
Micronesia 288	Solomon Islands 0811
Nepal ●▲ 0800-77-001	**Spain 900-99-00-11**
Netherlands ●...0800-022-9111	Sri Lanka 430-430
New Zealand ● 000-911	**Switzerland ●..0800-89-0011**
Pakistan ▲ 00-800-01001	**Taiwan..........0080-10288-0**
Palau 02288	Thailand ❮....001-999-111-11
Papua New Guinea...0507-12880	**U.K. 0800-89-0011**
Philippines ● 105-11	Vietnam ❤ 1-201-0288

FOR EASY CALLING WORLDWIDE

1. Just dial the AT&T Access Number for the country you are calling from.
2. Dial the phone number you're calling.   *3.* Dial your card number.

For access numbers not listed ask any operator for **AT&T Direct**® Service.
In the U.S. call 1-800-331-1140 for a wallet guide listing all worldwide AT&T Access Numbers.

Visit our Web site at: **www.att.com/traveler**

Bold-faced countries permit country-to-country calling outside the U.S.

  ● Public phones require coin or card deposit to place call.
  ▲ May not be available from every phone/payphone.
  ✔ Use U.K. access number in N. Ireland.
  ✚ Available from payphones in Phnom Penh and Siem Riep only.
  ❤ Available in select hotels in Ho Chi Minh City, calling centers in Hanoi, post offices in Da Nang, Ho Chi Minh City and Quang Ninh.
  ❮ When calling from public phones, use phones marked "Lenso."

When placing an international call *from* the U.S., dial 1 800 CALL ATT.

AP   © 8/00 AT&T

🎵 ENTERTAINMENT

Udaipur's charm isn't confined to lakeside palaces and museums. Traditional **Rajasthani folk dances** and music performances, involving a dazzling blend of local trance dances and circus-like balancing stunts, take place at **Meera Kala Mandir,** near the Pars Theater in Sector 11, a Rs25-30 rickshaw ride from the old city. (☎583176. Shows held M-Sa 7-8pm. Tickets Rs60. Book at Heera Cycle Store, Gangaur Marg, across the road leading to Lal Ghat. ☎523525. Open daily 7:30am-9pm.) For information about **puppet shows** at the Bharatiya Lok Kala Folk Museum and **folk dances** at Shilpgram, see p. 302. Mr. Virendra Bansal, the student of a student of Ali Akbar Khan, graciously invites travelers into his home every morning for free *sarod* and *tabla* music. (4A Shivaji Nagar. ☎485464. Open 7:30-11am.)

🛍 SHOPPING

Shopping here can be addictive. Countless clothing, jewelry, textile, and handicraft shops are crowded into the areas around Jagdish Mandir, Lake Palace Rd., and Bara and Bapu Bazaars. They sell wares from all over Rajasthan at inflated but negotiable prices. **Miniature painting** is an Udaipuri speciality, and there are many shops where skilled artists can be watched at work without any obligation to buy. It's best to buy from shops that are run by the artist himself, rather than by a middleman. Be wary of invitations into shops by anyone—rickshaw-*wallahs*, children, "friends" you have just met. These will inevitably mean higher prices and greater hassles for you, as they will expect a commission. **Hare Krishna Arts,** City Palace Rd., has an excellent selection of high quality work. **Ashok Art,** inside Hotel Gangour Palace, also has a wide variety at fixed, clearly labeled prices.

🎫 DAYTRIPS FROM UDAIPUR

EKLINGI AND ENVIRONS. Twenty-two kilometers north of Udaipur, in the heart of marble-producing territory, is the village of **Eklingi,** home to a magnificent Shaivite temple. The temple itself is vanilla-colored marble and encloses a four-faced solid black image of Shiva. Silver doors, silver lamps, silver parcels, and a solid silver bull adorn the interior. The exterior and the surrounding shrines are decorated with impressive stonework. The complex, erected in 734, houses a total of 108 temples, one for each of the 108 names for Shiva. *(Open daily 4:30-6:30am, 10:30am-1:30pm, and 5:30-6:45pm, though times vary depending on the season. Photography is not permitted.)* Many tours stop at Eklingi, which is also accessible by **bus** from Udaipur *(every 30min., 5am-9:30pm, 45min., Rs13).* Just 2km from Eklingi are the **Sas Bahu Temples** of Nagda. Built during the 10th century, these well-preserved temples are idyllically situated amid palm trees and agricultural fields. Several temples have been submerged by the nearby lake, but it is possible to see the tops of a few peeking above the water. *(Just off the road from Eklingi to Udaipur. Best reached by bike from Eklingi.)*

NATHDWARA. Forty-eight kilometers north of Udaipur is the important Vaishnava pilgrimage site of **Nathdwara,** built entirely around its incredible **Sri Nathji Mandir,** a temple dedicated to Krishna's *avatar* as the baby Sri Nathji. Legend maintains that, during the 17th century, a chariot carrying Krishna's image from Mathura to Udaipur became trapped inexplicably in the mud; the bearers interpreted the situation as a divine signal and built a temple on the spot. The image of Sri Nathji, with blazing diamond-studded eyes and Mughal dress, is found on decorative items in households all over India. The stalls outside the temple have commercialized the image—the assortment of Krishna paraphernalia is vast, and prices are high. Although the temple's architecture is a visual feast, far more interesting are the evening (5pm) ceremonies following the ritual feeding, bathing, and putting-to-bed of the image. For each *darshan*, a different backdrop is displayed behind the statue in order to depict various scenes from Krishna's life. After 3pm,

MIRABAI Visitors from far and wide come to Chittaurgarh to visit Meera Mandir, a tribute to the mystic poetess Mirabai, whose *bhajans* (devotional songs) grace the airwaves nationwide. Born in the 15th century to a Rajput family in the village of Kurki, outside of Jodhpur, Mirabai displayed an early affection for the Lord Krishna—she claimed him as her husband at a tender age. When she was matched with a mortal spouse, Raltan Singh of Chittaurgarh, Mirabai persisted in her devotion. She defied her new family (staunch Shiva devotees) and Rajput customs by leaving the fort to worship Krishna. The final straw for the royal family was her refusal to commit *sati* upon her husband's death. She claimed her true spouse was Krishna, citing his immortality as a reason for not mourning. Members of the enraged royal family plotted to take her life, first by sending her poison to drink and then by releasing a black cobra to kill her. Mira consumed the poison as if it were a *lassi*, and the cobra became a garland of flowers around her neck. After the attempts on her life, Mirabai took her statue of Krishna and fled to Dwarka in Gujarat. When Udai Singh came to power, he attempted to redress his family's transgressions and invited Mirabai back to Chittaurgarh. Legend has it that, after a visit to the Krishna temple that housed her statue, she was never seen again—she disappeared into the statue. Mirabai's cherished Krishna icon is now the personal property of the royal family of Udaipur. The songs Mirabai composed out of her devotional love (*bhakti*) remain a popular means of Krishna worship.

the temple only re-opens at 4:45 for just 15 minutes of viewing. The mad rush that ensues is enough to make even the most crowd-loving Krishna-fan claustrophobic. It also serves pick-pockets well, so guard your belongings. Photography is strictly prohibited in the temple. (*Nathdwara is a stop on many tours and is accessible by bus from Udaipur every 30min., 5am-9:30pm, 1hr., Rs26. RTDC runs a bus to Haldighati, Eklingi, and Nathdwara. The bus leaves from the Kajri Tourist Bungalow in Chowk Circle. M-F 2pm, which returns at 7pm for Rs90. ☎410501. Make reservations in advance at Kajri.*)

NEAR UDAIPUR: RANAKPUR रनकपुर   ☎ 02934

Eighty kilometers northwest of Udaipur, roads snake through the green valleys of the Aravalli range to Ranakpur's superb Jain temples, a complex rivaling Dilwara on Mt. Abu. The main, white marble **Chaumukha Temple,** built in 1439, is dedicated to Adinath, the first *tirthankara* (Jain teacher). Inside, each of the 29 halls, 80 domes, and 1444 pillars (no two of them alike) is intricately carved and sculpted—every last bead on a dancer's earring is rendered meticulously in stone. The temple's most intricate carvings surround a four-faced image of Adinath in the innermost sanctum. Within the complex are smaller shrines to Parshvanath and Neminath and a Hindu temple to Surya. A rickshaw to the temple is about Rs35. The temple is open to visitors daily noon-5pm, but menstruating women are not supposed to enter at any time. (Camera fee Rs25.)

Most **buses** from Udaipur to Jodhpur stop at Ranakpur (3hr. Rs35-40, see Udaipur, p. 297). Make sure the driver knows that you want to be dropped off in Ranakpur. Private bus companies in Udaipur arrange frequent departures and tours to Ranakpur as well. Private buses bound for Jodhpur, Jaipur, and Udaipur leave Ranakpur from in front of the *chai* stand on the main road (every 2hr.).

There are only two accommodations options in Ranakpur. The **dharamsala** offers simple lodgings and plentiful veg. lunches and dinners. Alcohol and smoking are prohibited; lights-out is at 10pm. (☎85019. Rs5 per bed; doubles Rs50; donations appreciated. Meals Rs15.) The **Shilpi Tourist Bungalow,** just up the road from the temples, has spacious, clean rooms—all with attached baths. (☎85074. Singles Rs150-300; doubles Rs250-400.) The **Roopam Restaurant,** 2km past the Tourist Bungalow, is an open-air establishment set among several forest villages. (☎85321. Most dishes Rs35-55. Open daily 7am-10:30pm.)

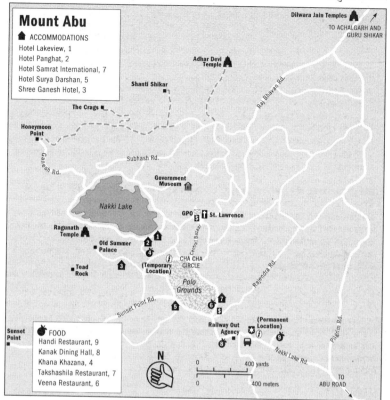

Mount Abu

⬛ ACCOMMODATIONS
Hotel Lakeview, 1
Hotel Panghat, 2
Hotel Samrat International, 7
Hotel Surya Darshan, 5
Shree Ganesh Hotel, 3

Dilwara Jain Temples
TO ACHALGARH AND
GURU SHIKAR

Adhar Devi Temple

Raj Bhavan Rd.

Shanti Shikar

The Crags

Honeymoon Point

Ganesh Rd.

Subhash Rd.

Government Museum

Nakki Lake

GPO St. Lawrence

Central Bazaar

Ragunath Temple

Old Summer Palace

Toad Rock

(Temporary Location)

CHA CHA CIRCLE

Polo Grounds

Rajendra Rd.

Sunset Point Rd.

Railway Out Agency

(Permanent Location)

Pilgrim Rd.

Nakki Lake Rd.

Sunset Point

🍎 FOOD
Handi Restaurant, 9
Kanak Dining Hall, 8
Khana Khazana, 4
Takshashila Restaurant, 7
Veena Restaurant, 6

N

0   400 yards
0   400 meters

TO ABU ROAD

MOUNT ABU माऊँट आबु
☎ 02974

Situated 1220m above sea level, on a temperate plateau with lush vegetation and bearable temperatures year round, Mt. Abu, Rajasthan's only hill station, is a popular destination for Indian families and honeymooners. Some are drawn by the ecological richness of the area—the most impressive natural sights are the winding rivers flanked by palm trees and shadowed by mammoth rock outcroppings. Others come to Mt. Abu with a more divinely inspired mission. Once part of the kingdom of the Chauhan Rajputs, the hill station is now an important Hindu pilgrimage site. Thought to be the home of Vashishta, the sage whose sacrificial fire gave rise to the five Rajput clans, Mt. Abu also contains the holy waters of Nakki Lake, held to be as purifying as those of the Ganga. Jains also make spiritual journeys here to worship at the architecturally breathtaking Dilwara temples. Despite the strongly religious atmosphere, though, sacred Mt. Abu does not inhibit frolicking honeymooners in their more worldly enjoyments; bangle stores, milkshake shops, and galloping ponies cater to the multitude of Gujarati tourists who come to Mt. Abu to enjoy a liquor-filled weekend of leisure. During the annual **Summer Festival** (June 1-3), tourists from nearby areas come here to cavort amid folk dances and music.

🏳 GETTING THERE AND GETTING AROUND

Trains: Trains depart from **Abu Road Railway Station** (☎ 22222), 27km from town. **Railway Out Agency,** Nakki Lake Rd. (☎ 38697), next to the bus stand, handles reservations to Delhi and Bombay. Open M-Sa 9am-1pm and 2-4pm, Su 9am-noon. To: **Ahmedabad** (5 per day, 4:20am-11:30pm, 4hr., Rs52); **Delhi** (2:40 and 9:30pm, 12-13hr., Rs250); **Jaipur** (3 per day, 11:15am-9:30pm, 7½hr., Rs99).

Buses: Main Bus Stand (☎43434). To: **Ahmedabad** (10 per day, 6am-9pm, 6hr., Rs81); **Jaipur** (9:45am, 12hr., Rs180; deluxe, 6:30pm, 12hr., Rs246); **Jaisalmer** (6:15am, 11hr., Rs155); **Jodhpur** (6:30am, 7½hr., Rs105); **Udaipur** (4 per day, 8:45am-4pm, 6hr., Rs66; deluxe 7pm, Rs125). **Private bus companies** lining the main road service Rajasthan and Gujarat. **Shobha Travels** (☎38302) is near Hotel Samrat. Open daily 7am-10:30pm. All bus transportation arranged in Mt. Abu departs from Mt. Abu proper, but arrangements made in other cities for service to Mt. Abu may only come as far as Abu Road, 1hr. away—be sure to check in advance.

Local Transportation: Buses to **Abu Road** depart frequently from the Main Bus Stand (every 30min., 6am-9pm, 1hr., Rs11-14). Jeeps and vans serving as local **taxis** leave from the taxi stand. A shared **jeep** to Abu Road costs Rs15 per person; private taxis are Rs250 one-way. To the Dilwara Temples, private taxis cost Rs50-60; shared jeeps, leaving from Cha Cha Circle, are Rs3 per person.

⚹🛈 ORIENTATION AND PRACTICAL INFORMATION

The small town can be crossed from one side to the other in 25 minutes. Buses will drop you off within walking distance of several hotels, but too far from the lake. The main drag, **Nakki Lake Rd.,** leads into town from Abu Road, passing the Tourist Reception Centre, Main Bus Stand, police station, and Railway Out Agency on the way. Just before Nakki Lake Rd. passes the **Polo Grounds,** you will find the taxi stand. At **Cha Cha Circle,** on the northern tip of the Polo Grounds, the road forks. The right branch leads through the **Central Bazaar;** the left fork takes you to **Nikki Lake.** The **Dilwara Jain Temples** are northeast of town on Raj Bhavan Rd.

Tourist Office: The main tourist office, near the bus stand, is currently undergoing renovations, but should resume service soon. Meanwhile, the temporary **Tourist Reception Centre** (☎43151) is in the RTDC youth hostel, off Nakki Lake Rd., at the north end of the Polo Grounds closest to the lake. Open M-Sa 10am-1:30pm and 2-5pm.

Currency Exchange: Bank of Baroda (☎43166), near the taxi stand, gives cash advances on AmEx, MC, Visa. Open M-F 10am-2pm, Sa 10am-noon.

Market: The **Central Bazaar** is Mt. Abu's main market. Open daily 9am-10pm.

Police: Main Police Station (☎43333), near the Main Bus Stand. Open 24hr.

Hospital: J. Watumull Global Hospital and Research Centre (☎38347 or 38348), 1km out of town on the road to the Dilwara Temples, is an ultra-clean, ultra-modern private facility. Open M-Sa 9am-1pm and 3-5pm. Open for emergencies 24hr.

Telephones: The **Telecom Centre** (☎43107; fax 38900), near the taxi stand, has STD/ISD, fax, and telegraph services. Open M-Sa 8am-8pm.

Post Office: GPO (☎43170). Open M-F 9am-3pm, Sa 9am-2pm. **Postal Code:** 307501.

⌂ ACCOMMODATIONS

Visitors arrive here in droves from April to June and September to December, whenever there is a holiday or a school break, and especially around **Diwali** (see **Holidays and Festivals,** p. 821). Prices of accommodations fluctuate depending on demand and at least triple during these peak times. Don't be surprised if you're asked for no less than Rs1000 for any room during peak season. Reservations are essential. Call ahead for rates. In the low season (Mar.-Apr. and July-Sept.), room rates are more negotiable. The dozens of "youth hostels" around town are intended principally for students attending Mt. Abu private schools. Most hotels have a 9am check-out, travel agencies, laundry, and room service.

Shree Ganesh Hotel (☎43591 or 37292), near Nakki Lake, on the road to the Old Summer Palace. The staff works hard to maintain a relaxing atmosphere. They also keep a tourist quota (until 10pm) during peak times, for which they offer reasonable rates. Clean rooms with TVs and attached baths. Singles Rs175-200; doubles Rs250-300.

Hotel Samrat International (☎ 43173 or 43153), on the main road, opposite the Polo Grounds. Neither here-nor-there location, but the rooms are clean, bright and modern. Singles Rs70-80; doubles Rs250.

Hotel Panghat, Nakki Lake (☎ 38886). Adequate rooms, all with attached baths and TVs, are good values considering their lakeside location. Several rooms have a direct view of the holy waters, but the carnival vibes from the streets below might start to test your patience after a while. Singles Rs100-200; doubles Rs250-450.

Hotel Lakeview, Nakki Lake (☎ 38659). An odd, off-white building with a garden in front. Big, well-lit rooms with tie-dyed bed spreads and attached baths. Lakeside balconies have swings and excellent views. Hot water 7-11am. Rooftop restaurant. STD/ISD. Singles Rs150-250; doubles Rs350-450; lakeside rooms Rs500-700.

Hotel Surya Darshan (☎ 43165 or 37149). The best value of all the places by the western Polo Grounds. Rooms are slightly stuffy but big and clean, with attached baths. Several overlook the grasses below. Singles Rs250-500; doubles Rs300-600. Low season: singles Rs100-150; doubles Rs150-200.

FOOD

Thanks to the (over)abundance of Gujarati tourists in Mt. Abu, you'll find Gujarati food as often as you will the typical Rajasthani, Punjabi, and Chinese items.

Kanak Dining Hall, near the Main Bus Stand. Come around lunchtime to see stainless steel fly in this spacious, undecorated dining hall. Mmm-good all-you-can-eat Gujarati *thalis* Rs45. Open daily 11am-3pm and 7-10pm.

Handi Restaurant, in the marvelously-named Hilltone Hotel, south of the Main Bus Stand. Indoor or garden seating. The food is superb; most dishes are Rs50-80. Open daily 7-11pm. The **Kalali Bar** has domestic and imported drinks (Rs80-120). Open daily 11am-3pm and 7-11pm.

Takshashila Restaurant, in Hotel Samrat. The best veg. food in town, according to the locals. Indian, Chinese, and continental stuff Rs40-60; Gujarati *thalis* (Rs45). Open daily 8am-3pm and 7-10pm.

Veena Restaurant, Nakki Rd., opposite the Bank of Baroda. Good, fast meal and snack joint specializing in South Indian food. Twist your hips to Hindi pop as you munch on a *dosa* (Rs20-40) or dare to try a veg. cheeseburger (Rs30). Open daily 7am-midnight.

Khana Khazana, near Nakki Lake. Head upstairs to leave the crowds behind and enjoy a quick bite. Above-average quality. Open daily 9am-11pm.

SIGHTS

DILWARA JAIN TEMPLES. The simple, worn stone exteriors of these Jain temples house some of the most amazing marble sculptures in the country. Workers toiled on this colossal sculptural achievement for 14 years. At the foot of the doorway to each of the complex's temples and shrines you will find a pair of carved dragons, the symbol for anger, signifying that one is to leave all anger outside the serene temple walls.

The main temple, the **Vimal,** constructed during the 11th century by Vimal Shah, Chief Minister to the Solanki King, is dedicated to the first *tirthankara,* Adinath. Devotees of art and Adinath alike flock to Dilwara to see the exquisitely carved pillars of dancers and the spiraling lotus domes that adorn the halls. Fifty-seven *tirthankara* statues line these halls in a kind of Hall-of-Jain-Fame. Etched into the ceilings above are all kinds of mythical scenes. One playfully illustrates Krishna with his *gopis;* others depict soaring goddesses, rendered in minute detail, right down to the fingernails. The central dome is alive with more dancing, and a triumphant marble elephant who turns up his trunk in homage to Adinath. The balconies to either side of the main sanctuary, built by two brothers, are identically decorated save for the last figure on the left, who is bent in respect to the work of the elder. The dome and walls of the outer sanctuary were left undecorated to avoid distracting people trying to meditate. The statue of Adinath is modeled on a 3500-year-old granite statue housed in the back corner of the temple. According to legend, Vimal Shah discovered the statue on this very spot under a sweet-smelling *champa* tree revealed to him in one of his dreams. Even more intricate than the decoration on the main temple are the curling arches of the second largest temple, the **Tejpal Temple,** dedicated to Neminath, the 22nd *tirthankara* and a cousin of Krishna. Its tiered lotus dome was carved from a single block of marble. Both temples contain marble memorials to their patrons, depicted on top of the elephants who transported the building materials to the site.

There are three other temples in the complex, including a 16th-century shrine to Mahavira and another commemorating Adinath Rishabdeo. The third is a memorial to the skilled workers who contributed to the complex; they constructed it during their breaks from building the other temples using marble and stone scraps left over from the main temples. *(A peaceful 45min., 3km walk northeast of town. Jeeps from Cha Cha Circle head to the temples every 15min. for Rs3. Open to non-Jains noon-6pm. Free. Photography and leather items prohibited. Menstruating women are not supposed to enter.)*

NAKKI LAKE. Visiting Nakki Lake, where most of Mt. Abu's activity is focused, is a bit like attending a carnival—crowding the short street to the lake are small shops, alongside popcorn sellers, fast-food restaurants, photo stalls, and brightly decorated **ponies** *(rides Rs45 per 30min.).* Mobs are constantly clamoring for the paddle **boats** and rowboats available at the dock *(Rs25 per 30min.).* The festive atmosphere tends to obscure the religious significance of the lake, thought to contain holy waters because it was dug out by the nails *(nakh)* of a god. Take a scenic walk along the left bank, from where you can see **Toad Rock,** past the small **Ragunath Temple,** to the quiet bank opposite lined with huge estates and stately homes.

VIEWPOINTS. Sunset Point lies along the left fork from the main road past the taxi stand. Although it does offer a beautiful view of the setting sun, the constant rabble of tourists has made it a much better people-watching spot. A similar fate has befallen **Honeymoon Point,** off the road leading northwest behind Nakki Lake. The view from here is also superb and the name draws newlyweds by the dozen. From here you can see the **Crags** or hike up a little farther to the **Shanti Shikhar,** for dazzling panoramic views. A left off the northeast road to Dilwara leads to the base of a good 30-minute heart-pumping trek up 360 steps to the mountain-top **Adhar Devi Temple.** Dedicated to the patron goddess of Mt. Abu, the "temple" is a natural cleft in the rock that can be entered only by crawling on all fours. It commands a spectacular view of the green valleys below.

GOVERNMENT MUSEUM. Back in town opposite the GPO is the bizarre **Government Museum,** with its huge collection of stone chunks and slabs from various archaeological hunts. Most of the artifacts come from Jain temples built between the 8th and 12th centuries. *(Open Sa-Th 10am-4:30pm. Rs3, students Rs1, free on M.)*

▶ DAYTRIPS FROM MOUNT ABU

Eight kilometers past Dilwara is **Achalgarh,** where, amid the heavy, sweet scent of the abundant *champa* trees, there stands a small 9th-century temple to Achaleshwar Mahadev, an incarnation of Shiva. The temple marks a small, supposedly bottomless crater that was created by the impact of Shiva's big toe. The temple also contains a Nandi statue made of over 4000kg of silver, brass, gold, copper, and tin. Outside the temple is a tank that, according to legend, was once filled with *ghee*. Lard-loving demons, dressed as buffalo, attempted to lap up the grease, but the king, ever-vigilant when it came to clarified butter, killed them. The three stone buffalo flanking the tank are the beasts' remains. Another five minutes up this same road is **Guru Shikar** (1721m), the highest point in Rajasthan, marked by a small Vishnu temple. *(Buses head to Achalgarh from the main bus stand. 10am, 12:15, and 4pm; 30min., Rs5; return 10:30am, 12:45, and 4:30pm. The RTDC leads tours that stop at Dilwara, Achalgarh, and Guru Shikar. 8:30am and 1:30pm, 5½hr., deluxe Rs40. Tour buses depart from the main bus stand.)*

Jodhpur

⌂ ACCOMMODATIONS

Ajit Bhawan, 8
Durag Niwas Guest House, 6
Galaxy Hotel, 3
Ghoomar Hotel, 5
Govind Hotel, 12
Hotel Akshey, 7
Hotel Arun, 11
Shanti Bhawan Lodge, 14

🍴 FOOD

Agra Sweets, 10
Gossip Restaurant, 1
Kalinga Restaurant, 13
Midtown Restaurant, 14
On the Rocks, 9
Poonam Restautant, 4
Soft 'n' Soft, 2

JODHPUR जोधपुर

☎ 0291

Once the capital of the state of Marwar ("Land of Death") and home to the warrior clans of Rathore, Jodhpur (pop. 1,000,000) has a past rich in tales of royalty and valor. During the 18th century, the city was overrun by the Mughals, and Maharaja Ajit Singh was exiled to Afghanistan, where he was murdered. The Mughals tried to legitimize their rule by claiming that there was no one left to take the throne. Thirty years later, Maharaja Ajit Singh II—kidnapped as an infant and brought up secretly in a tiny Himalayan village—rode through the city gates at the head of an enormous army and drove out the Mughals, who never returned.

Modern Jodhpur is still haunted by the legends of its past. As the sun rises on the eastern edge of the Thar Desert, daylight gilds the towers of Jodhpur's ancient buildings, monuments to Rajasthan's vivid history of maharajas and princesses and of caravans crossing sand dunes. As daylight penetrates the streets below, Rajasthan's second-largest city comes to life, and the fairy tales mix with the realities of industry, grime, and poverty. Jodhpur, however, remains a vibrant place to visit: the city is awash with color, from the deep reds of *bandhani* cloth and the brilliant yellow of the scorching desert sun to the sea-blue walls of the old city houses which have earned Jodhpur its nickname, "The Blue City."

⬛ GETTING THERE AND GETTING AROUND

Flights: Jodhpur Airport (☎ 142 or 430617), 6km from the city center, down Airport Rd. 15min. from town by auto-rickshaw (Rs60-80) or taxi (Rs90-100). **Indian Airlines,** Airport Rd. (☎ 510757 or 512617). Open daily 10am-1:15pm and 2-4:30pm. To: **Bombay**

(Tu, Th, Sa, and Su; 7:20pm; 2½hr.; US$155) via **Udaipur** (40min., US$65); **Delhi** (M, 2pm, 2hr., US$105) via **Jaipur** (40min., US$65).

Trains: Jodhpur Railway Station, Railway Station Rd. (☎131 or 132). Most trains also stop at **Raika Bagh Railway Station,** on the east side of town. Reserve at the **Advance Reservation Office,** Station Rd. (☎636407), next to the GPO. Reservations for long trips should be made several days in advance. Open M-Sa 8am-8pm, Su 8am-2pm. Prices listed are for sleeper class. To: **Ahmedabad** (3-4 per day, 1am-3:30pm, 10hr., Rs159); **Bikaner** (5 per day, 10:45am-7:50pm, 4½hr., Rs59); **Delhi** (7:30 and 11pm, 12hr., Rs199); **Jaipur** (5-6 per day, 5:45am-12:35am, 5-6hr., Rs123); **Jaisalmer** (8:20am and 11:15pm, 6½hr., 1st class Rs323).

Buses: Main Bus Station, High Court Rd. (☎544686 or 544989). To: **Ahmedabad** (6 per day, 6am-7:30pm, 12hr., Rs159; deluxe 6 and 9pm, Rs201); **Ajmer** (every 30min., 5am-midnight, 3½hr., Rs71); **Bikaner** (15 per day, 5:30am-10:30pm, 6hr., Rs101); **Delhi** (9, 10am, and 3:30pm; 14hr.; Rs218; deluxe 4pm, Rs356); **Jaipur** (frequent, 5am-8:45pm, 8hr., Rs115; deluxe 10, 11am, 10:15, 11:30pm, Rs159); **Jaisalmer** (4 per day, 5am-1:30pm, 7hr., Rs85); **Mount Abu** (daily, 12:15pm, 7hr., Rs120); **Udaipur** (5 per day, 7am-10pm, 8hr., Rs94; deluxe 5:30am, noon, 3, and 10:30pm, Rs126). There are dozens of **private bus companies** around; most are along High Court Rd., near the main railway station. Their fares are generally lower than the government bus fares, but their departure times are even harder to predict.

Local Transportation: Small, convenient local **buses** run by the railway stations, the bus stand, and along all major roads every few minutes for Rs2-7. A/C **taxis** are available at all the major sights and in front of the tourist bungalow for around Rs3 per km; minimum Rs60. Smaller side streets are inaccessible by taxi, particularly in the old city. **Auto-rickshaws,** the best way to maneuver through the streets of the old city, congregate around the major sights and stations (Rs10-30 to most destinations). **Tempos** all over the city for Rs1-5. **Bicycles** are a fun way to explore the city. **Prem Cycle Store,** a few doors down from Kalinga Restaurant, opposite the railway station, charges Rs2 per hr., Rs10 per day.

✷ ORIENTATION

Winding streets dotted with traffic circles and the absence of street signs make Jodhpur difficult to navigate. **Jodhpur Railway Station** is in the southwestern part of town, along **Station Rd.** Nearby are the two most important gates in the old city—**Jalori Gate,** at the end of the road running perpendicular to the station, and **Sojati Gate,** to the right as you exit the station, along Station Rd. The busiest commercial centers surround these two gates. **Nai Sarak** leads through Sojati Gate to the old city's biggest shopping street and then to the market area and **Sardar Bazaar,** at the base of the **Clock Tower** that marks the center of Jodhpur. **High Court Rd.** is the main east-west avenue, running from Sojati Gate past the **Umaid Gardens** and the **Tourist Reception Centre** to the distant **Raika Bagh Railway Station.** Directly opposite, where High Court Rd. bends north toward **Paota Circle,** is the **bus stand.** The magnificent **Meherangarh Fort** and **Jaswant Thada** can be seen from almost anywhere in the city.

🛈 PRACTICAL INFORMATION

Tourist Office: Tourist Reception Centre, High Court Rd. (☎545083), next to Ghoomar Hotel. Open M-Sa 8am-5pm. Ask about the Dept. of Tourism's daily **tours** which include the fort, the Umaid Bhawan Palace and Garden, and Jaswant Thada. Daily 9am-1pm or 2-6pm. Rs75, plus entrance fees. For info on **village safaris,** see p. 313.

Currency Exchange: State Bank of India (☎544247), near Paota Circle in the grounds of the Rajasthan High Court. Changes currency and traveler's checks. **Bank of Baroda,** Sojati Gate (☎636539), just below Hotel Arun. Changes traveler's checks and does cash advances on major credit cards. Both open M-F 10am-2pm, Sa 10am-noon.

Luggage Storage: Jodhpur Railway Station. Rs8-10 per day.

Bookstore: Rathi's Media Centre, Ratanada Rd. (☎513580-2), on the bridge over the railroad tracks. Open daily 8am-9pm.

Library: Sumer Public Library, High Court Rd., in Umaid Gardens, has a small collection of English books and newspapers. Open daily 8am-7pm.

Market: High Court Rd., Nai Sarak, and **Sardar Bazaar** are the main shopping areas. Fresh fruit and vegetable stalls and stores are in Sardar Bazaar and along **Station Rd.** Most stores open daily 10am-9pm.

Police: Ratanada Rd. (☎633700). **Police Control Room** (☎547180), at the intersection of Nai Sarak and High Court Rd., is also helpful in an emergency.

Pharmacy: Most of the chemists near the hospitals, around Sojati and Jalori Gates, and along Nai Sarak are open M-Sa 8am-10pm. **Manoj Chhajer Medical Provision Store,** Nai Sarak, on the right, in front of Sardar Bazaar. Open M-Sa 8am-10pm, Su 8am-3pm.

Hospital: Mahatma Gandhi Hospital, Mahatma Gandhi Hospital Rd. (☎636437), between Sojati and Jalori Gates. Also accessible from the Station Rd. side. **Goyal Hospital,** Residency Rd. (☎432144), near the Medical College, is one of the best private hospitals. Both open 24hr.

Internet: Sweet-Dreams Internet (☎543952), inside Ghoomar Hotel. Open daily 9pm-11pm. **Shanti Bhawan Lodge** (☎621689) also has Internet facilities daily from 8am-11pm. Both charge Rs2 per min.

Post Office: Jodhpur Head Post Office, Station Rd. (☎636695), near Sojati Gate. Entrance on the left side, closest to the railway station. Open M-Sa 8am-7pm, Su 10am-5pm. **Postal Code: 342001.**

▚ ACCOMMODATIONS

Budget hotels choke Station and High Court Rd. Hotels close to Raika Bagh Railway Station offer rest from the clamor of the city but not from the rumble of incoming trains. The Tourist Reception Center can arrange homestays.

Govind Hotel (☎622758), opposite the GPO, a 5min. walk from the railway station. Modern, well-kept rooms, a central location, and a rooftop restaurant with views of the fort. Singles Rs200-250; doubles Rs250-600.

Hotel Akshey (☎510327 or 510181), behind platform 2 of Raika Bagh Railway Station. Though some of the rooms shake from the sound of an occasional passing train, the otherwise quiet locale, immaculate rooms (all with TV and attached bath), and pleasant garden area combine to create an aura of calm. Travel services, currency exchange, room service, STD/ISD at reception, running hot water. Check-out 24hr. Dorm beds Rs60; singles Rs200-450; doubles Rs325-550.

Durag Niwas Guest House, 1st Old Public Park (☎639092), south of the tourist office, near K.M. Hall Girls' College. Popular guest house with a homey atmosphere at good prices. The bathrooms outshine the rooms. Owned by "Mr. Desert" himself, who is very knowledgeable about the Jodhpur area. Rooms Rs200-500. Not to be confused with the neighboring **Durag Villas** (☎621300), which offers similar amenities and more ornate rooms for slightly more rupees.

Shanti Bhawan Lodge, Station Rd. (☎621689 or 637001), opposite the railway station. Former residence of Jodhpur's prime minister. Small, clean, basic rooms overlook a noisy main road and open courtyards. Friendly staff, STD/ISD, and travel agency. TVs, direct-dial phones, and air-cooling. Check-out 24hr. Singles Rs100-180; doubles Rs180-450; deluxe room Rs700.

Ajit Bhawan, Airport Rd. (☎437410 or 510410), before the Indian Airlines office. Peacefully located away from the commotion of the city, this hotel features walkways shrouded by latticed vines, footpaths that coil through lush gardens, and individually decorated cottages. Fantastic restaurant. Best enjoyed with a rich uncle on hand to pay the bill. Check-out 10am. Half-day village safaris Rs450. Singles Rs1895; doubles Rs2295. Rates negotiable off-season (Apr.-Sept.).

Ghoomar Hotel, High Court Rd. (☎544010 or 548010), by the tourist office. Big, simply decorated rooms with hot water. Craft shop, restaurant, travel agency, laundry, and fax. Check-out noon. Dorm beds Rs50; singles Rs300-700; doubles Rs400-800.

Hotel Arun (☎620238 or 621824; fax 634228), opposite Sojati Gate. Moderately sized rooms with great views of the crazy streets below. Quiet and clean, despite the location. 24hr. room service, dining hall (open 6am-10:30pm), travel agency, laundry, STD/ISD, fax, and massage services. Dorm beds Rs80; singles Rs120-170; doubles Rs180-250. Reservations recommended and accepted 8am-6pm.

Galaxy Hotel, Sojati Gate (☎620796), at the intersection of High Court and Ratanada Rd. Sparse rooms of varying quality. 24hr. room service, laundry, and 24hr. hot water. Singles Rs80-230; doubles Rs150-495.

◖ FOOD

Midtown Restaurant, in the Shanti Bhawan Lodge. A great introduction to Rajasthani cuisine, this veg. restaurant has a range of local specialties, including *kabuli* (Rs50) and *chakki-ka sagh* (Rs55) as well as the usual continental and Chinese stuff. The *Rajasthani maharaja thali* (Rs80) includes many Jodhpuri specialties. In-season rooftop seating has an amazing view of the fort and palace. Open daily 8am-10:30pm.

Kalinga Restaurant (☎627338), in the Adarsh Niwas Hotel, on the road straight ahead of the railway station. Indian, Chinese, and Italian food in an elegant setting. *Paneer khas-e-kalinga* Rs65; banana split Rs45. Open daily 11am-3pm and 6-10pm.

On the Rocks, adjacent to Ajit Bhawan Hotel, on Airport Rd. Excellent Indian, Chinese, and continental food for Rs40-170. Live Indian classical music Sa and Su. Well-stocked bar and beautifully illuminated courtyard in the evenings. Open daily 11am-11pm. When they have enough guests, the **Ajit Bhawan** also serves a delicious buffet dinner (Rs350) to the accompaniment of live Rajasthani folk music. Buffet breakfast Rs195; lunch Rs275. Check with reception for times.

Gossip Restaurant, 32 Nai Sarak, in the City Palace Hotel. Excellent Rajasthani veg. dishes for Rs38-50. Open daily 7am-10:30pm.

Poonam Restaurant, High Court Rd., near the intersection with Nai Sarak. Choose from over 200 dishes as you sit under fans in dark wood-panelled and mirrored rooms. All-Jain food (pure veg., and nothing that grows underground). Almost everything is Rs10-40. Open daily 8:30am-11pm.

Agra Sweets, directly opposite Sojati Gate. The oldest shop in Jodhpur, where mobs clamor for the best *makhania lassi* in town (Rs10 per glass)—*Gourmet Magazine* once wanted the recipe. Try *mava kachori* (Rs9) over a cup of *espresso* (Rs6). A wide range of sweets and Rajhasthani snacks is also available. Open daily 8am-10:30pm.

Soft 'n' Softy, on Nai Sarak, just around the corner from Agra Sweets, is perfect if you're craving sweet relief from the heat. Serves ice cream in every conceivable form. Excellent shakes Rs20-35. Open daily 7am-midnight.

◉ SIGHTS

MEHERANGARH FORT. Rising magnificently above Jodhpur, Meherangarh dominates the city's landscape. The fort is a blend of well-designed defense systems and amazing artistry. Eight *pols* (gates) mark the various entrances. The **Jayapol,** the main entrance, commemorates the military achievements of Maharaja Man Singh. The impressive **Fatehpol** (Victory Gate), created by Maharaja Ajit Singh after his return from exile, marks the original entrance into the fort. The **Lohapol** (Iron Gate), where 15 handprints mark the *sati* sacrifice of Maharaja Man Singh's widows, is particularly dramatic. The final gigantic **Surajpol** leads to the tiny **Fort Museum,** in the sculpted red sandstone palace. Filling its halls are extravagant howdahs, exquisite wood and ivory artifacts, a weapons room, the royal dumbbells of the maharani, a beautiful 250-year-old tent canopy, 150 types of cannon, fancy baby cradles, musical instruments, miniature paintings, and a 300-piece turban collection. Of particular interest is the **Phool Mahal** (Flower Palace), an elaborately mirrored hall, and the **Moti Mahal** (Pearl Palace), a conference room with a glass and gold ceiling. At the south end of the fort, you can stroll along the ramparts and catch some of the best views of the "Blue City." The **Chamunda Temple** is also at this end of the fort. As you exit, noisy "traditional" musicians will surround you, demanding baksheesh. (*Open daily 9am-5pm. Rs50; camera fee Rs50; video fee Rs100. Guided tours for Rs100 are available at the ticket counter but aren't really necessary.*)

UMAID BHAWAN PALACE. The Umaid Bhawan Palace is a majestic marble and sandstone palace that dominates the eastern part of the city. Built just before Independence, the palace is impressive enough, but lacks it some of the charm of Rajasthan's older palaces. A grandiose hotel and restaurant have eaten up half the palace, while an eccentric museum containing traditional art, weapons, trophies, and miscellaneous relics—all belonging to the maharaja—occupies the rest. (*Open daily 9am-5pm. Rs40. Cameras strictly prohibited.*)

JASWANT THADA. This marble memorial to the beloved Maharaja Jaswant Singh II was erected by his wife after his death. Locals liken it to a miniature Taj Mahal. (*10min. from the fort, down a windy road. Open daily 8:30am-5:30pm. Rs10. No photography.*)

OTHER SITES. The **Clock Tower** marks the center of the old city and the Sardar Bazaar. The **Umaid Gardens,** near the Tourist Bungalow, are a good place for an aimless wander. (*Gardens open Sa-Th 10am-4:30pm. Rs3. Zoo open daily 10am-6pm. Rs1.*)

ENTERTAINMENT

What little nightlife Jodhpur has is geared to foreign tourists. **On the Rocks** (see p. 312) and the **Classic Bar** inside the City Palace Hotel are popular for a dark night of drinking. There are **Hindi cinemas** everywhere; one of the most popular is Girdhar Mandir Cinema, on Nai Sarak. (☎547371; showings at noon, 3, 6, and 9pm; tickets Rs6-27.) The annual **Marwar Festival** (Oct. 31-Nov. 2, 2001; Oct. 19-20, 2002) showcases local culture, history, dance, art, and most of all, food.

SHOPPING

The **Sojati Gate** and **Nai Sarak** areas, especially **Sardar Bazaar** by the Clock Tower, are full of stalls, markets, emporiums, and department stores. You can find just about anything here, from handicrafts to toilet seat covers. The area leading toward the Umaid Bhawan Palace is filled with enormous handicraft emporiums.

Handicrafts are one of Jodhpur's largest industries, and art shops such as **Rajasthan Arts and Crafts** (☎639220; open M-Sa 9am-7:30pm) and **Ajay Art Emporium** (☎624636; open daily 9am-8pm), both near Circuit House on Umaid Bhawan Palace Rd., sell excellent selections of items in wood, brass, marble, iron, clay, papier mâché, and textiles—all hand-made in Rajasthan. Also available are the beautiful and fabulously colorful cloths and saris of Rajasthan, including the traditional *bhandani* (tie-dyed) saris. **Lovely Silk Palace,** Railway Station Rd. (☎621590; open M-Sa 9:30am-9pm) and **Lucky Silk Stores,** Sojati Gate (☎622221; open daily 10:30am-9pm), both sell cloth, silks, and handmade saris from all over India.

DAYTRIPS FROM JODHPUR

BISHNOI. Guided tours to the desert villages around Jodhpur allow visitors to witness and participate in traditional local crafts such as carpet-making, weaving, spinning, foraging, indigenous medicine, and cooking. The villages of the Bishnoi, which date back to the 15th century, are devoted to environmental protection and conservation. Tours can be arranged through most hotels and through the Tourist Reception Centre, which charges per vehicle (Rs750) rather than per person (guide Rs350 extra). Mr. Parbat Singh (☎543805) arranges tours and cross-desert camel safaris as far as Jaisalmer and Bikaner for Rs500-900 per person per day.

MANDORE GARDENS. Once the capital of Marwar, the town of **Mandore** is known for its beautiful garden complex, which still houses the *chattris* (cenotaphs) of the Rathore maharajas, including that of Ajit Singh. Near the garden where the cenotaphs stand is the **Hall of Heroes,** a series of 15 colorful, life-size statues of Hindu gods and Rajput warriors carved out of one large wall of rock. The vibrant gardens and peaceful atmosphere make it a welcome escape from the hum of the city. *(9km north of Jodhpur. Local buses from Jodhpur Rs2-4. Rickshaw Rs75-100 round-trip.)*

OSIAN. An ancient town surrounded by sand dunes, Osian is home to 16 finely sculpted Jain and Hindu temples from the 8th-11th centuries—some of the best in India. *(65km north of Jodhpur. Buses depart every 30min., 5am-9pm, 2hr., Rs19.)*

PICNIC SPOTS. For prime picnic spots, visit **Kailana Lake,** about 11km from town on Jaisalmer Rd., or **Balsamand Lake and Palace,** about 7km from town. Balsamand Lake is surrounded by 12th-century mango, guava, papaya, and date groves. *(Rs75-100 by auto-rickshaw.)*

JAISALMER जैसलमेर   ☎ 02992

In the heart of the Thar Desert, 285km west of Jodhpur and 100km from the Pakistan border, is the "Golden City" of Jaisalmer (pop. 40,000), named for the color imparted to its sandstone skyline by the setting sun. Once a dusty Rajput stronghold, Jaisalmer started out as a fort. After being sacked twice and conquered by Muslim invaders, the city took on a new guise during the 17th century as a prosperous trading center for camel caravans. Under the British, maritime trade eclipsed the desert trade routes, and Partition in 1947 cut them off altogether, diminishing Jaisalmer's wealth and importance. With the Indo-Pakistan tensions of the 1960s, Jaisalmer became a military outpost once again. Today, the heavy army presence is a source of income second only to the booming tourism industry. Jaisalmer is home to scores of peerless *havelis* (royal mansions) that retain sandstorm-sculpted memories of the city's golden years. More recently, Jaisalmer has become popular as a starting point for camel-back journeys into the sand-duned desert.

⬕ GETTING THERE AND GETTING AROUND

Flights: Jaisalmer Airport (☎ 50048 or 52960), 5km from the city center down Sam Rd., 15min. by auto-rickshaw (Rs30-40). **Crown Tours Limited,** Sam Rd. (☎/fax 51912), in the Moomal Tourist Bungalow, is an agent for **Indian Airlines.** Open daily 9:30am-8:30pm. Flights operate in season only (Oct.-Mar.) to: **Bombay** (3 per week, 2½hr., US$195) via **Jodhpur** (30min., US$70); **Delhi** (3 per week, 2hr., US$155) via **Jaipur** (55min., US$125).

Trains: Jaisalmer Railway Station (☎ 52354, enquiry 51301), 10min. out of Gadi Sagar Pol, on the left. Reservation counter open M-Sa 8am-8pm, Su 8am-2pm. To: **Jodhpur** (7am and 10:30pm, 7hr., Rs323).

Buses: Main Bus Stand (☎ 51541), near the railway station. Both private and government buses also pass through the **Private Bus Stand,** south of the city near Hotel Neeraj. To: **Ahmedabad** (5pm, 11hr., Rs184); **Bikaner** (4 per day, 6am-8pm, 7hr., Rs120); **Jaipur** (5pm, 12hr., Rs175) via **Jodhpur** (Rs80) and **Ajmer** (Rs138); **Mt. Abu** (5:30am, 11hr., Rs177).

Local Transportation: On foot, it takes 15-20min. to cross the city. Unmetered **Auto-rickshaws** are everywhere, except in the fort during peak tourist hours (8am-noon and 4-7pm), when they are not permitted to enter. Most charge Rs10-15. **Bicycles** are a convenient means of getting around. Try shops inside Amar Sagar Pol and near the fort gate. Rs2-3 per hr., Rs10-15 per day. **Jeeps** available at Hanuman Cir. are needed to get to places outside of the city. Expect to pay at least Rs5 per km. Travel agents and hotels will rent out their own jeeps at cheaper rates for fixed tours.

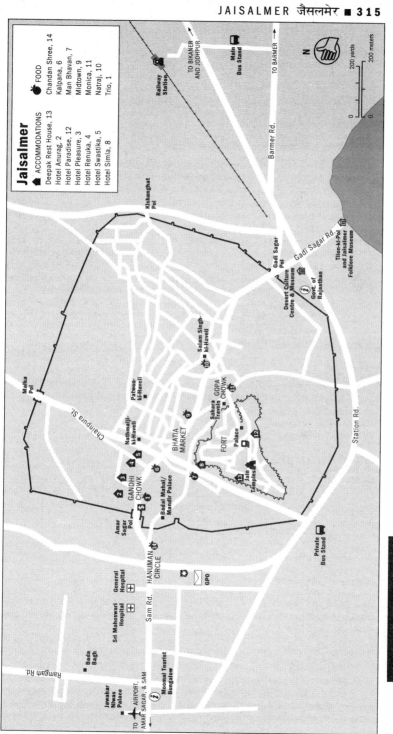

Jaisalmer

▲ ACCOMMODATIONS
Deepak Rest House, 13
Hotel Anurag, 2
Hotel Paradise, 12
Hotel Pleasure, 3
Hotel Renuka, 4
Hotel Swastika, 5
Hotel Simla, 8

● FOOD
Chandan Shree, 14
Kalpana, 6
Man Bhavan, 7
Midtown, 9
Monica, 11
Natraj, 10
Trio, 1

RAJASTHAN

✈ ☎ ORIENTATION AND PRACTICAL INFORMATION

Hanuman Circle is just outside **Amar Sagar Pol,** the main entrance to the old city. Littered with jeeps, buses, and taxis for hire, Hanuman Circle is easily identified by a strangely stationed jet fighter, a relic from a war with Pakistan. **Sam Rd.** heads east from Hanuman Circle into the city center. Just inside Amar Sagar Pol is **Gandhi Chowk,** the main market area. This narrow road leads through the market to **Jaisalmer Fort; Gopa Chowk** is at the base of the fort. The road continues east to **Gadi Sagar Pol,** the east gate of the city. From here, it becomes **Gadi Sagar Rd.,** which ends at Lake Gadisan, or Gadi Sagar. A left turn just outside of Gadi Sagar Pol leads to the **Main Bus Stand** and **Railway Station.**

Tourist Office: Tourist Reception Centre (☎52406). Exit Gadi Sagar Pol and turn right at the first intersection. Open M-Sa 10am-5pm. The RTDC-run **Moomal Tourist Bungalow** (☎52392; fax 52545), is on the other side of town, off Sam Rd.

Budget Travel: Safari Tours (☎51058), directly in front of Amar Sagar Pol. An excellent source of information on everything in and around Jaisalmer. Open daily 8am-8pm; May-Jun. 10am-5pm. For more information, see **Camel Safaris,** p. 319.

Currency Exchange: Bank of Baroda (☎52402), on the right, just inside Amar Sagar Pol. Currency exchange, traveler's checks, and cash advances on credit cards. Open M-F 10am-1pm, Sa 10-11am.

Bookstore: Bhatia News Agency, Gandhi Chowk (☎52671), on the right past Nachana Haveli, when coming from Amar Sagar Pol. Open daily 8:30am-8:30pm.

Market: Gandhi Chowk is the main commercial center. **Hanuman Circle** and **Gopa Chowk** are also shopping districts. **Vegetable markets** are in **Bhatia Market** and Gopa Chowk. Most stores open daily 8am-9pm.

Pharmacy: Government Pharmacy, outside the Government Hospital, is open 24hr.

Hospital: Sri Maheswari Hospital (☎50024), Sam Rd., on the right after the Government Hospital, past Hanuman Circle. Consultations M-Sa 9am-1pm and 5-7pm, Su 9-11am.

Police: Main Police Office (☎52322), south of Hanuman Circle. On the road that extends left out of Hanuman Circle as you walk away from Amar Sagar Pol.

Internet: Chirag Communications, near the palace. Open 24hr.

Post Office: GPO (☎52407 or 51377), south of the police station, 5min. from Amar Sagar Pol. Offices around the city. All open M-Sa 10am-5pm. **Postal Code:** 345001.

☗ ACCOMMODATIONS

Most of the hotels and guest houses in Jaisalmer are pretty much indistinguishable; those charging higher prices might offer a few more antique furnishings, but normally not much else to justify the high tariff. Staying inside the fort can be charming, and there are enough tourist facilities here to sustain you for days. Staying outside the fort, however, also has its advantages—there's more opportunity to mingle with the locals, and views of the fort at sunset are unbeatable. All hotels run **camel safaris** (see p. 319 for more information on the insanely competitive safari market) as well as other travel services. Expect rates to double (at least) during the **Desert Festival** (Feb. 6-8, 2001; Feb. 19-20, 2002).

If you are coming from Jodhpur, expect to be hassled all the way by hotel agents and touts, and absolutely mobbed once you arrive. You will be offered incredible deals (hotel rooms for Rs10), provided you go on that hotel's camel safari. If you ask for a particular hotel, touts will often tell you that the hotel is closed down or full, or that the management has recently been abducted by aliens—anything to get you to the hotel they are connected to. Some places do send their own vehicles to pick up travelers free of charge—look for hotel banners, not business cards.

▩ Hotel Paradise (☎52674 or 52417), in the fort. This beautiful *haveli* is built around a pleasant garden. The rooftop has many vantage points from which to look out onto the fort and city. Check-out 9am. Hot water 7am-noon, 5-10pm, and on request. Singles Rs80-850; doubles Rs120-850. Award-winning camel safaris Rs250-350 per day.

▨ **Hotel Renuka,** Chainpura St. (☎52757). Enter Amar Sagar Pol and turn left on Chainpura; it's 5min. down on the left. Family atmosphere and clean, basic rooms. The rooftop view is unparalleled. Rooftop veg. restaurant, where, for Rs500, the owners will arrange dance and music performances. Doors close at 11pm. Check-out 9am. Hot water 8am-noon and 6-9pm. Singles Rs30-150; doubles Rs40-200. Reservations recommended. Camel safaris to villages not visited by other safaris (1½ day Rs750).

Deepak Rest House (☎52665 or 52070), in the fort, near the Jain temple. Fantastic desert views from clean, modest rooms in the fort wall. Good rooftop veg. restaurant. Check-out 9am. Dorm beds Rs20; singles Rs30-80; doubles Rs60-450. Excellent camel safaris Rs450-750 per day.

Hotel Pleasure, Gandhi Chowk (☎52323). Simple, tiled rooms of moderate size. Breakfast-time room service, free storage while on camel safari (even a competitor's safari), free callbacks, refrigerator/freezer, and free washing machine. Rooms have air-cooling. Check-out noon. Singles Rs50-60; doubles Rs70-90. Camel safaris Rs350 per day.

Hotel Simla (☎53061 or 53113), in the fort. This renovated *haveli* has something for everyone, from lavish rooms with comfortable beds draped in silks to budget rooftop accommodations. Doors close at 10:30pm. Rs25 to sleep on roof, Rs50 with tent. Singles Rs100-350; doubles Rs150-550.

Hotel Anurag, Gandhi Chowk (☎50276). A small family hotel with rough-and-ready accommodations at very low rates. Rooms are clean, and the atmosphere is informal and welcoming. Rooftop snack shop in season. STD/ISD with free callbacks. Check-out 9am. Singles Rs50-125; doubles with bath Rs100-150. Camel safaris Rs350 per day.

Hotel Swastika, Chainpura St. (☎52483). Well-run, decently sized rooms with tatty rugs but tidy bathrooms around a courtyard. No restaurant, but they make a mean bread, jam, and tea breakfast. Laundry service. Free callbacks. Check-out 9am. Singles Rs100-150; doubles Rs150-250. May-June Rs50 discount. Reservations recommended. Camel safaris Rs300 per day.

◖▨ FOOD

The main reason to eat here is the rooftop view, but Jaisalmer also has its own desert cuisine not found elsewhere. Be sure to experience *ker sangri*, a mix of capers and beans (it looks like a bundle of gravied twigs); *gatte*, a *garam* flour preparation; and *kadhai pakoras*, a yogurt-based appetizer.

Monica Restaurant, Gopa Chowk, a betel-spit left of the fort gate. A local favorite, with a range of cuisines and a delicious *kadhai paneer* (Rs45). Local musicians play here nightly. Veg. Rs30-75, non-veg. Rs60-75. Open daily 8am-2pm and 6:30-10:30pm.

Natraj Restaurant, near the Salam Singh-ki-Haveli. Decorated with surrealist paintings and a striking rooftop view of the Salam Singh-ki-Haveli. A/C dining room. Standard range of dishes, all well-prepared. Rs35-60. Open daily 8am-11pm.

Midtown Restaurant, Gopa Chowk. Dim red lamps give it an atmosphere as intimate as the view of the fort. Popular with western tourists. The menu contains the usual items, in addition to some unusual desserts. Rajasthani *thalis* Rs50. Open daily 7am-11pm.

Trio Restaurant, Amar Sagar Pol (☎52733). Considered by many to be the best restaurant in Jaisalmer, Trio features great views, first-class service, well-prepared specialties (Royal Safari soup Rs45), and traditional Rajasthani music (7pm) at reasonable prices. Entrees Rs25-80. Open daily 7am-10:30pm. Reservations recommended in season.

Kalpana Restaurant, in the heart of Gandhi Chowk. Kalpana offers a rooftop view, specialty tandoori cuisine, and one of the best bars in the city. Popular with tourists and locals alike. Dishes Rs35-40. Open daily 7am-3pm and 6-11pm.

Man Bhavan (☎50408), at the base of the fort. Serves delicious South Indian, Bengali, Gujarati, and Rajasthani food for under Rs40. Open 7am-11pm.

Chandan Shree Restaurant, Amar Sagar Pol. Exit the old city and join locals as you enjoy cheap, filling *thalis* (Rs20-25). Open daily 8am-11pm.

RAJASTHAN

👁 SIGHTS

INSIDE THE FORT

Enter from Gopa Chowk, the commercial square outside the fort's main gate.

Jaisalmer's fort, founded in 1156 by Maharaja Jaisal, a king of the Bhatti clan of Rajputs, overlooks the city from the south. Its 99 circular bastions surround the labyrinth of houses and shops that winds its way around the old palace.

CITY PALACE. Just inside the fort, the City Palace is made up of five smaller palaces, one of which contains a dance hall decorated with blue Chinese tiles and green screens from the Netherlands. The old stone rooms are half-preserved; some even remain closed by their original locks. Others store decaying howdahs. A climb to the ramparts leads to great views of the fort and the old city. *(Open 8am-1pm and 2:30-5pm; in winter 9am-1pm and 2:30-5pm. Rs10; camera Rs10; video Rs50.)*

JAIN TEMPLES. A cluster of seven interconnected Jain Temples (two of which are open to tourists) lies within the fort. Built on a raised platform, the temples have low archways and tiny halls that display intricate sculpture covering every visible inch. A winding staircase leads to a circular balcony with an open view of the sanctuary and the temple domes below. *(Open daily 7am-noon. Free. Camera fee Rs50, video fee Rs100. Menstruating women are not supposed to enter.)*

OLD CITY HAVELIS. Any walk through the old city will bring you past numerous beautiful *havelis*, or mansions, but there are three particularly impressive ones open to the public. **Patwon-ki-Haveli,** the most remarkable of the three, is composed of five *havelis* built in the early 1900s. The single golden facade rises four dramatic stories, each fitted with stone balconies topped by arched stone umbrellas and exquisite latticed windows. The *haveli* is still owned by five different people. Parts of the mansion are given over to shops selling jewelry and cloth, but two doors still open to reveal stairs up to the building's towering rooftop views. The door to the left is operated privately. *(Open daily 8am-7pm. Rs 5; camera fee Rs10.)* The door on the right is government-run. *(Open daily 10am-5pm. Rs2.)* **Nathmalji-ki-Haveli** was built by two brothers, Lalu and Hat, who each took one half of the building's face. Inside, stairs lead up from a central courtyard to the elaborately carved dance hall. *(Open daily 8am-1:30pm and 3-8pm. Donations requested for maintenance.)* **Salam Singh-ki-Haveli,** with peacock buttresses adorning its exterior, was built by the infamous prime minister Salam Singh Mohta around 1800. Considered a tyrant for his crippling taxes, he attempted to add two additional levels to his own *haveli* to make it taller than the maharaja's. But the maharaja had the offending appendages torn down. Ultimately, Salam Singh's audacity got him killed, when the maharaja decided to have him assassinated. *(Open daily 8am-7pm; in winter 8am-6pm).*

MR. DESERT

Moustaches twisted to follicular perfection, camels dripping with shells, mirrors, and buttons, and turban-tying pros await those willing to brave the onslaught of tourists at the annual Desert Festival of Jaisalmer (Feb. 6-8, 2001). The event kicks off with a procession of "ships of the desert" and local bands followed by an odd assortment of competitions: tug-of-war, turban tying, a battle of the moustaches, camel racing, camel decoration, and, the high point of the festival, the "crowning of Mr. Desert." The prestigious and lucrative title is bestowed upon the man who best epitomizes Rajasthan—the one who exudes masculinity in his traditional dress, bushy beard, and gravity-defying moustache. Past winners include Mr. Shri Laxmi Narain Bissa, proud owner of Sahara Travels near the fort. After capturing the crown for four consecutive years, Shri Laxmi Narain Bissa hung up his turban and was bestowed with the title "Mr. Desert Emeritus." His face can now be seen staring out of *haveli* windows on posters promoting Rajasthani tourism and gracing advertisements for Jaisalmer Cigarettes, a stint that has earned him the title "The Indian Marlboro Man."

LAKE GADI SAGAR. A reservoir constructed in 1367, Lake Gadi Sagar was once Jaisalmer's only source of water. Today, it is frequented by bathers, *dhobi-wallahs*, and visitors who come to view the **Folklore Museum**, which contains quirky relics of Rajasthani art and culture. *(Open daily Aug.-Mar. 8am-6:30pm; Apr.-July 4:30-7:30pm. Rs10.)* Gadi Sagar's other attraction is a yellow sandstone gateway, the **Tilon-ki-Pol.** With its grand arched windows, this gateway once held beautifully carved rooms where the royal family stayed during the monsoon. Built by the king's chief courtesan, the gate was once a source of great controversy for the town's citizens, who refused to allow their womenfolk to walk beneath the "tainted" creation. As a compromise, a smaller entrance to the lake was built to the right. The lake is now decorated with royal stone *chattris*. **The Desert Culture Centre and Museum** holds a collection of 19th-century Ravi Varma paintings, petrified wood fossils, old coins, and regional musical instruments. *(Gadi Sagar Pol, next to the tourist office. Open daily Aug.-Mar. 10am-6:30pm; Apr.-July 9am-noon and 3-6pm. Free with stub from the Folklore Museum.)*

🐫 CAMEL SAFARIS

A wonderful way to experience the Thar Desert, camel safaris are the heart and soul of Jaisalmer's tourist trade. Not surprisingly, the camel safari business has become ruthlessly competitive. Every hotel offers camel safaris, as do several independent agencies, but few hotels actually have their own camels, and most safaris operate through independent agencies. Hotels pay the agencies about Rs100 per day just for the camels, with food and equipment costs added. For the hotels to make a profit, they must charge at least Rs200 per day. **Indeed, the tourist office recommends spending at least Rs350 per day on safaris.** If you're paying less, you won't get all of the basic amenities—blankets (it gets very cold in the desert at night), one camel per person, good food, English-speaking guides, etc. Deluxe safaris with tents, quality food, portable bars, dancing, music, and other goodies can cost over Rs2000 per day. Once you've chosen a safari, you still need to be on your guard. Cheap safaris often have **hidden costs** (e.g. Rs50 or more for bottles of mineral water). And as always, there are several scams designed to part you from your possessions, normally on the return trip. **Never accept offers to watch your luggage** while you explore a sight.

Of course, many hotels have honest, decent, and inexpensive safaris, but the most reliable safaris are booked through independent agents. **Safari Tours,** just inside Amar Sagar Pol, is excellent for general tourist information and safari specialties. They tailor their safaris to fit your schedule, and offer high-quality food and a night's stay in huts equipped with modern toilets for Rs1000-2000 per day. Safari Tours is one of the few companies that genuinely tries to keep the desert clean. (☎/fax 51158. Open daily 8:30am-8pm; May-Jun. 10am-5pm.) **Royal Safari** (☎52538), in Nachana Haveli, offers basic safaris for Rs450 per day, and deluxe safaris for Rs1050-2000 per day. **Sahara Travels,** near the Fort Gate, charges Rs500 per day for basic safaris and Rs800 per day for deluxe. (☎52609. Open daily 7am-10:30pm.) **Ask safari agents to specify all food and equipment; "deluxe" and "basic" can mean many things.**

Camel safaris often head to the spectacular Sam sand dunes, stopping at villages along the way. A round-trip takes 4½ days. All hotels and agents offer shorter jeep/camel combos for assorted prices, but you might not get the chance to sleep under the stars in the Thar Desert. Longer cross-desert safaris to Bikaner, Pushkar, or Jodhpur are also available from all of the safari companies listed above.

🎵 ENTERTAINMENT

Jaisalmer has little nightlife, but there is plenty to keep you occupied. For the wildest time in Jaisalmer, come to the annual **Desert Festival** (Feb. 6-8, 2001, Feb. 19-22, 2002; see **Mr. Desert,** p. 318). Prices double (at least) and tourists mob the place, but you'll still be able to enjoy traditional music and folk dance, camel races, camel polo, camel dances, puppeteers, **moustache contests,** and more. RTDC sets up a special tourist tent-village for accommodations.

Other diversions include **swimming** in Lake Gadi Sagar or at Narayan Niwas Palace's indoor pool (near Patwon-ki-Haveli, Rs100). Film fans can indulge at Hindi **cinemas,** including **Ramesh Talkies** (☎52242), near Patwon-ki-Haveli.

🛍 SHOPPING

Jaisalmer is a haven for **handicrafts,** including embroidery, patchwork, leather goods, and mirror work, as well as stone carving, silver, and pottery. Bargain hard, and don't even think about shopping during the Desert Festival. **Gandhi Chowk** and the main road connecting it to Gadi Sagar Pol are the primary commercial areas. The **Rajasthali Government Emporium,** just outside Amar Sagar Pol, south of Sam Rd., sells a vast selection of Rajasthani desert handicrafts in brass, silver, wood, and textiles, as well as carpets and paintings. (☎52461. Open daily 10am-8pm.) For a basic explanation of art, culture, and architecture in Jaisalmer, L.N. Khatri's *Jaisalmer: Folklore, History, and Architecture* (Rs75) can be bought at the author's craft store, the **Desert Handicraft Emporium,** Gandhi Chowk, on the right as you head away from Amer Sagar Pol. (☎50062. Open daily 9:30am-11:30pm.) Manak Lal Soni, owner of **Parmar Jewelers Emporium** (☎51373), in the fort opposite the palace, runs a wholesale and custom-made jewelry business from his home.

🔃 DAYTRIPS FROM JAISALMER

The areas surrounding Jaisalmer are as interesting as the city itself. Camel and hybrid camel/jeep safaris on their way to the dunes are the best way of getting to these sights. They are also accessible by bus, jeep, and (at a stretch) bicycle. Access to the area 45km west of Jaisalmer is restricted because of border disputes, and special permission (forget it) is required from the **District Magistrate Office,** near the police station.

BADA BAGH AND AMAR SAGAR. About 5km north of Jaisalmer is Bada Bagh, where 500-year-old sandstone cenotaphs stand next to the 300-year-old mango trees of the royal garden. To the far left is the most recent tomb, constructed in 1991 for the grandfather of the current maharaja. The gardens, which used to supply food to all of Jaisalmer, are a popular picnic spot. *(Open daily 8am-8pm. Rs10.)* Another well-known spot for tea and tiffin is **Amar Sagar,** 5km northwest of Jaisalmer, where a beautifully carved Jain temple, constructed under the orders of Majaraja Amar Singh, guards a lake and fertile gardens. *(Open daily 6am-9pm. Free. Camera fee Rs50, video fee Rs100. Menstruating women are not supposed to enter.)* The **Mool Sagar Garden Palace,** 7km to the north of Jaisalmer was once the picnic palace of the Maharaja. *(Open daily 8am-8pm. Rs10.)*

LODURVA. Once the capital of the region, Lodurva now lies in ruins 15km north of Jaisalmer. Restored Jain temples are all that remains of the town's former splendor. An amazing 1000-year-old archway from the original temple still stands in the courtyard. A cobra occasionally makes an appearance out of a small hole in the temple; glimpsing the snake is deemed auspicious. *(Open daily 7am-8pm. Free. Camera fee Rs50, video fee Rs100.)*

SAM. One way or another, most camel safaris end up in Sam, an expanse of rippling desert 42km west of Jaisalmer, whose growing popularity is quickly diminishing its appeal. Nevertheless, the dunes are beautiful, especially at sunrise and sunset. Most safaris spend the night on the dunes, under the stars or in a tent. The RTDC-run **Hotel Sam Dhani** is also available. There are two buses from Jaisalmer, one in the late morning or early afternoon and one in the early evening.

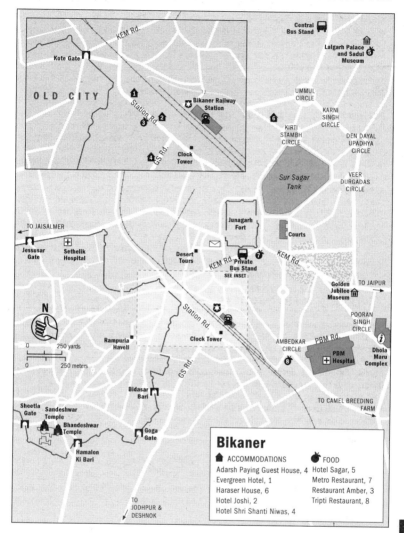

Bikaner

🏠 ACCOMMODATIONS

Adarsh Paying Guest House, 4
Evergreen Hotel, 1
Haraser House, 6
Hotel Joshi, 2
Hotel Shri Shanti Niwas, 4

🍴 FOOD

Hotel Sagar, 5
Metro Restaurant, 7
Restaurant Amber, 3
Tripti Restaurant, 8

BIKANER बीकानेर   ☎ 0151

The fourth largest city in Rajasthan, Bikaner has been trying to draw tourists, but its remote location and the competition from its higher-profile neighbors have been obstacles for the RTDC in this desert city. While maddening traffic circles and long stretches of road keep some visitors at bay, those who do trek here are rewarded with Jain temples, an enchanting fort, dozens of *havelis*, and (this is, after all, Rajasthan) lots of camels. For those weary of the tourists that descend upon the rest of the state, Bikaner is a relatively undiscovered oasis.

Founded in 1488 by Rao Bika, Bikaner was originally a stop on the Silk Route, as well as an important center for camel breeding. In the 16th century, its maharaja, Rei Singh, became one of the most successful generals in Emperor Akbar's all-but invincible army. By the 18th century, Bikaner had become a power to be reckoned with, a deadly enemy of Jodhpur, and the home of the legendary Bikaner Camel Corps.

RAJASTHAN

Since Independence, the city has been almost exclusively concerned with its own economic advancement, leading to its increased industrialization. Only recently has Bikaner looked to tourism as an avenue for economic development. The city's new interest in generating this industry is apparent in the grand show it puts on for the annual **Camel Festival** (Jan 8-9, 2001; Jan. 27-28, 2002), a celebration of food, music, and all things camel: races, contests, parades, trading, and safaris galore. Prices of everything double (at least), and Bikaner fills with tourists.

⌐ GETTING THERE AND GETTING AROUND

Trains: Bikaner Railway Station (☎131 or 132), a Rs20-30 auto-rickshaw ride from anywhere in the city. **Advance Reservation Office** (☎523132), next to the railway station. Open M-Sa 8am-8pm, Su 8am-2pm. To: **Delhi** (3 per day, 5am-4:30pm, 8½hr., Rs154); **Jaipur** (5am, 3:40, and 8:30pm; 7hr.; Rs138); **Jodhpur** (5 per day, 1am-12:30pm, 5hr., Rs59).

Buses: Central Bus Stand (☎523800), 3km north of the city, opposite Lalgarh Palace. To: **Ahmedabad** (1:30pm, 10hr., Rs249); **Ajmer** (frequent, 6am-11:30pm; deluxe 5pm; 7½hr.; Rs94); **Delhi** (5:45, 7:30am, and 7:15pm, 11hr., Rs166; deluxe 8:15, 10:25am, and 6:30pm, Rs177); **Jaipur** (frequent, 5am-10pm, 7hr., Rs96-120); **Jaisalmer** (4 per day, 7:30am-9:30pm, 7hr., Rs98; deluxe 5 and 6am, Rs110); **Jodhpur** (frequent, 4:45am-12:30am, 5½hr., Rs90); **Udaipur** (6:30pm, 12hr., Rs213). **Private buses** can be arranged through hotels, excursion agents, and the bus agencies that congregate around Goga Gate, south of Kote Gate, and behind the fort.

Local Transportation: Auto-rickshaws are unmetered and take you anywhere in the city for Rs15-30. **Bicycles** can be rented from cycle stores opposite the police station on Station Rd. (Rs2 per hr., Rs15 per day. Open daily 8am-9pm). **Jeeps** can be rented near the railway station and opposite the fort's front entrance for Rs3-5 per km.

✳🛈 ORIENTATION AND PRACTICAL INFORMATION

Station Rd., the hotel strip, runs parallel to the tracks in front of the **railway station.** To the right of the station, it intersects the main commercial thoroughfare, **KEM Rd.**, and then continues to the **Junagarh Fort** and the GPO. A left turn on KEM Rd. leads to **Kote Gate**, the main entrance to the **old city**. A left on Station Rd. from the station leads past the **Clock Tower** through two intersections. A left at the second intersection will lead you to **Ambedkar Circle**. Because of the distances involved, the city is best traversed by rickshaw.

Tourist Office: Tourist Reception Centre, Hotel Dhola Maru Complex (☎544125), near Pooran Singh Circle. Open M-Sa 10am-5pm.

Budget Travel: Desert Tours (☎521967), behind the GPO, provides tourist information. Mr. Kamal Saxena organizes horse and cart tours of the city: half day Rs120, full day Rs200. Camel tours Rs500-600. Open daily 8am-8pm.

Currency Exchange: Bank of Baroda (☎545053), opposite the railway station, changes currency and traveler's checks. Open M-F 10am-2pm, Sa 10am-noon.

Luggage Storage: Railway Station Cloak Room. Rs6-8 per item per day.

Bookstore: Nauyug Giranth Kuteer (☎520836), inside Kote Gate, on the right. Open daily 9am-9pm.

Market: The **vegetable market** is just south of the fort, opposite the Private Bus Stand.

Police: Main office (☎200840), next to the railway station. Open 24hr.

Pharmacy: PBM Hospital and MN Hospital (☎544423) both operate 24hr. pharmacies.

Hospital: MN Hospital (☎544122), near Karni Singh Stadium. **Sethelik Hospital** (☎528811), inside Jessusar Gate.

Internet: Vishal, Lalgarh Palace Rd. (☎522741), near Kirti Stambh Circle. Rs2 per min. Open daily 7am-11:30pm.

Post Office: GPO (☎524185), behind Junagarh Fort. Open M-Sa 10am-6pm. Branches near PBM Hospital, inside Kote Gate, and near State Bank of Bikaner and Jaipur. **Postal Code:** 334001.

ACCOMMODATIONS

Most of Bikaner's budget options are clustered on Station and GS Rd. Homestays with local families can be arranged through the tourist office (Rs80-750 per night). A lethargic tourist industry keeps hotel prices steady year round, but expect drastic jumps in fares during the annual Camel Festival.

Hotel Joshi, Station Rd. (☎527700), about 1½ blocks from the railway station. Modern and central, with clean rooms and attached baths. Good restaurant, STD/ISD, currency exchange, and laundry. Check-out 24hr. Singles Rs300-575; doubles Rs375-675.

Evergreen Hotel, Station Rd. (☎542061). Cheery rooms painted in ever-clean evergreen, at reasonable prices. Check-out 10am. Singles Rs80-125; doubles Rs125-175.

Hotel Shri Shanti Niwas, GS Rd. (☎521925 or 542320). No alcohol or meat allowed on the premises. Check-out 24hr. Singles Rs70-380; doubles Rs100-480.

Harasar House (☎527318 or 209891), north of Sur Sagar Tank. Enormous, carved wooden beds and sparkling bathrooms. Rooftop terrace with view of fort and palace. Good veg. restaurant. Singles 300-600; doubles 300-800. Reservations recommended.

Adarsh Paying Guest House, GS Rd. (☎548716). Basic rooms in a family environment. Check-out 24hr. Singles Rs50-100; doubles Rs60-150.

FOOD

Moomal Restaurant, Panch Sebi Circle, on the way to the Camel Breeding Farm. A large, air-cooled veg. restaurant serving everybody's favorite Chinese, continental, and Indian dishes: well worth the 20min. walk. Fast service. Rs30-45 for a full dinner. Open daily 11am-3pm and 6:30-10:30pm.

Metro Restaurant, at the front of the fort near Sadul Singh Circle. Air-cooled restaurant with booths on 3 levels. Old-friends menu Rs30-70. Open daily 8am-10:30pm.

Tripti Restaurant, near Ambedkar Circle. A popular local haunt with a dark and cavernous atmosphere. Meals Rs30-50; South Indian snacks Rs20-40. Open daily 9am-10pm.

Restaurant Amber, Station Rd., opposite Hotel Joshi. Red cushioned booths and dim lighting. *Dosas* Rs20-38; main dishes Rs40-65. Open daily 8am-10pm.

Hotel Sagar, Lalgarh Palace, opposite the bus station. A wide range of dishes, most for under Rs50. Unusual items include deep-pan pizza (Rs25-40) and apple onion soup (Rs45). Open daily 6am-10:30pm.

TURBAN LEGENDS Once upon a time, no one wore turbans in India; the idea of wrapping 7 to 10 meters of cotton cloth around the head had simply never entered the popular imagination. This changed forever when the turbanned Mughals poured into northern India in 1526, an invasion that sent shock waves through the world of South Asian fashion. Originally worn as a sign of respect when one appeared before a Mughal official, they soon became an indicator of status among high-caste Hindus and a symbol of the Sikh religion. In Rajasthan today, turban colors and styles vary according to region. In Bikaner, brahmins wear a yellow turban except when mourning, when they cut their hair off and switch to white head wear. Bikaner Rajputs, a *kshatriya* caste, wear brightly colored, striped, or *bandhani* (tie-dyed) turbans wrapped around one ear with a long tail in the back. Jats and Bishnois, the farming castes, wear enormous white turbans (called *safas*), and *vaishya* castes wear small turbans known as *pagoris.* Untouchables and *shudras* are not allowed to wrap their heads at all. But turbans can show shame as well as status—debtors and criminals often have their turbans forcibly removed in public.

🔍 SIGHTS

An essential part of any visit to Bikaner is a stroll through the **old city,** where narrow streets snake through metal, spice, sweets, bangle, and vegetable markets. The wealth brought in by camel caravans is reflected in over 200 towering *havelis*. Particularly interesting are those of the **Ramapuria Estate,** on Jail Rd., near Kotwali police station, fashioned out of Bikaner's red sandstone.

JUNAGARH FORT. Bikaner's grandest attraction, Junagarh Fort was built in 1589 by Rai Singh, and is of the few in the country that has never been conquered. The fort is a solid, densely packed ground-level structure whose 986m-long wall is capped with 37 bastions and surrounded by a 9m-wide moat. Try conquering that with a herd of camels. The fort entrance is on the east side through a succession of gates. Near the second gate, **Daulat Pol,** are 24 hand marks, left behind by the women who performed *sati* here after their husbands perished in an attempt to hold off a siege. The fort's main entrance is the **Suraj Pol** (Sun Gate), a large iron-spiked door flanked by two stone elephants.

The fort is an intricate complex of palaces, courtyards, pavilions, and temples (37 in all), added to the original structure by successive rulers. Each new addition was built to connect to the previous structures, so that there appears to be one elaborate but continuous palace. The **Karan Mahal,** built after an important victory over the Mughal army of Emperor Aurangzeb, features gold-leaf paintings and the silver throne of Lord Karan Singh. The **Chandra Mahal** (Moon Palace) is a beautifully painted *puja* room adorned with Hindu gods and goddesses. To the side is the **Sheesh Mahal** (Mirror Palace), the maharaja's bedroom studded with mirrors that provide a magnificent glitter—light a match or shine a flashlight to enjoy the dazzle. The **Shardaw Niwas** was the music room; it features old instruments and an ancient system of air-cooling. **Hanuman Temple** is filled with an array of swords, saws, spears, and nails, which are danced upon every January by *fakirs* from neighboring villages. The **Ganga Singh Hall,** the last portion of the fort, houses a **museum** whose collection of weapons and various relics includes a World War I biplane. *(Open daily 10am-4:30pm. Rs50, includes group guide; camera fee Rs30; video fee Rs100. Guides are not necessary.)*

LALGARH PALACE. This large, multi-tiered palace made of red sandstone was designed in 1902 for Maharaja Ganga Singh, in an attempt to fuse European opulence, "Oriental" majesty, and Rajasthani tradition—unfortunately, it falls short of every one of those ideals. The royal family of Bikaner still lives in part of the palace, a luxury hotel takes up some more space, and the **Sri Sadul Museum** occupies the rest. The museum houses every remaining personal item of Maharaja Ganga Singh and his son, Maharaja Karni Singh. Its seemingly endless corridors and halls are filled with everything from a picture of Ganga Singh signing the Treaty of Versailles to his son's personal effects, including his electric toothbrush, Ray Ban sunglasses, and a rifle from the 1960 Olympics, where he was a silver medalist in diving. *(3km north of the city, near the Central Bus Stand. ☎ 540201. Museum open Th-Tu 10am-5pm. Rs55. Guided tours Rs40-50.)*

TEMPLES. Following the main road through Kote Gate will eventually lead you to the base of the old city, where there are two extraordinary 16th-century Jain temples. The **Bhandeshwar Temple,** one of the most spectacular in India, is decorated with gilded floral motifs painted by Persian artists from Emperor Akbar's court. Fifty years, 500 laborers, and 40,000kg of *ghee* went into its construction. The *ghee* was used in place of water to make the temple's cement foundation; on hot days, the temple's base is said to ooze the clarified butter. *(Open daily 6am-7pm in season. Free. Camera fee Rs10.)* The **Sandeshwar Temple** also features intricate gold-leaf painting and sculpted marble rows of *tirthankaras.* The Hindu **Laxminath Temple,** behind the Bhandeshwar Temple, is a masterfully carved stone temple with superb views of the desert and city. *(Sandeshwar and Laxminath open daily 6am-8pm. Free. No socks, shorts, umbrellas, watches, cameras, or leather goods.)*

RODENT REVERENCE At the Karni Mata Temple in Deshnok, 30km from Bikaner, thousands of holy rats called *kabas* run rampant at the feet of worshippers, who bask in the auspiciousness of the fleeting footsteps of the *kabas*. Those lucky enough to see a white rat can consider themselves blessed. These rowdy rodent rapscallions consume massive quantities of grain and milk and play all day to work it off. According to local legend, the patron deity of Bikaner, Karni Mata, was once asked to resurrect her favorite nephew, who died drowning. She called up Yama, the god of death, who told her that the boy had already been reborn as a rat and that all her male descendants would first be born as rats in her temple at Deshnok. The *kabas* are fed *prasad* every morning—what's left is given to worshippers, who eat it without compunction, as the *prasad* anointed with the animals' spit is also considered auspicious. The best time to visit is during the Navratri festival in March, when the temple swarms with people as well as rats. The temple is not for the faint of heart, but it is worth visiting for its magnificent solid silver gate, donated by Maharaja Ganga Singh, and its ornate stone carvings. (The temple is accessible by taxi (about Rs200 round-trip) and by bus from Bikaner (every 15min., 5:15am-12:45am, 40min., Rs9-14), and is a stop on the city tours. Open daily 4am-10:30pm. Camera fee Rs20, video fee Rs50.)

CAMEL AND VILLAGE SAFARIS

Although nowhere near Jaisalmer proportions, **camel safaris** have recently become quite popular in Bikaner. Most of these begin with a tour of the city and nearby sights. A trek through the desert follows, with frequent stops at rarely touristed villages where you can witness local handicrafts in the making. Also common are **intercity safaris** to Jaisalmer and Jodhpur. As in Jaisalmer, the safaris often involve combinations of jeep, horse, and camel travel. Few hotels offer safaris, and those that do operate exclusively through independent agencies. **Vino Desert Safari**, near Gopeshwar Temple, organizes camel safaris for two to thirteen days at Rs600-900 per day. The agency is run by a group of musicians, teachers, and social workers who use the revenue to fund classes in Bikaner's slums. The knowledgable and friendly Vinod Bhojak is an excellent source for information on Bikaner and the surrounding area. (☎204445. Open daily 8am-5pm.) **Desert Tours** (☎521967), behind the Fort near the GPO, has a wide range of safaris for Rs500-1200 per day.

SHOPPING

Bikaner is a good place to shop for desert **handicrafts.** The main commercial areas are **KEM Rd.** and almost all of the **old city.** Just inside Kote Gate on the left are cloth and textile stores. There are several shops selling leather goods and other handicrafts. The government-approved **Abhivyakti** (☎522139), just inside the Fort, sells high-quality handicrafts from 115 villages around the city. Shop hassle-free, and rest assured that proceeds go to artisans and projects that promote health care, literacy, and women's rights. (Open daily 9am-6:30pm.)

DAYTRIPS FROM BIKANER

DEVIKUND SAGAR. This area contains the marble and red sandstone *chattris* (cenotaphs) of Bikaner rulers and their wives and mistresses, whose handprints commemorate their self-sacrifice. There is a *sati* temple where the spirits of the women who immolated themselves here are worshipped. It all surrounds a tranquil lake inhabited by pigeons and peacocks. *(8km west of Bikaner.)*

CAMEL BREEDING FARM. The largest of its kind in Asia, the nearby Camel Breeding Farm produces 50% of India's bred camels. In the early evening, hundreds of camels return here from the desert. During World War II, the Camel Corps of the British Imperial Army was drawn from the stock of this farm. Of course, during the Camel Festival, this place goes ballistic. *(10km south of the city. Round-trip auto-rickshaw Rs60-80. Open M-Sa 3-5pm. Free. Government authorized guides Rs50 per person. Photography permitted outside only.)*

GAJNER WILDLIFE SANCTUARY. Once the location of the royal hunting grounds and a resort for important visiting dignitaries, this area is now home to antelopes, black bucks, gazelles, and birds. The much twitched-over Siberian Imperial Sand Grouse migrates here every winter. The elegant palace on the lake has been converted into the upscale Gajner Palace Hotel. *(32km west of Bikaner. Buses depart the Central Bus Stand: 5 per day, 8am-6pm, 40min., Rs10-15. ☎ (01534) 55063-5 Wildlife Sanctuary Rs100 per person. Rs600 for guided jeep tour.)*

GUJARAT ગુજરાત

One of India's richest industrial regions, Gujarat has much to offer the visitor: magnificent mosque architecture, sublime and sweet cuisine, and all kinds of weird and wonderful wildlife. Gujarat sees far fewer travelers than its neighbors, Rajasthan and Maharashtra, allowing you to horde these wonders all to yourself.

Originally settled as part of the Indus Valley civilization around 2500 BC, Gujarat prospered under several empires, including the Solanki dynasty in the 11th and 12th centuries, which imbued the region with a culture influenced by a blend of Jainism and Hinduism. In 1299, the area was conquered by Muslims, who formed the Sultanate of Gujarat. The Portuguese stormed onto the scene in the 16th century, capturing the ports of Diu and Daman. During India's struggle for Independence, Gujarat came to prominence as the birthplace of Mahatma Gandhi, and as the home to Mohammed Ali Jinnah, architect of Pakistan.

Gujarat can be divided into three vastly different geographical regions. The eastern region, containing the capital Gandhinagar, the metropolis Ahmedabad, and the commercial cities of the mainland strip, is characterized by its modern industrialization. The northwestern quasi-island of Kutch is a dry and isolated area renowned for its traditional villages and handicrafts. The Kathiawar Peninsula (also known as Saurashtra), features lush land, breathtaking beaches, rich temples, forts, palaces, and all things Gandhi.

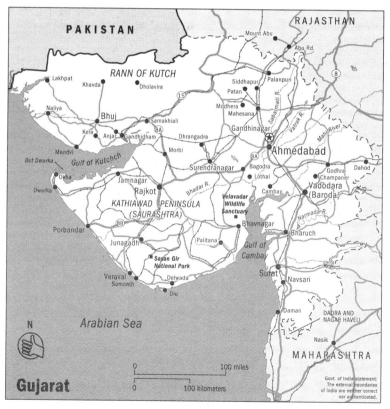

Gujarat

Gandhi and gingham combine in **Ahmedabad** (below), at the Mahatma's **Sabarmati Ashram** (p. 333) and the **Calico Museum of Textiles** (p. 333).

India sets its western compass point at **Dwarka** (p. 343), where pilgrims congregate and antique lighthouses afford sublime sunset vistas.

One of India's most isolated regions, beautiful **Kutch** (p. 345) is home to unique tribal cultures and the labyrinthine port of **Mandvi** (p. 348).

Bright-colored buildings, ancient Portuguese churches, isolated beaches, and serene streets await visitors to the Union Territory of **Diu** (p. 338). Most visitors come for the **booze**, however, available nowhere else in the state.

AHMEDABAD અમદાબાદ ☎079

Ahmedabad, the largest city in Gujarat, is one of the most eccentric and fascinating cities in all of Asia, as well as one of its most polluted and congested. Founded in 1411 by Sultan Ahmed Shah, the city expanded rapidly, attracting large numbers of traders, craftsmen, and artisans. The construction of countless mosques in the Indo-Saracenic style gave the city the decidedly Muslim character it retains today. Ahmedabad's prosperity waxed and waned over the centuries, and devastating famines periodically checked its growth. The city's strengths have always been in textiles and handicrafts—especially since the establishment here of the ashram that became the center of Gandhi's *swadeshi* movement. Today, Ahmedabad has the second largest textile industry in the country.

Much of Ahmedabad's appeal is well-hidden these days, covered up by hardboard signs advertising its various booming businesses. For those willing to dig a little deeper, though, much beauty still remains within the *pols* (self-contained neighborhoods) of the old city, where spectacular mosques, temples, and *havelis* await on nearly every corner. Wandering the streets of the old city, you can expect to see craftsmen adding the finishing touches to batiks put out to dry in the sun.

Across the river lies the new city and its expansive web of shopping arcades and cinemas, interrupted only by the occasional old-world ox cart or camel. Though not an area of much interest to the tourist, the new city operates at a more relaxed pace than the old city across the river and offers all the modern conveniences available in Delhi or Bombay.

▄ GETTING THERE AND GETTING AROUND

Flights: Ahmedabad International Airport, 10km northeast of the city center (☎642 5633). Taxis into the city cost Rs250, auto-rickshaws Rs125, and buses run to Lal Darwaja Bus Stand (every hr., Rs7). Bus #102 heads to the airport from Lal Darwaja, and bus #18 heads to the airport from the railway station, both during flight times. **Air India** (☎658 5633 or 658 5644; fax 658 5900), behind the High Court off Ashram Rd., west of the Gandhi statue. Open M-F 10am-1:15pm and 2-5:15pm, Sa 10am-1:30pm. **Jet Airways,** Ashram Rd. (☎754 3366), 1km north of Gujarat Tourism. Open M-F 10am-7pm, Sa-Su 10am-5:30pm. The *Times of India* Ahmedabad edition has up-to-date flight and train information. **Indian Airlines,** Lal Darwaja (☎550 3061; fax 550 5599), near the east end of Nehru Bridge. Open daily 10am-1pm and 2-5:15pm. To: **Bangalore** (6:45pm, 1½hr., US$220); **Bombay** (7:30am, 6:45, and 8:55pm, 1hr., US$75); **Delhi** (8:10am and 9:10pm, 1½hr., US$135); **Hyderabad** (M and F, 6:45am, 1½hr., US$170); and **Jaipur** (T, Th, and Sa, 6pm, 1hr., US$75).

Trains: Ahmedabad Railway Station (☎131 or 1331), on the east side of town. The **Reservation Office** (☎135) is in the building to the right as you face the station. Open M-Sa 8am-8pm, Su 8am-2pm. To: **Abu Road** (5 per day, 6am-12:30am, 4½hr., Rs53); **Bhopal** (1-2 per day, 7pm, 14hr., Rs205); **Bombay** (7 per day, 7am-11pm, Rs186); **Calcutta** (9:20am, 43hr., Rs422); **Delhi** (10am and 5pm, 17hr., Rs282); **Dwarka**

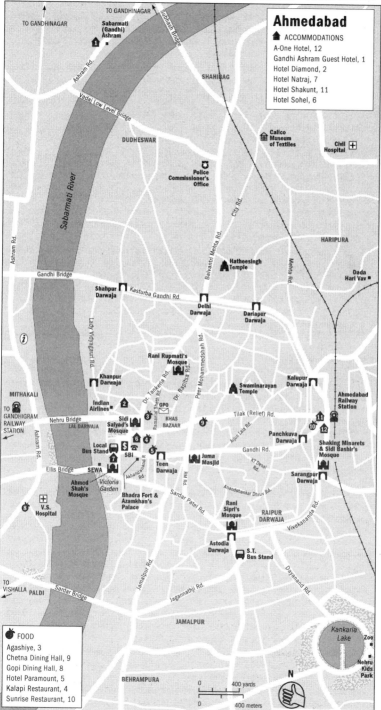

TO GANDHINAGAR

TO GANDHINAGAR

Sabarmati
(Gandhi)
Ashram

Subhash Bridge

Ashram Rd.

Vadaj Low Level Bridge

SHAHIBAG

Ahmedabad

🏠 ACCOMMODATIONS
A-One Hotel, 12
Gandhi Ashram Guest Hotel, 1
Hotel Diamond, 2
Hotel Natraj, 7
Hotel Shakunt, 11
Hotel Sohel, 6

DUDHESWAR

Calico
Museum
of Textiles

Civil
Hospital

Police
Commissioner's
Office

Sabarmati River

City Rd.

Balvantri Mehta Rd.

HARIPURA

Mehta Rd.

Ashram Rd.

Gandhi Bridge

Hatheesingh
Temple

Dada
Hari Vav

ℹ️

Shahpur
Darwaja

Kasturba Gandhi Rd.

Delhi
Darwaja

Dariapur
Darwaja

Lady Vidyaguri Rd.

Peer Mohammedshah Rd.

Rani Rupmati's
Mosque

Khanpur
Darwaja

Dr. Tankeria Rd.

Dr. Baghsa Rd.

Swaminarayan
Temple

Kalupur
Darwaja

MITHAKALI

Indian
Airlines

2

Ramanial Sheth Rd.

GPO

KHAS
BAZAAR

Tilak (Relief) Rd.

Ahmedabad
Railway
Station

TO
GANDHIGRAM
RAILWAY
STATION

Nehru Bridge

LAL DARWAJA

Sidi
Saiyad's
Mosque

3

9

11

Ajlun Lala Rd.

10   12

Panchkuva
Darwaja

Shaking Minarets
& Sidi Bashir's
Mosque

Ashram Rd.

Local
Bus Stand

SBI

6

5

Gandhi Rd.

Ellis Bridge

SEWA

7

Ahmand Anand R.
Rd.

Teen
Darwaja

Juma
Masjid

RM Rd.

KT Desai
Rd.

Sarangpur
Darwaja

Ahmed
Shah's
Mosque

Victoria
Garden

Bhadra Fort &
Azamkhan's
Palace

Sardar Patel Rd.

Anandshankar Dhruv Rd.

Vivekananda Rd.

V.S.
Hospital

8

Rani
Sipri's
Mosque

RAIPUR
DARWAJA

Jamalpur Rd.

Astodia
Darwaja

S.T.
Bus Stand

Dayanand Rd.

TO
VISHALLA   PALDI

Sardar Bridge

Jagannathji Rd.

JAMALPUR

Kankaria
Lake

Zoo

Nehru
Kids
Park

BEHRAMPURA

0   400 yards

0   400 meters

N

🍎 FOOD
Agashiye, 3
Chetna Dining Hall, 9
Gopi Dining Hall, 8
Hotel Paramount, 5
Kalapi Restaurant, 4
Sunrise Restaurant, 10

(6am, 10hr., Rs182); **Jaipur** (3 per day, 8:20am-5:30pm, 12-14hr., Rs225); **Madras** (6:30am, 35hr., Rs390); **Rajkot** (4 per day, 6am-2:30am, 5-6hr., Rs117); **Udaipur** (10:40pm, 9hr., Rs134); **Varanasi** (Tu, Th, and Sa 8pm, 42hr., Rs341); **Veraval** (2 per day, 10 and 11pm, 12hr., Rs174).

Buses: The **ST Bus Stand** (☎214 764) is near Astodia Darwaja (rickshaw Rs15 from Lal Darwaja). To: **Abu Road** (15 per day, 6:15am-9:30pm, 6hr., Rs70); **Bhuj** (12 per day, 8hr., Rs100; deluxe 8am and 9pm, Rs120); **Bombay** (5 per day, 2-8pm, 12hr., Rs202); **Chittaurgarh** (2 per day, 9am and 10pm, 9hr., Rs135); **Diu** (8am, 10hr., Rs89); **Dwarka** (3 per day, 6:15am-11pm, 11hr., Rs110; deluxe 8am and 7:30pm, Rs120); **Jaipur** (4:30 and 9:30pm, 15hr., Rs235; deluxe 6pm, Rs306); **Mt. Abu** (3 per day, 7-11am, 6hr., Rs81); **Rajkot** (express every 30 min. 5am-1am, 5hr., Rs67); **Udaipur** (11 per day, 5am-11:30pm, 6hr., Rs93; deluxe 3 per day, 11:30am-10:30pm, Rs115); **Una** (2 per day, 8am-8pm, 10hr., Rs90); **Veraval** (5 per day, 6:15am-8:45pm, 12hr., Rs100; deluxe 8pm, Rs120). Opposite the ST Bus Stand are dozens of **private bus** company stalls, but most are ticket agents only; most private buses depart from the main company office. Two good companies are **Punjab Travels,** Embassy Market, off Ashram Rd., north of the tourist office (☎658 9200. Open daily 6am-10:30pm); and **Shrinath Travels,** Shahi Bag, near the police commissioner's office (☎562 5351; fax 562 5599. Open daily 6am-midnight).

Local Transportation: Auto-rickshaws are the most convenient local transport. Insist on the meter, and ask to see the fare card. **Local buses** are cheap, and go just about everywhere. The **Lal Darwaja Bus Stand** (☎550 7739) is the local bus stand. #82 and 84 cross the river and run north up Ashram Rd.; #32 runs to the ST Bus Stand and southeast to Kankaria Lake; #34 and 112 run past the Civil Hospital; and #131 and 133-135 run to the railway station. Fares are never more than Rs7. A/C Ambassador **taxis** can be found at Lal Darwaja, at the two bus stands, the airport, the railway station, and the V.S. Hospital.

⊞ ORIENTATION

Ahmedabad is divided in two by the **Sabarmati River,** which cuts a north-south path—the river bed is usually dry and filled with grazing water buffalo—between the old and new sections of the city. The **Lal Darwaja (Red Gate)** opens into the old city on the east side of the river; the newer industrial and urban centers are to the west. The two parts of the city are connected by a series of five bridges.

East of the old city, the **Ahmedabad Railway Station** is connected to Lal Darwaja by **Relief Rd.** (officially known as **Tilak Rd.**) and **Gandhi Rd.,** both of which run through the heart of the old city. The **local bus stand** is in Lal Darwaja, near the end of Gandhi Rd. The **ST Bus Stand** is south of town near **Astodia Darwaja.**

Most of Ahmedabad's modern facilities are found in the ever-expanding **new city** to the west. **Ashram Rd.** runs north through this half of the city, leading past the Gandhi Ashram. **Panchwati Circle** and **CG Rd.** are bustling areas full of helpful services, but they are far away from the old city, the area of most interest to tourists.

⊡ PRACTICAL INFORMATION

Tourist Office: Tourist Information Bureau (Gujarat Tourism), HK House (☎1364 or 658 9683), off Ashram Rd. and down a side street opposite the South Indian Bank, between Gandhi and Nehru Bridges. Helpful English-speaking staff knows everything there is to know about the city. City maps Rs4, Gujarat maps Rs20. Open M-Sa 10:30am-1:30pm and 2-6pm. Closed 2nd and 4th Sa. The **tourist counter** at the airport has limited information. **City tours** depart from the tourist window at the Lal Darwaja Bus Stand (9am and 1:30pm; 4hr.; Rs60, A/C Rs75). Check out the **Ahmedabad city web site** for everything from emergency phone numbers to flight information to city tours and entertainment (www.ahmedabadcity.com).

Immigration Office: Foreigners Regional Registration Office (FRRO), Commissioner of Police, Dr. Tankeria Rd., 3rd fl. (☎563 0999; fax 562 4526), in Shahi Bagh 3km north of Lal Darwaja. Contact at least 15 days prior to visa expiration. Open M-Sa 10:30am-2pm and 3:30-6pm, closed 2nd and 4th Sa.

Currency Exchange: State Bank of India (☎ 550 6116), Lal Darwaja, near Lal Darwaja bus stand. **Bank of Baroda** (☎ 658 0362; fax 658 5175), Ashram Rd., south of the Gandhi statue, gives cash advances on Visa, MC. Open M-F 11am-2pm, Sa 11am-noon. **Dena Bank,** (☎ 658 4292; fax 658 8613), Ashram Rd., north of Nehru Bridge, 2nd fl. Open M-F 10am-2:30pm. All exchange currency and traveler's checks.

Luggage Storage: The railway station offers luggage storage. Rs5 per item for the 1st 24hr., Rs11 for the 2nd, and Rs18 per additional 24hr.

Market: Relief, Gandhi, Sardar Patel, Ashram Rd., and **Khas Bazaar** are the main commercial areas. Most stores open daily 9am-9:30pm. There is a **handicrafts market** along the western edge of the **Law Gardens** daily 6-11pm. The main **vegetable markets** are near the railway station on **Relief** and **Kasturba Gandhi Rd.**

Library: British Library (☎ 646 4693; fax 644 9493), Bhaikaka Bhawan, near the Law Garden. Open Tu-Sa 10:30am-7:15pm.

Bookstore: Crossword, Sri Krishna Shopping Centre, Mithakali, west of Ashram Rd. and south of Nehru Bridge. Includes a cafe. Open daily 10:30am-8:30pm.

Police: Major police stations are **Karanj** (☎ 550 7580), in Teen Darwaja; **Shaherkotada,** opposite the railway station; and **Ellis Bridge** (☎ 657 8202) at its intersection with Ashram Rd.

Hospital: One of the best private hospitals is **Chaturbhuj Lajpatrai Hospital,** also known as **Rajasthan Hospital** (☎ 286 6311), Dr. Tankeria Rd., south of the Police Commissioner's Office. English-speaking, modern, efficient. Well-stocked 24hr. **pharmacy.**

Internet: Random Access, Panchwati Circle, Agarwal Arcade, Ambavadi Rd. (☎ 646 4828). The city's first real cyber-cafe, with coffee and super-fast connections (Rs65 per hr.). Open daily 10am-midnight. **Cyber Valley** Sri Krishna Shopping Centre, Mithakali (☎ 640 9200), above Crossword Bookstore. Rs65 per hr. Open daily 10am-10pm.

Telephones: Central Telegraph Office, Lal Darwaja (☎ 550 2139; fax 550 0066), offers **STD/ISD,** telex, and telegraph services. Open 24hr.

Post Office: GPO, Mirzapar Rd. (☎ 550 0977), near Lal Darwaja. Open M-Sa 10:30am-6pm, Su 10:30am-3pm. Branches at the airport, Gandhi Ashram, and opposite the railway station. Open M-Sa 10am-5pm. **Postal Code:** 380001.

▚ ACCOMMODATIONS

The best budget hotels are conveniently scattered around the western half of the city center. Luxury hotels cluster around Khanpur Darwaja, between the Gandhi and Nehru Bridges on the east side of the river. All hotels add 10-15% luxury tax.

Hotel Sohel, Lal Darwaja (☎ 550 5465 or 550 5466), on a side street off Advance Cinema Rd. Well-kept, modern, and in the thick of things in Lal Darwaja. 24hr. hot water, TVs, and room service. Check-out 24hr. Singles Rs190-400; doubles Rs350-400.

Gandhi Ashram Guest House (☎ 755 9342), opposite Gandhi Ashram. Away from the city, this guest house catches some of the peaceful vibes that emanate from the ashram across the street. Grecian busts, phones, TVs and unbeatable 24hr. hot showers. Run by Gujarat Tourism. Good veg. restaurant. Check-out 9am. Singles Rs370-600; doubles Rs568-855. Breakfast included.

Hotel Shakunt (☎ 214 4615), opposite the railway station. A marble staircase lined with Rajasthani art leads up to this modern hotel, which also features a pleasant terrace garden and friendly staff. Rooms are slightly stuffy, but have TVs, phones, and baths. STD service in the lobby. Check-out 24hr. Singles Rs210-400; doubles Rs360-500.

Hotel Diamond, Gujarat Samachar Rd., Khanpur (☎ 550 3699). A good deal for the facilities. Well-kept rooms with baths, TVs, and phones, are well-insulated from the noise (and the air) outside. Check-out 24hr. Singles Rs190-310; doubles Rs270-390.

Hotel Natraj (☎550 6048), next to Ahmed Shah's Mosque south of the local bus stand. Rooms with balconies overlooking the gardens of the mosque next door offer the best view in the city proper. Rooms are large but aging rapidly. All have attached baths. Check-out 24hr. Singles Rs120; doubles Rs200.

A-One Hotel (☎214 9823), opposite the railway station. The undecorated, unfurnished, nondescript, and slightly grungy rooms are barely larger than the beds, but are OK if you just want to crash between train rides. Check-out 24hr. Dorm beds (men only) Rs60; singles Rs90; doubles Rs140-250.

🍴 FOOD

Ahmedabad has some of the best places to eat in all of Gujarat, often at very reasonable prices. Gujarati *thalis* blend several local specialties in a delightful, often sweet, mix. For quick and spicy stall food, **Khas Bazaar** can't be beat.

Gopi Dining Hall, off Ashram Rd. near V.S. Hospital on the west side of the river; look for the sign above the building. This packed little den of a place serves up excellent, enormous Gujarati *thalis* (Rs45) and sweets (Rs10). Come early, or be prepared to wait. Unparalleled service and prices. Open daily 10:30am-3pm and 6-10:30pm.

Chetna Dining Hall, Relief Rd., almost directly north of the Jama Masjid. Excellent *thali* house, with waiters rushing from table to packed table with pots of steaming vegetables. South Indian dishes (*dosas* Rs20-22) downstairs noon-10pm; *thalis* (Rs55) upstairs. Open daily 10:30am-3pm and 6:30-10pm.

Agashiye, on the roof of the red-and-white mansion opposite the Sidi Sayid Mosque. Scented candles and flower-filled fountains welcome you to this exquisitely decorated rooftop paradise. Incredible Gujarati *thalis* (lunch Rs125; dinner Rs155). Open noon-3pm and 7-11pm. Downstairs, the **Greenhouse Restaurant** serves juices, ice cream, and *lassis* (Rs25-35) as well as a few "light meals" (Rs40). Open daily 11am-11pm.

Sunrise Restaurant, Reid Rd., opposite the railway stations near Hotel Shakunt. A 6ft. high waterfall helps to drown out all the railroad noise from outside in this busy diner where the *dosas* are salty (Rs17-25) and the cold coffee ice cream floats (Rs30) are a bittersweet end to the meal. Open daily 6am-12:30am.

Kalapi Restaurant, near Advance Cinema, Lal Darwaja. One of the best bargains in town, as evidenced by the steady stream of locals that pours through the tinted glass door. Dim lighting, A/C, and no smoking. All-veg. food is excellent. Punjabi dishes Rs20-40. Open daily 11am-4pm and 6-11pm.

Hotel Paramount, near Khas Bazaar. Bland, vinyl-booth atmosphere, but dim lights and A/C make it comfortable. Good seafood dishes for under Rs50, veg. entrees under Rs45. Open daily 10am-11:15pm.

Tomatoes Restaurant, CG Rd., in the new city. If you miss Western food, this '50s style diner is your chance to splurge and satisfy your cravings as you pay tribute to the rock 'n' roll maharaja himself. Entrees Rs75-200. Open daily noon-3pm and 7-11pm. Upstairs, **RGs** serves "pizzas and more" (Rs114-149) to light jazz from 11am-11pm.

👁️ 🎵 SIGHTS AND ENTERTAINMENT

HERITAGE WALK. Created jointly by the Foundation for Conservation and Research of Urban Traditional Architecture (CRUTA) and the Ahmedabad Municipal Corporation, this walk was designed to "unveil" the city to tourists and residents alike. The guided tour takes you through the numerous *pols* (neighborhoods) and *ols* (markets) that make up the old city, explaining the rationale behind Ahmedabad's design and its architecture as well as outlining the city's history. Walk through the narrow streets and secret passageways, under 400 year-old gates, to the small temples and community squares that were once the focal point of daily life. The Heritage Walk takes you to parts of the city you would never see otherwise. *(Walk starts at the Swaminarayan Temple. Daily 8am, 2hr. Rs50.)*

LET'S GO FLY A KITE For three nights in January, the skies of Ahmedabad are speckled with kites of all styles, colors, and sizes. Enthusiasts from all over the world descend upon the city for the **International Kite Festival** (Jan. 13-15, 2001) also known as **Uttarayan,** the largest kite-related happening in the world. For the weeks leading up to the event, local shops and stalls sell an enormous variety of kites and kite-flying equipment, and experts roam the streets offering lessons on the finer points of the craft. In the festival itself there are competitions for kite size, original-ity, and beauty. At night, the skies light up with kites' illuminated tails. Dancing, sing-ing, shows, parades, and general merriment round out the festival, which ends with a highly competitive contest in which kite strings are coated with adhesive and ground glass, turning them into razor-sharp lines. Kites are then sent flying into one another to slash at each other's lines until one kite emerges victorious.

SABARMATI (GANDHI) ASHRAM. Every year thousands of admirers and follow-ers of Mahatma Gandhi descend upon Ahmedabad to visit this ashram, from which so much of Gandhi's spiritual and political influence emanated. Gandhi founded the original ashram in the middle of the city in 1915, upon his return from South Africa. A city-wide plague two years later, however, forced him to relocate to a plot of donated land on the banks of the Sabarmati River. Gandhi lived here until 1930, along with his wife, Kasturba, and 600 other residents. The Mahatma's sim-ple living quarters and several objects that once belonged to him are on display, as is an impressive exhibition on his achievements and philosophy. Narrated by Gan-dhi's own words posted alongside paintings, photographs, and political cartoons, the display touches not only on the political and spiritual sides of his life, but also on role that he played in the revitalization of the Ahmedabad textile industry. Don't miss the series of powerful portraits next to the ashram office. The museum library, open to visitors, holds a mammoth collection of over 36,000 of Gandhi's letters. Beyond **Vinoba/Mira Kutir,** the modest abode of two particularly fervent devotees, is a large building referred to as the "hostel," which was the first part of the ashram to be built. The room on the riverside was Gandhi's original dwelling and work room for three months. The building is now home to 2,000 orphans and children from impoverished families living in nearby slums. Also of interest is **Pasana Mandir,** a small plot of land overlooking the river, where Gandhi and his fel-low ashram inhabitants would recite their daily prayers. The ashram's current inhabitants also hold their evening prayer sessions in the same spot (6:30pm). Finally, Gandhi's main residence lies to the right as you face the mandir. Those interested in spending time at the ashram should contact the management directly by phone. For shorter stays, of one to two weeks, contact Jayesh Patel (☎755 1102; email safai@ad1.vsnl.net.in), next door to the ashram. The Department of Gandhian Studies of Gujarat Vidyapith offers classes structured after Gandhian principles. (☎ 755 1102. Ashram Rd., north of the Gandhi Bridge; take local bus #81, 82, 83, 84, 86, 87, 200, or 300. Open daily 8:30am-6:30pm. Free. Sound and light show Oct. 2-June 15 Su, W, and F 8:30pm.; 1hr.; Rs5.)

CALICO MUSEUM OF TEXTILES. Creatively housed in the *haveli* of the city's rich-est family, India's premier textile museum is worth a visit simply for the building itself, which is split into two sections surrounded by peacock- and fountain-filled gardens. The first of these displays non-religious textiles, and features an enormous collection of items made from every possible fabric, in every possible style, for every possible purpose, and from every part of India. The white-on-white translucent shadow work is remarkable, as are the lavish silk embroideries. Other highlights include beautiful saris (valued at Rs80,000 and up) made according to a highly com-plex method—one tiny mistake in the sewing ruins the entire piece—and clothes so heavily laden with gold lace that their weight exceeds 9kg. The second half of the museum displays textiles designed for religious use, and features an exquisite, 8m-long pictorial scroll, numerous old tapestries, and a series of rooms explaining the process of textile manufacture in excruciating detail—every knot, stitch, thread, and bead. *(Shahi Bagh, 3km north of Delhi Gate; take local bus #101, 102, or 106. ☎786 8172. Open Th-Tu. Guided tours of Foundation galleries 10:30am; of textile collection 2:45pm; both 2hr. Unguided visits 10:30am-12:30pm. Free. Photography permitted only in the gardens.)*

JAMA MASJID. Built in 1424 by Sultan Ahmed Shah I, the Jama Masjid centers on a large marble courtyard and a small pool often surrounded by devotees. The 15 domes of the mosque are supported by 256 pillars with detailed carvings, most of which are Hindu-themed. The curious black slab by the main massive archway is said to be an inverted Jain image. The twin minarets, which once towered over the main structure, collapsed in an earthquake and the broken stubs are all that remain. Through the left gate of the courtyard are the tomb of **Ahmed Shah** and the **Rani-ka-hazira,** the tomb of his queens. The cenotaphs, in vast pillared chambers, are covered with fancy gold-laced cloths. A guard can lift one for you, to reveal some fine stonework underneath. *(Gandhi Rd. Women are allowed to enter the main hall, except during prayer times, but are prohibited from entering the chambers that hold tombs of male members of the family.)*

SIDI SAIYAD'S MOSQUE. Constructed in 1573 by one of Ahmed Shah's slaves, Sidi Saiyad's Mosque, in Lal Darwaja, is the image that graces at least half of Gujarat Tourism's propaganda pamphlets. The interior of the mosque is impressive, with elaborately carved ceilings and domes, but the real highlight is the delicate latticework on the screens lining the upper walls. *(Women are not allowed to enter, but can view the screens from the gardens.)*

OTHER MOSQUES. Rani Sipri's Mosque is near the railway station, on Sardar Patel Rd. Also known as **Masjid-e-Nagira** (the "Jewel of a Mosque"), it was built in 1519. The central grave holds Rani Sipri, who ordered the mosque to be built after her son was executed for a petty crime. The mosque is known for its exquisite latticework. Near Sarangpur Darwaja are the famous **Shaking Minarets** and **Sidi Bashir's Mosque.** A huge arch supporting two 21m-high minarets explains half the name. These are balanced in such a way that if one minaret shakes, the other will move to counteract the tremor, allowing the mosque to survive jostles by earthquakes and colonialist bombardments alike. *Let's Go* does not recommend shaking the minarets. The **Dada Hari Vav** step-well, in the **Dada Hari Mosque,** was built in 1501 by (surprise, surprise) Dada Hari. Five stories and 100 steps descend into this cavern of stones, adorned with carvings and currently inhabited by a colony of bats.

TEMPLES. The **Swaminarayan Temple,** on the north side of the city, is dedicated to Vishnu and Lakshmi. Built in 1850, this rainbow of metallic colors contrasts dramatically with the rest of Ahmedabad's stonework. The temple's fine woodwork and bright, detailed painting rival the city mosques' in intricacy. *(Open daily 6am-8pm. Photography prohibited.)* The **Hatheesing Temple,** north of Delhi Lake, is one of several Jain temples in the city. Built in 1848 and dedicated to the 15th *tirthankara,* Dharamarath, this white marble temple, with detailed carvings of dancers and floral patterns, has a typical Jain design. *(Buses to the airport pass both Swaminarayan and Hatheesing Temples; be sure to let the driver know where you are going. Hatheesing Temple open to non-Jains daily 10am-noon and 4-7:30pm. Photography prohibited.)*

MUSEUMS. The **Mehta Museum of Miniatures** has a large collection of miniature paintings, most of them modern, from throughout India *(West of the city, near the university. ☎646 3324. Open Tu-Su 10am-5:30pm. Free).* Next door, the **L.D. Institute of Indology** offers more miniatures, manuscripts, and carvings. *(Bus #52 from Lal Darwaja and bus #56 from the railway station serve both museums. ☎644 2463. Open M-Sa 10am-5:30pm. Free.)* The **Shreyas Folk Museum,** west of the city, displays indigenous costumes, handicrafts, and textiles from all over Gujarat. *(Bus #41 from Lal Darwaja. ☎660 1338. Open Tu-Su 10:30am-1:30pm and 2:30-5:30pm. Rs40.)* The **Tribal Research and Training Museum** showcases similar crafts from regional tribal peoples and explains their customs. *(North of Ashram Rd., on the campus of Gujarat Vidyapith. ☎755 1148. Open M-Sa noon-6pm. Free.)*

THE INDIAN CULTURAL CENTRE. Call in advance to watch others as they get their groove on at the traditional folk dance rehearsals that take place here. *(Spandan G-11 Balaji Ave., Judge's Bungalow Rd. ☎ 675 7880).*

▓ DAYTRIPS FROM AHMEDABAD

VISHALLA. The Gujarati village mock-up of Vishalla, 4km south of Ahmedabad, offers a night of earthy village dining and rustic entertainment. Eat plentiful, spicy food from leaf plates and drink from clay cups while musicians play and attendants dressed in traditional village garb fan scented insect-repelling smoke in your face. The buffet dinner is Rs188-250, but snacks are also available. *(Open daily 7-11pm. Bus #31 from Lal Darwaja and #150 from the railway station run past the Octori check post—specify where you want to be let off. From the checkpoint, Vishalla is a 7-min. walk or a short rickshaw ride that will cost you Rs5-10).*

SARKHEJ. Eight kilometers southwest of Ahmedabad is Sarkhej, formerly the summer retreat of Gujarati sultans and today a peaceful suburb that feels farther away from the city than it really is. Set on one side of an artificial lake is the tomb of Sheikh Ahmed Khattu Ganj Buksh, the spiritual mentor and unofficial advisor of Ahmed Shah. The largest **mausoleum** in the state, it has a huge central dome supported by pillars and decorated with exquisite marble, brass, and wood ornamentation. Sultan Mohammed Beghada's mausoleum and that of his wife Rajabai are also interesting. It was Sultan Beghada who transformed the solemn Sarkhej complex in the 1500s by adding palaces, gardens, fountains, and courtyards. The area has declined over the years, but it is still a good place for a quiet walk. *(Bus #31 from Lal Darwaja and #150 from the railway station make the trip here.)*

ADALAJ VAV. Nineteen kilometers north off the road to Gandhinagar, the stepwell Adalaj Vav ranks among the most impressive in the state. Built in 1499 by Rani Rudabai as a summer retreat, it now serves mainly as a popular relaxation spot for locals. The gardens around it are pleasant enough, but the carvings on the well are the main attraction. Intricate lattices and detailed carvings of mythological scenes adorn the walls, pillars, and platforms of the five-story well. The best time to visit is just before noon, when sunlight illuminates the stonework all the way to the bottom. *(Buses going to Mehsama Kalol from the ST Bus Stand pass Adalaj Vav every 30min., 6am-10pm, 30min., Rs9.)*

GANDHINAGAR. Thirty-two kilometers northeast of Ahmedabad is Gandhinagar, the capital of Gujarat and the second state capital in India planned and constructed after Independence. Designed by Le Corbusier, the French architect who planned Chandigarh (see p. 258), the city might strike some as boring, with its perfect symmetry and regularly numbered sectors. *(Buses run to Gandhinagar from the ST Bus Stand every 30min., 4am-midnight, 1hr., Rs7.)*

MODHERA. The unassuming town of Modhera, 84km northwest of Ahmedabad, is home to an extraordinary, Jain-influenced **Sun Temple.** Built in 1026 by the Solanki King Bhimdev I, the temple was constructed and positioned so that, at the time of the equinoxes, sunlight falls directly on the image of Surya, the sun god, in the sanctuary—many worshippers come to see this sacred event. The main pillared entry hall is adorned on the sides with 12 *adityas* representing the sun's phases through the year. Guides (working for tips) will eagerly point out the multitude of sexy Kama Sutra-style carvings that are all over the inner sanctum and outer walls. The step-well in front of the temple contains over 100 smaller temples. *(Open daily sunrise to sunset. Rs2; video fee, Rs25.)* Stop for a nice cup of *chai* (Rs5) and *thalis* (Rs45) at the GTDC-run **Torah Garden Restaurant,** in front of the temple. *(☎ (0273484) 334. Open daily 9am-6pm. Buses run frequently to Modhera from the ST Bus Stand 9:30am-4pm, 3hr., Rs42 and from Mehsana, which is connected to Ahmedabad by rail.)*

LOTHAL. The discovery in 1945 of the archaeological site of Lothal ("place of the dead" in Gujarati), 90km southwest of Ahmedabad, was a major event, and the many objects unearthed here have been of immeasurable value in helping historians piece together a picture of what life was like in India's earliest civilizations. Lothal is what remains of a city of the ancient Indus Valley Civilization, dating from 2400 to 1900 BC. Lying in ruin are old roads, a bathhouse, a sewer, houses, and shops; the discovery of a dock and a cargo warehouse suggest that Lothal was a major port city. A **museum** showcases the findings of years of excavation. *(Open Sa-Th 10am-5pm. Free. To reach Lothal, take the bus to Bhavnagar, which runs every 30min., 7am-1am, 2hr., Rs33, and get off at Dholka. Take one of the frequent buses from there. Alternatively, catch a bus to Bagodra, which run every hr. 6am-7pm, 1hr., Rs35, and take a rickshaw from there to the site. Rs150 round-trip.)*

RAJKOT રાજકોટ   ☎ 0281

Rajkot is a clean, relaxed, typical Gujarati town, primarily of interest to travelers as a gateway to the Kathiawar Peninsula. Founded in the 16th century, it was the capital of the state of Saurashtra and an important administrative center for the Raj. Its recent fame is mostly due to its connection to Mahatma Gandhi, who spent his youth here. It was in Rajkot that Gandhi went to school, married, and received permission from his mother to go to England—the rest, as they say, is history.

▐▄ GETTING THERE AND GETTING AROUND

Flights: Rajkot Airport (☎ 454533), 4km northwest of town. **Indian Airlines,** Dhebar Rd. (☎ 234122; fax 233329), near the circle. Open daily 10am-1pm and 2-5:30pm. Purchase tickets before 4:30pm. **Jet Airways,** 78 Bilkha Plaza, Kasturba Rd. (☎ 479623 or 479624; fax 479624), opposite Lord's Banquet Restaurant. Open M-Sa 9:30am-7pm, Su 9:30am-6:30pm. Flights to **Bombay** (4 per week, 50min., US$75).

Trains: From **Rajkot Railway Station** to: **Ahmedabad** (8 per day, 6:30am-2:15am, 5hr., Rs97); **Dwarka** (11am, 6hr., Rs61); **Junagadh** (11:15am, 4hr., Rs33); **Veraval** (11:15am, 6hr., Rs53).

Buses: Main Bus Stand (☎ 235025). To: **Ahmedabad** (every 30min., 4hr., Rs68-77); **Bhuj** (16 per day, 4:45am-11pm, 6hr., Rs67-72); **Diu** (2:30pm, 6hr., Rs68-75); **Dwarka** (4 per day, 5:30am-1:30pm, 5½hr., Rs75-80); **Junagadh** (frequent, 2hr., Rs38-45); **Somnath** and **Veraval** (every hr., 5am-10pm, 4½hr., Rs55-65.) **Private bus companies** opposite the bus stand serve many cities in Gujarat and Rajasthan.

Local Transportation: Unmetered **auto-rickshaws** buzz to the airport (Rs15-20). **Local buses** can take you anywhere in the city (Rs5 or less)—though 'anywhere' might not always be where you wanted to go. **Chakka-rickshaws** (tempo-motorcycle hybrids) go to most points in the city (Rs5-10).

✳❓ ORIENTATION AND PRACTICAL INFORMATION

Everything of interest in Rajkot is sandwiched between the **railway station** to the north and the **bus stand** to the south. The bus stand is on **Dhebar Rd.,** which darts north to **Trikonbaug,** a major circle that marks the city center. East of the circle is **Lakhajiraj Rd.;** west is an intersection at the eastern edge of the **Playing Fields.** To the left, **Dr. Yagnik Rd.** heads south and circles the fields; to the right, **Jawahar Rd.** runs north past Jubilee Gardens to the Civil Hospital and **Junction Rd.** A right at Junction Rd. and a left onto **Station Rd.** takes you to the railway station. From the Civil Hospital, **Kasturba Rd.** leads to the **race course,** west of the Playing Fields.

Tourist Office: Tourist Information Bureau (☎ 234507), behind State Bank of Saurashtra at the south end of Jawahar Rd.; upstairs in the yellow brick building. Open M-Sa 10:30am-6pm; closed 2nd and 4th Sa.

Budget Travel: Jay Somnath Travels (☎474630 or 222630), Umesh Complex, near Chaudhri High School. Open daily 6am-midnight.

Currency Exchange: Bank of Baroda, MG Rd. (☎228396 or 225736), changes travelers checks. Open daily M-Sa 11am-3pm, Su 11am-1pm.

Police: Police Commissioner's Office (☎477220), opposite the race-course next to Galaxy Cinema. The **control room** (☎100) is open 24hr.

Hospital: Civil Hospital (☎440298; fax 445868), at the intersection of Kasturba and Jawahar Rd. 24hr. pharmacy. Clean facilities and English-speaking staff.

Internet: Wesphil C.C. (☎237290), upstairs in the Galaxy Building, just below the hotel. Rs60 per hr. Open daily 8am-midnight.

Telephones: Telegraph Office, Jawahar Rd. (☎180; fax 225752), opposite Jubilee Gardens. STD/ISD, fax, and telegraph services. Open 24hr.

Post Office: GPO, MG Rd. (☎228611), west of Jawahar Rd., opposite Jubilee Gardens. Open M-Sa 8am-7pm, Su 10am-4pm. **Postal Code:** 360001.

🔦 ACCOMMODATIONS

Budget hotels dot the railway station area and Lakhajiraj Rd. Business hotels surround the playing fields. There are plenty of both behind the bus stand.

Vishram Guest House, Lakhajiraj Rd. (☎230555 or 229208), the blue-and-white building opposite Rainbow Restaurant. The best deal in town, with spotless rooms, attached baths, and TVs to help you waste your time. Check-out 4pm. Singles Rs140-200; doubles Rs250-350. Reservations recommended.

Hotel Moon Guest House (☎225522), behind the bus stand. Don't be deterred by the betel-stained walls on the way up to the top floor. Sparsely decorated rooms with clean bathrooms and great city views from the terrace. All rooms have phones. Check-out noon. Singles and doubles Rs150-200.

Galaxy (☎222904), in the Galaxy Building overlooking the playing fields. Rajkot's "premier hotel" has room service, laundry, phones, TVs, currency exchange, nice bathrooms, and 24hr. hot water. Goodbye budget. Check-out noon. Singles Rs440-990; doubles Rs660-1485. 20% tax. AmEx, MC, Visa.

🍴 FOOD

Havmor Restaurant, Jawahar Rd., south of Jubilee Garden. Punjabi, Chinese, and continental entrees in a mirrored A/C, dining room. Havmor's food is renowned locally, so you might have to wait a while to taste it if they're busy. Veg. dishes Rs35-60, non-veg. Rs60-75. Open daily 9am-11pm.

Lord's Banquet Restaurant, Kasturba Rd. Gaudy chandeliers, cushy A/C booths, and an enormous selection of Chinese, continental, and Indian veg. specialties (Rs27-68). Open daily 11am-3pm and 7:30-11:30pm.

Rainbow Restaurant, Lakhajiraj Rd., under the Himalaya Guest House. Cheap South Indian veg. snacks (Rs15-30), Punjabi and Chinese dishes, and over 40 novelty ice cream confections. Dodge the flies and head upstairs (A/C). Open daily 10am-11pm.

👁 SIGHTS

Flanked by stone lions, the **Watson Museum** is dedicated, strangely enough, to Col. John Watson, a 19th-century British political agent. The museum houses artifacts from the ancient Indus Valley Civilization, exquisite miniature paintings, Gujarati handicrafts and metalwork, and classical Indian musical instruments. *(In the Jubilee Gardens. Open M-Sa 9am-1pm and 2-6pm. Closed 2nd and 4th Sa. Rs2.)* The **Kabo Gandhi no Delo** was the Gandhi family's residence when they moved to Rajkot in 1881. It now features a small collection of photographs and memorabilia. *(Ghitaka Rd. Open M-Sa 9am-noon and 3-6pm. Small donations appreciated.)*

DIU દીવ ☎ 02875

Local life on the small island of Diu, off the southern coast of Gujarat, revolves around the pursuit of fish and alcohol. For tourists, it revolves around the pursuit of sun, sand, and, well, alcohol. A Portuguese colony until 1961, when India reclaimed it, Diu is now considered part of Union Territory rather than part of Gujarat. As a result, Gujarat's alcoholic prohibition laws don't apply here, making it prime party ground for the thousands of Gujaratis who descend upon the island every weekend. Despite this weekly migration, Diu's streets are quiet, its beaches serene, and its people surprisingly accommodating.

▣ GETTING THERE AND GETTING AROUND

Flights: Diu Airport, 5km west of Diu Town, north of Nagoa Beach (auto-rickshaw Rs30). **Gujarat Airways** (☎ 52180; fax 52372), off Bunder Rd. next to the GPO is also an agent for **Jet Airways.** Open M-Sa 9am-1pm and 3-7pm, Su 9am-1pm and 3-6pm. Flights to: **Bombay** (50min., US$90). Departures often delayed or cancelled.

Trains: Delwada Railway Station (☎ 22226), between Una and Goghla, 8km from Diu Town (auto-rickshaw Rs100). To: **Junagadh** (1:30pm, 7hr., Rs32) via **Sasan Gir** (5hr., Rs18); and **Veraval** (6:30am, 4½hr., Rs19).

Buses: ST Bus Stand, just outside the city's northern gate. Buses depart from the Main Sq. until 6am. To: **Ahmedabad** (7am, 8½hr., Rs110); **Rajkot** (6 per day, 4:15am-2:15pm, 6½hr., Rs90); **Una** (every 30min., 6am-7pm, 40min., Rs7); **Veraval** (7 per day, 6am-10:30pm, 8hr., Rs105). The **Una Bus Stand** (☎ 31600) services: **Ahmedabad** (9 per day, 6am-10:30pm, 8hr., Rs105); **Junagadh** (6 per day, 4am-5pm, 5hr., Rs53); **Rajkot** (7 per day, 5am-7:45pm, 6hr., Rs68); **Veraval** (every 30min., 5:30am-8pm, 2hr., Rs34). **Private bus companies** surrounding the Main Sq. send buses to destinations around Gujarat and Bombay. **Gayatri Travels** (☎ 52346), next to the Bank of Saurashtra. Open daily 9am-noon and 3-8pm. Avoid Sunday night buses out of Diu; they're inevitably full of drunks.

Local Transportation: Auto-rickshaws travel within Diu Town (Rs5-10) and go to Nagoa Beach (Rs30) and Una (Rs80). A 3hr. tour costs about Rs150. Night travel out of Diu Town extra Rs20. **Local buses,** departing from the Main Sq., service **Nagoa Beach** (departs 8:15am, 10:15am, and 11:45am; returns 8:45am, 10:45am, and 12:15pm; Rs7.) **Private buses,** departing from the ST Bus Stand, go to **Delwada** (every 30min., 6:30am-7pm, Rs7). Buses from ST Bus Stand to Una (see above) also stop at Delwada (Rs5-10). Bikes, however, are your best bet for getting around the island. **Kismat Cycle Store** (☎ 52971), behind Main Sq. near the high school, rents **bikes** (Rs15 per day) and **mopeds** (Rs100 per day). Open M-Sa 9am-8pm, Su 9am-1pm.

◆▣ ORIENTATION AND PRACTICAL INFORMATION

You arrive in Diu via the port town of Una in Saurashtra, past the railway station in the town of Delwada, and through the little island of Goghla, off the northeastern tip of Diu Island. Diu town occupies the small eastern tip of the island. **Bunder Rd.** leads past the **ST Bus Stand** into town through the northern gate, then runs along the coast to the local bus stand and the **Public Gardens** before dead-ending at **Diu Fort,** which marks the extreme eastern tip of the town and island. The main road in the southern part of town runs east past **Sunset Point, Chakratirth Beach,** and **Jallandhar Beach,** bending past the hospital and St. Thomas' Church to Bunder Rd. **Nagoa Beach** and the **Diu Airport** are near the middle of the island, and are most easily reached by rickshaw.

Tourist Office: Tourist Information Bureau, Bunder Rd. (☎ 52653), near Main Sq., has maps and information. Open M-F 9:30am-1:30pm and 2:15-6pm, Sa 9:30am-1:30pm.

Currency Exchange: State Bank of Saurashtra (☎ 52135 or 52492), around the corner from the tourist office, behind the GPO. Open M-F 10am-2pm, Sa 10am-noon.

Market: Most markets and stores are closed M-Sa 1-3pm and on Su. The **fish market** is behind the Main Sq., and the **vegetable market** is farther down Bunder Rd., 200m past the Main Sq. Vegetable market open daily 8am-noon.

Police: Bunder Rd. (☎52133), past the Public Gardens on the left. Open 24hr.

Pharmacy: Manesh Medical Store, Dr. Ragaram Kelkar Rd. Open M-Sa 8am-1pm and 2:30-7:30pm, Su 8am-12:30pm.

Hospital: Government Hospital (☎102), in St. Francis of Assisi Church, 200m north of Jallandhar Beach. English-speaking. Open 24hr. for emergencies.

Internet: Nibble Nest Computer Centre, Gundi St. (☎52893), near Panchvati Rd. Once in the Old City, ask for Mr. Dhiren Shaw. Rs100 per hr. Open daily 8am-midnight.

Telephones: STD/ISD booths line Bunder Rd. Most open daily 8am-11pm.

Post Office: GPO, Bunder Rd. (☎52122), in Main Sq. Open M-Sa 8am-noon and 2-4pm. **Postal Code:** 362520.

▆▐ ACCOMMODATIONS AND FOOD

Considering that most visitors to Diu are only looking for a place to black out after a night of drinking, hotels here have no real incentive to impress. During low-season (roughly Feb.-Oct.) discounts can be substantial, but you'll need to bargain. Camping is no longer permitted on Diu's beaches. Free-standing bars are prohibited, so they parade as restaurants, providing only the minimum amount of food required by law; hotels are the best bet for decent food.

Ganga Sagar Rest House (☎52249 or 52501), Nagoa Beach. Relaxing, palm-shaded courtyard, right on the shore. Small rooms with mint green walls. Decent restaurant and bar offer limited room service. Check-out 10am. Singles Rs150-300; doubles Rs300-400. Low-season: Rs100-300.

Jay Shankar's Guest House (☎52424 or 52050), Jallandhar Beach. This guest house, diner, and bar caters to backpackers. Aging rooms, but wonderfully peaceful location. Restaurant serves Indian and Western dishes of all sorts—french toast is served all day—and the seafood is excellent. Check-out 9am. Dorm beds Rs50; singles Rs100-200; doubles Rs150-200. Low-season: Rs30/60-100/80-125.

Hotel Prince (☎52265), northwest of the Main Sq. Lacks character, but makes up for it in cleanliness. STD/ISD in lobby. Attached bar and restaurant. Check-out noon. Doubles Rs550-1200. Low-season: Rs200-600.

Hotel Mozambique, Burden Rd. (☎52223), in a Portuguese building in the heart of the vegetable market. Big, not-especially-clean rooms draw with balconies and seaside or market views. Check-out noon. Doubles Rs175-225. Off-season: Rs80-125.

Rio Restaurant (☎52209), in Fudam. A little out of the way, Diu's only luxury hotel, Kohinoor, has a good restaurant serving Indian and Chinese food (Rs35-100) and beer (Rs35-50). Open daily noon-3pm and 7-11:30pm.

◉▐ SIGHTS AND BEACHES

The massive **Diu Fort,** built between 1535 and 1541, is guarded by a tidal moat, which once made it virtually impenetrable. There is little to do here except wander through the cannons and the cannonballs and catch the beautiful sunset views over the sea and town. *(At the end of Bunder Rd. Open daily 7am-6pm.)* From the fort, you can also see the **Fortress of Panikota**, a once-white stone structure that now floats in the middle of the sea.

Wandering at random through the labyrinthine streets is the best way to see the Portuguese-influenced old city. **Nagar Seth's Haveli** is the most impressive and distinctively Portuguese building in Diu Town (ask for directions once you're in the old city). **St. Paul's Church** is badly weathered but still has grand ceilings and arches, excellent paintings, and a beautiful organ. Mass is still said here every Sunday. *(Open daily 8am-9pm.)* Nearby, St. Thomas' Church houses the **Diu Museum,** with its Catholic paintings and statues. *(Open daily 8am-9pm.)*

Travelers sick of (or from) drinking might enjoy one of Diu's excellent beaches. The island's longest and most famous is **Nagoa Beach,** 7km west of town. On the south side of Diu Town, **Jallandhar Beach** is rocky but great for wading. **Chakratirth Beach,** to the west of Diu Town, is better for swimming, and the nearby **Sunset Point** is a favorite local hangout. Across the bridge from Diu Town, **Goghla's** long beach is great for swimming, with fewer tourists, but also fewer palms, than Nagoa Beach. **Auto-rickshaws** shuttle from the bazaar to Jallandhar Beach and Chakratirth (Rs20), Goghla Beach (Rs20), and Nagoa Beach (Rs30).

VERAVAL વેરાવળ AND SOMNATH સોમનાથ ☎02876

The busy city of Veraval is Saurashtra's most important port, harboring over 1000 boats, and is home to a thriving *dhow*-building industry. The docks are an interesting-but-smelly area to stroll through, but Veraval is more important to travelers as a stepping stone to nearby Somnath, just 5km away. Known for its once-magnificent temple, Somnath, where old city streets laze in the shodow of the towering *mandir*, is a popular vacation spot for many Gujaratis.

▐ GETTING THERE AND GETTING AROUND. From **ST bus stand** (☎21666) **buses** go to: **Ahmedabad** (5 per day, 6:45am-10pm, 10hr., Rs105); **Diu** (3 per day, 7:30am-4:30pm, 3hr., Rs36); **Dwarka** (4 per day, 6:15am-4pm, 6hr., Rs67); **Junagadh** (every hr., 5:30am-10:30pm, 2hr., Rs35); and **Rajkot** (every hr., 7am-10:30pm, 4hr., Rs65). **Local buses** run from the clocktower to Somnath and back (every 30min., 6am-11pm, Rs5). **Auto-rickshaws** make the same trip for Rs25. **Veraval Railway Station** (☎20444; reservation office open M-Sa 8am-8pm, Su 8am-2pm). Fares listed are sleeper class. To: **Ahmedabad** (5 and 7:30pm, 11hr., Rs180); **Junagadh** (11:30am, 5 and 7:30pm, 2hr., Rs104); and **Rajkot** (11:30am, 5½hr., Rs82).

▐▌▊ ORIENTATION AND PRACTICAL INFORMATION. ST Rd., Veraval's main thoroughfare, runs roughly northwest-southeast past the **ST bus stand,** through the center of town and the **clock tower,** and comes to a dead-end at the port. At the clock tower, the left road heads northeast, past the **GPO** (☎21255; M-Sa 10am-6pm) down the first street on the left and forks just past the State Bank of India (no foreign exchange facilities). From the station, the road leads to another that bends around Veraval Harbor, past the Temple of Somnath to the **bus stand.** The **State Bank of Saurashtra,** Shubash Rd., past the clock tower and toward the port, changes currency and traveler's checks. (☎21266. Open M-F 11am-3pm, Sa 11am-1pm.) The **police station** (☎20003) is to the right of the tower. Open 24hr. **Postal Code:** 362265.

▐▛▐ ACCOMMODATIONS AND FOOD. Hotels line the route between the bus stand and the railway station. Although staying in Veraval might be more convenient, the two hotels in Somnath are cheaper and far more peaceful, if slightly spartan. **▨ Hotel Kaveri,** Akar complex, 2nd fl., is on the first side street to the left after you exit the Veraval bus station, and offers upscale hotel luxuries for budget hotel prices. The rooms here are not just the cleanest in the city; they also come fully equipped with TVs, phones, and 24-hour hot water. The hotel also has laundry service, 24-hour room service, and 24-hour STD/ISD service. (☎20842 or 43842. Check-out 11am. Singles Rs150-500; doubles Rs200-600.) The **Mayuram Hotel,** near the bus stand in Somnath, also has large, spotless rooms. Attached baths and noon check-out round out the pretty picture. (☎20286. Singles and doubles from Rs225.) **Hotel Ajanta,** on the right as you exit the Veraval bus stand, has quiet, moderately clean rooms in a central location with laundry and 24-hour room service. (☎23202. Check-out 11am. Singles Rs100-300; doubles Rs150-350.) Most restaurants in Veraval are between the bus stand and the clock tower. Somnath has many food stalls but no real restaurants. Though Veraval is a fishing town, pious Gujarati culture keeps seafood confined to a handful of hotels and Muslim restaurants—and meat, of any kind, is nowhere to be found in Somnath. **Jill Restaurant,** halfway between the bus stand and the clock tower, has an A/C dining hall with tall, cushioned booths, lively artwork on the walls, and a chef who's generous with the *ghee.* (Veg. Punjabi, South Indian, and Chinese dishes Rs30-50. Open daily 11am-3pm and 6-11pm.) Right around the corner from Jill is yet another **Sagar Restaurant.** Little differentiates this from any other Indian A/C restaurant chain. (Entrees Rs20-50. Open daily 9am-11pm.)

🔯 **SIGHTS.** Somnath is renowned throughout Gujarat for the **Temple of Somnath,** also known as **Prabhas Pratan Mandir,** one of India's 12 *jyotirlingas.* According to popular myth, the temple site was dedicated to *soma,* a hallucinogenic plant that appears often in the *Vedas* (see **Vedic Literature,** p. 77). People say the temple was built first of pure gold by Samraj, the moon god, then of silver by Ravana, the sun god, then of wood by Krishna, and finally of stone by the Pandava brother, Bhima (of *Mahabharata* fame). Boring old historians contend that the temple was built in the early 10th century AD, and that it has always been made of stone. The temple was once staffed by hundreds of dancers and musicians, and was so rich that its coffers were stuffed with gold and jewelry. The notorious Mahmud of Ghazni put an end to all that when he raided and destroyed the temple in the early 11th century, starting a cycle of sacking and rebuilding that persisted until Aurangzeb's final plundering in 1706. Sardar Patel, the philanthropist who funded the temple's reconstruction in 1950, is commemorated with a statue that stands outside the temple. The history of the temple is more interesting than the building itself; very little of the original structure remains. The stonework is quite elaborate in places, but the sea winds have worn down the carving on the ocean-side walls. *(Open daily 6am-9:30pm; puja 7am, noon, and 7pm. No cameras allowed inside.)* The **Prabhas Pratan Museum** holds the varied remains of the temple's past glories, including paintings, latticework, stone sculptures, and pottery *(Near the temple. Open M-Sa 9am-noon and 3-6pm; closed 2nd and 4th Sa. No discounts available on the Rs1 admission fee.)*

JUNAGADH જૂનાગઢ ☎ 0285

Less than 100km north of Diu, the lively town of Junagadh, also known as Junagarh, is refreshingly free of the corrupting influence of foreign tourists. From the 4th century BC until Emperor Ashoka's death, Junagadh was the capital of Maurya-ruled Gujarat. Control of the town then passed through several hands before falling under Muslim rule, where it remained until Independence. Although its rulers wanted to unite Junagadh with Pakistan, the town's Hindu majority insisted on joining India. Situated at the base of Mount Girnar, Junagadh's wealth of temples, *havelis,* mosques, and vibrant bazaars makes it a fascinating place to get lost. Expect crowds, however, when the town hosts a wild, four-day party replete with naked sadhus during **Shivaratri** (late Feb. or early Mar.).

📧 **GETTING THERE AND GETTING AROUND.** From the **ST Bus Stand** (☎ 630303), buses go to: **Ahmedabad** (4 per day, 6am-11pm, 7hr., Rs100); **Bhuj** (4 per day, 8am-4:30pm, 6hr., Rs82); **Dwarka** (5:40 and 10pm, 5hr., Rs72); **Rajkot** (every hr., 7am-11pm, 2hr., Rs35); **Una,** for buses to **Diu** (7 per day, 6am-4:30pm, 5½hr., Rs45); **Veraval** (every 30min., 6am-11pm, 2hr., Rs27). **Private bus companies** along Dhal Rd. run comfortable minibuses and buses to Bombay and to towns in Gujarat. **Junagadh Railway Station** (☎ 131) is on Station Rd. The reservation office is open M-Sa 8am-8pm, Su 8am-2pm. Trains run to: **Ahmedabad** (7 and 9pm, 9hr., Rs157); **Rajkot** (3 per day, 6:15am-1:30pm, 2½hr., Rs33); and **Veraval** (3 per day, 6:15am-2:20pm, 2½hr., Rs30). You can walk just about anywhere in 15 minutes, or **auto-rickshaws** can toot you around town for Rs5-10. **Rickshaws** to Mt. Girnar are Rs35. **Local buses** run to Mt. Girnar (every hr., 6am-5pm, Rs3) from the local bus stand on MG Rd.; early morning buses are the most reliable. **Bikes** (Rs5 per hr., Rs30 per day) can be rented from several locations around Chittakhana Chowk.

⚡🔀 ORIENTATION AND PRACTICAL INFORMATION. From the **ST Bus Stand, Dhal Rd.,** the main thoroughfare, runs east, passing through **Chittakhana Chowk** (marked by twin, pastel-painted minarets) on its way up to **Uperkot Fort.** At Chittakhana Chowk, **Mahatma Gandhi (MG) Rd.** branches south passing the **Government Hospital** (☎620652; open 24hr.), the **local bus stand,** the **GPO** (☎623701; open M-Sa 9:30am-5pm), the main **police station** (☎627001), and the **Bank of Baroda** (☎654684; open M-F 11am-3pm), on its way to Kalwa Chowk, another market area. Roughly halfway between Chittakhana Chowk and Uperkot Fork, **Jhalorapa Rd.** branches south off Dhal Rd. through Diwan Chowk, near the **State Bank of India.** (☎621094. Open M-F 11am-3pm.) **Pharmacies** are in Kalwa and Chittakhana Chowk near the Government Hospital. **Shree Medical Stores,** Dhal Rd., is just west of the railway crossing. (☎631820. Open 24hr.). **Postal Code:** 362001.

▐◪◩ ACCOMMODATIONS AND FOOD. Most hotels are on Dhal Rd. in and around Chittakhana and Kalwa Chowks, but there are also a few near the ST Bus Stand and the railway station. Reserve well in advance during Shivaratri. With a gracious and incredibly helpful staff, ◪**Hotel Relief,** Chittakhana Chowk, has unofficially assumed the role of the town's tourist information center. Above average rooms have attached baths with hot water. The hotel has a great city map on the wall, bus and train departure times, and information on all the sights in town. (☎620280. Check-out 10am. Singles Rs100; doubles Rs200-500.) **Hotel Anand,** Dhal Rd., between the ST Bus Stand and Chittakhana Chowk, has dimly lit, well-kept rooms with attached baths and TVs in a somewhat noisy area. (☎630657 and 631228. Check-out 9am. Singles Rs150; doubles Rs300.) **Hotel Somnath** is to the right as you exit the railway station. In the quieter outskirts of the town center, Somnath has well-furnished rooms and clean attached baths with hot water 5-9am. (☎624644. Check-out 10am. Singles Rs200-600; doubles Rs300-700.)

Although there are a number of food stalls and *dhabas* in Chittakhana and Kalwa Chowks, you'll find better food at the hotel restaurants in town. **Sagar Restaurant,** Riddhi Siddhi Complex, 1st fl., near Kalwa Chowk, serves standard but excellent food in its dimly lit A/C dining room. (☎623661. Entrees Rs20-40. Open daily 9am-3pm and 5-10:45pm.) **Swati Restaurant,** Jayshree Rd., Kotecha Complex, 1st fl., is near Jayshree Cinema. Hindi pop reverb fills the chilly air as friendly waiters serve deliciously spiced entrees (Rs25) in this ever-crowded veg. restaurant. (☎625296. Open daily 9am-3pm and 5-10pm.) **Santoor Restaurant,** MG Rd., near Kalwa Chowk, is another popular A/C place. Indian veg. dishes from Rs20. (☎625090. Open daily 9:45am-3pm and 5-11pm.)

▣ SIGHTS. The impressive **Uperkot Fort,** on top of a mini-plateau in the middle of the town, is one of the best in the state. Built in 319 BC, it was ignored for 1,300 years until it was rediscovered in 976 AD. Over the next 800 years, the fort was besieged 16 times; one ultimately unsuccessful siege lasted 12 years. A high stone *tripolia* gate marks the entrance to the fort and the start of the road that meanders to the **Jami Masjid,** built on top of a Hindu temple. Once an impressive edifice with 140 pillars supporting its high ceiling, the mosque has suffered from years of neglect. The fort also holds a 5m cannon cast in Egypt in 1531 and two step-wells *(vav):* the **Adi Chadi Vav** has 170 steps down into the darkness below, and the extraordinary **Navghan Kuva** has a unique 11th-century circular staircase that winds down to a depth of more than 50m below ground level. *(Fort open daily 7am-6:30pm. One whole rupee.)* From the fort, down the road and to the left through the double arched gate, is the **Durbar Hall Museum.** *(Open Tu-Th 9am-12:30pm and 3:30-5:30pm. Rs3.)* The **Babupyana Caves,** south of the fort, and the **Khapra Kodia Caves,** north of the fort, are also popular.

North of Chittakhana Chowk, on MG Rd., is the **Baha-ud-din-Bhar Muqbara,** with its spiraling minarets, curved grand arches, and numerous domes. The mausoleum's complex design and opulent interior, including carved silver doors, make it unlike any other in Gujarat. Also on the way to Mt. Girnar is a granite boulder inscribed with **Ashokan edicts.** Dating from the 3rd century BC, these edicts teach moral lessons of *dharma*, tolerance, equality, love, peace, and harmony. The Sanskrit inscriptions, which refer to flooding in nearby areas, were added by later rulers. Beside it stands the **Mahabat Maqbara,** which houses the remains of the nawab of Junagadh and the soft, pastel **Jama Masjid.**

Mount Girnar, 4km east of Junagadh, is an 1100m extinct volcano that has been sacred to several religions for more than two thousand years. Nearly 5,000 steps wind through forest outcrops of sun-scorched stone to the summit. Approximately half-way up the mountain (1½hr.), you'll come upon a cluster of intricately decorated Jain temples. The marble **Neminath Temple** is dedicated to the 22nd *tirthankara* who, according to legend, died on Mt. Girnar. A black marble image of him sits amid finely carved pillars, domes, and arches. Another 2,000 steps take you to the mountain's peak, where the small **Amba Mata Temple** and several other shrines offer a breathtaking view. Since a visit to the temple is said to guarantee a happy marriage, the summit sees many newlyweds. *(The hike takes approximately 5-6hr. round-trip. Begin your hike before 7am to avoid the heat. There are drink stalls along the way.)*

NEAR JUNAGADH: SASAN GIR NATIONAL PARK સાસાણ ગીર

Sasan Gir, 65km from Junagadh, is the last stronghold of the **Asiatic lion.** These great cats once roamed forests and grasslands all the way from Greece to Bengal, but by the turn of the 20th century, there were only 239 left on the planet. In 1900, the Nawab of Junagadh invited Lord Curzon, then Viceroy of India, to a lion hunt on his land, the only place outside Africa where wild lions could still be found. The two met a barrage of criticism for farther endangering the threatened species, and Lord Curzon cancelled the hunt, advising the Nawab to protect the lions. The forest became a wildlife sanctuary in 1969, and it now covers over 250 square kilometers. The lion population (today more than 300) is increasing at a healthy rate. The park's forests and grasslands are also a sanctuary for peacocks, hyenas, panthers, and several varieties of deer.

The park is accessible by **train** (*Delwara Local* 352, 6:10am, 3hr., Rs15) and **bus** (every hr., 6:30am-8pm, 2hr., Rs32) from Junagadh. **Shared jeeps** are required to tour the park (Rs500 for up to 6 people; departs 7am and 3pm). Sasan Gir is open from September 16 until the monsoon hits. Jeep and entry fees total about Rs215, and the camera fee is Rs40. Guides cost Rs430 for 6 people. An average trip through the park takes about 45 minutes, during which you are likely to catch a glimpse of at least one of the lions.

DWARKA દ્વારકા   ☎ 02892

Most Hindu legends are in agreement on the subject of Dwarka's holiness. The *Puranas* designate it as one of the seven holy cities in which pilgrims can attain *moksha;* Krishna set up his capital here, on the westernmost point of the Kathiawar peninsula, after being forced to flee Mathura in Uttar Pradesh; Vishnu descended to Dwarka in the form of a fish to battle local demons; and the 9th-century saint Shankara established a monastery here, marking it as India's western *dham.* Few tourists come here, and Dwarka is remarkable for its sense of peace, inspired by the town's active temple, its sea breezes, and mystical remoteness.

▐▐ GETTING THERE AND GETTING AROUND. Trains head from the railway station (☎34044; reservations office open M-Sa 8am-8pm, Su 8am-2pm) to: **Ahmedabad** (11:45am, 10hr., Rs183); **Bombay** (11:45am, 20hr., Rs287); and **Rajkot** (3 per day, 7:40am-9:40pm, 5-7hr., Rs61). **Intercity buses** run from the main bus stand (☎34204) to: **Ahmedabad** (5 per day, 8:45am-9pm, 10hr., Rs112); **Bhuj** (7pm, 9hr., Rs140); **Junagadh** (4 per day, 9:30am-2:45pm, 7hr., Rs90); **Mandvi** (7:30am, 10½hr., Rs150); **Rajkot** (14 per day, 5am-12:30am, 5hr., Rs82); and **Veraval** (7 per day, 5:45am-6:45pm, 6hr., Rs72). **Local buses** shuttle to **Okha** (every 10min., 6:45am-11pm, 45min., Rs10).

GUJARAT

⊞ ⊡ ORIENTATION AND PRACTICAL INFORMATION. The main road into the city bends right as it joins the road between the main gate into the **old city** and the **railway station.** Just before reaching the **main gate**, the road turns right, skirting a huge empty field, then bends left. After the bend on the right is a set of three arches—the second gate into the old city. Straight ahead is a road that runs along the coast, and the main road bends left, passing the main bus stand, and a small building that serves as the **GPO** (☎34529; open M-F 7:30am-12:30pm and 4-6pm, Sa 7:30am-12:30pm) on its way to **Okha**, the port for Bet Dwarka. The old city is a maze of tiny streets centered around the Dwarkadish Temple, with the main **police station** (☎34523) next door. Dwarka Lighthouse sits on the western outskirts of the old city. The best hospital in town, **Navajyot Hospital** (☎34419), 400m toward the coast from the main gate and has a **pharmacy.** (Open daily 9am-1pm and 4:30-8:30pm, 24hr. for emergencies.) Most **STD/ISD** booths in the old city open daily 8am-11pm. **Postal Code:** 361335.

⊡ ⊡ ACCOMMODATIONS AND FOOD. ⊠ **Hotel Rajdhani,** Hospital Rd., is on the first road to the right off the main road from the bus stand to the temple. The plush rooms feature marble bed frames, color TVs, phones, hot water 5-9am on request, and room service. (☎34070 or 34679. Check-out 3pm. Doubles Rs250-500.) **Hotel Meera,** near the main gate into the old city, has spotless whitewashed rooms and a whole family of friendly staff (☎34031. Check-out 24hr. Singles Rs100; doubles Rs200-575.) The **Toran Tourist Guest House,** near the coast, features big, well-kept rooms and attached bath (24hr. hot water). Mosquito coils and toilet paper provided. (☎34013. Check-out 9am. Dorm beds Rs50; singles Rs200-450; doubles Rs300-600.) **Shetty's Fast Food** offers cheap, tasty Punjabi and South Indian dishes (Rs15-35) and *lassis* for Rs8. (☎34512. Open daily 8am-3pm and 5:30-11pm). **Milan Restaurant,** Bhadrakali Rd., not to be confused with the Milan Dining Hall opposite the Hotel Rajdhani, serves fresh, delicious but seriously spicy entrees for Rs30-50. (☎34062. Open daily 9am-3pm and 7-11pm.) The **Meera Dining Hall** serves delicious never-ending *thalis* for Rs25. (Open daily 10am-3pm and 7-11pm).

⊡ SIGHTS. Dwarka's principal attraction is the staggering **Dwarkadish Temple,** also known as Jagat Mandir, or "Temple of the World," which marks the center of town with its six-story, 50m-high main spire. The temple was allegedly constructed over 1,400 years ago, and the spiky exterior stonework is a looking a bit weathered these days, but elaborate carvings of various incarnations of Vishnu are still visible on the temple's inner walls. Sixty columns support the main structure, which houses a black marble image of Krishna in a silver-plated chamber. Smaller shrines decorate the edges of the complex. *(Temple open daily 7am-1pm and 5-9:30pm. Non-Hindus must sign a release form to enter.)* The **Dwarka Lighthouse** offers spectacular views of the sunset over the Arabian Sea, though no cameras are allowed inside the lighthouse. *(Open daily 4:30pm-sunset; Rs1).* The long, clean **beach** nearby, which is rarely crowded (except Su), is great for wading past the small beach temples.

No pilgrimage to Dwarka would be complete without a visit to the tiny island of **Bet Dwarka** where Vishnu slayed the demon Shankasura. Right on the tip of the peninsula, Bet Dwarka has a number of Krishna temples, where devotees come for *prasad* and *puja.* The main temple, which marks the spot of Krishna's death, has a central well that is said to bring up sweet-tasting water, although it apparently draws from the surrounding ocean. Dwarka's real appeal, however, is its eery quiet, broken only by the howling of dogs and the chanting of old women. *(The island is accessible via the port at Okha, an hour north of Dwarka. Rickety, overloaded, pastel-colored boats make the crossing every 20min., 30min., Rs2.)*

KUTCH ५२४९

One of the most isolated regions in India, Kutch is bordered on the south by the Gulf of Kutch and the Arabian Sea, and on the north by the Rann of Kutch, a marsh in the Thar desert that is home to pink flamingoes and the (fortunately rare) wild ass. The Sultans who ruled Gujarat made repeated attempts to cross into Kutch, but it managed to remain independent, and developed its own customs, laws, and a thriving maritime trade with Muscat, Malabar, and the African coast. Kutch was absorbed into the Indian Union in 1948. During the monsoon season, floods in the Rann of Kutch cut the region off from its neighbors Saurashtra (Gujarat) and Sindh (Pakistan), causing varying degrees of damage every year. The Rann is a scenic place during the rest of the year. The dry northern part of Kutch is useless for agriculture, but the southern district of Banni used to be one of India's most fertile regions. Though drier today, Banni still produces cotton, castor-oil plants, sunflowers, and wheat. When climatic changes caused the people of Kutch to abandon agriculture, they turned to handicrafts—the villages of the region are famous for their mirrorwork, beaded embroidery, gold and silver jewelry, leather work (mostly in the villages of Dhordo, Khavda, and Hodko), woodcarving (in Dhordo), silver engraving (in Bhuj), and *bandhani* cloth (mainly in Mandvi and Anjar). Visitors to Kutch are also drawn here by the people themselves—the Harijans, Ahir, and the nomadic Rabari—and many make trips into the smaller villages, hoping for a closer look at these groups' traditional way of life.

BHUJ ભ્ય ☎ 02832

In the center of the region of Kutch, Bhuj is used by most tourists as a base for exploring outlying villages, but the city offers far more than just a place to leave your pack—maze-like old-city bazaars, interesting museums, and varied architecture, including an 18th-century palace and an array of interesting temples. Bhuj was founded in the 16th century as the capital of Kutch by Rao Khengarji, a Jadeja Rajput, and it remained the region's center of economic activity until the establishment of the city of Gandhidam and the port of Kandla to the east. Today, as the limits of the new city expand, the old city preserves the peaceful way of life that keeps those willing to brave the bus ride coming back, time and time again.

GETTING THERE AND GETTING AROUND

Flights: Bhuj Airport (auto-rickshaw Rs40-50, taxi Rs150). **Indian Airlines,** Station Rd. (☎50204 or 21433). Open daily 10am-5:30pm. **Jet Airways,** Station Rd. (☎53671 or 53674). Open M-Sa 8am-7pm, Su 8am-4pm. **Gujarat Airways,** ST Rd. (☎52286 or 52285), is an agent for both IA and Jet. Open daily 9-11:30am and 3-7:30pm. Flights to **Bombay** (2 per day, 1½hr., US$100-105).

Trains: Bhuj Railway Station (☎20950), 1km north of town (auto-rickshaw Rs20). Reservations office (☎131 or 132). Open M-Sa 8am-8pm, Su 8am-2pm. To: **Ahmedabad** (3 per day, 1:25pm-10:45pm, 6½hr., Rs140.) and **Gandhidham** (3 per day, 5:10am-8:15pm, 2hr., Rs11).

Buses: ST Bus Stand, ST Rd. (☎20002). To: **Ahmedabad** (10 per day, 5am-11pm, 8hr., Rs97; deluxe 7 per day, 5am-11pm, Rs110); **Dwarka** (10:45am, 11hr., Rs132); **Junagadh** (5 per day, 5am-9:30pm, 9hr., Rs98); **Mandvi** (every 30min., 5:30am-11:30pm, 1½hr., Rs14; deluxe 5 per day, 11am-10:30pm, Rs25); **Rajkot** (every 30min., 5am-10pm, 6hr., Rs76; deluxe 5 per day, 7:30am-11pm, Rs86). **Private bus companies** line ST Rd. **Ashapura Travels** (☎55661), opposite the bus stand. Open daily 6am-9pm.

Local Transportation: Auto-rickshaws around town cost Rs5-10. **Taxis** congregate around the bus stand, and compete to take you to villages around Bhuj (Rs3 per km).

GUJARAT

GUJARAT

✳🛈 ORIENTATION AND PRACTICAL INFORMATION

Bhuj's main **bus stand** is in the center of **ST Rd.,** which runs roughly east-west along the southern edge of the old city. From **Mahadev Gate** at the west end of ST Rd., **Uplipad Rd.** runs along the edge of Hamirsar Lake past the Swaminarayan Temple and the walled complex that contains the Prag and Aina Mahals. **College Rd.** leads south from the Kutch Museum, the **police station,** and the Folk Art Museum. Near the eastern end of ST Rd., **Waniawad Rd.** leads north to old city's **Shroff Bazaar.** From the northern edge of the old city, roads lead to the **railway station** and the **airport,** 6km away. **Station Rd.** borders the old city to the east and turns into **Hospital Rd.** as it runs south.

Tourist Office: In Aina Mahal (☎20004). Very helpful in planning rural tours. Open Su-F 9am-noon and 3-6pm.

Currency Exchange: State Bank of India, Hospital Rd. (☎56100). Open M-F 10am-2pm.

Market: ST Rd. and **Shroff Bazaar** are the main market areas.

Police: The main **police station** (☎53050), on the east side of College Rd., has English-speaking officers. To get permits for the sensitive border area north of Bhuj, go to the **District Superintendent of Police** (☎53593, ext. 132), east of College Rd.'s south end, down the road opposite the Collector's Office. Bring a copy of your passport and visa. Open M-Sa 11am-2pm and 4-6pm; closed 2nd and 4th Sa.

Hospital: Seth Gophandas Khetsey Hospital (☎22850), on the road to Gandhidam, is clean and modern with English-speaking doctors. Also has a 24hr. **pharmacy.**

Post Office: GPO (☎22952), off Station Rd. south of ST Rd. Open M-Sa 10am-5:45pm. Small branch on Langa Rd., opposite the City Guest House (☎22650). Open M-Sa 9am-5pm. **Postal Code:** 370001.

▟ ACCOMMODATIONS

▦ **City Guest House,** Langa St. (☎21067), in the main market. A backpackers' favorite, featuring small, spotless rooms livened up by bright linens. Indoor courtyard and 24hr. *chai* service. Check-out 24hr. Singles Rs60-170; doubles 140-170.

▦ **Hotel Annapurna,** Bhid Pol (☎20831). Also popular with the backpacking crowd, Annapurna offers well-decorated rooms with TVs and balconies. Outstanding restaurant downstairs. Check-out 24hr. Singles Rs50-90; doubles Rs70-150.

Hotel Jantaghar, ST Rd. (☎54456-7), east of the bus stand. Austere but clean rooms. A/C dining hall serves Gujarati *thalis* (Rs30). Check-out 5pm. Dorm beds Rs30; singles Rs50-100; doubles Rs75-150.

Hotel Abha, ST Rd. (☎54451-3). Jantaghar's slightly costlier next door neighbor has clean rooms with attached baths, 24hr. hot water, 24hr. room service, phones, and TVs. Singles Rs200-600; doubles Rs350-750.

◖ FOOD

Most restaurants in Bhuj open only for lunch and dinner with a hefty break between the two, making three square meals a day a virtual impossibility.

▦ **Annapurna Restaurant,** Bhid Pol, in Hotel Annapurna. Popular dinette allows you to custom make your own *thali*. Veg. dishes, sweets, rice, and *chappatis* are skillfully prepared. Also serves standard Punjabi fare (Rs15-25) spiced to taste. Open M-Sa 10:30am-3:30pm and 7-11:30pm, Su 10:30am-3:30pm.

Hotel Noorani Restaurant, near the vegetable market as you walk through the main bazaar from Aina Mahal. One of the few spots in Gujarat where meat is indulged in without remorse. Chicken tandoori (half-order Rs60), mutton *biryani* (Rs24). Open daily 9am-3:30pm and 6:30-10pm.

Hotel Anam Dining Hall, ST Rd., near the intersection with Station Rd. A very popular *thali* joint with black-and-white wildlife pictures all over the walls. Gujarati *thalis* Rs50. Open daily 11am-3pm and 7-10pm.

Resoi Restaurant, ST Rd., in Hotel Abha. A/C dining with Punjabi, Chinese, or continental (Rs35-55), or a bottomless *thali* (Rs60). Open daily 11am-3pm and 7-11pm.

Green Hotel Restaurant, Shroff Bazaar. One of the few places open in the morning, Green serves the standard set of South Indian, Punjabi, and continental dishes (Rs20-40). Open daily 9:30am-10:30pm.

🔍 SIGHTS

AINA MAHAL (PALACE OF MIRRORS). Maharao Lakhad (r. 1741-60) was renowned for his love of the Kutch regional art. His palace is a small, fortified structure in the old city. A raised platform here was once surrounded by a pool of water and fountains, where the maharao would sit as musicians entertained him. Inside the Aina Mahal, the beautifully designed **Maharao Madansinji Museum** is filled with artifacts and memorabilia from his reign. The maharao's bedroom has remained virtually untouched since his death. His *chakri* slippers still sit by the bed; they were designed to produce an olfactory warning of his proximity—with each step a flower at the toe of the slippers opens to release scented powder. *(Open Su-F 9am-noon and 3-6pm. Rs5. Photography prohibited.)*

PRAG MAHAL (NEW PALACE). Marble stairs ascend to the main hall beneath the curving arches and sandstone columns of the palace, built in 1816. The main hall is a macabre monument to death and is a taxidermist's nightmare—the floor is covered with the decaying heads of lions, tigers, leopards, deer, and wild cows. A spiral staircase leads to the top of the bell tower, where fantastic views await. *(Open M-Sa 9-11:45am and 3-5:45pm. Rs5; camera fee Rs15, video fee Rs50.)*

SHARAD BAGH MUSEUM. This beautifully kept museum at the southwestern corner of Hamirsar Tank was the residence of the last maharao of Kutch until his death in 1991. Built in the mid-19th century and styled after an Italian villa, the palace is much as the maharao left it, with his TV and VCR set among his hunting trophies and Chinese vases. *(☎ 20878. Open Sa-Th 9am-noon and 3-6pm. Rs5; camera fee Rs10, video fee Rs50.)*

OTHER MUSEUMS. Bhuj's museums are an excellent place to learn about Kutch culture before heading out to the villages. The **Kutch Museum,** the oldest in the state, has excellent anthropological and archaeological exhibits on the region. *(College Rd. ☎ 20541. Open Th-Tu 9am-noon and 2:45-5:45pm, closed 2nd and 4th Sa. Rs0.50, camera fee Rs2 per shot.)* The **Bharatiya Sanskriti Darshan,** also called the **Folk Museum,** contains a small collection of local textiles, embroideries, paintings, and bead work, supplemented by a library of related sources. The highlight of the museum is its reproduction of Rabari *bhungas* (huts) with their delicately decorated inner walls. *(Mandvi Rd., at the south end of College Rd. ☎ 25507. Open M-Sa 9am-noon and 3-6pm. Rs5; camera fee Rs50.)*

OTHER SIGHTS. On the way to Harmisar Tank from the Darbargadh Complex lies the **Swaminarayan Temple.** This early 19th-century technicolor temple consists of two single-sex temples and a third for men and women. *(Open daily 7-11am and 4-8pm.)* South of Hamirsar Tank, in the midst of a sandy, deserted plain, the eerie **Memorial Chattris** commemorate some of the previous maharaos of Kutch and their wives who committed *sati*. The red sandstone memorial to Maharao Shri Lakhpatji (1710-61) and his 15 wives is the biggest of the bunch.

🚩 VILLAGE TOURS

Many tourists use Bhuj primarily as a base from which to explore the nearby villages, renowned for the unique cultures that they have preserved for centuries.

These tours offer a glimpse of village life and provide plentiful opportunities for you to spend your money on local handicrafts, though the experience has been soured somewhat recently; many villages have responded to the tourist trade with aggressive merchandising and exorbitant prices. However, many of the villagers seem genuinely excited by the tourist traffic and seem to enjoy showing visitors around, sale or no sale. Tours can be made by **taxi** (Rs800-850 for up to 4 people for a full day tour to several villages) or, more slowly, by **bus** from Bhuj. Contact the tourist office for more information on arranging village tours.

The village of **Sumrasar,** just outside of Bhuj, is home to **Kala Raksha** (☎77238), a research institute and women artists' cooperative dedicated to the "preservation of traditional arts." Founded in 1993, the center has a large collection of embroidered textiles from around Kutch. A small store sells local work that has been adapted to a Western aesthetic. The items are of excellent quality, prices are reasonable, and profits go directly to the artists. For information on research opportunities and accommodations at Kala Raksha, contact Judy Frater, Project Coordinator (☎53697; fax 55500; email judyf@ad1.vsnl.net.in). From Bhuj, take a rickshaw (Rs100) or a bus (to nearby Hajipar; Rs6).

Kera, 22km south of Bhuj, is home to a Shiva temple thought to have been built in the 10th century (buses every hr., 6am-8:30pm, 45min., Rs6). Farther south is the Rabari village of **Tundawadh** (best reached by car), famed for its exquisite embroideries. **Anjar,** 40km southeast of Bhuj, is a major center for handicrafts enthusiasts, and specializes in weapons, nut-crackers, jewelry, and textiles (buses every 30min., 5am-11pm, 2hr., Rs12-20). For block printing galore, head to **Dhamanka,** east of Bhuj (buses every hr., 6am-9:30pm, 1½hr., Rs12-22). The village of **Khavda** specializes in pottery (buses 7 per day, 8:30am-6:30pm, 2hr., Rs16), and **Bhirandiyari,** on the way to Khavda, is known for its embroidery, weaving, and leather work (1hr., Rs13). **Zura,** home of the copper bell, and **Nirona,** specializing in Rogan painting, are accessible by the same bus (11 per day, 8am-6:30pm, Rs11-13.)

Those who can't bring themselves to look at another handicraft shop can head 60km northwest of Bhuj to the remote **Than Monastery** (bus at 5pm, 2hr., Rs20). The ruins of **Dholavira,** one of the largest sites uncovered in the Indus Valley, dates to around 2500 BC (bus at 2pm, 4½hr., Rs45).

MANDVI માંડવી ☎02834

Established by Maharao Khengarji in 1588, Mandvi rose to prominence as an important port, connected to South Africa, the Middle East, China, and Japan by trade. The Arab and European traders who settled here in the 18th century left grand mansions behind them in the winding lanes of the old city when they left, along with a dwindling boat-building industry. Pushcarts and auto-rickshaws almost seem to be propelled by the breeze, and hand-built wooden *dhows* lean lazily against the docks and the beautifully rusted anchors beached by the tide. Shop-owners rest quietly on the steps of medieval buildings, while blacksmiths and welders send dust and sparks into the salty evening air. Bordered by vast stretches of untainted shore and surrounded by a horizon studded with palm trees, Mandvi is the ideal place to sit back and do a whole lot of nothing.

📠 **GETTING THERE AND GETTING AROUND.** From the **ST Bus Stand** (☎20004), buses travel to: **Ahmedabad** (4 per day, 6:45am-7:15pm, 12hr., Rs117-125); **Bhuj** (every 30min., 6:15am-8:45pm, 1½hr., Rs14-29); **Dwarka** (9:30am, 11hr., Rs120); **Junagadh** (7:15am, 11hr., Rs125); **Rajkot** (5 per day, 6:15am-8:45pm, 7hr., Rs90-102).

📇🔀 **ORIENTATION AND PRACTICAL INFORMATION.** From the **bridge** that stretches over the salt flats, a left turn takes you down **ST Rd.** past the main **police station** (☎20008; open 24hr.) and the **ST Bus Stand,** coming to a dead-end at the port. The small road straight ahead from the bridge leads to the Rukmavati Guest House and, next door, is the **Shree Gokul Hospital** (☎20361), a very clean, modern facility with an English-speaking staff. (Open M-F 9am-1:30pm and 4-6:30pm for consultations, 24hr. for emergencies). There are many **pharmacies** near the hospital. (Open M-Sa 9am-9pm.) A right turn from the bridge takes you along the northern city wall to the **GPO**, 1km away (☎20266; open M-F 10am-6pm, Sa 10am-1pm), and leads eventually to Vijay Vilas Palace, 8km away. At the southern end of ST Rd., near the port, **Bandar Rd.** leads off to the right past the **State Bank of India** (☎20031; M-F 11am-3pm, Sa 11am-1pm) and past several sawmills to the southern end of **Bhid Chowk,** which is the central market area. **Postal Code:** 370465.

█▐▌ **ACCOMMODATIONS AND FOOD.** Far and away the best place to stay in Mandvi is the ▨**Rukmavati Guest House,** near the bridge. Enormous, elegant, well-furnished rooms open onto a plant-filled terrace with a porch swing. 24-hour hot water, laundry service, and kitchen available for use. (☎20557. Check-out 24hr. Dorm beds Rs75; singles Rs125-650; doubles Rs225-750.) The **Maitri Guest House**, Kanthawalo Gate, has bright, clean rooms in the heart of the old city. (☎20183. Check-out noon. Dorm beds Rs70; singles Rs150-200; doubles Rs200-250.) ▨**Hotel Nayna,** Azad Chowk, serves the best lunchtime *thalis* in town (Rs40), as well as Punjabi and South Indian dishes—the *masala dosa* with *sambar* is Rs17. (☎20183. Open daily 11am-3pm and 6-11pm.) The restaurant in the Osho Hotel, **Zorba the Buddha,** dishes out unlimited *thalis* (lunch Rs40, dinner Rs20) to a constant stream of locals. Don't let the slightly grungy atmosphere fool you—the food is fresh and delicious. (Open daily 11:30am-2:30pm and 7:30-9:30pm).

▨▐▌ **SIGHTS AND BEACHES.** Mandvi is blessed with many beautiful haunts—the old city walls, the port with its wooden ships moored on the salt flats, the canyon-like streets with their stone mansions, and the temples and mosques that crowd the eastern side of the city. But the **Vijay Vilas Palace,** 9km west of town, is Mandvi's biggest draw. A domed, latticed mansion set on 692 acres, the palace was built in 1927 as a summer home for the Maharao of Kutch. Spotless marble floors, walls delicately inlaid with floral patterns, and gorgeous carved rosewood and teak furniture decorate the inside. From the third floor, a rusting spiral staircase leads to a domed terrace with a view of the Arabian Sea and the coconut trees and windmills of the flat, green Kutch. Perhaps the highlight of the palace, though, is its private **beach,** 1km away. The nearly 2km stretch of sand is litter-free and blissfully unpopulated. Follow the road past the GPO and veer left at both forks. *(Open daily 9am-1pm and 2-6pm. Rs5; camera fee Rs50, video fee Rs200. Bike Rs5, rickshaw Rs15.)* Mandvi's seemingly endless shoreline draws many visitors. The town's main beach, called **Windfarm** because of the numerous windmills that line it, can get a bit crowded, but the farther west you go, the more isolated it becomes.

Kashivishvanath Beach is quieter and lies on the opposite side of the port. Cross the bridge and take your second right, following the road all the way to the water.

MADHYA PRADESH
मध्य प्रदेश

True to its name, Madhya Pradesh (the "Middle State") stretches right across the center of India. Although it covers a larger land area than any other state, its arid and inhospitable climate has given it a population of less than 80 million. Outside the fertile and heavily populated Narmada River Valley, the land is dominated by dense forests and scrubby hills and ravines, which provide refuge to *dacoits* (bandits) and tigers, and a rare unravaged homeland for the region's indigenous groups. Also hidden and protected by the forests are the ruined cities of Mandu and Orchha and the famous erotic temple carvings of Khajuraho.

The history of Madhya Pradesh dates back to the 3rd century BC, when the great Buddhist convert-king Ashoka founded Sanchi as a religious center. Mughal emperors ruled the region from the north until they lost control to the Marathas, whose leading families ruled until Independence. Today, 93% of the population is Hindu, and state politics are dominated by the BJP, but the landscape of Madhya Pradesh—from its great cities to its ancient Buddhist pilgrimage sites and its timeless national parks—preserves vivid reminders of a rich and varied past.

HIGHLIGHTS OF MADHYA PRADESH

Madhya Pradesh has the largest tiger population of any Indian state, and **Kanha National Park** (p. 368), of *Jungle Book* fame, is the best place to see them.

The middle-of-nowhere temple town of **Khajuraho** (p. 369), with its astounding erotic sculpture, is one of the great architectural marvels of the world.

The ruins of the town of **Mandu** (p. 361) open a window onto the Muslim Malwa culture of the 14th century.

The fort in **Gwalior** (p. 381) is one of the most impressive in India.

BHOPAL भोपाल   ☏ 0755

With well over a million inhabitants, a thriving arts community, and a lively Muslim quarter, the state capital of Bhopal serves up a rich slice of North Indian culture. Dost Mohammed founded modern Bhopal during the first half of the 18th century, laying its foundations on the site of an 11th-century city established by Raja Bhoja. The program of civic improvements embarked upon during the 19th century has left the city not only blessed with lakes and parks, but also adorned with the minarets of massive mosques. Bhopal, a good staging point for visits to the nearby Buddhist ruins at Sanchi and other sights in the state, is also a pleasant city in its own right. Mention Bhopal today, though, and many pale, remembering the city as the site of the worst industrial accident in history. In the middle of the night on December 2, 1984, a cloud of lethal methylisocyanate gas leaked from the Union Carbide fertilizer factory in the north of the city. Two thousand people died and thousands more were crippled for life.

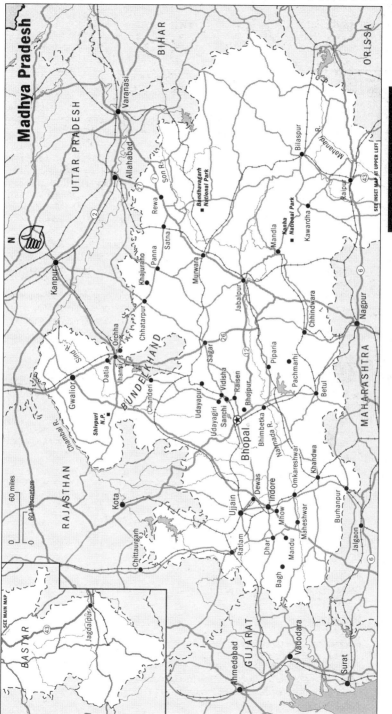

MADHYA PRADESH

SEE INSET MAP AT UPPER LEFT

Madhya Pradesh

N

ORISSA

BIHAR

UTTAR PRADESH

MAHARASHTRA

RAJASTHAN

GUJARAT

BASTAR

BUNDELKHAND

Varanasi

Allahabad

Kanpur

Rewa

Satna

Panna

Khajuraho

Chhatarpur

Orchha

Jhansi

Datia

Gwalior

Shivpuri N.P.

Chanderi

Kota

Chittaurgarh

Ujjain

Ratlam

Dhar

Bagh

Mandu

Mhow

Dewas

Indore

Maheshwar

Omkareshwar

Khandwa

Burhanpur

Jalgaon

Bhopal

Bhimbetka

Namada R.

Sanchi

Vidisha

Raisen

Udayagiri

Udaypur

Sagar

Piparia

Pachmarhi

Betul

Jabalpur

Chhindwara

Mandla

Kawardha

Nagpur

Bilaspur

Raipur

Kanha Natioal Park

Bandhavgarh National Park

Murwara

Son R.

Sind R.

Chambal R.

Mahanadi R.

Jagdalpur

SEE MAIN MAP

60 miles

0

60 kilometres

0

◻ GETTING THERE AND GETTING AROUND

Flights: The airport is on Agra Rd. (☎521789), 12km from the city center (taxis Rs100-150; rickshaws Rs80-100). **Indian Airlines** (☎770480), next door to the Gangotri Building in TT Nagar, 100m on the left, past the Rang Mahal cinema. Open M-Sa 10am-1pm and 2-5pm. To: **Bombay** (M and F, 5:10pm, 2hr., US$130); **Delhi** (Tu-Th and Sa-Su, 7:35 pm; M and F, noon; 2hr.; US$120); **Gwalior** (M and F, noon, 45min., US$80); **Indore** (M and F, 5:10pm; Tu-Th and Sa-Su, noon; 30 min.; US$55); **Madras** (Tu and Sa, 2:20pm, 3hr., US$195) via **Nagpur** (45min., US$80). **Sahara Airlines,** 196 Kamdhenu Complex, MP Nagar (☎765242).

Trains: The **railway station** (☎131) is down the street that leads off the bend in Hamidia Rd., 1km east of the bus station. Reservation office outside platform #1, on the far right as you face the station. Open M-Sa 8am-8pm, Su 8am-2pm. To: **Bombay** (4-6 per day, 6am-4:50pm, 16hr., Rs245); **Delhi** (16-20 per day, 12:40am-10:40pm, 8-12hr., Rs221) via **Agra** (6-8hr., Rs174), **Gwalior** (4½-6hr., Rs138), and **Jhansi** (3-4½hr., Rs72); **Hyderabad** (2-4 per day, 3:43am-11:35pm, 15-22hr., Rs267); **Indore** (5-6 per day, 3:10-9:40pm, 5-6hr., Rs67) via **Ujjain** (3hr., Rs52); **Jabalpur** (1-2 per day, 4 and 11pm, 7½hr., Rs81-126).

Buses: The **Nadra Bus Stand,** Hamidia Rd. (☎540841), west of the train station, 1km down on the right. Frequent departures for **Indore** (every 10min., 6am-6:30pm, 5hr., Rs58) and other cities around the state. Private operators run buses to **Sanchi** (frequent, 6am-6pm, 1½hr., Rs19).

Local Transportation: Metered **auto-rickshaws** will take you anywhere, including the airport (Rs80-100), but **minibuses** will take you almost as far for much less. Minibus #9 goes from the railway station to TT Nagar; #7 and 11 go by Sultania Rd.; #2 goes from Hamidia Rd. to New Market and MP Nagar.

✳ ORIENTATION AND PRACTICAL INFORMATION

The huge **Upper Lake** and smaller **Lower Lake** separate Old Bhopal in the northwest from the **New Town** in the southeast. **Hamidia Rd.** runs near the Taj-ul-Masjid (the city's largest mosque) on the western fringes of the old town, past the bus stand to the railway station in the east. If you arrive by train, exit via platform #5 for Hamidia Rd. From the station area, with its many cheap hotels and restaurants, Hamidia Rd. turns right and runs south toward the new town and government center. The MPSTDC, Indian Airlines office, and the banks are all in **TT Nagar.**

Tourist Office: MPSTDC main office, 4th fl., Gangotri Building, TT Nagar, New Town (☎774340), just past the Rang Mahal cinema. Staff can reserve rooms at all MPSTDC hotels in the state. Open M-F and 1st and 4th Sa 10:30am-5pm. Other branches are in the airport and the railway station. Open M-Su 7am-8pm.

Currency Exchange: State Bank of India, Parcharad Building, next to the Rang Mahal cinema in TT Nagar (☎528197). Open M-F 10:30am-2:30pm. **State Bank of Indore,** New Market Rd., beneath the Hotel Pachanan, TT Nagar. Open M-F 10:30am-2:30pm, Sa 10:30am-12:30pm.

Luggage Storage: In the railway station. Rs7 per piece. Open 24hr.

Bookstore: Variety Book House, GTB Complex, Bhadbhada Rd., TT Nagar (☎556022). Open Tu-Su 10:30am-9pm.

Library: British Council Library, GTB Complex, Bhadbhada Rd., TT Nagar (☎553767). Open Tu-Su 11am-7pm.

Market: The wholesale **fruit and vegetable market** stretches to the left off Hamidia Rd. and into the bazaars as you go from the railway station to the bus station. Open 4am-late. **Old Market,** directly behind it, is a lively market area selling clothes, buckets, and assorted engine parts. Closed Su. **New Market,** off Bhadbhada Rd., near TT Nagar, has more modern shops, including the bookstores and state emporiums. Closed M.

Police: Sultania Rd., Jehangirabad (☎555911).

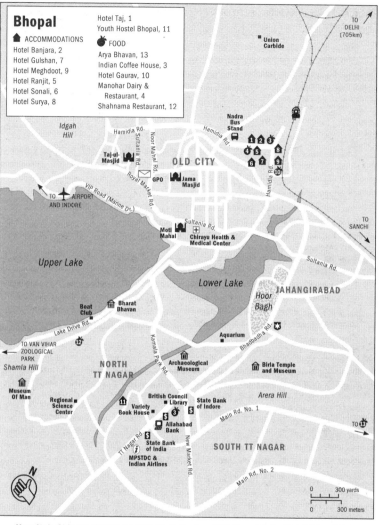

Bhopal

⌂ ACCOMMODATIONS
Hotel Banjara, 2
Hotel Gulshan, 7
Hotel Meghdoot, 9
Hotel Ranjit, 5
Hotel Sonali, 6
Hotel Surya, 8

Hotel Taj, 1
Youth Hostel Bhopal, 11

♣ FOOD
Arya Bhavan, 13
Indian Coffee House, 3
Hotel Gaurav, 10
Manohar Dairy &
    Restaurant, 4
Shahnama Restaurant, 12

Hospital: Chirayu Health and Medical Centre, 6 Malipur Rd. (☎531122), off Sultania Rd., near Peer Gate has a 24hr. **pharmacy** (☎737406).

Internet: Eventure.com, 31 Bhadbhada Rd., 1st fl., New Market, TT Nagar (220134), Rs40 per hr. Open 24 hr. Slightly cheaper but with slower connections is **Compquest Consultants,** 36 Bhadbhada Rd. (☎234440), just a couple of shops down the street. Rs35 per hr. Open daily 8am-midnight.

Post Office: GPO, Sultania Rd., opposite the Taj-ul-Masjid. Open M-Sa 10am-7pm. **Postal Code:** 462001.

⚑ ACCOMMODATIONS

Hotels in Bhopal cater to a largely male clientele of business travelers. There are not many good budget places around, and every place in town levies taxes and service charges of up to 20%. This does mean, though, that "luxuries" like TVs, telephones, and attached bathrooms are pretty standard.

▓ **Hotel Banjara,** Hamidia Rd. (☎544585), in an alley between the Alpana cinema and the Hotel Taj. Filling out the hotel register in triplicate and coughing up a huge advance is well worth it here. The modern rooms, complete with balconies and sparkling white marble bathrooms, are both spacious and spotless (especially the cheaper ones without carpets). Singles Rs300-500; doubles Rs400-600.

Hotel Sonali, Radha Talkies Rd. (☎533880), in the alley off Hamidia Rd., behind hotels Ranjit and Gulshan. The small but tidy rooms have attached balconies and hot showers. Check-out 24hr. Singles Rs210-450; doubles Rs285-525. AmEx, MC, Visa.

Hotel Surya, Hamidia Rd. (☎536925), south of the train station, on the right 200m before the turn. Modern rooms with all the usual perks. Check-out noon. Singles Rs250-500; doubles Rs300-600.

Youth Hostel Bhopal, North TT Nagar (☎553670), near the MPSTDC Hotel Palash. The cheapest choice in the New Town. Dorm beds Rs40; doubles Rs120. HI members get a 50% discount. Reservations essential.

Hotel Taj, 52 Hamidia Rd. (☎536261), opposite the Hotel Ranjit, toward the bus station. Atrium design insulates guests from the Hamidia hullabaloo. Check-out 24hr. Singles Rs200; doubles Rs350. AmEx, Discover, MC, Visa.

Hotel Gulshan, Hamidia Rd. (☎73506), in the alleyway next to Hotel Ranjit. Economic and basic. Singles Rs95; doubles Rs155.

Hotel Ranjit, Hamidia Rd. (☎533511 or 535211), between the bus and train stations, on the right 200m before the road turns. Small rooms share a building with Bhopal's busiest restaurant and bar. Check-out 24hr. Singles Rs150; doubles Rs200. Reservations necessary.

Hotel Meghdoot, Hamidia Rd. (☎534093), near the Hotel Surya. One of the cheapest deals in Bhopal, it has all the standard facilities and a noisy, betel-rich atmosphere. Check-out 24hr. Singles Rs130; doubles Rs170.

◖ FOOD

▓ **Manohar Dairy and Restaurant,** 6 Hamidia Rd., opposite the Hotel Taj. Good, cheap South Indian fare. Lively, with a quick turnover and a great menu. South Indian snacks Rs10-40; fresh juices Rs12-20; pizza Rs30-40; shakes and a wide variety of desserts Rs12-45. Open daily 6am-midnight.

▓ **Arya Bhavan,** MP Nagar, Zone II. Excellent vegetarian food and delicious desserts at reasonable prices. Most dishes Rs24-50. Lunchtime *thalis* Rs35-55; sweets Rs6-26; and South Indian snacks Rs6-28. Open daily 11am-3pm and 7-10:30pm.

Hotel Gaurav, Hamidia Rd., near Hotel Surya. The all-veg. menu (Rs20-45) features many *paneer* specialties. Pleasant atmosphere accented with French windows and Indian miniature paintings. Open daily 7am-11pm.

Shahnama Restaurant, in the Jehan Numa Palace Hotel, 157 Shamla Hills. The highest of haute cuisine in Bhopal. Dine to live evening *ghazals* in a former palace. The Indian non-veg. (Rs125-165) and continental selections (Rs120-190) are refined, but steer clear of the novelty-value-only Italian/Spanish/Mexican/Thai page of the menu. Open daily 1-3pm and 7-11pm.

Indian Coffee House, Hamidia Rd., opposite Hotel Ranjit, and on TT Nagar, opposite the Variety Book House. Open daily 7am-10pm.

Ranjit, 3 Hamidia Rd., inside Hotel Ranjit. A Bhopal institution, this fading dinner joint continues to draw in the crowds thanks to its reputation and location. Veg. Rs30-54; non-veg. Rs45-70; and beer Rs63-72. Open daily 11:30am-11pm.

♫ ◉ ENTERTAINMENT AND SIGHTS

BHARAT BHAVAN. A cultural center that produces exhibitions of theater, music, poetry, and the fine arts, the Bharat Bhavan is one of India's finest museums.

Architect Charles Correa crafted it into a charming public space with multi-layered courtyards overlooking the scenic Upper Lake. The three oddly shaped and even more oddly decorated protuberances are skylights that illuminate subterranean galleries featuring modern art. A repertory company performs throughout the year. The Bhavan also hosts classical music concerts and poetry readings; check at the ticket office for schedules. A library and cafe complete this culture vulture's oasis. *(Upper Lake Rd., in the new town. Auto-rickshaw from the old town Rs25-30. Open Tu-Su 1-7pm; Feb. 1-Oct. 31 Tu-Su 2-8pm. Rs5.)*

OLD TOWN. Bhopal's status as an independent, Muslim-ruled princely state until 1952 endowed the city with a strong Muslim character and a wealth of mosques. The old Muslim bazaar quarter, or **Chowk,** wedged in the crook of a turn in Hamidia Rd., has the strongest Islamic flavor. Many of the area's old buildings have disappeared, but skull-capped men returning from pilgrimages to Mecca and women in *chadors* continue to preserve Bhopal's Muslim traditions.

The **Taj-ul-Masjid,** Bhopal's biggest mosque, is a spectacular illustration of Bhopal's Islamic tradition. The plans of the original builder, Nawab Shajehar Begum, were so grandiose that they have still not been completed. The 18-story minarets, the vast courtyard, the three huge domes over the prayer hall filled with students of the Koran, and the river nearby combine to create a grand impression. Don't be fooled by the huge staircase on Sultania Rd.—the mosque can only be approached from Royal Market Rd. *(Open dawn-dusk. Free.)*

The **Jama Masjid,** built by Kudsia Begum in 1837, has impressive gold-spiked minarets. The **Moti Mahal,** constructed in 1860 by Kudsia Begum's daughter, Sikander Jehan, continues the Mughal tradition of small-scale, elegant, more "personal" mosques. Although less opulent than its big city counterparts, this mosque imitates many features (including striped domes) of the Jama Masjid in Delhi.

TRIBAL HABITAT (MUSEUM OF MAN). The Tribal Habitat reconstructs the dwellings of various indigenous Indian tribes and attempts to provide a glimpse of actual tribal life. The open-air exhibition matches the natural surroundings of the tribal villages. *(Shamla Hills, close to Bharat Bhavan. 1km auto-rickshaw ride to exhibition area. Open Tu-Su 10am-5:30pm; Mar. 1-Aug.31 Tu-Su 10am-5:30pm. Free.)*

OTHER MUSEUMS. The **Regional Science Center** is a science museum containing nearly 300 participatory exhibits in the "Invention" and "Fun in Science" galleries and planetarium. *(Shamla Hills. Open Tu-Su 11:30am-7pm. Rs2.)* The **government archaeological museum** has a small collection, including several noteworthy sculptures from around Madhya Pradesh, tribal art, and paintings from the Bagh Caves near Mandu. *(Banganga Rd. Open Tu-Su 10:30am-5:30pm. Free.)* The **Birla Museum** features a collection of 9th- and 10th-century sculptures from the Raisen, Sehore, Mandsaur, and Shahdol districts of MP *(Arera Hill. Open Tu-Su 9am-5:30pm. Rs3.)* Next door, the **Birla Temple** has another scenic view of the city, especially at night. *(Open daily 6-11:30am and 4-9pm; in winter 6:30-noon and 4-8:30pm. Free.)*

OTHER DISTRACTIONS. Locals enjoy strolling along VIP Rd.—Bhopal's answer to Marine Drive in Bombay—and Lake Drive in the evenings. Paddleboats and rowboats are available for hire at the **Boat Club.** *(Lake Drive Rd. Open 7am-8pm. Paddleboats Rs30 per 30min.; rowboats Rs40-50 per 30min.)*

SANCHI सांची
☎ 07482

In the 3rd century BC, the emperor Ashoka founded the Buddhist retreat at Sanchi as a haven for meditation, and 22 centuries have done little to undermine his purpose. Sanchi re-entered the limelight when a British officer stumbled across its ruins in 1818. The huge, white stupas, with later additions of exquisite sculpture, were named a UNESCO World Heritage site in 1989. Despite increased visibility, Sanchi remains a tiny village, rewarding visitors with a near complete compendium of Buddhist architectural history.

MADHYA PRADESH

GETTING THERE AND GETTING AROUND

Buses leave for Bhopal (at least every hr., 6am-6pm, 1½hr., Rs19), but some take the slow route through Raisen. Sanchi is on the main line from Bhopal to Delhi; express **trains** only stop here for 1st class or A/C passengers who have traveled at least 161km or 2nd class passengers in groups of 10 who have racked up 400km. The Bhopal station masters seem more officious in this matter than those at Sanchi, so although you may have trouble getting here by train, you should be able to snag a seat on the way back. If you're coming from **Agra** (Rs459), **Bombay** (Rs725), **Delhi** (Rs606), or **Gwalior** (Rs365), then you can invoke the 161km clause, as long as you have the extra cash to pay for A/C 3 tier sleeper class. Alternatively, you can get on or off the train at **Vidisha** (at least 3-4 per day, 9:20am-9:25pm, 1hr., Rs23) and take the bus to Sanchi (every 10min., 6am-10pm).

ORIENTATION

The two main roads in Sanchi intersect one another. One leads southwest from the **railway station,** past the few budget hotels and the **police station,** and up a hill to the **main gate** of the ruins. The road to Bhopal crosses this street at a right angle, continuing on to Vidisha, 10km to the northeast. The **small market** and **bus stand** occupy the quadrant on the station side of the main road and the Bhopal side of the crossroads. There's an **STD/ISD** booth at the bus stand.

ACCOMMODATIONS AND FOOD

Though many visitors see the sights in a couple of hours, accommodations are plentiful—most convenient is the (one) **railway retiring room,** complete with dressing room, shower-less bathroom, and mosquito nets (Rs120). The **Sri Lanka Mahabodhi Society Guest House,** on the left just outside the station, has a number of rooms with shared bath, though the Sri Lankan pilgrims for whom the guest house was built have first priority. (☎ 62739. Rs100 per person.) The **Tourist Cafeteria,** just before the museum, has bright, airy, spotless rooms. (☎ 62743. Singles Rs200; doubles Rs290.) The cafeteria serves the standard MPSTDC fare. (Snacks Rs12-25; soups Rs25-30; entrees Rs20-45. Open daily 7am-10pm.) Near the railway station, the **Pathak** and **Rohit** restaurants serve basic Indian meals.

SIGHTS

The main road from the railway station leads past a kiosk on the left that sells tickets for both the archaeological museum and the hilltop ruins. (Both Rs5. Free F.) The useful *Sanchi* guide, published by the Archaeological Survey of India, is also available here (Rs15). Past the museum, a road winds it way up the hill; if you're on foot, the steep staircase leading off to the right is the more direct route to the ruins.

THE GREAT STUPA

Even though the Enlightened One never visited Sanchi (as far as is known), the complex of temples and monasteries here chronicles the entire ancient history of Indian Buddhism. Mauryan Emperor Ashoka himself erected a pillar at the Great Stupa, and sculptures dating from the end of the Buddhist period resemble deities from the Hindu pantheon. Surprisingly, though Sanchi was an active Buddhist site for over 1000 years, only scattered references to it have been identified in the vast corpus of Buddhist literature. Archaeology provides the only hints about the history behind the hilltop ruins here. When the ruins were unearthed, archaeologists nearly destroyed the Great Stupa in their rush to find valuable artifacts before discovering that there was no treasure inside—the stupa was solid throughout. It was later restored, and today, along with its amazingly well-preserved gateways, the Great Stupa reigns over the crumbling edifices surrounding it on the hill.

In the first century BC, the Satavahanas tacked on Sanchi's richest addition: the four monumental gateways facing the cardinal directions. Archaeologists attribute the intricate sculpture to ivory carvers accustomed to making maximum use of minimum surface; the theory is borne out by a Pali inscription on the south gate. Since all the sculpture, except the four **seated Buddhas** inside each gate, dates from the Theravada period, no direct depictions of the Buddha appear on the gates. He is referred to only obliquely, with symbols such as the lotus flowers (for his birth), the pipal tree (for his enlightenment), and the wheel (for his sermons). Figures commonly depicted include six *manushis*—Buddha's predecessors who appear as stupas or trees, each of a different species. *Jatakas* (tales from the Buddha's previous lives) such as the **Chhadanta Jataka,** in which the Buddha, as an elephant, helps a hunter saw off his tusks, and stories from the subsequent history of Buddhism, particularly those detailing the distribution of the Buddha's relics, are also illustrated on the pillars of the temples.

SOUTH GATEWAY. The south gate, opposite the path to the ruins, was once the main entrance, as evidenced by the stump of a pillar erected by Ashoka. A local *zamindar* ("landlord") broke off the rest of the pillar to use in a sugarcane press. The middle rung of the south gate shows Ashoka's army arriving at the last of the eight original stupas containing the Buddha's relics at Ramagrama, but Ashoka is prevented from carting off the loot (as he had at the other seven) by the army of snake people to the left. On the inside, the middle rung depicts the Chhadanta Jataka, with the Buddha as the six-tusked elephant; above this scene are the trees and stupas of the *manushi* buddhas. The bottom rung shows the siege of Kushinagar (see p. 192), the prototypical story of Buddhist non-violence.

WEST GATEWAY. The front face of the west gateway features (from top to bottom) more *manushis*, the Buddha's first sermon (note the wheel), and more scenes of Chhadanta. Inside, the top two rungs show more wrangling over relics, and the bottom reveals the Buddha attaining enlightenment despite the distracting demons sent by Mara. On the south pillar of this gate, the **Mahakapi Jataka** depicts the Buddha as a monkey turning himself into a bridge so that his brethren can escape to safety over a river.

NORTH GATEWAY. The north gateway, less scarred by the ravages of time than its counterparts, shows the **Vessarkara Jataka** around both sides of the bottom rung. In the tale, Buddha successively gives up a magic elephant, his horse and chariot, and his wife and children before being reinstated to his princedom.

EAST GATEWAY. While the upper registers of the east gateway repeat earlier scenes, the south pillar depicts the Buddha walking on water (on the outside) and facing a fearsome cobra (on the inside). Below this scene is a depiction of villagers trying to make a sacrificial fire which won't light without the Buddha's permission.

MUSEUM. The small museum holds a modest collection of statues unearthed at Sanchi, including some impressive lion-headed Ashokan pillar capitals and a buxom *yakshi* swinging down from a mango tree.

INDORE इंदौर ☎ 0731

With a population of 1.2 million, Indore is the commercial center of Madhya Pradesh. More people pack its cityscape, more businesses clutter its buildings, more industries sear its escarpments, and more money flows through its coffers than any other city in the state. The old-town markets will reward travelers who wander its warrens long enough, but most people hurry to jump aboard the next bus to Mandu or Ujjain.

MADHYA PRADESH

▣ GETTING THERE AND GETTING AROUND

Flights: Airport (☎ 410452 and 413747) is 8km west of town center, along MG Rd. Auto-rickshaw Rs60-70. **Indian Airlines** (☎ 431595 or 431596) on Racecourse Rd. Open daily 10am-1:15pm and 2:15-5pm. **Jet Airways**, G-2 Vidyapati Bhawan, 17 Racecourse Rd. (☎ 544590-3). Open M-Sa 9:30am-6pm, Su 9:30am-1pm. **Sahara Airlines**, G-6 Industry House, Agra-Bombay Rd. (☎ 266299 or 266399.) Open daily 10am-6pm. To **Bhopal** (1-2 per day, 30min., US$55); **Bombay** (3 per day, 1½hr., US$90); **Delhi** (1-2 per day, 2hr., US$135); **Gwalior** (M and F, 2hr., US$105).

Trains: The **railway station** is on Station Rd. The **reservation office** is on the side street directly opposite the main entrance. Open M-Sa 8am-8pm, Su 8am-2pm. To: **Bhopal** (4-6 per day, Tu-F 6am-4:40pm, M and Sa-Su 6am-8:35pm; 5-7hr., Rs104); **Bombay** (3:45pm, 16hr., Rs244); **Calcutta** (M, Th, F, 8:30pm, 12hr., Rs374); **Delhi** (1 and 4pm, 14hr., Rs242); **Ujjain** (5-6 per day, 6am-8pm, 1½hr., Rs29).

Buses: Sarwate Bus Station, at the intersection of Nasia Rd. and Kibe Compound Rd., 500m south of the train station. Turn right and go under the Patel flyover as you exit the railway station. To: **Bhopal** (every 15min., 4:30am-12:30am, 4½hr., Rs58-88); **Omkareshwar** (frequent, 6am-4:15pm, 3hr., Rs35); **Ujjain** (every 15min., 6am-10pm, 2hr., Rs24). **Gangwal Bus Stand**, about 3km west of the train station, serves **Mandu** (frequent, 6:30am-11:30pm, 4hr., Rs32) via **Dhar**, but *not* Dhar Super. For a more comfortable ride to these and other destinations, including **Maheshwar,** try the private operators on the street opposite the train station, near the reservation office.

Local Transportation: English street signs are rare, and the old part of town is a labyrinth. Take advantage of the ubiquitous **auto-rickshaws.** Prices range from Rs10 for short rides to Rs25 to go across town. The meters are actually accurate in Indore, so make sure that your driver uses his. Or, jump aboard one of the **tempos** that ply the main thoroughfares (Rs3).

▣ ▣ ORIENTATION AND PRACTICAL INFORMATION

The train station is in the center of Indore, and the railway lines bisect the city down the middle into eastern and western halves. To the east, workshops and business hotels are built on top of each other; to the west is the older part of town, containing most of the city's sights. Two bridges link the two halves of the city. Shastri Bridge is 250m north from the railway station along **Station Rd.** From Shashtri Bridge, Mahatma Gandhi (MG) Rd. leads to the sights in the west and to the **Gandhi statue,** at the intersection with **RN Tagore Rd.,** in the east. A 500m walk south (right) from the railway station takes you under the Patel Bridge to **Sarwate Bus Stand.** A five-minute walk away from the railway lines from either the Patel Bridge or the bus stand takes you to the **Nehru statue** and to **Maharaja Yeshwantrao (MY) Hospital Rd.,** which leads southeast to the bank, GPO, and Central Museum.

Tourist Office: MPSTDC, RN Tagore Rd. (☎ 528653 or 521818), behind RN Tagore Griha Hall, just south of MG Rd., left of the Gandhi statue. Open daily 10am-5pm.

Currency Exchange: State Bank of India, Main Branch, Agra-Bombay Rd., on the left before the GPO and Central Museum. Turn right off MY Hospital Rd., heading out of town. Open M-F 10:30am-4pm, Sa 10:30am-1pm. **ATM: HDFC Bank,** G-F, U-V House, 9/1A South Tukhoganj. From the Nehru statue, it's 1km away from the city center, past the Landmark restaurant and Hotel Surya. AmEx, MC, Visa.

Bookstore: Sogoni Book House, G-F Rajan Bhawan, MG Rd., 200m from the intersection with RN Tagore Rd., behind the Gandhi statue. Open daily till 9pm.

Police: (☎ 464488 or 100 for emergencies), under the Patel flyover, between the railway station and Sarwate.

Pharmacy: MY Hospital Pharmacy, MY Hospital Rd., between the Nehru statue and State Bank of India. Open 24hr.

Hospital: Choithrom Hospital, Monik Barg Rd. (☎ 362491-8).

Internet: Cyber Point, Mahavir Empire Building, RN Tagore Rd., directly behind Gandhi's left shoulder. Rs50 per hr. Open daily 10am-midnight.

Post Office: GPO, Agra-Bombay Rd. (☎ 700244), between the State Bank of India and the museum. Turn right off MY Hospital Rd. Open M-Sa 8am-7:30pm, Su 10:30am-3:30pm. **Postal Code:** 452001.

ACCOMMODATIONS

Hotels in Indore fill up quickly with itinerant businessmen, especially at the beginning of the month. The cheaper places, which cluster between the Sarwate bus station and the Nehru statue, cater to the middle-class Indian entrepreneur, usually offering 24-hour check-out, TVs, phones, and *dhobi* service. Prices quoted do not include state taxes of 10%. The predominantly male clientele in these hotels and the abundance of workshops in the area mean that women may not feel comfortable walking around alone at night. Women might want to consider accommodations in the somewhat more expensive neighborhoods beyond RN Tagore Rd.

Hotel Neelam, 33/2 Patel Bridge Corner (☎ 466001), at the end of an alley opposite the Sarwate Bus Stand. The cleanest rooms and largest TVs you'll find in this price range. 24hr. check-out. Singles Rs145-295; doubles Rs195-345.

Hotel Sant Plaza, 9/1 Kibe Compound, Chhoti Gwaltoli Chouraha (☎ 463166 or 283203), opposite the small temple. Turn right as you exit Sarwate bus stand. Clean, standard business hotel, with good service. In-house Internet access. Singles Rs145–450; doubles Rs195-550.

Hotel Royal Residency, 225 RN Tagore Rd. (☎ 764633; fax 465377; email royalresidency@email.com), at the intersection with YM Hospital Rd., near the Nehru statue. Farther from the hubbub of the bus stand and workshops, Royal Residency is perhaps the best deal in town. Well-appointed rooms with sparkling baths and a range of services that would cost twice as much elsewhere. Singles Rs450-750; doubles Rs600-900. Check-out 9am. AmEx, MC, Visa.

Hotel Dayal, 10 Kibe Compound, Chhoti Gwaltoli Chouraha (☎ 462865 or 462866), next to Sant Plaza. This cheapie fills up quickly, so reserve in advance. Singles Rs80, with air-cooling Rs100; doubles Rs110/130.

Hotel Payal, 38 Chhoti Gwaltoli (☎ 463202 or 478460), in the row of hotels hidden behind the Patel flyover, just around the corner from the Sarwate bus station. Singles Rs150-200; doubles Rs200-250.

Hotel Ashoka, 14 Nasia Rd. (☎ 465991 or 475496), opposite Sarwate bus station, 100m to the right as you exit. Singles Rs150-310; doubles Rs200-360.

FOOD

Indore is not a city of culinary delights, and most restaurants are in the swankier hotels near RN Tagore Rd. Fortunately, prices tend to be quite reasonable. There is a wide range of bar-restaurants, juice bars, fruit stands, and sweet-sellers to the left as you leave the Sarwate bus station.

Woodlands Restaurant, Hotel President, 163 RN Tagore Rd., near the Nehru statue. A respite from the frantic frenzy of outdoor Indore, Woodlands serves breakfasts (Rs65-85), a great all-you-can-eat lunch buffet (Rs90), typical veg. dinners (Rs40-70), and snacks (Rs30-50). Open daily 7am-11pm; meals 7-11am, noon-3pm, and 7-11pm.

Landmark Restaurant, 163 RN Tagore Rd., between Woodlands Restaurant and the Nehru statue. This is *the* place to go to satisfy your salad cravings (Rs15-50). Landmark's menu proudly proclaims that it will take *at least* 20min. to prepare its French-inspired continental, Indian, and Chinese meals from fresh ingredients. Most entrees Rs50-70; chicken dishes Rs90-100. Open M-Sa 10am-11pm, Su 10am-10pm.

Indian Coffee House, MG Rd., 250m past Gandhi Hall, on the left inside a courtyard (look for the jeans ad on the archway), heading out of the city center toward Rajwada. A second location, opposite the MY Hospital, has outdoor tables in a small park. Open M-Sa 7:30am-10pm, Su 11am-10pm.

👁 SIGHTS

For most pilgrims, Indore is little more than a stopover point on the way to their next *yatra*. If you're stuck with time to kill in Indore, however, then there are worse ways of killing it then by checking out the following sights.

CENTRAL MUSEUM. Presenting religious sculptures from Madhya Pradesh, stone inscriptions, and Sanskrit copper plates from western MP, among other things, the Central Museum has a collection that is both beautiful and unique. Unfortunately, poor presentation does little to illuminate cultural context. Unlike in many other museums, however, it is OK to touch the sculpture, and the pieces scattered outside in the grass make the art accessible to all. Ask one of the attendants for a tour. *(On the Agra-Bombay Rd. beyond the GPO, Open Tu-Su 10am-5pm. Free.)*

LAL BAGH PALACE. This British-style manor was built by the Holkar Maharajas between 1886 and 1921. Along with the usual stuffed wildcats, the house features an underground tunnel connecting the main house with the kitchens on the other side of the river, as well as imposing gates that are replicas of the ones at Buckingham Palace. Don't jump out of your *chappals* when a statue of a definitely-not-amused Queen Victoria pops up at the exit to see you off the premises. *(Between the train station and Gangwal Bus Stand. Open Tu-Su 10am-5pm. Rs2. Guidebooks Rs3.)*

OTHER SIGHTS. On the western side of town, off MG Rd., **Rajwada** pays homage to the faded splendor of the Holkars. Wander the streets of the lively **Khajuri Bazaar** on your way to the nearby **Kanch Mandir**, a Jain temple made entirely of mirrored tiles. Finally, those interested in Raj-era architecture might want to visit **Gandhi Hall**, now a Municipal Corporation building, on MG Rd. just west of Shastri Bridge.

NEAR INDORE

MAHESHWAR महेश्वर

Both the *Ramayana* and the *Mahabharata* mention **Maheshvari,** once a glorious city and the capital of King Arjuna Kartavirya's realm around 200 BC. The city fell into oblivion until the late 18th century, when the Holkar queen, Ahilyabai, made it her capital, building a fortified palace and two richly decorated temples along the Narmada River. The queen also established a center for producing fine, hand-loomed saris, and legend has it that she created the simple but distinctive geometric border design that makes Maheshwari saris famous throughout India today.

To reach the sights, clustered inside the **fort,** turn left out of the bus station and straight across the main road. The right fork in the village road leads up to the fort. Past the main gate, a smaller gate leads into the palace grounds, where a two-room museum contains a jumble of broken statuary and Holkar dynasty paraphernalia. Through the gate to the left of the museum are steps down to the **sari workshop** and the temples and *ghats* below. The workshop at the top of the stairs, run by the Rehwa Society (established in 1978 to preserve Maheshwar's silk-cotton sari-weaving tradition), is set up for the benefit of tourists. In a dark, low, historic building lit by fluorescent tubes, workers, most of them women, spin and weave material in a stunning array of colors and designs. The manager, who sits just inside the door, will call somebody up to show you around. Though saris are most definitely *not* sold on the premises (perish the thought), they are available in town for Rs400-2500. *(Open W-M 10am-5pm. Free.)* Past the sari workshop, at the bottom of the stairs, Maheshwar's **temples** are pressed into small courtyards that make them seem larger than they are.

A three-hour bus ride from either Indore (via Dhamnod) or Mandu (Rs27) will drop you at the **bus stand. Buses** return to Indore every hour and leave for Mandu and Omkareshwar in the early morning and afternoon. **Ajanta Lodge,** on the main road 100m to the right of the bus stand, provides clean rooms. (☎07283 or 73226.

Singles Rs40-50; doubles Rs55-70.) For food, **VIP Cottage,** on the main road 400m to the left of the bus stand, just over the bridge, has all the usual stuff (Rs15-150).

OMKARESHWAR ओमकरेश्वर   ☎ 02780

For centuries, Omkareshwar, an island shaped like the holiest of all Hindu symbols, the "Om" (ॐ), has drawn pilgrims to its temples and *ghats*. With its endless night-and-day chants, repeated *"Hare Om"* greetings, and the incessant buzz of flies, Omkareshwar, with its seething crowds of devout believers, is a little like a miniature Varanasi. Its temples rise up over jagged cliffs, while the *ghats* climb serenely from the banks of the Narmada and Kaveri rivers.

To reach the temples, just walk through the village until you reach the bridge that spans the deep gully dividing the island. Otherwise, descend to the *ghats* and take a ferry across (Rs5). From the river you can see the town's two major temples: the remarkably detailed **Shri Omkar Mandhata,** home to one of only 12 *jyotirlingas* (manifestations of Shiva as brilliant columns of light) in India, and **Siddhnath Temple,** an early medieval brahmin temple.

Buses run directly to Omkareshwar from **Indore** (frequent, 5am-4:15pm; return from 10am; 3hr., Rs35), **Maheshwar** (early morning and afternoon; return 9:30am and 1pm; 3hr., Rs28), or **Ujjain** (1 per day; return noon and 1:30pm; 5hr., Rs59). Trains from Indore stop at the Omkareshwar Rd. **railway station,** but it is a 12km bus ride out of town back toward Barwaha (Rs7). The **police station** (☎ 344015; open daily 9am-5pm) and the **post office** (☎ 71222; open M-Sa 9am-5pm) are near the bus station. There is no place in town to change currency. From the bus station, a three-minute walk through the village takes you past the **Government Hospital** on the right (open daily 8am-noon and 5-6pm) and the **pharmacy** on the left (open daily 7:30am-9:30pm). The **Yatrika Guest House** is behind the bus station. (☎ 71308. Singles Rs100-180.) For nicer rooms and more scenic views try the **Hotel Aishwarya,** where prices are open to negotiation. Take the small side street directly across the bus station, and follow the signs. (☎ 71325 or 71326. Singles Rs250-300; doubles Rs350-450; 10% luxury tax.)

MANDU माण्डव   ☎ 02792

Mandu, the so-called "City of Joy," is the kind of agricultural idyll that India likes to promote in its tourist brochures. Goats munch their way through the grass that surrounds the ruins, while women sashay by with pots on their head, and children run over to say "hello." Stretched out on top of a narrow plateau in the Vindhya mountain range, the city was fortified as long ago as the 6th century. Mandu's golden age lasted from 1401 to 1526, when the Muslim rulers of the kingdom of Malwa called it their home, building walls, mosques, palaces, and pleasure domes in stone and marble across the length of the plateau. Five centuries later, their monuments still stand in a tranquil, underpopulated mountain region set against a backdrop of great natural beauty. The main tourist season is between July and March, but the monsoon season is perhaps the best time to visit, when the life-giving rains paint the surrounding countryside a lush green.

▐▀ GETTING THERE AND GETTING AROUND

Buses depart from the village square to: **Dhar** (14 per day, 7am-6:15pm, 1½hr., Rs15); **Indore** (5-6 per day, 6am-4:45pm, 3hr., Rs40); and **Maheshwar** (7:30am direct and 2:30pm via **Dhamnod**, 3hr., Rs27). Bus service is often less frequent during monsoon season. The easiest and most pleasant way of getting around is on **bikes,** which you can rent from several villagers living on the main road or from Ajay's Bicycle Shop, also on the main road, just south of the square (Rs3 per hr., Rs25 per day). Alternatively, Nitin Traders will wheel out the village **auto-rickshaw** (Rs150-200 for 3-4hr.) or lay on private **taxis** to Indore (Rs725, book 1½hr. before departure). They're just south of the square opposite the Jain temple; look for the sign. (Open daily 8am-8pm.)

✈ 🛈 ORIENTATION AND PRACTICAL INFORMATION

The **main road** runs south, past the **village square** and **Jama Masjid,** ending at the **Rewa Kund** ruins at the far end of town. **Jahaz Mahal Rd.,** next to Jama Masjid, loops back north to the **Royal Enclave.** The sights around town are well-marked, and there are signs in English to direct visitors to the ruins. All the hotels and restaurants, as well as the **post office** (☎ 63222; open M-Sa 9am-5pm), **police station** (☎63223), and the **pharmacy** (open daily 9am-7pm) are on the main road. There are several doctors' offices in Mandu, but the closest hospital is in Indore. There is no tourist office in Mandu, but the **MPSTDC** in Indore can help with hotel reservations (recommended in winter). **STD/ISD** calls can be placed from a market square stall (open daily 8:30am-9pm) or from the Rupmati Hospital. Power outages are frequent, and phone lines are often down during the monsoon. **Postal Code:** 454010.

🛏 🍴 ACCOMMODATIONS AND FOOD

Hotel Maharaja on Jahaz Mahal Rd., has small but clean rooms with attached baths, and is probably the best deal in town. (☎63288. Singles Rs100; doubles 200. Off-season: 75/100.) During the tourist season, the Nepalese kitchen staff whip up Indian, Chinese, continental, and, yes, Nepalese cuisine. SADA's **Tourist Rest House** (☎ 63234), at the corner of the main square and Jahaz Mahal Rd., has dark rooms with squat toilets (doubles Rs125). **MPSTDC** has two excellent but pricey hotels in Mandu. The **Travelers' Lodge,** 1km north of the square on the main road, has scenic views over the eastern ravine. (☎63221. Singles Rs290; doubles Rs390.) The **MPSTDC Tourist Cottages,** on the main road 2km south of the square, has better rooms in small cottages with lake views. (☎63235. Singles Rs350-750; doubles Rs450-850.) Both places charge 10% luxury tax but offer 25% discounts in May and June. Reservations can be made in any MPSTDC office (recommended in-season). Both have **restaurants** with the standard menu of snacks (Rs5-40), continental dishes (Rs30-100), and veg. (Rs20-45) and non-veg. (Rs30-100) options. (MPSTDC restaurants open daily 8-10am, noon-2pm, and 6-10pm; snacks available between meal times.) The **Rupmati Hotel,** the best in town, has views of the ravine, and large, clean rooms. (☎63270, or (in Indore) 702055. Doubles Rs375-750; 10% luxury tax.) The restaurant is more affordable than the rooms. The open-air pavilion overlooking a landscaped lawn, complete with swings and slides, serves veg. (Rs30-55) and non-veg. (Rs50-250) dishes. The restaurant also holds the only liquor license in town. (Beer Rs50-75. Open daily 7am-11pm.) The **Relax Point Restaurant,** in the main square, offers veg. *thalis* for only Rs30 (open daily 8am-10:30pm).

📷 SIGHTS

Ruins are everywhere in Mandu, dominating the landscape, from the gateways you pass on the way into town to the mosque and tomb in the market square; from the crumbling houses along the sides of the main street to the palace at the tip of the plateau. The attractions are in three main areas: the **central group** in the village center, the **royal enclave** in the north, and the **Rewa Kund complex** in the south.

THE CENTRAL GROUP. In the middle of both the plateau and the village, the central group includes the beautiful **Jama Masjid,** one of India's largest mosques. Like the other monuments here, it typifies the austere architectural style imported from Afghanistan by Hoshang Shah. Reputedly modeled on the mosque in Damascus, and completed in 1454, the Jama Masjid is remarkable for both its sheer scale and for the simplicity of its design. Hoshang Shah's son built a white marble **mausoleum** behind the Jama Masjid for his father. The structure so inspired Shah Jahan that he sent his architects to study it before they began work on the Taj Mahal. Opposite the Jama Masjid, the over-ambitious and underachieving **Ashrafi Mahal** proves, by contrast, that less patience and skill went into Mandu's other monuments. In the 15th century Mahud Shah Khilji tried to slap together a huge tomb and seven-story victory tower so carelessly that most of it has since collapsed, leaving only the remains of a *madrasa* (theological college) complete with students' cells.

THE ROYAL ENCLAVE. Sultan Ghiyas Shah constructed the huge **Jahaz Mahal** (or "ship palace"), just inside the gateway, to house his equally huge harem. The long, narrow design and the two artificial lakes on either side are what give the building its name, especially apt during the rainy season, when water comes cascading through the palace's complex system of pools and conduits. Behind the Jahaz Mahal stands the **Hindola Mahal,** an audience hall nicknamed the "Swinging Palace" because of its sloping buttresses, which look as if they're swinging out at an angle. Ghiyas Shah had a ramp built so that he could ride to the upper floor without the hassle of getting down from his elephant. Numerous other ruins, including **Dilwar Khan's Mosque** and **Gada Shah's Shop,** are also in this enclave. *(The Jahaz Mahal Rd., next to Hoshang Shah's tomb, continues to the Royal Enclave. Open dawn-dusk. Rs2; free F.)*

NIL KANTH TEMPLE. Originally a Mughal pleasure pavilion, complete with running water that flowed over ribbed stones in front of candles, the temple today has been taken over by the Shaivites. From this inspirational spot on the valley slopes just below the clifftop, they worship an incarnation of Shiva whose throat turned blue when he drank poison. *(At the southern end of the village, a fork leads right (west) from the main road to the Nil Kanth Temple, 3km away.)*

REWA KUND. The main road ends 5km from the square, at the **Rewa Kund** complex, named after the tank that used to supply water to the nearby palaces. Baz Bahadur, the last independent ruler of Mandu, built his **palace** in the 16th century to serve as a quiet retreat, with views of the surrounding greenery. But even this tranquil spot could not satisfy the stunning Rupmati, the sultan's favorite dancer. She was from the plains, and dreary luxuries of the high-life up on the plateau made her homesick. According to legend, Rupmati demanded that Baz Bahadur build her a pavilion on the crest of a hill, from which she could see her former village in the Narmada Valley far below. No sooner had the dutiful sultan completed **Rupmati's Pavilion** than the jealous Akbar marched on Mandu in order to seize the renowned dancer. Baz Bahadur fled, Rupmati swallowed poison, and Akbar, after a brief stay, let his testosterone guide him to the next desirable dancing girl (see **Orchha,** p. 376), leaving Mandu desolate. The views from the palace are superb.

UJJAIN उज्जैन ☎ 0734

Ujjain's long and varied history stretches back to the 3rd century BC, when the city was the imperial seat of Ashoka, Buddhism's first patron. Later, Ujjain served as a major center of Indian astronomy. Long before the days of the prime meridian, Hindu stargazers made Ujjain India's Greenwich. An 18th-century observatory on the southwestern side of town is still in use today. Ujjain is also among the holiest of holy Hindu cities; every 12 years during the festival of **Kumbh Mela** (see p. 209) Ujjain attracts millions of people with the promise of a hard-earned space along the city *ghats* for a dip in the sacred river Shipra. Ujjain's temples are not the most inspiring in the world; the best time to come is during Shaivite festivals or—if you can handle the crush of millions of pilgrims—during the Mela itself.

▐ GETTING THERE AND GETTING AROUND

Trains: The **railway station** is on Subhash Rd., 150m west of the bus station. To: **Bhopal** (6-8 per day, 1am-10:15pm, 3-4hr., Rs52); **Bombay** (daily, 5:33pm, 10hr., Rs228); **Delhi** (2:45 and 5:55pm, 17hr., Rs250); **Gwalior** (daily, 2:45pm, 10½hr., Rs190); **Indore** (10 per day, 2am-8:40pm, 2-3hr., Rs29); **Jaipur** (Th-Sa, 11:20pm, 9hr., Rs176). To get to **Orchha,** change trains in **Ahmedabad** (daily, 9:05pm, 10hr., Rs159).

Buses: **Mahakal Bus Stand,** on the corner to the right (northeast) as you leave the train station. To: **Bhopal** (frequent, 6am-9:30pm, 5hr., Rs58); **Indore** (frequent, 4:30am-9:30pm, 2hr., Rs24).

Local Transportation: Things are spread out, and most **auto-rickshaw** drivers refuse to use meters. Bargain; the longest ride should cost no more than Rs30-35. **Tempos** #2 and 9 go to the Mahakaleshwar Mandir; #4 and 10 go to the Gopal Mandir.

✦ ⁊ ORENTATION AND PRACTICAL INFORMATION

Hemmed in by the **Shipra River** to the west and the **railroad tracks** to the south, Ujjain's **old city** charms visitors with many small shops and drives them crazy with narrow lanes that frustrate even the most state-of-the-art navigation tools. There are no street signs, few landmarks, and countless little roads to nowhere. Most of the temples and *ghats* are within walking distance, but other places require a rickshaw ride. The railway station, bus stand, GPO, and most hotels are all clustered around one intersection.

Tourist Office: MPSTDC has a booth in the railway station that provides helpful maps of the city. Open daily 8am-3pm. The staff at the reception desk of the **MPSTDC Hotel Shipra,** Vishva Vidhyalaya Rd. (☎551495 or 551496), will also provide information. Exit the railway station through the stairway overpass. Cross the road and turn right; the hotel is 200m on the right. Ask here for Raju Pawar, the only government-licensed guide in Ujjain (Rs300-600 for a tour of the city).

Currency Exchange: The closest place to exchange currency is in Indore.

Police: ☎552140.

Pharmacy: Khandelaval Medical Store (☎554079), on the left, in the grounds of the Civil Hospital. Open 24hr. during the first 10 days of the month. **Radhaswami Medical Store,** opposite Civil Hospital, near the maternity home. Open 24hr. days 10-21. **Priya Medical Store** (☎559658), next to Khandelaval. Open 24hr. days 21-31.

Hospital: Civil Hospital, Ashok Rd. From the train station, it's 200m beyond Mahakal bus stand on the opposite side of street. For private medical assistance, the MPSTDC recommends Dr. Rita Shinde or Dr. Bishi (☎555067).

Post Office: GPO (☎551024), behind the bus stand at the 2nd gate on the left. Open daily 10am-8pm. **Postal Code:** 456001.

▐ ACCOMMODATIONS

Most of the budget hotels are near the railway station. Prices listed do not include state taxes of 5% on rooms Rs60-149 and 10% on rooms Rs150 and above.

Hotel Shipra, Vishva Vidhyalaya Rd. (☎551495 or 551496). Clean rooms have big windows, high ceilings, and desks. Check-out noon. Singles Rs350-690; doubles Rs390-790. AmEx, MC, Visa.

Hotel Rama Krishna (☎557012), opposite the train station to the left. No dead animals allowed. Avoid the stuffy interior rooms. All rooms have air-cooling and attached bathrooms. Check-out 24hr. Singles Rs130-450; doubles Rs170-250/550.

Hotel Chandragupta (☎561600), next to the Rama Krishna. Slightly cheaper (and less clean) than its neighbor. Attached bathrooms have squat toilets and wall faucets. Check-out 24hr. Singles Rs110-180; doubles Rs150-220.

Hotel Ajay, 12 Dewas Gate, Mahakaleshwar Rd. (☎550856 or 551354), on the street opposite the bus station. Small but clean rooms are a good deal. Singles Rs66-165; doubles Rs100-240.

◖ FOOD

A town of temples, Ujjain is a better place for fasting than feasting.

Nauratna Restaurant, inside Hotel Shipra. The standard MP Tourism menu made up of an uninspiring range of veg. and non-veg. Indian dishes (Rs15-175). Beer-drinkers are quarantined in a separate bar area. Open daily 8-10am, noon-3pm, and 7-10:30pm.

Sudama Restaurant, on Subhash Rd., opposite the railway station, next to Hotel Rama Krishna. Contemplate the fascinating cut-mirror decor while chowing down on veg. fare (Rs6-45). Dinner only after 7pm, but snacks (Rs6-32) and good veg. fried rice (Rs28) all day. Open daily 9am-11pm.

Chanakya Restaurant, on the ground floor of Hotel Chandragupta. The whole extended family can fit into one of the giant booths. Large selection of beer and spirits, and unmissable pseudo-erotic sculpture. Veg.-only dishes Rs6-40. Open daily 8am-11pm.

Ujjain

🏠 ACCOMMODATIONS
Hotel Ajay, 4
Hotel Chandragupta, 3
Hotel Rama Krishna, 2
Hotel Shipra, 5

🍎 FOOD
Chanakya Restaurant, 3
Nauratna Restaurant, 5
Sudama Restaurant, 1

👁 SIGHTS

Even with a map, start praying now—it's hard to find anything without faith. Thankfully, the largest temples and *ghats* aren't far from the railway station.

THE TEMPLES. The rosy *shikhara* of the **Mahakaleshwar Mandir** caps a series of long, narrow tunnels that eventually leads to an underground room containing one of the twelve *jyotirlingas*. These are believed to derive their power from within themselves; other *lingas* must have their power renewed from time to time by ritual. Amitabh Bachchan, the godfather of Bollywood cinema, was miraculously cured here after an accident in the movie *Shola*. *(From the bus stand, Mahakaleshwar Rd. leads 1½ km directly to the temple. Open daily 4am-11pm.)*

As its name suggests, the **Bada Ganesh Mandir** enshrines a gigantic sculpture of Ganesh. *(100m on the right down the road that goes around behind the Mahakaleshwar Mandir to the right.)* The **Harsiddhi Mandir,** the large temple complex behind high white walls to the right, is the focal point of Devi worship. It marks the spot where Parvati's arm was severed when Shiva pulled her from her *sati* pyre (see **Divine Dismemberment,** p. 692). A famous image of the goddess Annapurna is kept in the temple shrine. *(From the Mahakaleshwar Mandir, continue on the road past the Bada Ganesh Mandir into and over the marsh beyond; when you hit dry land, turn right.)*

Gopal Mandir (Ganesh Temple) sits behind a high, whitewashed, onion-domed fortification in the midst of a busy market square, where vendors display the season's most sought-after devotional paraphernalia. Inside, pilgrims lounge under the arched platforms that circle the complex's perimeter, while in the sumptuous main hall, a figure of Ganesh sits obediently between figures of his parents, Shiva and Parvati. *(In the center of town, head north 300m on Spiral Rd.)*

THE VEDHA SHALA. The instruments of the Vedha Shala (Veda School) sit in a compound behind a gate with a sign reading "Shree Jiwagi Observatory." The mathematically-inclined will wonder at the precision of gadgets like the parallel sundials on either end of a meter-high cylinder. Each side tells the time for exactly half the year. Others might wonder that such things exist at all. Located on top of a hill with a view of the river and fields beyond, the observatory would be a pleasant place to sit and admire the view, if it weren't for the non-stop truck traffic just outside the gate—the world of machines and modernity is never far away. *(On a road leading southwest from the back of the railway station, on top of the hill.)*

OTHER SIGHTS. There are any number of holy sights to see scattered throughout the city. If you have the patience and the fortitude to see them all, consult the encyclopedic MPSTDC mapguide. The **Ram Ghat** is the largest, although not always busiest, of the long row of *ghats* that lines both sides of the river. *(Take the road between the Harsiddhi Mandir and back down the slope toward the river.)* Toward the northern end of the row, the **Bhartirihari Caves** are home to the hoop-earringed Kanpatha yogis. Three kilometers north of town, worshipers still make offerings of sweets and alcohol at the Kal Bhairava Mandir.

JABALPUR जबलपूर ☎ 0761

The Madhya Pradesh tourism office tries to promote stays in this dusty town of just over a million people on the basis of some scenic white cliffs nearby. Basically, though, there is very little to see; as far as most tourists are concerned, Jabalpur is merely a staging point for Kanha and Bandhavgarh National Parks.

▬ GETTING THERE AND GETTING AROUND

Trains: The **railway station** (☎ 1311132) is a Rs15 rickshaw ride to the east of Russel Chowk. Reservation office open M-Sa 8am-8pm, Su 8am-2pm. Window #3 serves tourists. To: **Bhopal** (1-2 per day, 4:25am and 10:15pm, 7½hr., Rs126); **Calcutta** (2 and 11:40pm, 23hr., Rs300); **Delhi** (daily, 5 and 5:40pm, 23hr., Rs259); **Jalgaon** (5 per day, 4:45-9:45am and 3:20-11pm, 11hr., Rs190) for Ajanta; **Patna** (1-3 per day, 4pm-1am, 16hr., Rs289); **Satna** (frequent, 3hr., Rs60) for Khajuraho; **Umaria,** for Bandhavgarh N.P. (*Narmada Exp.* 8233, 6:20am, 1hr., Rs31); **Varanasi** (2-4 per day, 10am-5pm and 10pm-1:30am, 10hr., Rs182/1st class 546).

Buses: The chaotic **bus stand** has both public (MPSRTC) and private sections. To: **Bhopal** (every 30min., 5:30am-midnight, 9hr., Rs130); **Kanha National Park** (2 per day, 7 and 11am, 7hr., Rs50); **Khajuraho** (8:30pm, 10hr., Rs68). For Khajuraho, it is much quicker and easier to take the train to Satna first. For **Bandhavgarh,** take the train to **Umaria** and change to the Bandhavgarh bus there.

✴❓ ORIENTATION AND PRACTICAL INFORMATION

Collectorate Rd. curves north from behind the **railway station,** past the hospital and Gothic High Court to the **clock tower,** which marks the beginning of the **bazaar area.** Russel Chowk, the center of town, where the accommodations and bus stands are, is 200m to the left through the bazaar streets. **Station Rd.** is south of the station.

Local Transportation: Tempos run from the museum to the White Rocks for Rs10.

Tourist Office: MPTDC (☎ 322111), inside the railway station, makes reservations for MPTDC facilities at Kanha and Bandhavgarh. In season (Dec.-Mar.) bookings for accommodations in parks should be made at least 72hr. in advance from this or any other MPTDC office; full payment required. Open M-Sa 6am-8pm.

Currency Exchange: State Bank of India (☎ 322259), opposite Hotel Rishi Regency, near the railway underpass. Open M-F 10:30am-2:30pm.

Police: Collectorate Rd., Civil Lines (☎ 320352), in front of the clock tower.

Hospital: Medical College, Nagpur Rd. (☎ 322117), 8km south of the bus stand, has a 24hr. **pharmacy.**

Telephones: 24hr. **STD/ISD** booth at the railway station.

Internet: Honey's Cyber World, opposite Hotel Shivalaya on Russel Chowk. Rs50 per hr. Open 10am-10pm.

Post Office: GPO, Residency Rd. From the station, turn left on Station Rd. and then right on the next main road. The GPO is 500m down on the left. Open M-Sa 10am-6pm. **Postal Code:** 482002.

ACCOMMODATIONS AND FOOD

Most hotels are around Russel Chowk. Many have 24-hour check-out and slap on a 15-20% tax on top of already exorbitant charges for their miserable rooms.

Hotel Natraj (☎310931), near Karamchand Chowk. Heading north (away from Russel Chowk), cross the Navdra Bridge and then take the right fork. Turn left at the "Ask not what your country" quote; it's on the left, opposite the Indian Coffee House. Best budget place, but hopelessly booked most of the time. Rooms with attached baths have TV, air-cooling, and hand-held showers. Singles Rs58-80; doubles Rs115-145.

Lodge Shivalaya (☎325188), opposite Jyoti Cinema on Russel Chowk. Clean rooms with attached bath and color TV lead to enormous balconies overlooking the center of town. Singles Rs90-110; doubles Rs150-175.

Hotel President (☎401073), on Russel Chowk, employs a small army of uniformed waiters to deliver morning tea to a vast range of air-cooled rooms with TV and hot water. Singles Rs200-600; doubles Rs230-700.

Indian Coffee House, Malaviya Marg, near Karamchand Chowk, opposite Hotel Natraj. The mother ship of everybody's favorite chain. Sky-high ceilings, rock-solid tables, wicker chairs, and vintage advertisements make this a classic. *Dosas, utthapams* (Rs13), and other snacks. Great unsweetened coffee Rs4. Open daily 7am-9:30pm.

Hotel Republic Bar, just over Navdra Bridge, on the right. Rows of tall, straight-backed chairs and the no-nonsense Sikh owner behind the bar give the Republic a wild west feel. Butter chicken (Rs70) is their speciality. They also serve veg. dishes (from Rs15) and a full range of booze. Open daily 10am-11:30pm.

SIGHTS

On the road from Russel Chowk to the bus stand is a small **museum,** which contains temple sculpture from the region. *(Open Tu-Su 10am-5pm. Free.)* The star attraction in all MPTDC brochures are the **Marble Rocks,** 15km away from Jabalpur, which is where the Narmada River passes through a spectacular white-cliffed gorge and then drops 100 feet down a huge waterfall. The Marble Rocks are fully illuminated at night to maximize tourist viewing hours. Day and night, rowboats bob up and down in the river, allowing you to have an unadulterated view of the cliffs. *(Tempos go to Marble Rocks from in front of the museum for Rs100. Rowboats Rs10.)* On the way to the Rocks is the old grand fortress of **Madan Mahal,** testimony to Jabalpur's status as capital of the Gond kingdom from the 12th century on.

PROJECT TIGER Faced with a shocking drop in the tiger population caused by India's industrialization and continued hunting, Indira Gandhi inaugurated a drastic initiative to save tigers in 1973. **Project Tiger** set aside nine areas of tiger territory as national parks and hired a staff of armed guards to patrol the areas and thwart poachers. The plan was initially successful, and the tiger population grew from just a few hundred to several thousand. Ten more national parks were eventually set aside. Lately, however, poaching has increased as the forces protecting the sanctuaries have become less formidable. Tiger products—some believed to have healing and aphrodisiacal properties—fetch incredibly high prices on domestic and international markets. The tiger remains an endangered species and some fear it could soon face extinction again. The best places in India to catch a glimpse of the beasts are **Corbett** (see p. 150) and **Kanha National Park** (see following).

KANHA NATIONAL PARK

Beautiful Kanha and the animals that live here have had an up-and-down history. The same Brits who cantered across the continent with their rifles, driving game to the brink of extinction, also set aside Kanha as a hunting preserve, saving it from the encroachment of the local population. Kanha became a wildlife reserve in 1933, and the result of these preservation efforts is nearly 2000 sq. km of untainted jungle that served as the setting for Rudyard Kipling's *Jungle Book* and other stories. With 114 tigers in the park, sightings are frequent, and the number of tigers only keeps increasing (though not too quickly, as the males display a predilection to eat their own children). Once a tiger is spotted, it is held at bay by elephants until everyone in the area gets a look. Besides the well-fed tigers, you can also see their friends and their food: leopards, deer, sambar, wild boar, bears, pythons, porcupines, and over 300 species of birds. Your chances of seeing a tiger here are better than anywhere in India.

The park is open sunrise to sunset November 1-June 30; it closes down during the monsoon. Peak season is March to April. There is a one-time permit fee (Rs200) plus a camera fee (Rs25 for still 35mm), payable at Kisli and Mukki gates.

◪ GETTING TO THE PARK. The park has two main gates, one at **Kisli**, in the northwest, and another at **Mukki**, on the west side. **Buses** depart from Jabalpur to Kisli (7 and 11am, 6hr., Rs67), stopping on the way at Khatia gate near the **Visitor Centre,** where most non-MPTDC accommodations and food can be found. The daily bus from Jabalpur to Mukki no longer runs; ask in Jabalpur for most recent details. Beyond the Khatia Gate Visitor Centre, it is necessary to take a **jeep** (Rs10 per km); walking is out of the question as it's 4km from the Khatia to Kisli.

▛▟ LODGES AND FOOD. Two MPTDC-run accommodations exist in and around the park. The **Baghira Log Huts,** in the park, have posh singles for Rs590 and doubles with private baths for Rs690; the **Tourist Hostel** in Kisli offers dorm beds for an exorbitant Rs250 and also contains a depressing canteen with bland snacks. For information or reservations, contact one of the MPTDC offices in major Madhya Pradesh cities or in Bombay, Delhi, and Calcutta; the head office is in Bhopal (☎ (0755) 764397). It's a good idea to book MPTDC hotel rooms in advance during the in-season. The MPTDC requires prepayment in full for their accommodations, leaving last-minute visitors at a loss. Risk-takers will delight in the range of budget accommodations at nearby **Khatia,** most of which double as restaurants (*thalis* Rs25-30) and jeep stops. **◪Van Vihar,** 400m from the road, on the right as you walk away from the gate, has simple doubles with bucket showers. Surrounded by thatched huts and jungle, Van Vihar's village atmosphere and delicious home-cooked food have conspired to make many stay here much longer than they ever planned. (Rs50 per person; Feb.-Mar. Rs40.) Scattered around the woods by the gate are the huts of the forest department **Jungle Camp,** which has doubles with attached baths (and running water!) for Rs100 and an impersonal central dining hall. On the road near the gate is **Motel Chandan,** with its passable doubles and one "economy" room; prices fall dramatically off season and whenever else demand is low. (☎ 77220 or 77233. Doubles Rs300-600; economy Rs200.) The only **STD/ISD** booth in Khatia operates from here (open 8am-10pm). New tea stalls sprout up along the road like mushrooms after a thunder storm, allowing you to ignore more institutional options like the restaurant in Baghira, whose choices are at least better than the canteen (Rs50-100).

◪ OUT IN THE JUNGLE. Although you might catch one of the nightly man-eater films (7pm in English, at the Khatia Gate Visitor Centre) or take the somewhat disorienting 1.5km **jungle walk** from Khatia gate, you're really here to see the law of the jungle at work. Jeep trips, the only way to go, run through Sher Jahan-land for around Rs400-600 plus nominal sundry fees (Rs200 per trip), which can be split between a maximum of six passengers. Consult the manager of your hotel for a berth. Trips run in the morning (6am, 4-5hr.) and afternoon (around 3pm, 2-3hr.). The morning trip, which makes a breakfast stop (fritters and *chai* Rs9) in Kanha village at the heart of the park, is usually a better time for sightings. If there are tigers about, your jeep will take you to an **elephant** (an outrageous Rs300 for a 10min. ride) for closer, more silent viewing. Bring warm clothing and a blanket in winter, as the mornings are very cold and the evening chill sets in quickly.

BANDHAVGARH NATIONAL PARK

Although it tends to get overshadowed by the nearby Kanha Park, the small Bandhavgarh (170km northeast of Jabalpur) has the highest-density tiger population anywhere India. In 1952 the last white tiger in India was sighted here. Given its easier accessibility from places like Varanasi and Khajuraho, the park has been attracting an ever-larger number of tiger-seekers in recent years. The park is made up of two distinct habitats: one of jungle and one of sandy desert hills dotted with the ancient ruins of the maharajas of Rewa.

To reach the park from Jabalpur, take a train to **Umaria** (6:20am, 4½hr., Rs60) and then a connecting bus (1hr., Rs15). If you are coming from the north, you can catch the train to Umaria from **Katni Junction,** 18km south of Satna. The bus returns to Umaria at 3pm, in time to catch the 5:30pm train to Katni and Jabalpur. **Jeeps** depart at sunrise and three hours before sunset for 3-4 hour tours of the park (Rs400). When a tiger is spotted everybody leaps from the jeep and climbs on top of elephants (Rs300 a ride), which will take you within a safe shooting (by camera, that is) range. Pay the relevant fees beforehand at the park office: Rs200 per person per day; Rs100 vehicle fee; Rs80 guide fee. Accommodations are available close to the park entrance at the **Gitamjali Guest House** (doubles Rs150-200). MPTDC operates the overpriced **White Tiger Forest Lodge,** which must be booked and paid for several days (or, even better, years) in advance.

KHAJURAHO खजुराहो   ☎07686

The once-forgotten village of Khajuraho, stuck in the middle of nowhere in northern Madhya Pradesh, has become one of the most visited places in India, thanks to the remarkable erotic sculptures that adorn the walls of its temples. This dusty hamlet might not look like the kind of place that would inspire such uninhibited displays of passion, but nowhere else in India are so many couples shown so prominently copulating in every position imaginable. Each explicit detail is meticulously rendered in the sandstone facades, leaving nothing to the imagination but the question of what might have inspired it all in the first place. Surrounding the main temple area, the unavoidable souvenir stands are full of pocket paperback editions of the Kama Sutra translated into all of the world's major languages, and late-night conversation in the town's restaurants and cafes seems to focus on the advisability—and the possibility—of some of the things depicted here. But there is a lot more to Khajuraho's temples than a few exquisitely executed sex scenes. For all the attention they are given, the scenes represent only a small part of the cultural insight offered by these holy sites. From war to love, from joy to sorrow, the carvings cover the breadth of human experience.

▐ GETTING THERE AND GETTING AROUND

Flights: Khajuraho Civil Aerodrome, 6km south of the Western Group. **Indian Airlines,** Main Rd. (☎44035, airport office 44036), next door to the Clarks Bundela Hotel. Open daily 10am-1:15pm and 2-5pm. To: **Agra** (M, W, F, and Su; 45min.; US$80); **Delhi** (M, W, F, and Su; 1½hr.; US$100); **Varanasi** (M, W, F, and Su; 45min.; US$80). Advance reservations are essential year-round.

Buses: Buses are the only ground transport to Khajuraho. The station posts English schedules and has frequent departures for the nearest railheads at Satna, Mahoba, and Jhansi. To: **Agra** (9am and 4pm, 12hr., Rs170); **Bhopal** (6 and 7:15pm, 12hr., Rs180); **Gwalior** (9, 11:15am, and 4pm; 6hr.; Rs120); **Jabalpur** (6am, 12hr., Rs130); **Jhansi** (7 per day, 5:30am-4:30pm, 4-5hr., Rs75-85); **Mahoba** (every 45min., 7:30am-4:30pm, 3hr., Rs35) for trains to **Varanasi; Satna** (4 per day, 9:30am-4pm, 3½hr., Rs50) for trains to **Varanasi.** There is one direct bus to **Varanasi** (4pm, Rs175). **MPTC** runs a "luxury" coach that coordinates with the Shatabdi Exp., leaving Khajuraho at 4pm and continuing to Gwalior (Rs120). The last buses to Khajuraho leave Satna at 3:30pm, Jhansi at 1:15pm, and Mahoba at 5pm.

Local Transportation: Bicycles, the most practical mode of transport, can be rented at hotels or stands in the square for Rs15-30 per day. The few **auto-rickshaws** are overpriced. A **cycle-rickshaw** trip should cost between Rs5-10. It is a 20-25min. walk from the Western to the Eastern Group.

✈ 🅿 ORIENTATION AND PRACTICAL INFORMATION

You would have to try very hard to get lost in Khajuraho. There is only one main road, which leads up from the airport in the south to the **Western Group** (the main temple complex) and the mess of hotels, restaurants, and postcard shops that comprise the "new village." **Jain Temple Rd.** leads east from here to the **Eastern Group** (the second main group of temples) and then to the old village. The bus stand is on **Link Rd. Number Two,** South of Jain Temple Rd., a 10-minute walk from the main group of temples.

Tourist Office: Main Rd. (☎42347), opposite the Western Group. Open M-F 9:30am-6pm, Sa 9am-1pm.

Currency Exchange: State Bank of India, Main Rd. (☎42373), opposite the Western Group, cashes traveler's checks and changes many currencies. Open M-F 10:30am-2:30pm and 3-4pm, Sa 10:30am-1pm.

Police: (☎44032), in the booth opposite the Western Group. Also by the bus stand.

Hospital: The government-run **Community Health Centre** is on Link Rd. 2, after the police station. Open daily 8am-1pm and 5-6pm. Dr. R.K. Khare (☎44177, residence 42374) is recommended by local luxury hotels. His **clinic** is in the strip mall beside the bus station. Open M-Sa 10am-2pm and 6-9pm. There is a **24hr. pharmacy** (☎44453) to the right of Dr. Khare's clinic.

Post Office: Opposite the bus stand. Open M-Sa 9am-5pm. **Postal Code:** 471606.

▐ ACCOMMODATIONS

Prices are highly variable between seasons. There is a mini-boom during July and August, but rates drop off between April and June. The in-season runs from November to March, when most hotel owners drastically inflate their prices; it is common for a Rs50 room to go for Rs200, leaving budget travelers with no option but to fork over the money. Bargaining can sometimes bring prices within a reasonable range. Book in advance at peak times.

▨ **Yogi Lodge,** Main Sq. (☎44158), down an alley by the Terazza restaurant, on the left side of the square as you face away from the Western Group. Simple, clean rooms have baths with hot water. Air-cooling available. The owner runs another hotel, the **International Yogi Guest House,** 2km north of town on the main road, where he gives free meditation lessons daily at 7:30am. Prices for rooms are the same as the Yogi Lodge, and the house includes a kitchen, library, and fruit tree-filled garden for guest use. Inquire at the Yogi Lodge for details. Singles Rs50-70; doubles Rs80-120.

▨ **Marble Palace Hotel,** Jain Temple Rd. (☎44353), 50m before the Ristorante Mediterraneo. Designed by a Japanese architect; marble floors, tables, and sinks, sleek black beds, and maharaja-worthy arched doorways. The Marble Palace earns its name with class. Sheets changed daily. All rooms come with bathtubs. Singles Rs350; doubles Rs450-650. 20% off-season discount.

Hotel Surya, Jain Temple Rd. (☎44145), opposite Ristorante Mediterraneo. Spacious, spotless rooms, some with balconies overlooking the green lawn. Singles Rs200-350; doubles Rs250–550. May 1-July 15: 30-40% discount.

Hotel Casa Di William, Prem Sagar Lake Rd. (☎44244), on the 1st road that turns right after the Western Group. Clean rooms with tasteful furniture, writing desk, and bedside reading lamp. The three-leveled terrace offers 360° views of Khajuraho. 15% *Let's Go* discount; 25% off-season discount. Singles Rs300-500; doubles Rs400-600.

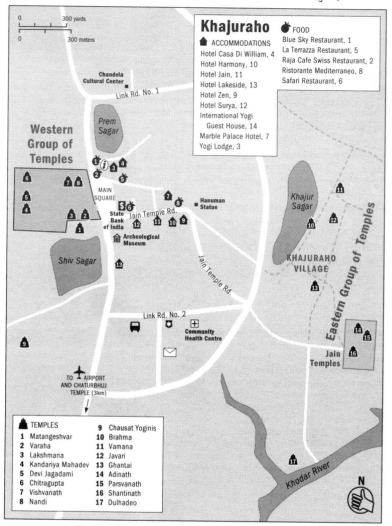

Khajuraho

🏠 ACCOMMODATIONS
Hotel Casa Di William, 4
Hotel Harmony, 10
Hotel Jain, 11
Hotel Lakeside, 13
Hotel Zen, 9
Hotel Surya, 12
International Yogi
   Guest House, 14
Marble Palace Hotel, 7
Yogi Lodge, 3

🍎 FOOD
Blue Sky Restaurant, 1
La Terrazza Restaurant, 5
Raja Cafe Swiss Restaurant, 2
Ristorante Mediterraneo, 8
Safari Restaurant, 6

Western Group of Temples

Chandela Cultural Center

Link Rd. No. 1

Prem Sagar

MAIN SQUARE

State Bank of India

Jain Temple Rd.

Hanuman Statue

Khajur Sagar

Archeological Museum

Shiv Sagar

Link Rd. No. 2

Community Health Centre

TO AIRPORT AND CHATURBHUJ TEMPLE (3km)

KHAJURAHO VILLAGE

Eastern Group of Temples

Jain Temples

Khodar River

N

🔺 TEMPLES
1 Matangeshvar
2 Varaha
3 Lakshmana
4 Kandariya Mahadev
5 Devi Jagadami
6 Chitragupta
7 Vishvanath
8 Nandi
9 Chausat Yoginis
10 Brahma
11 Vamana
12 Javari
13 Ghantai
14 Adinath
15 Parsvanath
16 Shantinath
17 Dulhadeo

Hotel Jain, Jain Temple Rd. (☎42352), next to Hotel Surya. Cheap, clean, friendly— what more do you want? Rooms with attached baths around a central courtyard. Dorm beds Rs30; singles from Rs60; doubles from Rs80.

Hotel Zen, Jain Temple Rd. (☎44228), farther down the road on the right-hand side from the Hotel Surya. A classy new place with well-furnished rooms, slippery pitter-pat marble floors, and a "zen" garden. Most rooms have a garden view. Off-season: doubles Rs100-200. In season, expect to pay at least double.

Hotel Harmony, Jain Temple Rd. (☎44135). Air-cooled rooms with wooden furnishings and attached baths. Pleasant garden open Apr. 1-June 30. Singles Rs200-650; doubles Rs250-750. Off-season: singles from Rs150; doubles from Rs200.

Hotel Lakeside, Main Rd. (☎44120), opposite Shiv Sagar Lake, next door to the museum. Popular budget place with good rooftop views of the lake and temples. In-season (July-Apr.): dorm beds Rs40; singles Rs150-500; doubles Rs250-700. Prices may be lower during the off-season depending on demand.

FOOD

Ristorante Mediterraneo, Jain Temple Rd., 200m from Main Rd., on the left, opposite Hotel Surya. 1000km from the nearest source of mozzarella, the Mediterraneo beats the odds. An Italian chef serves up pizza, pasta, and wine-sized bottles of well-chilled beer, to a European crowd that chatters the night away on the rooftop terrace. Spaghetti Arrabbiata Rs50; pizzas from Rs125; crepes Rs35-70. Open daily 7:30am-10pm.

Raja Cafe Swiss Restaurant, Main Rd., in a shaded courtyard directly opposite the Western Group. Run by a gregarious Swiss woman, the cafe dishes out full breakfasts (Rs80), Chinese food (Rs40-65), veg. au gratin (Rs60), and delicious semolina pudding (Rs25). Open daily 8am-10pm.

Blue Sky Restaurant, Main Rd., after the tourist office. The restaurant's two-story terrace offers some of the best views of the Western Group temples. Chef cooks a wide range of tasty Indian, continental and Japanese dishes. Spinach soups Rs25; cabbage roll *kofta* Rs50; ramen and vegetables Rs35. Open daily 8am-10:30pm.

La Terrazza Restaurant, just opposite the Western Group, on the left of the square at the corner that turns off toward Yogi Lodge. Another good rooftop place with views of the temples and terraces beyond. Menu includes usual breakfast items, *thalis* (Rs40), mutton *masala* (Rs60), and a selection of Chinese dishes (Rs50). Open daily 10am-10pm.

Safari Restaurant, Jain Temple Rd., on the left, 20m from the intersection with the main road. Street-level, open-air place offering no-nonsense breakfasts (omelettes Rs60) and standard Indian, Chinese, and continental food (Rs40-80). Open daily 7am-10pm.

SIGHTS

Construction of the temples at Khajuraho, which took place between 900 AD and 1100, was sponsored by the reigning Chandela dynasty, a Rajput clan claiming to be descended from the moon god. When Chandela power waned, the temples were forgotten and lay hidden deep in the jungle for 700 years before the outside world—in the form of the British officer T.S. Burt—stumbled across them in 1838 (see **Sex in Khajuraho,** p. 373). Of an original 85 temples, only 25 still stand today.

The morning is the coolest and quietest time to tour Khajuraho's temples. Since almost all the temples face east, the early light reveals sculptures and relief detail hard to see later on. Khajuraho's temples are conventionally divided into three groups; the Western Group contains the most famous and impressive of the temples, although all of them are stunning. For the biggest event in Khajuraho, the annual **Festival of Dance** in early March, the government flies in India's best classical dancers to perform in front of the temples.

THE WESTERN GROUP
Open sunrise-sunset. Rs5. Audio guide Rs50.

The Western Group of temples, in a grassy, fenced-in compound maintained by the Archaeological Survey of India, contains many of the best examples of Khajuraho's magnificent architecture. The custom of *pradakshina* dictates that you walk around the whole group clockwise and circle each temple the same way.

LAKSHMI AND VARAHA TEMPLES. The first stop on your *pradakshina* is the least impressive: the **Lakshmi Temple,** a small shrine that 19th-century repairs left with a jagged cement roof. Next door, the open-air, 10th-century **Varaha Mandap,** built for Vishnu's avatar as a boar, offers a more promising beginning. The huge sandstone boar is so well polished that it shines like glazed porcelain, and it is covered with hundreds of tiny gods and goddesses, including those of the sacred rivers Ganga, Yamuna, and Saraswati.

LAKSHMANA TEMPLE. Dating from around 941 AD, the magnificent Lakshmana Temple, across from the Lakshmi and Varaha temples, is one of the largest, oldest, and best-wrought in Khajuraho. A frieze depicting a military procession winds

SEX IN KHAJURAHO

The sculptor had at times allowed his subject to grow rather warmer than there was any absolute necessity for his doing; indeed, some of the sculptures here were extremely indecent and offensive.
  —T. S. Burt, describing Khajuraho, 1838

Ever since it was discovered by an itinerant Victorian officer, art historians and religious scholars have been trying to figure out why so much sex has been carved onto the walls of Khajuraho's temples. Some have suggested that the sculptures were used for sex education, while others maintain that they were offerings to the gods, especially Indra, the lord of lightning, who had to be entertained lest he destroy the temples. A more plausible theory argues that tantric cults used the temples for ritualized sex. Some Hindus read the sculpture as part of the wedding myth of Shiva and Parvati. The posing women, caught admiring themselves in the mirror, have stopped to watch the wedding procession. All the other gods are here as guests. Eventually, of course, the wedding is consummated—in a great lovemaking session that lasts 1000 god-years.

around the base of the temple; elephants, horses, and soldiers march together in riotous disorder. Here and there the carving is of scenes more reminiscent of an orgy than a goose-stepping drum-banging parade. The temple itself has four halls, which lead up to its *shikhara*, and secondary shrines at the four corners of its platform. A band of hulking elephants in the stonework supports the temple; higher up are several of the erotic scenes that put Khajuraho on the map and which continue to elicit giggles and blushes from visitors.

KANDARIYA MAHADEV TEMPLE. Straight ahead at the far end of the park, three temples stand together on the same platform. Built between 1025 and 1050 and dedicated to Shiva, the Kandariya Mahadev Temple, on the left, is the tallest temple in Khajuraho. It is also outstanding for the quality and variety of its sculpture. A waterfall of cascading rock pours down from the temple roof and over the perforated honeycomb stone to the lower walls, which are endlessly indented, projected, articulated, refracted, and retracted to create an intricate 3-D effect. A sex scene on the southern walls delights gaggles of gawkers, but the famous erotic scenes are really just one part of a wide variety of superlative sculpture here. A recent chemical treatment to remove the black mold that mars some other temples has enhanced the intricacy of the Kandariya Temple's adornments.

MAHADEV SHRINE AND DEVI JAGADAMI TEMPLE. On the same platform, next to the Kandariya Temple, is the **Mahadev Shrine,** which contains sculpture showing a human figure grappling with a lion. It has no religious significance; the scene is thought to be a Chandela symbol. The same pair of figures can be found all over Khajuraho. On the other side of the Mahadev Shrine is the **Devi Jagadami Temple.** Though smaller than the Lakshmana and Kandariya temples, it has some superb sculptures, most notably its directional guardians, who are stationed between boldly flirting women and delicate sensual scenes. The image inside is of Kali, but images of Vishnu cover the inside and outside walls.

CHITRAGUPTA TEMPLE. The overall shape of the Chitragupta Temple, Khajuraho's only temple to Surya (the sun god), is identical to that of Jagadami. Small processions run around the lower portion of the temple wall; higher up are many amorous couples. The damaged wall and roof were repaired with concrete. Most of the statues inside the temple have been decapitated, but the main image of Surya, driving his chariot across the sky, is missing only the arms.

VISHVANATH TEMPLE. Continuing around the circuit, you next come to the small and damaged **Parvati Temple,** but it is overshadowed by the more spectacular Vishvanath Temple next to it, a large Shiva temple dated to 1002 from an inscription inside. Notice the elephant guardians as you approach the stairs to the temple—

the mahout on the right side seems to have fallen asleep. The bawdy sculptures on the Vishvanath Temple are some of the best: depicted are whole scenes in which the couples' attendants also get caught up in the action. There are some fascinating sculptures of posing women here—look for the one on the south side twisting her hair to dry and the one on the ceiling inside holding a tiny baby. Some of the figures are sculpted in astonishing detail, down to the cuticles of their fingernails. The Vishvanath Temple originally had a shrine at each corner of its foundation, as the Lakshmana Temple does, but only two remain. In front of the temple is the **Nandi Mandap,** an open shrine where Shiva's bull, Nandi, gazes into the temple.

MATANGESHVAR TEMPLE. The two members of the Western Group that stray outside the fence are older and noticeably different from the others. Just over the fence from the Lakshmana Temple is the Matangeshvar Temple. Built around 900 AD, it is the only temple in the compound that's still in use—more people come here to worship than to view the architecture. It is a relatively plain temple with only thin stripes of carving. Inside, a *linga* sits on top of a huge stone platform. The temple's upper-level terrace has good views of the Lakshmana Temple.

CHAUSAT YOGINIS. Along the south side of **Shiv Sagar,** a lake bordered by the main road, a narrow, tree-lined path leads to the right and out to the temple of Chausat Yoginis ("Sixty-Four Goddesses"). The oldest temple in Khajuraho (built during the 9th century) is made of crudely cut blocks of granite piled together like sandbags. Scarcely more than a large stone platform, the top is ringed by a gallery of empty shrines—only 35 of the original 64 remain.

ARCHAEOLOGICAL MUSEUM. Across the street from the Western Group enclosure, the Archaeological Museum houses sculptures separated from their temples. A wonderful Ganesh dances in the entrance hall. In the center of the Miscellaneous Gallery on the right, a king and queen sit together making an offering; possibly a portrait of the sculptor's Chandela patrons. Also note the unfinished couple whose noses have been left stuck together, making them look like a pair of kissing Pinocchios. There are few pieces here to compare with the best sculpture still on the temples—the museum's main virtue is that it offers close-up views of sculptures otherwise hidden high up on the temple walls. *(Open Sa-Th 10am-5pm. Rs5.)*

EASTERN AND SOUTHERN GROUPS

Open sunrise-sunset.

Scattered in and about Khajuraho village, the temples of the Eastern Group are not as stunning as those in the Western Group. But since they are visited by fewer people, they have an atmosphere of relative quiet.and seclusion often missing from the temples of the main group. The so-called Southern Group comprises two temples farther apart from one another than from either of the other two groups.

EASTERN GROUP. Along Jain Temple Rd. is a **Hanuman Shrine** containing one of the oldest sculptures in Khajuraho, a large *sindur*-smeared Hanuman image that dates from the 9th century. Crossing the bypass road and entering Khajuraho village, the path veers to the left along the side of a seasonal pond called the **Khajur Sagar.** Not far along it on the left is the small **Brahma Temple,** misnamed by 19th-century art historians. A four-faced Shiva *linga* sits in the sanctuary, and Vishnu is carved on the lintel above the door. The **Vamana Temple,** at the end of this lakeside path, is as large as some of the temples in the Western Group. Simpler in design, it has slightly less impressive sculpture and decoration. Note the elephants, standing on little platforms of their own at the roof's corners, that seem ready to set off into the countryside surrounding the temple.

Down a path just south of the Vamana temple is the **Javari Temple,** which features a number of interesting pieces despite its small size and relatively simple design. The women dancing around the temple walls manage to look remarkably life-like and sprightly though most of them had their heads knocked off centuries ago. A section of the Eastern Group consists of several Jain temples walled into a Jain monastery complex on the far side of Khajuraho village. *(Entrance Rs2.)* The old temples here are interspersed with newer ones. This mixture is embodied in the **Shantinath Temple,** which was built recently but has heavy pillars and doorways taken from older temples. Inside the temple is a collection of photographs, posters of Jain pilgrimage sites, and plenty of sculptures and paintings of naked monks.

To the left of the Shantinath Temple is the best of the Jain temples, the **Parsvanath Temple.** It is notable for its simple design—there are no balconies—and the small shrine at the back. In addition to Jain *tirthankaras* (saints), the sculptures on the outside depict just about every major Hindu deity, so it is thought that this was once a Hindu temple. Some of the most famous sculptures in Khajuraho are here, including one of a woman putting on ankle-bells and another of a woman applying her make-up. On the other side of a big mango tree, the **Adinath Temple,** whose porch has been reconstructed in concrete, features supple women climbing up the walls. Shiny black *tirthankara* images sit inside both temples.

SOUTHERN GROUP. A paved road off to the right of Jain Temple Rd. (marked "Dhulade") leads to the **Dulhadeo Temple.** This temple dates from around 1100, by which time standards had started to slip in Khajuraho—the sculpture here is generally held to be inferior to that of the other temples. There are still plenty of interesting little scenes, though: numerous dragon-like mythical beasts and people shown going about their daily lives. At the southern end of the temple is a pair of dioramas showing first a man and then a woman unsuccessfully imitating one of the other sex-in-stone scenes so prevalent in Khajuraho. The *linga* inside the temple is overlaid with dozens of tiny replicas of itself, giving it a curiously scaly appearance. The *mahamandapam,* a hall with a great rotunda ceiling, has an elaborate star shape. By the time this temple was built, sculptors were getting so carried away with the ornaments and jewelry on their human figures that the quality of the sculptures themselves had begun to decline.

Chaturbhuj Temple is 3km south of Khajuraho down the main road. It's a trip best made in the late afternoon, since Chaturbhuj is the only big temple in Khajuraho that faces west. The evening light shines warmly on its 2.7m *dakshinamurti* statue: one stone, three deities. This huge image is a combination of Shiva, Vishnu, and Krishna. The sculptures around the outside feature another interesting hybrid: on the south side, an image of Ardhanarishvara (half-Shiva, half-Parvati) is split down the middle, illustrating the motif of male and female union that was so significant to those who produced the marvelous sculptures at Khajuraho. Chaturbhuj is the only temple at Khajuraho that does not contain any erotic sculptures.

JHANSI झांसी ☎ 0517

Jhansi is one of those places you only come to in order to get somewhere else. There are worse places than this in India, to be sure, but apart from those with a particular interest in dusty urban ugliness, most travelers would be well advised to take a good long look at the timetables before coming to Jhansi—this is not the kind of town you want to be stranded in. Jhansi draws tourists because of its proximity to Orchha and its function as a railhead for Khajuraho. Schedules may conspire to detain you here, in which case you can while away the hours in rapt contemplation of Maharani Lakshmi Bai's fort, the city's only attraction.

GETTING THERE AND GETTING AROUND. Buses for Khajuraho leave from the railway station (4 per day, 5:30-11am) and the bus stand (11:45am and 1:15pm, Rs75-85). Frequent Delhi-bound **trains** leave throughout the day, of which the fastest is the A/C *Shatabdi Exp.* 2001, which goes to: **Delhi** (5:55pm, 5hr., Rs565) via **Agra** (2hr., Rs295) and **Gwalior** (1hr., Rs200). Frequent trains also run to: **Bhopal** (*Shatabdi Exp.* 2002, 10:32am, 4hr., Rs480) and **Jabalpur** (*Mahakoshal Exp.* 1450, 11:05pm, 11hr., Rs107). **Tempos** for Orchha (Rs6) leave from the bus stand.

ORIENTATION AND PRACTICAL INFORMATION. Downtown Jhansi covers a 5km span from the **railway station** in the west to the **bus stand** in the east. About 1km north of the station, **Shivpuri Rd.** runs all the way across town. The **U.P. Tourism Main Office** is in the Hotel Veerangana on **Sipri Rd.** Take a left out of the railway station, go straight to Sipri Crossing, and take a right; the hotel is on the left. (☎441267. Open M-Sa 10am-5pm.) There is a **Madhya Pradesh Tourism** booth on platform #1 of the railway station. (☎442622. Open daily 10am-6pm.) The **State Bank of India,** at the center of town, near Elite Crossing, changes American Express traveler's checks. (☎443919. Open M-F 10am-4pm, Sa 10am-1pm.) The **GPO,** Sadarj Marg, Civil Lines, is across the street from the Jhansi Hotel. (Open M-Sa 10am-6pm.) The government **hospital** (☎440572) is on Manik Chowk, the market at the base of the fort. The **police station** is on the Main Rd. (☎440538). There's a 24-hour **STD/ISD** booth on platform #6 at the railway station. **Postal Code:** 284001.

█▟ ACCOMMODATIONS AND FOOD. Hotel Prakash, in Civil Lines, 1km from the railway station, is stretched out around a neglected lawn of grass and weeds. It offers somewhat dreary rooms with air-cooling and attached bathrooms. (☎448811. Singles Rs200-350; doubles Rs250-450.) **The Prakash Regency Guest House,** Sardari Lal Market, Civil Lines, north of the central road crossing, offers pleasant mid-range lodgings. The air-cooled rooms have wall-to-wall carpeting and twin beds. The Prakash Regency also boasts, wonder-of-all-wonders for a budget hotel, a clean, good-sized swimming pool. (☎330133. Singles Rs250-600; doubles Rs350-600.) **Hotel Veerangana,** run by U.P. Tourism, has clean dorms and large, clean rooms. (☎442402. Dorms Rs60; singles Rs200-300; doubles Rs275-375.) The downstairs restaurant has a small, dark, A/C bar. **Hotel Raj Palace,** next to the GPO, offers rooms with TVs and putting-green carpets. (☎470554. Singles Rs245-425; doubles Rs275-475.) The restaurant in the █Hotel Sita, Shivpuri Rd., serves first-rate food in a civilized and climate-controlled environment. (Open daily 6:30am-3pm and 7-11pm.) The Prakash Regency Guest House has a decent restaurant and bar called **Sagar,** where brave souls can sample *paneer pasendida* "stuffed with sultans" for Rs40. (Open daily 7:30am-11pm.) For a place with character as well as flavor, the restaurant in the colonial-era **Jhansi Hotel,** Sadar Marg, Civil Lines, is worth a visit. Stuffed animal heads hang from the walls, and the bar sees to the needs of the dress-for-dinner crowd. (Open daily 11am-3pm and 7-11pm.)

◙ SIGHTS. The **Jhansi Fort** has nothing much to recommend it apart from the views from its ramparts. The fort is dedicated to Maharani Lakshmi Bai; celebrated revolutionary, she joined the anti-British sepoys in the Mutiny of 1857. As the British recaptured the region, Jhansi was one of the last rebel holdouts. Dressed as a man, her guns blazing, the maharani rode out into battle to meet her demise 180km from Jhansi. Most of the fort itself is an empty and decrepit-looking home to bands of monkeys and bats, though the maze of archways, stairwells, turrets, and abandoned rooms can provide for some interesting exploration if you're stuck in Jhansi for few hours. Outside the fort, along the southern wall as you approach the main entrance, is a bizarre life-size model depicting a battle between heroic Indian freedom-fighters and their dastardly red-coat oppressors during the Mutiny of 1857. This stirring scene may quicken the pulse—"Who cannot remain unimpressed by this life-like picturisation?" asks a sign next to the diorama—but the nearby museum is sure to induce catatonia. *(Open July-Apr. 15 10:30am-4:30pm; Apr. 16-June 7:30am-12:30pm. Free.)*

ORCHHA ओरछा ☎07680

On a loop in the Betwa river, 16km from Jhansi, the wistful little town of Orchha sits in the shadows of an abandoned 17th-century city that rises out of the hills and trees, its crumbling towers still clinging to the rocky rubble. Raja Rudra Pratap Bundela chose Orchha as the capital of the Bundela kingdom in 1531. During its heyday in the 16th and 17th centuries, the Bundelas' fortunes grew as they continued to keep the Mughal Empire at bay. Raja Bir Singh Deo (r. 1605-27), the greatest Bundela king, befriended the emperor Jehangir and even had him to visit in 1606. Under Bir Singh Deo, the Bundelas controlled the whole region of Bundelkhand, which still bears their name. Later rulers were less successful at appeasing the Mughals, and once the emperor Shah Jahan attacked Orchha, the kingdom's long, slow decline was inevitable. Orchha was abandoned in 1783, when the onslaught of Mughal and Maratha attacks became too much for the city to withstand.

The Bundelas left a landscape filled with palaces and temples, and nothing but the forces of nature has disturbed them in two centuries since. Orchha, meaning "hidden," lives up to its name—when human rulers gave up the attempt to conceal the city from invaders, nature took up the challenge. The ruins are overgrown with trees and weeds, cracked walls are shrouded with vines, and empty palace court-yards echo to the screeching songs of squeaking bats.

ORIENTATION AND PRACTICAL INFORMATION

Tempos sputter to Orchha from Jhansi (Rs6) and from the intersection of **Orchha Rd.** with the highway running from Jhansi to Khajuraho, spitting out their passengers just south of the village's only **crossroads.** South past the bus and tempo stand is the pricey MPTDC Betwa Cottages complex, as well as some royal cenotaphs and the five-star Orchha Resort on the banks of the **Betwa River.** The right-hand (eastern) crossroad, heading up from the bus station, leads to the bridge that connects the main palace complex to the village. You'll first pass the **post office. Canara Bank** exchanges travelers checks. (☎52689. Open M-F 10:30am-2:30pm, Sa 10:30am-12:30pm.) Towering over the village are Orchha's best-preserved sights: the Jehangir Mahal and the Raj Mahal. From the crossroads to the left, on the way to Lakshminarayan Temple, are the MPTDC's Mansarovar Hotel, the Chaturbhuj and Ram Raja temples, and the Palki Mahal Hotel. Everything else is in Jhansi.

ACCOMMODATIONS AND FOOD

The MPTDC has converted an 18th-century palace in the middle of the ruins into the moderately priced **Sheesh Mahal Hotel** (☎52624), where only the most expensive suites are really palatial. The best rooms, decked out with rugs, carpets, and marble baths, have nooks and alcoves full of hookahs, tin drums, and TVs. Be prepared to shell out Rs2990 for the full maharaja treatment. (Singles with bath Rs490; doubles Rs590; suites with air-cooling Rs1990.) The hotel's **restaurant,** open to guests and non-guests, serves standard dishes, as well as breakfast and snacks (open daily 7am-11pm). Try to book at an MPTDC office up to a month in advance during busy times (email reservations to mail@mptourism.com). The local SADA runs two budget lodges, neither of which is anything special. **Palki Mahal,** buried inside the Phool Bagh Palace (next door to the Ram Raja Temple), combines dorm beds (Rs25) with history (don't be surprised if the manager is not around when you arrive) while the **Mansarovar,** by the crossroads, mixes threadbare sheets with tatty modernity (doubles Rs75). The **Shri Mahant Guest House,** next to the Mansarovar, has decent rooms with air-cooling and attached bath. (☎52715. Doubles Rs200-250.) There are plenty of *dhabas* in the market, but for anything more than a simple snack, you'll have to head down to the river. The **Orchha Resort's** shiny, A/C, all-veg. restaurant serves excellent meals for Rs85 and up. (Open daily 7am-9:30pm.) The **Betwa Cottages** restaurant is a bit cheaper. (Open daily 6am-11pm.)

SIGHTS: THE RUINS

All locations open 9am-5pm. Rs30 for a ticket that covers all the main sights, including the Lakshmi Temple and the chhattris. Walkman tour 2hr.; Rs50, Rs500 deposit.

The ruins of Orchha are scattered along a bend in the Betwa, and they spill across from the main "island" to the present-day village and beyond. Nothing much has happened in Orchha over the past 200 years to clear them away, and nothing of consequence has been built here since the Bundelas shut up shop and left the place to the winds. The old buildings still dominate the landscape, and abandoned palaces and temples stand undisturbed amid the grasses and trees. Slumping towers and overgrown archways are everywhere, most of them unnamed and unmarked. Hotel Sheesh Mahal offers a **walkman tour** that covers the three main palaces. This is well worth taking for the historical background, though you'll probably find your finger twitching over the fast-forward button from time to time as the breathless narrator launches into yet another dramatic "picture-the-scene" sequence. (If any of the ruins are closed and locked as you make the tour, a complaint at the ticket office can often prompt someone to find the keys to the gate.)

PALACES. The **Raj Mahal,** on the left side as you face the hotel (the Jehangir Mahal is on the right), was the king's residence, with a room for his private audiences and several chambers for his harem. One of the oldest buildings in Orchha, the palace lacks any notable ornamental features, though the walls and ceilings of many of the rooms are painted with intricate botanical patterns and murals depicting religious and mythical scenes. The top windows offer a good view of the town. The steps to the right of the Raj Mahal lead down to the **public audience hall,** after which the path veers down and to the right again through numerous unmarked ruins.

The next complete palace is the **Rai Praveen Mahal,** built and named for Raja Indramani's favorite dancing concubine. This palace was intended to be level with the treetops in the Anand Mahal gardens behind it. These can still be seen from the second floor, and, though neither the palace nor its gardens have exactly improved with age, it is still possible to imagine (as your audio-guide will constantly remind you) that this must once have been quite a nice place to kick back and relax after a long hard day spent wielding supreme executive power.

If you walk through the arch and head up the hill to the right (past the camel stables), you should be able to enter through the main door of the stunning **Jehangir Mahal** palace. Built for Emperor Jehangir when he visited Orchha in 1606, this palace surpasses anything else the Bundelas ever built in Orchha. Two elephants nod in welcome on both sides of the entrance, and inside, the Jehangir Mahal is filled with balconies, walkways, and railings. Traces of Islamic style can be seen in the stone screens and decorated domes. The views from the third-floor balconies are some of Orchha's best: the Betwa river curls through the countryside and into the village, winding its way past the ruins. Throughout the palace are fine carvings of peacocks, parrots, snakes, and other animals. There is also a tiny museum on the ground floor, whose most interesting piece is a tremendous metal pot.

TEMPLES. The north end of Orchha's island is reached by turning left after passing through the **Royal Gate,** then passing through another archway in a wall. This is a good place to fight back the thornbushes and explore—it's dotted with **old temples** that have been neglected, now surrounded by small wheat farms. People still dip into the ancient wells for their drinking water here, and, in some cases, the temples have become makeshift tool sheds, kitchens, and cow barns.

Back on the other side of the river, beyond the intersection with the main road, are several more minor palaces, as well as a number of important Bundela temples, the two most prominent of which share a connected history. The devout Raja Madhukar Shah had a dream in which Lord Rama appeared to him and ordered him to bring an image of the Lord to Orchha from Rama's holy hometown of Ayodhya. The king did as he was told, but arriving back in Orchha before his workmen had completed the temple designed to house the image, he decided to keep the holy image in his own palace until the temple could be completed. When the time came to relocate the image, though, Lord Rama refused to budge. The palace had to be given up, and it became the **Ram Raja Temple,** where Rama has been worshipped in his role as a king ever since. Painted pink and yellow and overlooking a cobbled square, Ram Raja is now a popular temple. (*Open daily 8am-12:30pm and 8-10:30pm.*) You'll have to leave your machine-gun and jackboots at home, though—no firearms or leather goods are allowed inside. The massive **Chhaturbhuj Temple** is defunct, left only with a great arching assembly hall and several large spires. Spiral staircases at each corner of the cross-shaped floorplan lead to high lookout points.

At the crest of a hill 1km west of town is the **Lakshmi Temple.** Its location seems fit for a fort, and the temple is built like one, with four high walls, turrets at the corners, and two mighty stone lions standing guard at the entrance. Inside the temple are the best paintings to be found anywhere in Orchha. Some of them date from as late as the 19th century, including one fabulous post-Mutiny scene of British soldiers swarming around an Indian fort. The lookout above the entrance offers a pleasant view of the temples and palaces. (*Open daily 10am-5pm.*)

Clustered along the peaceful, tree-lined banks of the Betwa river, just south of town and across from the Orchha Resort, is a series of box-like royal **chhattris** (cenotaphs). The Hindu Bundelas cremated their dead, but this did not stop them from borrowing the Mughal custom of mausoleum-building.

GWALIOR ग्वालियर   ☎ 0751

India is covered in ruins of one kind or another, but there are few anywhere that can rival those in Gwalior, the largest city in northern Madhya Pradesh. For centuries, Gwalior has been legendary for the massive fort that looks down upon the city from high above. Emperor Babur called the fort "the pearl amongst the fortresses of Hind," and generations of conquerors have gazed down on the world from here, from the Rajputs and Marathas to the Mughals and the British, to the Scindia family, who dominate local politics today. During the Raj, the Maharaja of Gwalior, in recognition of his loyalty during the Mutiny, earned one of only five 21-gun salutes granted to Indian potentates by the British. This stands in stark contrast to the fate of Maharani Lakshmi Bai, who resisted the British in such style from nearby Jhansi (see p. 375). The Scindia royal family is still the focus of Gwalior's civic pride: their palace, a 19th-century shrine to conspicuous consumption, offers a glimpse into a fairy-tale world of kitschy chaos and conforms to every stereotypical preconception of what a maharaja's house should look like.

▐ GETTING THERE AND GETTING AROUND

Flights: Bhind Rd. (☎470272), 10km northeast of the city. **Indian Airlines,** MLB Rd. (☎326872), opposite Shelter Hotel. Open M-Sa 10am-4:45pm. To: **Bhopal** (M and F, 2:45pm, 1hr., US$80); **Bombay** (M and F, 2:45pm, 3hr., US$160); **Delhi** (M and F, 1:15pm; Tu, Th, and Sa, noon; 45min.; US$70); **Indore** (M and F, 2:45pm, 2hr., US$105); **Jabalpur** (Tu, Th, and Sa; 8:25am; 1½hr.; US$130).

Trains: Railway Station, MLB Rd., Morar (☎341344). *Shatabdi Exp.* fares are for A/C chair-car; others are for sleeper class. To: **Agra** (several per day, 4am-2am, 2-3hr., Rs84); **Bhopal** (15-20 per day, 10:30am-2:30am, 6-8hr., Rs138; *Shatabdi Exp.* 2002, 9:15am, 4½hr., Rs545); **Bombay** (daily, 3:40, 10:30am, and 2:15pm; M and Sa 10:40pm; 21-24hr.; Rs300); **Delhi** (frequent, 3:45am-2am, 5½-7hr., Rs125; *Shatabdi Exp.* 2001, 7pm, 3½hr., Rs495); **Jhansi** (frequent, 3:45am-2am, 1½-2hr., Rs32); **Kanpur** (daily, 11:15am; also W, 4:15am; 7hr.; Rs125); **Lucknow** (daily, 11:15am; also W, 4:15pm; 9hr.; Rs140); and **Mathura** (frequent, 3:45am-1am, 3hr., Rs84).

Buses: State bus stand (☎340192), near the railway station, off MLB Rd. To: **Agra** (13 per day, 7:10am-7:30pm, 3hr., Rs55); **Bhopal** (7:30am and 8:45pm, 16hr., Rs187); **Delhi** (18 per day, 5am-9:30pm, 8hr., Rs139); **Jhansi** (every 30min., 3hr., Rs38); **Khajuraho** (7:25 and 8:30am, 8hr., Rs129). The **private bus stand** is in Lashkar, not far from Bada Chowk. From the railway station to Bada Square should cost about Rs20.

✱▐ ORIENTATION AND PRACTICAL INFORMATION

Gwalior is quite spread out, wrapped in an irregular "U" shape around the **fort.** The **Old Town,** containing the **railway station** and the **state bus stand,** lies to the east of the fort. The **Morar** area, dominated by the gaudy **palace,** is to the southeast, and the **Lashkar** area is in the southwest. Lashkar is the heart of modern Gwalior, with a bazaar area and **Bada (Jiyaji) Chowk,** where the GPO and State Bank of India are located. **Maharani Lakshmi Bai (MLB) Rd.** runs across town from the northeast, near the station, to Lashkar. Tuesday is Gwalior's **business holiday.**

Tourist Office: MPTDC (☎540777), platform #1 of the railway station. Open M-Sa 9am-8pm. The **main regional tourist office,** Gandhi Rd. (☎340370), is inside the Hotel Tansen. Open M-Sa 11am-5pm.

Currency Exchange: State Bank of India, Bada Chowk (☎336291). Changes traveler's checks and foreign currency. Open M-F 10:30am-4pm, Sa 10:30am-1:30pm.

Police: Jayendra Ganj (emergency ☎100).

Hospital: Royal Hospital, Kampoo (☎332711), near Roxy Cinema. Recommended private hospital, with doctors available 24hr. **Janak Hospital,** Jinsinala Number 3. With the Royal Hospital at your back, head left and then left again onto the next major road; Janak Hospital is 300m down on the right. **Pharmacy** open 24hr. **Kasturba Medical Stores,** 6 Kasturba Market (☎310953), is open 24hr.

Internet: Bhargava Computers, opposite the Miss Hill School, Lakshmi Bai Colony (☎428946). Turn through the eastern gate to the colony; the store is 100m down on the left. Web access Rs35 per hr.; after 5pm Rs25 per hr. Open daily 9:30am-9:30pm.

Post Office: GPO, Bada Chowk. Open M-Sa 8am-8pm, Su 10am-6pm. **Postal Code:** 474001.

ACCOMMODATIONS

In addition to the listings below, there are several acceptable budget hotels lining the market in front of the railway station. Most of these have 24-hour check-out. Many hotels charge 20% luxury tax in addition to the prices listed below.

Hotel Mayur, Paday (☎325559). Turn right out of the railway station and fly over the fly-over; turn back down the small service road to the right and look for the signs on the left. Check-out 24hr. Dorms Rs55; doubles Rs120-225.

Hotel Fort View, MLB Rd. (☎423409). One of a string of places along the main road in the shadow of the fort. Attached bar and restaurant. Good views of the fort from one side. Rooms all come with attached bath and TV. Check-out noon. Singles Rs250-375; doubles Rs300-425. Off-season: 10-15% discount.

Hotel Midway, MLB Rd. (☎424392), 2½km from the railway station, opposite the *gurud-wara*. A sterile complex with clean sheets and towels, satellite TVs, phones that work, hot water, and generator-powered email facilities. Clean, air-cooled rooms. Check-out noon. 10% discount for *Let's Go* readers. Singles Rs250; doubles Rs300-500.

Regal Hotel, Shinde Ki Chhawanii, MLB Rd. (☎334469). Another decent place facing the main road, with rooms for kings and queens of all shapes and sizes. Breezy garden terrace upstairs and airless beer bar downstairs. Check-out noon. Doubles Rs250-400.

Hotel Meghdoot, Padav (☎326148), next to the Indian Airlines office, just after the fly-over leading back to the railway station. Well-furnished rooms with wall-to-wall carpets and mural posters of tropical paradises that in no way resemble the chaotic street out front. Good location for rail access. Singles Rs200-250; doubles Rs250-350.

Hotel Surya, Jayendra Ganj, Lashkar (☎331183). Wood furniture, red carpet, color TVs, and balconies with views of the brick buildings next door. You can't ask for much more from a budget hotel in Gwalior. Singles Rs275-375; doubles Rs350-450.

FOOD

Volga Restaurant, Tayendra Ganj, inside Hotel Surya. The *malai-de-la-malai* of Gwalior society frequents this lair-like, chandeliered, A/C bastion of the *bourzhaozya*. Gentle lighting, soft music, and efficient service with a smile. All this and good food, too. Entrees around Rs50. Open daily 9am-11pm.

Indian Coffee House, Station Rd. In the strip of shops between the two exits of the railway station. Same old reliable veg. snacks as always. The old waiters-in-white-caps routine never fails. Just out of the fumy haze of Station Rd., it's a good place for a revitalizing cup of good coffee. Open daily 7am-10:30pm.

Kwality Restaurant, Deendayal Market, MLB Rd. Chalk up another one for the dim, non-descript, A/C chain with a spelling problem. Standard range of north Indian veg. (Rs28-50), chicken (Rs40-130), and mutton (Rs40) dishes. Open daily 10am-11pm.

Feeder's 2000 Restaurant, Gwalior Rd., on the left, just north of the intersection with MLB Rd. Welcomes everyone from young couples to parties of 20 or more. *Navratan* curry Rs38; veg. manchurian Rs50. Open daily 11am-11pm.

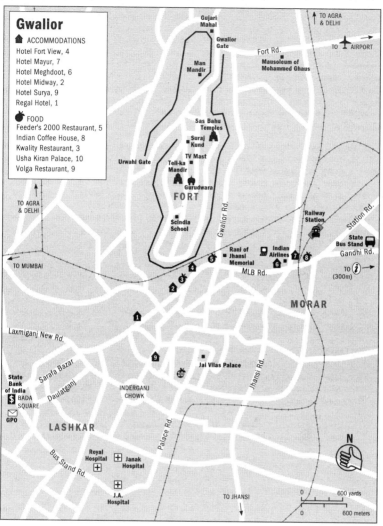

Gwalior

🏠 ACCOMMODATIONS
Hotel Fort View, 4
Hotel Mayur, 7
Hotel Meghdoot, 6
Hotel Midway, 2
Hotel Surya, 9
Regal Hotel, 1

🍎 FOOD
Feeder's 2000 Restaurant, 5
Indian Coffee House, 8
Kwality Restaurant, 3
Usha Kiran Palace, 10
Volga Restaurant, 9

(Map labels: Gujari Mahal, Gwalior Gate, Fort Rd., TO AGRA & DELHI, TO AIRPORT, Man Mandir, Mausoleum of Mohammed Ghaus, Sas Bahu Temples, Suraj Kund, Urwahi Gate, TV Mast, Teli-ka Mandir, Gurudwara, FORT, Scindia School, Gwalior Rd., Railway Station, Station Rd., TO AGRA & DELHI, TO MUMBAI, Rani of Jhansi Memorial, Indian Airlines, State Bus Stand, Gandhi Rd., MLB Rd., TO (i) (300m), MORAR, Laxmiganj New Rd., Sarafa Bazar, Daulatganj, Jai Vilas Palace, Jhansi Rd., INDERGANJ CHOWK, State Bank of India, BADA SQUARE, GPO, LASHKAR, Palace Rd., Bus Stand Rd., Royal Hospital, Janak Hospital, J.A. Hospital, TO JHANSI, N, 0 600 yards, 0 600 meters)

Usha Kiran Palace, Jayendraganj, Lashkar, next to the Jai Vilas Palace. This tasteful restaurant inside Gwalior's most beautiful hotel is the place to come if the luxury at nearby Jain Vilas palace has whetted your appetite for the finer things in life. *Haute cuisine* from around the world: everything from fish and chips (Rs200) to a pageful of "peony's favorites" (Rs100-200). Open daily 6am-midnight.

👁 SIGHTS

GWALIOR FORT

Open daily sunrise to sunset. Rs0.20. James Dean lookalikes admitted free of charge.

Gwalior's amazing fort, almost 3km long and at points 1km wide, dominates the city from 90m above, behind hulking 10m-high walls. It has been the center of the region's power for all of recorded history. According to legend, it was built during the first century AD by a king called Suraj, who was cured of leprosy here by a holy hermit named Gwalipa. Out of gratitude to his healer, Suraj named the fort Gwalior. Since then, the fort has been ruled by all of the region's succeeding dynasties: Rajputs, Delhi Sultans, Mughals, Marathas, and eventually the British. Since 1886, the fort has belonged to the Scindias, Gwalior's royal family. Through the ages, the fort has accumulated palaces and temples and, most recently, a prestigious boys' school, a TV relay station, and two post offices.

There are two entrances to the fort: **Gwalior Gate** on the northeast side, next to the Old Town, and **Urwahi Gate** on the southwest, which is approached through a long gorge. Both have long, steep ramps that must be climbed on foot, although cars and taxis (but not auto-rickshaws) can enter through Urwahi Gate. It's worth entering at Gwalior Gate for the view of the Man Mandir Palace's towers above.

THE PALACES. At the base of the hill just inside Gwalior Gate is the **Gujari Mahal Palace,** built by Man Singh Tomar for his favorite queen. Inside the palace courtyard is an **archaeological museum** with a melange of sculptures and paintings from the region. The curator keeps a miniature sculpture of the tree-goddess Gyraspur—a priceless piece of art history—under lock and key, but he might be coaxed into letting you see it. *(Museum open Sa-Th 10am-5pm. Rs2.)*

The northeastern ramp continues up through a series of archways past Jain and Hindu shrines. Looming overhead are the blue-splotched towers of the **Man Mandir Palace.** Inside the palace are many small rooms split by lattices carved into the shape of animals and dancers. These elaborate, perforated screens bear witness to the system of *purdah,* or veiling, that is customary among groups of Hindus and Muslims. Women would spend much of their time sitting behind these screens, peering through them at the world outside. A flashlight will show the way down to the bat-infested dungeon complex where, in the 17th century, the Mughal emperor Aurangzeb had his brother Murad chained up and slowly killed by starvation and intoxication, feeding him nothing but boiled and mashed-up poppies. Near the Man Mandir Palace is a **museum,** run by the Archaeological Survey of India. *(Open Sa-Th 10am-5pm. Rs2.)* On the other side of the Elephant Gate from the Man Mandir Palace are seats for the nightly **sound and light show.** *(Show at 7:30pm. Rs40.)*

To reach the north end of the fort, pass through the gate on your right as you exit the Man Mandir Palace. This area is a barren landscape where ruined palaces and dried-up tanks cling to the edge of the hill. There are four palaces here, two built by the Tomar Rajputs and two by the Mughals. The huge **Jauhar Tank** next to them is remembered for the *jauhar* (self-immolation) of Rajput queens here in 1232, when Sultan Iltutmish of Delhi was on the verge of capturing the fort.

THE TEMPLES. About halfway along the eastern edge of the hilltop are the **Sas Bahu** temples, built in 1093. The edge of the fort here offers a drab view of the city. You should be able to make out the big brown dome of Mohammed Gaus' tomb. The west side of the fort has better views of the huge city and its craggy landscape.

The **Bandi Chhor Gurudwara** is a Sikh pilgrimage site that marks the spot where the sixth Sikh Guru, Hargobind, was imprisoned for two years by Emperor Jehangir. Ritual cleansing is required, and cloths are provided for you to cover your head with before entering the *gurudwara.* Inside, men sit and chant Sikh scriptures above a sunken silver chamber marking the guru's jail.

Next-door to the *gurudwara,* the **Teli-ka Mandir** (Oilman's Temple) is a tall chunk of carved stone, though not tall enough to rival the nearby TV mast. The Mandir dates from the 9th century. It was once a Vishnu temple, but when the British occupied the fort in the 19th century, they turned it into a soda-water factory. There is nothing inside now but a fetid stink.

The southwestern entrance of the fort passes through the long Urwahi Gorge, a natural rift in the hillside. Its walls are decorated with rows of **Jain sculptures** dating from between the 7th and 15th centuries. These figures of *tirthankaras* still stand impassively above the road, despite the best efforts of Mughal conqueror Babur, who damaged many of the statues by smashing their faces and genitals to pieces. One statue, an image of Adhinath, is 19m tall. More of these carvings are on the southeastern side of the fort, including one still used as a Jain shrine.

COME ON BABY, FIGHT MY FIRE Legend has it that Akbar's greatest court singer, Miyan Tansen, learned the powerful *raga dipak* after seeing a twig spontaneously catch fire in a songbird's beak. The *raga,* when performed at full intensity, supposedly turns the performer's vocal chords into ashes. When Tansen's jealous rivals challenged him to sing *dipak* for the emperor, he welcomed the opportunity. Little did they know that the savvy musician had trained his wife in the rain-inducing *raga mahar* to counter *dipak*'s fiery impact. When the crooner began to ignite, his wife was called in, and the subsequent duet of fire and water so impressed Akbar that he aided Tansen's ascendancy in the imperial court.

OUTSIDE THE FORT

JAI VILAS PALACE. Maharaja Jiyaji Rao Scindia commissioned a British architect to build this great white whale of a complex for him in an attempt to impress the Prince of Wales (later Edward VII) on his state visit here in 1875. Generations of Scindias have since filled it with the most outrageous *objets d'art* and kitsch imaginable. Today, part of it is open as a **museum** (the rest is still the maharaja's residence). Furniture from Versailles, crystal and marble staircases, and a set of shimmering crystal furniture are just a few of the palace's notable features. Tatty stuffed tigers fill up the "Natural History Gallery." From the gilded ceiling of Durbar Hall hang two enormous Belgian chandeliers, each weighing 3.5 tons, and below them is the largest handmade carpet in Asia. To test the strength of the ceiling, ten elephants were led up ramps onto the roof. Downstairs, the dining table has tracks for a silver toy train that once wheeled around after-dinner brandy and cigars. *(Open daily Th-Tu 10am-6pm. Rs175 for foreigners. Keep your ticket stub for entry to both wings.)*

OTHER SIGHTS. To the east of the fort in the Old Town is the **Mausoleum of Sheik Muhammad Ghaus,** named for the Muslim saint who helped the emperor Babur capture Gwalior Fort. The walls of this fine early Mughal monument are made up of a series of cut-stone screens carved into beautiful geometric patterns. *(Open daily sunrise-sunset.)* The **Tomb of Tansen** is in the same graveyard; this 16th-century ragasinger was one of the greatest musicians in Indian history (see **Come on Baby, Fight My Fire,** above). Chewing the leaves of the tamarind tree near the tomb is supposed to make your voice as sweet as Tansen's. A classical music festival takes place here in November or December. Gwalior's newest big thing is its **Sun Temple,** in the Morar area. A scaled-down knock-off of the Sun Temple in **Konark** (see p. 618), it was built by the philanthropic Birla family. *(Open daily 6am-noon and 2-7pm.)*

MAHARASHTRA
महाराष्ट्र

Maharashtra, the "Great Country," straddles the Indian Peninsula, from the tropical coast to the arid Deccan Plateau, from the fringes of the hot and hectic Ganga Plain to the balmier, palmier, more easy-going South, and from isolated villages to metropolitan Bombay. From the sacred Godavari at Nasik and the giddy, red-robed, Birkenstock-clad acolytes of the Osho Commune to the businessmen and billboards of Bombay, Maharashtra has more than enough to keep you happy, whether you're a fan of the sacred and the sublime or whether you get your kicks at the low-brow altar of the ridiculous and profane. More than half of India's foreign trade and nearly 40% of its tax revenue flows from here, but two-thirds of Maharashtra's population still survives on subsistence-level agriculture. Many of the people here are proud of the the bold martial traditions of their state, and they are quick to emrace the fierce regional independence of their forbears, the Marathas, hardy fighters bred in the rocky hinterland. This heritage, embodied in the warrior-king and folk-hero Shivaji (1627-80), is currently exploited by the ruling Shiv Sena ("Shiva's Army") Party, a Hindu nationalist ally of the BJP.

HIGHLIGHTS OF MAHARASHTRA

The intricately carved **cave temples** at **Ajanta** (p. 423) and **Ellora** (p. 422), both UNESCO World Heritage Sites, are architectural wonders par excellence.

A hissing, buzzing helter-skelter of a city, **Bombay** (below) will make your head spin, with its sights, sounds, nightlife, and inexhaustible energy.

BOMBAY (MUMBAI) मुम्बई ☎ 022

India's largest city, in attitude if not in population, Bombay unites all of the country's languages, religions, ethnicities, castes, and classes in one heaving, seething sizzler of a metropolis. Bombay blends traditions and innovations from every region, city, and village in India and beyond, offering everything from *bhel puri* to bell-bottoms. Trade through the city accounts for 50% of India's imports and exports, its densest concentration of industry, and its largest stock exchange. Rupee and dollar billionaires, film stars, models, and politicians flock to frolic at the city's hotels, discos, and restaurants. But Bombay also harbors more of the desperate poor than any other Indian city; the endless shantytown at Dharavi has expanded into Asia's (and perhaps the world's) largest slum. As many as half of Bombay's 16 million residents live in shacks or on the street. An estimated 10,000 people flood into Bombay every day, hoping to make their homes and their fortunes in the country's commercial heart, the City of Gold.

The huge population, combined with arcane rent control provisions, has driven real estate prices in Bombay sky-high. A decent-sized, three-bedroom flat on the southern cusp of the city can cost up to US$2 million—this in a country in which the yearly per capita income is just US$350. Right-wing and sectarian politicians stoked this pressure-cooker of cramping and crowding, wretched sanitation, choking pollution, and religious tension until it exploded into riots and bomb blasts in 1992 and 1993. The city often serves as the arena for India's social struggles (witness a 1999 scheme by the Shiv Sena to deport all of the bazaar district's Bengali-speaking Muslims to Bangladesh) and as the lair of the nation's only urban crime syndicate. But none of the recent upheavals seem to be slowing Bombay down very much. The decade-long bull run on Dalal st. means that the Bombay Stock Exchange and its millions face the new millennium from uncharted heights.

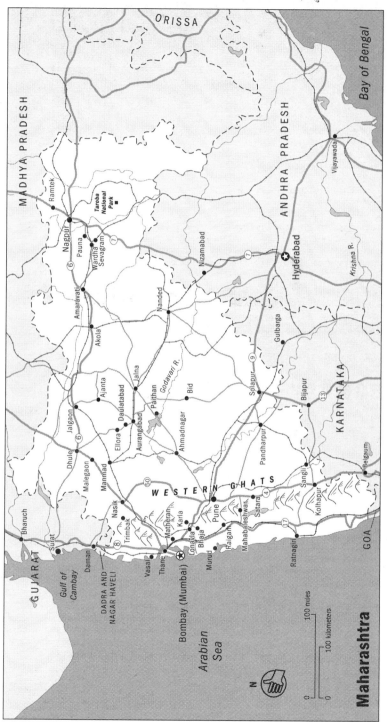

Maharashtra

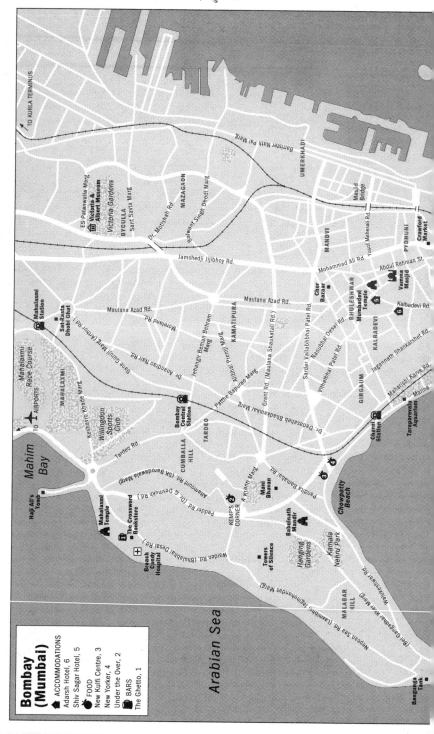

Bombay (Mumbai)

▲ ACCOMMODATIONS
Adarsh Hotel, 6
Shiv Sagar Hotel, 5

🍴 FOOD
New Kulfi Centre, 3
New Yorker, 4
Under the Over, 2

🍸 BARS
The Ghetto, 1

Arabian Sea

Mahim Bay

TO KURLA TERMINUS

Barrister Nath Pai Marg

UMERKHADI

Masjid Bridge

MAZAGAON

ES Patanwalla Marg
🏛 **Victoria & Albert Museum**
Victoria Gardens
Sant Savta Marg
Dr. Morishah Rd.
Balwant Singh Dhodi Marg

Jamshedji Jijibhoy Rd.

Mohammad Ali Rd.
Yusuf Meherali Rd.
Abdul Rehman St.
PYDHUNI

Crawford Market

Vanma Masjid

Chor Bazaar
BHULESHWAR
Mumbadevi Temple

Maulana Azad Rd.

KALBADEVI
Kalbadevi Rd.

🚉 **Mahalaxmi Station**
Sat-Rasta
Dhobi Ghat (Arthur Rd.)

Maulana Azad Rd.
Moreland Rd.
KAMATIPURA
Jehangir Beman Behram Marg

Sant Gunji Marg (Arthur Rd.)
Dr. Anandrao Nair Rd.

Grant Rd. (Maulana Shaukatali Rd.)

Sardar Vallabhbhai Patel Rd.
Manubhai Desai Rd.
Vyithalbhai Patel Rd.

GIRGAUM

Jagannath Shankarsheth Rd.

Maharishi Karve Rd.

🚉 **Charni Station**

Marine

Tarporevala Aquarium

Mahalaxmi Race Course

MAHALAXMI

Keshavro Khade Marg

Willingdon Sports Club

🛫 TO AIRPORTS

Tardeo Rd.

🚉 **Bombay Central Station**

TARDEO

Patthe Bapurao Marg
Dr. Dadasaheb Bhadkamkar Marg

CUMBALLA HILL

Altamount Rd. (SK Barodawala Marg)

A Karni Marg

Mani Bhavan

Pandita Ramabai Rd.

Chowpatty Beach

Haji Ali's Tomb

▲ **Mahalaxmi Temple**
📖 **The Crossword Bookstore**
➕ Breach Candy Hospital

Warden Rd. (Bhulabhai Desai Rd.)

Pedder Rd. (Dr. G Deshmukh Rd.)

KEMP'S CORNER

▲ **Babulnath Mandir**

🏢 Towers of Silence

Hanging Gardens

Kamala Nehru Park

MALABAR HILL

Nepean Sea Rd. (Laxmibai Jagmohandas Marg)

Walkeshwar Rd.

Wodehouse Rd.

Banganga Tank

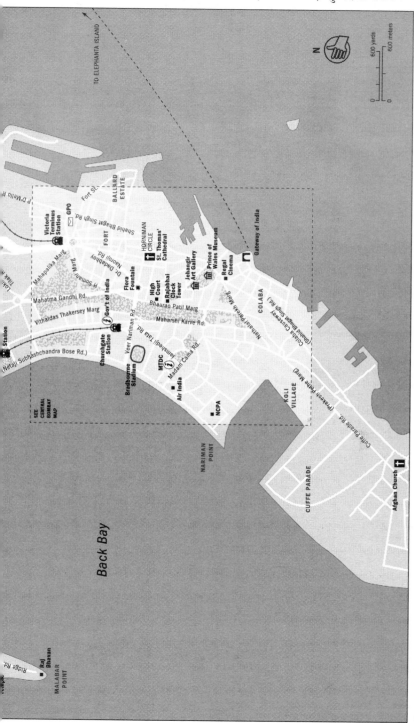

N

0   600 yards
0   600 meters

TO ELEPHANTA ISLAND

P D'Mello R.

BALLARD ESTATE

Fort St.

GPO

Victoria Terminus Station

Shahid Bhagat Singh Rd.

Dr. Naoroji Rd.

FORT

Mahapalika Marg

Somnath Marg

HORNIMAN CIRCLE

St. Thomas' Cathedral

Flora Fountain

Gov't of India

Mahatma Gandhi Rd.

Vithaldas Thakersey Marg

Station

(Netaji Subhashchandra Bose Rd.)

Churchgate Station

High Court

Rajabhai Clock Tower

Bhaurao Patil Marg

Maharshi Karve Rd.

Jehangir Art Gallery

Prince of Wales Museum

Regal Cinema

Gateway of India

Nathalal Parekh Marg

COLABA

Colaba Causeway (Shahid Bhagat Singh Rd.)

Veer Nariman Rd.

Jamshedji Tata Rd.

Brabourne Stadium

MTDC

Madam Cama Rd.

Air India

NCPA

NARIMAN POINT

KOLI VILLAGE

(Pravesh Pethe Marg)

SEE CENTRAL BOMBAY MAP

CUFFE PARADE

Cuffe Parade Rd.

Afghan Church

Back Bay

Raj Bhavan

Ridge Rd.

MALABAR POINT

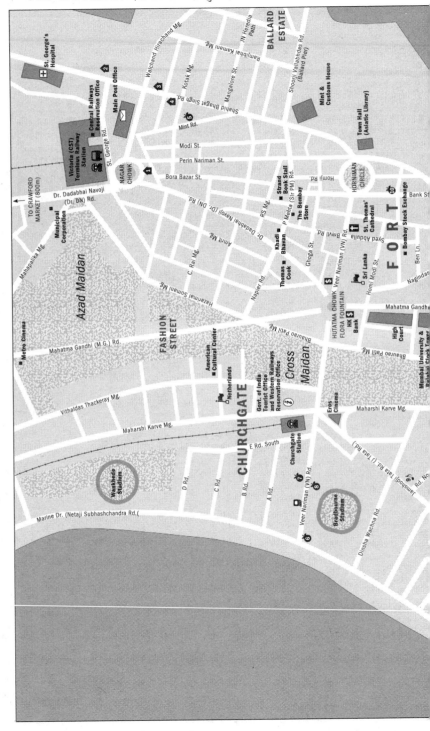

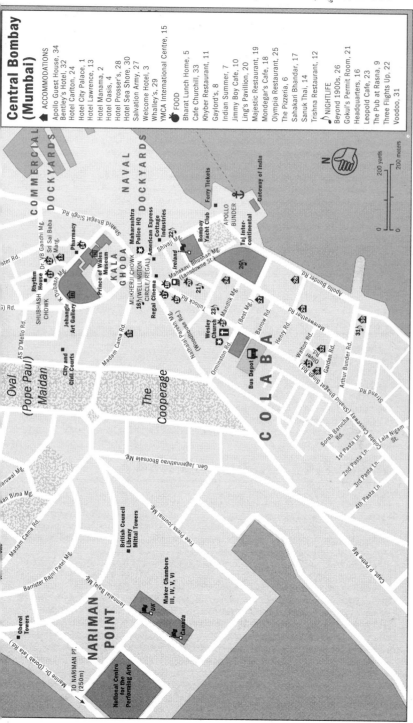

Central Bombay (Mumbai)

ACCOMMODATIONS
Apollo Guest House, 34
Bentley's Hotel, 32
Hotel Carlton, 24
Hotel City Palace, 1
Hotel Lawrence, 13
Hotel Manama, 2
Hotel Oasis, 4
Hotel Prosser's, 28
Hotel Sea Shore, 30
Salvation Army, 27
Welcome Hotel, 3
Whalley's, 29
YMCA International Centre, 15

FOOD
Bharat Lunch Home, 5
Cafe Churchill, 33
Khyber Restaurant, 11
Gaylord's, 8
Indian Summer, 7
Jimmy Boy Cafe, 10
Ling's Pavillion, 20
Majestic Restaurant, 19
Mondegar's Cafe, 18
Olympia Restaurant, 25
The Pizzeria, 6
Sahakari Bhandar, 17
Sanuk Thai, 14
Trishna Restaurant, 12

NIGHTLIFE
Beyond 1990s, 26
Gokul's Permit Room, 21
Headquarters, 16
Leopold Cafe, 23
The Pub at Rasna, 9
Three Flights Up, 22
Voodoo, 31

It all began modestly enough. Artifacts found in the suburb of Kandivli prove that the original seven islands that make up the city have been inhabited since the Stone Age. Successive dynasties ignored Bombay's potential as a port, but when the Portuguese acquired the islands in 1534, they called them Bom Bahia ("Good Port"). The British made good on the name after the dowry of Catherine of Braganza brought the islands to Charles II of England. The fourth East India Company Governor of Bombay, Gerald Aungier, set his dreams in motion by ordering a construction spree in 1672. Zoroastrians fleeing Persia built their first fire temple here in 1675, initiating a flow of affluent refugees. Bombay became the capital of the Company's regional holdings in 1687—and the rest is history.

The shortage of cotton in Britain during to the American Civil War prompted a boom in Bombay, resulting in an impressive array of late Victorian public works, including a massive land reclamation project that consolidated the city's seven islands into one. In 1885, a fledgling organization called the Indian National Congress held its inaugural meeting in Bombay. It was at another Bombay session in 1942 that the group first voiced its demand for full independence. After India realized that ambition in 1947, disputes between the Marathi- and Gujarati-speaking segments of the population ended in the partition of Bombay State into Maharashtra and Gujarat in 1960. Even during the conflict, the economy boomed, as it continues to do today. In 1995, the flick of a politician's pen gave the city a new official name—Mumbai, from Mumbadevi, the local version of the goddess Durga.

Despite all these changes, Bombay remains irrepressible. Bombay makes more movies than any other place in India, and India makes far more movies than any other place on earth. Cat-callers whistle at mini-skirted teens, while lunch delivery men overload their bicycles with pickles and *papads* for businessmen. Even the architecture expresses a uniquely urban schizophrenia: Victorian-Gothic vestiges share the streets with Art Deco apartments, Hindu shrines, and bamboo shacks.

The crowds of tourists who come to gawk at the city's insane extremes cause hardly a ripple. The manic mix of London double-deckers and bullock carts, sadhus and stockbrokers, and the perpetual motion of it all is enough to floor many first-time visitors. Bombay defies expectations of an India filled only with pot-bellied cows and ramshackle temples, although it has plenty of both. The city forces travelers to come face to face with an explosive fusion of development and despair. Whether it delights or disgusts, it cannot be denied that this unexpected, ebullient city is leading from the front as India charges into the new century. *Salaam* Bombay, indeed.

◪ GETTING THERE AND AWAY

INTERNATIONAL FLIGHTS

Sahar International Airport, Vile Parle (☎ 836 6700; Air India flight information 836 6767), is 20km north of downtown Bombay. This chaotic, mosquito-ridden complex prepares arriving travelers for the continent beyond. The **State Bank of India** and **Govt. of India Tourist Office** operate counters in the arrival hall for currency exchange and information (both open 24hr.). The easiest way to get from the airport to downtown Bombay is by **pre-paid taxi** (Rs250-290 to Colaba, depending on time of day, as opposed to Rs200 by meter; 1½hr.). Pay for a taxi at the counter in the arrival hall, and then go outside to the line of taxis and find the one whose number matches the number on your receipt. The non-pre-paid drivers at the airport are not to be trusted, but from Bombay to the airport, any metered cab will do. Allow two hours during rush hour (to the city 8-11am, from the city 5-8pm).

> **!** **NOTE.** There is a Rs500 **departure tax,** which all travelers must pay before going through customs and leaving India (Rs250 if you're headed to another South Asian country). Most airlines do not include this tax in their ticket prices. Set aside enough cash for the tax before exchanging your last rupees.

INTERNATIONAL AIRLINES. Air India, Marine Dr., Nariman Point (☎202 4142). Open M-F 9:30am-6:30pm, Sa-Su 9:30am-5pm. **Air Lanka,** Mittal Tower, C Wing, Nariman Point (☎282 3288). Open M-F 9am-5pm, Sa 9am-4pm. **Bangladesh Biman,** Airline Hotel Building, 199 J. Tata Rd., #32, Churchgate (☎282 4580). Open M-F 9am-5:30pm, Sa 9am-3pm. **British Airways,** 202-B Vulcan Insurance Building, Veer Nariman Rd., Churchgate (☎282 0888). Open M-F 9:45am-6pm, Sa 9:30am-5:30pm. **Cathay Pacific,** Taj Mahal Hotel, Apollo Bunder, Colaba (☎202 9113). Open M-Sa 9:30am-1pm and 1:45-5:30pm. **Delta,** Taj Mahal Hotel, Apollo Bunder, Colaba (☎288 3274 or 288 5652). Open M-Sa 9am-1pm and 1:30-5:30pm. **Emirates,** Mittal Chambers, 288 Nariman Point (☎287 1649 or 287 1650). Open M 9am-4pm, Tu-Sa 9am-5:30pm. **Lufthansa,** Express Towers, Nariman Point (☎202 3430 or 287 5264). Open M-F 9am-1pm and 1:45-5:45pm, Sa 9am-1pm. **Pakistan International Airlines,** Mittal Towers, Nariman Point (☎202 1598). Open M-Sa 9:30am-1pm and 2-5:30pm. **Royal Jordanian,** Jollymaker Chamber #2, Nariman Point, 4th fl. (☎202 2779). Open M-F 9am-1pm and 2-5:30pm, Sa 9am-3pm. **Royal Nepal,** 222 Maker Chamber SV, Nariman Point (☎283 6197). Open M-F 10am-6pm, Sa 10am-2pm. **Singapore Airlines,** Taj Mahal Hotel, Apollo Bunder, Colaba (☎202 3316 or 202 2747). Open M-Sa 9:15am-5:30pm. **Thai Air,** World Trade Center, Shop 15, Ground floor, Cuffe Parade (☎218 5426). Open M-F 9:30am-5:30pm, Sa 9:30am-2pm.

DOMESTIC FLIGHTS

Santa Cruz Airport is 20km northeast of downtown, 3km from Sahar International Airport. The new Terminal 1A is for Indian Airlines, and 1B is for all private carriers; **free shuttle buses** connect the two (every 15min., 4am-midnight). Free shuttle buses also depart from both terminals to the international airport (every hr.). Take a metered auto-rickshaw (about Rs40) from the airport to the Andheri Railway Station, buy a ticket for any **city-bound train** (45min., 2nd class Rs5), and get off at Churchgate Station, or vice versa. Exit on the east side of Andheri Station to get a rickshaw to the airports. There are no **pre-paid taxis** from the airport, but the ones at the stand outside should follow the meter one-way (Rs200 to downtown; under Rs75 to Sahar International Airport).

DOMESTIC AIRLINES. Indian Airlines, Air India Building, Marine Dr., Nariman Point (enquiry ☎140 or 141 for 24hr. service, reservations and reconfirmation ☎287 6161). Open M-Sa 8:30am-7:30pm, Su 10am-1pm and 1:45-5:30pm; ticketing office at domestic airport open 24hr. **Jet Airways,** Amarchand Mansion, Madam Cama Rd. (☎285 5788, reservations ☎836 6111). Open M-Sa 10am-5:30pm. **Sahara India Airlines,** Maker Chamber V, Nariman Point (☎83 5671 or 283 5672). Open M-Sa 10am-6pm. **Ahmedabad** (6-7 per day, 1hr., US$75); **Aurangabad** (2 per day, 45min., US$75); **Bangalore** (9-10 per day, 1½hr., US$140); **Bhopal** (1 per day Su-F, 2hr., US$130); **Bhubaneshwar** (3 per week, 3hr., US$250); **Calcutta** (5-6 per day, 2½hr., US$230); **Calicut** (3-4 per day, 1½hr., US$140); **Cochin** (4-5 per day, 2hr., US$150); **Coimbatore** (2 each per day, 2hr., US$150); **Delhi** (several, 2hr., US$175); **Goa** (4-5 per day, 1hr., US$85); **Hyderabad** (6-7 per day, 1½hr., US$120); **Indore** (2 per day, 1hr., US$90); **Jaipur** (2 per day, 3½hr., US$155); **Madras** (8-9 per day, 2hr., US$160); **Mangalore** (2 per day, 1½hr., US$115); **Trivandrum** (3-4 per day, 2hr., US$195); **Udaipur** (2 per day, 2hr., US$125); and **Varanasi** (1 per day, 5hr., US$235). Flights booked from abroad must be reconfirmed 72 hours before departure.

TRAINS

Western Railways connects Bombay to Gujarat, Rajasthan, and Delhi. Central Railways serves destinations to the east and Delhi. Some long-haul trains also leave from **Dadar, Kurla,** 15km northeast of downtown, or **Bandra** stations; all are accessible by local train from VT. For train **schedules,** arm yourself with a copy of *Trains at a Glance* (Rs25), available at railway station bookstalls.

CENTRAL RAILWAYS. Reservation Office, **Victoria Terminus (VT),** officially known as **Chhatrapati Shivaji Terminus** (enquiry ☎135 or 269 5959; automated info 265

6565). Head for **Window 7,** the Foreign Tourist Guide (open M-Sa 9am-1pm and 1:30-4pm). They sell tickets for US$ or UK£, or for rupees with an encashment certificate. They release tourist quota seats on a first-come, first-served basis on the day *before* departure for trains leaving before 2pm, or on the day *of* departure for trains leaving after 2pm. The following trains, which leave from VT, are just a select few of the many available. To: **Agra** (1 per day, 7:10pm, 22hr., Rs326; 1-2 trains per day from Dadar Station, 7:55am and 10:40pm); **Aurangabad** (6:10am and 9:20pm, 7½hr., Rs137); **Bangalore** (1-2 per day, 7:55am and 10:40pm, 24hr., Rs310); **Bhopal** (8am and 7pm, 14hr., Rs244; 1-2 per day from Dadar Station, 7:55am and 10:40pm); **Calcutta** (3 per day, 6am-9pm, 33hr., Rs393); **Ernakulam** (1-2 per day, 12:15 and 3:30pm, 28hr., Rs207); **Hyderabad** (12:35 and 9:55pm, 15-17½hr., Rs151); **Madras** (2 and 11:20pm, 24hr., Rs314; 1 train per day from Dadar, 7:50pm); **Margao** (5:15am and 10:30pm, 11hr., Rs225); **Pune** (16 per day, 4hr., Rs53); **Trivandrum** (12:15 and 3:35pm, 44hr., Rs256).

WESTERN RAILWAYS. Western Railways, Churchgate Reservation Office, Maharishi Karve Rd., Churchgate (enquiry ☎131, booking information 209 5959; arrivals from Delhi 132, from Gujarat 133). Across the street from Churchgate Station, in the same building as the Government of India Tourist Office. To get to the **Foreign Tourist Counter,** ignore the first reservation office and walk past the tourist office; it's the next door on your left, upstairs. Tourist quota procedures are the same as at VT (see above), but here an agent is specially assigned to help you. Open M-F 9:30am-1:30pm and 2-4:30pm, Sa 9:30am-2:30pm. The following trains leave from **Mumbai Central** (see **local trains**, p. 393). To: **Ahmedabad** (5-7 per day, 5:45am-9:50pm, 7-8½hr., Rs107; 4 per day from Bandra, 3-8:50pm); **Delhi** (5-6 per day, 7:25am-10:40pm, 17-22hr., Rs212/A/C 3-tier sleeper Rs1485; 1 per day from Dadar station, 10:40pm; 1 per day from Bandra, 10:25pm); **Jaipur** (7:05pm, 18hr., Rs184).

BUSES

State Transport Terminal, JB Behran Marg (☎307 4272 or 307 6622), opposite Central Railway Station, next to the Maratha Mandir Cinema. **Maharashtra State Road Transport Corporation** runs quiet, comfortable, and expensive buses to the major tourist destinations in the state; services are cut back during monsoon. To: **Aurangabad** (2 per day, 10hr., Rs190); **Mahabaleshwar** (2 per day, 7hr., Rs53). For other destinations in Maharashtra, you have to book at the ASIAD office (☎413 6835) in Dadar, or at an MTDC luxury service office, although trains are likely to be quicker and more convenient. **Goa State Transport** (Kadamba) runs a daily luxury bus to **Panjim** (5pm, 15hr., Rs240). **Gujarat State Transport** has at least 2 daily buses to **Ahmedabad** (3 and 7pm, 12hr., Rs168). **MTDC,** CDO Hutments, Madam Cama Rd. (☎202 6713), also runs buses to **Ganpatipule** (in-season 1 per day, 8-10hr., Rs230); **Mahabaleshwar** (in-season 7am, 7hr., Rs200); and **Shirdi** (in-season 1 per day, off-season 1 per week; 7hr.; Rs225). Their services change frequently, so check with them for up-to-date route information.

▐ GETTING AROUND

LOCAL BUSES

Trains are easier to deal with than buses, but if you're going to be in town for a while, it's worth the (Herculean) effort required to come to terms with the city's chaotic bus system. For a complete guide to stops and routes, pick up a city bus map (Rs20) from the bus terminal office on Colaba Causeway (open M-F 9am-5pm). Try to learn the Marathi numerals so that you can recognize the bus as it approaches (the Roman numeral and English destination are only written down on the side—often visible too late to allow you to clamber on board before the bus roars off again). Red numbers indicate "limited" services, which supposedly stop less frequently and cost marginally less. No fare within the city should exceed Rs3, limited or otherwise.

BUS #	MARATHI	ROUTE AND DESTINATION
1 ltd.	१	Colaba-Regal-Flora-VT-Crawford Market-Mahim
3	३	Afghan Church-Colaba-Regal-Flora-VT
6	६	Colaba-Regal-VT-Crawford-Byculla
62	६२	Flora-Metro-Marine Lines-Bombay Central-Dadar Station
61	६१	Regal-Metro-Opera House-Bombay Central-Dadar Station
81 ltd.	८१	VT-Kemp's Corner-Breach Candy and Haji Ali-Nehru Planetarium
91	९१	Bombay Central-Dadar-Kurla
106	१०६	Afghan Church-Colaba-Regal-Chowpatty-Kamala Nehru Park
108	१०८	VT-Regal-Chowpatty-Kamala Nehru Park
125	१२५	Colaba-Crawford Market-Haji Ali-Worli Village
132	१३२	Regal-Churchgate-Breach Candy and Haji Ali
188 ltd.	१८८	Borivli (E)-Sanjay Gandhi NP-Kanheri Caves
231	२३१	Santa Cruz (W)-Juhu Beach
321 ltd.	३२१	Airport-Vile Parle (E)
343	३४३	Goregaon (E)-Film City

LOCAL TRAINS

Bombay's commuter rail system runs along two lines. **Western Railways** runs one line, from **Churchgate** through Bombay Central, Mahalaxmi, Dadar, Bandra, Santa Cruz (for Juhu), Andheri (for the airports), and a dozen other stations before Borivli (Sanjay Gandhi NP) and beyond. The **Central Railways** line runs to and from **VT** (check the final destination; be sure you're on the right line) and tends to be of less use to the tourist. Most trains out of VT stop at Dadar, where you can cross the platform and change onto a Western train. One-way tickets (2nd class Rs3-10, 1st class Rs8-32) are sold at windows in each station. When boarding a train, check the illuminated display—the first letter code is the first letter of the final destination, the second code is the time, and the "F" or "S" indicates whether the train is (relatively) fast or (especially) slow. Fast trains skip the stations whose names are illuminated on the board below. That's right, the names that are lit up brightly are the **places it does not go.** There are special, less crowded cars exclusively for women on all trains.

TAXIS

Taxis rule in Bombay, since auto-rickshaws aren't allowed in the downtown area and public transport is so crowded. Set the meter and go—this shouldn't be too much of a struggle unless it's very late or the weather's very bad. You pay roughly 12 times what the meter shows—for the precise figure, consult the chart that the driver should carry. **Auto-rickshaws** only roam the suburbs; you pay about seven times the meter.

■ ORIENTATION

The city of Bombay reaches into the Arabian Sea like a cupped hand, the fingers and thumb forming a backward letter "c" off the western coast of India. For purposes of orientation, it is more important to familiarize yourself with the names of the city's different areas than specific street addresses, as most locals (and taxi drivers) navigate and give directions according to the names of neighborhoods and well-known landmarks. At the fingertip of **Colaba,** toward the southern end of the city, is the tourist ghetto. The area's main thoroughfare, **Colaba Causeway,** is where you'll find most of the budget accommodations and lost-looking backpackers. The Causeway ends in the north at a huge, circular intersection universally known as **Regal** because of the movie theater that presides over it. Directly west of Regal, jutting into the Bay, are **Cuffe Parade,** an elite residential area, and **Nariman Point,** Bombay's most prestigious corporate address, housing the offices of many

MAHARASHTRA

> **MUMBAI SAPPHIRE** Most tourists spin or stroll down Netaji Subhas Chandra Bose Rd. in Bombay several times without even realizing it. They, like all the city's residents, know this street by its colonial name, Marine Drive. No matter how civic-minded or patriotic the new designations chosen by the municipal corporation, people continue to rebel against today's authorities by refusing to relinquish the street names of past oppressors. Nepean Sea Rd. is never Laxmibhai Jagmohandas Marg; even the bus conductors say Ridge Rd. for Bal Gangadhar Kher Marg; Shahid Bhagat Singh Marg evinces blank stares from taxi drivers—but everyone recognizes Colaba Causeway. On the rare occasions when Bombay's citizens accept the new names, they inevitably abbreviate them beyond recognition: Sir Pherozeshah Mehta Rd. becomes PM Rd.; and Doctor Dadabhoy Naoroji barely escapes as Dr. DN.
>   Bombay's name game developed from small-scale civil disobedience to big-time politics, as the Hindu nationalist Shiv Sena party, senior partners in the state's coalition government at the time, decided that streets by any other name would smell more sweet. In 1995 the Sena dropped their biggest bomb, when they renamed the whole city Mumbai, in line with its perceived "traditional" Marathi name (Madras followed suit in 1996, switching its name to the hardly homophonic Chennai). But the struggle continues, as feeble-minded free-thinkers (such as the team that put this book together) stick stubbornly to the old name, and urbanites wryly refer to the city as "Slumbai."

international banks, airlines, and a few consulates. North of Regal, past the Prince of Wales Museum, stretches **Fort**, Bombay's oldest neighborhood and its main financial district. Banks cluster near its most prominent landmark, **Flora Fountain (Hutatma Chowk)**.

West of Fort and north of Nariman Point is the **Churchgate** neighborhood, where you'll find the Churchgate railway station and several trendy restaurants. **Marine Dr.** runs along the western edge of the city, curving from Nariman Point in the south to Churchgate in the north, and farther still to **Chowpatty Beach.** North of Chowpatty are the upmarket **Malabar Hill** community and the northern suburbs.

Most travelers arriving by train will enter Bombay at **Victoria Terminus (VT),** now officially called **Chhatrapati Shivaji Terminus (CST),** just north of the Fort. From VT, it's a Rs25 taxi ride to Colaba, though taxi drivers will try to charge more; stick to your guns. North of VT, **Crawford Market** marks the beginning of the **bazaar district.**

🛈 PRACTICAL INFORMATION

TOURIST AND FINANCIAL SERVICES

Tourist Office: Government of India Tourist Office, 123 Maharishi Karve Rd. (☎203 3144), 100m along the road running down the right of Churchgate Station as you face it. Open M-F 8:30am-6pm, Sa 8:30am-2pm. Also at Sahar International Airport (☎832 5331; open 24hr.) and at Santa Cruz Domestic Airport (☎615 9200; open during flight arrival times). **Maharashtra Tourism Development Corporation (MTDC),** CDO Hutments, Madam Cama Rd. (☎202 6713). From the Air India building, walk away from Marine Dr. along Madam Cama Rd.; it's on the left, after the giant Nehru statue. Open M-Sa 9:30am-5:30pm. Other offices at Santa Cruz airport, Sahar International Airport, Churchgate Station, and the Gateway of India.

Help Line: Ask Me (☎261 6666). Ask a silly question, get a silly answer.

Consulates: Australia, Maker Towers E., 16th fl. (☎218 1071), Cuffe Parade. Open M-F 9am-5pm. **Canada,** 41/42 Maker Chambers VI (☎287 6027), Nariman Point. Open M-Th 9am-5:30pm, F 9am-3pm. **Ireland,** Bombay Yacht Club, Apollo Bunder (☎202 4607), Colaba. Open M-F 9am-5pm. **South Africa,** Gandhi Mansion, Altamount Rd. (☎389 3725), near Kemp's Corner. Open M-F 9am-5pm. **Sri Lanka,** Jehangir Wadhwa, 1st fl., 34 Homi Modi St. (☎204 5861 or 204 8303), Fort. Most visas obtainable on arrival in Sri Lanka. Open for visas M-F 9:30-11:30am. **Thailand,** Malabar View Building

(☎363 1404), near Purandevi Hospital, Chowpatty Beach. 2-month vsisa Rs400; many nationalities can enter for up to 2 months without a visa. Open for visas M-F 9am-noon. **UK,** Maker Chambers IV, 1st and 2nd fl., 222 J. Bajaj Rd. (☎283 3602 or 283 0517), Nariman Point. Open M-F 8am-4pm. **US,** Lincoln House, 78 Bhulabhai Desai Rd. (☎363 3611 or 363 3617), Breach Candy. Open M-F 8:30am-1pm, 2-3:45pm.

Currency Exchange: Hong Kong Bank, 52/60 MG Rd. (☎267 4921), Flora Fountain. Cash advances on Visa and MC. On-site **ATM** is connected to the Plus network. Open M-F 10:30am-3:30pm, Sa 10:30am-1pm. **Standard Chartered,** Ismail Building, Dr. DN Rd. (☎204 5056), near Flora. On the right as you walk from Flora to VT. **24hr. ATM** connects to the Plus and Cirrus systems. Office open 9am-6pm. **Thomas Cook,** Dr. DN Rd. (☎204 8556), Fort. On the left, 2 blocks up as you walk from Flora to VT, with the bright red sign. Cashes Thomas Cook traveler's checks for free; Rs320 per transaction for other brands. Open M-Sa 9:30am-6pm. **American Express,** Regal Cinema Building, Shivaji Marg (☎204 8291), on Wellington Circle. Cashes AmEx traveler's checks for free; 1% fee on other brands. Open M-F 9:30am-6:30pm, Sa 9:30am-2:30pm.

LOCAL SERVICES

Luggage Storage: Cloak Room at VT, inside the station building, near platform 13. Rs7-10 per day, 31-day max. Similar facilities at all big stations. Bags must be locked closed (including the unlockable portion of backpacks). Don't lose the receipt. Limited space. Open 24hr. except 7:30-8am and 3:30-4pm.

Bookstore: The Strand Book Stall, Sir PM Rd. (☎266 1994), just above Horniman Cir., Fort. Favorite of the Bombay intelligentsia, the Strand's crowded collection is hand-picked. Search carefully for discounts. Open M-Sa 10am-7pm. **Crossword Bookstore,** Mahalaxmi Chambers, 1st fl., 22 Bhulabhai Desai Rd. (☎492 4882), Breach Candy. Look up for the yellow sign in the window. Open M-F 10am-8pm, Sa-Su 10am-6pm.

Library and Cultural Center: The Asiatic Society Library, Town Hall, SBS Marg (☎266 0956), Horniman Circle, Fort. A beautiful old cavern of a reading room in the old town hall; a great place to read and browse. Open M-Sa 10am-7:30pm. **American Center (USIS) Library,** 4 New Marine Lines (☎262 4590), Churchgate. The barricaded building on the right-hand side as you walk from Churchgate. For Rs10 per day, non-members may lounge in the A/C calm and read dated US papers. Open M-Tu and Th-Sa 10am-6pm. **British Council,** A Wing, Mittal Towers, 1st fl. (☎282 3560), Nariman Point. Open Tu-Sa 10am-6pm.

Bi-Gay-Lesbian Organizations: The Humsafar Centre, Vakola Market Building, 2nd fl., Santa Cruz E (☎618 7476; helpline ☎972 6913; www.humsafar.org). Take a train from Churchgate to Santa Cruz (Rs5); it's then a Rs10 rickshaw ride. Drop-in center with library and TV. Frequent lectures, workshops, videos and gatherings (call for details). Open M-Sa noon-8pm.

Market: M Phule Market, north end of Dr. DN Rd. Universally known as **Crawford Market,** despite the best efforts of several governments. Open M-Sa 6am-6pm.

EMERGENCY AND COMMUNICATIONS

Pharmacy: New Marine Lines is lined with late night chemists, such as **Mumbai Chemists** (☎200 1173), Churchgate, opposite Liberty Cinema and next to the Hospital. Open daily 7:30am-11pm. **Apollo Pharmacy,** 18/20 K. Dubash Marg (☎285 1873 or 282 9707), Kala Ghoda, behind Prince of Wales Museum. Open 24hr.

Hospital: Breach Candy Hospital, 60 Warden Rd. (☎363 3651), Breach Candy, just past the American Consulate and the Breach Candy Swimming Club. Not near Colaba, but one of the most modern hospitals in Bombay and accustomed to dealing with foreigners. Open 24hr. **Bombay Hospital,** 12 New Marine Lines (☎206 7676). Modern, established, and centrally located. Open 24hr. **Ambulance,** ☎102.

Police: Police Commissioner's Office, Dr. DN Rd. (☎100), Crawford Market. Opposite the market building, behind an iron fence. You can report thefts at this head office; expect an endless bureaucratic nightmare. Miracles have been known to happen.

MAHARASHTRA

Internet: L.S.M. PCO Service, Abubakar Mansion, Lansdowne St. (☎202 2452), Colaba. Coming from Colaba Causeway, go 20m down Lansdowne St. and turn into the burrow on your right. Rs60 per hr. Open daily 9am-11pm. **On-line Cyber Cafe,** VN Rd. (☎284 4723), Churchgate. Walk from Churchgate Station toward Marine Dr.; it's down an alley behind Berry's on the right. Rs80 per hr. Open daily 8am-midnight. **British Council Library** (see above). Rs60 per hr.

Post Office: GPO, W. Hirachand Marg (☎262 0956). The huge stone building next door to VT, off Nagar Chowk. Open M-Sa 9am-8pm, Su 10am-5pm. **Postal Code:** 400001.

▐ ACCOMMODATIONS

Most foreign tourists gravitate toward the peaceful, remodeled mansions of Colaba despite the area's proximity to Gateway of India touts and the (decidedly non-budget) Taj Mahal Hotel. Bombay real estate being what it is, "budget" means something entirely different in this city from what it means elsewhere in India. Even bottom-of-the-barrel digs charge rates that would mortify any self-respecting budget dive in a smaller Indian city. Reservations are a good idea at any time, especially in season (Nov.-Feb.). Check-out is noon unless noted otherwise.

COLABA

Hotel Lawrence, 3rd fl., ITTS House, 33 Sri Sai Baba Marg (Rope Walk Ln.; ☎284 3618), off K. Dubash Marg. The entrance is a few steps up from the Prince of Wales Museum, to your right. Nine clean, decent-sized rooms with shared bath and friendly staff. Singles Rs300; doubles Rs400. Breakfast included. Reserve 2 weeks in advance.

YWCA International Centre, 18 Madam Cama Rd. (☎202 5053 or 202 9161; fax 202 0445; email ywcaic@bom8.vsnl.net.in), 5min. from Regal, on the left. Entrance around right side of building. Although more expensive than most budget hotels, you get your money's worth at the Y—rates include all-you-can-eat buffet breakfast and dinner, TV lounge, daily room cleaning, telephones, and towels in spotless, spacious rooms with balconies. All have attached bath. Dorm beds Rs586; singles Rs689; doubles Rs1282. Additional Rs50 membership fee (good for 30 days). Reserve 15 days in advance.

Bentley's Hotel, 17 Oliver Rd. (☎284 1474 or 284 1733; fax 287 1846; email bentleyshotel@hotmail.com). A real treat—vintage rooms with hardwood floors, white-washed balconies, and mosaic tiling. Individual baths, TVs, and breakfast included in price. Doubles Rs650-1070. A/C Rs150-200 extra. Visa, MC.

Whalley's, Jaiji Mansion, 41 Mereweather Rd., Apollo Bunder (☎282 1802). Tiny, ordinary rooms in a big, breezy villa surrounded by greenery, where the birds make more noise than the traffic. Breakfast included. Singles Rs550-800; doubles Rs650-1200.

Salvation Army, 30 Mereweather Rd. (☎284 1824), behind the Taj Mahal Hotel. Pistachio-green walls make it as drab and institutional as you'd expect, but nothing beats it on a budget. Passable dorms and large, nondescript doubles. Max. 1 week stay. Check-in 10am. Check-out 9am. Dorm beds Rs130; doubles with bath Rs460-560.

Hotel Sea Shore, 1-49 Kamal Mansion, 4th fl., Arthur Bunder Rd. (☎287 4237 or 287 4238). From Regal, follow the Causeway to Arthur Bunder, 9 blocks down on the left. The entrance to Kamal Mansion is on the right, down an alley before Arthur Bunder hits the ocean. The rooms range from claustrophobic cubicles to large, airy, ocean-view suites. Sparkling common bath. Singles Rs320; doubles with TV Rs420-500.

Hotel Prosser's, Curzon House, 2-4 Henry Rd., Apollo Bunder Rd. (☎284 1715 or 283 4937), where Henry Rd. (the 6th left off the Causeway, south of Regal) meets the sea. High ceilings and spacious rooms. Common bath. Singles Rs400; doubles Rs600. Off-season: Rs350/400.

Hotel Carlton, Florence House, 12 Mereweather Rd. (☎202 0642 or 202 0259), 1 block north of the Salvation Army, behind the Taj. The veranda, equipped with tiny tables and red plastic chairs, allows residents to escape their cramped quarters for a glimpse of cathouse life across the street. Singles Rs350; doubles Rs500-950.

Apollo Guest House, Dhun Mahal, ground fl., Garden St. (☎204 1302). Turn left on Garden St.; it's on the left 8 blocks down Colaba Causeway from Regal. Beyond the plush lobby are tiny rooms off a cramped, noisy warren with a common bathroom. Singles with bath Rs350; doubles Rs400-1000.

BEYOND COLABA

Hotel Manama, P D'Mello Rd. (☎261 3412; fax 261 3860), opposite St. George Hospital. With your back to the GPO, head left on Hirachand Marg, then turn left on D'Mello; it's on the right. Good-value, crowded, middle-class hotel. Doubles Rs400-700.

Hotel Oasis, 276 Sahid Bhagat Singh Rd. (☎269 7886; fax 262 6498). With your back to the GPO, head left on Hirachand Marg, then right onto Sahid Bhagat Singh; it's on the right. Pleasant rooms with phones and TVs. Singles Rs410; doubles Rs600-875. No advance booking for singles.

Shiv Sagar Lodge, 144/146 Kalbadevi Rd. (☎240 4753 or 240 3938), 1km north of Metro Cinema, opposite the Cotton Exchange. A good location in the city's less touristy side. Nestled in the densely packed garment district of Bhuleshwar, the Shiv Sagar offers clean, well-appointed rooms with TVs, phones, and attached baths. Check-out 8am. Singles Rs450-650; doubles Rs550-750.

Adarsh Hotel, Kalbadevi Rd. (☎208 4989 or 208 4960), at PH Purohit Marg, 250m south of Shiv Sagar Lodge. Smallish, well-kept rooms with room service; some have TV, A/C, and attached bath. Check-out 8am. Singles Rs275-500; doubles Rs750-1000.

Welcome Hotel, 257 Sahid Bhagat Singh Rd. (☎261 2196 or 261 7474; fax 262 2715; email welcome_hotel@vsnl.com), opposite the Hotel Oasis. Glamorous and clean, with TVs and phones. Breakfast and morning and evening tea included. Singles Rs550-800; doubles Rs800-1100; rooms with bath Rs850-2000.

Hotel City Palace, 121 City Terrace, W. Hirachand Marg (☎261 5515 or 261 4759; fax 267 6890), opposite VT. Most rooms cost more than they're worth, but the ground-floor A/C cubicles with common bath are cheap. Prices include morning tea. Singles Rs500-1100; doubles Rs700-1250.

FOOD

Eating in Bombay can result in anything from gastronomical delight to gastrointestinal distress. The distinctive street food is a constant temptation, and the city's restaurants brim with the best international food in India, as well as every conceivable type of Indian cuisine, including a few (Parsi, Malvani) not to be found anywhere else. Not surprisingly, the Good Port of Bombay is also renowned for its seafood. There is no better place to splurge on your meals. Serious eaters should refer to the *Mid-Day Good Food Guide* (Rs50).

COLABA

Trishna, 7 Sri Sai Baba Marg (☎267 2176 or 265 9644). Follow Dr. VB Gandhi Marg past Rhythm House, turn left at the first intersection, and walk 2 blocks; it's on the right. Trishna started out as a food stall and, by word of mouth, became Bombay's trendiest seafood restaurant. Freakishly-sized shellfish at rock-bottom prices. Medium prawns with butter, pepper, and garlic are worth every paise of the Rs160. Pomfret (enough for two) Rs270; crisp calamari Rs130. Reservations essential for dinner. Open M-Sa noon-4pm and 6pm-midnight, Su noon-4pm and 7pm-midnight.

Sahakari Bhandar, to the right as you face the Regal Cinema. Fast and friendly snack joint. A convenient and safe place for *bhel puri* (Rs14) and *pao bhaji* (Rs22). Duck the fruit garlands on your way in, and don't miss the Chicu Milkshake (Rs24). Great, cheap South Indian tiffin (*dosas* Rs15). Open M-Sa 8am-9pm.

Ling's Pavilion, Mahakavi Bhusan Rd. (☎285 0023). Head north up the Causeway; it's the last street on the right before Regal. Ling's serves Chinese food free of mutation *a la masala* in an ultra-swanky, multi-colored fantasyland where iridescent fish frolic in a purple pond. Cantonese dishes include *dim sum* for two (Rs100) and a variety of tasty meat, seafood, and veg. options (entrees Rs100-200). Open M noon-3pm and 6-11:30pm, Tu-Su noon-11:30pm.

MAHARASHTRA

MAHARASHTRA

STREET EATS IN BOMBAY—HOW BRAVE

ARE YOU? Life in the streets of Bombay is tough—it takes guts of steel just to eat there. But a streetwise stomach is your passport to some of the city's best food. At every major intersection, food stalls, Bombay's truest "budget" food source, vie for the attention of passersby. One common sidewalk staple, **pao bhaji**, consists of batter-fried balls of potato and chilies served on white bread. Vendors also sell roasted peanuts, chickpeas, and **Bombay Mix** in small servings. The veggie sandwiches, spread with butter and green chutney, are stuffed with potatoes, cucumber, tomato, onion, and an optional slice of beetroot. But the most popular pavement peddling is the **bhel puri**. Puri, innocent-looking fried pastry shells, come in two varieties: flat and disc-like or hollow and spherical. The disc form serves to scoop up a sticky mixture of green chutney, tamarind sauce, chili paste, fried vermicelli, puffed rice, potato, tomato, onion, green mango, and coriander to create the full-blooded *bhel*. In **sev puri,** the crunchy frisbees act as platters for the same vegetable mix, minus the starch and plus *sev*: red, crunchy, and MSG-packed. *Chaat-wallahs*, as the snack merchants are known, fill the spherical version with a thin sauce or a spiced curd to create **pani puri** and **dahi puri,** respectively. Round off a full meal with fresh fruit or a slab of *kulfi*, and wash it all down with **coconut water, nimbu pani** (lemonade), or (if you're into typhoid roulette) **sugarcane juice.**

▨ **Cafe Churchill,** Colaba Causeway, between Walton and Garden Rd. This tiny, brightly colored cafe serves American snacks that taste better and cost less than those at the big tourist hangouts in the area. All-day breakfast skillets Rs50; sandwiches Rs40-55; brownies and cakes Rs25-40. Open daily 11am-11:30pm.

Olympia Restaurant and Coffee House, Rahim Mansion, opposite Mondegar's, SBS Marg, Colaba. Time stands still in this 2-tiered, turn-of-the-century, Iranian-style cafe. Today's owners are Bengali Muslims, but they've preserved the ancient carved chairs, marble-topped tables, and affordable Iranian cuisine that characterize one of Bombay's most distinctive genres of food. Brain *masala* fry (Rs27) is their most famous dish, but no-brainers will also be satisfied. Mutton *biryani* Rs14. Open daily 11am-11pm.

Majestic, Colaba Causeway, opposite Mondegar's, up a few stairs. Simple dishes (Rs18-40) and basic *thalis* (Rs20) served in a huge hall with low tables under whirring fans. And you thought there was no such thing as budget in Bombay. Open daily 7am-11pm.

Mondegar's Cafe, Metro House, Colaba Causeway. The first corner on the left after Regal. Bond with fellow backpackers grooving to the CD jukebox. Breakfast Rs50-65; dinner Rs45-80. Beer Rs90 per bottle. Open daily 8am-11:30pm.

Khyber Restaurant, 145 MG Rd. (☎267 3227). Where MG Rd. meets the Prince of Wales Museum. Lavish antiques-and-mirrors decoration; M.F. Hussain murals; intimate, multi-storied nooks and crannies; and, above all, the finest Mughlai cuisine in all the city. This expensive hotspot is Bombay's most popular restaurant. Chicken *makhanwala* (Rs225) swims in thick, tangy tomato sauce; chicken *badami* (Rs225) is superb. Reservations essential. Open daily 12:30-3:45pm and 7:30-11:45pm.

Sanuk Thai, 30 K. Dubash Marg (☎204 4233), behind the Prince of Wales Museum. Classy, authentic Thai food. Meat and vegetarian curries Rs180-280. *Pad thai* Rs120-220. Reservations recommended. Open daily noon-3pm and 8pm-midnight.

BEYOND COLABA

▨ **Indian Summer,** 80 Veer Nariman Rd., Churchgate (☎283 5445). You won't need to eat again for days after one of Indian Summer's upscale, sumptuous, all-you-can-eat Mughlai lunch buffets, which include appetizers, bread, meat, dessert, and a pint of beer (Rs270 plus 12% tax). Epic seafood buffet M night (Rs300 plus tax), and a large *a la carte* menu, too. Chicken and lamb dishes Rs165; veg. Rs140. Open daily noon-3pm and 7pm-12:45am.

Bharat Lunch Home (the Excellensea), 317 Mint Rd., Fort (☎261 8991), 3 blocks south of the GPO. Two restaurants in one. At Bharat, the budget option on the ground floor, tubfuls of live crabs await their cruel, creamy end (Rs150). Draft beer Rs35; fried squid *kolwada* Rs80. The A/C Excellensea offers longer menus, giant lobsters, and bigger bills. Open daily 11:30am-4pm and 7pm-midnight.

Rajdhani, Sheikh Memon St. (☎342 6919), opposite Mangaldas Market, near Crawford Market. From Crawford, look down the crowded lanes opposite Dr. DN Rd.; it's on the right of the lane with the turreted white building at the far end. Bombay's best, richest Gujarati lunchtime *thalis* (Rs85). Open daily 11:30am-3:30pm and 7-11pm.

New Kulfi Centre, opposite Chowpatty, near the pedestrian overpass where SVP Rd. meets Marine Dr. Locals stand on the sidewalk to wolf down creamy *kulfi* desserts in every possible flavor at this legendary street-side stall. Ask for *mutka kulfi*, served in small, earthen pots that you can take home. Open daily 10am-12:30am.

Jimmy Boy Cafe, 11 Bank St., Fort (☎270 0880), one block south of Horniman Cir., at Green St. A sleek Anglo-US fast-food conceit hides very Parsi roots. Burgers and sandwiches (Rs40-60) are good, but even better are the sweet-and-sour spiced Parsi veg. or non-veg. meals served on a banana leaf (Rs80-100), the *sassan-i-machli* (a spicy fish curry), and the *khir ghosh*, served in a bed of saffron rice. Open M-Sa 11am-11pm.

New Yorker, 25 Chowpatty Seaface (☎363 2923). America gets class in this A/C eatery opposite Chowpatty Beach. Trendsters down well-prepared plates of everything from pizza and sandwiches to nachos and falafal (Rs35-115). Open daily 11am-11:15pm.

Samrat, Prem Court, J. Tata Rd., Churchgate. From Churchgate, it's on the left side of the road that leads to the right of Eros. Fancy, pure-veg. restaurant specializes in slightly sweet Gujarati *thalis* (Rs100-130). You can wash down the all-you-can-eat *chappatis, dahl,* and vegetables with a bottle of beer (Rs80). Open daily noon-10:30pm.

Gaylord's, VN Rd., Churchgate (☎282 1259), on the left as you walk from Churchgate to Marine Dr. The sidewalk cafe, barricaded by potted plants, offers a pleasant compromise between indoor and out. Skip the overpriced menu (grilled sandwiches Rs80-95) in favor of the European pastries (Rs12-30) and freshly baked breads from the adjoining bakery as you linger over a cappuccino. Open daily 10am-11:30pm.

The Pizzeria, 143 Marine Dr., Churchgate (☎285 6115). Where VN Rd. meets Marine Dr. A cool bay breeze and pizza as authentic as anything Bombay can bake. Choices include margherita (8in. Rs100, 12in. Rs175) and the stuffed-crust Meat Ultimo (Rs270). Pasta dishes Rs150-185. Open daily noon-11:30pm.

Under the Over, 36 Altamount Rd., Kemp's Corner (☎386 1393), just beyond (and "under") the flyover at Kemp's Corner. Deep south shrimp gumbo, of all things, Rs255; pasta Rs150-200; chimichangas Rs165; brownies or cheesecake Rs110. Open daily 12:30-3:30pm and 7-11:30pm.

◉ SIGHTS

The Raj might have ended over half a century ago, but the most British-influenced area continues to dominate the sight-seeing scene in modern Bombay.

COLABA

THE GATEWAY OF INDIA. The quintessential starting point from which to lose yourself in the endless metropolis is the Gateway of India. Built to commemorate the visit of King George V and Queen Mary in 1911, this Indianized triumphal arch stands guard over the harbor next to the Taj Mahal Hotel. With a cosmopolitan nonchalance typical of Bombay, the gateway combines carved brackets derived from Gujarati temple architecture with Islamic motifs such as the minaret-like finials in a purely European building type. By day, the area is a sea of relentless tour touts. In the evening, however, the gateway is a favorite haunt of strolling couples, camera-happy tourists, peanut vendors, and snake charmers. In the small park nearby stands an imposing equestrian statue of the great 17th-century Maratha leader **Shivaji Bhonsle** (see p. 414). The reputation of this historical king and legendary hero has been hijacked by the right-wing Maharashtrian party, Shiv Sena, which decks out the unwitting image in marigold garlands and saffron flags.

TAJ MAHAL HOTEL. While modern tower of the Taj Mahal Hotel dwarfs Shivaji, the building's older wing is the real eye-catcher. Jamshedji Tata, one of India's first industrialists, built this Bombay landmark in 1899 in retaliation against the Europeans-only policies of other Raj-era hotels. Like all the other Tata enterprises, which dominate today's Indian economy, the Taj soared to success, monopolizing both the hotel industry and the city's early skyline. A self-assured expression wins even grubby backpackers access to the reverberant corridors inside.

AFGHAN CHURCH. Down at the southernmost end of the Causeway stands the 19th-century Afghan Church, built to commemorate the soldiers who died to keep the Khyber Pass British. This area also houses an old colonial cemetery and the now-defunct Colaba **lighthouse.**

KALA GHODA

PRINCE OF WALES MUSEUM. Opposite the Regal Cinema is the Prince of Wales Museum. The intervening gardens provide a buffer between the newly restored domed gallery and the relentless traffic outside. The most impressive exhibit is the collection of miniature paintings from the 16th to 18th centuries. These painstakingly detailed works showcase the various Rajasthani, Deccani, and Mughali schools in scenes of palace life, Hindu mythology, and animals. Other areas of the museum feature cluttered displays of everything from Mughal miniatures to stuffed animals and fourth-rate oil paintings. The first hall contains a trove of archaeological treasures dating back to the Indus Valley civilization. They include well-preserved stone tools and burial urns from both Harappa and Mohenjo-Daro. Another highlight is the collection of metal deities. (☎ 284 4484. Open Tu-Su 10:15am-6pm. Rs150.)

The **Jehangir Art Gallery,** just behind the Prince of Wales Museum, hosts temporary art exhibits. The displays focus on contemporary Indian painting, providing a counterpoint to the miniatures next door. The quality of the art here is mixed, but it's free and air-conditioned. (☎ 284 3989. Open daily 11am-7pm.) Inside the museum, **Cafe Samovar,** opening onto a garden, provides a peaceful escape, where you can munch on snacks and light meals. (Open M-Sa 10:30am-7:30pm.)

NEAR BOMBAY UNIVERSITY. The buildings of Bombay University and the **High Court** line the left side of MG Rd. from the Prince of Wales Museum to Flora Fountain. These Victorian-Gothic extravaganzas, centering on the 85m **Rajabai Clock Tower,** occupied the seafront until the Art Deco neighborhood opposite was built on reclaimed land in the 20s and 30s. Today, their finest facades face the Oval Maidan, one block to the west. The wide, grassy maidans, which now support enthusiastic cricket matches, used to separate the British residential communities in Fort from the Indian areas on the other side. (Open daily 11am-5pm.)

THE FORT AREA

Another area of sights stretches north from **Flora Fountain,** now renamed **Hutatma Chowk (Martyrs' Square)** in honor of the protesters who died agitating for a separate Marathi-speaking state in 1959-1960. Flora is lined by still more Raj-era Gothic buildings, now inhabited by foreign banks.

HORNIMAN CIRCLE. Horniman Circle strikes a calm, dignified note in the midst of the surrounding commercial hubbub. The elegant neoclassical colonnade faces the early-19th-century **Asiatic Society Library** (originally the Town Hall) across a small park complete with fountain. The neighboring **Mint and Customs House** also dates from the early 1800s. Bombay's oldest English building is **St. Thomas's Cathedral,** at the southwest corner of the circle. Although begun by East India Company Governor Gerald Aungier in 1672, when Surat was still the capital of the Bombay

THE GRRLS OF BOMBAY

The Koli fisherwomen of Bombay swear, spit, scream, and will seek retribution if you dare turn up your nose at them, let alone hold it as you walk by. In Marathi, Koli means "contentious woman." If you want icons of women's liberation, skip the bourgeois short-skirted babes of Breach Candy and extol these authentic anti-chicks instead. Utterly unrefined (every conversation starts with a profanity and sounds like a cat fight) and completely self-sufficient, Koli women will douse with reeking fish water those passersby who note, under their breath, the Kolis' putrid stench. They rise at dawn, head to the wharf to purchase the day's catch, and return home after the entire load is sold, only to be greeted by a slew of domestic duties. Indeed, amid the cosmopolitan chaos of Bombay, these "traditional" types perform, with superior agility, the working woman's balancing act. But then, most of Bombay's *Femina*-flaunting females are too busy holding their noses to notice.

Presidency, St. Thomas's remained incomplete until 1718. The interior reveals a fascinating slice of colonial life with its *punkahs* and endless marble memorials to long-gone English types. *(Open daily 6:30am-6pm.)*

NORTH FORT. At the northern edge of the fort area stand the grand colonial edifices of the GPO and **Victoria Terminus (VT).** Opposite VT, the **Bombay Municipal Corporation Building** comes as close to scraping the sky as any Victorian building could. The 76m dome can be viewed from the interior during office hours. **Crawford Market** sends a lesser, if equally improbable spire into the sky. Lockwood Kipling, Rudyard's father, designed the sculptures on the exterior during his tenure at the nearby art school. *(MJ Phule Market, a quick stroll up Dr. DN Rd. from VT, past the huge Times of India building and the Bombay School of Art.)*

CHURCHGATE AND BACK BAY COAST

NEAR CHURCHGATE STATION. The pink-and-white wedding cake of the **Eros Cinema** in the middle of this period-piece area exemplifies Bombay's unparalleled wealth of interwar architecture. Some of the surrounding buildings, on the same square as Churchgate Station, have been restored to their original waxy, zig-zag glory, but most have suffered from the damp, salty air and landlords constrained by rent control. Visitors strolling down the side of the maidan from Churchgate will find it hard to believe that these dilapidated apartments fetch millions of dollars on the rare occasions when they come up for sale.

KOLI VILLAGE. From the maidan, Maharishi Karve Rd. merges with Cuffe Parade Rd., where an abrupt gap in the land reclamation schemes has left a small bay between the towers of Nariman Point and the Cuffe Parade Extension. A fishing village, still populated by the original inhabitants of Bombay, the Kolis, lines the shore here (see **The Grrls of Bombay,** above).

MARINE DRIVE. In the opposite direction from Churchgate, Marine Dr. runs along the rim of the Arabian Sea, stretching all the way from Nariman Point to Chowpatty Beach at the foot of Malabar Hill. Near the beach, the Drive is lined with overflow from the supply of massive, gray "tetropods" that keep downtown Bombay from the waves below. At sunset, people come to stroll, power-walk, and jog along the sea front, chatting, buying snacks, and treating their children to rides on toy cars and merry-go-rounds while Chowpatty Beach comes alive with vendors, locals, and Kolis mending their fishing nets. During the monsoons, tremendous waves crash down on the street, but its roasted-corn hawkers, buses, and cars seem unperturbed. At night, neon ads and a long string of streetlights transform the seaside strip into what is still popularly known as the **Queen's Necklace.**

MALABAR HILL

Beyond the beach rises Malabar Hill, Bombay's wealthiest residential district.

MAHARASHTRA

BANGANGA TANK. The **Walukeshwar Temple** hides in one of the many old back streets that wind through Malabar, lined with bright flower stalls and renegade chickens. In local legend, the area harbored the banished hero of the *Ramayana*, Rama, and his brother Lakshmana, as they traveled south to free Rama's wife from captivity in Lanka. In order for Rama to perform his daily worship, Lakshmana had to bring a *linga* from far-off Varanasi. He was late one day, prompting Rama to make one from the only material he had, sand *(waluk)*, thus creating a *walukesh-war* ("sand god"). The temple's massive gray *shikhara* sits at the head of Banganga Tank, a huge rectangular pool of greenish water surrounded by jagged lines of rundown settlements and as full of legend as it is of bathers and *dhobis*. The thirsty Rama created the tank by shooting his arrow into the ground, and water began to gush forth to quench his thirst. What was once a celestial drinking fountain is now a glorified sink. Just behind the temple, the maze of *dhobi ghats* along the shore is crowded with row upon row of half-dressed washermen crouched low on the rocks, beating to smithereens the washables of everyone else in the city. The city has even more impressive *dhobi ghats* near the Mahalaxmi race course, but these are less accessible to most tourists.

THE HANGING GARDENS. The city's two most famous gardens are also at the top of Malabar Hill. Sir Pherozeshah Mehta Garden, locally known as the Hanging Garden, is at the terminus of buses #106 and 108. *(Open daily 5am-9pm. Free.)* The **Kamala Nehru Children's Park** across the street features a replica of the shoe that the old lady and all her children used to live in. *(Open daily 5am-8pm.)* Old people, families, and young lovebirds come to the park to relax, walking among topiary and penguin-shaped trash cans, lounging on lawns and benches, and taking in the views of the city. Crowning Malabar Hill are the seven massive **Parsi Towers of Silence**, where Zoroastrians set out their dead for vultures to eat. The whole complex is screened from sight by artful landscaping. The funerary customs of the Parsis nonetheless caused a stir a few years ago when the vultures threatened to contaminate the city's water supply by dropping leftover morsels in nearby reservoirs.

BABULNATH MANDIR. The entrance to **Babulnath Mandir** on Babulnath Mandir Rd. is an unassuming set of three small stone arches, seemingly held up by the throngs of flower sellers, holy men, and worshipers around their base. The gates open up to a world far removed from the jams of Marutis below, where a concert of blaring bells and chanting voices blankets the path up the stone stepped hill. The temple itself is loudly alive during worship. As you head back down, your ears still ringing, don't be surprised to find lines of women squatting beside baskets of coiled cobras asking for money to feed their serpents milk—feeding them on certain days of the week is considered an auspicious tribute to Shiva.

MANI BHAVAN. As the site of the first meeting of the Indian National Congress, Bombay pays tribute to the Father of the Nation and one-time citizen of the city, Mahatma Gandhi. The Mahatma stayed at Mani Bhavan during his frequent visits to Bombay. The building now houses a **museum** to the great man, with a huge research library on Indian history, Gandhi, and Independence. Along with a film archive, the museum includes a small collection of old photos and a "look-and-see" diorama version of the great moments in Gandhi's life and the struggle for independence. *(19 Laburnum Rd., a quiet lane in the streets behind the temple. Open daily 9:30am-6pm. Rs5.)*

MAHALAXMI AREA

MAHALAXMI TEMPLE. The Mahalaxmi Temple's patron goddess (like Bombay itself) devotes herself to wealth and beauty, making this *mandir* the city's most popular. In addition to a depiction of Lakshmi riding a tiger, the temple contains images of Kali and Saraswati, two other major goddesses of the Hindu pantheon. *(North past the flyover-ed shopping hub of Kemp's Corner, near the sea on Warden Rd., also called Bhulabhai Desai Rd.)*

TOMB OF HAJI ALI. Just beyond Mahalaxmi, on an island in the middle of the Arabian Sea, the shrine of the Sufi saint Haji Ali battles the waves daily. The bright white building stands out against the blue or gray of the sea like a beacon to all camera owners. The narrow causeway to the island disappears at high tide and during the monsoon storms, but at other times even non-Muslims can stride past the expectant rows of beggars as far as the outer chambers. On dry ground next to Haji Ali, the **Mahalaxmi Racecourse** cuts a green gash through the gray cityscape. The races run on weekends from December to May.

NEAR WORLI. Farther north still, on the edges of the upscale neighborhood of Worli, the **Nehru Centre** showcases Indian history, culture, and science. The theater offers both Indian and Western performing arts (see **Entertainment**, p. 404). The **Nehru Science Museum,** whose park is dotted with animal rides and old train cars, is mostly geared to children, but it also offers an exhibit on Indian contributions to science, from ancient ayurvedic medicine and the dawn of mathematics to current genetic discoveries by H.G. Khorana. (☎ 493 2667. Open Tu-Su 11am-5pm.)

CENTRAL AND NORTHERN BOMBAY

West of Crawford stretches an endless string of bazaars: first **Zaveri (Silversmiths) Bazaar,** then **Bhuleshwar Market** near the Mumbadevi Temple, and finally **Chor (Thieves) Bazaar,** northward by Johar Chowk.

BYCULLA. North again from Johar Chowk along Sir JJ Rd., in the neighborhood of Byculla, the **Victoria and Albert Museum** (now Veermata Jijabhai) sees relatively few foreign tourists. The exhibits on Bombay's history include the carved stone elephant that gave Elephanta Island its name. (Open Th-Tu 9:30am-5pm. Rs2.) For the real thing, head next door to Bombay's **zoo,** where mangy animals subsist in depressing surroundings. The adjacent **Botanical Gardens** are a more salubrious setting for a stroll. (Open Th-Tu 10:30am-4:30pm. Rs2.) The architecture in Byculla, in contrast to the examples farther south, is dominated by congested housing complexes known as *chawls,* which flourished during the first half of the 20th century when Bombay was enjoying its status as the country's premier cotton manufacturer and textile producer. The center of the city, where most of the factories were located, became the center of working class life, and the *chawls* served as a cauldron for labor unions to brew in. By the 1950s, however, rapid industrialization in other areas brought about a decline in textiles and with it a degeneration of Bombay's *chawls.* Today, 20 percent of Bombay's population lives in this tenement-style housing, where 10 families might share one room, a kitchen, and toilet.

JUHU BEACH. Scruffy palm trees and litter make this a less than idyllic sunbathing spot, but that doesn't stop crowds of city-dwellers from flocking here as the sun sinks down into the Arabian Sea. In a carnival-like atmosphere, you can bounce along in horse-drawn carriages, ride rickety ferris wheels, chow down at *chaat* stands, join in pick-up volleyball games, or simply stroll and wade along the water's edge. One of the best-known spots in the city, the Juhu area is also home to many a Bollywood star. The bungalow of the country's most famous actor, Amitabh Bachchan, is constantly surrounded by a small pack of curious crowds hoping to catch a glimpse of their hero. (Take a local train from Churchgate to Santa Cruz station. 45min., Rs5. Exit station on the west side, and take a rickshaw to Juhu Beach. Rs15.)

SANJAY GANDHI NATIONAL PARK. The Sanjay Gandhi National Park features over 100 rock-cut caves, although only a few amount to much more than holes in the wall. Nonetheless, those planning to hit Ajanta, Ellora, or Karla and Bhaja can come here for a quick prep course, while others can treat this as a kind of consolation prize. Cave 3, a *chaitya* hall guarded by two huge standing Buddhas, is the most interesting place to explore. (In the northern suburb of Borivili. Take the train to the Borivili stop. Open daily 9am-5:30pm. Rs2.)

ESSELWORLD. Esselworld, the larger of Bombay's two amusement parks, exhibits its middle-class urban life in its most packaged form for ruin-weary travelers. (From the Borivili railway stop, head to Gorai Creek (Borivili-W), where free ferries depart for Corao Island 10:30am-7:30pm. ☎ 492 0891 or 807 7321. Open daily 11am-7pm. Rs150; children Rs128.) Your ticket also gets you into the neighboring **Water Sports Complex.**

🎭 ENTERTAINMENT

Check *This Fortnight* or the *Bombay Times* section of the *Times of India* for the weekly bulletin of the latest concerts and plays at the **Tata Theatre,** the **Nehru Centre,** and a host of smaller venues.

Nehru Centre, Dr. Annie Besant Rd., Worli (☎ 492 8192 or 492 6042). In the same complex as the Nehru Planetarium, on the right just past the Mahalaxmi race course. Indian and Western classical music and theater. The **Planetarium** (☎ 492 0510) has English shows Tu-Su at 3 and 6pm, Rs10.

National Centre for the Performing Arts, Marine Drive (☎ 283 3737), at the very tip of Nariman Pt., just beyond the Oberoi. The compound houses a main theater, an experimental theater, and a third venue scheduled to open soon. More European and American offerings than at the Nehru, but good Indian music and theater, too.

Prithvi Theatre, Janki-Kutir, Juhu-Church Rd. (☎ 614 9546), along a lane that juts off the main road leading to the Juhu bus station. The theater hall here is a city legend and one of Bombay's most popular, with performances in many languages. Tickets Rs60. Call for dates and times of English shows.

🛍 SHOPPING

Like some enormous, quasi-tropical Mall of India, Bombay can fulfill every material need and wanton consumer desire in every price range. A two-minute walk north from Flora Fountain leads to a part of MG Rd. known as **Fashion St.,** an endless chain of street stalls selling cheap and disorientingly similar merchandise. The hawk-eyed hawkers of hackneyed, Western designer cast-offs can spot naive tourists a mile off, so bargain without shame. (Open daily roughly 10am-8pm.) For those who need a hiatus from haggling, **Cottage Industries Emporium,** Shivaji Marg, offers a government **fixed-price** alternative. Though it's unabashedly geared toward tourists and, compared to the chaos of the streets outside, rather sterile, you're guaranteed good quality and reasonably fair prices. The emporium is a pathetically convenient one-stop souvenir shop, proffering such wares as batik fabrics, handmade silk Nehru jackets and scarves, and all things sandalwood. (Open M-Sa 11am-7pm. Accepts major credit cards and exchanges money.)

The **Khadi Bhavan Village Industries Emporium,** at the corner of Dr. DN Rd. and Sir PM Rd. in Fort, offers hand-woven cotton cloth, *kurtas*, and traditional knick-knacks at reasonable prices. (☎ 207 3280. Open M-Sa 10:30am-6:30pm.) The more upscale **Bombay Store,** formerly known as the Bombay Swadeshi Store, is along Sir PM Rd. in Fort. The A/C store's gleaming glass cases and polished hardwood shelves bear little resemblance to the *swadeshi* movement's spinning wheels and simple, homemade cloth. Like a department store specializing in "ethnic" merchandise, this is sterile, spoon-fed shopping, but the quality and selection is hard to grumble about. (☎ 288 5048. Open M-Sa 10:30am-8:30pm, Su 11am-7pm. Major credit cards accepted.) Travelers with particularly fat wallets should head over to **Warden Rd.** near Kemp's Corner. This line of stores is the place to go if you want to match, thread for thread, the clothing worn by Bombay's hipsters.

🌙 NIGHTLIFE

Unlike most cities in India, Bombay knows how to party. International Bright Young Things pack the city's pubs and discos in search of the next "in" thing. Beware of the pervasive (though sporadically enforced) "couples only" policies on busy nights, and the occasional refusal of dirty-looking T-shirted or sandal-clad travelers. Bars and clubs in Bombay tend to close by 1am, causing a mass exodus to the all-night coffee shops at luxury hotels. If you're looking to splurge, try the **Taj Mahal Hotel**, Apollo Bunder (☎202 3366), in Colaba; the **Ambassador Hotel**, VN Rd. (☎204 1131) in Churchgate; the **President Hotel** in Cuffe Parade; or **The Oberoi**, Marine Drive (☎202 5757), in Nariman Point.

☒ **The Ghetto,** 30 Bhulabhai Desai Rd., Breach Candy (☎492 1556), in an alley on the seaward side of the road, just before Mahalaxmi. Bombay's most happening bar is full of yuppie kids every night. Blacklight, murals, a pool table, and a rockin' soundtrack make this hangout worth the trek. Beer Rs50; spirits Rs50 and up. Open daily 7pm-1:30am.

☒ **Headquarters,** Colaba Causeway (☎288 3982), upstairs from Cafe Royal, across the intersection from Regal Cinema. HQ is the young, hip hotspot for a crowd that drinks and dances the night away, especially on packed W, F, and Sa nights. W, F Rs400 cover per couple; Sa Rs500 per couple; other nights no cover. Draft beer Rs70; pitcher Rs200. Open daily 8:30pm-1am.

Three Flights Up, Shivaji Marg, Colaba (☎282 9935), next to the Cottage Industries. Swank, huge, and probably the least 'regional' club around. A neon trail down the mirrored black hallway leads up to the longest bar (40m) in the city. Half of the Rs200 cover goes toward beer (Rs75, pitcher Rs200) and cocktails. Semi-enforced 'couples-only' on the dance floor. Open daily 7:30pm-1:15am; busiest W, F, and Sa.

Beyond 1900s, in the Taj Mahal Hotel, Colaba (☎202 3366). Ushering in the new millennium with a major renovation and a new name, the disco formerly known as 1900s is priced to maintain its status as Bombay's most glamorous pretty-person nightspot. Cover Rs330 per head; Su-Th Rs300 goes toward drinks. Open daily 10pm-1am.

Gokul's Permit Room, Tullock Rd., parallel to the Taj, one street behind Colaba, next to Gokul's Communication Centre, this working man's beer-and-scotch joint is as authentic an Indian watering hole as can be. Escape the glitz and have a bottle of beer (Rs50) and a plate of fried Bombay duck (Rs45). Open daily 11am-midnight.

Voodoo, Arthur Bunder Rd., Colaba, 4 doors up on the left from the sea front. A dive for the desperate during the week, Voodoo transforms into Bombay's only above-ground gay disco on Saturday nights. India's most famous gay rights activist, Ashok Rao Kavi, is a regular. Beer Rs65. Cover Rs180. Open daily 7pm-1:30am.

Leopold Cafe, Colaba Causeway, Colaba (☎202 0131), 3 blocks down from Regal, on the left. A landmark stop for burnt-out escapees from both the West and the East. The dimly lit A/C upstairs hosts the serious drinkers. Beer Rs58, pitchers Rs200. Open daily 1pm-1am. Downstairs open daily 8am-11pm.

The Pub at Rasna, J. Tata Rd., Churchgate (☎282 0995), on the left side of the road that leads to the right of Eros from Churchgate, just after the small circle. Futuristic—if the future hinges on tall metal chairs, neon lights, streamlined decor, and a confusing floor plan. The children of Bombay's jet-set jam up against the aerodynamic bar, leaving breathing space only on the small dance floor. Beer Rs60. Open daily 7pm-1am.

M A H A R A S H T R A

THE THIRD SEX India has an entire subculture of **hijras,** which translates very roughly as "those between" or "shifters." Some *hijras* are hermaphrodites, others castrated or emasculated, while the rest have functioning male sex organs. They live with other *hijras* in modern-day harems. Their ambiguous sexual orientation and their dabbling in prostitution earn *hijras* little status in Indian society, and most Indians are reluctant or unable to explain exactly what they are. However, when a baby is born, a group of sari-clad *hijras* will show up at the hospital, where the proud parents welcome their blessing (which involves singing, dancing and, often, throwing the baby in the air) with baksheesh, for it is considered quite auspicious.

◪ DAYTRIP FROM BOMBAY

ELEPHANTA ISLAND

Elephanta is accessible by a one-hour ferry ride from the Gateway of India. It is not unheard of for the slow-moving ferries to ram into each other. Only luxury boats run during the monsoon months (roughly June-Sept.), and then only when waters are navigable. Enquiry ☎ 202 6364. Every 30min., 9am-2:30pm; return 11am-6:30pm. Round-trip Rs65-85. Open Tu-Su 9am-5:30pm. Rs5. Admission includes a group tour of the caves with government-approved guide.

About 10km northeast of the Gateway of India, Elephanta Island, in Bombay Harbor, offers travelers a fleeting glimpse of an Indian fishing village in its heyday. Well, almost—Elephanta is what happens to the quaint village when more tourists than fish are dragged in from the water. The island's 8th-century cave temples have lured in thousands of visitors, and locals haven't hesitated to capitalize. Point your Nikon at fisherwomen draped in emerald, magenta, and lime saris, and risk the repercussions—they will chase you, squawking demands for baksheesh (without upsetting the silver *mutkas* balanced on their heads). Also be prepared for the free-roaming monkeys ready to strip you of chips, Frootis, and bananas.

In spite of its hassles (the ferry ride itself is an adventure), Elephanta remains justly renowned for its truly extraordinary **cave temples.** The cave, at the end of a 125-step climb up the mountainside, covers over 5000 square meters, much of which is filled with moss and bats. The main chamber has a cross-like arrangement of massive pillars with no functional purpose. The image of Shiva as the cosmic dancer Nataraja is carved in detail near the entrance; the damage is due to the Portuguese, who reportedly used it for target practice when they occupied the island in the 1800s. A weathered and beaten-up panel of Lakulisha, a saint considered to be an incarnation of Shiva, stands opposite. The main **Linga Shrine** in the center of the cave is accessed by entrances on all four sides, each flanked by a pair of *dwarapalas*, guardians at least as vicious as the fisherwomen. The other attractions in the cave are the elaborate **wall panels** depicting assorted scenes from Shiva mythology in remarkable detail. On the north side is a lively panel of Shiva as Bhairava killing the demon Andhaka, who was attempting to steal a divine tree. The three panels on the south side of the temple are the caves' central attraction. The 6m-tall bust of Shiva as the three-faced Trimurti, Lord of the Universe, is also worth a look. To the sides, the descent of Ganga and Shiva as Ardhanarishvara (half male, half female) are shown. Near another entrance is a detailed panel showing Ravana's attempt to uproot Mount Kailasa.

MATHERAN माथेरान ☎ 02148

Once an exclusive retreat for Raj-era sahibs, the hill station of Matheran (95km east of Bombay) now swarms with Indian weekend vacationers. The village shuts down from mid-June to August, when the monsoon rains arrive. For frazzled Bombayites and city-weary travelers alike, the high-class, full-board resorts, open public spaces populated by wandering monkeys, red clay paths through leafy forests, and magnificent views are just the ticket for a few days of relaxation.

▣ GETTING THERE AND GETTING AROUND. The access point for Matheran is the small town of **Neral,** which lies at the base of the hill station. From Bombay's VT Station, local trains to **Karjat** stop at Neral Junction (approximately every hr., 6am-1am, 2hr., Rs16). Only a few of the Bombay-Pune express trains stop at Neral (*Deccan Exp.*, 6:40am; *Koyana Exp.*, 8:45am; 2½hr.; Rs30). From Neral, Matheran is 21km up the hill. It's a toss-up as to which option for this ascent is more nerve-wracking—a **taxi** hired at the station (Rs45 per person shared; Rs225 solo ride) or the **miniature train** (8:40, 11am, and 5pm; return 5:45am, 1:10, and 2:35pm;

2½hr.; Rs24). Tickets for the train can be reserved 3 days in advance, but not on the day of departure, at Pune and Bombay VT stations. During the monsoon, mini-train service is sporadic and may be cancelled entirely. Since motor vehicles are prohibited in Matheran, taxis cannot take you all the way into town. The taxi stand/drop-off is 2.5km north of the railway station; to complete the trip you're left with a 40min. hike (a *coolie* will carry your bags for Rs40), a rocky but fun horse ride (Rs80), or a hand-pulled rickshaw (Rs120). Matheran levies an entry tax on all visitors (adults Rs10, children Rs5).

ORIENTATION AND PRACTICAL INFORMATION.

The miniature train pulls into the **Matheran Railway Station,** on the main road, **Mahatma Gandhi Marg (MG Marg),** at the center of town. The **tourist office** is opposite the railway station and has town maps (open M-Sa 9:30am-5:30pm; closed during the off-season). Moving south down MG Marg—right if you're facing the railway—the **GPO** is on the left. Past the GPO, a fork to the right passes the **police station** before continuing on to Charlotte Lake. **Currency exchange** is available at **Union Bank of India,** on the right side of MG Marg as you walk south from the station. (☎30282. Open M-F 10am-2pm, Sa 10am-noon.)

ACCOMMODATIONS AND FOOD.

Matheran is a resort town, and prices can be high, especially in season, when reservations are required. In the off-season, many hotels close down or offer substantial discounts. Mid-week prices are generally open to a bit of haggling. Single rates are rare, and many family resorts will turn away solo travelers. Check-out times are distressingly early (7am is standard), and hotels will gleefully charge you for another half-day if you sleep in. The **Hotel Prasanna,** with all-Hindi signs, is opposite the train station. It contains tidier-than-usual bathrooms and warm showers. (☎30258. Doubles Rs600. Closed in the off-season.) North of the train station, on the opposite side of the tracks from MG Marg, the family-run **Hunjer House** offers one of the more pleasant budget options, with balconies on some of its basic-but-clean rooms and hot water in the mornings. (☎30536. Doubles Rs500-600. Off-season: Rs200.) The best room-and-board deal is the **Janata Happy Home,** on Kasturba Rd. Heading south from the station, take the first right, and then turn left onto Kasturba. (☎30229 or 30429; booking in Bombay (022) 619 3899. Doubles from Rs800; 30-50% discount off-season. Two night minimum stay.) For a more resorty option, with room service, a pool (with waterslide!), and a playground, try the **Gujarat Bhavan Hotel,** Maulana Azad Rd. Walk south on MG Rd., and then follow the signs. The five types of rooms range from Rs500-1500 and meals are included. All rooms are 40% less off-season. (☎30278; in Bombay (022) 203 0876. Two night minimum stay.)

There are several simple restaurants on MG Rd., south of the railway station. The amiable **Kwality Restaurant** has *bhel puri* for Rs18 and *dosas* for Rs18-22. (Open 9am-9:30pm; closed June 15-Aug. 15.) Many hotels offer full board—a good choice in the heavily discounted off-season, when non-hotel meals are few and far between. **Divadkar Hotel,** opposite the train station, serves non-guests. (Chinese and Indian dishes Rs40-80; beer Rs65. Open noon-2:30pm and 7-10:30pm.) Local specialties include *chikki*—a sweet, sticky, crunchy peanut brittle—and mango fudge, which tastes much better than it sounds (or looks, for that matter).

VIEWS.

The borders of the hill station are marked by numerous sheer cliff outcrops. Many of these have been set up as viewpoints. On the western side, **Porcupine and Louisa Points,** provide a glimpse of Neral in the distance. Also popular are **Monkey Point** to the north and **Alexandra Point** to the south. **Panorama Point** sits to the far north. The viewpoints are very romantic at sunset and sunrise: expect to feel left out if you're not here on honeymoon. Women are advised not to explore the more remote locales alone at night.

NASIK नासिक   ☎ 0253

Blackened bursts of diesel fumes, swirls of red and orange *kum kum* powder, and clouds of dust kicked up by thousands of bare feet all mingle in Nasik, along the banks of the sacred Godavari River. Nasik is believed to be the site where *Ramayana* bad-guy Ravana abducted Rama's wife Sita, igniting one of the greatest metaphysical match-ups in Hindu religious lore (see **The Ramayana,** p. 579). Today, Nasik's purity as a religious haven seems threatened by the growth of industrial plants all along the riverbanks. The jingle-jangle of temple bells and the hypnotic humming of the meditative syllable *om* combine discordantly with the chug and spit of smokestacks and exhaust pipes. Nevertheless, every year thousands of devotees head to Nasik to walk along the same pathways that their gods and goddesses once trod. Nasik plays host to the **Kumbh Mela** festival (see p. 209) every 12 years. During the Mela, one of the most auspicious moments in the Hindu calendar, millions come here to take a purifying dip in the waters of the Godavari.

▐ GETTING THERE AND GETTING AROUND

Trains: The **railway station** (☎ 561274) is 8km from the city center. As you leave the platforms, the booking office is on the left. To: **Bombay** (10 per day, 4hr., Rs53) and **Nagpur** (4 per day, 12:20am-11:45pm, 12hr., Rs225).

Buses: Central Bus Stand, Sharanpur Rd. (☎ 572854). To: **Ahmedabad** (5 per day, noon-1am, 12hr., Rs175); **Aurangabad** (every hr., 5:30am-2am, 4½hr., Rs97); **Bombay** (every hr., 5hr., Rs86); **Nagpur** (10pm, 15hr., Rs32); **Pune** (every 30min., 5hr., Rs103). Buses from Bombay arrive at **Mahamarga Bus Stand,** 7km away.

Local Transportation: Auto-rickshaws rule the road and are grudgingly subject to meters.

◼✳️▐ ORIENTATION AND PRACTICAL INFORMATION

Nasik's spiritual life centers on the banks of the **Godavari River.** Its commercial heart is a couple of kilometers away, near the **Central Bus Stand (CBS),** at the intersection of **Sharanpur** and **Old Agra Rd.** To the north, running parallel to Sharanpur Rd., is **Gangapur Rd.** To the south is **Trimbak Rd. MG Rd.,** providing access to the river area in the city's northwest corner, is off the northern end of Old Agra Rd. The **Nasik Road Railway Station** is 8km southeast of the CBS. Nearby is the chaotic **Dwarka Circle** (bus to CBS Rs4; auto-rickshaw Rs40).

Tourist Office: MTDC, T-1, Golf Club, Old Agra Rd. (☎ 570059). From the CBS, head down Old Agra, past the State Bank. Turn right at the 2nd major intersection; the MTDC is 5min. down on the right. Open M-F and 1st and 3rd Sa 10am-5pm.

Currency Exchange: State Bank of India, Old Agra Rd. (☎ 599935). Go right from the CBS; it's 200m after the intersection on the left. Open M-F 11am-5pm. **Trade-wings,** 1st fl., Manoram Arcade, Vakil Wadi (☎ 579556), off MG Rd., by Panchavati Hotel. Open M-F 9:30am-6pm, Sa 9:30am-3pm.

Police: Police Commissioner's Office (☎ 570183), off Sharanpur Rd.

Hospital: Lifeline, Wadala Rd. (☎ 591634 or 597904), near Dwarka Circle.

Internet: There are several cybercafes in **United Arcade,** on College Rd., opposite B.Y.K. College's main gate. Rs20-35 per hr. Open daily 9am-midnight.

Post Office: GPO, Trimbak Rd. (☎ 502141). Go down Old Agra Rd. from the CBS and turn left at the first major intersection. The GPO is on the right, beyond the next intersection. Open M-Sa 10am-6pm, Su 10am-2pm. **Postal Code:** 42001.

▐ ACCOMMODATIONS

Budget hotels cluster near the CBS on Shivaji and Old Agra Rd., and along Dwarka Circle. Most have noon check-out. Good luck finding a room during the Mela.

Hotel Siddharth, Nasik-Pune Rd. (☎553376 or 552620; fax 554288), near the Nasardi Bridge, 2km past Dwarka Circle, on the right. Sunny rooms with sparkling white walls, balconies, attached baths, TVs, and telephones. The expansive, well-maintained lawn in the back is ideal for evening lounging. Singles Rs350-500; doubles Rs500-700.

Raj Mahal Lodge, Sharanpur Rd. (☎580501; fax 571096; email rajmahallodge@vsnl.com), opposite the CBS. Basic rooms, unbeatable location, and relatively cheap rates conspire to fill the Raj's rooms early, so act fast. 24hr. STD/ISD in the lobby; TVs and telephones in all rooms. Singles Rs180; doubles Rs240-550.

Hotel Vaishali, Gole Colony (☎579910 or 573311; fax 575909). At its end farthest from the river, MG Rd. turns into a dirt alley; Vaishali is on this alley. Tidy, passable pink rooms in a location just close enough (and just far enough) from the chaos of the Goadvari. TV and phone in all rooms. Singles Rs300-525; doubles Rs430-675.

Hotel Basera, Shivaji Rd. (☎575616 or 575618). Cross the intersection from the CBS and head down the small alley on the left. Simple rooms in slight disrepair all have TVs and telephones. Singles Rs210-350; doubles Rs200-475. **Hotel Suruchi,** downstairs, dishes out dirt-cheap South Indian standbys. Open daily 6am-10:30pm.

FOOD

The **Samrat Restaurant,** in the Hotel Samrat, Old Agra Rd., opposite the State Bank, serves up pure veg. Gujarati *thalis* (Rs70) that are popular with locals. The canteen-like ambience is in step with the bus stand hullabaloo nearby. (Open daily 11am-3pm and 7-10:30pm.) **Nandinee Woodlands Restaurant,** Nasik-Pune Rd., in the plaza opposite Hotel Siddharth has a sleek decor, a Western clientele, and a real taste explosion in the form of excellent South Indian and Chinese dishes (Rs15-75). It also serves Western snacks like pizza (Rs50) and french fries for Rs25. (Open daily 9am-11pm. Meals 11am-3pm and 7-11pm.)

SIGHTS

GODAVARI RIVER. The easiest way to get to the sacred Godavari River is via the narrow, meandering alleys that shoot off from MG Rd. You don't have to walk far down the sloping pathways before you leave the thick traffic fumes behind you and are surrounded by the clatter of candy, *kurta*, and cloth vendors. Just beyond the Old Quarter, shallow squares of murky water can be seen next to the **Santar Gardhi Mahara Bridge.** Most mornings they are merely a gathering place for hundreds of *dhobi-wallahs* scrubbing clothes on the Godavari's stone steps, while huge groups of baksheesh babies tenaciously follow more moneyed visitors. Every 12 years, however, these *ghats* experience the onslaught of thousands of devotees who flood Nasik during the **Kumbh Mela.** Nasik's next Mela is in 2004, but it's not impossible to imagine the frenzied cacophony that ensues at this time—one glance at the sprawling **market** directly behind the *ghats* will give you an idea. Rickety stalls sell row upon cluttered row of religious paraphernalia as well as fruits, vegetables, nuts, lentils, steel jewelry, carved statuettes, and bronze vessels.

OTHER SIGHTS. Among the market stalls around the *ghats* are several sites steeped in mythology. Nasik's religious focal point, several meters to the left of the **Ram Sita footbridge,** is the **Ram Kund.** Thousands of people immerse themselves here in order to purify themselves of sin. The waters here are also supposed to have the unusual power to dissolve bones; the remains of several celebrities and top politicians (from members of the Nehru-Gandhi dynasty to Rama's father, King Dasharatha) languish here in the **Astivilaya Tirth** ("Bone Immersion Tank"). Up the hill from Ram Kund is **Kala Ram Mandir,** a temple at the site where, according to the *Ramayana,* Rama's brother Lakshman sliced off the nose (in Sanskrit, *nasika)* of Ravana's monstrous sister, Shurparnakha. The *mandir,* normally not open to Western visitors, houses ebony images of the myth's main protagonists. Sita's cave, or **Gumpha,** marks the site where Sita was abducted by the demon Ravana.

MAHARASHTRA

PUNE पुणे
☎ 020

As Bombay has become more and more congested and cosmopolitan, the steady trickle of daily commuters between Bombay and Pune (POO-nuh) has turned into a flood. In recent years there has been a mini-exodus to the cooler, more relaxed Pune, a four-hour climb up the Deccan Plateau. Birthplace of the Maratha hero Shivaji, capital of his successors, and an almost purely Marathi-speaking city, Pune lays a much more credible claim to son-of-the-soil status than its upstart cousin on the coast. Some of Bombay's urban sophistication (and dot-com-modernity) has made the trip to Pune, too, but without most of the characteristic Bombay madness. The city's biggest dose of internationalism springs from Pune's famous ashram, the Osho Commune International, established by the late "export guru" Rajneesh. The Birkenstock-clad crowd in their maroon robes (called *sannyasins*) come from all over the world to converge on Pune and undergo Osho's various meditation therapies. Pune's other attractions may not be as renowned as its ashram, but the city's biggest selling point is the easy-going and lively spirit of its people, which makes any stay among the city's crumbling, historic landmarks and pleasant parks worthwhile.

▶ GETTING THERE AND GETTING AROUND

Flights: Airport, Pune Nagar Rd. (☎6685591), 10km from the city. An Ex-Servicemen's bus leaves every hr. from outside the GPO (Rs25). **Indian Airlines,** Ambedkar Rd. (☎632140), near the Sangam Bridge, in Camp. **Jet Airways** (☎6137181). To: **Bangalore** (1 per day, 1½hr., US$145); **Bombay** (Indian Airlines, 1 per day M-Sa, US$45; Jet Airways, 2 per day, 35min., US$85); **Delhi** (Indian Airlines and Jet Airways, 1 per day, 2hr., US$205); **Madras** (Jet Airways, daily, 3hr., US$175).

Trains: Railway Station, MPL Rd. The booking office, on your left as you face the station, has sections for local tickets, reservations, and Bombay trains. Reservations upstairs. Fares listed are 2nd class. To: **Bangalore** (2 per day, 2:35am and noon, 20hr., Rs284); **Bombay** (5 per day, 6am-6:20pm, 4hr., Rs89); **Hyderabad** (4:45pm, 13hr., Rs194); **Miraj** for **Goa** (5:30pm, 9½hr., Rs109); and **Neral** for **Matheran** (2 per day, 6am and 3pm, 2hr., Rs104).

Buses: Pune has 3 main state stations and many private carriers. The most convenient station for tourists is right next to the railway station. To: **Bombay** (every 15min., 5am-10pm, 4½hr., Rs100); **Mahabaleshwar** (10 per day, 5:30am-6:30pm, 4hr., Rs76); **Panjim** (4 per day, 11hr., Rs331). Buses from **Shivajinagar Station** in Deccan head for: **Aurangabad** (12 per day, 5am-6pm, 6hr., Rs115); **Lonavla** (every hr., 2hr., Rs30); **Nasik** (every 30min., 5hr., Rs105). Go to **Swargate Station** for buses to **Bangalore** (2:30pm, 20hr., Rs300). It's worth shelling out the extra rupees for a private "deluxe" bus instead of the rickety old state machines. One reliable private carrier is **Bright Travels,** Connaught Rd., Sadhu Vaswani Square (☎6050879), a block south of MPL Rd.

Local Transportation: Auto-rickshaws are the best means of getting around Pune. The conversion rate is roughly 4-5 times the meter reading; ask to see a chart. Local **bus #4** goes to Deccan; #5, 6, and 31 go south toward Swargate bus station and the old town.

▰ ORIENTATION

Though quiet compared to Bombay, Pune is still a huge city, with a population of three million. The city is divided into two vaguely defined sections: the **Camp** and the **Old Town.** The railway station and one of the major bus stands rub shoulders in Camp, between **Sassoon Rd.** (formerly part of Connaught Rd.) to the east and **MPL Rd.** to the south. Camp's upscale shops and restaurants cluster around **MG Rd.** A 10-minute rickshaw ride west of here is the Old Town, where traditional *wadas* (mansions) surround the **Swargate Bus Terminal, Raja Kelkar Museum, Phule Market,** and the ruined **Shaniwar Wada Palace.** Farther west across the Mutha River is the middle-class neighborhood of **Deccan,** which stretches to Fergusson College Rd.,

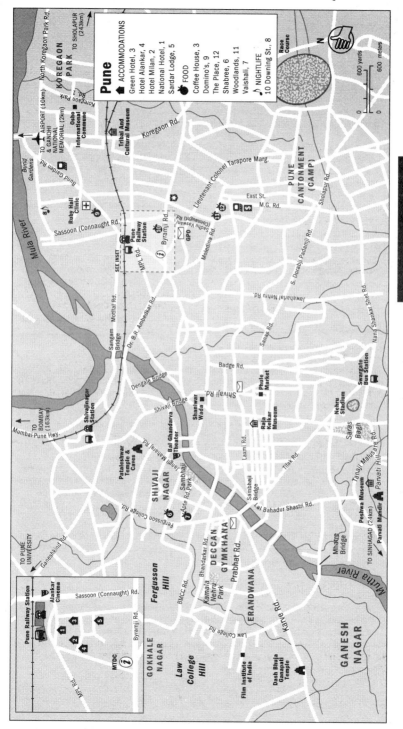

MAHARASHTRA

Pune

♠ ACCOMMODATIONS
Green Hotel, 3
Hotel Alankar, 4
Hotel Milan, 2
National Hotel, 1
Sardar Lodge, 5

● FOOD
Coffee House, 3
Domino's, 9
The Place, 12
Shabree, 6
Woodlands, 11
Vaishali, 7

♪ NIGHTLIFE
10 Downing St., 8

is where Pune's students hobnob in a string of restaurants and cafes. The Koregaon Park suburb to the northeast of Camp, home to the **Osho Commune,** occupies its own distinctive physical (and psychological) space.

Street names can be confusing in Pune. The old Connaught Rd. is now called Sassoon Rd. north of its intersection with Byramji, and Sadhu Vaswani to the south, even though it is essentially one street. Sassoon Rd. and Bund Garden Rd. flow into each other in a similar fashion, as do Ambedkar and Moledina Rd.

🛈 PRACTICAL INFORMATION

Tourist Office: MTDC, I block of Central Building Complex on Byramji Rd. (☎6126867). From the bus station, head south (right) on Sassoon Rd. Turn right at the first round-about onto Byramji Rd. The Central Building complex is about a 5min. walk down on the right. Enter through the main gate, and follow the road straight back. The MTDC is the first building on the left after the road curves. Not worth the walk, unless you're really desperate. Open M-F 10:30am-4pm. The **Bus Station Branch Office** (☎6125342) offers fifteen-point sightseeing tours of Pune (9am, 7½hr, Rs70).

Budget Travel: Apple Travels, Amir Hotel, Connaught Rd. (☎6128185), in Camp, at the junction of Sassoon and MPL Rd. Open M-Sa 9:30am-6pm.

Currency Exchange: AXE Central Bank of India, MG Rd. (☎6131413), in Camp, 5min. south of Moledina Rd. Up to US$500 cash advance on Visa or MC. Open M-F 11am-1:30pm. **Citibank,** East Rd., in Camp, 10min. south of Moledina Rd. has a 24hr. **ATM.**

Bookstore: Manney's Bookstore, 7 Moledina Rd., Clover Centre (☎6131683), in Camp. The best source for Pune maps. Open M-Sa 9:30am-1:30pm and 4-8pm.

Police: Bund Garden Station, Byramji Rd. (☎6123825). From MPL Rd., head south along Sassoon Rd. and make your first left onto Byramji. The station is the small house on the right, immediately after the first intersection. Open 24hr.

Hospital: Pune Medical Foundation, Ruby Hall Clinic, 40 Sassoon Rd. (☎6123391), in Camp. From MPL, turn left on Sassoon Rd., cross the railroad tracks, and follow the road to the right. On the left, immediately past Domino's Pizza. **Pharmacy** open 24hr.

Internet: Connect Cyber Cafe, Ashoka Mall, Bund Garden Rd. (☎6051918), opposite the Holiday Inn. Rs10 per hr. Open 24hr. There are many cybercafes in the MG Rd. area. A good, cheap one is **Cross Web Net Cafe,** MG Rd., two blocks south of Moledina Rd. On the right side of the street, inside a shopping center and up red, faux-marble stairs. Rs20 per hr. Open daily 9am-midnight.

Post Office: Sadhu Vaswani Rd. A domed stone building on the right, 5min. south of the intersection of Sassoon Rd. and MPL Rd. M-Sa 10am-6pm. **Postal Code:** 411001.

🛏 ACCOMMODATIONS

Almost all of the budget hotels in Pune are within the **Wilson Garden** area. Many of these buildings were once opulent personal *wadas*, though many of them are starting to crumble a bit these days. To get here, take the small lane to the left of the National Hotel and turn right at the corner.

National Hotel (☎6125054), opposite the railway station. Vast verandas sprout from the well-tended gardens of this 150-year old palace-turned-hotel. All rooms except singles have attached bath. Check-out noon. Singles Rs180; doubles Rs300-350.

Sardar Lodge, Wilson Garden (☎6125662), across the park from the main road. Friendly, and well-maintained. Check-out 24hr. Singles Rs110; doubles Rs160-325.

Green Hotel, 16 Wilson Garden (☎625229). Stained glass, wood finish, wrought iron, and old furniture make the Green unique among Pune's budget dives. Check-out 5pm. Singles Rs175; doubles Rs250-300.

Hotel Alankar, 14 Wilson Circle (☎6120484). Simple rooms (some with balconies) along long, quiet corridors. Check-out 24hr. All rooms with attached bath. Singles Rs250; doubles Rs325.

Hotel Milan, 19 Wilson Garden (☎6122024). One of the cheaper places with TVs and telephones. The rooms themselves are nothing extraordinary. Check-out 5pm. Singles Rs225–450; doubles Rs260-525.

⌔ FOOD

Lieutenant Colonel Tarapore Marg, which crosses Sadhu Vaswani Rd. a block before Moledina Rd., becomes a huge open-air cafe in the afternoons and evenings. Countless drink and *chaat* stalls lure revelers into street-side seats (or squats) to gossip and people-watch (closed on Sundays). The area between the bus stand and the railway booking office is full of fruit carts, providing perfect provisions for a peelable breakfast.

The Place: Touché the Sizzler, 7 Moledina Rd., Camp. The snappy, 2-tier Tudor interior packs in Pune's yuppies for "sizzlers"—iron skillets filled with vegetables, fries, and a choice of entree (veg. Rs90, non-veg. Rs110-175). Tandoori dishes also available (Rs70-125). A hotspot, indeed. Open daily 11:30am-3:30pm and 7-11pm.

Woodlands Restaurant, Woodland Hotel, Byramji Rd., Camp. Go south along Sassoon Rd. and turn right at the first intersection. Punjabi, Mughlai, and Chinese dishes Rs50-75. The Mysore *dosa* is magnificent. Open daily 7-11am, 12:30-3pm, and 7-11pm.

Coffee House, 2 Moledina Rd., Camp. Decent coffee and the standard array of Chinese and Indian dishes (Rs30-55). Tables are jammed with locals at peak times. Open daily for snacks 8am-11:30pm; meals 11am-3pm and 7-11:30pm.

Vaishali, Fergusson College Rd., Deccan, opposite Fergusson College. Tree-canopied backyard overflows during the day with students and at night with families, who all flock here for the *bhel puri* and South Indian snacks (Rs15-30), ice cream and shakes (Rs20-40), and the lively scene. Open daily 7am-11pm.

Shabree, Hotel Parichay, Fergusson College Rd., at the corner of Shola Rd., opposite Deendayal Hospital. One option—the ultimate, unlimited *thali* (Rs60)—is served up by majestically uniformed waiters. Open daily 11:30am-3:30pm and 7:30-11:30pm.

The German Bakery, North Koregaon Park Rd. From the Osho ashram, take a right at the gate, walk to the end of the road, and turn left; it's on the right. Homesick *sannyasins* spill *Apfelstrudel* crumbs (Rs22) onto their maroon robes in this popular, open-air, chill-out spot. More upbeat devotees can chat over cappuccino (Rs20) or "sterilized" pineapple juice, all the while pondering the merits of the acupuncture, *tai chi,* and Tao healing lessons advertised colorfully around them. Open daily 7am-midnight.

Domino's Pizza, Graficon Arcade, at the corner of Sassoon Rd. and Dhole Patil Rd. (☎6133022), opposite Ruby Hall clinic. Domino's will serve up a pie even better than the one you get at home, with an Indian twist on toppings like *paneer* and lamb (Reg. Rs50). And yes, they deliver within 30min. (within the 3km delivery area), or it's Rs30 off. Open daily 11am-11pm.

🎵🎦 ENTERTAINMENT AND NIGHTLIFE

One of the few disco-pubs around to cater to Bombay wannabes is **10 Downing St.,** Boat Club Rd. (☎6128343), off Bund Garden Rd., at the northern edge of town. Legions of students grind away on the strobe-lit upstairs dance floor, while a more mixed crowd throws back beers (Rs50) on the chill, ultraswank first floor. (Open daily 7pm-12:30am. Cover: W Rs150, Sa Rs250; ladies free on W. Dance floor is couples and single women only.) Huge crowds take in Bollywood flicks, afternoon and night, at numerous theaters in the city, including **Alankar Cinema,** Sassoon Rd. (☎6123333; Rs15-50) and **West End Cinema,** next to Touché the Sizzler on Moledina Rd., which also shows big Western releases. **The Film Institute of India,** Law College Rd., offers more high-brow stuff, but (at least in theory) you have to be a member to get in. **Nehru Memorial Hall,** Moledina Rd. (☎6128560) and **Bal Gandharva Theater,** Jangli Maharaj Rd. (☎5532959) stage performances of Indian drama, music, and dance. For more detailed listings and schedules, see the "Pune Plus" section of the *Times of India.*

SHIVAJI Pune is justly proud of its status as the birthplace of one of India's great national heroes, Shivaji Bhonsle. By the time of his birth in 1630, Muslims had dominated the subcontinent for 400 years, and persecution of Hindu subjects was widespread. Against this backdrop of oppression, the 16-year-old nobleman from the landholding Hindu Bhonsle family of the Maratha region of the Bijapur Sultanate declared his divine mission: the violent restoration of religious tolerance.

Shivaji's cunning and courage kept him one step ahead of his nemesis, the ardently Muslim Mughal emperor Aurangzeb. In 1659, Shivaji lured the Bijapur Sultan's Muslim general, Afzal Khan, into a "discussion" and ripped out his innards with his *wagh nakh*, or metal "tiger claws." Meanwhile, his troops dessimated the Bijapuri army. In 1666, Shivaji gave himself up at Agra, only to smuggle himself out of house arrest in a basket of sweets. On another occasion, he supposedly captured the sheer-walled fort of Sinhagad (see p. 415) by training lizards to carry ropes up the cliff face.

Shivaji ruled his Maratha Confederacy with religious impartiality, recruiting both Hindu and Muslim officers. Even after his death in 1680, the Confederacy continued to prosper until the British arrived. In the 1950s, Balasahek (Bal) Thackeray, a Bombay-based cartoonist, revived Shivaji's status as a folk hero and founded a political party in Maharashtra called the Shiv Sena in his honor. The party, however, does not share Shivaji's tolerance, opting instead for a doctrine of rigid Hindu nationalism and hostility toward Muslims.

🔎 SIGHTS

OSHO COMMUNE INTERNATIONAL. Upwardly mobile meditators worldwide flock to Pune's famous ashram, a weird synthesis of health-club luxury and hodge-podge of Eastern spirituality. Here, followers of the late, great, and intercontinentally controversial guru, Osho (also known as Bhagwan Shree Rajneesh), gather to practice his New Age meditation techniques among lush tropical plants. As the guru himself said: "The very air has a different vibe." Though most seekers come on a journey of self-transformation, the classy facilities, including an open-air meditation hall, swimming pool, library, bookstore, vegetarian canteen, jacuzzi, and "*zen*nis courts," don't hurt, either. However, these are only vaguely visible from the tour; to be a real part of the Osho Commune requires an HIV test (Rs125), two passport photographs, three robes, and Rs130 per day (Rs40 for Indians). Apart from six daily meditations—which encourage you to "become an empty vessel" or engage in the cathartic explosion of "shouting wildly the mantra 'Hoo!'"—all courses, food, and other services cost extra. (*17 Koregaon Park, in the northwest part of Camp.* ☎6218561; email commune@osho.com; www.osho.com. Visitors' Center open daily 9:30am-1pm and 2-4pm. Daily guided tours 10:30am and 2:30pm, 1hr., Rs10. One day advance ticket purchase recommended.)

SHANIWAR WADA. Amid the narrow winding streets of Old Town, the remains of the massive Shaniwar Wada Palace, built in 1736, are Pune's most celebrated and most decrepit landmark. At the height of its glory, the walls enclosed the multi-story home of the Peshwa rulers, the opulent bureaucratic center of the powerful Maratha empire that ranged across all of central India. Sadly, the inner structures burned down in 1828, leaving only the foundation and the palace's outer walls and gates for tourists and picnickers to explore. (*Shivaji Rd. Open daily 8am-6pm. Rs2.*)

RAJA KELKAR MUSEUM. The pack-rat passion of the late Dr. D.G. Kelkar, the museum's founder, has resulted in a vast collection that is as eclectic as it is eccentric. Enthusiastic guides lead groups through three floors of galleries, highlighting unique exhibits and their peculiarities: an elephant-shaped foot scrubber, eight images of Ganesh carved on a bean, and a painstakingly relocated and reconstructed 18th century royal palace room from Madhya Pradesh. More than just a random mish-mash of kitschy bric-a-brac, the exhibits here take obvious delight in the diversity of India's cultures in a light-hearted style often missing from more high-minded exhibits. *(Baji Rao Rd., Deccan Gymkhana. Open M-Sa 8:30am-6pm, Rs80.)*

TRIBAL AND CULTURAL MUSEUM. India has over 600 tribal communities, incorporating 67.7 million people—9% of the nation's population. This obscure gem of a museum celebrates those cultures and their craftwork with over 2000 artifacts, taken primarily from the 47 Maharashtran groups. The anthropologist staff more than makes up for the lack of English signs, offering unparalleled explanations of the "tribals'" cultural practices and survival concerns. *(Koregaon Park Rd., just south of the railroad tracks. Open M-F 10am-5pm. Free.)*

PATALESHWAR TEMPLE CAVES. Almost overshadowed by the modern temple next door, the 8th-century Pataleshwar Caves exude spirituality. A circular stone gazebo (a Nandi *mandapam*) stands by the entrance to the small underground temple, adding a marvelous escape from the Pune bustle to the peace and simple beauty of the site. *(On Jangali Maharaj Rd., near the intersection with Shivaji Rd.)*

OTHER SIGHTS. The **Ghandi National Memorial** is sadly neglected. The elegant architecture of the Aga Khan Palace, where Gandhi was once imprisoned, fades behind the crumbling paint and stained floors you see as you approach. A time-line of Gandhi's life, in similar condition, leads you through a few rooms and, outside, to the *samadhis* containing the ashes of Gandhi's wife. *(Aga Khan Palace, Pune-Nagar Rd., on the way to the airport. Open daily 9am-5:45pm. Requested donation Rs5.)* **Parvati Hill,** at the far southwest corner of Pune, has a pleasant view of the city and surroundings. A sloping staircase leads from a side street off Tanaji Malusane Rd. up to two temples, several outlooks, and the **Peshwa Museum.** *(Open 7:30am-8pm. Rs3.)*

DAYTRIP FROM PUNE: SINHAGAD FORT

Spread high atop the rugged green hills 24km southwest of Pune, Sinhagad Fort makes for a pleasant day's ramble away from the city. The fort is one of the most important historical sites in the area; its conquest by the great Maratha king, Shivaji, was an important step in the fierce drive to reclaim the area from the Mughals. There's not much left of the fort today. It is still possible to enjoy the awesome, sweeping views across the plateaus and to get a sense of the power and grandeur of the 17th-century warring empires. Locals make the weekend pilgrimage to their hero's mountaintop, wandering about the massive ruins, drinking the revered "sweet water" from the well, and snacking at the many ramshackle huts at the top of the fort area.

To reach Sinhagad from Pune, take public **bus** # 50 (Rs10) from the Nehru Stadium bus stop. If you have enough fellow travelers, it's worth taking a **tempo** (about Rs15 per person). From the bus drop-off, it's a 1½-2 hour uphill **hike** to the fort—bring plenty of food and water—or a Rs25 per person **jeep** ride.

NEAR PUNE: LONAVLA लोनावळा   ☎ 02114

Lonavla is a popular destination for both foreign and Indian tourists, thanks to its proximity to the **Buddhist caves** at Karla and Bhaja. It is also easily accessible by train and bus on the Bombay-Pune routes. The section of town of most interest to tourists lies north of the train station on the opposite side of the tracks.

GETTING THERE. Lonavla's **bus station** is at the intersection of **Shivaji Rd.** and **National Highway 4.** From the intersection, go straight, keeping the field on your right, and take the first left. The bus station will be on your right. (Reservations M-Sa 8am-2pm and 2:30-8pm, Su 8am-2pm.) **Buses** head to **Bombay** (every 15min., 3hr., Rs60); **Pune** (every 15min., 2hr., Rs40); and the Karla and Bhaja caves (see below). **Trains** to **Bombay** (3½hr., Rs39) and **Pune** (2hr., Rs26) depart frequently.

ACCOMMODATIONS AND FOOD. Most of the tourists in Lonavla are families from Bombay and Pune looking to splurge on resort-style, hill station living. Budget travelers have few accommodation options, especially in season (Apr.-

June). About 100m to the left of the bus station on Shivaji Rd., the **Hotel Chandralok,** with its clean bathrooms and friendly staff, is probably the best bet. (☎72294 or 72921. Singles Rs290; doubles Rs390.) A less tidy budget option is the **Adarsh Hotel,** across Shivaji Rd. from the Chandralok. (☎72353. Doubles Rs300.) The **Hotel Swiss Cottage** is neither Swiss nor a cottage, though it does have a vaguely homey lodge-like feel. From the train station, walk straight toward town. Take the first paved right, and follow the signs up the driveway on the left. (☎71320. Singles Rs300; doubles Rs600.) The area around the bus station has the best selection of restaurants, whereas the railway station neighborhood is dominated by shops and the market. The Chandralok (see above) serves big, bottomless Gujarati *thalis* (Rs70). The **Udipi Restaurant,** on the Bombay-Pune Rd., is popular with locals and has both South and North Indian food (Rs20-40).

☒ **SIGHTS.** Tourists come here not for the town itself (which is eminently forgettable), but for the exquisite 1st century BC Buddhist caves chiseled into the high, basalt cliffs at nearby **Karla** and **Bhaja.** Several buses per day cover the 12km from Lonavla's bus station to Karla (Rs5). At Karla, a steep staircase leads up from the small bazaar to the outcrop high above the plain, where the main cave is located. Several religions have claimed this outcrop as their holy space. The main *chaitya* (temple) hall—the largest in India—was carved out by Hinayana Buddhists. Mahayana Buddhists added sculptures of elephants and people, and a modern Hindu shrine obscures the entrance to the *chaitya.* The pipal-shaped window, which signifies learning, illuminates the Buddhist stupa. (Karla caves open daily 8am-6pm. Rs2.) It's a 5km walk or rickshaw ride from the Karla to the Bhaja steps. To walk, go back along the Karla road, cross over the main road, and keep going straight. Turn right immediately after you cross the Malouvil Station tracks, and follow the road to the Bhaja steps. A serene atmosphere prevails at these 18 cleaner, calmer, less-touristed, and better-preserved caves, which were carved in the 2nd century BC. *Viharas* surround the main *chaitya* and include a celebrated relief of a war elephant tearing up trees in its path. Past the main area, there is a cave containing 14 identical stupas, and a room with sculptured reliefs of the Buddha and Vishnu side-by-side. Farther still, down a narrow path, a lone stupa is tucked away behind a trickling waterfall. (Bhaja caves open dawn-dusk. Free.) If you have time after the caves, check out the Maratha-era **Lohagad** and **Visapur Forts,** visible in the hills behind Bhaja.

About 5km south of town is Lonavla's most popular attraction during the monsoons, the **Bhushi Dam.** The dam has rock steps along part of its face, and at the peak of the rainy season, it overflows, allowing foamy water to spill down these stairs, where tourists and locals delight in the bubbles.

MAHABALESHWAR महाबलेश्वर   ☎02168

Mahabaleshwar is Indian hill station life at its finest. Thirty viewpoints, several waterfalls, a lake, and numerous old temples call out to those eager to escape the hustle of Pune or Bombay.

▣ **GETTING THERE AND GETTING AROUND. Buses** run to: **Bombay** (5 per day, 9:15am-9pm, 7hr., Rs20); **Pune** (every hr., 6:30am-7:30pm, 4hr., Rs53); and **Satara** (for train connections; 11 per day, 5:30am-3pm, 2½hr., Rs28). **Taxis** loiter at the stand (☎60931) opposite the bus station; they offer tours (2½hr.; Rs280) of Mahabaleshwar and nearby Panchgari.

▣▪ **ORIENTATION AND PRACTICAL INFORMATION.** All visitors to Mahabaleshwar are charged a Rs10 entry tax. The main part of the town is south of Old Mahabaleshwar. **Dr. Sabane Rd. (Main St.)** runs east-west. On this road is the bazaar, the heart of Mahabaleshwar. The **bus station** is at the far western end of Main St. **Masjid Rd.** runs parallel to Main St. to the north, and **Murray Peth Rd.** is parallel to the south. **Exchange currency** at the State Bank of India, Masjid Rd., a 5-minute walk east and one block north from the bus stand (open M-F 11am-2:30pm,

Sa 11am-12:30pm). The **police station** is on the right, farther east on Main St. (☎60333. Open 24hr.) **Morarji Gokuldas Rural Hospital,** Shivaji Circle (☎60247), with a 24-hour **pharmacy,** is farther north. **Bicycle rental** is available at the east end of the bazaar (Rs5 per hr). The **GPO/Telephone Office,** FG Rd., is north of the bus station. **Postal Code:** 6061.

ACCOMMODATIONS AND FOOD. During the wet season, even the best hotels go for next to nothing and the whole town basically shuts down. In season, however, rates can more than triple. The closest thing to a budget option, especially in season, is the **MTDC Holiday Resort,** 2 km south of the bus stand, which has clean doubles with 24-hour hot water. (☎60318. Rs400; off-season 30% off.) **Hotel Nells,** Main St., offers the best cheap beds in town in spare but neat rooms with TVs. (☎60323. Doubles Rs500. Off-season: Rs100.) At the newly restored **Kalpana Excellency,** Murray Peth Rd., small rooms with TVs surround a gleaming stone and marble courtyard. (☎60419. Doubles Rs1200. Off-season: Rs250.) **Hotel Aman,** Masjid Rd., has clean rooms with 24-hour hot water (in-season), phones, and TVs. (☎61087 or 60417. Rs800; off-season Rs200.) Mahabaleshwar is famous for its berries, which can be found in-season all over town.

SIGHTS. In the dry season, you can see the ocean from **Arthur's Seat.** Other lookouts such as **Bombay Port** and **Kate's Port** provide good views out over the surrounding countryside. **Venna Lake** in the north offers boating and fishing, and nearby **Old Mahabaleshwar** enchants with its endless historic cobblestone streets and two ancient temples—**Panchaganga Mandir,** which is purported to contain the springs of five rivers, and the **Mahabaleshwar Mandir,** which encloses a natural rock *linga.* The historic **Pratapghad** and **Kamalghad Forts** are also nearby. During the particularly rainy monsoon season (mid-June to mid-Sept.), however, thick fogs make it hard to see anything more exciting than the mud beneath your feet.

AURANGABAD औरंगाबाद ☎0240

Cradled by the crags of the Deccan Plateau, Aurangabad isn't likely to win many Most Exciting City awards, but its strong tourist infrastructure makes it a good base from which to explore its celebrated neighbors, Ellora and Ajanta. Boulevards that are broad and clean run under 52 huge, 17th-century gates built by ultraorthodox Aurangzeb, the last of the Mughal bigshots to rule India. Right-wing Shiv Sena councillors recently renamed the city in honor of Sambhaji, Shivaji's son and a Maratha Hindu hero in his own right. To everyone else, though, the city is still named for Aurangzeb, and the old square, the stone houses, the sizeable Muslim population, and the special, silky *himroo* fabric still give the city a distinctly Islamic air. These days, the main empire in town is the evil of industrial capitalism, as Aurangabad enjoys the economic boom typical of Bombay's hinterland. The brewing capital of India, Aurangabad is a mellow place to throw back a few locally made "Australian" lagers after a long day touring the nearby ruins.

GETTING THERE AND GETTING AROUND

Flights: The **airport,** in Chikalthana, Jalna Rd., is 8km from the city center. Buses run to and from the city bus office at the railway station (Rs5). Taxis into town cost Rs125. **Indian Airlines (IA),** Jalna Rd. (☎485421 or 483392), 150m west of Rama International Hotel. Open daily 10am-1pm and 2-5pm. **Jet Airways,** opposite Indian Airlines (☎441770 or 441392). Open daily 9am-6:30pm. Both IA and Jet fly to **Bombay** (1 per day, 45min., US$75). IA also has service to **Delhi** (1 per day, 3½hr., US$175).

Trains: Railway station, Station Rd. (☎331015). Fares listed are 2nd class. To: **Agra** (12:25pm, 20hr., Rs357); **Bhopal** (12:25pm, 12hr., Rs251); **Bombay** (2 per day, 2:45 and 9:20pm, 10hr., Rs157); and **Delhi** (12:25pm, 25hr., Rs369).

Buses: Central Bus Stand, Dr. Ambedkar Rd. (☎331217), 2km north of the railway station, along the continuation of Station Rd. West. Schedules and fares are for regular

MAHARASHTRA

buses. The so-called "semi-deluxe" buses cost about 30% more; full-on "deluxe" buses are 60% more. To: **Ahmedabad** (9pm, 14hr., Rs175); **Bombay** (2 per day, 8:15am and 8:30pm, 10hr., Rs165); **Hyderabad** (3pm, 12hr., Rs200); **Jalgaon** (10 per day, 6am-6pm, 4hr., Rs50); and **Pune** (every hr., 5am-midnight, 6hr., Rs80). Frequent buses head to **Ajanta** (3hr., Rs42); **Daulatabad** (30min., Rs6); and **Ellora** (45min., Rs12).

Local Transportation: Auto-rickshaws are convenient, but make sure that they use the meters. Cost-effective **tempos** function as mini-buses, scooting up and down major city routes. **Bicycles** are for rent just outside the Railway Station, on your left as you face the station. Rs3 per hr.; Rs20 per day.

✳️ 🛈 ORIENTATION AND PRACTICAL INFORMATION

Tourist facilities are along **Station Rd.,** which has two branches: the western half runs north from the railway station to the bus stand; the eastern branch runs northeast past several hotels and restaurants to **Kranti Chowk,** a major business area. From Kranti Chowk, **Jalna Rd.** runs east to the airline offices and the airport. **Dr. Rajendra Prasad Marg** cuts back west to intersect Station Rd. North of this intersection, near the bus stand, Station Rd. becomes **Dr. Ambedkar Marg.** It ends at the north end of town near the Bibi-Ka-Maqbara and the Aurangabad Caves.

Tourist Office: Government of India Tourist Office, Krishna Vilas, Station Rd. (☎331217), on the right side of the main (western) branch of Station Rd., about 250m from the station. **MTDC,** MTDC Holiday Resort, Station Rd. E. (☎331513 or 331198).

Budget Travel: Classic Travel, MTDC Holiday Resort, Station Rd. (☎335598 or 337788), inside the lobby to the right. Open daily 7am-10:30pm. AmEx, MC, Visa.

Currency Exchange: State Bank of India, Dr. Rajendra Prasad Marg, Kranti Chowk, (☎351126) on NW corner. Open M-F 10:30am-4pm, Sa 10:30am-1pm. **Trade-wings,** Dr. Ambedkar Marg (☎332677), opposite Hotel Printravel. Open daily 9am-7:30pm.

Swimming Pool: Hotel Aurangabad Ashok (☎339468), Dr. Rajendra Prasad Marg, allows non-guests to use its pool for Rs100—the perfect diversion for hot Deccan days.

Market: The Aurangpura area is one giant market, selling everything from chandeliers to pomegranates—a much better shopping spot than the tourist bazaars near the caves.

Police: Kranti Chowk Police Station (☎331773), 150m west of Kranti Chowk on a parallel street. Turn north at the water tower and then left; the station is on the left.

Hospital: Kamal Nayan Bajaj Hospital (☎321329 or 334447), down a lane 100m west of Kranti Chowk; on the right if coming from the town center. **24hr. pharmacy.**

Internet: Uma Internet Cafe, Dr. Ambedkar Marg (☎358303), a few doors down from Trade-wings. Rs50 per hr. Open daily 10am-midnight.

Post Office: GPO, Juna Bazaar Chowk, Bazaar District. Open M-F 10am-4pm, Sa 10am-1pm. **Postal Code:** 431005.

🏨 ACCOMMODATIONS

Most budget hotels are around the railway station and bus stand. The Government of India Tourist Office also arranges homestays with local residents (Rs200-400).

Youth Hostel (HI), Station Rd. West (☎334892), 1km from the station, on the right just south of the intersection with Dr. Rajendra Prasad Marg. Well-run and spotless. Cheap, mosquito-netted dorm beds, warm water bathrooms, and cafeteria (breakfast Rs12; lunch and dinner Rs22). Check-in 7-11am and 4-8pm. Check-out 9am. Curfew 10pm. Dorm beds Rs25, non-members Rs45; doubles Rs110.

Hotel Shree Maya, Bharuka Complex (☎333093; fax 331043; email shrimaya@bom4.vsnl.net.in). Walking north on Station Rd. from the Government Tourist Office, take the first two right turns; it's 100m on the right. Freshly painted marble halls and attractive rooms with telephones, TVs, attached baths, and 24hr. hot water. Internet Rs60 per hr. Check-out 24hr. Singles Rs175-395; doubles Rs245-395.

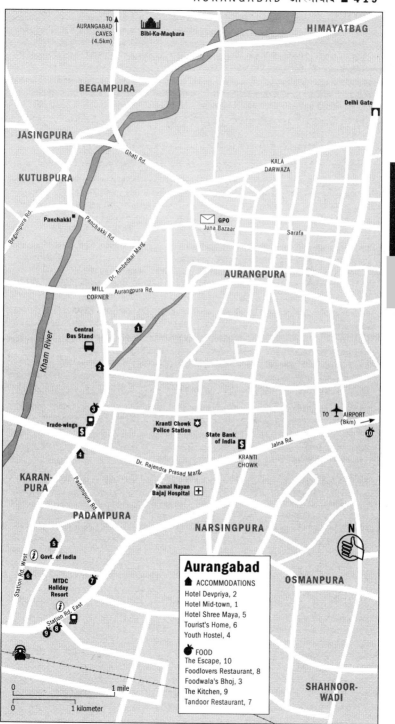

MAHARASH

TO
AURANGABAD
CAVES
(4.5km)

Bibi-Ka-Maqbara

HIMAYATBAG

BEGAMPURA

Delhi Gate

JASINGPURA

Ghati Rd.

KALA
DARWAZA

KUTUBPURA

Begampura Rd.

Panchakki

Panchakki Rd.

GPO
Juna Bazaar

Sarafa

Dr. Ambedkar Marg

MILL
CORNER

Aurangpura Rd.

AURANGPURA

Central
Bus Stand

Kham River

1

2

3

Trade-wings

Kranti Chowk
Police Station

State Bank
of India

TO ✈ AIRPORT
(8km) →

10

4

Dr. Rajendra Prasad Marg

Jalna Rd.

KRANTI
CHOWK

KARAN-
PURA

Padampura Rd.

Kamal Nayan
Bajaj Hospital

PADAMPURA

NARSINGPURA

N

5

Govt. of India

6

MTDC
Holiday
Resort

7

OSMANPURA

Station Rd. West

Station Rd. East

9 8

Aurangabad

🏠 ACCOMMODATIONS
Hotel Devpriya, 2
Hotel Mid-town, 1
Hotel Shree Maya, 5
Tourist's Home, 6
Youth Hostel, 4

🍎 FOOD
The Escape, 10
Foodlovers Restaurant, 8
Foodwala's Bhoj, 3
The Kitchen, 9
Tandoor Restaurant, 7

SHAHNOOR-
WADI

0 _____ 1 mile

0 _____ 1 kilometer

Hotel Mid-town, Nehru Place. Heading south from the Central Bus Stand, take the first lane on your left, turn left, and turn right at the sign. Finally, turn left, walk past the Shangrila Deluxe, and then turn right again. Spic 'n span tiled-floor rooms create an oasis amid the crud-haven that is the bus station budget scene. 24hr. check-out and hot water. Singles Rs150; doubles Rs250; triples Rs350.

Tourist's Home, Station Rd. West (☎337212), a 5min. walk from the railway station. Basic but solid and relatively clean—by far the best choice for tight budgets. All rooms with attached bath. Singles Rs100; doubles Rs150.

Hotel Devpriya, Dr. Ambedkar Marg (☎332344), just south of the Central Bus Stand. Despite all the bus station cacophony, this giant place has plenty of flavor. Attached baths and morning hot water. 24hr. check-out. Singles Rs150; doubles Rs250.

FOOD

The Escape, Jalna Rd., in Hotel Rajdoot. Yes, people in India *can* cook good Chinese food. This rare event occurs daily at the renovated Escape (formerly Mingling). Amid framed American vintage rock posters, savor noodles, veg. entrees, chicken, lamb, and seafood (Rs50-100). Large Indian selection, too. Open daily 11am-11:30pm.

Foodwala's Bhoj, Dr. Ambedkar Rd., in a big building 200m south of the bus stand, on the right, one floor up. Classy touches like a small rock fountain centerpiece mark this pure veg. joint as a hideaway for Aurangabad's elite. Tremendous *thalis* (Rs50) make up for the otherwise limited menu. Punjabi dishes Rs20-30; *dosas* and *uttapams* Rs12-18. Open daily 11am-3pm and 7-11pm.

Tandoor Restaurant, Shyam Chambers, Barsilal Nagar, Station Rd. East. Classy, civilized carnivores feast on tandoori specialities (Rs80-150). Mughlai (Rs80) and veg. (Rs35-65) dishes are also excellent. Open daily 11am-4pm and 6:30-11pm.

Foodlovers Restaurant, Station Rd. East, on the right, 250m from the station. Aurangabad's garden-restaurant fetish climaxes in this open-air thatched hall among bizarre, foaming, fake-tree fountains. Mammoth menu (353 items). Beer comes in a teapot. Open daily 12:30pm-midnight.

The Kitchen, Station Rd. E., by the train station. The budget trinity of good, cheap, and clean come together in Kitchen's South Indian snacks, bacon 'n' eggs breakfasts, and Bengali dishes. Entrees Rs15-50. Open daily 6am-11pm. Off-season: 7am-11pm.

SIGHTS

AURANGABAD CAVES. Aurangabad's cave temples are often eclipsed by the glamour that surrounds the caves at Ellora and Ajanta, but they remain a wonderful introduction to the breathtaking sculpture to be found all along Maharashtra's cave-trail and are blissfully free of tour groups and touts. Split into western and eastern sections, these important examples of Buddhist art and architecture were created by two great dynasties during the 6th, 7th, and 8th centuries. The western caves, numbers 1 through 5, are off the dirt road at the top of a treacherous climb up winding stone steps. The third and most beautiful cave was once a *vihara* (residence hall) for the wandering Buddhist monks *(bikshus)* of the time, who gathered in monastic communities in caves like these around the state. Some fragments of the original paintings depict stories about the Buddha's previous incarnations. The fourth cave is a *chaitya* hall, used for congregation and prayer. The eastern caves, numbers 6 through 9, are at the end of the right fork; they afford incredible views of the surrounding landscape, including the silhouette of Bibi-Ka-Maqbara against the city in the distance. The seventh cave greets visitors with lotus-framed *apsaras* (celestial dancing nymphs) at the entrance to the crypt. A shadowed Buddha sits peacefully inside the sanctuary, surrounded at his feet by the frozen faces of the disciples. Outside the final cave is a giant (broken) sculpture of the Buddha after his death. Visit the caves early in the morning when few tourists are there. *(In the hills behind the Bibi-Ka-Maqbara, up the dirt road that leads past the tomb; 10min. by auto-rickshaw or a 1hr. walk. Open dawn-dusk. Free. Bring a flashlight.)*

BIBI-KA-MAQBARA. Aurangzeb's son's milk-white monument to his mother, Begum Rabi'a Durani, has been the object of scorn as an inferior Taj Mahal knock-off. The Bibi-Ka-Maqbara was an important addition to the tradition of Mughal mausolea, but this relatively small tomb could never have challenged the Taj, even if cash shortages had not forced ungainly corner-cutting, such as the abandonment of marble for plaster a meter up the wall. *(Open daily dawn-10pm. Rs2; Free F.)*

PANCHAKKI. The Mughal water mill at Panchakki is a good stopover on the return trip from the caves or Bibi-Ka-Maqbara. The mill was built in 1624 in honor of Muslim saint Baba Shah Musafir to help feed the hundreds of orphans, paupers, and fakirs who were his devotees. From a well in the hills 11km away, water gushes through earthen pipes, is raised by a siphon, and then drops with intense force upon the blades of the water wheel. In the Panchakki's heyday, the output was almost four tons of finely ground grain. Today, Panchakki has been reduced to a breeding ground for hawkers and crafts shops specializing in the city's unique *himroo* fabric. *(Panchakki Rd. Open daily 7am-8:30pm. Rs3.)*

🚌 DAYTRIPS FROM AURANGABAD

DAULATABAD दौलताबाद AND KHULDABAD खुल्दबाद

There are several important sights along the road between Aurangabad and Ellora. The most impressive is the **Daulatabad fortress,** on top of a hill 13km from Aurangabad. In the 14th century, Muhammad Tughlaq, the Sultan of Delhi, decided this was just the spot for a capital. Rather than leave the development of a thriving city to chance, the not-so-savvy sultan decided to march the entire population of Delhi 1000km across India to people his new metropolis. Needless to say, the small proportion of the deportees who did not die on the way greeted life in the Deccan with a sullen resentment not conducive to prosperity. The Sultan abandoned his project after only eight years and marched the few survivors back home. Nevertheless, Daulatabad did grow to be an important city, and the fort itself is considered India's second most impregnable, after the Amber Fort in Rajasthan. Today, the ruins of the fort are inhabited only by monkeys, lizards, and tourists.

Through the first gates, spiked as usual to prevent elephant attacks, is a huge, ruined city. The **Chand Minar** victory tower, built in 1435, rises over a water tank and a mosque cobbled together with columns pillaged from temples. A series of steps leads up the hill past ruined palaces to the blue-tiled **Chini Mahal,** where the last king of Golconda met his end. On top of the small tower next door, a re-creation of a cannon called Qila Shikan (Fort Breaker) points menacingly out at the horizon. From here, the defenses begin in earnest; you have to cross a moat to get into the sheer-walled citadel. Inside the fort's walls is a night-dark passage designed as an ambush path for intruders. A guide will save you from attack and lead you through it with a kerosene lamp, in anticipation, of course, of a little baksheesh. Endless stairs lead upward, reemerging into daylight and to a farther series of palaces lining the slope to the fort's summit. From the top, there are magnificent views of Aurangabad and the surrounding countryside. *(Most buses from Aurangabad to Ellora stop at Daulatabad, Rs6. Open daily 6am-6pm. Rs2.)*

Back toward Aurangabad lies **Khuldabad,** or Rauza, a small, strongly Muslim town where the Emperor Aurangzeb finally found rest from the struggle to subjugate Maharashtra. In a departure from the grandiose mausolea of his Mughal forbearers, not to mention his wife, Aurangzeb asked for a modest grave funded by the proceeds from his own transcription of the Koran.

ELLORA इलोरा ☎ 02437

Ellora's Buddhist, Hindu, and Jain **"caves"** make up, along with similar structures at Ajanta, Maharashtra's most celebrated tourist attraction. Generations of India's most skilled artisans chiseled a series of temples and residence halls from the solid rock of the hills. Though still referred to as caves, they are actually man-made architectural and sculptural wonders. Also in Ellora is the **Ghrashneshwar Temple,** one of the *jyotirlingas*, where Shiva is said to have burst from the earth. The same square also houses three ancient temple-like structures said to be the tombs of Shivaji's father and grandfathers—locals maintain that this village, not Pune, is Shivaji's birthplace. A mere 29km from Aurangabad, Ellora usually gets relegated to daytrip status.

GETTING THERE AND GETTING AROUND

The main road runs west from the bus stand by the entrance site, concealing one budget hotel amid trinket stalls and cold drink stands. Frequent **buses** ply to Ellora via Daulatabad (6am-6pm, 45min., Rs12). **Shared taxis** run from the taxi stand opposite Aurangabad's Central Bus Station (Rs15). If you've ever wondered how many human bodies can squeeze into a jeep, you can find out by hopping into one of the many that cruise the Ellora-Aurangabad road for about the same prices as the bus, allowing you to see both Ellora and Daulatabad in a day.

ACCOMMODATIONS AND FOOD

The MTDC's **Kailas Hotel** is clean and well-run. (☎ 44543 or 44468. Dorms Rs100; singles Rs500; doubles Rs200-1000.) Food options in Ellora involve sodas and *pakoras* and a few minimalist restaurants. The **Kailas Hotel Restaurant** serves *thalis* for Rs50. (Open daily 7am-9:30pm.) Ellora's best restaurant, **Hotel Milan,** has veg. dishes for Rs15-50. (Open daily 8am-5pm and 8-11pm.)

THE CAVES

Caves open Tu-Su. Cave 16 open Tu-Su 6am-6pm. Rs5; video fee Rs25, exterior only. All other caves free.

Of the 34 caves, numbers 1 through 16 give the clearest impression of Ellora's development over the centuries, culminating in the masterpiece of the Kailasa Temple (number 16). Starting at the southernmost cave (on your far right as you face the caves, number 1 according to the Archaeological Survey of India) allows for a roughly chronological sequence.

CAVES 1-12. The first set of caves dates from the 6th to 8th centuries, the twilight years of Buddhist influence in India. The caves in this group grow increasingly elaborate as Buddhist influence fades. The popular revival of Hinduism is evidenced by the neighboring Shiva temples, whose construction began in the 7th century. Of the first nine *viharas* (monastery caves), **Cave 5** stands out. The flat, low ridges in the floor probably served as benches to make a community dining hall. The stern Vajrapani (the bodhisattva holding a thunderbolt) and the more forgiving Padmapani (flower-power in the form of a lotus-totin' bodhisattva) presided over the meals from the sides of the central shrine.

Cave 10, Ellora's only *chaitya* hall, echoes earlier structures at **Ajanta** (see p. 423), **Karla** (see p. 416), and elsewhere. The last Buddhist gasp at Ellora, **Cave 12** contains some beautiful sculpture on the third level. Bodhisattvas line the side walls, and the seven previous incarnations of the Buddha flank the main shrine. A different type of tree shades each Buddha, a symbolic technique developed at Sanchi (see p. 355) and other early Buddhist monuments. Traces of paint in the sanctum and chamber hint at the once bright decoration of the caves.

CAVES 13-29. Dating from Ellora's Hindu era, which lasted late into the 9th century, these more elaborate, densely sculptured temples share many motifs: Shiva appears most often on Mount Kailasa playing dice with wife Parvati while a demon tries frantically, in vain, to dislodge him; at other times he dances with both legs bent as Nataraja, whose gyrations shook the world into being and will one day destroy it. Vishnu crops up as Narasimha (the man-lion), Varaha (the boar), and, most commonly, as Narayan asleep in the coils of a serpent floating on the cosmic sea. From his navel grows a lotus, out of which Brahma emerges to create the world. The image of the Seven Mothers, buxom goddesses with children, flanked by Kala and Kali, also appears regularly. All of these sculptures are in **Caves 14** and **15**. The latter also depicts Shiva emerging from a *linga*, while Brahma and Vishnu kneel before him—testimony to Shiva-worship among Ellora's patrons.

Ellora's rock-cut temples reach their climax in **Cave 16**, the **Kailasa Temple**, one of the largest monolithic structures in the world. This massive 8th- and 9th-century building was created from the top down by several generations of incredibly skilled craftsmen. The sheer scale of this replica of Shiva's home in the Himalayas defies belief even before you consider the technical challenge of slicing it all out from just one solid rock. Traces of plaster and paint bear witness to further decorative complexity on top of the elaborate sculpture and architecture. The paved road in front of Cave 16 (to the left if you're facing the cave) leads to the remaining caves—don't let the stairs on the right fool you. At the first fork, a right turn takes you to caves 21-28, as does the second fork. **Cave 21** repeats Cave 14's iconographic scheme.

At the next fork in the road, a right turn leads to Cave 29. The left fork takes you on a 10-minute walk to Caves 30-34. **Cave 29**, with its view of a rainy season waterfall, contains perhaps the only mooner protected under UNESCO world heritage provisions: in another panel of Shiva ignoring Ravana's ruckus, you'll notice a dwarf baring his ass. Ellora's second-largest cave, it is also among the most structurally impressive, with three lion-guarded entrances protecting it. Cave 29 sees almost no tourists since the tours skip all the higher-numbered caves.

CAVES 30-34. Caves 30-34 date from Ellora's third and final phase of construction under Jain patrons during the 9th and 10th centuries. Though some sections remain unfinished, others hold some of the most intricately detailed carvings anywhere in Ellora. **Cave 32** depicts the *tirthankara* Gomatesvara so deep in meditation that he has not noticed the vines growing on his limbs or the animals surrounding him. This temple is dedicated to Indra, king of the gods, the pot-bellied god chilling under a banyan tree.

AJANTA अजन्ता ☎ 02438

Ajanta is almost as remote today as it was in the 2nd century BC, when it was a Buddhist retreat. Its architects chose a sheer cliff-face above a horseshoe-shaped canyon along the Waghora River to render their contemplative spiritual visions in painting and sculpture. During the 7th century AD, the monks abandoned their 29 *chaityas* and *viharas* (and the astonishingly life-like art with which they had filled them) to an even greater obscurity. Only the local people knew that these masterpieces even existed, prowled by tigers and overrun with creepers, until a red-coated hunting party spied Cave 10 from the opposite ridge in 1819. Two thousand years have chipped the paint, but Ajanta's colorful, meticulously detailed wall paintings continue to tell stories of the Buddha's past lives—known as the *Jataka* tales—and other legends.

▐ GETTING THERE AND GETTING AROUND

Visitors no longer have to beat back the brush, but they do have to suffer through a long, hot, jolting **bus** ride to get here. Many buses stop at Ajanta between Jalgaon (58km north) and Aurangabad (108km south), starting early in the morning and ending at 5:30pm from Aurangabad and 6:30pm from Jalgaon. You can come from one town, leave your well-locked bags to be guarded in the cloak room at the base of the caves (theoretically free), and proceed to the next town the same evening.

MAHARASHTRA

ACCOMMODATIONS AND FOOD

The MTDC, naturally, runs the **hotel** and **restaurant** at the caves themselves. Their rooms are clean but spare, with balconies and common bathrooms. (☎4226. Singles Rs200; doubles Rs250. Attached restaurant: entrees Rs22-50; open daily 9am-5pm.) For reservations, call the regional MTDC manager in Aurangabad (☎331198). A much better option is the **Forest Rest House**, 500m back down the road. It has two air-cooled doubles with hot water, a cook, mosquito nets, and a veranda. Book in advance with the Divisional Forest Officer, Opp. Government, Engineering College, Osmanpura, Aurangabad. (☎334701. Rs100 per person.)

THE CAVES

Open Tu-Su 9am-5:30pm. Rs5; additional Rs5 "light" fee for caves 1, 2, 16, and 17; video fee Rs25, exterior only; guide Rs100. The caves are up the steps behind the drink stands and over the rise.

The guided tours rely primarily on gimmicks: "See the expression of the Buddha change when I move the light" and "See the very first Bermuda shorts in history," but they also illuminate some of the murals' convoluted story lines.

CAVES 1-2. Cave 1, which dates from the 5th century, contains some of Ajanta's most naturalistic paintings. As with all of Ajanta's art, the life-like jewelry, clothing, and domestic objects are painted with an obsessive-compulsive attention to detail. On the left-hand wall, a king, newly converted to Buddhism, abandons earthly pleasures for a life of meditation. Just to the left of the rear shrine, a painting depicts the elegant Padmapani (the lotus-holding bodhisattva). Vajrapani stands sentry to his right with his thunderbolt. Four deer sharing a single head gaze out contentedly at the tourists from several capitals on the right-hand side of the hall. In **Cave 2**, paintings to the left show the dream of a six-tusked elephant which foretold the Buddha's conception and his miraculous birth directly into the arms of his mother. In the right-hand rear corner, a sculptural frieze of a classroom depicts an ill-behaved student pulling the hair of the girl in front. Above to the right, the demon Hariti dances furiously.

CAVES 9-26. The *chaitya* hall in **Cave 9** dates from an early era when the Buddha was not depicted directly. Instead of traditional images, there are oblique references to the Enlightened One, including the pipal-tree-shaped window in the facade, signifying learning, and the huge stupa in the apse, symbolizing the relics of the Buddha. The same goes for **Cave 10,** which dates from the 2nd century BC; thousands of years of sunlight and the scratching of graffiti artists have obscured most of the paintings here. In **Cave 16,** in the front left corner, the most celebrated fresco of all shows yet another princess swooning in distress as her husband throws in the worldly towel. *Jataka* stories about the Buddha's earlier incarnations fill the walls of **Cave 17.** On the left-hand wall, a well-intentioned prince gives away his father's magic elephant, his cart and possessions, and even his wife and children, renouncing all earthly ties before entering into the final life-phase of her-mitage. On the opposite wall, confusing tales of seductive beauties and blood-thirsty demons are depicted in remarkably accurate anatomical detail.

The elaborate sculpture in **Cave 19** indicates the Buddhist response to the Hindu renaissance of the 6th century AD. A columned *chaitya* hall, Cave 19 dates from a later period, when depictions of the Buddha were permitted. The most splendid example reclines along the left-hand wall of **Cave 26:** the Buddha on the verge of nirvana, surrounded by disciples. The path in front of Cave 16 leads down the hill to a bridge. From here, a path to the right leads to views of a rainy-season waterfall that surges over the cliffs. Visitors can head left and then climb to a **viewpoint** to relive the astonishment of the Brits who stumbled across the caves back in 1819. Wandering up to the cliffs, you can see the river's contribution to local sculpture, with gorges carved by its seven waterfalls. Backtrack down to the river bank; continuing along the river's edge opposite the caves will bring you to the parking lot.

NAGPUR नागपुर ☎ 0712

Smack dab in the center of India, Nagpur is the hub where virtually every major road and rail route meets. But it certainly doesn't *feel* as though an entire subcontinent revolves around this city of two million. The streets are filled with tattered *tongas* and auto-rickshaws rather than taxis and aggressive Tata two-tonners. The seat of the state legislature alternates between Nagpur and Bombay, but Nagpur lacks the skyscrapers and concrete that characterize many other cities of its size. In fact, with all its parks and playgrounds, Nagpur is one of the greenest cities in India. Most visitors are corporate types attending conferences. For tourists who find themselves at the center of things, however, Nagpur is a pleasant enough city, and a good starting point for excursions into the national parks nearby.

▐ GETTING THERE AND GETTING AROUND. The **airport** (☎ 260348 or 260433), is 8km from the city center. The **Indian Airlines office** is on Palm Rd., in Civil Lines. (☎ 523069. Open M-Su 10am-1pm and 2-5pm.) **Flights** go to: **Bhopal** (Tu and Sa, 1:05pm, 45min., US$80); **Bombay** (7:30am and 8:45pm, 1¼hr., US$130); **Calcutta** (W, F, Su, 7:30am, 1½hr., US$160); **Delhi** (10:30pm, 1½hr. US$150); **Hyderabad** (M, W, and F, 8pm, 1hr., US$160); **Madras** (Tu and Sa, 3:30pm, 1½hr., US$155); and **Rajpur** (8:45pm, 30min., US$80). **Trains** go everywhere, including: **Bombay** (5-7 per day, 14-18hr., Rs244); **Calcutta** (5-7 per day, 6:40am-8:15pm, 19-20hr., Rs297); **Delhi** (7-10 per day, 2:05am-11:05pm, 14-22hr., Rs290); **Hyderabad** (2-4 per day, 5:20-6pm, 8-12 hr., Rs190); **Madras** (4-5 per day, 6:05am-1:25pm, 15-21hr., Rs290); **Sevagram** (8 per day, 4:20am-3:55pm, 1hr., Rs29). The **local bus stand**, 1½km south of the railway station, has buses to: **Indore** (5:30am, 16hr., Rs224); **Jabalpur** (6 per day, 9:45am-11pm, Rs120); and **Wardha** (28 per day, 7:15am-8:30pm, 2½hr., Rs31).

▐▐ ORIENTATION AND PRACTICAL INFORMATION. Nagpur's pulse beats fastest around the **railway station,** on **Central Avenue;** the tracks split the city into eastern and western halves. Central Avenue becomes **Kingsway Rd.** after the station. South of Kingsway Rd. and parallel to it, is **Palm Rd.** Farther south is the tourist center, **Sitabuldi,** with shops and cheap hotels. North and west of Sitabuldi is **Civil Lines. Wardha Rd. (NH7)** runs parallel to the train tracks. The **MTDC tourist office,** Dr. Munje Rd. (☎ 533325), opposite the Laxmi theater in Sitabuldi, can provide information on area parks and lakes. (Open M-F and 1st, 3rd, and 5th Sa 10am-5pm.) The **State Bank of India,** Kingsway Rd., near the railway station exchanges currency and cashes traveler's checks at the **foreign exchange office** in the center of the left-hand building. (☎ 521196, ext. 416. Open M-F 10:30am-2pm.) **Mayo Hospital** (☎ 728621), on Central Ave., near the railway station, has a 24-hour **pharmacy.** Cyber Nook, opposite the Liberty Cinema, Residency Rd., in Sardar, has good **Internet** connections and Hindi *filmi* music. (Open daily 24hr., Rs25 per hr.). The **GPO** is on Palm Rd. (Open M-Sa 8am-10pm, Su 9am-1pm.) **Postal Code:** 440001.

▐▐▐ ACCOMMODATIONS, FOOD, AND ENTERTAINMENT. The large number of business travelers passing through has given the city an abundance of accommodations. A service charge of 10% and a luxury tax of 4% are often added to basic room rates. The thickest tangle of (disorientingly similar) budget hotels is on **Central Avenue** and its arteries. **Hotel Blue Diamond,** 113 Central Ave., Dosar Chowk, is a good bet if you think you can handle the huge psychedelic honeycomb. The cheap rooms share a common bath. (☎ 27461. Singles Rs100-130; doubles Rs150-200.) Nearby, **Hotel Midland** has tidy rooms, disinfected marble bathrooms, and funky-smelling hallways. (☎ 726131. Singles Rs225-300; doubles Rs400-550; A/C rooms from Rs650.) There is another cluster of cheapies in **Sitabuldi,** in the heart of Nagpur's market district. Head east along Mahatma Gandhi Rd. away from his statue and take the third left to reach **Hotel Amrta,** Modi No. 3. Even the "regular rooms" in this aqua oasis put most other places to shame. (☎ 543762; fax 553123. Check-out 24hr. Singles Rs400; doubles Rs450. AmEx, MC, Visa.) **Hotel Regal,** Buty (Main) Rd., in the alley opposite Parekh Arunkumar Bhogilal Jewelers near Modi No. 3, offers clean and tidy rooms off narrow marble hallways. (☎ 544956. Check-out 24hr. Singles Rs200-225; doubles Rs225-300.)

Nanking, Mount Rd., Sardar, is the best-known, best-value Chinese place in town. (Chicken Rs65-85; seafood Rs75-120; veggies Rs35-90. Open Tu-Su noon-3pm and 6-11pm.) **The Zodiac,** 24 Central Bazaar Rd., in the Hotel Centre Point, a popular spot among locals, is the most happening pub-cum-discotheque in town. (☎520910. Open for "jam sessions" W 2-6pm, Rs150 per couple; discotheque Sa 10pm-1am, Rs250 per couple.) **Ambajhari Lake and Garden,** on the western outskirts of Nagpur, is ideal for early morning or evening strolls (open daily 9am-sunset).

NEAR NAGPUR: SEVAGRAM ☎ 07152

Mahatma Gandhi founded an ashram in Sevagram, literally the "Village of Service," after he left his Sabarmati retreat in Ahmedabad, Gujarat (see p. 328) in 1936. From Sevagram, Gandhi directed the Independence movement, leading India to victory against the British in 1947 with his policy of non-violence. The community continues to thrive, the paradigm of simple living and self-sufficiency. The town is also the site of the **Nai Talimi Sangh,** the university founded by Gandhi to ensure that the town could meet its own aesthetic, spiritual, and intellectual needs. Far from the bustle of the rest of urban India, Sevagram is a breath of fresh air: clean, serene, and spiritual. Even people with little interest in Gandhi will find Sevagram a delightful place to relax for a few days.

Sevagram Ashram has kept all of its original buildings and Gandhi's personal belongings intact, complete with explanatory English signposts. Ashramites will also gladly answer questions and provide free pamphlets. *(Open sunrise to sunset.)* A shop near the entrance sells Gandhi's books and *khadi,* the hand-spun cloth that played an important role in the freedom movement, signifying *swaraj* (self-sufficiency) and a rejection of the reliance upon imported textiles. The *chakra* (wheel) that Gandhi used to spin the cloth now figures as the central motif on India's flag. Opposite the ashram, the **Gandhi Picture Exhibition** displays a photographic timeline of the Mahatma's life. *(Open Sa-Th 10am-6pm. Free.)* In the neighboring town of Wardha, **Magan Nadi,** the home of Gandhi's nephew, provides a history of *khadi.*

The Center of Science for Villagers, 4km away, devotes itself to explaining Gandhi's philosophy of village-based economics. *(Open daily 9am-1pm and 2-5pm. Free.)* Adjoining the center is the **Leprosy Home,** where sufferers engage in a variety of tasks including agriculture, shoe-making, weaving, and spinning.

The women who run **Vinobaji's Ashram** in Gopuri, 3km away, provide a living testament to the self-sufficient community that Gandhi envisioned. A fervent disciple of Gandhi, Vinoba Bhave was a social activist and reformer who advocated land reform and the eradication of caste hierarchy. **Vinobaji's Museum** has exhibits explaining Gandhi's and his efforts to get landlords to give land to the destitute. *(Open daily 9am-1pm and 2-5pm. Free.)*

Trains from Nagpur to Bombay and Madras will stop at Sevagram (8 per day, 4:20am-3:55pm, 1hr., Rs29) or at **Wardha** (an additional 4 per day, 11:50am-8:40pm, 1hr., Rs29), 8km away. Frequent MSRTC **buses** also run from Nagpur to Sevagram and Wardha (2½hr., Rs31). Shared auto-rickshaws travel between Wardha and Sevagram (Rs5). Buses also travel from Wardha to the ashram (every 10min., 7:30am-8pm, 15min., Rs2). Although the **MTDC** offers basic accommodations for Rs150-220, **Sevagram Ashram** is cheaper and nicer. (Dorm beds Rs30; doubles Rs80. Meals Rs7-80 per day.) **Yatri Nivas,** opposite the ashram, offers rooms and meals for the same price. **Vinobaji's Ashram** (☎43518), in Paunar (3km away), prefers to house only women and requires advance notification by mail (Vinobaji's Ashram, Paunar, District Wardha, Maharashtra, 442111) or by telephone. For food, **Goras Bhandar Wardha,** in the main square of Sevagram near the Central Bank (look for the cow on the sign), sells delicious bread and milk. Try the hot milk with cardamom (Rs5). Unless you're staying in a guest house or ashram, you'll have to make the trip to Wardha for a fuller meal.

GOA गोवा

Renowned for its sun-bathed white beaches, the lingering charm of its Portuguese colonial past, and its free and easy-going spirit, Goa has long been a prime destination for all kinds of travelers. Recently, however, the Goan idyll has begun to fall, beach by beautiful beach, before the advancing vanguard of an invading tourist culture. Battalions of red Coca-Cola umbrellas crawl up the shores, as regiments of middle-class Germans and Brits are marshalled off charter flights and into ritzy resort complexes, and as pan-European and Israeli techno junkies groove en masse to the pedestrian reveille of rave after identical rave. Goa is no longer Eden, but despite the development, you are never far from an unspoiled beach, where you can still revel in the simple splendor of it all, drinking from freshly fallen coconuts as fishermen fold their nets and the sun sinks down into the Arabian Sea. And while the parties and the raves and the raucousness have calmed down a bit recently under the influence of authorities desperate to bring order to chaos, the clouds of sweet-smelling smoke blown in all directions by the ocean breeze suggest that Goa is still a good place to come for an old-fashioned shot at a natural high. Homes converted into guest houses, restaurants whose chefs have mastered the art of banana pancakes, and five-star resorts with their capitalist megaplexes all share space with moss-covered Baroque churches, leafy coconut groves, soft-sanded shorelines strewn with fishing nets, platoons of Kashmiri rug sellers, and sun-lovers from all over the world.

The West has been encroaching on Goa since 1498, when the Portuguese explorer Vasco da Gama landed on the Keralan coast in search of spices. Portugal was looking to establish a foothold on the west coast of India, and in 1510, Goa became a Portuguese colony. During the 16th century, Goa developed as a prosperous trading city, where Portuguese soldiers and adventurers mixed with the locals, many of whom converted to Catholicism and married Europeans. Thanks to the guidance of the Jesuits and the "encouragement" of the Inquisition, Goa also became a stronghold of Christianity in India. The Portuguese made sure that Goa never became a part of the British Raj, and held on here until 1961, when Indian troops annexed the region. Goa holds the distinction of being both the first piece of subcontinental soil clutched by European colonizers and the last to be liberated. It first became a Union Territory and eventually, in 1987, an official state.

Some would say that the invasion of hippies and wealthy tourists in search of paradise has made Goa a colony once again. Others might say that there's no harm in a bit of fun. After five centuries of Portuguese rule, Goa is unique among Indian states: Portuguese-speaking Roman Catholics dressed in jeans and a muscle shirt are side by side with *lungi*-clad fishermen shouldering their day's catch. About 30% of Goa's inhabitants are Christian, and the state has literacy and income levels among the highest in India. Goa is small enough to explore thoroughly on a moderate stay, and the locals are usually eager to share their vanishing paradise with visitors. Go get yourself a tan....

HIGHLIGHTS OF GOA

India's most legendary (and most decadent) nightlife scene raves away all winter on the northern beaches of **Anjuna** (p. 441) and **Chapora and Vagator** (p. 444).

Time stands still in **Old Goa** (p. 435), home to Portuguese monuments, cathedrals, and the mortal remains of **St. Francis Xavier** (p. 436).

The northernmost and southernmost Goan beaches, **Arambol** (p. 446) and **Palolem** (p. 453), will do their best to seduce you into staying longer than you ever planned to, with their idyllic settings and tranquility.

WHEN TO GO

Goa's northern beaches are hopping from early November to late March, when near-perfect beach-bum weather (sunny, hot, and cloudless) draws sun-worshipers in droves. Beach fever is intense in the weeks before and after Goa's psychedelic Christmas; the months of December and January are considered peak season. Practically everything closes down during the monsoon (June-Sept.), and guest house prices bottom out as Westerners move out and head north to the grass-green fields of Manali (p. 233). The monsoon cools Goa down and fills up its wells, but the showers often cease for long sunny stretches. Other holidays well worth the trip are the **Carnival,** Panjim's pre-Lent revelry (Feb. 25-27, 2001), and the more solemn festivities in honor of Goa's favorite saint, Francis Xavier, held in Old Goa on December 3 every year.

⊠ GETTING THERE

Most travelers reach Goa from Bombay, 600km to the north.

DOMESTIC FLIGHTS. Dabolim Airport (info ☎ (0854) 512644), 29km south of Panjim. **Indian Airlines** and **Jet Airways** offer flights to and from: **Bangalore,** via **Bombay** (3 per day, 2½hr, US$245-310); **Bombay** (4 per day, 1hr., US$57-85); and **Delhi** (1 per day, 2½hr., US$167). There is a Rs750 airport tax for all flights. During peak season, seats on the Bombay-Goa flight can be difficult to obtain, but flights are normally available during the middle of the week; call a couple days in advance.

Dabolim's prepaid **taxi** counter, outside the airport's main entrance, will ferry you just about anywhere in Goa. A board to the left of the counter lists fares (to Panjim Rs300). Off season (May-Sept.), touts clutter the main exit, threatening to whisk you off to a plush hotel you've never heard of. **Local buses** run to nearby Vasco da Gama (8am-8pm, Rs5), with connections for Panjim and Margao.

TRAINS. After years of waiting and wondering, you'll be pleased to know that the **Konkan Railway** is finally complete. Traveling south from Bombay is now much quicker and more comfortable; as the tracks wind through lush tropical forests and over more than 100 bridges, the scenery is even more beautiful than ever. The only drawback is that the tracks were laid 15-20km outside city stations, so the railway only skirts major towns. *Mumbai-Madgaon Express* 0111 (1 per day, 10:30pm) trains from **Bombay** stop at four stations in Goa: **Pernem,** in the north, east of Arambol; **Tivim,** 20km due east of Vagator beach (arrives 9:15am, 10¼hr.); the centrally located **Karmali,** 12km due east of Panjim (arrives 9:35am, 10½hr.); and **Margao,** in the south, 5km outside the city (arrives 10:15am, 11¾hr.). All Bombay

---

DON'T MESS WITH GOA Goa's tourist boom has speckled its coast with huge resorts and small guest houses, all of which consume a hefty share of resources. The invasion of thirsty (and dirty) travelers depletes Goa's freshwater resources so much that village wells run dry or are contaminated by salty seawater. Hotels drilling private wells and filling Olympic-sized swimming pools deserve most of the blame for water waste, but backpackers can have an effect, too. There are simple ways to conserve water—take bucket baths, turn off the shower while soaping, and give clothes to a *dhobi* instead of washing them in your room. Beaches once trodden only by fishermen are now littered with Bisleri bottles, plastic bags, and light bulbs. Fishermen still work here, and people (including you) still eat the fish they catch. But now, in addition to fish, the ocean is violently vomiting up tourist trash—take the hint and don't litter. If you are considering a long stay, volunteering for one of Goa's Non-Governmental Organizations (NGOs) allow you to help on a local level. ECOFORUM in Mapusa publishes a book, *Fish Curry & Rice* (Rs200), which has a listing of Goa's activist groups. For more information, see **Environmentally Responsible Tourism,** p. 54.

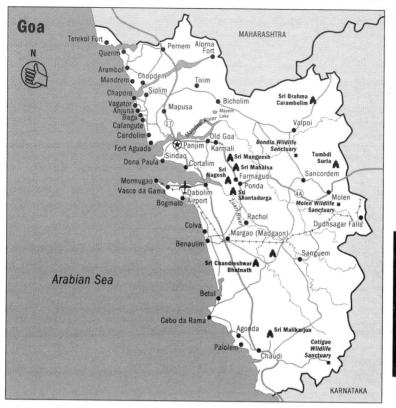

Goa

MAHARASHTRA

Terekol Fort
Querim
Pernem Alorna Fort
Arambol
Mandrem Chopdem
Tivim
Chapora Siolim
Vagator Bicholim Sri Brahma Carambolim
Anjuna Mapusa Mayem Lake
Baga Valpoi
Calangute 17 Mandovi River
Candolim Old Goa
Fort Aguada Panjim Karmali Bondla Wildlife Sanctuary
Siridao Sri Manguesh Tambdi Surla
Dona Paula Cortalim Sri Mahalsa
Sri Nagesh Farmagudi Sancordem
Mormugao Dabolim Ponda
Vasco da Gama Airport Sri Shantadurga Molen
Bogmalo Molen Wildlife Sanctuary
Rachol
Colva Dudhsagar Falls
Margao (Madgaon)
Benaulim Sanguem

Arabian Sea

Sri Chandreshwar Bhutnath

Betul

Cabo da Rama Agonda Sri Malikarjun
Paolem Cotigao Wildlife Sanctuary
Chaudi

KARNATAKA

fares are Rs251 for non-A/C sleeper and Rs696 for 3rd class 3-tier A/C with blanket and pillow. The *Mandovi Express* 0104 makes the return trip. Other trains continue down, eventually connecting Bombay with Mangalore, Bangalore, and Kanyakumari. Trains for **Delhi** leave daily from the coastal town of **Vasco da Gama,** near the airport (*Goa Exp.* 2779, 12:15pm, 41hr., Rs450/1750).

BUSES. Buses are the cheapest way to reach Goa from: **Bangalore** (16hr.); **Mangalore** (12hr.); **Miraj** (1 per day, 10hr., Rs112); **Bombay** (15hr.); **Mysore** (1 per day, 15hr., Rs212); and **Pune** (2 per day, 12hr., Rs173-250). In most cities, you can buy the tickets on the bus. **Private carriers** offer more extensive services, and their coaches are generally more comfortable (except for the infamous "video coaches," see p. 47). Book private coaches through a travel agency or at one of the shacks near the bus terminals throughout Goa.

⊑ GETTING AROUND

Traveling by bus along Goa's narrow roads is not as stomach-wrenching as it often is in other parts of the country; the popular routes are generally packed, but they are mercifully short.

BUSES. Intrastate buses go between the **Kadamba Bus Terminals** in the transport hubs of Panjim, Mapusa, and Margao. **Express buses,** available only for certain routes, are the fastest; others stop in every village and rice paddy as locals hop on and off. There are few real bus stops in the state, and most locals simply flag down non-express buses as they pass by. For more details on interstate bus travel, see listings for **Panjim** (p. 432), **Mapusa** (p. 437), and **Margao** (p. 448).

TAXIS AND RICKSHAWS. Tourist vehicles (expensive minivans) and **taxis** are available for short jaunts or longer-term rentals (Rs7 per km). **Auto-rickshaws** disinclined to set their meters zip between beaches or herd passengers in at rickshaw stands in town (Rs7 first km, Rs3.75 each additional km). Their fares tend to be a little more than half of what taxis charge. During the off-season and when heading to more remote areas, all require return fares. The distinctly Goan **motorcycle-rickshaws** (Rs4 first km, Rs2 each additional km) or **pilot taxis** are the cheapest options.

MOTORCYCLES. The simplest, riskiest, and sexiest transportation method employed by many visitors is an automatic Enfield, Honda Kinetic, or Yamaha **motorcycle,** which can be rented by the day or month through most hotels and guest houses in virtually every town and beach. Technically, you must obtain an Indian or international driver's license in order to drive one. Goan police have been known to keep themselves amused by busting unlicensed bikers in the cities, but license enforcement on the beaches is famously lax (except in Anjuna during Wednesday's flea market). If you are pulled over by a police officer and you do not have a valid license, keep your cool and remember that a little baksheesh might go a long way (see p. 15). **Helmets** can be hard to come by, but, with a little prodding and pleading, some official bike rental places might be able to find you one. An alternative is to pick up a helmet (with a visor to block dust) in Panjim or Bombay and keep it as a souvenir.

BICYCLES. Short distances, lack of direct bus service, and an overabundance of motorcycles make hitchhiking an attractive proposition. But riding with a stranger can be dangerous and *Let's Go* (of course) does not recommend it. **Bicycles** (Rs3-5 per hr., Rs30-50 per day) are a safer alternative, and can be hired from hotels and guest houses. You can pedal along the whole of Colva Beach when the tide is out, plan to get wet, and bring plastic bags for cameras and valuables. Cycling long distance is tough; rental bikes have one gear, and there are many, many hills.

NORTH GOA

PANJIM (PANAJI) पानाजी ☎ 0832

Panjim (pop. 100,000), the quiet state capital, covers the southern banks of the Mandovi River. Its Portuguese past is most obvious in the porticoed, red-tiled mansions that crowd the narrow streets of the Fontainhas area, the colonialist dream of a miniature Europe transplanted into the East. Shop signs in Portuguese and the whitewashed churches that speckle the countryside complete the image. In 1759, the viceroy moved his residence from Old Goa to Yusuf Adil Shah's old palace in Panjim (today's Secretariat), and from that point the city really began to grow, becoming the capital in 1843. Compared to the rest of the state, Panjim bustles with activity and has plenty of amenities for the beach-bound traveler. The city, though, deserves more than just a quick stocking-up stop, thanks to its proximity to lovely Old Goa and the hidden Hindu temples farther inland.

▣ GETTING THERE AND GETTING AROUND

Flights: Air India, 18th June Rd. (☎231101 or 231104), next to Hotel Fidalgo. Open M-F 9:30am-1pm and 2-5pm, Sa 9:30am-1pm. **Indian Airlines,** DB Marg (☎223826), at the northwestern edge. Open M-F 10am-1pm and 2-5pm. **Jet Airways,** Patto Plaza (☎221472 or 221479), just south of the Patto Tourist Hotel. Open M-F 9:30am-1pm and 2-5pm. **Jet Air,** 102 Rizvi Chambers, 1st fl. (☎226154 or 222438), at the corner of Gen. Bernarado Guedes and Heliodoro Salgado Rd., is an agent for **TWA, Gulf Air,** and **Air Canada.** Next door is **Air France** (☎420408). Both are open M-F 9:30am-1pm and 2-5:30pm, Sa 9:30am-1pm. **Alitalia,** 18th June Rd. (☎230940). Open 9:30am-1pm and 2-5pm, Sa 9:30am-1pm. **British Airways,** MG Rd. (☎420320 or 420320). Open M-F 9:30am-1pm and 2-5pm, Sa 9:30am-1:30pm. **Thakkers Travel Service,** Mahalaxmi Chambers (☎426678), on 18th June Rd. and up 4 flights of stairs, is an agent for **KLM.** Open M-F 9:30am-1pm and 2-5:30pm.

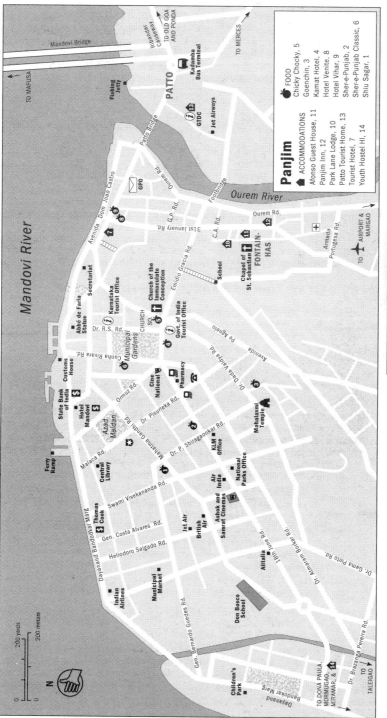

Panjim

▲ ACCOMMODATIONS
Afonso Guest House, 11
Panjim Inn, 12
Park Lane Lodge, 10
Patto Tourist Home, 13
Tourist Hotel, 7
Youth Hostel HI, 14

🍴 FOOD
Chicky Chocky, 5
Goenchin, 3
Kamat Hotel, 4
Hotel Venite, 8
Hotel Vihar, 9
Sher-e-Punjab, 2
Sher-e-Punjab Classic, 6
Shiu Sagar, 1

GOA

Trains: Karmali, 12km east of town, is the nearest station on the Konkan Railway (see **Getting There,** p. 428). Reservation office for **Konkan Railway.** Open M-Sa 8am-1:15pm, Su 8am-2pm. Buses and tourist taxis shuttle to Panjim.

Buses: Kadamba Bus Terminal, Patto. Prices listed are for regular/deluxe service. **Interstate buses** to: **Bangalore** (3 per day, 3:30-7pm, 14hr., Rs252); **Bombay** (2 per day, 4-5pm, 16hr., Rs240/307); **Mangalore** (2 per day, 6:15am-1:30pm, 10hr., Rs137); **Miraj** (10:30am, 10hr., Rs112); **Mysore** (2 per day, 2:30-5pm, 15hr., Rs212); **Pune** (2 per day, 6am-7pm, 12hr., Rs173/250). Advance reservations can be made at the **booking office.** Most counters open 9am-1pm and 2-5:30pm, but try to show up before 4pm, as some close early. **Private buses** departing for the same destinations can also be booked at many hotels and travel agents, or just show up at the bus stand along the river and hunt out a bus going the right way (north of Kadamba under the overpass). **Intrastate buses** zip to destinations throughout Goa 6am-8pm. To: **Calangute** (every 15min., 40min., Rs7); **Mapusa** (every 5min.; express 15min., regular 30min.; Rs5-6); **Margao** (every 5-10min.; express 30min., regular 45min.; Rs12).

Local Transportation: Taxis gather in front of the Hotel Mandovi, the Tourist Hotel, and at stands along 18th June Rd. **Auto-rickshaws** line up near the market and the Municipal Gardens. In good weather, budding capitalists hawk **motorbikes** across the street from the GPO. It's inadvisable to rent in Panjim without an international driver's license. Heavy, one-speed **bikes** are available at **Daud M. Aga** (☎222670), opposite the Cinema National entrance. Open M-Sa 9am-1pm and 2-7pm, Su 9am-noon.

■ ▐ ORIENTATION AND PRACTICAL INFORMATION

Situated at the intersection of the **Mandovi** and **Ourem Rivers,** Panjim is easy to get around on foot. On the east bank of the Ourem is the **Patto** area, enclosing the chaotic **bus terminal. Emidio Gracia Rd.** leads west uphill from the Ourem to **Church Square,** dominated by the white facade of the **Immaculate Conception Church.** From here, **18th June Rd.,** featuring many hotels, restaurants, and shops, leads southwest. **Dayanand Bandodkar (DB) Marg (Avenida Dom Joao Castro),** follows the bank of the Mandovi River. Most budget guest houses are in the old Portuguese quarter, **Fontainhas,** south of Emilio Garcia Rd. by the Ourem River.

Tourist Office: Government of India Tourist Office, Communidade Building, Church Square (☎223412). Open M-F 9:30am-1pm and 2-6pm, Sa 9:30am-1pm. **Dept. of Tourism, Government of Goa,** Patto Tourist Home (☎225583; fax 228819; email goatour@goa.goa.nic.in), between the traffic bridge and the footbridge on the bank of the Ourem River. Offers tours and the useful Goa Tourist Directory. **GTDC,** Trionara Apartments, Dr. Alvares Costa Rd. (☎226515; fax 223926; www.goacom.com/goatourism) arranges tours and sunset kitsch cruises on the river.

Currency Exchange: State Bank of India, DB Marg (☎224662), opposite the Hotel Mandovi. Open for exchange on the 1st floor M-F 10am-2pm and 3-4pm, Sa 10am-noon. **Thomas Cook,** DB Marg (☎221312), exchanges cash and all traveler's checks at better-than-bank rates. Open Oct.-Mar. M-Sa 9:30am-6pm, Su 10am-5pm.

Bookstore: In the **Hotel Mandovi.** Travel guides, novels, language books, and soft porn. Open daily 9am-6pm.

Pharmacy: Farmacia Salcete, 18th June Rd. (☎225959), just beyond the Municipal Gardens. Open M-Sa 9am-7:30pm.

Hospital: Dr. Bhandare Hospital, Fontainhas (☎224966). Go south on 31st January Rd., passing the Panjim Inn; bear left where the road forks, turn right at the People's High School, and take the first left. **Ambulance** (☎224824).

Police: Headquarters, Malaca Rd. (☎224488 or 223400), on the west edge of the Azad Maidan gardens. **Foreigner's Registration Office** is the second office on the left. Visa extensions are available in emergencies but take a long time. Open M-F 9:30am-1pm.

Telephones: Panjim has recently switched from 5- to 6-digit phone numbers. Replace the leading 4 with 22 or 42 in any 5-digit numbers you may stumble across.

Internet: There are plenty of email options. **Cosy Nook,** 18th June Rd., just beyond the Municipal Garden, provides a fast and consistent connection. Rs2 per min., Rs70 per hr. Open daily 8:30am-8:30pm.

Post Office: From the traffic bridge at the Ourem River, continue along the road into Panjim. The **GPO** is on the left behind a garden. **Postal Code:** 403001.

ACCOMMODATIONS

Guest houses and hotels do a brisk business, but since most people only stay a night or two before heading out to the beach, same-day accommodations are normally not hard to find. Standards (and prices) are high for the region. Tariffs often double around Christmas. Most of the best places are in Fontainhas, south of the footbridge by the Ourem River.

Afonso Guesthouse, Fontainhas (☎222359), on the same street as San Sebastian Chapel. A very pleasant guest house run by a lovely and helpful family. Eight clean, spacious rooms with attached baths. Try to snag one of the upstairs rooms. Check-out 9am. Rooms Rs350-400. Off-season Rs 250-350.

Park Lane Lodge, Fontainhas (☎227154 or 220238), near St. Sebastian Chapel. From 31st January Rd., walk to San Sebastian Chapel and turn right; it's up a flight of stairs. Cozy common TV room/study and terrace. Rooms with common bath are more spacious than those with attached bath. Lockers. Check-out 8am. Internet. Doubles Rs280-350. Off-season: doubles Rs190-235.

Panjim Inn, 31st January Rd., Fontainhas (☎226523; email Panjimin @goa1.dot.net.in), on the left when heading south from Emidio Gracia Rd. A beautiful 18th-century mansion with a vine-covered veranda and large rooms, all with gorgeous antique furniture. Internet service and A/C available. Hot showers in all attached baths. Flexible check-out, generally 9am. Singles Rs540; doubles Rs720. Off-season: Rs400-630. Rooms at the equally lovely adjacent annex, **Pousada,** 10% cheaper.

Tourist Hotel, Dr. Alvares Costa Rd. (☎227103), in a multi-storied white building a few blocks northwest after crossing Patto Bridge. This government-run hotel is the definition of institutional; even the welcome mats are issued by Big Brother. Rooms have attached baths as well as fans, phones, clean sheets, towels, and TVs. Check-out noon. Doubles Rs500, with A/C Rs600-800. Off-season: Rs450/530-700.

Patto Tourist Home (☎225715), near the bus terminal on the road along the Ourem River. Clean simple rooms with attached bath and television. Triples Rs400; 10-person dorm rooms Rs700. Off-season: Rs320/500.

Youth Hostel HI (☎22533), in suburban Miramar, a 45min. walk from the town center along DB Marg. Only worth the distance if you're all about pinching paise. There's a Marriott next door if you'd rather be pampered. Buses from town head out here; ask for Miramar. Meals Rs18. Check-out 8am. Dorm beds Rs40, HI members Rs20.

FOOD

Panjim's restaurants are a good reason to stay in the city longer than it takes to hail a beach-bound taxi. Visitors can pick from chow mein, lasagna, South Indian snacks, Gujarati *thalis*, Punjabi *dahl*, and Goan fish curry.

Shiu Sagar, MG Rd., in Shiu Sagar Hotel, opposite Centurian Bank. The most popular veg. fare in Panjim. Mobs of middle-class families and the occasional business group. North Indian veg. dishes Rs35-50; non-veg. under Rs30. Open daily 8am-11pm.

Kamat Hotel, 18th June Rd., in a prime location next to the Municipal Gardens, is busy all day serving up tasty samosas (Rs13) and generous *thalis* (Rs23) in a functional setting. Open daily 8am-9:30pm.

Hotel Vihar, MG Rd., north of Hotel Venite. This popular stainless steel and formica joint serves up meal-sized *dosas* (Rs12) and a veg. *thali* (Rs22). Open M-Sa 7am-9pm.

GOA

Sher-e-Punjab Classic, on the 1st fl. of Hotel Aroma, at the west edge of the Municipal Gardens. The delicacies that emerge from the restaurant's well-known *tandoor* (Rs50-90) will remind you why you eat meat in the first place. Open daily noon-3:30pm and 7pm-midnight. A cheaper and more low-key branch, **Sher-e-Punjab,** is on 18th June Rd., on the right as you walk away from the river. There's a lively bar scene at night. Beer Rs40. Entrees under Rs60. Open daily noon-11pm.

Hotel Venite, on 31st January Rd., near the river. A sign will direct you up a narrow staircase. Very mellow and airy space. While macaroni and cheese (Rs65) is available for the homesick, Venite's real crowd-pleasers are its fish curry (Rs80) and nightly specials (Rs60-100). Beer Rs40; coconut or cashew *feni* Rs20. Try the artery-clogging *bebinca* for dessert (Rs25). Open M-Sa 8am-3pm and 7-10pm.

Goenchin, Dr. Dada Vaidya Rd., on the left as you come from Church Sq. Look for a sign pointing uphill. Splurge on delicious Chinese food that is only slightly Indianized (you can even ask for chopsticks) in a lush setting. Entrees Rs90-150. Veg. choices Rs60-90. Open daily 12:30-3pm and 7:30-11pm.

Chicky Chocky, off Church Sq., to your immediate right with your back to the stairs. Indian variations on international fast-food delights. Grilled cheese and tomato roll Rs18; pizzas Rs35-50; and fried rice and noodles Rs25-40. Open daily 10am-10pm.

■ SIGHTS

Not even the tourist offices pretend that there are any real sights worth seeing in Panjim. Still, it's a pleasant enough place for idle meandering, particularly in the Fontainhas area on the west bank of the Ourem.

The bright white **Chapel of St. Sebastian,** dating from the 1880s, stands at the end of a short street opening off 31st January Rd. The life-sized statue of the crucified Christ that used to hang in the Palace of the Inquisition in Old Goa now hangs here, head unbowed. Towering over Church Sq. is the **Mary Immaculate Conception Church (Igreja Maria Immaculada Conceicao),** the top tier of a stack of white and blue criss-crossing staircases. The original chapel, consecrated in 1541, was the first stop for Portuguese sailors thanking God for a safe voyage. The chapel was renovated in the 17th century. This is the main place of worship for local Christians, and its musty, dark interior is heavy with silence and prayer. *(Open Su and holy days 10:30am-1pm and 6:15-7pm, other days 9am-1pm and 3:30-6pm.)*

The **Secretariat** sits on the banks of the River Mandovi. This grand white building was constructed in the 16th century as a palace and fortress for Yusuf Adil Shah of Bijapur. The Portuguese rebuilt it in 1615, and in 1759 it became the palace of the Portuguese viceroy.

You can reach the large, fairly unimpressive, **Mahalaxmi Temple,** by following Dr. Dada Vaidya Rd. southwest from Church Sq. Look for the red arch to the left.

■ ■ ENTERTAINMENT AND NIGHTLIFE

Panjim is well set-up to provide for the timeless recreational pursuit of consuming alcohol. Local brews are sold in small shops, and tiny bars dot the city, especially in Fontainhas. Try Kwality Bar & Restaurant, Church Sq., a place where Chinese flavor, wicker lanterns, Stevie Wonder tunes, and Goan hipsters all come together.

Government and private companies still organize **evening cruises** on the Mandovi River. The cruises feature traditional dancing—*denki, fijddi,* Portuguese, and *corredmino* styles—and, if you time it right, a stunning view of the sunset at sea. Book at any GTDC office, or just show up at the pier and look for the boat. Check an English-language newspaper to find what's showing at Panjim's three **cinemas:** the **Samrat** and the **Ashok** (which shows the dregs of English and American cinema) are in the same building on 18th June Rd., and the **Cine National** is behind the Hotel Aroma on Ormuz Rd.

During the peak season hotels organize events, but for the rest of the year options are slim for shaking your booty; head to the coast.

OLD GOA पुराना गोवा

Tourists who don't venture inland from the beaches might think European fascination with Goa began in 1970s Calangute. Old Goa, 9km east of Panjim along the Mandovi River, proves them wrong, evoking the 16th-century glory days of Portuguese rule, when the city of 200,000 was hailed as the "Rome of the Orient," and the (always unexpected) Inquisition was still in full swing. In 1510, Alfonso de Albuquerque, the original Portuguese man-o'-war, trounced the Bijapur Sultan, Adil Shah, and seized the city on the Mandovi, then known as Ela. Control of the city gave the Portuguese a virtual monopoly on regional trade. The city began to attract wealth, sailors, and the epic debauchery that was sparked off by the combination of the two. Galvanized into action by irresistible tales of terrible sin, the Jesuits arrived shortly thereafter, preaching and proselytizing to hedonists and heathens with the same zeal that built Old Goa's staggeringly ornate cathedrals. The city's decline, concurrent with the fading of Portuguese power in India, was hastened by malaria epidemics and silting in the Mandovi; by the 17th century the party was over for good, and the seat of government moved to Panjim. Today the city is looked after not by viceroys and aristocratic *hidalgos* but by the Archaeological Survey of India, which plasters the churches to keep them from crumbling in the monsoon. The churches are all that remain of the city, glorious yet forlorn reminders of the long-gone empire.

Auto-rickshaws (Rs50-70), **motorcycles,** and **bicycles** make the scenic 9km trip along the Mandovi riverbank from Panjim to Old Goa. **Buses** also shuttle from Panjim's bus terminal (every 15min., 7am-7pm, 20min., Rs5). If you bike, and want to avoid the main road melee, continue past the traffic circle beyond the Kadamba bus stand in Patto (the left fork goes directly to Old Goa) and go straight; take the smaller left-hand road parallel to the main road, then take the first fork to the left and follow the road through a small village. Take a left at the first chapel and the road will meet up with NH4 again. Finally, turn right into Old Goa. Unofficial guides, frequenting the churches in search of earthly reward, expect to be tipped in return for their knowledge of local history and legends. For eats, stands and "tourist restaurants" huddle at both ends of the Basilica Bom Jesus.

SIGHTS

SÉ CATHEDRAL. On the left, along the main road from Panjim, the yellow Sé Cathedral complex looms up from an expanse of green-trimmed lawn. After the decaying Chapel of St. Catherine on your left is the former **Convent and Church of St. Francis of Assisi.** The church floor is paved with coats of arms that mark family graves from as far back as the 16th century. Gold ornamentation and oil paintings adorn the walls, holding fast against the advancing orange water stains. Mary and Jesus are depicted with dark hair and complexions, similar to the dark-skinned cherubs in the Cathedral itself. *(Open daily 8:30am-5:30pm.)* The attached convent is now the none-too-thrilling **Archaeological Museum,** which exhibits portraits of the viceroys, currency from "India Portuguesa," Christian icons, and sculpture from Goa's Hindu temples. *(Rs5. Open Sa-Th 10am-5pm.)*

Beyond the museum is the **Cathedral** dedicated to St. Catherine. Erected by the viceroy in 1564, the vast, three-naved cathedral took 80 years to build. One of the twin towers was destroyed by lightning in 1775. The other houses the mellow-toned **Sino du Ouro (Golden Bell),** said to be the largest bell in Asia. Scenes from the life of St. Catherine are carved into the grand golden altar, and 14 smaller altars are set within the cavernous church. *(Open daily 8:30am-5:30pm.)*

AROUND THE SÉ CATHEDRAL. If you exit the cathedral grounds and take the road to the north, you come to the **Church of St. Cajetan.** According to local lore, Italian friars of the Order of Theatines built the church on top of an ancient Hindu temple in the 17th century. Today, the church is known for its dome (modeled after St. Peter's in Rome) and the elaborate woodwork of its interior. The ruined **gate** to Yusuf Adil Shah's collapsed palace rises in forlorn tribute to pre-Portuguese Goa by the entrance to the church grounds. Farther up the road toward the Mandovi River is the modest **Viceroy's Arch,** still waiting to receive the next Portuguese viceroy, who would be handed the keys to the capital as he passed ceremoniously under the arch. The gate bears an inscription left by Governor Francisco da Gama (r. 1597-1600) in memory of his great-grandfather, Vasco. *(Church open daily 8:30am-5:30pm but may close for a 12:30-3pm siesta.)*

BASILICA DE BOM JESUS. Built between 1594 and 1605 to house the remains of St. Francis Xavier, the Basilica de Bom Jesus (Cathedral of the Good Jesus), with its dark, orange stone walls, is perhaps Old Goa's most legendary site. Its interior is an explosion of gold. At the far end of the nave, above the altar, is a painting of St. Francis Xavier embracing Christ on the cross. The saint's mausoleum is off to the right of the altar behind a curtain of stars. Inside the windowed silver casket, a lightbulb shines on St. Francis' shriveled body, "donated" by Cosimo III de Medici in exchange for a pillow on which the saint's head had rested. A doorway to the left of the mausoleum leads to a small room with historical tidbits and photographs of the relic. Stairs lead to an **art gallery.** On the way out is a lovely cloister. *(Opposite the Sé Cathedral. Open M-Sa 9am-6:30pm, Su 10:30am-6:30pm. Gallery open Sa, M, W-F 9:30am-12:30pm and 2-5:30pm, Su 10:30am-12:30pm and 2-5:30pm.)*

AROUND THE BASILICA DE BOM JESUS. Up the hill to the west of the Basilica de Bom Jesus, on a road that runs parallel to and south of the main road, are the romantic ruins of the **Church of St. Augustine.** The 46m tower has been standing since 1602. Gravestones line the floor, and the knobby alcoves hint at carvings that have long since eroded. Below the church is the massive **Church and Convent of St. Monica Christon,** built in 1636. Its "miracle cross" was once well known for its tendency to open its eyes, bleed from its wounds, and speak. Miracles have recently been few and far between.

▟ DAYTRIPS FROM OLD GOA

A handful of Hindu temples near the Portuguese ruins of Old Goa are worth a look. Although far from India's finest, they remind daytrippers of the massive Hindu majority that always remained just behind coastal Goa's Portuguese facade.

Most of the temples hide along NH4, conveniently becoming less interesting the closer one gets to drab **Ponda.** When you get tired of the temples, just hop on a bus back to **Panjim** (every 15-20min. 6:30am-8:30pm, 45min., Rs12). Buses from Panjim are often full—tell the conductor where you want to get off, and be sure to stand near a door so you can fight your way out. The first temple is at **Mangeshi** (also called Priol) village (30min, Rs7). Head down the palm-tree lined path to the colorful arch that leads to the **Sri Manguesh** temple. Like most of the temples in this area, it was built in the 18th century to house deities smuggled inland in the 16th century from the Inquisition-ravaged coast. Less than a 15-minute walk south (1km) leads to the more sedately decorated **Sri Mahalsa,** acclaimed for the stunning wood carvings on the facades of its *mandapam* (sloping roof).

From Sri Mahalsa or the Mangeshi bus stop, get on a bus to Ponda for the 4km stretch to the Farmagudi junction. Reaching the **Sri Naguesh** temple is a 45-minute uphill slog in the burning sun for those with something to prove. At the roundabout, bear right down a narrow back road past a modern temple and through **Nageshi** village. Colorful woodcarvings in the entrance hall depict scenes from the **Ramayana** (see p. 579), though it's difficult to piece together the narrative. Ambling down the shady road for another 20 minutes will bring you to the red roof of the **Sri Shantadurga** temple. You'll know you've arrived when you spot the tourist taxis and the rows of stands hawking religious knick-knacks. Head back uphill to catch the bus back to Panjim.

MAPUSA मपुसा

The North Goan town of Mapusa is on a hillside 30km north of Panjim and 10km inland from the hopping beaches at Anjuna, Calangute, and Baga. Mostly of interest to travelers for its bus terminal, beach-seekers from Bombay or Bangalore jump off the bus at Mapusa and head straight for the sand.

⬛ GETTING THERE AND GETTING AROUND. Buses shuttle frequently from the **Kadamba Bus Terminal** to a variety of sinful locations. Most intrastate buses run from 7:30am to 7:30pm and travel to: **Anjuna** (every 10min., 30min., Rs5); **Arambol** (every 10min., 1hr., Rs10); **Baga and Calangute** (every 10min., 30min., Rs7); **Margao** (every hr. 6am-8:20pm, 1½hr., Rs17); **Panjim** (every 5min.; express 20min., local 40min.; Rs5-6); and **Siolim** (every 15min., 15min., Rs5). The express bus to Panjim leaves from the area across the parking lot that is by the ticket windows. If you're leaving Goa behind, there's no reason to go to Panjim to catch a bus—the area around Kadamba teems with private coach operators, and state-run buses also make the trip (long-distance booking office, opposite bus stall 8; open daily 6am-1pm and 2-8pm). Buses go to: **Bombay** (4:30pm, 12hr., Rs307); **Miraj** (10:45am, 8hr., Rs115); and **Pune** (7:30pm, 12hr., Rs215). **Motorcycle rentals** are hard to come by, thanks to Mapusa's police crackdown on foreigners without papers; easy-rider wannabes rent in the resort villages.

⬛⬛ ORIENTATION AND PRACTICAL INFORMATION. The **State Bank of India,** north of the bus terminal at the roundabout, changes money and does cash advances (open M-F 10am-2pm, Sa 10am-noon). The **police station** (☎262231) and the **GPO** are two blocks west. **Postal Code:** 403507.

⬛⬛ ACCOMMODATIONS AND FOOD. Staying in Mapusa should not be necessary. It might be worth taking a taxi to Calangute or Panjim rather than hanging around here. If you are forced to stay, try the well-staffed **Hotel Satya Heera,** north of the bus terminal with spacious rooms, spectacular views (on the upper floors), and even an antiquated TV. (☎262849; email satya@goa1.dot.net.in. Check-out 9am. Doubles Rs400. Off-season: Rs300.) The **Tourist Hostel,** at the Gandhi-statued roundabout, south of the bus terminal, has adequate rooms and will make you feel like the just-off-the-bus tourist that you are. (☎262694. Check-out noon. Doubles Rs300. Off-season: Rs260.) **Ruchira,** the Hotel Satya Heera's rooftop restaurant, serves Goan, Chinese, and standard Indian dishes. (Rs10-60. Open daily 7-11am and 11:30am-10:45pm.) Food stalls around the bus terminal serve delicious, greasy food, but Mapusa's **market,** southeast of the bus terminal, is an adventure: a more authentic version of the Anjuna flea market. It's at its busiest every Friday (early morning-late afternoon), but there's almost always something going on.

CALANGUTE कांलगुट AND BAGA बागा ☎0832

The twin villages of Calangute and Baga have your name written all over them. Beachfront shacks serve up mango *lassis* while vendors from Rajasthan and Kashmir peddle carved wooden elephants, sarongs, and mirrored purses to sunburnt tourists. Cafes fry your eggs however you want them, and bars play remixes of your favorite 80s hits. No, you haven't stumbled upon an undiscovered gem. This former winter hang-out of the backpacker set is now the favorite wintertime stomping ground of the package tourist. Not that there's anything wrong with that. The beach is still lovely, even if it has been narrowed a bit by all the guest houses and seafood shacks. This is no longer the Goa of legend—the hedonistic heyday of free drugs and free love is now long gone. Today the sunsets are rarely enhanced by anything stronger than an ice-cold Kingfisher beer, but the sun, sand, and surf remain. What more do you need? By late afternoon the crowds will start to trickle home, and you'll be left alone with the cows to watch the sun go down.

⌐ GETTING THERE AND GETTING AROUND

Buses: Buses from Mapusa stop at the **Calangute market** and at the main roundabout on the way to **Baga** (Rs3) and on their way back to **Mapusa** (Rs7). Buses to and from **Panjim** (Rs7) stop at the market and just beyond the roundabout before the beach.

Local Transportation: Tourist taxis go between Calangute and Baga for Rs40-50. **Rickshaws** and **motorbikes** make the same trip for about Rs25-30, and to Panjim (Rs70-150) and Anjuna (Rs50-100). **Motorcycle** rental is common in season. Off season, inquire near the gas station west of the market. For **bicycle** rental, try **Jay-Jay's,** on the road between Baga and Calangute (Rs50). Open daily 8am-7pm.

✳❓ ORIENTATION AND PRACTICAL INFORMATION

Most buses smoke their way into **Calangute market** at the bottom of the main road that heads west to the **beach.** They also stop about halfway down the main east-west road as their final stop on the way from Panjim. From the market stop, continue in the same direction as the bus until you come to the roundabout and Rama Books. With your back to the bookstore head north onto the main north-south road that runs between Calangute and Baga; the entire length of this road is lined with guest houses, restaurants, and souvenir stalls. The main east-west road leads from the **market** west to the **beach** and comprises Calngute proper.

Budget Travel: MGM Travels (☎/fax 276073), on the Calangute roundabout, sells plane and catamaran tickets. **STD/ISD** telephone services. Open M-Sa 9:30am-6pm.

Currency Exchange: State Bank of India, at Calangute market. Open M-F 10am-4pm, Sa 10am-1pm. **Thomas Cook** is inside the bank. Open M-F 10am-5pm, Sa 10am-1pm.

Bookstore: Rama Books & Jewelry, at the roundabout. Open daily 9am-7pm. **Jay-Jay's** (see **Local Transportation,** above) also sells used books.

Pharmacy: Walsons & Walsons Chemist and Druggist (☎276366), next door to Fatima Clinic, in the same building as the State Bank of India, stocks curative goodies. Open daily 8:30am-2pm and 3:30-9pm.

Internet: Everyone and their mother offers email services around here. **Squeeze Internet Email,** at the southern edge of Baga, is open 24hr. Rs100 per hr.

Post Office: In a cute pink building south of the market. Head east from the roundabout, turn right at the market, and then take the first left. Open M-Sa 9am-2pm and 2:30-5pm. **Postal code:** 403516.

▛ ACCOMMODATIONS

Most of the cheaper accommodations are around the main villages and the road between them. In general, the ones closer to Baga offer more pleasant surroundings, though most of the places between the villages are a fair distance from the beach. In season (Dec.-Jan.), prices can double. As usual, the taxi- and rickshaw-*wallahs* who claim a hotel is full are usually receiving commission from other places; insist on going to your first choice. Flats and houses for longer stays are usually still available in early December—the best of them are just north of Baga. Ask around; every other building has rooms to let.

▨ **Villa Fatima** (☎277418; email villa.fatima@sympatico.ca), on the main north-south strip, closer to Baga. Look for the sign on the left when coming from Calangute. A friendly family runs a cheerful complex, festooned with colored lights and plants. Spacious rooms with attached bath, hot water, and refrigerators all surround a courtyard restaurant. Safety deposit box. Check-out 10am. Rs200-600. Off-season: Rs150-400.

▨ **Alidia Cottages** (☎/fax 279041), just beyond Villa Fatima along the road to Baga. Behind a white church on the left. Another friendly, family-run establishment with lovely rooms, all with bath. Wander through the back gate, past the tiny fishing village, and out to the beach. Safety deposit box. Check-out 11am. In Sept., rates begin to rise, reaching Rs800 by Jan. and Dec. Off season, doubles drop to Rs100-150.

Joaquim's (☎279696), just off the east-west road that leads to Tito's. From the main north-south road, head east between the Sunshine Beach and Miranda Resorts and look for signs on your right to La Fantona, and continue north. Just seconds from the beach. Clean rooms with sparkling attached baths. Avoid the windowless room. Check-out 10am. Rs300. Off-season: Rs200.

Nani's and Rani's (☎277014), at the northern tip of Baga, across the river. From the main road bear right on the dirt path to the covered bridge. A bit of a haul but worth it for a tranquil backpacker-friendly spot. Splendid doubles with bath cluster around the popular restaurant. Doubles with bath and fan for Rs300. Off-season Rs250.

Albenjoh (☎276422), just north of Calangute on the inland side. A white-washed home with large rooms and shiny attached baths for Rs800-900. Off-season: Rs250-300.

West Horizon (☎276489), follow the main east-west road to the beach, and turn right just before the beach. Follow signs from the next east-west road; it's just north of Angelo's Inn. Clean rooms with attached bath. Bonus points for beach proximity. Doubles Rs250; 5-bed dorm Rs500; 6-bed dorm Rs600. Off-season: rooms half-price.

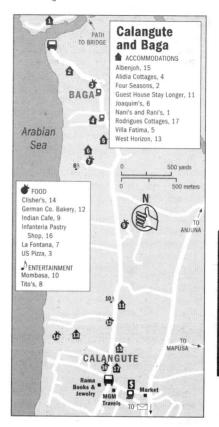

Calangute and Baga

⌂ ACCOMMODATIONS
Albenjoh, 15
Alidia Cottages, 4
Four Seasons, 2
Guest House Stay Longer, 11
Joaquim's, 6
Nani's and Rani's, 1
Rodrigues Cottages, 17
Villa Fatima, 5
West Horizon, 13

🍎 FOOD
Clisher's, 14
German Co. Bakery, 12
Indian Cafe, 9
Infanteria Pastry Shop, 16
La Fontana, 7
US Pizza, 3

♪ ENTERTAINMENT
Mombasa, 10
Tito's, 8

BAGA

Arabian Sea

0   500 yards
0   500 meters

N

TO ANJUNA

TO MAPUSA

CALANGUTE

Rama Books & Jewelry
MGM Travels
Market

GOA

Four Seasons (formerly Lucky Bar & Restaurant; ☎279474), along the main road in Baga. Rents rooms in a building near the beach or in brightly painted cottages with attached bath. Doubles Rs300. Off-season: Rs150–250.

Guest House Stay Longer (☎277460), on the inland side of the Calangute-Baga road. Decent rooms in a wide price range. Penny-pinchers can snag the windowless ground floor rooms with shared bath. Those who intend to stay true to the guest house's name should opt for the spacious rooms with attached baths upstairs. A pair of rooftop chairs are primed for sunset watching. Check-out 8am. Rs100-400. Off-season Rs50-150.

Rodrigues Cottages (☎276458), opposite the Calangute Association building. Basic rooms, all with attached bath, strung around a courtyard. Rooms Rs100-150.

🍴 FOOD

You can't please all the people all the time, but that doesn't stop the innumerable touristy seafood shacks in Calangute and Baga from trying. Copycat menus offer mediocre renditions of regional delights and favorites from home, whether that's Beijing, Bologna, or Bognor Regis. The seafood is good; if you're just looking for a good spot to meet fellow travelers over a cold beer and a sunset, try the popular **Britto's** or **St. Anthony's**, side by side on the Baga beachfront.

🍰 **German Co. Bakery,** opposite the Stay Longer Guest House. They swear they use purified water in all their drinks, so linger in the shade over fresh fruit juice (Rs10-40) and delicious home-made pastries (Rs8-35). Cinnamon rolls Rs15; omelettes Rs10-30. Open daily 8am-11pm.

Indian Cafe, midway between Calangute and Baga; look for the sign on the main north-south road. This excellent, quiet lunchtime retreat serves delicious *masala dosa* (Rs20) and fruit shakes. Best and cheapest Indian food in town. Open daily 8am-6pm.

Infanteria Pastry Shop, by the church, just north of the roundabout. Delicious pastries, donuts galore (plain Rs8, chocolate Rs12), and all the usual Chinese/Indian/ continental stuff. Open daily 8am-9pm. Table service stops 30min. before closing.

Clisher's, just west of the West Horizon Guest House. From the Calangute tourist complex, follow the large, fish-shaped sign. Excellent, moderately priced seafood in surroundings so quiet you can hear the waves on the shore. Indian dishes Rs30-50; seafood Rs30-60. Open daily 9am-11pm. Closed Jun. 1-Aug. 31.

US Pizza (formerly Joe's Cafe), on the southern outskirts of Baga, serves cheap, tasty breakfasts and fresh juice. Omelettes Rs20-30. For health nuts and those needing to dry out, a variety of fresh juice combos are available all day, with or without spirulina, whatever that might be (Rs20-50). Pizzas available during the afternoon (Rs60-200). Breakfast 8-11:30am. Open daily 8am-6pm.

La Fontana, next to Joachim, across the street from Tito's. Seafood, pasta, and veggies in a friendly atmosphere allow you to transcend your belly troubles and contemplate higher things at this outpost of Tibetan, Japanese, and Chinese culinary delights. Fresh pasta Rs35-60; fish Rs65-140. Open daily 8:30am-midnight.

⚡ BEACHES

> ⚠️ **WARNING.** The water on some beaches is off-limits during the monsoon season (roughly mid-June to late Aug.) because of rough waves and dangerous undertow. Ask before taking a dip, and watch for boulders and steep drop-outs.

It's hard to complain about the beach between Calangute and Baga. Despite all the development, the sand is still quiet in the morning, and the water always seems to be at an ideal temperature; the problem is the people. As the sun starts to climb higher in the sky, leather-skinned men in Speedos waddle out on to the sand and settle in for the day next to their women. Pallid children chase each other around and fry to a crisp, while their parents argue over souvenirs. As you head north, the bodies get younger, as the backpacker crowd strives to work up a credible tan before heading off to do the north Indian circuit.

South of Baga, a strip of beach has been set aside for water sports. **Goan Bananas** has a fleet of boats ready for just about anything (☎276362. Parasailing Rs1000; unavoidable Goan puns free). Next door, **Atlantis** will take you water-skiing (Rs650 for 15min.), set up wind-surfing lessons, rent surfboards (Rs250 per hr.), or drag you behind a boat on an inflatable banana (Rs300 for 15min.). In season, fishing boats, chartered by numerous companies, make the wet 'n' wild journey to the Anjuna flea market every Wednesday and offer dolphin-, crocodile-, and hippie-spotting tours for Rs200-500 per day.

📺 NIGHTLIFE

Despite a raucous past, nightlife in Calangute and Baga today tends to wind down early and errs on the side of resort-area hokeyness. While the more upscale hotels pack their bar-restaurants with the sort of live "musicians" who'd be confined to street-performing back home, there are worse places to begin or end a night of drunken revelry. Aside from surf-splashing and beer-swilling, there's little to do here—but isn't that why you came in the first place?

For nightlife without the schmaltz, the **Mombasa: Gateway to Africa** bar—a beach shack transplanted onto the main road—pounds drums late into the night. (Happy hour 7-9pm. Open 6pm-3am). There's only one real after-hours game in town: **Tito's,** a bar-restaurant on the Baga beach with a dance floor and boomin' hi-fi, serves expensive drinks (Rs60), often until the break of dawn. Outside the village proper, the **West End,** a somewhat tame party venue on the road between Calangute and Panjim, hosts parties regularly in season.

DAYTRIPS FROM CALANGUTE

Mocked by hipsters farther north, the resort-like village of **Candolim** is largely the preserve of middle-aged, middle-class package tourists, though there is also a burgeoning yoga scene. The hillside south of the Taj Holiday Village hides the impressive remains of the massive 17th-century **Aguada Fort,** which guards the mouth of the Mandovi. Follow the Candolim road south past the Taj and keep right as it winds 3km uphill. From the Calangute market, take the Mapusa bus via Sinquerim, and get off at Sinquerim, where the north-south road ends. Then, turn left at the bus stop and right at the chapel; a series of dirt paths winds to the top of the hill. The citadel commands an impressive view of the Mandovi and the southern coast.

Inside the remains of the fort is the **Central Aguada Jail,** filled with home-grown and imported drug offenders. From the citadel, follow the road east as it curves downhill and then make a sharp right, following the road to the prison. Charitable folks eager to perform good works (or those just hungry for juicy conversation) can show up to chat with inmates who don't already have another monthly visit scheduled (Tu and F, 9am-noon and 3-5pm). There are plenty of worse places then this to be locked away in a prison cell.

ANJUNA आंजना   ☎ 0832

Seaside restaurants and low, red-roofed cottages run along Anjuna's palm-fringed shoreline to the hill in the distance. Although Anjuna is slowing down a little as the party scene here approaches middle-age, for many a budget hedonist, the town remains the Goan ideal: long, lazy days on the beach, wild, raving nights, and liberal doses of cheap drugs to smooth the transition between the two. But the times they are a-gettin' different, and while Anjuna still buzzes with beach raves, full-moon parties, jungle boogies, and other breeds of psychedelic mayhem in peak season, much of the liveliest partying these days has moved to north Vagator or south to Gokarna. Regardless, the village's charms (or vices, for in Anjuna, they're one and the same) leave little room for complaint—each day is tagged by a beautiful sunset, each week brings free-market madness in the form of Anjuna's famous flea market (closed off-season), and each month is marked by the world-renowned full-moon raves. As Christmas approaches, the parties escalate in intensity and frequency. Though the scene isn't what it once was, Anjuna still plays host to a crazy cast of characters: from freaks to fishermen; package tourists to smacksters; Euro-yuppies to Kashmiri handicraft hawkers. Come join the fun.

> **! WARNING. Theft occurs frequently in Anjuna,** particularly on party nights. Carry important documents and valuables with you or (better still) lock them somewhere safe.

GETTING THERE AND GETTING AROUND

Buses: Buses stop at the end of the road above the beach, at the main intersection, and at several other places along the road heading away from the beach. To: **Mapusa** (20min., Rs5); **Vagator** (10min., Rs3). If your bus doesn't appear, hop on one to Mapusa and make your connection there.

Local Transportation: Taxis and **auto-rickshaws** wait near the beachfront bus stand. **Motorcycles and bicycles** can be rented along the main road.

GOA

✦ 🏧 ORIENTATION AND PRACTICAL INFORMATION

From the main intersection (crowned by the Starco Restaurant), roads lead west to the beachfront and bus stand, east to Mapusa and most banking facilities, south to the flea market and restaurants, and north to Vagator and some of the main party venues. For a small town, Anjuna sprawls over a surprisingly large area. Most get around by motor bike; be prepared for distances to be longer than you expect. Many places listed below have abbreviated hours in the off season.

Budget Travel: MGM Travels (☎ 274317) deals with plane tickets, reconfirmations, and car rentals. Open M-Sa 9:30am-6pm.

Currency Exchange: Orchard Food Stores. From the main intersection head east, and take the first right after Coutinho's Nest, and then the first left. Open daily 8am-9pm; closed Su in the off season.

Bookstore: Walk About Books, in the Oxford Stores. Open M-Sa 9:30am-9:30pm.

Telephones: Laxmi, just south of and behind Mary's Holiday Home, has 24hr. **STD/ISD.**

Internet: There are tons of email places in Anjuna. **Nehal Communications** and **Supriya Internet** flank the bus stand by the beach. Both Rs20 for first 10min. and Rs2 per each additional min.; minimum Rs20. Both open daily 8:30am-midnight.

Post Office: 2km up the road from the beach on the right. Open M-Sa 8:30am-1pm and 3-5pm. **Postal Code:** 403509.

🏠 ACCOMMODATIONS

Anjuna has acquired a somewhat undeserved reputation as a difficult place to find a bed, particularly during the peak season. A lack of phones in some guest houses makes getting reservations tricky, but you can normally find a room somewhere just by showing up. The large number of long-termers in Anjuna means that houses here aren't as prone to the insane Christmas price fluctuations of many of the places farther south. Guest houses hug the beachfront and the main east-west road. Room To Let signs are everywhere. South of the flea market is a veritable colony of long-term tourists, a good place to look for barebones lodgings for stays ranging from a week to several months. As usual, bargain away off season.

Mary's Holiday Home (☎ 273216), next to the beachfront bus stand. Clean, quiet, and close to the beach. Simple rooms with attached bath face inland. Satisfied customers sing the praises of the showers. Check-out 10am. Doubles Rs200-400.

Manali Guest House (☎ 273477), just south off the main intersection. This friendly spot in a central location offers email and a convenience store. All rooms have shared bath: Rs150-200. Off-season: Rs100-150.

Coutinho's Nest (☎ 274386), a 15min. walk east from the main intersection. An excellent, affable place with a rooftop terrace. Check-out 10am. Doubles Rs200–500.

Cabin Disco's (☎ 273254), on the south side of the road, just east of the main intersection. Cool clientele boogie-woogie their way into comfy rooms after a mellow evening in the groovy bar-restaurant. Check-out noon. Singles Rs200; doubles Rs300-500. Off season prices drop as low as Rs150.

Lolita's Guest House (☎ 273289), just north of the Orchard Store, a 30min. walk from the beach. Homey, freshly painted bungalows and immaculate doubles with bath, fridge, TV, and a sound system. Nymphets sold separately. Call ahead Dec.-Jan. Rs500. Off-season: Rs250. Discounts for longer stays.

Guru Bar-Restaurant and Guest House (☎ 273319), is one of the many basic cliffside options. Bare rooms are serviceable, but the outdoor common shower can get a bit muddy. The bar is a hub of the beachfront dope scene. Rooms Rs100-150.

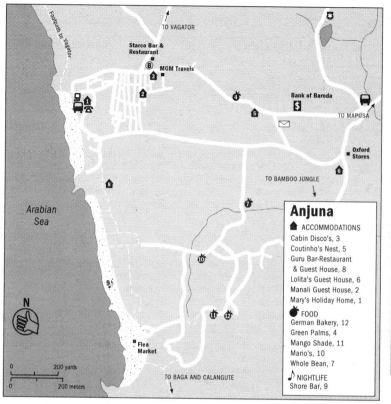

Anjuna

🏠 ACCOMMODATIONS
Cabin Disco's, 3
Coutinho's Nest, 5
Guru Bar-Restaurant
 & Guest House, 8
Lolita's Guest House, 6
Manali Guest House, 2
Mary's Holiday Home, 1

🍅 FOOD
German Bakery, 12
Green Palms, 4
Mango Shade, 11
Mario's, 10
Whole Bean, 7

♪ NIGHTLIFE
Shore Bar, 9

GOA

🍴 FOOD

The food served up at most of Anjuna's seaside restaurants is fast, cheap, greasy, and plentiful—perfect for snacks and sunset dinners. Those seeking variety will be better off at the restaurants that line the roads farther inland. Several vegan restaurants cater to the crunchy crowd, and falafal stands are everywhere. On Wednesday, a whole army of food vendors materializes out of nowhere to make the **flea market** Anjuna's premier spot for lunch or early dinner—the atmosphere is unbeatable. These places, and some of those listed below, are closed off-season.

■ **German Bakery,** Watch carefully for the sign; from the flea market road, cross the paved road and follow a worn dirt path east, or take the paved road east of Mario's. Not to be confused with the German Bakery at the Paradise Restaurant on the main road. Laid-back atmosphere comes complete with savory baked goodies every morning (Rs15-40). Veg. North Indian food at night Rs35-75. Open daily 7am-midnight.

■ **Mango Shade,** just west of the German Bakery, this often-packed spot offers cheaper food but has less atmosphere. Fresh fruit juices and *lassis* Rs20-40; sandwiches and toasts with delicious spreads (avocado, nutella, tuna) Rs30-40. Open daily 8am-5pm.

Mario's, on the paved road; from the flea market follow the road north and go right at the end. Spacious place serves up fresh seafood (Rs60-75) and Indian rice dishes (Rs35-50). Open daily 8am-noon and 6pm-midnight.

Whole Bean, along the road between town and the flea market. Vegan tofu shop pours out soy milkshakes in a variety of flavors (Rs30-45). Homemade tofu and tempeh sandwiches Rs60. Regular dairy delights and breakfast combos. Open daily 8am-5:30pm.

Green Palms, on the Mapusa road, about 1.5km inland. Delicious falafel sandwiches Rs40; banana milkshakes Rs15; and melancholic Israeli pop music (free). Open M-Sa 10am-11pm.

BEACHES

Not surprisingly, Anjuna's postcard-pretty shores draw huge crowds in season, when tanned and toned ravers in various states of tanked and stoned inebriation crash all along the strip. The beach is plagued with annoyingly persistent hawkers; practically the only things not for sale are tranquility and solitude. Packed with tourists, particularly on Wednesdays, this is the beach to sea and be scene on, but for peace and quiet, look elsewhere.

NIGHTLIFE

THE RAVES. The sloping hills of Anjuna have gained international renown in recent years as a hip and happening rave venue. The monthly full moon brings out the werewolf that lurks inside many of Goa's tourists, transforming them from placid beach-chillers into wild, snarling party-animals, especially during Goa's peak season. Christmas and New Year's Eve are the biggest nights, but things are pretty wild all year round. The roads are full of people cycling from party to party, and huge fields are flooded by rivers of ravers. Domestic and European DJs of varying quality broadcast the rave's techno soundtrack to a core of gyrating dancers, themselves surrounded by crowds of people resting and chilling, even as the Goan minions serve them tea, omelettes, chocolate, and smack. Understandably, many locals bemoan these monthly debauches. Recently, authorities have been doing their best to spoil everybody's fun, and at the time of writing had placed a ban on all music after 10pm. Whether the 24-hour party people will let a little legal technicality or two get in the way remains to be seen. By the time you read this, things could be back to business as usual.

OTHER NIGHTLIFE. If there isn't any scheduled action, most of the crowd heads to the **Shore Bar,** right in the middle of the beach. The terraced steps leading down to the beach are choked with beer-guzzling sunbathers or stargazers at most hours of day and night. Upstairs, the indispensable black lights flicker and imported DJs pilot the gargantuan sound system, while techno ravers go for broke on the small, sandy dance floor. Hours vary wildly by season. The **Sea Rock Restaurant,** just south of the bus stand, is another popular hangout, especially for Westerners. Don't worry if you're not hungry—only a few of the packed restaurant's occupants are dining at any one time; the rest are having coffee, tea, or juice, scoping each other out, or sneaking a joint. Farther south, the **Guru Bar,** with a much more relaxed drug policy, serves tall cold ones late into the night. However, much of the busiest partying these days goes on down the road in Vagator; those with motorbikes make the commute back and forth in search of fun fun fun.

VAGATOR वागातोर ☎ 0832

Of all the northern beach towns in Goa, Vagator comes closest to striking the perfect balance between hotspot and hideaway. Popular but not over-populated, scenic but not seedy, Vagator suns all day and raves all night without losing its cheerful, down-home vibe. The town houses a large number of long-term visitors, but the regulars here seem less jaded than their southern counterparts; the rigors of the tourism boom have yet to sap Vagator's easy, jubilant grace.

☞ GETTING THERE AND GETTING AROUND. Buses stop at the crossroads about 1km inland, where the road forks for Chapora and Ozran. They run to **Chapora** (every 15min., 6:30am-8pm, Rs5) and **Mapusa** (every 15min., 6:45am-7pm, Rs5). Buses also run between **Anjuna,** Chapora, and Vagator every hour (Rs3). **Prakash Motors,** on the main road, rents and repairs **motorcycles** at good rates. (Rs150-250 per day. Open daily 8am-8:30pm.) Touts along the road from Ozran Beach also rent motor bikes at similar rates. This area is also a good place for **bicycle rentals.** From behind Big Vagator Beach, taxis run to **Anjuna** (Rs50), **Chapora** (Rs30), and **Mapusa** (Rs150).

⚑ ORIENTATION AND PRACTICAL INFORMATION. Most resources for the budget traveler line the street that runs east-west from Big Vagator Beach. **Lalita Communications,** just inland, changes currency, provides travel services, and has computers for internet fun. (☎274481. Internet Rs90 per hour. Open daily 7am-11:30pm.) opposite the Primrose Bar, the **Rainbow Bookshop** sells and swaps used **books** (open daily 9:30am-10pm). The nearest **post office** is in Anjuna.

⚑ ACCOMMODATIONS AND FOOD. Vagator tends to cater to people here for the long haul. Guest houses line the main east-west road and the path to Ozran Beach, to the south. Off season, many restaurants and guest houses close. **Reshma Guesthouse,** on the south side of the road from Big Vagator beach, is cozy and communal (☎273568. Rs150-300. Closed Apr.-Sept.) Follow the yellow signs north of Big Vagator road to **Dolrina,** a large and popular guest house run by a friendly family (☎/fax 273382. Doubles Rs275-350. Off-season: Rs100-150. Book well in advance Dec.-Mar.) As the paved Big Vagator road curves in front of the beach and narrows to a dirt path, **Yellow House** is on the right, with basic, sparsely furnished rooms and common toilets and showers (Doubles Rs160. Closed Aug.-Sept.) For food, **Le Blue Bird,** near the seashore along the Ozran Beach road, is particularly mellow and comfy. Patrons lounge under the thatched roof and over delicious, reasonably priced veg. and non-veg. Indian and French cuisine. (Entrees Rs50-80. Open 8:30am-2pm and 5:30-11pm.) **Abu John's,** Big Vagator road, with its open kitchen, is a popular dinner spot for tandoori and barbecue dishes. (Entrees Rs40-60. Open daily 8am-noon and 6pm-midnight. Closed Mar. 31-Dec. 3.) Next door, the **Garden Villa** offers slightly better prices and food and nightly bootlegged American movies. (Entrees Rs25-40. Open daily 8am-11pm; movies 7:30pm.)

⚑ SIGHTS AND BEACHES. The southern **Ozran Beach** reigns as Vagator's most mellow and picturesque strip of sand—coconut palms, tranquil beach-shacks, and only a minimum of vendor-fuss and daytrippers. At the southern tip of Ozran is a small bay—deep, calm, and perfect for lazy swimming. Farther north, Vagator's distinctive, gently shelving hills lead, like giant steps, to the shore at **Little Vagator Beach.** Though nothing remarkable, this rocky bit is separated from the hills by a large, grassy field—the best place in the north for a seaside picnic. **Big Vagator,** just north past the hills, is the longest expanse of fine, white grains around; it is occasionally cramped by the big crowds it draws from Sterling Vagator Resort and the nearby bus stand. Towering over the whole scene to the northeast are the expansive ruins of the 17th-century **Portuguese Fort** that separates Chapora from Vagator. Today the ruins shelter only the occasional errant cow or enterprising cold drinks salesman, but it's worth a quick clamber for the view: a panoramic sampling of the whole Goa scene—beach blanket bingo to the south, fishermen hauling in their nets to the east, and lush, unspoiled territory looming across the Chapora River to the north. The southern scramble from Vagator to Anjuna, along rocky beaches and a pleasant path, is another enjoyable walk.

⚑ NIGHTLIFE. Vagator's bars bump and jive all night long in December and January; proprietors keep the beer flowing until there's no one left standing to drink it. The **Primrose Restaurant and Bar,** with black lights and techno DJs, is as good a place as any to start off the evening. Heading inland, it's the first right past the implausibly named See Green Little Tibet Cafe Brick Oven Pizza Olive Restaurant. (Entrees around Rs60; mixed drinks Rs40. Open 9am-1am.) The **Nine Bar** above Ozran Beach is another nighttime hotspot. Other places worth checking out are the **Millennium Bridge Lounge and Club,** just inland from the northern end of Ozran Beach, and **La Dolce Vita** to the south. Parties often break out between Vagator and Anjuna, with partiers commuting back and forth in search of the hippest scene. The cafes around Chapora market are usually a good source of info on where the next party will be.

NEAR VAGATOR: CHAPORA

Just a few hundred meters (and one old ruined fort) away from Vagator, Chapora isn't blessed with anything remotely resembling a beach, but it manages to more than make up for this lack by nailing hippie-chic fair and square. Tattooed and tanned back-packers suck down fresh juices in crowded cafes and muse where to bring the party next. If you are feeling out of place, **Queen of Hearts,** just down the road from Chapora market, will dread your locks for you. From Vagator, follow the turn-off for Chapora along the main road and bear right at the fork; the teeming market area is just up the road on the right. **Taxi drivers** huddle under the banyan tree on Chapora's main street when they're not hustling for fares to **Panjim** (Rs250), **Mapusa** (Rs150), **Anjuna** (Rs50-100), and **Vagator** (Rs50). **Buses** head to Mapusa, via **Vagator** (every 20min., Rs5). **Soniya Travels** in the **market** area, deals with **travel** arrangements and has **email** and **phone** services. (☎273344. Open daily 9am-midnight; off-season closes at 10pm.) **Guest houses** line the main road. One good option is **Helinda's,** just north of the market, which has spacious clean rooms around a welcoming restaurant (☎274345. Rs100-350.) **Private rooms** (inquire at the restaurants) are a good alternative; two can sleep well for under Rs150-200 per night. opposite Soniya Travel, **Yak Restaurant** has delicious fresh juices and generous veg. and non-veg. *thalis* (Rs25-30) as well as par-for-the-course Indian, continental, Tibetan, and Chinese delights. (Open daily 6am-10pm.)

ARAMBOL (HARMAL) आरामबोल ☎ 0832

If Arambol doesn't do it for you, then you're pretty hard to please. Pleasant and friendly, without the package tourists of Calangute and Baga, the aging, drugged-out hippies of Anjuna, or the hipper-than-thou party-people of Vagator and Chapora, Arambol might just be the beach of your dreams. Though a bridge over the Chapora river is slowly (*very* slowly) nearing completion, the village is currently accessible only by ferry or via a not-especially-frequent bus from Mapusa. Arambol's pristine beaches, freshwater lake, and lines of coconut palms are therefore reserved for a select bunch of persevering travelers who come in search of some tranquility, a few rays, and a little patch of the Arabian Sea to splash around in. Which is not to say that Arambol's long and sandy stretch of whiteness is all yours and yours alone. During peak season, Arambol's seaside cafes and bars swarm with daytrippers and fortnighters seeking solitude, driving the die-hard sociopaths south to Mandrem, north to Querim Beach, or up into the trees. At less crowded times of year, though—and always in the early mornings—you'll only have to share the beach with fishermen folding their nets.

 GETTING THERE AND GETTING AROUND. There are several ways to reach Arambol. The simplest is a direct **bus** from Mapusa (daily 8, 10am, and 1pm; 1hr.; Rs10). Buses arrive in **Arambol Junction** from Chopdem in the south. From the junction, backtrack south and take the first right, where the narrow road winds about 400m to the beach. Buses return from Arambol to Mapusa from in front of the Om Ganesh Guesthouse on the beach road (every hr. 7am-4pm, 1hr, Rs10 plus Rs7 for luggage). The main road heads north to the region's only **petrol station.** Fill up here before heading north to Querim or Terekol. If you are on the coast south of the Chapora River, a second option is to journey to Siolem (8km north of Chapora), from where a river ferry crosses to Chopdem. There is a **river ferry** to Chopdem (every 15min., 6:15am-10:30pm, 10min, Rs1; with bike Rs4). From the ferry dock in Chopdem, buses run at least every hour to Arambol (30min., Rs5). **Taxis** and **rickshaws** are all but unavoidable (Rs100-150). If you're on foot, just veer right from the dock and take a left at the first intersection (following the signs to Harmal). A third option is to take the **boat** from Anjuna during the Wednesday flea market (see **Entertainment,** below). A final option is to come by rail. The Konkan Railway station at **Pernem** is nearby (Rs200 by taxi; 2nd class train ticket to Bombay Rs231, first class Rs637). **Taxis** in Vagator, Chapora, Mapusa, and Siolem run to Arambol, though outside of December and January you'll have to pay for a round-trip (at most Rs400) even if you're only going one-way.

■🗗 ORIENTATION AND PRACTICAL INFORMATION. Tara Travels, at the corner where the beach road makes its final turn due west toward the beach, handles transport bookings and reconfirmations and does **currency exchange.** (☎297751. Open daily 8am-8pm.) There is a **police station** on the north side of the beach road, and a tiny **post office** just south of the beach road. (Open M-Sa 10am-1pm and 2-6pm.) **Postal code:** 403524.

▛🖰 ACCOMMODATIONS AND FOOD. Many visitors return here year after year and rent houses or rooms for several months. Guest houses lining the beach road are available for short-term stays, and even during peak season, accommodations can be arranged with a little legwork. Ask at restaurants and keep your eyes open for signs. During the monsoon, most lodges and restaurants are simply closed. **Tara Travels** (see above) can help arrange house and room rentals (Rs200. Off-season: Rs150.) **Houses** can be had for Rs200 per night or for Rs3000-4000 per month. Sizes and facilities vary as widely as the prices: many houses have no toilets or running water, just access to nearby bushes and wells. **The Ganesh Bar** has beautiful rooms dramatically situated on the cliffs midway between the two beaches. (☎287659. Doubles Rs400.) The very basic **Relax Inn,** on the beach, has few amenities, but rooms are big and the crashing of the waves will rock you to sleep. (☎207711. Rs150. Off-season: Rs100. Closed Jun. 15-Aug. 15.)

Restaurants line the road and beach front, but the cream of the crop is **▨Fellini,** an absolutely scrumptious Italian spot just inland on the beach road. Imported extra virgin olive oil and tomatoes makes a for a difference you can taste—*molto autentico!* Crowds of travelers pack the roof terrace for delicious pizzas (Rs40-75) and divine sandwiches for Rs25-60. (Open Th-Tu 10am-11pm, Su opens at 2pm and W 7:30-11pm.) For excellent Indian food and continental breakfasts, head to **21 Coconut Inn,** on the beach, one shack south of where the road intersects with the sand. Attentive waiters serve up rice dishes (Rs20-70), Goan specialities (Rs50-60), and excellent banana pancakes (Rs25). The **Ganesh Bar** on the cliffs offers food and drink. (Seafood Rs55-70; Indian Rs40-50. Open daily 9am-1am.) All of these restaurants are closed off-season.

▛🖰 BEACHES AND ENTERTAINMENT. Arambol's gorgeous beach stretches south as far as the eye can see. A shack toward the south of the main beach rents body-boards (Rs50) and wind-surfing equipment (Rs200, with lesson Rs250). You can walk as far south as the Chapora River on the lovely sandy expanse, though it would take a good part of your day to get there (2-3 hour walk). North of the main beach, along a rocky path negotiable only by foot, lies the smaller, more secluded **Paradise Beach.** Behind it is a lovely **freshwater lagoon** that defines picturesque. On Wednesdays, a fun and popular daytrip is to catch a boat to Anjuna for the **flea market.** The **Welcome Restaurant** near the beach sends boats there every Wednesday morning (Rs100 one-way, Rs150 round-trip). The northernmost boat on the main beach usually makes the trip. **Fellini** (see above) has live music most Saturday nights. The dozen-or-so bars along the main road pour fizzies to fuzz your mind.

🗗 DAYTRIPS FROM ARAMBOL: QUERIM BEACH. North of Arambol junction, virtually every trace of backpacker culture disappears. A couple of places stand out, though, beyond the pale of hippie settlement. The first is **Querim Beach,** a fir-backed strip of the white sand where you can vegetate from Noel to New Year's with hardly a Kodak or a dreadlock to disturb you. Querim (Keri) Beach is a two-hour walk north from Paradise Beach in Arambol. Alternatively, you can head north from the Arambol junction, following the signs to Keri (about 10km). Faint white writing on the road will point you to the beach, also known as Terekol Beach. Nowadays, **Terekol Fort,** as if tired of living a lie, has given up trying to be an impressive 400-year-old fort and has recently come out as a spruced-up, overpriced hotel and restaurant. Unless you have a special thing for modestly-sized immodestly-restored Portuguese forts, it's probably not worth making the trek. The journey north to Terekol has spectacular scenery, but is hard to manage without your own bike. **Buses** also make the trip from Chopdem/Arambol to Querim (every hr., 20min., Rs5), stopping at the Terekol ferry. **Ferries** cross the Terekol from Querim (every 30min.; 6am-10pm; 5min.; Rs1, with bike Rs4). From there it's just a few kilometers west—a 15-minute hike or Rs50 taxi ride—to the lonely fort (open 9am-6pm).

NEAR ARAMBOL: MANDREM मांडेरम

Over-endowed (even by Goan standards) with palm trees and white sand and overlooked by backpackers as they make their northward push to Arambol, the lucky vacationer who makes it here tends to linger. The town's innocence and unparalleled solitude will probably be lost someday, but for now there are already enough other destinations nearby to keep most of the tourists away from this hidden gem. "Beach" is a bit of a misnomer for Mandrem's seaside landscape—it's more like a desert. At its widest point, the vast expanses of sand stretch over 100 unspoiled meters, and it's rare to see more than a dozen beachcombers sauntering about, even on the busiest days.

Mandrem village lies on a short stretch of road that branches off from the main thoroughfare between Arambol and Chopdem. Travel amenities are scarce. For currency exchange, buses, or even rickshaws, you pretty much have to schlep 5km or so up the road to Arambol. **Rickshaws** from Chopdem (Rs80) and the **bus** to Arambol will stop at Mandrem. **Accommodations,** both short and long-term, are more plentiful in Arambol, but growing numbers of guest houses are sprouting up along the road at the Junuswaddo Junction—you'll be able to see the vast expanse of beach from the road for the first time here. At the very end of the road is the spectacular and unique ▨**Villa River Cat.** More of a retreat than a guest house, this is a sprawling, beautifully furnished home just off the beach. An international group of beautiful people is encouraged to light candles and bask in the Goan paradise, cooking and eating together. Kitchen available for guests. If you show up without a reservation and there's no room, you get a free hammock for the night. (☎297346; email sareka@p.p.phnet.fi. Doubles Rs 450-700 with spotless shared bath. 25% off during the monsoon for "artists." Reserve in advance by phone or email.) If you are on a bike take the Junuswaddo Junction road to the very end. If you are walking on the beach south from Arambol, after about 40min. you'll pass a cluster of beach shacks—the last is La Brasserie—and a creek heading inland. About 5-10min. later, beyond the large concrete building with two towers, there are a couple of tiny huts crowning sand dunes; head inland between them. The **Miau** restaurant is the Villa River Cat's back porch, but non-guests are welcome to join in the fantastic family-style meals. (Rs125-200. Breakfast 7-11am. Dinner served around 8pm. Book in person). The beach shacks a few hundred meters north and south of the Villa serve standard shack fare (meals Rs40-60).

SOUTH GOA

MARGAO (MADGAON) मारगांव   ☎0834

Capped with a shaking arterial highway, bounded by the glinting metal of the Konkan railway, and fed by the constant stream that oozes from the dusty maw of the gigantic KTC bus terminal, Margao is very much a transport hub. Most travelers spend only enough time here to catch their next connection, hurrying away as soon as possible. Tourist-hungry accommodations lie less than 30 minutes away in Colva and Benaulim. Margao doesn't exactly teem with attractions, but the bustling streets might come as a welcome reality check for anyone who has spent too many moons hopping from one other-worldly beach scene to the next.

GETTING THERE AND GETTING AROUND

Trains: Margao Railway Station, 4km southeast of the municipal gardens and 2km east of the old railway station, along Station Rd.—a brisk 15min. walk from the gardens. The Konkan Railway's major station has service to: **Bombay** (2 per day, 12:30 and 6:15pm, 11hr., Rs231 non-A/C sleeper) and **Mangalore** (1:50am, 7hr., Rs52). Helpful info desk (open 24hr.) and reservation desk (open M-Sa 8am-8pm, Su 8am-1pm).

Buses: KTC Bus Stand, 2km north along the road to Panjim, bound for: **Hubli** (5 per day, 6:15am-1:45pm, 6hr., Rs60); **Mangalore** (6pm, 8hr., Rs146); **Bangalore** (6:30pm, 14½hr., Rs246); **Bombay** (2:30pm, 16hr., Rs319); and **Pune** (5:15pm, 15hr., Rs260). Travel agents around the tourist hostels book frequent private buses to the same destinations. **Intrastate buses** depart from KTC for: **Chaudi** (every 10min. 6am-7pm, 30min., Rs12) and **Panjim** (every 5min. 6am-8:40pm; Rs10, express Rs12). Buses to and from **Colva** via **Benaulim** (every 30min. 7am-8pm, 30min., Rs5) also stop on the east side of the Municipal Gardens. Buses to other intrastate destinations stop on the western side of town, in front of the police station.

ORIENTATION AND PRACTICAL INFORMATION

The city's center, the **Municipal Gardens,** is bounded on the west side by **National Highway 17.** The bustling **Station Rd.,** the middle of three roads heading south, originates from the southeast corner of the gardens, diagonally opposite the Bank of India. The main railway station is southeast of the gardens.

Currency Exchange: State Bank of India, west of the Municipal Gardens. Open M-F 10am-4pm, Sa 10am-1pm, and Su 10am-2pm.

Bookstore: Golden Heart Emporium, take a right out of the GPO and then the first right on to Abade Fariard. Open M-Sa 9:30am-1:30pm and 3:30-9pm.

Pharmacy: Raikar Medical Stores, Station Rd. (☎ 732924). Open M-Sa 8am-8pm.

Police: Margao police station (☎ 705095) is just to the north of the bank.

Internet: Cyberlink (☎ 712079), 50m directly up the road from the Tourist Hotel. Go to the Rangavi Complex shopping center on the left. Cyberlink is shop #9 on the ground floor. Rs80 per hr. Open M-Sa 8:30am-6:45pm. There's also a crowded internet cafe upstairs at the Golden Heart Emporium, **Confident-Cyber Global Net.** Rs60 per hour. Open M-Sa 9:30am-1:30pm and 3:30-9pm.

Post Office: GPO, north of the police. Open M-Sa 7am-6:30pm. **Postal Code:** 403601.

ACCOMMODATIONS

Most foreigners stay one night at most in Margao; the steady influx from the trains and buses ensures that most hotels along Station Rd. fill up quickly each day.

Rukrish Hotel, Station Rd. (☎ 721709), in a tall once-yellow building diagonally opposite the Bank of India, just south of the Municipal Gardens. Has decent, spacious rooms. Singles Rs95-120; doubles Rs220.

Tourist Hotel, just south of the Municipal Gardens (☎ 721966), is overpriced but dependably institutional, and a good bet if you haven't reserved ahead. The attached bath in all the rooms will look pretty luxurious if you're coming from a spell on the beach-shack circuit. Singles Rs240; doubles Rs320-500. Off-season: Rs180/260-360.

Milan Lodge, Station Rd. (☎ 722715), is closer to the station than Rukrish; take the first left after Janata Hotel. Show up early or call ahead. Singles Rs100; doubles Rs175.

FOOD

Cafe Tato, one block east of the Municipal Gardens on the north-south Valaulikar Rd. in the Apna Bazaar Complex. Excellent, cheap vegetarian food can be enjoyed in air-conditioned comfort. *Thali* Rs22. Open M-Sa 7am-9:45pm.

GOA

Longuinhos, opposite the Tourist Hotel (☎ 739908), dishes up cheap Goan delights (Rs30-60), breakfast (Rs2-20), and copious cocktails. Open daily 8am-10:45pm.

Crislene Cafe, west of the GPO (☎ 721235), serves snacks to go in a compact setting. Samosas Rs6. Open 7:30am-8pm.

Kamat, in the Milan hotel, also does very good veg. delights. Samosas Rs10, *thalis* Rs23. Open daily 6:30am-9:30pm.

🔲 SIGHTS

Margao's "sights," more pleasant than impressive, can be seen at leisure within an hour. The central **Municipal Gardens** is a colorful public park, festooned with flowers, shrubs, and bronze busts of Portuguese dignitaries. Almost 1km north of the Gardens, at Largo de Igreja, stands the **Church of the Holy Spirit,** a classic Goan cathedral with carvings of the apostles and a history of religious conflict; it was built on the ruins of a Hindu temple sacked by Muslims and rebuilt by persistent Catholics. *(Open daily 6-9am.)* To the east is a narrow road leading up Monte Hill to **Our Lady of the Mount Chapel,** a 15-minute hike or quick drive leading to expansive views of Margao's hills.

One kilometer east of the KTC bus terminal looms the largest **football arena** in Goa, with a capacity of 40,000. Consult a daily paper or ask around for upcoming games, but be prepared to fight your way to the ticket windows.

The most interesting things to see in Margao are not really in Margao at all, but in smaller towns to the east, which are all accessible by bus. In **Rachol** *(7km from Margao, buses every 15min., 15min., Rs5),* the **Museum of Christian Art,** at the pretty white-washed Rachol Seminary, has an assortment of carefully labeled Christian artifacts from around Goa. The treasures include an 18th-century palanquin used to carry around ecclesiastical VIPs, a portable altar with accessories for mobile missionaries, and an enormous, kingfisher-shaped monstrance made out of silver and wood that was looted from the Sé Cathedral in Old Goa. *(Open daily 9am-1pm and 2-5pm. Rs5.)* On the kitschier side, **Ancestral Goa** (follow signs to Big Foot), in **Loutilim** *(10km east of Margao; buses every 30min., 30min., Rs5),* offers a presentation of Goan village life as it was in ye goode olde days, the Limca Book of World Records' longest laterite sculpture, a garden full of fruits and spices, and a surprisingly interesting and informative tour that somehow ties these wildly disparate elements together. *(Open daily 9am-6pm. Rs20.)* You can arrange at the reception to tour **Casa Araujo Alvares,** an old, Portuguese villa. *(Open daily 10am-12:30pm and 3-6pm. Rs100.)* To get from Rachol to Loutilim without going back to Margao, take the first right past the arch leading out of the seminary and then the bear left at the fork (ignore the driveway to the left); walk to a market, where you can pick up a motorcycle taxi to Loutilim *(Rs20-25).* If the return bus from Loutilim is being shy, head from the bus stand toward Ancestral Goa, taking the right fork. In 20minutes, you should hit the main road and a constant stream of buses heading to Margao *(Rs3).*

COLVA कोल्वा ☎ 0832

If first impressions told the whole story, any self-respecting backpacker would tuck tail and run after being dumped at Colva's beachfront. An unsightly mass of concrete pavement, garish resorts, and skeletal construction sights, Colva's beachfront is a prime example of the overdeveloped resort scene in Goa. As you move away from the beachfront, however, the concrete jungle recedes and the myriad gawking, daytripping Indian men, rich Bombayites, and extortionist scarf sellers are less of a presence. Though far and away the south's most touristed beach, Colva has far less traffic than in the north, but first impressions die hard. The sand is nice, but there is no reason not to push south where better things await. Colva's trash heaps and the rotting remains of the fishermen's morning catch give added incentive for you to follow your nose and head quickly on out of town.

COLVA कोल्वा ■ 451

◧ GETTING THERE AND GETTING AROUND. Buses from Margao stop at the crossroads and at the roundabout, going to Benaulim from the crossroads (every 30min., Rs3). For other destinations in Goa it is necessary to travel first to Margao. From the beach roundabout and the main road, **auto-rickshaws** go to **Benaulim** (Rs50) and **Palolem** (Rs300). **Taxis** charge almost twice as much. **Bicycles** (Rs50 per day) and **motorbikes** (Rs200 per day) can be rented at many shops and resorts, including **Maria Joanna Cycle Shop,** west of the crossroads (open daily 9am-6pm).

◪◲ ORIENTATION AND PRACTICAL INFORMATION. Colva's main strip, the east-west **Madgaon Rd.,** passes through **Colva Village,** and over a bridge to a crossroads leading south to Benaulim and north to Vasco da Gama; it then continues east, petering out 1km away at a beachfront **roundabout.** West of the church in the village, the **Bank of Baroda** gives cash advances on Visa (open M-Tu and Th-F 9am-1pm, Sa 9am-11am). Any resort with an ounce of pretension will also **exchange currency,** but their rates are less than ideal. Trashy and not-so-trashy paperbacks in various weird and wonderful languages can be bought cheaply or swapped at **Damodar's Books,** north of the roundabout (open daily 9:30am-9:30pm). Just east of Damodar's is the **tourist police** station and its crack detective squad (open daily 10am-6pm). Internet services are available along the east-west road. Try **WorldLinkers,** east of the roundabout on the main road. (☎732004. Rs2 per min., Rs100 per hr. Open daily 8:30am-midnight.) **STD/ISD** booths are scattered along the main road. A small **post office** is right behind the church (open M-F 9am-noon and 2-4pm). **Postal Code:** 403708.

◪▢ ACCOMMODATIONS AND FOOD. Transients holing up in Colva after a tour of duty in the north will be pleasantly surprised by the quality of the digs down here. Facilities vary widely, but prices are often much less than what you'd pay for comparable rooms north of Panjim. Outside Christmas week, only the most popular lodges fill up—bargain hard! The **Tourist Nest Hotel,** off the road north from the crossroads (follow signs), offers up some of the softest beds and pillows in Goa. The owner rents out the hostel to Westerners to run each season. Immaculate and spacious rooms welcome those who are tired after a long day of watching the surf. (☎723944. Singles Rs100; doubles Rs150-200.) From east of the roundabout, follow signs to Louguinho's to find **Fisherman's Cottages,** distinguished by a freshly whitewashed facade in view of the rolling surf. Look for a faded sign on your left. All rooms have attached bath. (☎734323. Doubles Rs150-200. Off-season: Rs100.) **Lucky Star,** north of the Colmar, off the next paved road north of the Fisherman's Cottages, is about on par with its competitor. Six attached rooms are on the 2nd floor above the eponymous bar and restaurant. (☎730069. Doubles Rs150-200. Off-season: Rs100. Restaurant open daily 8am-10pm. Seafood Rs80.)

The small road north from the beachfront roundabout heads toward the **Hotel Colmar** and its perks: cool and airy rooms surround a lush garden. (☎721253. Doubles Rs500; Christmas Rs800. Off-season: Rs250.) The pasta dishes (Rs35-75) at the attached **Pasta Hut** are better than the average Indo-Italian stuff (open daily 8:30am-11pm). From the crossroads head west toward the beach (bearing left at the fork) and follow signs opposite William's Beach Resort to the quiet area known as the **4th ward,** where **Vinson's Cottages** has pleasant clean rooms with bath and comes with an attached Goan restaurant. (☎736481. Doubles Rs200-300. Entrees Rs25-30.) **Rennie's Cottages** is a bargain. Six concrete blocks with attached baths sit beyond Vinson's—cut north across a field and continue 100m ahead. This place tends to attract those in need of privacy. (☎721926. Doubles Rs150.) **The Sea Pearl,** north on the road east of the roundabout leading to Fisherman's Cottages, draws good crowds for fresh seafood specials for Rs50-175. (Open daily 8:30am-2pm and 6-11pm; no kitchen orders past 10pm.)

GOA

◨◪ **NIGHTLIFE AND BEACHES.** Colva by night never slams, and outside Christmas week, it rarely works up more than a dull thud. The beach bars south of the roundabout host most of what action there is. The humdrum homogeneity of the beach pub scene has barmen wracking their brains to come up with amusements, from star-gazing to volleyball. **Splash's,** south of the roundabout, hosts a different theme party every night, but the crowd is usually in the young Indian male category. **Boomerang Bar,** also known as the **Malibu Beach House,** on the beach north of the roundabout, is another center of the so-called scene.

Colva village and its **beach,** lie midway along the longest strip of sand in Goa state. Decked out in 26km of sparkling white and emerald blue, the beach is long enough to make bicycles the best way of getting about. At low tide, it's possible to cycle along wet, packed sand along the whole length of the beach. Even when the beach gets crowded around Colva—what with Western package tourists and endless bus loads of Indian tourists—solitude awaits those willing to venture 1km north or south. Between Colva and Benaulim, the relatively quiet water makes for pleasant swimming. Balmy breezes and mildly rippin' tubes make **boogie boarding** and **windsurfing** popular here. Shacks south of Colva beach lease equipment (boogie board Rs30 per hr.; sailboard 200 per hr.).

BENAULIM बेनावलीम ☎ 0832

Just a 20-minute walk south of Colva, Benaulim is mercifully untouched by the daytripping hordes. Its beach is much more pleasant and less built up than Colva's; there are already signs, however, that its relative quiet won't last long. A rapidly disappearing buffer zone of small-scale agriculture that keeps the beach and the guest houses apart is being bought up by developers (and sometimes even seized illegally) to make room for exotic resort complexes, forcibly bending Benaulim into the shape of its northern neighbors. For now, though, the rooms are cheap and plentiful, the food is good, the nightlife is hip, and the long walk to the beach still affords pleasant encounters with local life.

◧ **GETTING THERE AND GETTING AROUND.** Buses stop at the eastern (Maria Hall) crossroads. Benaulim is on both the Margao-Mobor and Margao-Colva routes (every 30min. 7:30am-8:30pm), with departures to: **Colva** (15min., Rs3); **Margao** (25min., Rs4); and **Varca** (10min., Rs3). **Taxis** and **auto-rickshaws** wait at the drop spot to whisk you off to the shimmering sands 2km away (Rs20 by rickshaw), or to **Margao** (Rs150 by taxi) or **Colva** (Rs150 by taxi). Benaulim is a 50-minute taxi ride from Dabolim **airport** (Rs300). At the western crossroads, the north-south road faces the majority of guest houses and is cluttered with signs and entrepreneurs touting **motorcycle** (Rs150-200) and **bicycle** rentals (Rs50-65).

◪ ◨ **ORIENTATION AND PRACTICAL INFORMATION.** Two parallel north-south roads—comprising the heart of Benaulim Village—intersect the east-west Margao Rd. as it heads toward the beach. The Bank of Baroda, at the Maria Hall crossroads in town, only does cash advances on Visa and MC (open M-Tu and Th-F 9am-1pm, Sa 9-11am). **Currency exchange** is left to the travel agents, whose offices line the western crossroads. **GK Tourist Centre**, at the northwest corner of the western crossroads has good rates and **email** (Rs100 per hr.; open daily 9am-6pm). The **Benaulim Medical Store** (☎712124), right beside the Bank of Baroda, has medications, toiletries, and cheap film developing (open M-Sa 9am-1pm and 4-9pm, Su 9am-1pm). To get to the post office, walk south from the eastern crossroads 1km and bear west when the road turns just past the Holy Trinity Church (open M-Sa 9am-noon and 2-4pm). **Postal code:** 403716.

◪◩ **ACCOMMODATIONS AND FOOD.** If squatting in the half-finished beachside resort complexes isn't good enough for you, then try one of the cheap and comfortable guest houses that line the Margao road and the two north-south streets. To reach those listed below, head south from the western crossroads and watch for signs. **Diogo Con,** on the dirt road 100m east of the Meridian Restaurant, is one of Benaulim's best kept secrets, offering freshly painted, petite rooms with shiny, tiled baths (☎733749. Rs100-150.) Along the east-west beach road, west of the crossroads is the pleasant **Caroline Guest House.** All rooms have attached bath. (☎739649. Doubles Rs200. Off-season: Rs150.) **Casa De Caji Cottages** is in a lovely, quiet spot west of the western north-south road—watch for signs. (☎722937. Doubles Rs125-175. Off-season: Rs100-125.) **Cacy Rose**, on the main east-west road between the two crossroads, is a brightly painted house that has rooms with shared baths. (☎721813. Singles Rs100; doubles Rs150. Off-season: Rs70/100.)

Seaview Restaurant, on the beachfront south of the road, is particularly friendly and serves delicious sandwiches (Rs15-30) as well as breakfast (Rs10-30) and Indian standards for Rs30-60. (Open 8am-midnight.) Farther inland **Amal-M,** on the western north-south road, just past the Meridian Restaurant, serves up excellent entrees (Rs50-65) and breakfasts (Rs10-25) with Elvis and Kenny Rogers in the background. (Open daily 8am-midnight.) On the beachfront, north of the inland road, **Johncy's Restaurant** distinguishes itself by its late hours and good deals. The mussels *amotik* (Rs40), prepared with fiery chilies and whole cloves of garlic, is as subtle as a brick, and mercilessly mouth-watering. (Open daily 8am-midnight; closed intermittently during monsoon season.) **Pedro's,** right next door, does breakfast (French toast Rs20) as well as Chinese and tandoori dishes for Rs35-80. (Open daily 8am-midnight.) After dark, a few beach shacks south of the road play host to slacking off and mellowing out. The drinking, smoking, and debauchery continue until the wee hours. The partying is sporadic, but don't worry, for Colva and its theme parties are always just a 20-minute walk north along the beach.

PALOLEM पालोलेम ☎0832

When overworked desk jockeys daydream of telling the boss to shove it, quitting the rat race, and starting life anew in a tropical paradise, the place they have in mind often looks a lot like this. Strolling along its kilometer-long crescent of sand, you might find it hard to shake the feeling that you've walked into a dreamworld. The tiny cove flanked by forested hillocks and black rocks certainly makes the outside world seem a long way away. Hammocks strung between densely packed palm trees shelter guitar-strumming hippies, and the tide recedes to connect the northern end of the beach with an island inhabited by black-faced monkeys. The only tropical beach virtue Palolem doesn't offer is that of quiet, but the crowds, under the magical spell of the place, are mellower, happier, and more content than most: Palolem has plenty of paradise for everybody.

GETTING THERE AND GETTING AROUND. Buses run regularly to Margao (every 30-90min., 6:45am-4:30pm, Rs12). Fortunately, most guest house owners double as accurate bus timetables. If you miss the direct services, the bus from Chaudi to Margao (every hr., 8am-6:30pm, 1½hr., Rs10) is a viable option. At the time of writing, due to road construction, the Karwar-Margao bus runs through **Chaudi** (1½hr., Rs12). The Cancona **train** station is also in Chaudi (Margao 7:45pm, 40min). From Chaudi to Palolem you can take a **rickshaw** (Rs30), **taxi** (Rs100), or you can take a hike (4km). Signs on the road leading from the beach also tout **bike** (Rs3 per hr.) and **motorcycle rental** (Rs150-200 per day).

ORIENTATION AND PRACTICAL INFORMATION. The road from **Chaudi** zigzags 4km northwest to Palolem, running parallel to the surf midway along and intersecting the beach road at the northern end of the sand. There is a small **book exchange** at **Woody's Health Food** on the way to the village (open daily 9am-9pm). The Sun 'n' Moon offers **currency exchange** at decent rates and also offers **email** (Rs2 per min.; open daily 7am-midnight). The nearest **post office** is in Chaudi.

ACCOMMODATIONS AND FOOD. Compared to Colva and Benaulim, Palolem's accommodations are overpriced and underkept—expect to pay Rs200 in season for the privilege of crashing in a charmless double and using a common bathroom outside. A stay in one of the straw hut colonies on the beachfront provides a more picturesque alternative. Midway down the beach, south of where the road lets out, the **Deena Bar and Restaurant** rents simple huts with one light bulb, one bed, and one chair; they do have two toilets, though, and there's a safe for valuables. There's a bumpin' bar and restaurant out front. (☎643449. Rs150. Off-season: Rs100.) Just south of Deena, **Island View Cottages** offers similar accommodations plus bonus hammocks tied between palm trees. (☎634258. Rs150. Off-season: Rs120.) For the good old-fashioned four-solid-walls treatment, friendly **Blue Jays** offers basic but clean rooms with common bath. (☎643056. Doubles Rs150. Off-season: Rs100.) There's a pleasant attached restaurant (Rs20-50; open 8am-11pm) and beach access around the back. **Cocohuts,** at the southern end of the beach, offers huts raised up off the ground on stilts, along with lockers, electric fans, and a common toilet. (☎643296; email ppv@goa1.dot.net.in. Doubles with great sea view Rs500; Rs200 in back.)

Restaurants are fairly standard. **Blue Jays** and next door **Sun 'n' Moon** are both popular. (Seafood Rs65-95, breakfast Rs10-30. Both open daily 8am-10:30pm.) Beachfront restaurants, which win hands down on location, serve similar food. Folks can be found blowin' in the wind at **Dylan's**, circled by the circus sands. Once evening's empire has returned into sand, the rest of the town is Desolation Row.

🎆 **DAYTRIPS FROM PALOLEM.** Those who tire of sharing their paradise with others can wind their way northwest from Chaudi to the as-yet-uncontaminated **Agonda Beach** (Rs3 by bus from Chaudi). A cove almost as picturesque as Palolem's (although it doesn't match it palm-for-palm), Agonda lacks everything but surf and sand—wide-eyed refugees from Palolem stop their bikes, get agoraphobic, and leave. Supplies (petrol, cold snacks) are available from the garage-like complex of stores on the left as you head toward the beach (most close at 7pm). Cocohuts has a branch here, which is slightly cheaper than their place in Palolem.

Farther northwest (1hr. by scooter), the immense ruins of a Portuguese fort wait for the invasion that never happened in **Cabo de Rama,** a town consisting only of a name, a fort, and a few bars scattered along the one and only road. The ruins overlook an endless seafront and exude a quality of quiet grandeur that fits right in with a picnic. Neither the fort nor Agonda, however, are really worth the trip without a motorbike—taxis are expensive (Rs250-300 from Palolem), and though there are daily buses to Cabo de Rama from Margao and Agonda it takes two hours to complete the journey to a destination only really worth a half-hour visit.

KARNATAKA
ಕರ್ನಾಟಕ

Karnataka, with its beautiful beaches, ancient ruins, and fabulous palaces, embodies just about every romantic dream anybody ever dreamed about South India, and it has yet to be discovered by the sun- and fun-seeking foreign tourists who come in such numbers to the rest of the South. Though its residents are as mild as the climate, the attitude here is neither stubbornly traditional nor irritatingly mellow, and Karnataka is one of India's most progressive states. The region has been dominated for centuries by the city of Mysore, which rose to political and architectural prominence during long years of Muslim rule. Karnataka first prospered under the Muslim Sultanate, and it was ruled by Haider Ali and his son Tipu Sultan until the British took direct control of Mysore State in 1831. In 1956, Kannada-speaking regions in the north were added to the Mysore State, creating a Kannada-speaking state, renamed Karnataka in 1973.

Karnataka's coastline is dominated by the jagged Western Ghats, which shield the Deccan Plateau from the torrential monsoons of the coast. On the plateau, orange-red earth gives way to green fields and narrow waterways. The area upland from the Ghats is covered in dense teak and sandalwood forests. The rivers produce so much hydroelectric power that Karnataka used to sell its surplus energy to neighboring states. The rocky terrain around the Ghats provided the material for some of India's greatest architectural masterpieces: in the north, Chalukyan temples and the Vijayanagar ruins at Hampi; in the south, the temples at Belur, Halebid, and Somnathpur.

HIGHLIGHTS OF KARNATAKA

India's technology capital, **Bangalore** brims with pubs, gardens, unbelievable shopping, and all things cyber (p. 455).

The **Maharaja's Palace** is a fairy-tale vision set amid the laid-back, sweet-smelling chaos of **Mysore** (p. 467).

Hippie-tested and UNESCO-certified, **Hampi's** extensive **ruins** (p. 484) are enough to make you happy to be in the middle of nowhere.

Party hardy on **Gokarna's** gorgeous beaches (p. 493) with the holy town's hipster and hippie set.

BANGALORE ಬೆಂಗಳೂರು   ☎080

The city of Bangalore is where the West makes its cameo in the Deccan, dressed in Indian garb—a city where American and Indian execs down *dosas* streetside, where families open cybercafes in their backyards, and where auto-rickshaws bleat by with web addresses posted in their rear windows. A city of direct satellite links and three-*lassi* lunches, Bangalore is ground zero for India's technological revolution. A sizeable chunk of the world's software is written here, and in the conference rooms along MG and Residency Rd., India's wired elite drafts marketing strategies to sell the trappings of technology to the world's largest middle class—hundreds of millions of potential customers.

When Kempegowda, a petty chieftain under the Vijayanagar Empire, founded Bangalore in 1537, his son built four watchtowers to mark the boundaries of the city. Four and a half centuries later, the towers still stand, but modern Bangalore spreads far beyond these limits. The growth of India's fifth largest city has been accelerated by the huge influx of people from rural Karnataka, Tamil Nadu, Kerala, and north India, lured here by the city's mild climate and the prospect of making it big amid its metropolitan madness. Numerous lakes, parks, gardens, and broad avenues make Bangalore one of India's most pleasant cities.

▣ GETTING THERE AND GETTING AROUND

BY WINGS

The airport is 8km southeast of the city from the MG Rd. area (auto-rickshaw Rs60). It has a 24-hour pre-paid taxi booth (Rs250 to the city center).

Domestic Airlines: Indian Airlines, Cauvery Bhavan, Kempegowda Rd. (☎221 1914 or 141). Open M-Su 6am-5:30pm. Airport office (☎526 6233 or 140). Open daily 8:30am-8:30pm. **Jet Airways,** 22 Ulsoor Rd., Unity Building (☎227 6617-20), behind the Taj Residency. Open M-F 8:30am-7pm, Sa 9am-5pm. **Sahara,** 35 Church St. (☎558 4457 or 558 4507). Open M-F 8am-8pm, Sa 10am-5pm. Airport branch (☎527 1286 or 527 1287). To: **Ahmedabad** (1 per day, 3hr., US$220); **Bombay** (11 per day, 1½hr., US$140); **Calcutta** (2 per day, 2½hr., US$265); **Cochin** (2-3 per day, 10am and 6:50pm, 1hr., US$80); **Coimbatore** (2 per day, 40min., US$65); **Delhi** (7 per day, 2½hr., US$255); **Goa** (2 per day, 1hr., US$105); **Hyderabad** (3 per day, 1hr., US$95); **Madras** (7-10 per day, 45min., US$65); **Mangalore** (1-2 per day, 45min., US$80); **Pune** (2 per day, 1½hr., US$145); **Trivandrum** (1 per day, 2hr., US$120).

International Airlines: Air India, JC Rd., Unity Building (☎227 7747; fax 227 3300), a block from Corporation Building **Air Canada** (☎558 5394), **Air France** (☎558 9397), **Kuwait Airways** (☎558 9021), and **Gulf Air** (☎558 4702), are in Sunrise Chambers, 22 Ulsoor Rd., 1 block north of MG Rd., behind the Taj Residency. **British Airways,** 7 St. Marks Rd. (☎227 1205; fax 224 1503). **KLM,** West End Hotel (☎226 8703). **Lufthansa,** 42-2 Dickenson Rd. (☎558 8791), near Manipal Center. **Swissair,** 51 Richmond Rd., opposite BPL Plaza. Open M-F 9:30am-5:30pm, Sa 9:30am-1:30pm. **Quantas,** 13 Westminster Cunningham Rd. (☎225 6611), near Wockhardt Hospital. **Singapore Airlines,** Richmond Rd. (☎286 7868). **Thai Airways,** Imperial Court, Cunningham Rd. (☎226 7613). **United Airlines,** 12 Richmond Rd. (☎224 4620).

BY WHEELS

Trains: City Railway Station (24hr. arrival and departure information ☎131 or 133), at the end of Race Course and Bhashyam Rds. The **reservations counter** (☎132 or 1361), with special counters for women and foreigners, is in the building on your left as you face the station. Open M-Sa 8am-8pm, Su 8am-2pm. The **enquiries** counter (☎1361-3) is in the main building. Open daily 7am-10:30pm. Trains are often booked weeks in advance—if there is no space available, there are *tatkal* (immediate) and foreign tourist quotas for certain trains to major cities. Fares listed are for sleeper class for long journeys and 2nd class for short ones. To: **Bombay** (6am, 12:10, and 8:30pm, 24hr., Rs310); **Calcutta** (W and F, 37hr., Rs397); **Coimbatore** (6:15am and 11pm, 7-8 hr., Rs138); **Delhi** (6:25pm, 42hr., Rs436; *Rajdhani Exp.* 2429 M, W, Th, and Su, 35hr., Rs2205); **Hospet** (10pm, 10hr., Rs163); **Madras** (6-7 per day, 6:30am-11:30pm, 5-7hr., Rs87); **Mangalore** (6:40pm, 20hr., Rs235); **Mysore** (5 per day, 6:30am-6:15pm, 2-3hr., Rs41).

Buses: KSRTC Bus Stand, Bhashyam Rd. (☎287 3377 or 287 1261), has a reservation counter open 7am-11pm. To: **Badami** (5:30 and 9pm, 9hr., Rs151); **Bijapur** (7 per day, 6:15am-10:30pm, 11hr., Rs153-285); **Bombay** (2 and 4pm, 24hr., Rs350/400); **Cochin** (4 per day, 4-7:30pm, 12hr., Rs239); **Hassan** (every hr., 6am-11:40pm, 4hr., Rs55); **Hospet** (8:30am, 9:15, and 11pm; 8hr.; Rs105); **Hyderabad** (18 per day, 6:30am-9:30pm, 12hr., Rs276); **Kodaikanal** (9:15pm, 10hr., Rs146); **Madras** (9 per day, 9:30am-11:20pm, 7hr., Rs135); **Mangalore** (15 per day, 9am-11:40pm, 8hr., Rs124/149); **Mysore** (15 per day, 6am-9pm, 3hr., Rs43); **Panjim** (3:30, 4:45, and 5:30pm; 11hr.; Rs290); **Ooty** (8:30, 10am, and 10pm; 8hr.; Rs114); **Trivandrum** (2:30pm, 18hr., Rs334). **Private buses** to Bombay, Ooty, Mysore, and other destinations leave from the KSRTC bus stand area. These line the streets near the bus stand.

Local Transportation: Don't be shy about insisting that **auto-rickshaws** use their meters—it's the law and common practice. The auto-rickshaw stand in the northeast corner of the railway station parking lot has an armed policeman on hand to ensure compliance. From 10pm-6am expect to pay 1½ times the meter charge. Two kinds of **local buses** leave from the city bus stand: ordinary buses and the more expensive Pushpak

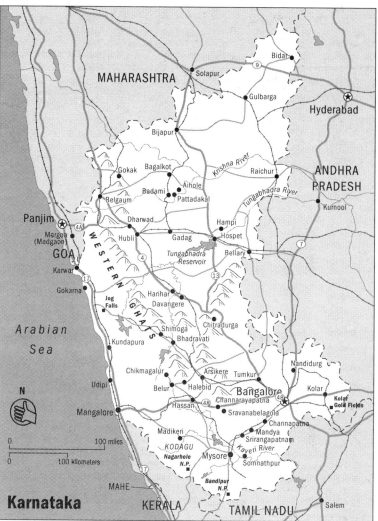

buses. Buses to MG Rd. leave from platforms 17 and 18 (frequent, 6:30am-10pm, Rs2-5). Route #7 serves the Corporation Building and MG Rd. (every 20min., Rs4). For **Whitefield,** take the #333E or 334 bus (1hr., Rs8).

ORIENTATION

The hub of modern, international Bangalore is the intersection of **Mahatma Gandhi (MG)** and **Brigade Rd.** South of MG Rd. are **Church St.** and **Residency Rd.,** home to hi-tech pubs, high-class hotels, and high-price shops. North of MG Rd., the aptly named **Commercial St.** leads west toward **Shivajinagar,** a bustling market district that is Bangalore's downtown. Most of the museums are in **Cubbon Park,** which stretches along **Kasturba (Gandhi) Rd.** from **Ambedkar Rd.** to MG Rd. The **Majestic** area, near the **City Railway Station** and **bus stand,** contains several good budget hotels. South of the Majestic is the frenetic **City Market** area, with its unpaved narrow roads, bullock carts, temples, and mosques.

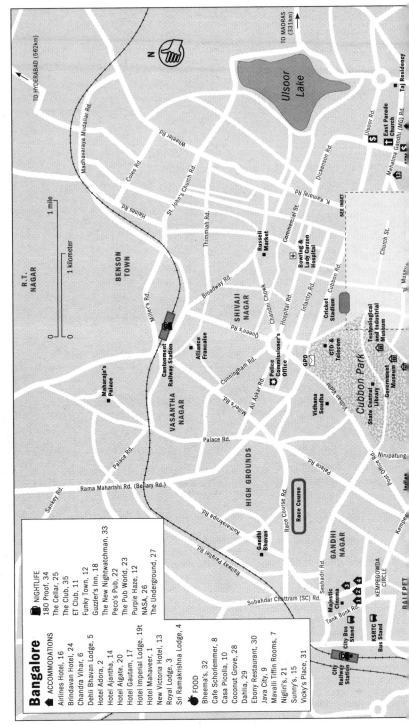

Bangalore

⚓ ACCOMMODATIONS
Airlines Hotel, 16
Brindavan Hotel, 24
Chandra Vihar, 6
Dehli Bhavan Lodge, 5
Hotel Adora, 2
Hotel Ajantha, 14
Hotel Algate, 20
Hotel Gautam, 17
Hotel Imperial Lodge, 19t
Hotel Mahaveer, 1
New Victoria Hotel, 13
Royal Lodge, 3
Sri Ramakrishna Lodge, 4

🍴 FOOD
Bheema's, 32
Cafe Schonlemmer, 8
Casa Picolla, 10
Coconut Grove, 28
Dahlia, 29
Ebony Restaurant, 30
Java City, 9
Mavalli Tiffin Rooms, 7
Nigiri's, 21
Sunny's, 15
Vicky's Place, 31

🍷 NIGHTLIFE
180 Proof, 34
The Cellar, 25
The Club, 35
ET Club, 11
Funky Town, 12
Guzzler's Inn, 18
The New Nightwatchman, 33
Peco's Pub, 22
The Pub World, 23
Purple Haze, 12
NASA, 26
The Underground, 27

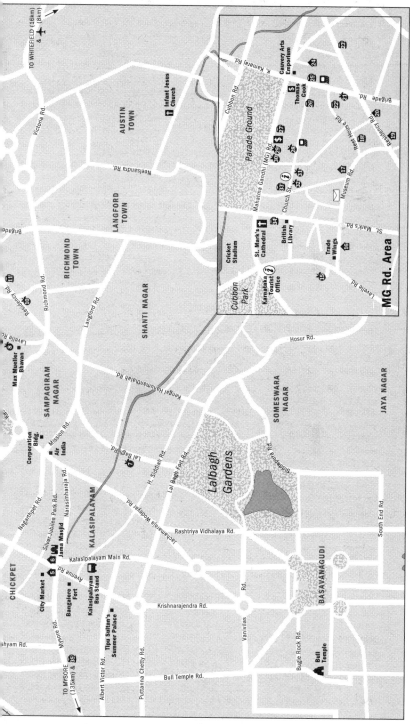

⚡ PRACTICAL INFORMATION

TOURIST AND FINANCIAL SERVICES

Tourist Offices: Government of India Tourist Office, KFC Building, 48 Church St. (☎ 532 1683 or ☎/fax 558 5417). From Brigade Rd., turn right; the office is on the right inside the KFC building. Ask for a copy of *Bangalore This Fortnight,* an excellent guide to the city. Open M-F 9:30am-6pm, Sa 9am-1pm. **KSTDC,** 104/1 Kasturba Rd. (☎ 221 2901), near the junction with MG Rd., opposite the Queen Victoria statue in Cubbon Park. Two flights up in a big, off-white building. Operates daily Bangalore **bus tours** (Rs75) and tours of Belur and Halebid. Open M-Sa 10am-5:30pm; closed 2nd Sa. Another KSTDC branch in Badomi House, opposite the City Corporation Office, N.R. Square (☎ 227 5869). **Tourist Information Centers** in the Railway Station (☎ 287 0068) and the airport (☎ 526 8012). The **Department of Tourism,** KG Rd., Cauvery Bhavan, F block, 1st fl. (☎ 221 5498).

Budget Travel: Travel agencies line the streets near the railway and bus stands, offering tours and coaches to Bombay, Mysore, Ooty, and other places. For car rental, bus, rail, air, and tour reservations go to **Trade Wings,** 48 Lavelle Rd. (☎ 221 4595), opposite the Airlines Hotel. Open M-F 9:30am-1pm and 2-5:30pm, Sa 9:30am-1pm.

Immigration Office: Foreigners Registration Office is at the **Police Commissioner's Office,** 1 Infantry Rd. (☎ 225 6242 ext. 251). Go north along Cubbon Park past the GPO onto Queen's Rd., then left 1 block later onto Infantry. Open M-Sa 10am-5:30pm. For visa extensions, head to Rm. 224 in Vidhana Soudha, the office of L. Shanmukha, Undersecretary to Government, Home and Transport Dept. Open M-F 3:30-5:30pm.

Currency Exchange: Thomas Cook, 55 MG Rd. (☎ 558 1340), just before the intersection with Brigade Rd., is the fastest place to change foreign currency or traveler's checks. Open M-Sa 9:30am-6pm. **Bank of Baroda,** Bluemoon Complex, 66 MG Rd. (☎ 559 6981-2), gives cash advances on Visa and MC. Open M-F 10:30am-2:30pm and 3-4pm, Sa 10:30am-12:30pm.

ATM: The **Citibank ATM** inside Nilgiri's, Brigade Rd., is conveniently located but is not open 24hr. Accepts Visa, MC, Citibank, and all Cirrus/Plus logo cards. 24hr. **Citibank ATM** at the Prestige Meridian Building, 2 MG Rd. The ATM in Manipal Center, 47 Dickenson Rd., outside the **HSBC** bank, is also 24hr. Walk east on MG Rd., 1 block past the parade grounds. At the East Parade Church, turn left Dickenson Rd. Accepts cards with Plus or Global Access logos; the bank gives cash advances on Visa and MC. Open M-F 10:30am-2:30pm and 3-4pm, Sa 10:30am-12:30pm.

LOCAL SERVICES

Market: Nilgiri's, 171 Brigade Rd., has fruit in outdoor stalls. Open M-F 9:30am-9:30pm, Sa 10:30am-1:30pm. **Russell Market,** 2km north of MG Rd., off Cunningham St., Shivajinagar, is an indoor market selling fruit, flowers, veggies, meat, antiques, and bric-a-brac. Generally open M-Sa 9:30am-1:30pm and 4-8pm. **City Market,** 1.5km southwest of City Railway Station, near the Jama Masjid, is a wholesale bazaar selling silk fabric in addition to food and flowers. Open dawn-dusk.

Library: State Central Library, Cubbon Park (☎ 221 2128). Approach Cubbon Park from Kasturba Rd. and follow Lavelle Rd. into the park; the library is in a red building with green sills. Open Tu-Su 9am-7pm. **British Library,** 29 St. Mark's Rd. (☎ 221 3485), off MG Rd., near Koshy's. Open Tu-Sa 10:30am-6:30pm. **Max Mueller Bhawan Library,** 3 Lavelle Rd. (☎ 227 5435). Open Tu-F 9am-noon and 3-5:30pm, Sa 2-5:30pm. **Alliance Francaise,** 16 GMT Rd. (☎ 225 8762).

Bookstore: Gangaram's Book Bureau, 72 MG Rd. (☎ 558 6189). Open M-Sa 10am-8pm. **Nationwide Books,** 39 MG Rd. (☎ 558 2080). Open M-Sa 10am-8pm, Su 10am-2pm. **Premier Bookshop,** 46/1 Church St. (☎ 558 8570), around the corner from Berry's Hotel. Open M-Sa 10am-1:30pm and 3-7:30pm. Sidewalk vendors are the cheapest option for books; there are a few near the Cauvery Arts Emporium.

EMERGENCY AND COMMUNICATIONS

Police: Commissioner's Office, 1 Infantry Rd. (☎225 4501). From the intersection of MG and Kasturba Rd., walk northwest with Cubbon Park on your left; follow Queen's Rd. to Infantry Rd. and turn left. **Headquarters,** Nirupatunga Rd. (☎221 1803), next to the YMCA. **Cubbon Park branch,** Kasturba Rd. (☎556 6242), next to the aquarium.

Pharmacy: Al-Siddique Pharmaceutical Centre (☎605491), opposite the Jama Masjid, near City Market. **Hosmat,** 45 Maganath Rd. (☎559 3796 or 559 3797), off Richmond Rd. Open 24hr.

Hospitals: The most respected government hospital is **Bowring and Lady Curzon Hospital** (☎559 1362), off Hospital Rd., 2km north of MG Rd. **Mallya Hospital,** 2 Vittal Mallya Rd. (☎227 7991); **Manipal Hospital,** 98 Rustumbagh Airport Rd. (☎526 6646 or 526 6441); and **St. John's Medical College and Hospital,** Sarjapur Rd. (☎553 0724 or 553 0734), offer excellent private care.

Internet: Bangalore has the best internet access in all of India, though connections may be slow. For the atmosphere, **Cafe Coffee Day,** 13 Brigade Rd. (☎559 1602) was Bangalore's first cybercafe and is still the best place to grab a cuppa and surf (30min., Rs30). Almost every major office or commercial building has at least one shop, but the **Brigade Gardens** building, 19 Church St., stands out, with five or six (Rs20 per hr.).

Post Office: The **GPO** is a stone colossus on the corner of Raj Bhavan and Ambedkar Rd. in Cubbon Park. Open M-Sa 8am-7pm, Su 10:30am-1pm. There is also a branch on Brigade Rd., between Church St. and Rest House Rd. Both branches open M-Sa 10am-6pm. **Postal Code:** 560001.

▚ ACCOMMODATIONS

It is difficult to find a decently priced room in the hip, hi-tech, and happening **MG Rd.** area. Book at least a week in advance. The area around the bus stand and railway stations has plenty of cheap places to stay, but they are a good 5km away from the center of town. The lodges in **City Market** are cheap but close to the traffic and noise. Prices do not include 5-12.5% taxes. Check-out is 24-hours.

MG RD. AREA

▨ Hotel Ajantha, 22-A MG Rd. (☎558 4321; fax 558 4780), 10min. from Brigade Rd. Clean, reasonably-priced rooms, helpful staff, and great location. Color TV and 24hr. hot water. Singles Rs190; doubles Rs325-600. Reserve up to 3 weeks in advance.

▨ Brindavan Hotel, 108 MG Rd. (☎558 4000), has pretty inexpensive rooms considering its great MG Rd. location. Singles Rs190-550; doubles Rs310-950. Reserve ahead.

Airlines Hotel, 4 Madras Bank Rd. (☎227 3783 or 227 3786), between Lavelle and St. Mark's Rds., 5min. from MG Rd. Rooms aren't sparkling, but they're well-furnished: towels, seat toilets, and hot water until 11am. Has its own internet parlor, bakery, and drive-in diner. Singles Rs300; doubles Rs500. AmEx, MC, Visa.

Hotel Gautam, 17 Museum Rd. (☎558 8764 or 558 8137), 5min. from Brigade Rd. Spacious rooms have hot showers 6-10am, Star TV, and balconies. There are a lot of rooms, making it more likely to find vacancies here than at other hotels in the area. Travel agency and attached veg. restaurant. Singles Rs400; doubles Rs450.

New Victoria Hotel, 47-48 Residency Rd. (☎558 4076 or 558 5028). Lost in trees and wildflowers, the New Victoria's bungalows were a British military canteen and library until about 1935. Attached baths have 24hr. hot water and seat toilets. Rooms are only average but, lucky for you, most have Star TV. Singles Rs400; doubles Rs1050. Service charge 10%. Credit card and traveler's checks.

Hotel Imperial Lodge, 93-94 Residency Rd. (☎558 8391 or 558 5473), has plain, functional rooms with large windows and a cheery atmosphere. Squat toilets; hot water in the morning. Singles Rs170; doubles Rs300.

Hotel Algate, 93 Residency Rd. (☎559 4786-89), at the intersection with Brigade Rd. These immaculate rooms are not cheap, but you get perks like A/C, HBO, and complimentary shampoo. Singles Rs759; doubles Rs900. AmEx, MC, Visa.

RAILWAY STATION AND BUS STAND AREA

▨ **Sri Ramakrishna Lodge,** SC Rd. (☎226 3041), next to Kapali Theater. Rooms have soft beds and immaculate bathrooms with squat toilets. Each floor has a pleasant veranda. 24hr. hot water, laundry, room service, TVs, and phones. Two adjacent restaurants (*thalis* Rs25), travel counter, and pharmacy. Singles Rs150; doubles Rs250.

Royal Lodge, 251 SC Rd. (☎226 6951). Basic rooms in a calm and welcoming atmosphere. Hot water 6:30-9am. Singles Rs110; doubles 149-275.

Hotel Mahaveer, 8-1 Tankbund Rd. (☎287 3670), on the corner of Chickpet Rd., by the station exit. Over 60 modern, boxy-but-clean rooms, with TV, phone, and attached bath with seat toilet. Friendly management provides hot water 6-9am, same-day laundry service, and foreign exchange. Singles Rs225; doubles Rs450-850. Visa, MC.

Hotel Adora, 47 SC Rd. (☎220 0324). Clean rooms with phones but the barest of furnishings. Veg. restaurant, laundry, and travel services. Singles Rs168; doubles Rs275.

CITY MARKET

▨ **Chandra Vihar,** MRR Ln. (☎222 4146), opposite City Market Building, west of Jama Masjid. All 50 of the modern rooms have desks, TVs, and phones. Deluxe doubles on higher floors have spectacular views of the market. Hot showers 6-10am. Singles Rs190; doubles Rs300-320.

Delhi Bhavan Lodge, Avenue Rd. (☎287 5045). Standard, clean rooms. Hot water 6-9am. Singles Rs70-125; doubles Rs149-205.

◑ FOOD

▨ **Sunny's,** 35/2 Kasturba Cross, off Lavelle Rd., near Trade Wings travel agency. A multicolored, multi-floor Mediterranean bistro extravaganza with an open-air terrace. Delicious pasta Rs150-250; Shrimp Diane Rs450; and freshly made desserts from the bakery downstairs Rs65-105. Bread and herb butter with every order. Rs200 min. per head, plus 10% service charge. Open daily noon-3pm, Tu-F 6-9:30pm, Sa-Su open until 10:30pm. AmEx, MC, Visa.

▨ **Mavalli Tiffin Rooms,** 11 Lal Bagh Rd. (☎222022). MTR is a local legend. Barefoot waiters in *lungis* serve Bangalore's best *dosas* (Rs18) and "full meals" (Rs60) that never seem to end. Open M 9am-4pm; Tu-Su: Tiffin section (*dosas*) 6:30-11am and 3:30-7:30pm, full meals section 12:30-3pm and 8-10pm.

▨ **Java City,** 24/1 Lavelle Rd. This popular cafe serves cappuccino (Rs20), multiple flavors of Italian sodas (Rs40-80), homestyle pizzas (Rs30-123), quiche (Rs30-35), croissant sandwiches (Rs42-54), and an array of fresh desserts (Rs30-40), including chocolate mousse. Open daily 11am-11pm. AmEx, MC, Visa. Branch on Cunningham Rd.

Casa Picolla, Devatha Plaza, 131 Residency Rd. (☎221 2907), at the intersection with St. Mark's Rd. Cheap food tastes surprisingly good in an airy setting complete with seaside murals. Lasagne *verde* Rs85; steak Rs85-95; sweet black forest crepes Rs35; profiteroles Rs40; cappuccino Rs20. Open daily 11:30am-10:30pm.

Ebony Restaurant, 84 MG Rd. (☎558 9333), top floor of the Hotel Ivory Tower. Spectacular views from an open-air terrace 14 flights up. Tandoori, Balti, Thai, and French cuisine. Entrees Rs100-250; lunch buffet M-F Rs155 for men, Rs110 for women. Open daily 12:30-3pm and 7:30-11:30pm. AmEx, Mc, Visa. Reservations essential.

The Coconut Grove, 86 Church St. Good prices and tropical decor; culinary curiosities from Kerala and Karnataka. Try the *kaikari kootu*, a dish of lentils and grated coconut (Rs45), or an unbeatable *thali* (Rs55-75). Seafood Rs110-125. Pineapple-based *kaidachakka halwa* (Rs35) is great for dessert. Open daily 12:30-4pm and 7-11pm.

Dalhia, G-37/38 Brigade Gardens, 19 Church St. (☎509 1293). Where else in India can you rub elbows with Japanese salarymen while slurping down a bowl of *udon* or *soba*

Here's your ticket to freedom, baby!

Wherever you want to go...
priceline.com can get you there for less.

- Save up to 40% or more off the lowest published airfares every day!

- Major airlines serving virtually every corner of the globe.

- Special fares to Europe!

If you haven't already tried priceline.com, you're missing out on the best way to save. **Visit us online today at www.priceline.com.**

(Rs200-250)? Sushi and sashimi (Rs120-450) on M and F. Open M-Sa noon-3pm and 6:30-9:30pm. AmEx, Mc, Visa.

Cafe Schorlemmer, Max Mueller Bhavan, 3 Lavelle Rd., opposite Hulkul Residency. Operated by a German expat, this rooftop bakery serves up probably the best apple strudel (Rs30) in all of South Asia and great homemade delights like kugel (Rs20). Full German lunch of the day (veg. Rs90, non-veg. Rs130-150). Sandwiches Rs30-40; freshly baked brown bread loaves Rs60; baguettes Rs30. Open M-Sa 9am-8pm.

Bheema's, 31 Church St. Popular Andhra-style restaurant. Veg Rs25-40; non-veg. Rs45-75. Open daily 11:30am-5:30pm and 7-11:30pm.

Nilgiri's Cafe, 171 Brigade Rd. Huge grilled sandwiches Rs38-60; doughy pizzas Rs65-90; hazelnut milkshakes Rs30; and ice cream Rs40. Open daily 9am-10pm.

Vicky's Place, 28 Church St. (☎558 4717). The friendly staff serves French and Italian cuisine in a laid-back veranda-like setting (veg. Rs130; non-veg. Rs150-200). Desserts too. Open daily 11am-3pm and 7-11pm. AmEx, Mc, Visa.

Karavalli, 66 Residency Rd., in the Gateway Hotel. Bangalore's most elegant coastal Keralan cuisine. *Appam*, with fish or veg. stew, is the specialty, but you shouldn't miss the coconut curries. Lunchtime *thalis* Rs215-250; French wine Rs120-125 per glass. Count on Rs300 per person. Open daily 12:30-3:30pm and 7:30pm-midnight.

The Only Place, 158 Mota Royal Arcade, Brigade Rd, was the first place in town to serve up hamburgers (Rs50-85), pizza (Rs70 and up), and steaks (Rs95-245). Open daily 11am-3:30pm and 7-11pm. AmEx, Mc, Visa.

Kamat, Unity Building, JC Rd. One of Bangalore's best-value Indian restaurants. Huge *thalis* noon-3pm (Rs40). Sweets counter, too. Open M-Sa 8am-11pm, Su 10am-3pm (snacks only) and 7-11pm.

👁 SIGHTS

CUBBON PARK AND MUSEUMS. Set aside in 1864 and named for the former Viceroy of India, Lord Cubbon, the park consists of 300 acres of fresh air and greenery in the center of the city. The park extends from the corner of MG Rd. to the Corporation Building, providing much needed shade and refuge from the city traffic surrounding it. The park also contains several museums. The **K. Venkatappa Art Gallery** exhibits watercolor landscapes by K. Venkatappa, the court artist who painted much of the Maharaja's Palace in Mysore. The second floor displays rotating exhibitions of contemporary Karnatakan artists. The **Government Museum,** one of India's oldest, is a fine example of monumental neo-classical architecture. The first floor houses some interesting archaelogical artifacts and stone Hoysalan sculptures. *(Museum and gallery open Tu-Su 10am-5pm. Rs4.)* Next door, the **Visveswaraya Industrial and Technological Museum** celebrates Bangalore's industrial progress from 1905, when City Market lit India's first light bulb, to the current boom in information technology. *(Open daily 10am-5:30pm. Rs10.)* The park also has an aquarium and a children's park, **Jawahar Bal Bhavan,** complete with boat, pony, and toy train rides, a doll museum, and a children's theater. *(Open daily 9:30am-6:30pm. Free.)* Across the park is the red **Attara Kachari,** which housed the 18 departments of the Secretariat until 1956 (*attara* means "eighteen" in Hindi).

VIDHANA SOUDHA. One of Bangalore's most recognizable landmarks, the Vidhana Soudha houses the Secretariat. In the early 1950s, a visiting Russian delegation pointed out the abundance of European architecture in Bangalore. Spurred to action by these remarks, the Chief Minister of Mysore state decided to build this spectacular neo-Dravidian temple-style structure. The Vidhana Soudha became not only an affirmation of Indian sovereignty but also an assertion of Bangalore's new legislative power. It was built out of pure granite by craftsmen from Andhra Pradesh (one of Bangalore's largest slums was formed by the displaced masons' families). On top of the main entrance sits Emperor

Ashoka's three-headed lion—the symbol of the Indian nation and the water-mark on all rupee notes. Statues of Jawaharlal Nehru and B.R. Ambedkar stand in the front lawn, gesticulating at each other beneath the self-congratulatory inscription, "Government Work is God's Work." The building is lit up every Sunday night. *(Across the street from Cubbon Park, to the northwest. Open Su 3:45-4:45pm and lit up 4:45-5:45pm.)*

BANGALORE FORT. Built in mud and brick by Chikkadevaraga Wadiyar during the late 1600s as an extension of another of Kempegowda's forts, the Bangalore Fort was refurbished by Haider Ali and Tipu Sultan during the 18th century. It originally encompassed the area between the Corporation Offices and City Market. Most of it was destroyed during the Anglo-Mysore War, but the remains are beautifully preserved, with ornately carved Islamic-style arches and turrets and an exquisite **Ganpati Temple** inside. *(Krishnarajendra Rd., opposite Vanivilas Hospital.)*

TIPU SULTAN'S SUMMER PALACE. Tipu liked to call his Summer Palace *jannat keliye jalan*, "The Envy of Heaven," but it is really just a low-budget replica of Daria Daulat in Srirangapatnam. Most of the original wall paintings have been obscured by brown paint. *(500m south of the fort. Open daily 8am-5:30pm. Rs2; F free.)*

BULL TEMPLE. The Bull Temple's massive black Nandi, over 500 years old, draws devotees from all around India. Legend has it that a raging bull used to torment local farmers by ravaging their fields at night. The frustrated farmers finally hired a night watchman to kill the bull with a crowbar. The next morning, they discovered that the carcass had transformed into a solid granite bull. Look closely, and you'll see the crowbar embedded in the poor beast's back. *(Bull Temple Rd., south of the Summer Palace. Open daily 8am-8pm.)*

LALBAGH GARDENS. Haider Ali laid out the botanical gardens in 1760. His son Tipu Sultan expanded the 16-hectare gardens to 96 hectares and added the mango grove. After Tipu's demise in 1799, the British took over. Prince Albert Victor of Wales built the Glass House in the late 1800s to resemble the Crystal Palace in London. The gardens are home to over 150 different varieties of roses and 1000 species of tropical and subtropical animals and plants, a giant floral clock, a lotus pond, a deer park, and countless walkers, joggers, cyclists, and monkeys. One of Kempe Gowda's four watchtowers, built in 1537 to mark Bangalore's city limits, can still be seen here. *(2km south of Cubbon Park. Open daily dawn-dusk. Rs2.)*

ULSOOR LAKE. The Ulsoor Lake spreads over northeastern Bangalore, its 1.5 sq. km of water speckled with tiny, picturesque islands. Enjoy a boat ride or swim in the Kensington pool nearby (see **Other Diversions,** p. 466). During the annual Ganesh Festival (Aug.-Sept.), devotees dunk a statue of Lord Ganesh, decked out in ceremonial regalia, into the lake. Local Bengalis follow a similar ritual during the Dussehra Festival in October when they submerge a statue of the goddess Durga. *(2 blocks north of MG Rd., on Gangadhana Chetty and Kensington Rd., near the Taj Hotel and Cottage Emporium. Open daily dawn-dusk.)*

OTHER SIGHTS. The **Jawaharlal Nehru Planetarium** was built to commemorate the 100th birthday of the freedom fighter and prime minister who called Bangalore "India's city of the future." *(T Chowdiak Rd., opposite Raj Bhavan. ☎ 220 3234. Open Tu-Su, closed 2nd Tu. English shows at 4:30pm. Rs15.)* The **Gandhi Picture Gallery,** on the second floor of **Gandhi Bhavan,** presents a well-organized journey through the Mahatma's life, with grainy blown-up photographs, quotations full of wisdom, and artifacts such as Gandhi's wooden *chappals*, drinking bowls, and letters to Franklin Roosevelt, Tolstoy, Gokhale, and Nehru. Since few people visit this place, there's no permanent staff; you'll need to ask to have the door unlocked. *(From Windsor Hotel, cross the Golf Course High Grounds, and head down Kumara Krupa Rd. ☎ 226 1967. Open M-Sa 10:30am-1:30pm and 3-5pm. Free.)*

🎭 🎵 NIGHTLIFE AND ENTERTAINMENT

BARS

Though plagued by water shortages, Bangalore is never dry. Its burgeoning pub culture has earned the city the title "Bar Galore." Most pubs are clustered around Brigade Rd., and the regulars who frequent them greet the pubs' godfather-esque owners with hearty hugs and know the bartenders by name. Pubs may serve alcohol only from 11am to 11pm. The police visit around midnight, suggesting that "good people sleep early" as stragglers exit quietly via the back door. Sometimes pubs refuse admission to unaccompanied women. Most accept major credit cards.

180 Proof, 40 St. Mark's Rd., south of MG Rd. The "heppest" meeting place for Bangalore's sophisticated set, complete with buff bouncers standing guard. This British colonial building-turned-loft is the place to see and be seen. Beer Rs80 per bottle. F-Sa Rs100 for solo sophisticates. Open daily noon-11:30pm.

Purple Haze, Residency Rd., opposite Black Cadillac. Dark and trendy pub whose Hendrix-only decor is let down a little by its soundtrack, which has been known to sink as low as Bryan Adams. Pitchers Rs170; mugs Rs35. Open daily noon-11:30pm.

The Cellar, 7 Brigade Rd., Curzon Ct., opposite the intersection with Church St. Wooden decor and cushy booths. The mellow afternoon might have been invented here. Proportionate representation of the sexes. Chinese, continental, and tandoori cuisine (Rs60). Pitchers Rs150, mugs Rs30. Open daily 11am-11pm.

The Pub World, 65 Residency St., opposite Galaxy Theatre. Marginally more snazz on display here than at most places, with oak banisters, lace curtains, and tapestried footstools. Well-lit, too, so you won't feel like a reprobate for drinking in the middle of the afternoon. Pitchers Rs200; mugs Rs40.

The New Night Watchman, 46/1 Church St., near Berry's Hotel. One of the few pubs that plays *bhangra*. Pitchers Rs165, mugs Rs33. Full lunch and dinner menus available. Open 11am-11:30pm.

Peco's Pub, 34 Rest House Rd., off Brigade Rd, one street south of Church St. Hendrix, Marley, Joplin, and Zeppelin grace the walls. 3 floors packed with college-aged guzzlers imbibing mugfuls (Rs30). Rooftop has relaxing chairs. Open daily 10:30am-10:30pm.

NASA, 1/4 Church St. Decorated with pictures of spaceships, astronauts, and...Michael Jackson? Enjoy beer (pitcher Rs175; mugs Rs25) while soaking in the out-of-this-world atmosphere—laser shows and other space-age exotica. Open 10:30am-11:30pm.

The Underground, 61/1 MG Rd., Bluemoon Complex. Mind the gap. Mugs Rs40; pints Rs80; pitchers Rs200. Veg. lunch Rs49; non-veg. Rs59; snacks Rs25-125. Open daily 11am-11:30pm.

Guzzler's Inn, 48 Rest House Rd., off Brigade Rd. Rock, tandoori, and beer (pitchers Rs150; mugs Rs30). Popular with a younger crowd. Open daily 10:30am-11:30pm.

DISCOS

Another much-loved city ordinance, the one against the late operation of discos, prevents a proper club scene from taking root. Of the few places that have managed to remain open, by far the most popular is **The Club,** Mysore Rd., outside of town. (Rs200-400 for a one-way rickshaw ride.) Five in-house DJs spin the latest techno, trance, and hip-hop beats, but The Club is much more than a discotheque. Site of MTV's launch into South Asia, the place draws up to 6000 revelers for its live gigs (past performers include such bright young luminaries as BoyZone, Shampoo, and Slash from Guns n' Roses) and sports a swimming pool, squash, tennis, and basketball courts, and even a 24-hour coffee shop serving snacks like "chicken 69." (☎860 0768 or 860 0769. Open M, W, and F-Sa until 5am. M and W Rs150 cover, F and Sa Rs175. Rs100 of the cover goes toward food.)

Four other clubs in town draw significantly smaller crowds. **Entertainment Terminus Club** (or **ET Club**), Cha Che Towers, 50 Residency Rd., above Black Cadillac, tries to do too much with a pub as well as a dance floor. (☎222 9321. Open daily noon-midnight.) Across the street, below Purple Haze, the new **Funky Town,** with its airbrushed fire and flames graphics, is what hell might look like if it were a disco. (☎221 3758. Open Tu and Th-Sa, Rs150 per couple; Tu-Su 7:30-11:30pm, Rs300 per couple.) The party doesn't start until past midnight at the more established **JJ's,** Airport Rd., just before the airport, above Air India. (☎526 1929. Open W and F-Sa 1-5am, Rs100; rest of the week 10:30pm-2am, Rs150.) A highlight is Sunday **jazz night,** where patrons relax to old rock and jazz. Farther out, **The Rocks,** Allasandra Bellamy Rd., is fun for weekend clubbing. (☎846 2776. Open F-Sa from 9:30pm. Rs150 per couple; beer Rs80.)

OTHER DIVERSIONS

A lot happens in Bangalore, so check the weekly listings in papers available at magazine stands; www.bangalorebest.com also has up-to-date information on current cultural events. Several cinemas in the MG Rd. area show English-language flicks. **The Galaxy,** Residency Rd. (☎558 2205), **The Plaza,** 74 MG Rd. (☎558 7682), **The Rex,** Brigade Rd. (☎571350), and **The Symphony,** 51 MG Rd. (☎558 5988), all show not-too-old American movies (showtimes noon/12:30, 3:30, 6:30, and 9:30pm; Rs25-60). Try to buy tickets at least an hour in advance. **Tak Residency,** 41/3 MG Rd. (☎225 558 4444) has a sauna, jacuzzi, and health club. The **Windsor Manor Sheraton,** 25 Sankey Rd. (☎226 9898), near the High Grounds, will let you use its outdoor swimming pool for Rs400 (open daily 7am-7pm). The **Taj West End,** Race Course Rd. (☎225 5055), will also let you use its pools for the same price and the same hours. If you don't mind a much less luxurious atmosphere, go for a dip in the public **Kensington Swimming Pool,** opposite Ulsoor Lake. (☎536413. Open daily 6am-5pm. Membership fee Rs100, plus Rs3 per hr.)

🛍 SHOPPING

Even if you've spent all your money in Bangalore's bars, you should still check out the city's arts and crafts emporiums, with handpainted or inlaid tables, saris fit for a *rani,* and life-size sandalwood Krishnas. The MG Rd. area is the emporiophile's paradise, with shops selling stuff from all over India at prices to match the superlative quality. Luckily, most accept credit cards, so you can rue the purchase of that antique jade Buddha later. The government-run **Cauvery Arts Emporium,** 49 MG Rd., near Brigade Rd., has fair prices and a decent selection. (☎558 1118. Open daily 10am-1:30pm and 3-7:30pm.) **Nateson's Antiquaries,** 76 MG Rd., sells unique art pieces of their own design. (☎558 8344. Open M-Sa 10am-8pm.) **Himalayan Dowry,** 72 MG Rd., sells Kashmiri and Tibetan handicrafts and donates a portion of its proceeds to anti-dowry campaigns. (☎559 7366. Open M-Sa 10am-9pm). On **Commercial St.,** you'll find *salwar kameez* and saris in unimaginable permutations of style, color, and price.

🏃 DAYTRIPS FROM BANGALORE

BRINDAVAN. Sathya Sai Baba's Karnataka ashram (Brindavan) is in the town of **Whitefield,** 16km from Bangalore. Although he spends most of the year at his main ashram in Puttaparthi, Andhra Pradesh, Sai Baba often spends the summer months at Brindavan. Affectionately referred to as "Swami," Sai Baba has established free hospitals, schools, and countless public aid projects, including "The Water Project" which brought running water to several neighboring villages. He normally gives morning and afternoon *darshan,* during which he meanders up and down through the crowds of devotees who have assembled here from all over the world. You can stay at Brindavan for a nominal charge. For information call the ashram office (☎845 2233). City **buses** #333E and 334 run to Whitefield (1hr., Rs7). **Trains** also service the town (7 per day, 6:45am-8:15pm, 45 min., Rs5).

THE BOY WONDER Photographs of **Sathya Sai Baba,** with his expansive coiffure, saffron robes, and beatific smile, decorate and bless restaurants, hotels, homes, and autos throughout India. Millions of faithful devotees worldwide believe that he is a living god and a reincarnation of an earlier saint, Shirdi Sai Baba. Born in the tiny village of Puttaparthi, the young Sathya first displayed his spiritual leanings at the tender age of 13. Some say he was stung by a scorpion and subsequently fell into a trance from which he awoke chanting Sanskrit passages. His parents thought him possessed and called in an exorcist who tried to beat the devil out of him, but Sai Baba responded by materializing sweets out of thin air. Finally his father cried, "Who are you?" to which his son answered, "I am Sai Baba."

Since then, Sathya Sai Baba has achieved renown by performing such variously impressive feats as raising the dead, healing the sick, and producing diamonds out of thin air. However, he considers the miracles secondary to his main task of promoting the values of truth, peace, non-violence, love, and righteousness. Thousands upon thousands of people flock to Sai Baba's ashrams in Andhra Pradesh and Karnataka, hoping to observe, learn, and bask in the peaceful aura that radiates from the master.

NRITYAGRAM DANCE VILLAGE. In Hessaraghatta, 35km from the city, on the Bangalore-Pune Highway, is the Nrityagram Dance Village (☎ 846 6313; fax 846 6312; www.allindia.com/nritya) established by the late Protima Gauri, one of the most respected *odissi* dancers of the 20th century. Dancers from all over India come to train here. Tours of the village include an hour-long lecture-demonstration of *odissi* and *kathak* dance, a lecture on Indian philosophy and culture, and an organically grown lunch. (Casual tours Rs20 per person.) During the first week of February, the dance village conducts an all-night dance and music festival. The festival is free, featuring performances by Gauri and her students as well as musical faves Zakir Hussain and Amjad Ali Khan. The audience usually numbers well over 25,000, so get there by 5:30pm if you want a seat. (Dance performance Rs1100, min. 10 people; advance booking required. Village open Sept.-May Tu-Su 10am-5pm.) **Buses** run regularly from Bangalore (#253, 253A, 253D, and 253E from City Market) to Nrityagram, but the village is 5km from the bus stand, and there aren't many auto-rickshaws around. It's easier to arrange a private **taxi** (about Rs500 round-trip) or book through either **Cosmopole Travels** (☎ 228 1591) or **Cox and Kings Travel** (☎ 223 9258).

MYSORE ಮೈಸೂರು ☎ 0821

The sandalwood capital of India and home to the breathtaking Maharaja's Palace, Mysore rises above the cliched tourist brochure blurb with its countless immaculately maintained sights and small-city charm. The Wadiyar dynasty ruled Mysore from the 15th century until Independence in 1947. As the capital of a princely state until 1956, when Bangalore claimed the title, Mysore is filled with grand old palaces and other maharaja ex-haunts, as well as monuments, temples, gardens, and parks. The city is home to a thriving incense industry, churning out hundreds of thousands of incense sticks and beauty products every year. The city explodes during the annual **Dussehra Festival,** a 10-day celebration (Oct. 17-26, 2001).

▣ GETTING THERE AND GETTING AROUND

Flights: Indian Airlines, Hotel Mayura Hoysala Complex, Jhansi Laxmi Bai Rd. (☎ 421846), 250m south of the station. Open M-Sa 10am-1:30pm and 2:15-5pm.

Trains: The **railway station** is at the intersection of Irwin and Jhansi Laxmi Bai Rd. The enquiry and reservations desks (☎ 131 or 520103) are open M-Sa 8am-8pm, Su 8am-2pm. To: **Bangalore** (9-12 per day, 6am-11:30pm, 3hr., Rs64); **Hassan** (6am and 6pm, 2-3hr., Rs58); and **Madras** (1-2 per day, 2:20 and 6pm, 7-10½hr., Rs166).

Buses: Long-distance buses leave from the **Central Bus Stand** (☎520853), on B-N Rd., near Wesley Cathedral. Reservations desk open daily 7:30am-8pm. Buses run to: **Bangalore** (every 15min., 5am-10:30pm, 3hr., Rs43); **Belur** (7am and 1pm, 5hr., Rs43); **Bijapur** (1pm, 18hr., Rs211); **Coimbatore** (11 per day, 6am-11:30pm, 6hr., Rs55); **Hassan** (every 30min., 6am-10:30pm, 3hr., Rs37); **Madikeri** (every 30min., 5:15am-11pm, 3hr., Rs37); **Madras** (5 and 7pm, 12hr., Rs147); **Mangalore** (every 30min., 5am-11pm, 7hr., Rs79); **Ooty** (every 30min., 7am-7pm, 5hr., Rs43). The bus to **Somnathpur** (11:45am, Rs13) leaves from the street in front of Wesley Cathedral, but you can also take a bus to **Bannur** (every hr., Rs10), 7km from Somnathpur, and catch a bus from there (every 30min., Rs3). Near the cathedral, **private bus** companies vie for space and customers. Most are open late into the night.

Local Transportation: Local buses leave from the **City Bus Stand** (☎425819), off K-R Cir. Fares are Rs3-6. To: **Brindavan Gardens** (Platform 6, #303, every 30min., 30min.); **Chamundi Hill** (Platform 7, #201, every 20min., 20min.); **Srirangapatnam** (Platform 7, #313 and 316, every 20min., 45min.). **Taxis** cluster in Gandhi Sq.; fares are subject to negotiation. Metered **auto-rickshaw** trips across town should cost Rs15 max.

▓ ORIENTATION

Although Mysore is dotted with rotaries and streaked with unforgiving twisty-turny roads, the city is actually quite compact and easily navigated. Running north-south, **Sayajit Rao Rd.** bisects Mysore into roughly equal halves, cutting through **K-R Circle,** the true center of the city. The **City Bus Stand** is off the southeast quarter of K-R Cir., near the outskirts of the gigantic **Maharaja's Palace.** Farther southeast looms the summit of **Chamundi Hill.** About 300m north of K-R Cir., just north of the copper-domed statue, is **Sri Harsha Rd.,** where you'll find a number of accommodations and restaurants. Sri Harsha Rd. leads east to a north-south thoroughfare, **Bangalore-Nilgiri (B-N) Rd.** North on B-N Rd., opposite Wesley Cathedral, is the **Central Bus Stand.** Farther north is **Irwin Rd.,** which leads west past the GPO, the government hospital, and the tourist office. One block farther west, set back from the road, is the domed **railway station.**

▓ PRACTICAL INFORMATION

Tourist Office: Karnataka Tourist Office, Old Exhibition Building (☎442096), at the corner of Irwin and Diwan's Rd., 1 block east of the railway station. Open M-Sa 10am-5:30pm; closed 2nd Sa. The **KSTDC** (☎423652), on Jhansi Laxmi Bai Rd., adjacent to the Hotel Mayura Hoysala, will book day tours of Mysore. Open 24hr.

Budget Travel: There are many travel agencies in the vicinity of Gandhi Sq. **Dasaprakash Travel Agency** (☎529949), in the same-name hotel complex off Gandhi Sq., books tours and air and rail tickets. Open daily 7am-10pm.

Foreigners Registration Office: Police Commissioner's Office, Lalitha Mahal Rd. (☎226203), 3km from the city center. May grant free 3-month visa extensions, which take 1 week to process, but a trek out to Bangalore is likely to be necessary.

Currency Exchange: The **State Bank of Mysore** (☎443866) has foreign exchange branches at the junction of Sayajit Rao and Old Bank Rd. and opposite the GPO. The **State Bank of India,** K-R Cir. (☎437650), changes US$, UK£, and traveler's checks. Both open M-F 10:30am-2:30pm, Sa 10:30am-12:30pm.

Luggage Storage: Railway Station. Rs7. Open daily 6am-11:30pm.

Bookstore: Ashok Book Centre (☎435553), on Dhanvantri Rd., near Sayajit Rao Rd. Open M-Sa 9:30am-2pm and 3:30-8:30pm.

Library: Mysore City Central Library, at the intersection of Irwin and Sayajit Rao Rd. Open M 10am-5:30pm; Tu-Su 8:30am-8pm. Closed 2nd Sa.

Market: Devaraja Market, tucked behind the glitzy sari shops on Sayajit Rao Rd. and the sandalwood shops on Dhanvantri Rd. Sells fresh vegetables and fruit, color film, and colorful *kum-kum* powder. Open daily dawn-dusk. **Pick 'n' Pack Mini Supermarket,** Hotel Luciya complex, Old Bank Rd. (☎425445), between Gandhi Sq. and Sayajit Rao Rd. Open M-Sa 9:30am-9pm, Su 9:30am-2pm.

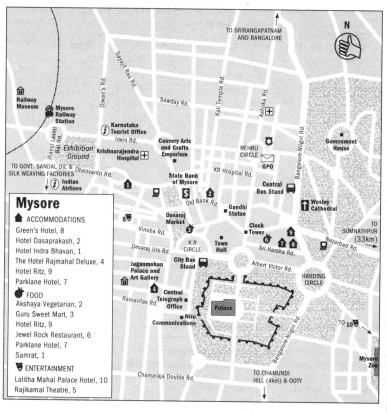

Mysore

🏠 ACCOMMODATIONS
Green's Hotel, 8
Hotel Dasaprakash, 2
Hotel Indra Bhavan, 1
The Hotel Rajmahal Deluxe, 4
Hotel Ritz, 9
Parklane Hotel, 7

🍎 FOOD
Akshaya Vegetarian, 2
Guru Sweet Mart, 3
Hotel Ritz, 9
Jewel Rock Restaurant, 6
Parklane Hotel, 7
Samrat, 1

🍷 ENTERTAINMENT
Lalitha Mahal Palace Hotel, 10
Rajikamal Theatre, 5

Police: Branch offices opposite the GPO and at the Central Bus Stand (☎ 522 2222).

Pharmacy: Janatha Bazaar Drug Unit, Dhanvantri Rd. (☎ 427678), on KR Hospital grounds opposite Indra Bhavan Hotel. Open 24hr.

Hospital: Krishnarajendra (KR) Hospital (☎ 443 3000), at the corner of Sayajit Rao and Irwin Rd., opposite Cauvery Emporium, is quite impressive-looking as government hospitals go, but the private **Holdsworth Memorial (Mission) Hospital,** Sawday Rd. (☎ 521650), is nicer and cleaner.

Telephones: 24hr. **STD/ISD** booths near Gandhi Sq. and at the **Central Telegraph Office,** south of K-R Cir., before Ramavilas Rd. Callbacks Rs1 per min.

Internet: Connections are slow in Mysore. Try **Cyber Net Corner,** 2/3 Indra Bhavan Building, Dhanvantri Rd. (☎ 446200). Rs2 per 30min. Open 8:30am-10pm. **Coca-Cola Cyber Space,** #2 Madvesha Complex, Nazarbad (☎ 565574 or 522740). Rs60 per hr. or Rs1 per min. Open M-Sa 10am-10:30pm, Su 10am-8pm.

Post Office: GPO (☎ 22165), intersection of Ashoka and Irwin Rd., 750m east of the tourist office. Open M-Sa 9am-6pm, Su 10:30am-1pm. **Postal Code:** 570001.

📷 ACCOMMODATIONS

Mysore is full of reasonably priced, centrally located hotels. Many have devoted followings, so reservations (a week ahead in season, a few days otherwise) are a good idea. There are state taxes of 5-10% on rooms Rs150 and up. Check-out is 24-hour unless otherwise noted.

Hotel Dasaprakash (☎442444 or 444455), on the corner of Gandhi Sq. and Old Bank Rd. Spacious and airy. Palm-fringed courtyard meets all your needs—an ice cream parlor, astropalmist, and a travel agency. Hot water 5am-11am; towels and soap provided. Seat or squat toilets. Veg. restaurant. Singles Rs145-335; doubles Rs300-625.

Parklane Hotel, 2720 Sri Harsha Rd. (☎434400 or 437370). Eight small but clean rooms. Popular restaurant on the terrace. Hot water 6-10am; squat toilet on the ground floor, seat toilet on the first floor. Singles Rs100-125; doubles Rs149. Visa, MC.

Hotel Ritz, 5 B-N Rd. (☎422668), 100m south of the Central Bus Stand, on your right as you exit. The four high quality, batik-decorated rooms are usually booked solid. Attached baths have seat toilets and 24hr. hot water. Terrific restaurant/bar. Check-out noon. Doubles Rs300. Visa, MC.

Green's Hotel, 2722/2 Sri Harsha Rd. (☎422415), next to Parklane hotel. Decent and inexpensive rooms. Mostly Indian clientele. Bucket hot water. Attached restaurant and bar open 10:30am-2:30pm and 5:30-11pm. Singles Rs60; doubles Rs90.

The Hotel Rajmahal Deluxe, Lakshmivilas Rd. (☎421196), to the right as you walk out of Jaganmohan Palace. Large, spotless rooms have huge windows, baths with seat toilets, and hot water 6:30-8:30am. Some have TVs. 24hr. room service, friendly staff, laundry service, and travel counter. Singles Rs140-175; doubles Rs200-225.

Hotel Indra Bhavan, Dhanvantri Rd. (☎423933), on the SR Rd. side. Manned by cordial and sweet old men who are inflexible about 3 rules: no alcohol, no meat, and no dirt. Attached baths. Good restaurant. Singles Rs150; doubles Rs190-330.

🍴 FOOD

Mysore is famous for its *masala dosas* and *pak*, a sweet made out of *ghee* and corn flour. The cheapest, tastiest, and most authentic *dosas* can be had at one of the myriad "meals" or "tiffin" cafes, where dingy painted signs proclaim "Meals Ready!" in Kannada and English. Mysore *pak* can be found at any of the sweet shops in the city, but locals jockey for space at the counters of the tiny **Guru Sweet Mart,** Sayajit Rao Rd., at Devaraja Market, to savor the best in town—still warm from the oven and dripping with *ghee* (Rs7 per piece).

Parklane Hotel, Sri Harsha Rd., near New Statue Circle. The menu solemnly notes that "disposable vomit bags are available on request in case of need, and as a consideration to fellow diners." Secluded booths are ideal for twilight wining and dining. Great *kadai paneer* (Rs55), tandoori items (Rs70-160), and veg. *pulao* (Rs40). Beer Rs37-62. Open daily 10:30am-3:30pm and 6:30-11:30pm. Live music 8-10pm. Visa, MC.

Jewel Rock Restaurant, 2716 Sri Harsha Rd., at Hotel Maurya Palace. Serves delicious tandoori, *tikkas*, and *ghee*-laden *biryanis* (Rs38-60). Dim lighting and jazz muzak. Try the Jewel Special: a sampling of chicken, mutton, and fish kebabs (Rs80). Open daily 11am-3:30pm and 6:30-11pm.

Hotel Ritz, 5 B-N Rd. Standard fare well spiced and well crafted. Candle-lit dining and garden patio. *Rumali* rolls Rs35-60; kebab platter Rs75; veg. dishes Rs36-55. Meals with drinks from Rs100. Open daily 7am-11pm. Bar open daily 11am-11pm.

Akshaya Vegetarian Restaurant, in the Hotel Dasaprakash, serves brimming *thalis* (Rs25-40) to hordes of locals and travelers. Open daily noon-3pm and 7:45-10pm. Tiffin 6-10:30am and 4-10pm.

Samrat, Dhanvantri Rd., inside Hotel Indra Bhavan. The North Indian veg. menu will satisfy your penchant for *paneer*—16 varieties may well be a Mysore record! North Indian *thali* Rs55. Open daily noon-3pm and 7-10:15pm.

👁 SIGHTS

THE MAHARAJA'S PALACE. The home of the current maharaja and the jewel of the dusty Mysore plateau, the Maharaja's Palace (Amber Vilas) is impressive for its girth (it covers more than 3.5 sq. km) as well as its worth (construction cost Rs4.2 million, not a small sum 100 years ago). The palace is visited daily by slow-moving streams of tourists. In 1897, during the reign of Krishnaraja Wadiyar IV, who had been reinstated as ruler by the British 16 years earlier, the original wooden palace burned to the ground. A certain Henry Irwin was immediately commissioned to rebuild it. The task took him and his team of artisans 15 years to complete. Durbar Hall is plastered with murals depicting scenes from the Dussehra Festival, complete with scores of cavalry in various stages of uniform. The museum is a must-see for those with an itch for kitsch: gold chariots, slightly androgynous Wadiyar family portraits, a weapons room with sharpened scythes, Ganesh-stained windows, and a wax effigy of the maharaja himself. Visible from the palace exit, the **Maharaja's Residential Palace,** with its tarnished cutlery and shabby school uniforms, is rather disappointing. On Sundays and government holidays, the palace is illuminated with 80,000 light bulbs. *(Purandara Dasa Rd. Open 10am-5:30pm. Rs10; Residential Palace Rs15. Camel rides Rs10; elephant rides Rs25; horse carriage ride Rs25.)*

CHAMUNDI HILL. Even if you're not religious, a visit to Chamundi Hill can be a spiritual experience. The ride affords a divine view of the Deccan plain, with its squares of saffron and green, and of Mysore city—even at a distance, you can see the Maharaja's Palace in all its splendor. At the top of the hill, 16m-high **Mahishasura,** the buffalo demon who plagued Mysore (and from whom the city takes its name) greets you in all his god-awful gaudiness. The **Sri Chamundeswari Temple,** with its 40m *gopuram,* derives its name from Chamundi, an incarnation of the goddess Durga who brought Mahishasura down to size. The area is a bit of a madhouse (mind your shoes!), but the rest of the hill is quite peaceful. *(Temple open 7:30am-2pm and 4-8pm.)* The tiny **Godly Museum,** near the Mahishasura statue, is filled with dioramas depicting various stages of spiritual life. One exhibit delineates "Today's Problematic World," in which most troubles seem to stem from overpopulation. Note the picture of a family of seven on one bicycle and the prophetic sketch of the crowded bus you'll take down the hill. This is also a good place to stock up on those holographic Om stickers. *(Open daily 10:30am-7pm. Free.)* Ascending or descending Chamundi Hill's 1000 steps—a journey that takes at least two hours—will have you exclaiming "My-sore feet!" at the end of it all. If you do opt to hike it, don't miss the **Shiva Temple** one-third of the way up. A granite statue of a corpulent Nandi, Shiva's loyal bull, guards the temple. Nandi has been protecting the temple for 300 years, and it's whispered that each year he, like all of his stone friends, grows just an itsy-bitsy bit bigger. It is expected that in another 300 years, Nandi will have grown so large that he'll cover the whole of Mysore—but that might just be a lot of bull. *(Southeast of town. City bus #201 and special buses, Rs4. Taxis Rs150-200 round-trip. Shiva Temple open 7:30am-2pm and 3:30-9pm.)*

OTHER SIGHTS. The **Jaganmohan Palace,** containing the **Jayachamarajendra Art Gallery,** holds a jumble of ill-exhibited *objets d'art.* There are a few gems are on display: Rabindranath Tagore watercolors and Raja Ravi Varma oils; a collection of tablas, sitars, and veenas; a series of Buddhas carved onto an elephant tusk; and ancient silk game boards. *(2 blocks west of the Maharaja's Palace. Open daily 8:30am-5pm. Rs10.)* Indian tourists flock to the **Brindavan Gardens** and **Krishnarajendra Dam** on the weekends. The gardens lack flowers, but the fountains are let loose at night, with an over-hyped light show accompanied by Hindi and Kannada music. The dam was built across the Kaveri River at the turn of the century by Maharaja Krishnaraja Wadiyar Bahadur. *(City bus #303, Rs5.50. Open M-F 7am-8:30pm, Sa-Su 7am-9:30pm. Rs5; camera fee Rs15. Light show M-F 7-7:55pm, Sa-Su 7-8:55pm.)* As Indian zoos go, the **Mysore Zoo,** which spreads over 250 green acres, is rather pleasant. Plenty of tigers (including the endangered white tiger) prowl about their enclosed grounds. Pure white peacocks, languid emurs, ponderous pachyderms, and elegant emus eke out an existence here amid expertly groomed topiary and unruly crowds of *homo sapiens.* Efforts to house animals in their most natural habitats led to the 1994 escape of two vagrant crocodiles into rural Karnataka. *(Open W-M 8am-5pm. Rs15.)*

KARNATAKA

♫🛍 ENTERTAINMENT AND SHOPPING

Rajkamal Theatre, Vinoba Rd., screens English-language films (Rs35; showtimes 11am, 3, 6:15, and 9:30pm). After the flick, unwind at **Bure's Concert Pub,** Balajee Complex, next to the theater, where the selection of booze attracts foreigners and locals alike (open 11am-midnight). You no longer have to be the Maharaja's personal guest to use the **swimming pool** at the opulent, massive-domed **Lalitha Mahal Palace Hotel** at the base of Chamundi Hill. (☎571265. Rs175 per hr. Open daily 7am-7pm.) Mysore produces half of India's **sandal oil** as well as massive quantities of **silks** and **jewelry.** The state government's **Cauvery Emporium,** Sayajit Rao Rd., is a giant warehouse of such things. They accept AmEx, MC, Visa and traveler's checks, and will arrange packing and export for an extra charge. (☎521258. Open daily 10-1:30am and 3-7:30pm.) Cauvery has an open-air annex near the palace (open M-Sa 10am-1:30pm and 3-7:30pm). Cheaper mini-emporiums crowd Dhanvantri Rd. near its intersection with Sayajit Rao Rd. Farther down Sayajit Rao Rd., near K-R Cir., silk stores sell enough saris to clothe an army of elephants. Many tailors will alter dresses or shirts in an afternoon. The **Government Silk Weaving Factory** in Vidyaranyapuram, allows tours. Here, you can watch your silk being woven and buy it later at mill prices. (☎481803. Open M-Sa 10am-noon and 2-4pm.) Next door is the **Government Sandal Oil Factory,** where, with permission, you can schedule a tour. (☎481803. Open M-Sa 10am-noon and 2-4pm.) Take the bus (# 9, 3, 8, 11, 13, 14, or 44; every 10 min.; 15min.) to Vidyaranyapuram.

🏃 DAYTRIPS FROM MYSORE

SOMNATHPUR

To get to Somnathpur, take a private bus from near Wesley Cathedral (See Buses, p. 468), or hire a taxi.

A tiny village 38km east of Mysore, Somnathpur is the site of the beautiful **Keshava Temple,** built in 1268. The village was established and the temple commissioned by Soma, a high officer under the Hoysala King Narasimha II—hence the name Somnathpur. Legend has it that when the temple was completed, the gods deemed it too beautiful and too grand (despite its height of only 10m) for this earth and wanted to transport it to heaven. The temple quaked and began to levitate. In horror, the chief sculptor mutilated some of the images on the outside wall to avert such a catastrophe. The slightly disfigured temple came crashing back down to earth. These events explain why the *garudagamba* (stone pillar depicting the divine mount, the eagle Garuda) is not exactly opposite the entrance, as is traditional, but skewed to the northeast. The Keshava Temple contains six layers of carved friezes; elephants, scrolls, geese, and scenes from the *Bhagavad Gita, Mahabharata,* and the *Puranas* border the exterior, and dozens of images fill the interior. *(Open daily 9am-5:30pm. Rs2; video fee Rs25.)*

SRIRANGAPATNAM

To reach Srirangapatnam, take a bus from Mysore. #313 and 316, every 20 min., 6am-8pm, 30min., last return to Mysore 9pm. Rs5.

Srirangapatnam, 16km from Mysore, was the site of Tipu Sultan's island fort and the seat of his vast kingdom until the fourth Anglo-Mysore war in 1799. Tipu's father, Haider Ali, defeated Mysore's Hindu raja in 1761. In 1782, Tipu inherited the throne, along with his father's rivalries with the Marathas, the French, and the British. He proved especially fearsome to the East India Company, to whom he dealt two sound defeats before the colonialists finally managed to turn the tide against him. Tipu met his final defeat here in 1799, ending his subcontinental conquest and opening up the path for the East India Company's expansion into South India. Today, Srirangapatnam is a history buff's heaven—this is, after all, where the roguish ruler met his demise after a series of legendary events. Barraged by redcoat bullets, Tipu toppled off his horse into a pile of the dead and dying. A British soldier, catching a glimpse of Tipu's ostentatious gold belt buckle, tried to snatch it for booty. But the barely-breathing Tipu lanced the soldier with his ever-ready sword. Alas, the soldier was merely injured and was still sharp enough to lodge a bullet in Tipu's temple. It is rumored that, in the depths of night, the ghost of Tipu still wanders around his former digs in search of his stolen belt buckle.

Turn left from the bus stand to reach the **Jama Masjid,** the mosque Tipu built on the grounds of an old Hindu temple. Remnants of walls put up to keep the British out surround the area. According to the Archaeological Survey of India, they are "protected and ancient monuments," but this doesn't stop local woman from using them to dry cow-dung patties on. **Daria Daulat,** Tipu's summer palace, is about 1km from the village. Tipu's main palace was destroyed in 1807 by Colonel Wellesley, and its timbers went to build the maharaja's palace in Mysore and St. Stephen's Church in Ooty. The manicured lawns and splendid palace still carry the whiff of that bygone era of pomp and luxury. The palace, built in 1784 in an Indo-Islamic style, is now a **museum** housing some marvelous murals of Tipu's battles and portraits of the entire Tipu Sultan clan, including a portrait of Tipu wearing his signature tiger stripes, which gave him the title "Tiger of Mysore." *(Rickshaw Rs20. To walk, turn right out of the bus stand platform and take the immediate left; the palace is on the left. Open Sa-Th 9am-5pm. Rs2.)* Beyond Daria Daulat, another 1km down the road, lies **Gumbaz,** the mausoleum where Tipu and his father lie. The **Sri Ranganatha Temple,** the town's namesake, dates from the Hoysala age. *(Open daily 8am-1pm and 4-8pm.)*

MADIKERI
☎08272

Formerly known as Mercara, Madikeri is the capital of the tiny coffee-growing district of Kodagu (Coorg). Roughly halfway between Mysore and Mangalore, Madikeri is well off the beaten path and sees few foreign visitors. With extensive cardamom plantations, coffee estates, and pepper vines covering the up-and-down hills of the surrounding terrain, Madikeri offers unrivaled opportunities for trekking. The city is also a good base for exploring the nearby settlements and monasteries run by Tibetan exiles. Madikeri's season runs from October to May. The best time to visit is between October and March.

▐▌ GETTING THERE AND GETTING AWAY. The steep road to the left of the bazaar leads down to the KSRTC **bus stand.** Buses go to: **Bangalore** (every 30min., 5:30am-11pm, 6hr., Rs81-105) via **Kushalnagar** (45min., Rs11) and **Mysore** (3hr., Rs37-50); **Coimbatore** (8pm, 15hr.); **Hassan** (every 30-60min., 6am-7:30pm, Rs80); **Mangalore** (every 30-60min., 5:30am-8:30pm; 10 night buses after 11:30pm, 4hr., Rs43-56); and **Ooty** (7:30am and 8:30pm, 9hr.). The unmetered **auto-rickshaws** that line the bazaar charge at least Rs15 for a trip around town; bargain hard.

▐▌ ORIENTATION AND PRACTICAL INFORMATION. Winding along the base of a series of hills is Madikeri's main thoroughfare, **General Thimaya Rd.** (also known as Mysore Rd. or Main Rd.). It runs roughly southeast-northwest past General Thimaya (GT) Circle and the fort before reaching the town bazaar and the bus stand. At the first intersection, 200m past Thimaya Circle, **MG Rd.** heads southwest (left) toward **Raja's Seat** and several hotels. Just past the bazaar, **School Rd.** (Junior College Rd.) loops northeast (right) and back around to rejoin General Thimaya Rd. The main road continues onward to **Abbi Falls** and Mangalore. The **tourist office,** a 5-minute walk south of Thimaya Circle, is pretty useless. (Open M-Sa 10:30am-5:30pm.) For information on **trekking,** contact Ganesh Aiyanna at the **Hotel Cauvery Capitol** (☎25492) or **Coorg Travels** (☎25817) at the Hotel Vinayaka Lodge. The closest place to **change currency** is Mysore. The **police station** (☎29333) is on the main road opposite the fort. Several **pharmacies** cluster around GT Circle; **Gautham Pharma** is the cleanest and friendliest of the bunch. (☎25768. Open daily 8:30am-8:45pm.) The **Cauvery District Hospital** (☎23444) is 50m southeast of the General's statue. The **Head Post Office** is on General Thimaya Rd., just up the hill from the bazaar. (☎25413. Open M-Sa 9:30am-5:30pm.) **Postal Code:** 571201.

KARNATAKA

ACCOMMODATIONS AND FOOD. The **Hotel Cauvery Capitol,** hidden below its restaurant in the bazaar, is probably the best place to stay if you can stand to listen to the same Hindi film songs blaring from the nearby theater all night. The rooms have clean lilac sheets, pink curtains, and color-coordinated walls. (☎25492. Check-out 24hr. Singles Rs200; doubles Rs350. Off-season: Rs150/Rs250). The **KSTDC Hotel Mayura Valley View,** past Raja's Seat at the end of MG Rd., is noteworthy for its spectacular views. (☎28387. Singles Rs300; doubles from Rs400. Off-season: Rs275/Rs330.) The newly-built **Hotel Amrita,** JC Rd., is much more luxurious. The sparkling, if characterless, rooms all have TVs and phones. (☎23607. Doubles Rs500. Off-season: Rs400.) **Vinayaka Lodge,** next to the bus stand, is the cheapest place in town. The rooms with squat toilets are passable, though the balcony looks out onto the town sewer. (☎29830. Singles Rs160; doubles Rs325.)

Restaurants are mainly confined to the hotels, but **Hotel Veglands,** near the police station, is a popular local "meals" joint. (Meals Rs12-17. Open M-Sa 7am-9pm.) **Santrupti,** 116/2 MG Rd., in the Hotel Rajdarshan, is the best restaurant in town. (Indian and Chinese dishes Rs38-120. Open daily 7:30am-3pm and 4-11pm.)

SIGHTS. A favorite of the long-gone kings, the views from **Raja's Seat,** on MG Rd., are now popular with tourists, especially at sunset. The **fort** at the center of town houses a life-size pair of elephant statues as well as **St. Mark's Church,** now a small museum of British memorabilia and local archaeological finds. *(Open Tu-Su 9am-5pm; closed second Sa.)* Accessible from the steps leading down from the police station, the lilac **Omkareshwara Shiva Temple,** School Rd., combines Hindu, Gothic, and Islamic architectural styles. The gilded domes of the **tombs** of the Rajas glint over the town, 1km northwest of the bazaar. Note the Hindu statuettes of bulls on the Islamic-style minarets. The path, well labeled with signposts, continues 7km through coffee plantations, cardamom estates, and cow pasture to **Abbi Falls.** The walk is pleasant, but auto-rickshaws will take you there and back for about Rs200.

NEAR MADIKERI: KUSHALNAGAR AND SERA JE

Kushalnagar is easily reached from Madikeri—all buses running between Mysore and Mangalore stop at the town's bus stand. The area around Kushalnagar, 22km east of Madikeri, is dotted with **Tibetan settlements,** making it one of the largest expatriate Tibetan communities in the world. Some 10,000 refugees were relocated here during the 1960s and early 1970s after subsisting for ten years behind the barbed-wire fences of a former British internment camp in the jungles of Assam. Within this group were about 200 monks who had escaped when Lhasa's Sera Je Monastery was destroyed in 1959. They set about rebuilding it 6km southwest of Kushalnagar. Today the new **Sera Je Monastery** serves as a university for more than 3000 monks. A stone pillar in front of the three-story main hall recounts the history of the monastery, and the grounds are constantly abuzz with monks praying and debating. On the road to Sera Je is the **Nyingmapa Monastery.**

From Kushalnagar, **auto-rickshaws** charge Rs30 to go to Sera Je, but you can probably share one with some monks. The **Sera Je Guest House,** established to raise money for the monastery, is the only place to stay in town. The manager's friendliness more than makes up for the lack of English-speaking ability, and the restaurant is always filled with monks slurping *thukpa* and gobbling *momos*. (☎54672. Doubles Rs125.) Another monkish fave is the **Norling Hotel,** opposite the monastery, serving only chow mein (Rs15) and *momos* (Rs10).

Kushalnagar has more accommodations options, but there are no gems here. **Radhakrishna Lodge,** Mysore Rd., to the right as you exit the bus stand, is not the cleanest place, but the rooms have seat toilets and showers. (☎74822. Singles Rs75; doubles Rs100.) The nearby **Ganesh Lodge** offers minimal amenities. (☎74528. Singles Rs80; doubles Rs120.) Young monks enjoy the **Tibet Restaurant,** IB Rd., 200m across from the bus stand; look for the green sign. (Chow mein Rs20-30; *thukpa* Rs15-25; *momos* Rs25-35; and *mothuk* Rs20-25. Open daily 9am-9pm.)

HASSAN ಹಸನ

☎ 08172

The busy industrial city of Hassan has little tourist appeal and no sights of its own, but its location 40km from the temple villages of Halebid and Belur has ensured it a place along South India's tourist trail. Hassan's railway station, bus stands, hotels, and modern conveniences make it a practical place to spend your nights while visiting these nearby areas.

⊏ GETTING THERE AND GETTING AROUND

Trains: The **railway station** serves **Arsikere** (10:50am, 3:30, and 9pm, 1½hr., 2nd class Rs10) and **Mysore** (6am and 6:30pm, 3hr., Rs56). Both connect to **Bangalore,** but the Mysore connection is faster.

Buses: The **bus stand** (☎ 68418) is opposite Maharaja's Park. To: **Bangalore** (every 15min., 5am-9pm, 4hr., Rs57) via **Channarayapatna** (1hr., Rs12); **Belur** (every 15min., 6:15am-8:30pm, 1½hr., Rs12); **Halebid** (every 30min., 7am-7pm, 1hr., Rs8); **Mangalore** (20 per day, 6am-6:30pm, 3½hr., Rs50); **Mysore** (every 30min., 5:15am-9:30pm, 3hr., Rs40). From **Channarayapatna** connections can be made to **Sravana-belagola** (every 20min., 15min., Rs4). For **Hospet/Hampi,** head to **Shimoga** (every 15min., 5am-10:45pm, 4hr., Rs45) and transfer. Hordes of **private bus** companies go to Bangalore (Rs60). **Tempos** also service Belur and Halebid; from the bus stand, make a left onto Church St., take the first right, and proceed for a few blocks.

✈🛈 ORIENTATION AND PRACTICAL INFORMATION

Most of the hotels are within 500m of the **bus stand,** which is on the southwest corner of the intersection of **Bus Stand Rd.** (north-south) and **Church Rd.** (east-west). Running parallel to Bus Stand Rd., 200m to the east, is **Race Course Rd.** It intersects the second east-west thoroughfare, the **Bangalore-Mangalore (B-M) Rd.,** 300m to the south. The **railway station,** on B-M Rd., is 2km to the east. The city center hugs the bus stand and the intersection of Race Course and B-M Rd.

Tourist Office: Regional Tourist Office, Vartha Bhavan, B-M Rd. (☎ 68862). From the bus stand, walk 1 block south, turn left onto B-M Rd., and continue for a few blocks; it's on the left. Open M-Sa 10am-1:30pm and 2-5:30pm.

Immigration Office: Foreigners Registration Office, B-M Rd. (☎ 68000), at the **police station,** in the women's grievances office. Open M-F 10am-5:30pm.

Currency Exchange: State Bank of Mysore (☎ 68407), on the corner of Bus Stand and B-M Rds. Changes US$, UK£, and traveler's checks. Open M-F 10:30am-2:30pm, Sa 10:30am-12:30pm.

Market: The market to the south and west of the bus stand has pyramids of tangerines, grapes, apples, and mangoes alongside *chaat* carts, *chai* stalls, and omelette fryers.

Pharmacy: Gopal Medicines, Bus Stand Rd. (☎ 68678), opposite Karnataka Bank. Open 9am-9:30pm.

Hospital: CSI Redfern Memorial Hospital, Race Course Rd. (☎ 67653), 1 block north of the intersection with Church Rd.

Internet: Cyber Park, above Vaisnavi Lodging. Rs35 per hr.

Post Office: Bus Stand Rd. Open M-Sa 10am-6pm, Su 10am-1pm. **Postal Code:** 573201.

⚑ ACCOMMODATIONS

▨ **Sri Ganesha Lodge,** Devaraj Market, Subhash Square (☎ 32736). Exit the bus stand using the alley next to Hotel Ashraya. The cherry-red paint is hardly dry on the doors to the new rooms here. The proprietor is cheerful. The doubles have good views of the market below. Sit *or* squat on the funky toilets. Hot water 6-9am. Check-out 24hr. Singles Rs125-150; doubles Rs200-225.

KARNATAKA

Vaishnavi Lodging, Harsha Mahal Rd. (☎ 63885-9). Turn left out of the bus stand, turn right onto Church Rd., and take the first left. Big rooms with clean sheets, fluffy pillows, phones, and attached baths (squat, baby, squat). Hot water 6-9am. Check-out 24hr. Singles Rs110; doubles Rs170.

Hotel Suvarna Regency, B-M Rd. (☎ 64006). From Bus Stand Rd., turn right after the police station and follow B-M Rd. to where it turns south; look for the Suvarna Regency's towers. Star TV, phones, seat or squat toilets, travel services, and towels. Check-out 24hr. Singles Rs275; doubles Rs400-550. Amex, MC, Visa.

Abiruchi Lodge, B-M Rd. (☎ 67852). From the bus stand, walk 2 blocks south on Bus Stand Rd. and take a right after the police station. Clean rooms and spotless bathrooms. Sit or squat; shower or bucket. Attached restaurant. Hot water 6-9am. Check-out 24hr. Singles Rs80-145; doubles Rs140-200.

🍴 FOOD

▨ **Suvarna Sagar,** B-M Rd., attached to Hotel Survarna. Dishes out costly *thalis* (Rs18-55) and small-portioned North Indian selections (Rs24-50). The spices are blended harmoniously and the fresh *paneer* is so soft it practically melts in your mouth. They've scooped the competition when it comes to ice cream (Rs9-35). 10% surcharge to sit in the A/C section. Open daily 7am-10:30pm.

Hotel GRR, Bus Stand Rd., opposite the bus stand. Excellent banana-leaf *thalis* (Rs15). Open daily 11:30am-4:30pm and 7:30-11pm.

Hotel Sanman, M-O Rd. From the bus stand, head south on Bus Stand Rd. and take the last road before B-M Rd. The fresh and steam-filled *puris* are piled mile-high. Open daily 6am-9:45pm. *Thalis* (Rs15) served 11:30am-4pm and 7-9:45pm.

Golden Gate, behind Suvarna Sagar. For those who can't handle another *thali,* this pricey restaurant offers food such as spaghetti "nepolitine" (Rs50). Tandoori/Mughlai Rs30-140; Chinese Rs30-70. Booze Rs30-120. Open noon-3pm and 7-11pm.

NEAR HASSAN: SRAVANABELAGOLA ಶ್ರವಣಬೆಳಗೊಲ ☎ 08176

Sravanabelagola's 17m-high statue of the Jain saint Bahubali is said to be the world's tallest monolithic statue. The beatific smile that plays across the face of the naked holy man, also called Gomateshvara, blesses the tiny town with serenity. The streets are clean and empty, the air is suffused with calm, and the touts are less aggressive than their postcard-pushing buddies in most temple towns. While the main attraction is, of course, the towering statue, Sravanabelagola is also the site of some important and even older *bastis* (temples).

📧 TRANSPORTATION AND PRACTICAL INFORMATION. The **bus stand** is on Bangalore (CR Patna) Rd., opposite the hilltop *basti.* **Buses** leave for **Bangalore** (4 per day, 6:45am-3pm, 3hr., Rs46); **Chanayapatna** (every 15min., 6am-9pm, 15min., Rs4); **Hassan** (6:30, 9am, and 3pm, 45min., Rs16); and **Mysore** (6:15, 7:30am, and 2:15pm, 2½hr., Rs31). Make a right from the station onto Bangalore Rd.; your first right will be **Kalyani Rd.,** which fronts many small stores and cold-drink shops and leads to **Temple Rd.** The hill where Bahubali and many of the *bastis* stand is to the right, with the KSTDC **tourist office** at its base. The staff speaks little English, but their tours are helpful. (☎ 57254. Open M-Sa 10am-5:30pm. Tours Rs100.)

📧 ACCOMMODATIONS AND FOOD. Most visitors make Sravanabelagola a daytrip, but the town has plenty of places to stay, in part because of the Mahamastakabhisheka ceremony, which attracts thousands of Jain pilgrims here every 12 years. Visitors should respect the Jain prohibitions on meat and alcohol. The Jain **lodging houses,** which must be reserved through the central **Accommodation Office** (☎ 57258), have quiet, clean doubles with attached baths (seat toilet) for Rs125. Turn left from the bus stand; they're on the left. Farther down the street, **Yatri Nivas** has bigger, slightly more luxurious rooms that can also be reserved through the Accommodations Office (singles Rs60; doubles Rs80-160).

⊡ SIGHTS. Built around 980 AD, the **Bahubali statue,** on top of Indragiri Hill, is a relatively recent fixture in Sravanabelagola. Son of the first Jain *tirthankara* and a saint in his own right, Bahubali wears an enlightened smile and not much else. Vines creep up his legs, snakes coil around his feet, and anthills fester at his ankles, all symbolizing his detachment from the world of the senses. The 620 steps leading up to the statue require about 15 to 20 minutes of dedicated climbing. Wear a pair of thick socks if your soles are not ascetically hardened to the touch of burning granite. A group of tired-looking old men can carry you up in a chair for Rs85. *(The temple housing the statue is open daily sunrise-sunset. Puja 8am. Visit in the morning to avoid the crowds and the heat.)*

Every 12 years the Jain mega-festival of **Mahamastakabhisheka** is held here. On the eve of the ceremony, scaffolding is erected behind the monument and 1008 pots of sacred colored water are placed in front of the statue. Priests and wealthy devotees chant mantras as they anoint Bahubali with water, milk, dates, bananas, curds, sugar, almonds, and gold and silver flowers. Thousands of pilgrims attend the ceremony in pin-drop silence. The next is scheduled for 2005.

Tall, naked ascetics tend to get all the attention, and Bahubali is certainly no exception. However, the hills surrounding him have been a Jain pilgrimage site long before the statue was carved. The Jain *bastis* scattered throughout the town were built over several centuries, forming an architectural history of the hills. The Mauryan emperor Chandragupta came to Sravanabelagola in 300 BC, when he abdicated his throne to retire here as an ascetic. His guru Bhadrabahu attained enlightenment here and passed away in a cave on Chandragiri Hill. Chandragupta, after whom the hill is named, faithfully spent days inside the cave worshipping the footprints of his deceased teacher until he, too, died of starvation. The site still attracts pilgrims who believe that viewing the prints can cure all illness.

HALEBID ಹಳೇಬೇಡು ☎ 08177

Visitors might find it difficult to imagine Halebid during its 12th and 13th century heyday, when it was "Dwarasamudram," the capital of the magnificent Hoysala Empire. Halebid's current name means "Destroyed City," a fitting description; today, the village of 12,000 is home to more cows and goats than kings and sculptors. With the Western Ghats in the distance, small children playing in the road, and cows grazing along the edges of sunflower fields, Halebid indulges all romantic stereotypes of India's long-lost simplicity. That is, until one of the sweet children morphs into an insistent soapstone tout and wretches you back to reality.

⊡ GETTING THERE AND GETTING AROUND. The **bus stand** is opposite the Hoysalesvara Temple. Buses go to: **Arsikere** (10 per day, 7am-5:30pm, 3hr., Rs18); **Belur** (every 30min., 7am-6:30pm, 45min., Rs6); and **Hassan** (15 per day, 6am-7pm, 1hr., Rs8). Private **maxicabs** going to Hassan and Belur bid aggressively for customers in front of the temple.

⊡⊡ ORIENTATION AND PRACTICAL INFORMATION. Halebid has more 12th-century shrines than banks, police stations, and hospitals put together. The **Hoysalesvara Temple,** the only star-shaped soapstone edifice in town, is hard to miss. An energetic, safari-suited employee at the **Tourist Help Desk** will supply you with information on every conceivable subject. (Open M-Sa 10am-5:30pm.) The **Jain Temples** and the Kedareshvara Temple are 500m down the road. The **Primary Health Center** (☎73022) is directly behind the bus stand; exit to the left and take an immediate left. The **police station** (☎73201) is just beyond, on the right. The **post office** is opposite the bus stand (Open M-Sa 8:30am-4:30pm). **Postal Code:** 573121.

⊡⊡ ACCOMMODATIONS AND FOOD. Halebid's **Hotel Mayura Shantala,** run by the Department of Tourism, is the only lodging in town. The four rooms have attached baths and 24-hour hot water. (☎73224. Singles Rs100-150; doubles Rs150-200.) The attached **restaurant** serves the standard menu. (*Thalis* Rs20. Open daily 7am-11pm.) The bus stand also has a **restaurant,** with *thalis* for Rs15 and good *dosas* for Rs9. (Open 5:30am-8:30pm.)

> **ROAD WRITING** The backsides of Indian motor vehicles make for interesting recreational reading. Even the most fume-filled of city drives can be brightened up a bit by a simple game of "guess-the-rickshaw-driver's-religion-from-his-bumper-stickers." Similarly, road trips offer the treat of those humorously ominous warnings painted on the backs of lumbering Tatas and Ashok-Leylands. The most pervasive genre of this lorry literature is the proper-horn-use statement: "Soundhorn," "No Horn!," and the ubiquitous and inane "Horn OK Please." This last phrase has its origins in the days when many Indian goods carriers had a centered, cyclops-like brake light. The "Horn Please" directed drivers to signal if they wished to pass the larger, slower vehicle. If the truck driver saw fit to allow such a maneuver, he would tap his brake, and the center light, labeled "OK," would flash. Eventually the one tail-light became two, but by then the order had stuck. "Horn OK Please" was fixed in the mind, and the tailgate, of Indian automotive consciousness.

◉ SIGHTS. The largest of the Hoysalan temples, **Hoysalesvara Temple** overlooks the vast Dwarasamudra Lake and is surrounded by immaculately tended gardens. Construction began in 1121, but before it could be completed, the armies of the Delhi Sultanate sacked the temple and ravaged the town. By the time of India's Independence, only 14 of the original 84 large statues remained, and only one of the "bracket figures" (the mini-statues for which Belur's temple is famed) was left. Those that were not destroyed or vandalized were stolen—British museums display quite a few of them.

The temple is actually composed of two Shiva temples on a single, star-shaped platform. The larger of the two was commissioned by the Hoysala king Vishnuvardhana, and the smaller one by his senior wife, the famed dancer Shantaladevi. Like all Hoysalan temples, the deities face east toward the sunrise. Over 20,000 elaborate figures remain in and around the temple. The unusually funny and well-informed ASI-sanctioned **guides** will point out the best and the brightest. *(Guides Rs30 for up to 5 people.)*

Six levels of **frieze work** border the base of the temple. Images include elephants, lions, geese, horsemen, scrolls, and stories from the *Puranas* and the epics. Larger, more gory engravings of gods and goddesses line the upper exterior walls: Shiva killing an elephant demon by severing his trunk and then dancing on the poor thing's stomach in celebration; Vishnu peeling off the face of a demon as you might peel a banana; and Bhima tossing elephants over his shoulders like long-nosed grenades. One scene, for example, depicts a monarch peering through a surprisingly modern-looking telescope. The temple also houses two *lingas* and a platform once used for devotional dances. Leave your shoes at the entrance. *(Open dawn-dusk. Free; Rs1 for shoe storage.)*

The **Archaeological Museum**, a pebble's throw from the temple, houses deity statues from the town's temples and nearby ruins. Half of it is outdoors, and some of the statues sit in a pretty garden with a fountain. *(Open Sa-Th 10am-5pm. Rs2.)* The 12th-century **Jain Bastis**, built by King Vishnuvardhevna before he converted to Hinduism, are styled much like the town's Hindu temples. The most prominent of these is the **Parswanathasamy Temple,** held up by 12 columns. Their simple design—so smooth you can see your own reflection—is meant to convey the serenity of meditation and worship. *(500m south of the bus stand. Open 10am-5pm. Puja 9am.)* The **Kedareshvara Temple,** a smaller cousin of the Hoysalesvara, is 300m farther on.

BELUR ಬೇಲೂರು   ☎ 08177

Belur, a little town on the banks of the Yagachi River, was the capital of the Hoysalan Empire until Halebid deprived it of the honor in the 12th century. Seven hundred years and several dynasties later, Belur has become a blink-and-you'll-miss-it kind of town, betraying none of its gilded history. Only the Chennakeshava Temple, set apart from the town by its tall *gopuram*, reminds visitors of Belur's glorious past. Although Belur has more hotels and restaurants than Halebid, most prefer Halebid's peaceful village feel to Belur's rough, small-town vibe.

🔄 GETTING THERE AND GETTING AROUND. Buses run to: **Arsikere** (every 30-45min., 6am-7pm, 1½hr., Rs16); **Halebid** (every 30-60min., 6am-9pm, 45min., Rs6); **Hassan** (every 30min., 5:30am-11:30pm, 1hr., Rs12); **Mangalore** (6:45 and 8:15am, 5hr., Rs70); and **Mysore** (every 30-60min., 7:30am-11pm, 4hr., Rs42). **Auto-rickshaws** head to the temple (Rs5), but you can walk there in less than 10 minutes.

🔳🔢 ORIENTATION AND PRACTICAL INFORMATION. There are two roads in Belur. **Main Rd.** is roughly perpendicular to **Temple Rd.,** which runs from the **bus stand** to the Chennakeshava Temple. From the bus stand, turn right out of the exit opposite the platform onto Temple Rd. Services include the brand-new **Government Hospital** (☎ 22333), just past the the **Tourist Office** (☎ 22209; open M-Sa, 10:30am-5:30pm), inside the Mayura Velapuri Hotel Complex; the **State Bank of Mysore,** opposite, which changes currency (open M-F 10:30am-2:30pm, Sa 10:30am-12:30pm); the **police station** (☎ 22460), on Main Rd., opposite the bus stand; and the **post office,** farther down Main Rd. (turn left out of the main entrance of the bus stand building). **Postal Code:** 573115.

🔳🔳 ACCOMMODATIONS AND FOOD. The limited lodging options in Belur range from cheap and functional to cheaper and less functional—no air-conditioning or TVs here. Dining is best done in one of the hotels. You are unlikely to find roaches scuffle across the clean floor of the **Hotel Mayura Velapuri,** the priciest hotel in town. (☎ 22209. Singles Rs135-168; doubles Rs168-200.) Its **restaurant** dishes up *thalis* (Rs25) and snacks (open daily 6:30am-10:30pm). **Swagath Tourist Home,** a few minutes' walk down Temple Rd., is cheaper, cheerier, and more intimate than its neighbors. Owned by the family that runs the market below, the Swagath has pink balconies overlooking a tiny courtyard. (☎ 22159. Check-out 24hr. Doubles Rs60.) **Hotel Annapoorna** serves a good *thali* for Rs15 (open daily 6am-10pm) and has decent doubles with bath (Rs150).

⬛ SIGHTS. Perhaps Vishnu's fearsome eagle-mount Garuda, who guards the famous **Chennakeshava Temple,** saved it from the brutal ransacking that Halebid suffered. Along with those at Somnathpur and Halebid, this temple is considered one of the best examples of Hoysalan architecture. The Hoysala king Vishnuvardhana commissioned the temple to commemorate his conversion from Jainism to Hinduism, and even though three generations of sculptors devoted their lives to its construction, the Chennakeshava Temple was never finished.

Like the temples at Halebid and Somnathpur, Chennakeshava has a base covered with astoundingly detailed horizontal friezes. To bear the weight of the temple, 644 stone elephants, each one unique, stand at the bottom. Nine statues of Vishnu surround the exterior. The emblem of the Hoysalan empire—its first emperor smiting a half-lion, half-tiger beast—also stands outside. When he was a boy, the emperor Sala and his guru were sitting under a tree when this ferocious animal appeared. Sala stared the beast down as his guru shouted **"Hoy, Sala"** ("Kill, Sala"). The courageous boy founded the great Hoysalan Empire, which ruled over Karnataka and parts of Tamil Nadu from the 10th to 14th centuries.

The temple is renowned for the 42 mini-statues, or **bracket figures,** that line the interior ceilings and exterior walls. The detail of these sculptures is incredible. Voluptuous women with jingling bangles and head pendants are carved out of a single stone. One wears an expression of longing as she holds a letter to her faraway lover while a lusty monkey tugs at the edge of her sari. The famed **Thribhanghi Nritya,** a classical dancer, contorts her body in such a way that a drop of water from her right hand grazes the tip of her nose, then her left breast, and then hits the thumb of her left hand before it lands at the arch of her right foot.

Inside the temple is a platform once used by the *devadasis* (temple dancers), a waiting area for the audience, and several four-ton columns, which were so heavy that they had to be turned by elephants while sculptors detailed them. The **Narasimha Pillar** at the center of the temple contains miniature replicas of all of the temple's other carvings. One square is left empty, to indicate that, despite the efforts of the earthly artists, God can never be truly depicted.

KARNATAKA

Two images of Vishnu sit inside the **sanctum**—a large, silver-plated image that pilgrims still pray to every day, and a smaller wooden sculpture used in temple processions. Carved on the wall in front of the image is a creature with a peacock's tail, a boar's body, a lion's feet, a crocodile's mouth, a monkey's eyes, an elephant's trunk, and a cow's ears. The animal possesses the best part of each of the animals, making it more perfect than any single animal and, thus, fit to guard Vishnu himself. *(Non-Hindus may view the images. Puja 9am and 7pm.)*

The Vijayanagar Dynasty constructed the temple's original **gopuram**, which has since been rebuilt after it was destroyed by fire. At the bottom right-hand corner, as you exit the temple, are some erotic engravings. Leave your shoes and inhibitions at the door. *(Temple open daily 8am-8:30pm. Inner sanctum closed 1-3pm and 4:30-5:30pm. Free; Rs1 for shoe storage.)*

MANGALORE ಮಂಗಳೂರು ☎ 0824

An important trading port for centuries and a major shipbuilding center during the 18th century, Mangalore today retains much of its mercantile feel but little of its former glory. Mangalore's main claim to fame today comes from its position as India's biggest cashew and coffee processor and a major *bidi*-production center. It's little wonder that Mangalore isn't exactly a tourist magnet. Nevertheless, it's a modern city with plenty of budget hotels and cheap restaurants. As a transport node between Goa and Kerala, Mangalore makes a decent stopover and, with the completion of the Konkan railway, its importance to travelers will only increase.

▐▌ GETTING THERE AND GETTING AROUND

Flights: Bajpe Airport (info ☎ 142), 22km from town, can be reached by local buses #47B and 47C or by taxi (Rs225). **Indian Airlines** (☎ 455259) is on Hat Hill. Head west from Lalbagh Circle and take the first right (rickshaw Rs12 from KS Rao Rd.). Open daily 9am-1pm and 1:45-5pm. **Jet Airways,** KS Rao Rd. (☎ 440694). Open M-Sa 8:30am-5:30pm, Su 9am-2pm. To: **Bangalore** (1-2 per day, 1hr., US$70); **Bombay** (3 per day, 1hr., US$115); **Madras** (Tu, Th, Sa; 2hr.; US$95).

Trains: Railway station, 300m south of the intersection of KS Rao and Lighthouse Rd. From Hampankatta, take the road going south in between Maiden Rd. and Falnir Rd. Reservations open M-Sa 8am-8pm, Su 8am-2pm. To: **Calicut** (5-6 per day, 3:15am-8:10pm, 5hr., Rs95); **Ernakulam** (3:15am and 4:30pm, 10hr., Rs148); **Madras** (11:15am and 8:10pm, 18hr., Rs250); **Margao** (8:30pm, 5hr., Rs154); and **Trivandrum** (3:15am and 4:30pm, 15hr., Rs205).

Buses: KSRTC Bus Stand, in Bijai, 3km from the center of town (Rs15 by autorickshaw from Hampankatta). Reservations open daily 7am-9:30pm. To: **Bangalore** (14 per day, 8hr., Rs109-133); **Hassan** (every 30min., 4hr., Rs65); **Mysore** (15 per day, 7hr., Rs79-115); and **Panjim** (8am and 9:30pm, 10hr., Rs122-168). **Private buses,** at the new bus stand near the intersection of Maidan and Maidan Cross Rd., are more convenient to the city center and run more frequently. Many companies have offices at the old bus stand, in the alley near the intersection of Lighthouse Hill and KS Rao Rd. **Ganesh Travels** (☎ 441277; open daily 5am-10:30pm) sends buses to: **Bangalore** (9 per day, 8hr., Rs165-180); **Cochin** (8:10pm, 10hr., Rs210); **Margao** (9 and 9:30pm, 9hr., Rs170); **Mysore** (10pm, 7hr., Rs135); **Panjim** (9:30pm, 9hr., Rs170); **Udipi** (frequent, 1¼hr., Rs19); books seats to **Bombay** (7:30am and 2pm, 22hr., Rs350-400).

Local Transportation: Most **local buses** stop on Dr. UP Maliya Rd., near Town Hall. In general, buses are numbered in front or on the side, and many stands list the buses that stop there. **Auto-rickshaws** are the easiest way to get around. Except for those around the bus and railway stations, most will use the meter with a Rs7 flag-fall.

✳🛈 ORIENTATION AND PRACTICAL INFORMATION

Mangalore's mangled street plan can make navigation tricky. The monthly *Mangalore Today* (Rs10) available at newsstands usually includes a map. In the heart of the city, **Hampankatta** consists of a chaotic traffic circle from which six major thoroughfares radiate. Heading northeast and sharply uphill from Hampankatta is **Lighthouse Hill Rd.** Forking east off Lighthouse Hill Rd. is **Balmatta Rd.** Just west of Lighthouse Hill Rd., **KS Rao Rd.** heads due north and is cluttered with budget hotels and restaurants. To the southwest, **Maidan Rd.** passes the **Town Hall** and heads to **Shetty Circle.** Branching west off Maidan Rd. is **Maidan Cross Rd.** Due east off Hampankatta is **Falnir Rd.**, and going southeast between Falnir and Maidan, is the road leading 300m south to the **railway station.**

Tourist Office: Department of Tourism Information Office, Lighthouse Hill Rd. (☎442926), in Hotel Indraprastha. Open M-Sa 10:30am-1:30pm and 2:30-5:30pm.

Currency Exchange: Bank of India, KS Rao Rd., exchanges cash and traveler's checks. Open M-F 10am-2pm, Sa 10am-noon. **Travel Wings,** Lighthouse Hill Rd. (☎426225) also exchanges money at good rates. Open M-Sa 9:30am-1pm and 2:30-5:30pm.

Bookstore: Higginbothams, Lighthouse Hill Rd. (☎427585), near the intersection with KS Rao Rd. Open M-Sa 9:30am-1:30pm and 3:30-7:30pm. **Athree Book Centre,** 4 Sharavathi Building, Balmatta Rd. (☎425161), just beyond the University Medical Centre. Open M-Sa 8:30am-1pm and 2:30-8pm.

Police: (☎426426), by the central post office, just beyond Shetty Circle. **Foreigner's Registration Office** open M-F 10am-1:30pm and 3:30-5:30pm.

Pharmacy: Sharavu Medicals (☎442197), just off KS Rao Rd. Open M-Sa 8:30am-10pm, Su 9am-9:30pm.

Hospital: City Hospital (☎217424), in Kadri, 3km from Hampankatta, and **Father Muller's Hospital** (☎436301), in Kankanady (3km), are both good and privately-run.

Telephones: A few 24hr. **STD/ISD** booths on KS Rao Rd. allow callbacks. The main **Telegraph Office,** Dr. UP Maliya Rd., next to the GPO, allows collect calls. Open 24hr.

Internet: Check email to the beat of classic and techno rock at **I-net 107 The Cyber Cafe,** KS Rao Rd. (☎424639), in the Classique Arcade. 10 terminals. Rs50 per hr., Rs45 after 8pm. Open daily 10:15am-11pm. **Kohinoor Computer Zone,** Lighthouse Hill Rd., close to Hotel Indraprastha. Rs50 per hr. Open M-Sa 8am-2am, Su 10am-2am.

Post Office: Dr. UP Mallya Rd., southwest from Town Hall, past Shetty Circle. Open M-Sa 8:30am-6pm. **Postal Code:** 575001.

🛏 ACCOMMODATIONS

Weary travelers need look no farther than KS Rao Rd., where the hotels are fairly cheap, clean, and pleasant. Most own back-up generators, so you can lounge in well-fanned, Star TV bliss all night long. The places below have 24-hour check-out.

Hotel Naufal, Mission St. (☎428085). With the Town Hall on your left, follow Maidan Rd. to Mission St.; it's on your right. Convenient to the bus and train stations. Bathrooms with seat toilets and hot water 6-10am. The waterfront is a short walk away. Jasmine Restaurant downstairs serves basic fare. Singles Rs100; doubles Rs150.

Hotel Shaan Plaza, KS Rao Rd. (☎440312). Large, well-kept hotel with huge rooms. Restaurant, phones, seat toilets, and Star movies. Singles Rs270; doubles Rs370-600.

Hotel Manorama, KS Rao Rd. (☎440306), next door to Hotel Shaan Plaza. Spacious rooms with seat toilets and fans. Singles Rs185; doubles Rs275.

Hotel Roopa, Balmatta Rd. (☎421271), Hampankatta. A good alternative to "hotel central" on KS Rao Rd. From the Hampanketta traffic circle, start up Lighthouse Hill Rd. and bear right almost immediately. Singles Rs125; doubles Rs184-450.

FOOD

Janatha Restaurant, in the Hotel Shaan Plaza. This busy restaurant serves up North and South Indian dishes (Rs20-48) and ice cream treats (Rs8-28). Meals 11:30am-3pm and 7-10:45pm. Open daily 7am-10:30pm.

Pai Cafe, in Hotel Navaratna. An excellent veg. restaurant. Good *puri thalis* Rs20; South Indian breakfasts Rs8-14; and Bengali sweets Rs7-15. Meals 7am-noon and 3-8pm. Open daily 6am-10pm.

Tai Chien, in Hotel Moti Mahal, Fahir Rd., just beyond Milagres Church. An impeccable spread of silverware, porcelain, linens, sauces, and pickles is only vaguely discernible in the dim light of Chinese lanterns, but the food is so good you won't need to see it. Szechuan pork ribs Rs75. Beer and liquor available. Open daily 7pm-midnight.

The Galley (☎ 420420) in Manjuran Hotel. Don your last clean t-shirt and take a rickshaw (Rs10 from KS Rao Rd.) or walk due west from Shetty Circle (10min.) to Mangalore's fanciest address. Pricey, but the food and atmosphere are both worth the investment. Enjoy the tasty Mangalore fish curry (Rs100) as you sway to the sounds of Urdu love songs, performed live Th-Su evenings. Frequent fixed-price specials (Rs150-200). Open daily 12:30-3pm and 7:30-11pm.

SIGHTS

LIGHTHOUSE HILL. The **Lighthouse** itself, orange racing stripe and all, is not worth the walk up the hill, but it is surrounded by lovely gardens with fine views of the city—a fair reward for a bit of sweat. Just beyond the lighthouse, off the road to the left, is the Jesuit **St. Aloysius College Chapel,** whose lovely painted ceilings date from 1899. *(Chapel open daily 8:30-10am, noon-2pm, and 3:30-6pm. English mass M-Sa 6:30 and 7am, Su 6:30 and 8am. Ceiling-oglers not welcome during Sa-Su services.)*

KADRI TEMPLE. Once a center for the Shaiva and tantric Natha-Pantha cult, the temple is notable for its bronze figures, including a 10th-century seated Lokeshvara, considered among India's finest. The gabled, towered temple complex is surrounded by nine tanks. A steep staircase opposite the temple entrance leads to several shrines and the **Shriyogishwar Math,** whose tantric sadhus are depicted contemplating Kala Bhairawa (a terrifying aspect of Shiva), Agni, and Durga. *(5km north of the city center, at the bottom of Kadri Hill. Various city buses go there, including the #14, 21, 22, and 30; rickshaws Rs25 round-trip. Open daily 6am-1pm and 4-8pm.)*

OTHER SIGHTS. Sultan's Battery, on the headlands of the old port, is a fort constructed by Tipu Sultan. There's not a great amount to see here besides the modest ruins of the tiny fortress, but it's a peaceful river scene. *(5km north of the city center; take the #16 bus or a rickshaw for about Rs40.)* **Mangaladevi Temple,** built in 1000 AD, was named for the same Malabar princess who gave the the city itself its name. *(3km south of the city center. Take bus #27, 27A, or 15 or a rickshaw for Rs20.)*

HOSPET ಹೋಸಪೇಟ್   ☎ 08394

The famed Vijayanagar king Krishnadevaraya built Hospet between 1509 and 1520, and it soon became one of his favorite haunts. The last traces of the Vijayanagar Empire were long ago trampled into the dust, and Hospet today is typical of humdrum Karnataka, treading the line between heavy industrialization—blaring, barreling trucks transporting the products of a burgeoning steel industry—and village life—pigs, roosters, and dogs sifting through the streetside trash. Regular buses run from here to Hampi, where most of the remaining ruins are. Although food and lodging can also be found in Hampi, Hospet offers easy access to transportation and a modicum of luxury unavailable in Hampi.

GETTING THERE AND GETTING AROUND

Trains: Hospet Junction Station (☎131), 750m from the bus stand, at the end of Station Rd. Reservation counter open daily 8am-8pm. To: **Bangalore** (8:10pm, 11hr., Rs88); **Gadag** for **Bijapur** (3per day, 5:15-10:40am; 1½-2½hr.; Rs47; and **Guntakal** for **Delhi** and **Bombay** (3:25 and 8:10pm, 1½hr., Rs55).

Buses: Bus station, Station Rd. (☎28802), opposite Hotel Vishwa. Reservation counters open daily 8am-noon and 3-6pm. To: **Badami** (1pm, 5hr., Rs60); **Bangalore** (frequent, 9hr., Rs107-139); **Bijapur** (5:30 and 8am, 5hr., Rs72); **Hassan** (7:30am, 10hr., Rs90); **Hyderabad** (6:45 and 9pm, 11hr., Rs134); **Mangalore** (7:30pm, 13hr., Rs150); **Mysore** (10am and 7:30pm, 8hr., Rs134). Deluxe **KSTDC** tourist buses to **Bangalore** (10pm, 7½hr., Rs160).

Local Transportation: Auto-rickshaws (Rs60-80 to Hampi) are unmetered. **Cycle-rickshaws** (Rs10 to the railway station) are easily found. **Local buses** go to **Hampi** from platform 10 (every 30min., 5:30am-7:30pm, 30min., Rs4). **Khizer Cycle Market,** Station Rd., Thaluk Office Complex, rents **bikes** (Rs3 per hr., Rs20 per day). Open daily 7:30am-7:30pm.

ORIENTATION AND PRACTICAL INFORMATION

Life in Hospet revolves around **Station Rd.** (occasionally called MG Rd.), which runs roughly north to south from the **railway station,** passing the **bus station,** and turning into **Main Bazaar Rd.** in Hospet's commercial area. Station Rd. bridges two canals in the process as well as the northeast-running **Hampi Rd.** and the **Tungabhadra Dam Rd.,** which runs west and skirts the market area.

Tourist Office: Karnataka Dept. of Tourism and **KSTDC,** whose commercial wing organizes tours, share an office (☎28537) at the corner of College and Old Bus Stand Rd. From the bus station, turn left onto Station Rd.; take your first left onto College Rd. and then your first left onto Old Bus Stand Rd. **Tours** of Hampi and the Tungabhadra Dam (9:30am, return 5:30pm; Rs75.) Dept. of Tourism open M-Sa 10am-5:30pm. Closed 2nd Sa. KSTDC open daily 7:30am-10pm.

Budget Travel: Monika Travels, Station Rd. (☎27446). Turn left from the bus station; it's on the left. Open daily 9:30am-9pm.

Currency Exchange: State Bank of India, Station Rd. (☎25478), a few steps north of Hotel Priyadarshini. Changes US$ and UK£ only. **State Bank of Mysore,** Station Rd., Thaluk Office Compound (☎24918), changes traveler's checks and US$ and UK£. Both open M-F 10:30am-2:30pm and 3-4pm.

Pharmacy: Several cluster around Hotel Priyadarshini.

Hospital: Government General Hospital (☎28444, emergency 28199). Head west on College Rd. and turn left immediately after the college. Cross the canal and continue ahead; the hospital is on the right. **Medinowa,** 35/G-1 ISR Rd. (☎55789), is a new private hospital.

Post Office, Station Rd. (☎28210), 400m south of the bus stand. Open M-Sa 8am-6pm. **Postal Code:** 583201.

ACCOMMODATIONS

Malligi Tourist Home, 6/143 JN Rd. (☎28101; email malligihome@hotmail.com), 250m south of the bus stand; turn left before the 2nd intersection. Regular rooms are good value; the luxury rooms are spectacular. New pool open Tu-Su 7am-7pm (Rs25 per hr. for non-deluxe room guests). 24hr. hot showers. Check-out 24hr. Singles Rs140-200; doubles Rs140-250; deluxe Rs550-2250. AmEx, MC, Visa.

Hotel Vishwa, Station Rd. (☎27171), opposite the bus stand, in a nook set back from the street. The single rooms with squat toilets are a good value (Rs80). The double rooms have seat toilets and balconies (Rs149).

Hotel Karthik, Sardar Patel Rd. (☎08394 or 24938). From the bus stand, turn left onto Station Rd.; take the first left onto College, then the next right. Spic 'n' span rooms in a new concrete block. Running hot water 5:30-11am and by request. Check-out 24hr. Singles Rs100-225; doubles Rs225-300.

Hotel Priyadarshini, V/45 Station Rd. (☎28838), 500m south of the railway station. 82 spacious rooms with phones, fans, room service, and same-day laundry. Each has a balcony, some with nice views. Hot water 6:30-10am. Two good attached restaurants. Check-out 24hr. Singles Rs140-205; doubles Rs195-250. A/C rooms Rs500-650.

Hotel Shalini, Station Rd. (☎28910), 300m south of the railway station. With flowering trees in front of its tiny pink facade, the place makes up in character (and cheapness) what it lacks in convenience or cleanliness. Squat toilets and bucket hot water 7-9am. Bring your own sheets. Check-out 24hr. Singles Rs60; doubles Rs90.

◖ FOOD

■ **Waves Restaurant,** in Malligi. This ultra-slick restaurant overlooking a swimming pool could just as easily be Bangalore's hippest hot-spot. Expect to pay Rs100 for a meal. Kashmiri *pulao* Rs50; chicken *tikka* Rs55; delicious pancakes with honey Rs30. Open daily 6:30am-11:30pm.

Manasa, in Hotel Priyadarshini, fulfills your cravings for home with shepherd's pie (Rs55), farmer's bake (Rs40) and fruit trifle (Rs20), but it also offers Indian and Chinese dishes (non-veg. Rs35-60; veg. Rs25-30), beer (Rs50-60), and spirits (Rs17-60). Open daily noon-3pm and 7-11pm.

Shanbhag Restaurant, Station Rd., next to the bus stand. This popular travelers' watering hole serves *idli* (Rs5.50) and *masala dosas* (Rs11) as well as delicious sweets like the special Mysore *pak* (Rs7.50) or fruit *burfi* (Rs3.50). Open daily 6am-11pm.

Naivedyam Restaurant, also in Hotel Priyadarshini, dishes out huge, fresh portions. North and South Indian *thalis* (Rs20) with choice of *chappati* or *puri*. *Aloo* and *palak* prepared a million different ways (Rs18-24). Open daily 11am-3pm and 7-10:30pm.

HAMPI ಹಂಪೆ   ☎08394

It is said that gold once rained down on Hampi. The city was awash in rubies and diamonds, and wealth dripped from its rooftops, flowing into its gutters and filling its sacred tanks. The Vijayanagar king would regularly distribute his weight in precious metals to the area's needy. But riches eventually led to ruin. Five dynasties ruled the kingdom and its resplendent capital from 1336, building all manner of temples, pavilions, aqueducts, and palaces, until a confederacy of Muslim sultans from the north annihilated the empire in 1565 and soaked up Vijayanagar's wealth, leaving the once thriving capital dry and desolate.

Today, Hampi is one of India's hottest hippie hang-outs. After the Christmas raves in Goa, the crew packs up and heads to the banks of the Tungabhadra River and, much to the chagrin of the town's residents, brings the acid parties with it. Hampi's season runs from October to March, peaking between December and February. More than a few expats have turned a week's stay into years, using the ruins for drug dens or eloping with locals and settling down on the other side of the river to avoid the police. Isolated from time and urbanity, Hampi is an alluring permanent oasis for travelers seeking to slow down; the chance you take by going to Hampi is that you might decide never to leave.

> ▌ **WARNING.** Muggings and rapes have been reported recently in the area near Vittala Temple, on Matanga Hill, and along the foot path leading from Vittala Temple to the Royal Center (Zenana Enclosure). **Foreigners are asked to register with the police at Hampi** when they arrive in town.

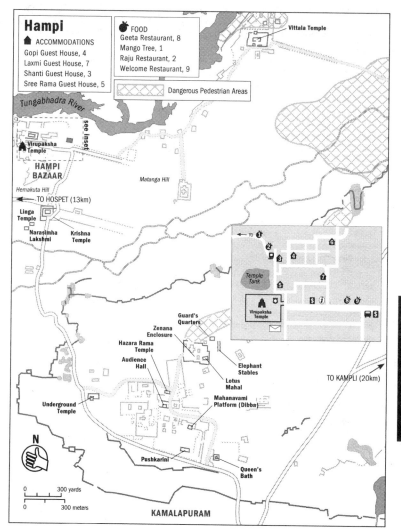

Hampi

🏠 ACCOMMODATIONS
Gopi Guest House, 4
Laxmi Guest House, 7
Shanti Guest House, 3
Sree Rama Guest House, 5

🍎 FOOD
Geeta Restaurant, 8
Mango Tree, 1
Raju Restaurant, 2
Welcome Restaurant, 9

Dangerous Pedestrian Areas

Vittala Temple

Tungabhadra River

Virupaksha Temple

HAMPI BAZAAR

Hemakuta Hill

Matanga Hill

see inset

TO HOSPET (13km)

Linga Temple

Narasimha Lakshmi

Krishna Temple

Temple Tank

Virupaksha Temple

Guard's Quarters

Zenana Enclosure

Hazara Rama Temple

Audience Hall

Underground Temple

Elephant Stables

Lotus Mahal

Mahanavami Platform (Dibba)

TO KAMPLI (20km)

N

0 — 300 yards
0 — 300 meters

Pushkarini

Queen's Bath

KAMALAPURAM

KARNATAKA

🚌 TRANSPORTATION AND PRACTICAL INFORMATION

The road from **Hospet** skirts banana plantations, coconut groves, sugarcane fields, and boulder formations before reaching **Hampi Bazaar.** The bazaar is actually a clump of guest houses, restaurants, and bauble shops clustered around the **Virupaksha Temple** and its 53m *gopuram*. The ruins of Vijayanagar spread across 26 sq. km and are concentrated into three distinct groups. The **Virupaksha Temple,** ruins of the **Krishna Temple,** and many other shrines directly above the bazaar on Hemakuta Hill make up the **Sacred Center.** The **Royal Center** includes the **Palace Area** and the **Zenana Enclosure,** 3km southeast of Hampi, along the paved road to Kamalapuram. About 2km to the northeast of the bazaar lies the other major area of ruins, including the **Vittala Temple.**

Local Transportation: Buses to Hospet depart from the intersection of Hampi Bazaar and the road to **Hospet** (every 30min., 6:15am-8:15pm, 30min., Rs4). **Auto-rickshaws** run between Hampi Bazaar and Kamalapuram (Rs5) and Hospet (Rs50). Prices double at night. Another way to get around is to rent a **bike** at Guru's Bicycle Shop, 25m behind the tourist office (Rs3-5 per hr., Rs25-30 per day). Open daily 6am-7pm.

Tourist Office (☎ 41339), 100m toward the Virupaksha Temple from the bus stop. Get a detailed map of the ruins or hire an approved **guide** (in-season Rs150-700; off-season Rs150-500). Government of India guides charge Rs500-600. Open M-Sa 10am-5:30pm. Closed 2nd Sa of the month.

Currency Exchange: Canara Bank (☎ 41243) exchanges only AmEx and Thomas Cook traveler's checks in US, British, and French currencies. Open M-Tu and Th-F 11am-2pm, Sa 11am-12:30pm. In season, various travel agencies exchange currency—try **Modi**, next to the tourist office.

Police: (☎ 41241), inside the Virupaksha Temple, immediately to your right. Registering here when you get in town takes 2min. Open 24hr. There's also a branch in Kamalapuram (☎ 41240), 4km southeast of the bus stand.

Hospital: The nearest medical services are in Hospet.

Telephones: The bazaar's **STD/ISD** booths are open 24hr. in-season.

Internet: There are several internet places along the main strip of Hampi's Bazaar. Try **Net-Cafe** (☎ 41465), next to Shanthi Guest House. Access, however, is expensive (Rs80 per hr.). Open 24hr. in-season.

Post Office: (☎ 41242), just outside the temple, beside the *gopuram*. Open M-Sa 9:30am-3:30pm. **Postal Code:** 583239.

ACCOMMODATIONS

To 15th-century traveler Domingo Paes, the Hampi Bazaar was "a broad and beautiful street, full of rows of fine houses and *mantapas*…[where] you will find all sorts of rubies, and diamonds, and emeralds, and pearls, and every other sort of thing there is on earth that you wish to buy." To many 20th-century tourists, however, Hampi Bazaar is more important for its cheap rooms, pancakes, spaghetti, and hash. Staying in the guest houses behind the bazaar, most of which are portions of homes, often requires a lack of concern for cleanliness, a fondness for squat toilets, and a tolerance for bugs, dogs, and frogs. The guest houses listed below are open all year; many others open only during the tourist season.

Shanthi Guest House (☎ 41568). From the bus stand, walk toward the Virupaksha Temple, turn right, and go around the Sree Rama Lodge. Enclosed garden, cheerful exterior, and clean common baths (cold showers) make it a wellspring of tourist camaraderie. As an added treat, the guest house takes orders for cakes (various banana cakes Rs25-30; apple pie Rs40), made by Island Bakery across the street. Check-out 10:30am. Singles Rs100; doubles Rs150. Mar.-Dec.: Rs50/70.

Gopi Guest House (☎ 41695). Clean rooms have flowered sheets, large windows, and pink mosquito nets. Friendly proprietor ensures a pleasant atmosphere. Rooftop restaurant with good views. All rooms with attached baths. Check-out 11am. Singles Rs100; doubles Rs150. Off-season: Rs60/80.

Laxmi Guest House (☎ 41287 or 41728), behind the tourist office. The mattresses are hard but the sheets are clean. Common trough baths. Bring your own padlock. Check-out noon. Internet access. Doubles Rs80. Mar.-Nov.: Rs50.

Vicky Guest House (☎ 41694), 200m behind the tourist office. Huge beds, fans, and attached baths. The rooms downstairs, super-modern for Hampi, are a great bargain. Restaurant operates in-season. Check-out 11am. Doubles Rs125. Mar.-Nov.: Rs80.

Sree Rama Tourist House (☎ 41219). The beds and rooms are decent enough. Fickle lighting. Attached musty bathrooms with squat toilets and showers. Check-out 24hr. Singles Rs60; doubles Rs100 year-round.

FOOD

Raju Rooftop Restaurant, near Shanthi Guest House. Falafal *chappati* (Rs30) and tomato pasta (Rs25) combined with the spiked punch of a sangria (Rs30) capture the delightful oddity of Hampi's restaurant menus. Open daily 7am-10pm.

Mango Tree, behind Virupaksha Temple. Follow the path around the temple past Shanthi Guest House. Just past a white temple building on the right, two stone monoliths mark the dirt path to the cafe. Set under a stand of mango trees amid a banana plantation, this restaurant serves the standard backpacker fare of pancakes (Rs20-25), *momos* (Rs35-40), and pasta (Rs25), but the riverside view is spectacular. Open daily 7am-10pm. Bring a flashlight if you plan on staying late.

Welcome Restaurant, Hampi Bazaar. Popular for its pasta (Rs30-40), pancakes (Rs20-25), hummus (Rs30), and falafal. Also offers the rare Indian *thali* (Rs25), rice pudding (Rs20), and espresso (Rs35). Open daily 7am-9:30pm. Off-season: 7:30am-9pm.

Gopi Rooftop Restaurant, above Gopi Guest House. Special *thalis* (Rs35), *dahl makhani* (Rs30), coconut (Rs30) cashew (Rs35) curry. Open daily 7am-10pm.

Geeta Restaurant, Hampi Bazaar. Everything here is "Recommended in Lonely Planet." Nevertheless, the "cornflesh and banana milk" (Rs25) and the lunch and dinner options (Rs25-40) are a treat, and are recommended by us, too. Open daily 7am-9:30pm.

Hotel Mayura Bhuvaneswari, Kamalapuram. Take the road toward Kampli. The only enclosed restaurant in the whole area, it has *thalis* (Rs25-37) and veg. (Rs18-32) and chicken (Rs40-48) curries all the time. Beer Rs55-60. Open daily 6:30am-10pm.

SIGHTS: VIJAYANAGAR RUINS

Though it won't enable you to see every sacred inch of the 26 sq. km of ruins, you can squeeze most of the major sights into one foot-sore, back-aching, thigh-throbbing day. Renting a bike in Hospet, Kamalapuram, or Hampi Bazaar will help you see everything except the Vittala Temple area to the northeast, where the path is too rocky to ride; you can lock your bike and leave it with the tourist office or approach Vittala from the southeast, along the tour bus route. There have been reports of robbers lurking along this road. **Avoid walking along the river or behind the Vittala Temple alone.** The path to the temple from Hampi Bazaar is considered safe.

THE SACRED CENTER. At the west end of Hampi Bazaar is the imposing **Virupaksha Temple,** once the king's personal temple. Inside is a marriage hall and an assembly hall. To the rear is a small room where an upside-down image of the *gopuram* is projected onto the wall. Walk back toward the *gopuram* and take a right before exiting. Hike up the stony hill past the **Jain Temples** on your right. There are beautiful views of Hampi from the top. The road below eventually leads to Kamalapuram and the ruins of the Royal Center, but before you see these, you will pass the **Krishna Temple** on your right. Make a right on the dirt path to reach the **Narasimha Lakshmi statue.** When Muslim sultans sacked the city, they sliced open Narasimha's belly to see if the 7m-high monolith had eaten any gems, but they found nothing. Although the Narasimha remains disfigured, he is one of Hampi's most striking figures. Around the back you can see the hand of his consort Lakshmi, who was probably depicted resting on Narasimha's thigh. The Arcaeological Survey of India is trying to restore Narasimha to his original wholeness. Beside the statue is the **Linga Temple,** which contains the second-largest *linga* in India.

THE ROYAL CENTER. From the main road, continue on to the Royal Center until you see a sign for the Lotus Mahal. On your right will be the **Underground Temple,** which fills up with rainwater and fish during the monsoon season. Follow the signs to the Lotus Mahal at the end of the road. Make a left, walking away from the Hazara Rama Temple (see below), past the pink Archaeological Camp House. Here you'll see the **Zenana Enclosure,** a stone wall where the ladies of the court used to live, protected from male ogling. *(Open daily 8am-6pm. Rs5; free F.)* To the right is the pink stucco **Lotus Mahal,** a fine example of Indo-Saracenic architecture. Opposite the Lotus Mahal are the **Guard's Quarters.**

KARNATAKA

To the east and through the stone walls are the 11 domed **Elephant Stables,** where more than 15,000 of the royal beasts slept, rested, and ate a whole lot of elephant food back in the 15th century. Backtrack to the sign pointing to the Mahanavami Dibba and take that road south; on your right will be the **Hazara Rama Temple,** or the Temple of One Thousand Ramas. The enclosure walls are carved with scenes from the *Ramayana* on the inside and with a parade of horses, elephants, dancing girls, and soldiers on the outside. Two rare images of Vishnu incarnated as the Buddha are inside the sanctum.

Continue on the road and just as the path veers east (to your left), you will see a large platform that was once the **Audience Hall.** The **Mahanavami Platform,** also on your right, is crossed by ancient aqueducts and now-dry stone canals. This platform, where the gala Dussehra Festival was held, is one of the tallest and most ornate around. The throne inside is covered with gold and gems. South of the platform is the recently excavated **Pushkarini,** a deep, sacred water tank with remarkably regular steps. On the left, just before the dirt road joins the main paved road to Kamalapuram, you will see the **Queen's Bath,** a giant stone enclosure surrounded by a moat. Inside is a huge pool where the queen used to kick back after a hard day. *(Open daily 8am-6pm. Rs5. Free F.)*

Kamalpuram is another 600m down the road. There, you will find an Arcaeological Survey of India museum, which contains all the things that ASI museums usually contain. *(Open Sa-Th 10am-5pm. Rs5.)*

VITTALA TEMPLE. Though Vittala seems small and unimpressive from the outside, the clutter of cold-drink dealers and tourist buses around the temple make it hard to miss. Construction of the temple, which was never finished or consecrated, was begun around 1513 by the Vijayanagar king Krishnadevaraya, and the work was halted when the city was destroyed in 1565. A competing bit of lore has it that Vittala, an incarnation of Vishnu, came to look at the temple, found it too grand for him, and hightailed it back to his humbler home in Maharashtra. Indeed, the carvings here are certainly the most ornate of any around the ruins. Each of the 56 musical pillars inside the temple sounds a different note when tapped, but the security guards glare sternly at tourists who try to play a tune. Outside the temple is the massive stone chariot of Vishnu's mythical bird Garuda. *(From Kamalapuram, ride the paved road 5km north to the Vittala Temple, or backtrack to the Hampi Bazaar and walk 2km along the river to the temple. It is unsafe to travel on the road from Kamapalpuram to Vittala Temple alone at night.)*

▶ DAYTRIP FROM HAMPI: ANEGUNDI

The ancient cave temples at Anegundi are seldom visited by tourists. The Archaeological Survey of India isn't in charge here, and getting to the caves is an adventure in itself. Because there are no signs, it is best to solicit the assistance of a certified **guide** at Hampi's tourist office (see p. 486).

From the Vittala Temple, continue on the main paved road along the Tungabhadra River. Eventually the road deteriorates into a path leading to the river bank, where two boats shuttle people, bicycles, and (more perilously) motorcycles to and from Anegundi. Once you reach the other side, walk straight up a small slope and you'll see the village. A left turn at the first opportunity and then a left at the next fork will lead you past the Andhra Bank and under a small gate. After the gate, turn left onto the paved road that cuts through the rice paddies. A dirt path veers off to the left; take it and you'll be at the base of a rocky hill. Midway up the hill is a **Durga Temple,** supposed to be the site where Rama killed the monkey king Vali. The temple is especially favored by soldiers who perform *puja* here to gain strength. A *bidi*-smoking *swami* offering *chai* and other treats will point you past his shrine and up the hill to the **Lakshmi Temple.** Here, Sita prayed for Rama's forgiveness after she had been banished, demonstrating her devotion to her doubting husband as well as the purity of her mind, body, and soul. The nearby **Pampasarovara Pond** is believed to be the site where Parvati prayed for a husband—the reward for her efforts was Shiva himself. A small 7th-century temple marks **Hanuman Hill,** the monkey-god's birthplace.

BADAMI ಬಾದಮಿ
☎08357

Badami, a jumping little town in the middle of nowhere, was the capital of the mighty Chalukyan Empire from 543 to 757. The town's ancient cave temples are high in the mountains and surround an ancient Chalukyan tank. Badami is also the town closest to Pattadakal, 20km away, where Chalukyan kings were crowned, and Aihole, 44km away on the Malaprabha River, the first Chalukyan capital. Together, these three towns are a fascinating study in the development of Indian temple architecture. Aihole is considered the birthplace of the now-dominant style—its structures were built up rather than carved out, as older cave temples were. The cave temples of Badami and the later temples at Pattadakal illustrate the evolution of an increasingly sophisticated style. Though less impressive than what you'll find in Belur, Halebid, and Somnathpur, the Chalukyan temples served as a template for styles which later emerged throughout the country.

▤ GETTING THERE ANDGETTING AWAY

Buses run from Hampi to: **Aihole** (8 per day, 7am-12:30pm, 2hr., Rs10) via **Pattadakal; Bagalkot** (frequent, 6am-8:45pm, 2hr., Rs12); **Bangalore** (8 per day, 5am-8:30pm, Rs165); **Bijapur** (12 per day, 7am-6:45pm, 4hr., Rs43); **Gadag** (12 per day, 5:30am-10:45pm, 4hr., Rs25) for connections to **Hospet** and **Bangalore; Pattadakal** (7 per day, 8:35am-6:30pm, 45min., Rs6.50); and **Solapur** (6 per day, 6am-8pm, 7hr., Rs90) for train connections to **Bombay. There is a super-deluxe bus** service to **Bangalore** (9:30pm, 9hr., Rs193); book through Hotel Mookambika Deluxe (☎20067). Private **maxicabs** are another way to reach Pattadakal (Rs5-8). **Trains** run north to **Bijapur** and **Solapur** for connections to Bombay and south to **Gadag** for connections to Hospet and Bangalore.

✴❓ ORIENTATION AND PREACTICAL INFORMATION

Badami's main road, **Station Rd.,** is probably the only straight path in the entire village. From the **railway station** in the north, it runs 5km south to the **bus stand** and eventually to the routes to Pattadakal and Aihole. **College (Ramdurg) Rd.** runs west from Station Rd., south of the bus stand, and winds around to the KSTDC hotel and **Tourist Information Center** 1km later. (☎20414. Open M-Sa 10am-5:30pm; closed second Sa.) The private **hospital,** Karudagmath Nursing Home (☎20191), is north from the bus stand, along Station Rd., toward the railway station. Several **pharmacies** line Station Rd. between the bus stand and GPO. The **police station** (☎20133) is opposite the bus stand. The **GPO** (open M-Sa 7-11am and 2-5pm) and the **Telegraph Office** (☎65030) are just south of the bus stand. **Postal Code:** 587201.

▥ ACCOMMODATIONS AND FOOD

Compared to Aihole and Pattadakal, Badami has plenty of places to stay, most of which are near the bus stand. **Hotel Mookambika Deluxe** is the cheeriest and cleanest in the area. Windows look out upon the Chalukyan hills, and an in-house travel agency will help get you there. (☎20067. Singles Rs200-600; doubles Rs250-750.) The attached restaurant serves food made-to-order. Cheaper options include **Hotel Anand,** opposite Hotel Mookambika (☎20074; singles Rs50-70; doubles Rs120-150), and the somewhat brighter **Hotel Satkar,** across the street. (☎20417. Singles with bath Rs70; doubles Rs100.) If *paise*-pinching is not your top priority, you might want to consider the **Hotel Mayura Chalukya,** College Rd. Turn right from the bus stand, walk 500m, and turn right onto the first wide paved road; the hotel is 1km down on the right, next to the PWD Inspection Bungalow. The huge, relatively clean rooms look out on overgrown gardens. Seat and squat toilets are available. 24hr. hot water. The attached restaurant serves all the usual mediocrities. (☎20046. Check-out noon. Singles Rs168; doubles Rs200.) For cheaper food, try the no-nonsense, no-chairs **Geeta Darshini,** just north of the bus stand, where nothing on the menu costs more than Rs7 (open M-Sa 6:30am-9pm). Next door, the **Hotel Parimal** serves cheap *dosas* and omelettes. (Open M-Sa 6:30am-9pm.)

KARNATAKA

◉ SIGHTS

The **South Fort Cave Temples,** carved out of the red sandstone and connected by steps, are some of the most important cave temples in India. The first three temples are Hindu, though both Jain and Buddhist influence is also apparent. **Cave 1,** the oldest of the bunch, is dedicated to Shiva in his different guises. On the right front wall is an 18-armed dancing Shiva. There is a *linga* protected by granite cobras in the back of the cave. **Cave 2** is dedicated to Vishnu, as is **Cave 3,** the largest and best-sculpted of the group, dating from 578. The facade of Cave 3 is carved with figures of humans, gods, and dwarves, as are the pillars and the steps leading to the foundation. In one scene, Vishnu is depicted as Narayan, reclining on the serpent Sesa's lap at the dawn of creation. Though the caves were once painted, the only traces of color that remain are on the ceiling of Cave 3. The path up to Cave 3 leads past a natural cave once used as a Buddhist temple; the Buddha image has since been defaced. **Cave 4,** probably the only cave here ever used as a Jain temple, overlooks the lake. The pillars appear to be held up by an assortment of creatures, including one that bears a startling resemblance to Yoda from Star Wars. *(From the bus stand, head right on Station Rd., past College Rd.; facing the Dr. Ambedkar statue, turn left and follow that road to the end. Temples open daily 6am-6pm. Rs2; F Free. Guides Rs175 for a 2-3hr. tour; Rs350 for a full day.)*

Across the lake from the cave temples are several other *mandirs.* The **Upper Shivalaya Temple** is one of the oldest of the group at Badami, and its carvings depict scenes from the life of Krishna. The most spectacular of the temples is the **Malegetti Shivalaya,** with its pillared hallway, flanked on one side by Shiva and Vishnu on the other. The temple is on top of the hill and has spectacular views of the village and the fields below. In town, by the 6th-century **Agastyatirtha Tank,** is the **Jambulinga Temple,** which was built by the Vijayanagars in 699. The peaceful **Bhutanatha Temples** are on the opposite side of the tank. To reach the temples and the **Archaeological Museum,** head right from the bus stand and follow a sign. This will lead you along narrow stone paths through a tiny neighborhood. You can also take the path from the South Fort cave temples along the tank; signs point the way. *(Museum open Sa-Th 10am-5pm. Rs2.)*

▣ DAYTRIPS FROM BADAMI

PATTADAKAL

Since there is nowhere to stay here, you will have to daytrip from Badami or Aihole. Buses (every 45min. 6am-7pm, Rs7) and private maxicabs (Rs5-8) make the 45-minute trip to Badami. Buses also go to Aihole (4 per day, 10am-1pm, 1hr., Rs6).

Pattadakal, between Badami and Aihole, was the Chalukyan capital during the 7th and 8th centuries. Its temples, the most stylistically advanced in the region, are clustered at the base of a pink sandstone hill. Pattadakal's only active temple, the **Virupaksha (Lokeshvara) Temple,** has a three-story spire with a stone Nandi sitting in front of it. Passages lead around the shrine past carvings that depict episodes from the *Ramayana* (see p. 579) and *Mahabharata* (see p. 79), as well as scenes of Chalukyan martial triumphs. Other prominent temples in the compound include the **Mallikarjuna Temple** and the **Papanatha Temple.** The **Jain Temple,** 1km south of the compound, has an upper-story sanctuary accessible by a staircase and guarded by a crocodile-carved gate. *(Temple compound open daily 6am-6pm. Rs5. Guides Rs50.)*

AIHOLE ಐಹೊಳ

Buses run between Aihole and Badami (5 per day, 7:15am-4pm, 2hr., Rs10-11), most via Pattadakal.

Aihole, 44km northeast of Badami on the banks of the Malaprabha River, is full of spectacular temples. The litter of beautiful, half-finished temples here was once the playground of a civilization determined to build the greatest architecture around. Aihole's 100 temples combine elements of both Dravidian and northern Nagar styles—there are *gopurams* of both kinds. The temples' square pillars and flat roofs, gently sloping downward on the periphery, reflect a distinctly Chalukyan element.

The most impressive temple within the main compound is the **Durga Temple**, dedicated to Vishnu and named because it sits next to a fort, or *durga*. The temple's Islamic-style windows are similar to the later latticework found in Fatehpur Sikri and Ahmedabad, while the circular apse is evocative of Buddhist *chaitya* halls. *(Open daily 6am-6pm. Rs2. Free on F.)* The Jain **Meguti Temple** has a stone inscription in Old Kannada script that has been dated to 634 AD, making it one of the oldest dated temples in India. A relatively unadorned Buddhist temple is just below. Farther south in the main compound, the **Ladh Khan Temple** is named after a 19th-century Muslim who set up house in the sanctuary. This temple was once thought to date from the 5th century, which would have made it one of the oldest in India; now it is believed to have been built between the late 6th and the early 8th centuries. The compound also has a less than inspiring two-room **Archaeological Museum**, but if you're waiting for the next bus out, you might as well have a look. (Open Sa-Th 10am-5pm. Rs2.) Outside the compound and off the main road, but still within walking distance, is **Ravan Phadi**, a precursor to the more sophisticated cave temples of Badami.

The **KSTDC Tourist Home** (☎ (03851) 34541) is the only place for non-locals to lay their weary heads. The manager is gracious, the food is cooked to order (*thalis* Rs20-25), and there are no postcard touts hanging around. Standard, clean rooms cost half of what they would in Badami. (Singles Rs35; doubles Rs60.)

BIJAPUR ☎ 08352

With its multitude of mausoleums, minarets, and museums, Bijapur has some of India's most remarkable Muslim architecture, most of which dates from the 15th to 17th centuries. Ruled from 1482 by the Adil Shahi kings, Bijapur was the capital of one of five splinter states that later reunited to sack Hampi. Unlike the Vijayanagar kings, who decorated Hampi with opulent rubies and gold, the Adil Shahis preferred to surround themselves with fortifications and austere monuments. Today, only the Golgumbaz receives much attention, but the other ruins are also worth visiting, especially for those seeking a bit of peace and quiet.

▐▆ GETTING THERE AND GETTING AROUND

Trains: The **railway station** serves **Gadag** (5 per day, 4:15am-6:25pm, 3hr., Rs53) via **Badami** (2hr., Rs37) on slow meter-gauge lines for connections to **Bangalore** and **Solapur** (3:30, 9:45am, and 4:35pm; 3hr.; Rs34).

Buses: The KSRTC **bus stand** is in the center of town, at the intersection of Bagalkot and Bus Stand Rd., just west of the citadel. Reservations can be made 3 days in advance at the computerized reservation counter. (Open daily 7am-1:30pm and 2-8pm). To: **Aurangabad** (6, 6:30am, and 9:15pm; 14hr.; Rs170); **Badami** (5:30, 10am, and 5pm; 4hr.; Rs43-47); **Bangalore** (9 per day, mostly evening departures, 12hr., Rs180); **Bombay** (10 per day, 8am-10pm, 12hr., Rs198) via **Pune**; **Gadag** (6:30, 10am, and 2:30pm; 5½hr.; Rs80); **Hospet** (5 per day, 5:30am-4pm, 5hr., Rs72); **Hyderabad** (5 per day, 6am-9:30pm, 11½hr., Rs172); **Mangalore** (2pm, 12hr., Rs190); **Mysore** (5pm, 15hr., Rs211); **Solapur** (every 30min., 3hr., Rs40). **VRL Vijayanand Travels,** Padmashri Complex, Bagalkot Cross Rd. (☎35220), runs luxury buses with reclining seats that are well worth the extra expenditure. To: **Bombay** (8pm, Rs230); **Bangalore** (every 30min., 7:30-9:30pm, Rs200-220); **Mangalore** (5pm, Rs230).

Local transportation: Bijapur's light traffic and simple layout make **biking** an ideal way to get around. Bicycles can be rented to the left of the bus stand, opposite Golgumbaz, and at Gandhi Chowk (Rs2 per hr.). Unmetered **auto-rickshaws** are readily available (Rs20-25 for a hop across town). Horse-drawn **tongas** are more scarce and more expensive. A local **bus** (Rs2) runs along Station Rd. from the train station to the western walls on the other side of town.

✈ 🔁 ORIENTATION AND PRACTICAL INFORMATION

The Adil Shahis built 10km of massive fortified walls around their capital, but modern Bijapur is fairly compact and easily navigated. **Station Rd.** (also known as MG Rd.) runs the length of the town, connecting the railway station and the **Golgumbaz** mausoleum, along the eastern ramparts, to the **Ibrahim Rauza,** 6km away, beyond the western wall. **Jama Masjid Rd.** runs parallel to and south of Station Rd. Between Station Rd. and Jama Masjid Rd., the **citadel** once served as the royal enclave of the sultans. Here Jama Masjid Rd. connects to **Bagalkot Rd.,** which leads 500m farther west to the bus stand. From the bus stand, roads run north to **Gandhi Chowk,** the market center, and the GPO on Station Rd.

Tourist Office: KSTDC, Station Rd. (☎50359), behind the KSTDC Mayura Adil Shahi Annex. Open M-Sa 10am-5:30pm; closed 2nd Sa.

Currency Exchange: Canara Bank, Azad Rd. It's a 400m walk up the left-most of the three streets radiating north from Gandhi Circle. Only accepts traveler's checks in US$ and UK£. Open M-F 10:30am-2:30pm, Sa 10:30am-12:30pm. **Girikand Tours and Travels,** 1st fl., Nishant Plaza, Ram Mandir Rd. ☎35510), opposite the Union Bank of India, changes 32 currencies and traveler's checks. Rs25 fee.

Market: Gandhi Chowk, MG Rd., west of the citadel. Some shops close W, others F.

Police: Gandhi Chowk Police Station (☎50033), on the southern side of MG Rd., opposite Shastri Market.

Pharmacy: Pharmacies are all along Station Rd. Most close by 9pm.

Hospital: The government **City Hospital,** Hospital Rd. (☎50709), is 2km west outside of town, beyond Atke Gate.

Internet: Cyber Park, opposite the GPO on MG Rd., is in a cloth shop, but the connection is reasonably fast. Rs50 per hr. Open daily 9:30am-11pm.

Post Office: GPO, MG Rd. (☎50224), 50m west of the citadel. Open M-Sa 8am-6pm. Postal Code: 586101.

🔁 🖸 ACCOMMODATIONS AND FOOD

Most hotels are along Station Rd. between the Golgumbaz and Gandhi Chowk. Standards tend toward the shabby side; insist on seeing rooms before booking. Dining options are not much better, with most restaurants restricted to the hotels. Unless otherwise noted, hotels have 24-hour check-out.

Hotel Sagar Deluxe, Barakaman Rd. (☎59234), near the Shivaji statue at the intersection of Station Rd. and Bus Stand Rd. Clean sheets, soft pillows, and a central location make this the best option in town. Seat toilets; hot showers in the morning. Singles Rs125-175; doubles Rs150-200.

Hotel Blue Diamond, Bus Stand Rd. (☎52941), in an alley behind Bharat Petroleum, near Laxmi Talkies Rd. New budget alternative with small rooms and minimal amenities, but very clean. Squat toilets and bucket baths. Singles Rs80-125; doubles Rs125-170.

Hotel Samrat, Station Rd. (☎51620), halfway between the Golgumbaz and stadium. Huge attached baths with squat toilets and showers. Singles Rs120; doubles Rs150. The **restaurant** is popular with local families. Eat *thalis* (Rs17-40) or choose from 12 kinds of *dosas* (Rs6-15) under a painting of Ganesh, whose belly looks strikingly like someone's buttocks. Most dishes Rs20-45.

Hotel Madhuvan (☎55571), Station Rd., down a side street 150m east of Hotel Samrat; look for the signs. The rooms are exorbitantly priced, but the **restaurant** is the best in town. The wide-ranging vegetarian menu includes all the standards. *Thalis* Rs20-50; North Indian and Chinese dishes Rs25-45. Open daily 8am-11pm; *thalis* 11am-4pm.

🔆 SIGHTS

Robust souls with resilient soles see all the sights by foot in one strenuous day, but renting a bicycle is probably the best method for getting between the monuments.

GOLGUMBAZ. As you approach it from Station Rd., the mausoleum is an awesome sight. Towering over the city's eastern fortifications, the cubic structure is reinforced by four octagonal minarets and crowned by an enormous dome, 38m across, supposed to be the second largest in the world—after St. Peter's in the Vatican. Built in 1659, the hall contains the gravestones of Mohammed Adil Shah, several of his family members, and his favorite court dancer and mistress, Rambha. Seven stories above the hall, at the base of the dome, is the famous Whispering Gallery, where sounds are said to echo over ten times. If too many noisy visitors are testing the acoustics, step outside for some stunning views of Bijapur and the Deccan plains. Also on the grounds is an Archaeological Museum—one of the country's finest—featuring Jain *tirthankaras*, ancient stone inscriptions, 17th-century copies of the Koran, and Chinese porcelain collected by the Adil Shahis. *(Open daily 6am-6pm. Rs2, F free; video cameras Rs25. Museum open Sa-Th 10am-5pm. Rs2.)*

IBRAHIM RAUZA. Built by Ibrahim Adil Shah II, this graceful mausoleum is the last resting place of the sultan himself, his queen, Taj Sultana, his mother, and three of his children. On the other side of a small reservoir and fountains, an equally elegant mosque lends balance to the walled compound. Together the two structures are one of the finest examples of Islamic architecture in India. The walls are covered with fine stone latticework made up of elaborate inscriptions from the Koran. Local belief holds that the minarets here inspired the Taj Mahal. *(1km beyond the western walls, 500m south of Station Rd. Open daily 6am-6pm. Rs2, F free.)*

JAMA MASJID. One of the finest mosques in India, the Jama Masjid was built by Ali Adil Shah I to commemorate his victory over the Vijayanagars in 1565. The massive prayer hall is covered with more than 2000 rectangular spaces for individual prayer mats. The Mughal emperor Aurangzeb added these, apparently to atone for hauling away the velvet carpet and other valuables that originally covered the hall. Today, only the prayer niche remains adorned with gold leaf and elegant inscriptions. *(Directly opposite the Golgumbaz, Shanmukharudh Mahadwar Rd. leads under a large arch 500m to Jama Masjid Rd. Turn right (west) toward the town center, the Jama Masjid is another 500m down on the left.)*

OTHER SIGHTS. Another 500m west on Jama Masjid Rd., the ornate **Mithari Mahal** serves as a gateway to a small mosque. Today it is not much more than a beautiful facade. **Asar Mahal** can be reached by taking the wide dirt road opposite the Mithari Mahal to the end and turning left. Dating from 1646, it served as a Hall of Justice and later housed hairs from the Prophet's beard. The **citadel** is just to the west. Most of the buildings have collapsed, but the ruins of **Gagan Mahal** and **Sat Manzil,** the sultan's durbar hall and pleasure quarters respectively, still stand.

Along the western walls 1½km west of the citadel is a gigantic cannon, aptly named **Malik-I-Maidan,** or "Lord of the Plains." The cannon was cast around 1550. It took ten elephants, 400 oxen, and hundreds of men to haul it up to its emplacement on top of the ramparts. Visible just behind Malik-I-Maidan to the northeast, **Upli Burji** features more cannons and views of the city and plains.

GOKARNA ಗೋಕರ್ಣ ☎ 08386

Gokarna and its two separate personalities will play games with your mind. On the one hand Gokarna is a small, vibrant, South Indian village, where people bustle through streets lined with vendors selling kitchenware, bangles, and bright skirts (and not a mirrored halter top in sight). A Shiva temple welcomes pilgrims and worshipers to one of the most holy spots in India. And then there are the beaches. Hippies drift south from Goa searching for the unspoilt beach, and here's where they strike gold. A string of beaches lines the coast south of town and—if there is no party going on—the isolated coves define tranquility. A few hipsters snooze in hammocks while *chai* shops provide them with the bare necessities. Gokarna's independent town life is a breath of fresh air after the tourist resorts in Goa and Kerala, and sun-worshipers will be pleased with the sand and surf.

📧 **GETTING THERE AND GETTING AROUND. Trains** run from Gokarna station, 10km out of town, north to **Goa** (11:30am, 2hr., Rs30) and south to **Mangalore** (4pm, 4hr., Rs46). For other destinations, take a bus to **Kumta** (every hr., 1hr., Rs12). **Buses** run to: **Bangalore** (7:30pm, 12hr., Rs185); **Hospet** (12hr., Rs102); **Margao** (8:15am, 4hr., Rs45); **Mangalore** (6:45am, 12hr., Rs158); and **Panjim** (8:15am, 4hr., Rs60) via **Hampi** (7am and 2:45pm, 10hr., Rs100). **Vaibhav Nivas** (see below) can help book train and private bus tickets. **Minibuses** shuttle bags and bodies from the train station to town (Rs25). Local buses depart from in front of the bus station parking lot and head to the railway crossing, 1km from the station (15min., Rs20).

🔁 **ORIENTATION AND PRACTICAL INFORMATION.** Gokarna's main road runs north-south from in front of the **bus station** parking lot and intersects with **Car St.** Another road runs behind (west of) the bus station and also intersects Car St. Car St. runs past the **Mahabaleshwara Temple** and west to the **town beach.** South of the temple is a path leading to Gokarna's **beaches: Kudle, Om, Half-Moon,** and **Paradise.**

It's best to **change money** before arriving, but **Om Lodging Bar,** on the road west of the bus station, has tolerable rates. (Open daily 9am-noon and 5:30-11pm.) **Hegde Medical Stores,** along the north-south stretch of Main St., can fulfill your pharmaceutical needs. (☎56394. Open daily 8:30am-2pm and 4-9:30pm.) The **police station** (☎56133) is up a hill on a road heading east off Main St. **STD/ISD phone** booths are along the main roads; a storefront, **C-TECH,** along the way to the post office promises to bring **email** soon, but at the time of writing the town is a rare internet-free zone. The main **post office** is a 5-minute walk north from the bus station along Main St.; a second branch is above a vegetable store where Main and Car St. meet. (Both open M-Sa 9am-5pm.) **Postal code:** 581326.

📷 **ACCOMMODATIONS AND FOOD.** Although there are several places to stay in town, most people prefer to flop down in huts on the beach. In town, the friendly **☒Viabhav Nivas** has some small but clean rooms. It's just east off the north-south Main St., north of the bus station; take a left out of the front of the bus station, and you'll see signs. (☎56714. Singles Rs50; doubles Rs100-125. Off-season: Rs30-40/75-100.) More snazzy accommodation is available at the **Hotel Gokarna International,** north of the bus station, along Main St. Gloriously clean rooms have balconies and hot water; for a few extra rupees you can even have a bathtub and a TV. (☎56622. Check-out 4pm. Singles Rs150; doubles Rs200-300.) If you are staying for a while it makes sense to settle down in a **beach hut.** Lone travelers may want to stay in town a night and check out how many people are on the beach before committing to a deserted strip of sand. Accommodations on Kudle Beach run the gamut—an unmarked **chai shop** just north of the German Bakery has huts in a lovely garden (Rs60). On Om Beach, people string up hammocks (Rs150 along the main road in Gokarna) or rent thatched huts (Rs30) from a row of identical *chai* huts; Om Beach is by far the hippest address. The **Sea Shore Chai Shop** on Paradise Beach has huts from Rs25. Bring a floor mat—you'll be sleeping on a sand or clay floor. Vaibhav Nivas will store your luggage if you don't want to haul it with you down to the beach.

On all the beaches, *chai* huts turn out snacks (Rs10-25) and the usual range of *thalis* (Rs30), eggs, and sandwiches, often overpriced. In town, **Viabhav Nivas** does nice breakfasts (Rs8-30) and snacks, including a great *chappati* with cheese, onion, and tomato for Rs20. (Open 8am-9:30pm.) The **Downtown Bar and Restaurant,** in the Hotel Gokarna International, has excellent food (Rs40-65) and cheap beer (Rs45) but very slow service. (Open 9am-4pm and 5pm-1am.)

☷☾ SIGHTS AND BEACHES. Gokarna is packed with temples. The main east-west road, Car St., leads to the **Mahabeleshwara Temple,** which houses a venerated Shiva *linga*. Two massive chariots sit outside and get dragged through Gokarna's streets for Shiva's birthday (Shivaratri) in late February or early March. Foreigners are not allowed inside, but they can wander to the massive bathing **tank** and watch the washing. *(From the temple, take a left at the sign for the Shankarling Arts Studio and follow the narrow path as it turns inland or from Main St. Don't turn west on Car St.—continue south.)*

The road to the temple continues straight to the **town beach,** which isn't really anything to put your clogs on and do a dance about. The first beach worth taking your clothes off for is **Kudle Beach** to the south. From the temple, take the path west of the lane that leads to the bathing tank; it quickly climbs uphill to a rocky, barren landscape and follows a string of telephone poles before heading to the sand. When the road forks, bear right and cut left through a *chai* shop to the beach (25min.). From the wide Kudle beach it's another 20-minute walk to the more picturesque **Om Beach,** made up of two narrow, semi-circular beaches lined with trees and *chai* shops. You can also take a rickshaw to Om, as a paved road connects it to Kudle. Behind the last *chai* shop a narrow path leads up along the ridge of the black cliffs to **Half-Moon Beach** (20min.), where there is a restaurant and not much else. If you are scared of heights turn back now. Beyond the tiny cove, a rocky scramble (15min.) brings you to **Paradise Beach.** The views along the paths are stunning, and long strips of white beach stretch south as far as the eye can see.

As the authorities toughen up in Goa some of the party scene is migrating south to Gokarna. Keep your ears open; most take place on Om Beach and, in true party fashion, the international drugged-out hippie set grooves to pounding techno and trance all the live-long night while *chai* vendors serve up overpriced tea, coffee, and bottled water. If there is no party, nightlife is restricted to guitar strumming around a jingle-jangle bonfire. Things could be worse.

NEAR GOKARNA: JOG FALLS

Jog Falls are the highest waterfalls in India; the Sharavathi River falls in four separate cascades known as the Rani, Raja, Roarer, and Rocket, the tallest of which plummets 253 meters. The Sharavthi Dam limits the amount of water that can be released, but more water is let through to please daytrippers on the weekends. The falls are at their most dramatic after the rainy season. Pleasant (if indistinct) trails twist throughout the area. There are several places to stay in Jog Falls, including the comfortable government-run **Hotel Mayura.** (☎ (08186) 44732. Doubles Rs300.)

From Gokarna, take a bus to Talguppa (7 and 10:45am, 4hr., Rs31.50) and then pick up one of the frequent buses to Jog Falls. There are also frequent buses from Gokarna to Kumta (1hr., Rs10), where buses go onward to Jog Falls (4hr., Rs31). Connections can also be made through the town of Honavar. A direct bus runs from Udipi to Jog Falls (2pm, 5hr., Rs52).

UDIPI   ☎08252

Unless you have a thing for Krishna temples, there is no real reason to visit Udipi. The small, busy city's only claim to fame is the revered **Sri Krishna Temple.** The temple itself isn't particularly stunning, but the giant chariots and the constant hubbub—drumming, chanting, and general carrying-on—in the surrounding **Car St.** is definitely worth a look if you are forced to make a stopover here.

⊏ GETTING THERE AND GETTING AROUND. There are three **bus stands** in Udipi. To the northeast end of KM Marg is the local bus stand; to the southeast, behind the State Bank of India, a bus stand sends vehicles to Jog Falls. Most private and public buses go from the central bus stand at the end of KM Marg. **Government buses** run to: **Gokarna** (2:45pm, 4hr., Rs61); **Mangalore** (5 per day, 1hr., Rs18); and **Mysore** (7 per day, 8hr., Rs130-188). **Private companies** send buses to these destinations and more, including **Mangalore** (every 15min., 1½hr., Rs19). Bus companies and travel agencies cluster between the three bus stands. The **train station** is

KARNATAKA

due east of the town center. If you are a glutton for punishment, head east from the north end of KM Marg and hike 30 minutes; a sign on your right points the way to the station, 1km south of the main road. Local buses run to the junction (Rs3). Incoming trains are met by buses (Rs3) and taxis (Rs75) who will compete for the pleasure of driving you into town. **Trains** head from the station to: **Gokarna** (8:30am, 2hr., 2nd class Rs32); **Margao** (4 per day, 8:30-12:20am, 4hr., Rs128); and **Mangalore** (6am and 7pm, 1½hr., Rs47).

■■ **ORIENTATION AND PRACTICAL INFORMATION.** Udipi is slightly inland, just east of NH-17. The city's main road, **KM Marg** (occasionally called Church St.), runs south from the three bus stands. From the main stand, the second left at the Hotel Triveni will put you on **Kanakadas Rd.,** which leads down to the temple complex. The **Sri Krishna Mutt Enquiry counter** provides a **map** of the town; ask for the Udipi District Information booklet. On Kanakadas Rd., the **Canara Bank** will change cash and traveler's checks. (Open M-F 9:30am-1:30pm, Sa 9:30-11:30am.) Also on Kanakdas Rd., **Navayuga Press** caters to fans of Danielle Steele and Jane Austen alike. (Open M-Sa 9am-8pm.) On KM Marg, **Medical Emporium** can provide the goods to cure what ails you. (☎20401. Open daily 8:30am-9:30pm.) A **police outpost** is by the temple on Car St. Check **email** at **Cyberdhama,** behind the Alankar Theater, on KM Marg. (☎73969. Open M-Sa 9:30am-2pm and 4-9pm, Su 10am-4:30pm. Rs60 per hr.). The head **post office** is on Kanakadas Rd., east of KM Marg. **Postal code:** 576101.

■■ **ACCOMMODATIONS AND FOOD.** Udipi's accommodations cater to business travelers, so you get a lot of bang for your buck. **Hotel Vyavahar Lodge,** on Kanakadas Rd., right by the temple, is great value, with large rooms with bath and almost-hot water. A resident astrologer on the second floor offers guidance of all kinds. (☎2256. Check-out 24hr. Singles Rs85; doubles Rs150.) **Kalpana Residency** is a litle more swish; take KM Marg to its southern end and bear left. (☎20440. Check-out 24hr. Singles Rs90-140; doubles Rs195.) You'll be hard-pressed to find a banana pancake in Udipi—revel in authenticity and do a lot of pointing. **Sudheshna,** in the Hotel Swadesh Heritage, on MV Rd., just south of Kanakadas Rd., does mean veggie delights. (Veg. dishes Rs18-30; rice dishes Rs15-35. Open daily 7am-10:30pm; snacks only 3-7pm.) Right by the temple and all the action on Car St., **Davarika** does elaborate ice cream drinks, South Indian snacks, and sandwiches for Rs10-20. (Open daily 9:30am-10pm.)

■ **SIGHTS.** If you end up staying in Udipi, head to **Malpe,** which has a fairly clean beach and a thriving fishing industry that provides Karnataka with most of its seafood. **Buses** leave the Udipi local bus stand frequently for Malpe (15min., Rs3.50). From Malpe, you can take a boat to the picturesque **St. Mary's Island.** This uninhabited island is reputed to be where Vasco da Gama landed before hitting Calicut. **Anushka,** at the southern end of the beach in Malpe, sends **boats** to the island but waits until 30 people arrive before setting sail; if you show up on the weekend, you won't have to wait as long for a full boat. (☎22844. 30min. Rs30, advance booking of entire boat Rs900. No service during monsoon season.)

KERALA കേരളം

The locals call it "God's own country," and there is no denying that Kerala is a pretty spectacular part of the world. Lined with palm trees and golden beaches, the state's famous backwaters are quite stunning. Forty lazy rivers run through canals and rice paddies from the Western Ghats down to the sea, channeling their way through tiny fishing villages and islands of palm groves. Beautiful beaches have made the state second only to Goa as a coconut-oil haven for sun-worshipers and beach bums from around the world. Renowned for its unique *kathakali* dance and its age-old ayurvedic medicine, as well as for its beautiful scenery, Kerala deserves to be even more popular with tourists than it already is.

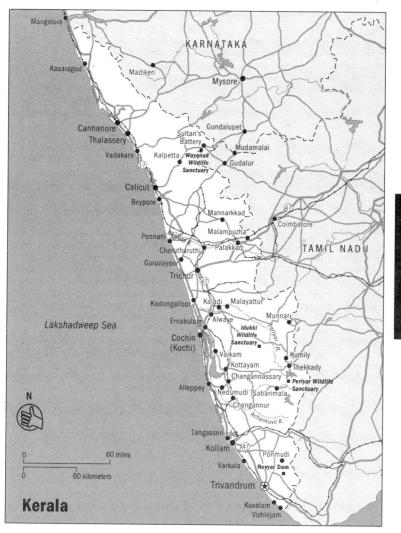

Kerala

But Kerala's history stretches back to long before the first tourists ever hungered after banana pancakes. Legend tells that when Parashoram, an incarnation of Vishnu, threw his axe into the sea at Gokarna, the oceans retreated to reveal the land that is now Kerala. The foreign presence here is older than anywhere else in India. As early as the 3rd century BC, travelers from China and the Middle East had set up trade routes with Kerala, and people came here from around the ancient world in search of spices, ivory, and sandalwood. Jews fleeing Roman persecution in Palestine landed here as long as 2000 years ago, and many believe that St. Thomas the Apostle was the first to bring the Christian gospel to Kerala, less than 20 years after the death of Jesus. Arabs dominated the spice trade for centuries, spreading Islam throughout the region, until the Portuguese landed at Calicut in 1498 and gun-boated their way to exclusive trading rights. Rivalry between the port cities of Cochin and Calicut weakened both, and Dutch and British forces ejected the Portuguese from their forts early in the 17th century. Kerala became a part of the Raj during the 18th century.

After Independence, the princely states of Cochin and Travancore were combined to form the state of Kerala, and in 1956 Kerala's boundaries were redrawn along linguistic (Malayalam) lines to include Malabar. A year later, Kerala became the first state in the world to elect a communist government. The state's leftist tradition has brought many advantages to its citizens: reforms have given Kerala the most equitable land distribution in India, and Kerala's literacy rate—around 90%—is the highest in the country. Vestiges of ancient matrilineal, polyandrous systems, such as those still practiced by the Nayar people, have given women a somewhat higher status in Kerala than elsewhere in India, and the UN has commended the state for its exemplary women's rights record. The relative prosperity of Kerala makes it a pleasure to travel in—so crack open a coconut, grab a straw, and enjoy.

Kerala's biggest festival is Onam, held in September to celebrate the harvest, when carnivals, elephant processions, and dance performances are held all over the state. Kerala is renowned for its elephant pagents; the most famous is the Trichur Pooram in May. The Nehru Trophy Boat Race, the most popular of the many backwater boat races, is held on the second Saturday in August.

TRIVANDRUM (THIRUVANATHAPURAM)
തിരുവനന്തപൂരം ☎ 0471

While most foreign tourists consider it nothing more than a piddling stop-off on the way to the balmy beaches of Kovalam and the backwaters of Alleppey, Kerala's state capital is worth a closer look. Speckled with parks, palaces, monuments, and museums, it is a good place to gain some insight into Kerala's culture. By the time it became the capital of Kerala when the state was formed in 1956, Trivandrum had already been the capital of Travancore for two centuries. It still retains its trademark red-tiled, pagoda-roofed houses, winding streets, tiny cafes, and beautiful gardens. The city's Malayalam name refers to Anantha, the serpent who holds the reclining Lord Vishnu (Lord Padmanabha) in the Shree Padmanabha Swami Temple. A welcome break from beach-hopping, Trivandrum is a good place to begin or end any trip through South India.

▐ GETTING THERE AND GETTING AROUND

Flights: Trivandrum's **international airport** (☎ 501537 and 501542) is 6km outside town. Buses for the airport leave from the city bus stand at East Fort (every 30min., 30min., Rs5). Auto-rickshaws cost Rs50. **Indian Airlines,** Museum Rd. (☎ 531 8288), 1 block west from the intersection with MG Rd. Open M-Sa 10am-1pm and 1:35-5:35pm. **Jet Airways,** Ashkay Towers (☎ 321018), Sasthamamgalam Junction, about 1½km east of the museum compound along Museum Rd. Open M-Sa 9am-5:30pm, Su 9am-3pm. To: **Bangalore** (1:50pm, 5hr., US$170); **Bombay** (3-4 per day, 2hr., US$195); **Delhi** (2 per day, 5½hr., US$360); **Madras** (2 per day, 1hr., US$105). Also international flights to **Male** in the Maldives (Tu-Th and Sa-Su, 12:15pm, 1hr., US$75) and **Colombo,** Sri Lanka (M-Sa, 2hr., Rs2560). Up-to-date schedules of trains and planes are published every Tuesday in a supplement to The Hindu.

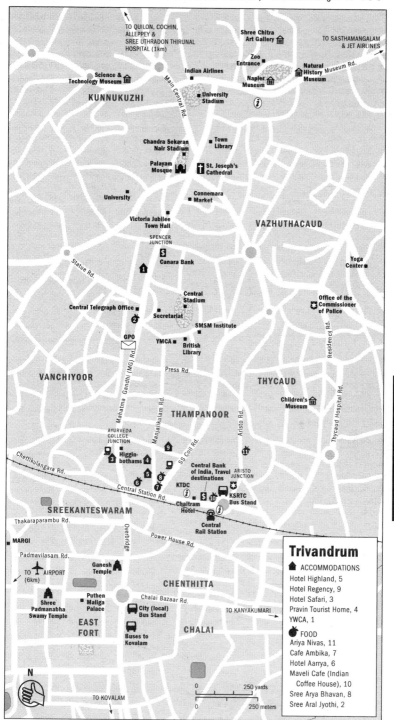

TO QUILON, COCHIN,
ALLEPPEY &
SREE UTHRADON THIRUNAL
HOSPITAL (1km)

Shree Chitra
Art Gallery

TO SASTHAMANGALAM
& JET AIRLINES

Science &
Technology Museum

Indian Airlines

Zoo
Entrance

Napier
Museum

Natural
History Museum Rd.
History
Museum

KUNNUKUZHI

Main Central Rd.

University
Stadium

Chandra Sekaran
Nair Stadium

Town
Library

Palayam
Mosque

St. Joseph's
Cathedral

University

Connemara
Market

VAZHUTHACAUD

Victoria Jubilee
Town Hall

SPENCER
JUNCTION

Statue Rd.

Canara Bank

Yoga
Center

Central
Stadium

Office of the
Commissioner
of Police

Central Telegraph Office

Secretariat

SMSM Institute

Residency Rd.

GPO

YMCA

British
Library

Mahatma Gandhi (MG) Rd.

Press Rd.

VANCHIYOOR

THYCAUD

Children's
Museum

Thycaud Hospital Rd.

THAMPANOOR

Manjalikulam Rd.

Aristo Rd.

AYURVEDA
COLLEGE
JUNCTION

SS Coil Rd.

Chettikulangara Rd.

Higgin-
bothams

9

Central Bank
of India, Travel
destinations

ARISTO
JUNCTION

KTDC

KSRTC
Bus Stand

Central Station Rd.

10

Chaitram
Hotel

SREEKANTESWARAM

Central
Rail Station

Thakaraparambu Rd.

Overbridge

Power House Rd.

MARGI

Padmavilasam Rd.

TO ✈ AIRPORT
(6km)

Ganesh
Temple

CHENTHITTA

Chalai Bazaar Rd.

Shree
Padmanabha
Swamy Temple

Puthen
Maliga
Palace

City (local)
Bus Stand

TO KANYAKUMARI

EAST
FORT

CHALAI

Buses to
Kovalam

N

0   250 yards

0   250 meters

TO KOVALAM

KERALA

Trivandrum

🏠 ACCOMMODATIONS
Hotel Highland, 5
Hotel Regency, 9
Hotel Safari, 3
Pravin Tourist Home, 4
YWCA, 1

🍴 FOOD
Ariya Nivas, 11
Cafe Ambika, 7
Hotel Aarrya, 6
Maveli Cafe (Indian
   Coffee House), 10
Sree Arya Bhavan, 8
Sree Aral Jyothi, 2

Trains: The **railway station,** Station Rd., a few min. east of MG Rd. Reservations counter open M-Sa 8am-8pm, Su 8am-2pm. Fares listed for sleeper class. To: **Alleppey** (3-8 per day, 9:30am-4:20am, 3½hr., Rs43); **Bangalore** (1-2 per day, 9:20am-3pm, 20hr., Rs245); **Bombay** (3-5 per day, 3am-10:30pm, 46hr., Rs397); **Cochin** (3-5 per day, 8:40am-9:30pm, 5hr., Rs90); **Delhi** (2-4 per day, 11am-7:15pm, 63hr., Rs506); **Kanyakumari** (2-3 per day, 2:45pm-1:30am, 2hr., Rs84); **Kollam** (several per day, 5am-9:40pm, 1½hr., Rs26); **Madras** (4-5 per day, 8:40am-4:20pm, 20hr., Rs260); **Madurai** (4:30am and 8:40pm, 8hr., Rs80); **Mangalore** (5-7 per day, 6am-8:30pm, 16hr., Rs205); **Varkala** (several per day, 5am-9:45pm, 1hr., Rs21).

Buses: The **long-distance KSRTC Bus Station** is on Station Rd. (☎323886), opposite the railway station. To: **Alleppey** (every 30min., 4hr., Rs57-70); **Cochin** (every 30min., 5½hr., Rs100); **Kanyakumari** (8 per day, 2½hr., Rs30); **Kollam** (every 30min., 2hr., Rs35); **Thekkady** for Periyar (4, 6, and 8:45am, 8hr., Rs95); **Varkala** (10 per day, 7:45am-9:30pm, 2hr., Rs20). The **Tamil Nadu Transport Office** (☎327756), at the far east end of the KSRTC bus station, runs buses to cities in Tamil Nadu. Open daily 10am-6pm. To: **Madras** (9 per day, 11:30am-8pm, 17hr., Rs237-260); **Madurai** (13 per day, 10:30am-10:30pm, 7hr., Rs102); **Pondicherry** (4pm, 16hr., Rs204). The **local bus stand,** MG Rd., is a few min. south of the train tracks at East Fort. Buses to **Kovalam** (every 20min., 5:50am-8:30pm, 25min., Rs5.50) depart from the bus stand on Overbridge Rd., 100m south of the local stand.

Local Transportation: Auto-rickshaws should use meters; base Rs6. Rs100 to Kovalam.

🛈 ORIENTATION AND PRACTICAL INFORMATION

The streets tangle over 74 sq. km of coastal hills, but navigation is easy if you stick to the few main roads. The north-south **MG Rd.** dumps all its traffic onto **Museum Rd.,** at the north end of town. To the south, MG Rd. cruises downhill to a hectic intersection with the city's other main drag, **(Central) Station Rd.** One hundred meters east on Station Rd. from MG Rd., **Manjalikulam Rd.** leads north to the budget hotel district. Farther down Station Rd., the **KSRTC Long-distance Bus Station** is on the left, opposite the **railway station.** MG Rd. becomes **Overbridge Rd.** when it heads south over the railway tracks to the **East Fort** area. A great white gate marks the entrance to **Shree Padmanabha Swamy Temple,** opposite the **local bus stand.** Behind the stand, **Chalai Bazaar Rd.** leads east through the bazaar.

TOURIST AND FINANCIAL SERVICES

Tourist Office: Tourist Facilitation Centre, Museum Rd. (☎321132), in the Directorate of Tourism, opposite the museum compound. Ask for the useful *Kerala Companion* and the list of festivals. Open daily 10am-5pm. Smaller branches at the **KSRTC Bus Stand** (☎327224) and the **train station** (☎334470) also have maps. Both open M-Sa 10am-5pm. **KTDC Reception Centre,** Station Rd. (☎330031), in front of Chaitram Hotel, next to the bus stand, promotes KTDC tours. Open M-Sa 6:30am-9:30pm.

Budget Travel: Travel Destinations, Chaitram Hotel, Station Rd. (☎330702), between the intersection with MG Rd. and the KSRTC bus stand. Open M-Sa 9am-9:30pm.

Immigration Office: Foreigners Registration Office, Residency Rd. (☎321399), in the Office of the Commissioner of Police. Extensions for student and entry visas "with proper documents." The process should take 2 weeks, but "urgent" applications might be processed in 7 days. Open M-Sa 10:15am-1:15pm and 2-5:15pm. Closed 2nd Sa.

Currency Exchange: Central Bank of India (☎330359), in the Chaitram Hotel lobby. Exchanges foreign currency and traveler's checks. Open M-F 10am-2pm, Sa 10am-noon. **Canara Bank,** MG Rd. (☎331536), at Spencer Junction just north of the Secretariat, gives cash advances on Visa, and exchanges cash and traveler's checks. Open M-F 10am-2pm and 2:30-3:30pm, Sa 10am-noon.

LOCAL SERVICES

Market: Chalai Bazaar Rd., which intersects MG Rd. at the local bus station. The smaller and more sedate **Connemara Market** is north of Spencer Junction on MG Rd.

Library: British Library, on the right off Manjalikulam Rd., where the street swerves left to MG Rd. Open Tu-Sa 11am-7pm. The **town library,** the "Victoria Diamond Jubilee Library," is on MG Rd., south of Museum Rd. Open daily 8am-8pm.

Bookstore: Higginbothams, MG Rd., north of Station Rd. Open M-Sa 9:30am-7:30pm.

EMERGENCY AND COMMUNICATIONS

Police: Thampanoor Police Station, Station Rd. (☎326543), near the KSRTC bus station, before Aristo Junction. Outpost inside the museum compound (☎315096).

Pharmacy: Darsana Medicals (☎331398), on Station Rd., just west of Manjalikalam Rd. Open daily 8am-9:30pm.

Hospital: Sree Uthradon Thirunal Hospital (☎446220), in Pattom, north of the city center (Rs25 rickshaw from Station Rd.), is considered the best private hospital here.

Internet: Orbit Cybercafe, Vasantham Chambers, SS Coil Rd., just north of Station Rd. Air-conditioned and fast. Rs60 per hr. Open daily 9:30am-10pm. **Starnet Communications,** Old Sreekanteswaram Rd. (☎464550), south of Ayurveda College Junction, is also good. Rs60 per hr. Open M-Sa 9am-9pm.

Telephones: The **Central Telegraph Office,** MG Rd. opposite the Secretariat, allows collect calls. Open 24hr.

Post Office: GPO, MG Rd., south of the Secretariat. Open M-Sa 8am-8pm, Su 10am-4pm. **Postal Code:** 695001.

ACCOMMODATIONS

Manjalikulam Rd. is the real budget hotel district, though MG and Station Rd. also have plenty of large hotels.

Pravin Tourist Home, Manjalikulam Rd. (☎330443), a 3min. walk north from Central Station Rd. Spacious rooms with big windows and attached bathrooms (seat and squat toilets). TV in the lobby. Check-out 24hr. Singles Rs110; doubles Rs195.

Hotel Highland, Manjalikulam Rd. (☎333200 or 333421), near Central Station Rd., on the left. Large, posh, and popular hotel has big airy rooms with TV. Seat toilets. Check-out 24hr. Singles Rs292-670; doubles Rs344-820.

Hotel Regency (☎330377). Follow Manjalikulam Rd. to the first cross-street, then turn right. Big clean rooms with satellite TV. Seat toilets and hot water. Several restaurants (including one on the roof), room service. Currency exchange. Check-out 24hr. Singles Rs300-600; doubles Rs475-700. MC, Visa.

YWCA (☎477308), 4th fl., Indian Overseas Bank Building, opposite the Secretariat. Lovely, clean rooms with attached baths. No unmarried couples allowed. Singles Rs155; doubles Rs205-355.

Hotel Safari, MG Rd. (☎477202), a few min. north of Central Station Rd. Standard accommodations plus TVs. Restaurant has city views. Lone women might want to steer clear of the hotel bar. Singles Rs185-500; doubles Rs198-550.

FOOD

It's difficult to find authentic Keralan food in Trivandrum, as most South Indian restaurants dish out a more Tamil-influenced menu. But at least it's authentic Indian—you are no longer at the mercy of banana pancakes and spaghetti.

▨ **Sree Aral Jyothi,** MG Rd., opposite the Secretariat. Crowded restaurant serves authentic Keralan "raw rice meals" (Rs19) and *masala dosas* (Rs12.50). Windowless A/C space in the back, or heart-of-town street views in front. Open daily 6:30am-10pm. Meals served 11am-3pm and 7-10pm.

▨ **Sree Arya Bhavan,** on the corner of SS Coil and Station Rd., 100m west of Hotel Chaitram. This hole-in-the-wall serves terrific North Indian veg. food. Often crowded and sometimes slow. Exellent menu changes daily. Open daily 8:30am-3pm and 7-11pm.

Hotel Aarrya, Central Station Rd., between Manjalikulam and the intersection with MG Rd. Simple but smashing South Indian meals. Good *masala dosas* (Rs12) and Keralan meals (Rs19). Open daily 6am-10pm.

Cafe Ambika, MG Rd., where Manjalikulam and SS Coil meet, turns out good veg. and non veg. meals at unbeatable prices (Rs12; *parotha* Rs2). Open daily 5:30am-1am.

Maveli Cafe (Indian Coffee House), facing the KSRTC long-distance bus station; it's the red, spiraling building on the left. The coolest structure in Trivandrum, it must be seen to be believed. Standard *dosas* (Rs8) and coffee. Open daily 7:30am-10pm.

Ariya Nivaas, around the corner from the station, toward Aristo Junction. Popular up-market veg. restaurant caters to middle-class families. Fancy *thali* served on a banana leaf (11am-3pm, Rs45 in the A/C upstairs). Open daily 7am-10pm.

◉ SIGHTS

MUSEUM COMPOUND. A big red gate marks the entrance to the lovely, 20-hectare public gardens, with its two museums, two galleries, a zoo, and crowds of moon-eyed couples. The **Natural History Museum** features dioramas of natural history, a model of a traditional upper-class house in Travancore, dolls dressed in traditional styles from all over India, and a life-sized, ivory model of a human skeleton made for Marthandavarma Maharaja in 1853. To the left as you come out of the Natural History Museum is the **K.C.S. Paniker Gallery,** which features paintings by the 20th-century Indian artist. Better maintained is the **Shree Chitra Art Gallery,** across the grounds, decked with Western-style portraits by the famed Raja Ravi Varma (1848-1906), Tibetan *thankas*, Japanese, Chinese, and Balinese paintings, 400-year-old Rajasthani miniatures, and modern Indian works.

In the center of the grounds is the **Napier Museum,** which looks suspiciously like a Walt Disney spin-off—florid gables and red, black, and pink bricks and tiles decorate the outside, while the inside is striped in yellow, pink, red, and turquoise. In fact, the building is an Indo-Saracenic experiment by Robert Fellowes Chisholm, who attempted to combine traditional Keralan and colonial architectural styles. The museum, along with the mandatory *kathakali* figures, includes Southeast Asian and Balinese art. Some choice pieces of kitsch on display, including an engraved plate to mark Kuwait Airlines' inaugural flight to Trivandrum, were gifts from foreign rulers to First Ministers of Kerala. (*Museum Rd. From Station Rd. follow MG Rd. north until it comes to a dead end, and then go right (east). The complex will be on your left (2.5km total). Galleries open Tu and Th-Su 10am-4:45pm, W 1-4:45pm. Rs5 for all four museums. Purchase tickets at the Natural History Museum from 10am-4pm.*)

The compound also contains a **zoo.** Though the animals probably live better than fellow-sufferers elsewhere in India, many are kept in frighteningly small cages. It might be worth a visit, however, for the impressive roost of wild fruit bats. (*Open Tu-Su 9am-5:15pm. Rs5; camera fee Rs10, video Rs500. Tickets sold until 5pm.*)

PUTHEN MALIGA PALACE (KUTHIRAMALIKA OR HORSE PALACE). Every inch of this palace of Prince Swati Tirunal, also a famed musician and court composer, is exquisitely decorated. Its beautiful wooden carvings took four years to complete, after which the surly Swati Tirunal occupied the palace for just one year before he left in a huff. The Puthen Maliga Palace or "Horse Palace," named for the 122 horse sculptures beneath its eaves, provides some fascinating insight into how the other half once lived. The palace also functions as a museum (i.e. "repository of old stuff"), featuring life-size *kathakali* figures in full regalia, paintings of the rajas and ranis of Travancore, weapons, and thrones in ivory and Bohemian crystal. (*Open Tu-Su 8:30am-12:30pm and 3-5:30pm. Rs20; camera fee Rs15, photography prohibited inside. Official museum guides are required to accompany you.*)

SHREE PADMANABHA SWAMY TEMPLE. Marked by a large white gate, the Shree Padmanabha Swamy Temple features a 6m-high statue of the reclining Vishnu. The whole of the god's body is made visible by the opening of three doors—one at the head, one at the midsection, and one at the feet. The *gopuram* was built in 1566, but the structure was not completed until 1733. The temple itself is open only to Hindus, but non-Hindus can climb the steps and peek in at some of the less sacred images. The lane leading up to the temple, through a thicket of handicraft sellers, houses a large green **tank** used by bathing pilgrims.

🌺 FESTIVALS

The Attukal Bhagavathy Temple, 2km south of East Fort, holds the **Festival of Attukal Pongala** in late February or early March, corresponding to the day of the Makom star. Tens of thousands of women converge on Trivandrum during this time, each one setting up a miniature kitchen on the streets in the center of town. The women offer Pongala, a sweet rice porridge, considered the goddess's favorite food, which they cook in earthenware pots over sanctified fires from the temple. Men are not permitted in the vicinity of the temple during the festival. Trivandrum's center is closed to traffic and takes on an uncharacteristically peaceful air as the smoke from thousands of cooling fires drifts up into the heavens. The **Swati Music Festival** (late Jan.-early Feb.) presents evenings of classical music on the lawn of the Puthen Maliga Palace. The annual **Nishagandhi Dance Festival,** with outdoor classical performances, takes place during the last week of February. Contact the Tourist Facilitation Centre for a complete festival schedule.

🎵 DANCE AND THEATER

MARGI (☎478806), a school at West Fort, occasionally performs **kathakali dance drama** and **kutiyattum theater** (Keralan martial arts) in the evenings. Follow MG Rd. south over the train tracks, turn right at the corner temple, and walk 10 minutes into West Fort. When the street comes to a final "T," turn right. MARGI is behind Fort High School on your left—look for the big banyan tree. The sign on the door is in Malayalam, but the image of a dancer gives it away. Performances are not regularly scheduled and often take place in local temples; call for details. Trivandrum has 18 **movie theaters.** Sree Kumar and Sree Visakh (☎321222), both near the Chaitram Hotel), and New Theatre (☎323244; walk east on Central Station Rd., turn left in front of the railway station) screen English-language films.

KOVALAM കോവളം   ☎0471

The pounding of hammers and the pouring of concrete have forever altered the calm landscape of Kovalam's black sands and turquoise waters. Since the arrival of the first sun-seekers back in the 1930s, Kovalam has become Kerala's most touristed beach resort and one of the most popular in India. The busy beachfront has been consumed by hotels, swallowed up by persistent touts, and spat out again by thieves dressed up as tailors and handicraft sellers. Enjoy the carnivalesque atmosphere—it was created just for you. The water's still wet, the sun's still hot, and the orange juice is cold, sweet, and fresh-squeezed. Things could be much worse. Beyond the tourist enclave, local fishing boats still ply the bays, and life continues as it always has, amid thatched huts and rice paddies.

📁 GETTING THERE AND GETTING AROUND

Buses: The **bus stand**, at the top of the path from the north end of Eve's Beach, has no ticket office, but the Tourist Facilitation Centre (see below) can give bus schedules. To: **Cochin** (7, 10:30, and 11am, 5½hr., Rs82) via **Kollam** (2hr., Rs41) and **Alleppey** (4hr., Rs62.50); **Kanyakumari** (5 per day, 9:25am-6pm, 2½hr., Rs32) via **Nagercoil** (1½hr., Rs25); **Trivandrum** (frequent, 5am-9:30pm, 20min., Rs5.50-7.50).

Local Transportation: Rickshaws and **taxis** hover at the bottom of Lighthouse Rd., the bus stand, and Kovalam Junction. A rickshaw to Trivandrum should cost less than Rs100, one to the airport Rs150-200.

🛈 ORIENTATION AND PRACTICAL INFORMATION

Kovalam Beach is made up of three coves divided by rocky promontories. A lighthouse marks the southernmost **Lighthouse Beach.** From here, **Lighthouse Rd.,** crawling with seafood restaurants, leads down to the water and the budget hotels favored by foreign tourists. **Eve's Beach** is north of a rocky promontory. The headland is home to the **Kovalam Ashok Beach Resort,** north of which is **Samudra Beach.** A road leads up from Eve's Beach past several travel offices, handicraft shops, and tailors to the **bus stand** at the entrance to the Ashok Beach Resort. From there, the road that leads southeast goes first to **Kovalam Junction,** 2km away, where a left turn at the fork brings you to the **post office,** and 14km later to Trivandrum. Between Lighthouse Rd. and the road to the bus stand, paths twist through the palm trees, connecting the beach to some of the quieter restaurants and hotels. The power shuts down at 8pm or 8:30pm every night for 30 minutes. Some hotels have back-up generators, but don't count on it.

Tourist Office: Tourist Facilitation Centre (☎ 480085), near the bus stand toward Ashok Beach Resort. Arranges tickets for the backwater cruises (see p. 506). Keeps current copies of international newspapers. Open in-season daily 10am-5pm.

Budget Travel: Western Travels (☎ 481307), next to the bus stand. Organizes **sightseeing tours** in season. Currency exchange and cash advances on credit cards. Taxis for hire. Open daily 6:30am-12:30am. Off-season: 7am-9pm. Amex, MC, Visa.

Currency Exchange: Several shops on the beach exchange currency. The reception desk at **Wilson's Tourist Home,** behind Hotel Neelakanta, offers bank rates. Open M-Sa 9am-5pm. The **Central Bank of India** has a small branch in the Kovalam Hotel shopping complex. Open M-F 10:30am-1:30pm, Sa 10:30am-noon.

Bookstore: Shops along the beach sell musty used books. The German Bakery has a decent (if overpriced) selection. Books bought and exchanged 9am-noon. Open daily 8am-10pm. **Anjana Emporium,** in the Ashok Hotel, has more expensive books, magazines, and postcards. Open daily 10am-9pm; off-season M-Sa 10:30am-8pm.

Police: (☎ 480255), left off the road to Kovalam Junction, 10min. from the bus station on the left. In season, the **Tourist Aid Post** is on the beach. Open daily 9am-7pm.

Hospital: Upasana Hospital (☎ 480632), a right off the road to Kovalam Junction, a 10min. walk from the bus stand. **Pharmacy** open M-Sa 9:30am-1pm and 4:30-8:30pm, Su 9:30am-1pm. In an emergency, you can call Dr. Chandrasenan (☎ 457357) or Dr. Will (☎ 480270 or 480277).

Internet: There are lots of email places; almost all charge Rs120 per hr. and are relatively small but fast. **Alpha Internet Services** (☎ 481926), right on Lighthouse Beach, close to the southern end, has 2 terminals. Rs120 per hr. Open daily 8am-9:30pm.

Post Office: Branch next to Tourist Facilitation Center. Open M-Sa 9am-3pm. The **main office** can be reached by taking a left at Kovalam Junction. Open M-Sa 9am-1pm and 1:30-5pm. **Postal Code:** 695527.

🛈 ACCOMMODATIONS

Prices peak in December and January. Off-season and during the monsoon, bargain hard—don't let persistent touts determine where you will stay. In general, the quality of rooms is high; most places don't have a separate price for singles—at best expect to pay 25% less. All the places listed below are on Lighthouse Beach, and come with attached bathrooms and (usually) hot water.

Green Valley Cottages (☎ 480636). From the beach, walk straight past Hotel Neptune and follow signs back to the paddies. Forsaking the beachfront has its advantages—lower prices and dreamy views of the paddies, for instance. Each immaculate room has a private balcony and chairs to loll around in. Doubles Rs450. Off-season: Rs200. The same friendly folks run **Silent Valley Inn** (☎487928) right behind. Gorgeous rooms, with balconies you can see the sea from. Doubles Rs500. Off-season Rs250.

Sandy Beach Resort (☎480012; sandybeach@vsnl.com), opposite Hotel Neptune, about 75m in from the beach. Sparkling and spacious rooms with balconies around a courtyard. Singles Rs250; doubles Rs500-600. Off-season Rs150/250.

Wilson's Tourist Home (☎480051). From the beach turn inland at the Palm Beach Restaurant and take your first right, close to Hotel Neelakanta. Rooms with massive beds and balcony. Friendly female staff is a draw for women traveling alone. Doubles Rs350-900. Off-season Rs200-600. Visa.

Hotel Suriya (☎481012). From the beach, turn inland betwen the Coconut Grove Restaurant and the Coral Reef Cafe, near the Hotel Jeevan House. A little back from the beach, but the price is right, rooms are clean and spacious, and the staff is pleasant. Doubles Rs300. Off-season Rs150.

Hotel Neptune (☎480222), about halfway down the beach; follow signs a little inland. Your average (clean) rooms, around a pretty greenery-filled courtyard. Singles Rs375–1100; doubles Rs450-1100. Off-season: Singles Rs200-600; doubles Rs250-750.

Hotel Jeevan House (☎480662), on the sand midway down the cove, next to the Coral Reef Cafe. Pleasant, airy rooms with balconies, though you'll have to pay for a sea view. Doubles Rs300-1200. Off-season Rs150-1000.

⬤ FOOD

Restaurants stretch in an almost uninterrupted sweep all the way along the beaches. What little Indian food there is has been de-spiced to appease Western palates. Alcohol is served at many beachfront establishments (beer Rs70).

◼ **Red Star Restaurant.** Though little more than a bamboo hut at the south end of the beach, this is the best place in Kovalam to get a feel for the old days. The size of this tiny place means you get to hang out and chat with the owner, Mani. *Masala dosa* Rs15; excellent Keralan meal Rs20, with a tasty fried fish Rs34. Open daily from 6am.

◼ **German Bakery,** toward the south end of Lighthouse Beach. There's always a breeze at this rooftop spot. Though you're a long way from home, but you wouldn't know it after a bite of that cinnamon-apple strudel (Rs25). Open daily 7:30am-11pm.

Leo's Restaurant, toward the north end of Lighthouse Beach, is a popular choice, and makes a mean cheese tomato onion garlic omelette (Rs25; no kissing afterward). Fish and chips Rs100; spaghetti with mussels Rs60. Open 7:30am-11:30pm.

Lonely Planet Restaurant. Follow directions for Green Valley cottages (above) and take a left at the fork; it's on your right, in a lovely, tranquil spot. Shame about the name. Mainly Indian veg. food. No liquor allowed. Open daily 6am-midnight.

Swiss Cafe, near the northend of Lighthouse Beach. Beautifully designed restaurant where satisfied costumers linger over sandwiches and imported Swiss cheese (Rs25). Open 7:30am-11:30pm.

Garzia, on the northern end of the beach. Fresh pasta is a treat. Fresh seafood Rs100; cheese, tomato, and garlic pasta Rs77. Open daily 7am-11pm.

Udaya Hotel, by the bus stop. When the beach gets too sandy, head inland to where the real people eat their meals (Rs10). Open 6am-9:30pm.

⬤ ♫ SIGHTS AND ENTERTAINMENT

BEACHES. Well you're here for the sand—no two ways about it. The most popular beach among foreign tourists is **Lighthouse Beach,** the most southern. Here you can rent boogie boards and fend off hawkers of edibles and durables. Always swim near the lifeguard. Almost as popular is **Eve Beach.** North of the headland is **Samudra Beach,** delightful but largely ignored by the crowds.

KERALA

> ❗ **WARNING.** The undertow and rip currents here can be very strong, so follow the warnings of the signs, flags, and whistle-toting lifeguards. Also, proximity to Trivandrum means there are daytrippers; though many Western women wear their bikinis with pride, some opt to swim in T-shirts to avoid unwanted attention.

MASSAGE AND YOGA. Tired of the waves? Kiss your aches and pains good-bye with an **ayurvedic massage.** Kerala is touted as an ayurvedic haven, and there are numerous establishments in Kovalam providing treatment. **Wilson's Tourist Home** has a masseur for men and a masseuse for women. (☎480051. Open M-Sa 9am-5pm. Rs200 per hr., Rs300 to have your head seen to as well.) **Amritha Ayurvedic Health Centre,** adjoining Hotel Neptune, does a full body massage. (☎401769. Open daily 8am-9pm. Rs250.) Peak season also means that **yoga** is in full swing at many hotels and private institutions. Hotel Neptune offers classes (1hr. session Rs200).

NIGHTLIFE. During peak season, "cultural nights" featuring **kathakali dance** (see p. 520) take place at the Hotel Ashok (☎480101; Tu and F; Rs150) and Hotel Neptune. (☎480222; M, W, and Sa; Rs125. Make-up starts at 5pm; the dance program begins at 6:45pm.) Pirated **movies,** complete with laughter from the original audience, are shown nightly at several restaurants, including the Coconut Grove Restaurant (☎480481) and the Hawah Beach Restaurant (☎484031).

SHOPPING. Knick-knacks, fabrics, and tapestries from the whole sub-continent await you here, ripe and ready for your "just for looking" pleasure and convenience. Tailors with skeins of silk busily churn out attire to your specifications. Bargain hard. Ask around if you are making big purchases (such as the pashmina scarf for Great Auntie Bertha).

BACKWATER CRUISES. The Tourist Facilitation Centre arranges **backwater cruises** around an island 5km from Kovalam. The Rs300 fee covers transportation to the boat, three hours of cruising time, and the return trip to Kovalam. Unlike in the Alleppey-Kollam tour, the boat used in season is a traditional, non-motorized vessel with a rattan shade; off season, an uncovered boat is used. The Tourist Facilitation Centre can book tickets for the Kollam-Alleppey backwater cruise as well. Western Travels (see p. 504) offers a four hour backwater cruise along some of the Alleppey-Kollam backwaters. (7:30am-6:30pm; Rs550.)

OTHER SIGHTS. It's worth wandering up to the landscaped grounds around the Tourist Facilitation Centre and the Kovalam Ashok Beach resort, part of which is housed in the 250-year-old **castle** that was once the Maharaja's summer retreat. The views are gorgeous, and if you're lucky no one will try to sell you anything. If, after spending too much time in Kovalam, you've forgotten that you're in India, take the 20-minute stroll along the coastal road to the ramshackle village of **Vizhinjam** (VEER-in-yam). Only ruins of some small shrines remain in this former capital of the Ay Kings. Brightly painted fishing boats fill the harbor, crowned at the north end by a dizzying pink-and-yellow **mosque.**

FESTIVALS. Kovalam's biggest to-do is **Gramam** (Jan. 14-23) when a Keralan village is recreated on Eve's Beach, complete with the traditional *nalukettu* (square house with courtyard), where an arts and crafts fair is held.

KOLLAM (QUILON) കൊല്ലം ☎0474

Kollam is one of the oldest ports on the Malabar Coast. Called "Kaulam" Mall by ancient Arabs, and "Coilum" by Marco Polo in the 13th century, the town was the center of the "heroic rebellion" against British rule led by Veluthambi Dalava. Today, however, the prosperous city is the center of the country's cashew trade, and its location on the sprawling Ashtamudi lake makes it an excellent base for exploring the backwaters. Though little remains from its glory days—shopping malls and modern storefronts have obliterated ancient palaces and most of the ancient streets—it is worth staying a night or two in the lovely Government Guesthouse and taking a cruise through the backwaters before heading to the coast.

GETTING THERE AND GETTING AROUND

Trains: The station is about 1km southeast of the center of town. Fares listed are sleeper class. To: **Alleppey** (2-3 per day, 4:50am-11:15pm, 1½hr., Rs30); **Bangalore** (1-2 per day, 10:55am and 4:20pm, 5hr., Rs147); **Bombay** (1-2 per day, 4:45 and 8:40am, 46hr., Rs256); **Delhi** (1-2 per day, 12:20-4:20pm, 53hr., Rs319); **Ernakulam** (several, 4:30am-11:15pm, 3hr., Rs42); **Kanyakumari** (2-3 per day, 9:55am-9:25pm, 4hr., Rs46); **Madras** (2-4 per day, 5:35am-3:20pm, 16hr., Rs158); **Mangalore** (2 per day, 7:15am and 7:20pm, 14hr., Rs120); **Trivandrum** (9 per day, 6:35am-8:45pm, 1½hr., Rs26); **Varkala** (5 per day, 6:35am-8:45pm, 30min., Rs18).

Buses: KRSTC bus station (☎ 752008), Jetty Rd., north toward the river and the boat jetty. To: **Alleppey** (every 20min., 2hr., Rs32); **Ernakulam** (every 20min., 3½hr., Rs55); **Trivandrum** (every 20min., 1½hr., Rs26-35); **Varkala** (10 per day, 7:30am-8:30pm, 1½hr., Rs12). A Varkala bus leaves at 6:50pm, scooping up most passengers disembarking the backwater cruise from Alleppey.

ORIENTATION AND PRACTICAL INFORMATION

Kollam's streets follow the bends of the canals and turn at confusing angles. **National Highway (NH) 47** runs southeast to northwest through town. Beginning in the southeast end of town, NH47 passes the **railway station** before crossing the tracks to the congested center of town. At the junction of Chinnakkada, marked by the **clock tower**, it intersects with the east-west **Main Rd.** Just beyond is the large junction of NH47 with the wide north-south **Tourist Bungalow Rd.** From there NH47 twists in a northwest direction past the **post office**, the sprawling **Bishop Jerome Nagar Shopping Centre**, and the wild Shrine of Our Lady of Velankanni. The next junction is with **Jetty Rd.**, which leads to the right (north) to the **KSRTC bus station** and the **ferry jetty**, 100m away. A 10-minute walk to the left (southwest) leads to the fruit and vegetable **market**.

Tourist Office: District Tourism Promotion Council (DTPC) has outposts at the railway station. Open M-Sa 9am-5:30pm. The bus station branch (☎ 745625), open M-Sa 6am-6pm, is especially helpful. Backwater tour booking, hotel reservations, and, at the bus station, foreign exchange. Expect heavy promotion of *their* backwater tour (over ATDC's version). Across the street from the bus staion is a small **ATDC** branch (☎243462). Open daily 8am-6:30pm.

Currency Exchange: State Bank of Travencore, in the Bishop Nagar Shopping Centre, changes currency. Open M-F 10am-2pm and 2:30-3:30pm, Sa 10am-12:30pm. Toward the jetty, **Bank of Baroda** does cash advances. Open M-F 10am-2pm, Sa 10am-noon. The tourist information office at the bus station also changes currency occasionally. Open M-Sa 10am-5pm.

Bookstore: Chani Bookseller, NH47 (☎743973), in the Bishop Jerome Nagar Shopping Centre. Open M-Sa 9am-8pm.

Market: A fruit and vegetable market occupies a few blocks of the road that leads southwest from the boat jetty into town. A 15min. walk from the boat jetty.

Police Station: (☎742072), right from the railway station, next to the large temple.

Pharmacy: Kochappally Medicals, Tourist Bungalow Rd. (☎749286), just southwest of the main intersection with NH47 and Main Rd. Open daily 8am-9pm.

Hospital: Nair's Hospital (☎742413), 1½km northeast of the jetty, east off Tourist Bungalow Rd.

Internet: Net4you (☎741266), 2nd fl. in the Bishop Jerome Nagar Shopping Centre. 6 terminals in shiny new A/C room. Rs60 per hr. Open daily 9am-9pm. **SilverNet** on the ground floor is not as posh, but does the job. Rs60 per hr. Open M-Sa 10am-8:30pm.

Post Office: Head Post Office, NH47, northeast of the intersection with Tourist Bungalow Rd., on the left. Open M-Sa 7am-8pm. **Postal Code:** 691001.

BILE BALANCE The predominant medical tradition in Hindu culture is associated with *ayurveda*, which translates as the "knowledge of long life." Practitioners of this wisdom are called *vaidyas*. Ayurvedic medicine takes a holistic approach to diagnosis (a broken heart is as much an ailment as a broken leg) and to treatment (a combination of herbal potions and worthy notions). The earliest known herbal prescriptions date back to the *Atharva Veda* (c. 1000 BC), when *vaidyas* were already performing surgery on external wounds. Ayurvedic medicine, however, is primarily associated with maintaining a balance between the three bodily essences or *doshas: vatta* (wind), *pitta* (bile), and *kapha* (phlegm). *Vatta*, associated with the nervous system and movement, represents kinetic energy. *Kapha*, potential energy, is associated with lymph and mucus, and opposes *vatta*. Finally, *pitta* mediates between these two forces, governing digestive and metabolic processes. Balance between the three *doshas* is essential to good health.

ACCOMMODATIONS

The Tourist Bungalow (Government Guest House), Tourist Bungalow Rd. (☎743620), a few km outside of town (rickshaw Rs25). This beautiful old British mansion with its huge, echoing ballroom hung with quietly mildewing prints, has rooms with 3m high ceilings and sparse antique furniture. Recently refurbished, it's more gorgeous than ever. Wonderfully romantic and often full—come for a look around even if you can't get a room. Attached bathrooms (seat toilets). Only government officials can make reservations, but call call ahead to see if it's booked. Singles and doubles Rs164.

Yatri Nivas (☎745538), opposite the lake from the boat jetty. Phone from there for a pickup in their speedboat (Rs20); otherwise, hire a rickshaw (Rs10). Standard rooms have attached baths and great views of the water. Singles Rs110; doubles Rs165.

Hotel Shah International, Tourist Bungalow Rd. (☎742362), 100m from NH47. A quiet and conveniently located large place with grand aspirations it doesn't quite live up to. All rooms have balconies and attached baths with seat toilets, towels, and soap. Singles Rs210-480; doubles Rs260-480.

FOOD

Jala Subhiksha, next to the boat jetty, is a floating restaurant in a lovely traditional *kettuvallam* (boat). Delicious Chinese and Indian dishes: *saiwoo* chicken Rs55; Manchurian tofu Rs45. Open daily 6pm-10pm.

Indian Coffee House, Main Rd., tucked away on the right. From the post office, turn right on NH47, then take the second right. Once a franchise, always a franchise. Banana fry Rs9. Open daily 8am-9pm.

Supreme Bakers, from the post office, turn right onto NH47, then take an immediate right; it's on the left. Spic-n-span bakery serves fresh cakes, bread, and pastries for Rs4-20. Cold drinks, snacks, and A/C offer relief. Open M-Sa 9am-8pm.

SIGHTS AND ENTERTAINMENT

The highlight of Kollam's calender is the **Ashtamudi Craft and Art Festival** in late December and early January, when craftsmen from all over India come to demonstrate their skills. There are also demonstrations of traditional dance and music.

BACKWATER CRUISES. The backwater cruises to Alleppey are the main attraction in Kollam. The boat can take both you and your luggage, making this a convenient and beautiful mode of transport north up the Keralan coast. Many of the cruises make several stops along the way, including one at the Mata Amrithanandamayi Mission (see below). Cruises are run by the District Tourism Promotion Council (DTPC); though others offer similar service, discounts are available by booking through the DTPC. For more information, see p. 512. *(Tours depart 10:30am from the DTPC office near the KSRTC bus stand and the boat jetty, and arrive in Alleppey 6:30pm. Report to the office by 10am. Rs150, Rs100 for ISIC holders.)* The KDTC office at the bus station organizes additional backwater tours, including a justifiably popular **village tour** that winds through barely 3m wide canals in Munroe Island in a traditional wooden boat. *(Departures daily from KDTC 9am and 2pm; 3hr.; Rs300, Rs75 discount for students and seniors. Book online at www.dptc-quilontourism.com or by contacting the DTPC directly.)* There is also a range of cheap **houseboat tours** starting at Rs2000 for 2 people for the 14-hour Starnight Cruise. *(Can be booked online at www.dptc-quilontourism.com, or by contacting the DTPC directly.)*

MATA AMRITHANANDAMAYI ASHRAM. Backwater cruises frequently stop to pick up and drop off passengers at the ashram of one of India's few female gurus, Mata Amrithanandamayi, usually known as Amma, the Hugging Mother. Particularly popular with Westerners, the ashram houses hundreds of residents and vistors in pink skyscrapers that look somewhat incongrous against the surrounding backwaters. There are many amenities at the ashram including a general store, a hospital, and 24 hour STD/ISD phones. Ask in Alleppey or Kollam, or call the ashram to see if Amma is in residence and not on tour. The backwater cruise boats honor partially used tickets—a single ticket will take you from Kollam to the ashram and, a few days later, on to Alleppey (or vice versa). *(☎ (0476) 621279; mam_hq@vsnl.com. Rs125 per day in a room with attached bath and 1 or 2 roommates; meals included.)*

SHRINE OF OUR LADY OF VELANKANNI. This towering polygonal shrine rises above everything else in Kollam. Festooned with bright plastic flowers and tinsel, the shrine occupies a central place in Kollam's religious life. Although a mere 13 years old, the shrine has already gained a reputation for healing and performing miracles. On Wednesdays, crowds line up inside, fingering rosaries and praying for hours. *(NH47, near Jetty Rd. Mass W 8am and noon; 5pm mass usually in Malayalam.)*

VARKALA ☎ 0472

The town of Varkala, with its quiet beach and towering cliffs, just might rescue South India's reputation for over-commercialized beaches. Though Varkala, 25km from Kollam, is slowly developing an affinity for tourist dollars, it still retains some of the beauty and tranquility for which Kovalam was once famed.

GETTING THERE AND GETTING AROUND. Buses stop at the temple junction, a short walk from the beach. To: **Kollam** (every hr., 1-2hr., Rs15.50) and **Trivandrum** (5 per day, 6am-5pm, 1½hr., Rs16). A direct bus heads to **Kovalam** (4:30pm, 2hr., Rs20) via **Trivandrum. Trains** are faster and more reliable, if less conveniently located; the **railway station** is a couple of kilometers from the temple junction (Rs15-20 auto-rickshaw ride). Trains run to: **Kollam** (10 per day, 7:25am-10:30pm, 40min., Rs28) and **Trivandrum** (9 per day, 7:15am-6:30pm, 1hr., Rs33).

PRACTICAL INFORMATION. The **DPTC** has opened a branch at the end of Beach Rd. The office has train and bus schedules, books backwater cruises, and, in its incarnation as the private tourist office **JK Tours and Travels**, exchanges **currency.** (Open daily 9am-7pm.) Another **JK Tours and Travels** is at the temple junction (☎ 600713. Open daily 9am-6:30pm.) A **DPTC** of Trivandrum is near the helipad. (Open daily 8am-6pm.) There are several **book exchanges** along the cliff road. On Beach Rd. in Nikhil Beach Resorts there are four terminals to check **email.** (Rs70 per hr. Open daily 7am-11pm.) Email at the Seaview Restaurant is available 24 hours. (Rs80 per hr.) The tiny Janardhanapuram **post office** is at the temple junction (open M-Sa 10am-2pm). **Postal code:** 695141.

ACCOMMODATIONS AND FOOD. The cliff-top overlooking the beach is crowded with hotels; follow Beach Rd. west and head north uphill for a sweaty

KERALA

15minutes. Views cost money in Varkala, so wander inland if your budget is tight. Turn east from the cliff road at the Virgin Vegetarian restaurant to find the pleasant **Greenhouse**. Look for the purple walls with the name painted sporadically and apparently at random along several buildings. The big, clean rooms with attached bath are just in from the cliff. (☎604659. Doubles Rs200; off-season Rs100.) The **Clafouti Bakery** (☎601414) lets rooms at the north end of the cliff. Slightly inland rooms with bath are small but decent (Rs200-300; off-season Rs50-75). Posher rooms are closer to the cliff and the bakery's freshly baked bread. (Doubles Rs500. Off-season: singles Rs150; doubles Rs250.) On the cliff, the aptly named **Seaview Restaurant and Cliff House** has views of the sea. (☎601019. Doubles Rs400-800; off-season Rs100-200.) Varkala's restaurants, which open early and close late, have lengthy menus featuring everything from hash browns to *pad thai*. The ◪**Clafouti Bakery** has delicious banana-pineapple muffins (Rs15), brownies (Rs20), and assorted fresh bagels, as well as the usual array of eggs, *dosas*, rice, and noodles. (Open daily 8:30am-11pm). At the south end of the cliff the popular **Sunset Restaurant** does breakfast by nationality. (Indian Rs30, English Rs90, French Rs75, Italian Rs40, Israeli Rs60, and just plain Special Rs40. Open daily from 8am.)

◉ SIGHTS. The town's only real **beach**, Papanasham, is at the base of a dramatic cliff, which shoulders the burden of most of Varkala's tourist infrastructure. From the cliff, steep narrow paths scramble down to the surf. There are dangerous riptides; always swim near the lifeguard and ask about conditions. The cliff-top **path** winds north for quite a distance, with superb views of the rocky coastline. Beach Rd. leads west from the **Sree Janardhana Swami Temple,** a Hindu pilgrimage site— one of the seven most important Vaishnavite shrines in India. The road passes the large **tank.** From the beach, rickety bridges lead up the cliff to the **Kerala Kathakali Centre,** which stages **kathakali dance** performances (daily; make-up 5pm, show 6:30pm; Rs100). Operations all along the beach specialize in ayurvedic treatments and assorted curative programs. Other places on the cliff-top north of the beach, including the **Scientific School of Yoga and Massage** (1¾hr. massage Rs300), promise a combination of spiritual and physical rejuvenation, and offer yoga classes.

ALLEPPEY (ALAPPUZHA) ആലപ്പുഴ ☎ 0477

The two canals that dominate the center of Alleppey were once the major arteries of a great shipping center. Today, tangles of water lilies fill the waterways, and most of the town's activity revolves around all the *coir* (woven coconut fiber) products shipped through here on small boats propelled by pole. Partly because of its fading economic importance, Alleppey is a prime example of a traditional Keralan town, complete with steeply-pitched, red-tiled roofs. The town's snake-boats (traditional Keralan battle vessels) compete several times a year, especially during the annual **Nehru Trophy Boat Race** (2nd Sa in Aug.). The popular backwater cruises between Alleppey and Kollam bring tourists here from all over the world.

▐ GETTING THERE AND GETTING AROUND. The **railway station** is near the beach, 4km southwest of the town center. Trains go to: **Bombay** (Su 6:30am, 44hr., Rs386); **Ernakulam** (8 per day, 6am-7:20pm, 1-1½hr., Rs11); and **Trivandrum** (2-3 per day, 7:20am-3am, 3hr., Rs43). An auto-rickshaw from the train station to the boat jetty or bus station will cost you Rs25-35. Privately operated local buses leave from the street directly opposite the most eastern footbridge over the North Canal to the train station (Rs2). The **KSRTC bus station** is at the east end of **Boat Jetty Rd.,** which runs along the south bank of North Canal. Buses go to: **Cochin** (every 20min., 2hr., Rs23); **Kollam** (every 20min., 2hr., Rs32); **Kottayam** (every hr., 5:50am-9pm, 1½hr., Rs19), for buses to **Periyar;** and **Trivandrum** (every 20min., 4hr., Rs59). Public and private boats leave from the jetties 200m west of the bus station, just before the Mullackal Rd., the large street that bridges the North Canal.

⬛🔳 ORIENTATION AND PRACTICAL INFORMATION. The town is sand-wiched between two east-west canals: the **North Canal** and the **South Canal,** about a 10-minute walk apart. The streets between the two canals are laid out in a grid. The helpful **District Tourism Promotion Council (DTPC),** on Boat Jetty Rd. (☎253308 or 251796), next to the boat jetties, sells tickets for boat rides and the Nehru Trophy Boat Race. (Open M-Sa 9am-6pm.) To get to the equally helpful **ATDC Tourist Office,** take Mullackal Rd. north, turn right immediately after crossing the canal, and then turn left; the office will be on your left. (☎243462. Open daily 8am-8pm.) The **Indian Bank,** on Mullackal Rd., south of North Canal, past the intersection with Cullen Rd., exchanges cash and traveler's checks. (Open M-F 10am-2pm, Sa 10am-noon.) A **market** lines Mullackal Rd., both north and south of the canal. For **Medical College Hospital** (☎251611), head south along the road one block west of Mullackal Rd., continue south across the Iron Bridge and the South Canal, and take the third left after the canal. **Haifa Medicals** is just south of the North Canal on Mullackal Rd. (☎251365. Open M-Sa 8:30am-9pm, Su 9am-8pm.) Follow the street opposite the eastern footbridge south to Stone Bridge, over the South Canal, to **Atlanta Computers.** (Email Rs90 per hr. Open M-Sa 9:30am-7:30pm, Su 2-5pm.) On the way to Atlanta Computers but with only one terminal is **N&G Communications.** (Rs90. Open 9am-11pm.) Take Mullackal Rd. south until it ends at the South Canal, then turn right to reach a branch of the **post office.** (Open M-Sa 9am-5pm.) For the **Head Post Office,** continue to the west and take the second right on Exchange Rd. (Open M-Sa 9:30am-5:30pm.) **Postal Code:** 688001.

🔳🔳 ACCOMMODATIONS AND FOOD. Hotels line Boat Jetty Rd., 10 minutes from the bus stand, just north of North Canal. The **Arcadia Hotel,** next to the bus station, is the most convenient. It has comfortable rooms with seat toilets and a popular restaurant and bar. (☎251354. Singles Rs150; doubles Rs300-600.) Just east of the boat jetty, **Hotel Raiban Annexe** is also very convenient and the price is right. (☎261017. Attached baths with seat toilets. Singles Rs86; doubles Rs172-385.) **Mutteal Holiday Inn,** Nehru Trophy Rd. (☎242955), north of the North Canal and east of the footbridge, has double rooms with character for Rs300. The **Komala Hotel,** Mullakal Rd., is north over the North Canal traffic bridge. Turn right, then left; the hotel is set back on the right, just beyond the ATPC. (☎243631. Attached baths with squat toilets. Singles Rs118-495; doubles Rs172-605.) **Karthika Tourist Home** is 50m north over the North Canal traffic bridge. The friendly staff lets some-what scruffy, blue rooms at great prices. Attached baths have squat toilets. (☎245524. Singles Rs60; doubles Rs100.) **Hotel Annapoorna,** Boat Jetty Rd., near the boat jetty, next to Hotel Raiban Annexe, serves standard South Indian veg. fare for Rs14-18. (Open daily 7am-9pm. Meals 12:30-2pm.) **Cafe Venice,** next to the DPTC, named for its location overlooking the fetid but picturesque canal, serves Keralan meals (Rs20) and chicken *masala* (Rs50). It is also a convenient breakfast stop for departing backwater trippers. (Open daily 8am-10pm.) The standard ruffle-clad waiters at the **Indian Coffee House,** Mullackal Rd., a few blocks south of the North Canal, serve the standard snacks and coffee. (Open daily 8am-9pm.) Bakeries line Boat Jetty Rd. Most of Alleppey's hotels also have restaurants.

🔳🔳 SIGHTS AND ENTERTAINMENT. The main reason people come to Alleppey is to leave it again via some means of backwater transport, but the palm-lined town is pretty enough to be an attraction in its own right. Much of the tradi-tional architecture still stands, and has yet to be converted into concrete block constructions. Wandering along the South Canal takes you by many of Alleppey's traditional, red-roofed houses, with their deep, shady eaves and decorated gables. The **beach,** to the west, is decent. At **Seaview Park,** just north of South Canal by the beach, you can rent a **boat** for solo jaunts down the canals. *(Rs10-25 for 10min.)*

The highlight of Alleppy's tourist calendar is the annual **Nehru Trophy Boat Race,** held in the lake east of town on the second Saturday of August, which finds hundreds of oarsmen crewing 65m-long snake-boats. The first race was held in

KERALA

honor of Prime Minister Jawaharlal Nehru during his visit here in 1952. Nehru was so flattered and fascinated by the race that he awarded the winners a trophy; the event soon developed into an Alleppey institution. *(Tickets, between Rs10-500, are available from the ATDC and DTPC and may be purchased up to one week in advance or on the day.)* Other races are held throughout the year, including the **Moolam Boat Race** at Champakulam in July. The ATDC runs boat rides to the race. *(Rs100 round-trip.)*

For most of the year, daily **backwater cruises** run the 80km of green canals that separate Alleppey from Kollam. From the boat, you can see an 11th-century statue of the Buddha, temples, churches, *coir*-producing villages, and an ashram. A traditional Keralan meal is served on a banana leaf for lunch *(Rs40-50)*. Drinks are available for sale on board the boat. The ATDC and DTPC both operate cruises. *(10:30am departure, 6:30pm arrival; tours operate in both directions. Make reservations one day in advance or on the day, before 10am. During the off-season months of June and July, trips with fewer than 10 people will be cancelled. Both the ATDC and DTPC charge Rs150, and give a Rs50 discount to ISIC cardholders and children under 12. If you break your trip, your ticket will be honored whenever you pick up your journey.)* The ATDC and other private agencies along Boat Jetty Rd., including **Penguin Tourist Service** *(☎ 261522. Open daily 8am-6pm)*, north of Mullackal Rd., arrange shorter trips.

Private agencies, including Penguin Tourist Service, also arrange stays on traditional cargo boats—converted **houseboats** with tiny bedrooms, bathrooms, dining areas, and two men to pole the boat around. *(Rs5000 for 2 people for 24hr.; Rs7500 for 4 people.)* The DPTC and ATDC can also arrange **village stays** for Rs300-500. The budget backwater cruise is the public **ferry ride** to and from Kottayam *(7 per day, 7am-5:30pm, 3hr., Rs9)*. Most Kottayam ferries stick to the wide canals, but those via Nedumudi *(11am and 2:25pm)* and Changansherry *(1pm)* go on the narrow canals and are lovely and very cheap. *(From Kottayam a 2:30pm ferry goes to Mannar; get off at Nedumudi and catch a local bus for the 15min. ride to Alleppey.)*

PERIYAR TIGER RESERVE ☎ 0486

Situated in nearly 800 sq. km of high, misty woodlands on the border of Tamil Nadu, Periyar Tiger Reserve surrounds the picturesque Periyar Lake. Set aside as reserved forests in 1899, the woods became the Nellikkampatty Sanctuary in 1934, and were incorporated into **Project Tiger** in 1979 (see p. 367). Tigers are elusive, but a twilight boat cruise usually turns up herds of wild elephant. Surrounded by spice plantations, the streets of Kumily, where most tourists stay, are suffused with the sweet smells of cardomom, cinnamon, cloves, and nutmeg. Kumily's religious fervor makes it a lively contrast to Thekkady; the mosque and temple keep up a steady stream of chanting, singing, and bell-tolling.

▣ GETTING THERE AND GETTING AWAY

Buses: Both private and state buses operate out of **Kumily Bus Stand** on the Tamil Nadu border, but you must walk across the border for Tamil Nadu buses. From Kumily to: **Alleppey** (11:15am, 5hr., Rs55); **Ernakulam** (every hr., 5:30am-10:30pm, 6hr., Rs70); **Kottayam** (every 30min., 2am-11pm, 4hr., Rs35); **Munnar** (6, 9:45am, and 1:30pm; 5hr.; Rs39). From the Tamil Nadu side of the border, buses go to: **Madurai** (every 30min., 4hr., Rs30). From Thekkady (buses stop in Kumily 15min. later) to: **Ernakulam** (6:30am and 2:30pm); **Trivandrum** (8am, 3, and 3:30pm; 8hr.; Rs79).

Local Transportation: Taxis, jeeps, and **auto-rickshaws** to the boat jetty in Thekkady are available from the Kumily bus stand. A **park bus** runs between the bus stand in Kumily and the Thekkady boat landing about every 30min., but waits for a full bus (first bus from Kumily 8:30am; last bus to Kumily waits for the boat tour at 6pm; Rs2). There's a lot to be said for walking through the reserve; even in the middle of the day, the road is well shaded, and you stand a good chance of seeing some of the wildlife.

🔢 ORIENTATION AND PRACTICAL INFORMATION

Periyar is made up of the reserve itself and a small collection of hotels at the town of **Thekkady.** Most park activities, including the boat rides, originate here. Most tourists, however, stay in **Kumily,** northwest of the park. The cheap hotels are along **Thekkady Rd.,** which runs from the Kumily bus station, on the border of Tamil Nadu, to the boat jetty at the end of Thekkady. The entrance to the reserve is about 1½ km from the bus stand; it's another 3km to the boat jetty. Walking through the park is permitted as long as you stay on the road, but you may not enter the forest without a guide. Unless otherwise noted, the following listings are for Kumily.

Tourist Office: Idukki District Tourism Information Office, Dept. of Tourism Gov. of Kerala (☎322620), 10min. from the bus station toward the reserve. It's on the left, away from the road, up the stairs in a yellow building. Arranges private tours of local spice plantations (2hr., Rs550 for 2 people). Open M-Sa 10am-5pm. **Rickshaw drivers** also offer budget tours of spice plantations; it should cost Rs250 for 3hr. For information on activities in Periyar, see the **Wildlife Information Centre** (☎322028), at the boat jetty in Thekkady. Open daily 6:30am-5pm. The **tourist police** at the bus stand are also helpful. Open daily 8am-8pm.

Currency Exchange: The State Bank of Travancore, behind the bus station, exchanges foreign currency and traveler's checks. Open M-F 10am-2pm, Sa 10am-noon.

Bookstore: DC Books, a bit beyond the tourist office. Open daily 9:30am-9:30pm.

Police: (☎322049), past the bus station toward the border. **Tourist Police Office,** Thekkady Rd., before the Ambadi Hotel and at the bus stand. Open daily 8am-8pm.

Pharmacy: High Range Drug House (☎322043), about 5min. away from the bus stand toward the reserve. Open M-Sa 8:30am-8:30pm.

Hospital: St. Augustine Hospital, Spring Valley (☎322042), 3km from the town center. Take a rickshaw (Rs25) or any bus toward Kottayam. The smaller **Kumily Central Hospital** (☎322045) is on the road to the reserve.

Internet: Rissas Communication (☎322103), opposite the Lake Queen Tourist Home. 8am-10pm, Rs90 per hr.; 10pm-8am, Rs60 per hr. Open 24hr.

Post Office: Near the bus stand on the main road. Open M-Sa 9am-5pm. There is also a branch at the park entrance. Open M-Sa 9am-5pm. **Postal Code:** 685509.

🏠 ACCOMMODATIONS

There are only three hotels inside the reserve, and all are run by the KTDC. Expect to spend more to stay there; otherwise, plan to shack up in Kumily.

Hotel Regent Tower (☎322570), 50m from the bus stand on the main road. Big, functional rooms with access to balconies overlooking the beautiful bus station (and those mountains all around). Attached baths with seat toilets. Buckets of hot water. Singles Rs150; doubles Rs250-350.

Lake Queen Tourist Home (☎322084), 200m down the main road. Run by a charitable foundation and managed by a retired military man. "Special" doubles feature mosquito nets, towels, and soap. All rooms have attached baths with seat toilets. Singles Rs130-270; doubles Rs320.

Coffee Inn (email coffeeinn@satyam.net.in), 500m before the park entrance. Six cottages and 2 bamboo shacks with attached baths. Singles Rs150; doubles Rs200-250.

Hotel Ambadi (☎322193), 1km from the bus stand. Slightly dark cottages are a good deal. Rooms have beautiful furniture and attached baths with seat toilets, towels, and toilet paper. Check-out noon. Cottages Rs425; rooms Rs690-990. Visa, MC.

Periyar House (☎322026), 2km inside the reserve, is the cheapest of the KTDC hotels in the park. High-ceilinged rooms with attached baths and seat toilets. Breakfast and dinner included. Singles Rs500-1300; doubles Rs700-1500. Off-season: Rs300-750/ 500-950. Visa, MC.

⬥ FOOD

Stalls opposite the bus stand set up large griddles and cook up stacks of delicious, piping hot *parothas* (Rs2) every night.

Hotel Maharani, on the first floor of the Regent Tower Hotel, packs them in for the mid-day Keralan meal (Rs20, with an excellent fish curry Rs32). Watch Indian soap operas while you eat. Egg breakfasts Rs15-25. Open daily 7am-10pm.

Hotel Ambadi Restaurant, offers all the standards. The "Kerala meal" (Rs25) is delicious. Open daily 6:30am-10:30pm.

Cafe Periyarenis, near the Thekkady jetty. Run by the park staff cooperative society, Periyarenis is the only non-hotel restaurant in the reserve. A chalkboard lists breakfast and lunch selections. Curries and *dosas* Rs6-10. Open daily 8am-6pm.

Coffee Inn, 500m before the park entrance. This tourist favorite features new age music, colorful murals, porridge (Rs30), homemade brown bread (Rs10), and tasty sandwiches (Rs20-35). Open 7am-9:30pm.

Cafe Machan, by the turn-off for the tourist police. Coffee and tea in a chic setting. Full English breakfast Rs60; sandwiches Rs25; lunch Rs30. Open daily 8:30am-8:30pm.

Sabala Restaurant KTDC, Karthika Tourist Home on the road to Thekkady. Though Sabala does good, cheap South Indian food, the clientele prefers a liquid diet—it may not be an ideal hang-out for women. Beer Rs50, *thalis* Rs19-25. Open daily 7am-10pm.

⬛ THE RESERVE

Open daily 6am-6pm. Rs50 per multiple-entry day. **KDTC Boat Tours** *(7, 9:30, 11:30am, 2, and 4pm; Rs100 top deck, Rs50 lower deck). Park boats (9:30, 11:30am, 2, and 4pm; Rs15). The boat rides last 2hr. Purchase tickets at Wildlife Information Centre for their more modest boats, or at the KTDC ticket booth at the boat jetty. The KTDC ticket booth is just up the stairs toward Aranya Nivas. Only same-day advance bookings. If a boat cruise is sold out, enquire at the reception desk of the Aranya Nivas Hotel, up the steps behind the jetty; the hotel allocates a number of spots for its guests, many of whom don't show up, and in case of demand occasionally sends out an additional boat.* **Jungle walks** *(7:30am, 3hr., Rs10);* **elephant rides** *(every 30 min., 11am-12:30pm and 2-4:30pm, 30min., Rs30). Book jungle walks and elephant rides at the Wildlife Information Centre.*

The reserve is home to a wide variety of animals, including wild boar, monkeys, the Nilgiri Langur, Malabar Giant Squirrels, Barking Deer, and gaur. Most people, however, come to Periyar to see its main attractions: wild elephants and (extremely elusive) tigers. Periyar claims to be home to at least 49 of the world's 3700 remaining wild tigers, but you would have to be very lucky to stand much chance of seeing any of them. At a cool and breezy 900m above sea level, Periyar is a good place to relax, take a leisurely boat cruise, and watch herds of wild elephants bathe. September to March is the best time to visit; January through April are the dry months, when animals come down to the lake to drink. During the monsoon you should come prepared to encounter leeches.

> ⬛ **WARNING.** So-called "official" guides often approach tourists with offers of jungle walks and jeep tours. Contracting them is illegal, and you may be fined.

The two main ways of exploring the reserve are by boat tour and trekking. Early morning and evening are the best times to see the animals. Jungle-walking groups are usually small. To see as much as possible in one day and max out on your Rs50 daily entrance fee, take the pleasant morning jungle walk and do the tranquil afternoon cruise. If you want more variety, some of the fancier hotels—including the KTDC hotels in the park and Hotel Ambadi—have government permission to lead jungle treks. The Wildlife Information Centre can also organize additional walks for small groups. On both the walk and the boat rides you are likely to see wild elephants, herds of boar, and tons of birds.

Elephant rides are purely for entertainment, and so you probably won't see very much. One of the best ways to see the wildlife is to spend a night in one of two **observation towers.** The Wildlife Information Centre handles the necessary reservations. The tower houses a maximum of two people, who must provide their own food, water, and bedding. The center will arrange transportation by boat (Rs50 per person, park boat fee Rs15).

COCHIN (KOCHI) കൊച്ചി ☎ 0484

Cochin's history stretches back thousands of years. St. Thomas the Apostle is believed to have stopped by in 54 AD, and Jews fleeing Jerusalem landed nearby in 70 AD. Trade links were established with the Chinese and Arabs at least 2000 years ago. In 1341, torrential floods from the Western Ghats hollowed out Lake Vembanad, and gave Cochin a perfect harbor that would become known as the "Queen of the Arabian Sea." Vasco da Gama arrived in the late 15th century, initiating an international scramble for access to the Malabar Coast and the lucrative spice trade. The Portuguese were followed by the Dutch and then the British, who briefly ruled the Madras Presidency from here. During its long history, the quiet fishing village spread over a cluster of islands and narrow peninsulas and was transformed into a rich and cosmopolitan port.

Cochin's cultural mix is alive and well today. The area of Fort Cochin is renowned for its tangle of different traditions and architecture: Chinese fishing nets line the harbor's mouth, Dutch-style houses cram narrow streets, and sacks of spices fill the air with the same evocative smells that drew merchants and explorers. Jew Town is a five minutes from the raja's palace. Known as the Dutch Palace, it was built by the Portuguese, remodeled by the Dutch, and filled with murals depicting scenes from the Hindu epics. Ernakulam plays the part of modern alter-ego, its frantic, brash, and polluted streets contrasting with the archaic, vaguely European feel that Fort Cochin has managed to preserve.

▐ GETTING THERE AND GETTING AROUND

Current plane, train, and bus schedules can be found in the very useful *Hello, Cochin* (free; at most hotels and tourist offices) or *Jaico Timetable* (Rs5; at bookshops and stations).

Flights: Airport, at the south end of Willingdon Island. Taxis run to Ernakulam (Rs300) and Fort Cochin (Rs400). From the Indian Airlines office a private shuttle transports passengers to the airport (Rs125). **Indian Airlines,** DH Rd., Ernakulam (☎370242), near the Foreshore Rd. intersection. Open daily 10am-1pm and 1:45-5pm. **Jet Airways,** MG Rd. (☎369423), across the street and just south of Thomas Cook. Open M-Sa 9am-5:30pm, Su 9am-4pm. To: **Bangalore** (2-3 per day, 1hr., US$80); **Bombay** (4-5 per day, 2hr., US$150); **Delhi** (1 per day, 4hr., US$330); **Goa** (M and F, 1hr., US$110); **Madras** (1-2 per day, 1hr., US$110).

Trains: Cochin has 3 stations. **Ernakulam Junction Railway Station,** 2 blocks east of Jos Junction, is the best. To: **Alleppey** (7 per day, 6:15am-11:50pm, 1½hr., Rs39); **Bombay** (1:30 and 2:50pm, 26hr., Rs337); **Trivandrum** (6 per day, 4am-5:15pm, 4½hr., Rs95). **Ernakulam Town Railway Station,** 4km north of the Junction Station along Banerji Rd., is far from MG Rd. Sleeper class to: **Bangalore** (2:35pm, 13hr., Rs193); **Calicut** (4-5 per day, 10:55am-2:10am, 11pm, 4½hr., Rs83). **Cochin Harbour Railway Station,** on Willingdon Island, is serviced by few trains.

Buses: KSRTC Bus Stand (☎372022), central Ernakulam, 2 blocks east of Senoy Junction. To: **Alleppey** (every 30min., 1½hr., Rs25); **Bangalore** (8 per day, 6am-9:30pm, 14hr., Rs240); **Calicut** (every hr., 5hr., Rs95); **Coimbatore** (frequent, 4½hr., Rs73); **Madurai** (7:45pm, 10hr., Rs130); **Munnar** (6:30am, 5hr., Rs52); **Mysore** (8 per day, 6am-9:30pm, 10hr., Rs190); **Trivandrum** (frequent, 5hr., Rs100). Tamil Nadu State Transportation services, around the corner from the main KSRTC enquiry desk goes to:

Madras (3:30pm, 15hr., Rs243) and **Madurai** (8:15am, 10hr., Rs130) via **Kumily** (6hr., Rs77). **Private bus companies** also run long-distance buses from several terminals in Cochin: Ernakulam South, opposite the Ernakulam Junction Railway Station, and High Court Junction, at the end of Shanmugham Rd. Several agencies have offices around Jos Junction, Ernakulam. *Hello Cochin* lists departure times.

Ferries: The most scenic—and often only—way to move from one island to another (frequent, 6am-9pm, no services from Ernakulam's Main Jetty to Fort Cochin noon-1pm and none from Fort Cochin to Ernakulam 1:20-2:55pm, Rs2). Ferries hop between islands along a variety of routes; the most useful are listed below. From **Ernakulam: Main Jetty,** mid-town, to Vypeen Island and Fort Cochin (last boat 9:10pm; buy tickets at the SWTD counter); **High Court Jetty** to Vypeen Island and to and from Bolghatty Island. From **Fort Cochin: Customs Jetty** (from the bus stand follow River Rd. east to just beyond Hotel Seagull) to Ernakulam's Main Jetty (last ferry 9:30pm); **Vypeen Island Jetty** (opposite the bus stand) to Vypeen Island. From **Mattancherry** (the jetty is opposite the Dutch Palace) to Ernakulam (sporadic). From **Vypeen Island:** to Ft. Cochin, Willingdon Island's Embarkation Jetty, and Ernakulam's High Court Jetty. The most frequent ferries run between Vypeen and Ernakulam and Vypeen and Fort Cochin; if the Fort Cochin ferry is a long wait, you can go via Vypeen.

Other Local Transportation: Local buses are cheap (under Rs5) and orderly. In Ernakulam, local buses depart from the KRSTC bus station, and can also be nabbed as they pass through town. Buses to Ft. Cochin leave from the east side of MG Rd., just south of Jos Junction (last bus 9pm). In Ft. Cochin, local buses run from the bus stand (opposite the Vypeen Island jetty), over the bridge onto Willingdon Island, past the airport, across the bridge to Ernakulam, and up MG Rd. In Ernakulam, **auto-rickshaws** are plentiful during the day but scarce at night. There are no buses or taxis in Ft. Cochin, but cycle- and auto-rickshaws can be found near the jetties. Auto-rickshaw-*wallahs* often refuse to use their meters; most in-town fares should be under Rs15. For rickshaws from Ernakulam to Fort Cochin you will be charged round-trip fare for a one-way trip (at least Rs80; more after dark). The peninsula is navigable by foot, and **bike** rentals are available from the **Vasco Hospitality Center** (Rs5 per hr., Rs35 per day).

✳ ORIENTATION

Cochin is spread around **Lake Vembanad** and is made up of **Ernakulam** on the shore of the mainland, **Fort Cochin** and **Mattancherry** on the peninsula, **Vypeen Island,** and the smaller islands of Willingdon, Vallarpadam, Gundy, and Bolghatty. The central railway and bus stations and many of the hotels are along the eastern shore of Lake Vembanad in Ernakulam, but tourists generally devote their waking hours to the other side of the lake and the sight-filled peninsula.

Ernakulam's three main streets, **Shanmugham, Mahatma Gandhi (MG),** and **Chittoor Rd.,** run north-south, parallel to the shore. MG Rd. is intersected by three major cross-streets that lead to the lake shore: **Convent Rd.** intersects at **Shenoys Junction,** a couple of blocks west of the **central bus station;** three blocks south of Shenoys Junction, **Hospital Rd.** runs to the lake-front; farther south, **Jos Junction** marks the intersection with **Durbar Hall (DH) Rd.** The **main jetty** is midway between **Press Club Rd.** (the western extension of Convent Rd.) and Hospital Rd.

The north-south **Princess St.** is Fort Cochin's main drag. It extends to **Calvathy Rd.** (called River Rd. in the west and Bazaar Rd. in the east), which skirts the shore. **Jew Town** and Mattancherry, home of the Dutch Palace, are on the eastern side of the peninsula. In the early 20th century, a mammoth dredging project created **Willingdon Island,** sandwiched between Ernakulam and the peninsula. Willingdon is home to the **airport** and, 2km south, the **Cochin Harbour Railway Station.** With a 270° view of the harbor, the Taj Malabar Hotel is at the northern tip of the island.

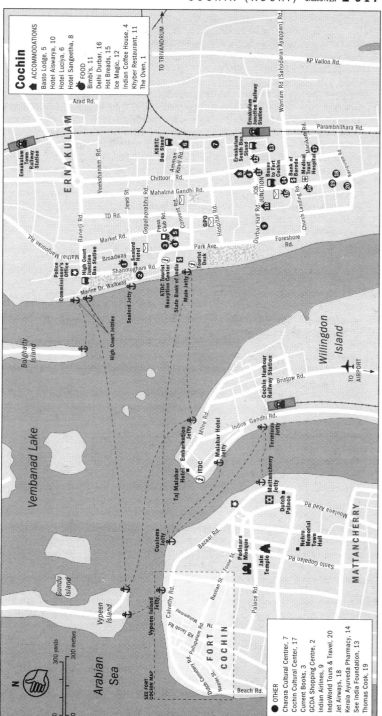

Cochin

ACCOMMODATIONS
Basto Lodge, 5
Hotel Aiswarya, 10
Hotel Luciya, 6
Hotel Sangeetha, 8

FOOD
Bimbi's, 11
Delhi Durbar, 16
Hot Breads, 15
Ice Magic, 12
Indian Coffee House, 4
Khyber Restaurant, 11
The Oven, 1

OTHER
Charara Cultural Center, 7
Cochin Cultural Center, 17
Current Books, 3
GCDA Shopping Centre, 2
Indian Airlines, 9
IndoWorld Tours & Travel, 20
Jet Airways, 18
Kerala Ayurveda Pharmacy, 14
See India Foundation, 13
Thomas Cook, 19

KERALA

🛈 PRACTICAL INFORMATION

Tourist Office: There is a privately run **Tourist Desk,** Ernakulam (☎371761), at the dock-side ticket office of the Main Jetty in Ernakulam. For information on their **Backwater Cruises,** see p. 524. Open daily 9am-6pm. **KTDC Tourist Reception Centre,** Shan-mugham Rd., Ernakulam (☎353234), next to the State Bank of India, just northwest of the end of Press Club Rd., offers backwater tours. Open daily 8am-7pm. There are a number of privately run tourist offices in and around Princess St., Ft. Cochin, including the helpful **Vasco Information Centre** (☎229877), which distributes the informative map and brochure *Walking Through Ft. Cochin.* Open daily 9:30am-11pm.

Budget Travel: Indoworld Tours and Travels, MG Rd. (☎367818), at the intersection with Ravipuram Rd. Open M-Sa 8am-7pm, Su 8am-2:30pm.

Currency Exchange: Thomas Cook, MG Rd., Ernakulam (☎373829), near the Air India build-ing. Open M-Sa 9:30am-6pm. **Bank of Baroda,** MG Rd. (☎351205), a few blocks south of Jos Junction, on the west side of the street, gives cash advances. Open M-F 10am-2pm and 2:30-3:30pm; Sa 10am-12:30pm. In Ft. Cochin, **Canara Bank,** TM Mohammed Rd. (☎225467), at Kunnumpuram Junction, one block east of where Bastian and KB Jacob Rd. meet, gives cash advances and changes traveler's checks. Open M-F 10am-2pm, Sa 10am-noon.

Bookstore: Current Books, Press Club Rd., Ernakulam, has a wide selection. Open M-Sa 9:30am-7:30pm. **Idiom,** Mattancherry, opposite the Pardesi Synagogue. Open daily 10am-6pm. They've opened a new branch at Bastion and Princess St., in the center of Ft. Cochin. Open M-Sa noon-9pm.

Market: In Ernakulam, there are shops of every stripe at Jos Junction and a lot of shop-ping action on and around Broadway. The area near the jetty features roadside hawk-ers, used-book kiosks, and fruit stands. In Ft. Cochin, beach shacks near the bus stand sell fresh fish and fruit.

Police: For the Ernakulam central **police station** (☎394500), head inland from Shan-mugham Rd. and take the first left onto Erg Rd. Then, turn right onto Banerji Rd. **Fort Cochin Police** (☎224055) is behind the bus station, opposite the Vypeen Island Jetty.

Hospital: Medical Trust Hospital, MG Rd., Ernakulam (☎371852), 3 blocks south of Jos Junction, is newly renovated. The **pharmacy** inside is open 24hr. **Gautham Hospital** (☎223055), 3km from Ft. Cochin, to the southeast in Chullickal.

Pharmacy: In Ft. Cochin, **Jeny Medicals,** Kunnumpuram Junction (☎224253), at the intersection of TM Mohammed and Bastian Rd. Open daily 8:15am-10pm.

Internet: In Ernakulam, **Times,** DD Angadi Building, (☎381892), at the corner of Press Club and Market Rd. Rs 50 per hr. Open M-Sa 9am-9pm, Su 10am-9pm. **Campus Web,** Press Club Rd., is only Rs30 per hr. but has fewer terminals. Open M-Sa 9:30am-10pm. In Ft. Cochin email is ubiquitous but costs more. **Call'n'Fax/Shop'n'Save,** Princess St. (☎223438), next to Elite Hotel is relatively fast. Rs90 per hr. Open M-Sa 8am-11pm; in-season also Su 5-11pm.

Post Office: Ernakulam's **GPO,** Hospital Rd., between Foreshore and MG Rd. Open M-F 8:30am-8pm, Sa 9:30am-8pm, Su 10am-5pm. **Kochi Head Post Office,** Ft. Cochin. Open M-Sa 9am-5pm. **Postal Code:** 682011.

🏠 ACCOMMODATIONS

ERNAKULAM

Ernakulam's rooms tend to be characterless and overpriced, but they are more convenient to the stations and restaurants.

Hotel Luciya (☎381177), behind the KRSTC bus station, is well-run. Its enormous size almost ensures room availability. Singles (squat toilet) Rs130-305; doubles (seat toilet and balcony) Rs260-440.

Basoto Lodge, Press Club Rd. (☎352140), close to Market Rd. Comfortable, with basic facilities and high ceilings very popular with foreigners. Check-out 24hr. Singles Rs60; doubles with bath (squat toilets) Rs120.

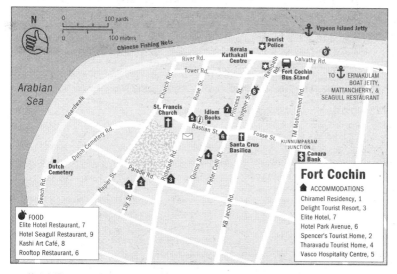

Fort Cochin

♠ ACCOMMODATIONS
Chiramel Residency, 1
Delight Tourist Resort, 3
Elite Hotel, 7
Hotel Park Avenue, 6
Spencer's Tourist Home, 2
Tharavadu Tourist Home, 4
Vasco Hospitality Centre, 5

🍴 FOOD
Elite Hotel Restaurant, 7
Hotel Seagull Restaurant, 9
Kashi Art Café, 8
Rooftop Restaurant, 6

Hotel Aiswarya, Warriam Rd. (☎364454), near Jos Junction, where Warriam meets DH Rd. Cool marble floors and decent furnishings. All rooms have TV and bath with hot water and seat toilets. Check-out 24hr. Prices do not include 7.5% tax. Singles Rs300-650; doubles Rs400-650. Visa, MC.

Hotel Sangeetha (☎368487). From the railway station, take your first right. Clean rooms with Star TV and soft beds. Breakfast included. Check-out 24hr. Singles Rs350-760; doubles Rs550-850. Visa, MC.

FORT COCHIN

Flee the bustle of Ernakulam for the old world tranquility of Ft. Cochin, where you'll get much more quality for your rupees. In season (Dec.-Jan.), accommodationse are limited. Most hotels double as tourist offices, offering backwater cruises, ayurvedic massages, and tickets for dance shows. Things are much cheaper off-season (roughly late-Mar.-Nov.).

▨ **Spencer's Tourist Home,** Parade St. (☎225049). Turn right off Rose St.; Spencer's is the handsome, rambling old house on the left, at the intersection with Lily St. Big common room with cable TV, couch, and reading materials. Large, clean rooms with huge soft beds. Dorm beds Rs40; singles Rs100-150; doubles with bath Rs200.

Chiramel Residency, Lily St. (☎227310), close to the intersection with Parade St. A small, attractive, family-run guest house. Mosquito-proof and beautifully furnished; if you give advance warning, you can get home-cooked meals. Check-out noon. Singles Rs100-150; doubles Rs200-600. 25% less off-season.

Delight Tourist Resort, Rose St. (☎228658), south from St. Francis Church; on the left, just before the end of the field. Hardly qualifies as a resort, but it's certainly a delightful place to stay. Large rooms with attached baths set in a lovely house with a large library. Check-out noon. Doubles Rs200-700. Off-season: 50% discount.

Vasco Hospitality Centre (☎229877), on the corner of Bastion and Rose St., offers 7 basic rooms in a tired old house. Local legend has it that Vasco da Gama expired here on Christmas Eve, 1524. Provides tourist information, bike rentals (Rs5 per hr., Rs35 per day), and Internet access (Rs75 per hr.). Singles Rs75; doubles with bath Rs125-200. Off-season: Rs60-100.

Elite Hotel, Princess St. (☎225733), has 15 rooms ranging from basic to spacious with tiled floors. Most rooms have attached bath. Check-out noon. Singles Rs125; doubles with bath Rs150. Extra person Rs50.

KERALA

Hotel Park Avenue (☎222671), at the intersection of Princess and Bastion St. A marble-faced monstrosity that is nevertheless a great place to stay. Modest-sized rooms have attached baths, and everything works. Rooftop restuarant. Check-out noon. Add 7-15% tax. Singles Rs175-500; doubles Rs250-750. Off-season: knock off 30%.

Tharavadu Tourist Home, Quiros St. (☎226897). From the south end of Princess St., turn right, and then left. Well-maintained, 400-year-old house with 8 clean rooms, two with common bath (seat toilet and shower). Rooms Rs135-205.

FOOD

ERNAKULAM

Ernakulam's eateries serve a mishmash of international cuisines. Try local foods like *appam* (a thick *dosa* served with fish stew), and coconut dishes. Excellent bakeries and tempting juice bars (no water, no ice) line the streets.

- **Delhi Durbar,** MG Rd., a few blocks south of Jos Junction. Here you'll find Ernakulam's best slice of North Indian cuisine: succulent chicken *tikka masala* (Rs50) and great garlic *naan* (Rs15) in A/C comfort. Open daily noon-3:30pm and 6pm-1am.

- **Bimbi's,** Jos Junction. The chaotic ambience of this local landmark is mesmerizing, its food good and cheap. Pay at the register, claim your food at the counter, then sit down and watch the world whizz by. Excellent *masala dosa* Rs15. Huge selection of sweets at the front. Open daily 8am-9:30pm.

- **Hot Breads,** Warriam Rd. Follow MG Rd. south from Jos Junction and turn right; it's on the right. Fresh pastries and cakes, including chocolate croissants (Rs10) and brownies (Rs10). Pizza, burgers, and sandwiches, too. Open daily 9am-9pm.

- **Ice Magic,** South Railway Station Rd., toward MG Rd. from the station—one in a row of enticing juice bars. Select the fruit of your choice to be blended up (Rs10-15) or go for the mean mango milkshake (Rs20). Open daily 10am-11:30pm.

- **Khyber Restaurant,** Jos Junction, upstairs from Bimbi's. Dimly lit, marble-floored, and significantly more expensive than its downstairs neighbor, the mildly A/C-ed Khyber offers Chinese and Indian food. Luscious *kadai paneer* Rs55; incredible garlic *naan* Rs20; and smooth, creamy *lassis* Rs20. Open daily 11am-10:45pm.

- **The Oven,** Shanaugham Rd., just north of the Sealord Hotel, plays country tunes and serves up tasty Indian snacks (Rs7-12), grilled sandwiches (Rs15-25), and delicious sweets (Rs7-20) to the crowds. Open daily 10am-9pm.

- **Indian Coffee House,** one opposite Main Boat Jetty, the other in Jos Junction, opposite Bimbi's. Beloved by purists and tourists alike, ICH is convenient and fast. Veg. *biryani* Rs15; banana fry Rs3; and *dosas* Rs8. Open daily 7:30am-9pm.

DON'T MAKE THAT FACE OR IT'LL STICK

THAT WAY Kathakali, which means "story play," is one of India's four major schools of classical dance. Transformed into gods and demons by the application of wildly colored make-up, massive golden headdresses, and skirts bright and full enough to put any ballerina to shame, the performers, who are traditionally men, have studied scripture, Kalaripayatu, ayurvedic massage, and music for eight years, beginning at the age 10 or 12. They are then trained in dance for four years. Emphasis is given to proper lifestyle and the deep understanding of archetypes portrayed in the *Vedas.* The dancers communicate through the use of 24 *mudras,* hand gestures augmented by convulsive movements of the eyes and facial muscles and the pounding of *ghungroo*-laden feet. By using combinations of these *mudras*—signifying "love," "courage," "bee drinking from a lotus flower," etc.—the dancers depict stories from the *Ramayana* and *Mahabharata* while piercing drums and classical vocals provide narration. Although traditional *kathakali* was—and still is on special holy days—performed as part of a temple ritual, modern-day shows last only one hour and are given in theaters filled with tourists who come to "watch the Gods dance."

KERALA

FORT COCHIN

Fort Cochin has few restaurants, but there are shacks on the sea-front that grill fish to order and serve the usual fried snacks. Bakeries and vegetable stores are at the intersection of Bastian St. and TM Mohommed (one block east and parallel to KB Jacob), and fruit is sold near the bus stand. Bakeries are along Fosse and Pullupalam Rd., the eastern extensions of Bastian Rd.

Kashi Art Cafe, Burgher St., one block from Princess St. A little pretentious and over-priced perhaps—all that art on the walls—but you can reacquaint yourself with *real* coffee (Rs30) and make lots of tourist friends. Light Western meals, including breakfast (Rs45-55). For Rs5 fill up your water bottle with boiled and purified water and spare the street another piece of plastic. Open M-Sa 8:30am-6:30pm, Su 8:30am-2:30pm.

Hotel Seagull Restaurant, Calvathy Rd., on the waterfront. Enter through the east entrance to the Family Garden Restaurant, where you'll be served fresh seafood and cold beer to wash it all down (Rs60) on an open air patio overhanging the sea. Excellent ginger fish Rs80; crab fry Rs60; mixed vegetable curry Rs30. Open daily 7am-10:30pm.

Rooftop Restaurant, in the Hotel Park Avenue, is quiet and calm and serves tasty and affordable Keralan seafood dishes (fish masala Rs35). Open daily 7am-10:30pm.

Elite Hotel Restaurant, Princess St., on the ground floor of the hotel. Locals eat, drink, think, and wink while tourists catch up on the latest news from Goa and try the seafood of the day with finger chips (Rs50). *Dosas* (Rs15) served after 5pm. Egg breakfasts Rs10-20. Open daily 8am until the crowd trickles out (10 or 11pm).

SIGHTS

FORT COCHIN

Ancient church bells toll while fishermen haul up Chinese fishing nets and the heavy orange sun sinks down into the Arabian sea—all the hoary old fantasies come true in Fort Cochin. The brochure *Walking Through Fort Cochin*, available at tourist offices, offers informative details about the area.

ST. FRANCIS CHURCH. Believed to be the first church built by Europeans in India, St. Francis Church (locally called the Vasco da Gama Church), was built in 1503 by Franciscan friars from Portugal. The stone version, constructed a few years later, still stands among the houses built by British traders and Dutch farmers. When Vasco da Gama died in Cochin in 1524, his remains were buried under the church floor. Fourteen years later, the remains were transferred to Lisbon, but his tombstone remains here. Cochin fell to the Dutch in 1663, and the church was Protestantized in 1779. Although the British occupied Cochin in 1795, the church remained a Dutch stronghold—the walls are still lined with Dutch memorials. The church became Anglican in 1864, and the Church of South India, which now carries the ecclesiastical baton, has since dedicated it to St. Francis. Pre-electricity fans hang from the ceilings; some very sweaty soul had to pull constantly at the cords to keep the flaps flapping and a breeze blowing down on the worshipers below. *(Open M-F 9:30am-1pm and 2:30-5:30pm.)*

SANTA CRUZ BASILICA. A church was first built on this site in 1505 and replaced by a cathedral in 1558. The current cathedral, consecrated in 1905, is new by Ft. Cochin standards, but its painted ceiling merits a quick look around nevertheless. *(Bastian St.; follow Princess St. south and turn left. English mass Su 4:30pm.)*

OTHER SIGHTS. Crumbling tombs disintegrate beside the beach at the overgrown **Dutch Cemetery.** *(Turn left from the gates of St. Francis Church, then right onto Dutch Cemetery Rd.)* A driveway next to PWD Guest House leads to the **beach,** where the crowd consists of fishermen, fish-sellers, fish-buyers, and fish. The skeletal **Chinese fishing nets** nearby were brought to Kerala by traders between 1350 and 1450. As massive cargo ships pull into the harbor, fishermen return from the sea in long canoe-like boats with the day's catch. Linger to watch teams of men pull up the nets; high tide is the time to see them in action.

KERALA

MATTANCHERRY

A 45-minute stroll from Ft. Cochin brings you to the heart of Mattancherry, a historical center of the international spice trade. Follow Calvathy Rd. to the Customs Jetty and keep going as it turns into Bazaar Rd.—it's a pleasant walk past rows of export warehouses, where rich smells of tea, pepper, and spices waft out of every alley. The olfactory kaleidoscope can also be sampled, along with exhaust fumes, in an auto-rickshaw. *(Rs25 from Ft. Cochin.)*

THE DUTCH PALACE. The **Mattancherry Palace** (a.k.a. the Dutch Palace) was built by the Portuguese in 1555 for Raja Virakerala Varma; its construction was a "goodwill gesture," probably in exchange for trading rights. During their occupation in 1663, the Dutch renovated and renamed the palace. Two **temples,** one dedicated to Krishna and the other to Shiva, were built on the palace grounds by the Portuguese, but today only Hindus may enter. Beautiful, detailed **murals** depicting scenes from the *Ramayana* and the *Puranas* in distinct Keralite style cover nearly 300 square meters of the palace walls. In one, Krishna uses six hands and two feet to pleasure a group of admiring *gopis* (milkmaids) and two more hands to play the flute. Downstairs, a number of less detailed paintings show divine sexual scenes set in a beautiful forest. Rooms without murals make up a **museum** and house oil portraits of Cochin rajas with their palanquins, robes, weapons, Dutch drawings, and umbrellas. *(Palace open Sa-Th 10am-5pm. Rs2. No photography permitted.)*

PARDESI SYNAGOGUE. Originally built in 1568 (though the current structure dates from 1664), the synagogue is lit by 19th-century oil-burning chandeliers suspended over a floor of blue-and-white Cantonese tiles given in 1762. Though they bear a common willow pattern, the 1100 tiles are each unique. The synagogue's Torah is written on sheepskin scrolls and stored in ornate metal canisters, one of them a gift from the Raja of Cochin. The true antiquity of the Jewish community in Kerala can be witnessed in a Helnas-inscribed stone set into an outside wall of the synagogue; it comes from a now-defunct synagogue built in 1344 in Kochangadi. Gravestones with Hebrew inscriptions are propped around the outside of the synagogue. You can still visit the synagogue, in **Jew Town,** tucked in an alleyway parallel to Bazaar Rd. The area is teeming with stores selling curios and antiques—bargain hard. *(5min. from the Dutch Palace. Walk away from Ft. Cochin until the road makes a right turn and make a sharp right there; the synagogue is at the end of the street to the right. Open Su-F 10am-noon and 3-5pm. Rs2.)*

JEW TOWN It is believed that the first Jews came to Kerala during the 10th century BC as traders from King Solomon's Israel. The destruction of the Second Temple in Jerusalem by the Romans in 70 AD led to the dispersion of the Jewish people, some of whom landed in Shingly (30km north of Cochin, now known as Cranganore) a few years later. In 379 AD, Joseph Rabban was made a prince of Anjuvanam, establishing a Jewish Kingdom. Around 500 AD, another large group of Jews immigrated here from Iraq and Iran. With the onset of Portuguese persecution in the 16th century, the Jews were expelled from Shingly. Legend has it that Joseph Azar, the last surviving Jewish prince, swam to Cochin with his wife on his shoulders. The Jewish Keralans placed themselves under the protection of the Raja of Cochin, who gave them a parcel of land for a synagogue next to his palace (see p. 522).

Emigration to Bombay and Israel has pared Cochin's Jewish population down to a geriatric 14, but you'll still see menorahs in some of the windows. There has been no rabbi here for several years, so the elders of the synagogue conduct ceremonies and make decisions regarding Jewish law. Happy to discuss their future with visitors, the remaining Jews seem unconcerned about the survival of their community. Sixty or seventy Jews remain in Kerala, along with some four to five thousand in India as a whole, most of them in Bombay.

VYPEEN ISLAND

Miles of ignored **beaches** roll along the Arabian Sea on Vypeen Island, passing a **Lighthouse** at Ochanthuruth (1.5km west of the main road; open daily 3-5pm) and the early 16th-century **Palliport Fort** (open Th 10am-5pm). The beaches are empty, except for herds of sunbathing cows and a few fishing boats, until the in season, when scattered foreigners arrive. Men come from the nearby villages to see the show—women are advised to swim in a t-shirt and shorts or pants. **Cherai Beach,** just a few kilometers shy of the northern tip of the island, is more frequented by foreigners and is probably safer for women than the others. From Vypeen Island catch a frequent bus (50min., Rs5.75) to the Cherai Junction. From there continue away from Vypeen and bear left (west) onto Cherai Beach Rd. for a scenic walk (15min.; Rs20 by rickshaw). Sprinkled along the main road are bakeries and produce stands; just before Cherai Beach, the tranquil Kadaloram serves the usual snacks for Rs10-20 and Chinese and Indian cuisine for Rs20-60. (Open daily 8am-9:30pm.) **Ferries** run between Vypeen Island and Ernakulam's Main Jetty (every 20min. 5:30am-10:30pm). Ferries from Ft. Cochin to Vypeen (6:30am-9pm) depart from the launch opposite the bus stand.

🦆 BACKWATER CRUISES

Beyond the city lie magical green fields, towering palms, and lazy backwaters—some of India's most remarkably green and pleasant landscapes. Kerala's tourist industry has capitalized on all this, offering backwater tours on non-motorized boats through the maze of lagoons, lakes, canals, and streams. A guide paddles the vessel, which can hold no more than 6 people, for several enchanting hours, stopping for a fresh coconut break and a stroll through paddy fields. The whole scene is enthralling, especially for bird-watchers. The tours also offer a unique opportunity to see Keralan village life up close. **Moonlight cruises** on full-moon nights are offered in season. The **Tourist Desk,** Main Jetty, charters daily tours. In season, reserve at least one day in advance; off season, show up 30 minutes before departure. (☎371761. Tours 9am-1:30pm and 2-6:30pm. Rs275; save Rs50 by booking directly at the Tourist Office.) The **KTDC** also provides backwater tours on country boats (8:30am and 2:30pm, Rs315, minimum 2 people). Most hostels can also arange backwater cruises.

🎭 ENTERTAINMENT

For those with an itch to twitch and tremble, the resident band in the Princess Room at the **Sealord Hotel,** Shanmugham Rd., cranks out a good "Mustang Sally." Ice cream *and* booze are available (☎382472. Band plays 8-11pm, beer Rs90). The **Sridar** movie theater (☎352529), opposite the GCDA Shopping Centre, screens English-language films in Dolby stereo and A/C comfort.

The **Cochin Cultural Centre** (☎380366) teaches dance, yoga, music, costume making, and more (for directions, see below). The traditional Keralan martial art of Kalaripayatu, dating from medieval times, is taught at the **ENS Kalari Centre** (☎700810), 9km from the city center; call for directions.

The **Kerala Ayurveda Pharmacy,** Warriam Rd., just east of MG Rd., is one of many places in Cochin offering **ayurvedic massage.** (☎361202. Rs350, with steam wash Rs450. Open M-Sa 8am-7pm, Su 8am-4pm; men only M-Sa 4-7pm.) The **Sree Narayana Holistic Clinic,** on Vypeen Island, offers a full body ayurvedic massage and steam bath as well as an excellent home-cooked Keralan meal for Rs600. (☎502362. Open for appointments daily 9:30am-5pm. The doctor will pick you up from the Vypeen ferry jetty. Both Spencer's and Delight Tourist Homes can set up appointments.) Since it's an important component of *kathakali*, several dance centers also offer ayurvedic massage by appointment: Cochin Cultural Centre (☎380366), Chavara Cultural Centre (☎368443), and Kerala Kathakali Kendra (☎740030). For more on **Ayurvedic Medicine,** see p. 508.

KERALA

DANCE PERFORMANCES

Cochin offers spectacular nightly performances of **kathakali dance** (see p. 520). Geared toward tourists, these performances are usually prefaced by elaborate make-up demonstrations, an explanation of the music and hand-symbols, and a synopsis of the tale to be enacted. Performances last from one hour to 90 minutes.

Cochin Cultural Centre (☎ 380366). From Jos Junction, head south on MG Rd., turn left on Sahodaran Ayappan Rd., right on Chittoor Rd., and, finally, left onto Manikath Rd. Make-up 5:30pm, performance 6:30pm; Rs125.

See India Foundation (☎ 369471). From MG Rd., head east on Warriam Rd. for 2 blocks; the Foundation is on the right under the painted face. Director Devan has been performing here for 30 years. Make-up 5:45pm, performance 6:45pm; Rs100.

Kerala Kathakali Centre (☎ 221827), near the Ft. Cochin bus stand at the end of Princess St., has a young troupe of artists. Make-up 5pm, performance 6:30pm; Rs100.

Kerala Kathakali Kendra, Bolghatty Island (☎ 355003), in the Bolghatty Palace Hotel near the jetty. A good pretext for visiting this palace built by the Dutch in 1744. Make-up 6pm, performance 7pm; Rs100.

MUNNAR വ്വന്നാർ ☎ 0486

At an elevation of 1500m, Munnar is an invigorating antidote to the steamy heat of the plains, and it has scenery superlative enough to match Mt. Anaimudi (2700m), the highest peak in India south of the Himalayas. It was a Scot, J.D. Munro, who kicked off the town's development during the 1870s, creating a fiefdom for generations of Scottish tea-planters. Munro and his friends left town long ago, however, leaving their rolling oceans of tea in the hands of Tata Tea Ltd., an offshoot of the same Parsi-owned mega-company that built the bus that brought you here. These days, Munnar is rapidly reinventing itself as a hill station, and its attractive mix of climate, wildlife, and scenery will not go unnoticed for long.

🚌 **GETTING THERE AND GETTING AROUND. Buses** depart from the KSRTC bus station, 2km south of town; east-bound buses also stop in town. To: **Cochin** via **Alway** (3 per day, 6:30-11:30am, private bus 10:30am, 4hr., Rs60); **Coimbatore** (6:30am and 3:30pm, 6hr., Rs48); **Kottayam** (3 per day, 6am-noon, 4hr., Rs60); **Madurai** (2:30pm, 5hr.) or via **Theni** (7:30am and 9:30am). **Jeeps** and **rickshaws** (Rs15 to New Munnar) are hard to miss; bargain hard. **Matha Cycle Shop,** in the middle of the bazaar, rents bikes for Rs3 per hour. (Open daily 9am-6pm).

🏛️🛈 **ORIENTATION AND PRACTICAL INFORMATION.** In Tamil, Munnar means "Three Rivers," and the heart of the town centers on the point where the three rivers meet. The road from Cochin enters the relatively flat valley alongside the main river 3km south of Munnar's town center. Several budget hotels, restaurants, tourist offices, and local bus stands are compacted into this area and are overlooked by the **Tata Tea Regional Headquarters** on Cochin Rd. At this point, the road leads out to the mid-range hotels of **New Munnar** and the **KRSTIC bus stand.** In the other direction, to the left of the temple, are the bazaar and the road to **Eravikulam National Park.** Joseph Iype, in his tiny **tourist information shop** close to the bazaar end of the footbridge, is Munnar's local action hero. Keen to share the delights of the region, he can provide bus times, tours, and hand-drawn maps to waterfalls. He also offers lodging in his cottage and will find you a doctor if you need one. Batteries sold separately. (☎ 531136, or at home 530349. Open daily 9am-1pm and 3-6pm.) Other services include the **State Bank of Travancore,** opposite the Tata Tea Headquarters (open M-F 10am-2pm, Sa 10am-noon), the **hospital,** opposite the Government Guest House, and the **post office,** across the river from Tata Tea. (Open M-Sa 9am-5:30pm.) **Postal Code:** 685612.

ACCOMMODATIONS AND FOOD. Most of the cheap eating and sleeping options are in the center of town. **Hilltop Lodge** is probably the best of Munnar's basic lodges. Clean, compact rooms come with attached squat toilets. (☎530616. Singles Rs110; doubles Rs160.) **Krisna Lodge,** on the opposite side of the river, has singles with shared bath (Rs100) or doubles with clean, attached bath and seat toilets (Rs200). **Hotel Hajrath,** in the market, is a popular place to eat. (Veg. entrees Rs12. Open daily 6:30am-9:30pm.) **Aiswarya Restaurant,** under the Hilltop Lodge, offers mountain views and down-home cooking. (Veg. entrees Rs12; meat Rs20. Open daily 7am-9pm.) **Brothers Restaurant,** by the temple, is little more than a dark shed, but they grill tasty fish for Rs30 (open daily 6am-9pm).

SIGHTS AND HIKING. Munnar is all about strolls through tea fields, and splashing around in waterfalls. Large cascades can be found just off Cochin Rd. They are accesible by foot with the option of returning by local bus. Fifteen kilometers away is a lake with boating and (land-bound) elephants.

The major attraction in Munnar is **Eravikulam National Park,** 15km away, which was established in 1978 to protect the spectacular Mt. Anaimundi (2694m), the highest Indian peak south of the Himalayas. The mountain and surrounding area is home to the endangered Nilgiri tahr (only 2500 are left), a species of mountain goat that's a lot more interesting than it sounds. The park's ecosystem also supports tigers, Nilgiri Marten, Asiatic Elephants, sambar, ganr, Nilgiri Langur, wild dogs, jungle cats, mongoose, and barking deer. Surrounded by beautiful tea fields, visitors can stroll by waterfalls and the mountainside fields of grass, where the wild goats are. Visitors are requested not to stray from the road, especially during February and March, when the tahr are busy breeding. Take an auto-rickshaw from town to the second forest check-point (one-way Rs80, with 1hr. wait Rs130), the farthest a rickshaw can go. From there, it is a 2km walk up to Rajamalai Gap on the mountain's shoulder and then another 4km down to a tea factory. Unless you have a rickshaw waiting for you, walk down the hill from the check-point to catch a local bus on Munnar Rd. *(Park admission Rs50, rickshaw fee Rs5. Local buses leave Munnar every 30min. from Marayoor station, across the bridge from the back of the bazaar, and drop you off at the park around 45 min. later.)*

Lockhart Mountain offers another superb mountain ridge hike. Take a bus (Rs3) or a rickshaw (Rs120) to Lockhart Gap. The round-trip hike takes about three hours and offers some spectacular views. A lazier way to soak in the scenery is to bus it to **Top Station.** The first bus of the day (7:15am, 1½hr.) should get you there before the clouds come down and the haze comes up. You can also make a three-day trek to **Kodaikanal** (see p. 586) from Top Station; two villages along the way provide basic accommodations.

ENTERTAINMENT AND NIGHTLIFE. Munnar doesn't have much of a nightlife, but a visit to the **High Range Club,** at the end of a footbridge across the river from the SN Tourist Home, is an excellent substitute. The club is formally open to members and high-paying guests only, but proper dress (a collar and long sleeves are required of men in the evening) and a polite word with the Club Secretary might just be enough to gain you access to the planters' social world. The walls of the "Men Only" bar (women admitted occasionally) sag under the weight of hunting trophies and a collection of ancient headgear (beer Rs50).

With all that tea around, you might start to wonder how those cute, tubby little green bushes get twisted and squeezed into a Tetley's tea bag. While Tata Tea isn't too keen on conducting **tours** of its factories, a little polite persistence or a word with Joe Iype might prove fruitful.

KERALA

LOCO FOR COCONUTS
In Malayalam, the coconut tree is called *kalpa vrishka*, "the heaven-gifted tree." The coconut tree and its products are everywhere, from the leaf you eat your breakfast on to the bed you go to sleep in at night. A coconut tree takes 7-8 years to mature. A new bud appears every 40 days, and each bud will yield 10-12 coconuts. The buds contain a sticky liquid, which after 12-14 hours of fermentation, turns into toddy, a sweet little drink with a nice kick to it. Let the buds blossom, and in 3-6 months you'll have young green coconuts filled with sweet water. If you let the coconuts mature for a year, the water inside dries and condenses into the white coconut meat. This is grated and used in cooking. The coconuts can also be dried; they are cut in half and laid out for a week. Look out of bus windows and the mats of drying coconuts are hard to miss. The dried whites, *copra*, are sent to a processor to be squeezed for coconut oil, which is used in cooking, ayurvedic massages, and Kathakali make-up. The husks of the coconut shells are used to make *coir* ropes and mats. The shells themselves are used to make spoons, cups, bowls, and vases, and as a fine charcoal for cooking sweets. The palm leaves are woven to thatch roofs and build huts and fences. The stems of the fronds are used as brooms. And after 80 years (the average life span of a tree is 60-70 years) the bark of the coconut tree becomes very hard and is used to make furniture.

TRICHUR (THRISSUR) തൃശ്ശൂർ ☎ 0487

With its high concentration of universities, museums, and temples, Trichur bills itself as the "cultural capital of Kerala," but most foreign visitors only come for the annual **Puram Festival,** held in April and May. During Puram, deity-bearing revelers from neighboring villages descend on the town, heralded by musicians and brightly decorated elephants. Trichur isn't worth a detour during the rest of the year, though its temple and park make it a pleasant enough stopover.

⬚ GETTING THERE AND GETTING AWAY

Trains: The **railway station** (☎ 423150) is on Railway Station Rd. Fares listed are 2nd class. To: **Bangalore** (2 per day, 4:30 and 9:25pm, 12hr., Rs113); **Bombay** (1-2 per day, 9:30am and 2:10pm, 26hr., Rs369); **Calicut** (6 per day, 4am-6pm, 3hr., Rs56); **Delhi** (4-5 per day, 2:30-9:25pm, 43hr., Rs495); **Ernakulam** (several, 1½hr., Rs44); **Madras** (5 per day, 12hr., Rs204); **Mangalore** (2 per day, 12:45am and 12:30pm, 10hr., Rs247); **Margao** (2-3 per day, 11:35am-7:55pm, 12hr., Rs235); **Trivandrum** (8 per day, 6hr., Rs111).

Buses: The **KSRTC bus stand,** Masjid Rd. (☎ 421150), near the railway station, south of Railway Station Rd. Frequent buses to: **Alleppey** (3½hr., Rs70); **Calicut** (3hr., Rs45); **Ernakulam** (2hr., Rs30); **Kottayam** (3hr., Rs50); **Mangalore** (7:30am and 9pm, 12hr., Rs147); **Trivandrum** (7hr., Rs105). **Sakthan Thampuran Bus Stand,** TB Rd., 1.5km south of the Round (follow MO Rd. south), has frequent private buses to **Guruvayur.**

Local Transportation: Most of Trichur's sights and accommodations are within walking distance. **Auto-rickshaws** are plentiful. Rs6 first km, Rs3 per km thereafter.

✴⑦ ORIENTATION AND PRACTICAL INFORMATION

Trichur is laid out like a wheel. The hubcap is the vast, green **Swaraj Round,** the site of the **Vadakkunathan Temple.** The major roads are the spokes: moving clockwise from the western edge, these are **Mahatma Gandhi (MG), Shornur, Palace, College, High, Municipal Office (MO), Chembottil, Kurrappam,** and **Marar Rd.** Most hotels and restaurants are on these thoroughfares, near the Round. The KSRTC **bus stand** and **railway station** are both 500m south of the Round; head down Kurrappam Rd. until you pick up **Railway Station Rd.**

Tourist Office: KTDC (☎ 332333), at the Yatri Nivas Hotel reception desk. Follow signs north from the intersection of Palace and Museum Rd. Open daily 6am-10pm. **DTPC,** near the corner of Palace and Museum Rd., is defunct, despite the huge sign and the large numbers of people sitting in the office.

Currency Exchange: State Bank of Travencore, on Town Hall Rd., just off Round East, changes cash and AmEx traveler's checks. Open M-F 10am-2pm and 2:30-3:30pm, Sa 10am-12:30pm.

Bookstore: Current Books, MG Rd., on the Round. Open M-Sa 9am-8pm. **Higginbotham's,** at the train station. Open daily 6am-10pm.

Library: Public library in the Town Hall, Palace Rd. Open M-Sa 8am-8pm, Su 8am-noon.

Pharmacy: Girija Medical Stores (☎ 421571), Round South. Daily 8:45am-8:45pm.

Hospital: Jubilee Mission Hospital (☎ 420361), East Fort, northeast of the city center, is the best private hospital. Auto-rickshaw from city center Rs10.

Police: East Police Station (☎ 421400), off MO Rd., just south of Railway Station Rd.

Internet: Bhavana Systems and Communications, MO Rd. (☎ 424708), 3rd fl. of the building opposite the Municipal Office. Rs60 per hr. Open M-Sa 9am-6pm.

Post Office: GPO, south of the Sakthan Thampuran Bus Stand. Open M-Sa 8am-6pm. More convenient is the **Trichur City Post Office,** Railway Station Rd. at MO Rd. Open M-Sa 9am-5pm. **Postal Code:** 680001.

ACCOMMODATIONS

During Puram, the room rates listed below triple or quadruple. Check-out is 24hr.

Alukkas Tourist Home (☎ 426067), in an alley off Railway Station Rd., opposite the bus station. The dribbling waterfall outside makes for an irresistible welcome to this busy hotel. Basic rooms with seat toilets. Singles Rs210; doubles Rs268.

Chandy's Tourist Hotel, Railway Station Rd. (☎ 421167), between the bus and train stations. Simple rooms with attached bath. Singles Rs95; doubles Rs170.

Hotel Elite International, Chembottil Ln. (☎ 421033), off the Round South, between Kurrappam and Municipal Office Rd. Comfortable place with 24hr. hot water, phones, seat toilets, and balconies with city and parking lot views. Attached restaurant. Singles Rs255-495; doubles Rs365-644.

FOOD

Delite Sweet Parlour, on Round South at the corner of Chembottil Ln., turns out excellent sweet and savory snacks (Rs3-10). Open daily 9am-8:30pm.

Hotel Bharath Restaurant, on Chembottil Ln., between Round South and Railway Station Rd., has cheap South (*thali* Rs18) and North Indian veg. fare (*aloo gobi* Rs19). Frenetic at mealtimes and justly popular. Open daily 6:30am-10:30pm.

Ming Palace, opposite the Hotel Elite, on the 2nd fl. of the Pathans building. Chinese and Thai dishes (Rs25-50) served by a courteous staff. Open daily 11am-10pm.

SIGHTS AND ENTERTAINMENT

Most tourists know Trichur only by its association with the annual **Puram Festival** in April and May. Featuring a multitude of elephants, masses of onlookers, and noisy bands, the festival is Indian pageantry at its very best. Hotels fill up fast and charge extravagant rates during the festival, so plan well in advance. It is held on the grounds of the **Vadakkunathan Temple,** the oldest (and largest) temple complex in the state. Dedicated to Shiva, the temple sits on the site where Nandi, Shiva's bull, is said to have rested. The temple is closed to non-Hindus.

There is a local **zoo** in the northeast corner of Trichur, 2km from the Round, but unless you're into watching school children gawk at depressed animals in tiny

KERALA

cages, the zoo is not for you. (Open Tu-Su 9am-5:15pm. Rs5.) The art museum on the same grounds has some decent sculptures and carvings. There is also a "multi-purpose" **museum** that contains plenty of dusty *kathakali* dance costumes, dried leaves, and what are presumably the stuffed remains of erstwhile zoo occupants. (Open T-Su 10am-5pm. Free.) You'll find more carvings at the **Archaeological Museum,** 100m farther along Museum Rd. (Open Tu-Su 9:30am-5pm. Free.) The **market area** behind Municipal Office Rd. is worth exploring; colorful vegetable and spice stands pack the narrow streets. The pretty **Puttanpalli Church,** just off High Rd., is also worth a look-see. (Open for toursits M-Sa 9am-5:30pm, Su 2-4pm.)

CALICUT കോഴിക്കോട   ☎ 0495

Once among India's most celebrated seaports, Calicut was the the harbor of choice for Chinese and Middle Eastern spice traders as early as the 7th century. In 1498, Malabar-man Vasco da Gama tread his first subcontinental steps just north of here, inadvertently initiating three centuries of mercantile mayhem that culminated in Tipu Sultan's trashing of the region in 1789. The British took over three years later, and immortalized Calicut by coining the word "calico" for the locally produced fabric. Those who imagine a city filled with ruined forts, wharfside temples, and cartloads of black pepper have probably been reading too much Salman Rushdie (part of his *The Moor's Last Sigh* is set here) and will be disappointed to find a complete lack of cute and colorful Kodak moments in Calicut, which serves mainly as a stopover for tourists between Cochin and Mysore.

▐ GETTING THERE AND GETTING AROUND

Flights: The **airport** is in Karipur, 28km from Calicut. Taxis cost Rs150-200. **Air India,** Eroh Centre, Bank Rd., 1st fl. (☎ 766669). Open M-Sa 9:30am-5:30pm. To: **Bombay** (5 per week, 1½hr., US$100). **Indian Airlines** (☎ 766243), is next door. Open M-Sa 10am-5:35pm. To: **Bombay** (2 per day, 1½hr., US$140); **Coimbatore** (1 per day, 30min., US$40); **Madras** (4 per week, 1½-2hr., US$90).

Trains: The **railway station** (☎ 703822), 1km south of the park; follow Town Hall Rd. To: **Delhi** (1-2 per day, 3:15am-7:40pm, 36hr., Rs489); **Ernakulam** (3-4 per day, 6:40am-11:15pm, 5hr., Rs83); and **Mangalore** (5-6 per day, 12:55am-6pm, 5hr., Rs95).

Buses: There are several bus stands in town. **KSRTC Bus Stand,** Mavoor Rd. (☎ 723796), not far from the intersection with Bank Rd. To: **Bangalore** (9 per day, 8½hr., Rs118-170); **Cochin** (30 per day, 5½hr., Rs95); **Mangalore** (4 per day, 7hr., Rs97); **Mysore** (19 per day, 5½-6½hr., Rs73); **Trivandrum** (15 per day, 10½hr., Rs195). Cleaner and cheaper **private buses** run from the bus stand farther down Mavoor Rd., at the intersection with Stadium Rd. To: **Cochin** (6 per day, 6hr., Rs73); **Devala,** near Ooty (2:15pm, 10hr., Rs56); **Mangalore** (5 per day, 6hr., Rs73); and **Mysore** (6 and 8:30am, 6hr., Rs73).

Local Transportation: Auto-rickshaws are your best bet (Rs6 per km). **Taxis** are unmetered and everywhere. **Local buses** run around town, to Beypore, and to the beach.

▌✈▐ ORIENTATION AND PRACTICAL INFORMATION

At the center of town is **Ansari Park,** flanked to the north by **Town Hall Rd.** and **Bank Rd.,** which turns into **GH Rd.** From the south of the park, SM Rd. runs south between Town Hall Rd. and GH Rd. **Mavoor Rd. (Indira Gandhi Rd.)** veers east off Bank Rd. in the north, leading to the KSRTC and private **bus stations.** To the south, GH Rd. intersects with **MM Ali Rd.,** which leads east to an older part of the city, and runs west to the beach as **Palayam Rd.** The **railway station** is on Town Hall Rd., southwest of the park. The **beach,** 2km west of the town center, is unsafe at night.

Tourist Office: The **KTDC** office (☎ 7222392), at the reception desk of the Malabar Mansion, on the south side of the park. The **Kerala Tourism information booth** (☎ 702606) at the railway station can also be helpful. Open M-Sa 10am-1pm and 2-5pm.

Budget Travel: PL Worldways, Lakhotia Computer Centre, 3rd fl. (☎ 722564), at the intersection of Mavoor and Bank Rd. Books airline reservations and processes foreign visas. Open M-F 9:30am-1pm and 2-5:30pm, Sa 9:30am-1:30pm.

Currency Exchange: State Bank of India, Bank Rd. (☎ 721321), changes currency and traveler's checks. Open M-F 10am-2pm, Sa 10am-noon. **PL Worldways** (see above) also cashes traveler's checks.

Bookstore: TBS Publishers, GH Rd (☎ 720085), south of the park. M-Sa 9am-8pm.

Library: Kozhikode Public Library, west of Malabar Mansion, has a decent selection and an original painting by Kerala homeboy M.F. Hussain. Open Tu-Su 2-8pm.

Market: There is an extensive fruit and vegetable market around the old bus station, on the left side of MM Ali Rd., as you head away from GH Rd.

Police: (☎ 722673), Manachira, on the east edge of the park.

Hospital: National Hospital, Mavoor Rd. (☎ 723061 or 723062), near the intersection with Bank Rd., is the best in town. Its **pharmacy** is open daily 8am-midnight.

Internet: Netshare Internet Zone, south of the park, just west of Malabar Mansion in the Public Library Building. **Metropolitan Internet Point** (☎ 310904), Bank Rd. On the 2nd fl., above the Cochin Bakery. Both places Rs50 per hr. Open M-Sa 10am-10pm.

Post Office: (☎ 722663), on the west edge of the park. Open M-Sa 10am-7:45pm, Su 2-4:45pm. **Postal Code:** 673001.

ACCOMMODATIONS

Sasthapuri Tourist Home (☎ 723281), down MM Ali Rd. from GH Rd, on the left. Good value in a lively part of town, convenient to the train station. Attached bath. Check-out 24hr. Singles Rs75-350; doubles Rs100-400.

Malabar Mansion (☎ 722391), on the south side of the park. KTDC-run, with a tourist reception desk, snackbar, restaurant, and beer parlor. All rooms have TV, phone, and attached bath. Check-out 24hr. Singles Rs185-360; doubles Rs225-400.

Kalpaka Tourist Home (☎ 720222), Town Hall Rd., just south of the park. Looks like a mental institution, run by a cadre of efficient women. Big beds, in big rooms. Hot water 24hr. Check-out 24hr. Singles Rs322-450; doubles Rs430-660. MC, Visa.

Metro Tourist Home (☎ 766029), at the junction of Mavoor and Bank Rd. In the whizzing, grinding heart of town. All rooms have seat toilets and A/C. Doubles Rs500.

FOOD

Woodlands Restaurant, in the Hotel Whitelines on GH Rd., not far from the intersection with MM Ali Rd. Feels more like a diner than a *dhaba,* but its excellent all-veg. food is the real thing. *Thalis* Rs25-40. Open daily 8am-10pm.

Dakshin-The Veg, Mavoor Rd., near the intersection with Bank Rd. Good food, great name. Self-service downstairs; A/C and non-A/C restaurants upstairs. North Indian veg. dishes Rs35; South Indian *thali* Rs25. Open daily 6am-11pm.

Cochin Bakery, opposite the State Bank of India. Spicy snacks, cold drinks, and pastries from Rs4. Open daily 7am-10pm.

Malabar Mansion Restaurant, in KTDC hotel, 1st fl., serves up the usual assortment of dishes (Rs25-35), and has eggs for breakfast (Rs12-15). Open daily 7am-10pm.

SIGHTS AND ENTERTAINMENT

ANSARI PARK. Ansari Park, also known as **Manchira Maidan,** brings well-maintained greenery to Calicut's center. The lovely **tank** on the western edge of the park is all that remains of a palace built by one of the local rulers, the Zamorin king Manavikrama. The public **library** on the south edge of the park is a good example of traditional Keralan architecture. Every evening at the park, a little guy in a box madly flips switches to manipulate a **Music Fountain** choreographed to Hindi pop. *(Show at 7:15pm, 30min., Rs3.)* The art deco **Crown Theatre,** Town Hall Rd., at the southwest corner of the park, screens Western films.

BEACH. The city's long, sandy **beach,** just 2km from the city center, is worth a visit. The areas close to town are best overlooked, but farther to the north, fishermen and their colorful boats take over the scene.

SHOPPING. Calicut has always been a trading city, and indulging in a bit of bartering and haggling can provide plenty of entertainment. The **Comtrust Store,** south of the park and just off Town Hall Rd., is the outlet store for the Raj-era factory next door, which produces hand-loomed fabrics. *(Open M-Sa 10am-1pm and 2:30-7pm.)*

MUSEUMS. The **Pazhassiraja Museum** is one of those all-purpose Indian museums that contain everything anyone ever thought of putting in a museum and lots of other stuff too. Most of it is junk, but downstairs there are a number of well displayed stone carvings. *(East Hill, 5km from Calicut; rickshaw Rs35. Or take a bus from in front of the Hotel Malabar Mansion to West Hill (15min., Rs2), get off at the stop opposite St. Michael's Church, take the first right, then left where the street ends, and right at that street's end. Head uphill on the left fork to the museum. Open T-Su 10am-1pm and 2-4:30pm. Free.)* Around the back, the **Krishna Menon Museum** houses the personal belongings of the late Indian president (b. Calicut 1896, d. Delhi 1974), including his Seiko watch and a couple portraits of Lenin. The **Art Gallery** upstairs contains a collection of paintings by Raja Ravi Varma and Raja Raja Varma. *(Museums and gallery open Tu-Su 10am-5pm.)*

BEYPORE. Ten kilometers—and 100 years—away from Calicut is the ship-building town of **Beypore.** Under thatched roofs, but otherwise exposed to the elements, master woodworkers carve, scrape, and pound huge beams into 200-ft. barges. All work is done by hand—even the vast trees destined to become the boats' beams are shifted using only a few crowbars. These ocean-going monsters are made for a life of trading between India's west coast and the Arabian peninsula, providing an extraordinary glimpse of living nautical history. Get Uncle Ed a model ship in a bottle as a souvenir. *(Ask in Calicut whether construction is currently underway. Auto-rickshaws Rs6 one-way. Or, take a bus (25min., Rs3) from in front of the Hotel Malabar Palace.*

TAMIL NADU
தமிழ் நாடு

The southernmost state in mainland India, Tamil Nadu is the heartland of Dravidian culture and a stronghold of traditional Hindu practice. For more than 3000 years, Tamil Nadu has cultivated a spirit and a heritage uniquely its own. The people are friendly and welcoming, the roads are safe, and the food is delicious.

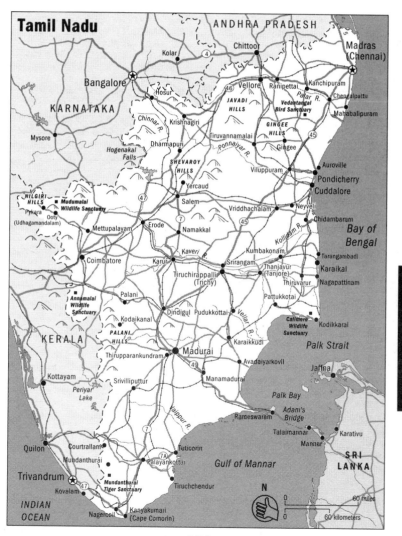

Travelers here can lose themselves in the local culture without worrying about falling victim to overzealous trinket-dealers, mudslides, or undercooked vegetable chowmein. Some of the finest temples in India are in Tamil Nadu; vividly colored towers and gateways soar over huge temple-city complexes, with dusty streets spiraling around a central shrine abuzz with worshipers. The state moves to the pulsing rhythms of *bharat natyam*, India's most popular classical dance form. Most of the population is Dravidian, the descendents of the earliest inhabitants of the subcontinent. Since the first century, the state has nurtured South India's oldest literary tradition in its mother tongue, Tamil. The refusal to welcome the Hindi language into its schools and administration has tinged the state's history with separatism and linguistic pride.

During the last few centuries BC, Tamil Nadu was ruled by three rival dynasties: the Cholas, the Pandyas, and the Cheras. By the 4th century AD the Pallava kingdom had risen to power, and it ruled until the 9th century, when it was toppled by the Cholas, who eventually came to rule the whole of South India. Under the British, Tamil Nadu was part of the Madras Presidency, which included parts of present-day Andhra Pradesh, Kerala, and Karnataka.

Today, Tamil Nadu is a peaceful patchwork of pilgrimage sites, hill stations, and small cities. From the green paddy-fields and the red, tilled earth of the coastal plains to the welcome cool of the Nilgiri hills and from the sun-drenched beaches of Pondicherry to the southernmost tip of the Indian subcontinent at Kanyakumari, surrounded by the waves of the Arabian Sea, the Bay of Bengal, and the Indian Ocean, Tamil Nadu is a country to itself.

HIGHLIGHTS OF TAMIL NADU

A fascinating cultural mix distinguishes **Pondicherry** (p. 554), the former capital of French India, now home to the famously surreal **Aurobindo Ashram** (p. 558).

Thousands flock to the **Meenakshi Amman Temple** in **Madurai** (p. 573), where some 30 million sculptures provide an artistic counterpoint to a lively city.

Kodaikanal (p. 586), in the Western Ghats, has all the standard hill station amusements, set against some of India's finest film-grade scenery.

MADRAS (CHENNAI) சென்னை ☎044

Dubbed the "Gateway to the South" by its champions, Madras is India's fourth largest city and most travelers' first stop in Tamil Nadu. The capital of the state, Madras is a bastion of South Indian culture, with its dance and music festivals attracting bigger crowds than the few sights sprinkled within the city limits. Madras's cityscape is punctuated with large patches of greenery, which provide welcome relief from the burning heat and complement the lazy stretches of sand along the Bay of Bengal.

Madras's climb from humble fishing village to overwhelming metropolis began in 1639, when East India Company worker Francis Day founded a trading outpost here. Forts and churches went forth and multiplied, and the Company continued to buy up huge tracts of land. French forces stormed, seized, and sacked the city in 1746, but Madras continued to develop as a thriving economic center. During the late 19th and early 20th centuries, its factories spun out thousands of bales of cotton clothing for export throughout the Empire.

Although the city lacks the attractions to make it much more than a gateway for tourists, its beaches, mini-malls, and new coffeehouses offer a slice of quintessentially Indian life for those just discovering the South.

Recently, Madras has been swept up in India's wave of politically motivated name changes. Many of the town's major thoroughfares have been stripped of their colonial names and renamed in honor of Tamil leaders. In 1996, the city's old name, "Madras," was officially replaced by "Chennai," a Tamil name that evokes the original Indian settlement of Chennaipatnam.

✈ GETTING THERE AND AWAY

FLIGHTS

Chennai Meenambakkam is not as heavily used as the airports in Bombay and Delhi, making Madras a relatively peaceful port of entry and exit. The city center is 16km north of the airport, and there are a number of ways of getting there. **Local buses** (#21G, PP21, 52B, and 60E; Rs13) are too crowded to be useful unless you are carrying all your luggage in your pockets. The **minibus service** running between the airport and the major hotels (Rs100) is a slow but sure and comfortable way of making it into the city. Tickets are sold at a counter in the international terminal. The **pre-paid taxi booth** inside the international terminal will fix you up with a taxi downtown for about Rs200; regular taxis charge upward of Rs250. **Auto-rickshaws** can be brought down to Rs150 with some fierce haggling. Another option is the urban **train** system; it runs from Tirusulam Station (a short walk from the terminals) to Egmore Station, the site of a number of cheap hotels. Expect a few exasperated stares if you squeeze into a crowded train car with a bulging pack.

INTERNATIONAL AIRLINES. American Airlines and **TWA** share an office at 43-44 Thaper House, Montieth Rd. (☎859 2915 or 859 2564). Both open M-F 9am-1pm and 2-5:30pm, Sa 9am-1pm. **Air France** is also at Thaper House (☎855 4894). **Air India,** 19 Marshalls Rd. (☎855 4488 or 233 4654). **Air Lanka,** 76 Cathedral Rd. (☎826 1535), opposite Chola Hotel. Open M-Sa 9am-5:30pm. **British Airways,** Alsa Mall Khaleeli Centre, Montieth Rd. (☎855 4752 or 855 4726). **Delta Airlines,** 47 White's Rd., Royapettah (☎852 5655 or 852 5647). Open M-F 9:30am-5:30pm, Sa 9:30am-1:30pm. **Gulf Air,** 52 Montieth Rd. (☎855 4417 or 855 3101). **Lufthansa,** 167 Anna Salai (☎852 3272). **Malaysia Airlines,** 498 Anna Salai (☎434 9651). **Singapore Airlines,** 108 Dr. Radhakrishnan Salai (☎852 2871). **Swiss Air,** 47 White's Rd. (☎851 4337 or 4339). Open M-F 9:30am-5:30pm, Sa 9:30am-1:30pm. **Thai Airways** (☎433 0098), **United Airlines** (☎822 6290), **SAS** (☎822 6149), **Air New Zealand,** and **Varig Airlines** share an office at the Malavikas Centre, 144 Kodambakkam Rd. (☎822 6150). All open M-F 9:30am-5:30pm, Sa 9:30am-1pm. Air Lanka and Air India both fly to **Colombo, Sri Lanka** (4-5 per day, 1½hr., US$90).

DOMESTIC AIRLINES. Jet Airways, Thaper House, 43-44 Montieth Rd. (☎841 4141). Open daily 8:30am-8:30pm. **Indian Airlines,** 19 Marshalls Rd. (☎855 5200). Daily fights to: **Bangalore** (7-8 per day, US$65); **Bombay** (7-9 per day, US$160); **Calcutta** (2-3 per day, US$220); **Cochin** (1-3 per day, US$120); **Coimbatore** (2-3 per day, US$90); **Delhi** (6-7 per day, US$260); **Hyderabad** (3-4 per day, US$105); **Pune** (1 per day, US$175); and **Trivandrum** (11:40am, US$105).

TRAINS

Madras has two main train stations: **Egmore,** for travel within Tamil Nadu, and **Madras Central,** for trains to other parts of the country. Both are in the north of town near Periyar EVR Rd. (Poonamallee High Rd.). For **arrival and departure information,** ☎1361 and dial the train number after the beep. Southern Railways maintains an extremely useful and up-to-date website of schedules and route maps that finally relegates *Trains At A Glance* to the status of an ancient abacus. Ride the rails at www.srailway.com or www.southernrailway.org.

MADRAS CENTRAL. Long-distance trains arrive and depart from Madras Central, in George Town, near the Buckingham Canal, also fairly close to the hotels of Gandhi Irwin Rd. The reservation counter is upstairs in the administrative building—the 10-story, yellow concrete structure to the left of the huge red station. On the first floor, a special desk attends to tourists. (General inquiries ☎132. Open M-Sa 8am-8pm, Su 8am-2pm.) To: **Ahmedabad** (*Navjivan Exp.* 6046, 9:30am, 35hr., Rs390); **Bangalore** (8 per day, 5am-10:45pm, 8hr., Rs166); **Bombay** (3 per day, 6:50am-9:30pm, 30hr., Rs315); **Calcutta** (6 per day, 7:35am-10:45pm,

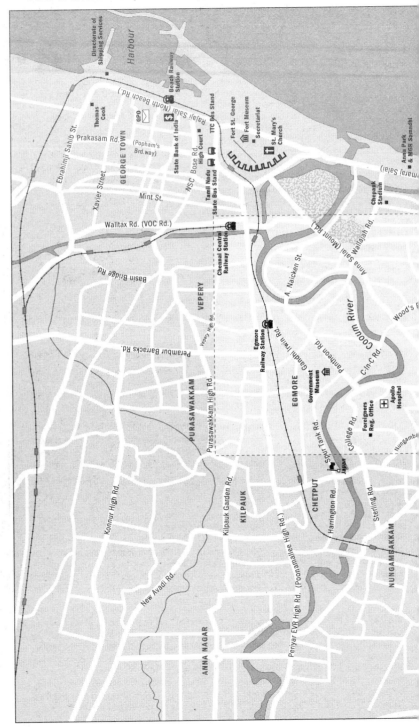

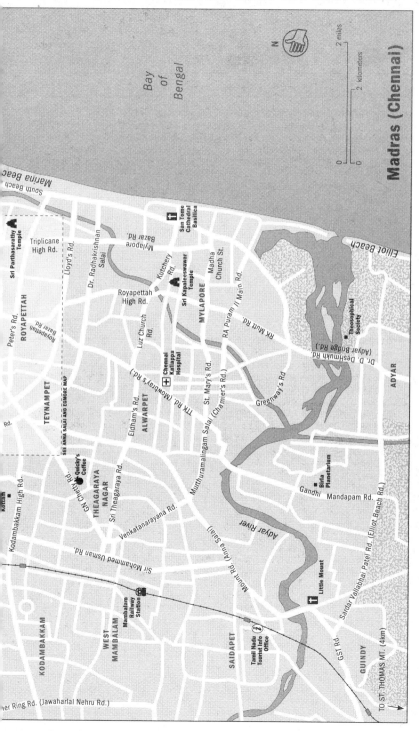

Madras (Chennai)

Bay of Bengal

N

2 miles
2 kilometers

South Beach
Marina Beach
Elliot Beach

San Tome Cathedral Basilica

Sri Parthasarathy Temple

Triplicane High Rd.

Lloyd's Rd.

Mylapore Bazar Rd.

Dr. Radhakrishnan Salai

Kutchery Rd.

Sri Kapaleeswaar Temple

Madha Church St.

MYLAPORE

Peter's Rd.

ROYAPETTAH

Royapettah Bazar Rd.

Royapettah High Rd.

Luz Church Rd.

RA Puram / Main Rd.

RK Mutt Rd.

Theosophical Society

TEYNAMPET

Rd.

SEE ANNA SALAI AND EGMORE MAP

Chennai Kaliappa Hospital

Eldham's Rd.

TTK Rd. (Mowbray's Rd.)

St. Mary's Rd.

ALWARPET

Dr. D. Deshmukh Rd. (Adyar Bridge Rd.)

ADYAR

Greenway's Rd.

Kodambakkam High Rd.

Kottam

Quicky's Coffee

GN Chetty Rd.

THEAGARAYA NAGAR

Sri Theagaraya Rd.

Murthuramalingam Salai (Chamier's Rd.)

Venkatanarayana Rd.

Birla Planetarium

Gandhi Mandapam Rd.

Adyar River

Sir Mohammed Usman Rd.

Mount Rd. (Anna Salai)

Sardar Vallabhai Patel Rd. (Elliot Beach Rd.)

Little Mount

KODAMBAKKAM

WEST MAMBALAM

Mambalam Railway Station

SAIDAPET

Tamil Nadu Tourist Info Office

GST Rd.

GUINDY

TO ST. THOMAS MT. (4km)

ner Ring Rd. (Jawaharlal Nehru Rd.)

33hr., Rs366); **Coimbatore** (14 per day, 4:25am-2:55am, 8½hr., Rs166); **Delhi** (5:30am and 10pm, 35hr., Rs410); **Ernakulam** and/or **Cochin** (11 per day, 4:10am-2:25am, 13¼hr., Rs211); **Hyderabad** (4 and 6:10pm, 14½hr., Rs236); **Kanyakumari** (6:16 and 8:30pm, 16hr., Rs228); **Mangalore** (1-2 per day, 4:40am-2:55am, 19hr., Rs250); **Mysore** (10am and 1pm, 9½hr., Rs166); **Tirupati** (3 per day, 9:30am-7:50pm, 3hr., Rs72); **Trivandrum** (5 per day, 4:30am-2:55am, 17hr., Rs252); and **Varanasi** (5:30pm, 39hr., Rs407).

EGMORE RAILWAY STATION. Most trains to destinations within Tamil Nadu depart from the Egmore Railway Station, though some trains now run from Tambaram, an hour away (see below). Egmore Station is north of Gandhi Irwin Rd. The reservation counter is to your left as you enter. (☎ 135. Open M-Sa 8am-2pm and 2:15-6pm, Su 8am-2pm.) To: **Chidambaram** (7:30pm, 6hr., Rs97); **Kodaikanal** (4 per day, 6:15-8pm, 9½hr., Rs159); **Madurai** (5 per day, 12:15-8pm, Rs166); **Thanjavur** (10pm, 9½hr.,138); and **Trichy** (8 per day, 12:25-10pm, 7½hr., Rs126).

TAMBARAM. Schedule changes made in July 2000 mean that some trains within Tamil Nadu now run from Tambaram, about an hour away from Madras. Shuttle buses are supposed to link the two stations. Destinations served from Tambaram include: **Chidambaram** (3 per day, 8:45am-10:45pm, 5½hr., Rs95); **Kumbakonam** (3 per day, 8:45am-10:45pm, 7½hr., Rs123); **Rameswaram** (3 per day, 1-9pm, 17½hr.); and **Thanjavur** (3 per day, 8:45am-10:45pm, 8½hr.).

BUSES

Buses to most tourist destinations leave from the **State Express Transport Corporation Bus Stand** (☎ 534 1835), on the south side of George Town, in an area officially known as Park Town. Open daily 7am-9pm. To take any inter-city bus, you'll need a reservation form (Rs0.25, or one salted peanut) from the reservations counter upstairs. SETC runs buses to: **Bangalore** (#831, every 30min., 8hr., Rs119) via **Kanchi** or **Vellore; Chidambaram** (#300 and 324E; 1:30, 3:30, and 5pm; 6hr.; Rs60); **Coimbatore** (#460S and V, every 2hr., 12hr., Rs173); **Kanyakumari** (#282, 8 per day, 19hr., Rs165); **Kodaikanal** (#461, 5:45pm, 14hr., Rs109); **Kumbakonam** (303, #303F, 303V, 308, 332S, 336S; every hr.; 7hr.; Rs99); **Madurai** (#137, every 30min., 10hr., Rs140); **Mysore** (#863, 5 and 8pm, 10hr., Rs186); **Ooty** (#468S, 7pm; #860, 6pm; 14hr.; Rs145); **Pondicherry** (#803 and 803E, every hr., 4hr., Rs49); **Rameswaram** (#166, 5:45pm, 13hr., Rs177); **Thanjavur** (#323, 323F, and V; every 30min.; 8hr.; Rs103); **Trichy** (#123, 123F, and V; every 30min.; 6hr.; Rs112); **Tirupati** (#902 and 911, every hr., 4hr., Rs67); and **Vellore** (every 30min., 5hr.). **Broadway Terminal,** opposite the State Express stand, is somewhat nightmarish and thankfully necessary only for travelers headed to **Kanchi** (#76, 79, and 130; every 30min.; 3hr.; Rs16) or **Mahabalipuram** (#19C, 119, 188, and 189; every 30min.; 2½hr.; Rs16).

BOATS

There are three sailings a month from Madras to Port Blair in the **Andaman Islands.** Fares are Rs1100 for a bunk, Rs2700 for a 2nd class cabin, Rs3500 for a 1st class cabin. To purchase tickets, foreigners need four passport photos (get them done at one of the shops on Anna Salai). Contact the Deputy Director of Shipping Services, Andaman & Nicobar Administration, NSC Bose Rd. (☎ 532 1401. Open daily 8am-5pm.) See p. 705 for more information. Don't forget the special permit needed for travel to this restricted area (see p. 539).

⚑ GETTING AROUND

AUTO-RICKSHAWS

The streets of Madras are infested with buzzing swarms of auto-rickshaws, probably the best way to get about. Though the minimum charge is supposed to be Rs1 per km (Rs7 min.), many drivers tamper with the meters or ask for more money. It is sometimes easier just to agree on a price before getting in, though the first price you're offered will almost always be about double the going rate. Rs40 is a typical fare between two downtown destinations; significantly cheaper prices normally involve a stop at "my cousin's shop" on the way. Most rickshaw-*wallahs* will meet you at your hotel in the morning or will take you around town for the day—simply discuss your plans beforehand and agree on a lump sum (Rs80-200). If you have serious trouble with a driver, threaten to take down his number (on the back of the vehicle or on a black pin worn on his shirt) and report him to the police.

TAXIS

Taxis are much less common and about twice as expensive as auto-rickshaws. Most have meters, but again, it's often best to fix a price beforehand. Expect to pay at least Rs100 from the railway stations to Anna Salai or to Triplicane.

LOCAL BUSES

The very thought of getting onto an Indian city bus is enough to make some people ill. Compared to some of the horrors you might have experienced in other places, though, the bus system in Madras is efficient and reliable. It is also (marginally) less crowded than those in Bombay, Calcutta, and Delhi. Many public buses are green and have their final destination printed on the side. There is a bus stand every few blocks throughout the city. Rush hour (7:30-10:30am and 5:30-7pm) is for masochistic crowd-lovers only.

Sneak up on your bus and board it from behind. The conductor will soon amble along and extract payment (usually Rs2-3). Many buses are unofficially segregated by sex—women on one side, men on the other. There are also special "ladies' buses" every 10-20 minutes between 8-9am and 4-5pm. "Deluxe" blue-and-white buses also operate on the hour (Rs5). Regular bus service runs 5am-10pm. Night buses follow the same routes 10pm-5am for double the rupees.

BUS #	ROUTE
22, 27, 27B, 29A	Egmore-Triplicane
PP23C	Egmore-Anna Salai-Adyar Depot
9, 10, 17, 17E, 22	Egmore-Central
9, 9A, 10, 17D, 17K	Broadway-Egmore
21G, PP21, 60E	Broadway-Guindy National Park-Airport
9, 10	Parry's Corner-Central-Egmore
9A, 17D	Parry's Corner-Nungambakkan
18A, A18, 52B, 60, 60A	Parry's Corner-Anna Salai-Airport
21G	High Court-Adyar-Guindy National Park-Airport
4, 23C, PP23C	Anna Salai-Besant Nagar (Adyar)
1A, 3A, 5, 19M, 21	Anna Salai-Mylapore
17A, 17G, 25B, 25E	Anna Salai-Nungambakkan
25B, 27A, 40	Anna Salai-Triplicane-Egmore
23A, 23B, 23C, PP23C	Adyar Bus Depot-Anna Salai-Egmore

MOPEDS

You need an international license to rent a moped (Rs75 per day). If you're craving your own pair of wheels, check out **U-Rent Services Ltd.,** 36 II Main Rd., in the Gandhi Nagar district in the southern part of town, past the Adyar River. (☎491 0838. Open daily 8:30am-8pm.)

TAMIL NADU

✚ ORIENTATION

Madras is a massive, sprawling city, extending more than 15km along the western shores of the **Bay of Bengal**. The city can be divided into three distinct sections. Northernmost is **George Town**, an area of long, straight streets running south to **Fort Saint George** and the **Central Railway Station**. George Town's major east-west artery is **NSC Bose Rd.**, which runs north-south along the shoreline, parallel to **Prakasam Rd. (Broadway)**, until it ends at its intersection with **Rajaji Rd. (North Beach Rd.)**. **Parry's Corner**, at the intersection of NSC Bose and Rajaji Rd., is the wheeling, dealing market area. The city's **bus terminals** are here.

The southernmost section is 10km south of George Town and stretches from **Mylapore** in the north to the residential areas south of the **Adyar River**. This area is pleasant but has little of interest besides the **Guindy National Park,** south of Adyar in the city's nether regions.

Between George Town and Mylapore is the real center of the city, including **Egmore** and **Anna Salai (Mount Rd.)**, the longest and busiest street in Madras. Many of the city's tourist services are along Anna Salai, which runs northeast to southwest. North of Anna Salai is the congested Egmore area, full of cheap hotels. Egmore's northern boundary is **Egmore Railway Station**, just off hotel-rich **Gandhi Irwin Rd. Pantheon Rd.** runs parallel to and south of Gandhi Irwin Rd. **Periyar EVR Road (Poonamallee High Rd.)** is to the north. Perpendicular to both are **Commander-in-Chief Rd. (C-in-C Rd.)** and, farther southwest, **Nungambakkam High Rd. (NH Rd.)**, two busy streets where many of Madras's businesses are. Triplicane is a mix of hotels, residences, and buisnesses in a central location near the coast and just south of Anna Salai. Nungambakkam, T. Nagar, and Dr. Radhakrishnan Salai are good areas for coffee shops, stores, and restaurants.

🔁 PRACTICAL INFORMATION

For the most up-to-date information, tourists should pick up a copy of **Hallo! Chennai,** which details everything from practical information to sights and shopping.

TOURIST AND FINANCIAL SERVICES

Tourist Office: Government of India Tourist Office, 154 Anna Salai (☎851 0459; fax 852 2139), at the corner of Clubhouse Rd. The best place to start collecting informational pamphlets on Madras, Tamil Nadu, and the country beyond. Open M-F 9:15am-5:45pm, Sa 9am-1pm. There's also an **information counter** (☎234 0569) in the domestic airport. Open daily 6am-9:30pm. **Tamil Tourism Development Corporation (TTDC) Office** (☎535 3351), near Madras Central RW Station, books TTDC tours. Open daily 7am-7pm. **Kerala Government Tourist Information Office,** 28 C-in-C Rd. (☎827 9862). Open M-Sa 10am-5pm (closed second Sa of the month).

Budget Travel: Global Nest Travels & Tours (☎573 3101; email taraniglobal@hotmail.com) can arrange just about any kind of outdoor activity or special-interest tour. They run half-day boat trips (US$50 per person) and full-day trips to Pulicat Lake (US$60 per person), as well as overnight treks (with treehouse lodging) to waterfalls all over South India (US$75 per person per night). The extremely professional outfit, run by B. Tharaniselavam, specializes in finding off-the-beaten-path sites, as well as catering to special-interest groups such as artists or boatbuilders. They have even been known to host company retreats.

Consulates: Australia, 115 Mahatma Gandhi Rd. (☎827 6036). Open M-F 9:30am-2pm. **France,** 202 Prestige Point Building, 16 Haddows Rd. (☎826 6561). Open M-F 10am-3pm. **Germany,** 22 Ethiraj Salai (☎827 1747). Open M-F 8am-noon. **Netherlands,** Catholic Center, 64 Armenian St. (☎538 5829). Open M-F 10am-4pm. **Sri Lanka,** 9D Nawab Habibullah Ave. (☎827 0831). Open M-F 9am-5:15pm. **UK,** 24 Anderson Rd. (☎827 3136, 24hr. coverage). Open M-F 8:30am-11:30am. **US,** 220 Anna Salai (☎827 3040), at Cathedral Rd. Open M-F 8:15-5pm, 24hr. emergency.

Immigration Office: Foreigners Registration Office, Sastri Bhavan Annex, 26 Haddows Rd. (☎827 5424), off NH Rd. 3-month visa extensions take about a week and cost Rs900. The office also issues special permits for restricted areas such as the Andaman Islands. Submit forms M-F 9:30-11:30am; open for info 2:30-5pm.

Currency Exchange: Bank of America, 748 Anna Salai (☎855 2121), 2 blocks west of the tourist office and across the street. Open daily 10am-7pm. **CitiBank,** 768 Anna Salai (☎852 2484), opposite the government tourist office, has 24hr. ATM machines that accept international cards. Open M-F 10am-2pm, Sa 10am-noon. **State Bank of India,** 46 Cathedral Rd. (☎827 8091). Open M-F 10am-2pm, Sa 10am-noon. **Thomas Cook,** Eldorado Building, 112 NH Rd. (☎827 2610). Open M-F 9am-6:30pm, Sa 9am-6pm. **Forexpress,** 1 Prestige Point, 16 Haddows Rd. (☎855 2020), guarantees 5min. exchange. Open daily 9am-7pm. **American Express** (☎852 3628), Anna Salai, 1st fl. of Spencer Plaza Mall. Open M-F 9:30am-6:30pm, Sa 9:30am-2:30pm.

LOCAL SERVICES

Bookstore: Landmark, Apex Plaza, 3 NH Rd., is a huge store with a wide selection. Open daily 9am-9pm. **Higginbothams,** 814 Anna Salai (☎852 2440). Open M-Sa 9am-7pm. **Odyssey,** 6 First Main Rd., Adyar, Gandhi Nagar (☎442 0393). Open daily 10am-8:30pm. **Fountainhead,** Laxmi Towers, 27 Dr. Radhakrishnan Salai (☎828 0867). Open Tu-Su 9:30am-8:30pm.

Libraries: American Library, US consulate building (see **Consulates,** above). Day membership Rs10. Open M-Sa 9:30am-6pm. **British Council,** 737 Anna Salai (☎852 5002). 1-month membership Rs100. Open Tu-Sa 11am-7pm.

Cultural Centers: Alliance Francaise, 40 College Rd., Nungambakkam (☎827 2650), brings that neo-imperialist *je ne sais quoi* to Madras. **Max Mueller Bhavan,** 13 KN Khan Rd. (☎826 1314), ist der beste Ort in der Stadt, einen deutschen Film zu sehen. Bibliothek offen M-F 9am-mittag und 4-6:30pm, Sa 11am-6:30pm.

Markets: You can find everything form carnations to computers at **Parry's Corner,** NSC Bose Rd., in George Town, northeast of the city center. The nearby **Burma Bazaar** flogs imported goods. **Spencer Plaza Mall** provides a more bourgeois shopping experience, including Foodworld. Open daily 9am-9pm.

EMERGENCY AND COMMUNICATIONS

Police: Stations in **Adyar** (☎491 3552); **Anna Salai** (☎852 1720), just opposite Spenser's; **Egmore** (☎825 0952); **Guindy** (☎234 1539); **Kodambakkam,** 28 VOC St. (☎483 8902); and **Mylapore** (☎498 0100).

Pharmacy: Emsons Medicals, 114 Poonamallee Rd. (☎825 5232). Open daily 8am-10pm. **Spencer & Co.,** Spencer Plaza, Anna Salai (☎826 3611). Open M-Sa 8am-7pm. **Apollo Pharmacies.** Open 24hr.

Hospital: Apollo Hospital, 320 Anna Salai (☎433 1741, emergency 829 1111). Pharmacy attached. Reputed to be the best in Madras. Open 24hr. **K.J. Hospital,** 496 Periyar EVR Rd., Egmore, near Hotel Blue Diamond (☎641 1513, 515, 517). Attached pharmacy open 24hr. **Malar Hospital,** 52 1st Main Rd. (☎491 2878, emergency 491 4737), near Adyar Bridge, Gandhi Nagar. Attached pharmacy. Open 24hr.

Internet: Above Landmark Books (☎826 4626). Rs40 per hr. Open 10am-8pm.

Post Office: GPO, Rajaji Salai (☎524 4338, enquiries ☎514289). **Mount Rd. Head Post Office,** Kennet Ln., Egmore (☎852 1947). **Anna Salai Head Post Office,** Madras 600002. Open M-Sa 10am-4pm. **Postal Code:** 600001-600099.

ACCOMMODATIONS

Hotels in Madras cater to virtually every budget, but this is a big city, and if you've been on the road a while, you'll find Madras pricey. Budget hotels are concentrated on or around Gandhi Irwin Rd., Kennet Ln. in Egmore, and in Triplicane. Many of the really cheap ones have a strict "no foreigners policy." There are still good deals to be had. Reserve in advance. Check-out is 24-hour.

TAMIL NADU

Dayal-De Lodge, 486 Pantheon Rd. (☎822 7328), just west of the intersection with Kennet Ln. Driveway leads to a villa removed from the hectic Pantheon Rd. High-ceilinged, pastel rooms with French-style windows. Bathrooms have either squat or seat toilets. Singles Rs185; doubles Rs300.

Hotel Regal, 15 Kennet Ln. (☎823 1766), behind Hotel Masa. Get your daily fix of Doordarshan TV. Squat toilets, but would you have it any other way? Attached restaurant. Singles Rs258; doubles Rs330-480. AmEx, MC, Visa.

Hotel Pandian, 9 Kennet Ln. (☎825 2901; fax 825 8459). More upscale, but it won't break the bank. Eager staff shows off the "luxuries" that come with the plain rooms: soap, TV, towel, phone, and seat toilet. Attached restaurant and bar are above standard (open 11am-11pm). Singles Rs400-750; doubles Rs600-850.

Hotel Dasaprakash, 100 EVR Periyar Salai (☎825 5111), parallel to Gandhi Rd., north of Egmore Station. This sleepy old favorite has dark but clean rooms, complete with daily newspaper, change of towels, seat toilets, and balcony views. Attached restaurant and ice cream parlor. Singles Rs300-575; doubles Rs575-720. 20% luxury tax.

YWCA International Guest House, 1086 EVR Periyar Salai (☎532 4234; fax 532 4263). Removed from the noisy streets by a tree-filled courtyard, the YWCA has bright white rooms and spotless bathrooms. Comfy wicker settees and large TVs in common areas. Attached restaurant. If you're not a member, you can buy a month's YMCA membership (Rs20). Breakfast included. Singles Rs450-630; doubles Rs580-750.

Broadlands, 16 Vallabha Agraharam, Triplicane (☎854 8131), opposite Star Theaters. Steeped in backpacker lore, this labyrinthine villa has been around for nearly 50 years. Passport required. 10pm curfew. Singles Rs120-175; doubles Rs150-390.

Paradise Guest House (☎854 7542), next to Broadlands Bright rooms with sparkling bathrooms. Phone and TV. Cool breezes and chit-chat on the rooftop. Singles Rs20.

◙ FOOD

EGMORE

For the most part, budget dining in Egmore is a strictly proletarian experience. So roll up your sleeves, wash your hands, and plunge your fingers into that *thali*.

▨ **Tulsi Restaurant,** 6 College Rd. (☎827 2119). Rockin' American faves and student-friendly prices keep the people rollin' in. Good food keeps 'em satisfied. Mouth-melting mango milkshakes (Rs35) and *kadai paneer* (Rs50). Chinese and Western dishes too. Fast-food atmosphere. Open 11am-11pm.

Vasanta Bhavan, at the corner of Gandhi Irwin Rd. and Kennet Ln. The South Indian restaurant that follows you wherever you go. *Thalis* (Rs20) and *dosas*. A tempting array of Indian sweets is sold in the front. Open daily 7am-11pm.

Ceylon Restaurant, 15 Kennet Ln., in front of Hotel Mass. A popular cross between the whirring *thali*-joint and the A/C hotel restaurant, Ceylon is calmer than the places opposite the railway station. Fruit salad Rs12; *biryani* Rs32. Open daily 7am-11:30pm.

Raj, 9 Kennet Ln., attached to Hotel Pandian. Typical mid-range hotel restaurant with classical music. Tandoori and Chinese dishes as well all the usual stuff. Entrees Rs30-75. Open daily 6am-11pm.

Jewel Box Restaurant, 934 EVR Periyar Salai, next to Hotel Blue Diamond. Continental breakfasts (Rs45) and savory garlic chicken (Rs70) served Italian style, on red-and-white checkered tablecloths by candlelight. Open daily 7:30am-11pm.

ANNA SALAI AND TRIPLICANE

Some of the city's classiest restaurants are along its main thoroughfare. With the prime location and extra pampering, however, come prices more bloated than than a maharaja's elephant.

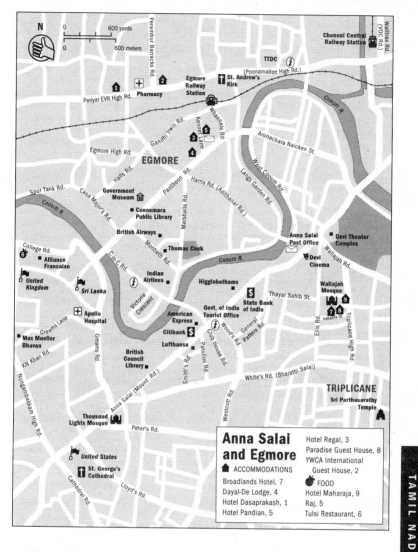

Anna Salai and Egmore

▲ ACCOMMODATIONS

Broadlands Hotel, 7
Dayal-De Lodge, 4
Hotel Dasaprakash, 1
Hotel Pandian, 5
Hotel Regal, 3
Paradise Guest House, 8
YWCA International
Guest House, 2

🍴 FOOD

Hotel Maharaja, 9
Raj, 5
Tulsi Restaurant, 6

House of Dasaprakash, 806 Anna Salai, in a white building set back from the street. Best known for its ice creams (Rs50-175). Excellent soups and salads Rs125; spaghetti Rs90; and ravioli Rs90. Open daily 12:30-3pm and 7-11pm.

Buhari's, 83 Anna Salai, opposite the Tarapore Towers, near where Anna Salai veers slightly to the right. Their specialty is tandoori cooking (9pm-midnight). At night, you can take in the cityscape from the terrace. Open daily 8am-11pm.

Hotel Maharaja, Triplicane High Rd., at the Wallajah end. Quality breakfast *idlis*, lunch *thalis* (Rs21) and dinner *dosas* for the backpackers camped out in Triplicane. Veg. tandoori Rs15-30. Open daily 7am-11pm.

Southern Chinese Restaurant, 683 Anna Salai (☎852 2515). Small and romantic, with red decor and tables for two. Delicious food and attentive service. Non-veg. options include dead cows (Rs55-70). Open daily 11:30am-3pm and 6-10:30pm.

Aavin, on Anna Salai, between the GOI and Tamil Nadu tourist offices. Get to know the name of this ice-cream/flavored-milk bar; you'll be seeing its blue-and-white stalls all across the city. Rich dairy goodies like mango ice cream (Rs12) and "African delight" (Rs75). Open daily 6am-8pm.

Cakes 'N' Bakes, 22 NH Rd. (☎827 7075), off Anna Salai's southern end. Try a slice of black forest cake (Rs15) or some mango pudding (Rs20). Tasty milkshakes (Rs30) wash down the heavy desserts. Open daily 10am-10pm.

Fruit Shop on Greams Road, 11 Greams Rd., north of Anna Salai. Other branches in Besant Nagar and Kilpauk. A cool, colorful rest from the blistering heat. Fruit cocktails made with mineral water before your eyes. Sit upstairs and try the "Sheikh shake" (Rs65) or the "Jughead Special" (Rs50). Open Su-F 11am-midnight, Sa 11am-1:30am.

The Galloping Gooseberry, 11 Greams Rd. (☎829 1077), upstairs from the Fruitshop. Can't stand another *dosa?* This pleasant Italian eatery has burgers (Rs75), sandwiches (Rs65), and pasta galore. Open daily 11am-11pm.

MYLAPORE, ALWARPET, AND T. NAGAR

The restaurants that dot the Mylapore/Alwarpet area are hidden gems—less crowded, they often have a menu and an ambience that even the more upscale competition on Anna Salai can't match.

■ **Quiky's Coffee,** 93 GN Chetly Rd. (☎825 5275), next to the Residency T. Nagar. From the la-la land of your auto-rickshaw, you catch a glimpse of a sign suspiciously like Starbucks. A moccachino in Madras? Almost—Quiky's has got the caffeine and good sandwiches too. Don't forget to ring the cowbell on your way out. Also at 151 Village Rd., Nungbakkam. Open daily 7am-11pm.

■ **Kabul,** 35 TKK Rd. This place gets rave reviews from locals, with good reason: waiters move at the drop of a napkin, serving kebabs (Rs120) so soft that you could cut them with a straw, and savory *biryani* (Rs90-120). Open daily noon-3pm and 7pm-midnight.

Hotel Saravana Bhavan, 57 Dr. Radhakrishnan Salai. *Idlis* (Rs10) and *thalis* (Rs20) served in a sparkling clean environment. Watch them squeeze the pulp out of fresh mangoes to make your juice (Rs8-21). Open daily 5am-midnight.

Woodlands, 72/75 Dr. Radhakrishnan Salai, attached to the New Woodlands Hotel. Efficient, prompt service in cool surroundings. South Indian *thali* Rs45; *idli* Rs10; *vadai* Rs15; and *dosas* Rs18-50. Open daily 7am-10pm.

Coastline, Kaaraikudi, The Dhaba, and **Shogun,** at the Kaaraikudi Complex, 84 Dr. Radhakrishna Salai, is a good place to mix-and-match. Seafood, kebabs, Chinese food, and South Indian dishes (Rs60-Rs120). Open daily 11:30am-3:30pm.

Gem Restaurant, at the corner of Peter's Rd. and Anna Salai. Candlelight, gilded swans, and excellent food. Succulent Reshmi kebab Rs70; non-veg. selections Rs70-100; and fruit drinks Rs40. Open 11am-midnight.

COFFEE?, 10 Greenways Rd., RA Puram. (☎495 7820). No hassles aside from all the teeny-boppers on their cell phones. Thai, choccacino (Rs40), "Spice Girls," and more. Fries Rs25. Open 10am-11pm.

◎ SIGHTS

For a city of six million, Madras has a surprisingly small number of things to see. If you're in town for a day, avoid overdosing on unimpressive monuments—head for Marina Beach or have a peek in the museum and do a bit of shopping.

FORT ST. GEORGE. Foremost among the city's traditional attractions, the huge Fort St. George was once an enclave of British power, where the British Regiment and the East India Company were housed in 1640. Many of the original buildings were damaged or destroyed during mid-18th century French attacks, though some remain. These days, the fort complex is home to Tamil Nadu's state government, which closes most of it to tourists. *(Rs2.)*

Amid the everyday workings of the Tamil Nadu Legislative Assembly and Council, the ghost of the fort's colonial past lingers in the **Fort Museum**, which displays an assortment of items from Raj days, including uniforms, weapons, coins, lithographs, and a collection of Robert Clive's writings. *(Open Sa-Th 10am-5pm. Rs2.)*

South of the museum, **St. Mary's Church**, consecrated in 1679 is the oldest Anglican church east of the Suez. The church was built with a bomb-proof ceiling to withstand the frequent attacks on the fort. *(Open daily 9:30am-5pm. Services Su 9am.)*

MARINA BEACH. This city beach is spectacular at dusk; the setting sun casts an iridescent glow as peddlers hawk everything from roasted peanuts to balloons and ice cream and hundreds of people amble along the shore. Palm readers lure customers, telling fortunes with the aid of seashells and tarot cards. Few locals swim here, in part because of the dangerously strong tides, in part because of the social current—wearing a swimsuit in public is frowned upon. Near the beach are **Anna Park** and the antenna-like **MGR Samadhi**, memorials to former Tamil Nadu Chief Ministers C.N. Annadurai and M.G. Ramachandran. There is also a slimy aquarium and several decrepit swimming pools. Deserted areas of the beach are often unsafe, especially at night.

GOVERNMENT MUSEUM. A string of six buildings, the Government Museum covers everything from archaeology to modern art. A highlight is the free-standing **bronze gallery.** The unparalleled collection of Chola bronzes includes a complete set of characters from the *Ramayana* and a succession of excellent dancing Shivas. West of the bronze gallery is the less-than-thrilling **Children's Museum** and its large plastic dinosaurs. Next door is the **National Art Gallery,** housed in a splendid Indo-Saracenic edifice, built in 1906, that is more impressive than most of the stuff inside. The **Museum of Contemporary Art** contains a collection of contemporary art. Hence the name. *(Pantheon Rd., south of Egmore Station. Open Sa-Th 9:30am-5pm; ticket booth closes at 4:30pm. Rs3; camera fee Rs10. Free tours at 10am, noon, 2, and 4pm.)*

SRI PARTHASARATHY TEMPLE. Originally raised by the Pallavas in the 8th century and renovated by the Cholas and the Vijayanagar Kings, this temple is dedicated to Krishna. Its distinguishing feature is that it contains the images of no fewer than four of Vishnu's avatars: Varaha (boar incarnation), Narasimha (lion incarnation), Rama, and Lord Venkatakrishna. *(Triplicane, west of South Beach Rd. Open daily 7am-noon and 4-8pm. Inner sanctum Rs3.)*

SRI KAPALEESWARAR TEMPLE. The Vijayanagar Kings built the present structure in the 16th century and the majestic 37m *gopuram* (gateway) at its entrance after an earlier temple on the same site was destroyed by the Portuguese. The great saint Ugnanasambandar sang a hymn here to Lord Kapaleeswarar in order to bring back to life a girl who had died of a snake bite; a shrine and statue in front of the temple commemorate the event. The temple's name is derived from a meeting of Brahma and Shiva on top of Mount Kailas. When Brahma failed to show Shiva the respect and courtesy due to him, an angry Shiva plucked off one of his *kapalams* (heads). In an act of regretful penance, Brahma came to Mylapore and installed Shiva's *linga* himself. Non-Hindus are allowed only as far as the outer courtyard, which houses a shrine to Parvati in peacock form. *(Mylapore, off Kutchery Rd. Open daily 5:30am-noon and 4-9:30pm. Puja every hr.)*

SAN THOME CATHEDRAL BASILICA. Built over the tomb of the apostle St. Thomas, the basilica is an important pilgrimage site,. It is believed that Thomas arrived in India from Palestine in 52 AD and was killed 26 years later. A millennium later Thomas's remains were moved inland, and a new church was built, probably by Madras's Persian Christian community. In 1606, the church was refurbished and made into a cathedral, and in 1896 it was rebuilt as a basilica. San Thome is more interesting for its history than for its aesthetic appeal, although the pleasant and peaceful church sanctuary bears a large stained glass window depicting the apostle's life. A **museum** on the premises contains a 16th-century map of South Asia. *(Eastern Mylapore, 6km south of Egmore. Open daily 6am-6pm. Museum open M-F 9:30am-12:30pm and 2-5:30pm.)*

TAMIL NADU

LITTLE MOUNT AND ST. THOMAS MOUNT. Just south of the Adyar River is **Little Mount,** a complex of mildly interesting caves where St. Thomas led the life of an ascetic, occasionally offering sermons from his rocky pulpit. According to local lore, the impressions in the caves are St. Thomas's handprints. Little Mount has two churches, both of which attract plenty of pilgrims. The older church was built in 1551 by the Portuguese. The newer one, Our Lady of Health, was consecrated in 1971. *(Little Mount is 10km south of the city center. Auto-rickshaws from downtown Rs60.)* About 5km southwest of Little Mount, 160 steep steps lead up to **Saint Thomas Mount (Great Mount),** where St. Thomas is said to have been killed after fleeing his home at Little Mount. The Portuguese church at the top of the Mount was put up in 1523 on the site of a church built by Armenian traders nearly 1000 years earlier. The altar is supposed to stand on the very spot where St. Thomas died, and legend holds that the paintings over the altar were done by St. Luke. The altar cross is named "the bleeding cross," since the red stains on the carving are believed to be patches of blood that reappear annually on the 18th of December. The hilltop offers a pleasant respite from Madras's bustle, but it is far away (45-60min.). Those with an interest in Madras's present-day Christian community can visit the largest church in India—the 15,000 member congregation of New Life Assembly of God. *(Near Little Mount. English services Su 8am and 4pm.)*

OTHER SIGHTS. Guindy National Park is a peaceful, though increasingly scruffy, place. Popular with families, its zoo is home to some deer and the occasional jackal, mongoose, and monkey. *(1km south of Little Mount. Open daily 8:30am-5:30pm. Rs3.)* Also on the premises is the popular **Snake Park.** *(Open daily 9am-5:30pm; demonstrations every hr. 10am-5pm. Rs2.)* Eastern Adyar harbors the headquarters of the **Theosophical Society,** a spiritual movement founded by a pair of Americans in 1875. The mansion is surrounded by elaborate gardens, containing "The Great Banyan Tree." *(☎ 491 7198. Open M-Sa 8:30-10am and 2-4pm.)* Not far from Fort St. George rise the minarets of the **High Court** and the **Law College,** constructed in an Indo-Saracenic style in the mid-19th century and still in use today.

🎬 ENTERTAINMENT

Madras is home to India's second-largest film industry; taking in a Tamil talkie is a fun way to spend a couple of hours. You don't need to know much Tamil—none at all, actually—to figure out the plot (there's only one), and you'll probably leave the theater having learned *something*. Cinemas are on nearly every corner; many screen English-language movies. The following cinemas all show four films per day: **Sathyam,** 8 Thurni Vika Rd., off Peters Rd., near New College; **Woodlands,** Royapettah High Rd. (☎ 852 7355); and **Devi,** Anna Salai (☎ 855 5660). Women should be careful—dark cinemas are popular hang-outs of dirty old men. *The Hindu* has listings of films, special screenings, and cultural events.

Performances are often given at the city's various music and dance academies. The **Carnatic Music and Dance Festival** takes place every year from early December to mid-January. **The Music Academy,** 115 E. Mowbray's Rd. (☎ 827 5619), often gives away free tickets for shows.

🛍 SHOPPING

Before you bust your wallet, take a moment to reflect on your itinerary. Many crafts and silks can be had for considerably less in smaller towns, where you can purchase goods directly from the artisans. **Street shopping,** however, can be rewarding since hawkers are common and often offer good deals. Dozens of makeshift shops line the streets in **Luz** (directly south of city center in **Alwarpet**). **Radha Silk House (RASI),** 1 Sannadhi St., Mylapore, next to the Kapaleeswarar Temple, is a hot favorite, with silk fabrics and saris of all kinds in a profusion of colors. The basement has a decent selection of gift items, wooden carved boxes, brassware, and paintings. (☎ 494 1906. Open daily 9am-9pm. Accepts all major credit

I'M NOT A POLITICIAN, BUT I PLAY ONE

IN REAL LIFE Residents of Tamil Nadu have long had a penchant for electing members of the immensely popular local film industry to positions of power. In 1977, the film star M.G. Ramachandran ("MGR") won a landslide victory on behalf of the All-India Anna Dravida Munnetra Kazhagam (AIADMK), a breakaway faction of the ruling DMK. That was only the beginning. In 1990, the most (in)famous of AIADMK's leaders, Jayalalitha Jayaram, came to power. The former actress and dancer quickly became embroiled in a veritable mini-series of corruption and scandal. She was forced to make a hasty exit in 1995 as her unfolding political drama was too much for her fans (or was it voters?) to handle. Her successor, the DMK-backed N. Karunanidhi, is the happy-looking bald man in dark glasses, whose pretty little mug grins out from statues and billboards in every town in the state. A former screenwriter for Tamil films, Karunanidhi is often depicted alongside Rajnikant, a feather-haired, mustachioed actor who shares his buddy's deep concern for a variety of social causes. For now, Karunanidhi runs a fairly clean ship, but locals jokingly wonder what sort of high-stakes *filmi* scandal this writer will dream up.

cards.) Also of interest are more glitzy shopping plazas, such as **Alsa Mall,** 149 Montieth Rd., Egmore, where you can buy beautiful *salwaar kameez.* Spencer Plaza Mall on Anna Salai sells name-brand Western clothes at Indian prices.

🎵 NIGHTLIFE

Tamil Nadu only recently repealed its prohibition laws, and there is still a stigma attached to alcohol consumption. Most bars have heavily tinted windows and doors, as if to obscure the shameful goings-on inside. Nearly every three-to-five-star hotel has its own permit room. But don't expect to find your poison of choice, since most permit rooms are stocked with whatever IMFL the owners can get their hands on. Near Egmore, are some decent hotel bars, including **Sherry's,** in the Hotel Imperial, 6 Gandhi Irwin Rd. (☎ 825 0376), and **Bon Sante,** in the Hotel Chandra Towers (☎ 823 3334). Both are open 11am-11pm. **Tinto,** at the Residency in T. Nagar, has a graceful and relaxing atmosphere, with classic wooden and wicker furniture, and 4 muted TVs. (Snacks Rs50; full meals Rs110-240; beer Rs85; and cocktails Rs110. Open daily 11am-11pm.) For the serious action, posh hotels are the venues to look into. Only the trendiest frequent **Socko,** Ambassador Pallava, 53 Montieth Rd., Egmore, a popular disco that churns out techno rhythms for gyrating pre-collegiate types. (☎ 855 4476. Rs300 per couple.) University angels and devils frolic together at **Hell Freezes Over (HFO)** at the Quality Inn in Aruna. Also popular are Saturday nights at **ED-41** on the Beach Rd., next to VGP (getting there and back may be difficult and expensive).

KANCHIPURAM காஞ்சிபுரம்   ☎ 04112

From the dusty streets to the towering *gopurams,* Kanchi is a city of temples, "the Varanasi of the South." One of Hinduism's seven most sacred cities, Kanchi derives its name from the words *Ka* (another name for Brahma, the creator) and *anchi* ("worship")—Brahma worshiped Vishnu and the goddess Kamakshi here. Some magnificent temples were built in Kanchi between the 4th and 8th centuries, when the city was the capital of the Pallava kings. Kanchi was also the seat of the guru Shankara (780-820 AD) and has been a center of philosophy and learning ever since. The city is divided into two parts: Little Kanchi houses the important Vishnu temples and Big Kanchi has over a thousand temples dedicated to Shiva. Modern Kanchi is a place where the temple bells and dazzling silks conspire to create a sensory assault. Look for the elegant threads worn by Tamil women—Kanchipuram silk saris are famous all over India.

GETTING THERE AND GETTING AROUND

Trains: Railway station (☎23149), on Station Rd., east of the Vaikuntha Perumal Temple. Take E. Raja Veethi north and follow the signs. 2nd class only to **Madras** via **Chengalpattu** (7, 8:25am, and 6pm; 3hr.; Rs16).

Buses: The chaotic **bus stand,** hidden behind storefronts, is at the intersection of Kamarajar and Nellukkara St. To: **Chengalpattu** (#212H and 212B, every hr., 1½hr., Rs8); **Madras** (#76B and 76C, every 30min., 2½hr., Rs15) or Point-to-Point (PP) bus (every 30min, 1½hr., Rs17); **Mahabalipuram** (every 15min., 2hr., Rs12); and **Vellore** (every 30min., 2½hr., Rs12). Frequent buses to **Pondicherry** depart from Chengalpattu.

Local Transportation: Auto-rickshaws can be flagged down on Kamarajar St. or Gandhi Rd. or picked up next to the bus stand. A ride from the bus stand to the outskirts of town should cost no more than Rs25. **Bikes** can be rented from the shop outside Vaikuntha Perumal Temple and at the stall near the railway station (Rs15 per day).

ORIENTATION AND PRACTICAL INFORMATION

The **bus stand** has one main entrance on **Kamarajar St.** (formerly known as Kossa St.), which runs north-south through the center of town, where many shops and eating places are located. You can also find food and lodging on **Nellukkara St.,** which runs perpendicular to Kamarajar St. at its northern end. **Gandhi Rd.** runs parallel to Nellukkara St., about 500m down from the bus stand, turning into **T. Nambi Koil St.** Most of Kanchi's famous silk emporiums are along these roads. One block east of the Nellukkara-Kamarajar intersection, **East Raja Veethi** shoots northward out of town.

Tourist Office: There is no official tourist office, but you can get basic info and maps at the TTDC-sponsored **Hotel Tamil Nadu,** Railway Station Rd. (☎22553 or 22554). Take E. Raja Veethi north from the bus station, turn right at the sign, and follow the street to its end at Railway Station Rd. Turn right again; the main entrance is ahead.

Currency Exchange: The nearest place to change foreign currency is in Madras.

Market: Rajaji Market, at the intersection of Railway and Gandhi Rd., sells all the fruit, vegetables, and mutton you could want. Open daily 7am-7pm.

Police: Police Control Room, Kamarajar St. (☎22000 or 22805).

Pharmacy: Tamil Nadu Medicals, 25 Nellukkara St. (☎22285), west of the intersection with Kamarajar St. Open M-Sa 8am-11:30pm.

Hospital: Manohar General Hospital, Railway Rd. (☎22102), is a private facility.

Post Office: GPO, Railway Rd. Open M-F 9am-5pm. **Postal Code:** 631502.

ACCOMMODATIONS

Kanchi's budget hotels, mostly near the bus station, tend to be dank and windowless and fill up quickly.

Hotel Jaybala International, 504 Gandhi Rd. (☎24348). The better rooms have towel, soap, satellite TV, phone, safe deposit box, room service, and a doctor on call. Seat and squat toilets. Check-out 24hr. "Ordinary" singles Rs125; singles Rs300; doubles Rs340; quad Rs525. 15-20% luxury tax.

Rajam Lodge, 9 Kamarajar St. (☎22519), near the bus stand entrance. Ask for a double on the 2nd floor—in return you'll get windows (a scarce commodity in this town). Squat toilets. Singles Rs70; doubles Rs110.

Hotel Abirami & Lodge, 109B Kamarajar St. (☎20797). Bathtub-like rooms with phones but no windows or sheets. Seat and squat toilets. Rooms Rs70-145.

Hotel Baboo Surya, 85 E. Raja Veethi (☎22555 or 22556), near the Perumal Temple, a 5min. walk from the bus stand. You get what you pay for: immaculate rooms, seat toilets, and the morning paper. All rooms have Star TV. Attached restaurant. Singles Rs300-375; doubles Rs350-450. 15-20% luxury tax. AmEx, MC.

Kanchipuram

ACCOMMODATIONS
Hotel Abirami & Lodge, 3
Hotel Baboo Surya, 1
Hotal Jaybala Int'l, 5
Rajam Lodge, 4

FOOD
Hotel Abirami, 3
Hotel Saravana Bhavan, 6
Hotel Shakti Ganappatti, 2
Kanchi Woodlands, 1

FOOD

Hotel Saravana Bhavan, 504 Gandhi Rd., next to Hotel Jaybala International. Suited officials bring order to the masses by way of an intricate token system and assigned seating. The most popular spot in town—with good reason. Splendid "rice meals" (Rs28) from 10am-4pm. Sweet *badam halwa* Rs10. Open daily 7am-10pm.

Hotel Shakti Ganappatti, on E. Raja Veethi St., about 2min. north from the bus stand. All your old favorites. *Masala dosa* Rs12; steaming hot *idli* Rs3 per piece. Open daily 5:30am-8:30pm.

Kanchi Woodlands, inside Hotel Baboo Surya, serves veg. meals in a silent, slightly chilly atmosphere. Pick from a wide variety of *dosas* (Rs10-16), *paneer* (Rs33), and rices (Rs20-40). Open daily 6am-10:30pm.

Abirami, 109B Kamaraj St., underneath the hotel of the same name. Despite its somewhat run-down appearance, the *thali* (Rs15) gets good reviews from locals. Cheap *dosas* (Rs3) and *idlis* (Rs8). Open daily 6am-10pm.

SIGHTS

The temples here rank among India's most sacred places for Hindus. For most tourists, however, a daytrip from Madras or Mahabalipuram is enough. The temples are fairly spread out. Auto-rickshaw drivers will ask for Rs150-200 for a tour, including "waiting charges." An alternative is to rent a bicycle for the day. Below, the temples are arranged in a roughly clockwise order.

SRI KAILASANATHA TEMPLE. Built by Rajasimba Pallava in the first quarter of the 8th century, this temple is the oldest building in Kanchi. Its relatively modest size and the use of soft amber sandstone are both characteristic of Pallava temples; the famous shore temple at Mahabalipuram was built by the same team at about the same time. The quiet temple sees relatively little traffic since most visitors opt for either the Kamakshi Amman or Sri Ekambaranathar temples in the center of town. The interior of the wall that surrounds the shrine is marked by a row of 58 small meditation chambers, where sadhus mull things over in quiet solitude. In some of these cubbyholes, traces of the temple's frescoes can still be seen. Most of the wall paintings were destroyed by the British in their attempt to "preserve" the monument by encasing it in plaster and stripping it of its fragile artwork. On the rear wall of the sanctum are carvings of Shiva performing the Urdhwa Tandava dance of destruction. The inner sanctum (closed to non-Hindus) houses a *linga* to which it is believed Vishnu prayed for help in defeating the demon Tripurantaka. To walk around the image, worshippers must first crawl on all fours through a hollow. (*1½km out of town. Follow Nellukkara St. westward until it becomes Putteri St. Sri Kailasanatha is on the right past a small lake. Open daily 8:30am-noon and 4-6pm. To make the most of your visit, arrive before sunset. Free.*)

SRI EKAMBARANATHAR TEMPLE. The magnificent white *gopuram* of the Sri Ekambaranathar Temple dominates the skyline all across the northern part of town, dwarfing everything around it and mesmerizing visitors. The origins of the temple are recorded in the *sthalapurana*, which recounts an incident when Parvati jokingly covered the eyes of her soon-to-be hubby Shiva, upsetting the process of creation and destruction. So angered was Shiva that he ordered Parvati down to earth. On earth, Parvati came to a mango tree on the banks of the river Kampa in Kanchi and fashioned a *linga* out of sand. To test her devotion, Shiva placed before her numerous obstacles, all of which Parvati overcame. Finally, Shiva let the Ganga flow from his hair, hoping to inundate Kanchi and wash the *linga* away. But Parvati's devotion was so great that that she held tight, protecting the *linga* through the torrent. Pleased by this, Shiva took her back.

Shiva and Parvati were married underneath the same mango tree which is now inside the temple. It is from this tree that the temple derives its name—the root "Eka" means "mango tree." Each of its four branches—they represent the four books of the Vedas and are supposedly 3500 years old—is said to produce a different type of leaf, as well as fruit of a different taste. Locals believe that eating the fruit cures women of infertility. Women hang brightly colored ribbons and offerings from the branches, and sometimes Parvati answers their prayers. Also within the inner sanctum is the *linga* that Parvati fashioned, one of five in Tamil Nadu devoted to the five elements. A cavernous hallway surrounding the sanctum houses many *lingas* and statues of the 63 Alvar poet-saints. These colorful works are displayed during the temple's car festivals in April and July. Shiva and Parvati's wedding anniversary is celebrated during the full moon in March. (*Puthupalayam St. leads directly north to the temple. Open daily 6am-12:30pm and 4-8pm. Puja 6, 7am, noon, 4, 5, and 9pm. Free; camera fee Rs3.*)

KAMAKSHI AMMAN TEMPLE. *Gopurams* cast in soft shades of yellow, green, and pink and capped with tiny wooden spires adorn this temple, dedicated to Kamakshi, an incarnation of the goddess Devi and the town's resident deity. The temple is one of the sacred *shakti pithas* of India, sites devoted to the worship of the female element in creation *(shakti).* The inner sanctum (inaccessible to non-Hindus) is a squarish chamber with inscriptions on all sides. Outside, a golden *vimana* glows blindingly bright beneath the sharp South Indian sun. The sacred tank in the back is also steeped in legend—Vishnu sent two servants-turned-demons to bathe here to cleanse them of their evil ways. (*From W. Raja St., turn right onto Amman Koli St. Open daily 5am-12:30pm and 4-8:30pm. Free. Photography not permitted.*)

VAIKUNTA PERUMAL TEMPLE. This temple, dedicated to Vishnu, is deserted, and its sculptures have been repaired with plaster by the Archaeological Survey of

India. Legend holds that a Pallava king performed an elaborate *puja* at the Sri Kailasanatha Temple on the holiday of *Maha Shivaratri*. Ancient texts proclaim that those who worship devotedly on this holiday will have sons who will be followers of Vishnu. The courtyard surrounding the inner sanctum is lined with granite pillars and carvings depicting the Pallava kings, battle scenes, and musicians. The back left corner has a panel showing Xuanzang, the Chinese Buddhist pilgrim who traveled all over India during the 7th century.

The inner sanctum (with its images of Vishnu) is usually locked, but a bit of baksheesh to the key-wielding guard can work wonders. The central spire contains three images of Vishnu, one on top of the other. On the ground floor he is seen sitting; on the second floor, reclining on the serpent *ananta;* on the top, standing in an ascetic pose. A small walkway around the *vimana* is filled with well-preserved panels of Vishnu and his consort Lakshmi. *(From E. Raja St., turn right; the temple is several hundred meters ahead. Open daily 8am-noon and 4-8pm. Free.)*

SHOPPING

Each Kanchi sari is woven by hand and takes 15 days to a month to complete. Kanchi silks start from around Rs1000 and skyrocket into the tens of thousands for elaborate wedding saris. Expect to pay at least Rs3000 for a good quality sari with a fair amount of *zari* (pure gold thread) and an intricately woven *pallu* (the part that drapes over the shoulder). Store owners should give you at least a Rs1200 "discount" off the first price named. The biggest and most reputable of Kanchi's silk sari shops is **Nalli Silks**, 54 Nellukkara St. (Open M-Sa 9am-11pm.) You can also try **Srinivasan Silk House**, 17A TK Nambi St. (Open daily 8:30am-11pm.) Most owners will gladly take you to the back of the stores to show you silk yarn and demonstrate the process of adding *zari* designs onto saris. Turn right onto the road perpendicular to Sannadhi St. (outside Varadaraja Perumal Temple), and take a left at **Ammangar St.**, full of silk weavers eager to demonstrate their craft. Weavers' cooperatives cluster near temple entrances, and you'll probably be accosted by salesmen wielding business cards.

VELLORE வெல்லூர் ☎ **0416**

Vellore, 145km southwest of Madras, is not for the claustrophobic. Vendors crowd every inch of the narrow streets, and masses of pedestrians and bicycles scramble toward the famous hospital, which dominates the city center. Hundreds of people come here every day in hope of a cure. For the traveler, Vellore's well-preserved relics provide insight into its past as a medieval city of the Vijayanagar kingdom.

GETTING THERE AND GETTING AROUND. Buses run from the bus stand on PTC Road to: **Madras** (every 10min., 3½hr., Rs28) and **Trichy** (5 per morning, 5hr., Rs60). PATC goes to: **Bangalore** (12 per day, 6am-11pm, 6hr., Rs57); **Kanchi** (every 30min., 2hr., Rs14); **Madras** (every 15min., 4hr., Rs31.50); and **Tirupati** (every hr., 7am-11pm, 3hr., Rs18).

ORIENTATION AND PRACTICAL INFORMATION. Everything you need is in the immediate vicinity of the **CMC Hospital,** at the center of town. (☎222102. Open 24hr.) Most restaurants are on **Ida Scudder Rd.,** which runs directly parallel to the hospital. **Babu Rao St.,** parallel to and south of Ida Scudder Rd., and **KVS Chetty St.,** south of Babu Rao St., front most of Vellore's hotels and lodges. The **Main Bazaar,** two streets south, and parallel to KVS St., leads straight to the fort and temple entrances. The temple's major cross street is **PTC Rd.;** turning right onto it from the Main Bazaar will bring you to the **bus stand.** The **pharmacy** (☎222121), attached to the hospital, and the **North Vellore Police Station** (☎200021), on the corner of PTC Rd. by the bus station, are both open 24 hours. The nearest place to **exchange currency** is in Madras. The **post office** is on Katpadi Rd. (Open M-F 10am-6pm, Sa 10am-4pm.) **Postal Code:** 632004.

▛▟▛ ACCOMMODATIONS AND FOOD. Hotel vacancies increase the farther you get from the hospital. **VDM Lodge,** on Beri Bakkali St., has small but clean rooms. (☎224008. Check-out 24hr. Singles Rs60-70; doubles Rs90.) **Srinivasa Lodge,** opposite VDM Lodge, has slightly bigger, well-lit rooms, all with attached bath and free hot water from 5 to 8am. (☎226389. Singles Rs90; doubles Rs135.) Vellore's grimy diners are not to be trifled with. **Hotel Susil Classic,** 64 Arcott Rd., past the hospital in the direction of the hills, is dimly lit and has A/C. Vegetable soup (Rs13) and South Indian staples such as *dosa* (Rs14) and *idli* (Rs7) are among the picks. (Open daily 6:30am-10:30pm.) At **Chinatown,** on Arcott Rd. above Hotel Susil Classic, bow-tied waiters serve fried rice (Rs35), wonton soup (Rs30), and *naan* (Rs18) in a small, cool dining room. (Open daily noon-3pm and 6-11pm.)

◪ SIGHTS. Legend has it that the **Vellore Fort** was built in an attempt to lift a curse placed on the temple that previously stood on this site. Put up during the 13th century under the rule of the Vijayanagar kings, this huge granite fortress and its beautiful moat were the nucleus around which the town of Vellore grew. For several turbulent centuries, control of the fort changed hands regularly, beginning in the 1600s when the Bhamini Sultans occupied it. The Sultans were ousted by the Marathas, who held power until they were booted out by the Mughals. In the 18th century, the British took over. The fort was the scene of the short-lived **Vellore Mutiny,** in which South Indian troops in the British Army protested changes in headgear and uniform by storming the fort. Several British officers were killed before the mutiny was put down by the no-nonsense Colonel Robert Gillespie, who had the mutineers blown to pieces. Today, there are several government offices, schools, and businesses inside, as well as a **museum** containing some interesting stone carvings. *(On PTC Rd. Fort open daily 6am-8pm. Free. Museum open Sa-Th 9:30am-5pm. Free.)* The beautiful limestone **Jalakanteshwara Temple** was built just before the fort, and its white statues and carvings remain in superb condition. On top of the *gopuram* above the main entrance is a small carving of the fort's builder and his wife. To the left of the entrance, a series of spectacularly carved outer pillars, all carved from one stone, supports a great hall. *(The temple is inside the fort.)*

NEAR VELLORE: TIRUVANNAMALAI திருவண்ணாமலை

Tiruvannamalai's main attraction is the **Siva-Parvati Temple of Arunachaleswar** (open daily 6am-8pm), a truly awe-inspiring monument, though the town's tranquility also comes as a welcome relief from the bustle of other South Indian cities. A peaceful morning can be had watching the sun rise over the ivory-colored *gopurams* and exploring the five gigantic courtyards. **Buses** go to and from **Vellore** (every 15min., 2hr., Rs18) and **Villapuram** for connecting buses (every 15min., 3hr., Rs18). Opposite the eastern temple wall—the first one you'll see when coming from the bus stand—the **Sri Kalaimagal Lodge,** N. Othavadai St., has large rooms with floors as clean as *thali* plates. (☎24215. Singles Rs100; doubles Rs150.) Down the street, near the temple entrance, is the **Hotel Dibum,** one of the town's few non-grimy, open-air restaurants. If you don't like *dosa* (Rs29) and *idli* (Rs9) you're in for a hungry day. (Open daily 6:30am-10:30pm.)

MAHABALIPURAM மஹாடவிறம் ☎04114

Officially known as Mamallapuram, the village of Mahabalipuram rests comfortably on the shores of the Bay of Bengal, awash in the pungent odors of the fishermen's catch and the "herbal" aromas left in the wake of the tourists who drift up and down the sandy beaches. The town's tourist appeal is so great that there is even a festival devoted to its foreign visitors: the **Tourist Dance Festival** (Jan. 15-Feb. 15). Behind just about every door on E. Raja St. seems to be a hotel, restaurant, or overzealous tour operator. The air is filled with the hammer and clang of artists carving stone, a tradition with deep roots in Mahabalipuram, dating back to the reign of the Pallavas during the 4th-8th centuries. Today, it is rivaled only by the art of salesmanship. With sunset, calm descends on Mahabalipuram, and the incessant push and thrust of tourists and touts are softened by the beauty of the evening sea—fresh fish and cool breezes keep cafes and rooftops pleasant and popular until the early hours.

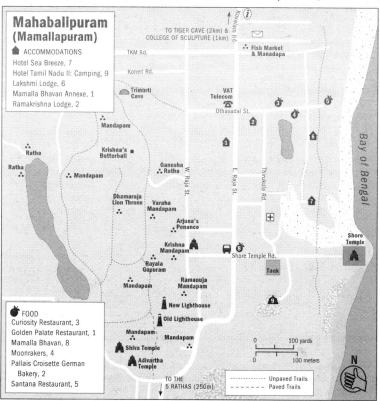

Mahabalipuram (Mamallapuram)

🏠 ACCOMMODATIONS
Hotel Sea Breeze, 7
Hotel Tamil Nadu II: Camping, 9
Lakshmi Lodge, 6
Mamalla Bhavan Annexe, 1
Ramakrishna Lodge, 2

🍅 FOOD
Curiosity Restaurant, 3
Golden Palate Restaurant, 1
Mamalla Bhavan, 8
Moonrakers, 4
Pallais Croisette German Bakery, 2
Santana Restaurant, 5

TO TIGER CAVE (2km) & COLLEGE OF SCULPTURE (1km)

TKM Rd.
Koneri Rd.
Trimurti Cave
Mandapam
Ratha
Ratha
Mandapam
Krishna's Butterball
Ganesha Ratha
Dharmaraja Lion Throne
Varaha Mandapam
Arjuna's Penance
Krishna Mandapam
Rayala Gopuram
Mandapam
Ramanuja Mandapam
New Lighthouse
Old Lighthouse
Mandapam
Mandapam
Shiva Temple
Adivartha Temple
TO THE 5 RATHAS (250m)

Kovalam Rd.
Fish Market & Manadapa
VAT Telecom
Othavadai St.
W. Raja St.
E. Raja St.
Thirikula Rd.
Shore Temple Rd.
Shore Temple
Tank
Bay of Bengal

0   100 yards
0   100 meters

----------- Unpaved Trails
- - - - - Paved Trails

N

GETTING THERE AND GETTING AROUND

Buses: The **bus stand** is on E. Raja St. To: **Chengalpattu** (#212H and 108B, every 30min., 45min., Rs6); **Kanchi** (#157M and 212H, every 45min., 2hr., Rs13); **Kovalam** (#117, 118, and 188V, every 30min., 30min., Rs4); **Madras** (every 30min., 2hr., Rs18); **Tirupati** (#212H; 5:20am, 1:20, and 3pm, 2½hr., Rs13); **Pondicherry** (every 30min., 2½hr., Rs19).

Local Transportation: Auto-rickshaws and tourist taxis wait outside the bus stand, but you won't need them in this small town unless you stay at one of the beach resorts outside Mahabalipuram. **Nathan Cycle Works,** opposite TTDC, rents bicycles (Rs15 per day) and mopeds (Rs175 per day).

ORIENTATION AND PRACTICAL INFORMATION

Finding your way around in Mahabalipuram is a cinch. From the **inter-city bus stand,** it's a five-minute walk north (left) along **East Raja St.** to the **tourist office.** On the way, you'll cross three east-west streets. The first, unmarked, small street to the right (look for Baskin-Robbins) leads to the hospital and several lodges and restaurants on Thirikula St., which runs parallel to E. Raja St. The second, larger, unmarked street is **Othavadai Rd.,** which leads east to more lodges and restaurants. A bit farther north, **TKM Rd.** cuts across E. Raja St. on its left-hand side, leading to the **bank** and **pharmacy.** At the tourist office, E. Raja St. becomes **Kovalam Rd.,** which stretches out of town, to the beach resorts and Tiger Cave. To get to the **Shore Temple** and the beach, take a right from the bus stand onto E. Raja St., and then a left onto **Shore Temple Rd.** If you want to see the **mandapams** and surrounding caves, take a right on Shore Temple Rd. and W. Raja St., which runs parallel to E. Raja St. on the opposite side of the temple from the bus station.

> ⚠ **WARNING.** The Bay of Bengal can be very dangerous, and many people drown every year. Ask at the tourist office and at your hotel about the advisability of swimming. Even if you are an experienced swimmer, don't underestimate the force of the undertow. And don't even *look* at the water if you've been drinking.

Tourist Office: TTDC (☎42232), has bus schedules posted on the wall. Open daily 10am-5:45pm.

Currency Exchange: Indian Overseas Bank, TKM Rd. (☎42222). North on E. Raja St.; turn left onto TKM. Changes traveler's checks. Open M-F 10am-2pm, Sa 10am-noon.

Police: Vandavasi Police Station, Kovalam Rd. (☎42221), north of town. Open 24hr.

Hospital: Suradeep Hospital, Thirukula St. (☎42389 or 42448), next to Baskin Robbins, has a 24hr. **pharmacy.** Still, your best bet is to go to Madras if seriously ill.

Telephones: The booth at the intersection of Othavadai St. and E. Raja St. is open 24hr.

Internet: There are several places along E. Raja St. **VAT Telecom Center** (☎42711), just north of Othavadai St., is the most reliable. Rs50 per hr. Open 8am-10pm.

Post Office: E. Raja St. (☎42230), near the tourist office. Open M-Sa 9am-4pm. **Postal Code:** 603104.

▐ ACCOMMODATIONS

Plenty of cheap hotels have sprung up to cater to the droves of tourists who descend on Mahabalipuram during high season. Most of the cheapest places are on or near E. Raja, Othavadai, or Thirakua St. A number of resorts line Kovalam Rd., offering private beaches and extravagant buffet feasts to anybody with a few extra rupees to burn. Many of these places offer bargain rates during the off-season. From Kovalam Rd., the town is just a short, invigorating bike ride away.

Ramakrishna Lodge, 8 Othavadai St. (☎42331 or 42431), in a pink and red painted building. Wide rooms with big beds and mosquito screens. Attached bath, seat toilets, and hot water. Singles Rs75; doubles Rs125.

Lakshmi Lodge, 29/A2 Othavadai St. (☎42463), down the dirt road on the right of Moonraker's Restaurant. Sea-side lodge full of foreigners. Rooms vary in price according to view (patio or beach). Most bathrooms have seat toilets. Staff will arrange practically anything for guests, including bikes, massage, and astrology readings. Attached rooftop restaurant. Singles Rs100-200; doubles Rs400.

Hotel Tamil Nadu II: Camping Site (☎42287), off Shore Temple Rd. You can't miss the billboard. Government-run hotel, with the cheapest dorm beds in town. You can pitch a tent out back. Dorm beds Rs50; cottages Rs300-450.

Hotel Sea Breeze (☎43035), down the dirt road to the right, off Othavadai St., past Moonraker's. Mosquito netting, marble floors, wooden furniture and breezy balconies. Pool can be used by non-guests for Rs75. Singles Rs250; doubles Rs450-700.

Mamalla Bhavan Annexe, 104 E. Raja St. (☎42060). The most luxurious hotel in town, with an eager team of blue-uniformed employees. Spacious rooms have marble-tiled floors with double beds and cable TVs. Attached restaurant. Doubles Rs350-700.

▐ FOOD

Mahabalipuram is full of restaurants offering European "health food" and seafood. You'll have a difficult time finding straightforward Indian food. Beer is not difficult to find, though it's not on most menus; just ask.

▨ **Moonrakers,** Othavadai St. European breakfasts are popular (*muesli* and yogurt Rs40), but the mellow vibes keep travelers here throughout the day. Fish and chips with salad Rs60; chicken in lime-mint sauce Rs60; honey crepes Rs25. All in all, an excellent choice, Mr. Bond. Open daily 7am-1am.

Pallais Croisette German Bakery, Othavadai St., on top of the Ramakrishna Hotel. Airy rooftop restaurant serving excellent rice pudding (Rs20) and golden pancakes (Rs15-25). Open daily 7:30am-10:30pm.

Curiosity Restaurant, Othavadai St., near Hotel Sea Breeze. Excellent vegetable *biryani* (Rs25) and banana shakes (Rs15). Open daily 7am-10pm.

Mamalla Bhavan, E. Raja St., opposite the bus stand. If you can't stand the tourists any more, come here for your daily fix of *thali* (Rs15). Open daily 7am-10pm.

Golden Palate Restaurant, 104 E. Raja St., inside Mamalla Bhavan Annexe. A more upscale place serving enormous, elaborate *thalis* (Rs50) and ice cream sundaes (Rs45-70) in A/C cool. Open daily 7am-10:30pm.

Santana Restaurant (☎ 43145), at the end of Othavadai St., at the beach, is an unpretentious place run by 3 lively old men. Tables set in the sand overlook the sea. Fish Rs75-150; prawn fried noodles Rs55. Open 11am-11pm.

🔆 SIGHTS

Mahabalipuram has an incredible collection of well-preserved sculpture, weathered by hundreds of years' worth of sun, sand, and surf. Scholars agree that most of these masterpieces were sculpted under the patronage of the 7th-century Pallava leader Narasimhavarman I, who went by the fearsome name Mamalla ("Great Wrestler")—hence the town's (official) name. The sights are conveniently all near the southern part of town.

SHORE TEMPLE. Dedicated to Shiva and Vishnu, this temple was built at the turn of the 8th century, and is thought to have been the first South Indian temple built entirely of stone. The Pallavas' maritime exploits helped spread their culture far and wide around the region; echoes of the Shore Temple's lion carvings and stocky spires can be seen throughout South Asian temple architecture of the period. Inside the temple are a flower-strewn image of Vishnu reclining on the serpent Sesa and a broken, fluted granite Shiva *linga*. Outside the temple, carved panels depict scenes from the lives of its Pallava creators. There has been speculation that the Shore Temple once served as a lighthouse, which would explain its oddly elongated *vimana*. It is now protected and kept litter-free by the Archaeological Society of India. *(On Shore Temple Rd., jutting into the Bay of Bengal, 1km to the right of the bus stand. Open daily 6am-5:30pm. Rs5 includes admission to the 5 Rathas; Free F.)*

ARJUNA'S PENANCE. One of the world's largest bas-relief sculptures, Arjuna's Penance is the most impressive sight in town. Particularly engaging are the elegant, humorous depictions of animals and birds—the delightful renderings of an elephant family and an ascetic, meditating cat surrounded by dancing rats. It is easy enough to admire the visual spectacle, but scholars are still scratching their heads trying to figure out what it's all supposed to mean. According to one widely accepted theory, Arjuna's Penance depicts a well-loved story from the *Mahabharata*—the scrawny man standing on one leg is the penitent archer Arjuna, who is gazing through a prism and imploring Shiva to give him the *pashupatashastra*, a powerful magic arrow. Other historians believe that the images represent Rama's ancestor, Bhagiratha, begging the gods to give the Ganga River to the people of the world (see **Ganga Comes to Earth,** p. 149). The gods have agreed to comply with Bhagiratha's request, and the whole of creation—including the elephants—has turned out to watch the miracle of Ganga gushing down from the Himalayas. *(In town, just behind the bus stand on W. Raja St.)*

MANDAPAMS AND SURROUNDING MONUMENTS. The hilly area behind the bus stand and Arjuna's Penance is strewn with massive boulders and 10 small **mandapams** (cave temples), which depict tales from Hindu mythology. Finding your way from one *mandapam* to the next can be difficult, and making a systematic tour is next to impossible. But getting lost and stumbling upon *mandapams* at random is half the fun. Just around the corner to the right from Arjuna's Penance is the **Gane-**

sha Ratha, a free-standing monolith dedicated to the elephant-headed son of Shiva and Parvati. North of the *ratha* and off to the left is **Krishna's Butterball,** a massive boulder balanced on the side of a hill. The name comes from popular stories of Krishna's youth, which recount an incident when the baby Krishna was caught stealing *ghee* from an urn. North of the Butterball and next to a Pallavan water tank is the **Trimurti Cave,** which contains shrines to Shiva, Vishnu, and Brahma; all are depicted with their right hands in the *abhya,* or blessing, pose. The **Kotikal Mandapam,** dating from the turn of the 7th century, is down the hill to the left. A small cell in the back is guarded by stone carvings of female attendants.

Heading south back toward the bas-relief, you'll first pass the 7th-century **Varaha Mandapam.** Its four panels represent the goddess Varaha raising the earth from the ocean. Most impressive is the one on the left, which depicts Vishnu in the form of a boar with the goddess Bhumidevi (Earth) seated in his lap. Another panel depicts the goddess of wealth, Lakshmi, accompanied by elephants. The trough in front of the *mandapam* was used by worshippers to wash their feet before entering the temple. From the Varaha Mandapam, walk 150m southeast to the exquisite **Krishna Mandapam,** a large mid-7th-century bas-relief that shows Krishna holding up Mount Govardhana to protect his relatives from the floods brought on by the god Indra. Other panels illustrate scenes from Krishna's life, including his flirtatious play *(lila)* with the milkmaids *(gopis).*

Up the steep hill directly west of the Krishna Mandapam is the decaying **Rayala Gopuram.** This uncompleted construction bears slender vertical panels that portray the 10 incarnations of Vishnu. From the Krishna Mandapam, it's a short walk south to the **Ramanuja Mandapam,** built in the mid-7th century and almost completely ruined by vandals who chiseled away at many of the temple's elaborate panels. From here, you can see the 100-year-old **New Lighthouse.** Next to the New Lighthouse is the **Old Lighthouse,** a Shiva temple at an especially high elevation that was used as a lighthouse with a bonfire on top until the turn of the last century.

FIVE RATHAS. A collection of worn but still stunning monoliths, known as the **Pancha Pandava Rathas,** was carved during the reign of Narasimhavarman I Pallava, and are full-size models of the temples known to the Dravidian builders of the 7th century. The five temples influenced by Buddhist temple architecture and named for the five Pandava brothers, the heroes of the *Mahabharata.* The largest, the **Dharmaraja Ratha,** is adorned with various carvings of demi-gods and Narasimhavarman. The complex also includes life-size animals carved out of stone. *(About 1½km south of town along E. Raja St. Rs5, including admission to the Shore Temple.)*

GOVERNMENT COLLEGE OF SCULPTURE AND ARCHITECTURE. Hundreds of artists in training learn their craft at this always-lively seaside complex. Contact the tourist office or college directly to make an appointment to have a look around. *(About 3km north of Central Mahabalipuram along Kovalam Rd. ☎ 42261.)*

CROCODILE PARK. Vodanammali, a small town north of Mahabalipuram, is home to a privately owned "collection" of over 3500 specimens of crocs and alligators that snap at one another in various water holes and pools throughout the park. Next door to the croc farm is the government-run **Snake Venom Extraction** facility. *(15km north of Mahabalipuram. Crocodile Park open daily 8am-5:45pm. Rs15. Snake facility open W-M 9:30am-5pm. Rs5.)*

PONDICHERRY பாண்டிச் சேரி ☎ 0413

Many visitors to Pondicherry expect the one-time capital of French India to be an unadulterated enclave of European culture, but this coastal town's claim to fame is somewhat tinged with hyperbole: Pondicherry isn't Paris. It's a decidedly divided town, split geographically and culturally by a narrow canal. To the west, is plain old Pondy, your basic, bustling, mid-sized South Indian city. To the east of the canal is *Pondicheri.* The streets here are well-kept, the *flics* sport red *képis,* restaurants serve French food, and the architecture is European.

Pondicherry

🏠 ACCOMMODATIONS
Ajantha Guest House, 10
Aristo Guest Hosue, 3
International Guest House, 5
Garden Guest Hosue, 1
Park Guest Hosue, 13

🍴 FOOD
Ajantha Sea View, 10
Ashram Dining House, 6
Hot Breads, 4
Hotel Aristo, 2
La Terasse, 12
Le Café, 7
Le Club, 11
Rendezvous, 9
Satsanga's, 8

TO AUROVILLE (12km) & QUIET BEACH (VIA EAST COAST RD.)

Sangara Dess St.
Thiyaga Raja St.
North Boulevard (Sardar Vallabhai Patel Salai)
P. Koil St.
MA Koil St.
ID Koil St.
KA Koil St.
Sri Aurobindo St. (Aravindar St.)
Supraya Chettiar St.
C Koil St.
AH Madam St.
Jawaharlal Nehru (JN) St.
Market
Ranga Pillai St.
Vellaja St.
Nidarajapayer St.
Baharati St.
St. Theresa St.
Petit Canal St.
Sinna Pappara St.
Lapporth St.
Monthorsier St.
C Mudhallar St.
Lal Bahadur Shastri St.
SS Pilai St.
West Boulevard (Anna Salai)
Mahatma Gandhi (MG) Rd.
Mission St.
Canteen St.
Capt. Xavier St.
Gingy Salai
V. Simonel St.
L. Thollandal St.
B Derichemont St.
Dupuy St.
Sri Aurobindo Ashram
Marine St.
F. Martin St.
Compagnie St.
France
Canal
Higginbothams
Pondicherry Museum
Romain Roland Library
Raj Nivas
Old Lighthouse
Government Place
Gandhi Memorial
Mahe de la Bourdonnais St.
Surcouf St.
State Bank of India
Dumas St.
Bussy St.
Bazar Saint Laurent St.
Alliance Française
Bay of Bengal
Botanical Gardens
South Boulevard (Subbaiyah Salai)
VOC St.
Ellai Annan Covil St.
Cazvar St.
Rue Suffren
Romain Roland St.
Beach Rd. (Goubert Salai)
Eglise de Sacre Coeur de Jésus
Water Tower
TO
N
0   500 yards
0   500 meters

   The streets are populated from early morning until late evening with magistrates in flowing robes, barefoot joggers, and hip wayfarers holidaying in the sun. Most of the city's elaborate architecture was built during the French occupation, begun in 1673 by François Martin, who hoped to gain a commercial advantage for his country over the roving Dutch and English. Over the next two centuries, the French ruled their South Asian colonial enclaves from Pondicherry. In 1954, they handed over their scattered territories to India; with Ponidcherry as their capital, these became a semi-autonomous Union Territory. Today, the overwhelming influence on the city is the Sri Aurobindo Ashram, established in 1926. The French artist Mirra Alfassa (later known as "the Mother") helped the Bengali mystic Sri Aurobindo Ghose popularize his spiritual teachings among thousands of devotees worldwide. The fruits of their efforts are readily apparent today: the ashram occupies a sizeable chunk of real estate in Pondy, and at the Mother's request, fllowers have established the experimental community of Auroville, 12km north of the city. Like everything else in Pondicherry, the Aurobindo Ashram is a multifaceted entity—for many locals, the Mother is "The French God," complementing "The Muslim God," "The Hindu God," and all the other powers in the local pantheon. For several thousand devotees, Auroville is a meaningful alternative lifestyle. For everybody else, it's just a good place to come and giggle. Lingering French influence has molded Pondy into a relaxing, chic, and decidedly pricey city.

GETTING THERE AND GETTING AROUND

Trains: The **railway station** (☎36684), on South Blvd., serves **Villupuram** for connections to the Madras-Rameswaram line (4 per day, 5am-7:20pm, 1hr.).

Buses: The massive bus station is on Lal Bahadur Shastri. There are several reservation and inquiry counters, including **SETC (State Express Transport Corp.), TNSTC (Tamil Nadu State Transport Corp.),** Pondicherry, and "local." Compare departure and journey times before boarding a bus. **Bangalore** (SETC 9am and 10pm, 7hr., Rs105; TNSTC 7:20am and 11:15pm); **Chidambaram** (every 15min., 2hr.); **Coimbatore** (SETC 8 and 8:45pm, 9hr., Rs106; 9 and 10pm, Rs 33); **Kanchi** (TNSTC 5 per day, 7:30am-8:10pm; 4hr.); **Madras** (every 30min., 4hr., Rs47; SETC has direct service every hr., 6-10am and 2-6pm, 3½hr.); **Mahabalipuram** (every 30min., 2hr., Rs22); **Trichy** (TNSTC direct 4 per day, 4:45am-10pm); **Trivandrum** (SETC 4pm, 16hr., Rs204); **Vellore** (TNSTC direct 7am, 5 and 9:15pm).

Local Transportation: Auto-rickshaws line up at the stand on Capt. Xavier St. and wait in packs outside every major tourist spot. Pay no more than Rs25 for a trip between the bus stands and the French side of town.

ORIENTATION

Pondy is a well-planned city. It is bordered on the east by the **Bay of Bengal,** and divided into eastern and western sections by a covered canal. Its streets are laid out in a simple grid. Three major commercial thoroughfares (from north to south), **Jawaharlal Nehru (JN), Rangapillai,** and **Lal Bahadur Shastri St.,** run east-west. Lal Bahadur Shastri leads past the **bus stand.** West of the canal, the major north-south avenue is **Mahatma Gandhi (MG) Rd.** East of the canal, the major north-south roads are **Rue Suffren** and **Romain Roland St.,** both of which end at the centrally located **Government Place. Beach Rd.** (Goubert Salai) runs along the shore and hooks west as it heads south, becoming **South Blvd.** (Subbaiyah Salai). The **railway station** is off Subbaiyah Salai. As Subbaiyah Salai heads north, it passes the Botanical Gardens and becomes **West Blvd.** (Anna Salai). To the north, **North Blvd.** (Sardar Vallabhai Patel Salai) links West Blvd. and Beach Rd.

PRACTICAL INFORMATION

Tourist Office: Pondicherry Tourism and Transport Development Corporation (PTTDC), 40 Goubert Salai (☎334978), north of Lal Bahadur Shastri St. **Tours** depart from the office (2pm; Rs50). Make reservations by 1pm. Open daily 8:45am-1pm and 2-5pm.

Currency Exchange: State Bank of India, Surcouf St. (☎36208), at Rue Suffren. Open M-F 10am-2pm, Sa 10am-noon. On the western side of town, **Souvenir,** on Mission St., near JN St., changes currency and traveler's checks. Open M-Sa 9am-1pm and 3-7pm.

Cultural Centers: Alliance Française, 38 Rue Suffren (☎334351), has a French library and sponsors cultural events and art displays. Open M-F 8:30am-12:30pm and 2-8pm; Sa 8:30am-noon.

Bookstore: Higginbothams, Gingy St. (☎333836), just north of Rangapillai St. **French Bookshop,** Rue Suffren (☎38062), just south of the Alliance Française. Open M-Sa 9am-12:30pm and 3:30-7:30pm.

Pharmacy: National Medicals, JN St. (☎333073), east of MG Rd. Open 7am-10pm.

Police: 14 Goubert Ave. (☎337243).

Hospital/Medical Services: The best place to go is **Jawaharlal Institute of Medical and Educational Research** (☎372380), a few km north of town; take NH 45 straight. **St. Joseph's Hospital,** 16 Romain Roland (☎339513), is also good. Emergency ward open 24hr. Consultations 8-11am and 4-6pm.

Telephones: The communications megaplex next to the GPO is open 24hr.

Internet: Bussy Fax Pt., on Bussy St., to the west of the canal. There are also two places on Captain Xavier St., behind Higginbothams.

Post Office: GPO, Rangapillai St. (☎33050). Open M-Sa 10am-7:30pm. **Postal Code:** 605001.

■ ACCOMMODATIONS

Apart from a couple of overpriced "luxury" hotels, accommodations in Pondy fall into two basic categories: standard Indian lodges and ashram guest houses. The ashrams are probably the most appealing options in town. Run by the followers of Sri Aurobindo, the ashram guest houses, all on the French side of town, have serene, immaculate rooms. The guest houses tend to abide by a strict curfew and prohibit smoking, drinking, and drugs. Guests are entitled to extremely cheap meals in the ashram dining hall. Only two of the larger ashrams are listed here, but any ashram facility can provide a list of over a dozen lodging options.

Park Guest House, Goubert Salai (☎334412; email parkgh@auroville.org.in). No, you're not dreaming—this hotel really *is* paradise. Lush gardens surround the building, and balconies have stunning views of the ocean crashing against the rocks. Cleaned daily, rooms have couch, desk, comfy bed, mosquito net, and bureau. Attached baths with seat toilet, towels, soap, and showers. Bike rental Rs20 per day. Attached restaurant. Check-out noon. Singles Rs200; doubles Rs400.

Garden Guest House, Akkasamy Madam St. (☎20797). Phenomenally inexpensive and clean ashram guest house set in a very Indian neighborhood. Rooms Rs45.

International Guest House, 17 Gingy St. (☎336699). A sense of purity and calm reigns in the spacious white rooms. Small "dressing rooms" lead into gleaming bathrooms. Communal meditation room and indoor garden. Check-out noon. Often full, so call ahead. Singles Rs90; doubles Rs120-350.

Aristo Guest House, 50A Mission St. (☎336728), just north of JN St. Management, up a flight of stairs. Pink painted rooms are cool and clean. Stroll on the upper balcony for fresh air. Check-out 24hr. Singles Rs100-550; doubles Rs150-650.

Ajantha Guest House, 22 Goubert Salai (☎38898), south of the tourist office. Musty rooms could use some light, but the morning breeze compensates. Attached baths with clean seat toilets. Check-out 24hr. Singles Rs250; doubles Rs300-450.

○ FOOD

Eating out in Pondicherry comes as a welcome change of pace. Pondy's colonial legacy includes a handful of glitzy continental restaurants featuring gourmet French food and ample drinks menus. You can find better-than-average Indian food at inflated prices on both sides of the canal.

Satsanga's, 13 Bussy St., around the corner from Rendezvous Restaurant. Quite the lovers' nest at night, with its high arches, potted jungle plants, and candlelight. Enjoy fresh arugula salad with grated parmesan, and crave more of the chewy, perfectly cooked homemade pasta (Rs90) for days to come. Open Tu-Su 8am-2pm (breakfast till noon) and 5-10pm. Tea salon open 8am-noon and 3-7pm.

La Terasse, 5 South Blvd., a short jaunt westward from the southern end of Goubert Salai. Relax in a small courtyard beneath a thatched roof as the musty scent of the wood-fire oven wafts into the dining area. Thin-crust pizza from Rs50; fresh fruit juices Rs20; fried banana Rs22. Open Th-Tu 8:30am-2:30pm and 6-10pm.

☒ **Le Café,** on the Goubert Salai promenade. A small ring of tables on the ocean front. Food is simple but hearty; eat an omelette (Rs18) or *dosa* (Rs16) while your coffee (Rs10) is being brewed, then sip at it with the waves at your feet. Open daily 24hr.

Rendezvous, 30 Rue Suffren, on the corner with Bussy St., east of the canal. Tuxedoed waiters and elegantly folded napkins. *Très chic,* man. Pasta with sauce Rs60-100; rich mousse Rs25. Open W-M 8-10:30am, 11:30am-3pm, and 6-10:30pm.

Hot Breads, Gingy St., next to Higginbothams. The closest thing to a Parisian cafe you'll find in Pondicherry. Croissants, baguettes, and pastries. Open 10am-9:30pm.

Ajantha Sea View Restaurant, 22 Goubert Salai, upstairs from the hotel of the same name. Immensely popular with locals. Chicken *biryani* Rs32; Indian and continental dishes Rs50-150. Attached bar (beer Rs35-40). Open daily 10am-11pm.

Hotel Aristo, 714 JN St., between Mission St. and MG Rd., west of the canal. Rooftop restaurant with chirping birds and dangling vines. A variety of salads (Rs30) and fish dishes (Rs65-75). Open daily 9-10:30am and 6-10pm.

Le Club, 33 Dumas St. French open-terrace restaurant with a lush foyer and gracious service *en français ou en anglais.* Delicious but small portions. European desserts include chocolate mousse and apple fritters (Rs70-85). Excellent continental breakfasts Rs100-150. Open Tu-Th 8-10am, noon-2pm, and 7-10pm. AmEx, Visa.

Ashram Dining House, on Ranga Pillai St., right before the post office. Yet another perk of staying at one of the ashram guest houses: for Rs20 you get a voucher entitling you to 3 meals here. Piles of *basmati* rice and fresh fruits will be heaped upon your metal platter. Daily serving times: 6:40-7:45am, 11:30am-12:30pm, dinner as posted. Vouchers must be obtained in advance from your guest house.

◉ SIGHTS

SRI AUROBINDO ASHRAM

Marine St. Open daily 8am-noon and 2-6pm. Free. Children under 3 not permitted. Photography allowed only with prior permission.

Bengali mystic **Sri Aurobindo Ghose** created the method of "integral yoga" in an attempt to realize a new consciousness by mingling the principles of yoga with the findings of modern science. Born in Calcutta in 1872, he was educated in England, where he earned a degree in Classics from King's College, Cambridge. Sri Aurobindo returned to India soon afterward, where he headed an Indian nationalist newspaper; his staunch opposition to British rule led to his imprisonment in 1908. Within his prison cell he underwent a spiritual evolution, and in 1910 he gave up politics and headed for French-ruled Pondicherry. Here, Sri Aurobindo met "the Mother," French artist **Mirra Alfassa,** who had come to India to further her spiritual development, and who eventually became his constant companion.

The ashram was founded in 1926, as Sri Aurobindo writes, "not for the renunciation of the world but as a centre and field of practice for the evolution of another kind and form of life which would in the final end be moved by a higher spiritual consciousness." To this end, the ashram includes small-scale businesses, educational centers, farms, and health care among its facilities.

It was largely the charisma and energy of The Mother that brought these projects to life, as she oversaw the tremendous growth of the ashram during Sri Aurobindo's later life as a hermit and after his death in 1950. After her death in 1973, the ashram faced tumultuous times, as internal struggles developed about the direction the ashram would take; tensions were especially high with regard to the fate of Auroville, the ashram's experimental community (see p. 559). These days, the ashram houses the flower-strewn **samadhis** (mausoleums) of Sri Aurobindo and the Mother. At any time of the day, devotees mill around the perimeter of the *samadhis,* bowing their heads in silent prayer. The ashram is full of people from all over the world who have chosen to follow the teachings of Sri Aurobindo. You can get a good map and brochure at any ashram shop, guest house, or from the Bureau Central, on the western side of the canal, around the corner from Telecom Complex. **Autocare**, 3 blocks north, conducts morning tours of ashram industries and afternoon tours of the Matrimandir (see p. 559) in Auroville (Rs42).

OTHER SIGHTS

Aside from the ashram, most of Pondicherry's attractions are clustered around **Goubert Salai**, the promenade where locals go to see and be seen in the evening hours. During the day, the street is peaceful and deserted, disturbed only by tourists and the occasional ice cream vendor. The 1500m-long rocky beach is pretty to look at but not safe for swimming. Along the beach is a 4m-high statue of Mahatma Gandhi, surrounded by eight elaborately sculpted monoliths, as well as some splendid French architecture, including a monument built in memory of Indians who died fighting on the French side during World War I.

Just west of Goubert Salai is the **Government Place**, a grassy quadrangle framing a solemn, neo-classical monument dating from the time of Napoleon III. On the northern edge of the park is the elegant, French-built **Raj Nivas**, now the plush residence of Pondicherry's Lieutenant Governor. Next door is the **Pondicherry Museum**, which displays dusty 19th-century French furniture, a small collection of Chola bronze sculpture, and an assortment of pottery and other objects dug up at the nearby site of Arikamedu. *(Museum open Tu-Su 10am-5pm. Rs1.)*

Follow Goubert Salai to South Blvd. to reach the **Botanical Gardens**. Planted in 1826, the gardens contain species from around the world. *(Open daily 9am-5:30pm.)* On your way to the gardens, have a look at the **Eglise de Sacre Coeur de Jésus**, where the altar is flanked by three stained-glass panels depicting the life of Christ.

🎵 ENTERTAINMENT

By Tamil Nadu's conservative standards, alcohol flows quite freely in Pondicherry, and bars are relatively common on the French side. Most of the bars attached to hotels—including the **Ajantha Bar** and the **Bar Qualithé Hotel**, on the southern edge of Government Place—are frequented by local men, and are not the most comfortable place for foreigners, especially women. Many tourists spend the evening at the waterfront restaurants, including the **Ajantha Sea View Restaurant** and **Le Café**.

Chunnamber Boat House, 10km out of town on the backwaters of the Bay of Bengal, offers boat rentals (kayak, paddle, sail, water scooter Rs10-75). It is also possible to take a dolphin-watching **sea cruise**. Contact the tourist office (☎339497) for more information.

NEAR PONDICHERRY: AUROVILLE ஆரோவல்

The ethereal "aura" of Auroville can be attributed to Sri Aurobindo's companion—the Mother—who, in a dream, envisioned a crystalline sanctum where ultimate levels of meditation could be achieved. She also visualized a peaceful international city of the future, arrayed in the shape of a galaxy around this sanctum, in which the ideals of integral yoga could come to fruition.

At the community's inauguration in 1968, delegates from 126 countries gathered to place handfuls of their native soil in a large urn. Today, there are around 1500 people living here, including some of those original delegates. Citizens are grouped into small rural settlements around the urn and the **Matrimandir**. A geodesic dome housing the envisioned meditation chamber, the solar-powered Matrimandir symbolizes the goals of The Mother and Auroville: the integration of science and meditation within a peaceful, industrious international community. However, the temple has been a source of tension in the striving-to-be-harmonious community, as some residents feel the considerable money and energy funneled into the project has been misdirected. Like the rest of Auroville, it is both literally and figuratively still under construction.

For now, the real center of the community is the **Solar Kitchen,** where many residents gather for lunch or an afternoon cappuccino and email in the rooftop cafe. Residents live in small settlements named after development goals such as Utility and Amity. The many entrepreneurial and research institutions include a Building Research Center dedicated to new, low-cost housing technologies, and Aurelec, the town's computer company. There are also innovative agricultural and environmental projects, schools, and a village development program. Over 2000 Tamil villagers are employed in Auroville. Many build businesses on its outskirts and a few have become permanent residents. The community is still very much in its formative stages; currently, membership, growth, housing, and the role of money are pressing concerns.

■ **VISITING AUROVILLE.** Understandably, residents are unappreciative of tourists who lack sincere interest in their way of life and come to gawk at them as a relic of the 1960s. If you're interested in a brief visit to Auroville, consider joining the **tour** (Rs42) sponsored by the tourist office in Pondicherry or by Autocare (Rs40). As part of a group, you'll avoid the hassles of transportation and the bureaucracy of getting to see the Matrimandir, but you may feel rather herded. The tour goes first to the Visitor's Information Centre, which sells various brochures and displays photos and exhibits detailing Auroville's mission and development, including a model of the proposed town. An 11-minute video about the community is shown at 10:30am and 3:30pm every day except Sunday. Just across from the exhibits is a larger version of the Boutique d'Auroville, selling all things New Age. (Open M-Sa 9am-1pm and 2-5:30pm.) A **cafeteria** is undergoing renovation and may be closed. The Matrimandir itself is open for viewing only from 4-4:45pm, and for meditation from 5-6pm. Passes must be obtained from the Visitor's Information Centre between 3:30 and 4:30pm. During the viewings, a strict code of silence is enforced as visitors are ushered down a gravel path and up a ramp past construction work to glance inside the other-worldly meditation chamber, which houses a large crystal ball surrounded by a ring of slender white columns. The crystal is illuminated by sunlight deflected from a mirror on top of the dome; when the sky is overcast, lamps lit by solar power provide the necessary light. Entering the Matrimandir is a bit like entering another dimension—don't be surprised if even this quick peek leaves you dazed; but to truly enter the next dimension you need a separate ticket for the meditation hour. Access to the gardens and banyan tree next to the Matrimandir is only possible from 9am-3:30pm.

To get to Auroville on your own, you can employ one of the many eager rickshaw-*wallahs* in Pondy (Rs100 plus waiting charges) or brave the East Coast Rd. on a **bike**. You can rent one from the Park Guest House in Pondicherry and pedal the 12km to Auroville. One advantage to visiting the community on your own is that you'll have a better chance of actually meeting Auroville settlers, though it is a good idea to proceed to the Visitor's Centre first to gain a bit of background on the community and obtain a map and newspaper. It is also possible to eat lunch at the Solar Kitchen (12:15pm) if invited by a resident, or sometimes by contacting Guest Services above the kitchen around 9:30am (Rs35).

■ **STAYING ON.** If you are intrigued by Auroville, you might consider a longer stay in one of the guest houses, which range from Rs100 to Rs500. Many of the accommodations include kitchen facilities, bath, laundry services, and breakfast. The Visitors' Information Centre will provide a list and make arrangements. For more information, contact **La Boutique d'Auroville,** 12 JN St. (☎37264), Pondicherry. Alternatively, you can contact the **Visitor's Information Centre** in Auroville directly (☎62239; fax 62274. Open daily 9:30am-5:30am.) If you'd like to plan your trip before you leave for India, contact **Auroville Guest Programme,** Visitor's Information Centre, Auroville 605101 (email guests@auroville.org.in).

CHIDAMBARAM சிதம் பரம்   ☎ 04144

History has heaped affection on Chidambaram, entwining its past in legend and lore. It was here that Shiva descended from the divine firmament as Nataraja ("King of Dance") and performed the *ananda tandavam* ("Cosmic Dance"). The forested clearing where Nataraja danced became sacred ground; the town that grew around it was dubbed "Chit Ambaram," the "Hall of Wisdom." With Nataraja as their patron deity, the Cholas made Chidambaram their capital in 907 AD.

The **"car festivals"** in mid-January and June, when ritual chariots glide through the four streets bearing their names, attract thousands of revelers, as does the Tamil New Year (April 14th every year). Every February, prominent dancers from throughout the country converge in Chidambaram to present dance-offerings to Nataraja in the Natyanjali Festival. The town itself, despite its prominent university, is small and sleepy, but the magnificent *murti* of Shiva Nataraja makes it worth a trip from Pondicherry or Thanjavur.

GETTING THERE AND GETTING AROUND

Trains: The small station is uncommonly quiet. Most travelers opt for buses to avoid the longer train routes. To: **Madras** (5 per day, noon-3:30am, 6hr., Rs220); **Rameswaram** (daily, 2am and 7pm, 11hr., Rs148); **Trichy** (5 per day, 2:10pm-2:20am, 5hr., Rs157) via **Kumbakonam** and **Thanjavur; Tirupati** (6:15pm, 12hr., Rs82).

Buses: The **bus stand,** just off the eastern end of S. Car St., services all parts of Tamil Nadu. To: **Kumbakonam** (frequent, 2hr.); **Madras** (every 30min., 5-6hr., Rs65); **Madurai** (5 per day, 3:45am-5:30pm, 8hr., Rs65); **Pondicherry** (every 30min., 2hr., Rs12); **Thanjavur** (every 30min., 3hr., Rs18); **Trichy** (every 1-2hr., 5½hr., Rs40).

Local Transportation: Rickshaws are an unnecessary extravagance in a town where everything can be reached by foot in under 15min. Still, the little buggers are everywhere—especially in front of the bus stand, hospital, and East Temple Gate.

ORIENTATION AND PRACTICAL INFORMATION

Chidambaram is small and easy to find your way around. **North, South, East,** and **West Car St.** form a rectangular border around the temple. To reach them from the bus stand, turn right (north) toward the Hotel Afson Plaza; then take your immediate left onto Venugopal, a.k.a **VGP St.** After three major intersections, VGP St. turns into S. Car St. To get to the **Tourist Office** from the bus stand, take a left and then another left about 200m later onto **Pillaiyar Koil St.** Cross over the **Khan Sahib Canal** before making your first right onto **Railway Feeder Rd.,** where, at the end of the street, you will find the railway station.

Tourist Office: TTDC (☎ 38739), at the beginning of Railway Feeder Rd., next to Hotel Tamil Nadu, on the way to the railway station. Open daily 10am-5:45pm.

Currency Exchange: The nearest place to change money is in Pondicherry.

Police Station: Chidambaram Police Station, W. Car St. (☎ 22201). Open 24hr.

Pharmacy: Vani Pharmacy, W. Car St. (☎ 22252). Open 9am-11pm.

Hospital: Raja Muthandi Medical College and Hospital (emergency ☎ 38147), is just outside town.

Telephones: Deluxe Telecom, on W. Car St., has free callbacks.

Post Office: A tall, cream-colored building covered by a patchwork of orange squares on the western end of N. Car St. Open M-F 10am-5pm. **Postal Code:** 608001.

ACCOMMODATIONS

Ganesha Bhavan Hotel, 115 W. Car St. (☎ 22985). Spic 'n' span rooms with lots of cubby space. Bathrooms are a bit musty. Padlocks on doors. Attached restaurant. Singles Rs65; doubles Rs95.

Hotel Akshaya, 17-18 E. Car St. (☎20191). Basic attached baths with seat or squat toilets. Rooftop terrace offers a spectacular aerial view of the temple. Excellent attached restaurant. Singles Rs160; doubles Rs195-480.

🍴 FOOD

▩ **The Regency,** 2 VGP St., in Chidambaram's best hotel, The Hotel Afsan Plaza. Indulge in a full range of Indian, continental, and Chinese cuisine in A/C luxury. The tandoori chicken (Rs55 for a half a bird) and *ghee naan* (Rs8) are superb. Open 24hr.

Aswini Restaurant, 17-18 E. Car St., in the Hotel Akshaya. Quiet dining in cushioned chairs, with piped-in soul and jazz. The golden *dosas* are wonderful. Open daily 7-10am, 11am-3pm, and 6-10pm.

Hotel Saradharam, opposite the bus stand. Four different restaurants, each with its own distinct flavor. In the front, **Pallavi** has *thalis* and other veg. delights. Open 24hr. **Annu Pallavi,** in back, serves up spicy, meaty meals. Open daily 11am-11pm. **Moon Shadow** is a seasonal barbecue grill. Open daily July-Dec. 6-11pm. **The Pizza Shop** serves pizza and burgers (Rs30) and has Internet access (Rs60 per hr.). Open 11am-11pm.

Bombay Sweets, W. Car St., sells a wide range of sweets and savories.

🔭 SIGHTS: SABHANAYAKA NATARAJA TEMPLE

Open daily 6am-noon and 4-10pm. Puja at 7, 9, 11am, noon, 6, 8, and 10pm.

Distinctive not only as an amazing architectural achievement, but also because it is one of the few temples where Shiva and Vishnu are enshrined together, the Sabhanayaka Nataraja Temple draws daily crowds of thousands. It was here that the dance duel between Kali and Shiva, the Nataraja, took place. The temple is also one of the five Shiva temples in South India dedicated to the five Vedic elements (earth, air, water, fire, and ether); Chidambaram, as it is situated on a major energy vein, is dedicated to the "Ether of Consciousness."

Covering more than 54 hectares, the temple dominates central Chidambaram. Though scholars believe that work on the temple began during the 10th century, local tradition holds that there has been a temple on this site for thousands of years. The modern Nataraja Temple, it is said, was built in the 6th century, when the Kashmiri monarch Simhavarman II (r. 550-575) made a pilgrimage to Chidambaram, hoping that bathing in the tank of the ancient Nataraja Temple would cure his leprosy. When he recovered soon after his bath, the king—thereafter known as Hiranyavarman, or the "golden-bodied one"—ordered the temple enlarged and modernized. In addition, Hiranyavarman decreed that the holy entourage of 3000 brahmin priests *(Dikshitars)* who had accompanied him from Kashmir should remain behind at Chidambaram to serve the temple. Today, lepers still come to the temple for its holy healing powers, and descendants of the *Dikshitars* still live in Chidambaram. You'll recognize them by the knot of hair at the front of their heads.

TAMIL NADU

RAT RACING The depiction of Ganesh (also known as Vinayakar) on the east side of the Sabhanayaka Nataraja Temple in Chidambaram is taken from a story in which Lord Shiva held a contest between his two sons, Ganesh and Kartikkeya. A delicious mango was to be given to the son who could go around the universe and return first. Kartikkeya immediately mounted his peacock and set off, confident of victory. The short, plump Ganesh had only a little mouse for a mount. He thought for a while and then rode around his parents, Shiva and Parvati. When Shiva asked his son what he was up to, the clever Ganesh replied: "Going around the supreme Lord Shiva and Goddess Parvati who create and contain the universe is equivalent to going around the universe." Shiva smiled in satisfaction and presented the mango to his slow-footed but quick-witted son.

THE OUTERMOST EDGE. Most visitors enter through either the eastern or western **gopuram** (gateway), where **guides** immediately accost any foreign-looking person. Their level of knowledge varies tremendously—hiring one is something of a crap-shoot. Also beware of English-speaking individuals trying to usher you to a priest who will anoint you with *kumkum* for a "voluntary" donation. To avoid most of the general hassle, enter instead through the northernmost gate.

The temple's four massive, pyramidal *gopurams* are painted every 50 years in a rainbow of pastel tones, and each has a distinctive character. The eastern *gopuram* is supposed to invoke a feeling of love, with the worshipper approaching the Nataraja as he would approach his beloved. From the south, the soul approaches as a child, and from the west, as a friend. One enters the northern *goparum* in a position of subservience. The 42m-high northern *gopuram*, erected in the 14th century, bears an inscription claiming that it was built by a 16th-century Vijayanagar king. Its interior is embellished with carvings of the 108 dance poses associated with *bharat natyam*. The southern *gopuram*, put up in the 12th century, contains a set of impressive carvings of the goddess Lakshmi. Each of the four *gopurams* still has its original granite base, although the brick towers have been replaced numerous times, often falling victim to the winter monsoon. Across the front of each base are carvings of Shiva and Parvati.

As you enter through the western gate, the **Shivaganga Tank** is in the far corner to the left. This is where King Simhavarman bathed, emerging with golden-hued skin. Opposite the tank is the **Shivakumarasundari Temple**, dedicated to Shiva's consort Parvati. On the other side of the tank, in the northeast corner of the temple grounds, stands the 103m-long **Raja Sabha**, the temple's "1000-pillared corridor" where the victory processions of the Pandavas, Cholas, and other local powers were held. The corridor has only 999 pillars; Shiva's leg serves as the 1000th.

THE INNER CHAMBERS. The inner chambers are accessible from the north and south. On the eastern side of the enclosure, the **Devasabha**, or "Hall of the Gods," is where images of deities are stored when they are not being used; this is also where temple meetings are held. In the southwest corner of the second enclosure, the **Nritta Sabha** (Dance Hall) marks the spot where Shiva and Kali had their famous dance duel. The hall is adorned with 56 pillars representing various dance poses.

The holy **Inner Sanctum**, accessible from the southern side of the second enclosure, is off-limits to non-Hindus. It is possible to get a glimpse of the gold-tiled **Chit Sabha** and **Kanaka Sabha** from the outside. Five silver-plated stone steps lead to the Chit Sabha; they represent the five Sanskrit letters that spell out the famous Hindu Panchakshara mantra, "Nama Shivaya." The Chit Sabha contains small images of Nataraja and Parvati. To the right, behind a string of leaves, is the Chidambara Rahasyam ("Secret of Chidambaram"); the **Akasa Linga,** representing the elusive and invisible element *akasa* (ether). In the passageway to the sanctum is a hallway that leads to the **Govindaraja Temple,** dedicated to Vishnu.

KUMBAKONAM கும் பகோணம்   ☎ 0435

The name of this 2000 year-old town is derived from the holiday for which it is famous, the Kumbh Mela. Every 12 years, hundreds of thousands from across India descend upon the town's Mahamakham Tank, into which the waters of nine sacred rivers are believed to flow. Kumbakonam provides access to an abundance of holy sites, including five major temples within the city and two others in the towns of Darasuram and Gangaikondacholapuram. When not inundated by pilgrims or sacred streams, Kumbakonam's significance as a religious center takes a back seat to its role as a center of silk production and small-scale industry.

◤ GETTING THERE AND GETTING AROUND

Trains: The **railway reservations counter** (☎ 433134, reservations 430052) is open M-Sa 8am-noon and 3-7pm, Su 8am-2pm. To: **Madras** (4 per day, 10hr., 10am-1am,

Rs151); **Thanjavur** (4 per day, 1am-9pm, 1½hr.); **Trichy** (4 per day, 3:55pm-4:15am, 3hr., Rs65; all trains to **Rameswaram** go via Trichy); **Villupuram** (4 per day, 10am-1am, 5hr., Rs61.)

Buses: To reach the **bus stand,** follow Ayikulam Rd. to its end and take a right. To: **Bangalore** (6:30pm, 11hr., Rs130); **Karaikal** (every 45min., 2hr., Rs13); **Madras** (superdeluxe with video every hr., 6am-3pm, 6hr., Rs99; other buses 4am-2:30pm and 8-10pm, 7hr., Rs76); **Pudukottai** (frequent); **Thanjavur** (every 30min., 1½hr., Rs15); **Trichy** (every 30min., 2½hr., Rs22); **Tirupati** (9am and 9pm, 10hr.).

ORIENTATION AND PRACTICAL INFORMATION

Kumbakonam is a somewhat confusing place; every street seems to end at a temple gate. To get from the train station to the center of town, turn right out of the station, take your first left on **Kamaraj Rd.,** and walk straight for 1km. From the bus stand, exit left, and then take a right onto Kamaraj Rd., which runs into **Head Post Office (HPO) Rd.** near the large **Mahamakham Tank.** Turn right on HPO Rd., and head toward Hotel Raya's to Kumbakonam's main east-west street, known as **Thanjavur Rd.** in the town's eastern end, as **Nageswaran Rd.** in the middle, and as **Ayikulam Rd.** in the west. **TSR Big St.,** marked by VPR Hotel Siva and many banks, runs parallel and to the north of the main street.

Currency Exchange: City Union bank Ltd., 140 TSR Big St. (☎420088), or **State Bank of India,** also on TRS Big St. Both open M-Sa 10am-2pm, Su 10am-noon.

Police: Thanjavur Rd. (☎421450), opposite Potramai Tank.

Hospital: ST Hospital, HPO Rd., between Ayikulam Rd. and Hotel Raya's. The head doctor is Dr. S. Thiyagarajan (☎430839 office, 430139 home, pager 9628 5078390). Attached **pharmacy** open 24hr.

Telephones: STD/ISD booths are plentiful on TSR Big St. and HPO Rd. Many open 24hr.

Internet: Universal Computer Ed., 7 TSR Big St. (☎421163), 2 blocks east of City Union Bank. Rs40 per hr. Open 8am-10pm.

Post Office: The **Head Post Office,** on HPO Rd., next to Hotel Rayas. Open M-F 6am-6pm, Sa 6am-1pm. **Postal code:** 612001.

ACCOMMODATIONS

Femina Lodge (☎420369), up two flights of stairs in the red-tiled building opposite Hotel Raya's. The best bet in town. Good location. Large beds in small, modest rooms, all with spotless bathrooms (squat or seat toilets). Doubles Rs150; quads Rs250.

VPR Lodge, 102/3 TSR Big St. (☎421949), at the very end of the road. Older lodge with functional rooms. Singles Rs90; doubles Rs120.

Hotel ARR, TRS Big St. (☎421234), opposite City Union Bank Ltd. Rooms have color TVs, sofas, and seat or squat toilets. Attached bar. Check-out 24hr. Prices include 20% luxury tax. Doubles Rs375-660.

Hotel Athityaa (☎421794), south of Sarangapani Temple on the "Thanjavur" end of Ayikulam Rd. Friendly management and well-furnished rooms with towels and TVs. Both seat and squat toilets. Restaurant and bar. Singles Rs325-500; doubles Rs350-500.

Hotel Rayas, 28/29 HPO Rd. (☎423170), north of the post office and clock tower. Carved doors open on to pretty rooms with the firmest beds in town. Attached baths have 24hr. hot water and seat or squat toilets. Color TV with music channels. **Sathars** restaurant (see below) downstairs. Doubles Rs450-630.

FOOD

Arul, near the Sarangapari Temple, opposite Pandiyar Hotel. Whirring floor fans and dim lighting create a relaxed setting for the best *thalis* in town (Rs18-45). The "ordinary" *thali* comes with 6 extraordinary chutneys and a dessert. Open 6am-10pm.

Pandiyar Hotel, opposite Arul. Ground-floor cafeteria teems with hungry pilgrims. If you can find a seat, a banana leaf will be slapped down before you as your *thali* (Rs15) is constructed one heaped spoonful at a time. Open daily 11:30am-2pm and 4-10pm.

Arogya, in the Hotel Athityaa (see above). Serves veg. staples such as *poori* (Rs12), North and South Indian snacks, and Chinese dishes (Rs15-60). Booze served at the adjoining **Nattiya** permit room. Open daily 11am-11pm.

Sathars, inside Hotel Raya's, on HPO Rd. Chicken, mutton, seafood, and beef dishes from across India (Rs30-115). Count on delicious *naan* (Rs8-15), *basmati* rice (Rs15), elaborate *thalis* (Rs25-36, 11am-4pm only), and excellent *dahl* garnished with cilantro. Attached bar. Open daily 11am-11pm.

👁 SIGHTS

KUMBESHWARA TEMPLE. Facing east, the Kumbeshwara Temple is the largest and most important Shiva temple in Kumbakonam; the *linga* inside is believed to have been shaped by the hands of Shiva himself. According to legend, Brahma anticipated the Great Deluge, "Mahapralaya," and entreated Shiva to save creation from destruction. Shiva instructed him to place a pot, or *kumbh*, containing sacred nectar and the seed of creation on top of Mt. Meru. The Great Deluge carried the sacred *kumbh* south to rest at Kumbakonam, where Lord Shiva, in the guise of a hunter, broke the pot with an arrow and spilled the potent nectar. He then gathered up the wet sand and shaped the **Mahalinga.** Unlike most other *lingas*, the one at Kumbeshwara is not made of granite, and the ritual of *abisheka* cannot be performed with watery substances in case they dissolve its shape. Nectar from the broken pot trickled to 5 other places within a 10-mile radius of Kumbakonam, as well as to the site of the Mahamakham Tank. Traditionally, pilgrims visit these shrines before coming to Kumbeshwara. *(Western end of Thanjavur Rd. Open daily 7am-1pm and 4-9pm. Puja at 7, 8:30am, noon, 5, 7, and 8:30pm.)*

SARANGAPANI TEMPLE. Sarangapani is one of the three most sacred Vishnu shrines in India, along with Srirangam near Trichy (see p. 572) and Tirupati in Andhra Pradesh (see p. 608). On the left of the main sanctum is a golden shrine to Lakshmi, the goddess of prosperity, which depicts her seated on a thousand-petal lotus, worshipping Vishnu; legend holds that she was discovered in this position in the temple's tank. It was only later that Vishnu came to Kumbakonam to marry her. It is customary for visitors to stop at the goddess' shrine before proceeding to the **inner sanctum.** During certain holidays, devotees are required to use the southern entrance; it was from here that Vishnu and Lakshmi emerged after their marriage. Around the inner sanctum are fine carvings of Vishnu's 10 avatars. In the sanctum itself, a monolithic Vishnu reclines, ornamented with silver and watched over by his two wives, Lakshmi and Saraswati. *(Take a left at the end of TSR Big St. Open daily 7am-noon and 4:30-9pm. Puja 9, 10am, noon, 6, 8, 9pm.)*

NAGESHWARA TEMPLE. Built during in the 10th century, the Nageshwara Temple, dedicated to Shiva, is thought to be the oldest temple in Kumbakonam. The sculpted figures adorning the *gopurams* are some of the best examples of early Chola workmanship. Many of the temple's finest sculptures are within the

THE ANTI-BEAUTY MARK If it's your first time in India, you might be wondering why so many small Indian children seem to have identical black birthmarks—one on the forehead, the other on the left cheek. Actually, it's no genetic similarity that causes these marks—they are, in fact, dots of charcoal placed on the child by its mother. This practice of *drishti* is performed in order to protect the beautiful baby from the envy of others. Jealousy, it is feared, could jinx the child and bring misfortune upon it, so the mother uglifies her offspring with these black smudges in an attempt to thwart the "green-eyed monster."

sanctum itself; all around are niches containing carvings of Shiva and Parvati. The temple has been constructed so that sunlight passes through the opening in the *gopuram* three times a year and illuminates the shrine's image. It is believed that Surya (the sun god) worships Shiva at these times. *(From the bottom of HPO Rd., take your first left and then your first right. Open daily 6am-noon and 4:30-8pm. Puja on the hr.)*

MAHAMAKHAM TANK. A multi-functional pond where people go to swim, do laundry, or worship, the Mahamakham Tank is especially pleasant in the evening, when you can rent paddle-boats. The sacred nectar of Brahma's *kumbh*, broken by Shiva, was collected here. Every 12 years, the tank's tranquility is disrupted by the **Kumbh Mela** (see p. 209), when thousands of pilgrims descend on Kumbakonam to bathe in the waters here. When Jupiter passes Leo, the waters of the Ganga and eight other sacred Indian rivers—the Yamuna, Kaveri, Godavari, Narmada, Krishna, Saraswati, Sarayu, and Tungabhadra—are believed to flow into the tank. During the 1992 festival, over one million devotees came to Kumbakonam. When controversial political leader, Jayalalitha, went to take her purifying dip, a stampede ensued that killed 60 pilgrims. *(At HPO Rd. and Kamarajar Rd. Open 24hr.)*

🖼 DAYTRIPS FROM KUMBAKONAM

DARASURAM

There are frequent local buses from Kumbakonam to Darasuram (20min.). An auto-rickshaw should cost about Rs30.

Just 4km from Kumbakonam, Darasuram is famous for its **Airavateshwara Temple,** a modestly sized example of 12th-century Chola architecture. The granite temple gets its name from Airavata, the white elephant mount of Indra, who worshipped Shiva here in the hope of changing its skin, turned black by an angry god, back to white. Near the base of the inner wall are some remarkably well-preserved carvings, depicting gymnasts, *bharat natyam* dancers, and even a woman giving birth. Today, the temple grounds look a bit like a halted construction site, as the Archaeological Survey of India waits for funds to continue its refurbishment.

GANGAIKONDACHOLAPURAM

There are frequent buses from Kumbakonam (1hr., Rs6-10).

Gangaikondacholapuram, whose name means "the city of the Chola who conquered the Ganga," was built by King Rajendra I (r.1012-1044), son of Raja Raja of Tanjore Temple fame, when he defeated the kingdoms to the north. To commemorate his victory, the king had water from the Ganga transported to the temple's tank. The temple is dedicated to Shiva—a large Nandi guards the entrance—and among the most impressive carvings is a frieze that depicts Shiva and Parvati crowning King Rajendra. The upper stories served as a fortress and are accessible to visitors (and bats!). The exquisitely maintained grounds also contain temples to Parvati, Ganesh, and Kali.

KARAIKAL AND VELANKANNI

*The bus stand in Karaikal services **Chidambaram** (every 20min., 2hr., Rs45); **Kumbakonam** (every 30min., 2hr.); **Madras** (every 30min., 8hr.; express deluxe 9:45 and 11am, 7hr.); **Mylar** (for train connections, every 45min., 1hr., Rs20); and **Pondicherry** (every 2hr., 4hr.). From Karaikal, take a bus to **Nagapattinam** (every 5min., 45min., Rs3), and switch to a bus going to **Velankanni** (every 5min., 20min., Rs3).*

The medium-sized town of **Karaikal** is in a constant state of pandemonium, thanks to its proximity to several holy cities. The only reason to come to Karaikal is to visit **Velankanni** or to pay homage to the female Shaivite saint, Punithavathi, in the **Darbanyeswar** or **Ammaiyar** temples, on Bharathiar Rd. The **Tourist Office,** Nehru St., is about nine side streets west of Hotel Paris (open daily 9am-1pm and 2-5:30pm). The **State Bank of India,** 14 Thirumallar Rd., changes money. (☎22524. Open M-F 10am-2pm, Sa 10am-noon.) For lodging, try the friendly **City Plaza Lodge** (singles Rs80; doubles Rs120-375). The more upscale **Hotel Paris** is also a good bet. (☎20304. Single Rs175; doubles Rs300-400.) Its attached **Tasty Restaurant** is clean, cool, and cheap (open daily 6-9pm).

The gleaming white spires of the **Roman Catholic Church of our Lady of Good Health** in **Velankanni** twinkle a shining answer to the question, "Why did I go to Karaikal?" Thousands of pilgrims visit the church and adjoining tank every day, drawn by the site's legendary curative powers. The Virgin Mary and the infant Jesus appeared to a boy selling buttermilk here, and also saved Portuguese sailors from shipwreck. *(Church and Museum of Offerings open daily 5am-9pm. English mass daily 10am, and Sa 5:45pm with car procession.)*

THANJAVUR (TANJORE) தஞ்சாவூர்   ☎ 04362

Though only an hour from the burgeoning urban center of Trichy, Thanjavur remains laid-back and provincial. Thanjavur's bronze handicraft trade and strong agricultural focus, evidenced in the thatched farming huts and plowed fields that surround the town, are remnants of the Chola Empire, which ruled the area between the 10th and 14th centuries. The spectacular architecture of the Brihadishwara Temple, along with the Chola bronzes on display at the museum, are well worth a stop when traveling between the coast and the western hills.

▐ GETTING THERE AND GETTING AROUND. The **railway station** is on the aptly named Railway Station Rd., 600m south of the canal (rickshaw to the center of town Rs15-30). To: **Chidambaram** (8 per day, 3:30am-10:45pm, 2½hr., Rs53); **Madras** (*Cholan Express* 6154, 9:20am, 9hr., 2nd class Rs84); 4 night trains including the 8:20pm express, 10hr., 2nd class Rs151); **Madurai** via **Trichy** (5 express trains per day, 3hr., 2nd class Rs73); **Rameswaram** (5:20am and 9:50pm, 9hr., Rs123); **Trichy** (all trains from Madras or to Madurai go through Trichy, 1hr., Rs35).

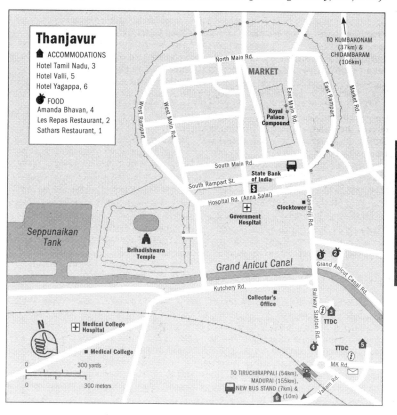

Thanjavur

🏠 ACCOMMODATIONS
Hotel Tamil Nadu, 3
Hotel Valli, 5
Hotel Yagappa, 6

🍎 FOOD
Amanda Bhavan, 4
Les Repas Restaurant, 2
Sathars Restaurant, 1

The **Old Bus Stand** is in the city center, where Gandhiji Rd. turns into East Main Rd. The **New Bus Stand** is 7km from the city center. Buses from Trichy and other points south and west arrive at the new stand. Local buses #41, 60, 74, 74A, 74B, and 74D travel between the two stands. Auto-rickshaws between the two bus stands cost around Rs40. Buses run to: **Chidambaram** (every 2hr., 4hr., Rs30); **Kumbakonam** (every 15-30min., 1½hr., Rs10); **Madras** (every 30min., 6am-1pm, 9hr., Rs110; "superfast" buses, 10am, 9:30, and 10pm, 8hr., Rs110); **Pondicherry** (every 2hr., 3:40am-9:30pm, 6hr., Rs50); **Trichy** (every 15-30min., 1½hr., Rs15).

▮▮ ORIENTATION AND PRACTICAL INFORMATION. Thanjavur is divided into northern and southern sections by the **Grand Anicut Canal.** From the station, **Railway Station Road** curves slightly as it heads north, passing a branch of the **tourist office** (☎30984; open daily 10am-2pm and 4-8pm) and several hotels before reaching the canal. As it crosses the canal, Railway Station Rd. becomes **Gandhiji Road,** which is dominated by upscale silk shops. The busiest part of town is the area around the bus stands, immediately north of the intersection of Gandhiji and **Hospital Road,** where the **Raja Merusudad Government Hospital** (☎31323) is situated. The **State Bank of India** is opposite the government hospital. (☎30082. Open M-F 10am-2pm, Sa 10am-noon.) The **Thanjavur Medical College Hospital,** Medical College Rd. (☎22459), is a 15-minute rickshaw ride from the station toward Tamil Nadu University. The superintendent of **police** (☎38450) is on Collector Office Road. The head **post office,** MK Rd., is off Railway Station Rd. in the southern part of town. (☎31022. Open M-Sa 10am-5pm, Su noon-4pm.) **Postal Code:** 613001.

▮▮ ACCOMMODATIONS AND FOOD. Accommodations south of the canal are much quieter than those that overlook the bus stand. All hotels have a 24-hour check-out policy. The best of the lot is **Hotel Tamil Nadu,** in the large white complex on Railway Station Rd. Good-sized rooms have phones, comfy beds, and attached bathrooms with seat toilets and hot water. There is a restaurant and bar downstairs. (☎31421. Doubles Rs330-600. Book in advance.) **Hotel Valli,** 2948 MK Rd., is on a well-shaded side-street east from the railway station. Rooms have attached baths with squat and seat toilets; the hotel has an attached restaurant. (☎31580. Singles Rs165; doubles Rs199-265.) **Hotel Yagappa,** off Trichy Rd. (☎30421), south of the station has clean rooms with attached squat toilets and bucket bath for Rs150. Sheets and hot water are available.

There are plenty of indistinguishable vegetarian restaurants around the bus stand. **Ananda Bhavan,** Railway Station Rd., up the street from the railway station, serves good old-fashioned South Indian *masala dosa* (Rs10) on banana leaves. Its location makes it a key stop for locals headed to work, so expect morning crowds. (Open daily 6:30-10:30am and 11:30am-10pm.) The popular **Sathars Restaurant,** 167 Gandhiji Rd., is north of the canal. The red-brick, open-air area upstairs gives relief from the dusty streets below. Garnished chicken, beef, and vegetarian dishes are Rs26-105. (Open daily noon-11:30pm.) **Les Repas,** at the Hotel Parisutham, 55 Grand Anicut Canal Road, showcases a large multicuisine menu in a formal setting, complete with waterfall. Various chicken dishes for Rs90-140, grilled cheese Rs100, and soup Rs40-60. (☎31421. Open 6am-11pm. Bar downstairs; cocktails Rs100-140, beer Rs100. Poolside food service extra 15% charge until 7pm.)

▮ SIGHTS. The **Brihadishwara Temple,** the pride of Thanjavur, is recognized by the United Nations as a World Heritage Site. The temple stands as an impressive reminder of the splendor and opulence of the city's glory days during the reign of the Chola king Raja Raja I (r. 985-1013). Legend has it that he built the temple to save his own life. Unable to find a cure for his leprosy, Raja Raja turned to his religious tutor for guidance, who advised him to build a temple to Shiva using a *linga* from the Narmada River. Raja Raja rushed off to the river and pulled a *linga* from the water; as he pulled, the *linga* grew and grew, and Raja Raja had no choice but to build a massive temple to enclose it.

Above the *linga* rises the stepped superstructure, called a *vimana*, that represents Mt. Meru, the cosmic mountain around which the Hindu universe is centered. In an inversion of the traditional South Indian architectural order the *vimana* soars over the *gopurams*, or entry gates. The set of exquisite carvings on the frontal face, depicting Shiva, Parvati, and other gods on top of Mt. Meru, has earned the temple the local nickname "Himalaya of the South." The monolithic stupa that caps the *vimana* was raised via a ramp over 6km long. Also within the temple's courtyard walls are a 16th-century temple to Krishna, famed for its intricate, miniature carvings, and another to Ganesh and Parvati. The temple complex is guarded by a giant sculpture of Nandi (Shiva's bull sidekick). This massive sculpture weighs in at 25 tons, making it one of the largest in India. Over 1000 little Nandis and 252 *linga* also keep careful watch from the walls.

Awe-inspiring by day, the temple acquires an added aura of magic at sunset as couples stroll and families picnic in its park-like atmosphere. When night falls, artfully placed lights bring the sculptures into sharp relief. Outside the temple, a pathway on the left leads to the **Shivaganga Tank** and garden. (☎ 22317. Open daily roughly 6am-noon and 4-9pm. Religious dances 2nd and 4th Friday evening of the month. Elephant ride and blessing Rs30. Shiva's birthday March 30-April 18, 2001. Guides at the tourist booth by the temple parking lot. Half day guide Rs250.)

The large **Royal Palace** was built as a residence by the Nayaks in the 16th century and was subsequently refurbished by the Marathas. These days, the palace has been colonized by a number of incongruous outfits, including a secondary school, an agricultural office, and a martial arts academy. The only real reason to come here is the excellent collection of Chola bronzes and stone sculptures, in the **Durbar Hall Art Museum.** (Once inside the palace, follow signs for the art gallery. Open daily 9am-1pm and 3-6pm. Rs3.) The **Saraswati Mahal Library,** also in the palace, houses thousands of palm-leafed manuscripts. With 33,433 holdings (24,627 in Sanskrit, 953 in Marathi, 1206 in Tamil, 816 in Telugu, and 5831 others—we counted), the collection is one of the world's finest. The museum is open to the public, but the stacks are not. (Open Tu-Th 10am-1:30pm and 2:30-5:30pm. Free.)

TIRUCHIRAPPALLI திருச் சிராய்ப்ள்ளி ☎ 0431

For a growing industrial center of 700,000, Tiruchirappalli (commonly called Trichy or Tiruchi) remains remarkably clean and relatively tranquil. The city has been occupied for over 2000 years, controlled at various times by the Cholas, Pandyas, Pallavas, and Nayaks, whose prosperous reign brought about the creation of the imposing Rock Fort. Since the late 19th century, when British-designed railroads brought industry to South India, Trichy has been ruled by manufacturing—today, the city is home to a large working-class population that produces staggering quantities of *bindis* and costume jewelry. Trichy's greatest attraction is the temple city of Srirangam, 4km north of town. Trichy is also a convenient stop en route to destinations farther south, with the railway station, bus stand, and a whole range of hotels all within comfortable walking distance of each other.

▣ GETTING THERE AND GETTING AROUND

Flights: The **airport** is 8km south of the city, 25min. by direct "airport" buses (every 15min., Rs2) or taxi (Rs100). **Indian Airlines,** Dindigul Rd. (☎ 481433, airport ☎ 420563), 500m southwest of the intersection with Junction Rd., has flights to **Madras** (3 per week, 1hr., US$70). **Air India** (☎ 481200). **Air Lanka,** Williams Rd. (☎ 460844), Hotel Femina Complex. Open M-Sa 9am-5:30pm. To **Colombo, Sri Lanka** (3 per week, 45min , US$75).

Trains: The user-friendly **Trichy Junction Railway Station** in the south of town, off the intersection of Junction and Madurai Rd. The **Reservations Building** (☎ 461362) is the small white structure to your left as you approach the main station complex. Open M-Sa 8am-8pm, Su 8am-2pm. Fares listed are 2nd class. To: **Chidambaram** (6 per day, 8am-

11:05pm, 5hr., Rs104); **Kollam** (4:15am and 4:15pm, 12hr., Rs174); **Madras** (6 per day, 6:30am-11:45pm, 5½-7hr., Rs146); **Madurai** (12:30 and 5:45pm, 3hr., Rs104); **Rameswaram** (4 per day, 6:50am-12:30am, 7½hr., Rs124); **Tirupati** (2pm, 15hr., Rs127) via **Thanjavur** (1½hr., Rs57).

Buses: The **State Bus Stand** at the intersection of Rockins and Royal Rd. To: **Bangalore** (4 per night, 10hr., Rs150); **Coimbatore** (every 30min., 6hr., Rs60); **Dindigul** (every 15min., 3½hr., Rs18); **Kodai** (3 per day, 6:40-11am, 6hr., Rs50); **Madras** (every hr., 7hr., Rs100); **Madurai** (every 15min., 3½hr., Rs28); **Pondicherry** via **Villupuram** (every hr., 5hr., Rs40); **Thanjavur** (every 10min., 1½hr., Rs15). Charter buses to Bangalore (Rs200), Madras (Rs185), and Madurai (Rs50) are also easy to find.

Local Transportation: The tourist office raves about Trichy's **local bus** system, probably the most efficient in all of Tamil Nadu. A fleet of brand-new, shiny silver buses, each equipped with a deafening sound system, shuttles passengers around the city. The **#1 bus** is every tourist's best friend; it passes the railway station, the State Bank of India, and the Head Post Office on its way to the Rock Fort (Rs2) and the Srirangam Temple (Rs4). Buses depart every few minutes from the State Bus Stand. As a result, Trichy has hordes of hardly-used **rickshaws,** which congregate in the bus stand/tourist office area. They aren't really necessary, unless you need to get to the airport (Rs50).

ORIENTATION AND PRACTICAL INFORMATION

With the **Kaveri River** forming its northern border, Trichy is split into two segments by the **Woyakondan Channel.** The northernmost portion (nearest to the Kaveri River) is Trichy's industrial area, full of textile shops and marked by the **Rock Fort** and the town's **railway station.** To the south of the channel is the busy **Trichy Junction Railway Station.** The streets around the railway station are full of hotels and banks. This area also contains the GPO, the tourist office, and the town's two **bus stands.** From the station, **Madurai Road** runs northeast, forming a "V" with the northwest-bound **Lawson's Road. Dindigul Road** connects to Lawson's Rd., looping around the western streets up to the eastern side of the Woyakondon Channel, where it intersects with **Big Bazaar Road,** northern Trichy's main street.

Tourist Office: Government of Tamil Nadu Tourist Office, 1 Williams Rd., Cantonment (☎460136), diagonally opposite the central bus stand. Decent city maps for Rs10. Open M-F 10am-5:45pm. Info counters also at the airport and railway junction.

Currency Exchange: State Bank of India (☎460172), off a courtyard on Dindigul Rd., around the corner from Jenney's Residency. Open M-F 10am-2pm, Sa 10am-noon.

Swimming Pools: Head over to **Jenney's Residency** (see below), where you can do doubletime laps in the not-quite-Olympic-size pool for Rs100. Open daily 7am-7pm.

Police: Cantonment, Trichy 1 (☎461683). Open 24hr.

Pharmacy: Subasree Medicals (☎410228) or **Vasam Medical** (☎792206) near the central bus stand. Open M-Sa 9am-10:30pm.

Hospital: The private **Sea Horse Hospital,** 6 Royal Rd. (☎415660) is open 24hr.

Telephones: 24hr. **STD/ISD** booths opposite the bus stand on McDonald's Rd.

Internet: MasNet, McDonald's Rd., opposite the bus stand. Open 7am-11pm.

Post Office: Head Post Office, Barradiar St. (☎460575). Open M-Sa 10am-6pm. **Postal Code:** 620001.

ACCOMMODATIONS

The Trichy Junction area has plenty of hotels, all with 24-hour check-out.

Ashby Hotel, 17-A Junction Rd. (☎460652 or 460653), near the intersection with State Bank Rd., is packed with personality. Rooms are old and dim, but spacious enough; wooden floors impart a mellow, homey feel. Leafy courtyard keeps things cool. Attached restaurant and bar. Singles Rs175, with A/C Rs480; doubles Rs300-630.

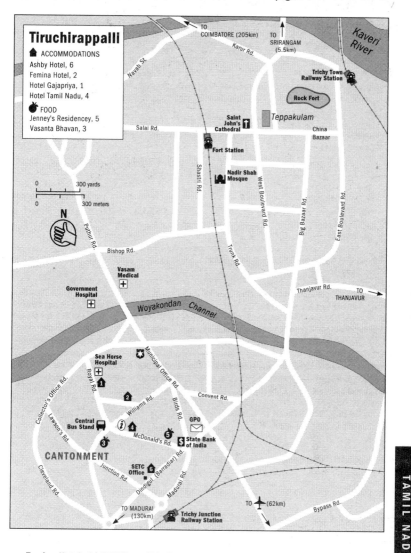

Tiruchirappalli

♠ ACCOMMODATIONS
Ashby Hotel, 6
Femina Hotel, 2
Hotel Gajapriya, 1
Hotel Tamil Nadu, 4
🍴 FOOD
Jenney's Residencey, 5
Vasanta Bhavan, 3

Femina Hotel, 14-C Williams Rd., Cantonment (☎414501). The cavernous lobby sparkles with the polish of a professional businessman's welcome. The basic rooms are a cut above the best of the rest, and cool luxury breezes through the A/C rooms. Singles Rs225-600; doubles Rs400-900. 15-20% luxury tax. MC, Visa.

Hotel Tamil Nadu, McDonald's Rd. (☎414346), next to the tourist office. A notch above most TTDC offerings, its well-kept rooms are covered with amber tiles and dressed with gleaming white sheets and dark, billowing curtains. Singles with A/C Rs300; doubles Rs225-600. 15-20% luxury tax.

Hotel Gajapriya, 2 Royal Rd. (☎414411). Look for the sign in the sky. Spacious rooms have modern furnishings, TVs, and attached bathrooms with seat toilets and hot water. A laid-back place with an equally laid-back staff. Attached Chinese restaurant and bar. Singles Rs190-450; doubles Rs330-600. 20% luxury tax. Diner's Club, MC, Visa.

🍴🎵 FOOD AND ENTERTAINMENT

Vasanta Bhavan, on the ground floor of Hotel Abhirami, opposite the bus stand. Enjoy a filling banana-leaf *thali* (Rs20), or choose from a number of typical options, including delicious coconut rice (Rs10) and *gobi masala* (Rs16). Open daily 6am-11pm.

Amaravathi Restaurant, Ramyas Hotel, near the tourist office. Dark and cool, with decent food. *Biryani* Rs35-45; chicken *masala* Rs55; and veg. fried rice Rs35. Open daily 11am-3:30pm and 7-11pm.

Golden Rock, inside the Femina Hotel. With window shades closed and A/C in overdrive, this little cafe certainly helps you chill out, serving *idlis* (Rs9), heavenly *masala dosas* (Rs22), and all the rest. Open 24hr.

Jenney's Residency, 3/14 McDonald's Rd. Recently bought out by Park Sheraton, this swanky hotel contains two restaurants. The formal **Suvia** serves a killer lunchtime *thali* (Rs60) until 3pm and sublime chicken *chettinand* (Rs90). Open daily 6am-11pm. **Peaks of Kunlun** serves the same multi-cuisine menu. Open 7pm-midnight. Jenney's also has the most original watering hole in town, the **Wild West Bar,** an old-fashioned saloon complete with swinging doors and a well-watered cowboy clutching an economy-size bottle of liquor. Open daily 11am-11pm.

👁 SIGHTS

THE ROCK FORT. One of the oldest lumps of rock anywhere in the world, this site was developed as a citadel long ago by the Pallavas and later by the Nayaks. Today, most people who reach the summit are Hindu pilgrims visiting the temple or camera-happy tourists on the hunt for good views. Four hundred rock-cut steps lead to the top. At the foot of the staircase is a small shrine to Ganesh; remove your shoes before you ascend. A little way up is the official entrance, where you can deposit your shoes. Most of the shrines along the side of the staircase are off-limits to non-Hindus. At the top (whew!) the view is just spectacular—you should be able to make out the *gopurams* of the Sri Ranganathaswamy and Jambukesh-wara temples in nearby Srirangam. A final crooked staircase leads to the white-washed Vinayaka (Ganesh) temple, where there is a viewing platform at the very top. The temple is closed to non-Hindus. *(Take bus #1 (Rs2) and get off when you see Saint John's Cathedral; from here, turn right, walk through the arch, and follow the street on your left for about 5min. to the Fort. Open daily 6am-8pm. Rs1; camera fee Rs10.)*

OTHER SIGHTS. Saint John's Cathedral, a Catholic church modeled after the Basilica in Lourdes, is worth a stop on your way to the Rock Fort. Between 7 and 11am, the banks of the **Kaveri River** are the site of a series of ceremonies and rituals, as pilgrims bathe for good fortune, priests pray for childbirth, and mourners scatter ashes. *(Take the #1 bus and ask to be let off at Amma Mandapam, Rs4.)* For a more detailed explanation of the goings-on, see **Srirangam,** below.

NEAR TIRUCHIRAPPALLI: SRIRANGAM

Five kilometers north of Trichy, on a peninsula formed by the Kaveri River and its tributary, is **Srirangam,** home of the **Sri Ranganathaswamy Temple.** The sheer size of the temple, which is dedicated to Vishnu in his role as "Director of the Universe," makes it unique—the seven concentric walls have, over the centuries, come to absorb an entire town. Most of the significant buildings were initiated by the Vijay-anagar and Nayak dynasties. Construction has continued into the modern era; the largest of the temple's 21 *gopuram* was completed in 1987.

Unusually, the entrance to the temple complex faces south rather than east; the reason, like so many things in India, is the stuff that legends are made of. Vibish-ana, the good brother of the demon Ravana (see **Ramayana,** p. 579), was awarded a reclining statue of Vishnu in recognition of his valor in war, under the stipulation that the *murti* should never be allowed to touch the ground. When Vibishana stopped by the Kaveri River to bathe, he gave the statue to a young boy who, of course, proceeded to drop it. Vibishana, infuriated, chased the boy to the spot where the Rock Fort stands today and bopped him on the head, at which point, the boy transformed into a statue of Ganesh. The fallen Vishnu statue was stuck forever to the place where it had fallen and bade Vibishana to rule Sri Lanka wisely with the words, "I will watch over you to the South."

You don't need to remove your shoes until you reach the fourth wall, beyond which are the elaborate sculptures that make this temple a rewarding masterpiece even for non-Hindus denied access to the sanctum itself. The fantastical *yali* (face of lion, body of horse, legs of tiger, trunk of elephant, and tail of cow) that greet you are a Nayak invention representing Hinduism and its victory over Buddhism, symbolized by the elephant crouched under the yali. A little farther along is access to the roof, with its fantastic views and large statue of Garuda, Vishnu's vehicle. On the eastern side of the fourth enclosure of the complex is the "1000-pillared hall," containing 936 columns carved in the shape of horsemen riding rearing steeds. The 16th century Vijayanagara horse pillars portray the battle between the Hindus (horses) and Muslims (tigers). Behind them are the 10 avatars of Vishnu.

The **Amma Mandapam**, by the banks of the Kaveri, is on the way to the **Sri Ranganathaswamy Temple.** Pilgrims come here to purify themselves before offering further *puja* at the temple. Many of the ceremonies take place on the 10th day after birth or death; you may also see a plantain ceremony aimed at preventing second marriages, or small bags tied to trees in hopes of pregnancy. This site has been sacred since ancient times, and the older Dravidian gods and goddesses of the earth are remembered in the worship of snake sculptures placed under a spreading tree. *(Take the #1 bus from Trichy Bus Stand and get off at Amma Mandapam. Rs4.)*

The **Vaikunta Ekadasi Festival** (Dec.-Jan.) draws thousands of pilgrims to the site; during the festival, a procession enters through a doorway called the "Gateway of Heaven" to ensure everlasting afterlife. *(Bus #1 leaves from Trichy's bus stand. Temple open daily 6am-9pm.)* S. Murali, 43C Ragavendrapuram, Srirangam (☎434095 or 431741) and his colleague, N. Suresh (☎434095), are two extremely knowledgeable guides, who offer tours in several languages. *(A half-day tour, including Amma Mandapam and both temples, is negotiable at Rs255.)*

The **Sri Jambukeshwara Temple,** shrine of the submerged *linga*, lies 2km east of Srirangam. One of the oldest and largest Shiva temples in Tamil Nadu, it is significant as one of five Shaivite temples in southern India dedicated to the five elements; this one is dedicated to water. The temple, with five enclosures, contains an 800-pillar *mandapam* and a tank fed by a natural spring. At around 11:30 every morning, a priestess, clad in sari and crown and representing Parvati, proceeds with an elephant from the sanctuary of the goddess to that of her husband, Shiva, and back again. *(Regular #1 bus service is currently interrupted by construction, making it easier to take a rickshaw for Rs20 from the Vishnu temple to the Sri Jambukeshwara. Then, from the main street near the Sri Jambukeshwara, take any one of a number of buses going back to Rock Fort or to Trichy's Central Bus Stand. Temple open 6am-noon and 4-9pm.)*

MADURAI மதுரை ☎0452

According to legend, Shiva himself once stood over Madurai to dry his matted hair; the nectar that fell from his holy locks soaked the city and gave it its name, derived from the Tamil word *madhuram* (sweetness). The sugar buzz is still going strong in modern Madurai, a small but turbulent temple town that energizes the thousands who visit it every day. Madurai has thrived as a cultural center ever since it was founded as the capital of the Pandya kingdom that ruled central South India back in the 4th century BC. The powerful Vijayanagar Kingdom reigned from here throughout the 15th and early 16th centuries, when the temples and towers of the city's famous Meenakshi Amman Temple were built. From 1559 onward, Madurai was ruled by the Nayak dynasty, which built the modern city's attractions—the Teppakkulam and the Raya Gopuram. The Nayak Empire lost power in 1736 when the East India Company bought out and de-fortified the city, tearing down its walls and filling in the moat that once stood where the Veli streets run today.

Madurai has survived to become an important commercial hub, with a population of well over one million. Huge electronic signboards illuminate the night sky, and large volumes of traffic (both cars and cows) surge through the streets. For all its vibrant clamor, Madurai still moves to the rhythm of the temple's activities, and the festival season sees the traditional procession through town of crowds of gods, residents, and visiting pilgrims.

▐ GETTING THERE AND GETTING AROUND

Flights: (☎670433), 15km south of the city center. A taxi into town costs upward of Rs170. Hourly buses leave from the exit. **Indian Airlines,** 7A W. Veli St. (☎741234), opposite the railway station. Open daily 10am-5pm. To: **Bombay** (daily, 1:20pm, 3hr., US$190) via **Madras** (1hr., US$90). **Jet Airways** (☎522077), in Rajam Plaza in Talakallam area, across the river, also has flights to Madras.

Trains: Madurai Junction Railway Station, W. Veli St. (☎743131). Reservations open M-Sa 8am-1:30pm and 2-8pm, Su 8am-2pm. To: **Bangalore** (8pm, 12hr., Rs182); **Chidambaram, Thanjavur,** and **Tirupati** via **Trichy** (5-7 per day, 6:45am-10pm, 3hr., Rs84); **Coimbatore** (3 per day, 6am-2:20pm, 5hr., Rs95); **Kanyakumari** (2-3 per day, 4am-2pm, 6hr., Rs97); **Madras** (6 per day, 6:45am-10pm, 10hr., Rs166); **Rameswaram** (6am and 2pm, 5-5½hr., Rs65).

Buses: There are two interstate bus stands. Buses (Rs2-3) or auto-rickshaws (Rs50) connect the two. **Mattu Thavani Bus Stand** serves **Bangalore** (6 per day, 10hr., Rs142); **Cochin** (9am and 9pm, 8hr., Rs112) via **Munnar** (5hr.); **Madras** (every 30min., 10hr., Rs118); **Pondicherry** (8:45 and 10pm, 8hr., Rs90); **Rameswaram** (every hr., 4hr., Rs25); **Thanjavur** (every 30min., 4hr., Rs25); **Trichy** (every hr., 5:30am-9pm, 4hr., Rs26). **Arapalayam Bus Stand** serves the north. To: **Coimbatore** (every 30min., 5hr., Rs47); **Kodai** (frequent, 5:40am-4:45pm, 4hr., Rs26); **Munnar** (8am, 6hr.). **Palanganatham Bus Stand** deals mostly with buses to Kerala. To: **Kanyakumari** (every hr., 6hr., Rs50); **Trivandrum** (every hr., 8hr., Rs75).

Local Transportation: Local buses leave from the **Periyar Bus Stand** on W. Veli St., a 2min. walk south from the railway station. The stand is so congested that a small overflow lot has been set up east of the bus stand between W. Veli and W. Perumal Maistry St. Auto- and cycle-**rickshaws** are everywhere; the main stand is right outside the railway station. A pre-paid rickshaw booth opens when trains arrive.

◆✶⁊ ORIENTATION AND PRACTICAL INFORMATION

Madurai stretches north and south of the **Vaigai River.** The city is bordered on the south and west by railway tracks, and is dominated by the **Meenakshi Temple.** The **Periyar Bus Stand** and **Madurai Junction Railway Station** are off **W. Veli St.,** 1km west of the temple. To reach the city center and the budget hotels from the railway station, follow **Town Hall Rd.** east; from **Periyar bus stand,** follow the wider **Nethaji (Dindigul) Rd.,** marked by the Hotel Empee. Streets are arranged concentrically around the temple, forming an irregular grid. Closest to the temple are North, East, South, and West **Chittrai St.** Farther from the temple are North, East, South, and West **Avani Moola St.** North, East, South, and West **Masi St.** are encircled by North, East, South, and West **Veli St.** To cross the Vaigai River, head 1km northeast of the temple and across **Victor Bridge.** The road leading northeast from the bridge, **Alagar Koil Rd.,** is intersected by **Tamukkam Rd.**

Tourist Office: Tamil Nadu Tourism Development Corporation (TTDC), 180 TB Complex, W. Veli St. (☎734757). Exit Periyar bus stand to the south; the tourist office is on the opposite side of the street, on the right. Open M-F 10am-5:30pm, Sa 10am-2pm. There are also offices at the airport and railway station.

Currency Exchange: State Bank of India, 6 W. Veli St. (☎742127), Sangam Towers, north of the railway station and across the street. Open M-F 10am-4pm, Sa 10am-1pm.

Bookstore: Malligai Book Centre, 11 W. Veli St. (☎740534), opposite the railway station. Open M-Sa 9am-1pm and 3:30-9pm.

TAMIL NADU

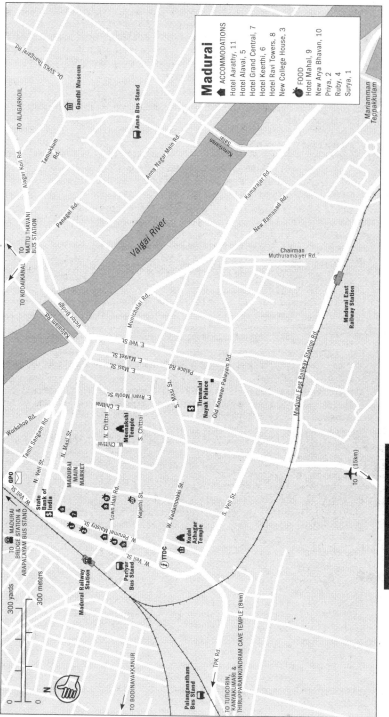

Madurai

ACCOMMODATIONS
Hotel Aarathy, 11
Hotel Alavai, 5
Hotel Grand Central, 7
Hotel Keerthi, 6
Hotel Ravi Towers, 8
New College House, 3

FOOD
Hotel Mahal, 9
New Arya Bhavan, 10
Priya, 2
Ruby, 4
Surya, 1

Mariamman
Teppakkulam

Dr. SVKS Thangaraj Rd.

TO ALAGARKOIL

Gandhi Museum

Anna Bus Stand

Alagar Koil Rd.

Tamukkum Rd.

Anna Nagar Main Rd.

Panagal Rd.

Kamarajar Rd.

New Ramnad Rd.

Valgai River

Kumar Sangam

Chairman
Muthuramaiyer Rd.

TO MATTU THAVANI
BUS STATION

TO KODAIKANAL

Victor Bridge

Kanjalam Rd.

Munichalai Rd.

E. Veli St.

Madurai East Railway Station Rd.

Madurai East
Railway Station

TO (15km)

Workshop Rd.

Tamil Sangam Rd.

N. Veli St.

E. Chittrai

E. Masi St.
E. Market St.

E. Avani Moola St.

S. Masi St.

S. Chittrai

Palace Rd.

Old Kosavar Palayam Rd.

Trimalai
Nayak Palace

N. Chittrai

Meenakshi
Temple

N. Masi St.

W. Chittrai

S. Chittrai

MADURAI
MAIN
MARKET

GPO

State
Bank of
India

N. Veli St.

Town Hall Rd.

Kejethi St.

W. Perumal Maisty St.

W. Vadamoolki St.

S. Veli St.

Kutal
Azhagar
Temple

TDC

W. Veli St.

Periyar
Bus Stand

Madurai Railway Station

TO MADURAI
BRIDGE STATION &
ARAPALAYAM BUS STAND

300 yards

300 meters

N

TO BODINAYAKKANUR

TO TUTICORIN,
KANYAKUMARI &
THIRUPPARANKUNDRAM CAVE TEMPLE (8km)

TPK Rd.

Palanganatham
Bus Stand

TAMIL NADU

Police: The main station (☎538015) is on the north bank, on the road to Natham. The E-1 station, on W. Veli St. next to the tourist office, is the closest to the hotel area.

Pharmacy: Suresh Medicals, 63 Town Hall Rd. (☎741625). Open M-Sa 7:30am-10:30pm.

Hospital: The private **Jawahar Hospital,** 14 Main Rd., KK Nagar (☎650021 or 650022), on the northern bank of Vaigai, has a 24hr. pharmacy.

Internet: Global Net, Nethaji St., near W. Perumal Maistry St. Rs35 per hr. Open 24hr.

Post Office: Head Post Office (☎740756), on N. Veli St. Open M-Sa 9am-7pm, Su 9am-4pm. **Postal Code:** 625001.

▌ ACCOMMODATIONS

Nearly all of Madurai's hotels are within walking distance of the Meenakshi Temple and the city's transportation hubs. Good budget options do exist, though rooms under Rs150 are an endangered species.

Hotel Keerthi, 40 W. Perumal Maistry St. (☎741501), 1½ blocks north of Town Hall Rd. Polite staff and tiny whitewashed rooms with spotless sheets, ample lighting, TVs, and phones. Clean attached baths with warmish water. A/C rooms have seat toilets. Attached restaurant. Singles Rs175; doubles Rs220-300. 15% tax.

Hotel Grand Central, 47 W. Perumal Maistry St. (☎743940). Reasonable rooms with clean sheets and TV. Attached bath with seat toilet. 24hr. check-out. Singles Rs175-250; doubles Rs195-450.

Hotel Ravi Towers, 9 Town Hall Rd. (☎741961; fax 743405), 2 blocks east of W. Perumal Maistry St. Neat, cool rooms. 24hr. hot water, reality-numbing Star TV, and STD/ISD phone service. Some rooms have clean attached baths and seat toilets. Room service. Check-out 24hr. Singles Rs125; doubles Rs195-350.

Hotel Alavai, 86 W. Perumal Maistry St. (☎740551). Simple rooms containing the usual combo: rickety bed, plastic chair, and attached bathroom with squat toilet. Singles Rs85; doubles Rs115-140.

New College House, 2 Town Hall Rd. (☎742971). Big enough so that rooms—large, clean, with attached bath—are almost always available. Offers some relief from the congestion of the area. Sheets available. Single Rs135; doubles Rs195-500.

Hotel Aarathy, 9 Perumal Koil, W. Mada St. (☎731571). Walk south of the bus stand on W. Veli St. until you see the sign on the right. Turn left, and then right again. A well-maintained establishment with restaurant. Sparkling attached bathrooms with seat or squat toilets. Check-out 24hr. Singles Rs195-300; doubles Rs300-450.

PIECES OF FATE In these modern times of high-tech gizmos and Internet heart-break, the hand-cast horoscope looks set to go the ill-starred way of the wind-up automobile and the beehive hairdo. Thanks to computers, you can now have your horoscope (*jadhagam*) plotted just by specifying your date of birth, which will be checked against a database of planetary positions and twinkle-star migrations. The result is spooled out unceremoniously in barely-legible dot matrix. All very scientific. In some parts of India, though, you can still get your fortune told the good old-fashioned way: by *kili josyam* (parrot astrology). The human astrologer (merely the hands and mouth of the parrot itself, you understand) has a number of cards placed face down in front of him, marked with pictures of deities. To determine a client's fortune, he releases a highly-trained parrot from its cage, and the bird grabs one of the cards in its beak. Each deity corresponds to a chapter in the *Agastya Arudal*, an ancient fortune-telling treatise written by the sage Agastya. The astrologer then divines the punter's fortune from the designated chapter. The prognosticating polly is re-caged, but the game continues, as the same astrologer is usually also a palmist and has a million ways to clarify or elaborate upon the parrot's prediction.

FOOD

The best restaurants in Madurai are in and around the hotels on W. Perumal Maistry St. and Town Hall Rd. Many of the hotels have rooftop dining, which usually means quiet surroundings, cool breezes, and great temple views.

New Arya Bhavan, 241-A W. Masi St., at Kejethi Rd. A large, calm oasis on a busy street, this local favorite serves up delicious *masala dosas* (Rs15), *pakoras* (Rs10), and all the rest. Efficient, smiley service. If the mango ice cream (Rs9) doesn't cool you down, the A/C banquet booths certainly will. Attached sweet shop. Open 6am-10:30pm.

Surya, 110 W. Perumal Maistry St., on the roof of Hotel Supreme. Relax with a few beers as the sun sets to the west and the *gopurams* of the Meenakshi Temple glitter to the east. Extensive veg. menu has the usual Indian, Chinese, and continental favorites (Rs30-70). Beer Rs75. Open 6am-11pm.

Priya, 102 W. Perumal Maistry St., in Hotel Prem Nivas. Phenomenal Indian food: huge *masala dosa* (Rs8) and delicious *thalis* (Rs25-30). Quick service. Munch on cornflakes (Rs18) for breakfast. Open daily 6:30am-10pm.

Hotel Mahal, 13 Town Hall Rd., next to the Taj Restaurant. The most varied dining options in town, served amid tanks of tropical fish. North Indian *thali* Rs35; tandoori Rs30-40; pasta Rs65; lamb Rs60. Open daily 7am-11pm.

Ruby Restaurant, W. Perumal Maistry St., next to Ruby Lodge. One of Madurai's main foreigner hubs. Standard menu. Open daily 11am-11pm.

SIGHTS

MEENAKSHI AMMAN TEMPLE

Enter the temple complex from East Chitrai St., through the eastern gopuram, or from S. Chittrai St., through the southern gopuram. Open daily 5am–10pm. Sanctum closed 12:30-3pm. Free; camera fee Rs30.

The Meenakshi Amman Temple, drawing more than 10,000 people every day, is probably the most splendid in all of Tamil Nadu. Besides dazzling visitors with the vivid colors and vibrant energy of the 30 million sculptures that adorn the complex, the temple is also impressive for its sheer size—it covers an incredible 65,000 square meters, and the tallest of the temple's twelve *gopurams* is nearly 50m high.

Dedicated both to the goddess Meenakshi and to Shiva, the temple was originally a humble shrine built by the Pandyas. It was enriched and enlarged by the patronage of the Vijayanagar kings. In the 16th century the Nayaks came to power and continued this work by expanding the complex even further, building the temple's massive *gopurams*. The temple was opened to Untouchables after Gandhi initiated a boycott and made a crucial visit here in 1946.

Legend has it that Pandya King Malayadwaja was childless, and desperately sought a male heir. The king appealed to the gods by performing a series of *yagnas*, or fire sacrifices. To his great surprise, during one of these ceremonies, a three-year-old girl emerged from the flames. Named Meenakshi, the "fish-eyed" goddess (fish-like eyes being considered a mark of beauty), the child was born with three breasts and a whole lot of divine attitude. The king was a little troubled by his daughter's appearance, but a voice from above assured him that her third breast would disappear when she met the man who would become her husband. After growing up to become a beautiful princess, Meenakshi set out to conquer the world. She wasted little time in defeating one god after another, until only Shiva was left. When Meenakshi confronted Shiva (known in Madurai as Sundareswar, the "good-lookin' lord"), her heart turned to *ghee*, her third breast disappeared, and she was easily domesticated. Meenakshi and Sundareswar were married in Madurai and ruled the Pandya kingdom together from here. The **Meenakshi Kalyanam** is the festival commemorating the wedding and usually takes place in May.

ASHTA SHAKTI AND MEENAKSHI NAYAKKAR MANDAPAMS. In the southeastern corner is the brightly painted Ashta Shakti Mandapam (Eight Shakti Corridor), where hawkers peddle postcards, curios, and *puja* offerings. The passage was named for the eight *avatars* of the goddess Shakti carved on its pillars. Other sculptures and paintings depict the miracles *(tiruvilayadal)* of Shiva. The Meenakshi Nayakkar Mandapam has two rows of pillars carved with images of the *yali*, mythological beasts with the body of a lion and the head of an elephant, which were commonly used to express Nayak power.

POTRAMARAI KULAM. The corridors surrounding the Potramarai Kulam (Golden Lotus Tank) are often crowded by devotees relaxing in the shade or taking in the spectacular view of the temple's southern *gopuram*. The tank itself is frequented by pilgrims seeking a purifying bath in its light green waters, following the tradition of Indra, who is said to have bathed here. In ancient times, the Tamil Sangam (Academy of Poets) met in the area around the tank. Locals claim that the Sangam judged the merit of literary works by tossing submissions into the tank. If a work sank, the aspiring writer's hopes went along with it. If a work floated, however, it was deemed worthy of the Sangam's attention.

KILIKOOTU MANDAPAM. The northwest corner of the tank leads directly to the Meenakshi Shrine, which is closed to non-Hindus; the corridor surrounding the shrine, however, is open to all. Called the Kilikootu Mandapam, or Parrot Cage Corridor, the space was once used to keep the lucky green parrots—trained to repeat Meenakshi's name—that would be used as offerings to the goddess.

OONJAL MANDAPAM. The golden images of Meenakshi and Sundareswar are carried into the neighboring 16th-century Oonjal Mandapam (Swing Corridor) to be placed on a swing and sung to every Friday at about 5:30pm. The shrine has a three-story *gopuram* guarded by two stern *dwarapalakas* (watchmen) and is supported by golden, rectangular columns that bear the mark of a lotus. Along the perimeter of the chamber granite panels of the divine couple overlook the crowds.

KAMBATHADI MANDAPAM. North of the Oonjal Mandapam is the **Sundareswar Shrine,** with its eight-foot image of Ganesh (Mukkuruni Vinayakar). The idol was discovered in the 17th century when King Tirumalai Nayak began digging the Mariamman Teppakulam in the southeastern corner of the city. To the right, in the northeast corner of the enclosure, is the Kambathadi Mandapam, adorned with elegant pillars, each of which bears a sculpture of Meenakshi or Shiva. Sculptures of Shiva and Kali trying to out-dance one another are pelted with balls of *ghee* by devotees who hope to soothe their competitiveness. On the left are two sculptures of Shiva killing the demon child. A golden flagstaff with 32 sections symbolizes the human backbone and is surrounded by various gods, including Durga and Siddhar. The inner chamber contains the image of Sundareswar as well as an image of Nataraja, unique for having his *right* foot raised.

AYIRAKKAL MANDAPAM. East of the Kambathadi Mandapam is a lively market, where vendors sell postcards and religious trinkets. These stands surround the Ayirakkal Mandapam (Thousand Pillar Hall), which contains 985 carved pillars (no word on the other 15). It has been converted into a quiet **museum** with a substantial collection of sculptures. Outside the museum entrance is a set of pillars that plays seven notes when tapped. *(Open daily 7am-7:30pm. Rs2; camera fee Rs10.)*

OTHER SIGHTS

GANDHI MUSEUM. The Mahatma visited Madurai several times, but the museum does much more than merely chronicle his stops. One section presents a stirring version of the events leading up to Independence. The other part focuses on samples of Gandhi's correspondence and houses relics such as the loincloth he was wearing when he was killed. *(Bus #3 from Periyar to Anna Bus stand. Auto-rickshaw Rs20. Open 10am-1pm and 2-5:30pm. Free.)*

TIRUMALAI NAYAK PALACE. All that remains of Tirumalai's grand 17th-century palace is the cavernous **Swargavilasam** (Celestial Pavilion), an arcaded courtyard where the Nayak rulers held public audiences. Although heroic efforts are being made to renovate the courtyard, there is no undoing the damage wrought by Tiru-malai's grandson, who looted the palace to outfit his own in Trichy. Parts of the interior have been fully restored; the deep crimson hue, along with the cream-col-ored carvings and figures in relief, hints at the palace's former grandeur. The pal-ace now houses a small collection of stone carvings and early terra-cottas. *(1.5km southeast of the Meenakshi Temple. Open daily 9am-1pm and 2-5pm. Rs1.)*

VANDIYUR MARIAMMAN TEPPAKULAM. This square water tank has a tree-sur-rounded **shrine** in the center. The tank was built in 1646 by Tirumalai Nayak, who retired with his harem to the central shrine. These days the tank is usually dry, and the only activity in the area is boys playing cricket. Every year, a colorful float fes-tival (Jan.-Feb.) commemorates the birth of its builder. *(Kamarajar Rd., 5km south-east of the railway station. Bus #4 or 4A.)*

THIRUPPARANKUNDRAM. Though not as awe-inspiring as Meenakshi Amman, Thirupparankundram is an impressive cave-temple dedicated to Lord Subramanya and guarded by sculptures of prancing horses. The **inner sanctum** is carved right out of the rock in the side of a mountain and is accessible to non-Hindus. *(8km south of town from Periyar Bus Stand. Bus #5, 30min. Open 5am-12:30pm, 4pm-9:30pm.)*

THE RAMAYANA
Arguably the most culturally influential work of litera-ture in India, the *Ramayana* (literally, "the romance of Rama") has inspired thousands of dances, paintings, shadow puppet shows, inter-religious riots, and even its own TV mini-series. The epic's main characters, Rama and Sita, are revered as archetypes of those who unwaveringly follow their *dharma* (duty or fate). The Sanskrit poet Valmiki is thought to have composed the *Ramayana* around 400 BC, basing it on events that took place between 1000 and 700 BC.

Act I, Scene 1: Rama is born to King Dasaratha's wife Kausalya in Ayodhya, capital of Kosala. Dasaratha's other wives, Kaikeyi and Sumithra, bear him Bharata and the twins Lakshman and Shatrugna, respectively. **Scene 2:** Rama journeys with his guru Viswamitra to the kingdom of Mithila, where he falls in love at first sight with King Jan-aka's beautiful daughter, Sita. But winning her hand is not an easy task. Fearing he will lose his daughter to an unworthy man, Janaka declares that only he who is able to break Shiva's divine bow can have her hand in marriage. **Scene 3:** Rama successfully breaks the bow, and the two kingdoms delight in the wedding of Rama and Sita. **Scene 4:** the aging Dasaratha names Rama as his successor, but his wife Kaikeyi refuses to accept Rama as king and forces Dasaratha to banish Rama to the forest for 14 years. Kaikeyi's son Bharata is crowned king instead.

Act II, Scene 1: Rama, Sita, and Rama's faithful brother Lakshman leave Ayodhya for the forest. The sorrowful Dasaratha soon dies, and Bharata rushes to the forest, beg-ging Rama to return to claim the throne. Unwilling to break his promise to his father, Rama stays in the forest for the next 14 years. **Scene 2:** Ravana, chief of the *asuras* (demons), abducts Sita to his island kingdom of Lanka. **Scene 3:** Rama and Lakshman journey in search of Sita, encountering en route the clever monkey Hanuman, son of the wind god. Rama sends Hanuman to Lanka to assess the situation and deliver a token to his beloved wife. Hanuman sets fire to the entire capital of Lanka before he leaves. **Scene 4:** With the help of a Lankan spy, Rama and his army of monkeys advance on Lanka. The valiant monkeys build a bridge to Lanka, and a celestial battle ensues. Rama emerges victorious, vanquishing Ravana and winning back Sita. **Scene 5:** 14 years are up, and Rama, Lakshman, Sita, and Hanuman return to Kosala. Rama is crowned king, and Ayodhya erupts in celebration upon the revelation that Rama is an avatar of Vishnu. **Scene 6:** Sita's fidelity during Rama's absence is questioned. Subordinating his trust in Sita to his princely duty, Rama subjects her to an ordeal of fire, from which she emerges unscathed and vindicated. The end.

🎵 🛍 ENTERTAINMENT AND SHOPPING

There are several **cinemas** near the Periyar Bus Stand. *The Hindu* has the latest listings for English-language films. Check with the tourist office for **cultural programs** such as classical dancing and music in Lakshmi Sundaram Hall, Tallakulam (☎530858). Madurai is full of **textile shops** and sari showrooms. You will be accosted repeatedly by tailors offering to sew an exact copy of whatever you're wearing for a nominal cost. As always, beware of auto-rickshaw drivers who force you to check out a particular handicraft store—they're just after the commission. Even if you don't plan on buying anything, you may find yourself slurping down yet another free 7-Up as a smooth-talking salesman tries to talk you into buying that Rs500 parakeet-embroidered pillowcase you never knew you wanted. **Parameswari Stores,** 21 East Chittrai St., just outside the southern *gopuram* of the Meenakshi Temple, is well-known for its silk-cotton blends. **Cooptex Sales Emporium,** W. Chittrai St., sells fabric as well as saris. **Khadi Emporium,** Town Hall Rd., is a good place to buy gifts and wooden carvings. Handicraft enthusiasts should visit the **Madurai Gallery,** Cottage Expo Crafts, 19 N. Chittrai St. (☎627851); as always, bargain like your grandmother. **Meenakshi Treasures,** also on N. Chittrai St., has a beautiful but expensive jewelry collection upstairs.

RAMESWARAM இராமேசுவரம்   ☎04573

The setting of the epic *Ramayana* (see p. 579), Rameswaram is the venerated spot where Rama, the epic's hero, launched an attack on Ravana's fortress on the island of Lanka. According to a later myth, Rama, after defeating Ravana in their cosmic battle, made a *linga* of sand here to honor Shiva and expiate the sin of murder. This remote island off the country's southeastern coast draws thousands of Hindu pilgrims from all over India. Rameswaram marks the southern holy *dham* (abode), one of India's four sacred places marking the cardinal directions. (The others are Dwarka in the west, Badrinath in the north, and Puri in the east.) A number of festivals are held in Rameswaram, including **Thai Amavasai** (Jan.), **Masi Sivarathiri** (Feb.-Mar.), and **Adiammavasai** (Jul.-Aug.).

🚍 GETTING THERE AND GETTING AROUND

Trains: Rameswaram Station (☎21226), 1km southwest of the temple. To: **Coimbatore** (4pm, 12hr., Rs140); **Madras** (noon and 3:10pm 17hr., Rs210); **Madurai** (2 per day, 7:30am and 9:50pm, 5-7hr., Rs84); **Trichy** (1pm, 7½hr., Rs104).

Buses: The **bus stand** is on Bazaar Rd., 2km west of the temple. A short auto-rickshaw (Rs25) or bus (Rs1) ride from the temple. **SETC** runs buses to: **Madras** (5pm, 13hr., Rs177); **Madurai** (every 20min., 5am-midnight, 4hr., Rs44); **Salem** (2 per day, 7:40am and 7:40pm, 10hr., Rs110). **Non-SETC** buses also run to: **Madurai** (frequent, 4hr.); **Thanjavur** (4 per day, 6:55am-4:30pm, 7hr.); **Trichy** (every hr., 6hr.).

Local Transportation: Unmetered **auto-rickshaws** whiz around Rameswaram, and silver-and-red **local buses** shuttle between the bus stand and E. Car St. Shops on the Car Streets rent **bikes** for about Rs3 per hr.

✳ 🛈 ORIENTATION AND PRACTICAL INFORMATION

Navigating Rameswaram involves wandering the four **Car Streets**—North, East, South, and West—surrounding the **Ramanathaswamy Temple.** Most of the hotels and restaurants are on these four streets and on **Sannadhi St.,** which runs east from the middle of E. Car St. to the Bay of Bengal. To reach the temple from the railway station, walk out of the main entrance and follow the road for about 300m as it curves slightly, then turn left (north) when you hit the principal north-south thoroughfare. Walk north for 500m until you reach **Middle St.,** which leads east to the middle of W. Car St. and the western entrance to the temple.

Tourist Office: 14 E. Car St. (☎21371), has rudimentary maps of Rameswaram. Open M-F 10am-5:45pm. The Tourist Information Centre (☎21373), inside the train station, and the Temple Information Center, inside the temple, are helpful.

Currency Exhange: The nearest place to change currency is Madurai.

Police station: (☎21246), in a red brick building at the junction of East and N. Car Sts.

Pharmacy: Sri Meenakshi, W. Car St. Open daily 8am-10pm.

Hospital: Government Hospital (☎21233), near the railway station; toward the temple and left off Bazaar St., before the Township Office. Open daily 8am-7:30pm. You can also try the **Temple Trust Ayurvedic Dispensary,** near the temple police station. Open daily 8am-noon and 3-6pm.

Post office: One branch on Middle St., toward the bus stand. Smaller office on E. Car St.

▚ ACCOMMODATIONS

Except for the TTDC Rest House, most hotels are in the immediate vicinity of the Ramanathaswamy Temple. Accommodations are very basic, catering to pilgrims looking for a cheap place to crash for the night. Rameswaram's tap water can be salty, and showers are extremely rare, so test the plumbing before checking in. Reserve ahead during the pilgrimage season (July-Aug.).

Hotel Maharaja's, 7 Middle St. (☎21271), has pleasant, well-maintained rooms with cable TV and a view of the temple's *gopurams*. Attached squat toilets are the cleanest you'll get; hot water available. Check-out 24hr. Singles Rs120; doubles Rs195.

Hotel Venkatesh (☎21296) on W. Car St., is another good option. Large, clean rooms have attached bath with squat toilets. Doubles Rs170-350.

Hotel Tamil Nadu, on the beachfront, just past the holy bathing spot, is more expensive, but farther from the temple noise. Attached bar and restaurant. Doubles Rs350-500.

◖ FOOD

Ganesh Mess, near Hotel Maharaja's and the western gate, has perfectly spiced lemon rice for Rs6 and masala dosa for Rs10. (Open 6am-10pm.) **Hotel Abirami,** on Sannadhi St., serves piping-hot *chappatis* for Rs8 and *sabjis* for Rs10. (Open daily 6am-10pm.)

▨ SIGHTS

THE RAMANATHASWAMY TEMPLE. Bathing in the bay of Bengal and the 22 tanks of the Ramanasthawamy Temple forms part of one of the most sacred pilgrimages a Hindu can make—its spiritual power is akin to jumping in the waters of the Ganga at Varanasi (see p. 193). Before taking *darshan* of the temple's resident deities, pilgrims first bathe in the sea at **Akini Theetum** ("Holy Fire Water") and then proceed to the temple where they are led from holy tank to holy tank. To expedite the process, temple employees are on hand to dump buckets of salty water on devotees. Taking part in the ritual is a once-in-a-lifetime experience; contact a tour guide to avoid the hassles of getting into the inner sanctum, which is usually inaccessible to non-Hindus. *(Contact Kannan at the Hotel Tamil Nadu or M. Selvam, 25 N. Car St. ☎21353 or 21501. Full ritual Rs250.)*

The inner sanctum houses two *lingas*, one of which was fashioned out of sand by Rama himself. According to a later version of the *Ramayana*, Rama returned to Rameswaram after he had killed Ravana in Lanka, only to discover that Ravana had been a brahmin and that his murder was therefore a grave sin. Rama sent Hanuman to bring back a *linga* with which Rama could worship Shiva and expiate his guilt, but the monkey was slow in returning, and Rama had to make do with a *linga* of sand. When Hanuman finally returned and tried to replace the makeshift *linga*, it would not budge; the new *linga* was installed to the left of it.

Construction of the temple, famous for its sculpted pillars that form huge, long corridors, began in the 12th century under the Chola empire; the last major alterations to the temple were made in the mid-18th century by the Raja of Ramnathapuram, Muthuramalinga Sethupathi. The eastern *gopuram* was completed during the 20th century, causing some cement corridors to look shockingly new. *(Temple open daily 4am-8pm. Rs2. Bathing at dawn. Inner sanctum closed noon-4pm.)*

OTHER SIGHTS. Dedicated to Rama, the **Kothandaramar Temple** is said to mark the site where Ravana's brother, Vibhishana, was crowned king of Lanka after Ravana's death. *(20km along the road toward Sri Lanka. Open daily 8am-5pm.)* The **Gandamadana Paravtham**, a simple, white-washed temple on top of the highest hill in town, houses an imprint of Lord Rama's feet and commands splendid views of the sandy island terrain. *(3km north of the Ramanathaswamy Temple.)* The southeastern end of the island forms a great finger of sand that points toward Sri Lanka. The railway line to **Dhanushkodi** was destroyed by a cyclone that roared through in 1964, but it is accessible today by bus. Take bus #3 (leaves from E. Car St., 30min., Rs3.50) to the "new" Dhanushkodi; from there it's 3km of sand, seashells, and blue surf to the smaller village. **Boats** can be hired at **Sangumal**, 2½km northeast of the temple. A guide will strap a mask onto your face and take you snorkeling in the beautiful **coral reef**, about 2km from the shore. *(Boats Rs300 for 4hr.)*

KANYAKUMARI கன்னியாகுமாரி ☎ 04652

Kanyakumari (Cape Comorin), the southernmost tip of the Indian subcontinent, is particularly auspicious for Hindus because it is the meeting place of three major bodies of water—the Arabian Ocean, the Bay of Bengal, and the Indian Ocean. Hindu pilgrims come in thousands to sacred Kanyakumari to watch the sun set into one ocean and rise from out of another. Just as South India's beach resorts provide sun, sand, and tropical fruits in one easy-to-swallow package for consumption by Western tourists, so Kanyakumari provides an equally irresistible dose of patriotism, spirituality, and tacky shell art for Indian tourists. As well as monuments to Gandhi and Swami Vivekandanda, Kanyakumari is also the site of the Kumari Amman Temple, dedicated to Devi Kanya—a virginal incarnation of Parvati (*kanya* means virgin). The holiness that Kanyakumari's monuments impart to the town is hard to spot by day, however, as tour buses parked along the seafront disgorge masses of pilgrims into the waiting arms of beach vendors hawking cheap souvenirs. Screeching families, scores of scantily clad men (wearing only *lungis*), and children shooting their plastic guns all push and shove their way through the monuments. But when the sun goes down and the hyperactive pilgrims slow down to munch on deep-fried peppers and bananas at lit-up street stalls, the carnivalesque air just about manages to mitigate the town's grimness.

Weekends are a peak of activity; avoid them if at all possible.

▌ GETTING THERE AND GETTING AROUND

Trains: Railway station, on Main Rd., a 15min. walk from the sea. Reservations open M-Sa 8am-noon and 2-4pm, Su 8am-2pm. To: **Bangalore** (6:30am, 20hr., Rs252); **Bombay** (4:45am, 48hr., Rs402); **Ernakulam** (2-3 per day, 12:45-6:30am, 10hr., Rs405); **Madras** (5:45am and 3:40pm, 17hr., Rs228); and **Trivandrum** (2-3 per day, 12:45-6:30am, 2½hr., Rs84).

Buses: The **bus stand** posts schedules in English. All buses also stop on Main Rd.; save yourself the walk and get off opposite the Government Hospital. **Tamil Nadu State Express Transport** (☎ 46019) runs buses to: **Coimbatore** (5:45pm, 11hr., Rs146); **Kodai** (daily, 8:45pm, 10hr., Rs101); **Madras** (8 per day, 9:30am-8:30pm, 16hr., Rs217-238); **Madurai** (frequent, 9:30am-8:45pm, 6hr., Rs82); and **Ooty** (5:45 and 6:30pm, 14hr., Rs152). Buses also go to **Nagercoil** (every 5min., 30min., Rs4.50), from where there are frequent connections to many other cities. Kerala's state buses, KRSTC, leave from platform #4 of the bus station and go to: **Ernakulam** (7:15 and 9am, 8hr., Rs89); **Kovalam** (6:30am and 1pm, 3hr., Rs35); and **Trivandrum** (11 per day, 5:45am-9:15pm, 2½hr., Rs20). The Kovalam schedule is particularly variable; it may be easiest to go to Trivandrum and take a local bus from there.

⚹📝 ORIENTATION AND PRACTICAL INFORMATION

Buses from Trivandrum and Madurai head south down **Main Rd.** past the **railway station.** Buses stop on Main Rd., just north of S. Car St. and then turn west onto **Bus Stand Rd.**, past the **lighthouse,** to the **bus stand.** Main Rd. continues south past the junction to the **tourist office** and peters out at the seafront by the **Gandhi Memorial.** Running east from Main Rd. Junction, Bus Stand Rd. crosses **Sannadhi St.** before ending at the **ferry service station.** Sannadhi St. heads south through the stalls to the **Kumari Amman Temple,** at the very tip of the subcontinent.

Tourist Office: Main Rd. (☎46276), on the right, in a circular building north of the Gandhi Memorial. Open M-F 10am-5:45pm. Open for shorter hours some weekends.

Budget Travel: Several small offices north of the temple on S. and E. Car St. sell private bus and train tickets.

Currency Exchange: Canara Bank, Main Rd., a 5-10min. walk north of Main Rd. Junction, on the left. Changes AmEx and Thomas Cook traveler's checks. Gives cash advances on AmEx, MC, Visa. Allow at least 1hr. Open M-F 10am-2pm, Sa 10am-noon.

Bookstore: Shamus Book Centre, Sannadhi St., opposite and a little beyond Hotel Saravana. Sells maps. Open F-W 8:30am-9pm.

Police: Main Rd. (☎46224), next to the GPO.

Pharmacy: Sastha Pharmacy, Main Rd. (☎46455), halfway between the railway station and the tourist office, just beyond Hotel Sangam. Open daily 8:30am-9:30pm.

Hospital: Government Hospital, off Main Rd., close to the police station. Since it has no phone, tourists might want to call **Dr. Arumugam's** clinic, E. Car St. (☎46349), between Hotels Manickham and Maadhini.

Telephones: All Kanyakumari phone numbers that began with 71 now begin with 46.

Internet: LS Computers, Middle St., in Hotel Ashoka, parallel to E. Car St. Rs90 per hr. Open M-Sa 9:30am-11pm, Su 10:30am-11pm.

Post Office: GPO, Main Rd., just south of Canara Bank. Open M-Sa 8am-noon and 1:30-4:30pm. **Postal Code:** 629702.

📍 ACCOMMODATIONS

Every second building in Kanyakumari provides lodging of some kind. Prices begin to soar in August and peak between October and February. There is no such thing as tranquility here—families wake up noisily at 5:30am to catch the sunrise. All hotels listed have attached restaurants.

Manickam Tourist House, N. Car St. (☎46387), near Hotel Maadhini. Decent amenities and views of the sea. Facilities are a little tired, but cheap. Clean rooms with attached bathrooms and balconies. Buckets of hot water upon request. Check-out 24hr. Singles Rs160-250; doubles Rs250-350.

Hotel Maadhini, E. Car St. (☎46787), on the shore, 200m north of the temple. Carpeted rooms with bright lighting and large disinfected baths with soap and towels. Balcony views of the ocean and fishing villages. 24hr. hot water. Doubles Rs350-900.

Hotel Sangam, Main Rd. (☎46351), opposite the GPO. Less-than-tranquil location. Clean, well-lit rooms have sea views and spotless baths with seat toilets and towels. Roof-top viewings of the sunrise. 24hr. room service. Singles and doubles Rs380-900.

Kerala House (☎46229), on the seaward side of Bus Stand Rd., between the bus stand and Main Rd.; look for signs. A sort of upscale government guest house, with dining room tables, separate dressing rooms, and ocean views. Slightly faded, but still an elegant option. Doubles Rs500-750.

Hotel Narmadha, Bus Stand Rd. (☎71365), close to Main Rd. Junction. Clean, spacious doubles. Attached baths have squat toilets. Rooms Rs150-250.

FOOD

Since people come to attend to spiritual affairs and buy souvenirs, it's perhaps not surprising that material matters, like food, lean toward simple and uninspiring. The stalls, which set up at night at the junction of Main and Bus Station Rd., will slap down a banana leaf in front of you and serve excellent fast meals (chicken or fish fry with a veg. curry and *parathas*) for less than Rs25.

Hotel Saravana has two very popular branches: one on Sannadhi St., 50m in front of the temple, and another around the corner toward Main Rd. Junction. South Indian breakfasts (excellent *masala dosa* Rs16), as well as Gujarati, Rajasthani, Punjabi, and South Indian veg. *thalis* (Rs25). *Thali* meals served 11am-3pm. Both open daily 6am-10pm.

Hotel Sangam, Main Rd., opposite the GPO. One of the few places with Chinese and non-veg. fare. A wide range of slightly misspelled tasties. Most dishes Rs25-70; eggs and sandwiches Rs15-25. Open daily 6:30am-11:30pm.

Sree Bhagavath Amman Canteen, right next to the temple entrance, serves up basic food to hungry pilgrims. *Masala dosa* Rs12; veg. meal Rs15. Open daily 6am-9pm.

Anila Restaurant (or Hotel Alana depending on the sign), Bus Stand Rd., next to Hotel Narmadha, close to Main Rd. Junction. Decent, if basic, source for North Indian veg. dishes. *Aloo gobi* Rs12; meals Rs20. Open daily 7am-10:30pm.

SIGHTS AND ENTERTAINMENT

KUMARI AMMAN TEMPLE. The seaside Kumari Amman Temple, with its unmistakable red-and-white vertical temple stripes, is at the very tip of India. Dedicated to Kanya Devi, an incarnation of Parvati, the temple celebrates the penance she did in the hope of winning Shiva's hand in marriage. Shiva consented and set off for the midnight wedding ceremony. The other gods, wanting Kanya Devi to retain her divine *shakti* by remaining a virgin, hatched a plot to spoil the wedding. The sage Narada, assuming the form of a rooster, crowed for dawn long before sunrise to make Shiva think he was late for the ceremony. Shiva fell for the trick and went home, leaving poor, heartbroken Kanya Devi an eternal virgin.

Foreigners should expect to pay an entrance fee and will find it difficult to shake amateur guides. All visitors must remove their shoes to enter, and men must also shed their shirts. *(Open daily 4:30am-noon and 4-8:15pm. Rs10; camera Rs2.)*

GANDHI MANDAPAM. This unusual rendition of Orissan-style architecture overlooks the southernmost tip of India. A black marble box marks the spot where the ashes of Mahatma Gandhi were stored before being scattered seaward. The *mandapam* rises 79 ft. (23m), one for each year of Gandhi's life. It was designed so that it is hit by rays of sunlight at noon every year on October 2, his birthday. *(At the seaward end of Main Rd. Open daily 7am-7pm.)*

VIVEKANANDA MEMORIAL. Accessible only by ferry, the two rocks marking the Vivekananda Memorial sit in the Bay of Bengal east of Kanyakumari. The Hindu reformer Swami Vivekananda swam here and meditated on top of the rocks for several days in 1892 before heading to Chicago for the 1893 World Religions Conference. The glossy Vivekananda Memorial temple commemorates the event. Arrows mark a path around the island, which also houses a temple built around one of **Parvati's footprints.** The notice board at the ferry terminal on the mainland gives information on sunrise times. Expect a wait for the ferry on weekends. *(Ferries daily 7:45am-4pm. Rs10. Memorial entrance fee Rs10.)*

WANDERING MONK EXHIBITION. Infinitely more tranquil, if a little less picturesque than the other monuments, this small museum is devoted to the life of Swami Vivekananda. Panels chronicle his life, his wanderings, and his goals. For those with little prior knowledge of the Swami, it is well worth a wander. *(At the junction of Bus Stand and Main Rd. Open daily 8am-noon and 4-8pm. Rs2.)*

FISHING VILLAGE. Although the sections of Kanyakumari near the temple and the cape overflow with cheap lacquered seashells, Ray-Ban-*wallahs*, and nondescript hotels, the village on the east coast north of the hotel district has many charms—bright yellow- and lavender-colored houses, small church-shrines, and a thriving catamaran fishing business. The elegant and imposing **Holy Land of Ransom Church,** with its impressive facade, towers over the southern edge of the village.

THIRUVALLUVAR STATUE. Impossible to miss, this impressive stone statue rises from a rocky island next to the Vivekananda Rock Memorial and commemorates the Tamil poet who lived over 2000 years ago. His *Thirukkural* consists of 1330 couplets on ethical and moral themes. Accordingly, the statue stands 133 ft. high.

❀ FESTIVALS

Kanyakumari's **Pongal Festival** (Jan. 10-15) marks the end of the rice harvest with the ritual cooking and offering of South India's beloved sweet (sticky rice in earthern pots) to the Goddess. The tourist office heads trips to nearby villages to watch the festivities. The tourist office also organizes the **Cape Festival,** a celebration of Tamil culture, especially *bharata natyam* dance. Finally, **World Tourism Day** (Sept. 27) is a party of free cultural shows, free food, and free garlands for foreigners.

⚑ DAYTRIPS FROM KANYAKUMARI

Both Suchindram and Padmanabhapuram can be visited by taking bus #303 from Kany-akumari.

SUCHINDRAM TEMPLE. The beautifully carved Suchindram Temple, 13km from Kanyakumari, is dedicated to the holy trinity of Hinduism—Shiva, Vishnu, and Brahma—and contains large numbers of sculptural odds and ends, including India's only depiction of a female Ganesh. Also of note are several hollow pillars, each sounding a different musical note when hit, and a huge Hanuman statue. *(Take a rickshaw or taxi from Kanyakumari. All buses leaving Kanyakumari also pass through Suchindram (Rs3.25, 25min.). Open daily 4:30am-noon and 4:30-8:45pm.)*

PADMANABHAPURAM. Located 45km from Kanyakumari on the way to Trivandrum, Padmanabhapuram was the capital of Travancore until 1790. Padmanabhapuram's grand **palace** spans more than half of the 6½ acre grounds of the town. The original palace dates from 1550; the other buildings date from the 17th century. The mostly wooden palace has exquisitely carved teak ceilings designed by Chinese architects and a smooth black floor that has stood the test of time remarkably well considering that it is made out of charcoal, egg, coconut oil, river sand, lime, and sugar. The Travencore dynasty was matrilineal—the king's wife lived in a separate building, and the dynasty was passed on to the eldest son of the king's eldest daughter. Or something like that. The famous murals in the meditation room are being restored, but the beautiful grounds and building are definitely worth the trek. *(Bus #303 from Kanyakumari goes to Thuckalai (every 15min., 1¼hr.). From Thuckalai bus station, backtrack, head left downhill at the fork, turn right at the next fork, and then right again to the palace (20min.); or take a rickshaw or local bus #13D. Frequent buses head back to Kanyakumari. Open Tu-Su 9am-4:30pm; ticket counter closed 1-2pm. Rs6, camera fee Rs16. Knowledgeable guides accompany you through the palace; circumvent the large groups and have a small English tour—guides expect baksheesh.)*

HILL STATIONS

KODAIKANAL கொடைக் கானல்   ☎ 04542

Set apart from major cities by towering cliffs and protected forests, the flower-filled haven of Kodaikanal rises above the flatlands as one of Tamil Nadu's most popular hill stations. The heady scent of eucalyptus mingles with the fresh breezes that blow across Kodai's mountainside, covered in blue-gums and *kurinji* blossoms. During the hottest months of the year (Apr.-June), the town swarms with foreigners and middle class Indian tourists, who descend en masse to stroll along the gentle slopes to breathe the crisp country air. It was the Brits who kicked off this trend in the 1840s, when they designed Kodai as an antidote to the sweltering, malaria-infested plains. Today, Kodai remains largely free of noise and pollution, and its surroundings are arguably the most beautiful of any hill station. Thankfully, the daily temperature is usually 10-20°C cooler than in Madras, and the nights are often nippy enough for warm shawls and fireplaces.

▐ GETTING THERE AND GETTING AROUND

Trains: Kodaikanal Road Station (☎ 4543) 38226) is a 3hr. bus ride from town. Fares listed are 2nd class. From Kodaikanal Rd. to **Madras** (4 per day, 8-11pm, Rs159).

Buses: The **bus stand** is a dirt lot just off Anna Salai, on Wood Will Rd. A very helpful reservations and inquiry booth is open daily 9:30am-5:30pm. To: **Bangalore** (6pm, 12hr., Rs165); **Coimbatore** (8:30am and 4:30pm, 6hr., Rs35); **Dindigul** (every hr., 3hr., Rs22); **Kanyakumari** (8:30am, 9hr., Rs96); **Madras** (6:30pm, 12hr., Rs157); **Madurai** (every 30min., 6:45am-9:30pm, 4hr., Rs26); **Ooty** (8:30am, 9hr., Rs55); **Palani** (every hr., 3hr., Rs15); **Trichy** (3 per day, 1:30-5:30pm, 6hr., Rs45). A number of **private bus** operators with offices on Anna Salai offer deluxe bus service to Bangalore, Madras, Madurai, Ooty, and Coimbatore (Rs100-700).

Local Transportation: The best way to get around is on foot or by bike. **Bike rental** is available in the lake area (Rs10 per hr.; Rs50-75 per day). **Taxis** are also available outside the bus stand to help you deal with Kodai's hilly roads (minimum charge Rs50).

✴❷ ORIENTATION AND PRACTICAL INFORMATION

Kodai is all about elevation. Buses pull into a lot on the corner of **Anna Salai Rd.** and **Wood Will Rd.,** by the Hotel Astoria. Going uphill on Wood Will Rd. (toward the bus reservation booth), leads to **Coaker's Walk,** the Youth Hostel, and to **Pillar Rocks** and other scenic points. Downhill on Anna Salai are most of the budget hotels and the post office. Flat along Anna Salai in the other direction is a large intersection with restaurant-rich **Hospital Rd.** From here, the lake is down the hill to the left.

Tourist Office: (☎ 41675), on the northern side of Anna Salai, a 2min. walk east of the bus stand; look for the glut of tourist vans. Open daily 10am-5pm.

Budget Travel: For bus, train, and airline bookings, try the **Almond Travel Agency** (☎ 43376) near Hilltop Towers Hotel, Club Rd. Open M-Sa 9am-9pm.

Currency Exchange: State Bank of India (☎ 41068), next to the tourist office, changes traveler's checks in US$ and UK£. Open M-F 10am-2pm, Sa 10am-noon.

Bookstore: CLS Bookstore (☎ 40465), opposite the tourist office. Sells maps of the area. Open M-Sa 9am-1pm and 2-6pm.

Market and Pharmacy: Kurunji Mini Super Market, next to the post office, or **Spencer's** next to Hilltop towers.

Hospital: Government Hospital (☎ 41292). From the Seven Road Junction, follow PT Rd. north for about 250m; the hospital is on the right, before Law's Ghat Rd. **Van Allen** (☎ 40273) is a reputable private hospital near Coaker's Walk.

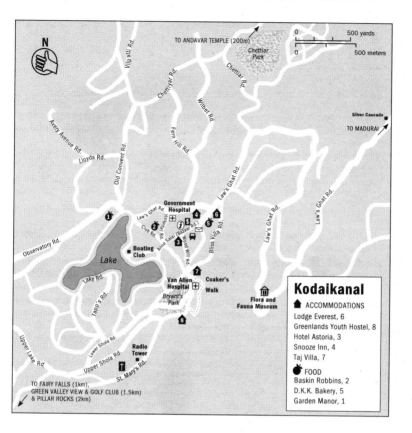

Kodaikanal

🏠 ACCOMMODATIONS
Lodge Everest, 6
Greenlands Youth Hostel, 8
Hotel Astoria, 3
Snooze Inn, 4
Taj Villa, 7

🍎 FOOD
Baskin Robbins, 2
D.K.K. Bakery, 5
Garden Manor, 1

Police: (☎ 40262 or 100), diagonally opposite the post office on Anna Salai.

Post Office: (☎ 41267), a huge yellow building on Anna Salai, opposite Snooze Inn. Open M-F 8:30am-5pm. **Postal Code:** 624101.

🔥 ACCOMMODATIONS

Every other building in Kodai seems to have rooms for rent. The cheapest lodgings are along Anna Salai. As you move away from the town center, quality and prices increase exponentially. The high season runs from April to mid-June.

🔲 **Greenlands Youth Hostel,** St. Mary's Rd. (☎ 40899). From the bus stand go uphill on Wood Will Rd. and past Coaker's Walk on St. Mary's Rd. for about 10min. Situated in a secluded little spot near a cliff, the grassy terraces and welcoming porch of the appropriately-named Greenlands command absolutely stunning views of the plains and ridges in the distance. The staff is friendly, the manager is knowledgeable, and the travelers who chat over morning coffee never want to leave. Clean, private rooms with attached bath; some with fireplace. Hot water in the mornings for Rs10. Dorm beds Rs75; doubles Rs350. Off-season: Rs55/175-300.

Taj Villa, St. Mary's Rd. (☎ 43556), at the start of Coaker's Walk. The view from the patio almost rivals the one from the Youth Hostel. Tastefully furnished, spotless rooms with 24hr. hot water, telephone, and TV. The white-washed deluxe rooms in the old stone building are an off-season steal. Doubles Rs490-790. Off-season: Rs250-490.

Lodge Everest, Anna Salai (☎40100). A wood-paneled lobby leads to two levels of green, cave-like rooms. Small attached bucket baths, some with seat toilet. Hot water in the morning. Doubles Rs350-350. Off-season: Rs125-150.

Hotel Astoria (☎40524), at the intersection of Wood Will Rd. and Anna Salai. Upscale, popular place retains a homey feel. Large beds, seat toilets, and satellite TV. Hot water all day. Doubles Rs690. Off-season: Rs350. 20% luxury tax, 15% off-season.

Snooze Inn, Anna Salai (☎40837). Beds with cushioned headrests, surrounded by soft red carpet. Tiny TVs in all rooms. Ultra-clean, tiled bathrooms have seat toilets and hot water. Doubles Rs575. Off-season: Rs300. 20% luxury tax, 15% off-season.

▐ FOOD

Kodai's restaurant scene caters to the culinary tastes of its cosmopolitan visitors. If you don't leave town a kilo or two heavier, you've probably missed out. Many excellent restaurants line Hospital Rd., north of the Seven Road Junction.

Tibetan Brothers Restaurant, PT Rd., 2nd fl., on the left. Mouth-watering cuisine served by a Tibetan family. Crispy vegetable *momos* (Rs35), lemon tea (Rs25), Tibetan bread (Rs10), and steaming hot chocolate (Rs12) are perfect for a cool day in Kodai. Open daily noon-4pm and 5:30-10pm.

Hotel Astoria. See **Accommodations,** above. This popular people-watching spot is famous for Indian favorites at reasonable prices. Rajana curry Rs25; *channa patura* Rs24; onion *oothapam* Rs15; and lunchtime *thali* Rs23. Open daily 7am-9:30pm.

Hotel Punjab, Hospital Rd., visible from Seven Road Junction. Classy restaurant serving lip-smackin' tandoori dishes: chicken *tikka* kebab Rs60; Punjabi chicken Rs80; and cucumber *raita* Rs18. Open daily 10am-10pm.

Kavi Bala Cafe, opposite the bus stand. Well-priced vegetarian delights, including a green salad, in the dim, refined aura of a classy hotel restaurant. Entrees Rs35-45; soup Rs25. Open daily 6:30am-10:30pm.

Green Manor Restaurant, Lake Rd. near Convent Rd. When the sun sets over the lake, and you can't take one more plastic cafeteria-like setting, wander over to this quiet, romantic garden overlooking the lake. Indian and Chinese entrees Rs45-60.

Chef Master, Hospital Rd., Gratifyingly grease-free Chinese and Indian food draws locals and foreigners alike. Assortment of chow mein (Rs30-40), soups (Rs18-35), and chicken dishes (Rs50-70). Open daily 9:30am-10pm.

D.D.K. Bakery, Anna Salai, by the big stone wall. The sweetest of sweets and the most savory of savories, all baked fresh daily. Open 7:30am-10pm.

Eco-Nut, Hospital Rd. Crunchy munchies galore. Almonds, walnuts, health nuts (Rs45 per 100g), whole grain muffins (Rs12), and dried fruits (Rs60 per 100g).

◉ ▟ SIGHTS AND SCENERY

THE LAKE AND ENVIRONS. Tourist activity centers on the man-made lake; the 5km path that leads around it is a pleasant bike ride. There are **bike rental** places and **horseback riding** between the boat club and Bryant Park on Lake Rd. *(Bike rental Rs100 per hr.)* Those cute, little paddleboats can be rented at the historic **Kodaikanal Boating Club.** *(Rs8 per person per 30min.; rowboat Rs40 per 30min; canopy boats Rs80 per 30min. Open 9am-noon and 2-6:30pm.)* Boats are also available at the **T.T.D.C. Boathouse** *(2-seat paddleboat Rs40 per 30min; rowboat and 4-seat paddle Rs80 per 30min. Open 9am-5:30pm.)* Just south of the lake is **Bryant's Park** with a **botanical garden** founded in 1902. Expertly trimmed and clipped by a a staff of 45, the gardens are ablaze with flowers, trees, and cacti. *(Open daily 8:45am-6pm. Rs5; camera fee Rs25.)*

COAKER'S WALK. Kodai's most famous scenic promenade is Coaker's Walk, a 10-minute stroll along a paved precipice that traces an arc from Taj Villa to Green-land's Youth Hostel. On clear mornings, the views of the surrounding hills and plains are amazing—you can see as far as Madurai. A small **telescope house** near the far end gives you a closer look at the surrounding countryside. *(Open daily 7am-7pm. Rs2; camera fee Rs5; telescope house Rs1.)*

PILLAR ROCKS, GREEN VALLEY VIEW, AND BERIJAM LAKE. Get a taste of Kodai's best scenery at **Pillar Rocks,** a series of hulking cliffs that plunge down into the valley below. For the Kodak moment of your dreams, stop at **Green Valley View**, a roadside promontory that doubles as tour bus central. *(From town, bike 8km up Upper Shola Rd. past Fairy Falls and the Golf Club. Garden park open 8am-8pm.)* Farther uphill is **Moir Point,** where the road splits to continue downhill to town via Observatory Rd., or to **Berijam Lake.** *(Permission from the District Forest Officer in Kodai is required for travel to the lake by car or to Silent Valley or Cap Play View. Get a permit at least one day in advance.* ☎ *40287. Open daily 10am-5:30pm. Free.)*

DOLPHIN'S NOSE AND VELLAGAVI VILLAGE. A pleasant hour's stroll through a hillside village and shimmering eucalyptus stands leads to the breathtaking prom-ontory known as **Dolphin's Nose.** The gorgeous views continue as the rocky path winds downhill, eventually reaching the terraced farms of Vellagavi, which has only three streets and friendly residents who offer coffee. *(From Coaker's Walk, follow signs to La Salette shrine, continue on the cobbled road until it dips, and then take the dirt path to the left. Cross the bridge when you come to it and stay left. Make another left at the sign for Voyce. Keep left through the village of turquoise houses. One hour down to Dolphin's Nose. For Vellagavi, allow at least 7hr. and 2 bottles of water.)*

CHETTIAR PARK. A secluded spot, Chettiar Park is the center of attention every 12 years, when the chronically shy *kurinji* plant springs into colorful bloom; blos-soms are next scheduled for 2006. Don't call the police if you see some flower before then, though—there are a few plants whose biological clocks are off-kilter. Just past Chettiar Park is the simple **Kurinji Andavar Temple** (dedicated to Murugan), with a viewing platform. *(3km northeast of the bus stand.)*

OTHER SIGHTS. The **Flora and Fauna Museum,** on the grounds of the Sacred Heart College, features a fine orchid house. *(Follow Law's Ghat Rd. southeast and out of town for 3km. Open M-Sa 9:30am-noon and 3-6pm. Rs1.)* About 800m past the museum is **Silver Cascade**, a small waterfall along the road to Madurai.

COIMBATORE கோயம் டுத்தூர் ☎ 0422

Perhaps it is the city's proximity to Kerala, the lights that impose some degree of order on the traffic, or the protective ring of the surrounding mountains. Somehow, Coimbatore manages to maintain an air of organized calm even as its bus stands and railway stations bulge with travelers, most of them on their way either to or from Ooty, Kerala, or Karnataka. Most travelers are quite happy to stop here just long enough to check their email and grab a few hours of sleep before hopping onto their next bus, leaving most of this pulsating industrial city unexplored.

◪ **GETTING THERE AND GETTING AROUND.** Coimbatore's **airport** is 10km northeast of the city center. Indian Airlines (☎399833) has daily flights to: **Bombay** (8:25pm, US$150) and **Madras** (8:25pm, US$90) via **Bangalore. Jet Airways** (☎212034) offers daily service to: **Bombay** (2:35pm, 2hr., US$150) and **Madras** (12:35pm, 1hr., US$90). **Coimbatore Junction Railway Station** is on Bank Rd., in the southern part of the city. (Reservations ☎131. Open M-Sa 8am-8pm, Su 8am-2pm). Fares listed are 2nd class. To: **Bangalore** (3-4 per day, 4:45am-noon, 7hr.; Rs138); **Bombay** (2-3 per day, 5am-11:30pm, 23hr., Rs343); **Cochin** (2-5 per day, 6am-6:45pm, 5hr., Rs95); **Delhi** (8:20pm, 20hr., Rs572); **Kanyakumari** via **Trivandrum**

(5-11 per day, 5am-1:20am, 12hr., Rs149); **Madras** (8-12 per day, 6am-10:45pm, 8hr., Rs132); **Madurai** (3 per day, 7:40am-11:30pm, 6hr., Rs115); **Ooty** (5am, 2hr., Rs40; connects in Mettapalayam to toy train, 7:30am, 5hr.).

Three of the city's four **bus stands** are at the northern end of Dr. Nanjappa Rd., 1½km from the railway station. The **Town Bus Stand** (known as **Gandhipuram** to the locals), marked by the pedestrian flyover on Nanjappa Rd., provides efficient local service, including buses to the railway station (#55, 57, or 24; Rs1). Behind Gandhipuram, on Cross Cut Rd., is a station with reservation desks for Tamil Nadu, Kerala, and Karnataka State Buses. (☎434969. Reservation desks open daily 7am-10pm.) There is a distinct whiff of rivalry and a sorry lack of communication between state systems—doublecheck everything. Buses go to: **Bangalore** (5 per day, 6:30am-10pm, 11hr., Rs99); **Cochin** (every 2hr., 6hr., Rs45); **Madras** (every hr., 6am-10pm, 11hr., Rs158); **Madurai** (every hr., 6hr., Rs42); **Mysore** (10 per day, 7:30am-11pm, 6hr., Rs55). Buses to Bangalore and Madras also leave from the **State (Central) Bus Stand,** just south of Gandhipuram, on the opposite side of Dr. Nanjappa Rd. It also serves **Ooty** (every 30min., 3hr., Rs21). A fourth stand, **Ukkadam,** 1½km south of the other three, services smaller towns to the south. Buses from Kerala and other southern destinations arrive here. Buses to: **Madurai** (5 per day, 6am-5pm); **Munnar** (8:15am and 2:25pm); **Thrissur** (4 per day, 5:30am-2pm, 3½hr., Rs40). From Gandhipuram, **local buses** #3, 15, 47, 69, 91 run to the State Bus Stand. Bus #38B runs from Ukkadam to the railway station.

◼️🛈 ORIENTATION AND PRACTICAL INFORMATION. Coimbatore's city limits expand almost daily with the influx of new residents, but the area of interest to travelers is fairly self-contained. Home to a number of tourist services, the north-south thoroughfare of **Bank Rd.** heads north from the bank; it forks 200m before it hits **Mill Rd.** (called **Avinashi Rd.** farther east). The right fork feeds into Avinashi Rd. The left fork hits Mill Rd. and continues north as **Dr. Nanjappa Rd.,** Coimbatore's congested main drag. **State Bank of India,** Bank Rd., changes money. (☎803251. Open M-F 10am-2pm, Sa 10am-noon.) **Pharmacies** dot the bus stand and train station area. **KG Hospital** (☎212121), open 24 hours, is near the railway station on Art College Rd. There is a **police station** (☎216749) on Bank Rd., near the railway station, and another (☎302005) close to the bus stands. The **Head Post Office** is on Railway Feeder Rd.; from the intersection of Mill and Dr. Nanjappa Rd., head west and take the first left after Hotel Sri Thevar (open M-F 10am-5pm). Access the **Internet** at **Krisan Business Center,** 1 Art College Rd., 300m to the right as you face the hospital (☎214716; Rs40 per 30min.) or at **Netsea** in Raj Rajeswara Tower, opposite Gandhipuram bus stand. **Postal Code:** 641001.

🏠🍴 ACCOMMODATIONS AND FOOD. Coimbatore's best hotels and restaurants are around the bus stands, but there are a few cheaper hotels near the railway station. The best option if you need to catch an early train might be the **railway retiring rooms,** upstairs in the station building, opposite the computerized reservation area. Immaculate (and often full), the enormous blue rooms with attached baths are set along a shiny hallway; the only drawback is the noise. (Rooms Rs250-300, with A/C Rs300-350.) A small path directly across the street from the railway station entrance leads to several good budget options, including **Hotel Anand Vihar,** which has basic rooms with baths and squat toilets. (☎300580. Singles Rs60; doubles Rs110.) **New Vijaya Lodge,** also in this area, is a good option, with freshly painted rooms. (Singles Rs95; doubles 150-250). **Hotel Tamil Nadu,** down the street from the town bus stand, on Dr. Nanjappa Rd., has standard rooms. (☎302176. Singles Rs195; doubles Rs325-600; 20% luxury tax.) There are also plenty of high-rise hotels in the same price range along Nehru St. and Sastri Rd., opposite the central bus stand. For cheap food, head to **Sree Annapoorna,** at the State Bus Stand on Dr. Nanjappa Rd., where you will probably

Hmm, call home or eat lunch?

With **YOU**^{SM}

you can do both.

Nathan Lane for YOU^{SM}.

No doubt, traveling on a budget is tough. So tear out this wallet guide and keep it with you during your travels. With YOU, calling home from overseas is affordable and easy.

If the wallet guide is missing, call collect 913-624-5336 or visit www.youcallhome.com for YOU country numbers.

Pack the Wallet Guide
and save 25% or more* on calls home to the U.S.

It's lightweight and carries heavy savings of 25% or more*
over AT&T USA Direct and MCI WorldPhone rates. So take this
YOU wallet guide and carry it wherever you go.

To save with YOU:
- Dial the access number of the country you're in (see reverse)
- Dial 04 or follow the English voice prompts
- Enter your credit card info for easy billing

Service provided by Sprint

find every traveler in town slurping *sambar* by the bucketful. (Meals Rs21. Open daily 7:30am-10pm.) **Cloud Nine,** at the Hotel City Tower, tosses up Indian, Chinese, and continental dishes ranging from Rs60 to Rs105 and has stunning views of the mountains. (Open daily 11am-3pm and 7-11:45pm.) Next door, the **Heritage Inn** has an excellent breakfast buffet for Rs97 (open daily 7:30am-10:30pm). For dessert, do not pass **New Kosikori Pure Ghee Sweets,** on the corner by the State Bus Stand, without buying something!

OOTY (UDHAGAMANDALAM) உண்டி ☎0423

Cotton wool-wrapped in layers of movie mystique, the hill station of Ooty is a favorite backdrop for Indian filmmakers and something of a promised land for many of the country's holiday-makers too. Established in 1821 by John Sullivan, an enterprising collector with the East India Company, Ooty quickly earned a reputation as a high-class getaway. No longer the exclusive retreat of the gin-and-tonic-at-sundown crowd, Ooty is often overrun with tourists: exhaust fumes dirty the crisp mountain air, sewage clogs the once-pristine lake, and the booming hotel and package-tour industries do their best to make a mess of Ooty's quiet charm.

It's not hard, however, to escape the crowds, and a bit of off-the-beaten-track exploring will soon bring you face-to-face with what made Ooty special in the first place: the laid-back locals; the tea, potato, and carrot plantations; and the mighty Mt. Doddabetta, which, at 2638m, is about as close as you can get to heaven in South India. Ooty's season runs from April to mid-June and from September to October, when temperatures hover around a dry 25°C during the day, and the nights can be chilly. Monsoon season runs from July to August. Ooty's cold, relatively dry winter stretches from November to March.

▐ GETTING THERE AND GETTING AROUND

Trains: Railway Station, North Lake Rd. Reservations counter open daily 10am-noon and 3:30-4:30pm. The Blue Mountain Railway (the "toy train") chugs through tea and potato plantations and past waterfalls; like the rest of Ooty, it is often crowded. Fares listed are 2nd class. To **Coonoor** (9:15am, 12:15, 3, and 6pm; return 7:45, 10:40am, 1:35, and 4:30pm; Rs5) and **Mettupalayam** (9:15am and 3pm; return 7:10am and 1:15pm; Rs10).

Buses: The **bus stand** is 100m south of the railway station. Regular and private buses operate out of one dusty lot. The departure bays are labeled in English (wow!), and the buses actually use them, most of the time. The **TSTC** reservations counter (☎494969) is open daily 9:30am-1pm and 1:30-5pm. Make reservations for long-distance buses 2 days in advance. To: **Bangalore** (every 30-90min., 9:30am-2pm and 8:30-10:30pm, 8hr., Rs109-128); **Calicut** (4 per day, 6:30am-3:15pm, 6hr., Rs54); **Coimbatore** (every 10min., 6:45am-5:20pm, 3hr., Rs30); **Hassan** (10am, 8hr., Rs91); **Kodaikanal** (6:15am, 8hr., Rs70); **Madikeri** (11am and 6pm, 8hr., Rs82); **Madras** (5:45pm, 8hr., Rs133); **Mysore** (8am and 3:30pm, 5hr., Rs45). **Karnataka State Road Transport Corporation (KSRTC)** has a reservations counter open daily 6:30am-10:30pm. To: **Bangalore** (6:30, 8:30am, and 10:30pm; Rs125); **Hassan** (11:30am and 3pm, Rs90); **Mysore** (9am and 1:30pm, Rs50). Local **TTRC** buses go to: **Coonoor** (frequent, 5:30am-11pm, 30min., Rs5); **Doddabetta Junction** (every 30min., 20min., Rs4); **Doddabetta Peak** (11:30am, 30min., Rs5); **Mettupalayam** (every 15min., 5:30am-8:30pm, Rs14); **Mudumalai** (every 30min., 3hr., Rs31); **Pykara** (every 30 min., 6:30am-4:30pm, 30min., Rs6).

Local Transportation: Unmetered **auto-rickshaws** charge at least Rs15 for a ride from the railway station to Charing Cross.

⚡ 🔢 ORIENTATION AND PRACTICAL INFORMATION

Getting around Ooty can be tricky because its streets snake about the valley and surrounding mountainsides. Not to worry—the town is fairly small, and locals are used to directing tourists. Ooty's expansive **lake** is in the southwest of town, a 200m walk west from the **railway station** and the **bus stand** along **North Lake Rd.** From the railway station, walk northeast for 1½km along **Upper Bazaar Rd.** to get to **Charing Cross** in the town center. From the bus stand, you can reach Charing Cross by skirting the fruit market via **Lower Bazaar Rd.**, which becomes **Commercial Rd.** 750m before it hits Charing Cross. From Charing Cross, follow **Garden Rd.** 1km north to reach the **Botanical Gardens.** Climb the hill 500m behind Charing Cross to reach **Town West Circle.** From there, **Hospital Rd.** makes a steep and lengthy westward descent to the railway station area.

Tourist Office: The new **Government of Tamil Nadu Tourist Office,** Wenlock Rd. (☎443977), 200m from Charing Cross. Open M-F 10am-5:45pm. For trekking information and reservations for government accommodations at **Mudumalai Wildlife Sanctuary** (see p. 595), contact the **Wildlife Warden** (☎444098), between the tourist office and Town West Circle, next to the Superintendent of Police Office. Open M-F 10am-5:45pm. Trekking requires a permit, obtainable 1 to 2 weeks in advance from the Udhagamandalam Forest Department, behind the tourist office. The Deputy Forest Officer (north; ☎443968) issues permits for the northern and eastern Nilgiris; the DFO (south; ☎444083) handles the southern Nilgiris.

Budget Travel: Tourist agencies are as common as *paan* stalls, and they all offer the same unimaginative tours of Ooty and environs. **Thomson Tours and Travels** (☎443111), in the strip of stores at Hotel Charing Cross, books plane tickets and bus tours to nearby cities (from Rs75). Open daily 9am-5:30pm.

Currency Exchange: State Bank of India, Town West Circle (☎444099). Changes AmEx and Thomas Cook traveler's checks in US$ and UK£. Open M-F 10am-2pm and 3-5:50pm, Sa 10am-noon.

Bookstore: Higginbothams, Commercial Rd. (☎443736), next to the tourist office. Open Th-Tu 9:30am-1pm and 3:30-7:30pm.

Market: K. Chellaram's, Commercial Rd. (☎442229), has cheese, toilet paper, and Nilgiri tea. What more could you want? Open daily 9:30am-1:30pm and 3-7:30pm.

Police: Town West Circle (☎443973), near the collector's office.

Hospital: Government Hospital, Jail Hill, Hospital Rd. (☎442212). **Vijaya Hospital,** Ettines Rd. (☎442500), behind Alankar Theatres.

Internet: Globalnet, Commercial Rd., 50m past Tandoor Mahal, on the opposite side of the street. Rs60 per hr. Open daily 8:30am-10:30pm.

Post Office: Town West Circle (☎443791). From the traffic circle, head northwest up the steep staircase on the side of the hill. Open M-Sa 9am-5pm. **Postal Code:** 643001.

▮ ACCOMMODATIONS

Seeing that this *is* a resort town, it should come as no surprise that most of Ooty's buildings are hotels. The lake area has more spacious and quieter lodging options.

▧ **Hotel Mount View,** Ettines Rd. (☎443307 or 444182). Colonial house-turned-hotel with spacious rooms and pine-wood floors—very Raj-reminiscent. Seat toilets; hot water in the morning. Doubles Rs300-700. Off-season: Rs199-300. 15% luxury tax.

▧ **The Reflections Guest House,** North Lake Rd. (☎443834), 500m west of the bus stand. The proprietress, Mrs. Dique, is legendary in backpacker circles for her home-cooked meals and maternal disposition. Soft beds, wild flowers, and a lake view. Clean bathrooms with seat toilets. Heat in the winter; hot water 6-11am. Check-out noon. Reserve 14 days ahead in-season. Rooms Rs400-500. Off-season: Rs250-350.

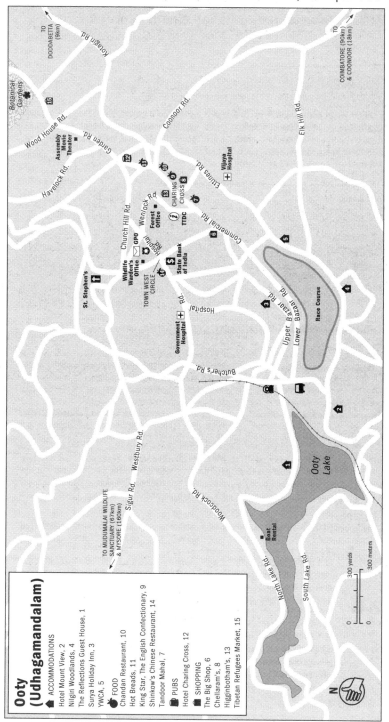

Ooty (Udhagamandalam)

▲ ACCOMMODATIONS
Hotel Mount View, 2
Nilgiri Woodlands, 4
The Reflections Guest House, 1
Surya Holiday Inn, 3
YWCA, 5

● FOOD
Chandan Restaurant, 10
Hot Breads, 11
King Star, The English Confectionary, 9
Shinkow's Chinese Restaurant, 14
Tandoor Mahal, 7

▲ PUBS
Hotel Charing Cross, 12

■ SHOPPING
The Big Shop, 6
Chellaram's, 8
Higginbotham's, 13
Tibetan Refugees Market, 15

TO MUDUMALAI WILDLIFE
SANCTUARY (67km)
& MYSORE (160km)

TO
DODDABETTA
(9km)

TO
COIMBATORE (90km)
& COONOOR (18km)

Botanical
Gardens

Assembly
Movie
Theater

Vijaya
Hospital

Wood House Rd.
Garden Rd.
Havelock Rd.
Wenlock Rd.
Church Hill Rd.
Coonoor Rd.
Elk Hill Rd.
Ettines Rd.
CHARING
CROSS

Forest
Office
TTDC
GPO
Wildlife
Warden's
Office
TOWN WEST
CIRCLE
State Bank
of India

St. Stephen's

Government
Hospital
Hospital

Butcher's Rd.
Sigur Rd.
Westbury Rd.
Woodcock Rd.
Upper Bazaar Rd.
Lower Bazaar Rd.

Race Course

Ooty
Lake

Boat
Rental

North Lake Rd.
South Lake Rd.

0   300 yards
0   300 meters

N

TAMIL NADU

Surya Holiday Inn, Upper Bazaar (☎442567). One of the few decent hotels in the Bazaar and Commercial Rd. area. The best deal in town. Hot water 7:30-8:30am; squat toilets. Check-out noon. Singles Rs150; doubles Rs250.

YWCA, Ettines Rd. (☎442218), 500m from the racetrack. Sparkling cottages with wicker chairs and seat toilets. Sunlit sitting room in the main building with TV and piano. Grungy dorms are best avoided. Attached restaurant. Check-out 11:30am. Dorm beds Rs77; cottages Rs300-1040. Off-season: Rs66/195-655.

Nilgiri Woodlands, Ettines Rd. (☎442551 or 442451), on top of the hill, on the southern side of the racetrack. Spacious rooms with high ceilings, antique furniture, and carpets. Clean attached baths with seat toilets and 24hr. hot water. Check-out noon. Rooms Rs450-1150; cottages Rs950. Off-season: Rs300-900/500. AmEx, MC, Visa.

◖ FOOD

Chandan Restaurant, Commercial Rd., in Hotel Nahar at Charing Cross. Carefully prepared vegetarian selections (Rs45-60) served in heated *kadhais* in a wood-paneled room. Popular with Indian families. Open daily noon-3:30pm and 7-10:30pm.

Shinkow's Chinese Restaurant, 38-42 Commissioners Rd. (☎442811), opposite the State Bank of India, Town West Circle. Serving mouth-watering but overpriced stir-fry to locals and tourists since 1954. The food includes sliced beef (shhhh!) with broccoli (Rs50-70) and cashew chicken (Rs80-100). Open daily 9am-4pm and 6-10pm.

Hot Breads, Charing Cross (☎445333), near the international school. Warm, freshly baked breads, pizzas, and pastries. Butter buns Rs10; chicken burgers Rs40; and exquisite slices of chocolate truffle cake Rs16. Open daily 10am-8:30pm.

King Star, The English Confectionery, Commercial Rd. (☎445742), a few hundred meters from Charing Cross. Milk chocolate walnut, fudge, or mango-flavored chocolate Rs 30-45 per 100g. Open F-W 11:30am-8:30pm.

Tandoor Mahal, 69 Commercial Rd. Efficient service. Tandoori and Chinese food Rs20–125. Open daily 9:30am-3:30pm and 6:30pm-midnight.

◖ SIGHTS

BOTANICAL GARDENS. Ooty's Botanical Gardens were originally established in 1847 and spruced up again in 1995. A century and a half after they were opened, they are as green as ever. With more than 2000 species on display, the gardens have come a long way from their original purpose of producing "English vegetables at reasonable cost." From the vivid colors of the rose garden to the quiet, well-sculpted knolls that surround the park, the whole area is gorgeous. *(Open daily 8am-6:30pm. Rs5; camera fee Rs25, video Rs500.)*

OTHER SIGHTS. Just west of the railway station and bus stand is Ooty's lily-filled, sewage-stopped **lake,** constructed in the 1820s by good old John Sullivan. *(Rowboats and pedal boats Rs50 per 30min.; boat house admission Rs3; camera fee Rs10.)* Near the boat house is a **miniature train.** *(Rs5 a whirl.)* **Horse rentals** near the lake are officially Rs150 per hour, though you should be able to bargain them down.

♫ ▮ ENTERTAINMENT AND SHOPPING

If occupied at all, **bars** in Ooty usually have just a few sorry-looking men mumbling to each other in a darkened corner. A slightly more cheerful watering hole is the bar at **Hotel Charing Cross.** (☎444387. Kingfisher Rs40. Open daily 11am-11pm.)

Atari-nostalgics can satisfy their urges at one of several **arcades** along Commercial Rd. **Moodmaker's** is near the Hotel Charing Cross, beyond the brandy shop. (Open daily 10am-9:30pm.) Farther down the street is the underground **Missing Link,** 49 Commercial Rd, where bug-eyed boys dish out Rs1 for a game of

Pac-Man, Super Mario Bros., or Tetris. (Open daily 10am-6pm.) About 750m up from Moodmaker's on Garden Rd. is the **Assembly Movie Theater,** which screens dated American flicks. (2:30 and 6:30pm; Sa 2:30, 6, and 8:30pm. Rs2-12.) The **Race Course,** near the bus stand, is a 1¼-mile loop where jodhpured jockeys run their horses to the delight of riotous but low-betting crowds. Races are held from April to June.

Shopping in Ooty revolves around locally made body oils and textiles. **The Big Shop,** halfway between Charing Cross and the Lower Bazaar on Commercial Rd., sells Toda tribal shawls (Rs200-300), silver jewelry, and handicrafts. (☎444136. Open daily 8am-8:30pm. Traveler's checks, MC, Visa, and AmEx accepted.) A **Tibetan Refugees' Market,** along Garden Rd., near the Botanical Gardens, has stands selling mohair sweaters and colorful wool blankets. (Open daily 6am-8:30pm.)

★ DAYTRIP FROM OOTY: PYKARA டைகாரா

Twenty kilometers west of Ooty is the tranquil village of **Pykara,** the perfect place for anybody longing for the hills. A small boathouse on Pykara's lake rents out boats and sells snacks for visitors to munch on as they float on the waters. *(Boats Rs50-100 per 30min.)* Near the lake is **Pykara Dam,** 2½km downstream, with an attractive series of rocky **waterfalls,** especially impressive during July and August. *(All buses to Gudalur from Ooty pass through Pykara every 30min., 6:30am-9pm.)* If you're up for the climb, the 9km hike up **Mt. Doddabetta** gives you views you won't get from an aisle seat of a tour bus. *(Trail open daily 8:30am-5:30pm, 2hr. long.)* No visit to Ooty's surroundings would be complete without a **Filmy Chakkar** ("Film Trip"), a tour of scenic spots where romantic pairs have frolicked before Bollywood's cameras.

NEAR OOTY: COONOOR குன்னூர்

Deep in the tea-growing region of the Nilgiris, the quiet and calm of Coonoor come as a welcome break from the commercial bustle of Ooty, only 18km away. Coonoor is easily accessible (see **Ooty: Getting There and Getting Around,** p. 591); it's getting out to the spectacular panoramic views that takes a bit of effort.

▆ GETTING THERE AND GETTING AROUND. Trains creak along narrow-gauge tracks to: **Mettupalayam** (10:35am and 4:15pm, 2hr., Rs8) and **Ooty** (4 per day, 7:45am-4:30pm, 1½hr., Rs5). **Buses** go to: **Coimbatore** (frequent, 6:30am-8pm, 2hr., Rs16) via **Mettupalayam** (1hr., Rs9); **Dolphin's Nose** and **Lamb's Rock** (every 2hr., 7:30am-6:30pm, 30min., Rs4); **Ooty** (frequent, 5:30am-10:30pm, 45min., Rs5). It is probably easier to hire a **taxi** for the sights (Rs250-400), so that you can take your time and not be at the mercy of mass transport. **Auto-rickshaws** run between Lower and Upper Coonoor (Rs20-25); the **local buses** along Mount Rd. follow the same route for less (Rs2).

▆▆ ORIENTATION AND PRACTICAL INFORMATION. The town is separated into two parts: the railway station and bus stand are in the town center of Lower Coonoor, down in the valley; most of the attractions are in Upper Coonoor, around **Bedford Circle.** The **railway station** and **bus stand** are on the Ooty-Mettupalayam Rd., near **Mount Rd.,** which winds 2km up to **Upper Coonoor.** The **police station** (☎30100), the **post office** (open M-F 9am-2pm, Sa 9am-noon), and **Sagayamatha Hospital** (☎31919) are all on Balaclava Hill. From the bus stand, go straight across the railway tracks past the Gandhi statue, 200 meters up the road, and take the steps up the steep slope to the left.

▆▆ ACCOMMODATIONS AND FOOD. Most of the places to stay are in Upper Coonoor. The **YWCA "Wyoming" Guest House,** on the road between the bus stand and Mount Rd., up the hill past the Mar Thoma Syrian church, is one of the most congenial places in the whole of South India. Rooms overlook tea and flower gardens from a bluff above the bazaar. Home-cooked meals (Rs40-60) and 24-hour hot water are provided. (☎34426. Singles Rs200; doubles Rs400.) The **Quality Restaurant,** Mount Rd., near Bedford Circle, serves decent Indian and Chinese food. (Most dishes Rs35-70. Open daily 8am-10:30pm.) The **railway retiring rooms** in Lower Coonoor are convenient. (Mar.-June and Aug.-Oct.: doubles Rs200; off-season: Rs125.) **Anupam Restaurant,** 25A Mount Rd., near the bus stand, serves cheap meals for Rs15 and good *idlis* for Rs5. (Open daily 8am-10pm.)

■ **SIGHTS.** Coonoor's response to Ooty's Botanical Gardens is Sim's Park, high on a hill on the road to Kotagiri, 3km from the Coonoor bus stand. Set in a small ravine, the park displays varieties of flowers and plants not found in Ooty. *(Open daily 8am-6:30pm. Rs5, children Rs2; camera fee Rs5, video Rs25.)* Travel around Coonoor invariably involves tramping across tea plantations; for those with piqued pekoe passions, the **Highfield Tea Estate** will let you frolic in the fields and tour the factory. (☎30023. Open daily 8am-7pm.) From Sim's Park, the estate is 2km up Kotagiri Rd., but it is only a short walk from the park via a shortcut along the park's eastern edge; see the map of the grounds just inside the park. In January, there's a week-long Tea and Tourism Festival. **Lamb's Rock,** 12km from Lower Coonoor, overlooks the Coimbatore plains far below. Four kilometers farther is Dolphin's Nose, a rock formation with views of a gaping, waterfall-filled gorge.

MUDUMALAI WILDLIFE SANCTUARY

The 32 square km of **Mudumalai Wildlife Sancutary and National Park** is only a fragment of the protected area which includes **Bandipur** in Karnataka and **Wyanad** in Kerala. However it's an excellent fragment; complete with friendly monkeys, herds of wild elephants, pleasant facilities, a healthy does of tranquility, and the occasional distant roar of a very big cat—in short all you need to live out your *National Geographic* wildlife fantasies. The park is at its most lush in the monsoon season (Aug.-Nov.) and occasionally closes down from Feb.-Apr. if it is too dry. The best time to visit is at the beginning of the wet season (mid-Apr. to mid-June) or just after it (mid-Dec. to mid-Feb.). Though the park sees quite a few daytrippers from Ooty, in general it stays quiet. There are usually just a handful of tourists, the gurgling Moyar River, the chirpings of myriad birds, and you.

■ ⁊ ORIENTATION AND PRACTICAL INFORMATION

Mudumalai sits at the border between Tamil Nadu, Karnataka, and Kerala. It is along the Ooty-Mysore bus route (90km from Mysore; 36km from Ooty via Masinagudi and 67km via Gudalor). The modest cluster of buildings at the official reception area of the park is known as **Theppakadu;** 7km east is the nearest proper village, **Masinagudi,** complete with mosque, temple, and church. **Buses** run every hour (7am-5:30pm) to Ooty (via Masinagudi, 1½hr, Rs10; via Gudalor, 2½hr., Rs25) and Mysore (2hr., Rs30). For other destinations, take an Ooty bus or any other sporadically appearring bus west to Gudalor (17km; 30min., Rs5.25) or north 30km to Gudelpet. Taxis will also make these trips. Buses run occasionally between Masinagudi and Theppakadu—a jeep **taxi** will cost Rs50.

The first place to head in Theppakadu is the **Reception Center** where you can book accommodations, elephant rides, peruse the library, and get transportation info. (☎(0423) 56235. Open daily 6:30am-6:30pm.) Short of a tea stall, all other services are in Masinagudi. Private **tours** and **treks** can be organized by **Wild Ways Eco Tours** (☎(0423) 56340; open daily 8am-10pm) and **Jungle Tours and Travels** (☎(0423) 56336; open daily 9am-8:30pm), both in Masinagudi. They offer similiar services (prices per person; 1 hr. trek Rs100; 1hr. night ride Rs225). The ubiquitous

Vishnu and friends linger at the reception center to snag clients; they charge Rs50 per hour per person for their adventures.

The nearest place to exchange money is Ooty; bring enough cash. In Masinagudi, **Lakshi Medicals** can see to your pharmaceutical needs (☎(0423) 56372; open M-Sa 9am-9pm). The **police** (☎(0423) 56227) are at the edge of town. **STD/ISD phones** are opposite the Masinagudi bus stop. **Postal code:** 643 223.

ACCOMMODATIONS AND FOOD

There are ten **lodges** and **dormitories** within the actual sanctuary. They can be booked in advance at the **Wildlife Warden** in Ooty (☎(0423) 44098) but if head to the reception center in Theppakadu without a booking you can usually at least get a dorm bed. All the sanctuary dormitories have shared bath and four beds to a room (Rs25 per bed; Rs100 for the room). The lodges and resthouses all have double rooms with attched bath (Rs320). In Theppakadu proper, the **Minivet Drmitory,** down the road from Hotel Tamil Nadu, has a particularly nice proprietor. Beyond it the **Sylvan Lodge** and **Log House** are much posher. Next to the reception center is the **Morgan Dormitory,** right on the main road. The park's other offical accommodations are sprinkled 5-7km away from Theppakadu and are accessible by jeep taxi or sporadic bus. In all sanctuary operated accommodations there is a two night maximum stay that can be waived depending on availability. Check-out is noon. The other option within the sanctuary is **Hotel Tamil Nadu,** the Tamil Nadu Tourist Development Corporation offering. All rooms have four beds and attached bath and can be booked in advance from TTDC hotel (☎(0423) 56249; Rs350 plus 20% tax). If you want the bustle of town, albeit a pretty low-key bustle, or are coming up dry in Theppakadu, there are a handful of options in Masinagudi. The brand-spanking new **Kongu Lodge** has a very friendly owner and cosy rooms with great views and multiple sheets on the bed (☎(0423) 56131 or 56411; singles and doubles Rs200; with bath, hot water and TV singles Rs300, doubles Rs600).

For eats, all accommodations run by the sanctuary offer **meals** (around Rs35) and snacks, chai, etc. for guests. Many cooks will take requests. **Hotel Tamil Nadu's restaurant** will serve non-guests as well (open daily 6am-9pm, *dosas* Rs10, meals Rs35). In Masinagudi shops offer snacks and produce and restaurants do meals for around Rs15. **Kongu Lodge** has an attached restuarnt (open daily 8am-10pm).

SIGHTS

The sanctuary is officially open only from 6:30am-9am and 4-6pm, and walking within the park is prohibited. However just sitting by the river you'll see and be forced to interact with crowds of brown Bonnet Macaques and the black-faced Common Langur (we're talking monkeys here). Peacocks, spotted deer, and the dangerous wild boar wander around, unperturbed by traffic or gawkers. There are two official ways to get into the park. One is by **elephant ride** (book in advance through the Ooty warden or try your luck at the Reception Center; 6:30-8am and 4-5pm; 1hr., Rs100, 4-person max.)—surprisingly comfortable and pleasant—and you'll probably spot a few more birds and a giant squirrel, but your best bet for wild elephant sightings is by taking the sanctuary **bus tour.** Though often packed with snapshot-taking-daytripping Indian nationals, the bus covers more ground so you may see more (6:30-8am and 4-5pm, 30min., Rs25, Rs5 camera fee). The odds are just as much in your favor, though, of seeing a herd of elephants during the bus ride to Mysore, Masinagudi, or west to Kerala where you'll pass through Wyanad and Bandipur. The bus need not be booked in advance, but for both the elephant rides and bus ride show up at 6:30am or 4pm as there isn't usually enough demnad for a second bus, and the elephants are sent out on a first-come, first-served basis to those who have booked ahead. If domesticated elephants float your boat there is an evening **elephant show** in Theppakadu where the elephants perform *puja* (Rs20, Rs5 camera fee).

If you want to do some walking or check out some of the waterfalls your only option is to head out with a **private guide** (see above). In general they are fairly knowledgable—be clear about what you want to do and what they have planned and it will probably be well worth your rupees. Keep your eyes peeled for the tiger.

ANDHRA PRADESH

ఆంధ్రదేశము

The state of Andhra Pradesh occupies a large portion of southeastern India, from the dry Deccan Plateau to the coast of the Bay of Bengal, where the Krishna and Godavari Rivers feed into rich, cyclone-drenched deltas. The state is named for the kingdom of the Andhras, who ruled most of the Deccan from the 2nd century BC until the 3rd century AD. As part of Emperor Ashoka's vast kingdom, the region was also a major Buddhist center. Beginning in the 16th century, Andhra Pradesh was ruled by Muslims, first under the Golconda Sultanate, then as part of the Mughal Empire, and finally under the Nizams, who ruled from Hyderabad under British protection from 1723 until 1948. In spite of the religious differences that might separate them, the people of Andhra are bound together by their language, Telugu. When India gained Independence in 1947, the Nizam of Hyderabad refused to cede his lands. After a year-long standoff, the Indian government forcibly annexed the territory, which was later merged with other Telugu-speaking areas to form Andhra Pradesh. Though one of the least touristed destinations in India, the state is home to a number of superb attractions well worth visiting.

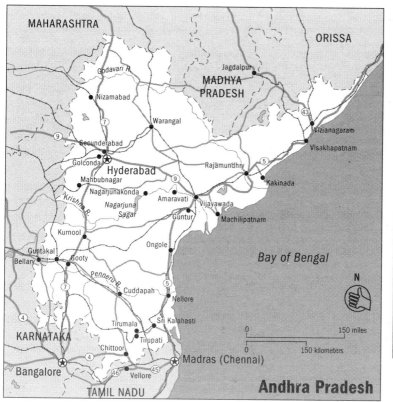

HIGHLIGHTS OF ANDHRA PRADESH

Hyderabad's bazaars and monuments (p. 605) complement the nearby spooky ruins of **Golconda Fort** (p. 604) and the gorgeous marble **Birla Mandir** (p. 606).

A visit to **Tirupati's** hilltop temple frenzy (p. 608) provides an insight into contemporary Hinduism, and then thrills with a harrowing bus ride down to calmer climes.

HYDERABAD హైదరాబాదు   ☎ 040

> Let millions of men and women of all castes, creeds, and religions make it their abode, like fish in the ocean.
> —Muhammad Quli Qutb Shah, upon laying Hyderabad's foundation

The story of Hyderabad's origins stands as a sweet testament to the overwhelming power of love. The city was founded in the late 16th century by Muhammad Quli Qutb Shah, Sultan of Golconda. Though he was to ascend to the throne of one of the greatest kingdoms in India, the young Muhammad had fallen in love too hard and too fast to heed religious and social barriers. His love, Bhagmati, was a beautiful Hindu dancer and singer. Muhammad risked his life and inheritance for his sweetheart, making midnight journeys on horseback from Golconda to a village on the banks of the Musi River to tryst with the beautiful Bhagmati. Upon discovering the depths of his son's infatuation, Muhammad's father relented and allowed his son to marry the common Hindu girl. The boy became king and founded a new city on the banks of the Musi, which he named Bhagnagar.

Today, this metropolis of five million has the highest proportion of Muslims of any city in the south. The soulful Islamic call to prayer crackles over loudspeakers in the streets, adding its echo to the blaring cacophony of motorcycle and rickshaw horns. The last Nizam was reputedly the wealthiest man in the world, and he liked to show it—the city's architecture is a highly impressive example of the Indo-Saracenic style. Hyderabad used to be known for its relatively clean streets and mellow pace, but no more—recent years have seen increasing congestion and urbanization, with all the related benefits and problems. A huge new bus station and plans for an international airport have confirmed the city's status as the travel and tourism hub of Andhra Pradesh—you won't need to take a midnight horseback ride to get here—but the increased traffic has quickened drivers' tempers and dirtied the streets. None of this has been able to spoil the city's still-beautiful Muslim monuments, however, or the bazaars of the Old City.

▐ GETTING THERE AND GETTING AROUND

Flights: Begumpet Airport (enquiry ☎ 140, recorded flight info ☎ 142), on the north side of Husain Sagar, off Sardar Patel Rd., 8km north of Abids. Auto-rickshaws go to Abids (Rs65 fixed). Taxis cost twice as much. **Air Canada, Air France** (☎ 230947), **Gulf Air** (☎ 240870), **Kuwait Airways** (☎ 234344), **Royal Jordanian,** and **TWA** (☎ 598774) are all in the same building, 500m north of Basheer Bagh. **Bangladesh Biman** (☎ 598775), Flat 202, Gupta Estate, Basheer Bagh. **Lufthansa,** 3-5-823 Hyderguda Rd. (☎ 235537), to the right off Basheer Bagh Circle. **Delta Airlines, Jet Airways** (☎ 330 1222), **Singapore Airlines** (☎ 331 1144), and **Swissair** are all in the Navbharet Chambers, Raj Bhavan Rd. **KLM Royal Dutch Airlines,** 3-6-284 Hyderguda Rd. (☎ 322 7351). All open M-F 9:30am-5:30pm, Sa 9:30am-1:30pm. **Air India,** 5-9-193 HACA Bhavan (☎ 237243), opposite the Public Gardens. Open M-Sa 9:30am-1pm and 1:45-5:30pm. **Indian Airlines,** Secretariat Rd. (☎ 236902 or 141), opposite Assembly Saifabad. Open daily 10am-1pm and 2-5:15pm. Flights to: **Ahmedabad** (W, Th, Sa, and Su; 1½hr.; US$165); **Bangalore** (daily, 1hr., US$105); **Bombay** (daily, 1hr., US$120); **Calcutta** (daily, 2½hr., US$210); **Delhi** (daily, 2hr., US$205); **Madras** (daily, 1hr., US$105); **Tirupati** (M and F, 1hr., US$85).

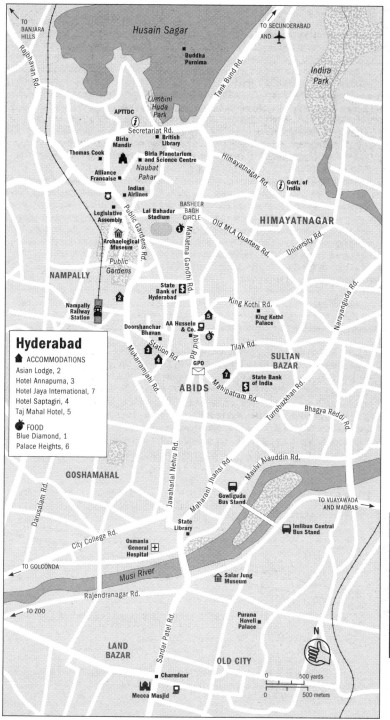

TO
BANJARA
HILLS

Rajbhavan Rd.

Husain Sagar

■ Buddha
Purnima

TO SECUNDERABAD
AND ✈

Tank Bund Rd.

*Indira
Park*

*Lumbini
Huda
Park*

APTTDC
(i)

Secretariat Rd.

Birla
Mandir

■ British
Library

Thomas Cook ■

■ Birla Planetarium
and Science Centre

*Naubat
Pahar*

Alliance
Francaise ■

■ Indian
Airlines

Lal Bahadur
Stadium

BASHEER
BAGH
CIRCLE

Himayatnagar Rd.

(i) Govt. of
India

Legislative
Assembly

🏛 Archaeological
Museum

Public Gardens Rd.

Mahatma Gandhi Rd.

Old MLA Quarters Rd.

University Rd.

HIMAYATNAGAR

*Public
Gardens*

NAMPALLY

State
Bank of
Hyderabad 💲

King Kothi Rd.

Narayanguda Rd.

Nampally
Railway
Station

2

Doorshanchar
Bhavan

AA Hussein
& Co.

5

6

King Kothi
Palace

Tilak Rd.

**SULTAN
BAZAR**

Mukarramjahi Rd.

Station Rd.

Abid Rd.

3

4

GPO
✉

7

State Bank
of India
💲

ABIDS

Mahipatram Rd.

Turrebazkhan Rd.

Bhagya Reddi Rd.

Jawaharlal Nehru Rd.

Hyderabad

🏠 **ACCOMMODATIONS**
Asian Lodge, 2
Hotel Annapurna, 3
Hotel Jaya International, 7
Hotel Saptagiri, 4
Taj Mahal Hotel, 5

🍴 **FOOD**
Blue Diamond, 1
Palace Heights, 6

GOSHAMAHAL

Darusalam Rd.

Maharani Jhansi Rd.

Maulvi Alauddin Rd.

Gowliguda
Bus Stand 🚌

TO VIJAYAWADA
AND MADRAS

🚌 Imlibun Central
Bus Stand

City College Rd.

State
Library

Osmania
General
Hospital ✚

TO GOLCONDA

Musi River

Rajendranagar Rd.

🏛 Salar Jung
Museum

TO ZOO

Sardar Patel Rd.

Purana
Haveli ■
Palace

N

**LAND
BAZAR**

OLD CITY

■ Charminar

🕌 Mecca Masjid

0   500 yards
0   500 meters

Trains: There are tourist quotas at each of the three **stations** (centralized enquiry ☎ 783 3541): **Secunderabad, Nampally** (in Abids), and **Kachiguda** (east side of Sultan Bazaar). Secunderabad and Nampally are the most useful for tourists. Nampally (the main Hyderabad station) is most convenient to budget hotels. Many trains stop at both stations. Reservations open M-Sa 8am-8pm, Su 8am-2pm. To: **Bangalore** (5:40pm (Secunderabad) and 5:58pm (Kachiguda), 13½hr., Rs255); **Bombay** (2:30 and 8:40pm, 15½hr., Rs255); **Delhi** (6:40am and 9:30pm, 26hr., Rs200); **Madras** (3:50 and 7pm, 13½hr., Rs255); and **Tirupati** (5-6 per day, 5:30am-7pm, 13½hr., Rs245).

Buses: The new **Imlibun Central Bus Stand** (enquiry ☎ 461 4406), across the Musi River from the old station, proclaims itself Asia's largest. You'll believe it as you wander its 73 platforms. Open 24hr. Deluxe to: **Bangalore** (every 30min., 4:30am-9pm, 12hr., Rs281); **Bombay** (10:30am and 9:30pm, 16hr., Rs320); **Hospet** (11am and 5:30pm, 8hr., Rs230); **Madras** (4:30pm, 14hr., Rs344); **Nagarjunakonda** (every hr., 4hr., Rs69); and **Tirupati** (5 per day, 4:30-10pm, 14hr., Rs281).

Local Transportation: Buses are typically packed to overflowing—you'll need turbo-*chappals* to catch one. Terminals at **Nampally, Nurkhan Bazaar,** near the **Charminar,** and **Secunderabad** Railway Station. The Nampally terminal is north of the railway station on Public Garden Rd., at the entrance to the public gardens. From Secunderabad Station to Nampally: #2 and 8A. From Nampally to Golconda Fort: #119 and 142N. **Auto-rickshaws** cost Rs6 for 1km, Rs3 per km thereafter; most drivers are (surprise surprise) reluctant to use the meter. **Taxis** are unmetered and twice as expensive.

✈ ORIENTATION

The **Musi River** divides the **Old City**—containing the Charminar, the Mecca Masjid, and the bazaars—from the **New City,** with its government offices, glitzy downtown shops, and glimmering Birla-commissioned landmarks, to the north. The **Abids** area, the heart of the New City, is about 1½km south of the gargantuan, Gautama-guarded **Husain Sagar,** the artificial lake built back in the days of the Golconda empire. Abids contains **Hyderabad (Nampally) Station.** The other main transportation hub is in Hyderabad's twin city, **Secunderabad,** to the northeast of Husain Sagar, where the **railway station** sends travelers in and out of the area.

⚡ PRACTICAL INFORMATION

TOURIST AND FINANCIAL SERVICES

Tourist Office: Government of India Tourist Office, 2nd fl. Sandozi Building, Himayatna-gar (☎ 763 0037). From Basheer Bagh, the office is 750m down the road, on the left. Free Hyderabad city map. Open M-F 9:30am-5:30pm. The **Andhra Pradesh Travel and Tourism Development Corporation Ltd. (APTTDC)** has its main office at the Yatri Nivas Hotel, Sardar Patel Rd., Secunderabad. Open daily 6:30am-8pm. Another branch is next to Lumbini Park, Tank Bund Rd. (☎ 345 3036). Open daily 6:30am-8:30pm. Both offices book local sightseeing tours (daily 8am-5:15pm, Rs125). They also offer tours to Nagarjunasagar (Sa-Th 6:45am-9:45pm, Rs225), Tirupati (4 days, Rs850 includes one night's accommodation), and other destinations in South India.

Budget Travel: Sita World Travel, 3-5-874 Hyderguda Rd. (☎ 233629; fax 234223), next to Apollo Hospital. Turn right coming from Abids Circle to Basheer Bagh. Open M-F 9:30am-6pm, Sa 9:30am-1:30pm. **Omega Travels,** 13 Buddha Bhavan Complex, MG Rd., Secunderabad (☎ 782 5111).

Immigration Office: Foreigners Regional Registration Office, Commissioner of Police, Purana Haveli Rd. (☎ 809715), 500m southeast of the Salar Jung Museum. Registra-tion fee Rs150. Visa extensions US$5-100. Open M-Sa 10am-5pm. Closed 2nd Sa.

Currency Exchange: State Bank of Hyderabad, MG Rd. (☎ 320 1594), 700m north of Abids Circle. Open M-F 10:30am-2:30pm, Sa 10am-noon. **Thomas Cook,** 6-1-57 Saifa-bad (☎ 329 6521), near the junction of Secretariat and Public Gardens Rd. Both change currency and traveler's checks. Open M-F 9:30am-5:30pm, Sa 9:30am-5pm.

LOCAL SERVICES

Bookstore: AA Hussein & Co., 5-8-551 Arastu Trust Building, Abid Rd., Abids (☎320 3724). Sells Hyderabad guides and maps. Open M-Sa 10am-8:30pm. **Walden,** 6-3-871 Greenlands Rd., Begumpet (☎331 3434), between Abids and the airport, in the Vivekananda Hospital complex. Open W-M 9am-8:30pm.

Library: State Central Library, Turrebaz Khan Rd. (☎500107), near Osmania General Hospital. Open daily 8am-8pm. **British Library,** 5-9-22 Sarovar Centre, Secretariat Rd. (☎230774). Open Tu-Sa, 11am-7pm.

EMERGENCY AND COMMUNICATIONS

Police: Abids Circle Police Station (☎230191), to the right as you face the GPO.

Pharmacy: Apollo Pharmacy (☎360777, ext. 2020), in the Apollo Hospital Complex (see below). Open 24hr. **Medwin Hospital Pharmacy** (☎320 3820), off Station Rd., on Chirag Ali Ln., in a tall building visible even from the Nampally Railway Station. The pharmacy is inside the lobby to your left. Open 24hr.

Hospital: Apollo Hospital Medical Center, Jubilee Hills (☎360 777), 8km northwest of Abdis. Open 24hr. **Gandhi Hospital** (☎770 1089), near Secunderabad Station.

Telephones: Telegraph Office, Abids Circle, adjoins the GPO on the left. Open 24hr.

Internet: Web Alert Cyber Cafe (☎475 5186), in an alley just before King Kothi Rd., on your right as you head north from the GPO on Abid Rd. in Abids. Open daily 9am-11pm. Rs50 per hr. **Compu Care,** East Charminar, Old City (☎456 8793). 500m down the road that heads east from the Charminar (in the opposite direction from Laad Bazaar), on the right side. Rs30 per hr. Open daily 10:30am-midnight.

Post Office: GPO, Abids Circle (☎474 5978). Open M-Sa 8am-8:30pm. **Postal Code:** 500001.

▐ ACCOMMODATIONS

Budget dives are 10-paise-a-dozen in the upscale Abids area. There are a few lodges around the Secunderabad Railway Station, but the area is grungy and there's no reason to stay there unless you have a morning train to catch. Almost all hotels have attached restaurants. All have 24-hour check-out.

ABIDS

Hotel Jaya International, 4-1-37/A&B Reddy Hostel Rd. (☎475 2929). Facing the GPO in Abids Circle, bear left along Mahipatram Rd., then take the first left at the Dhanalakshmi Bank. The best value for its price, with huge windows, seat toilets, and showers. Singles Rs300-600; doubles Rs400-750. AmEx, MC, Visa.

Taj Mahal Hotel, 4-1-999 King Kothi Rd. (☎475 8221). Walk away from the GPO in Abids Circle and veer right after 200m. One of Hyderabad's most popular hotels. Large, well-kept rooms with TVs, phones, seat or squat toilets, and 24hr. hot water. Singles Rs350-500; doubles Rs500-750. AmEx, MC, Visa.

Hotel Saptagiri, 5-4-651 Nampally Station Rd. (☎460 3601), down a narrow dirt road opposite the CLS Bookshop. Scrubbed and polished through and through. Well-lit rooms with TVs. Balconies, telephones, seat toilets. Singles Rs215; doubles Rs270.

Hotel Annapurna, 5-4-730 Nampally Station Rd. (☎473 2612), near Hotel Saptagiri, sandwiched between electronics stores. Overwhelmingly pink (but otherwise unexciting) place has TVs, direct-dial phones, and towels. Star-shaped rooms have faux-leather couches and seat toilets. Check-out 24hr. Singles Rs220-240; doubles Rs300-530.

Asian Lodge, Public Garden Rd. (☎650 6050). Turn left as you come out of the station; it's one block up on the left. Cheap and dusty. Singles Rs60-100; doubles Rs100-150.

SECUNDERABAD

Hotel Sitara, 7-1-2 SPG Church Complex (☎770 0308). From the Secunderabad station, veer diagonally left. By far the cleanest and friendliest hotel in the area. Broad, well-lit hallways, tiled bathrooms with squat toilets, balconies, and spacious rooms. 24hr. hot water. Singles Rs165; doubles Rs225-270.

National Lodge, 9-4-48 Syed Abdulla St. (☎ 770 2622), opposite Secunderabad station. Basic, clean rooms with narrow beds and no hot water. Doubles with bath Rs100.

◐ FOOD

Traditional Andhra cuisine demands either iron taste buds or stubborn stoicism. Either way, you'll never have clogged sinuses in Hyderabad. To ease your pain, delve into one of the ubiquitous bakeries that have popped up in the past few years or gorge at one of the many four-star cosmopolitan restaurants in the Abids area.

▨ **Taj Mahal,** in the Taj Mahal Hotel, King Kothi Rd. off MG Rd., is a Hyderabad legend, and with good reason: it's cheap, comfortable, and generous with portions of South and North Indian favorites. No smoking or alcohol. Tiffin 7am-9:30pm. Open daily 11am-3:30pm and 7-10:30pm.

Palace Heights, 8th fl., Triveni Complex, Abids Rd., 500m north of the GPO, down an alley on your right, just before King Kothi Rd. Opulent decor matches the paintings of past maharajas on the walls. Fabulous city views and an elaborate array of Chinese, Indian, and continental dishes (Rs85-160). Open daily 11:30am-3pm and 7-11pm.

Blue Diamond, 100m south of Basheer Bagh circle. Chinese food as authentic as it gets round here. Wide selection includes Manchurian prawns (Rs100), Hong Kong chicken (Rs90), and sweet-and-sour pork (Rs80). Open daily 11am-3:30pm and 6-10:30pm.

The Terrace, adjoined to the Birla Science Museum. Outdoor dining patio and elegant enclosed area. An impressive array of Chinese and Indian food (most dishes Rs50-90). Garlic kebab Rs115; Cantonese chicken Rs125. Open daily noon-3pm and 7-10pm.

Minerva Coffee Shop, 3-6-199/1 Himayat Nagar; from MG Rd., on the right. Servers weave between the rows of potted plants as locals gossip away. Veg. cheese *dosa* Rs23; huge *puris* Rs18; ice cream Rs45. Open daily 7am-11pm.

👁 SIGHTS

GOLCONDA FORT

8km west of the city. From the bus stand outside the Public Garden in Nampally, take bus #119 or 142. Open daily 7am-8pm. Sa-F Rs2, Su free; video fee Rs25. One-hour sound and light show daily 7pm, Nov.-Feb. 6:30pm; Rs25. English show on W and Su.

Headquarters of the Qutb Shahi kingdom from 1512 to 1687, the fort is Hyderabad's most popular attraction. At its peak, the Golconda empire stretched as far as the Bay of Bengal; now the circumference of the fort is a mere 7km. The kingdom was a thriving center for the arts and learning, as well as a bastion of religious tolerance, until it was crushed and annexed after two sieges by the Mughal emperor Aurangzeb. Durbar Hall is a 1000-step ascent that takes about a half-hour to climb. At the top is a panoramic view over the ramparts below and Hyderabad's other landmarks; if you squint hard enough, you should be able to make out the Birla Mandir and the Charminar in the distance to the east.

The fort is best toured counter-clockwise. On the way up, visitors follow the path used by the common people during the fort's active days; the steep descent leads down a route once used exclusively by the king and the poor chumps who had to carry him wherever he went. You first pass through the heavily studded **Balahisar Gate,** which served as the first line of defense against invaders. Just ahead is the **Grand Portico,** where guides are often seen clapping to demonstrate the fort's acoustics: Golconda was engineered so that a clap at the summit of Durbar Hall would reverberate at five places along the inside perimeter of the fortress wall; a clap at the center of the Grand Portico can be heard at the summit, 1km away. This built-in communication system was used to notify the king of any visitors while they were still far away. Straight ahead are the covered **bodyguard barracks.** Ahead and to the right is the **Nagina Bagh,** a royal garden. From the gardens, a stone staircase begins the ascent to the summit. At the foot of the steps, on the right, you can see the 12m deep **water tank,** one of three within the fort. The water came from a natural spring and was transported by a complex system of limestone pipes, the stumps of which can still be seen today.

Durbar Hall commands spectacular views of Hyderabad and Secunderabad. The summit is also home to the 12th century Hindu **Sri Jagadamba Temple.** From Durbar Hall, you have to go almost all the way down the king's staircase before you get to the next sight. At the foot of the hill is a water tank; around the corner are the **Rani Mahals,** a series of buildings once occupied by the king's harem. There is a somewhat functional fountain in the central courtyard, where the daily sound and light show is held. Once upon a time long ago, these buildings were decorated with curtains, mirrored glass, and jewels. Now, a colony of bats occupies the main building, and the gardens have been overtaken by weeds. Passing through the Rani Mahals takes you past the **Taramati Mosque** to the three-story **arsenal,** which contains more dusty guns and cannon balls than you can shake a stick at.

QUTB SHAHI TOMBS. Containing the remains of seven of the dynasty's patriarchs (each of whom supervised his own tomb's construction), the Qutb Shahi tombs play an undeserved second fiddle to the more frequently visited Golconda Fort. They are magnificent buildings in amazing condition. Locals come here to stroll or picnic in the gardens. Each tomb is built on a square base and capped with a Muslim-style onion dome, but is adorned with Hindu motifs such as lotus friezes and leaves. The cenotaph in the center of the tomb covers the crypt below. Though the tombs all have a similar shape, each bears the distinctive mark of its designer. The grandest tomb is that of **Sultan Muhammed Quli Qutb Shah,** which is surrounded by gardens criss-crossed by waterways. Farthest from the entrance, the tall, thin tomb of **Jamshid Qutb Shah** commands views of Golconda and other ruins from its terrace. The complex also contains a mortuary bath, where bodies were ritually cleansed before being buried. Next door, a small **museum** displays a variety of artifacts from Qutb Shahi times: ceramics, weapons, hand-written texts, and portraits of the kings who have their tombs here. *(1km north of Golconda Fort. Open 9am-4:30pm. Rs2. Museum open Sa-Th 9am-1pm and 2-4:30pm. Rs2. Camera Rs5, video Rs25.)*

OLD CITY

The back streets of the Old City, with their distinctive Muslim flavor, are arguably the most characteristic part of town. Along these streets are several pilgrimage sites sacred to Shi'a Muslims, each one housing a revered *alam*, a heavy banner into which gold, gemstones, and precious objects are woven. Ask a local to show you to the **Biha ka alawa,** which protects a bright green shrine within its whitewashed walls. The *alam* contains pieces of a wooden plank upon which the Prophet Muhammad's daughter is believed to have bathed. Not far away is the **Sar tauq ka alawa,** which houses an *alam* containing portions of the shackles and chains in which the fourth *imam* was bound.

PISCINE PLACEBO Every year in early June, thousands of asthmatics flock to the outskirts of Hyderabad to the home of the Battina Gowd brothers. The reason: they dispense an ancient ayurvedic cure that involves ingesting a live fish wrapped in herbs. According to a loose interpretation of Vedic texts, the live fish squirms around inside the body, clearing up breathing passages. But there's an added benefit: the fish is said to be a heat-generating agent and a preventive measure for the coughs and colds that accompany the beginning of the monsoon season in early June. To accommodate the demand for this treatment, the Indian government has arranged extra trains to Hyderabad during the fish camp season. It's difficult to gauge the fish's effectiveness, but many patients report a decrease in attacks and return annually to have the slimy little suckers shoved down their throats. The treatment is free, so the masses will probably continue to come.

CHARMINAR. The four-minaret Charminar is Hyderabad's oldest and most recognizable landmark. The edifice was built by Muhammed Quli Qutb Shah in 1591 to celebrate the end of an epidemic that had been plaguing the city. An image of the four towers graces every packet of Charminar cigarettes—it's said that the last Nizam of Hyderabad refused to smoke any other brand. There's not much to see in the building, since you're no longer allowed to climb the 149 steps to the small mosque on top, but a prime bazaar area surrounds it. The **Laad Bazaar** (see **Shopping,** p. 607) stretches west from the Charminar.

MECCA MASJID. Like the Charminar, the Mecca Masjid was built during the sultanate of Muhammad Quli Qutb Shah, but after Golconda's fall, completion of the mosque was left to Aurangzeb. It took fourteen hundred bulls to haul the granite slabs that form the colonnaded entrance from a quarry 11km away. Named for the few bricks from Mecca embedded in its central arch, the mosque is the largest in Hyderabad, accommodating up to 10,000 people at Friday prayers. Before entering the Mecca Masjid, check your *chappals* at the podium on the left and walk through a pavilion containing the tombs of various Hyderabad *nizams. (2km south of the Musi River on Sardar Patel Rd., just south of Charminar.)*

SALAR JUNG MUSEUM. The impressive Salar Jung Museum is touted as one of the world's largest collections amassed by a single individual, but it is actually the work of three generations of Salar Jungs, each of whom served as the *nizam*'s *wazir* (prime minister). The huge museum is stocked with everything from gorgeous Chola sculptures to mediocre European oil paintings. Room 14, the Ivory Room, displays a solid ivory chair given to Tipu Sultan by Louis XV. Room 17 has some marvelous modern paintings by premier Indian artists such as Ravi Varma and K. Hebbar. In Room 18, next door, you can trace the chronological and regional evolution of Indian miniature painting. *(CL Badari Malakpet, south of the Musi River. ☎ 523211. Open Sa-Th 10am-5pm. Rs150.)*

HUSAIN SAGAR AREA

ALL THINGS BIRLA. The spectacular **Birla Mandir,** dedicated to Lord Venkateshwara, crowns Naubat Pahar hill. Commissioned by the industrial kings of India and built over 10 years, it has awesome views of Hyderabad and Secunderabad, especially at sunset. The temple's elevation and the pure white Rajasthani marble against the blue of Husain Sagar combine to paint a quite sublime picture. For once, the serenity is unmarred by shoe-touts or alms-driven priests. At night, the whole structure is illuminated. *(Open daily 7am-noon and 2-9pm.)* The **B.M. Birla Science Centre and Archaeological Museum** is opposite the temple. Downstairs is an impressive archaeological section, with excavations from Vaddamanu dated between 100 BC and 200 AD, wood and stone sculptures, and miniature paintings. *(Open daily 10:30am-8:30pm, closed last Tu. Rs10.)* Exit to the right and climb the stairs to the domed **Birla Planetarium.** *(☎ 241067. Three English shows per day. Closed last Th. Rs13; combined ticket to the planetarium and the museum Rs20.)*

HUSAIN SAGAR. Visitors to Hyderabad cannot escape Husain Sagar, the 6½km by 800m tank whose blue waters provide a pleasant backdrop to the cityscape. Historians say that the tank was constructed during the days of the Golconda Empire. Legend says that the tank was promised hundreds of years ago by a sadhu who collected large sums of money from the thirsty populace. Weeks passed and no construction had begun, prompting the people to confront the sadhu, who then promised to undertake the project or return their money. The next morning, a shimmering tank was in place, and the sadhu had disappeared. The magic continued in the 1980s, when a monolithic **Buddha statue** was built (amid a lot of hype) and then placed on a barge for transport across the artificial lake. It promptly sank into the water, dragging down seven people with it. Several years ago, the statue was retrieved from the bottom intact, no damage having been inflicted by the accident. The only real park on the lake is **Lumbini Huda Park,** which is small but nicely landscaped and well-maintained. Boats are available for tours or do-it-yourself jaunts. A musical fountain chimes away three times every night. *(Just off Secretariat Rd., near Public Gardens Rd. Open Tu-Sa 9am-9pm. Rs2. Boats available Tu-Su 9am-6pm; paddleboats Rs10 per person.)*

🎵 ENTERTAINMENT

Hyderabad is not just a political capital, but a cultural one too, hosting countless dance programs, *ghazal* sessions, and plays. **Ravindra Bharati** (☎233672), in the Public Gardens, stages about four events per week. **Bharatiya Vindya Bhavati** (☎237825), off Basheer Bagh Circle, holds classical and popular dance and music concerts, often for free. Hyderabad claims to have more than 100 **cinemas.** The best English theaters are **Sangeet,** 23 Sardar Patel Rd., Secunderabad (☎770 3864), and **Skyline,** 3-6-64 Basheer Bagh Rd., Hyderabad (☎231633). There are usually three shows per day, and balcony seats cost Rs25. The **Alliance Francaise** (☎236646), next to the Birla Science Centre, screens two flicks per week: one in French, the other in German or English. The **Hyderabad Film Club** (☎290265) has weekly screenings at the Sarathi Studio Preview Theatre in Ameerpet, north of Banjara Hills. *Channel 6*, a weekly publication available at local bookstores, is the best source of information for upcoming events.

As Andhra Pradesh only recently repealed its prohibition law, the **bar scene** is still struggling to get off the ground. **One Flight Down** (☎320 4060), in the Residency on Public Garden Rd., is fairly popular, and many other five-star hotels are planning their own watering holes. For a different kind of liquid refreshment, try the **Ritz Hotel,** Hill Fort St., Basheer Bagh, where you can swim in the same **pool** as the Nizam's privileged guests. (☎233570. Open daily 3-7pm. Rs60 per hr.) If you can't handle the sultry mid-mornings, there is also a pool at the **Taj Residency,** Rd. No.1, Banjara Hills. (☎339 9999. Rs150 per hr. Open daily 7am-7pm.)

🛍 SHOPPING

The bazaars around the Charminar in the Old City are the best places to hone your bargaining skills. The **Laad Bazaar,** extending west from the Charminar, is renowned for its bangles and wedding fashions, luring people from all over India for pre-nuptial purchases. Step into a shop and take a look at the heavily embroidered *kamdani* dresses for women or the regal, sultan-esque caps for men. If you're not into buying jewelry (strands of imperfect pearls for Rs100-500) and armfuls of bangles (around Rs25 per set), you can always just stroll around and look into the stalls where craftsmen hand-pound sheets of silver foil, which is used to coat Indian sweets. Most of the shops in the Old City are open from 10am to 7pm; some observe Friday as a holiday. Emporiums line the roads in the Abids area. **Kalanjali Arts and Crafts,** Hill Fort Rd., opposite the Air India office, is not too expensive. (☎231147. Open daily 9:30am-8:30pm.)

NAGARJUNAKONDA (NAGARJUNASAGAR) నాగార్జునకొండ   ☎08680

The ruins of one of the largest Buddhist monasteries and learning centers in South India lie 150km southeast of Hyderabad and about 20m underwater. Excavations in 1926 first revealed evidence of stupas, *chaityas*, and other artifacts dating back to the 2nd century BC. Much later, in the 1950s, plans to build a dam on the Krishna River adjacent to the site spurred government archaeologists to resume digging. The most important ruins were evacuated, brick-by-brick, to a nearby hill before the dam was finished in 1966. Today, a lake occupies the original site, and the island of Nagarjunakonda now supports both the rebuilt structures and a museum. Nagarjuna, a first-century Buddhist scholar, had no problem meditating in the sleepy village of Nagarjunasagar nearby, and neither would you, but don't expect to find much else to do.

ANDHRA PRADESH

□ GETTING THERE AND GETTING AROUND. The nearest **train station** is in Macherla, 13km east of the dam, but Vijayawada is better serviced. **Buses** leave from Nagarjunasagar (14km from the ruins in Nagarjunakonda) to **Hyderabad** (every hr., 4hr., Rs69); **Tirupati** (7:30am and 1:30pm, 13hr., Rs150); and **Vijayawada** (7am and 1pm, 4hr., Rs60). Buses into town will drop you off (on request) at the **boat launch** on the opposite end of the dam at Vijayapuri South (ferries Sa-Th 9:30am and 1:30pm, 45min., Rs30). More ferries are added throughout the morning if there's enough tourist demand. The ferries stay at Nagarjunakonda for an hour before returning—enough time for a visit to the museum and a (quick) look at the ruins; if you want to stay longer, ask about the next ferry back to the mainland. Buses are your best bet for getting back to Hill Colony.

■☑ ORIENTATION AND PRACTICAL INFORMATION. The **Nagarjunasagar Dam** is the village's main axis. The lake is to the west, and the **Krishna River** runs to the east. To the north is **Hill Colony**, where you'll find the better tourist hotels and the **bus stand.** The APTTDC **tourist office** is opposite the bus stand in Project House (Sagara Paryataka Vihar). They operate guided minivan tours to Nagarjunakonda, the dam, and Ethipothala Waterfall for Rs100 per person. (☎76634. Open Sa-Th 9am-6pm.) APTTDC bus tours from Hyderabad, also available subject to demand, visit the same sites; they leave Hyderabad at 6:45am and return at 9:45pm (Rs225). About 6km south of Hill Colony, just before the dam, is Pylon Colony, with a number of **STD/ISD** booths. The **police station** (☎76533) and **post office** are on the main road from Hill Colony to the dam. **Postal Code:** 508202.

▮☖ ACCOMMODATIONS AND FOOD. The best rooms in town are those in Hill Colony run by the APTTDC. **Project House** has an acceptable **restaurant** and large, clean doubles. (☎76540. Check-out 24-hr. Rs250.)

☎ SIGHTS. After taking a ferry from Nagarjunasagar to the island, visitors typically head from the ferry straight to the **museum,** which features a range of sculpture, friezes, and other artifacts, all accompanied by detailed description in several languages (open Sa-Th 9am-4pm, Rs2). The rebuilt **ruins** are somewhat disappointing. Each has a sign describing the purpose of the original structure. The **Ethipothala Waterfall,** a popular picnic spot, is 16km away from the boat launch, and is reachable by shared tempo.

TIRUPATI తిరుపతిAND TIRUMALA తిరుమల ☎08574

Red rock hills covered with greenery form the backdrop to the temple of the Sri Venkateshwara at Tirumala, the most popular pilgrimage site in South India. Built in the 11th century by the founder of the Sri Vaishnava sect, the temple draws in thousands upon thousands of Hindu pilgrims every day. The task of housing, feeding, and moving the masses falls to Tirupati, the little boomtown 20km down the hill. Sri Venkateshwara is one of the few temples in India that allow non-Hindus into the inner sanctum, but it is not visited by many foreigners. Wading through the crowds for *darshan* of the image can be nerve-racking and exhausting, but it will give you a unique perspective on the impressive phenomenon of Hindu pilgrimage. The amount of hassle that devotees will put up with for one fleeting brush with the sacred is incredible. If you're not a devout Hindu, make your trip on a weekday, preferably Tuesday, in order to escape the weekend rush; avoid the months of June and September and any public holidays.

□ GETTING THERE AND GETTING AROUND. Tirupati's **airport** is 12km from the city. **Indian Airlines** (☎25349; open daily 10am-5pm), in the Hotel Vishnupriya complex opposite the Tirumala bus stand, flies to **Hyderabad** (Th and Su, 1hr., US$85) and **Madras** (M and F, 20min., US$40). The **railway station** (enquiry ☎131) is in the heart of town, near the Govindaraja Temple. The reservations counter is opposite the station, next to the bus stand (☎25850. Open M-Sa 8am-8pm, Su 8am-

2pm.) **Trains** run to: **Bombay** (M and F, 9:40pm, 24hr., Rs321); **Chidambaram** (3:40pm, 10hr., Rs148); **Hyderabad** (4-5 per day, 5:30am-7pm, 15hr., Rs245); **Madras** (4 per day, 6:30-7:45pm, 3hr., Rs176); **Thanjavur** (3:40pm, 12½hr., Rs182); and **Tiruchirappalli** (3:40pm, 14hr., Rs194). The **APSRTC Central Bus Station** (☎22333) is 500m from the center of Tirupati. To get there, stand with your back to the train station and follow the road that leads to your right. Bear right when you reach the mis-shapen Gandhi statue; the bus station will be on your left. Buses travel to: **Bangalore** (every 30min., 5:45am-2:15am, 5½hr., Rs258); **Hyderabad** (4 per day, 12hr., Rs240); **Madras** (every 15min., 4hr., Rs55); **Nagarjunasagar** (6pm, 12hr., Rs165); **Pondicherry** (3pm, 6hr., Rs56); and **Vijayawada** (4 per day, 10hr., Rs142). The **Tirumala bus stand,** 250m from the railway station, sends a constant stream of buses up the hilltop along Alipiri Rd. (Rs18). Be prepared for a long wait, and buy a round-trip ticket to avoid waiting again on the way back. To dodge the crowds, you can also catch a bus to Tirumala from Tirupati's Central Bus Station. The Tirumala terminal is in a separate building at the back right corner of the bus station complex. The bus ride to Tirumala takes 45 minutes on curvy roads (57 hairpin turns) with insane driving—you might consider taking a taxi (Rs50 shared).

▓▌ ORIENTATION AND PRACTICAL INFORMATION. The **tourist office,** near the bus stand, has daily tours. (☎43602. Tours Rs125, not including admission fees. Open daily 10am-5pm.) The **State Bank of India** takes major traveler's checks. Follow the road opposite the Bhimas Deluxe Hotel and take the first right. (☎20699. Open M-F 10am-2pm, Sa 10am-noon.) Gandhi Rd. fronts the **police station** (☎20352) and the **post office** (☎22103; open M-F 10am-5pm, Sa 10am-2pm).

▛▟ ACCOMMODATIONS AND FOOD. All the decent hotels are in Tirupati. The only option in Tirumala is the **Devasthanam dormitory rooms,** which offer the bare minimum. Rooms are free but usually full. The **Bhimas Hotel,** 42 G Car St., about a block from the railway station, is popular with Indian pilgrims because of its reasonable price and prime location. The rooms aren't spectacular, but the place is generally clean, and fans keep it cool. (☎25744. Singles Rs75-150; doubles Rs175-550.) One kilometer away are the white towers of **Hotel Bliss,** Renigunta Rd., the town's most luxurious hotel, with four-star accommodations and a swimming pool. (☎21650; fax 20657; email blisstpt@vsnl.com. Singles Rs475-775; doubles Rs550-925. AmEx, MC, Visa.) Aside from some grubby *dhabas*, the best **restaurants** are attached to the hotels in Tirupati. Budget dining in Tirumala is only for those eager to wait in line with thousands of others to eat questionably hygienic (but free) food slapped onto a banana leaf. The **Bhimas Deluxe,** next to the Bhimas Hotel, has a popular restaurant serving the usual North and South Indian food. (Open daily 6am-10pm.) **Surya,** Hotel Mayura's restaurant, serves vegetarian dishes for Rs20-45. (Open daily 6am-10:30pm.) **Hotel Bliss** has a 24-hour coffee shop.

⬚ SIGHTS. Receiving the *darshan* of Lord Venkateshwara (Balaji) at the **Sri Venkateshwara Temple** in Tirumala is something that most devout Hindus hope to experience at least once during their lifetime. It is believed that any wish made at the temple will be granted by Lord Venkateshwara, an avatar of Vishnu. Visits to the temple begin in Tirupati, where buses shuttle passengers along a winding mountainside road to Tirumala and deposit them at the top of the hill. From there you can float along with the crowds through broad, clean, and exuberant bazaar-lined paths to the temple. Don't be surprised to find a lot of people with shaved heads; pilgrims here often make a sort of barber-barter deal with the gods: hair for favors. If you're willing to lose your locks, tonsuring stations will gladly do the job. (Not surprisingly, the area around Tirupati is home to a flourishing wig industry.)

At the temple, two types of *darshan* are available. Regular *darshan* comes at no cost, but often entails a wait of 12 hours or more. The "special *darshan*" queue (Rs50) will reduce your waiting time to 2-4 hours, depending on the crowds. You can buy "special *darshan*" tickets at either the Pilgrim Amenities Center near the bus drop-off or at the counter near Rambagicha Guest House no. 3 near the temple. After buying a ticket, follow the "Special Entrance" signs around the right side of the temple. Do not rely on middlemen to purchase your tickets, as scams are common. Before entering the temple grounds, leave your shoes with a shop owner for a few rupees. The wait to enter the temple—even in the "special *darshan*" line—involves pressing through a network of narrow wire cages and constriced passageways with hundreds of other pilgrims. Once you've entered the line, you'll have little idea of where you're going or how much farther you have to inch along. Rest assured that a few hours later, you'll round the corner to the home stretch.

The temple's interior contains some impressive sculpted columns. The *vimana* is fully covered with gold, and its dazzling brilliance is testimony to the wealth of the temple. After the long wait, *darshan* will seem exceptionally short. At the moment of truth, bare heads crane toward the holy image for one transcendent glimpse, while temple workers yank your arm to force your exit. If they recognize you as a (wealthy) foreigner, the workers may pull you aside, giving you extra *darshan* time in exchange for baksheesh. The impressive image wears a gold crown and is covered with flowers so that not much is visible, apart from the mask of Vishnu drawn clearly on its forehead. The last leg of the visit takes you to the *prasad* line, where workers dish out free food consecrated by Lord Venkateshwara. Opposite the temple is a small, unremarkable **museum.** *(Open M-F 8am-8pm; Rs3. Temple open daily 24hr.)*

ORISSA ଓଡ଼ିଶା

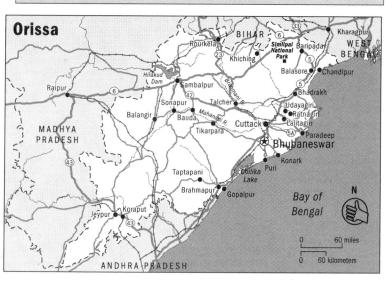

In October 1999, the state of Orissa was ravaged by one of the worst cyclones ever to hit India. The cyclone killed over 10,000 people, uprooted villages, home, trees, telephone cables, and caused untold damage to a prosperous past. The people of Orissa have begun to rebuild their lives, but the extent of the devastation is frightening, and the path to recovery is likely to be a long and painful one.

The state's coastline stretches for almost 500km, and nearly all of Orissa's urban residents live within a stone's throw of the Mahanadi River Delta. Most of the rural population work in rice paddies; the rest can be seen every morning in the fishing fleets that fight the pounding surf in narrow wooden boats—a far cry from the maritime prowess of the Kalingas and other local dynasties that once ruled these seas and sent colonists as far as Java. The thick forest cover of the Eastern Ghats has allowed *adivasis* (indigenous peoples) to survive relatively undisturbed.

Orissa has defended its independence for thousands of years. The Kalingas held out against the expanding Mauryan Empire during the 3rd century BC, capitulating only after a battle so bloody that it convinced Emperor Ashoka to renounce violence and convert to Buddhism. Orissa withstood Muslim rule until 1568, almost 400 years after surrounding regions had been conquered. The state's cultural autonomy throughout the centuries led to the development of several distinctive art forms, including its glorious temple architecture and the *odissi* form of dance.

HIGHLIGHTS OF ORISSA

On the coast of the Bay of Bengal, **Puri** (p. 620) juggles dual roles as religious center and beach-side resort.

Temple-packed **Bhubaneswar** (below) showcases the unique beauty of the region's varied and intricate Hindu architecture.

Konark (p. 618), the third point of Orissa's "Golden Triangle" of tourism, is the site of the spectacular **Sun Temple** and a wonderfully tranquil beach.

BHUBANESWAR ଭୁବନେଶ୍ୱର ☎ 0674

Bhubaneswar, the apex of Orissa's "Golden Triangle," has the finest collection of Hindu temples anywhere in India. The city's role as the major center of three different religions is reflected in the city's skyline, dominated by the spires of Shiva's *lingaraj* temple, the Buddhist peace pagoda on Dhauli Hill, and the pink Jain temple on Khardagiri Hill.

As the capital of the powerful maritime dynasties that ruled the coast of the Bay of Bengal, Bhubaneswar was for over a thousand years the center of trade and commerce in the area now known as Orissa. Members of the Hindu ruling classes erected the finest devotional structures money could buy; under their patronage, temple architecture grew into a highly developed art form. Under Muslim and British rule, however, neglect reduced many of the monuments to rubble. But when Bhubaneswar became the new capital of Orissa in 1950, it received a cosmetic makeover; urban planners built monumental, bureaucratic warrens along wide, shaded avenues, and the preservation of the old town's remaining temples became not only a religious but also a civic imperative. Today, this city exhibits both the outward characteristics of a modern state capital and the enduring spirit of the majestic kingdom that was classical Orissa.

▐▅ GETTING THERE AND GETTING AROUND

Flights: Bhubaneswar Airport (☎ 406472 or 401084), northwest of the temples in the Old Town. **Indian Airlines** (☎ 400533 or 400544), across the street from Capital Market. Open daily 10am-1pm and 2-4pm. To: **Bombay** (Tu, Th, and Sa; 1:40pm; 2hr.; US$250); **Calcutta** (M, W, F, Su, 2:30pm; Tu, Th, Sa, 8am; 1hr.; US$85); **Delhi** (daily, 3:20am, 2hr., US$215); **Hyderabad** (Tu, Th, and Sa; 7:25pm; 2hr.; US$160); **Madras** (M, W, F, and Su; 1:15pm; 2hr.; US$200).

Trains: Bhubaneswar Railway Station, Station Sq. (reservations ☎ 502042). To: **Calcutta** (15-18 per day, 4am-11pm, 8hr., Rs154); **Delhi** (3-6 per day, 8:15am-9:50pm, 32hr., Rs400); **Hyderabad** (3 per day, 1:50-7pm, 19hr., Rs300); **Madras** (4-10 per day, 6:30am-3:50am, 20-25hr., Rs312); **Puri** (frequent, 1½hr., Rs50).

Buses: Baramunda New Bus Station, NH5 (☎ 526977). To: **Balasore** (every 10min., 4:30am-10pm, 4hr., Rs55); **Berhampur** (6 per day, 5-11am and 3pm, 4hr., Rs50); **Calcutta** (4, 6, and 6:30pm; 13hr.; Rs120); **Cuttack** (frequent, 1½hr., Rs6); **Konark** (every 30min., 6am-5pm, 2hr., Rs14); **Puri** (frequent, 1½hr., Rs13). Buses to nearby towns also depart from **Kalpana Sq.**

Local Transportation: Minibuses cover all the major streets (Rs2-3). A useful route runs from the front of Kalinga Ashok Hotel to the Baramunda Bus Stand, passing the bank and airline office on the way. **Cycle-** and **auto-rickshaws** zip across town (Rs50). Although auto-rickshaws are unmetered, drivers will grudgingly take Rs5 per km.

✳ ORIENTATION

Bhubaneswar consists of the well-planned and spaced-out **New Town** to the north and the temple-packed **Old Town** to the south. Large roads like the north-south **Jan Path** and **Sachivalaya Marg** and the east-west **Raj Path** cut the New Town into neat squares called **nagars**, or **units**. Units have numbers; *nagars* have names. **Station Square,** in front of the railway station with a horse statue in its roundabout, is the closest thing to a city center. To the west and north of Station Sq. are **Ashok** (Unit 2) and **Kharavela Nagar** (Unit 3), containing most shops and services. There are some hotels around Station Sq., but most of the budget places are at **Kalpana Square,** at the junction of **Cuttack Rd.** and Raj Path, to the south. The haphazard Old Town, south of Kalpana Sq., has no main road. The **Bindu Sagar** tank is at its center and the tall **Lingaraj Temple** lies south of it.

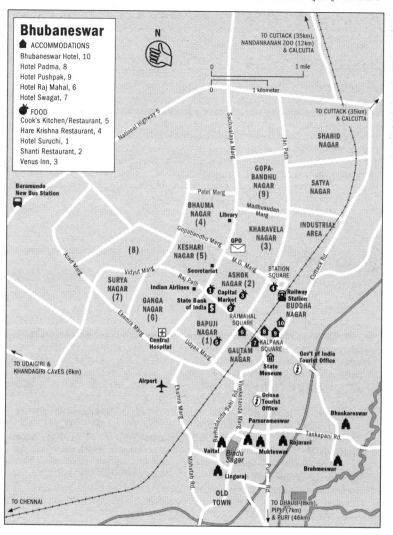

Bhubaneswar

🏠 ACCOMMODATIONS
Bhubaneswar Hotel, 10
Hotel Padma, 8
Hotel Pushpak, 9
Hotel Raj Mahal, 6
Hotel Swagat, 7

🍴 FOOD
Cook's Kitchen/Restaurant, 5
Hare Krishna Restaurant, 4
Hotel Suruchi, 1
Shanti Restaurant, 2
Venus Inn, 3

⚡ PRACTICAL INFORMATION

Tourist Office: Government of Orissa Tourist Office, 5 Jayadev Nagar (☎431299), off Puri Rd. to the south, 50m down on the left. Open M-Sa 10am-5pm. Counters at the airport (☎404006) and railway station (☎530715) are open 24hr. **ODTC** (☎432282), on the corner of Puri Rd. and Jayadev Nagar, behind the Panthanivas Tourist Bungalow, arranges cheap but rushed tours of Bhubaneswar, Puri, and Konark. **Government of India Tourist Office,** B-21 Kalpana Sq. (☎432203). From the railway station, take the last left before the fork that leads to Puri Rd.; it's on a side road 750m down on the right. Open M-F 9am-6pm.

Budget Travel: Swosti Travels, 103 Jan Path (☎508526), next to the Hotel Swosti. From Station Sq., walk north on Jan Path. Open M-Sa 7am-7pm.

Immigration Office: Foreigners Registration Office, District Intelligence Bureau, Sahid Nagar (☎403399). Open M-Sa 10am-5pm.

Currency Exchange: State Bank of India, Main Branch, Raj Path (☎403810). A short walk from Raj Mahal Sq., on Raj Path, opposite Capital Market. Open M-F 10am-3:30pm, Sa 10am-12:30pm.

Bookstore: Modern Book Depot (☎502373), on the right side of Station Sq. Open M-Sa 9am-1pm and 4-9pm.

Library: Harekrishna Mahtab State Library and **Bhubaneswar Public Library,** Sachivalaya Marg (☎404315). From Station Sq., head northwest on MG Marg and turn right on Sachivalaya Marg; the complex is 300m on the left, opposite Keshari Talkies. Open M-F and alternate Sa 9am-8pm.

Market: Capital Market, Unit 2, Raj Path, opposite Indian Airlines. Handicrafts, clothing, and fresh produce. Open Tu-Su 10am-8pm.

Pharmacy: Iswar Medical, Ashok Nagar (☎400359), half a block north of Raj Mahal Sq. Open daily 9am-10pm. **Capital Hospital's** pharmacy is open 24hr.

Hospital: Capital Hospital, Unit 6 (☎400688 or 401983). From Raj Mahal Sq., go south on Jan Path. After 1 long block, turn right (west) on Udyan Marg past Sachivalaya Marg. To the left is the 24hr. **government hospital. Ayurvedic Hospital,** Malisha Sq. (☎432347), east of Vivekananda Marg, opposite the Brahmeswar Temple.

Telephones: The **STD/ISD** booth in the station is open 4am-midnight. **Central Telegraph Office,** inside the GPO. Open daily 8am-8pm.

Internet: Com-Cyber Tech, Ashoka Market (☎425180), on the southeast corner of Station Sq. Internet (Rs2 per min.) and email (Rs20 per page). Open M-Sa 9am-6:30pm.

Post Office: GPO, PMG Sq. (☎406340), on the corner of MG and Sachivalaya Marg. Head across Jan Path from the horse statue in Station Sq. Open daily 10am-5pm. **Postal Code:** 751001.

ACCOMMODATIONS

■ **Hotel Padma,** 67 Budha Nagar, Kapana Sq. (☎416626 or 416628), to the right of Hotel Swagat. Friendly staff, clean and comfortable rooms, and a pleasant garden on the grounds. Singles with shared bath Rs60; doubles with bath Rs160-200.

■ **Hotel Swagat,** Cuttack Rd. (☎416686 or 425879). Exit the east side of the railway station (not the main exit facing Station Sq.), turn right, and walk for 5min. Clean rooms, clean prices. Restaurant inside. Singles Rs175; doubles with bath Rs200-550.

Hotel Raj Mahal, Raj Mahal Sq. (☎532448), at the corner of Jan and Raj Path. Centrally located. Airy hallways lead to clean, cool rooms with balconies and attached baths. Singles Rs150-200; doubles Rs200-300.

Hotel Pushpak, Kalpana Sq. (☎415545 or 415943). At the corner of Raj Path and Cuttack Rd. Restaurant and bar downstairs, complete with color TV blaring Hindi hits (open 11am-11pm). Room service brings drinks until midnight. Singles with bath Rs100; doubles with bath Rs200-500.

Bhubaneswar Hotel, Cuttack Rd. (☎416977 or 425518), past Swagat. This deservedly popular hotel won Bhubaneswar's best budget accommodation award in 1997. Small, well-appointed rooms. Attached restaurant (*thalis* Rs40-60) and travel counter (air and train bookings). 24hr. check-out. Singles with bath Rs125-150; doubles Rs175-550.

FOOD

Bhubaneswar is the perfect place to sample traditional Orissan cuisine, served in small *ginas* arranged on a large *thali*. This toned-down version of South Indian food is lightly spiced. The whole of Jan and Raj Path, and especially the Kalpana Sq. area, offers delicious veg. and non-veg. food for under Rs50.

Hotel Suruchi, Market Building, Capital Market, several blocks northwest of Raj Mahal Sq., opposite the State Bank of India. Highly recommended by locals. The perfect place to refuel after browsing the wares of the daily market. Speedy service. Try the Suruchi Special—a scoop of rice with *puri* and *ginas* swimming in spicy, strictly veg. South Indian sauces (Rs30). Open daily 7am-10:30pm.

Venus Inn, Ashok Nagar, behind Auroopa. The best place in town for South Indian food. *Dosas* Rs18-35, *idlis* Rs20, *uttapanis* Rs30, and A/C Rs0.

Hare Krishna Restaurant, Lalch and Market Complex, Master Canteen, opposite Hotel Jajati. From the railway station, head toward Station Sq. and turn right. Reputedly the best veg. deal in town. Full veg. *thalis* Rs20-40; other veg. dishes Rs20-50. No alcohol. Open daily 11am-3pm and 7-10pm.

Cook's Kitchen/Restaurant, 260 Bapuji Nagar. Head south on Jan Path from Station Sq. and take the third left past Raj Mahal Sq. Street-side "take away" kitchen offers full-flavored curries (from Rs18). The vividly clean, A/C restaurant (1st fl. of Blue Heaven Hotel) has tasty curry (Rs25). Open daily 10:30am-10:30pm.

Shanti Restaurant, 50 Ashok Nagar, Jan Path (☎531041). Quiet, A/C family restaurant. Bar upstairs. A huge menu with a variety of soups (Rs20-40), *dahl* fry (Rs18), and kebabs (from Rs60), as well as Chinese and eurotrash. Open daily 10:30am-11pm.

SIGHTS

It is said that there are more ancient temples in Orissa than in the rest of North India put together. There are more famous and more monumental temples in Puri and Konark, but for sheer range and number, Bhubaneswar is the place to be. Carved between the 7th and 12th centuries, the temple sculptures tell the story of Hinduism's resurgence—the frequent depiction of a lion pouncing on an elephant represents Hinduism's triumph over Buddhism. Lakulisa, a 5th-century Shaivite saint who converted many Orissans, also appears frequently on temple walls. Most of Bhubaneswar's temples are dedicated to Shiva, whose cult remains an important part of the lives of most in the region. The temples, in the middle of the Old Town around Bindu Sagar, can be explored in a few hours. Guides prowl the temple circuit soliciting customers, but they are of little use. Certified guides can be hired from the state tourism office and will describe the history and carvings in excruciating detail. Be wary of the men with a "temple register" listing contributions made by foreign visitors—it's a scam. The temples are all are open from dawn to dusk, with the exception of the Lingaraj temple (see below).

LINGARAJ TEMPLE. The Lingaraj is one of Orissa's great temples, notable for the balanced placement of sculpture on its 45m spire. Built around 1100, it has a full, four-chambered temple structure: a sanctum (under the spire), a porch, a dance hall, and an offering hall. Shiva is worshipped here in the form of Tribhubaneswar (Lord of Three Worlds), hence the city's name. Devotional songs have been sung here without a pause since the temple was built nearly 1000 years ago. The compound contains a jungle of ornate stonework—more than 50 smaller temples surround the main one. The second-largest temple in the compound, to the right in front of the main temple, is devoted to Shiva's consort, Parvati. The entire compound is closed to non-Hindus, but the British built a **viewing platform** right next to the wall, providing tourists with a peek inside. *(Open 6am-3pm and 6-9:30pm.)*

PARSURAMESWAR TEMPLE. The oldest and best-preserved of the early group of Orissan temples, the 7th-century Parsurameswar Temple exhibits many of the features common to the early temples, including a small, squat *shikhara* and an uncarved roof over the porch. Note the latticed windows that frame many of its sculptures. These derive from an even earlier artistic element used in Buddhist temple architecture. Standing sentinel at the back of the temple, on the left side of the rear entrance, is a *linga* with 1000 other tiny *lingas* carved into it—photography is not permitted. *(From the New Town, turn down the road to the left just before the Bindu Sagar; the temple is on the left not far from here.)*

MUKTESWAR TEMPLE. In contrast to the Parsurameswar Temple, the Mukteswar Temple built 300 years later, is comprised of a series of small monuments rather than a single building. A bold U-shaped archway sits in front of the complex, and a lotus is carved into the porch's ceiling. Look for the story of the monkey and the crocodile from the *Panchatantra* depicted on the eastern outer wall of the main temple. The Mukteswar is considered one of the finest temples in Orissa, both for its carvings and its well-preserved condition. *(A short walk down the road from the Parsurameswar Temple.)*

KEDARESWAR TEMPLE. From the Mukteswar Temple, turn left past the trinket stands and cold drink shops to reach the whitewashed **Kedareswar Temple,** the most active temple in Bhubaneswar after Lingaraj.

RAJARANI TEMPLE. Originally named for the *raja* (red) and *rani* (yellow) stones from which it was built, this now-defunct 11th-century temple is looked after by the Archaeological Survey of India. The temple is famous for its *shikhara*, built in the *shekhari* style, with miniature temple spires clustered around the main tower. Though common in other parts of India, this style of building is rare in Orissa. Also remarkable are the carvings of the guardians of the eight directions *(dikpalas)*, ancient Vedic gods who stand stiffly holding flags, thunderbolts, and nooses. *(Up the road behind the Mukteswar Temple, after a right on Tankapani Rd.; after a 5min. walk, you'll see the temple on the right, at the back of a rectangular park.)*

BHASKARESWAR AND BRAHMESWAR TEMPLES. The chunky **Bhaskareswar Temple** is no artistic triumph, but it does contain a 3m-high *linga* encased in what is thought to be an Ashokan column from the 3rd century BC. Wander down a cow-trampled lane to the right after the Bhaskareswar Temple to the 9th-century **Brahmeswar Temple.** The temple walls are carved with a miniature version of the Lingaraj temple. Some of the carvings depict the temple dancers who served as consorts to the deity here. The temple has smaller Shiva shrines at the four corners of its compound. *(A short rickshaw ride down Tankapani Rd., via the scenic route along the pretty sewage canal. Rs20 from OTDC)*

VAITAL TEMPLE. The Vaital Temple, sunk in the ground at a crossroads on the western side of the Bindu Sagar, struts a style unlike those found in Bhubaneswar's other temples. Its oblong, rounded *shikhara* was adapted from principles of Buddhist temple design that had gone out of fashion by the time the other temples were built. Take a light with you to illuminate the gory carvings inside, depicting scenes of human sacrifice and the skull-clad goddess Chamunda with her attendant owl and jackal. Beside the Vaital Temple is the **Sisireswar Temple,** a near-duplicate of the nearby **Markandeswar Temple.** In both temples, images were carved directly into the walls, a technique that was later discontinued.

ORISSAN TEMPLE ARCHITECTURE
Orissa's Kalinga kings staved off temple-razing Muslim invasions until 1568, allowing a distinctive style of architecture to develop unmolested. Orissa has some of the best examples of old stone Hindu temple design anywhere in northern India. The most important part of the temple, the *deul* (inner sanctum) housed an image of the deity. It was crowned by a huge, pyramidal *shikhara* (spire) and, above that, a lotus-shaped stone called an *amlaka*. On top was a small pot and the deity's weapon—a trident for Shiva and a discus for Vishnu. Adjoining the *deul* was a rectangular *jagamohana* (assembly hall). Larger temples added more rooms in single file behind the *jagamohana:* first a *nata mandir* (dance hall), then a *bhoga mandir* (offering hall). Aside from the consecrated images in the sanctum, the symbols depicted in temple sculpture were either specific to the temple itself (as with images of guardian figures) or illustrations of legends.

BINDU SAGAR. Central to the city's religious life is this Old Town landmark, a large green tank at the foot of Vivekananda Marg. The waters of the Bindu Sagar (Ocean-Drop Tank) are believed to contain droplets from all of India's holy pools and streams. Early-morning bathers come here to take advantage of the blessings the waters bestow. An image of Lord Tribhubaneswar is dipped in the tank during the **Rath Yatra** (see **Gods on Wheels,** p. 623).

MUSEUM. The **State Museum** contains a small collection of illuminated palm leaf manuscripts, a room full of Orissan musical instruments, ethnographic exhibits on Orissa's indigenous peoples, and heaps of orphaned temple sculptures and friezes. *(Puri Rd., a short walk from Kalpana Sq. ☎ 430870. Open Tu-Su 10am-1pm and 2-4pm. Rs2.)*

🚌 DAYTRIPS FROM BHUBANESWAR

UDAIGIRI ଉଦୟଗିରି AND KHANDAGIRI ଖଣ୍ଡଗିରି CAVES

Auto-rickshaws from Bhubaneswar Rs80. Caves open daily 8am-6pm. Rs2. Guides Rs80 for both hills.

More vestiges of antiquity can be found at the Udaigiri and Khandagiri Caves, 6km west of Bhubaneswar, less than 1km off National Highway 5 past Baramunda Bus Station. Cut into the hillside are 33 small niches that functioned as sacred retreats for Jain ascetics during the first and 2nd centuries BC. King Kharavela of the Kalinga Dynasty also took refuge here after the bloody Kalinga War at Dhauli. A road now divides the Udaigiri caves (on the right) from the Khandagiri caves (on the left). An explanation of the various carvings and paintings decorating the caves is in the "Inscription of Kharavela" at Udaigiri, near Cave 12.

The best sculptures are found in and around Cave 1 at Udaigiri, otherwise known as **Rani Gumpha** (Queen's Cave). Originally ten stories high, the cave is now reduced to the bottom two stories; the rest were wiped out by earthquakes. The central area of the first floor contains hiding places that were used by the king and his ministers. Large holes in the ceiling seamed with thin fissures served as communication channels, air tunnels, and water drains. Intricate carvings inside the caves depict the marriage of the gods. Cave 12 is carved as the gaping mouth of a tiger, Cave 13 as a cobra. Cave 14, the **Hathi Gumpha** (Elephant Cave), has a ceiling inscription from the reign of King Kharavela of the Chedi Dynasty, perhaps the greatest of Kalinga kings and patron of the caves. Images from Jain legends, mythology, and iconography decorate **Rani Nur** and **Ganesh Gumpha** (Cave 10).

Though the caves of Khandagiri are not as well-carved, they do house an old temple with 26 sadhus and 26 goddesses carved in two rows, one above the other. At the entrance to the temple is what is thought to be the only pair of carvings of Durga and Kali facing each other. This temple is still an active religious center; the pundits are extremely friendly, but beware of their fanatical pursuit of donations. An active **Jain temple** at the top of the hill offers great views down to Bhubaneswar, including the Lingaraj Temple and Dhauli Hill. The best preserved carvings at Khandagiri are in **Cave 3.** Crawl into the caves at your own risk—they are home to hundreds of hanging bats. If you don't bring peanuts, be prepared to face down the tiny, hungry baby monkeys, many of whom are as persistent at pursuing hand-outs as the priests and *chai-wallahs.* If you're interested in the history of the caves, hire a certified guide.

DHAULI ଧଉଲି

You can visit Dhauli as part of an ODTC guided bus tour. Auto-rickshaws cost Rs100 round-trip; buses, Rs4, drop you off 3km from the hill. Open daily 5am-8pm. Free.

The hill of Dhauli (also known as Dhauligiri), 8km south of Bhubaneswar on the Puri road, is Orissa's main claim to fame; it reflects the Buddhist influence in this predominantly Hindu region. The Mauryan emperor Ashoka the Terrible defeated the Kalingas in a horrific battle here in 261 BC. He was so appalled by the bloodshed that he renounced violence forever, converted to nonviolent Buddhism, and changed his name to Ashoka the Righteous. A long-winded rock edict in Brahmi script at the foot of Dhauli Hill explains Ashoka's theory of governance according to the principle of *dharma* (an English translation is posted near these inscriptions). In the rock above is one of the earliest stone carvings from Buddhist India—a gently and elegantly sculpted head of an elephant commemorating the emperor's conversion. On the summit of Dhauli hill, affording fantastic views of Bhubaneswar and the sandy River Durga, is the **Shanti Stupa** (Peace Pagoda), built in 1974 by the same team of Japanese Buddhists who created the almost identical stupas in Vaishali, Lumbini, and Milton Keynes.

NANDANKAN ZOOLOGICAL PARK

This zoo and wildlife park, in a vast expanse of the Chandaka forest, has a huge collection of animals from all over the world. The zoo shot to fame (or shame) in July 2000, when several of its prized Bengal White Tigers died under mysterious circumstances. Zoo officials first claimed the tigers died of sleeping sickness, but animal rights advocates pointed to tainted meat or overcrowding as possible causes. Most of the animals are squeezed into cages and artificial ponds, but several lions and what's left of the tiger collection can be seen on a **bus safari** (Rs10) through the park's fenced-off game preserve. It's not exactly "Wild Kingdom;" most of the "vicious predators" here look pretty bored. **Paddleboats** (Rs10) take you around the large, artificial lake; a **toy train** (Rs22) runs through the park and **cable cars** (Rs10) ride high above it. *(Buses from Bhubaneswar cost Rs5 for the 1½hr. trip; auto-rickshaws Rs90 round-trip. Open daily 8am-5pm. Rs20, vehicles Rs20.)*

KONARK ଚକାଶାର୍ଗ ☎ 06758

Konark, named for the god who was "sun of the corner," sits along an isolated stretch of Orissa's coast. Little is known of the town's ancient history, but its Sun Temple is hailed today throughout India as one of the country's great architectural marvels. Even in ruins, the Sun Temple is magnificent, and it is completely accessible to non-Hindus. Since the temple's excavation and restoration in the early 20th century, Konark has become a popular daytrip destination, especially during the annual **Odissi Dance Festival** (December 1-5).

◼◗ ORIENTATION AND PRACTICAL INFORMATION

Konark's street plan looks like the letter Z. The diagonal stroke is the main street, which contains the temple entrance and many small shops; the top stroke is the road to Bhubaneswar; the bottom is the Marine Rd. to Puri, which passes beautiful deserted beaches along the way. **Buses** depart from the middle of the intersection before Yatri Nivas to **Bhubaneswar** (every hr., 5am-6pm, 3hr., Rs15) and **Puri** (every 15min., 8am-8pm, 1hr., Rs9). Labanya Lodge rents **mopeds** (Rs150) and **bikes** (Rs20), and the **Orissa State Tourism Office,** inside the Yatri Nivas Hotel, arranges **taxis.** (☎35821. Open M-Sa 10am-5pm.) Labanya Lodge has **STD/ISD** phones (open 24hr. for guests, 6am-11pm for non-guests). **Canara Bank,** past the post office, changes traveler's checks. (☎35828. Open M-F 10am-2pm, Sa 10am-noon.) **Police:** ☎35825. The **post office** is just past the Archaeological Museum, on the right (open M-Sa 9:30am-5pm). **Postal Code:** 75211.

◖◗ ACCOMMODATIONS AND FOOD

Labanya Lodge, a few minutes out of town on the road to Puri, is a salmon-colored box framed by palm trees. (☎35824; fax 35860. Singles Rs75; doubles with bath Rs100-150.) The state-run **Pantha Nivas,** next to the museum on the road to Bhubaneswar, has small, clean rooms around green courtyards. (☎35820. Doubles Rs300-350.) **Konark Lodge,** on the right as you enter town from Puri, has dark, basic rooms. It's cheap, and you get what you pay for. (☎75221. Doubles with bath

Rs70.) Konark's food is nothing to write home about, but the **Geetanjali Restaurant,** set back in the trees next to the Pantha Nivas, has great, cheap breakfasts (open daily 6am-10pm). **Sharma Marwad Restaurant,** next to Geetanjali, is a popular veg. restaurant with various *thalis* for Rs15-50 (open daily 6:30am-10:30pm). The **Sun Temple Hotel,** on the right, just past Pantha Nivas, has the most wide-ranging menu in town (veg. curry Rs15) but achingly slow service (open daily 8am-10pm).

👁 SIGHTS

THE SUN TEMPLE

The ticket booth is up to the left of the gated entrance. Another entrance to the grounds, the next left after the Archaeological Museum, brings you to the outer wall of the complex, but you still have to walk around to the booth to pay. Open dawn-dusk. Rs5, free on F.

Konark's Sun Temple, dedicated to the sun god **Surya,** is built in the form of a huge chariot. With its intricate carvings and raunchy imagery, it is the best example of Orissan temple architecture. The Sun Temple once stood on the shoreline and was used as a navigational aid by European sailors on their way to Calcutta, who called it the "Black Pagoda" to distinguish it from the "White Pagoda"—the Jagannath Temple in Puri (see p. 623). There has been a Surya temple in Konark as far back as the 9th century, but most of the existing structure dates from about 400 years later. Over time, the shoreline has receded more than 3km, and today, a wall of tall pines conceals the Sun Temple from the sea. Though still undergoing restoration in places, the temple remains the central feature in the geographic—and economic—landscape of the area. Every year, during the first week of December, the Konark Festival, which features renowned Odissi dancers, takes place in an open air auditorium with the temple as the backdrop. Half the town, it seems, freelances as "guides" to the temple's racy iconography. The other half aggressively hawks trinkets from the street-side stalls surrounding the temple entrance.

JAGAMOHANA. Whichever direction you come from, the *jagamohana* (porch), a step pyramid that rises up from the middle of the compound, is the temple's most prominent feature. The eastward-facing door was originally designed to catch the light of the rising sun and to reflect it into the sanctuary behind the porch. The sanctuary is now in ruins, and the doorway and interior of the porch have been filled in to support the crumbling structure.

PLATFORM AND PORCH. The sanctuary and the porch are mounted on an ornate platform carved with 24 giant wheels and seven horses, simulating Surya's chariot ride across the sky. The clock-like spokes of the chariot wheels represent the hours of the day, and the images carved on them follow the progress of a typical day. Toward the front of the porch on the south side, the first six spokes are decorated with images of a woman bathing and performing housework, while the last six spokes—the nighttime hours—show her making love to her husband.

The porch itself is also carved with erotic images, some tiny and intricate, others blocky and larger-than-life. Behind the porch, steps lead up to three stone images of Surya in stone on the south, north, and west sides. Two modern staircases lead from the statues to the remains of the sanctuary itself. Before the temple fell into ruin, the sanctuary could only be reached through the porch, but engineers created the alternate route when the porch was filled in.

SANCTUARY. Considering the breathtaking appearance of the Sun Temple as a whole, the sanctuary itself is rather plain. The Surya statue that once presided here no longer exists, and archaeologists can only speculate about its design. Some tour guides claim that the statue floated in the air, suspended by powerful magnets lodged in each corner of the sanctuary. It seems more likely that it rested on the ornate pedestal that still exists. The frieze on the east side of the pedestal shows King Narasimha, the temple's patron, and his queen. The north and south faces depict the retinues of the queen and king, respectively.

MAYADEVI TEMPLE. Behind the sanctuary of the Sun Temple and to the southwest are the remains of a **Mayadevi Temple.** Once thought to be dedicated to one of Surya's wives, it is now considered to be an older Surya temple. Erotic images decorate the exterior. In front of the main sanctuary is a huge **platform** with four columns rising up in the corners, each decorated with carvings.

OTHER SIGHTS

ARCHAEOLOGICAL MUSEUM. Sculptures from the temple were scattered about the site by successive waves of plunderers and collectors. Some of the finest fragments, cleaned and polished, are now on display in the Archaeological Museum. (Other fragments from the temple's sculptures are kept in the Indian Museum in Calcutta and the Victoria and Albert Museum in London.) Well worth a visit, the museum sells the Archaeological Survey's informative guide to the Sun Temple for Rs15. *(On the road to Bhubaneswar, down from Yatri Nivas. ☎ 35822. Open Tu-Su 10am-5pm.)*

BEACHES. Sunset and sunrise are quite spectacular on Konark's beaches. Narrow paths lead to wide open expanses of ocean, and superb views of the sun's rays stretch endlessly across the horizon. The beaches may be beautiful to look at, but don't jump in! **The fast currents and uneven sea bed make it dangerous for swimmers.**

PURI ପୁରୀ ☎ 06752

Despite the multitudes that have descended upon it over the years, the tranquil little seaside town of Puri has somehow managed to age more or less gracefully. Since the 12th century, the skyline has been dominated by the immense temple of Jagannath, Lord of the Universe, which rises above the crowded old town. But it is the peaceful white sand beaches that lure crowds of vacationers and sun-worshipers here from landlocked cities all over India. In the 1960s and 1970s, Puri's permissive attitude toward (and plentiful supply of) drugs made it a popular stop along India's well-established hippie trail. Today, three distinct categories of visitors hang out here almost year-round, with little interaction among them. Hindu pilgrims tend to occupy the moral high ground up by the Jagannath Temple (closed to non-Hindus) and the eight *dharamsalas* that line Grand Avenue, Indian tourists populate the busy downtown boardwalk area, while the penny-pinching foreigners wallow in expatriate grunge resorts that lines the quieter beach east of town. East of the international commune area is a friendly and vibrant fishing village whose residents still farm the seas in boats from a bygone era.

▟ GETTING THERE AND GETTING AROUND

Trains: Puri Railway Station, Station Rd. and Hospital Rd. Open M-Sa 8am-8pm, Su 8am-1pm. Foreign non-reserved tickets at window #7. To: **Calcutta** (6:45 and 9:15pm, 12hr., Rs140); **Delhi** (6:45am and 8:45pm, 33hr., Rs325). There are regular trains to **Bhubaneswar,** but the bus is more convenient.

Buses: New Bus Stand, Grand Rd., past Canara Bank. Buses to **Konark** (frequent, 7am-7pm, 1hr., Rs10). Numerous **private companies** operate interstate buses; tour agencies and hotel desks make arrangements. To: **Bhubaneswar** (frequent, 2hr., Rs18); **Calcutta** (7am, 16hr., Rs150); and **Cuttack** (frequent, 2½hr., Rs20).

Local Transportation: Cycle- and **auto-rickshaws** tinkle and hoot their way from one corner of Puri to another for less than Rs20—the going rate is Rs5 per km; expect to be charged more. **Local buses** (under Rs5) rarely run properly, if at all. One useful route runs from the New Bus Stand to the Jagannath Temple, to the beach, and back (Rs3). **Aju's,** east on CT Rd., opposite the Holiday Home, has **bikes** (Rs20 per day), **scooters** (Rs200 per day), medium-sized **motorcycles** (Rs250-300 per day), and attractive Enfield Bullets for the motorcycle-experienced (Rs300 per day). Passport required for rentals. Open daily 7am-8pm.

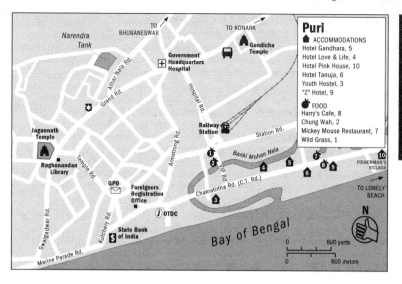

▚▞ ORIENTATION AND PRACTICAL INFORMATION

Puri's busiest area is **Grand Avenue,** which runs east-west through the northern (inland) part of town, arching southwest near the **Jagannath Temple** to become **Swargardwar Rd.** On the southern side of town is the Bay of Bengal. Along the shore runs **Chakratirtha (CT) Rd.,** with a number of budget hotels, restaurants, and tour agencies. As it runs west, CT Rd. intersects with **VIP** and **Marine Parade Rd.**

Tourist Office: Government of Orissa Tourist Office, Station Rd. (☎22664). From the railway station, follow Station Rd. west for 500m. The office is on the right just before VIP Rd. Upstairs, a tiny branch of the State Museum displays local handicrafts and photos of the Rath Yatra (see **Gods on Wheels,** p. 623). Both open M-Sa 10am-5pm.

Budget Travel: Om Travels, CT Rd. This ashram, travel agency, and religious bookshop offers standard tours run by Orissa Tourism. Open daily 6am-10pm. MC, Visa. **Gandhara International** (☎24623), in front of Hotel Gandhara, provides a wide variety of services including train and international flight booking and "tribal tours." Open M-Sa 8am-8pm, Su 8am-1pm. AmEx, MC, Visa.

Currency Exchange: State Bank of India, VIP Rd. (☎23995 or 23682). From the station, head west on Station Rd., turn left onto Armstrong Rd., left again onto VIP Rd., and follow it south past the Bose statue. Open M-F 10am-2pm, Sa 10am-noon. **Hotel Gandhara** changes traveler's checks for a fee. Open M-Sa 8am-8pm, Su 8am-1pm.

Bookstore: Loknath Bookshop and Library, CT Rd., toward the fisherman's village, next door to Raju's Restaurant. Books can be rented (Rs10 per day, with a Rs300 deposit) or purchased (Rs200-900). Passport photos (Rs20 for 3) and stamps are also sold. Open daily 9am-9pm; May-Aug. 8am-noon and 3-8pm.

Library: Raghunandan Library, Grand Rd. (☎22252), opposite the Jagannath Temple. Historically a monastery and library, it houses books and palm-leaf manuscripts on the 1st fl. Open daily 8am-noon and 4-7pm.

Market: Laxmi Market, west on Grand Rd. Farther east on Grand Rd. is the smaller **Municipality Market.** Both open daily 10am-10pm.

Police: Town Police Station, Grand Rd. (☎24059), near Jagannath Temple. The control room is open 24hr. **CT Rd.** area police station (☎25208). Contact **City Beach Police** (☎22025, emergency ☎100) in case of a beach emergency.

Hospital: Government Headquarters Hospital, Grand Rd. (☎23742), is the place to go only if you're dying. A visit might speed the process along. **Emergency:** ☎22094.

Internet: Harry's Cafe (☎23852 or 27032; open daily 8am-10pm) and **Gandhara International** (☎24623; open M-Sa 8am-8pm, Su 8am-1pm) offer full Internet access. Rs3 per min. **"Z" Hotel** is cheaper. Rs100 per hr. Open daily 9am-5pm.

Post Office: GPO, Kutchery Rd. (☎22051). From CT Rd., walk west past the Bose statue and turn right after the State Bank of India. Proceed north on Kutchery Rd.; the GPO is down the first street to the left. Open M-Sa 9am-6pm, Su 3-5pm. **Postal Code:** 752001.

ACCOMMODATIONS

> **WARNING.** Rickshaw-*wallahs* play a commission game with some hotel owners, who kick back up to 50% of the rent—ignore their claims that the hotel you are looking for is closed, full, very expensive, or has changed its name.

Budget accommodations for foreigners are concentrated around CT Rd., a small stretch of beach most easily accessed by rickshaw.

Hotel Gandhara (☎24117), at the end of CT Rd., opposite a path to the beach. The 19th-century bungalow in front contains a dorm and some budget rooms; the 5-story building behind it has pricier accommodations. Friendly and well-run, with a travel agency and restaurant serving Japanese food for Rs100. Make reservations by noon. Check-out 9am. Dorm beds Rs50; singles Rs120; doubles Rs150-750. AmEx, MC, Visa.

"Z" Hotel (☎22554), east of the Hotel Gandhara, past Restaurant Peace. Draws tourists for its sea-view rooms, garden, and direct beach access. Once home to the maharaja of Puri, "Z" (pronounced "zed" by everyone but the bloody Americans) is run by a former Chief Minister of Orissa. Excellent cook, 24hr. room service, and accommodating staff. Dorm beds (women only) Rs50; singles Rs150; doubles Rs250-450.

Hotel Pink House (☎22253), 5min. south of CT Rd. A bit run-down from constant sea winds, this ultra-budget cottage offers views onto the Bay of Bengal for next to nothing. Rooms opening directly onto the beach make for beautiful sunrises and sandy floors. Mosquito nets, coils, and insect spray available. Road-weary Suny cycles for rent (Rs100-175). Doubles Rs100-120.

Hotel Love & Life (☎24433; fax 26093), next to Hotel Gandhara. A long-term favorite with travelers, but less romantic than the name suggests. Dorm beds Rs30; singles Rs90-125; doubles Rs100-250; cottages (double occupancy) Rs200-250.

Hotel Tanuja (☎24823 or 24974), opposite Harry's Cafe and the Mickey Mouse Restaurant. Alcohol, smoking, and visitors are allowed in the rooms. Yippee. Mosquito nets, TV room, laundry service, in-house postal service, and Tanuja Tribe Tour agency complete the offerings. Singles Rs90; doubles Rs80-300.

Youth Hostel (☎22424), closer to town. Although it might look a bit like a haunted house from the distance, don't be spooked: the hotel is clean and popular with both Indians and foreigners. Check-out 8am. Dorm beds Rs30, non-members Rs50.

FOOD

Food in Puri is cheap and tailor-made for foreign tourists, with a wide array of non-Indian options on CT Rd. Fish (and lobster) is as fresh as you'd expect it to be.

Mickey Mouse Restaurant, diagonally across the street from the "Z" Hotel. A reggae-playin', international-copyright-violatin' hippie holdover. Try 11 different *lassis* (Rs10-30), made with in-season fruits, 18 varieties of custard (Rs10-30), or one of 46 pancakey permutations (Rs10-40). Complete *thalis* Rs12-52. Booze is not sold here but may be brought in. Open daily 6am-11pm.

■ **"Z" Hotel Restaurant.** The kitchen staff does a superlative job cooking up a spicy fish curry (Rs35). The *navaratan* (Rs25) and *aloo dum* (Rs14) are also outstanding, and the beer (Rs60) is always chilled. Open daily 7am-3pm and 6-10:30pm.

Harry's Cafe, near the "Z" Hotel. Perhaps Puri's best-known and most popular tourist trap. Better for dessert than for dinner. Coconut milkshakes Rs12; chocolate pancakes Rs20. No alcohol. Open daily 8am-10pm.

Wild Grass, VIP Rd., around the corner from Chung Wah. An extraordinary garden setting with ordinary South Indian dishes at non-local prices (*thalis* Rs40-90). Thatched roofs and tribal drawings evoke Orissa's "primitives." Cheap snacks (veggie burger Rs15) available daily 4-6pm. Open daily 11:30am-10:30pm.

Chung Wah, VIP Rd. Head west on CT Rd. then right on VIP Rd.; it's less than 1km down on the left. One of the cleanest and coolest spots in Puri. Veg. dishes Rs20-25. Garlic fish (Rs52) by request. Open daily 11am-3pm and 6-10:30pm.

SIGHTS

JAGANNATH TEMPLE. Constructed in the early 12th century by the Ganga king Anantavaram Chodaganga, the Jagannath Temple is a stunning example of the Kalinga style of Orissan temple architecture. Every pilgrim's entrance into Puri begins with a short devotional stop in front of the main **simhadwara** (lion gate)—the most important entrance to the east of the spectacular temple—which rises to 65m. It's *the* feature of the Puri skyline, symbolizing the power that the charcoal-faced Jagannath, the "Lord of the Universe," continues to wield over the town below.

GODS ON WHEELS Sweating, singing, shouting, and praying, exuberant crowds move en masse to enact an event of cosmic proportions. Though the **Rath Yatra** (Cart Festival) of Puri is celebrated two days after the new moon in the month of Ashadha (June-July), preparations begin a month beforehand. New *raths* (chariots) are built every year. Lord Jagannath's is the largest chariot, at nearly 14m tall, with 16 wheels, and draped in red and yellow cloth. His brother Balabhadra's chariot is 13.2m high; it has 14 wheels and red and blue cloth. Poor little sister Subhadra's, dressed in red and black cloth, is a relative titch, at a mere 12.9m, and with only 12 wheels. On the full moon of the previous month, Jyesththa (May-June), the deities are bathed and retired from public view for 14 days of treatment and rest. They reappear, refreshed, reinvigorated, and ready to roll three days before the festival day kicks off. The grand day begins with the divine procession **(Pahandi Bije),** during which the gods are carried from the temple to their chariots in a rhythmical march called *Pahandi,* accompanied by beating cymbals and drums and thousands of devotees chanting prayers. This is followed by the **Gajapati** (the King of Puri) making a gesture of *chhera paharna*, ritually "sweeping" the chariots to symbolize humanity humbling itself in preparation for the mercy and goodwill of the gods. As the mesmerizing chants and ecstatic shouts of "Jai Jagannath" fill the air, some 4000 people pull the three newly constructed chariots from the main gate of the temple east along Grand Ave. As if propelled by divine force, the *ratha* carriers proceed forward on a 3km journey. The three gods spend seven days at **Gundicha Ghar** (Garden House), where they are dressed anew each day and eat specially prepared rice cakes. Their symbolic tour of the universe, as erratic and intensely delirious as the trip to Gundicha Ghar, is completed with a repeat processional performance back to the temple on the tenth day of the new moon during Ashadha. The deities are dressed in golden clothes the following day, before taking up their places in the temple again. Nineteenth-century British observers reported that people would sometimes throw themselves under the wheels of the carts to obtain instant *moksha*. The word "juggernaut" (an object that crushes everything in its path) comes from Jagannath's name.

The three roughly hewn divinities are abstractly depicted: dense, rectangular wooden blocks represent the bodies of **Jagannath** (a form of Krishna), his brother **Balabhadra,** and his sister **Subhadra.** Tiny arms extend from stumpy legless abdomens; enormous eyes glare out from disproportionately sized, perfectly round heads. It is said that Lord Jagannath has no eyelids so that he can continually look after the well-being of the world. His small arms stretch outward in a gesture of unconditional love. Temple priests cite ancient myths to explain the peculiarly shaped forms, while academics suggest that the deities have their origins in the cults of Orissa's indigenous people.

Patterned on the same architectural principles as the older Lingaraj Temple in Bhubaneswar (see p. 615), Jagannath's abode is structurally aligned from east to west. Built in white sandstone, the temple is also known as the **White Pagoda,** a name given by the British who used it as a navigation point for sea travel. The *bhog mandir* (offering hall) and *nritya mandir* (dance hall) nearest to the entrance were 15th- and 16th-century additions to the original *jagamohana* (assembly hall). The *deul* (inner sanctuary), crowned by a 65m roof, signifies the presence of the divine trio. Earlier these three structures were surrounded by water and only accessible by boat. Over the years the moat was filled up to make the structure more stable and better protected from the cyclones that sweep in from the Bay of Bengal. Almost one fourth of the temple is underground. There is a model of the temple as it would originally have looked near the Western Gate—it shows the extent to which the temple is buried.

Surrounded by a 6m-high wall, the massive temple compound hosts action-packed days of *darshan* and treats worshippers to devotionals and sacred dances at night. The complex employs approximately 6000 specially trained priests to care for the deities (waking, cleaning, feeding, and dressing them). Communities of artists work to produce ritual materials and thousands prepare *prasad* daily for Jagannath himself. The kitchen to the left of the temple, supposedly the largest in the world, serves meals of **mahaprasad** to 10,000 people every day and up to 25,000 during festival times. The temple is strictly closed to non-Hindus—even Prime Minister Indira Gandhi was denied access because of her marriage to a Parsi.

OTHER SIGHTS. A full view of the eastern gate, the Jagannath Temple, and the surrounding smaller temples can be had from on top of the **Raghunandan Library,** across the street. Travelers are ushered in by a palm leaf manuscript expert and a congregation of temple monkeys. *(Open daily 8am-noon and 4-7pm.)* The **Lokanath Temple** is a bit of a "poor man's" Jagannath: smaller, less beautiful, and farther out of town. Still, it merits a look since its Hindus-only rule is not strictly enforced. *(1km away. Open dawn to dusk.)*

◪ BEACHES

> ❗ **ACHTUNG!** The beaches here are generally free of violent crime, but locals advise against going alone at night. Always leave your valuables in your hotel.

Puri's beaches have a reputation as the most beautiful in Eastern India. A bit like a pointillist painting, though, they tend to show their spots when seen from up close. If it's brown and it floats, it isn't a horseshoe crab! Still, for those who successfully dodge the debris, the beaches are all the entertainment most travelers need. A short walk away from the hotels will take you to cleaner sand where there are fewer sweaty massage-*wallahs* offering their oily services. At the main beach near the town center, Indian tourists wade in their customary fully-clothed style; east of CT Rd., children sell coral necklaces. For a few rupees, fishermen can often be talked into providing a boat ride or fishing excursion—though rough waters and tricky tides can make this a risky business.

🌿🎵 FESTIVALS AND ENTERTAINMENT

In a pilgrim city like Puri, festivals are common throughout the year, although locals don't always make them well-known. The grand-daddy of them all is the **Rath Yatra Festival,** when Lord Jagannath, his brother Balabhadra, and his sister Subhadra are paraded through the city on large chariots (see **Gods on Wheels,** p. 623). Puri's **Beach Festival** (late Mar. or early Apr.), showcases the best of Orissan folk dancing, music, and handicrafts. The Government of Orissa Tourist Office also arranges **dance and theatrical programs** (check their bulletin board for current information). You can always take an evening stroll along Marine Parade through the Swargadwar area and the **night market** of western Puri. Saris color the market landscape, and the bright lights from Puri's burning *ghats* glow in the distance.

CUTTACK କଟକ ☎ 0671

Cuttack might be at the top of the Mahanadi River Delta, but it's at the bottom of the charts of Orissa's most attractive and exciting destinations. Not much of interest seems to happen in this crowded town of quarter of a million people. Cuttack had an inauspicious beginning—not long after King Anangabhima Deva III founded the city, it was sacked by Muslim invaders. The Marathas and the British took their turns at sacking the town, too, but Cuttack's most recent sacker has been the Orissan government, which took away the city's one distinguishing feature by moving the state capital to Bhubaneswar, 35km away. Tourists seldom stay here for long, usually just passing through on their way to the Buddhist sites at Lalitagiri, Udayagiri, and Ratnagiri or to shop for silver and gold filigree work.

📧 **GETTING THERE AND GETTING AROUND.** Passenger **trains** run to: **Bhubaneswar** (1:54pm, 1½hr., Rs14); **Calcutta** (6 per day, 8hr., Rs95 for 2nd class); and **Puri** (3 per day, 8am-7:30pm, 3hr., Rs30). You can also catch one of the many trains on the Calcutta-Madras line that swing by the coast, but you'll pay more (Rs81 for 2nd class to Puri or Bhubaneswar). **Buses** run from the Badambadi Bus Stand to: **Bhubaneswar** (every 15min., 6:15am-10:30pm, 1hr., Rs11). Private buses to **Puri** (frequent, 2½hr., Rs20) depart from **private bus stands,** most of which are opposite the Badambadi. **Cycle-rickshaws** go almost anywhere (under Rs10), and harder-to-find **auto-rickshaws** cost twice as much.

🏛📱 **ORIENTATION AND PRACTICAL INFORMATION.** Cuttack is crammed onto a skinny finger of a peninsula that points northwest. **National Highway (NH) 5** and the railway line cut across the southeast; the fort-like **railway station** is to the east of the **Badambadi Bus Stand.** In the center of town are Cuttack's main **bazaars;** the **fort** and **dock** to Dhabaleshwar are both in the less crowded northwest. The **Tourist Office** is on Link Rd., 1km from the bus stand, on the front, left side of the Arunodag Market complex. (☎612225. Open M-Sa 10am-5pm.) It has an outpost at the railway station. (☎610507. Open daily 10am-5pm.) Local services include: the **State Bank of India,** west of Choudhury Bazaar, next to the High Court (☎618235; open M-F 10am-2pm, Sa 10am-noon); the **police** control room (☎621477); the **Popular Nursing Home,** Ring Rd. (☎614026), and its 24-hour **pharmacy;** and **Cyber Zone,** Dolmundai Square, which has Internet access for Rs3 per minute (☎611207; open daily 6am-11pm). There is an **STD/ISD** booth in the railway station, opposite the tourist office (open 5am-11pm). The **GPO** is 50m from Buxi Bazaar's main intersection. (☎620150. Open M-Sa 10am-5pm.) **Postal Code:** 753001.

🏠🍴 **ACCOMMODATIONS AND FOOD.** Seedy hotels surround the bus stations, and there are a few more hidden away in the bazaars. **Hotel Adarsh,** Choudhury Bazaar, halfway between the mosque and the jewelers, has tiny cubicles with ceiling fans and hot water in winter. (☎619201. Singles Rs50-60; doubles with bath Rs70.) That famous smile greets you at the **Hotel Mona Lisa,** rising high over Badambadi Bus Stand. The hotel has hot water buckets and 24-hour check-out.

(☎621109. Singles Rs120; doubles Rs150-300.) **Panthanivas** (☎621916 or 621867), in the middle of Buxi Bazaar, is your safest bet. **Orissa Tourism's** clean, well-maintained hotel has large rooms overlooking a courtyard, though the 8am check-out is enough to put many people off. (☎621109. Rooms Rs300-575.) The A/C **Panthanivas Hotel Restaurant** dishes up a thick, rich vegetable *korma* (Rs20). Though their official policy is to serve only guests of the hotel, it's enforced with a "don't ask, don't tell" vigilance. (☎621916. Open daily 7am-11pm, though they claim to serve guests at any time.) **Hotel City Light,** opposite the GPO, makes delicious rolls (veg. Rs8, chicken Rs12) in front of an open window. (Open daily 4pm-midnight.)

🔲 **SIGHTS.** Even the tourist office here admits that Cuttack does not contain any must-see sights. **Dhabaleshwar,** the most prominent feature in the State Tourism's pitch, is an island on the Mahanadi River. A Shiva temple, a state-run hotel, and an excuse to get out of the house make it a popular outing for locals. *(Take a town bus to Bidanasi, where small private launches at Cuttack Ghat cross the river to Dhabaleshwar.)* The road to the *ghat* passes the once-leafy **Deer Park.** Since the cyclone, the poor deer are often seen searching for grass in their small barren compound. The ruins of **Barbati Fort,** built by the Maharaja of Cuttack, are near a park in the northwest of town. Demolished by the British, the fort is now only a small pile of stones remains from what was once a nine-story palace marred by graffiti. Unless you're an avid student of history, you don't want to come here.

NEAR CUTTACK: LALITAGIRI ଲଳିତଗିରି, UDAYAGIRI ଉଦୟଗିରି, AND RATNAGIRI ରତ୍ନଗିରି

Orissa's "Golden Triangle" of tourism might be shaped by the towering temples of Bhubaneswar, Konark, and Puri, but the state has a rich Buddhist heritage as well. Forming their own triangle of sorts, Udayagiri, Lalitagiri, and Ratnagiri stand as remarkable ancient monuments to a religious culture steeped in art and learning. Excavations on the ruins, only discovered in 1984, are ongoing, providing great opportunities to view ancient relics before they get bundled away to museums and have labels stuck on them. **Lalitagiri's** 12th-century ruins are the smallest site and include a large brick monastery, stupas, and numerous other artifacts in various stages of discovery and recovery. The site at **Udayagiri,** dating from the 9th century, has a stupa, a brick monastery, a beautiful stone step-well, and some splendid hilltop sculptures. **Ratnagiri,** the largest Buddhist site in Orissa, also features monasteries, shrines, sculptures, a statue of the Buddha, and a huge collection of stupas at its entrance. There is also an Archeological Survey of India **museum** here that displays artifacts found at the three sites. *(Open M-Th, Sa and Su 10am-5pm. Rs2.)*

All three sites can be visited on a daytrip from Cuttack, with lots of gorgeous natural scenery to feast your eyes on along the way. From the **private bus** yard, take the 60km (1hr.) ride to **Chandikol. Tempos** from the bus stand make the journey to Ratnagiri and stop at Udayagiri on the way back (Rs250 round-trip, add Rs100 for Lalitagiri). You can also climb aboard a tempo ferrying locals to villages near the sites. It's possible to complete the entire circuit in this way for less than Rs20, but you will need very good karma to find tempos when you need them. Bring plenty of water—*dhabas* are ubiquitous in Chandikol, but bottled water is scarce. *(All sites open daily dawn-dusk. Free.)*

BIHAR बिहार

Bihar is justly proud of its past. Some of India's most formative events took place in its
once-thick forests. The region gets its name from the word *vihara* (monastery), refer-
ring to the secluded centers of Buddhist learning that flourished here more than a thousand years ago. The Buddha attained enlightenment under a tree in Bodh Gaya, and the
Mauryan and Gupta Empires both grew from the city of Pataliputra (modern-day Patna).

BIHAR

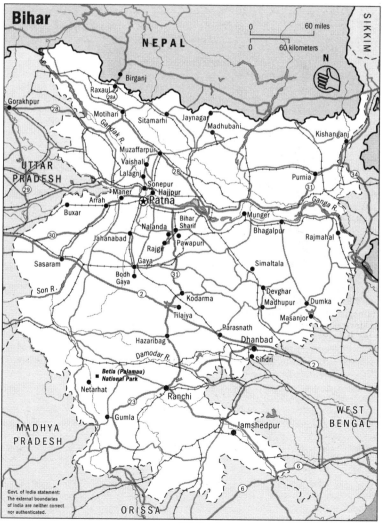

Bihar

NEPAL

SIKKIM

60 miles
60 kilometers

N

Birganj
Raxaul
(28A)
Gorakhpur
(28)
Motihari
Gandak R.
Sitamarhi
Jaynagar
Madhubani
Kishanganj
Muzaffarpur
Vaishali
UTTAR
PRADESH
(29)
Lalganj
Sonepur
Purnia
(28)
(31)
(34)
Maner
Hajipur
Ganga R.
Arrah
Patna
Buxar
Bihar
Sharif
Munger
Nalanda
Bhagalpur
Rajmahal
(30)
Jahanabad
Rajgir
Pawapuri
Sasaram
Gaya
Simaltala
Son R.
Bodh
Gaya
(31)
Devghar
Dumka
Kodarma
Madhupur
Tilaiya
Masanjor
Parasnath
Hazaribag
Dhanbad
Damodar R.
Sindri
(2)
Betla (Palamau)
National Park
Netarhat
WEST
BENGAL
(23)
Ranchi
MADHYA
PRADESH
Gumla
Jamshedpur
(6)
(6)
Govt. of India statement:
The external boundaries
of India are neither correct
nor authenticated.
ORISSA

HIGHLIGHTS OF BIHAR

The so-called **Lotus Circuit** traces the Buddha's footsteps through several of Bihar's towns—**Bodh Gaya** (p. 636), where the Buddha attained enlightenment; **Rajgir** (p. 632), where his teachings were first compiled; **Nalanda** (p. 634), a major center of learning and philosophy, and **Vaishali** (p. 641), where some of his ashes are interred.

However, few tangible traces are left of Bihar's past glories—the state is now the poorest and least urbanized in India. Bihari politics have seen an unending stream of controversy and periodic outbreaks of caste-based violence over the years. In 1997, Bihar's Chief Minister, Laloo Prasad Yadav, stepped down after a series of corruption scandals; in his place, he appointed his illiterate wife Rabri Devi and promised to continue his rule via mobile phone from his prison cell. In the February 2000 state assembly elections, everything indicated that a broad anti-Laloo coalition was finally going to oust the cowherd couple from power. Defying poll predictions and common sense, the master of caste politics managed to emerge victorious, and his party remains the strongest force in the state. Much of the Bihari countryside is effectively ruled by *goondas* (thugs) with under-the-table connections to politicians, and *dacoits* (bandits) are still part of Bihari life.

Traveling in Bihar can be a frustrating business; conditions are basic, electricity cuts are frequent, and journeys of just a few kilometers can take most of the day. Partly because of these logistical inconveniences and the state's general lawlessness, Bihar draws few Western tourists. Some come to visit its important Buddhist sites, and many simply pass through on their way to Nepal, but it is worth putting up with Bihar's many hassles for the insight it offers into an India outside the big baksheesh cocoon of the major tourist circuit.

PATNA पटना   ☎ 0612

Most visitors catch their first glimpse of Patna from the railway station—one of the dirtiest and most chaotic places in the whole of India—and vow to head out to another destination as soon as the congested station will allow. Many find Patna's essence captured in the name of one of its major streets: Boring Road. There is little to see here and even less to do; most travelers opt to stay in this

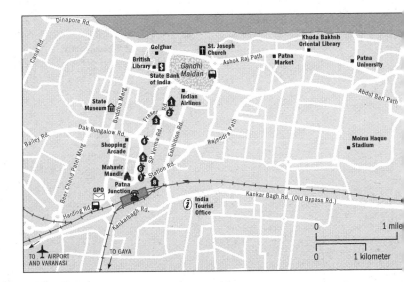

energy-sapping sump of a city for as little time as possible before heading out to Nepal or the next stop on the Buddhist pilgrim circuit. All this is in spite of Patna's illustrious history. The Mauryan empire had its center here, and the Guptas, too, made this their capital. Pataliputra, as it was called back then, was abandoned after the decline of the Guptas, but it rose again during the 17th century to become a regional center for the Mughals. The birth of the last guru Gobind Singh turned a narrow lane in the north of the city into a major Sikh pilgrimage destination. The East India Company had its largest opium warehouses here, now converted (vice for vice) into a state government printing office. Though the city continues to serve Bihar and the rest of northeast India as a major industrial center, the glory days are long gone and there is not much here to draw camera-toting tourists.

⬛ GETTING THERE AND GETTING AROUND

Flights: Patna Airport, 6km from the railway station (taxi Rs150, auto-rickshaw Rs50, cycle-rickshaw Rs25). **Indian Airlines,** Gandhi Maidan (☎222554). Open daily 10am-1pm and 2-4:30pm. To: **Bombay** (4:50pm, 4 hr., US$162); **Calcutta** (8:25pm, 1 hr., US$75); **Delhi** (8:55am and 4:50pm, 2 hr., US$109). **Necon Air,** in the Ashoka Hotel, on Fraser Rd. (☎224511), flies to **Kathmandu** (M, W, F, Sa; 1hr.; US$79).

Trains: To: **Bombay** (1-3 per day, 1-11:20pm, 33hr., Rs223); **Calcutta** (6-9 per day, 2:20am-9:40pm, 7-11hr., Rs154); **Delhi** (8-11 per day, 4:40am-11:55pm, 13-25hr., Rs252); **Gaya** (4 per day, 9:50am-10:40pm, 2-4hr., Rs30); **Guwahati** (2-4 per day, 5:30am-10:15pm, 21-25hr., Rs270); **Rajgir** (daily, 7:15am and 4:30pm, 5hr., Rs16); **Varanasi** (1-2 per day, 6:15-11am, 3-5hr., Rs61).

Buses: You can get anywhere in Bihar from **Harding Rd.,** 500m west of the railway station. To: **Bihar Sharif** (every 10 min., 4:30am-8pm, 3hr., Rs30); **Gaya** (4 per day, 5:30am-2:30pm, 3hr., Rs40); **Rajgir** (every 2hr., 5am-5pm, 4hr., Rs40); **Raxaul** (every 1½hr., 6am-noon, and 11:30pm, 6 hr., Rs100); and **Vaishali** (4 per day, 5am-1:30pm, 2hr., Rs25). Frequent buses run to **Rajgir** (1hr., Rs12) from Bihar Sharif. From the intersection of Gandhi Maidan and Ashok Raj Path, buses head to **Siliguri** (3:30pm, Rs140).

Local Transportation: Shared **tempos** ply the main city arteries (Rs2-5 per ride) between the railway station and Gandhi Maidan.

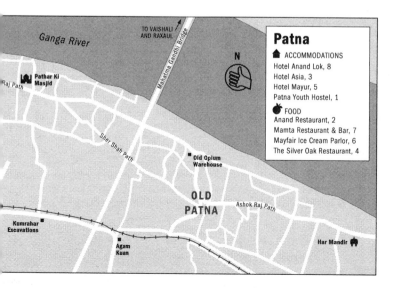

Patna

🏠 ACCOMMODATIONS
Hotel Anand Lok, 8
Hotel Asia, 3
Hotel Mayur, 5
Patna Youth Hostel, 1

🍴 FOOD
Anand Restaurant, 2
Mamta Restaurant & Bar, 7
Mayfair Ice Cream Parlor, 6
The Silver Oak Restaurant, 4

✈ 🛈 ORIENTATION AND PRACTICAL INFORMATION

Patna sprawls along the south bank of the mighty Ganga. Getting from east to west across the city is a road trip in itself. **Ashok Raj Path** is the main thoroughfare, sticking close to the river the whole way. **Kankar Bagh Rd. (Old Bypass Rd.)** covers the same distance on the southern side of the city, just south of the railroad tracks. The east end of town is Old Patna. Most trains stop at **Patna Junction Station,** in the west. **Fraser Rd.,** where Patna's hotels, restaurants, and other conveniences are concentrated, runs straight north from the station. The **Gandhi Maidan,** a large park north of Fraser Rd. (touching Ashok Raj Path), is a major landmark and local transportation hub. Next to the railway station, **Station Rd.** leads west to the **bus station** and various government buildings.

Tourist Office: State Government Tourist Office, Fraser Rd. (☎225295), 300m up on the right, on the 2nd fl. of the Silver Oak Restaurant and Bar. Open M-Sa 10am-5pm. **Government of India Tourist Office,** Sudama Palace Complex, 3rd fl., Kankarbagh Rd. (☎345776), near the Jasmine Hotel. Tall building on the right by the petrol pump; no sign on the street, only on the 3rd fl. balcony. Open M-F 9am-6pm, Sa 9am-1pm.

Budget Travel: Royal Nepal Airlines, Dunlop Compound, Fraser Rd. (☎231946), just before the road makes a right bend. Ultra-knowledgeable staff.

Currency Exchange: State Bank of India, Gandhi Maidan (☎226134), on the left. Open M-F 10:30am-4pm, Sa 10:30am-12:30pm.

Luggage Storage: On the right as you exit the railway station. Rs7 per piece, per day.

Bookstore: Tricel, Fraser Rd. (☎221412), opposite the Satkar International Hotel. Open M-Sa 10:30am-8:30pm.

Library: British Library, Bank Rd. (☎24198). Open Tu-Sa 10:30am-6:30pm.

Market: Colorful market lanes along Ashok Raj Path sell everything from bananas to books and electronics. Station Rd. sells the essentials, but without the color.

Police: Control Room (☎223131), on N. Gandhi Maidan, next to the white-domed Shri Krishna Memorial Hall.

Pharmacy: Popular Pharmacy (☎226393), on the left of the railway station, opposite the mosque on the far side. Open daily 8:30am-10:30pm.

Hospital: Raj Lakshmi Nursing Home, Kankarbagh Rd. (☎352225 or 354320), 4km east of the Government of India Tourist Office.

Internet: Cyberzone, SP Verma Rd. (☎224717), before the intersection with Fraser Rd., opposite the Ruby Hotel. Rs70 per hr. Open M-Sa 10am-8:30pm.

Post Office: GPO, Station Rd., to the left, opposite the railway station. Open M-Sa 10am-4pm, Su 10am-1pm. **Postal Code:** 800001.

▟ ACCOMMODATIONS

Fraser Rd. is the only place in Patna to find hotels, all of which are run down and dirty. Are you having fun yet?

Hotel Anand Lok, Station Rd. (☎223960), is a large white building towering over the railway station. A gate by the luggage office leads right to the door. Excellent service. Despite the noise, this is your best bet for a hassle-free night's sleep. Spacious rooms have attached baths. Check-out 24hr. Singles Rs214-321; doubles Rs294-428.

Patna Youth Hostel (☎211486), Fraser Rd., after it jogs right, then left. Basic concrete rooms, some with beds. Rs20 per bed (or floor space), plus Rs50 annual membership.

Hotel Mayur (☎224142), on the right, 500m up Fraser Rd. from the railway station. Classical statuettes and a great wooden peacock are just a few of the tasteful *objets d'art* arranged around the Mayur's reception lobby, where busy fans clack like castanets and compete with the around-the-clock entertainment of the hotel's favorite TV. Clean but dark rooms with attached baths. Singles Rs268; doubles Rs332-642.

Hotel Asia (☎227702), on Fraser Rd., between the right and left bends. Sandwiched between a school, a restaurant, and another hotel, the rooms don't get much air, but the management tries to keep them painted and bearable. Attached bath with squat toilets. Singles Rs150; doubles Rs200.

FOOD

Patna is a good place to try *lithi,* made from a mixture of wheat and bean flour, spiced with onions and green peppers, served with curry vegetables or lentils. *Khaja,* a deep fried biscuit with both salty and sweet variations, is another Bihar specialty. Pyramids of this crisp dough adorn shops in front of the museum.

Anand Restaurant, on the 2nd floor of the new building at the intersection of Fraser and S.P. Verma Rd. The menu, loaded with *Kiev shashliks* (Rs65), is a bold attempt to be different. It works. The intimate lighting and cushioned sofas make Anand popular with college students who—without exception—come here in pairs. Open 10am-11pm.

Mayfair Ice Cream Parlor and Restaurant, Fraser Rd., opposite the Bansi Vihar, 5min. from the railway station. With all the dark, subterranean charm of an aging army mess hall, the Mayfair is packed most nights with young people sucking in the cool air and slurping down ice cream (Rs15). Flavors include vanilla, strawberry, and blind love. Lengthy veg. (Rs18-42) and non-veg. (Rs22-60) menus too. Open daily 8am-10:30pm.

Mamta Restaurant and Bar, Fraser Rd., next to Mayfair Ice Cream Parlor. A friendly, well-cooled oasis to recuperate after a day spent struggling in the smog and noise. Fish bubble away in the bar-side aquarium, and a welcome air of calm and quiet pervades. Good food at decent prices. *Kashmiri korma* Rs40. Open daily 10am-10pm.

The Silver Oak Restaurant and Bar, Fraser Rd., on the right toward Gandhi Maidan, just before the road veers right and merges with SP Verma Rd. From finger chips and fried *chappatis* to peanuts and *paneer pakora,* the Silver Oak packs in the locals on a nightly basis for beer (Rs65) and bar snacks to the background hum of American light rock. Open daily 11:30am-10pm.

SIGHTS

PATNA MUSEUM. The Patna Museum contains a superb collection of stone and bronze sculpture, much of it dating from the Mauryan (3rd century BC) and Gupta (4th-6th centuries AD) periods. Most of the rest of the exhibits can be safely skipped. *(Buddha Marg. Open Tu-Sa 10:30am-4:40pm. Rs2.)*

HAR MANDIR. In the twisting lanes of Old Patna is Har Mandir, a Sikh *gurud-wara* that marks the birthplace of the 10th and last Sikh guru, Gobind Singh (b. 1666). The second-most important throne of the Sikh religion (after the Golden Temple in Amritsar), Har Mandir is an impressive, white-domed building set among the busy bustle of the old town's *chowk.* The present building was built after a 1954 earthquake destroyed the original temple. You can climb a set of steps inside the temple up to the roof, which offers a good view of the city. A one-room museum gives a brief introduction to the Sikh holy book and the guru Granth Sahib, displaying the bloody story of the guru's life in detailed pictures. *(Share a tempo from Sri Krishna Hall on Gandhi Maidan (Rs6). Visitors need to cover their heads to enter. Open 5am-9pm; museum 8am-noon and 3-8pm. Free.)*

GOLGHAR. One of Patna's most bizarre landmarks is the Golghar, an egg-shaped grain storage bin near Gandhi Maidan. Built in 1786 to protect against famine, it was never used and now sits like a great stone space helmet just to the left of Gandhi Maidan. Two staircases spiral high above the street and offer one of the quickest ways for people to get up out of the smog and dirt at ground level, hence its otherwise inexplicable popularity.

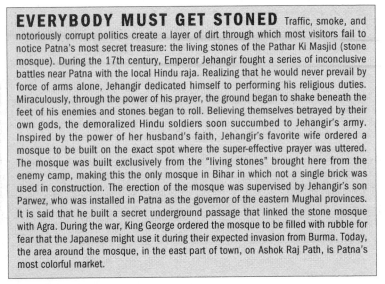

EVERYBODY MUST GET STONED Traffic, smoke, and notoriously corrupt politics create a layer of dirt through which most visitors fail to notice Patna's most secret treasure: the living stones of the Pathar Ki Masjid (stone mosque). During the 17th century, Emperor Jehangir fought a series of inconclusive battles near Patna with the local Hindu raja. Realizing that he would never prevail by force of arms alone, Jehangir dedicated himself to performing his religious duties. Miraculously, through the power of his prayer, the ground began to shake beneath the feet of his enemies and stones began to roll. Believing themselves betrayed by their own gods, the demoralized Hindu soldiers soon succumbed to Jehangir's army. Inspired by the power of her husband's faith, Jehangir's favorite wife ordered a mosque to be built on the exact spot where the super-effective prayer was uttered. The mosque was built exclusively from the "living stones" brought here from the enemy camp, making this the only mosque in Bihar in which not a single brick was used in construction. The erection of the mosque was supervised by Jehangir's son Parwez, who was installed in Patna as the governor of the eastern Mughal provinces. It is said that he built a secret underground passage that linked the stone mosque with Agra. During the war, King George ordered the mosque to be filled with rubble for fear that the Japanese might use it during their expected invasion from Burma. Today, the area around the mosque, in the east part of town, on Ashok Raj Path, is Patna's most colorful market.

KUMRAHAR EXCAVATION PARK. Two solitary pillars—one standing, one broken—and a mound indicate that Ashoka's splendid capital of Pataliputra once stood here. There is not much to see, but the park's vegetation does offer a break from Patna's modern bustle. *(5km out of town. Take a Rs4 tempo from the railway station along Kankar Bagh Rd. Open Tu-Sa 8am-4:30pm. Rs2.)*

KHUDA BAKHSH ORIENTAL LIBRARY. The library houses a vast collection of Arabic and Persian manuscripts as well as the only books rescued from the plunder of the University of Cordoba. Display cases show off a few illuminated manuscripts, 19th-century astronomical and astrological equipment, and a manuscript copy of a poem by Rabindranath Tagore. *(Ashok Raj Path. Open Sa-Th 9:30am-5pm.)*

RAJGIR राजगीर ☎06112

Although the centuries have reduced the capital of the once-powerful Magadha kingdom to rubble, the impressive mountain walls that once marked the boundaries of the inner city continue to evoke the past glory of Rajgir, Mountain of Kings. Since the town figured prominently in the life of the Buddha, pilgrims flock here during the winter months to climb Vulture Peak, where the Buddha delivered many of his most famous sermons. The first Buddhist Council took place in Rajgir, and the extensive ruins of the university at Nalanda nearby convey a sense of the success and scale of Buddhist learning that thrived here for nearly a thousand years. Jain influence in Rajgir was also strong; Jain temples dot the low hills around the town center, commemorating the 14 seasons that Mahavira spent in this tranquil valley. Surrounded by mountains, scattered with ruins, and still very much alive as a major pilgrimage site for three religions, Rajgir is the most scenic and most relaxed of all Bihar's Buddhist towns.

▐ GETTING THERE AND GETTING AROUND. Jeeps and **buses** from Bihar Sharif pass Nalanda and then, 15km later, arrive at the bus stand in Rajgir. From here, buses run to **Gaya** (every 30min., 6:30am-6pm, 3hr., Rs24); **Nalanda** (every 10min., Rs4); and **Patna** (2 per day, 3 and 6pm, 4hr., Rs28). For Patna, take a jeep or bus to **Bihar Sharif** first (frequent, 5am-7pm, 1hr., Rs10) and catch a bus from there (3hr., Rs25). **Trains** go to **Patna** (2 per day, 5:30am and 3:30pm, 4hr., Rs16).

◼◪ ORIENTATION AND PRACTICAL INFORMATION. From the **bus stand,** the **bypass road** continues to the hot springs and on to the ropeway. A dirt street lined with shops leads left from the bus stand, and after 200m, hits the **main street,** which connects with the bypass road at the hot springs. The **post office,** the **New Popular pharmacy** (open 6am-9pm), and the **police station** (☎25228) are all next to each other on the main street. **Postal Code:** 803116.

▛▟ ACCOMMODATIONS AND FOOD. Two monasteries offer flawless lodging over the dried channel of a mythical river and the ruined ramparts of an ancient fort. In January and February, Burmese nirvana-seekers occasionally fill these places, sending you spinning out to the darkest reaches of samsara in search of good alternatives. Good luck. The **Burmese Buddhist Temple,** at the end of the main road, is a good, friendly place away from the noise, with views of the fields and hills. Plaques attesting to the karma-improving effects of the place adorn everything from the fridge to the ceiling fans to the crockery. (☎5024. Beds in single, double, and triple rooms with clean common baths are Rs50.) The **Bengali Buddhist Society Temple,** next to the Burmese temple, overlooks the dwindling stream that is still considered a sacred river. Rooms lack views but feature tiled, geyser-equipped bathrooms capable of pleasing gods, bodhisattvas, and backpackers alike. (Rooms Rs100-200.) If your karma is bad enough to get you shut out of both these places, there is always the **Hotel Gautam Vihar,** also known as Government Bungalow #1, on the main road between the bus stand and the railway station. This has large, high-ceilinged rooms around a pleasant garden. (☎55273. Dorm beds Rs50; doubles Rs321-535. Off-season: Rs25/221-535.) In the evenings, the **Blue Beer Bar,** on the main road opposite the all-singing, all-dancing Raj Hotel, offers a lively environment for the mostly mustachioed crowd to engage in drinking and spitting competitions. Particularly atmospheric during power cuts.

◪ SIGHTS. Rajgir's sights are spread out over a 5km long stretch of road best covered by **tonga** (Rs35-50). Centers of Buddhist interest are on **Ratnagiri,** at the far end of the road. A creaking **chair lift**—the "pride of Rajgir"—leads up to the top, where the huge Japanese-built **Vishva Shanti Stupa** (world peace stupa) casts its shadow over the valley below. (Chair lift open 8am-1pm and 2-5pm. Rs15.) Banging drums and voices chanting the Lotus Sutra echo out over the hills from the small temple next door. From the stupa, a small path winds around the side of the mountain back down to the road; take the first left onto a series of stony steps that leads up and down until it arrives at **Gridhrakuta,** or "Vulture's Peak." Once a favorite rainy season retreat of the Buddha, Gridhrakuta marks the site of two caves where the Buddha gave sermons. The remains of a monastery from the Gupta period are also here. At the foot of Ratnagiri are the remains of **Jivakamra Vana,** an early monastery built in the mango garden that was another of the Buddha's favorite spots.

Near the intersection with Gaya Rd. is **King Bimbisara's jail,** where the Buddhist convert-king was imprisoned and eventually executed by his son and successor, Ajatasatru. Legend says that the king chose the site of his own incarceration; from here he could look out from his cell and watch the Buddha as he meditated and taught on the mountainside. One kilometer back toward Rajgir are the remains of **Manyar Math,** believed to have been a temple dedicated to cobra worship. Along the dirt road that passes the *math* are two chambers carved out of the cliff-face, known as the **Swarna Bhandar,** which are said to mark the location of Bimbisara's treasury. A "secret" doorway is supposed to lead from the cave through the rock into the still-intact treasure trove.

At the foot of Mt. Vaibhara, on the outskirts of town, is **Brahma Kunj,** where a half-dozen hot springs have been incorporated into the design of a Hindu temple. A sign at the entrance warns non-Hindus not to enter, but this rule is not always strictly enforced. A stone stairway past the baths leads up to **Pippala Cave,** a rectangular piece of rock that was once a hermits' refuge. The stairway continues up to the **Saptaparni Cave,** where 500 of the Buddha's disciples held the first Buddhist

Council. The surrounding hills are home to over 40 Jain shrines, most of them connected by stone paths. Visiting the temples on the five principle mountains of the area—in clockwise direction, Vipulachal, Ratnagiri, Udaxgiri, Savrangiri, and Vaibhargiri—is an arduous task but well worth the stunning views and the insight they give into Jainism. Bring enough change to leave as an offering with the temple keepers or the gods will curse you to the point of no return.

DAYTRIPS FROM RAJGIR

NALANDA. Built by the Guptas during the 5th century, and with a reputation as a center of learning that dates back to the 1st millennium BC, Nalanda is the site of one of the oldest universities in the world. By the time the Buddha made his visits here, the town was already a teeming and prosperous population center. Other religious VIPs came to Nalanda: Jainism's founder Mahavira used it as a retreat from the monsoon, and Sariputra, the Buddha's earliest disciple, was born and also died here. Legendary Chinese traveler Xuanzang, known for his detailed accounts of the places he visited on his sutra-collecting journeys around India, studied at the university during the 7th century along with 4000 other students studying everything from Buddhist and Vedic philosophy to logic, grammar, chemistry, and medicine. As Nalanda's fame grew during the centuries that followed, so did its size. New buildings soared to the height of nine stories, and with the aid of King Harsha of Kannauj, Nalanda amassed a library of over nine million manuscripts. By the 13th century, though, successive waves of Muslim invaders had chased out all the students and reduced the library's collection to cinders.

Today, it is possible to walk through the excavated remains of a dozen monastery buildings, all situated within a peaceful, evocative, and well-kept **park** run by the Archaeological Survey of India. Guides offer their services at the gate *(Rs50)*, but you can guide yourself by reading the plaques flanking each monument. *(Open daily 7:30am-5pm. Rs2; Free F.)* There is a small **museum** opposite the entrance 200m down the road, containing stone and bronze Pala sculpture. *(Open Sa-Th 10am-4:40pm. Rs2.)* Continue along this road, past the park and museum, to admire the detailed carvings on a recently constructed Jain temple. In the middle of the village behind the temple is the **Surya Mandir** (Sun Temple), which houses a number of black stone images that predate even the ruins of the university. The remains of a **main temple** are at the south entrance. A **smaller temple** to the right of the monasteries is plastered with 6th-century wall paintings. A **museum** here houses a collection of Buddhist images and other archaeological finds unearthed nearby. *(Frequent jeeps and buses leave for Nalanda from the bus stand at Rajgir (Rs4). From Nalanda's bus stand, you can share a tonga (Rs5), or walk 2km to the site. Open Sa-Th 10am-5pm. Rs2.)*

PAWAPURI. Revered as a sinless city, Pawapuri is the holiest pilgrimage site of the Jains. Mahavira delivered his last sermon and was cremated here. The white marble Jalamandir and Samosharan temples in Pawapuri are supreme examples of Jain craftsmanship. From Rajgir, take a bus or jeep to Bihar Sharif (1hr, Rs10); from there, catch the next flying pig to Pawapuri (30min, Rs5).

GAYA गया   ☎ 0631

According to folklore, the name Gaya derives from the demon Gayasura, who purified himself through a rigorous series of yoga poses and received as a reward this sacred tract of land along the River Phalgu. As an additional reward, Gaya was also imbued with the power to absolve ancestral sins—it is said that one *shraddha* (funeral rite) in Gaya is equivalent to 11 *shraddhas* anywhere else. Hindu pilgrims visit each of the 45 shrines in Gaya (including the Bodhi Tree in Bodh Gaya), offering prayers for the dead and rupees for the *gayaval* (attending priests). The in-season comes in September when the Phalgu swells with the monsoon rains and thousands of pilgrims descend the *ghats* to perform their ritual ablutions. Gaya is almost as important to devout Hindus as its sister city is to Buddhists.

Unfortunately, many of the most important sites are closed to non-Hindus. Besides the shrines, Gaya has little to recommend it. Thirty-six kilometers north are the **Barabar Caves,** a series of rock-hewn Jain temples dating from the 3rd century BC, that were featured as the "Marabar Caves" in E.M. Forster's *A Passage to India*.

GETTING THERE AND GETTING AROUND

Trains: Trains leave from **Gaya Junction Station.** The railway reservation office is to the right of the station. Open M-Sa 8am-8pm, Su 8am-2pm. To: **Bela** (10 per day, 1hr., Rs17); **Calcutta** (4-6 per day, 3:20am-11:20pm, 6-7½hr., Rs104); **Delhi** (2-5 per day, 1:30am-10pm, 12-16hr., Rs270); **Patna** (2:17am in theory, 2½hr., Rs31; frequent, slower "passenger" trains); **Varanasi** (4 per day, 2am-9pm, 4-5½hr., Rs61). From Bela to the **Barabar Caves,** it's a 12km tempo or tonga ride (Rs20-25) plus a 5km walk.

Buses: Depart from the **Zila School Bus Stand** to Bodh Gaya (frequent, 30min.-1hr., Rs6). The **Manpur Bus Stand,** across the Phalgu River, near the bridge, has buses to **Nalanda** and **Rajgir** (every hr., 6am-6pm, 3hr., Rs24).

Local Transportation: Rickshaws go to the Zila School Bus Stand; to the Vishnupad Temple or Shaktipith (Rs10). Shared **tempos** run between the railway station, Gandhi Chowk, and the Manpur Bus Stand (Rs6).

ORIENTATION AND PRACTICAL INFORMATION

Gaya is on the western bank of the Phalgu River. At the northern end of the town is the **Gaya Junction Station,** connected to the main bazaar and **Gandhi Chowk** via the twisting **Station Rd.** The southern edge of the city is marked by **Shaktipith, Brahmyoni Hill,** and **Vishnupad Temple. Gautama Buddha (GB) Rd.** runs here from Gandhi Chowk and continues another 10km south to reach **Bodh Gaya.**

Tourist Office: Inside the railway station. Has a wall map of Gaya. Open M-Sa 6am-8pm.

Currency Exchange: The nearest banks that change currency are in Bodh Gaya. The **Siddharth International Hotel** (☎436243) will change major currencies and traveler's checks at alarmingly low exchange rates.

Luggage Storage: Platform 1, Gaya Junction Station. Rs7 per day. Open 24hr.

Market: Saris, fruits, beer, watches and pink plastic telephones—all this and more can be yours in the lanes that converge on Gandhi Chowk's clock tower.

Police: Control Room (☎223131 or 223132). **Emergency:** ☎20999.

Hospital: The **Magadh Medical College** (☎22410) is a government hospital. Bihar's government services being what they are, Gaya is an awful place to be sick.

Telephones: There is a 24hr. **STD/ISD** booth is inside the railway station.

Post Office: HPO, GB Rd., one block east of Zila school bus stand. Open M-Sa 10am-4pm. There is a smaller post office on Station Rd., 150m right of the station, on the left. **Postal Code:** 823001.

ACCOMMODATIONS

Hotel Buddha, Laxman Sahay Ln. (☎423428), straight back from the railway station, at the end of a long road perpendicular to Station Rd. Much quieter than the hotels along Station Rd. Small, sunny, clean doubles have comfortable mattresses, TVs, and attached baths with decent showers. Singles Rs150; doubles Rs200.

Ajatsatru Hotel, Station Rd. (☎434584), opposite the railway station. One of the largest hotels along the crowded Station Rd. strip and the least spartan in terms of facilities. Check-out 24hr. Singles from Rs160; doubles Rs195-595.

Pal Rest House, Station Rd. (☎436753). Turn right out of the station; 250m down on the left-hand side, after the post office. Simple rooms around a central stairwell. This is an unremarkable little place, but it passes the all-important "clean, cheap, and friendly" test. Singles Rs65-90; doubles Rs120.

Hotel Saluja, Station Rd. (☎436243), 50m past Pal Rest House. Crams dark but surprisingly comfortable rooms into a narrow passageway that faces its twin, the Punjab Hotel. TV, fans, and the occasional carpet. Singles Rs125; doubles Rs225.

🕐 FOOD

Haji Market, a block south of Gandhi Chowk, next to Chatta Masjid, is the place to taste the local speciality of *bakharkhani,* a crisp, round, Muslim bread that can be savored crisp with an afternoon tea or downed in larger quantities as an accompaniment to curry. The **Sujata Restaurant,** in the Ajatsatra Hotel, has great food and good service, and serves the best meals in Gaya. (Vegetable curry Rs25; chicken *biryani* Rs45. Open 7am-11:30pm.)

🔎 SIGHTS

Though Gaya is one of Hinduism's most sacred cities, its temples lack the splendor and atmosphere of those in other large pilgrimage centers. The shrines listed below are within easy walking distance from each other.

VISHNUPAD TEMPLE. Towering over the bank of the Phalgu River, this golden-spired temple contains a 2m-long footprint of Vishnu in the form of the Buddha that is enshrined in a silver basin. Non-Hindus may not enter the main shrine, but they can try to get a closer look at the sanctum (but not the footprint) by climbing the stairs at the back of the first shop to the left of the temple entrance.

BRAHMYONI HILL. One-thousand steep stones twist up to the Shiv Mandir at the top of this hill, where you are rewarded with a rare lungful of fresh air and views over Gaya, Bodh Gaya, and the surrounding countryside. There is also a small goddess temple with an image of Vishnu's foot at the door. The hill is sacred to Buddhists, as it is associated with Gayasirsan, the mountain where the Buddha delivered several important sermons. (*1km southwest of the Vishnupad Temple.*)

DURGA TEMPLE. In this rather mundane temple, non-Hindus can observe and even participate in the *shraddhas* (funeral rites). Pilgrims wishing to perform the *shraddha* at Gaya must first circumambulate their own village five times. Once in Gaya, a *gayaval* (priest trained in the *shraddha*) guides them in a complicated ritual involving Sanskrit prayers and offerings of *pinda* (water and rice kneaded into a ball). (*1 km east of the Vishnupad Temple.*)

SHAKTIPITH. Sati's breast fell here after she was cut to pieces (see **Divine Dismemberment,** p. 692). Images of the goddess are housed in a squat, cavernous mausoleum, inscribed on the front with the epic verse of Sati's destruction. (*Open daily 6am-noon and 1pm-midnight.*)

BODH GAYA बोध गया ☎ 0631

Of all the holy Buddhist sites scattered around northern India, Bodh Gaya is the holiest by far. One of the most significant events in the history of Asia took place here in the 6th century BC, when Prince Siddhartha Gautama gained enlightenment after prolonged meditation under the famous pipal tree, a descendent of which still stands on the same spot today. For Buddhists, this is the most important pilgrimage site in the world, and Bihar's other Buddhist sites, most of which consist of little more than piles of rubble, pale in comparison.

The Buddhist presence in Bodh Gaya, however, is quite new and mostly foreign. Although Buddhist monasteries thrived here long ago, they were left to sink into the mud after Buddhism faded out of India in the 12th century. It wasn't until the 19th century that Bodh Gaya was reborn as an important religious center, when British-led archaeological teams persuaded monks from Sri Lanka and Burma to raise the funds necessary to restore the Mahabodhi Temple to its former glory.

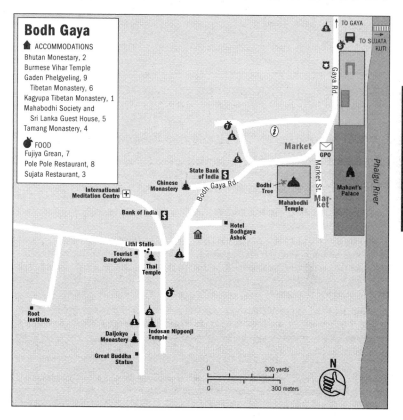

Bodh Gaya

▲ ACCOMMODATIONS
Bhutan Monestary, 2
Burmese Vihar Temple
Gaden Phelgyeling, 9
   Tibetan Monastery, 6
Kagyupa Tibetan Monastery, 1
Mahabodhi Society and
   Sri Lanka Guest House, 5
Tamang Monastery, 4

🍲 FOOD
Fujiya Grean, 7
Pole Pole Restaurant, 8
Sujata Restaurant, 3

TO GAYA

TO SUJATA KUTI

Gaya Rd.

Market

GPO

Phalgu River

BIHAR

State Bank
of India

Bodhi
Tree

Chinese
Monastery

Bodh Gaya Rd.

Mahabodhi
Temple

Market St.

Mahant's
Palace

Market

International
Meditation Centre

Bank of India

Hotel
Bodhgaya
Ashok

Lithi Stalls

Tourist
Bungalows

Thai
Temple

Root
Institute

Daijokyo
Monastery

Indosan Nipponji
Temple

Great Buddha
Statue

0   300 yards
0   300 meters

N

The winter (Dec.-Feb.) is the busiest and most vibrant time to visit, when students, pilgrims, and monks from around the world (the Dalai Lama included) congregate here. The monasteries fill up, visiting teachers offer meditation courses, tent restaurants spring up to see to the pilgrims' more secular needs, and monks from around the world intone sutras in monasteries and temples built in their own national styles. By April, however, the crowds thin out, many of the restaurants and hotels close down, and the streets of Bodh Gaya again take on the air of meditative quietude that has reigned here for thousands of years.

📇 GETTING THERE AND GETTING AROUND

Buses leave for **Gaya** from the stand near the Burmese Temple (every 30min., 5am-6pm, Rs6), with the bus stopping every 10m for passengers to embark, disembark, and sometimes just bark. Shared tempos and jeeps ply the route for the same price. A bus to **Varanasi** (5:30am, Rs60) stops in front of the Mahabodhi Society.

🗺️🛈 ORIENTATION AND PRACTICAL INFORMATION

It would require real effort to get lost in Bodh Gaya. The main road from Gaya runs through town, linking all the major sights and hotels before stopping by the **market** just in front of the **Mahabodhi Temple.** The area immediately in front of the temple has recently been converted into a paved pedestrian zone closed to traffic. Rickshaw- and postcard-*wallahs* congregate to the right of the temple, where the main road resumes again in front of the Tibetan monastery. This road turns left at the **Chinese Temple** and passes the **museum** and the **Thai Temple,** on either side of which smaller roads lead down to many of the other monasteries. The main road continues past the **Root Institute** and on to the future site of the new Maitreya statue.

Tourist Office: (☎ 400672), in the tourist bungalow compound, just after the Thai Temple on the main road out of town. There's no real reason to come here, unless you're keen to add to your collection of tourist pamphlets. Open M-Sa 10am-5pm.

Budget Travel: Middle Way Travels (☎ 400648), opposite the main temple, next to Weston Shoes. Extremely helpful and well-informed. This the best place in the area to arrange your tickets out of town. Offers all-inclusive tours of Buddhist sites in northern India and provides information on meditation courses in the area. Major credit cards accepted. Open daily 9am-9pm.

Currency Exchange: State Bank of India, Bodh Gaya Rd. (☎ 400852), in the new hotel compound next to the Chinese temple. Open M-F 10:30am-4pm, Sa 10:30am-1:30pm.

Library: Temple Management Committee of Bodh Gaya and Library (☎ 400735), at the end of the pedestrian precinct. Daily newspapers and a comprehensive range of Buddhist texts and periodicals. Open daily 9am-5pm. Adjacent bookshop open 6am-6pm.

Market: At the intersection of Gaya and Bodh Gaya Rd., a small lane to the left leads to a bazaar where you can buy fruit, handicrafts, and umbrellas.

Police: (☎ 400741), 200m past the Burmese Temple.

Hospital: Conditions at the **government hospital,** on the left on the way into town, are far from ideal. Doctors at the **Japanese temple's clinic** will see tourists in an emergency.

Telephones: Opposite the Mahabodhi Temple and in front of the Thai temple. Open 24hr.; off-season 7am-9:30pm. The Burmese Vihar's booth is open 24hr. year-round.

Internet: Several travel agents in front of the Mahabodhi Temple have computers with Internet access. Given the state of Bihar's communications, however, even brief moments online require a great deal of effort and prayer. Rs3 per min.

Post Office: Gaya Rd. (☎ 400472), on the left, as you enter town. Open M-Sa 10:30am-5pm. **Postal Code:** 842231.

ACCOMMODATIONS

Bodh Gaya is full of hotels, but the temple- and monastery-run guest houses are the best options. During the winter months, they fill up very quickly. Remember to respect the rules of the religious community—no drinking, smoking, devil-bating, or "improper sexual conduct" allowed.

▨ **Mahabodhi Society and Sri Lanka Guest House** (☎ 400742), set back from the road, across the street from the Mahabodhi Temple. Spotlessly clean and conscientiously managed place offers accommodations ranging from dorms (Rs100) to deluxe doubles with attached baths (Rs450). Book 2 months in advance for Oct.-Mar. Check-out 24hr.

▨ **Bhutan Temple,** Temple Rd. (☎ 400710), near the Great Buddha image. In a beautiful garden dominated by a colorful Bhutanese-style temple. Rooms are clean and spacious and have mosquito nets. Gates close 9:30pm. Doubles Rs100-200. Fills up Nov.-Dec.

Gaden Phelgyeling Tibetan Monastery, next to the Mahabodhi Society. An ever-expanding universe overrun by Tibetan monks Oct.-Feb. Gates close 9:30pm. Tiny singles Rs50; larger rooms with bath Rs100.

Kagyupa Tibetan Monastery, near Temple Rd. (☎ 400795). The more remote and peaceful of the two Tibetan temples, Kagyupa is less likely to be full during the packed winter months. Clean common bath with running hot water. Doubles Rs250.

Tamang Monastery, Bodh Gaya Rd. (☎ 400802), on the left side of the main road, just past the museum. Miniscule rooms facing a tiny temple are filled to the brim Nov.-Jan. by Nepalese pilgrims. In an open field near a crossroad and too exposed to permit a peaceful state of mind. Rs100-150. Off-season: Rs50-100.

Burmese Vihar Temple, Gaya Rd. (☎ 400721), on the right as you enter town; opposite
the bus station. Simple rooms with mosquito coils and nets look out onto quiet fields
and rice paddies on one side and the busy Gaya road on the other. Packed Nov.-Jan.;
in-house travel agents provide services that attract more tourists than pilgrims. Gates
close 9:30pm. Common bath. Singles Rs45; doubles Rs80.

⌂ FOOD

Seasonal stalls in front of the Mahabodhi Temple and Burmese Vihar provide *lassis* and cakes. A few evergreen places in the market lane sizzle fritters year-round.
The *lithis* served in the family-operated tea stalls in front of the Thai temple have
been known to transport hungry pilgrims to higher states of consciousness.

◪ **Fujiya Green,** near the Tibetan Temple. Leaving the pedestrian precinct with the Mahabodhi Temple to your left, make a right and follow the signs around to the left. Lamps-and-shades shack serves up simple dishes to the lamas from the monastery next door.
Authentic *thukpas* Rs10; vegetable chop suey Rs25. Open daily 7am-9pm.

◪ **Pole Pole Restaurant,** Gaya Rd., opposite Deep guest house. Exhaustive Italian and Japanese menu borders on a spiritual experience. The bakery (operating Nov.-Feb.) supplies Bavarian village essentials. Open 5-11pm.

Sujata Restaurant, inside Hotel Bodh Gaya Ashok, next to the museum. Of the few
perennial places, this is the best but also the most expensive. Offers the standard antiseptic, A/C atmosphere with Indian veg. and non-veg. dishes (Rs125-145). To ditch the
asceticism, pig out on the in-season all-you-can-eat lunch and dinner buffets (Rs300).

Kalyan Restaurant, opposite the main temple, 70m down a small lane on the left-hand
side. Simple, open-air place serves the usual range of dishes as well as vegetable
gyoza for Rs25. Open daily 7am-10pm.

👁 SIGHTS

MAHABODHI TEMPLE. The main point of interest in Bodh Gaya is the Mahabodhi Temple, referred to simply as "the stupa" by most Buddhists. Built right next
to the site of the Buddha's Enlightenment, the temple rises up from peaceful
flowery gardens to tower above the sacred Bodhi Tree that marks the spot
where Siddhartha Gautama meditated through the night and awoke to Buddhahood. Smaller shrines throughout the grounds mark different stages in the
Buddha's meditations; he is supposed to have spent a total of 49 days here deep
in thought after deciding that the practice of extreme asceticism was getting him
no closer to a true understanding of life's suffering. Emperor Ashoka built the
first temple on this site during the 3rd century BC, but the present temple, which
has been through layers and layers of restorations, probably dates from the 6th
century AD. Much of the rescue work was initiated in 1882 by Burmese monks
after the temple was found neglected and overrun by squatters. Over the last 30
years, many statues have been stolen from the temple's circular niches. The
oldest structure left on the site is a stone railing built in the 1st century AD to
keep out wild animals; a good quarter of it, however, has been removed and
whisked away to museums in London and Calcutta.

At the back of the temple is the sacred **Bodhi Tree** (see p. 640), a direct descendent of the tree under which the Buddha attained enlightenment *(open daily 6-8am
and 6-8pm)*. The **Vajrasana**, or "diamond throne," between the tree and the
temple, is thought to be the precise spot where the Buddha sat. A large gilded
image of the Buddha is kept behind glass in the temple, and another is on the
first floor, which is only open in the evenings for meditation. A part of the first
floor is permanently closed off, due to one man's recent attempt to saw off a
branch of the sacred tree as a souvenir. *(Temple compound open daily 5am-10pm. Free;
camera fee Rs10.)*

BIHAR

THE TREE OF KNOWLEDGE

THE TREE OF KNOWLEDGE As with any object of religious reverence worth its offerings of flowers and gold leaves, the Bodhi Tree at Bodh Gaya has been the subject of countless legends and stories over the years. Central to the mystique and holiness of this particular pipal tree that stands in Bodh Gaya today is the belief that it is a direct descendent of the one under which the Buddha meditated more than 2500 years ago. Some believe that the original tree was cut down by Emperor Ashoka before his famous conversion to Buddhism. The tree was miraculously restored to life, only to be hacked down again by Ashoka's wife, jealous of the attention and respect her husband had started to bestow upon the tree since its remarkable recovery. But the tree once again sprang up from its roots. Suitably impressed by its hardiness, Ashoka and his wife sent a sapling from the original tree to Sri Lanka, where it is believed to still prosper today. The centuries to come were to witness a series of attacks on the tree at Bodh Gaya, which weakened it to such an extent that it finally fell to a storm in 1876. The incarnation that is the object of such veneration today was grown from a seedling taken from the original tree's offspring in Sri Lanka.

SUJATA VILLAGE. In the winter, you can cross the dry river bed from the Mahant's palace in Bodh Gaya to the peaceful village on the other side (in summer, use the bridge 200m downstream). Here, 500m through the eastern fields, grows a descendant of the banyan tree under which the Buddha feasted on *kheer* (sweet rice milk) offered by a local woman named Sujata. This was his first meal after six years spent in ascetic solitude. The tree has since been converted into a shrine. The **Matang Rishi Ashram** is the banyan's neighbor. In the middle of the village is a grass mound believed to mark the site of Sujata's house.

OTHER TEMPLES AND MONASTERIES. The **Thai Temple**, Bodh Gaya's second-most prominent landmark, is 500m after the main road takes a sharp left. A large *wat* with classic claw-like tips on its orange roof, the temple opened in 1957 (year 2500 in the Buddhist calendar). Side-roads branch off the main road on either side of the Thai Temple. To the left are the **Bhutan Monastery** and the Japanese **Indosan Nipponji Temple.** The lane on the right side of the Thai Temple leads to the **Kagyu-pa Tibetan Monastery,** which contains brightly-colored, larger-than-life murals depicting the life of the Buddha. Next door is the **Daijokyo Temple,** another Japanese construction with an oppressive concrete exterior. Just up the road is the 25m **Giant Buddha Statue,** which was built by Japanese monks and inaugurated by the Dalai Lama in 1989. The chapel walls of the **Gelug-pa Tibetan Monastery,** next to the Mahabodhi Society, are painted with *thanka*-style clouds, wheels, and bodhisattvas. Be sure not to neglect the **Mahant's Palace,** on the left just before you reach the center of town. Now a working Hindu temple, it offers rear views of the Niranjna Ganga River and the Mahakala Mountain beyond, making it a great spot for meditation, contemplation, or just plain chillin' out. *(Most temples open daily dawn-noon and 2pm-dusk.)* The Archaeological Survey of India has a small **museum,** just off the main road, which contains images unearthed nearby. *(Open Sa-Th 10am-5pm. Free.)*

BUDDHISM AND COMMUNITY SERVICE

During the in-season, meditation courses are a major industry in Bodh Gaya. Teachers from all over the world jet (or rickshaw) in to provide training to Buddhists and aspiring Buddhists in the *dharma*-rich atmosphere of this temple town. A few permanent institutions in Bodh Gaya dedicated to the dissemination of the Buddha's word also conduct courses; though the peak season runs from October to March, a couple of places remain open and active throughout the summer. **The Root Institute for Wisdom Culture** (☎400714; fax 400548), at the edge of town down a dirt path to the left, offers 10-day courses during the winter with guest lamas and Western teachers in a quiet, intimate setting (Rs2900-4600, including room and board). Room and board is also available for non-meditators and, although they don't provide instruction in the off-season, visitors are welcome all year. During the winter, daily meditation sessions are open to outsiders on a walk-in basis, conducted at 3-4:30pm. The institute also has a good library of Buddhist literature (open 9:30-11:30am and 1-4pm). **The International Meditation Center,** opposite the Thai monastery, offers courses in the Vipassana Method year-round. The 10-day course is free, but a donation of Rs75-100 per day will defray the costs of a dorm bed in a double or triple and three meals. Shorter courses are also available. The **Vipassana Meditation Center** (☎400437), behind the university, has 10-day courses every month except July. They will house and feed you for a donation. A branch of Goenha, the **Dhamana Bodhi Meditation Center** (☎400437), 1km past the big Japanese Buddha, also holds classes in season, as does the **Burmese Vihar.**

There are a number of charitable organizations in Bodh Gaya. The **Root Institute,** which sponsors tree planting in addition to year-round leprosy and polio projects, is always looking for volunteers and donations. The Mahabodhi Society runs a number of charitable programs, including a free pharmacy, a primary school, an ambulance service, and a rehabilitation center. They also have information on the many charitable organizations that pop up during peak season.

VAISHALI वैशाली

Fifty-five kilometers from Patna, Vaishali is a tiny, one-cow town, surrounded by rice paddies and home to a handful of farming families, a scattering of small street stalls, and the ruined remains of the world's first republic. As the capital of the Licchavis during the 6th century BC, Vaishali was renowned for its peace and prosperity and for its elected system of government. Birthplace and hometown of Jainism's founder Mahavira, Vaishali also featured prominently in the life of the Buddha. He is thought to have preached one last sermon here before announcing his approaching *parinirvana.* Also mentioned in the *Ramayana* as the place where the gods and demons pow-wowed before churning the oceans, Vaishali today is a quiet, friendly place off the well-trodden tourist path. During the in-season (Oct.-Feb.), Vaishali occasionally attracts tourists of Bihar's Buddhist sites; off-season, you will almost certainly have the place to yourself.

▐▀ GETTING THERE AND GETTING AROUND. Direct **buses** go to Vaishali from the main bus stand in Patna (4 per day, 5am-1:30pm, 2hr., Rs25). Alternatively, after crossing the MG Bridge in Patna, hop on one of the frequent buses to **Hajipur** (Rs8), get on another bus to **Lalganj** (Rs7), where many shared **taxis** (Rs10) ply the road that passes through Vaishali. Ask to be let off at the Government's Tourist Lodge. Highly erratic direct buses from Vaishali to **Patna** (theoretically 5 per day, 6:45am-3pm, Rs25) pass by the Tourist Lodge, and there are regular jeeps and trucks to Lalganj, where connections to Patna are frequent. Trains can also get you from Vaishali to **Raxaul,** on the border with Nepal, via **Bakhra.** Take a **jeep** north from Vaishali to **Muzaffarpur** (Rs10), and then take a train (6 per day, 4hr., Rs28) or bus straight through to Raxaul (4hr., Rs40).

▐▛ ACCOMMODATIONS AND FOOD. The **Tourist Lodge** on the main road has simple rooms, with fan and attached bath. (Singles Rs50; doubles Rs75.) Alongside the Coronation Tank off the main road, through the gateway by the tourist lodge is the luxurious **Tourist Complex.** (Doubles Rs350.) A gate to the left just after the tourist lodge leads back to most of the ruins and to the **Youth Hostel.** (☎29425. Dorm beds Rs20; doubles Rs75.) At the Youth Hostel, **Dilip's Cafeteria** serves 24-hour hot food and cold drinks. Tea stalls on the main road also supply the basics for food.

▨ SIGHTS. Through a gateway to the left, just after the Tourist Lodge and a 15-minute walk off the main road, is the large rectangular pond known as the **Coronation Tank,** once used to anoint the town's leaders during inaugural ceremonies. Today, it's a favorite soaking spot for local farmers and their buffalo. A small **museum** on the right side of the tank showcases some of the stone and terra-cotta pieces dug up from nearby sites. *(Open Sa-Th 10am-5pm. Rs2.)* Down a small lane to the back of the museum, a well-maintained garden encloses the **relics stupa,** thought to contain a portion of Buddha's ashes, which were divided up after his cremation and distributed among the leaders of the eight major kingdoms of northern India. Today, a shallow circle of stones covered by a conical green tin roof is all that remains of the stupa. *(Open dawn-dusk.)* On the other side of the tank is the **Japanese Temple** *(open dawn-dusk)* and the great crowned white dome of the new **Vishwa Shanti Peace Stupa,** consecrated here in 1996. *(Open 7am-5pm.)*

Fifty meters down the highway from the tourist lodge is a fork, which goes left through fields and villages to the walled compound containing the **Ashokan Pillar** (locally known as **Kolhua Lat**). Circled by a pinkish brick wall, the well-preserved pillar and its lion capital, cut from a single piece of limestone, dominate the remains of a major monastic complex. The lion faces Kushinagar, where the Buddha died (see p. 192). An age-withered **stupa** and a small tank lie in the pillar's shadow, both commemorating the spot where a monkey once presented honey to the Buddha. On the other side of the main road, a 10-minute walk through the village, is the ancient **Chaumukhi Mahadev Mandir,** a four-faced Shiva *linga*.

RAXAUL रक्सौल ☎ 06255

Raxaul ain't pretty, but it's probably better than the alternatives. Mercifully, direct trains run from here to Delhi and Calcutta. Birganj, on the Nepalese side of the border, is a quick rickshaw ride away. **Trains** run from Raxaul to: **Calcutta** (daily, 10:20am, 19hr., Rs214); **Delhi** (1-2 per day, 12:45 and 8am, 26-29hr., Rs285); and **Muzafarpur** (2-3 per day, 7:15-12:45am, 4hr., Rs28), where more train connections are available. Erratic **buses** to **Patna** leave from the Old Bus Stand just off the main road by the railroad tracks (every hr., 4am-6pm, 9hr., Rs90).

Raxaul's main street leads straight over the bridge into Nepal, cutting through the market area and the tangle of alleyways to the east and west. **No bank changes money in Raxaul**—Birganj and Patna are the closest places to do so. A row of money changers by the railroad tracks will do the job at emergency-only rates. The **police station** (☎61021) and the **post office** (open M-Sa 9am-5pm) are on the main street, next to the Sun Temple. **Postal Code:** 845305.

! WARNING. Whether you are coming from India or Nepal, make sure you stop at *both* immigration offices. You need a Nepal departure stamp to be allowed into India and an India departure stamp to get into Nepal. The **Indian Immigration Office** is hidden below the bridge, to the left when coming from Raxaul. (Open daily 6am-8pm.) **Indian visas are not issued here.** The closest place to get one is Kathmandu, and even there, it's not easy. If you are leaving India and your visa has expired, you will be sent to the closest Superintendant of Police (in Motihari), who will fine and reprimand you. The Nepalese Immigration Office is next to the gate and is open daily 7am-7pm. You will need **one passport-size photo and US$30 for a single-entry 60-day visa (US$55 for double entry).** If this is your second Nepalese visa within one calendar year, the cost rises to US$50 for a single entry 30-day visa (US$75 double entry). Only US dollars are accepted, and the closest official exchange on the Indian side is in Patna. You are also supposed to stop at the respective customs offices, but nothing horrible will happen if you saunter past them. The cheapest way of getting across the border is to take a rickshaw from the main market in Raxaul to the Indian Immigration Office (Rs3-5), and then walk 200m across the bridge to Nepalese Immigration. From here, you can share a tonga to Birganj bus station (NRs5). Alternatively, you can hire a rickshaw to take you the whole way, but all the "waiting" causes the price to jump to IRs40. The bridge sometimes gets so clogged that rickshaws cannot even pass through. The whole border crossing ritual should be over in 30 minutes.

   Hotel Ajanta, Ashram Rd. (☎61019), down a quiet lane east of the main road, is a tolerable enough place. All rooms have fans, but only those with attached baths have mosquito nets. The hotel has its own generator. (Doubles Rs100-321.) The **Hal Chal Meet House,** on the same lane, serves good mutton curry and kebabs (Rs40).

WEST BENGAL

পশ্চিম বঙ্গ

West Bengal is India's most densely populated state, with nearly 800 people to every one of its 90,000 square kilometers. With this crush of humanity comes a history and a culture that has dominated India for hundreds of years and which continues to thrive today. In the 19th century, Bengal was at the center of literary and religious revival and a hotbed of national activism—the Bengali Renaissance produced India's finest writers, thinkers, and social reformers, including Rabindranath Tagore, India's first Nobel laureate for literature, and Swami Vivekananda, a spiritual leader who attempted to infuse Hinduism with Western ideas of material progress. As the state's capital, Calcutta still maintains its position as India's artistic and intellectual epicenter. Bengalis have developed a reputation of robust character, captured in pride for their cultural heritage, their language, and their unique religious traditions.

West Bengal's location, spanning the Gangetic delta, made it a rich agricultural and commercial region that began to attract European plunderers during the 17th and 18th centuries. The province came to prominence after the Battle of Plassey in 1757, when Robert Clive defeated Nawab Siraj-ud-Daula and his French allies to claim Bengal for Britain. The British would eventually make Calcutta their capital. The year 1905 saw the infamous Partition of Bengal, which divided the state along religious lines: East Bengal (later East Pakistan, then Bangladesh in 1971) and Assam held a strong Muslim population, and West Bengal, together with Bihar and Orissa, was largely Hindu. The tragic and bloody partition directly paved the way for the even bigger bloodier tragedies to come with the Partition in 1947. Today, Bengal revels in its enlightened Marxist traditions—the Communist Party of India has ruled since the 1960s.

West Bengal is home to a collage of landscapes and cultures. At its northern end, in the foothills of the Himalayas, is Darjeeling, India's most famous hill station. The southern end of the state drops right down to sea level at the swampy mangrove forests of the Sunderbans, home to the Royal Bengal Tiger. One hundred kilometers inland is the choked, crowded, and utterly captivating city of Calcutta.

HIGHLIGHTS OF WEST BENGAL

India's most famous hill station, **Darjeeling** (p. 665) seduces heat-weary travelers with tea plantations, toy trains, and superb views of the Himalayas.

Calcutta's temples, monuments, museums, and parks (p. 655) are rivaled only by the unchecked exuberance of the city's denizens.

CALCUTTA কলিকাতা ☎ 033

Oh Calcutta! Bursting at the seams with 13 million people, Calcutta is India's largest city, encompassing a mind-boggling 853 sq. km. Even to its own residents, Calcutta sometimes seems like a human cyclone. You don't just walk down the street here—you step into it, jump over it, and try to scoot your way around the worst parts of it. Wherever you go, you can't avoid breathing in layers of black soot. Old men trot with the traffic by day, hauling behind them the world's last fleet of handpulled rickshaws; families sleep by the thousands on the pavement at night. And yet the same people who lament the city's overpopulation and pollution also speak of their hometown as a "City of Joy" (the name of Calcutta's most famous slum).

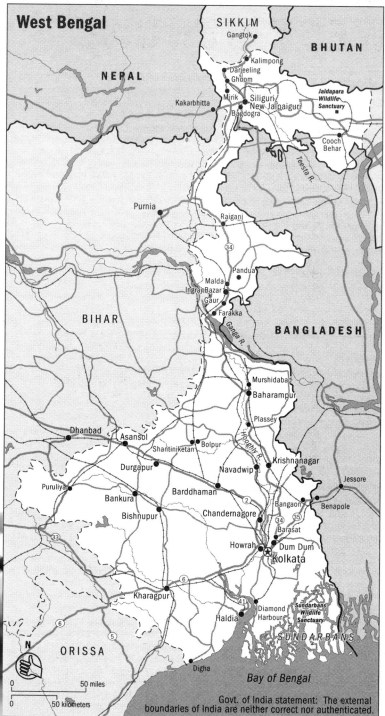

West Bengal

SIKKIM
Gangtok
BHUTAN
Kalimpong
Darjeeling
Ghoom
NEPAL
Mirik
Siliguri
New Jalpaiguri
Kakarbhitta
Bagdogra
Jaldapara
Wildlife
Sanctuary
Teesta R.
Cooch
Behar
Purnia
Raiganj
(34)
Pandua
Malda
Ingraj Bazar
Gaur
Farakka
BIHAR
Ganga R.
BANGLADESH
Murshidabad
Baharampur
Plassey
Dhanbad
Asansol
Shantiniketan
Bolpur
Hooghly R.
Durgapur
Navadwip
Krishnanagar
Jessore
Puruliya
Barddhaman
Bankura
(2)
Bangaon
Benapole
Bishnupur
Chandernagore
(34) (35)
Barasat
Howrah
Dum Dum
Kolkata
(33)
(6)
Kharagpur
(41)
Diamond
Harbour
Sundarbans
Wildlife
Sanctuary
Haldia
SUNDARBANS
(6)
(5)
ORISSA
N
Digha
Bay of Bengal
0   50 miles
0   50 kilometers

WEST BENGAL

For years the city has enjoyed a position at the vanguard of Indian culture, dictating intellectual trends for the entire country. The city churns out poets, painters, and saints and is deservedly proud of its magnificent parks and palaces.

The city's name derives from the word "Kalikshetra" (Ground of Kali), and the worship of Kali is an essential part of the city's character: the Durga Puja in October is the highlight of the year for many. Despite the scores of Indian temples scattered along the River Hooghly, Calcutta still bears the indelible imprint of the Raj. Competing with the temples for attention are monuments to monarchs, governors-general, and martyrs. In 1690, East India Company agent Job Charnock bought the fertile land and helped to build it up into a prosperous trading post and industrial base. Though captured in 1756 by Bengal's nawab, Siraj-ud-Daula, the fortified city became the centerpiece of British India soon after Robert Clive's victory at Plassey, and Calcutta became the capital of the Raj in 1773. Under the first governor-general, Warren Hastings (r. 1774-1785), Bengalis got their first taste of English-style education. The new literati proved too proud to submit to assimilation under a foreign power, and the 19th century witnessed the elite-led Bengali Renaissance. Ram Mohan Roy (1774-1833) started the movement by pushing for social and religious reform with his Brahmo Samaj, a theistic movement that called for reform within Hinduism. Calcutta's upper-class salons hosted a revolution in literature, music, dance, and painting that culminated in the work of the Nobel Prize-winning poet Rabindranath Tagore. Calcutta also became a center for anti-British politics; when the British moved to partition Bengal in 1905, their efforts were met with bombs and boycotts.

By the end of the 19th century, Calcutta had plenty of critics, including the British colonialists who had built the city in the first place. A series of blows, from the transfer of the capital to Delhi in 1911, to the opening of the Suez Canal (which made Bombay a much more prosperous port), to the disasters of Partition in 1947, gave the city a reputation for squalor and seediness. Increasing migration from Bangladesh and the rest of India and the silting of the increasingly unnavigable Hooghly, have only made things worse. The Communist government has worked wonders in the countryside, but has failed to rid the city of all its problems. In 1984, Calcutta opened its Metro, the first anywhere in India, and the government is currently developing Salt Lake to the east as a "second Calcutta." Untroubled by the rioting that has plagued other Indian cities, Calcutta's residents appear unified in their unmatched love for their home town.

◼ GETTING THERE AND AWAY

FLIGHTS

Officially known as the Netaji Subhas Chandra Bose Airport, **Dum Dum Airport** (☎511 8070 or 511 8079), is 2km northeast of the city. The **pre-paid taxi** stand in the domestic terminal is the best place to catch a ride into downtown Calcutta (40min., Rs150). City buses #46, 303, and 510 (Rs4) and the less direct E3 (Rs5) all run between the Esplanade and the airport. Minibus #151 (Rs18) goes from BBD Bagh to the airport. The airport has a **currency exchange counter,** a **post office,** and **tourist offices.** The **train ticket counter** serves Delhi, Bombay, and Madras only. The Airport Manager in the domestic terminal can arrange beds in the waiting room for tired travelers with a layover of 24 hours or less.

> **WARNING:** Many of Calcutta's taxis (even pre-paid ones) are operated by touts attached to a particular hotel, who receive a hefty commission for every tourist they deliver. **Insist on going to the hotel you want,** and ignore claims that it has been closed down, destroyed by floods, or packed up in boxes and sent to Venezuela. If you arrive late at night and feel threatened by the chaos all around you, spend the night in the airport and take a taxi in the morning, when there is much less danger of muggings and other kinds of nastiness.

INTERNATIONAL AIRLINES. All carriers have offices at the airport, as well as downtown. **AeroFlot,** 58 Chowringhee Rd. (☎242 1617). Open M-F 10am-1pm and 2-5:30pm, Sa 10am-1pm. **Air France,** 41 Chowringhee Rd. (☎296 6161). Open M-Sa 9am-5:30pm. **Air India,** 50 Chowringhee Rd. (☎242 2356 or 242 1187). Open daily 9:30am-5:30pm. **Alitalia,** 230A AJC Bose Rd. (☎247 7394). Open daily 9:30am-5:30pm. **American Airlines,** 2/7 Sarat Bose Rd. (☎747622). Open M-F 9am-1pm and 1:30-5:30pm, Sa 9am-1:30pm. **Air Canada, Gulf Air,** and **TWA,** 230A AJC Bose Rd. (☎247 7783). Open M-F 9am-1pm and 1:30-5:30pm, Sa 9am-1:30pm. **Bangladesh Biman,** 33C Chowringhee Rd. (☎293709). **British Airways,** 41 Chowringhee Rd. (☎293450). Open M-Sa 9:30am-5:30pm. **Canadian, SAS, South African,** and **United Airlines,** 2/7 Sarat Bose Rd. (☎747623). Open M-F 9:30am-1pm and 2-5:30pm, Sa 9:30am-1pm. **Cathay Pacific,** 1 Middleton St. (☎240 3211). Open M-F 9:30am-1pm and 2-5:30pm, Sa 9:30am-1:30pm. **Delta,** 13D Russell St. (☎246 3873 or 246 3826). Open M-F 9am-5:30pm. **Japan Airlines,** 35A Chowringhee Rd. (☎226 7920). Open M-F 9am-1pm and 1:30-5:30pm, Sa 9am-1pm. **KLM** and **Northwest,** 1 Middleton St., Jeevan Deep (☎240 3151). Open M-F 9am-5pm, Sa 9am-1pm. **Kuwait Airways,** 2/7 Sarat Bose Rd. **Lufthansa,** 30A/B Chowringhee Rd. (☎249 5777; fax 246 4010). Open M-F 9am-1pm and 1:30-5:30pm. **RNAC,** 41 Chowringhee Rd. (☎298549). Open M-F 9am-1pm and 2-4pm, Sa 9am-1pm. **Singapore Airlines,** 1 Lee Rd. (☎280 9898). Open M-F 9am-1pm and 2-5pm. **Swissair,** 46C Chowringhee Rd. (☎282 4643). Open 9am-1pm and 2-5:30pm. **Thai Airways,** 18G Park St. (☎229 9846). Open 24hr.; tourist window (#12) open M-F 9am-1pm and 2-5pm.

DOMESTIC AIRLINES. Indian Airlines and **Alliance Air,** 39 Chittaranjan Ave. (☎236 0870 or 236 4433; fax 236 5391). Open 24hr. Great Eastern Hotel branch, 1-3 Old Court House St., 2nd fl. (☎248 0073 or 248 8009). Open M-Sa 10am-1:30pm and 2-5pm. **Jet Airways,** 18D Park St. (☎229 2660). Open daily 9am-7pm. **Sahara Airlines,** 2A Shakespeare Sarani (☎282 8969 or 282 7686). Open M-Sa 10:30am-5pm.

To: **Agartala** (1-2 per day, 1hr., US$40); **Ahmedabad** (M-Sa, 2½hr., US$160); **Aizawl** (M, W, and F; 1hr.; US$65); **Bagdogra** (M, W, F; 1hr.; US$70); **Bangalore** (2 per day, 3½hr., US$185); **Bhubaneswar** (daily, 1hr., US$60); **Bombay** (6 per day, 3hr., US$205); **Delhi** (4 per day, 2hr., US$140); **Dibugarh** (M, W, F, and Su, 1½hr., US$85); **Dimapur** (Tu, Th, Sa-Su; 2hr.; US$85); **Guwahati** (daily, 1hr., US$50); **Hyderabad** (2 per day M-Sa, 3hr., US$150); **Imphal** (2 per day, 2hr., US$65); **Jaipur** (daily, 2½hr., US$160); **Jorhat** (Tu, Th, Sa-Su; 1½hr.; US$85); **Lucknow** (2 per day, 2½hr., US$100); **Madras** (3 per day, 2hr., US$160); **Nagpur** (M, W, F; 1½hr.; US$100); **Patna** (daily, 1hr., US$70); **Port Blair** (M, Tu, Th, Sa-Su; 2hr.; US$195); **Dhaka, Bangladesh** (daily, 1hr., US$50); and **Kathmandu, Nepal** (Tu and F, 1½hr., US$100).

TRAINS

Calcutta has two stations: **Sealdah Station,** northeast on AJC Bose Rd., for trains going north, and **Howrah Station,** across the Hooghly River from Calcutta, for trains going to the rest of India. The best way to get to or from Howrah Station is by bus. If you're going to the Sudder St. area, take a bus to the Esplanade (Rs2) and walk five minutes. There is a **pre-paid taxi** stand at the station (Rs40 to downtown Calcutta) as well as a **West Bengal Tourist Office** (open M-Sa 7am-1am, Su 7am-12:30pm). Tickets can be purchased at the **Railway Booking Office,** 6 Fairlie Pl. (☎220 3496), near BBD Bagh. The **Foreign Tourist Office** is on the first floor. Foreign currency or rupees with an encashment certificate are accepted. (Open daily 9am-1pm and 1:30-4pm.)

From **Howrah Station** to: **Bhubaneswar** (9-11 per day, 8:25am-3:50am, 7½-9hr., Rs154); **Bombay** (4-5 per day, 10:40am-8pm, 32-36hr., Rs390); **Delhi** (9:15, 9:45am, and 7:15pm; 23hr.; Rs343; *Rajdhani Exp.* 2301, 5pm, 18hr.); **Madras** (4 per day, 1:15-10:20pm and 3:50am, 28-34hr., Rs366); **Patna** (6-9 per day, 9:15am-11pm, 8-10hr., Rs182; *Rajdhani Exp.* 2305, 1:45pm, 7hr., Rs915, 3-tier A/C only); **Puri** (6:05 and 9:45pm, 11hr., Rs166); **Varanasi** (3-5 per day, 9:15am-11pm, 8-17hr., Rs235). **Sealdah Station** to: **New Jalpaiguri** (6:25am, 1:40, 7:15, and 9:15pm; 13hr.; Rs190).

WEST BENGAL

BUSES

Private buses go to Siliguri (12hr.), a departure point for Darjeeling. West Bengal Tourism runs the most direct bus which leaves Calcutta at 6pm, reaching **Siliguri** at 6am and **Jalpaiguri** at 6:15am (Rs195). Buses also run to **Dingha** (7am, 6hr., Rs55) and **Jaigon** (6pm, 19hr., Rs235). Tickets must be purchased in advance at the booth at the Esplanade: to get there, take a left from Chowringhee Rd. onto SN Banerjee Rd.; the booth is on the right just before the tram tracks. Other private bus company booths are to the left (follow the tracks).

BOATS

Two to three ships sail each month to **Port Blair** in the Andaman Islands; the exact schedule depends on the weather. Tickets and a tentative schedule for the month are available from the **Shipping Corporation Office,** 13 Strand Rd. (☎246 2354), two blocks south of the Railway Booking Office. Enter through the mail entrance, go through the back door and up one floor (open M-F 10:30am-1pm). Arrivals and departures are announced about a week in advance. Ticket sales begin seven days before the scheduled departure, often selling out in the first couple of days. Bring three passport photos to purchase tickets. (3-4 days. Bunk Rs955; 2nd class Rs2243; 1st class Rs2852. Food per day Rs50 in bunk; Rs100 in 1st and 2nd classes.) Boat conditions are suspect.

▐ GETTING AROUND

Locals joke that the quickest way of getting around town is to walk. Traffic in Calcutta is chaotic, and the only thing that keeps the vehicles on the right side of the road (well, sometimes) is the equally chaotic stream of opposing traffic.

BUSES

Buses in Calcutta are cheap and always crowded. It's important to let go of the "bus stop" concept: you can get on just about anywhere—just put your hand out and the driver will slow down. If the bus is moving too fast for you to feel comfortable running alongside and jumping aboard, shout *"asthe!"* The key to finding your bus is identifying a major destination that's in the same direction. On your way out, make your way to the door one stop before or else you'll never make it in time.

TRAMS AND SUBWAYS

Trams leave from the central Esplanade to major destinations throughout south Calcutta and to Sealdah and Howrah Bridges (Rs1-2). They are slow and sometimes crowded. A list of routes can be purchased at any bookstand. India's first **subway (metro)** extends in a virtually straight line from Tollygunge, up Chowringhee Rd., to Dum Dum Station. From this station, a taxi or auto-rickshaw to the airport takes 45 minutes, with traffic (Rs70). The metro is relatively quick and uncrowded—the fastest and most reliable mode of transportation available. (Rs3-7. Open M-Sa 8am-9:30pm, Su 2-9:30pm.)

TAXIS AND RICKSHAWS

Though expensive, **taxis** are the most convenient way to cover long distances in Calcutta. Drivers must use the meters; don't ride in a cab if the driver won't turn on the meter. The meter begins at Rs5, and the fare is 2.4 times the meter reading. The prepaid taxi counters at the airport have long lines, but they are worth the wait (Rs150). Calcutta's **hand-pulled rickshaws** fight for space on the congested roads. In most cases, you can walk faster than they can pull. **Auto-rickshaws,** though quite efficient, leave you open to breathe all the exhaust fumes. They are cheaper than taxis but aren't metered; negotiate beforehand.

◼ ORIENTATION

Expansive as it is, Calcutta's layout is relatively straightforward; it shouldn't take you long to get your bearings. The **River Hooghly** cuts through town, separating Calcutta proper from **Howrah**; these areas are linked by one of the world's most heavily used bridges, **Howrah Bridge**, and, farther south, by the new **Vivekananda Bridge**. Howrah's centerpiece is the frenetic **Howrah Station**, easily accessed from Calcutta by the Howrah Bridge. The main road in Howrah is the **Grand Trunk Rd.**, which runs parallel to the river and connects the Botanical Gardens in the south with the Belur Math up north.

Flanking the river's east bank is the **Maidan**, a grassy field cut through by streets and sprinkled with monuments. The central city hugs the maidan; **Strand Rd.** cuts between the maidan and the river. At the maidan's northeast corner is the **Esplanade**, the central bus and train terminus. A couple of blocks north is **BBD Bagh**, around which are the tourist office, GPO, railway and shipping companies, and several banks. To the east of BBD Bagh is **Old Court House Rd.**, which continues north to become **Netaji Subhas Rd.** Along with **Chittaranjan Ave.** to the east, it is the major thoroughfare leading to north Calcutta.

Running along the east side of the maidan is **Chowringhee Rd.** Several smaller streets wind their way east from Chowringhee. These include Park St., with fancier restaurants, hotels, and shopping areas, and (two blocks north of Park St.) **Sudder St.**, home to the vast majority of budget accommodations. At the eastern end of Sudder St. is the north-south **Free School St.** (now **Mirza Ghalib St.**), with a range of eating and shopping facilities. Even farther east is **Acharya Jagadish Chandra (AJC) Bose Rd.**, which used to circle the city—to the south it curves back westward and leads to St. Paul's Cathedral and the Victoria Memorial, both at the maidan's southeast corner. East of it all is the only clean and efficient **Eastern Metropolitan Bypass** (the Chief Minister's route to work, hence its excellent upkeep). This is the route taxi drivers should take to bring you into town.

In the south, Chowringhee Rd. becomes **Ashutosh Mukherjee Rd.**, which continues into southern Calcutta. To the west is the upmarket area of **Alipur**, which also contains the zoo and the National Library; south of Alipur is the Kalighat Temple.

◪ PRACTICAL INFORMATION

TOURIST AND FINANCIAL SERVICES

Tourist Office: Government of India Tourist Office, 4 Shakespeare Sarani (☎242 1402 or 242 5318). Provides an excellent map of Calcutta and *Calcutta This Fortnight,* a free pamphlet detailing cultural events. The West Bengal Chamber of Commerce publishes *Calcutta: Gateway to the East* (Rs25), a smart, honest, and comprehensive introduction to the city and its sights. The office also provides a list of host families and *dharamsalas* for those seeking alternative accommodations. Open M-F 9am-6pm, Sa 9am-5pm. **Airport Branch** (☎511 8299), in the domestic terminal of Dum Dum Airport. **West Bengal Tourist Bureau,** 3/2 BBD Bagh E. (☎248 8271), provides city tours (full day Rs100), information and tours for all of West Bengal, and passes for wildlife parks and the Marble Palace. Open M-Sa 10:30am-1pm, Su and holidays 7am-1pm. Counters at the airport and Howrah Station (☎660 2518) both open daily 7am-1pm.

Consulates: Bangladesh, 9 Circus Ave. (☎247 5208). Open M-Sa 10am-5pm. **Bhutan,** contact **Bhutan Tourism,** 35A Chowringhee Rd. (☎246 8370). Open M-F 10am-5pm. **Germany,** 1 Hastings Park Rd. (☎479 1141). Open M-F 10am-5pm. **Nepal,** 19 National Library Ave. (☎479 1224). Open M-F 9:30am-12:30pm and 1:30-4:30pm. **Sri Lanka,** Nicco House, 2 Hare St. (☎248 5102). Open M-F 10am-5:30pm. **Thailand,** 18B Mandville Gardens (☎440 7836). Open M-F 9am-noon. **UK,** 1 Ho Chi Minh Sarani (☎242 5171). Open M-F 9am-noon. **US,** 5/1 Ho Chi Minh Sarani (☎242 3611). Open M-F 8:30am-12:30pm and 2-4pm.

Immigration Office: Foreigners Registration Office, 237 AJC Bose Rd. (☎247 3301). Provides visa extensions and work visas only. Open M-F 9am-1pm and 2-4pm.

Currency Exchange: 24hr. **ATMs** are all over Calcutta, and all major banks have attached ATMs unless noted. **American Express,** 21 Old Court House St. (☎248 2133 or 248 9555; fax 248 8096), has travel services and currency exchange. Open M-Sa 9:30am-6:30pm. **ANZ Grindlays,** 41 Chowringhee Rd. (☎248 3371). Open M-F 10am-3pm, Sa 10am-12:30pm. **Banque National de Paris,** 4A BBD Bagh E. (☎248 2166 or 248 0197). Open M-F 10am-5pm, Sa 10am-2pm. **Citibank,** 43 Chowringhee Rd. (☎249 2484). Open M-F 10am-2pm, Sa 10am-noon. **HSBC,** 8 Netaji Subhas Rd. (☎248 6363), also holds mail. Open M-F 9am-4pm. **State Bank of India,** Dum Dum Airport, international terminal. Open 24hr. **Thomas Cook,** 230A AJC Bose Rd. (☎247 4560; fax 247 5854), Chitrakut Building, 2nd fl., side entrance, offers travel services and currency exchange. No ATM. Open M-Sa 9:30am-1pm and 1:45-6pm.

LOCAL SERVICES

Luggage Storage: Howrah Station, track 12. Rs5-8 per day. Note "Beware of Rats" sign.

Bookstore: Landmark, Emami, 17 Lord Sinha Rd., has the best selection of books. **Oxford Book Store,** Park St. (☎297662). Open M-Sa 10am-8:30pm. **College St.** is lined with book stalls. **Survey of India Map Sales Office,** 13 Wood St., has a good selection of trekking maps. Open M-F 10:30am-1pm and 2:30-5pm.

Library: National Library, Alipur Rd., near the zoo. India's largest library—2 million books in all of India's official languages. Open M-Sa 9am-8pm, Su 10am-6pm. **Asiatic Society of Bengal,** 1 Park St. (☎226 0355). A Calcutta institution dating back to 1784 and the best place to study Persian manuscripts and 19th-century academic tomes. Adjacent museum contains paintings by Rubens and Reynolds. Open M-F 10am-6pm. **British Council,** 5 Shakespeare Sarani (☎282 5378). Open Tu-Sa 10:30am-6:30pm.

Cultural Centers: Alliance Francaise, 24 Park Mansions, Park St. (☎282 8793). **British Council,** 5 Shakespeare Sarani (☎242 5378). Open Tu-Sa 10:30am-6:30pm. **Academy of Fine Arts,** Cathedral Rd. (☎248 4302). **Rabindra Sadan,** corner of Cathedral Rd. and AJC Bose Rd. stages Bengali plays and classical music concerts.

Market: New Market, north of Lindsay St., sells everything from Kashmiri carvings and *filmi* cassettes to fruit, vegetables, and animals. Open dawn-dusk. Don't miss the **flower market,** just before Howrah bridge, on the left. Open M-Sa 8-11am. For **books,** head to **College St.** where second-hand and new book stalls line the pavement.

EMERGENCY AND COMMUNICATIONS

Police: Police Headquarters (☎479 1311-5), Lal Bazaar. **Emergency: Police,** ☎215 5000.

Pharmacy: Dey's Medical Store, Ltd., 6A Nell Sengupta Sarani (☎249 9810), on the left where Madge St. intersects New Market. Open M-F 8:30am-9pm, Sa 8:30am-5pm.

Hospital: B.M. Birla Heart Research Centre, 1/1A National Library Ave. (☎479 4003, 4024, or 4012). Open 24hr. Highly recommended English-speaking doctors.

Internet: Rishi's Cyber Cafe, 9A Lord Sinha Rd., off Shakespeare Sarani, offers the cheapest service. Rs3 per hr., Rs20 per 30min.

Post Office: GPO, BBD Bagh (☎220 1451). Open M-Sa 7am-8:30pm. **Branch post offices:** Airport, Russell St., Park St., and Mirza Ghalib St. **New Market Post Office,** Free School St., opposite Sudder St. **Postal Code:** 700001.

▛ ACCOMMODATIONS

Prices in Calcutta tend to be high. Most of the budget accommodations in town are around the Sudder St. area. The location is central and the prices reasonable, though the hotels are a little shabby. There are a few other cheap hotels off Chittaranjan Rd., south of the Indian Airlines office, and to the northeast of New Market. Hotels often fill up before noon; most have a noon check-out policy. Contact the Government of India Tourist Office for a comprehensive list of host families willing to take in paying guests. (Rs200-400 per night. Breakfast.)

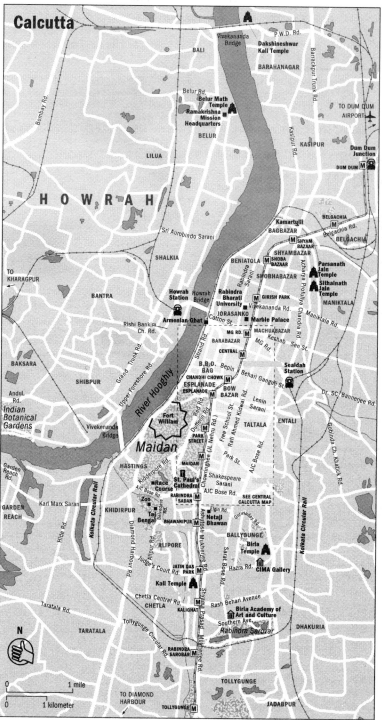

Calcutta

P.W.D. Rd.

Vivekananda Bridge

Dakshineshwar Kali Temple

BALI

BARAHANAGAR

Bombay Rd.

Belur Rd.

Belur Math Temple

Ramakrishna Mission Headquarters

BELUR

LILUA

Barrackpur Trunk Rd.

TO DUM DUM AIRPORT

Kasipur Rd.

KASIPUR

Dum Dum Junction

DUM DUM M

H O W R A H

Sri Aurobindo Sarani

SHALKIA

BELGACHIA

M BELGACHIA Rd.

BELGACHIA

Kamartulli

BAGBAZAR

SHYAM BAZAR

M SHYAM BAZAR

Parsanath Jain Temple

TO KHARAGPUR

BENIATOLA

BANTRA

Howrah Station

Howrah Bridge

Rabindra Bharati University

JORASANKO

Cotton St.

Rishi Bankim Ch. Rd.

Armenian Ghat

Strand Rd.

Grand Trunk Rd.

Upper Foreshore Rd.

SHOBHABAZAR

Acharya Profullya Chandra Rd.

Sithalnath Jain Temple

MANIKTALA

Maniktala Rd.

M GIRISH PARK

Vivekananda Rd.

■ **Marble Palace**

MG RD.

MACHUABAZAR

Keshab Sen St.

MG Rd.

BARABAZAR

CENTRAL

Bepin Behari Ganguli St.

Sealdah Station

Dr. SC Bannerjee Rd.

BAKSARA

SHIBPUR

River Hooghly

B.B.D. BAG

CHANDNI CHOWK M

ESPLANADE M

ESPLANADE

AnduI Rd.

Indian Botanical Gardens

Vivekananda Bridge

Garden Reach Rd.

GARDEN REACH

Karl Marx Saran

Hide Rd.

KHIDIRPUR

Maidan

HASTINGS

Kolkata Circular Rail

Diamond Harbour Rd.

Kidderpore Rd.

A/C Bose Rd.

Race Course

Zoo

Taj Bengal

ALIPORE

Allpur Rd.

Judge's Court Rd.

Kali Temple

CHETLA

Chetla Central Rd.

Fort William

BOW BAZAR

Free School St.

Rafi Ahmed Kidwai Rd.

Lenin Sarani

TALTALA

ENTALI

Gobinda Ch. Khatick Rd.

Dufferin Rd.

Red Rd.

Chowringhee (J.L. Nehru Rd.)

PARK STREET M

Park St.

AJC Bose Rd.

MAIDAN M

Shakespeare Sarani

AJC Bose Rd.

SEE CENTRAL CALCUTTA MAP

RABINDRA SADAN M

Ashutosh Mukherjee Rd.

Netaji Bhawan

BHAWANIPUR

Elgin Rd.

Gurusaday Rd.

BALLYGUNGE

Birla Temple

Sarat Bose Rd.

Hazra Rd.

CIMA Gallery

Shyama Prasad Mukherjee Rd.

JATIN DAS PARK M

KALIGHAT

Rash Behari Avenue

Birla Academy of Art and Culture

Southern Ave.

Rabindra Sarovar

DHAKURIA

Tollygunge Circular Rd.

Taratala Rd.

TARATALA

N

0 _____ 1 mile

0 _____ 1 kilometer

RABINDRA SAROBAR M

TO DIAMOND HARBOUR

TOLLYGUNGE M

TOLLYGUNGE

JADABPUR

WEST BENGAL

■ **YMCA,** 25 Chowringhee Rd. (☎ 249 2192; fax 249 2234). From Sudder St., turn right; it's immediately on the right. Enormous, clean rooms with attached bath; dorm rooms are also clean. Breakfast included. Reserve 10 days ahead. Dorm beds Rs110, with a not-worth-it dinner Rs220; singles Rs300-500; doubles Rs460-730.

■ **Salvation Army Red Shield Guest House,** 2 Sudder St. (☎ 245 0599). Turn left after The Great Eastern Hotel (on J.L. Nehru Rd.); it's the big red building on the right. One of the most popular hotels with the backpacker set and volunteers at Mother Teresa's Missionaries of Charity (see p. 660). Large grungy dorm rooms and bathrooms that don't exactly sparkle. Separate lounges for Indians and foreign guests. Lights-out 10pm; gate closes at midnight. Check-out 10am. Reservations not accepted; rooms are usually available. Dorm beds Rs60; doubles Rs150-350.

■ **Classic Hotel,** 6/1A Kyd St. (☎ 290256), just off Mirza Ghalib St., next to Mehfil restaurant. Walking bare-foot in its cool marble interior is a welcome break from the hot city streets. Generator in case of power cuts. Singles Rs150; doubles Rs300-650.

Modern Lodge, 1 Stuart Ln. (☎ 244 4960). From the east end of Sudder St., opposite Astoria Hotel and down a street on the left. Popular with Missionaries of Charity volunteers. Clean bathrooms. Moderately sized rooms have desks and tables. Check-out 10am. Singles Rs85; doubles with bath Rs120-300.

Gujral Guest House, Lindsay St. (☎ 244 0392 or 245 6066). Circle around the right side of Lindsay Hotel and turn left onto an alley behind it; look for the painted signs. Enormous, comfortable rooms await on the third floor; some doubles have Star TV. Potted plants, nature paintings, telephones. Common TV room. Tea and breakfast available. Singles Rs220; doubles with bath Rs450-650.

Hotel Galaxy, 3 Stuart Ln. (☎ 246 4565), opposite the Modern Lodge. Only slightly more expensive than other budget places, Galaxy is a steal. The staff is very friendly. Huge rooms have color TV, A/C, and wooden furniture. Singles Rs420; doubles Rs520.

Hotel Astoria, 612 Sudder St. (☎ 244 9679), in the middle of Sudder St. Large clean rooms. Doubles have clean bathrooms. Singles Rs200; doubles Rs300-450.

Hotel Plaza, 10 Sudder St. (☎ 2446411 or 2492435), on its western end. Medium-sized rooms with clean beds, baths, and carpets. Sweet tea and toast for breakfast. Singles Rs300; doubles Rs450.

Shilton Hotel, 5A Sudder St. (☎ 245 1512 or 245 1527). Set back away from the bus-tle on Sudder St.; look for signs. Huge rooms have spotless bathrooms, good lighting, and desks. Dark but friendly TV room. Singles Rs200; doubles Rs300.

YWCA, 1 Middleton Rd. (☎ 297033; fax 292494), right off Park St. **Women only.** Simple but spacious and clean rooms. Meals are included, as is access to table tennis and badminton tables (lawn tennis Rs20 extra). The staff is friendly and keeps the place safe. Singles Rs325-570; doubles Rs600-800. Reserve at least a week in advance.

Central Calcutta (Kolkata)

🛏 ACCOMMODATIONS
Classic Hotel, 26
Gujral Guest Hosue, 16
Hotel Astoria, 20
Hotel Galaxy, 24
Hotel Plaza, 14
Modern Lodge, 22
Salvation Army Red Shield Guest House, 18
Shilton Hotel, 21
YMCA, 19
YWCA, 7

🍴 FOOD
Abdul Khalique & Sons, 23
Aheli, 3
Amina, 15
Anand Vegetarian Restaurant, 2
Bar B-Q, 8
Flurys, 6
Haldiram Bhujiawala, 12
Hare Krishna Bakery, 9
How Hua, 25
Indian Coffee House, 1
Khalsa Restaurant, 17
Nizam's, 4

♪ ENTERTAINMENT
Anticlock, 13
Nandan, 11
Rabindra Sadan, 10
Someplace Else, 5
Tantra, 5

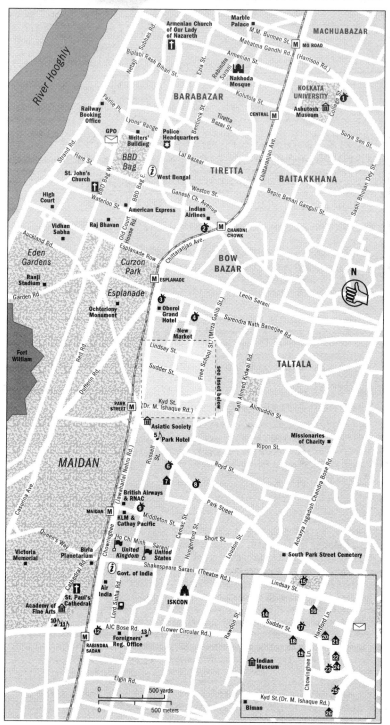

WEST BENGAL

☐ FOOD

Bengali cuisine is sizzling on the scene with its mix of mustard-seasoned rice and fish (avoid seafood in monsoon season), and is best enjoyed at the street stalls that dot the city, particularly on Park St. Calcutta's thriving Muslim population has seen kebab shops open up all over town, serving Kathi roll (a *paratha* with a layer of egg and stuffed with spicy chicken, lamb, or egg). Try the tiny street shops on Chitpur Rd. or slide into more hygienic establishments. There is a thriving Chinese colony in Tangra near Salt Lake, the hottest place in town for Chinese food.

- **Aheli,** in The Peerless Inn, 12 J.L. Nehru Rd. The best Bengali *thalis* around (Rs225). Waiters don traditional *dhotis* and *kurtas*. Open 12:30-2:30pm and 7:30-10:30pm.
- **Nizam's,** 22/25 New Market, northeast of New Market, just southwest of the large red municipal building. Ask for directions—everyone knows where it is. The "pioneer of kebab rolls in India" sells chicken, mutton, and beef kebabs for Rs15-25.
- **Amina,** New Market, near Eliot Cinema. This joint is quickly displacing Nizam's as the best kebabs 'n' rolls joint. Excellent *biryani* Rs35.
- **Abdul Khalique and Sons Restaurant,** 32 Marique Amir St., a block south of Sudder St., near Jamuna Movie Theatre. Squeeze onto a bench and watch your food being cooked. Beef stew Rs9; mutton *masala* Rs16; fish curry Rs10. Open daily 5am-11:30pm.
- **Anand Vegetarian Restaurant,** 19 Chittaranjan Ave., between the Indian Airlines office and Chowringhee Rd. Excellent South and North Indian food on 2 floors behind tinted glass. Popular with the bourgeoisie for post-cinema jaunts. Dishes Rs20-40.

Suruchi, Elliot Rd., near Mallik Bazaar. Open for lunch only. Delicious mustard fish.

Haldiram Bhujiawala, AJC Bose Rd. at the corner of Chowringhee Rd., next to the Aeroflot office. A neon sign advertises this eat-and-run sweet and snack chain, popular with Calcutta's middle classes. Try the cutlets (Rs15) and puffs (Rs10-20). The *kulfi* (Rs20), which comes with *faluda,* is famous.

Flurys, 18 Park St., the large white building on the corner. A Calcutta landmark, popular with foreign tourists. Relaxed cafe with an enormous sweets shop specializing in buns and chocolate pastries. Ask for a pastry assortment (Rs9) with your tea while you decide what to take home. Open daily 7am-8pm.

Indian Coffee House, 15 Bankim Chatterjee St., 1st fl., just off College St., near Calcutta University. Popular haunt for students and Calcutta's intelligentsia. A portrait of Rabindranath Tagore presides over the scene. Coffee Rs7; chicken *hakka* Rs25.

Hare Krishna Bakery, at the corner of Russell and Middleton St., 2 blocks west of the US consulate. No longer features sadhus and shaved heads; only the background music serves as a reminder that the profits go to the International Society for Krishna Consciousness. All the food—breads, pastries, samosas (Rs10-15)—is *prasad* (blessed), so don't leave any on your plate. Open daily 10:30am-8pm.

BENGALI SWEETS Bengal is famous for its mouth-watering and artery-clogging sweets *(mithai),* most of which are made of milk and *paneer* (cottage cheese). **Rossogullah,** huge white balls of *paneer* immersed in sugar syrup, are sweet and light, and are best eaten cold. For **sandesh,** cottage cheese is boiled with sugar until it forms tiny balls. These are ground and then set in different-sized molds. They are flavored with lemon or saffron and decorated with pistachios. **Mishti dahi,** literally "sweet yogurt," is sold in small earthenware pots (Rs2-3 per pot) and is a welcome treat in the scorching heat of summer. **Ras malai** is cottage cheese boiled with sugar and shaped into ovals flavored with saffron and pistachio. This is served cold, in a thick milk syrup. There are sweet shops on just about every corner. Particularly good are **Haldirani Bhujiawala,** AJC Bose Rd. at the corner of JL Nehru Rd., next to the Aeroflot office, and **Ganguram Bengali Sweets,** the original Bengali sweet shop chain, scattered all over town and known by every local.

Call the USA

"feel free to call"

1-800-COLLECT

When in Ireland
Dial: 1-800-COLLECT (265 5328)

When in N. Ireland, UK & Europe
Dial: 00-800-COLLECT USA (265 5328 872)

Member of
Dublin Tourism

Australia	0011	800 265 5328 872
Finland	990	800 265 5328 872
Hong Kong	001	800 265 5328 872
Israel	014	800 265 5328 872
Japan	0061	800 265 5328 872
New Zealand	0011	800 265 5328 872

How Hua, Mirza Ghalib St. Opposite Hotel Paramount, south of Sudder St. People from northern China lovingly prepare their native cuisine in a classy, quiet, A/C dining hall. Their specialty is *chimney* soup, which can be made with chicken, crab, or bean curd (Rs45). Delicious, freshly-made noodles. Open W-M 11am-11pm.

Bar B-Q, 43/47 Park St. (☎299916). This elegant, spacious restaurant with extensive Chinese and Indian (dinner only) menus rewards the weary backpacker with an escape from the grime. Don't order your food spicy unless you've got coolant in your belly. Szechuan chili chicken Rs70. Open noon-3pm and 7-10:30pm. Major credit cards accepted. Reserve ahead on weekends.

Don Giovanni's, Park St., opposite the petrol pump. Expensive but thick crust pizza with any topping tastes just like the real thing (small Rs180). Bacon, ham, anchovies, mushrooms, chillies, fish, sausage, capsicum...the toppings are endless!

Khalsa Restaurant, Madge Ln., just north of the Salvation Army Guest House, serves the best economy meals around. Thick *dahl* Rs10; *paratha* Rs7; mixed vegetables Rs20. Open daily 4:30am-10pm.

Tulika's Ice Cream Parlor, Russell St., next to the post office, opposite the Royal Calcutta Turf Club. Probably the best ice cream in Calcutta. *Idlis, dosas,* and pizzas (Rs30-60). Open daily 8am-11pm.

🎬 SIGHTS

The best way to experience Calcutta and to see the sights is by **walking.** If it's not too hot, equip yourself with a copy of Prosenjit Das Gupta's *10 Walks in Calcutta* and take to the streets for a few hours every day. Or, join renowned architect and conservationist Manish Chakrabovti on a conducted walking tour of north Calcutta (contact **Footsteps** ☎337 5757). If you're in a hurry, hop on the West Bengal Tourism's **day tour** (Rs100). They rush you around the city in just ten hours, but it's a good way to catch a glimpse of everything and decide what to revisit.

MAIDAN, PARK STREET, AND NEW MARKET AREA

VICTORIA MEMORIAL. The southern end of the maidan is dominated by the infamous Victoria Memorial, the most impressive (and outlandish) reminder of Calcutta's past as capital of the British Raj. The British spent 15 years (1906-21) putting together this strange hybrid cross between Buckingham Palace and the Taj Mahal, designed to stand in loving memory of the self-proclaimed "Empress of India." Untouched by the pollution and chaos of the rest of Calcutta, this overpowering monument to British imperialism seems quite out of place among the poverty-stricken streets of the "City of Joy." Four minarets surround a central dome of white marble, lugged at great expense from the same Rajasthani quarries that furnished the material for the Taj Mahal. But unlike Agra's great white monument, the "VM" is shaped by the angles and spheres of the Italian Renaissance, with a bronze winged statue of Victory on top of it. A statue of an aging Queen Victoria waits at the entrance to the complex, greeting the crowds who come to wander through her gardens and pools. A much younger Victoria stands inside the building, now a **museum** chock full of British war memorabilia and state portraits. Much of the colonialist artwork and finery on display still provokes resentment among Bengali tourists, but their malice doesn't extend to the ever-popular queen, whose name has remained affixed to the building despite decades of political efforts to change it. The most impressive exhibit is undoubtedly the cool **Calcutta Gallery,** a timeline that chronicles the city's history and features examples of artwork, literature, and craftsmanship by leading Bengali figures. Be sure to check out the letter written by Rabindranath Tagore that asks for his knightship to be revoked after the Jallianwallah Bagh Massacre (see p. 675). The entire monument is beautifully illuminated at night. *(Museum open Tu-Su 10am-5pm; Nov.-Feb. 10am-4pm. Rs2. Photography not permitted. Sound and Light Show Tu-Su 8:15pm. Rs10. Garden open 24hr.)*

WEST BENGAL

ST. PAUL'S CATHEDRAL. This cavernous center of Anglican Calcutta was built by Maj. Gen. William Nairn in 1847. The white Gothic architecture is patterned on Norwich Cathedral. Old paintings of the Cathedral (at the Calcutta Museum) show a large spire, which fell during an earthquake in the 1930s. In its place, a new spire, modeled on the Bell Harry Tower at Canterbury Cathedral, was erected. There are some splendid stained glass windows, especially the one overlooking the west portico. *(At the south end of Chowringhee, on Cathedral Rd., opposite the Victoria Memorial. Open M-Sa 9am-noon and 3-6pm; services Su 7:30, 8:30, 11am, and 6pm.)*

BIRLA PLANETARIUM AND ACADEMY OF FINE ARTS. For celestial viewing, head to the **Birla Planetarium,** a stupa-esque edifice just south of St. Paul's Cathedral. *(English show at 1:30pm. Rs10.)* The **Academy of Fine Arts** is part of Calcutta's ongoing cultural buzz, holding exhibitions of local artists' work. The permanent collection here features many works by Rabindranath Tagore and the Bengal School of painters. *(South of St. Paul's. Permanent collection open Tu-Sa noon-6:45pm. Rs2. Local artists' exhibition open M-Sa 3-8pm. Free)*

INDIAN MUSEUM. Housed in an Italian-style building, the nation's largest and oldest museum contains a remarkable collection of sculpture from around India. Though the exhibits are poorly organized and displayed, it's well worth the patience to sift through the enormous collection, which includes several Mauryan and Shunga capitals and a large section of railing from the stupa at Bharhut in Madhya Pradesh. The painting collection (in the rooms on the terrace) is usually closed, but a bit of persuasion and a little baksheesh can work wonders. The central courtyard, adorned with flowers and fountains, is a welcome refreshment spot. *(At the corner of Sudder St. and Chowringhee Rd. Open Tu-Sa 10am-5pm; Dec.-Feb. Tu-Sa 10am-4:30pm. Rs50.)*

PARK STREET CEMETERY. The final resting place of British colonialists since 1767, the cemetery is one of the city's most serene spots. Among the most notable of the many huge gravestones here are those of Maj. Gen. Sir Charles Stuart (built like a small temple in black granite and complete with a *shikhara* and lotus motifs) and Rose Whitworth Aylmer, which has a spiralled obelisk and a romantic poem-epitaph by her admirer Walter Servage Landor. Also note the graves of Henry Vansittart, one of the first governors of the East India Company, and Sir William Jones, the first president of the Asiatic Society. Ask for the guidebook (Rs30) at the gate and remember to give a small donation in the box in the office. *(Southeast end of Cemetery Rd., near AJC Bose Rd. Open daily 7am-4pm. Free.)*

THE MAIDAN. Unquestionably the best spot in town to get a taste of Calcutta's public life, the maidan is a mix of unkempt nature and splendid gardens. Robert Clive cleared this vast field to give his soldiers a clear shot, and the old cannons that dot the ground are reminders of the maidan's military past. Unfortunately, **Fort William** itself remains closed to the public. During the Raj, the maidan was the site of a posh, year-round cocktail party, where the good old boys of the East Asia Company would sit back and watch cricket games. These days it belongs to the masses. Tram and bus lines run straight through the maidan, which is also the site of daily community rallies of workers announcing various grievances and *bandhs* (strikes). At the northwest corner of the maidan, near the river, are the **Eden Gardens,** the pride of India's cricket fans. The stadium has hosted World Cup matches and is notorious for the rowdy nationalistic fervor of the Indian fans. These take place in the shadow of the enormous Ranji Stadium, which has a capacity of over 100,000. The maidan is also the site of many local festivals and parades. Near the northern edge of the maidan is the **Shahid Minar** (Martyrs' Tower), built by the British in 1817 as the **Ochterlony Monument.** Originally designed as a tribute to David Ochterlony, who led royal forces against Nepal in 1814-16, the obelisk—renamed in 1969—is now a symbol of fierce Bengali pride.

THE BLACK HOLE OF CALCUTTA
Rumor has it that the silver-domed General Post Office, in BBD Bagh, is built over the site of one of the most infamous events in the history of Calcutta. The original Fort William once stood on this very spot, its past shadowed with grim misdeeds and suffering. In 1756, the Nawab of West Bengal, Siraj-ud-Daula, attacked Calcutta when the city's patron, the East India Company, neglected to protect the city during the Seven Years' War. The nawab imprisoned city council member John Holwell along with several other Europeans in the local penitentiary, dubbed the "Black Hole"—it was a room 18 feet long and 14 feet wide, with two small windows. According to Holwell, 146 were imprisoned, of whom only 23 emerged alive; he was one of the lucky few not to have been suffocated. Later researchers would claim that Holwell must have been exaggerating, since a room of such small dimensions could not have held that many people. Further research indicated that the death toll was significantly less, and that any casualties were due purely to the nawab's negligence. The topic is still controversial; it's one of the few colonial incidents where the Brits were not the bad guys.

BBD BAGH (DALHOUSIE SQUARE) AREA

Most of Calcutta's historic buildings are near its center, north of the maidan. **BBD Bagh,** the hub of this area, previously known as Dalhousie Sq., was renamed for Benoy, Badal, and Dinesh, three freedom fighters hanged by the British during protests following the 1905 partition of Bengal. The Lal Digha ("Red Tank"), is in the center. Up Netaji Subhas Rd. to the left of the Writers' Building is Calcutta's financial district. On **Lyons Range,** *bakda-wallahs* sell stocks in the street. To the southwest of the Writer's Building is the GPO, alleged site of the infamous Black Hole of Calcutta incident (see p. 657). To the east of the Writer's Building is Lal Bazaar, home to fascinating music stores that sell everything from Hawaiian guitars to brass *ghungroos.*

WRITER'S BUILDING. Spanning the north side of BBD Bagh is the red-brick caterpillar of the Writer's Building. No great literary figures toiled here, other than the clerks of the East India Company, for whom it was built in 1780. It's now the lair of the West Bengal state government—hidden inside are unthinkable catacombs of bureaucracy. The elevators recently got a full makeover after the Chief Minister got stuck in one, and, upon his rescue, ordered upgrades.

ST. JOHN'S CHURCH. With its clumsy-looking spire, St. John's is the oldest church in Calcutta. The octagonal mausoleum of Job Charnock, founder of Calcutta, is tucked away in the yard. Some belongings of Warren Hastings, the first governor-general of India, are kept inside the church. *(Down Government Place W. Open M-F 9am-noon and 4-6pm. Weekday services 9am, Su 8am.)*

RAJ BHAVAN AND HIGH COURT. Formerly home to British governors-general and viceroys, the vast grounds of Raj Bhavan (Government House) are the official residence of the Governor of West Bengal. The inside is suitably palatial, but it's not open to the public, so enjoy the walk in the shade of the barbed wire. Nearby, on the other side of Government Place West, are the State Legislature and the cheerful tricolor Gothic High Court. *(Diagonally opposite St. John's.)*

NORTH CALCUTTA

One of the oldest and most fascinating parts of the city, North Calcutta was home to the educated Bengali elite of Calcutta—the Tagores, Chakrabovties, Mullicks and Debs—during the colonial period. Tourists can visit many of the area's sprawling bungalows with permission from the owners. **Chitpur Rd.** (now officially Rabindra Sarani) is a narrow and crowded street lined with all kinds of shops—metalworkers, shoe-menders, wig-makers, and tailors. Just ahead is the red sandstone Nakhoda Masjid. The shops around the mosque sell *attar,* oil-based perfumes, and *surma,* a thick yet cooling eyeliner. There are also shops selling *sherwanis* and Lucknawi pyjamas. At the end of Chitpur Rd. (a *long* way) is Kamartulli, a colony of craftsmen carving out statues of your favorite Hindu deities.

BENGALIS IN THE AGE OF KALI

While the rest of the world has made a smooth transition into the 21st century, Bengalis continue to live in the age of Kali. Come October (during 2001, the festival will be held during Oct. 17-25, along with Navaratri), the whole state's affairs come to a screeching halt to celebrate the coming of Durga, Kali's maternal alter-ego. The Durga Puja festival is the most important time of the year for Bengalis, and it's a spectacle not to be missed by any visitor to the area. The preparations for the festival start with the onset of the monsoon. A small colony of idol-makers in Kumartulli (on Chitpur Rd., after Shyani Bazaar) starts hammering away at all the granite they can collect. By early September, the hammering has given life to a million Durgas, and people rush to get their hands on one before they are sold out. At the same time, most stores have a month-long 20-50% sale. People all over the city put together *pandals*, street shows, exhibitions, and melas, as the excitement mounts and the anticipation rises. Finally, the four-day festival begins when Durga returns to earth with her children to visit her parents, Himalaya and Menake. Tied into this familial reunion is the story of the *Ramayana*: it was Durga who gave Rama the energizing *shakti* that helped him kill Ravana. The next two days are spent rejoicing and worshiping her arrival. On the fourth day, as Durga gets ready to bid farewell, the whole city heads to the river to send her off. At dusk, people launch their statues of Durga onto the water, adorned with candles and garlands of flowers, and watch as she makes her way to the sea.

MARBLE PALACE. Built in 1835 as a mansion for the *zamindar* Raja Rajendro Mullick Bahadur, the Marble Palace features 13 different types of marble in all kinds of colors—green, grey, brown, and white. The Mullick family still lives in parts of the house. The guide will point out every single image of Victoria (and there aren't just two or three) including a massive wooden statue of the Empress on the ground floor. Highlights include the intricate ceiling and the solid gold clock on the first floor. Don't miss the sprawling lawns, where gray pelicans fish in the lake (on the right-hand side as you enter). You can get a free **gate pass** from the Tourist Office, on BBD Bagh, or the Government of India Tourism Office, on Shakespeare Sarani. A little baksheesh has been known to work just as well. Remember to leave the guide and the guards separate tips. *(Muktaram Babu Dr., off Chittaranjan Ave. Open Tu-W and F-Su 10am-4pm. Free.)*

RABINDRA BHARATI UNIVERSITY. One of several universities founded by Bengal's most famous son, Rabindranath Tagore, Rabindra Bharati University is built on the site of his lifelong home. The old mansion of the prolific Tagore family has been expanded and turned into an arts college, and the house itself has been preserved as the Rabindra Bharati **museum.** Beginning with the room where Tagore died, the museum traces the story of the Tagores and the Bengal Renaissance through a large collection of art and memorabilia. There is an entire section devoted to paintings by Rabindranath himself. *(Dwarakanath Tagore Ln., near the Marble Palace. Museum open M-F 10am-5pm, Sa 10am-1pm. Free.)*

PARASNATH JAIN TEMPLE. Built by a jeweler in 1867, this shimmering palace is dedicated to Sithalnath, the tenth Jain *tirthankara*. The building is full of colored glass and mirrors, set with sparkling and intricate designs. In one corner is an "ethereal lamp" that has been burning constantly since the temple was founded. *(Open daily 6am-noon and 3-7pm. Free.)*

DAKSHINESHWAR TEMPLE. It was here that the Hindu spiritual leader Sri Ramakrishna had his vision of the unity of all religions. One day, a brash, urbane, young agnostic walked into the compound and asked for proof of the existence of God. Promising revelation, Ramakrishna led him into an adjacent chamber, where the young follower was shown God—in his heart. Later, he came to be known as Swami Vivekananda, a spiritual leader who traveled around the world spreading the message of spiritual unity. The temple consists of three parts: the smallest chamber is devoted to Vishnu; the more impressive building next to the nearby sacrificial platform is dedicated to Shakti; directly opposite, built in traditional Bengali style, are five domes, each of which houses a Shiva *linga*. *(10km from the city center. Bus #32 from the Esplanade, Rs5. Open daily 6am-9pm. Free.)*

NICCO PARK AND SCIENCE PARK. Amuse yourself at Nicco Park with all your thrill-seeking Indian friends—a collection of amusement park rides waits here to jolt you out of India and into fantasy land. Science Park is a huge complex with several large buildings and exhibits. From space travel to dinosaurs, this is India's finest science museum. *(Off the East Metropolitan Bypass; Nicco Park is 2km from Science Park. Buses from BBD Bagh Rs5, taxis Rs40. Both open daily 9am-9pm. Science Park Rs15; Nicco Park Rs25. Nicco admission includes 10 ride tickets.)*

HOWRAH

BELUR MATH. This site served as the center of the movement founded in 1897 by Ramakrishna's disciple Swami Vivekananda, who aimed to unite all religions. The soaring temple dominates the grounds, but the most peaceful spot on the compound is at the end of the field, in the small cottage where Vivekananda spent his last days. His bedroom has been preserved, and an attached museum contains some of his belongings. Each one of the temples' four facades is designed to represent a different place of worship—church, temple, mosque, and *gurudwara*. Just before Belur Math is the headquarters of the Ramakrishna Mission. *(Taxis from BBD Bagh Rs50. Open Tu-Su 7-11am and 4-7pm; Oct.-Mar. 7-11am and 4-6pm. Free.)*

BOTANICAL GARDENS. This is one of Calcutta's most relaxing spots—if you go during the week, you'll have few companions other than storks, cranes, insects, and an amazing range of plants from every continent. The **Great Banyan Tree** is supposed to be the largest in the world, with roots stretching out nearly a mile from the treetop. A series of storms destroyed the trunk decades ago, but its standing roots still survive and flourish under the expansive canopy. *(20min. by taxi from Howrah Station. Ferries from Armenian Ghat Rs3. Open dusk-dawn. Free.)*

SOUTH CALCUTTA

KALI TEMPLE AT KALIGHAT. Calcutta's most important temple, Kalighat, is where the goddess Sati's little toe is said to have fallen to earth after being hacked off by Vishnu (see **Divine Dismemberment,** p. 692). Pilgrims have streamed in and out of the temple since its construction in 1809, but the authorities have recently decided to close it to foreigners. Nevertheless, a bit of charisma and baksheesh (probably the most you will ever dish out, so start bargaining cheap at Rs50) might be enough to get you inside the striking building built in the medieval Bengali style. Inside you can gaze into the goddess's wise and terrifying red eyes, reproduced on dashboards and refrigerators all over Bengal. During Durga Puja and Kali Puja in October, goats are sacrificed here. *(Open daily 6am-10pm. Free.)*

NETAJI BHAVAN. For many, the non-violent tactics of Gandhi are no way to bring about real progress. Their hero is Subhas Chandra Bose, erstwhile leader of the Indian National Army, which sought to wrest control of the country from the British by force. Netaji Bhavan was the home of Bose, who collaborated with the Japanese and led troops against the British during WWII. It features a museum with Bose's belongings and a history of his achievements. Every January 23rd, his birthday is celebrated here. *(Elgin St., near Chowringhee. Open Tu-Sa noon-4pm. Rs2.)*

ZOOLOGICAL GARDENS. Calcutta's zoo contains India's foremost collection of predatory felines; the centerpiece is the large island home of the zoo's Bengal Tigers. Sightings are rare during the hot season, but don't fret—the lions and tigers are also on display in cages, where they laze in the open more frequently. Avoid the weekends when the zoo is absolutely heaving. *(Near the Taj Bengal. Taxi from Park St. Rs25. Open F-W 9am-5pm. Zoo Rs5; camera fee Rs250. Aquarium Rs2.)*

THE BIG CATS OF BENGAL Catching a glimpse of the Bengal Tiger, a majestic beast with a deep reddish tan, black stripes, and white-furred belly, is a rare event. Most of the tigers in West Bengal are found only in the swampy mangrove forests of the Sunderbans, though they have occasionally been known to stray. In 1974, a tiger made it all the way to a village 50 miles outside Calcutta, where it killed a local woman. Only about 4% of tigers are "man-eaters," but all will attack if disturbed. Forest guards wear fiberglass head and neck protectors—these are the parts most vulnerable to attack. Honey-gatherers wear masks on the back of their heads since tigers tend to attack only when people are looking away. Researchers are trying to train tigers to stay away from humans by positioning electrified dummies in the forest—a 300V shock is administered if the tiger attacks. The experiment has been successful so far, but some people still look to the gods for protection. Many wood-cutters and honey-farmers refuse to enter the Sunderbans without being escorted by *fakirs*, religious men who have the power to ward off tiger attacks. *(West Bengal Tourism conducts tours to the Sunderbans; the best season to visit is Nov.-Feb.)*

⚑ ENTERTAINMENT

The **Calcutta Information Centre,** in the same complex as the Nandan, provides information on theater, film, and other cultural events. (☎248 1451. Open M-F 1-8pm.) Check newspapers for listings and go early for tickets.

PERFORMING AND FINE ARTS. Calcutta supports a thriving tradition of performing arts. Bengali music, dance, and drama are staged at several venues throughout the city. The Drama Theater at the back of the **Academy of Fine Arts** has daily performances. (☎223 4302. 6:30pm, Sa 10am and 3pm. Rs10-25.) On the corner of Cathedral and AJC Bose Rd. is **Rabindra Sadan** (☎223 9936 or 223 9917), an important concert hall dedicated to Tagore. Other playhouses, such as the **Kala Mandir,** are also along AJC Bose Rd. **CIMA** (Center for International Modern Art), Sunny Towers, 43 Ashutosh Chowdhari Ave., has regular exhibitions of contemporary and traditional art.

CINEMAS. Although Calcutta is home to India's artsiest film industry, its cinemas, such as the **Globe Theater** on the corner of Madge and Lindsay St., tend to show the usual Indian and American bilge. The gigantic **New Empire** and **Light House Cinema** movie theaters, side by side just west of New Market, both favor recent hits. **Nandan Theater,** south of the Academy of Fine Arts, has both English and Bengali productions. (Shows 2, 4, and 6pm. Rs5-12.)

NIGHTCLUBS. Most nightclubs are open till early in the morning and are choc-a-bloc with boogying Calcuttans of all ages. **Tantra,** Park Hotel, Park St., plays new-age and techno, with hardly enough room to shake a leg. (Cover Rs200. Open 8pm-4am.) **Anticlock,** Hotel Hindustan, the first disco in Calcutta, is still a popular haunt when Tantra gets too full. (Cover Rs200.) **Someplace Else,** Park Hotel, Park St., is a nice, ritzy place to grab an early drink before the late night cruisers arrive. (Beer Rs130. Cover Rs300. Open Th-Sa 7pm-2am.)

🖪 VOLUNTEER OPPORTUNITIES

Even after her death, Mother Teresa's organization continues to care for the destitute and dying. Now headed by Sister Nirmala, the **Missionaries of Charity** have bases around the city. Their **Mother House,** 54 AJC Bose Rd., is the place to go if you're interested in learning more about volunteering. While the Sisters always welcome those willing to help, they do expect a certain degree of dedication, commitment, and fortitude. Sister Nirmala registers all volunteers, and is available before 9am and later on in the afternoon (3pm). No prior arrangements have to be made, and you can volunteer for as long as you want, either at the home for destitute girls in Kalighat or Shishu Bhawan or for orphans at AJC Bose Rd.

SILIGURI শিলিগুড়ি AND
NEW JALPAIGURI ☎ 0353

Since Siliguri and New Jalpaiguri function as the main transit point to Nepal, Sik-kim, and the Northeast, most travelers can't avoid stopping here at some point. Linked by urban sprawl, these two indistinguishable cities have managed to cap-ture all the congestion, noise, and filth of urban India with none of the beautiful scenery or fresh air that their location might seem to suggest. Because of their low elevation, the climate of Siliguri and New Jalpaiguri (114m) has much more in common with Calcutta's scorching heat than with the cooler temperatures of nearby Darjeeling (80km north). This self-proclaimed "gateway to the Indian Himalayas" offers hardly a hint of the natural splendor that awaits just up the road.

GETTING THERE AND GETTING AROUND

Airport: Bagdogra Airport, 16km west of Siliguri. Take the Hill Cart Rd. bus, which leaves from NJP Station, stopping in front of Tenzing Norgay Bus Terminal before arriving in Bagdogra (Rs3); then hop on a rickshaw to the airport (Rs10). The trip takes 1hr. **Jeeps** also run to the airport from Hill Cart Rd. in front of the bus terminal (30 min., Rs30). **Indian Airlines,** 2nd fl., Mainak Hotel, Hill Cart Rd. (☎431493), a 5min. walk north from the bus station. Open M-Sa 10am-5:30pm. MC, Visa. Flies to: **Calcutta** (M, W, and F; 12:40pm; 1hr.; US$80) and **Delhi** (M, W, and F; 12:40pm; 3hr.; US$185) via **Guwa-hati** (45min., US$50). **Jet Airways,** 1st fl. Hotel Vinayak, Hill Cart Rd. (☎450589), 200m south of the bridge, has flights to **Calcutta** (M, W, and F; 2:10pm; 1hr.; US$80) and **Delhi** (M, W, and F; 2:15pm; 3hr.; US$185). Open M-F 10am-5pm.

Trains: All trains stop at **New Jalpaiguri Station,** Hill Cart Rd., before continuing on to the Northeastern States. The **Central Rail Booking Office** (☎423333) is near the Hospital Rd./Hill Cart Rd. police traffic booth, 30m up the road headed diagonally northeast. Open M-Sa 8am-8pm, Su 8am-2pm. To: **Bombay** (M and Th, 2:15am; Tu, 11pm; 39hr.; Rs444); **Calcutta** (4-5 per day, 3:45pm-8:45pm, 12hr., Rs210); **Delhi** (3 per day, 12:15-10:50pm, 33hr., Rs363). The **Toy Train** runs from NJP station to **Darjeeling** (6:30am, 9hr., 2nd class Rs20, 1st class Rs200).

Buses: Government buses leave **Tenzing Norgay Bus Terminal,** 250m north of the bridge. **Private buses** congregate on Hill Cart Rd., next to the main bus station, and are slightly more expensive, more frequent, and faster than the public buses. **Jeeps** gather in the square area, on the opposite side of the road, and are the fastest but most expensive option. Fares listed are for private buses, and change frequently. To: **Calcutta** (4 per day, 12hr., Rs200); **Darjeeling** (every 30min., 6am-8pm, 3½hr., Rs45); **Kalim-pong** (every 30min., 6am-5pm, 4hr., Rs40); **Kurseong** (every hr., 6am-5pm, 1hr., Rs35); **Mirik** (every 30 min., 6am-5pm, 3hr., Rs45). **Sikkim Nation Transportation (SNT) Centre** is on Hill Cart Rd., a short walk south from the bus station. To: **Gangtok** (every hr., 7am-2pm; 4hr.; Rs70, Rs90 deluxe); **Geyzing** (12:30pm, 4½hr., Rs70); **Pel-ling** (11:30am, 5hr., Rs84). Buses for **Kathmandu** leave from Kakarbhitta, Nepal. Take a jeep to the border at **Panitanki** (1hr., Rs30), and then walk across the bridge or take a cycle-rickshaw (Rs10). **Jeeps** run to the same places all day. To: **Gangtok** (3½hr., Rs80); **Kalimpong** (3hr., Rs45); **Darjeeling** (3hr., Rs50); **Kurseong** (1hr., Rs40).

ORIENTATION AND PRACTICAL INFORMATION

The bustling centers of these joined-at-the-armpit cities are Siliguri's **Tenzing Nor-gay Bus Terminus** (named for Edmund Hillary's Everest climbing partner) and, 6km south (cycle-rickshaw Rs30, auto-rickshaw Rs60), the **New Jalpaiguri Railway Sta-tion.** For the most part, the area is oriented along the north-south axis defined by **Hill Cart Rd. (Tenzing Norgay Rd.),** a bustling "miracle mile" connecting the cities. The most useful landmark is Siliguri's **Mahananda River Bridge,** just south of the bus station. Budget accommodations cluster north of the bridge near the bus station. Most shops and services line **Hill Cart Rd.,** just south of the bridge.

Tourist Office: West Bengal Tourism (☎511974; fax 511979), in the big orange building, 100m south of the bus terminal on the east side of the road. Does advance booking for Jaldapara Wildlife Sanctuary. Open M-F 10am-5pm. There's a smaller branch at the NJP Railway Station (☎561118). **Sikkim Permit: Sikkim Tourist Office** (☎432646), SNT Centre, opposite the bus station, issues basic Sikkim permits for free, but requires a passport photo. Open M-Sa 10am-4pm.

Passport Photo: Studio Ellora, Hill Cart Rd. (☎432028), 150m south of the bridge, next to the State Bank, does 4 photos for Rs60. Necessary for Sikkim permit and Nepal visa. Open M-Sa 8:30am-8pm.

Currency Exchange: State Bank of India, Hill Cart Rd. (☎431364), 150m south of the bridge, changes cash and Thomas Cook and AmEx traveler's checks. Rs20 commission up to Rs5000, Rs25 above Rs5000. Open M-F 10am-2pm, Sa 10am-noon. Many banks and hotels on Hill Cart Rd. change money.

Luggage Storage: Tenzing Norgay Bus Terminal, on the right as you enter; or **NJP Station,** on track 4. Both charge Rs3 per day.

Pharmacy: Medical booths dot the city. Look around or ask a local. Most close by 11pm.

Police: (☎520453) on Hill Cart Rd. opposite the bus station and 50m north.

Internet: The most convenient is **Biswadeep Communications** (☎531724), opposite the bus terminal, 20m down the road behind the jeep lot. Rs2 per min. Open daily 6:30am-10:30pm. The cheapest is **Weblink,** Hill Cart Rd. (☎537244), 200m south of the bridge on the 2nd floor. Rs1 per min. Open daily 9am-9pm.

Telephones: Most STD/ISD booths close by 11pm.

Post Office: GPO, Hospital Rd. (☎421965). Turn left at the third police traffic booth south of the bridge on Hill Cart Rd., and follow it for 200m. Open M-Sa 7am-7pm. **Postal code:** 734401.

ACCOMMODATIONS AND FOOD

The warm, family-like **Siliguri Lodge,** north of the bridge on the east side of Hill Cart Rd. and opposite the bus station, has a garden, complete with mini-gazebo, a TV in the lobby, and a choice of squat or Western-style communal toilets. (☎533290. Check-out noon. Singles Rs100; doubles Rs140-200.) Two blocks north on the same side of the street is the more up-market **Hotel Mount View,** Hill Cart Rd., which has large, institutional rooms, all with private bath and TV. The TVs range from hi-fi to diorama-in-a-microwave, so make sure to check what you're getting. Reservations are recommended. MC, Visa. (☎425919 or 531598. Check-out noon. Singles Rs175-400; doubles Rs250-650.) The cheapest alternative is the **Rajasthan Guest House,** 100m west of Hill Cart Rd., on the road that diverges just where the train tracks cross Hill Cart Rd. It's easiest to take a cycle-rickshaw. Bare, basic rooms and an inconvenient location conspire against it, but the bathrooms are clean and the price is right. (☎525163. Dorms Rs60; singles Rs90-100; doubles Rs150-200.)

ANIMAL HOUSE Tourists aren't the only ones starved for nightlife in early-to-bed, early-to-rise Northeast India. The natives are apparently getting restless as well. In fact, in recent years drunken gallivanting and late-night carousing are on the rise among local populations...of elephants. Last call at many of the popular pachyderm watering-holes comes in late November when Jaldapara's streams fall victim to the winter dry season. Rather than resort to a winter on the wagon, wild elephants have been hitting the human hot spots (usually people's huts) in search of Hariya, a locally micro-brewed rice wine. But the hedonism does not stop there. With their booze-fed libidos primed, the wild male elephants, or tuskers, cruise for chicks at the makeshift brothel which hosts domesticated, female touring elephants. After having their way, the tuskers stagger back to the jungle—presumably to sleep the bender off.

There are a few decent restaurants on Hill Cart Rd., south of the bridge. **Anand Restaurant,** about 50m south on the east side of the road, serves an outstanding tandoori *paratha* for Rs35. (Open daily 7:30am-10pm.) The **New Ranjit Restaurant,** in the Ranjit Hotel, less than 1km south of the bridge, on the west side of Hill Cart Rd., is popular for its all-veg. dishes. (Rs24-60. ☎431758. Open daily 9am-11pm).

🔟 JALDAPARA WILDLIFE SANCTUARY

Jaldapara is truly a site fit for kings—or so the kings of Bhutan and Coochbhear (now part of West Bengal) believed some 100 years ago, when each jealously coveted the land as a royal rhinoceros-hunting ground. Along came the British to "settle the dispute" in true imperial fashion by claiming the entire Dooras ("gateway") region as their own, gradually converting thousands of acres of lush jungle into vast tea plantations. This ecological upheaval left only a few large pockets of dense forest; and the well-preserved Jaldapara Wildlife Sanctuary, officially designated a national park in 1985, is one of them. Though it's one of India's smaller wildlife sanctuaries, Jaldapara is one of a handful of parks left in India with a sizable population of rhinos. It also contains over 100 species of birds and is home to an impressive community of monkeys, deer, and elephants.

Jaldapara is just about the only reason not to flee straight into the hills from Siliguri. Jaldapara's well-run services ensure a comfortable, safari-like experience. Best of all, the park is still relatively undiscovered by the tourists that flock to India's other wildlife sanctuaries. (In-season Oct.-Apr., closed June 15-Sept. 15. Entrance fee Rs20. Camera fee Rs20.)

The most popular and fun way to take in what the park has to offer is via an **elephant ride** (Rs150). Other options include a drive (Rs200) and trek to the **tiger reserve,** where you'll be lucky to see a tiger. Jeeps (Rs150) tour the area's **tea gardens,** which include a few monasteries and well-preserved British colonial forts.

There are two lodges in the area. Both are excellent, though prices are very high. Rooms should be booked in advance through the tourist office in Siliguri. At the edge of Madarihat, the **Jaldapara Tourist Lodge** has large, comfy rooms and a huge yard. All meals are included. The staff is friendly and attentive. (☎03563 or 62230. Dorm beds Rs275; doubles Rs650-950.) The alternative is the **Hollong Forest Lodge,** within the confines of the park. Its location and garden make it even more expensive than the other place. (☎62228. Doubles Rs2000. Meals included.)

Jaldapara is about 125km east of Siliguri, which provides the only major access point to the park. The journey is picturesque, as road and rail wind their way through green foothills and tea fields. **Madarihat,** the town near the park's entrance, is accessible by **buses** running to and from Siliguri (every 2hr., 6am-7pm, 4hr., Rs35). If direct buses to Madarihat are not available, any bus going to **Alipurduara, Hashimara, Joygoin,** or **Phuntsholling** can drop you there. There is an overnight bus from Madarihat to **Guwahati** (9pm, 8hr., Rs200).

SUNDERBANS NATIONAL PARK

Tucked into the extreme southeastern corner of West Bengal, the Sunderbans National Park covers more than 4000 sq. km of mangrove forests and water channels, and is home to one of India's largest tiger populations. The estuarine crocodile is another full-time resident, though it doesn't get out much these days. Although your chances of seeing the predators are relatively slim, you are certain to spot plenty of their prey, such as barking deer and spotted deer, turtles, monkeys and villagers. Large heron populations dominate the birdlife here. The sound of birdsong, along with the deep green of the mangroves and peaceful flow of the tides is enough to make you feel you've taken a long rickety ride to paradise after frantic Calcutta. The journey to the park takes you deep into the heart of the Bengali countryside, dotted with rice paddies and thatched roofs. Although the park is open all year long, the best season to visit is November-February.

⊡ GETTING TO THE PARK. The park is accessible from **Sajmekhali,** roughly 85km southwest of Calcutta. Reaching the park involves a fascinating (and long) journey through dusty piles of Indian bureaucracy, crowds of urban commuters, and some very beautiful and very peaceful countryside. The description that follows is likely to sound complicated and painful. Once you are in motion, however, it's almost as easy as falling off a bus (or running away from a tiger). The first step involves getting your hungry hands on a permit from the magestically-titled **Principal Chief Conservator of Forests,** who spends much of his time hanging out on the third floor of the new CIT Building, P16 India Exchange Place, next to the Telegraph Office. (☎225 4514; official working hours M-F 11am-5pm). All you need is your passport, and if you can manage to track down the man you're looking for, you ought to be able to get a permit issued within 30 minutes (free). If, however, the officer's niece happens to be getting married on the day you arrive, then you're right out of luck. With the permit in safely in hand, you can continue over to the Southern Railways terminal at **Sealdah** station to catch a commuter train to **Canning** (17 per day, 90min., Rs10). In Canning, follow your fellow passengers through the bazaars to the river, where a *bodhooti* will ferry you over to the Dok Kart (Rs1). In Dok Kart, try to squeeze yourself a bit of breathing space in one of the shared tempos to **Somakhali** (45min., Rs8). The next step is to catch a ferry to **Gosaba** (90min., Rs7.50). From there, take a rickshaw to **Pakhinda** (45min., Rs15) and (just one more) ferry to Sajmekhali (Rs3). The entire journey takes six hours.

⊡⊡ FOOD AND ACCOMMODATIONS. In Sajmekhali, the only available accommodation is the expensive **Tourist Lodge,** which needs to be booked in advance through any West Bengal Tourism Office. (☎(03219) 52562. Dorm Rs200; double Rs525.) Across the great divide in Pakhirala is the **Krishnakunja Hotel,** where luxuries include concrete rooms with attached bath (Rs300-400). The cheapest option is to ask for a bed at the general stores in Pakhirala. With a bit of luck, you will be directed to one of the straw huts and provided with a mosquito net (Rs50). If everything is full, turn back and return to Gosaba. In the bazaar here is the **Kumor Kamini Hotel,** with simple rooms with fans and mosquito nets (Rs80-150); the **Anapuran Hindu Hotel** has rock-bottom singles (Rs25) and doubles (Rs50), which share a miserable common toilet. There is also the semi-luxurious **Surya Tapa Lodge,** where the rooms come with showers. (☎(03219) 52509. Rs300.) The bazaar in Gosaba is also the best place to stock up on food—there are a number of decent Bengali eateries and sweet shops. In Pakhirala, there are a few tea stalls and a store, but no restaurant. The canteen in the Sajnekhali Tourist Lodge is overpriced. The nearest **pharmacies** selling ointments for tiger bites are in Gosaba and so are the STD/ISDs to make next-of-kin calls from.

DISORIENT EXPRESS Ninety kilometers in nine hours? Sounds like a fast-paced trek, but the toy train uses every minute to lug some 80 passengers up more than 2000m of vertical ascent from Siliguri to Darjeeling. This little engine that can (most of the time) hauls three cars and manages the climb (and descent) by traversing the main auto road at least 100 times. Service is sporadic, due to seasonal weather variations and constant mechanical problems. However, if the train is running, the breathtaking views make the experience one that should not be missed. The two time-saving alternatives are to ride the train to Kurseong, roughly the mid-point, and then catch a bus (2hr., Rs25) or a jeep (1½hr., Rs35) the rest of the way; or experience the train for the one-hour ride between Darjeeling and Ghoom (although this may be the most boring part of the trip). And don't worry if part of the train slips from its 60cm tracks (this has been known to happen); locals will emerge from the woods bearing poles to lever the carriage back on course.

☗ **WATCHING FOR TIGERS.** The only way to see the park is by taking a boat tour. First you need to obtain a clearance from the **Park Office** in Sajnekhali (open sunrise-sunset). This will be given upon display of your permit and payment of the Rs5 per person per day and Rs10 per camera per day fees. Boats depart 7-8am from in front of the office. Book the day before, or else take your chances and try to join a group in the morning. **Sudharnokali** reportedly has the best chances of tiger sighting (4 hr., Rs500 plus Rs200 compulsory guide fee). **Burit Dabri** is the most popular with Bengali tourists and takes you within earshot of the Bangladeshi border (8½hr., Rs800 plus Rs200 guide fee). The **Natidupani** tour takes you through the heart of the park (8hr., Rs700 plus Rs200). The boats seat up to 35, bringing the cost down as low as Rs20-50, per person depending on the number participants. In Sanjekhali there is a watchtower and a nature observation center (open 8am-5pm). Try to come on weekdays to avoid crowds of picnicking local tourists. February and March are the quietest time to come.

DARJEELING दार्जिलिङ दार्जलिनि   ☎ 0354

The most famous of the British hill stations, Darjeeling in every way lives up to the grand expectations its legendary name conjures up. Tottering along a knife-edged ridge, the city looks out over the Himalayan foothills and all the way up to Kanchenjunga, the third-highest mountain in the world, while on the other side the ridge drops away to the tropical valley floor literally thousands of meters below. When the British chanced upon this wooded ridge in 1828, they were so enraptured with the cool climate and majestic mountain views that they convinced the king of Sikkim into letting them use it as a health resort. Darjeeling's popularity as a getaway for heatstruck colonials grew and grew; by 1861 Sikkim was forced to cede this great playground of colonial India to the British. Today, Darjeeling is as famous for being the staging point for the earliest Everest expeditions and a center for tea production as it is for the spectacular scenery. Its infrastructure is under constant strain to meet tourists' demands for electricity, water, and transportation. The region's Gorkha inhabitants, most of them brought over from Nepal as laborers, never abandoned their language, dress, or blend of Hinduism and Buddhism. The Gorkha National Liberation Front's war for secession culminated in the 1958 formation of the Gorkha Hill Council, which now governs the area. Tensions persist, and the Council occasionally holds *bandhs* (strikes), during which the entire town and the road to Siliguri are closed for a day.

▐ GETTING THERE AND GETTING AROUND

Trains: The **Reservation Booth** (☎ 52555) at the **railway station** issues quota tickets for major trains leaving NJP (Siliguri) Station. Open 10am-1pm and 2-4pm. The station services the **Toy Train,** which traverses the route between Siliguri and Darjeeling (from Darjeeling 8:25am; 2nd class Rs20/1st class Rs200) and also makes an overpriced daily "joy ride" to Ghoom and back (11:30am, Rs250).

Buses and Jeeps: Most buses, including private ones, and jeeps headed out of Darjeeling leave from the main bus stand at the Chowk Bazaar on Hill Cart Rd. Other jeeps leave from the intersection of Laden La Rd. and Hill Cart Rd., and from the area around the clocktower. **Buses** to: **Gangtok** (4 per day, 8am-2pm, 5hr., Rs75); **Kalimpong** (7am, 4hr., Rs37); **Rimbik** (3 per day, 7am-2pm, 5hr., Rs55) via **Manebhanjang** (1½hr., Rs20); **Siliguri** (frequent, 6am-5pm, 3½hr., Rs45). **Jeeps** to: **Gangtok** (frequent, 7am-3pm, 4hr., Rs120); **Ghoom** (frequent, 7am-6pm, 10min., Rs8); **Jorethang** (every 30min., 7am-9am, 1½hr., Rs75), where service is available to points farther north; and **Kalimpong** (frequent, 7am-3pm, 2½hr., Rs60).

▌! Do not accept passage on vehicles with white numbers on black license plates; **they are not authorized to carry passengers** and may be detained by the police.

✦ ORIENTATION

Darjeeling is draped like a blanket on a clothesline over either side of a narrow, north-south ridge, and its steep, tangled streets, alleys, and stairways will strain both your legs and your sense of direction. Fortunately, locals are very knowledge-able and helpful with directions. The town's belly is **Hill Cart Rd.**, on the west side near the bottom. The **railway** and **bus stations** are here, as is the motor entrance to town. It's quite a climb from Hill Cart Rd. to **Chowrasta**, the town's central plaza near the top of the ridge. The Chowrasta intersection has a bandstand at the north end and a fountain and tourist office at the south. To the right of the fountain descends **Nehru Rd.** (also called **The Mall**), one of the town's main avenues for shops and restaurants. **Laden La Rd.** runs right below, connecting Nehru Rd. and Hill Cart Rd. At the intersection of Nehru and Laden La Rd. sits the **clocktower.** The road to the left of the fountain in Chowrasta (past the ponies) leads to the TV tower area, home of many of the cheap hotels are.

⏚ PRACTICAL INFORMATION

Tourist Office: West Bengal Tourist Office, Chowrasta (☎ 54050), south side, just above the Indian Airlines office; enter around to the right, up the ramp. Friendly, English-speak-ing staff provides a map of Darjeeling (Rs3), good transportation information, and free luggage storage. Runs a bus to Bagdogra Airport (3½ hr., Rs65) if there are enough pas-sengers (min. 12). Open M-F 10am-4:30pm. Transport desk open daily during tourist season. The **Darjeeling Gorkha Hill Council Tourist Office** (☎ 54879), 50m north of Chowrasta on Mall Rd. West, also has maps and brochures and arranges rafting expedi-tions on the Rangeet and Teesta rivers. Open M-Sa 10am-5pm.

Sikkim Permit: The process of securing a **Sikkim permit** is a bureaucratic hassle that may take hours (it's much easier at the office in **Siliguri**—see p. 662). You need your passport at every step. First go to the **District Magistrate's Office,** 7min. down Hill Cart Rd., north of the bus stands; look for the "Sikkim Pass" sign. Office is on 1st fl. of central building. Open M-F 10:30am-1pm and 2:30-4pm. With the stamped form, go to the **Foreigners' Registration Office,** Laden La Rd. (☎ 54203), next to ANZ Grindlays Bank, for a police sig-nature (or stamp). Open M-F 10am-4pm. Then, return to the District Magistrate's Office for the final signature. It's worth the effort, though; the permit is free and valid for 15 days.

Currency Exchange: ANZ Grindlays Bank, Laden La Rd. (☎ 54551), just down from the Nehru Rd. intersection. Changes traveler's checks, cash, and gives cash advances on MC and Visa (Rs100 fee). Open M-F 10am-3pm, Sa 10am-12:30pm; traveler's checks only M-F 10:30am-1pm. **State Bank of India,** Laden La Rd. (☎ 53589), 50m south of Grindlay's Bank, changes traveler's checks M-F 10am-2pm, Sa 10am-noon. Rs20 fee up to Rs5000, Rs25 fee above Rs5000.

Luggage Storage: Free at the tourist office, most hotels, and trekking companies.

Bookstore: Oxford Bookshop, Chowrasta (☎ 54325), overlooking town. Open M-F 9:30am-7:30pm, Sa 9:30am-2:30pm, Su in-season. AmEx, MC, Visa.

Police: Police assistance booths are all over the shop; there's one in Chowrasta, one at the intersection of Nehru and Laden La Rd., and one opposite the GPO.

Pharmacy: Economic Pharmacy, Laden La Rd. (☎ 52174), opposite the GPO, at the bend. Open daily 8am-7:30pm.

Hospital: Sardar Hospital (☎ 54077), above the main bus stand. Many pharmacies, par-ticularly along Nehru Rd., also have private doctors for consultation.

Internet: Compuset Centre, Gandhi Rd., on the right side, about 200m south of the clock-tower. Rs2 per min. Open daily 9am-6pm.

Telephones: Most **STD/ISD** booths close around 11pm.

Post Office: GPO, Laden La Rd. (☎ 52076), halfway down, just after sharp bend. Open M-F 9am-5pm, Sa 9am-2pm. **Postal Code:** 734101.

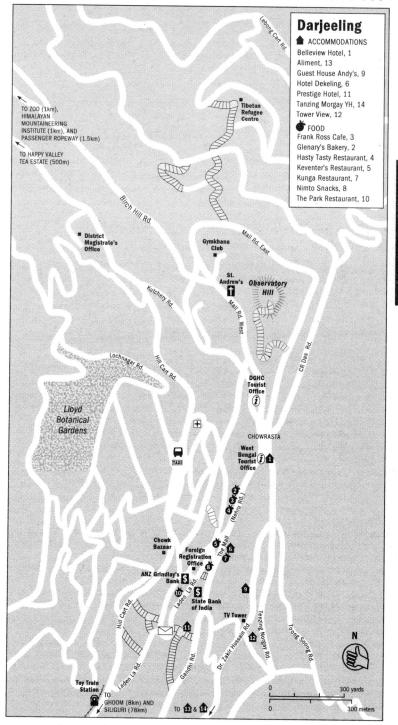

Darjeeling

🏠 ACCOMMODATIONS
Belleview Hotel, 1
Aliment, 13
Guest House Andy's, 9
Hotel Dekeling, 6
Prestige Hotel, 11
Tanzing Morgay YH, 14
Tower View, 12

🍴 FOOD
Frank Ross Cafe, 3
Glenary's Bakery, 2
Hasty Tasty Restaurant, 4
Keventer's Restaurant, 5
Kunga Restaurant, 7
Nimto Snacks, 8
The Park Restaurant, 10

WEST BENGAL

TO ZOO (1km),
HIMALAYAN
MOUNTAINEERING
INSTITUTE (1km), AND
PASSENGER ROPEWAY (1.5km)

TO HAPPY VALLEY
TEA ESTATE (500m)

Lebong Cart Rd.

Tibetan Refugee Centre

Birch Hill Rd.

District Magistrate's Office

Gymkhana Club

Mall Rd. East

Kutchery Rd.

St. Andrew's

Observatory Hill

Mall Rd. West

CR Das Rd.

Lochnagar Rd.

Hill Cart Rd.

Lloyd Botanical Gardens

DGHC Tourist Office ℹ️

CHOWRASTA

West Bengal Tourist Office ℹ️ 1

TAXI

2
3
4
(Nehru Rd.)

Chowk Bazaar

The Mall

6
7
8

Foreign Registration Office

ANZ Grindlay's Bank 💲

Laden La Rd.

10

State Bank of India 💲

9

TV Tower

Tenzing Norgay Rd.

Toong Soong Rd.

11

Gandhi Rd.

Hill Cart Rd.

Dr. Zakir Hussain Rd.

12

N

Toy Train Station

Laden La Rd.

TO GHOOM (8km) AND SILIGURI (78km)

TO 13 & 14

0   300 yards

0   300 meters

ACCOMMODATIONS

Darjeeling is home to a wide array of high quality, cheap hotels; there's no need to settle for the wrong place or price. Off season (mid-June to Aug. and Dec.-Feb.), there's plenty of space, and discounts of up to 50% are sometimes available; in season (Oct.-Nov. and Mar.-May), you may have to hunt a bit for a room.

■ **Aliment,** 40 Dr. Zakir Hussain Rd. (☎55068). From Chowrasta, take the road to the left of the fountain and bear right when it splits into three. After the TV tower (on the right), bear right up the hill and follow Dr. Z's around to the left. An unassuming but expertly run hotel with an excellent restaurant. The owner's tips and the detailed tourist log are helpful in planning treks. All rooms have private bath. Laundry service. Dorm beds Rs40; doubles with bucket shower Rs120, with hot shower Rs200.

■ **Tower View,** 8/1 Dr. Zakir Hussain Rd. (☎54452; fax 54330). It is actually just off Dr. Z's Rd. The friendly owner, a former Gorkha soldier, welcomes foreigners, sharing his regional knowledge and the tourist log, which has good trekking tips. Rooms look out over Kanchenjunga, facing the sunrise. Backpacker-filled restaurant serves good meals. STD service. Dorm beds Rs40; singles Rs60-80; doubles Rs120-150.

■ **Belleview Hotel,** Chowrasta (☎54075), on the south side of the plaza. Although a real step up in price, the cozy ski-lodge atmosphere, central location, private baths in every room, and fantastic views make it worth the extra rupees. For real decadance, snatch up the top-floor corner room, complete with panoramic views, a wood burning stove, and a bathtub (Rs1000). Rs80 for 10 kilos of stove wood. Singles Rs385; doubles Rs500-1000. Off-season Rs300/400-900.

Guest House Andy's, 102 Dr. Zakir Hussain Rd. (☎53125). Close to Chowrasta, 150m past the *puri* stalls. Huge doubles with great views. Quiet and spotlessly clean, with large seat toilet. Viewing platform on roof provides unparalleled vistas. Top priced rooms have hot shower. Doubles Rs200-300. Off-season: Rs150-250.

Hotel Dekeling, 51 Gandhi Rd., above the Nehru-Laden La intersection. Prime location in the center of town, a quality restaurant downstairs (10% discount for guests), and private baths in every room, but with a price tag to match. Hot showers, hot water bottles, and extra blankets free of charge. Doubles Rs800-1100. Off-season: Rs480-660.

Prestige Hotel (☎53199), on the steps between Laden La and Gandhi Rd. No views, but clean, inexpensive rooms with 24hr. hot water. Kerosene heat and color cable TV (both Rs80 per night) available on request. A la carte breakfast. Dorm rooms Rs250 for 4 people; singles Rs88-132; doubles Rs132-165.

Tanzing Norgay Youth Hostel, Dr. Zakir Hussain Rd. (☎56794), 100m up the hill from the Aliment. Sterile, institutional dorm rooms are compensated for by the expansive balcony circling the building. Dorm beds Rs40; doubles Rs120.

FOOD

Darjeeling is crammed with restaurants, with **Aliment** and **Tower View** being the best of the hotel variety. The choicest **street stand food** is on Dr. Zakir Hussain Rd., just as it leaves Chowrasta, although you'll have to suffer the hungry stares and smelly deposits of the adjacent horses.

■ **Hasty Tasty Restaurant,** 13 Nehru Rd. Darjeeling's widest selection of all-veg., the monumental menu covers everything from Indian to Chinese to continental to American, and the service is quick and friendly. Dishes Rs25-80. Open daily 8am-8:30pm.

■ **The Park Restaurant,** Laden La Rd., opposite the State Bank of India. While the prices are a little high, the consensus is that the Park serves the best Indian food in town. Savory chicken *tikka masala* Rs85; vegetable curry Rs30. Open daily 8am-9pm.

■ **Glenary's Bakery,** Nehru Rd., 100m uphill from the Hasty Tasty. The self-proclaimed master baker lives up to his own billing. Donuts, scones, macaroons, and rolls for Rs10-40. Request a window seat for great mountain views. Open daily 6:30am-7pm.

Keventer's Restaurant, 9 Nehru Rd. Those in search of a taste of Raj-era Darjeeling need look no farther than "Kev's," famous for its hearty English breakfasts (Rs25-60). Their rooftop deck also makes for a fantastic brunch spot. Open daily 7:30am-7pm.

Kunga Restaurant, Gandi Rd., above the Nehru-Laden La intersection. Excellent Tibetan fare at competitive prices, and quite popular with locals. *Thukpa* (veg. noodle soup) Rs30, *momos* (plate of ten) Rs27. Open daily 7:30am-8:30pm.

Nimto Snacks, at the intersection of Nehru and Laden La Rd., opposite the police booth. A tiny eatery carved out of the wall, with an intimate, relaxed atmosphere. The all-veg. snacks and sweets are clean, cheap, and tasty. Excellent Tibetan *momo* (4 pieces with hot soup Rs6). Open daily 9am-8pm.

Frank Ross Cafe, Nehru Rd., just up the hill from the Hasty Tasty. This recently opened eatery is a good lunch stop, if only to see a menu offering tacos (Rs35) and enchiladas (Rs30). Standard Italian and American dishes are also served, as well as cinnamon mocha and "expresso" coffee (Rs14-18). Open daily 8am-9pm.

🔲 SIGHTS

TIGER HILL. Darjeeling's most popular sight is **Kanchenjunga**, the world's third-highest mountain. On the border between Nepal and Sikkim, some 70km from Darjeeling, its 8586m cone can be seen on a clear day. For Kanchenjunga views, nothing beats the sunrise on **Tiger Hill,** which has become something of a pilgrimage site for Indian tourists. An observation tower on top of the 2590m rise offers views stretching from the flood plains of the Ganga delta to the snowcaps of the Himalayas, each peak lighting up in turn as the sunlight inches west. Everest and its neighbors are occasionally visible. Beginning in June, however, such views become elusive, and you may end up taking pictures of fellow backpackers among the clouds. Most hotels and agencies organize morning excursions, but it's just as easy to catch a jeep from among the hordes idling at the Nehru-Laden La intersection. *(11km out of Darjeeling. Jeeps leave 4-5am. Rs50.)*

OBSERVATORY HILL. A fine spot from which to take in Darjeeling's unavoidably magnificent views, Observatory Hill is more importantly a sacred site for both Hindus and Buddhists. It is also closely tied to the origin of Darjeeling's name, as it is believed to be the resting place of Indra's scepter, or *dorje*. Protected by a grove of stately pines, woven together by thousands of prayer flags, and tirelessly guarded by an army of fearless monkeys (they'd make Hanuman proud), the hill is a world apart from commercial Chowstra only minutes below. Don't miss the cave below and to the left, complete with carvings of Vishnu, Ganesh, and company. *(Stairs to Observatory Hill begin 50m north of Chowrasta on Mall Rd. East.)*

ZOOLOGICAL PARK. Darjeeling has more to offer than just mountains. At the north end of the ridge is a complex containing the Padmaja Naidu Himalayan Zoological Park, the Snow Leopard Breeding Center, and the Himalayan Mountaineering Institute (see below). Though pitifully small, this park gives its animals much leafier spaces than most Indian zoos and has species rarely seen elsewhere, including Siberian tigers and Red pandas. Animal lovers may be upset by the conditions. Farther down the ridge, is the **Snow Leopard Breeding Center,** where an ambitious program that began with two cats is attempting to produce a sustainable population. *(20min. walk from Chowrasta on Mall Rd. West, which becomes Birch Hill Rd. Both open F-W 8am-4pm. Zoo entrance Rs5, camera fee Rs5. Breeding Center entrance Rs10.)*

HIMALAYAN MOUNTAINEERING INSTITUTE (HMI). Above the zoo's Siberian tigers is the cenotaph of **Tenzing Norgay,** a Sherpa from Darjeeling who co-conquered Everest with Sir Edmund Hillary in 1953. Tenzing was the long-time director of the HMI, and his ashes now rest here. HMI organizes climbing courses for Indians only; its main function is to instruct Indian Army soldiers. Darjeeling has had a long connection with mountaineering: when Nepal was a closed country, the earliest Everest trips took off from here. HMI's **Everest Museum** is full of relics. The displays in the affiliated **Mountaineering Museum** range from butterflies to ice picks to relief models of the Himalayas. Around the corner, a telescope is set up to catch views of Kanchenjunga; it was given to one of Nepal's Rana prime ministers by Adolf Hitler. *(Museums open F-W 8am-4:30pm. Rs4.)*

RANGEET VALLEY PASSENGER ROPEWAY. Clockwise around the ridge from the HMI is the starting point for the Rangeet Valley Passenger Ropeway. The cable car no longer makes the full trip to Singla Bazaar in the north, but it does go for a scenic half-hour dip over the tea shrubs. They won't operate the cars until full (10-20 people), so service can be erratic. *(Cars run daily 9:30am-5:30pm. Round-trip Rs50.)*

HAPPY VALLEY TEA ESTATE. This is the best place to see a tea plantation, where pickers work through the shrubs on the hills around you and the "factory" is open to visitors. Except during the off-season (late Jun.-Aug.), a worker will guide you through the tea leaf's four-day metamorphosis from flora to flavoring; don't forget to give a small tip. *(Hill Cart Rd., 2km past the District Magistrate's Office, down a rocky road that diverges to the left. Open Tu-Sa 8am-noon and 1-4:30pm, Su 8am-noon. Free.)*

GYMKHANA CLUB. This dilapidated Raj-era recreational facility, just north of Observatory Hill, gives a glimpse of British Darjeeling, plus 50 years and a few cobwebs. And, for a small price, they also allow you to use the arcane facilities. From old standbys like billiards and snooker, to more active games including squash and tennis, to the downright odd like roller-skating, it's all available for the price of a day membership and equipment rental. Don't miss the library, chock-full of dusty literature and tales of imperial conquest. *(On Mall Rd. West, 300m north of Chowrasta. Open daily 8am-8pm. Day membership Rs50. Week membership Rs250. Equipment for activities Rs5-7 per game.)*

GHOOM MONASTERY. Founded in 1850, Yiga Choling Ghoom is the region's most famous monastery. The Ghoom Monastery's large shrine contains a 5m golden statue of the Maitreya Buddha (the future Buddha). The murals inside have been recently refurbished and appear beautifully reborn. Don't confuse this with the new and not terribly interesting Samten Choling Ghoom Monastery below the road to Ghoom. *(In Ghoom, 8km from Darjeeling. Buses and jeeps run here throughout the day for Rs5-10. In Ghoom, turn right onto the road opposite the "Ghoom Boys' H.S. School" gate and follow the road for about 1km to the monastery.)*

ARE YOU A TEA SNOB?

Knowing and distinguishing the different varieties of tea can set your average tea-drinker apart from the connoisseur. In Darjeeling, the manufacture and consumption of tea has become an art, available to both the masses as well as an elite group of tea fans.

The Basics: The two types of black tea grown in India and Nepal are known as **orthodox tea** (or leaf tea), from the Darjeeling's temperate slopes, and **Cut-Tear-Curl (CTC) tea**, which is grown in the lowlands around Siliguri. The strongly flavored and inexpensive **lowland tea** is used in *chiya*, the omnipresent milk tea. The high altitudes ensure slower growth, which limits production but enhances the quality—**highland teas** are hailed as top notch for their lighter orange-colored liquors and delicious aroma.

Manufacture: Green leaves are **withered** for 16 hours to extract moisture. Next, the dried leaves are **rolled** for 45 minutes on a large rolling machine. **Fermentation** follows for a couple of hours as the rolled leaves are laid out on aluminum trays or ceramic tiles. Then the leaves are **dried** at 220°F in a large oven for over 20 minutes. Finally, they are sorted according to grade, and the stalks are removed.

Tea terms: Unscrambling the acronyms of once-British tea industries can be confusing. Strictly speaking, there are four grades of black tea. The first is denoted as **FTG-FOP**, for "Fine Tippy Golden Flowery Orange Pekoe." The second is **TGBOP**, for "Tippy Golden Broken Orange Pekoe." The third and fourth are dust-like teas used in tea bags for speedier brewing: **GOF** for "Golden Orange Fannings" and **PD** for "Pekoe Dust."

OTHER SIGHTS. Below the Gymkhana Club is the **Bengal Natural History Museum,** which has an extensive collection of stuffed creatures, particularly birds. *(Open F-W 10am-4pm. Rs2.)* Below the bus stand are the expansive and well-maintained **Lloyd Botanical Gardens,** which specialize in alpine foliage. *(Open daily 9am-4pm. Free.)*

NIGHTLIFE

Darjeeling is essentially dead after 8pm. One exception is **Joey's Pub,** an oasis of familiarity for bar-starved Westerners. Joey, a Darjeelingite who spent two years in London in the 70s, has succeeded in recreating the British pub scene—Indian style. Relax with a cold pint of your favorite...OK, they only have Indian beers, but the music (classic American and British rock) and ambience (bar stools and Guinness posters) are a great cure for homesickness, and there are rumors that Guinness may in fact soon arrive. They even serve traditional pub fare, including fish and chips for Rs30. (Open daily 10am-11pm.)

SHOPPING

Darjeeling's main product is its excellent **tea,** available in shops and stalls all over town. For the best (but most expensive) stuff, head to Nehru Rd., which is lined with tea shops. Cheaper tea, along with everything else imaginable, is available at the **Chowk Bazaar,** the market surrounding and engulfing the main bus station. **Hayden Hall,** Laden La Rd. (☎53228), opposite the State Bank of India, is a women's cooperative that sells locally made handmade blankets, rugs, bags, and sweaters. Proceeds go to needy women in Darjeeling. (Open M-Sa 9am-5pm.) A larger collection of handmade goods is available at the **Tibetan Refugee Self-Help Centre,** beyond and below Observatory Hill. From Chowrasta, take CR Das Rd. (which departs near the police booth and runs below Mall Rd. East) north and west around the ridge. Follow the right fork and descend to the right until you reach the center. Established by Tibetans who fled here in 1959, the workshop produces carpets, sweaters, woodcarvings, and other crafts. (Open M-Sa 9am-4pm.)

TREKKING AROUND DARJEELING

Trekking is the best way to get around the Darjeeling and Western Sikkim regions from October to early December and from March to early June. Treks consist of six- or seven-hour long hikes between villages, where small hotels (usually Rs35-50) and food are available. On the trail itself, provisions are unavailable and should be packed along with a sleeping bag, warm clothes, and rain gear. Trekkers must also bring their **passports,** which are required at Manebhanjang and sometimes at Sukia Pokhri. The routes are often old jeep roads that are bypassed in several sections by trails. For the most recent information, consult **West Bengal Tourism** (see p. 662) and tourist logs at the Belleview, Tower View, and Aliment hotels.

The most common starting point for treks is **Manebhanjang,** a stop on the road from Darjeeling to Rimbik. **Buses** going to Rimbik (7am, 12:30, and 2pm; 5hr.; Rs55) can drop you off (1½hr., Rs20). A popular two-day excursion starts at Manebhanjang and climbs steeply up to **Tonglu** (9km, altitude 900m), where lodging is available and the mountain views are spectacular, and then returns to Manebhanjang the following day. This trek can be extended, however, into a loop that goes on from Tonglu to **Gairibas** (9km, -400m), and from there to **Bikhebhanjang** (6km, 400m) before climbing up to **Sandakphu** (6km, 600m). From Sandakphu, this trail heads to **Phalot** (23km, 0m) and from there to **Gorkhey** (15km, -600m), then to **Ramram** (9km, -400m), to the **Siri Khola River** (10km, -500m), and then ends in **Rimbile** (9km, 400m), where buses head back to Darjeeling (6am and noon, 5hr., Rs55). Another popular option is to head from Rimbik to Gorkhey, Phalut, Sandakphu, and back to Rimbik—each leg takes a day. The direct trail from Sandakphu to Rimbik has many bifurcations, and it's easy to get lost; it's better to go from Sandakphu to Rimbik via Gurdum and Siri Khola, which has a nice trekkers' hut. Numerous modifications are possible on these routes, and a helpful guide is West Bengal Tourism's free "Himalayan Treks" pamphlet.

KALIMPONG কালিমপং কালিম্প ☎ 03552

Largely neglected by tourists, Kalimpong (1250m) is the black sheep of the Indian Himalayan family. However, this small but lively center of the Gorkha independence movement has grown in recent years, in population as well as popularity among travelers. For many, the breathtaking ride from Darjeeling to Kalimpong makes this often-overlooked town worth the trip. The road drops steeply off Darjeeling's ridge into the lush, tropical Teesta River Valley below, before twisting and turning its way up the opposite side to Kalimpong. And while the town itself lacks some of Darjeeling's majesty and charm, the surrounding countryside certainly does not. Panoramic vistas, intricately decorated monasteries, and extensive orchid nurseries are all within walking distance, and all are relatively untouched by the hordes of tourists swarming to other towns in the region.

▐ GETTING THERE AND GETTING AROUND

Trains: The closest station is NJP in Siliguri, but there is a **booking office** (☎55643) in Kalimpong, 100m from Main Rd.'s north intersection. Head up the diagonal road to the right; the office is in a yellow building on the right. Quota seats are available on major trains, but reservations must be made a few days in advance. Open M-Sa 10am-1pm and 4-5pm, Su 10am-1pm.

Buses and Jeeps: Buses and jeeps depart from Market Sq., with booking offices along the perimeter. **Buses** to: **Darjeeling** (noon and 12:30pm, 3hr., Rs42); **Gangtok** (7:30 and 8am, 3hr., Rs42); **Siliguri** (every 30min., 6am-5pm, 2hr., Rs40). **SNT** runs two daily buses to **Gangtok** (8:30am and 1pm, 3½hr., Rs55). Reserve in advance. Open daily 7:30am-1pm. **Jeeps** run throughout the day (7am-5pm) to: **Darjeeling** (2½hr.; front Rs70, back Rs65); **Gangtok** (2½hr.; front Rs65, back Rs60); **Siliguri** (1½hr.; front Rs45, back Rs40).

✦▐ ORIENTATION AND PRACTICAL INFORMATION

The **bus stand** consumes most of **Market Sq.** in the center of town. On the east of Market Square is Hotel Cosy Nook; on the west is a corrugated-roofed building. **Sikkim Nation Transport (SNT)** is just to the left of this building, and the Himilashree Lodge is to the right. Just south of Market Square is the old **football field**, also known as the **Mela Grounds**. **Ongen Rd.** crosses the square at the west end. Parallel to Ongen Rd. is **Main Rd.**, the town's major thoroughfare and primary axis. Main Rd. is capped at both ends by traffic intersections—at the north intersection is **Gompu's Restaurant,** and at the south intersection is the police station. Main Rd. continues past those intersections where it's known as **Rishi Rd.**

Tourist Information: The **DGHC Tourist Office,** 30m north of Main Rd.'s north intersection, has free pamphlets and maps of Kalimpong. Open daily 8am-6pm.

Budget Travel: Shangri-La Services, Rishi Rd. (☎55109), 50m north of Main Rd.'s north intersection, is an authorized agent for Jet Airways, Blue Dart Express, and Sita World Travels. Open daily 8am-6pm. **Mintri Transport,** Main Rd. (☎55741), books airline tickets and runs daily buses to Bagdogra Airport (7:15am, Rs120) and NJP Station (1-4 per day, Rs55). Open M-Sa 8am-7pm, Su 8am-5pm.

Immigration Office: Because Kalimpong is so close to the Chinese border, foreigners are technically required to register at the **Foreigners Registration Office** (☎55312), opposite the post office. Not to worry though—all hotels in Kalimpong automatically take care of this for you. In fact, there's no reason to go to the office itself, as they can't issue either visa extensions or Sikkim permits. Open daily 9:30am-6pm.

Currency Exchange: None of Kalimpong's banks changes currency. **Shangri-La Services** (see **Budget Travel,** above) will change US$, UK£, and francs at pretty reasonable rates.

Bookstore: Kashi Nath and Sons, opposite the tourist office, has a good selection of everything from Hardy to the Hardy Boys. Open daily 7:30am-7:30pm.

Police: (☎55268). On the corner at the south intersection of Main Rd.

Pharmacy: Shree Tibet Stores, Main Rd. (☎55459), opposite Snow White Fashion near Gompu's Restaurant. Open daily 8:30am-8:30pm. Doctor available 9:30am-6pm. If it's an after-hours emergency, knock loudly on the door.

Hospital: Sadar Hospital (☎55245), northeast of town. Take your first left north of Main Rd.'s north intersection, then a right at the fork in the road.

Internet: Odyssey Internet Cafe, Main Rd. (☎57977), on the 1st fl. of the supermarket at Main Rd.'s south intersection. Four terminals (Rs2 per min.). Free tea. Open F-W 9am-7pm. **Delta Communications,** Main Rd. (☎55911), 20m west of Main Rd.'s south intersection. Rs2 per min. Open M-Sa 8:30am-7pm.

Telephones: Most **STD/ISD** booths are open 6am-11pm.

Post Office: GPO, Main Rd. (☎55990), at the end of the football field. Open M-F 10am-4pm. **Postal Code:** 734301.

ACCOMMODATIONS

Shangri-La Guest House, Tripai Rd. This aptly named hotel is worth the 45min. walk from town along the road to Dr. Graham's School. Beautiful, secluded, and friendly, with kitchen facilities, private baths in each room, and a surrounding garden that provides the meals. Check with Shangri-La Services (see **Budget Travel,** above), in town about availability and directions before making the long trip. Singles Rs200; doubles Rs250. Extra people Rs50 each.

Deki Lodge, Tripai Rd. (☎55095). From Main Rd.'s north intersection head north on Rishi Rd. for about 600m; Tripai Rd. branches left, and Deki is visible from here. Peaceful location, perpetually smiling staff, and relaxed backpacker atmosphere set Deki apart. Spacious rooms and hot showers. Set off for treks armed with the owner's extensive local knowledge. Singles Rs100-130; doubles with bath Rs180-600; triples with bath Rs350-450; quad Rs380. Off-season (Jul.-Sept.): 10% discount.

Himalshree Lodge, Market Sq. (☎55070), just to the right of the corrugated-roofed building and overlooking the bus stop. It's worth the walk up several flights of stairs. Six comfy rooms are often full, but no reservations are taken. The noise outside starts early. Meals available on advance order. Hot water buckets Rs6. Doors lock at 9pm. "Dorm beds" (actually two beds in the lobby) Rs60; doubles Rs120; triple with bath Rs200.

Gompu's Hotel (☎55818), 10m west of Main Rd.'s north intersection. Clean, green rooms, mountain views, and a quality restaurant downstairs. All rooms have attached baths. Singles Rs150; doubles Rs300. Off-season: Rs150/200.

Cosy Nook, Market Sq. (☎55541), on the east side of the bus stop. The *betel*-chewing owner offers advice on seeing the sights. Rooms are small and basic, but all have attached bath (bucket hot water Rs4). Singles Rs150; doubles Rs200; triples Rs300.

ONE MO MONASTERY Kalimpong's Tharpa Choling Monastery, of the Geluk-pa (Yellow Hat) sect, exhibits a particularly strong blend of Chinese and Tibetan influences. Most striking, perhaps, is the practice of Mo, a form of fortune-telling closely related to the I-Ching. Visitors are welcome to watch and join in. The first step is the casting of the Sho, a large seed split into two parts. While kneeling and thinking of a particular question or problem, the supplicant casts the seed onto the ground. If both sides land face up or face down, they aren't ready to continue. Only if one side is face up and the other face down may they proceed. They're allowed three tries at this. Next, they are given the Tonje, a large bamboo cup filled with a hundred numbered bamboo sticks. The Tonje must then be shaken back and forth until one of the hundred sticks pops out. The number of this stick is then taken to the enormous Chinese (and corresponding Nepali) text, where the often enigmatic fortune is read. Like the I-Ching, these fortunes are heavy on symbol and light on specifics. So if you can't decide what to do with your life, or maybe just where to go to dinner, check with Mo. Mo knows fortunes.

⚡ FOOD

Kalimpong has a scant selection of good restaurants, but some Chinese eateries have popped up around Market Square. Main Rd. is lined with veggie snack stalls.

▨ **Kelsang Restaurant,** by the football stadium, 20m from the bus stop. Follow the path toward the field, then go down some steps into a kind, Tibetan family's home. Cheap, delicious, and authentic Tibetan food. *Momos* Rs10; beef chow mein Rs25; *thukpa* Rs15. Open daily 7am-7:30pm.

▨ **Glenary's,** Main Rd. and Rishi Rd. The master baker rears his doughy head at two locations in Kalimpong: one on Main Rd., 30m south of the intersection, the other on Rishi Rd., 100m north of the north intersection. Same great pastries as Darjeeling—swiss rolls Rs8; macaroons Rs8; donuts Rs10. Both open daily 8am-7pm.

Kalash Vegetarian Snacketeria, Main Rd., opposite the State Bank of India. The best menu of veg. snacks in town. Specializes in North and South Indian as well as continental favorites. Great *dosas* Rs15-30; curries Rs20-40. Open daily 8:30am-8pm.

Gompu's Restaurant, Main Rd. (☎55818), west of Market Sq. Centrally located and hopping with fast service. Chinese (Rs25-40) and chicken (Rs50-60) dishes. Order ahead for large, well-prepared *momos* (Rs30-60). Beer Rs55. Open daily 7am-8:30pm.

📷🎵 SIGHTS AND ENTERTAINMENT

Kalimpong has a bountiful bouquet of orchids, amaryllises, roses, gladioli, and dahlias, most impressive from March to June. Nurseries are scattered all around the outskirts of town. **Ganesh Mani Pradhan Nursery,** 4km north of town on Rishi Rd., specializes in orchids; calling ahead is recommended. (☎57217. *Open daily 9am-5pm.*) Also on the premises are beautiful but expensive guest cottages (*doubles Rs1500*). The **Tharpa Choling Monastery,** a Geluk (Yellow Hat) monastery, was founded in 1892 and is still in the process of renovation; visitors are likely to see wood carvers and other artisans at work. The monastery retains obvious evidence of its Chinese influences, particularly in the first temple on the left as you enter the compound, with Chinese script adorning the entry pillars, a distinctly Chinese central statue (Ling Cesar), and all the tools and texts necessary for Mo divination (See **"One Mo Monastery,"** p. 673). While renovations in the main temple may never be completed, the sections of the temple not under construction are still worth the walk. (*A 20min. walk uphill east of town beyond the Deki Lodge, off Tripai Rd.*) Farther along the same road, you will find the complex of **Dr. Graham's Home,** which was built in 1900 when a Scottish minister set up a home for six orphaned students. The school eventually acquired the whole hilltop and became largely self-sufficient. Almost entirely funded by alumni donations, it now has over 1200 students from as far away as Calcutta and is the model for many schools for orphaned and handicapped children. (*20min. beyond the Tharpa Chaling Monastery on the same road.*) If you continue even farther on this road, it eventually leads to the top of **Deolo Hill,** the highest point in the area. The views are without equal—from the top you can see Kanchenjunga, Darjeeling, Sikkim, Kalimpong, the confluence of the Teesta and Rangit rivers, and east to the border of Bhutan. The DGHC has built a number of free (and garishly painted) gazebos perfect for a picnic lunch. A 200-meter footpath leads to a more secluded and less mowed side of the hill.

At the bottom of Deolo Hill is the brilliant yellow **Bhutanese Monastery,** or Thongsa Gompa. Established in 1630, the monastery is Kalimpong's oldest. Home primarily to Bhutanese students and monks, it also draws local Tibetan and Nepali worshippers, particularly on Sundays. The monastery is in constant need of volunteers; at its age things often need repair (see **Volunteer Opportunities,** below).

The **Kanchan Cinema Hall** often shows somewhat stale Hollywood films to go along with the standard Hindi attractions. (*On Rishi Rd. 300m north of Main Rd.'s north intersection. Showings 11am, 2, and 5pm. Rs6-12.*) The **Snooker and Pool Hall** is a local hang-out, but as there's only one table you may wait a while for your turn. (*On Rishi Rd. 50m north of Main Rd.'s north intersection, next to Shangri-La Services. Open daily 8am-9pm. Pool Rs10 per frame, snooker Rs20 per frame.*)

RABINDRANATH TAGORE

The Bengali poet Rabindranath Tagore (1861-1941) towers over modern Indian literature and Bengali life. The youngest son in the large family of the prominent *zamindar* and Brahmo Samaj leader Debendranath Tagore, Rabindranath dropped out of school at an early age, and taught himself English and Sanskrit. He began writing poetry as a boy, and before long broke new ground, introducing English forms previously unknown in Bengali. He traveled around Bengal looking after his family's estates; many of his poems and stories concern the lives of villagers in Bengal, and his songs draw from the melodies of Bengali folk music. Tagore translated many of his verses into rhythmic English prose, catching the attention of Western readers. In 1913 he received the Nobel Prize for *Gitanjali* (Song Offerings), a collection of poems expressing his longing to become one with God. Tagore was knighted by the British in 1915, but renounced his title after the 1919 Jallianwallah Bagh massacre in Amritsar. In his later years Tagore experimented with novels, plays, and elaborate songs; toward the end of his life he took up painting as well. Gandhi and other political leaders considered Tagore an inspiration, and frequently visited him at Shantiniketan, the school he founded in 1901. Verses by Tagore now constitute the national anthems of both India and Bangladesh. His plays are widely produced, and his songs have become a genre of their own. The filmmaker Satyajit Ray has produced interpretations of several of Tagore's novels.

VOLUNTEER OPPORTUNITIES

The **Bhutanese Monastery** (see above) is often in need of volunteers for everything from manual labor to medical care to teaching English and gratefully accepts any help. Contact **Lama Kunzang** at the monastery or, in the likely event he's not around, with **Tsheltrum,** the resident Bhutanese painter who speaks English.

WEST BENGAL

SIKKIM सिक्किम

Shambala, Tazik, Shangri-La; whatever you want to call it, most people agree that Sikkim is heaven. The natural beauty is without compare—the tropical valleys, sheltered and watered by the surrounding peaks, support rice, mustard, papaya, wheat, and millet farming, while the sheer, vertical ridges stacked one against the other all the way to the horizon are home to small villages, monasteries, and some of the most ambitious farming terraces in India. Bordered by Nepal, Tibet, and Bhutan, the state's cultural bounty is similarly appealing; the native Lepchas peacefully coexist with Tibetan Bonpos and Bhutanese businessmen. Sikkim is so peaceful, in fact, that it once appeared in the *Guiness Book of World Records* for going 10 years without a single criminal case. Perhaps the most charming aspect of the state, however, is the privacy. Because foreigners are only allowed to visit for a limited period of time (see **Sikkim Permits**, p. 677), the state has so far been spared the crushing tourist influx of neighboring Nepal.

The Hindu Nepalese currently represent 75% of the population, although Sikkim, home to over 250 monasteries, is historically a Buddhist kingdom, closely linked to Tibet. The earliest known inhabitants of Sikkim were the Lepchas, who arrived sometime around the 13th century. They were joined in later years by a steady stream of new residents. In the 15th and 16th centuries, following conflicts between Buddhist sects in their own country, many Tibetans immigrated to North India, and the first *chogyal* (king) of Sikkim was appointed in the 17th century. Under the British protectorate, which began in 1861, Hindu Nepalese were brought to Sikkim to work on tea plantations, and they soon came to outnumber the Lepchas and Tibetans. The result of all this ethnic diversity is a remarkably friendly confluence of cultures. People from the flatlands to the south are "Indian," while those who grew up in the mountains identify themselves according to their ancestry: Nepalese, Bhutanese, Tibetan, or Lepcha.

When India became independent in 1947, Sikkim was made a semi-independent Indian protectorate. In 1975, 97% of the Sikkim's electorate voted to join India, and the territory became the country's 22nd state. Sikkim has managed to maintain a degree of regional distinctiveness since joining the Indian union. Though it has gradually begun to open its borders to tourists, the people of Sikkim take its new status as a tourist destination in stride; travelers can expect a refreshingly hassle-free and tranquil stay. The best times to visit are from late March to May, when the flowers are in bloom, and October to November, when clear views are guaranteed. **Visitors to Sikkim must first obtain permits** (see **Special Permits**, p. 10).

HIGHLIGHTS OF SIKKIM

Peaceful **Pelling** (p. 682) is a good place to relax and soak up the views, or to begin the scenic, four-day **Local Trek** (p. 685).

Headquarters of the *karma-pa* sect of Tibetan Buddhism, the beautiful hilltop village of **Rumtek** (p. 681) is a get away from it all and watch the vegetables grow.

GANGTOK गातोक ☏ 03592

Carved out of the hillside, Sikkim's capital is dwarfed both in altitude and scenic beauty by its spectacular surroundings. Still, Gangtok has its own appeal with friendly, helpful people, relatively clean streets, and easy travel connections to Sikkim's most picturesque spots. The mighty tourist infrastructure dominates the town's activity, and Gangtok is the state's best bet for store-bought goods and supplies, as well as practical services. This is the place to come to organize treks, extend Sikkim permits, stock up on equipment, and send off a batch of emails. Perhaps the most charming aspect of the city, though, is its intermittent power

Sikkim

TIBET (CHINA)

NEPAL

Kanchenjunga
(8586m)

Yumthang

Teesta River

Rangit River

Mangan

Phensang

Yuksam

Phodong

Khechopalri
Lake

Tashiding

Rumtek

Tsomgo
Lake

Pelling

Geyzing

Kewzing

Gangtok

Legship

Singtam

Namchi

Rangpo

BHUTAN

Jorethang

Melli

WEST BENGAL

Kalimpong

N

0   10 miles
0   10 kilometers

Govt. of India statement:
The external boundaries
of India are neither correct
nor authenticated.

SIKKIM PERMITS. The ins and outs of the Sikkim permit process can seem endlessly bureaucratic, but in fact, most of it is pretty simple. Most people only need the basic permit, called a **RAP (Restricted Area Permit).** These are good for **15 days,** and are available at Sikkim Tourist Offices in Calcutta, Delhi, Siliguri, and Darjeeling. Easiest, however, is to apply for it **along with your Indian visa,** as it's then stamped onto the visa and starts whenever you arrive in Sikkim. Regardless of where you obtain the permit, it's free and allows you travel to: Gangtok, Mangan, Geyzing, Namchi, Soreng, Ravangla, Pakyong, Rongli, Singhik, Yuksam, and Tashiding, as well as other towns inside this rough boundary. **Extensions** of this permit are available only from the tourist office in Gangtok. The maximum number of extensions (each 15 days) is two, allowing a total stay of 45 days. Unless you have a good reason, apply for an extension only a few days before the last has run out. Permits, as well as passports and visas, are checked at the Sikkim border. If, however, you're reading this for the first time on a Sikkim-bound bus and are permit-less, don't panic. The border post at Rangpo is authorized to issue a **two-day permit,** allowing absent-minded travelers to continue on to Gangtok and apply for an extension. Beyond a basic RAP, all permits *must* be handled through a tourist agency. Briefly, there are two sorts—a **PAP (Protected Area Permit)** and a **Trekking Permit.** Both are **only available in Gangtok** and also require a **minimum of four people.** The PAP covers destinations like Tsomgo Lake (one-day) and Yumthang (five-day). Finally, it's important to remember that *all* Sikkim permits are issued expressly for **tourism only,** so even if you're here for something else (religious pilgrimage, studying the flowers), it's best to just lump it all under "tourism."

supply—Gangtok blinks into and out of the modern era many times a day, and shops and hotels are all prepared with candles, flashlights, and occasionally, generators. The refusal to electrify completely is a pleasant reminder that technological progress has yet to tame Gangtok entirely.

⊏ GETTING THERE AND GETTING AROUND

Flights: The nearest airport is **Bagdogra,** near Siliguri. **Josse and Josse,** MG Rd. (☎24682), next to Raj Enterprise, are authorized agents for Jet Airways, Sahara, and Skyline NEPC. Open daily 9am-7pm. The proprietor of the **Green Hotel,** MG Rd. (☎24049; fax 23354), is a sub-agent for Indian Airlines and Jet Airways.

Trains: The **railway reservations window,** at the south end of the SNT Bus Terminal, has quota tickets on major trains leaving New Jalpaiguri. Open M-Sa 8am-2pm, Su 8-11am.

Buses: Sikkim Nation Transport **(SNT) Bus Terminal** (☎22016), down from the National Highway at the north end of town. Book tickets early at the far left window. Open daily 6:30am-3pm. The crowded, subsidized buses are the cheapest, although slowest, mode of transport. To: **Darjeeling** (7am, 5hr., Rs78); **Geyzing** (7am, 5hr., Rs45); **Jorethang** (7am and 2pm, 3hr., Rs60); **Kalimpong** (7:15am and 1pm, 3hr., Rs55); **Mangan** (8am and 3pm, 5hr., Rs45); **Namchi** (7:30am and 2pm, 5hr., Rs55); **Rumtek** (4pm, 1hr., Rs15); **Siliguri** (6 per day, 6am-12:15pm, 4hr., Rs70). **Private buses** gather along the highway around Naya Bazaar. **Shared jeeps,** available below Lal Bazaar just above the highway, run to all the same destinations as the SNT throughout the day, but are faster and costlier. To: **Darjeeling** (Rs120); **Kalimpong** (Rs65); and **Siliguri** (Rs130). Make sure you are sharing a jeep; solo rides cost over Rs1000.

Local Transportation: Taxis run up and down the National Highway and idle along the north end of MG Rd. Negotiate prices first; it shouldn't cost more than Rs30 for the length of the city.

✴ 🔁 ORIENTATION AND PRACTICAL INFORMATION

The **National Highway** cuts northeast, diagonally up the hill, with roads branching off horizontally above and below. The **SNT Bus Terminal** is 100m off the highway at the northern end of town. **Mahatma Gandhi (MG) Rd.,** which effectively serves as the center of town, branches south off the highway, 50m downhill from the intersection that leads to the SNT Bus Terminal. The large, impossible-to-miss **tourist center** sits at the intersection of MG Rd. and the highway. Farther south on MG Rd., **Lal Bazaar Rd.** branches off to the right, leading down to the bazaar itself and to a lot full of private buses and jeeps. Other private buses and jeeps depart from the lot on the National Highway just above Hungry Jack restaurant.

Tourist Office: National Tourist Centre (☎23425 or 22064), on the corner of MG Rd. and the highway. Useful maps of Gangtok and Sikkim. Open M-Sa 10am-4pm. Issues Sikkim permit extensions, trekking permits, and protected area permits (see **Sikkim Permits,** p. 677).

Tours: Tour companies provide comprehensive trek services, including permits, guides, and equipment. Tours cost around US$30 per day. One very popular and professional operation is **Modern Tours and Treks,** MG Rd. (☎27319), opposite the tourist office. Run by the proprietors of the Modern Central Hotel, the tours are mid-range in price and well equipped (and fed). Open daily 7:30am-9:30pm. **River rafting** in the Teesta river is becoming popular; tour agencies, including several along MG Rd., organize such trips. **Brothers Tours and Treks** (☎24220), 50m along the road that climbs up from MG Rd. opposite the tourist office, on the west side of the jeep lot, runs trips on the Teesta and Rangit from Sept.-May. Four person min. Daytrips Rs550 per person; Rs750 with food and transport. Two-day trips Rs1850, all equipment, food, and transport included.

Currency Exchange: State Bank of India, MG Rd. (☎26091), opposite the tourist office. Cashes AmEx traveler's checks on the 3rd floor. Open M-F 10am-2pm, Sa 10am-noon.

Police: (☎22033), 60m up the road that climbs up from MG Rd., opposite the tourist office, on the left side of the road. Helpful policewomen.

Pharmacy: Many along MG Rd. and Naya Bazaar. Locals like **Chiranjilal Lalchand Pharmacy,** MG Rd., opposite the Green Hotel. Open daily 8am-8pm.

Hospital: Sir Thutab Namgyal Memorial (STNM) Hospital, National Highway (☎22944), 50m north of the tourist office. Enter via the footbridge overpass.

Internet: Gokul Communications, Yama Building, MG Rd., 50m south of the tourist office. Web access Rs1.50 per min., Rs30 minimum. Open M-Sa 9am-7:30pm.

Telephones: Most **STD/ISD** are open until 11pm.

Post Office: (☎23085), halfway between the SNT Terminal and the National Highway. Open M-F 9:30am-5pm, Sa 9:30am-noon.

ACCOMMODATIONS

Many of Gangtok's hotels are new but tend to be oriented toward wealthier Indian tourists. The few budget places are usually crowded. Always ask for a discount—many managers take pity on well-behaved travelers. Consider staying near the **Rumtek Monastery** (see p. 681), 24km across the river valley. During peak season (Sept.-Dec. and Mar.-May), prices rise and hotels fill up fast.

Modern Central Hotel, Tibet Rd. (☎24670). Go up the road that climbs up from MG Rd. opposite the tourist office. At its end, turn left on Tibet Rd and walk 100m up. Very popular with backpackers, and for good reason. Sonam, the manager/owner, is a wellspring of information. The front rooms have very nice views of the valley, there's a TV room upstairs, and the restaurant serves tasty meals. Dorm beds Rs40; doubles with bath Rs120-200. Prices subject to bargaining, particularly off season.

Kewzing House, Upper Sichey Busty Rd. (☎23702). Follow the road to the SNT Bus Terminal farther north, and take the upper fork around the bend; it's the four-story yellow house with the prayer flags on top. Kewzing's four rooms are exquisite, with attached bath, hot water, TV, and gas lamps for power outages. More important, though, is the family atmosphere—guests are invited to eat with the family and then relax in the living room with a gigantic steaming mug of millet *chang*. Smaller rooms: singles Rs350; doubles Rs500. Larger rooms: singles Rs400; doubles Rs600.

Green Hotel, MG Rd. (☎24049 or 25057; fax 23354). Provides every amenity imaginable—STD, fax, Internet access, travel agency, money changer, restaurant, TV, and a generator for those rare power outages. Jam-packed with tourists. Singles Rs150-200; doubles Rs250-475; triples Rs450. Off-season discounts up to 50%. MC, Visa.

Hotel Mig-Tin, Tibet Rd. (☎24101), 200m south of the Modern Central. Still in the process of remodeling, the rooms that are available have immaculate attached baths with hot water. The upstairs rooms have terrific views. Attached restaurant (see below). Dorm beds Rs120; singles Rs350-400; doubles Rs550. Off-season Rs100/220/400.

Travel Lodge, Tibet Rd. (☎23858), 50m south of the Modern Central. Huge rooms have balconies and hot showers. Black and white TV in some rooms. Doubles Rs450; triples Rs600; quads Rs700. Off-season Rs250/400/500.

FOOD

Food can be expensive in Gangtok. Bulk foods for hiking are available along Naya Bazaar, which has the best selection in Sikkim. The best of the hotel restaurants is the **Modern Central Hotel,** with its five cozy booths and boisterous clientele.

Parivar Restaurant, MG Rd., in the basement of the Yama building, 100m south of the tourist office. This all-vegetarian restaurant is popular with locals, and it serves up all the standard favorites at very reasonable prices. *Paneer kofta* Rs28; *dosas* Rs18; veg. *momos* Rs20. Open daily 9am-8:30pm.

> **KEEPING SIKKIM GREEN** With the central government understandably preoccupied by pervasive poverty, disputed borders, and inter-ethnic conflict, it is little wonder that India's environmental health is often overlooked. Token clean-up efforts such as the "Keep India Green" postering campaign in India's urban centers have proven unsuccessful as the mounds of refuse keep growing. In Sikkim, however, environmental action is no joke. In 1999, the state's Chief Minister Pawan Kumar Chamling was honored by environmentalists as India's most green-friendly state head for instituting a complete ban on the use of plastic and polyethylene bags. In recognizing Chamling, the non-governmental organization Centre for Science and Environment expressed its hope that the rest of India might soon follow suit.

Hungry Jack Restaurant, National Highway, south of the lower taxi/private bus stand, beyond the gas pumps. Clean, spacious, westernized restaurant and bar. North Indian, Sandwiches Rs35-65; Sikkim-brewed Dansberg beer Rs40. Open daily 7:30am-9pm.

Crispy Cuisine, MG Rd., 10m south of the Tibet Rd. intersection, on the 1st fl. Overlooks a busy corner of MG Rd. and pumps out hour after hour of Western pop music. Veg. corn soup Rs20; veg. chow mein Rs25. Local dishes available on 8hr. advance order (rice with *sisno makhu* Rs150 per person). Open daily 8am-7pm.

Sagar, Durga, and **Laxmi Sweets,** MG Rd., across and a bit south from the Green Hotel. A popular trio of adjacent snack shops. Pastries Rs5-10 each. Open daily 6:30am-8pm.

Khampie Restaurant, Tibet Rd., in the Mig-Tin Hotel. Try Khampie for a little bit of everything: North Indian, Chinese (chicken chow mein Rs40), excellent Italian (lasagna Rs50), and even, for the brave, Mexican (tacos Rs45). Open daily 7am-8:30pm.

SIGHTS AND SHOPPING

Though not much of a destination in itself, Gangtok is surrounded by lakes, parks, and monasteries that make ideal daytrips. Many of the sights can be visited on foot or by cab, and many tour agencies also operate whirlwind tour-of-attractions daytrips (Rs400-600). Contact the Tourist Department (see p. 678) for more information. Also look for the artfully rendered and enormously helpful *Gangtok in a Nutshell*, a map guide available in some stationery stores around the city.

ENCHEY MONASTERY AND TSUGLA KHANG. The **Enchey Monastery** is on the landing spot of Lama Druptob Karpo, who is said to have flown over from Maenam Hill over 200 years ago. The building itself dates from 1909 and has beautiful views of Kanchenjunga, Gangtok, and the river valleys on either side of the ridge. *(A 30min. walk from downtown Gangtok; head uphill to Ridge Rd. and walk north past the White Hall. The road branching right after the Mintok Gang leads to the monastery.)* The mural-covered walls of the **Tsugla Khang,** or Royal Chapel, enclose huge collections of scriptures. Officially, the monastery and chapel are closed to tourists, but you may be able to charm your way in as long as you're not toting a camera. *(At the south end of Ridge Rd., overlooking Bhanu Path and the government offices of Tashiling.)*

FLOWERS. Only a few hundred meters north of the chapel is the appropriately named **Flower Show Venue** where Gangtok shows off its bounty of blooming buds. The highlight of the year comes in March during the orchid show, but other flowers, including a full spectrum of rhododendrons, are displayed from April to December. *(On Ridge Rd., just south of the White Hall.)*

MORE FLOWERS. A couple kilometers south and downhill from town sits a peaceful hilltop complex containing the enormous **Do Drul Chorten,** the **Sikkim Institute of Tibetology,** and an adjacent flower garden brimming with orchids and giant ferns. The Do Drul Chorten, surrounded by 108 prayer wheels, is one of the largest and most important stupas in Sikkim, and it occupies the very top of the hill. Down the hill is the Sikkim Institute of Tibetology, with an extensive library and museum open to the public. Founded by the Dalai Lama in 1957, it now houses roughly 30,000 volumes of Tibetan documents (mostly wooden boards called xylographs) and a large collection of ornate *thankas*, as well as some more gruesome ritual items—a number of *kanglings* (trumpets made from human thighbones), a *kapala* (ritual bowl made from a human skull), and a pair of *damarus* (two-sided drums also fashioned from the tops of human skulls). Directly below the institute is a small but well-kept flower garden, with a number of benches perfect for resting your feet after the walk from Gangtok. *(The entire complex sits just above the Deorali Bazaar, which is 2km south and downhill from Gangtok along the National Highway. Institute ☎ 22525. Open M-Sa 10am-4pm. Rs2. Chorten and Garden free.)*

GOVERNMENT INSTITUTE OF COTTAGE INDUSTRIES. The Government Institute of Cottage Industries serves as a "factory" for handicrafts and furniture and a display center where colorful crafts are sold *(20min. north of the tourist center on the National Highway, on the left. Open M-Sa 10am-5pm.)* The best local market for everything from prayer flags to potatoes is Lal Market, which reaches its commercial peak every Sunday. *(Below MG Rd., beyond the taxi lot.)*

NEAR GANGTOK: RUMTEK रुम्तेक

Rumtek is a quiet, lovely hillside village only 24km away, on the opposite side of the valley from Gangtok. The SNT **bus** (4pm, 1hr., Rs15) is the cheapest option, followed by a **shared jeep** (morning departures, 45min., Rs30), and finally by a **taxi** (round-trip Rs300, including one-hour wait).

The centerpiece of the town is the **Rumtek Monastery,** the headquarters of the Karma-pa (Black Hat) sect of the Kagyu-pa order of Tibetan Buddhism. Built in the 1960s, the monastery is modeled on the main Kargyu-pa monastery in Chhofuk, Tibet. In a back room is an impressive collection of golden statues of the 16th Gwalpa who fled Tibet when China invaded. Turn on the charm, and a monk might let you have a peek. The building directly behind the main monastery houses the much-venerated **Golden Stupa,** protected by a glass window in front and surrounded on the other sides by elaborate *thankas*. Step outside and you can get a cup of tea (Rs3) and challenge the monks to a game on the carrom board.

A 30-minute walk downhill is the impressive **Old Monastery,** visible from behind the Kunga Delek; ask a young monk to show you the path. The not-to-be-missed sight here is the collection of sometimes uplifting, sometimes horrifying (think disembowelment) wall paintings. Two days before Losar, the Tibetan New Year in February, and on the 10th day of the 5th month of the Tibetan calendar in July.

Accommodations around Rumtek are cheaper, more peaceful, and less crowded than those in Gangtok, but are less convenient for those with business in the capital. The best value in town is the almost-impossible-to-find **Hotel 93,** tucked away (without any sign) behind the Kunga Delek, just south of the courtyard in front of the monastery. If you survive the tornado of fur and teeth that is their dog, you're in for a treat. Pristine attached baths, hardwood floors, hot water showers, and majestic views grace every room. (☎ 52250. Doubles Rs100.) Another good option is the **Sun-gay Guest House,** just above the guarded checkpoint. Beautiful, spacious rooms with attached bath are a great value, and the spacious balcony overlooking the vegetable garden is ideal for sitting. (☎ 52221. Doubles Rs100-150.) The **Sangay Hotel,** just up the hill beyond the checkpoint for the monastery, is run by a friendly family that serves good, cheap food. (☎ 52238. Singles Rs60; doubles Rs120.)

NEAR GANGTOK: TSOMGO LAKE

Cradled at the top of some of Eastern Sikkim's highest peaks, **Tsomgo Lake** (3700m), also known by its aliases Tsonga Lake or Changu Lake, feels like the top of the world. Just a two-hour jeep ride east (and straight up, at times) from Gangtok, this sacred site is jaw-droppingly beautiful. The lake is frozen from December to January, ringed with snow until late March, and surrounded by wildflowers in the warmer seasons. The jeep tour is well worth the price. (Round-trip US$12; 4 person min. Book with any local travel agent.) For the energetic, a short but steep hike up to the ridge overlooking the lake (4000m, 1hr. up, 20min. down) gives a spectacular, 360° panorama which includes (in clockwise order) the lake, the Kanchenjunga range, the mountains of Tibet and Bhutan. Tsomgo lake may be above the treeline, but it's not above the snack-bar line (*momos* Rs10 at any of the cafeterias). A special permit is required for Tsomgo (see **Sikkim Permits,** p. 677), but your tour company should take care of it.

WESTERN SIKKIM

This once tightly restricted area has opened up considerably over the past few years. Nowadays, most general Sikkim permits are stamped with extensions for Western attractions like Yuksam, Pemayangtse, and Khechopalri Lake. To secure a permit to trek in Northern Sikkim or north of Yuksam, you will need to get paperwork processed in Gangtok (see **Sikkim Permits,** p. 677). The easiest way to enter Western Sikkim is to take a jeep or bus from Gangtok or Darjeeling. Transportation to the region will usually stop in Geyzing or Pelling, ideal transit points for treks or rides to the rest of Western Sikkim. Most towns are five or six hours apart on foot, and only slightly less if you travel over the winding roads by bus or jeep.

GEYZING गेज़िन्ग AND PELLING पेल्लिन्ग ☎03595

Geyzing is a necessary transportation stop for many travelers. As the district headquarters of Western Sikkim, it is the departure point and destination for many of the local buses and jeeps. An hour's walk up the hill, on the opposite side of the ridge, is Pelling, the real gem of Western Sikkim. The starting point for paths to Yuksam, Tashiding, and Khechopalri Lake, the town caters to foreign trekkers; its accommodations are excellent sources for hiking information. Pelling is also surrounded by a number of attractions all within a day's hike, including monasteries, waterfalls, archaeological ruins, Lepcha villages, and jungle treks. Both towns have plenty of friendly hotels, up-close and personal views of Kanchenjunga, and lots of sunny terrace space. No wonder so many travelers have a hard time leaving.

■ ⊠ **ORIENTATION AND PRACTICAL INFORMATION.** Geyzing's **SNT Bus Terminal** is down the main road from the central square at the bend in the road. Buses run to: **Gangtok** (7:30am, 5hr., Rs70); **Jorethang** (4 per day, 7am-2pm, 2½hr., Rs28); **Pelling** (3 per day, 2-3:30pm, 30min., Rs10); **Siliguri** (7:30am, 5hr., Rs78). **Jeeps** leave from the lot just uphill from the SNT Terminal; the ticket offices are above the lot. They depart intermittently throughout the day for: **Kechopalri Lake** (1½hr., Rs4); **Pelling** (20min., Rs16); **Tashiding** (2hr., Rs35); **Yuksam** (3hr., Rs55). The **Tourist Office** in Pelling, just up the street from the Hotel Garuda, has free booklets about the area and the most current transportation information (open daily 6:30am-9pm). **Currency exchange** is not available. For medical attention, contact the private **Chapagais Medical Hall** (☎50317). The **police** (☎50833) in Geyzing are 25m up the hill to the left of the post office. **STD/ISD** services are available in the booth next to the No Name Hotel in the Geyzing central square (open 6am-9pm) and at **Hotel Window Park,** next to Hotel Garuda in Pelling. The Geyzing **post office** is up the main street from the central square, next to the Kanchenzonga Hotel; in Pelling, it is on the side of the Sikkim Tourist Centre building (both open M-F 9am-4pm, Sa 9am-2pm). **Postal Code:** Geyzing 737111, Pelling 737113.

⌐⌐ **ACCOMMODATIONS AND FOOD.** Accommodations in Geyzing are limited. Unless you're catching an early bus or jeep, there's no reason to stay the night. Most hotels are in the central square area. The best bet is **Hotel No Name,** on the end of the square closest to the SNT bus station. The attached restaurant (also nameless) serves decent food (curry chicken Rs35). Rooms are large and clean, but hot water comes only in buckets. (☎50722. Doubles Rs80.) Another option is the **Kanchenzonga Hotel,** 20m up the main road from the central square. The big, high-ceilinged rooms all have common bath. (☎50789. Doubles Rs120.)

A BON-AFIDE RELIGION
Among its many wonders, Sikkim is home to Bon, one of the oldest and least understood religions in Asia, which predates Buddhism by hundreds if not thousands of years. Followers of Bon (known as Bonpo) adhere to the teachings of their own enlightened one, **Tonpa Shenrab.** Bon was the original religion of Tibet, but the arrival of Buddhism in the 8th century did not bode well, and Bonpos were forced to convert or be driven from the country. Time, however, has mended the wound, and today the two religions are so remarkably similar that Bon is often considered the "5th Sect" of Mahayana Buddhism. Many of the rituals are similar to, if not the same as, their Buddhist counterparts; both sides claim that they invented them. But there is one obvious difference in the direction of ritual motion: Bonpos do everything counter-clockwise, opposite the Buddhists.

Over the years, the number of Bonpos has dwindled, and the number of contemporary adherents outside of Tibet is very small. Sikkim, though, harbors a sizeable population, and it is in fact home to one of the three Bon monasteries in India. The **Kundrung Kundrakling Bon Monastery,** just outside of the town of Kewsing, houses a small community of monks and struggles to preserve a vanishing tradition. While the monastery is small and its facilities modest, the monks are very welcoming and cater to show visitors around. They'll even let you sit in on their morning and evening rituals (daily 6am and 6pm), which last about half an hour. At the monastery, ask for **Kalsang Nyima,** the resident painter, who speaks English.

Kewzing sits on the front road between Gangtok and Legship. From Gangtok, any Kewzing-, Legship-, Geyzing-, Pelling-, or Jorethang-bound bus or jeep will pass right by the monastery, about 5km before town. While in Gangtok, you can often meet with the monastery's head Lama, **Yungdrung Lama,** at his own photo-developing store on MG Rd. opposite the tourist office.

Pelling, on the other hand, is full of new accommodations, but the tourism boom has inflated prices considerably. The backpacker's choice award goes to **Hotel Garuda,** at the first sharp bend in the main road, below the tourist office. They hand out copies of a very helpful area map, and have a detailed logbook of trekking information as well as a well-stocked book exchange. An attached restaurant serves Sikkimese, Chinese, and continental food (dishes Rs20-40). You can leave your gear here, and grab a packed lunch before while you go traipsing about the hills. (☎50614. Dorm beds Rs80; singles Rs120-250; double with bath Rs480. Off-season: Rs40/70-120/200.) If they're full, the owner will direct you to the nearby and nearly identical **Sister Guest House.** (☎50569. Common bath. Prices same as at Garuda.) **Hotel Kabur,** just uphill from the tourist office, has a similar setup, with great views, attached baths in every room, and decent meals. (☎50685. Singles Rs200; doubles Rs550. Off-season: 100/300.) If these prices seem a little steep, try the **Ladakh Guest House,** 20m down the road from the tourist office, near the football field. Rooms are basic but clean; common baths are outside. (Dorm beds Rs40; doubles Rs100.) For a change from hotel menus, try the **Alpine Restaurant,** on the road behind and below the Hotel Garuda has an intimate ambiance and outstanding food. (Chow mein Rs20; beer Rs35. Open daily 6:30am-9pm.)

E! VOLUNTEER OPPORTUNITIES. Up the hill from Pelling, about halfway to the Pemayangtse Monastery (see below) on the main road, is the **Denjong Padma Choeling Academy,** a school for disadvantaged Sikkimese children, many of whom are orphans. The school is desperately in need of English-speaking volunteers to teach the children everything from math to art, as well as anyone else willing to help with carpentry, computers, medical aid, or baking. The school provides food and housing for its volunteers, and Sikkim Permit extensions (see **Sikkim Permits,** p. 677) are easy to get for this purpose. To find out more, just drop by the school, or contact the headmaster, Yapo S. Yongda. (DPC Academy, Yongda Hill, Drakchong Dzong 737113, West Sikkim, India. ☎(03595) 5056; fax (03592) 24802; email netuk@sikkim.org.)

NEAR PELLING: PEMAYANGTSE पमयान्गटसे

Founded in 1705 by Lhatsun Chenpo, one of the three "Great Lamas" of Yuksam, the **Pemayangtse Monastery** (Monastery of the Sublime Perfect Lotus), is the third-oldest monastery in Sikkim. Currently the key Nyingma-pa (Red Hat) monastery, it is also one of the most artistically stunning in the region. Intricate wall paintings incorporate everything from fiery, wrathful deities to serene and detached bodhisattvas. An enormous pair of terrifying Dorje Taras guard the main room, while an enlightened Guru Padma Sambhava looks on from the top of a lotus. The monastery's centerpiece, though, is the **Sang Thog Palri.** An endlessly detailed, seven-meter-high wooden rendering of the Maha Guru's paradise, the Sang Thong Palri is encased on all sides by glass, and occupies the whole of the monastery's top room. *(Open daily 7am-5pm. On occasion, a Rs10 entrance fee is requested.)*

Just below the monastery are the **Rangdentse Palace Ruins,** the remains of Sikkim's second capital. The second king of Sikkim, Tenzing Namgyal, moved the capital from Yuksam to this area in 1670. It served as the seat of royal power until 1814. The entrance to the ruins is on the main road from Pemayangtse down to Geyzing. From the main road, take a left onto a small path just before the 3km marker. The path crosses a small meadow before it climbs to the principal ruins. On the right as you climb through the ruins is what remains of the stable and military headquarters; on the left is the site of the main throne. The view from here takes in the holiest areas of Western Sikkim, including Yuksam and Tashiding.

NEAR PELLING: SANGA CHOELING MONASTERY

Even older than Pemayangtse, the less flashy and less popular **Sanga Choeling Monastery** is more peaceful and sedate, with a real charm of its own. Ancient pine forests surround the hilltop complex, and the breathtaking (literally) climb alone is worth the trip. Inside the main building are three central statues—the Buddha on the left, Dorje Sempa in the middle, and Guru Padma Sambhava on the right. Behind the elevated row of white stupas on the far side of the main building are a pair of rocks covering a hole. Local legend has it that this hole leads all the way out to a cave near Legship, and that this cave is the source of the eerie wind that emanates from the hole. Whatever its actual source, the gusts are real enough—drop a few blades of grass in and watch them blow back out. The monastery is about a 45-minute hike from town, in the opposite direction from Pemayngtse. From the tourist office head to the football field, bear left around the small hill, and continue straight up to the monastery. The same trail continues past Sanga Choeling (it's easy to miss; watch for the faded wooden sign) into the forested ridge behind, a popular destination for day hikes.

TREKKING IN WESTERN SIKKIM

The best way to take in the culture and natural beauty of Western Sikkim is on foot. Though the most popular sites are connected by road, the most enjoyable (and most challenging) routes are the unmarked "short-cuts." It's easy to get lost since these trails have many branches, but there are plenty of farmers around who will help you find your way. Keep in mind that while finding dinner and a place to sleep is rarely a problem, lunch or bottled water is generally unavailable along the trail. Many hotels will provide a packed lunch (Rs20-30). There is no phone service in Western Sikkim north of Pelling.

There are two extremely popular trekking routes in Western Sikkim, which differ greatly in duration, difficulty, price, and the degree of advance planning required. The **Local Trek** (3-4 days) hits many of Western Sikkim's top destinations. It is not too difficult, requires no advance booking or additional permits, and should cost roughly Rs150-250 per day. For serious trekkers, the more challenging (and more costly) **High Altitude Trek** (6-9 days) leaves from Yuksam and ascends well above 4000m. It must be booked ahead of time in Gangtok and can cost anywhere from US$15 per day (roughing it) to US$80 per day (bring your hair dryer, and a porter will carry it for you). The trek goes from **Yuksam** (1780m) to **Dzongri** (4024m) over a period of four days. Some trips continue for three more days to **Goeche La** (4940m) before returning to the "lowlands." Although most of these treks are guided and relatively safe, read up on Acute Mountain Sickness (AMS) before you go (see p. 35).

NEAR PELLING: THE LOCAL TREK

An exhilarating three- to four-day circuit from Pelling, the local trek winds its way along rivers and up mountains, through villages and past monasteries, into the dense jungle and terraced farmland of Western Sikkim. The three biggest attractions along the way are **Khechopalri Lake,** the town of **Yuksam,** and the monastery at **Tashiding.** The term "trek," however, is used loosely, as each leg of the trip is also linked by road, intermittent **jeep service** is available between any two points, and all major points are within a day's walk of Pelling. From some points along the trek, **buses** also travel to Pelling or Geyzing. It's easy to customize an itinerary to fit any length of time and level of energy. The route described is the longest and proceeds in the more popular (and more auspicious) clockwise direction.

DAY 1: PELLING TO KHECHOPALRI LAKE. (4½-6½hr.) From the tourist office in Pelling, the road bends sharply and heads down the north side of the ridge past the Alpine restaurant. Follow this road into lower Pelling until you see the sign for the Mondol Lodge. Immediately in front of this sign, the concrete path descends to the right, heading down to the river. The concrete soon disappears, and the path begins to fork regularly. Almost all of the forks will eventually take you where you want to go, but when in doubt, favor the more downhill option. The descent to the Rimbi river takes 45 minutes to 1.5 hours. At the river, there's a rickety bamboo bridge, and then the trail climbs quickly to the road. Follow the road east to the intersection where a faded road sign points the way to Khechopalri, 10km away. Numerous shortcuts traverse the road's initial switchbacks, but it's easiest to stay on the road since it eventually levels out. The road winds up the valley, crosses the stream, and then spins back out and around the next ridge before reaching the lake. Snacks and bottled water are available at some of the roadside villages.

Khechopalri Lake is considered the holiest lake in Sikkim, and legend says that if even a single leaf falls on its surface, a bird will pluck it up. The lake's wish-granting abilities are also considerable (make your wish wisely!), and the eerie calm that graces the lake's surface, along with the multicolored prayer flags give the place a special atmosphere. Swimming is not allowed. On the eastern side of the lake is the main shrine, where a small platform extends down to the lake's edge. A "trail" of sorts continues on and circles the lake, but it's hard to follow in some places. Also accessible from the lake are the **Chubuk** and **Dupuk** caves, where religious ceremonies are performed by local monks, and the site of the **"footprint rock"**—legend tells that a monk's foot was imprinted here when he stepped on it. Ask at the trekkers' hut (see below) for directions.

The best accommodation at the lake is the privatized **trekkers' hut,** on the road 200m before the lake. The serene atmosphere and friendly staff are complemented by the huge communal dinners for Rs25. (Dorm beds Rs30; doubles Rs100.) The **pilgrims' hut,** at the monastery, on the ridge overlooking the lake, offers more basic amenities at a cheaper price (dorm beds Rs20). Jeeps running this stretch from Pelling to Khechopalri leave Pelling every afternoon (3pm, Rs35) and will drop passengers right at the trekker's hut.

DAY 2: KHECHOPALRI LAKE TO YUKSAM. (3-5 hr.) From the lake, a shortcut trail descends off the main road just opposite the trail leading up to the monastery. Dropping past a few houses and some long rows of white prayer flags, the trail soon crosses a stream on a springy bridge. From there, you can follow the downhill road around the next ridge or take the much steeper path straight over the ridge. Either way, you eventually have to join the path that crosses the crystal-clear Rathong River on the suspension bridge. The brutally steep shortcut to Yuksam climbs up from the road just a few hundred meters past the bridge. This trail zig-zags through terraced fields all the way up to an unused stretch of road, which leads the rest of the way at a more relaxed pitch.

Yuksam itself is relatively built-up; as the starting point for the popular **Dzongri Trek,** the town sees a fair bit of tourist traffic. Yuksam (Lepcha for "three lamas") became the first capital of Sikkim in 1641 when three lamas, Lhatsun Chenpo, Rigdzin Chenpo, and Nadak Sempa Chenpo, met here to consecrate the first king of Sikkim, Phontsog Namgyal. The spot of the ceremony, a white stone throne, is still intact, and is known as the **Norbugang Chorten.** The capital has long since moved on, but Yuksam still has some basic services. There are no telephones, but there is a **police outpost** on the main road, 150m north of the Wild Orchid Hotel, and a **hospital** another 100m north on the road that curves to the right.

The best place to stay is the ▓**Hotel Yangrigang,** at the bend in the main road, just south of the bazaar. The rooms are clean, the lobby features comfy couches, and the restaurant dishes out outstanding veg. chow mein for Rs25. (Dorm beds Rs50; doubles with bath Rs150. Off-season: Rs40/100.) Though not quite the seductive paradise its name suggests, **Wild Orchid Hotel** is another reliable option, just south of the main bazaar. All rooms have a common bath and hot water is available at Rs10 per bucket. (Singles Rs75; doubles Rs100.) For a good meal outside the hotels, try the **Gupta Restaurant,** just north of the Wild Orchid Hotel. (Veg. *momos* Rs10; beer Rs35. Open daily 6am-8pm.) The nearby **Dubdi Monastery** is the oldest in Sikkim. A well-maintained trail (1hr.) leads to the monastery from just below the hospital. **Jeeps** for this leg of the trip depart very early from in front of the trekkers' hut in Khechopalri (before 6:30am, Rs30).

DAY 3: YUKSAM TO TASHIDING. (4-7hr.) The walk from Yuksam to Tashiding is long but not strenuous; practically all of it is downhill, and much of it is along the road. The only shortcut worth taking comes at the very start. From Yuksam, a trail descends off the main road, beginning just before the Hotel Yangrigang. This trail cuts diagonally downhill for about 2km; at every fork, opt for the more downhill path. Eventually, the trail intersects with the road. From this point on, the hike sticks to the road, and while the route is lovely (and without much traffic), many trekkers choose to hop on a jeep for this leg. Shortly after the intersection, you'll pass **Phamrong Falls,** a good place for a break. Farther along, the path passes through the village of **Gerethang,** where the bottled water and snacks are available. Forty-five minutes to 1 hour before you reach **Tashiding,** you will round a site where the town and the local monastery (see below) are visible for the first time. Tashiding is on top of the ridge; it looks down on the Rathong River to the west and the Rangeet River to the east.

The **Tashiding Monastery,** the real attraction of the day, is an hour's hike from town up the stupa-dotted hill to the south. (You have to walk this stretch, even if you come by jeep.) The monastery dates from 1716 and now houses about 50 monks and the **Bhumbhu,** a sacred water vase that is the center of a local festival every March. During the festival, the water case, sealed empty a year beforehand, is opened to reveal a miraculous bounty of fresh water, which is then diluted with regular water and divided up for everyone to sample. Also on the premises is the **Thong Wa Rang To Chorten,** considered the holiest *chorten* in Sikkim—simply beholding its glory is supposed to wash away all sin. Behold it well.

If you are looking for a place to stay in Tashiding, keep your eyes peeled for the **Hotel Blue Bird,** just north up the hill from the main intersection. Rooms are simple and slightly dingy, all sharing a common bath, but there's a comfortable sitting area upstairs and free buckets of hot water. (Dorm beds Rs20; singles Rs40; doubles Rs50.) The restaurant serves cheap meals (veg. rice Rs20; chicken rice Rs40).

Jeep service for this part of the trek runs mostly in the early morning (before 6:30am, 1hr., Rs30); it is possible to visit Tashiding early and then continue on to either Legship or Pelling in the evening.

DAY 4: TASHIDING TO PELLING OR LEGSHIP. (5-7hr. or 3-5hr.) You have two options from Tashiding: one is to take the shortcut trail directly down to the river and up the other side to Pelling; the other is to follow the road down to **Legship,** where buses and jeeps run up to Pelling, Gangtok, Jorethang, and Siliguri.

Heading straight to Pelling requires more energy. The shortcut trail departs directly from the town of Tashiding (ask at the Hotel Blue Bird, see above) and meanders steeply down to the Rathong River (1½-2½ hr.) and the suspension bridge. Across the river, the trail leads up the hill; at the few forks in the trail, veer toward the more uphill path. This eventually leads to **Naku Chumbong Village** (2½-3hr.), where a number of paths converge. Use that keen trekking sense you've cultivated, and take the most uphill trail, which will take you to Pelling (1-1½ hr.).

The other option is to follow the descending course to Legship, a more convenient choice for those headed to other parts of Sikkim or West Bengal, as most area buses and jeeps pass through this town. Navigation is easy—just follow the road. But keep in mind that there is no food or water available along the way. The road crosses the Rangeet River (1½-2½hr.), then winds its way downstream, crossing the river again at Legship (1½-2½hr.). It's a long walk, but it is downhill nearly all the way. **Jeeps** run from Tashiding to Legship in the morning (before 7am, 1hr., Rs25), and the trucks plying the route will often stop for trekkers (Rs10).

In Legship, **buses** run from the terminal to: **Gangtok** (7 and 8am, 4hr., Rs45) and **Siliguri** (6:30 and 7:30am, 4½hr., Rs50). **Jeeps** head to: **Gangtok** (every hr., 7:30-11:30am, 3½hr., Rs60); **Pelling** (every hr., 7am-2pm, 1hr., Rs30) via **Geyzing** (30min., Rs20); and **Siliguri** (7:30 and 8am, 4hr., Rs80). The only real accommodation in town is at the **Hotel Trishna,** up the street from the bus terminal, at the main intersection. Their rooms are clean, and they'll wake you up for early buses and jeeps. (☎ 50887. Doubles Rs100-200). Ask the hotel for directions to the **hot springs,** a half-hour walk from town.

SIKKIM

NORTHEAST INDIA

Northeast India consists of seven states connected to the rest of the country by a narrow isthmus and an even narrower thread of cultural similarity. At the heart of the region is the Brahmaputra Valley state of Assam, which until recently encompassed the entire region. The Northeast is largely inhabited by *adivasis* (indigenous peoples) who have had little or no exposure to the myriad wonders of industrial civilization. In 1963, these peoples' struggles for autonomy led to the splintering of Assam and the creation of six new states: Arunachal Pradesh, Nagaland, Manipur, Mizoram, Tripura, and Meghalaya, which together make up the mountainous regions bordering China, Burma, and Bangladesh. All kinds of turmoil accompanied the changes, and instability still threatens many regions today. The capital of Assam was officially moved from Shillong to Guwahati in 1974, two years after Meghalaya became a separate state.

The tradition of armed insurrection in Mizoram, Nagaland, and Assam continues only partially abated, and political violence is still common in the Northeast. Dissidents claim that India takes advantage of the region's rich natural resources while ignoring its chronic underdevelopment. Political instability, coupled with Indian fears of a Chinese invasion (China still claims Arunachal Pradesh), kept the entire region closed to foreigners until 1995. However, the long-promised easing of restrictions is finally becoming a reality—in some parts of the region, at least. Assam, Meghalaya, and Tripura are now open to unrestricted tourism. The other states require permits, which can theoretically be obtained in Delhi, but which are practically impossible to get hold of. Your best bet is to apply as a group (of four or more) and to find an organization or travel agent willing to "recommend" you for a permit. Miracles have been known to happen, but the limited-time, place-specific permits are not worth the effort, hassle, and frustration involved unless you are looking for long-lost relatives or writing a dissertation on Naga culture.

Fortunately, Assam and Meghalaya offer opportunities enough to experience the natural beauty and indigenous cultures of the Northeast. Tripura has a proud cultural legacy and is a good gateway into rarely visited Bangladesh. The Northeast's lack of any real infrastructure makes exploration here that much more exciting, and makes for a feeling of remoteness only rarely encountered elsewhre in India these days.

HIGHLIGHTS OF NORTHEAST INDIA

Assam's **Kaziranga National Park** (p. 695) teems with wildlife, including a large population of protected rhinos.

One of the wettest places on earth, **Meghalaya** (p. 699) showers visitors with hospitality, sublime scenery, and well-watered greenery.

ASSAM অসম

Stretching 800km through the low-lying Brahmaputra Valley, present-day Assam is the largest of the seven northeastern states. Despite mentions in both the *Mahabharata* and the *Puranas*, Assam didn't really enter recorded history until early in the 13th century, when a group of Buddhists from Thailand called the Ahom conquered the area's indigenous peoples and established a capital in Sibsagar. The cultural victory, however, belonged to the Hindus who quickly converted their conquerors. Even today, East-Asian-looking Assamese speakers perform *puja*

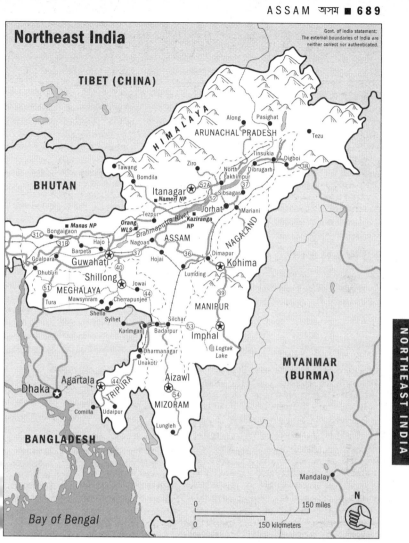

Northeast India

Govt. of India statement:
The external boundaries of India are
neither correct nor authenticated.

TIBET (CHINA)

BHUTAN

ARUNACHAL PRADESH

HIMALAYA

Along
Pasighat
Tezu

Tawang
Ziro
Tinsukia
Digboi
38

Bomdila
North
Lakhimpur
Dibrugarh

Itanagar ✪
52A
52
37
Sibsagar

■ Nameri NP

Tezpur
Jorhat
Mariani

Kaziranga
NP

Brahmaputra River

■ Manas NP

Orang
WLS

ASSAM

NAGALAND

31C
Bongaigaon

31B
Hajo
Nagaon
36
Dimapur

Barpeta

Goalpara
Guwahati ✪
37
Hojai
Kohima ✪

40

Dhubri

Shillong ✪
Lumding

51
Jowai

MEGHALAYA
44
39

Tura
Mawsynram
Cherrapunjee
MANIPUR

Shella

Sylhet
Silchar
53

Karimganj
Badarpur
Imphal ✪

Dharmanagar
Logtak
Lake

Unakoti

Agartala ✪
44
Aizawl ✪

Dhaka ✪
TRIPURA
54
MYANMAR
(BURMA)

Comilla
Udaipur
MIZORAM

BANGLADESH
Lungleh

Mandalay ●

Bay of Bengal

0   150 miles
0   150 kilometers

N

alongside Aryan Indian pilgrims. A weak central government opened the door to power shifting in the 19th century, first to the Burmese and then to the British, who built Asia's first oil refinery and seized advantage of the hilly terrain (Assam means "uneven") and unfaltering seasonal rains to establish plantations that today produce over half of India's tea.

Adding to the influx of outsiders, the last two decades have brought migrants from West Bengal and illegal immigrants from Bangladesh, adding a substantial Bengali-speaking population and leading to tension between the new arrivals and the native Assamese. In addition, frustration over the region's poor economy and the sense of being neglected by the central government have led to the formation of groups such as the United Liberation Front of Assam (ULFA), whose nefarious tactics include bombings, kidnappings, and financial racketeering. The dream of autonomy has also spurred the indigenous people into an unprecedented attack on the state's remaining areas of unspoiled jungle: the extent of their settlement would demarcate the area of any autonomous region.

Geographically as well as culturally, Assam is divided into three main regions. In the north, the Brahmaputra Valley combines alluvial lands and islands, hilly tea plantations, and patches of pristine jungle and wilderness. Unfortunately, in the last three years, forests have been slashed and burnt down at an alarming rate, without so much as a squeak from politicians afraid to upset potential voters. The Cachar Hills, in the middle area of the region, are inhabited by indigenous peoples and are the best alternative to a visit to the states of Nagaland, Manipur, and Mizoram, all of which require special permits. Close to the border with Bangladesh in the south, the Barak River Valley is home to a sizeable Muslim population, the majority of whom speak a dialect of Bengali.

> **WARNING.** Over the past few years, there have been occasional terrorist attacks on trains and buses in Assam. In June 1998, explosions temporarily severed all road and rail links between the Northeast and West Bengal. Since then, there have been sporadic clashes between government forces and the ULFA. Travelers are advised to keep abreast of the news and to avoid traveling at night.

GUWAHATI গুয়াহাটি ☎ 0361

Referred to in ancient texts as Pragjyoyishpur, or "Eastern Ray of Light," Guwahati derives its present name from its much more earthly function as a betel-nut (*guwa*) market (*hatt*). As the Northeast's main crossroads and only connection to the outside world, Guwahati sees people of all the region's diverse races pass through its crowded lanes, bazaars, and stations. Just a few steps away from the bustle of the bazaars flows the majestic Brahmaputra, overshadowed by the Nilachal Hill at its holiest point. This is the site of the Kamakhya Temple, one of the most sacred of all Hindu *tirthas*. Despite its attractions, both sacred and mundane, for most of the few travelers that come here, Guwahati is little more than a gateway to the remote areas to the south and east. It is the most distinctly "Indian" town of the region and a good place to sit back for a few days and get acclimatized to the massively different regional culture that begins just east of here.

▣ GETTING THERE AND GETTING AROUND

Flights: Gopinath Bordelai Airport (☎ 840221), 24km from town in Borjhar. **Taxis** run from Paltan Bazaar (Rs60 per person if you share, Rs300 for the whole car). Buses go from Judge Field, next to Nehru Park, to VIP Point (every 30min., Rs3), 2km from the airport, where you can pick up an auto-rickshaw (Rs10-20). To get to Judge Field from the railway station, take a rickshaw (Rs5) or city bus, or walk straight through 2 major traffic circles. The **Indian Airlines** office (☎ 564425) is a 15-min. ride along Shillong Rd. Open M-Sa 9am-1:15pm and 2-4pm. To **Calcutta** (noon, 1hr.), **Delhi** (daily, 2:30-4pm, 2½hr.), and **Imphal** (Su and Th, 1pm, 50min., US$50).

Trains: The main railway station in the Northeast, **Guwahati Junction,** is centrally located next to Paltan Bazaar. To book sleeper tickets, go to the **North Eastern Railways Reservation Building** (☎ 541799), on the right, 200m in front of the railway station. To: **Calcutta** (2-4 per day, 7am-10pm, 20-23hr., Rs270); **Delhi** (3-4 per day, 6-8:30am and 12:30-8pm, 36hr., Rs461); **Dimapur** (for buses to Kohima and Imphal, 4-5 per day, 2:30pm-1am, 5-6hr., Rs100); and **Jorhat** (7pm, 13hr., Rs126).

Buses: Throughout the Northeast, private buses, which depart from **Paltan Bazaar,** are of better quality, more frequent, and more reliable than the state transport companies. For booking and schedule inquiries, go to one of the many agencies nearby, including **Network Travels** (☎ 522007). **Assam and Meghalaya State Transport** buses depart from the decrepit depot between the railway station and Paltan Bazaar and head to: **Agartala** (3:30pm, 24hr., Rs300); **Dimapur** (7pm, 10-12hr., Rs100); **Imphal** (7pm, 16hr., Rs220); **Jorhat** (frequent, 6:30am-8pm, 9hr., Rs100); **Shillong** (every hr., 6am-4pm, 4hr., Rs50); **Silchar** (6am and 5pm, 12hr., Rs180); and **Tezpur** (every hr., 7:30am-4pm, 5hr., Rs66). For **Kaziranga,** take the **Jorhat** bus to **Kohora** (6hr., Rs80).

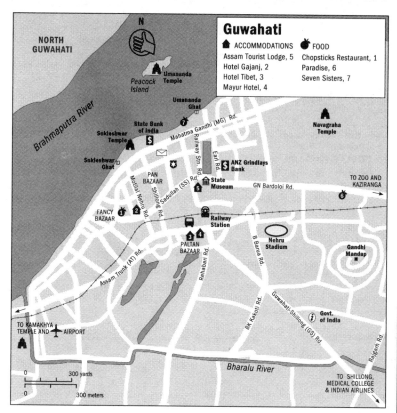

Guwahati

🏠 ACCOMMODATIONS   🍎 FOOD

Assam Tourist Lodge, 5   Chopsticks Restaurant, 1
Hotel Gajanj, 2   Paradise, 6
Hotel Tibet, 3   Seven Sisters, 7
Mayur Hotel, 4

Local Transportation: Cycle-rickshaws and **auto-rickshaws** park on either side of the railway station. City **buses** run on MG, AT, Shillong, and GS Rds. (Rs1-3 within the city). You can catch a bus going west along MG Rd. to the base of Nilachal Hill and the Kamakhya Temple. **Ferries** run to Umananda (Rs10 per person), unless the river's too high. **River cruises** also leave from the ferry landing (11am and 4pm, Rs35).

> **WARNING.** Before you get into any vehicle, try to make sure that your driver is not dead drunk. Alcoholism is a serious problem all over Assam, and although it is fairly unlikely that you will ever manage to find a 100% sober rickshaw-*wallah*, you can at least pick one who is more or less in control of the most basic bodily functions. It is not unknown for travelers to end up peddling themselves to their destination, while their driver sleeps off his hangover.

◼◼ ORIENTATION AND PRACTICAL INFORMATION

The **Guwahati Jct. Railway Station** is the heart of the town. South of it lies **Paltan Bazaar,** the departure point for both private and state buses. A 10-minute bus ride along **Shillong Rd.** brings you to **Dispur,** where you will find the government offices of Assam and other Northeastern states. Northwest of the station are the **Pan** and **Fancy Bazaars** (Rs5 rickshaw ride or a 10-minute walk), the liveliest areas of town. **Mahatma Gandhi (MG) Rd.** runs behind Pan Bazaar along the river's edge; government buses ply this route to the Kamakhya Temple, 8km to the west, and the Navagraha Temple, 1km to the east.

Tourist Office: Government of India Tourist Office, in G. L. Publication Complex
(☎547407), just off Shillong Rd. From Paltan Bazaar, take a bus to Lachit Nagar; the
office is in the tall building on the left. The staff is surprisingly helpful and supplies up-to-
date information on permits and travel throughout the Northeast. Open M-F 9:30am-
5:30pm, Sa 10am-1pm. The **Assam State Tourist Office** (☎544475), inside the
tourist lodge, is absolutely useless. Open M-Sa 10am-5pm, closed 2nd and 4th Sa.

Currency Exchange: ANZ Grindlays Bank (☎540597), opposite the Assam State
Museum, cashes traveler's checks and gives credit card advances. Open for exchange
M-F 10am-3pm, Sa 10am-12:30pm.

Police: Stations in Pan Bazaar (☎540106) and Paltan Bazaar (☎540126). The **Superintendent of Police** (☎540278), near the District Court, registers foreigners for long term
stays. Open M-Sa 10am-4:30pm.

Hospital: Down Town Hospital, GS Rd., Dispur (☎560824 or 562741), near Capitol
Complex, has fluent English speakers on staff and is the best place for extended stays.

Internet: Cyberzone, on B. Barua Rd., opposite Nehru Stadium. Open 10am-11pm. Rs1
per min.

Post Office: GPO, Meghdoot Bhawan (☎543588), near Pan Bazaar. Open M-Sa 10am-
5pm. **Postal Code:** 781001.

ACCOMMODATIONS

There are a number of decent places in the Paltan Bazaar if you're just passing
through. To groove with the pulse of local life, you'd be better off staying in one of
the slightly more expensive lodges in the Pan Bazaar.

■ **Mayur Hotel** (☎541115 or 541116), behind the bus station on AT Rd., in Paltan Bazaar.
Surprisingly cheap modern rooms with seat toilets. The restaurant serves good vegetarian dishes. Singles Rs110-140; doubles Rs160-250.

■ **Assam Tourist Lodge** (☎544475), in front of the railway station. Spacious doubles with
bathroom, balcony, and dressing room. Singles Rs100; doubles Rs170.

Hotel Tibet (☎610600), next to the Mayur, on AT Rd., is sparklingly new and clean. Each
bed is equipped with a mosquito net. Singles Rs130-170; doubles Rs200-250.

Hotel Gajnaj (☎525070), SS Rd., near Pan Bazaar. Somewhat cramped but still the
best value in the core of the market town. Singles Rs150; doubles Rs230.

FOOD

Assamese cuisine—fish, rice, and heavy mustard seasoning—is available around
Pan Bazaar.

DIVINE DISMEMBERMENT
Legend has it that the beautiful
goddess Sati fell in love with an uncouth ascetic insolent enough to dare to marry her.
Her disapproving father, Daksha, decided to hold a sacrifice, and invited every god to
the celebration, except for the vagabond bridegroom, Shiva. Incensed by her father's
treatment of her husband, Sati flung herself on the sacrificial pyre. When Shiva learned
of his wife's demise, he lifted up her blackened body and began to sob convulsively,
shaking the entire universe. In the interest of saving the cosmos, Vishnu stepped in
and began hacking off bits of the charred corpse with his *chakra* (discus). Literally and
figuratively, this action relieved Shiva of the burden of Sati's death, and he ceased his
sobbing. The holy places where fragments of Sati's body fell to earth became known as
shakti pithas. These sacred sites, which number 4, 51, or 108, depending on who's
counting, began as independent goddess shrines, but the myth of Sati's dismemberment provides a unifying thread. The most important *shakti pithas* are those which
came from the most potent parts of Sati—the **Kamakhya Temple** in Guwahati is the
greatest of them all.

▨ **Paradise,** GN Bandoloi Rd., Silpukuri. From in front of the museum, take a bus toward Silpukuri. Excellent Assamese dishes in a soothing environment. The *thali* (Rs55) has 11 different varieties, including fried fish and chili chicken; the veg. version (Rs50) is equally impressive. Beer Rs55. Open daily 10am-3:30pm and 6-9:30pm.

▨ **Chopsticks Restaurant,** on SS Rd., in the Dynasty Hotel. Serves specialties from every region of India in a classy setting. The *nilgini korma* (Rs95) will carry you to the hills of Kerala in a matter or minutes. Croissants and donuts for breakfast. Open 7am-11pm.

Seven Sisters, on Kacheria Ghat, next to the Umananda Ferry. The food isn't great, but the peaceful river setting is a good enough reason to pass a few hours here.

Madras Cabin, Paltan Bazaar, near Mayur Hotel. A shot of southern comfort to complement the northern grit of the surrounding *dhabas*. Open daily 5am-10pm.

👁 SIGHTS

NILICHAL AND KAMAKHYA TEMPLE. The Blue Hill is the highest peak in the area and is crisscrossed by paths leading up to 10 shrines, each dedicated to a different form of Kali, the bloodthirsty goddess. By far the most important site is the Kamakhya Temple, the principle *shakti pitha* for Hindus. It is said that the goddess Sati's *yoni* (vulva) fell here when she was cut into pieces by Vishnu (see **Divine Dismemberment,** p. 692). After it was burned down by a brahmin priest who converted to Islam, the temple, with its beehive-shaped spire, was rebuilt in 1665 by King Naranarayana. The king is said to have inaugurated his new temple by offering no fewer than 140 human heads to the goddess Kamakhya. Inside, the Mother-Goddess is worshipped in the form of a crack in a rock, rather than as a sculpted image. The ancient stone bleachers that rise up from the base of the temple provide seating to spectators eager to see animal sacrifices. Male goats tied to the posts at the main temple gate each morning are decapitated by the evening. The shrine inside the temple is open to non-Hindus, but you will need to have a good deal of change on you to satisfy all the guardian priests. *(The bus from Guwahati will drop you on MG Rd. From here, you can walk up the path to the temple in 30 min., or catch a taxi up the winding road. From Kamakhya, a 20 min. scenic walk leads up to the peaceful Bhubaneshwari Temple, under a pipal tree at the top of the hill. Last bus from Kamakhya leaves 6pm.)*

BRAHMAPUTRA RIVER. The mighty Brahmaputra ("Son of Brahma") surges past the city in the north, often overrunning its banks during the rainy season and flooding the riverside settlements. From its banks, or from any of the adjacent hills, the river (incidentally, the only river classified in Hindi as a male) might look serene or even sluggish, but its undercurrents are swift. The river's vast hydroelectric potential has not yet been exploited, but engineers claim that the Brahmaputra could satisfy 30% of India's energy needs. Ferries run between 7am and 4pm (Rs10) from Umananda Ghat, near the Brahmaputra Ashok Hotel, to the Umananda Temple, on a small island in the middle of the river. The temple is in a state of disrepair, but it offers the best views of the river. Along the way to the temple is the **Urbashi Kharti,** a yardstick that measures the level of the water during the monsoon; according to legend, it is a beautiful woman, transformed into a rock.

NAVAGRAHA TEMPLE. The small Navagraha ("Nine Planets") Temple is a reminder that Guwahati was once a great center of astronomy and astrology. An echo chamber holds nine *lingas*, dedicated to the nine heavenly bodies that ancient Indians were able to identify without the aid of astronomical equipment: the sun, the moon, the ascending and descending nodes of the moon, Mercury, Venus, Mars, Jupiter, and Saturn. The dark, dank temple now seems more abandoned than mysterious. *(On a hill in east Guwahati. Open daily 10am-6pm.)*

OTHER SIGHTS. The Assam State Museum, **Dighali Pukhi,** has a large collection of Assamese cultural artifacts, as well as a fascinating photography exhibit on the Independence movement. The library next door is stocked with literature on regional cultures. *(Behind the tourist lodge and opposite the lake. Both open Tu-Sa 10am-*

5pm; in winter 10am-4:15pm; closed 2nd and 4th Sa. Rs2.) A new cultural center, the **Sarkardev Kalashetra Complex,** opened recently on the 6th mile of GS Rd. Named for a famous Assamese artisan who devoted his life to the promotion of regional culture, the center is a veritable theme park of all that is Assamese, complete with reconstructions of temples, an open air amphitheater, and a beautifully landscaped "Heritage Park," which contains sculptures, paintings, and mosaics depicting scenes from rural Assamese life. *(Take a bus along GS Rd., or hire an auto-rickshaw from the Paltan Bazaar (Rs60). Open daily 10am-7pm. Rs5.)*

TEZPUR   ☎ 03712

Tezpur, the "city of blood," is a pleasant little town with a grim mythological past. The site of the legendary battle between Hari (Krishna) and Hara (Shiva, in the form of Banasura), Tezpur was drenched in blood by the vicious conflict. The red stains have been washed away, but if you search hard enough you might still manage to find a few hints of its great past. At **Da-Parbatia,** an astonishingly small gate is all that remains of one of the oldest temples in Assam. In **Agnigargh,** 5km out of town, on a hillside facing the river, are the ruins of a rampart. The main reason to come to Tezpur, though, is its location on the northern bank of the Brahmaputra, close to Orang Nameri and Kaziranga, making it an ideal launching point for these national parks. Also nearby is the breathtaking Bomdila road, which ends at the **Tawang Gompa,** a real gem of a place. Tezpur is also the gateway to the western part of Arunachal Pradesh. **Permits** are required and foreigners can obtain them only from the Home Ministry in Delhi (extremely difficult and frustrating) or through a local travel agent. Permits are issued to groups of four or more, and the cost is US$150 per person per day (US$50 to the state government, US$100 to the tour operator). Tsering Wange of **Himalayan Holidays** in Bombdilla can work wonders with Indian bureaucracy (☎ (03782) 22017; email wange10@hotmail.com).

Buses arrive near Cole Lake, a 10-minute walk from the town center. Buses run to: **Guwahati** (every hr., 7am-4pm, Rs70). The town centers on the **Main Rd.,** which ends at a fish and fruit market near the mosque. **Shambala Tour/Himalayan Holidays** runs Tata Sumos to Bomdila. (☎ 52108. Two per day, 5:30am and 1pm, 6hr., Rs120.) The **police station** is in the middle of the main road, and the **post office** is three blocks southeast (☎ 540238; open M-Sa 7am-5pm; **postal code** 754001). **No currency exchange** is available in town. Travel companies are gathered on **Kabarkhana Rd.,** which runs parallel to the Main Rd. from the state transport bus stand. **Hotmail,** Main Rd. next to Basant Hotel, and **Nice Internet Services,** in front of Hotel Luit, are proud local Internet providers for Rs80 per hour (open 10am-9pm).

Durbar Hotel on Kabarkhana Rd., is bright and new. (☎ 4276. Singles Rs200; doubles Rs300.) **Basant Hotel** (☎ 30831) on the main road, is the best value, with clean rooms from Rs132-287. Both have restaurants, but locals are committed to the **Flora Restaurant and Bar,** on Jonaki Cinema Rd., near the police station, which has the best food and the cheapest beer (Rs45 per bottle. Open 10am-10pm).

NATIONAL PARKS

NAMERI NATIONAL PARK

Together with the Pakhui Wildlife Sanctuary in Arunachal, Nameri constitutes a vast area of over 1000 sq. km of evergreen forests that reaches uninterrupted all the way from the northern bank of the Jia Bhoroli River to the Himalayas. Ideal elephant country, it is also well known for its orchids, its steadily increasing tiger population, and the endangered White Winged Wood Duck. To reach the park from Tezpur, take a Tata Sumo (3 per day, 6am-1pm, 1hr., Rs40) or bus (3hr., Rs20) heading from Bomdila to **Hathiket.** From the road it is a 2.5km walk to the **Forest Ranger Office** and the **ECO Camp,** on the southern bank of the Bhoroli river. The camp is run by the Bhoroli Angling Association and fills up with members on weekends, so try to **come during the week.** The best way to visit the park is to go for a two-hour walk at either sunrise or sunset—the only times you stand any chance of seeing some of the wildlife. Pay the Rs175 fee at the Forest Ranger Office (open daily 8am-5pm), and the ranger will arrange a ferry across the river, as well as a guide. There are "luxury tents" (Rs720-880), as well as few beds in double rooms with common bath (Rs120). Meals are served here. Call ahead to reserve a place (☎(03714) 44246) or to get permission to camp. Managers Mr. Phukan and Mr. Agarwala are very knowledgeable and can arrange rafting trips (Rs750) or visits to the nearby **Missing indigenous villages.** If you want to fish, you'll need to bring your own equipment and secure a permit from the DFO office in Tezpur.

ORANG WILDLIFE SANCTUARY

This "mini-Kaziranga" packs rhinos, elephants, a small population of tigers, and rare birds (including the Bengal Florican) into just 76 sq. km. At the edge of a village of Bangledeshi Muslims—150km from Guwahati and 32km from Tezpur, on the northern bank of the Brahmaputra—remote, quiet Orang makes a great one-night getaway. From Tezpur, take the Guwahati bus to the village of **Orang** (1hr., Rs10). From here, another bus goes to Silbari, a 2km walk from the park. Alternatively, a car can be hired in Tezpur (Rs200). Before you go, contact the BFO office in Tezpur (☎(03712) 20803) to get permission to stay in the park. Accommodations consist of two basic forest bungalows, the better of which is within the confines of the park. (For booking call ☎(03713) 22065. Doubles Rs120.) Bring your own food; the ranger might help you cook.

MANAS NATIONAL PARK

Manas is supposed to be quite a place. One of the most beautiful wildlife parks in the whole of Asia, it is a UNESCO World Heritage Site that is home to rhinos, elephants, and tigers. Sadly, it also home to a particularly violent group of BODO rebels. Even the poachers are afraid to enter the park these days. For all purposes, the park is closed to visitors, unless you can talk somebody into providing you with a heavy-duty police escort.

KAZIRANGA NATIONAL PARK

The Kaziranga National Park, in the tea-country 217km from Guwahati, is Assam's top tourist attraction and the undisputed heavyweight champion of wildlife parks in the Northeast. Most visitors come here to see the Indian **one-horned rhinoceros**—Kaziranga is home to 65% of the world's population of this endangered species. Since 1966, the park's rhino population has increased threefold, despite the best efforts of horny horn hunters (the phallic proboscis is a much-coveted aphrodisiac). There is no doubt that the rhinos are the stars of the show, but Kaziranga's cast of supporting characters is also impressive. Your chances of seeing a tiger are close to nil, but Asiatic wild buffalo (or *gaur*), equipped with mammoth horns, are all over the place. The park is also home to four kinds of deer and packs of wild elephants. For bird-lovers and twitchers, there are Fish Eagles, Gray-headed Pelicans, and even the rare and much sought-after megatick, the Bengal Florican.

The 430 sq. km sanctuary, only a small part of which is open to visitors, is a hodgepodge of habitats. Swampland gives way to jungle, which rises up to deciduous forests and eventually to the evergreen slopes of the Karbi Anglong Hills. The best view of the animals is from the back of an elephant—each seats up to four people—since they are able to get much closer to the animals than the jeeps can. The sanctuary is open from late October to late April; during the monsoon, animals flee the flooded marshland for the muddy roads, making passage through the park dangerous or impossible.

■ ⚄ **ORIENTATION AND PRACTICAL INFORMATION.** Kaziranga is 217km from Guwahati and 96km from Jorhat, the closest airport. From Guwahati take a Jorhat bus to **Kohora,** the gate of the park (every 30min.; 7-10, 11:30am, 12:30 and 8pm, 6hr., Rs80). From Tezpur, take the bus to Jorhat via Kohora (7am-2pm and 8pm, 2hr., Rs30). From Horhat it takes three hours and costs Rs40. The bus drops you off on the main road by the Park View Restaurant, the only decent place to eat in all of Kaziranga. (Open 6am-10pm.) Take the road behind the restaurant and past the police station (☎62426). After a 10-minute walk, you will find the Kohora village where the Park Office and all the accommodations are situated. Assam Tourism runs four different lodges. To the left is the Bonani Lodge, with spacious rooms and enormous bathrooms. (☎(03776) 62423. Singles Rs250; doubles Rs350). The reception at Bonani also deals with bookings for Bonoshree, which has basic doubles (Rs170), and Kunjaban where you get what you pay for, which is not much (dorm beds with no linen Rs15-30). To the right of the road is Aranya, which has the most expensive but not the best rooms. (☎62429. Singles Rs350; doubles Rs450.) Another 15-minute walk along the road takes you to the recently opened Soil Conservation Guest House, facing a tea plantation and protected by a muzzle gun. (☎62409. Dorm beds Rs25; doubles Rs200-300.)

⏹ VISITING THE PARK. There are two ways to visit the park—by jeep and by elephant. Either way, you will start your trip from the Forest Range Office in Kohora, where you pay a Rs175 entrance fee per person per day and a Rs175 daily camera fee, as well as Rs575 for the elephant ride. (Open 7:30-9:30am, 2-3:30pm, and 8-9pm to reserve elephant seats for the next morning.) Jeeps (Rs30-100) depart from the office at 5:30 and 6:30am to the elephant-mounting point in the central region of the park. The elephant ride lasts an hour and gets you within sniffing range of wild buffalo and rhino. Jeep safaris depart from the office at 8:30-9:30am and at 2:30pm. There are three routes available. The **Central Region route** is the shortest and most popular of these (3hr., Rs680). There are normally enough people around to share the cost. Sightings of elephants and eagles are pretty much guaranteed, both from the jeep and from the numerous look-out towers. The **Western Range route** has good chances to see elephants and rhinos (4hr., Rs700). The **Eastern Range route** leads through a pelican colony and other major bird habitats (7hr., Rs1100). It is generally more difficult to find people to share the cost for these two routes. You might spot a tiger on any of the rides. But it's not very likely.

JORHAT   ☎0376

Though it's not much of a destination itself, you might have to spend a night in Jorhat on your way somewhere else. Buses stop here on their way to Sisagar, the capital of Ahom kings, to the Gibbon Wildlife Sanctuary, and to Majuli, a huge island and the site of several prominent *satras* (Vaishnava monasteries).

⛴ GETTING THERE AND GETTING AROUND. Rowriah Airport, 5km from Jorhat, has flights to **Calcutta** (1 per day, 1½hr., US$50) and **Dimapur** (1 per week, 1½hr., US$65). **Trains** run to **Guwahati** (8:30pm, 11hr., Rs150). Consider getting off at **Lumding** and taking the scenic narrow-gauge railway through the **Cachar Hills** to **Haflong** and **Silchar** (7:15am, 11hr., Rs60). The **bus stand** is on MG Rd., between AT Rd. and Rd. Buses run to **Guwahati** via **Kohora** (every hr., 6am-9pm, 9hr., Rs120); **Mariani** for the **Gibbon Wildlife Sanctuary** (every hr., 7am-4pm, 1hr., Rs10); **Nimati Ghat** for the ferry to **Majuli** (9am for the 10:30 ferry, 2pm for 3:30pm ferry; 1hr.; Rs5); **Sibsigar** (every 30min., 6:45am-4:30pm, 2hr., Rs20).

▦🛈 ORIENTATION AND PRACTICAL INFORMATION. Jorhat is 80km east of Kaziranga, on the southern banks of the Brahmaputra. The town centers on a quadrant defined by **AT Rd.** and **KB Rd.,** running east-west, and **MG Rd.** and **Gar Ali,** running north-south. The **tourist office** is on MG Rd., a 3-minute walk from the bus stand (☎321579). The **Police station** is next door (☎320022). **Pelican Travels** on MG Rd., opposite the police station, books flights (☎321128. Open M-Sa, 10am-5pm). The **State Bank of India** exchanges foreign currency (open M-F 10am-2pm, Sa 10am-noon). The **post office** is near the bus stand. (☎320045. Open M-Sa 10am-5pm.) **Postal Code:** 785001.

■■ **ACCOMMODATIONS AND FOOD.** The **Assam Tourist Lodge,** in the same building as the Tourist Office, has spacious doubles with mosquito nets. (☎321579. Singles Rs100; doubles Rs170.) A growing number of hotels cluster on AT Rd. **Hotel Paradise,** AT Rd., is leader of the pack, with luxury rooms and a restaurant-bar featuring a funky dancing platform. (☎331521. Singles Rs300; doubles Rs400.) The **Food Hut** near the Tourist Office on MG Rd., serves good Indian, Chinese, and continental food. (Dishes Rs25-50. Open daily 9:30am-9:30pm.)

■ **SIGHTS.** Jorhat is at the heart of world's largest tea-growing belt; the **Toklai Tea Research Station** is the oldest and largest institution of its kind in India and illuminates visitors on the magic ingredients of the *chai* taste. (Contact tourist office for more information).

NEAR JORHAT: MAJULI ☎ 03775

The world's largest river island, Majuli is populated by a number of local indigenous groups, who are isolated from the mainland by the swelling Brahmaputra. The peaceful remoteness of the island was perhaps what attracted Shankardeva, the prominent 16th-century Vaishnava saint, who established a number of *satras* (Vaishnava monasteries) here. Today, the largest of them, **Auniati Satra,** has more than 300 residents and gives an insight into the song-and-dance-oriented Vaishnava cult, a sharp contrast to the individualistic, Shiva-devoted sadhus that hang out along the banks of the Ganga. Walking between the *satras* takes you through a number of Missing villages, where a cup of *chai* with the locals might prove to be more fun than a *bhajan* sing-along with the priests.

■ **GETTING THERE AND GETTING AROUND.** Buses leave Jorhat for the **Nimiti Ghat** at 9am (for the 10:30am ferry) and 2pm (for the 3:30pm ferry). The ferry lands at the **Kamalabasi Ghat** (1½hr., Rs10), from where buses cross the burning sands to **Kamalabari,** the largest town on the island (30min., Rs7). The bus continues to **Garamur** (6km) and then onto another ferry to **Lahkimpur** in northern Assam. To get back, buses depart from Kamalabari for the Kamalabari-Nimiti ferry at 8am (for the 9am ferry) and at 1pm (for the 2pm ferry).

■■ **ORIENTATION AND PRACTICAL INFORMATION.** At Kamalabari, you are required to report at the **police station** (☎73429) by the bridge, perhaps because the officer is so fond of chatting with the rare foreign visitor. There is a **post office** in Kamalabari and a number of **STD booths. Postal Code:** 785106.

■■ **ACCOMMODATIONS AND FOOD.** There are two guest houses on the island. To reach the **Kamalabari Satra Guest House,** take the dirt road opposite the police station and walk 15 minutes along the river. Contact *Ensign Swami* (the head priest) for reservations. The monks are friendly and fond of dancing. (☎73302. Rs60 per person.) In the **Circuit House,** in Garamur, on the other hand, you are likely to come face-to-face with stern Indian officialdom. (☎74439. Singles Rs100; doubles Rs200.) You can walk to Garamur (6km), or hope for a bus.

■ **SIGHTS.** One kilometer from the Circuit House is the **Garamur Satra,** historically the most famous of the island's *satras* because of the patronage of Sibsagar's Ahom kings. Today, however, only fallen store pillars, a hidden Boxtop gun, and a richly adorned Vishnu altar sheltered in a shack testify to the glories of the monastery's past. The community (one of the few non-celibate ones on the island) is undergoing a major transition, and debates continue about the future of the once great *satra*. At the **Auniati Satra,** on the other hand, the compounds are clean and the monastic community is flourishing. Ask for the head priest, who speaks excellent English and enlightens visitors with tales from local history. Auniati *satra* is a 5km walk from the town of Kamalabari. The other large monastary, **Dakhimpat Satra,** is a long 18km walk from Kamalabari, but the route is worth the effort, as it leads through some of the island's most interesting villages. Trucks and motorcycles occasionally motor along this stretch and will usually give you a ride.

NORTHEAST INDIA

SIBSAGAR

For over six hundred years, Assam was ruled from Sibsagar by the Ahom kings. Today, the seven-storied **Gargaon Palace** and the **Shivadol,** the highest Shiva temple in India, stand witness to the area's glorious past. Frequent buses (7am-4:30pm, 1½hr., Rs15) connect Sibsagar with Jorhat, and the trip can be made in a day. If you do decide to spend the night, the **Assam Tourist Lodge** (☎ (0377) 22394; singles Rs100; doubles Rs170) and a number of private hotels are around to put you up.

GIBBON WILDLIFE SANCTUARY

Twenty kilometers south of Jorhat, the Gibbon Wildlife Sanctuary is home to the largest number of primate species anywhere in India. Seven different kinds of monkeys swing from the jungle branches here, making this the best spot to catch a glimpse of the rare macaques and Capped Langurs. To reach the sanctuary from Jorhat, take a bus to Mariami (1hr., Rs10) and then hire a rickshaw or walk the remaining 5km to the ranger's office, following the signs for the Indo-US Primate Project. There is a two-room Forest Department's Bungalow on the premises, but you need a permit from the District Forest Official in Jorhat to stay here. It's worth the hassle; wildlife is best observed at sunrise and sunset, and you'll miss it if you're just daytripping.

SILCHAR

In the middle of the Barak River valley, Silchar, the biggest town in southern Assam, is a strategic transit point for the lucky Manipur and Mizoram inner-line permit-holders, as well as for anyone bound for Tripura and Bangladesh.

CACHAR   ☎ 03482

The Cachar Hills—a four-hour train ride north of Silchar—is the best place to experience the culture of the indigenous groups of the northeastern hills. Foreigners need a **permit** before they can travel to Imphal from Silchar or have any hope of getting near the restricted area of Mizoram. Contact the Home Ministry in Delhi. The check posts are heavily guarded.

GETTING THERE AND GETTING AROUND. Given the inaccessibility of Nagaland to foreign visitors and the precarious condition of the Silchar-Imphal road, flying is the only practical way to get into Manipur. The **Indian Airlines** office is on Blub Rd., by the police circle. (☎45649. Open M-Sa 10am-4:30pm.) **Flights** connect Silchar to **Calcutta** (M-Sa, 1hr., Rs2085). There is also an unbelievably cheap connection to **Imphal** (Tu, Th, Sa, 15min., Rs680). **Trains** go via **Haflong** to **Lumding,** where connections can be made to **Guwahati** (*Barak Valley Exp.* 5812, 7:30am; *Cachar Exp.* 5802, 6:30pm, 11hr., Rs60). Private **buses** leave from Club Rd. for: **Agartala** (7am, 12hr., Rs155); **Aizwal** (7pm, 9hr., Rs140); **Guwahati** via Shillong (5 per day, 6:30am-6pm, 12hr., Rs180); and **Imphal** (3:30am, 12hr., Rs195). **Sumos** are a much better option if you want to get to **Aizwal;** they leave from Club Rd. (frequent, 7:30am-7pm, 5hr., Rs180). Any company will do, but **Capital Tours** (☎34425) on Club Rd., by the police circle, provides the most reliable Sumo service.

ORIENTATION AND PRACTICAL INFORMATION. The **State Bank of India** on Park Rd., next to Borail View Hotel, exchanges foreign currency (open M-F 10am-3:30pm, Sa 10am-1pm). The **Superintendant of Police** (☎45866) lives on Park Rd., and should be able to answer permit-related questions. **Kaycee Nursing Home** (☎34145) is a good place to take your dog if it gets sick. **Postal code:** 788001.

ACCOMMODATIONS AND FOOD. **Assam Tourist Lodge,** Park Rd., is a Rs5 rickshaw ride from the train station and has rooms with mosquito nets and bathroom. (☎32376. Singles Rs100; doubles Rs170.) **Hotel Ellora,** near the police circle on Club Rd., has a remarkable variety of rooming options. (☎47412. Bare dorm beds Rs50; passable singles Rs100; luxury doubles Rs250.) **Hotel Borail View,** on Park Rd., near the tourist lodge, offers sheer comfort, complete with elevators. (☎35077. Singles Rs300; doubles Rs400.) The area is devoid of culinary delights, but **Bholanath Bakery,** near the train station is an exception, creating fresh and crisp pastries and breads of all shapes and sizes. (Open 8am-10pm.)

MEGHALAYA

Travelers who take the hilly roads from Assam into Meghalaya soon discover why the region is called the "Abode of Clouds." The state's seven ranges of hills seem to be perpetually swaddled in a cool, cloudy mist that occasionally bursts into violent rains, dousing the valley and swelling the Brahmaputra River. The region is home to Cherrapunjee and Mawsyn, two of the wettest places on earth—from 1860 to 1861, 1042 inches of rain fell into Cherrapunjee—as well as a wealth of vegetation ranging from steaming jungles to pineforests in the north.

Two distinct ethnic groups inhabit Meghalaya: the Hynniewtrep people who live in the Khasi Hills to the east and the Achiks (or Garos) in the Garo Hills to the west. In the 19th century, Welsh and Italian missionaries and the officers of the British Raj were added to the melting pot. By the time they had vacated the region in the 1960s, the missionaries had left behind a strong legacy of Christianity—75% of Meghalayans remain Christian—and one of the highest literacy rates in India. The British were more keen on the hills as an escape from the torturous heat of the Brahmaputra plains. Having defeated (and beheaded) the local independence hero, Raja of Nongkhlaw, during the 1830s, they established a hill station in Cherrapunjee, only to be driven out by the rains. They decamped to Shillong, which they converted into the capital of Assam, and furnished it with essential modern amenities, including a golf course and tennis club. To this day the missionaries are remembered with fondness while the British are resented, especially for their discouragement of human sacrifice.

In 1972, Meghalaya gained independence from Assam and became India's 21st state. Despite the various outside influences, Meghalayans have managed to hold onto their unique traditional institutions such as matrilineal descent and property inheritance. Today, offices, families, and bazaars are run primarily by women. Democratic values are deeply rooted by regional *syiem* (kings) who have long allowed and pushed for self-government through public discourse and referenda.

Opened to unrestricted tourism only in 1995, Meghalaya has just begun attracting foreign discovery. Most people come to enjoy the cool weather of Shillong and the Khasi Hills and to visit the wildlife sanctuaries of West Meghalaya. The bumpy road that cuts west from Shillong to Phulbari gives the more adventurous an opportunity to explore the hill cultures in greater depth.

SHILLONG ☎ 0364

Although the capital of Assam was moved to Guwahati after Meghalaya became an independent state, Shillong is still a major cosmopolitan center. The city, named for an incarnation of the Khasi creator god Shullong, is still marked by its British past, which is visible in the churches, botanical gardens, and colonial cottages that still dominate the old European center of town. People come to Shillong from all over the Northeast and Bengal, drawn to the city by its excellent schools, cool climate, and lively cultural scene. Shillong is also blessed with extraordinary natural surroundings. The area glows with a sense of prosperity and well-being that has yet to draw the throngs of tourists that flock to other hill stations such as Darjeeling or Shimla. Today the Iewduh Market (Bara Bazaar), the biggest in the Northeast, is alive with traditional local color. The city is a good base for walking expeditions through the local hills, and, with a solid infrastructure that you won't find elsewhere in the Northeast, Shillong is a pleasant spot to kick back and refuel.

NORTHEAST INDIA

GETTING THERE AND GETTING AROUND

Flights: The closest **airport** is in Guwahati. **Jais Travels** (☎222777), MG Rd., 100m from the State Bank of India, is connected to the Indian Airlines and Jet Airways reservation terminals. Open daily 10am-5pm. **Sheba Travels** (☎221834), by police point, runs a bus to Guwahati airport (6:30am, Rs125). Open M-Sa 10am-5pm, Su 10am-noon.

Trains: Shillong has no train service, but reservations for trains elsewhere can be made at the booth in the **MTC building** (☎221303). Open daily 8am-3pm.

Buses: Government buses depart from the **MTC bus stand** in Police Bazaar; tickets can be bought at the MTC building. To: **Guwahati** (every hr., 6am-4pm, 4hr., Rs46); **Tura** and **Williamnagar Wildlife Preserve** (5pm, 12hr., Rs180). For **Aizwal** and **Imphal,** go to **Silchar** to make a connection (7am and 7pm, 8hr., Rs134). Government buses also go to **Ranikor;** you can jump off on the way and walk 2km to **Mawsyn.** Frequent **private buses** for Guwahati and Silchar depart from the Polo Ground; make reservations at any travel agency in Police Bazaar. **Sumos** and buses for **Cherrapunjee** depart from Bara Bazaar (6am-4:30pm, 2hr., Rs25). **Capitol Travels** (☎225674) on Jowai Rd., near the cathedral, runs a direct bus to **Agartala** (6pm, 23hr., Rs275).

Local Transportation: Shared taxis, Rs5 per head, barrel through the city streets without even coming to a complete stop to pick up passengers. Taxis can be hired for trips to more remote tourist spots for about twice the local rate.

ORIENTATION AND PRACTICAL INFORMATION

Shillong is a hilly mess. Tiny, nameless roads snake out from around the MTC bus stand in the **Police Bazaar. Guwahati-Shillong (GS) Rd.,** lined with budget hotels, bends westward and eventually leads to **Bara Bazaar,** a web of narrow lanes littered with pineapple tops and animal fat. **MG Rd. (Kacheri Rd.),** winding southeast away from Police Bazaar, fronts many government offices. Along this wide, tree-lined boulevard you'll find the Shillong Club, the State Bank of India, and, at its southern tip, the State Museum. Apart from **Ward Lake,** most of Shillong's natural wonders—waterfalls and parks—are on the outskirts of town.

Tourist Office: Government of India Tourist Office, GS Rd. (☎225632), near Police Bazaar. Open M-F 9:30am-5:30pm, Sa 9:30am-2pm. **Meghalaya Tourist Information** (☎226220), at the bus stand, Police Bazaar, opposite the MTC building. Open M-Sa 7:30am-4:30pm, Su 7:30-11am.

Currency Exchange: State Bank of India, MG Rd. (☎223520), accepts AmEx travelers checks in US$ only. Open M-F 10am-3pm, Sa 10am-noon.

Library: State Central Library, MG Rd., next to the State Museum, is the best in the Northeast. Open M-Sa 11am-5pm. Closed 2nd and 4th Sa.

Bookstore: The Modern Book Depot, GS Rd., next to Broadway Hotel. Open M-Sa 10am-7pm.

Market: The **Bara Bazaar** is an endless maze of market lanes, selling everything from pineapples and star fruit to cow hooves and electronic equipment.

Superintendant of Police, MG Rd. (☎224150), next to the Secretariat, is empowered to deal with foreigners. Open M-Sa 10am-4:30pm.

Pharmacy: Economic Medical Hall (☎224237). Open 24hr.

Hospital: Woodlands Nursing Home, Dhanketi, South Shillong (☎225240 or 224885), is a private hospital with the most up-to-date equipment.

Telephones: Central Telegraph Office, Vivekananda Marg, European Ward (☎226288), opposite the hostel. Free callbacks. Open 7am-midnight; holidays 8am-6pm.

Post Office: GPO (☎222768), opposite Raj Bhavan. Open M-Sa 10am-7pm. **Postal Code:** 793001.

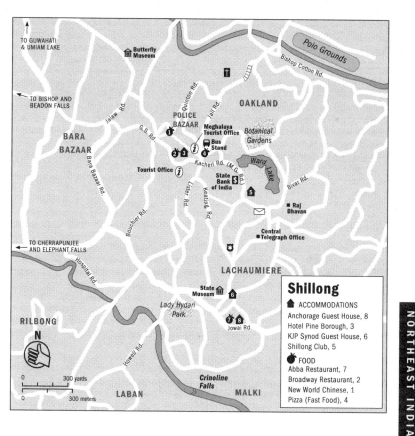

Shillong

▲ ACCOMMODATIONS
Anchorage Guest House, 8
Hotel Pine Borough, 3
KJP Synod Guest House, 6
Shillong Club, 5

🍴 FOOD
Abba Restaurant, 7
Broadway Restaurant, 2
New World Chinese, 1
Pizza (Fast Food), 4

ACCOMMODATIONS

Rooms in the many hotels between GS Rd. and Police Bazaar are uniformly cramped and dark. For space, light, and peace, you are better off hopping into one of the black-yellow cabs and heading out of the jostling heart of the city.

KJP Synod Guest House, MG Rd. (☎228611), opposite the State Museum. Run by a tiny Khasi woman and an army of her nieces. Clean dorm beds in spacious rooms with fireplaces. Breakfast, heater, and buckets of hot water are all standard issue. Hearty Khasi lunches also available. Beds Rs75.

Shillong Club, MG Rd. (☎227497). Recent renovations have returned some of the Club's British-era polish. Each room has a state-of-the-art bathroom, 32-channel TV, a fireplace, and a balcony overlooking Ward Lake. For Rs25, guests get access to billiard tables and the red clay "lawn tennis" court. Singles Rs312-478; doubles Rs565.

Anchorage Guest House, Jowai Rd., near the cathedral (☎225233). Another "Jewel in the Crown" Raj-nostalgia place. Singles Rs350; doubles Rs400.

Hotel Pine Borough, Police Bazaar (☎220698), the best option in the center of town. Small rooms have thick carpets, hot water, and music TV. Popular with Indian tourists, it fills up quickly. Room service 7am-10pm. Singles Rs200; doubles Rs330.

FOOD

Decent Chinese food is available in the Police Bazaar. The stalls along the Bara Bazaar serve the meat- and fish-loaded cuisine particular to the Khasi Hills.

■ **Abba Restaurant,** GS Rd., by the Monsoon Hotel. There is another branch on Jowai Rd., just below the Anchorage Guest House. Authentically Chinese dishes include such wonders as the Mapo-style beancurd from Szechuan. Open daily 10am-7pm.

New World Chinese Restaurant, at the end of the Police Bazaar, has invented some amazing Szechuan/Thai/Korean noodle mixtures. Enjoy these dishes by windows that are among the best places around for watching the town stroll by. Open 10am-7pm.

Pizza (Fast Food), Jail Rd., Police Bazaar, on the right before the bus stand. American food with an Indian twist. Veggie burger (Rs20) is fat, filling, and flavorful. Popular with local teenagers. Open daily 9am-7:30pm.

Broadway Restaurant, GS Rd., in the Broadway Hotel. Delicate curry and tandoori flavors. Mutton curry Rs60; vegetable shish kebab Rs50. Open daily 10am-9:30pm.

SIGHTS

Shillong's wooden colonial houses are scattered over crooked hills and ridges; each hill has its own church and its own identity. Several sights on the outskirts of town make decent half-day excursions. It is also possible to take the MTDC's half-day tour (8:30am-2:30pm, Rs80) around to some of the sights.

SHILLONG PARK. Although hard to reach, Shillong Park is one of the most spectacular of the sights near the city proper. Follow Howell Rd. up through Laban, where it turns into a stone path as it enters a pine wood. The path through the woods takes you up to the **Shillong Observation Point** (1hr.). From here, you can follow the road right through the Northeastern Air Command military installation, past a heavily guarded gate, and through potato fields. **Bara Peak,** the highest point in Meghalaya, is off the road to the left, about 1km after the gate (1-2hr. from Shillong). To get back to town, follow the same road for another 3km through the woods until you hit the Shillong-Cherrapunjee road. Turn left and walk for 600m to the **Elephant Falls.** Buses and jeeps running along this road will give you a lift down to Shillong (6am-7pm, 30min., Rs10).

THE BUTTERFLY MUSEUM. Started by a Mr. Wankhar in the 1930s, the Butterfly Museum, now looked after by his grandson, includes such priceless items as a collection of 30cm-long poisonous stick bugs and the world's heaviest beetle. From the Police Bazaar, take GS Rd. and walk past the Grand Hotel on your right. Take the first soft right onto Umsohsun Rd.; at the fork, go left and follow the curving residential street for 500m. The museum is on the right, though the sign is difficult to see. (☎ 223411. Open M-F 10:30am-4pm, Sa 10:30am-1pm. Rs5.)

OTHER SIGHTS. The "Gleneagles of the East," the **Golf Course** used to be a favorite open-air retreat for homesick Brits in need of a revitalizing bit of rain. Walk down Jail Rd., pass the jail, and continue behind the Polo Grounds. Equipment and caddies are available year-round (Rs200 per 18 holes). Non-golfers can stroll along the course. On a hill to the right, at the end of the course, is the wooden **St. Joseph's Church,** run by Italian priests. Back in the town center is **Ward's Lake.** Couples, families and the occasional loner can rent rusty paddleboats (9:30am-4pm, Rs15 per 20min.) The **State Museum** contains a weird mixture of stones, silkworms, and wax figurines. (Open M-Sa 10am-4pm, closed 2nd and 4th Sa. Free.)

DAYTRIPS FROM SHILLONG

JOWAI

Buses (Rs40) and jeeps (Rs350, or Rs50 per person) leave for Jowai from the private bus stand in Shillong opposite Anjalee Cinema Hall.

Meghalaya is a popular spot for caving, and the town of Jowai, 64km from Shillong, is the home the longest cave in India, the **Krem Um Lawan.** For more information and tours, contact the Meghalaya Adventurers Association (☎243059), near the Synod Complex in the Mission Compound, in Shillong. B.O. Kharpran Daly (General Secretary), c/o Hotel Centre Point, Police Bazaar, Shillong. During July, the Jaintas of Jowai celebrate a festival to stomp out epidemics and pray for a healthy crop by dancing in a pool of muddy water. For more information on festivals in Meghalaya, contact the Shillong branch of the Government of India Tourist Office or the MTDC.

CHERRAPUNJEE

Buses and Sumos leave from the Bara Bazaar in Shillong for Cherrapunjee (7am-5pm, 2hr., Rs25). The last bus from Cherrapunjee to Shillong leaves around 4:30pm. The bus arrives next to the Ramakrishna Mission in Cherrapunjee. The easiest way to reach Cherrapunjee's major attractions is to take the MTDC's tour. Tours depart from the MTDC office in Shillong daily at 8am, as long as at least 15 people sign up. Returns at 4:30pm. Rs100.

Until recently, the town of Cherrapunjee, 56km south of Shillong, held the world record for the most rainfall within a 24-hour period. An unbelievable 104cm of rain fell here on June 16, 1876. The southern ridges of the Khasi Hills are so wet that trees cannot grow here, making it a rare case of a "wet desert." The road that runs up to the left of the Mission High School leads to the **Nohkalikai Falls** 4km away. The path down from the bus stand takes you to the **Welsh Mission**—Cherrapunjee was the site of their first church in the area. The **Circuit House,** 500m farther down to the left off the main road, is the only "hotel" in the area. (Contact the Sub-Divisional Officer next door for reservations. ☎(0927) 35222 or 35326. Rs35 per person in mosquito-netted rooms.)

Two kilometers past the Circuit House, along the main road, is the **Mawsmai Village,** known for its cave and waterfalls. The cave gives you the chance you've always been waiting for—to crawl through a dark 100m-long passageway to the jungle on the other side. If you don't have a flashlight, stalls by the parking lot rent both functioning and broken ones *(Rs10).* The **Nohsngi Thiang** (Seven Sisters) **Falls,** the second highest in India, are a few meters off the main road past Mawsmai Village. They dry up during the winter, and the run-down Orchid Tourist Restaurant nearby won't do much to raise your spirits. Another 10km from here is the **Trop U Rambah,** an enormous rock that Hindus regard as the world's largest Shiva *linga.* Close by, **Thangkhang Park** is a popular picnic spot.

TRIPURA

The tiny state of Tripura is a narrow finger of land poking into Bangladesh. At the southwestern corner of Northeast India, the region is distinct from its neighboring states. The Manikya, the traditional rulers of Tripura, submitted to the Mughal authority, but regained and retained control of the state during the Raj. Tripura was a princely state until 1949, when it joined the Indian Union. Several ethnic groups continue to inhabit the state, but the majority of the population today is Bengali. Tripura has several beautiful forests and wildlife sanctuaries, but expansive development is threatening these precious ecological preserves. Most of the few who visit Tripura are drawn by its cultural attractions, which are all close to one another.

Agartala is the sleepy capital of Tripura. There's not much to do in here—it's really just a small administrative center—but the relaxed pace of life here has been enough to charm some visitors, and a few have been known to stay for weeks. **Buses** connect Agartala with Silchar in Assam. There are also buses that run directly to Guwahati. You can also fly into the city, which is connected to Calcutta and Guwahati. The town is dominated by the **Ujjayant Palace** at its center. This sprawling white structure was built in 1901 by Radhakishore Manikya; it now houses the State Legislature. Go around to the back for the **Tripura Tourist Office**

(☎225930 or 223893). This is the place to make your accommodation inquiries. The staff can also direct you to **currency-exchange** facilities and the Bangladesh **visa** office on Kanjuban Rd. (Open M-Sa 9am-4:30pm.) The fee is between US$5-50, depending on nationality, and is processed within a day. A short **rickshaw** ride will take you to the Bangladeshi town of **Akhoura.** Frequent buses and two trains a day (12:20 and 6:30pm, 2½hr., taka130) leave from here to **Dhaka.** From Dhaka there are frequent buses to Calcutta (taka500).

The famed **Water Palace** at Neermahal is 53km south of Agartala. Built in 1930 as a summer resort for Bir Bikram Kishore Manikya, the palace is an exquisite example of Indo-Saracenic architecture. The red-and-white structure lies in the middle of a large lake. A **tourist lodge** and a few restaurants dot the shore: the area is left blissfully deserted at night. Neermahal is 1km from **Melaghar,** which is connected by **bus** to Agartala (2hr., Rs50).

OTHER STATES

Travel to the states of **Manipur, Mizoram, Nagaland,** and **Arunachal Pradesh** involves huge amounts of red tape, and requires permits, which must be obtained in Delhi. It is threoretically possible to get a permit from the **Minsitry of Home Affairs** in Khan Market (☎4611434. Open M-F 10:30-noon). The officers, here, though, like to direct foreigners to the **Foreigners Registration Office,** 1st Fl., Hansa Bhavan, Tilak Marg, whose employees appear to take great delight in denying any knowledge of the permits, and laugh at the absurd suggestion that they might be able to issue one. **Mizoram** and **Manipur** State Houses are far more approachable. In **Manipur House,** Sardar Patel Marg, Chanakyapuri (☎687 3009. Open M-F 10am-5pm), Mr. Varghese can use his miraculous powers of persuasion to get one-week permits issued within hours (!) to groups of four or more. In **Mizoram House** (☎301 5951. Open M-F 10:30am-4:30), the Resident Commissioner Rajpal Rana is friendly, but less than all-powerful. If you bother him persistently enough, and the gods are on your side, then you might be able to persuade him to issue your permit within 2-3 weeks. The political situation in **Nagaland** is hairy and unpredictable, and permits are impossible to obtain. **Arunachal Pradesh** includes the highly sensitive areas along the borders with China and Burma. Only organized group travel is allowed here. The most in-demand destinations are the Tibetan towns of Bomdila, and Tamang near the border with Bhutan. Mr. Tsering Wange in Bombila can arrange everything from permit and accommodation to a pick-up from Tazpur in Assam for roughly US$90 per day. Write to wange10@hotmail.com a few weeks in advance.

For detailed information on these states, contact the relevant State Houses in Delhi, or the well-stocked Government of India Tourist Office in Guwahati. **Foreigners must obtain the necessary permits in Delhi.**

THE ANDAMAN ISLANDS

अंदमान द्वीपरूसमूह

Beautiful, secluded beaches, rich, green rainforests, mangrove swamps, and pristine marine and bird life—you can find them all in the idyll that is the Andaman Islands, an area only recently opened to tourism and still largely untouched by commerce. The *Ramayana* identifies the brawny monkey-god Hanuman as the first visitor to the islands; he used them as stepping stones on his way to Burma. In later years, the British built a penal colony here to imprison agitators against colonial rule. Since Independence, the Indian government has tempered further efforts to colonize the islands with an anthropological interest in the indigenous inhabitants, but people here have still been forced to watch their land succumb to settlement and deforestation. The Andaman and Nicobar Islands (the latter of which are off-limits to foreigners) are administered directly from Delhi, and the quality of the roads and infrastructure here is far above the Indian average. The population is a mishmash of different ethnic groups from around the subcontinent; Telugu and Bengali speakers are the most numerous. Rising awareness of the importance of the islands' natural wealth has led to increased efforts to make sure that it survives. Open-fire camping was banned in 1999, though this restriction has not always been enforced. Temperatures are about 30°C (86°F) throughout the year. The monsoon lasts from late May-September.

PORT BLAIR पोर्ट ब्लैअर ☎ 03192

Port Blair hasn't changed much since its days as a British penal colony, leaving nothing much to see or do in the capital. As the only thing approaching city-status on the Andamans, Port Blair is the major air and water transportation hub. Anywhere else in India, Port Blair would be considered a pleasant, quiet town, but by Andaman standards, this is about as big, bad, and bustling as it gets. Most people stop here just long enough to secure a permit and book boat tickets out of town.

▐▌ GETTING THERE AND GETTING AROUND

Flights: The **airport** is on Junglighat Rd., on the left past the Government of India Tourism Office. Public buses leave from the bus stand (every 30 min., 5am-8:30pm, Rs3). Taxis to the airport run from downtown (Rs40). **Indian Airlines** (☎ 33108) is across the street from the tourist office. Open M-Sa 9am-1pm and 2-4pm. To: **Calcutta** (Sa-Tu and Th, 8:10am, US$148) and **Madras** (M, W, F, and Su; 8:15am; US$148). **Jet Airways** flies to **Madras** (9:15am, 2hr., US$195).

Ships: Enhance your Andaman experience with a voyage across the Bay of Bengal. Four sailings per month connect the Islands to **Calcutta** (70hr.), three to **Madras** (65hr.), and one to **Vishakapatnam** in Andhra Pradesh (60hr.). Prices are the same for all crossings (bunk Rs1100; 2nd class cabin Rs2700; 1st class cabin Rs3500). It's worth shelling out a bit of extra cash and getting a cabin: rough seas coupled with weak stomachs make the toilet-less bunks an unpleasant place to be cooped up in. The **Directorate of Shipping Services,** in the Phoenix Bay Jetty, sells tickets for Madras four days before departure. The **Shipping Corporation of India** office, in Aberdeen Bazaar, sells tickets for Calcutta and Vishakapatnam three days in advance. (☎ 33590, fax 33778. Open 9am-12:30pm.)

From October to March, tickets sell out within a day. For exact sailing details, consult the tourist office. The ticket booth at the **Phoenix Bay Jetty** (☎32426 or 33690), a 5min. walk north past Lighthouse Cinema, is open 9am-noon. Tickets for in-state destinations are available a day in advance and can also be bought on board for double the price. To: **Diglipur** via **Mayabunder** (Tu, 6am; F, 4pm; 14hr.; Rs70); **Havelock** via **Neil Island** (6 per week, 6:15am, 4hr., Rs16); **Rangat** (Tu, W, F, Sa; 6am) via **Long Island** (W and Sa, 8hr., Rs36); **Ross Island** (Th-Tu, 4 per day, 20min., Rs16). Boats to **Mahatma Gandhi National Marine Park** leave from **Wandoor Jetty,** 30km from the city (Tu-Su, 10am, 24hr., Rs32). The *Daily Telegrams* has up-to-date ship schedule information.

Buses: Government bone-shakers leave from the bus station in Aberdeen Bazaar (☎32278), and private "deluxe" coaches depart from outside the bazaar. Ask the ticket-*wallahs* on the buses for route information. Prices are regular/deluxe. **Mayabunder** via **Rangat** (5-6am, 9hr., Rs70/130). Super deluxe for: **Rangat** (11am and noon, 6hr., Rs130); and **Wandoor** (5:30, 8:30am, 1:40, and 5pm; 1½hr.; Rs10). The ferry connects with the bus in Mayabunder for **Diglipur** (2hr., Rs20). Unlike in the rest of India, buses tend to depart *ahead* of schedule on the Andamans.

Local Transportation: Most distances are walkable, though the terrain is hilly. **Taxis** don't use meters and charge Rs20-50 depending on the distance. **Jagganath Guest House** rents **motorbikes** (Rs120 per day) and **cycles** (Rs35). **TSG Autos,** Aberdeen Bazaar, also rents motorbikes. (☎32894. Rs120 per day, Rs500 deposit; mopeds Rs90.) **Patel Cycle Center,** behind the bus stand, has the best bicycles for hire in town—but still only 1 gear (Rs35 per day). Open M-Sa 8:30am-7pm.

✶🛈 ORIENTATION AND PRACTICAL INFORMATION

Three main roads converge at the **clock tower** in the middle of **Aberdeen Bazaar.** The road uphill and southwest leads to the tourist office and the airport. Downhill to the west is the **main market** area; this road runs past the **bus stand** and turns right to the **Phoenix Bay Jetty.** The level road east leads to **Netaji Stadium,** from where the road curves along the coast for 5km to **Corbyn's Cove.**

Tourist Office: The **A&N Islands Tourism Office** (☎32747 or 32694; fax 30933) is the tall, spiffy-looking building at the top of a hill. Bookings for all government accommodations on the Andamans *must* be made through this office or through the branch at the airport. Open M-F 8:30am-4:45pm, Sa 8:30am-12:30pm.

Permits: For those arriving by air, a 30-day permit issued upon arrival covers all of the Andaman Islands except the indigenous Jarwa reserve and several wildlife sanctuaries (such as Smith Island). The latter require a special permit, issued by the respective Forest Ranger Office. Those arriving by sea should contact the **Deputy Commissioner** (☎33089), next to the ADN Tourism Office. The Nicobar Islands are off-limits to foreigners.

Currency Exchange: The **State Bank of India** is opposite the bus stand. Open M-F 10am-2pm, Sa 10am-noon. **Island Travels** (☎33358), 110m east of the clock tower, is a better bet. Open daily 9am-6:30pm. Off-season: 3-4pm.

Library: Post Office Rd., next to the Telegraph Office. Open M-Sa 12:30-7:45pm. Closed 2nd Sa. There's a decent library upstairs in the **Zonal Anthropological Museum,** but you'll have to convince the head office (on the left, 100m down Junglighat Jetty) that you're a "researcher."

Police: Aberdeen Bazaar (☎33077).

Pharmacy: Devraj Medical Store, Hospital Rd. (☎34344), in the bazaar opposite the stadium. Open daily 8am-1pm and 2-8pm.

Hospital: G.B. Panth Hospital (☎32102) has ambulance service.

Post Office: GPO, Post Office Rd. (☎32226). From the tourist office, go downhill and turn right at the first intersection; the post office is on the right. Open M-Sa 9am-12:30pm and 1-3pm. **Postal Code:** 744101.

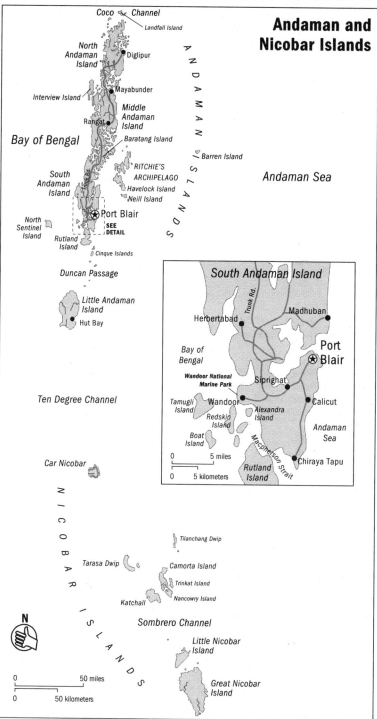

Andaman and Nicobar Islands

Coco Channel
Landfall Island
North Andaman Island
Diglipur
ANDAMAN
Mayabunder
Interview Island
Middle Andaman Island
Rangat
Baratang Island
Barren Island
Bay of Bengal
ISLANDS
RITCHIE'S ARCHIPELAGO
Andaman Sea
South Andaman Island
Havelock Island
Neill Island
North Sentinel Island
Port Blair
SEE DETAIL
Rutland Island
Cinque Islands
Duncan Passage
Little Andaman Island
Hut Bay
Ten Degree Channel

South Andaman Island
Trunk Rd.
Herbertabad
Madhuban
Bay of Bengal
Port Blair
Wandoor National Marine Park
Siprighat
Tamugli Island
Wandoor
Calicut
Redskin Island
Alexandra Island
Andaman Sea
Boat Island
Macpherson Strait
Chiraya Tapu
0   5 miles
0   5 kilometers
Rutland Island

Car Nicobar
NICOBAR
Tilanchang Dwip
Tarasa Dwip
Camorta Island
Trinkat Island
Katchall
Nancowry Island
ISLANDS
Sombrero Channel
N
Little Nicobar Island
Great Nicobar Island
0   50 miles
0   50 kilometers

ANDAMAN ISLANDS

ACCOMMODATIONS

Private guest houses are springing up in the busy parts of town to meet the rising demand. If your confinement to Port Blair is expected to last long, the luxurious government nests are worth a try for their scenic setting and surprisingly good value. **All government accommodation on the islands require prior booking (either in person or via phone) through the tourism office.** All hotels have early-morning check-out policies. There is a 25% discount May-Sept.

Central Lodge (☎ 33632 or 33634). From the tourist office, walk toward the airport, then turn right downhill toward Goalghar. Retired professor R.K. Sharma was inspired by his army barracks to build this ultimate budget guest house. Bare, uncarpeted rooms offer little sensory stimulation, but they are clean and comfortable. Camp on the lawn or in the jungle-like "garden." Often packed in season. Camping Rs20; singles Rs60; doubles Rs90-120.

Teal House (☎ 34060 or 340611), up Moulana Azad Rd., away from the center of town; look for the signs. Sweet-smelling, carpeted rooms with a wonderful hilltop view. Telephones, bamboo furniture, mosquito nets, and big bathrooms with hot showers. Book in advance. Doubles with bath Rs250-400.

Jagganath Guest House, Moulana Azad Rd. (☎ 33140). Well-kept by a kind, thoughtful manager. Rooms have balconies, sometimes-hot showers, bathrooms, and 24hr. water. Free bottles of filtered water. Snorkeling equipment (Rs50 per day), bicycles (Rs35 per day), and motor bikes (Rs120 per day) for rent. Singles Rs200; doubles Rs300.

Hornbill Nest (☎ 33018). From Netaji Stadium, follow the coastal road for 2km toward Corbyn's Cove on the east coast. All by itself amid greenery, the Nest is the only peaceful seaside place to stay in Port Blair. With its open-air, spider-shaped atrium, Hornbill appears to have been teleported straight from of the 1950s. The price you pay is a one-hour trek to the nearest store and STD booth. Dorm Rs75; doubles Rs250.

Atlanta Cottage, on Medical Rd. (☎ 36739), over-looking Netaji stadium and the sea. Meticulously clean rooms—the front ones are light and open to ocean breezes. The back rooms are dark and cramped. Multi-windowed second floor restaurant ensures you won't miss the ocean view, even if your room does. Doubles Rs300-400.

N.K. International, by the Phoenix Bay (☎ 33382). Thirty unremarkable double rooms with 24hr. running water and TV will save you if you get stranded in season without a roof over your head. Rooms Rs400-500.

FOOD

■ **Ananda,** Aberdeen Bazaar, 50m uphill from the clock tower, on the left, opposite the police station. Crabs, prawns, fish, chickens...half the animal population of the islands can be found here, lightly killed and spiced with a thousand seasonings. Chicken Rs65; ice-cold curds Rs10. Open 6am-11pm.

New India Cafe, on the left, 40m before Jagganath Guest House. Frequented by the foreign crowd and globe-trotting Indian sailors, this is the place to go to pick up hand-drawn maps of treasure islands and hear accounts of stormy sailings. Food and music selection are equally cosmopolitan. Fish *thali* Rs20; prawn coconut curry Rs45. Open 6am until the last customer drops.

Mona Jyoti Rubber Stamp Shop and Eatery, 20m down the road from the New India Cafe. One tiny room packed with locals gulping down egg curries and fried fish along with *sambar*-soaked *parathas* and *sabji*-laden rice. Open 6am-11pm.

The Waves, at Corbyn's Cove, across the street from the beach. Lounge around in plastic chairs in front of the ocean at this two-story bar and restaurant. Snacks Rs5-12; prawn *pakora* Rs55; beer Rs65. Open daily 6am-10pm.

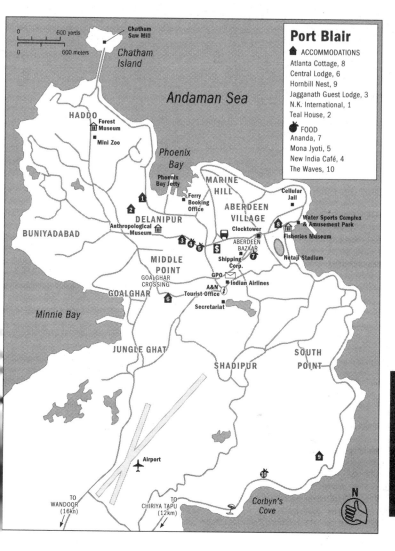

Port Blair

🏠 ACCOMMODATIONS
Atlanta Cottage, 8
Central Lodge, 6
Hornbill Nest, 9
Jagganath Guest Lodge, 3
N.K. International, 1
Teal House, 2

🍎 FOOD
Ananda, 7
Mona Jyoti, 5
New India Café, 4
The Waves, 10

ANDAMAN ISLANDS

👁 SIGHTS

CELLULAR JAIL AND MUSEUM. Believing that rebel activists were less of a threat if they couldn't rile up fellow prisoners on the mainland, British colonial authorities used the Andamans to isolate and imprison unruly natives. The Cellular Jail, where many early freedom fighers once languished, has transformed into a monument to India's struggle for independence. The museum's two ground-floor galleries chart the history of the prison and document the broad base of Indian resistance to colonialism. One room upstairs is devoted to the life and work of Subhash Chandra Bose, who was imprisoned here. *(From the clock tower, go down toward the ocean. Bear left and head uphill. ☎ 30117. Jail open daily 9am-5pm; museum open Tu-Su 9am-noon and 2-5pm. Sound and light show Tu-Su 7:15pm, weather permitting.)*

OTHER SIGHTS. The **Zonal Anthropological Museum** is one of the few places where you can find photos and information on the islands' indigenous peoples. *(Open Tu-Su 9:30am-12:30pm and 1-4pm.)* Don't expect too much, though. A better bet for getting information about the indigenous cultures of the Andaman and Nicobar Islands would be to attend one of the Tourism Department's **free documentary screenings.** *(M-F 5:30pm; M and Th at the Teal House, W and F at the Megapode Nest, and Tu at the Hornbill Nest.)* A 15-minute bike ride along the coast from the Netaji Stadium leads to **Corbyn's Cove,** a white sand beach surrounded by green palms—a good place to get in the mood for the stupendous beauty of the rest of the Andamans. *(From the clock tower, go west, turn right, and follow the road along the coastline.)* The **Water Sports Complex and Amusement Park** offers evening fun. *(Open M-Sa 4pm-8pm, Su 8am-noon and 2-8pm.)*

NEAR PORT BLAIR

SOUTH ANDAMAN ISLAND. On the northeastern side of South Andaman island, **Ross Island** was once the center of operations for the British penal colony. The ruins are a great (and surreal) place to wander around for the day. **Ferries** leave from Phoenix Bay Jetty (Tu-Th 8:30, 10am, 12:30, and 2pm; 2hr.; Rs15). The last ferry back to Port Blair leaves at 5:30pm. **Viper Island,** like Ross Island, is dominated by the hauntingly overgrown ruins of the British penal project. You can reach Viper on the general **Harbour Cruise,** which leaves daily from Phoenix Bay Jetty (Th-Tu 3pm, 2hr., Rs25). **Chiriya Tapu** is a fishing village at the south end of South Andaman, 30km from Port Blair. The road winds through countryside and jungle until it reaches mangroves and wooded mountains that rise from the sea. Most people come on a day trip from Port Blair to the Mundapahar beach and wildlife area, 2km past the village. But decent accommodation overlooking the islands in the bay is available in the air-conditioned rooms (Rs200) of the **Forest Department Guest House,** provided you obtain the permission of the Chief Wildlife Warden, Van Sadan, Haddo, Port Blair. (☎ 33549. Open M-F 8:30am-4:30pm.) The area is excellent for snorkeling; hire a motorboat in Chiriya Tapu to take you to the coral. Be sure to bring equipment from Port Blair.

MAHATMA GANDHI NATIONAL MARINE PARK. The Mahatma Gandhi National Marine Park is probably what Jacques Cousteau would dream about in his sleep. A fantastic kaleidoscope of living coral, the marine park is also home to all kinds of wildly colored marine life including angel fish, clown fish, starfish, butterfly fish, parrot fish, sea anemones, and shark. From the Port Blair bus stand, the 8:30am bus to Wandoor connects with the 10am boat to either Jolly Buoy or Red Skin Island (Rs60). A park permit costs Rs15 and snorkel equipment rental is Rs50, but equipment gets scarce during season—you should bring your own or rent from it from a Port Blair hotel. Although glass-bottomed boats are available for undersea sight-seeing, you might prefer to go solo. Coral and shell collecting is forbidden. Bharat Hotel, a shack 50m from the boat dock, rents snorkels and serves excellent fish curry (Rs8) and *chappatis* (Rs2). You can also rent one of its tiny rooms for Rs50-80. The road here leads a few kilometers past the boat dock to a beautiful beach with drift-logs perfect for setting up a tarp. Beer (Rs65) and basic food can be had at the government-run restaurant a few yards away.

RITCHIE'S ARCHIPELAGO

Havelock Island is the most popular tourist getaway on Ritchie's Archipelago. **Neil Island, Long Island,** and **North Passage** are also open for overnight stays. Ships from Phoenix Bay Jetty stop at Neil Island (3-4 per week, 6:15am, Rs8) and Long Island (2 per week, 6:15am, Rs13).

HAVELOCK ISLAND

Havelock Island has white sand, white sand, more white sand, and an occasional dolphin leaping up out of the sapphire blue water. Much of the island is jungle, but the northern part has been cleared, to make way for a few villages surrounded by coconut, banana, and mango plantations. No special permits are required to stay on Havelock Island; your Andaman permit suffices.

GETTING THERE AND GETTING AROUND. Ferries leaving Port Blair (6 per week, 6:15am, 4hr., Rs16) arrive at the **jetty** (also known as Govindanagar or Village #1). **Boats** leave Port Blair for Havelock Island from the Phoenix Bay Jetty (3-4 per week, 6:15am, 4hr., Rs16) and return from Havelock the next day. It's a bumpy ride, so have motion sickness pills handy. Once you arrive, a government bus will shuttle you to your accommodation. Ferries from Havelock sail to **Port Blair** (10:30am) and **Rangat** (Tu, W, F, Sa; 11:30am). Check with the guards on the dock for exact timings and to find out if the ship stops at Long or Neil Islands. An unpredictable **bus** chugs between the jetty and Beach #7. Your best bet is to hire a **bicycle** (Rs50 per day) or **moped** (Rs150 per day) at your guest house or at **Krishna Tours** (☎82457), in the jetty market. For gas, ask at the shops in Village #3.

ORIENTATION AND PRACTICAL INFORMATION. The jetty acts as the island's main **bazaar.** There are several restaurants here and even a **post office** (open M-F 10am-5pm). A metal-topped road extends 3km to the romantically named **Village #3,** referred to as "the capital" by islanders. This heaving metropolis has the only **STD/ISD** booth on Havelock. In #3, the road forks 2km to the left and leads to **Beach #5,** spoiled only by a government lodge. The road to the right winds for another 11km to reach **Village** (and Beach) **#7,** on the edge of the jungle.

ACCOMMODATIONS AND FOOD. Over the last five years, increasing numbers of visitors have been coming here, making Havelock the most popular spot in the Andamans. Guest houses have sprung up to meet the demand. Most of the best places to eat and sleep are around the jetty, just a peanut's throw from the dock. The ban on camping is strictly enforced on Havelock. ▓ **Jungle Lodge,** hidden in the jungle off the stunningly beautiful Beach #7, is managed by a Port Blair native who returned from Switzerland to become a local pioneer in eco-awareness when he heard that the islands had been opened to tourism. Simple straw huts come with breakfast and dinner (Rs600) and 40% of profit goes into island development projects. Jeep transportation to and from the jetty is complimentary. During the monsoon, volunteers are welcome to plant trees in exchange for room and board. Reservations can be made through **Travel World** (☎37656; fax 37657), in Port Blair. A few other places are usually available on a walk-in basis. **Sea View Tourist Complex** takes its name seriously; it's a mere 10m roll from your bed to the edge of the sea. (☎82367. Doubles with attached bath Rs150-250.) **M.S. Lodge,** 100m farther along the coast, has spacious doubles with 24-hour showers. The straw huts have mattresses and mosquito nets. (☎82439. Huts Rs50 per person; rooms Rs300.) **Gongrongo Lodge** is 2km from the jetty, under banana trees and coconut palms, just before Village #3. A narrow strip of beach is just 50m away. (Bare doubles Rs200; 4-bed dorm with shared toilet and bucket shower Rs70.) **Tent Resorts** is a government-run accommodation available on Beaches #5 and 7. (Double-bed Rs300, with food Rs500.) **Dolphin Yatri Ninas** is another government place on Beach #5 (☎82411. Doubles with showers Rs300-800.) Both government hotels must be booked through the tourist office in Port Blair. ▓**Anjana Restaurant** in the jetty bazaar does ginger prawns (Rs45) and garlic crabs (Rs50) as well as fish curry and *paratha* for Rs15. (Open 6am-1:30pm and 4-9:30pm.)

SNORKELING. The best place for snorkeling is **Elephant Beach.** Take the road toward Beach #7 until you pass a school. Leave your bike by the road and turn left onto the path through the woods. A 45-minute walk leads to the coral. To go farther afield, you will have to arrange a *dungee* with your hotel manager. In season, you can rent diving gear from the **Jungle Lodge** (see above) for Rs2200 per day, including boat, or take a 5-day diving course for Rs14,000. The **Gongrongo Lodge** also rents snorkeling equipment (Rs50) as well as bicycles (Rs50) and mopeds (Rs150, Rs500 deposit).

INDIGENOUS PEOPLES OF THE ANDAMAN
AND NICOBAR ISLANDS Outside of the bustle of Port Blair,

the Andaman Islands seem beautifully and peacefully underpopulated. But there is a sizable (though still precariously small) indigenous population here, and their recent history has been far from peaceful. Troubles began with the British penal colony established on Viper Island. Western diseases, deforestation, and armed skirmishes (spears vs. rifles) initiated a decimation of the Andaman and Nicobar indigenous populations that began to level off only in the 1980s. By then, the entire Andamanese population, which has now been relegated to Strait Island, had been reduced to just 28 survivors. With the exception of the Nicobarese, who have fared better by "integrating" themselves in government development programs, other indigenous groups have suffered declines of similar magnitude.

Since Independence, the Indian government, in shifting its policy from colonize-or-bust to colonize-with-scientific-curiosity, has set aside indigenous reserves. Still, quite understandably, some indigenous groups have opted for zero communication with the bungling invaders. The Sentinelese of North Sentinel Island (64km southwest of Port Blair) have been a target of government anthropological excursions since 1967. Government boats would pull up to the island, leave gifts of plastic buckets, roasted pigs, and sacks of coconuts in an attempt to establish contact. The Sentinelese would take the gifts—and then fire arrows at the anthropologists. The Jarawa, who occupy much of the busier Middle Andaman, have had a more contentious time resisting, and many have been shot while trying to deter poachers and loggers (in one case by chopping off the offenders' hands). Buses plying Trunk Rd., which runs directly through "reserve" land, now carry armed guards—an arrow or two still occasionally crashes through the windows. For more information on the Andaman and Nicobar indigenous peoples, see the exhibits at the Zonal Anthropological Museum (see p. 710).

NEIL ISLAND

Neil Island is, esentially, a miniature version of Havelock. The **Shanti Guest House** has doubles with private balconies and common bathrooms for Rs150. In the government-run **Hanabill Nest** (☎82630), doubles with shower and air-conditioning are Rs400. Dorms are Rs75. Camping is still a viable option on Neil, although Long Island is a better choice for the wilderness experience.

MIDDLE ANDAMAN

RANGAT AND MAYABUNDER

Rangat and Mayabunder are merely transit points on the way to the wild north, but there are a few decent beaches nearby. **Ships** sail from Rangat to **Port Blair** via **Havelock** (W, Th, Sa, Su; Rs16), stopping at Neil and Long Islands (Th, Su). **Buses** run to: **Port Blair** (4 per day; 7am-noon; 6hr.; Rs60, deluxe Rs130) and **Mayabunder** (5:30am-5pm, 3hr., Rs16). Rangat Bay is 8km from the town itself; minibuses run back and forth. **Hotel Avis**, on Church Rd., has tiny rooms with snow-white sheets and showers. (☎74554. Singles Rs70; doubles Rs120.) **Hawksbill Nest** is on the beach, 15km from Rangat on the road to Mayabunder. (Dorm Rs75; doubles Rs250.)

MAYABUNDER

Mayabunder is useful for its ferry to **Kalighat** on North Andaman (8am and 2:30pm, 2hr., Rs20). From Kalighat, a bus connects to **Diglipur** (30min., Rs3). Once a month, a Calcutta-bound steamer pulls into the Mayabunder port. Tickets can be purchased in the office at the jetty—if you're lucky, you can avoid the hassles of Port Blair. Buses run to **Port Blair** (7-10am, 9hr., Rs70-130) and **Rangat** (5:30am-5pm, 3hr., Rs16). The town's pride—Karmatang Beach—is 7km from town. The **Swiflet Nest** is the local government's bid to bring you bliss. (Dorms Rs75; doubles Rs250.)

The **P.W.D. Guest House** is the only option if you get stranded in the town. (Rs75 per person). **Pharmacies, post offices,** and **STD** phones are available in Mayabunder.

NORTH ANDAMAN

North Andaman is the most isolated as well as the most spectacular of the main islands, with the mist-veiled Saddle Peak (2431ft.) towering over deep jungles and a coastline dotted with hundreds of unexplored off-shore islands.

▣ GETTING THERE AND GETTING AROUND. Ships sail for **Port Blair** (W 6am, Sa 4pm; 14hr.; Rs70). Tickets can be bought either from the Tehsil office in the Diglipur Bazaar (open M-F 9-11am) or aboard ship, for double the price. The bus to **Kalighat** (3am, 1hr., Rs6) connects with the 5am ferry to Mayabunder, which is greeted by a fleet of Port Blair-bound buses. The only other ferry leaves at noon, and gets you into Mayabunder too late to catch anything going any farther than Rangat. **Buses** also run to **Diglipur** (9am-8pm, 30min., Rs3) and **Kalipur** (6 per day, 6:30am-5:30pm; last bus returning at 6pm; 30min.; Rs2).

▣▣ ORIENTATION AND PRACTICAL INFORMATION. Aerial Bay, the fishing village that acts as Diglipur's port, is a merciful 12km from the busy town and is an ideal base from which to explore. In the **bazaar** at Aerial Bay, you will find just about everything you could need for life in the jungle: mosquito nets, plastic sheets, strings, kerosene, pots, rice, Beatles wigs, and a 24-hour **STD booth** to get in touch with the outside world. The **Forest Range Office** in Aerial Bay grants permits for Smith Island, Ross Isalnd, and a few other islands, upon presentation of your passport, an Andaman permit, and the Rs10 fee (open M-Sa 6am-2pm). The nearest doctor and **pharmacies** to treat your malaria and snake bites are in Diglipur.

▣▣ ACCOMMODATIONS AND FOOD. The two doubles in the wooden **P.W.D. Guest House,** set on top of a hill overlooking the bay, are fit for Elvis himself (Rs150). If they are full, the noisy rooms above the shops down in the bazaar will disappoint even the hardiest of the hard core (Rs100). **Mohan Hotel,** on the way to the jetty, serves good versions of the staple *paratha* and fish curry.

▣ ISLANDS. Across the bay from the dock are **Smith** and **Ross Islands,** connected to a flawless stretch of sand and empty of permanent inhabitants, except for one drunken forest ranger. Coral reefs and long stretches of white sand have made this the ultimate dream of any nature-loving camper; millions of crabs crawl straight from the sea into the depths of the jungle. The growing number of visitors has, however, started to concern environmentalists in the Andamans, and it is uncertain how long the administration will allow free camping to continue.

As of 2000, the F.R.O. in Aerial Bay is granting permits to stay on **Smith Island.** You can ask at any house in Aerial Bay for a *dungee* to Smith (1hr., Rs150). There is a water spring on the island, but all food and shelter needs to be brought with you. Smith is one of the last places on earth where you can camp in pristine tropical jungle. Remember to take all your trash with you when you leave, burn your toilet paper (or better still, do without it entirely—it's such a dirty habit, anyway). Jackals and wild dogs hunt through the night, so don't expect anything you leave out overnight to be there when you wake up in the morning.

Twelve kilometers from Aerial Bay, in the shadow of Saddle Peak, **Kalipur** has a passable beach and miles of walks along the craggy shore. For those less inclined to play Tarzan or Jane in the jungle, the government-run **Turtle Resort** features hot-shower luxury, balconies, and Swiss Alps posters. (☎72553. Dorms Rs75; doubles Rs250.) An impatient bus streaks between Kalipur and Diglipur during the day. Alternatively, the 3-hour walk back to Aerial Bay takes you through Bengali villages and banana and mango plantations.

ANDAMAN ISLANDS

NEPAL नेपाल

GEOGRAPHY

Nepal has some of the most dramatic mountain terrain in the world. The massive Himalayan mountain range was thrust up out of the ocean 50 million years ago when India collided with the rest of the Asian land mass. Today, Nepal is nearly 75% mountain, and it contains eight of the world's 10 highest peaks. And they just keep on getting bigger—tectonic plate movements means that the mountains continue to grow at the rate of several centimeters per year.

At the northernmost reach of the Indo-Gangetic Plain, the relatively flat **Terai** is fertile, low-lying (200m), hot, and humid. This whole area was once covered in dense stretches of malarial forest that supported only wild animals and hungry mosquitoes, but recent years have seen vast deforestation, and today it is the hub of Nepal's growing population. Jutting out from the Terai to altitudes of over 1500m, the forested **Chure Hills** run parallel to the 3000m Mahabharat Range farther north. Between the Chure and the Mahabarat Hills are the broad basins of the **Inner Terai,** cut by the deep, north-south river gorges of Nepal's three biggest rivers—the Karnali, the Narayani, and the Kosi. At altitudes of 500 to 2000m, the **Pahar** region, north of the Mahabarat, is marked by flat, fertile valleys, including the Kathmandu, Banepa, and Pokhara Valleys. This region has been inhabited and cultivated longer than anywhere else in Nepal. Over 40% of the population lives in this region today.

The mighty **Himalayas** are inhabited only in scattered pockets. Human settlements are sparse after about 4000m. Nepal's plant life thins out as altitudes increase, with the dense timber forests yielding to alpine pastures of spruce, birch, rhododendron, which stretch to the snowline. Beyond 4900m, nothing but mountains grow. Ten mountains in Nepal are higher than 8000m, including **Mount Everest** (8848m), the highest point on earth. North of the peaks is the high desert plateau of the **Trans-Himalaya.**

The Terai is inhabited by tigers, leopards, *gaur* (wild oxen), elephants, and several species of deer. The Rapti Valley is one of the last refuges of the endangered Indian rhinoceros. The Himalayas are also home to the fantastically rare and surprisingly docile **yeti** *(Homo nivosus abominabilis)*, of four-toed footprint fame.

PEOPLE AND LANGUAGE

Nepal is home to approximately 24 million people, representing more than 60 ethnic, linguistic, and caste groups. The country's cultural variety is largely the result of its rugged and often impassable terrain, which has kept different areas isolated from one another. While the many cultures of Nepal have ancient roots in the land, the country itself is a young one. Until a couple of hundred years ago, a "Nepali" was somebody from the Kathmandu Valley, and it is still normal for people to identify themselves by the region that they come from: as *pahari, madeshi,* or *bhotia* (hills, plains, or northern-border dwellers), rather than as Nepalis.

Nepal is a nation of villages, and about 90% of the population lives in small market towns and rural settlements. Settlement is thickest in the fertile Terai, Nepal's bread-basket and a booming industrial region. Up in the highlands and the Trans-Himalayan valleys, less than 1% of land is under cultivation, and these areas remain sparsely populated, with most people leading a nomadic lifestyle.

The official language is **Nepali,** also called Gorkhali. The mother tongue of 50% of the population, Nepali is understood by nearly everyone. As a descendent of Sanskrit, like the languages of North India, it uses the Devanagari script. (For basic Nepali vocabulary, see the **Phrasebook,** p. 830.)

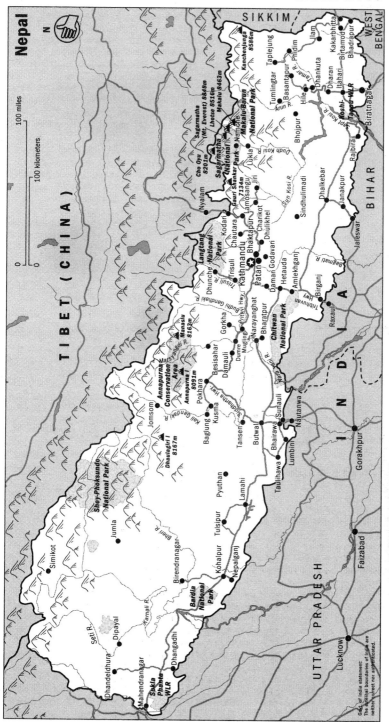

Nepal

N

100 miles

100 kilometers

SIKKIM

WEST BENGAL

TIBET (CHINA)

Kanchenjunga 8586m

Ilam

Kakarbhitta

Phidim

Birtamod

Bhadrapur

Taplejung

Tumlingtar

Basantapur

Dhankuta

Dharan

Itahari

Koshi-Tappu WLR

Biratnagar

Cho Oyu 8201m

Sagarmatha (Mt. Everest) 8848m

Lhotse 8516m

Makalu 8463m

Makalu-Barun National Park

Namche

Arun R.

Bhojpur

Hile

Nyalam

Gauri Shankar 7134m

Sagarmatha National Park

Lukla

Jiri

Lamosangu

Dudh Kosi R.

Sun Kosi R.

Sindhulimadi

BIHAR

Dhalkebar

Rajbira

Kodari

Chautara

Bhaktapur

Charikot

Dhulikhel

Langtang National Park

Dhunche

Tatopani

Trisuli

KATHMANDU

Patan

Daman

Godavari

Hetauda

Amlekhganj

Bagmati R.

Janakpur

Jaleswar

Budhi Gandaki R.

Prithvi Hwy

Gorkha

Narayanghat

Bharatpur

Chitwan National Park

Birganj

Raxaul

INDIA

Tribhuvan Hwy

Manaslu 8163m

Mars Yandi R.

Mugling

Dumre

Annapurna Conservation Area

Annapurna I 8091m

Besisahar

Damauli

Pokhara

Kali Gandaki R.

Kusma

Jomsom

Baglung

Siddhartha Hwy

Tansen

Butwal

Bhairawa

Sunauli

Nautanwa

Dhaulagiri I 8167m

Shey-Phoksundo National Park

Pyuthan

Lamahi

Taulihawa

Lumbini

Gorakhpur

Simikot

Jumla

Bheri R.

Tulsipur

Kohalpur

Nepalganj

Bardia National Park

Karnali R.

Birendranagar

Faizabad

UTTAR PRADESH

Dhandeldhura

Dipayal

Seti R.

Karnali R.

Dhangadhi

Lucknow

Mahendranagar

Sukla Phanta WLR

NEPAL

Most Nepalis are Hindus of Indo-Aryan ancestry, though Buddhist influence is also strong. The **Newari** people, the earliest known arrivals in Nepal and the original settlers of the Kathmandu Valley, practice a religion made up of a mixture of Buddhism and Hinduism. The Newari language is Tibetan in origin, although it uses the Devanagari script and takes half of its vocabulary from Sanskrit. Only 4% of the total population today, the Newari have produced some of Nepal's most celebrated art. The Eastern hills are inhabited by **Rais, Limbus,** and **Sunwars,** and the Terai is populated by **Tharus, Yadavas, Safars, Rajvanshis,** and **Dhimlas,** who speak dialects of Hindi such as Bhojpuri and Maithili. In west-central Nepal, the **Gurungs** and **Magars** are also thought to be among Nepal's earliest inhabitants.

Recent large-scale migrations from Tibet have brought Tibeto-Burmese languages and Tibetan Buddhist culture to Nepal. Today, 45% of the population claims Tibeto-Burmese descent. The Tibeto-Burmese settled mostly in the higher altitudes of the north, where Buddhist culture still predominates. Among the most recent immigrants from Tibet are the **Tamangs,** the most populous of Tibeto-Burmese ethnic groups, and the **Sherpas.** Tibetan refugees continue to seek asylum in Nepal, and the use of Tibetan, a Sanskrit-based script, is not uncommon. English is also spoken quite widely, and it's not hard to get around knowing nothing more than "*namaste*," a Sanskrit term meaning "I salute the God in you."

GOVERNMENT AND POLITICS

Nepal became a constitutional monarchy with a parliamentary system of government on November 9, 1990. The power of the sovereign, a position held since 1972 by **King Birendra Bir Bikram Shah,** is limited, and real power is in the hands of the prime minister (currently **Krishna Prasad Bhattarai**), chosen by a the 205-member House of Representatives. Members are elected by universal suffrage for a term of five years. An upper house, the 60-seat National Assembly, is made up of both appointed and elected members.

The main political parties in Nepal are the moderate Nepali Congress (NC), the Communist Party of Nepal-United Marxist-Leninist (CPN-UML), and the right-wing National Democratic Party (NDP). Also on the scene is the Nepal Sadhbhavana Party (NSP), a regionalist party from the Terai.

ECONOMICS

With 90% of its population depending on subsistence farming, Nepal is one of the poorest countries in the world. Hillsides are used for terrace farming, but landslides and erosion make it difficult to cultivate crops. In the more fertile Terai, where farming is potentially more lucrative, high population growth makes even subsistence farming difficult. Many people's hopes for the future hinge on the hydroelectric potential of Nepal's raging rivers, but development stands at odds with the bankable tourist appeal of pristine valleys for rafting and hiking. Meanwhile, roads are expensive to build and maintain, and the Indian border is the only easily negotiable channel of trade. Heavy industry is concentrated in the Terai, and most manufactured goods and machinery have to be imported from India.

Nepal's biggest source of foreign exchange is the export of wool and international aid. Foreign assistance over the past four decades has been a mixed blessing. Aid donors have made many mistakes—development programs unsuited to the region, uneven distribution of aid, corrupt and unregulated rural NGOs (nongovernmental organizations), and assistance given in return for political favors. Environmentalists wonder whether industrial "development" is a good idea at all in a country that has until now managed to maintained its way of life without any need for floods of consumer goods.

HISTORY

Despite everything that it has borrowed from its neighbors, Nepal has a history and a culture that are as unique and diverse as the land itself. Nepal's closeness to India has led to Indian influence in the Terai, while the central hills and mountain valleys, including Kathmandu, have tended toward independence but not isolation. Deep in the heart of the mountains, life has always gone on without much outside influence at all.

ORIGINS AND EARLY DYNASTIES (200,000 BC–1200 AD)

Nepal's early history is shrouded in myth and mystery. Stone Age settlers are thought to have arrived around 200,000 BC, and written references to the region appear as early as the first millennium BC. The **Kiratis,** a Mongoloid people who migrated into Nepal during the 8th century BC, were the first known rulers of the Kathmandu Valley. Small kingdoms began to develop in the Terai region around 500 BC in response to the growth of powerful Aryan kingdoms to the south. **Siddhartha Gautama,** the man who would become the Buddha, was born into one of these early tribal confederations, the Sakya clan, during the 6th century BC. Three centuries later, the Indian Buddhist emperor **Ashoka** came on a pilgrimage to the Buddha's birthplace, and built one of his famous pillars in **Lumbini** (see p. 785). The region was greatly influenced by the culture of the mighty Mauryan empire, both politically and culturally (see p. 64).

Buddhism spread throughout Nepal during Ashoka's lifetime, and the concept of the king as upholder of *dharma*, borrowed from the Mauryas, began to play a major role in Nepal. Early kingdoms found it hard enough just to guard their own borders and control their own land, and none of them ever expanded very far. Most of what is known of Nepal's early history comes from the Kathmandu Valley, the historical heartland of Nepal and the source of its most distinctive culture.

During the 4th and 5th centuries AD, the **Licchavis** arrived from the Indian plains and overthrew the Kirati kings. They brought Hinduism and the caste system to Nepal, and began the tradition of Hindu upper classes ruling over mostly Buddhist masses. Under the Licchavis, the Kathmandu Valley enjoyed an era of economic and artistic growth, which continued despite the wars and poor administration that characterized the reign of the **Thakuris,** who rose to power in the 9th century.

MALLA KINGDOMS (1200–1742)

A new dynasty emerged in the Kathmandu Valley in 1200, when the **Mallas** came to power. Despite shaky beginnings, they ushered in a golden era in Kathmandu Valley culture and ruled for over 500 years. After the death of Yaksha Malla, the greatest of the Malla kings, in 1482, the kingdom he had ruled from Bhaktapur was split among his three children. Kathmandu, Patan, and Bhaktapur developed into rival city-states. Despite constant feuding over trade with Tibet, all three kingdoms reached new heights in art and culture—the great wood-screened temples and the many cobbled **Durbar Squares** of the valley date from this time.

UNIFICATION AND THE SHAH DYNASTY (1742–1816)

It all began with the small hill-state of Gorkha, 50km west of Kathmandu. Gorkha was ruled by the **Shahs,** the most ambitious of the many immigrant Rajput clans that had come to Nepal between the 14th and 16th centuries, driven out of India by Muslim invaders. In 1742 King Prithvi Narayan Shah ascended to the throne of Gorkha, and within two years he set out to conquer Nepal's richest region, the

NEPAL

Kathmandu Valley. After 25 years of war and attrition, the three cities of Kathmandu, Patan, and Bhaktapur surrendered. When Prithvi Narayan Shah invaded Kathmandu, King Jaya Prakash Malla asked the British East India Company for help, but to no avail. The victorious Shah became the founder of the modern nation of Nepal, and his Gorkha army proceeded to conquer the eastern Terai and hills. Prithvi Narayan closed the doors of his new nation to the outside world, a policy that would keep Nepal isolated until the 1950s. Calling his kingdom a "garden of many flowers," he respected the country's institutions and rewarded his officials according to their merit. Prithvi Narayan's kingdom began to deteriorate soon after his death in 1775, however, as the monarchy passed from one infant Shah to another, and members of the nobility battled one another to act as regent.

Eventually the shrewd chief minister **Bhim Sen Thapa** took control, and he found that he could unite Nepal by launching a war against the west, annexing Garwhal and Kumaon (now part of Uttar Pradesh) and Himachal Pradesh, in modern India. But the government mishandled its new lands and soon found itself in trouble with foreign powers. From 1788-92 it fought a war with Tibet and China, and in 1814 its expansion into the Terai provoked the hostility of the East India Company.

The Anglo-Nepalese War was not the easy victory the British expected. In spite of superior numbers and weaponry, the British were beaten back again and again by the Nepalese soldiers, who held their hilltop forts and charged at the redcoats with *khukuri* knives. It was two years before the British were able to break through and finally defeat Nepal in 1816. The **Treaty of Segauli** stripped Nepal of Himachal Pradesh, Garhwal, Kumaon, and much of the Terai, fixing the eastern and western borders of the country where they remain today. The prospect of another insurrection encouraged the British to adopt a more sensitive stance toward Nepal; it survived as one of the few countries in Asia that was never colonized. Eventually, the British Army would begin to recruit Nepalese soldiers for its new **Gorkha** (or Gurkha) regiments.

STAGNATION AND COUP D'ETAT (1816-46)

Prime Minister Bhim Sen Thapa kept the country stable by strengthening the army, but chaos ensued when he fell from grace in 1837, and various palace factions struggled for power. On September 14, 1846, a powerful minister was murdered, and the queen assembled the entire royal court in an attempt to discover the culprit. The personal guards of **General Jung Bahadur,** cabinet minister for the army, surrounded the court and opened fire, killing 32 of Kathmandu's most powerful nobles. Over the next few hours, Jung Bahadur and the queen came to a secret agreement, and the general was appointed prime minister.

THE RANA REGIME (1846-1951)

Jung Bahadur took the title of **Rana,** and under this name his family would keep an iron hold on Nepal for 105 years, amid countless family feuds and outrageous nepotism. Jung Bahadur eventually stripped the king, Rajendra, of his last few vestiges of power, taking total control for himself. After visiting London in 1850, Jung Bahadur kicked off a series of reforms designed to drag Nepal into the modern world. He began to bureaucratize the government—he did away with patronage and started to keep track on who was spending what and why. Land tenure was registered, and landlords could no longer arbitrarily evict tenants from their land. In 1856, Jung Bahadur gave himself the title of Super-Minister and promoted himself to the position of "Maharaja of Kaski and Lamjung," which gave him the right to overrule the king. The title was made hereditary, and the Shah kings became mere figureheads.

The Indian **Mutiny of 1857** provided an opportunity for Nepal to flex its muscles and win British support. Jung Bahadur sent 10,000 men to aid the British. In return, the British gave back the Terai lands they had taken in 1816. The British gave Nepal "guidance" on its foreign policy, but Nepal remained independent, scoffing at British demands for trading rights and keeping strict tabs on Gorkha recruitment. The Rana prime ministers, however, proved to be more interested in advancing their family fortunes than in helping their country. When Jung Bahadur Rana died in 1877, his successors turned out to be just as venal as he had been and a whole lot less competent.

Chandra Shamsher Rana, who ruled from 1901-29, was a better administrator than most, but his motivation—social conscience or rampant egotism—is still the subject of controversy. He began his reign by building the enormous Singha Durbar palace for himself and his hangers-on. This one project alone was enough to swallow the whole of the national public works budget for the first three years of his rule. During WWI, Chandra Shamsher began to implement changes to appease the 100,000 Nepalese Gorkha soldiers who had fought overseas and had returned home with all kinds of new ideas in their heads. The introduction of a transportation system and a whole range of social reforms, such as the banning of slavery and *sati*, were among the first of the changes. Nepal's first college, was founded, and tenant farmers were made the owners of the lands they had rented for centuries. The Treaty of Friendship with Britain formally recognized Nepal's independence in 1923. Fewer trade restrictions, however, made Nepal more economically dependent on imported British and Japanese goods. Prime Minister Judha Shamsher Rana (r.1932-45) returned Nepal to military rule, and dissatisfaction with Rana rule became ever more widespread.

Indian Independence in 1947 gave Nepal a new neighbor to deal with, and Indian Prime Minister Jawaharlal Nehru disapproved of the Rana regime. In 1947 the **Nepali Congress** was formed, in the tradition of the Congress that had led India to freedom. Several renegade members of the Rana family who favored democratization fled to India and joined the growing anti-Rana resistance. The turning point came in 1950 when **King Tribhuvan,** a palace figurehead since 1911, also fled to India. By this time, he had captured popular support. The king, the prime minister, and Congress leaders met in Delhi, where Nehru engineered the **Delhi Compromise of 1951,** effectively bringing the Rana regime to an end.

NEPAL AFTER THE RANAS (1951–1990)

After the Ranas' defeat, Nepal's foreign policies underwent a dramatic change for the better. The Delhi Compromise was replaced in 1959 by a new constitution that called for a democratically elected assembly. The Nepali Congress won a large majority in the elections, and its leader, **B.P. Koirala,** became prime minister. But the state of affairs was fragile. King Tribhuvan had died in 1955, and his son **Mahendra,** was less enthusiastic about political reforms, believing that Nepal wasn't developed enough to handle them. He dismissed the Congress government almost as soon as it took power, throwing its leaders in jail. In 1962, a new constitution replaced the national assembly with a system of *panchayats* (village councils) to elect members to district councils, which, in turn, elected a National Panchayat. Political parties were banned, and the new system, supposedly a "special" kind of democracy uniquely suited to Nepalese traditions, effectively marked a return to absolute monarchy. Mahendra opened Nepal to foreign aid and set in motion the controversial process of development that cntinues to transform Nepal today.

King Birendra, who came to power in 1972 (although for astrological reasons he wasn't crowned until 1975), was a committed supporter of the *panchayat* system. Early in his career Birendra declared Nepal a "Zone of Peace" (a declaration of neutrality that angered India) and tightened visa restrictions for foreigners. The *panchayat* system continued to provoke dissent, however, and resistance came to a head in 1979 with riots in Kathmandu and Patan. In response, Birendra called for a national referendum to decide between the *panchayat* system and multiparty democracy. The *panchayats* won by a 10 percent margin, and the monarchy hung on another decade, kept in place by massive censorship and police brutality.

DEMOCRACY RESTORED (1990-PRESENT)

Inspired by the previous years' revolutions in Eastern Europe and provoked by an economic blockade imposed by India, the outlawed opposition parties banded together in 1990, and pro-democracy demonstrations filled the streets of Kathmandu. When the king realized that mass arrests would not quell the uprising, he gave in and lifted the ban on political parties on April 8. A week later the major parties formed an interim government and wrote a new constitution. A parliamentary democracy came into effect, with Birendra as constitutional monarch.

Elections gave a majority to the Nepali Congress, which had led the democracy movement. The **Communist Party of Nepal-United Marxist-Leninist (CPN-UML)** became the main opposition. The new prime minister was **G.P. Koirala,** brother of the late B.P. Koirala. Rising inflation gave rise to general discontent (again), and an agreement with India over the Mahakali Dam project on Nepal's western frontier brought accusations of selling out to India. Unimaginative and stubborn, Koirala alienated many in his own party and was forced to resign in 1994.

The elections that followed brought the Communists to power in a minority government. Prime Minister **Man Mohan Adhikari** launched a series of populist schemes, including the "build-your-own-village" program, which gave large cash grants to local governments. Adhikari then resigned, hoping to gain a parliamentary majority for his government through another election. The king approved Adhikari's call for elections, but the Supreme Court ruled against the maneuver. No elections were held, and the Congress party took power by allying itself with the right-wing **National Democratic Party (NDP).**

New Congress Prime Minister **Sher Bahadur Deuba's** efforts to bolster ties with the NDP were waylaid by intra-party dissent, and a March 1997 no-confidence motion brought the government down. The breakaway NDP faction led by **Lokendra Bahadur Chand** formed a coalition government with the CPN-UML, pushing Nepal into a new era of instability. In 1998, guerillas from the Communist Party of Nepal-Maoist turned violent and killed several NGO workers, alleging that they had mishandled funds. The assassination of an opposition party member of parliament brought strikes and rioting. When **Girija Prasad Koirala** refused to allow elections in December, the king dissolved parliament. In the May 1999 elections, the Nepali Congress won 110 seats to the Communist Party's 68. The Congress Party candidate in the Kathmandu district, **Krishna Prasad Bhattarai,** is the current prime minister. The country's Maoist insurgency is now in its 6th year, and continues to gain support. More than 1,300 people have lost their lives in violence related to the struggle to overthrow the monarchy and set up a Communist government.

RELIGION

Nepal's religious diversity reflects its position at the cultural crossroads between India and Tibet. Nepal is about 90% Hindu and 5% Buddhist, with small Muslim, Christian, and Jain minorities. A defining characteristic of life in Nepal, however, is its unique breed of mix-and-match religious syncretism. Although Nepal is the only country in the world with Hinduism as an official state religion, most Nepalis follow some combination of Hinduism and Buddhism, with plenty of local traditions thrown in for good measure. Asked if they are Hindu or Buddhist, many Nepalis will reply that they "don't know," or that they're "both." That people can at once follow a religion of 33 million gods and one that originally recognized no gods at all baffles many visitors, but it seems to work nonetheless.

In general, the northern regions close to the border with Tibet tend to be Buddhist, while the lands closer to India are Hindu. The areas in between (including the Kathmandu Valley) have the most complex blend of the two.

HINDUISM

Hinduism first came to the Kathmandu Valley with the Licchavi dynasty during the 4th and 5th centuries AD. Introduced to the hills by conquerors, it has long been Nepal's religion of status—**brahmins** (the priestly caste) and **chhetris** (the Nepalese warrior caste) have traditionally been at the top of the social hierarchy. Various legal reforms long ago tried to force lower-class Buddhists into an occupational caste system; this social practice still survives, though few Buddhists recognize the legitimacy of the caste system.

Shiva is the most popular Hindu god in Nepal; he is a fitting lord for this mountainous land, since he began his career as a Himalayan wanderer. He commonly appears in Nepal as Bhairava or "Bhairab," a ghoulish figure who chases away demons, though he is also the compassionate Mahadev, worshiped out of love and devotion. In his form as Pashupatinath, the benevolent Lord of Animals, Shiva is Nepal's patron deity, and Nepal is often referred to as Pashupatinath Bhumi (Land of Pashupatinath). The temple of Pashupatinath near Kathmandu is the most important Hindu site in Nepal (see p. 746).

Vishnu, the cosmic "preserver," is also popular. In Nepal he is often called Narayan, a name that comes from his role in the Hindu creation myth—he sleeps on the cosmic ocean while the creator god, Brahma, sprouts from his navel. Goddesses are also worshiped, and Nepal's grandest festival, **Dasain,** is held in honor of **Durga.** Nepal also holds a special place for **Annapurna,** goddess of abundance and distributor of food. Each goddess is an individual in her own right, but the goddesses are also important as the consorts of the male deities, embodying the female aspect *(shakti)* of each god. In the Nepalese religious tantras, this *shakti* is considered the most powerful and active force in the cosmos. (For a (slightly) more detailed introduction to **Hinduism,** see p. 76.)

BUDDHISM

The Buddha was born during the 6th century BC in Lumbini, within the borders of modern Nepal. Although he left Lumbini as a young man, and did most of his traveling and teaching farther south in India, his doctrines eventually returned to the land of his birth, spreading deep into the mountains.

Most Nepali Buddhists follow the **Mahayana** (Great Vehicle) school, which differs from the older **Theravada** (Way of the Elders) school. Mahayana Buddhism, with its doctrine of salvation for all, developed in India during the 1st century AD and came to predominate in Tibet, China, Japan, and other parts of East Asia. The more orthodox Theravada school persisted in Sri Lanka and most of Southeast Asia. While Buddhism in India was subsumed by Hinduism, a particularly Indian-influenced Mahayana Buddhism survived in Nepal, where it is still practiced today.

Mahayana Buddhism initially developed after a disagreement over monastic law *(vinaya)* in Buddhist communities. The Mahayana doctrines put less emphasis on the individual quest for nirvana, stressing instead the need for compassion for all beings. The Buddha was more than just a wise teacher and holy man in the Mahayana tradition—he is a cosmic being with magical powers and countless incarnations. The concept of a bodhisattva, who vows to put off his own enlightenment for the sake of saving all sentient beings, is very important in the Mahayana tradition, and a number of bodhisattvas are worshiped alongside the Buddha. (For a more detailed introduction to **Buddhism,** see p. 65.)

TIBETAN BUDDHISM

In Tibet, a unique form of Buddhism developed when the Mahayana and Vajrayana (Thunderbolt Vehicle) traditions blended with the indigenous religion, Bon (see p. 683). Although Buddhism was originally brought to Tibet via Nepal, Tibetan traditions exerted a greater influence on the religion as it is practiced in Nepal than the other way around. As a result of the Chinese occupation of

NEPAL

Tibet, many Tibetan Buddhists have immigrated to Nepal, bringing prayer wheels and prayer flags blowing the mantra *Om Mani Padme Hum* ("Hail to the jewel in the lotus") all across Nepal's mountains and hills. Tibetan Buddhism divides the Buddha's nature into five "aspects," reflected in each of the five elements (earth, water, air, fire, and space). It is also noted for its monastic tradition—before the Chinese take-over, 25% of all Tibetans belonged to some kind of religious order. Of the 6000 Tibetan monasteries in existence at the time of the occupation, only five remain. **Tibetan monasteries** are headed by teachers called lamas, addressed by the title *rimpoche* (precious one). Lamas are believed to have cultivated wisdom over many lifetimes, transmitting their knowledge to each reincarnation. The reincarnated lama is identified by using astrology, consulting the Tibetan oracle, and having the young candidates identify the former lama's possessions.

TANTRA

Tantra holds that polar opposites are merely two different manifestations of the same consciousness, and that the true nature of the mind can be realized by transcending opposites. Acts that are typically condemned, such as the consumption of meat fish, and alcohol are prescribed as ways of transcending dualities. Tantric rituals also involve the harnessing and release of different energies in the body through sexual intercourse.

Tantra has much in common with the Hindu traditions of *shakti* and yoga. Between the 7th and the 9th centuries, tantra became popular throughout India as part of both Hinduism and Buddhism, and its influence can still be seen today in Tibetan Buddhism, though it died out in India long ago. Some aspects of Tibetan Buddhism can be classified as **Vajrayana** (Thunderbolt Vehicle), a separate sect from the Mahayana and Theravada schools. Vajrayana inherited much of its symbology from the tradition of tantra—the major symbols of Vajrayana are the *vajra* or *dorje* (thunderbolt) and the *ghanti* (bell), meant to represent the male element of compassion and the female element of wisdom, respectively. The conscious release of bodily energy, achieved by meditation upon goddess figures, is also prominent. Vajrayana couples the *dhyani* Buddhas and the major bodhisattvas with *taras*, female consorts of great power and strength. These figures are often depicted in sexual intercourse, symbolic of the reconciliation of dual energies.

INDIGENOUS TRADITIONS

Nepal has its own pantheon of indigenous gods, and most people worship these local heroes, quite regardless of any other religion they might follow. Common in the Kathmandu Valley is the worship of the **Kumari,** a young girl recognized as an incarnation of the Hindu goddess Durga. The living goddess stays secluded in a palace for her entire childhood until she reaches puberty, at which point she reverts to the status of a mortal (see **The Living Goddess: Kumari,** p. 740). The Newaris also worship **Macchendranath,** a god born of a fish and identified both with Lokesvara, Shiva's form as "Lord of the World," and with the Bodhisattva of Compassion, Avalokitesvara. Macchendranath's towering chariot makes his festivals distinctive highlights of the religious calendar. The Newari craftsmen of the Kathmandu Valley have also turned **Bhima** (or Bhimsen), the hero of the *Mahabharata* epic, into their patron deity. Also prominent in the valley is **Manjushri,** the valley's creator god, associated with Saraswati, the Hindu goddess of learning.

Outside the Kathmandu Valley, different ethnic groups preserve many of their local beliefs despite the widespread acceptance of Buddhism and Hinduism. The local gods are worshiped in return for good harvests and healthy children, and animal sacrifices to the gods are common. Many of Nepal's local religions are led by shamans, who mediate between the human and supernatural worlds.

CLIMB (ALMOST) EVERY MOUNTAIN Since large-scale mountaineering began in the Himalayas during the 1950s, many climbers have come close enough to see the summits and have then returned to the bottom without actually standing on top, in deference to the deities and sacred powers that live there. Hindus believe mythical Mt. Meru to be the center of the universe and the axis of all power. Mt. Kailash in Tibet is Shiva's stomping ground, and the Gauri-Shankar and Annapurna mountains in Nepal are both named after gods. Most of the Himalayan peaks, including those with more mundane names—such as Macchapuchare, which means "fish tail," and Kanchenjunga, which means "five treasures"—are considered sacred. In fact, the Himalayan range itself is said to be the father of Shiva's consort, Parvati. Soaring to heights of over 8000m, the Nepalese Himalayas contain eight of the world's top 10 highest peaks. It's not difficult to understand how they came to be seen as the abode of the gods.

THE ARTS

The Nepalese artistic tradition emerges from the synthesis of different regional styles. Absorbing elements of Indian and Tibetan aesthetics, the Newari artisans of the Kathmandu Valley developed a distinct style and sensibility. Many older works, made mostly of wood, disappeared long ago, but many of the valley's masterpieces still remain in their original settings. Nepalese art has generally been inspired by religion, funded by kings, and executed by anonymous craftsmen.

Thanks to the boost in tourism, just about anything made in Nepal can be bought in Kathmandu, but many handicrafts are cheaper and available in a better and wider selection in their place of origin. For woodcarving and pottery, head to Bhaktapur; for papier-mâché masks and puppets, go to Thimi; for metalwork, Patan; and for Tibetan crafts like *thankas*, the best place to go is Boudha.

THE VISUAL ARTS

ARCHITECTURE

The oldest remaining structures in the Kathmandu Valley are **stupas,** sacred mounds of earth layered with centuries of plaster. They are large hemispherical domes, usually marking Buddhist holy places or enclosing sacred relics. Nepalese stupas, typified by the amazing Boudha Stupa (see p. 755) in the Kathmandu Valley, display distinctive symbols on the square, golden spire at their top. These **chakus** are usually painted with the Buddha's eyes surveying the four cardinal directions and a number one (?) to represent universal unity. Stupas are often accompanied by **chaityas,** small stone shrines holding written mantras or scripture.

The greatest architectural achievements of the Kathmandu Valley, though, are its wood and brick **pagodas,** many of which resemble elaborate *chakus*; it is possible that they evolved from this earlier architectural form. Nepal is considered the birthplace of the pagoda—a 13th-century architect named Arniko is said to have exported the pagoda to Kublai Khan's Mongolia, from where it later spread to the rest of Asia. Most of Nepal's pagodas are Hindu temples, built around a central sanctum housing the temple's deity. The sanctum is made of brick, with intricately carved wooden doors, window frames, and pillars. The pillars and struts on the outside support the tiered, sloping, clay-tiled roof. The upper portions of the temple are not separate stories as they might appear; they are left empty since there is to be nothing above the deity except the roof and the heavens. The whole structure usually sits on a terraced stone base resembling a step pyramid.

NEPAL

The Newaris also planned and built **bahals**, blocks of rooms surrounding a rectangular courtyard. These compact community units were used either as monasteries or as blocks of houses. *Bahals* are designed to be perfectly symmetrical, and the main doors and windows usually appear along the group's central axis.

Despite their xenophobic foreign policy, the Rana prime ministers, who reigned from 1846 to 1951, embraced a European neoclassical style of architecture for the buildings they put up as part of their various modernization drives. Parts of Kathmandu's Durbar Square would not look out of place in Trafalgar Square. Modern architecture in Nepal is mainly utilitarian, using brick and concrete block.

SCULPTURE

Early work in the Kathmandu Valley was influenced by North Indian styles of stone sculpture. Newari artisans of the Licchavi period made devotional images of Vishnu and the Buddha that strongly resembled the work of the Mathura school. Written accounts indicate that wood sculpture also flourished at this time, though none has survived.

Stone sculpture in Nepal reached its height from the 7th to 9th centuries and virtually disappeared after the 10th. Metal became the medium of choice for medieval Nepalese sculpture, again as a result of Indian influence. During the 17th and 18th centuries, the dominant influence was Tibetan. Newari artisans made bronze images of tantric aspects of the Buddha, which were exported to Tibetan monasteries—many "Tibetan" bronze sculptures were actually made in Nepal. Nepalese artists of the Malla period also created fantastic wood sculptures as architectural ornaments. Temple roof struts and window grilles were made of wood ornately carved with plant and animal forms.

Over the last two centuries, the crafts of bronze-casting and wood-carving have declined somewhat because of a lack of patronage. Foreign-funded restoration projects have recently given sculptors some business, and the demand created by tourism has encouraged the mass production of consumer-oriented crafts.

PAINTING

The earliest paintings to have survived in the Kathmandu Valley were painted onto palm leaf manuscripts. A few examples have survived from as far back as the 10th century, but most are badly decayed. More common in Nepal today are Tibetan *thankas* (intricate scroll-paintings of deities) and *mandalas* (circles symbolizing the universe in Hindu and Buddhist art). During the medieval period, a distinctive Newari style of *thanka* developed, called a *paubha*. These were painted on coarser cloth and without the landscape background of a traditional Tibetan *thanka*. Later paintings in Nepal were heavily influenced by the detailed miniatures of the Indian Mughal and Rajasthani styles.

MUSIC

Music in Nepal is a part of everyday life. The **gaine,** a caste of musician-storytellers, once wandered the hills, accompanying themselves on the *sarangi* (a four-stringed fiddle). Music of a traditional *panchai baja* (five-instrument) ensemble is often played for weddings, processions, and rituals. The women of most Indo-Nepalese castes are usually excluded from music-making, though they are allowed to sing in public during rice-planting and at the *teej*, an annual women's festival.

Several traditional styles of hill music still exist. Most popular is the *maadal*-based (double-sided drum held horizontally) *jhyaure* music of the western hills. The Jyapu farming caste developed an upbeat rhythmical style that uses numerous percussion instruments, including the *dhime* (a large two-sided drum) woodwinds to accompany nasal singing. The *selo* style, developed by the Tamangs but shared by others, keeps rhythm with the *damphu* (a flat one-sided drum).

Music is vital to Hindu and Buddhist ritual. In traditional Newari communities, most young men complete a musical apprenticeship that enables them to participate in festival processions. Newari Buddhist priests chant ancient tantric verses as part of meditation exercises, and, on sacred occasions, ritual dancing accompanies these hymns. The music of the Sherpas derives much of its character from the ancient rituals of Tibetan Buddhism.

The continued presence and influence of Indian classical music in Nepal is a relic of the days when it was all the rage at the court of the Malla kings. The Rana prime ministers were such fervent patrons of Indian classical musicians that they banned Nepalese folk performers from their courts altogether.

DANCE

Nepalese dance, in both folk and classical styles, is usually based on the dramatic retelling of sacred Buddhist and Hindu stories. The Newaris of the Kathmandu Valley are the chief exponents of **classical dance**. Newari performers enter a trance and become vessels possessed by the spirit of the deity. They gyrate and gesture and generally put on quite a show, dressed in elaborate costumes and ornately painted papier-mâché masks. On the tenth day of the Dasain festival (in Sept. or Oct.), the *nawa* dancers of Bhaktapur perform the vigorous dance-drama of the goddess Durga's victory over the buffalo demon.

Tibetan Buddhism also engages music, dance, and dramatic forms in festivals, ceremonies, and sacred rites. Performances often involve intricate hand gestures, ritual objects, and the contributions of many unusual and symbolic musical instruments. **Cham** is a dance-drama specific to Tibetans and Bhotiyas, in which monks don masks and costumes to enact various Buddhist tales.

FOOD AND DRINK

Dal bhat tarkari (lentils, rice, and curried vegetables) is the staple dish for most Nepalis, as it is for people in large parts of North India. Indeed, *bhat*, the word for cooked rice, is often used as a synonym for *khana* (food). Food in Nepal differs little from Indian food, with the exception of a few Tibetan dishes that have made their way onto many Nepalese menus and dining tables. Ravioli-like **momo** and **thukpa**, a soup made with noodles, are popular dishes. Newari food is based largely on buffalo meat, which is commonly served instead of beef. **Choyala** is buffalo fried with spices and vegetables.

The most popular breads in Nepal are **chappati**, identical to the ones you see in India. Most Nepalis don't really eat breakfast, but it is commonly served in tourist restaurants and hotels. Vegetarians are well looked after, and they will probably have a better time with the food than meat-loving tourists.

Milk, or **dudh**, is an important staple of the Nepalese diet, and is often served hot, making it safe to drink. **Chiya** (tea) is served hot with milk and lots of sugar. Yogurt *(dahi)* forms the base for **lassis** and for the Newari delicacy **juju,** made from yogurt, cardamom, and cinnamon. Most sweets, including **barfi** and **peda**, are milk-based.

Alcohol is drunk in Nepal primarily in the form of beer and *chang*, a homemade Himalayan brew. *Raksi* is a stronger version of *chang* that bears a resemblance to tequila in both taste and potency. *Tong-ba* is a Tibetan brew made from fermented millet and sipped through a straw.

FURTHER SOURCES

GENERAL

Culture Shock! Nepal, by Jon Burbank (1992). A guide to Nepali customs and etiquette especially aimed at those planning to live and work in Nepal. Advice for all sorts of social situations and business hassles.

Nepal: Profile of a Himalayan Kingdom, by Leo E. Rose and John T. Scholz (1980). Covers the history, politics, culture, and economics of Nepal. Very sensibly written, though somewhat out of date.

TRAVEL AND CULTURE

Life and Death on Mt. Everest, by Sherry B. Ortner (1999). An exploration of the world of the Sherpas and their mountaineering culture.

Into Thin Air: A Personal Account of the Mount Everest Disaster, by Jon Krakauer (1998). Intimate and thought-provoking first-hand account of the highly publicized May 1996 Everest expeditions, in which 12 lives were lost.

Trekking in the Nepal Himalaya, by Stan Armington (1997). The most comprehensive trekking guidebook available. It includes maps, day-by-day descriptions, and altitude charts for the most popular treks.

Trekking in Nepal, by Stephen Bezrucha (1997). Detailed route descriptions and a comprehensive section on planning and health concerns. Especially rich in historical, cultural, and biological commentary on Nepal's trekking routes.

The Snow Leopard, by Peter Mathiessen (1978). Travelogue interspersed with contemplations of the existential variety. Sold everywhere in Nepal, *The Snow Leopard* sums up a lot of the soul-searching and nature-gazing that draw tourists to Nepal.

HISTORY AND POLITICS

Nepal: Growth of a Nation, by Ludwig Stiller (1993). An account of the period from the unification of Nepal until 1950. One of the few histories of Nepal that doesn't slobber all over the Shah dynasty.

Politics in Nepal: 1980-1990, by Rishikesh Shah (1990). Once banned by the government (always a good sign), these essays look at Nepal's more recent political history.

RELIGION

Short Description of Gods, Goddesses, and Ritual Objects of Buddhism and Hinduism in Nepal. Published by the Handicraft Association of Nepal, this short but comprehensive book includes illustrations and is a valuable (and portable) reference. Available in Kathmandu bookstores (Rs80-100).

The Festivals of Nepal, by Mary M. Anderson (1988). A month-by-month description of the legends and practices surrounding Nepal's major festivals; you'll be in the right place at the right time.

LITERATURE

Himalayan Voices: An Introduction to Modern Nepali Literature, by Michael Hutt (1991). The best of a limited number of English translations of Nepali poetry and prose.

Nepali Visions, Nepali Dreams: The Poetry of Laxmiprasad Davkota, translated by David Rubin (1980). A good introduction to Nepal's most prominent modern poet.

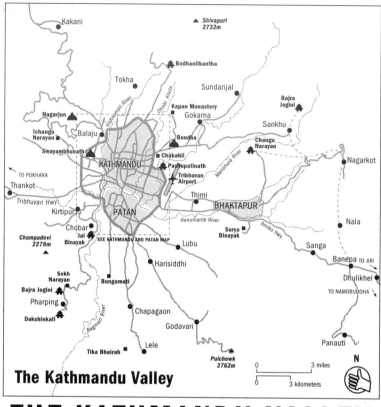

The Kathmandu Valley

THE KATHMANDU VALLEY

A great stretch of flatness surrounded by mountains, the Kathmandu Valley is the heart of Nepal and the focal point of any visit. Though many travelers stay only long enough to get ready for a trek, the Kathmandu Valley is home to no fewer than seven UNESCO World Heritage Sites, all set against a backdrop of green hills and the awe-inspiring peaks of the Himalayas. Before Prithvi Narayan Shah's unifying conquest in 1768, Kathmandu, Patan, and Bhaktapur were individual city-states that vied for control of the valley. Today, each one retains traces of its days as a tiny kingdom—a Durbar (Palace) Square filled with towering temples and the unrivaled metalwork of the indigenous Newari people, among South Asia's foremost artisans. Between the cities, set amid lush farmland, are surprisingly urban red-brick towns with tightly packed, multi-storied houses. The valley's hilltops have quite amazing views and a pollution-free quiet and calm, a million miles away from the city commotion just a bus stop away. A network of trails winds through the hills, offering countless opportunities for short treks and bike rides. It only takes a few days to see the valley's most popular sights, but those with the time and inclination to explore a little will be richly rewarded.

HIGHLIGHTS OF THE KATHMANDU VALLEY

Most cities in Nepal have a Durbar Square, but **Patan's** (p. 761), with its temples, palaces, and pavilions, sets the standard by which all others are judged.

Bhaktapur's cobbled streets and restored temples (p. 758) are a window into valley life before backpackers and brownie sundaes arrived.

A visit to the monumental stupa at **Boudha** (p. 755) provides a glimpse into Tibetan Buddhism in Nepal.

KATHMANDU काठमाण्डौं

☎ 01

A half century after Nepal opened its borders to the world, Kathmandu has become a hippie haven, a mecca for trekkers, and a thriving cosmopolitan cultural center. As Nepal's largest city, Kathmandu has a gravity that pulls together tourists, sadhus, Tibetan refugees, and work-seeking Nepalis. For all its world heritage sites, this bustling city is no fossil, nor is it just another anonymous South Asian metropolis. The indigenous Newari culture and centuries of turbulent history have left Kathmandu with an unmistakably Nepali fingerprint.

Founded as Manju-Patan around AD 723, Kathmandu was not always the valley's pre-eminent city. In Malla days, when it was known as Kantipur, it stood on a level with Patan and Bhaktapur, though it was more successful than the others at controlling trade with Tibet. Prithvi Narayan Shah made Kathmandu his capital when he unified Nepal in the 18th century, and it has dominated the valley ever since. Bursting into the new millennium as the fast-growing capital of a desperately poor country, present-day Kathmandu bears both the scars and the trophies of rapid economic growth. The latter includes an array of imported goods, arts, institutions, diplomatic missions and foreign aid agencies, and, of course, planeloads of tourists. But in spite of all this and the optimism inspired by the 1990 movement for democracy, Kathmandu faces plenty of problems. The city suffers from oppressive pollution, a chronic shortage of resources, and a crippling lack of infrastructure, as its government languishes under corrupt politicians.

For the tourist, Kathmandu is a fascinating city where pagodas crowd the traffic into narrow cobbled lanes and neighborhood boys kick soccer balls around dusty stone shrines. Myth and history mingle at every corner—glazed-over, time-worn shrines stand alongside ancient shops. Of course, not everything in Kathmandu is remote or mysterious; there's plenty of dust here too, as well as rancid trash and faceless concrete. But it's all part of a unique package.

◤ GETTING THERE AND AWAY

INTERNATIONAL AND DOMESTIC FLIGHTS

If you're flying into Kathmandu from the east, try to sit on the right side of the plane to get a good view of the mountains. Flights land at **Tribhuvan International Airport,** 5km east of the center of town. Planes are small, seats are limited, and facilities are so basic that even slightly bad weather can delay flights. Bring a book. As you leave the airport, you will find yourself at the left edge of a large parking lot; to get to the bus stop, walk to the far right and follow the downhill road through the huge archway to Ring Rd., where you'll wait for a bus heading to your left. **Bus #1** goes to **Ratna Park** (frequent, 30min., Rs4), but not all buses are numbered and not all buses heading this way go to Ratna Park, **so be sure to ask the driver or conductor.** Alternatively, **pre-paid taxis** (to Thamel Rs200; Freak St. Rs250) can be arranged at a counter just before the airport exit or at a booth outside.

Visas are issued upon arrival to anybody with a passport, photograph, and hard currency (payable only in US dollars). For more information, see **Visas: Nepal,** p. 10. There is a **departure tax** of Rs660 to South Asian countries and Rs1100 to others. **RNAC** and **Indian Airlines** fly to **India.** International flights to: **Bombay** (Th and Sa, 4pm, 2hr., US$257); **Calcutta** (Th and Su, 1:30pm, 40min., US$96); **Delhi** (8am and 6pm, 1hr., US$142); **Varanasi** (Su, Tu, and Th; 3pm; 55min.; US$71). If you're under 30, RNAC will give you a 25% discount on tickets to India bought in Kathmandu.

Fares on domestic flights are virtually identical across airlines. **RNAC,** Kantipath (☎220757), at New Rd. Open daily 9am-1pm and 2-5pm. **Necon Air,** Sinamangal (☎473860; fax 471679). Open Su-F 9am-5pm. To: **Bhadrapur** (12:50pm, 1½hr., US$109); **Bhairawa** (2:50pm, 1hr., US$79); **Bharatpur** (Tu, Th, and Su; noon; 30min.; US$50); **Biratnagar** (8:50am, 1:30, and 4pm; 1hr.; US$85); **Janakpur** (Su and Tu, 12:50pm, 1hr., US$61); **Jomsom** (4 per day, 55min., US$101); **Lukla** (in-season 1-15 per day, 40min., US$83); **Nepalganj** (10:10am, 2hr., US$109); **Pokhara** (8:30, 11:10am, and 3:10pm; 40min.; US$61). Mountain-viewing flights from Kathmandu cost US$99.

BUSES

The cheapest way into town is by **bus.** To get to Thamel from Ratna Park, turn right after leaving the bus park, walk north along Durbar Marg all the way to the end, turn left and walk three long blocks. The walk takes 20 minutes without heavy luggage. Most buses to destinations outside the Kathmandu Valley leave from the **New Bus Park,** Ring Rd., in Balaju. Almost all city buses make a stop at the New Bus Park. Bus #23 from Ratna Park takes one of the most direct routes; it also stops along Kantipath, north of Rani Pokhari (every 5min., 5am-8pm, 30min., Rs3-6). You can also take a taxi (Rs58 from Thamel, Rs65 from New Rd.). The departure bays are not labeled in English, but the staff of the 24-hour "Police Room" will direct you to the right counter; most of the ticket vendors speak English.

There are no express or deluxe distinctions here, and even tourist buses sometimes pick up locals along the way. Most buses that leave after noon are night buses—for these you should book 1-2 days in advance in season. Unless otherwise noted, prices are for morning/night buses.

PRIVATE BUSES. To: **Bhairawa** (every hr., 5am-8pm, 8hr., Rs150/198); **Birganj** (every hr., 5am-8pm, 8hr., Rs120/165); **Dharan** (5am and 3:30pm, 12hr., Rs275/321); **Gorkha** (every hr., 5am-2pm, 6hr., Rs95); **Ilam** (2pm, 20hr., Rs460); **Janakpur** (6am, 6, 7, and 7:30pm; 11hr.; Rs160/226); **Kakarbhitta** (5am and 3-6pm, 16hr., Rs330/365); **Lumbini** (6am and 7pm, 10hr., Rs165/220); **Pokhara** (frequent, 5am-8:30pm, 7-8hr., Rs105/144); **Tansen** (6am and 4:30pm, 11hr., Rs180/240); **Tardi Bazaar** (frequent, 7:45am-1:45pm, 7hr., Rs90) for **Sauraha**.

GOVERNMENT BUSES. Sajha, the government bus corporation, runs mostly day buses; reserve 2 days in advance. Sajha buses are slightly cheaper and faster than other buses. To: **Bhairawa** (7:15am and 7pm, 8hr., Rs135/168); **Birganj** (8 and 8:30am, 8hr., Rs130); **Gorkha** (6:30 and 7:45am, 5hr., Rs70); **Janakpur** (6:30am, 10hr., Rs179); **Lumbini** (6:45am, 9hr., Rs158); **Narayanghat** (8am and noon, 4hr., Rs77); **Pokhara** (7:30am and 7pm, 7hr., Rs105/120); and **Tansen** (7:30am, 10hr., Rs148).

TOURIST BUSES. Tourist buses are slightly more expensive minibuses, with clear aisles and comfortable seats. Tickets for tourist buses to **Chitwan, Pokhara,** and **Nagarkot** can also be booked through travel agencies in Thamel. Fares include a commission, but the stops are much more conveniently located on Kantipath at the intersection with Tridevi Marg. **Greenline Buses** (☎ 253885 or 257544), at the corner of Tridevi Marg and Kantipath, has A/C coaches to **Pokhara** (8am, 7hr., Rs600) and **Chitwan** (8am, 5½hr., Rs480), with breakfast included. Tickets should be bought one day in advance (AmEx, MC, Visa).

▛ GETTING AROUND

LOCAL BUSES

By far the cheapest means of getting around the Kathmandu Valley, the bus ensures that you rub shoulders with locals—just when you thought another wailing child couldn't possibly squeeze in, five more people and seven roosters climb on board. Despite their appearance, Kathmandu buses do work; many are even painted with route numbers these days. **Always confirm that the bus is going to your destination.** The valley bus station is known as **Ratna Park** (named for the park across the street); Nepalis also call it *purano* (old) bus park. Bus #7 (to Bhaktapur) leaves from **Bagh Bazaar,** one block north of Ratna Park. Buses generally leave as soon as they're full.

#	DESTINATION	LENGTH	COST
1	Tibhuvan Airport	40min.	Rs4
2	Boudha (Boudhanath)	40min.	Rs4
2	Pashupatinath	30min.	Rs4
4	Sankhu	2hr.	Rs10
5	Budhanilkantha	1hr.	Rs6
7	Bhaktapur	45min.	Rs8
9	Old Thimi	30min.	Rs5
9	Bahaka Bazaar	1hr.	Rs6

#	DESTINATION	LENGTH	COST
12	Dhulikhel	2hr.	Rs17
14	Jawlakhel and Lagankhel	20min.	Rs4
19	Swayambhu	45min.	Rs4
21	Kirtipur	1hr.	Rs4
22	Dakshinkali	1½hr.	Rs13
23	New Bus Park	30min.	Rs3
23	Balaju	30min.	Rs3
26	Patan	30min.	Rs4

TROLLEYBUSES

Haggard, Chinese-built electric trolleybuses creak between Kathmandu and Bhaktapur (frequent, 45min., Rs6). The first stop is on **Tripureswar Marg,** just south of the National Stadium. Trolleybuses tend to be less crowded than buses, and they are a far more pleasant (and environmentally friendly) ride.

TAXIS AND RICKSHAWS

Shiny new red, green, or yellow **taxis** are all metered, as are the older ones (identifiable by their black license plates). Rates typically start at Rs7-9. Fares within the city should be less than Rs150: Rani Pokhari to Swayambhu or Pashupathi costs around Rs75; shorter trips like Thamel to New Rd. will cost around Rs40. An all-day sight-seeing tour around the valley costs about Rs1000. After 9pm, rates go up by over 50%, and drivers may be reluctant to take you where you want to go. Taxis queue on Tridevi Marg near the entrance to Thamel. **Auto-rickshaws** are cheaper than taxis, if you can persuade the driver to use his meter. Aggressive **cycle-rickshaw** drivers bargain hard, charging almost as much as auto-rickshaws. Rickshaws are not allowed on some major streets (e.g. Durbar Marg).

TEMPOS

Tempos, larger, sturdier versions of auto-rickshaws, can be flagged down anywhere along their routes; to request a stop, bang on the metal ceiling and honk like a mongoose. Tempos use the same route numbers as buses but leave from different places. Tempos leave from **Sundhara,** just outside the GPO: #2 to **Boudha** via **Pashupatinath** (30min., Rs6). Others depart from just north of **Rani Pokhari:** #5 to **Budhanilkantha** via **Lazimpath** (45min., Rs6) and #23 to **Balaju** (40min., Rs6).

BICYCLES

Bicycles can be rented from shops in Thamel, especially around Thamel Chowk and Chhetrapati. Mountain bikes (Rs150 per day) are better for trips outside the city; heavier, bell-equipped one-speeders (Rs60 per day) are fine for the city.

✴ ORIENTATION

Kathmandu is quite small, and navigation is pretty straightforward. The shrines of **Swayambhunath** and **Pashupatinath** are at the western and eastern edges of the city, respectively. Almost exactly halfway between them, the two main roads of **Kantipath** and **Durbar Marg** run parallel to each other, north to south. Kantipath is where you'll find the post office and plenty of banks; Durbar Marg has its share of airline offices, trekking agencies, luxury hotels, and restaurants as well as the **Royal Palace** at its north end. Between the two streets farther south is the **Tundikhel** parade ground around which Kantipath and Durbar Marg become one-way streets.

Kantipath and Durbar Marg divide Kathmandu into two halves—most of the older, more interesting parts of the city are to the west of Kantipath. The area east of Durbar Marg is mainly new neighborhoods. The year-round tourist carnival that is **Thamel** is west of Kantipath, in the northwestern corner of town. Thamel is joined to Kantipath and Durbar Marg by **Tridevi Marg.** Kathmandu's old center, **Durbar Square,** filled with magnificent architecture, is west of Kantipath, close to the banks of the **Vishnumati River. New Rd.,** built in 1934 out of the rubble left behind by an earthquake, runs east from Durbar Square to Kantipath. New Rd. is the city's top commercial district, with rows of jewelers and electronics sellers. A nameless narrow lane that sprouts northeast from Durbar Square used to be the main trading center. It cuts through **Indra Chowk,** one of Kathmandu's most interesting neighborhoods, and **Asan Tol,** the seething center of Kathmandu's main bazaar.

Tripureswar Marg is the biggest road in the southern half of town, running east-west and leading to the **Patan Bridge.** The capital's twin city, Patan, is across the **Bagmati River,** the southern limit of Kathmandu. **Ring Rd.** encircles Kathmandu and Patan, connecting them with the suburbs that have grown up around them.

❼ PRACTICAL INFORMATION

TOURIST AND FINANCIAL SERVICES

Tourist Office: The Nepal Tourism Board's main office, the **Tourist Service Center, Bhrikuti Mandap** (☎256909), is south of Ratna Bus Park, just east of Durbar Marg. Open Su-F 9am-5pm. They also have an office at the **airport** (☎470537). Open daily 9am-5pm. The **Thamel Tourism Development Committee** (☎429750) has an office north on Thahity, near the small Bhagwati temple. Open Su-F 9am-4pm.

Trekking Information: Himalayan Rescue Association (HRA), P.O. Box 4944 (☎262746; email hra@aidpost.mos.com.np), Thamel Mall at Jyatha-Thamel. Focuses on mountain safety, providing information on altitude sickness and free safety talks in the spring and fall. Talks Su-F 2pm. HRA also runs 2 clinics in Manang (Annapurna circuit) and Pheriche (Everest trek); they appreciate donations of medicine and money. **Kathmandu Environmental Education Project (KEEP),** P.O. Box 9178 (☎259567; fax 256615; email tour@keep.wlink.com.np), Thamel Mall, in the same complex as HRA, has slide show presentations on low-impact trekking twice a week. Both offices keep logbooks for trekkers to record their experiences and to read about those of others. Fill out an embassy registration form at one of these offices (or at your embassy) before you go trekking. Both open Su-F 9am-6pm; off-season 10am-5pm.

Budget Travel: Visit one of the well-established agencies on Durbar Marg: **Annapurna Travels, Everest Express,** or **Yeti Travels.** For bookings on tourist buses to places like Pokhara and Chitwan, most agencies offer similar prices—make sure you're getting the going rate. For plane tickets, go directly to the airline offices, as travel agencies take commission on flights (see **Getting There and Away,** p. 728).

Embassies: Australia, Bansbari (☎371678; fax 371533), on Maharajgunj, just past Ring Rd. Open M-Th 8:30am-5pm, F 8:30am-1:15pm. **Bangladesh,** Maharajgunj (☎372843; fax 373265), on Chakrapath, near Hotel Karnali. 2 photos required for a 15-day tourist/transit visa. Open M-Th 9am-5pm, F 9am-noon and 2-5pm. Apply for a visa M-F 9:30am-noon and pick it up the next day between 4 and 5pm. **Burma** (Myanmar), Chakupat, Patan (☎521788; fax 523402), near Patan Gate. One-month tourist visa requires 4 photos and US$20. Apply M-F 9:30am-1pm and 2-4:30pm; visas ready in 24hr. **Canada,** Lazimpath (☎415389; fax 410422), down the lane opposite Navin Books stationery shop. Open M-F 9am-5pm. **China,** Baluwatar (☎411740, visa services ☎419053). Visas Rs2200; bring your passport and 1 photo. Allow 4 days for processing. Visas to **Tibet** available only to organized groups of 5 or more and only obtainable through a travel agency (see **Surrounding Countries,** p. 11). Open M-F 10am-5pm. Visa dept. open M, W, and F 9:30-11:30am. **India,** Lainchaur (☎410900; fax 413132). Walk north up Lazimpath and veer left before the Hotel Ambassador. 15-=day transit visas require 1 photo and Rs350 and can be picked up the same day from 4:30-5:15pm. 6-month tourist visas require 1 photo and Rs2100, and you must wait to be cleared by your home embassy, which can take up to a week. US citizens must pay an additional Rs1400. Apply for visas M-F 9:30am-noon. **Malaysia:** Visas to Malaysia are administered through the UK's consular services (☎410583). 3-month tourist visa

(Rs2300) requires 2 photos, traveler's checks, plane ticket, and occasionally a hotel reservation slip. Apply Tu and Th 8-11:30am; processing takes 2 days. Many nationalities do not require visas for travel to Malaysia. **Pakistan,** Chakrapath (☎374024; fax 374012), near the intersection of Ring Rd. and Maharajgunj, northwest quadrant. 3-month tourist visa requires 2 photos. Australia Rs1124; Ireland Rs1000; New Zealand free; US and Canada Rs3853; UK Rs4238. Apply M-F 9am-1pm; visas ready the next day. **Sri Lanka,** Baluwatar (☎413623; fax 435428). Visas require 2 photos, and Rs3210. Apply M-F 10am-12:30pm. **Thailand,** Bansbari (☎371410; fax 371408). Turn east just north of the Australian Embassy. Visas require 2 photos and a copy of your plane ticket. One-month transit visas Rs450; 2-month tourist visas Rs700. Apply M-F 9:30am-12:30pm; visas ready in 24hr. **UK,** Lainchaur (☎410583; fax 411789). Open M-Th 8:15am-12:30pm and 1:30-5pm, F 8:15am-1:15pm. **US,** Pani Pokhari, Maharajgunj (☎411179; fax 419963). Open M-F 8am-5pm.

Immigration Office: The **Department of Immigration** (☎494273), is in New Baneswor, a fair distance from central Kathmandu. This is the place to get your **visa extended** or to purchase a **trekking permit.** Permits are no longer required for the major areas of Everest, Annapurna, Langtang, or Rara. For **Humla** (US$90 for the 1st week, US$15 per day thereafter); **Lower Dolpa** and **Kanchenjunga** (US$10 per week for the 1st month, US$20 per week thereafter); **Manaslu** (US$90 per week for treks Sept.-Nov.; US$75 for treks Dec.-Aug.); **Upper Mustang** and **Upper Dolpa** (US$700 for the 1st 10 days, US$70 per day thereafter). Treks to Dolpa, Kanchenunga, Makalu, and Upper Mustang must be organized by a registered trekking agency. Visa extensions and trekking permits require a passport and a photo. Apply M-F 9am-3pm (9am-2pm in winter); pick up before 5pm (4pm in winter). There is an additional fee of Rs1000 for treks through a national park or conservation area (Rs2000 for Kanchenjunga). To avoid hassles during your trek, pay these entry fees in advance at the **Entry Fee Collection Centre** (☎225395, ext. 363), in the basement of the Himalayan Bank Building, by Fire and Ice. Open M-F 9am-4pm, Su 9am-3pm.

Currency Exchange: Nepal Bank Ltd., New Rd. (☎221185), has the lowest commission around for traveler's checks (0.5%). Open daily 8am-1pm and 1:30-6pm. **ANZ Grindlays** (☎421787), on Tridevi Marg, opposite Fire and Ice, gives cash advances on MC and Visa and sells AmEx traveler's checks. Commission on traveler's checks Rs200 or 1.5%. Open Sept.-May Su-F 9:30am-7:30pm; June-Aug. M-F 9:30am-4:45pm. The several official **exchange counters** around Thamel generally charge 2% commission. **Western Union** is at Annapurna Travel and Tours, Durbar Marg (☎223530; fax 222966), on the east side of the street. Money can be wired here within a minute. Open daily 9:30am-7:30pm. **American Express: Yeti Travels,** Hotel Mayalu, Jamal, P.O. Box 76 (☎226172; fax 226152). Open Su-Th 10am-1pm and 2-5pm, F 10am-1pm and 2-4:45pm. The **Easylink Cybercafe,** in Thamel, also has **Moneygram** service for quick money transfers.

LOCAL SERVICES

Bookstore: Pilgrims Book House, Thamel (☎425919). Browsing here is one of the joys of being in Kathmandu. An enormous place that not only has every book you never knew you wanted, but also CDs, handicrafts, classical music concerts, and yoga classes. Open daily 8am-10pm.

Library: Kaiser Library, Ministry of Education compound (☎411318), on the corner of Tridevi Marg and Kantipath. Open M-F 9am-5pm. **American Center,** Gyaneswar (☎415845). Open M-F 11am-6pm.

Market: Asan Tol, in front of the Annapurna Temple, has fresh fruits and vegetables. **Open Market** (also called Hong Kong Market), south of Ratna bus park, is a large tarpaulin congregation of food, clothing, and other products. Snacks, toiletries, and trekking supplies are at the **Best Shopping Centre,** where Tridevi Marg narrows into Thamel. Open Su-F 8am-8pm, Sa 10am-8pm.

Laundry Service: Almost all guest houses have laundry service, but independent establishments sometimes charge less. **The 1 Hour Laundry,** next door to the Khukuri House, also does dry cleaning and has the quickest service around. Open daily 8am-8pm.

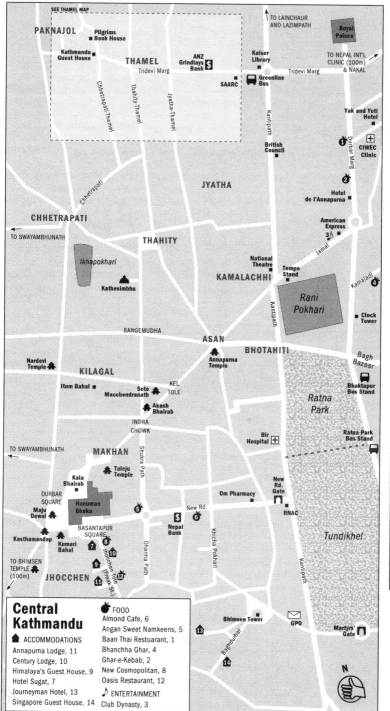

SEE THAMEL MAP

PAKNAJOL

Pilgrims Book House

Kathmandu Guest House

THAMEL

Tridevi Marg

ANZ Grindlays Bank

Kaiser Library

TO LAINCHAUR AND LAZIMPATH

Royal Palace

TO NEPAL INT'L CLINIC (100m) & NAKAL

Tridevi Marg

SAARC

Greenline Bus

Chhetrapati-Thamel

Thahity-Thamel

Jyatha-Thamel

Kantipath

British Council

Yak and Yeti Hotel

Durbar Marg

CIWEC Clinic

JYATHA

Hotel de l'Annapurna

Chhetrapati

CHHETRAPATI

TO SWAYAMBHUNATH

Ikhapokhari

THAHITY

American Express

Jamal

Kathesimbhu

National Theatre

KAMALACHHI

Tempo Stand

Rani Pokhari

Kamaladi

BANGEMUDHA

Kantipath

Clock Tower

ASAN

BHOTAHITI

Bagh Bazaar

Nardevi Temple

KILAGAL

Annapurna Temple

Itum Bahal

Seto Macchendranath

KEL TOLE

Bhaktapur Bus Stand

Ratna Park

Akash Bhairab

INDRA CHOWK

Bir Hospital

Ratna Park Bus Stand

TO SWAYAMBHUNATH

MAKHAN

Shukra Path

New Rd. Gate

Om Pharmacy

Kala Bhairab

Taleju Temple

DURBAR SQUARE

Hanuman Dhoka

New Rd.

RNAC

Maju Dewal

Nepal Bank

Khicha Pokhari

Tundikhel

Kasthamandap

BASANTAPUR SQUARE

Kumari Bahal

TO BHIMSEN TEMPLE (100m)

JHOCCHEN

Jhochhen Tole (Freak St.)

Dharma Path

Baghdurbar

Bhimsen Tower

GPO

Martyrs' Gate

N

Central Kathmandu

🏠 ACCOMMODATIONS
Annapurna Lodge, 11
Century Lodge, 10
Himalaya's Guest House, 9
Hotel Sugat, 7
Journeyman Hotel, 13
Singapore Guest House, 14

🍴 FOOD
Almond Cafe, 6
Angan Sweet Namkeens, 5
Baan Thai Restuarant, 1
Bhanchha Ghar, 4
Ghar-e-Kebab, 2
New Cosmopolitan, 8
Oasis Restaurant, 12

🎵 ENTERTAINMENT
Club Dynasty, 3

NEPAL

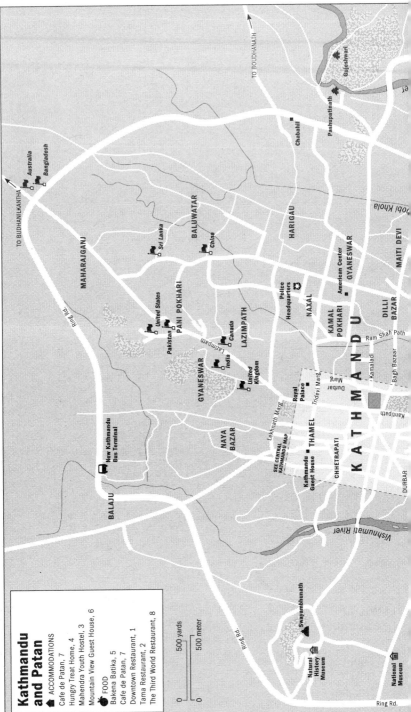

Kathmandu and Patan

ACCOMMODATIONS
Cafe de Patan, 7
Hungry Treat Home, 4
Mahendra Youth Hostel, 3
Mountain View Guest House, 6

FOOD
Bakena Batika, 5
Cafe de Patan, 7
Downtown Restaurant, 1
Tama Restaurant, 2
The Third World Restaurant, 8

0 ──── 500 yards
0 ──── 500 meter

TO BUDHANILKANTHA

TO BOUDHNATH

Australia
Bangladesh

Sri Lanka

BALUWATAR
China

MAHARAJGANJ

Ring Rd.

Chabahil
Pashupatinath
Guješhwari

HARIGAU

Pobi Khola

United States
Pakistan
PANI POKHARI

Canada
Lazimpath

India
LAZIMPATH

United Kingdom

GYANESWAR

Police Headquarters
NAXAL
American Center
GYANESWAR

KAMAL POKHARI

DILLI BAZAR

MAITI DEVI

Ram Shah Path

Kamaladi
Bagh Bazaar

New Kathmandu Bus Terminal

BALAJU

NAYA BAZAR

Royal Palace
Tridevi Marg

SEE CENTRAL KATHMANDU MAP

Lekhnath Marg

Durbar Marg

K A T H M A N D U

THAMEL

Kandpath

Kathmandu Guest House

CHHETRAPATI

DURBAR

Vishnumati River

Ring Rd.

Swayambhunath

Natural History Museum

National Museum

Ring Rd.

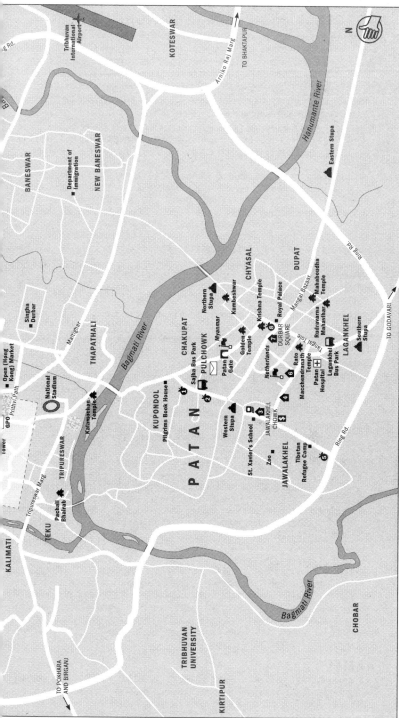

EMERGENCY AND COMMUNICATIONS

Emergency: Ambulance, ☎228094 (Red Cross). **CIWEC** (☎228531 or 241732) has 24hr. emergency service.

Police: The **Tourist Police** handles petty thefts and rip-offs and can be reached at any of the city's tourist offices: Bhrikuti Mandap (☎256909), Tribhuvan Airport (☎470537), and Thamel (☎429750). Contact the city police for more serious issues (☎100).

Pharmacy: Om Pharmacy, New Rd. (☎244658), opposite RNAC. Open daily 8am-9pm. Several other pharmacies are opposite Bir Hospital.

Hospital/Medical Services: Kathmandu has numerous reliable **clinics** geared toward Westerners. In case of illness, visit one of these first. **CIWEC Clinic** (☎228531 or 241732), off Durbar Marg, behind the Yak and Yeti sign, to the right. US$45 per consultation, US$65 after hours or on weekends. Open M-F 9am-noon and 1-3:30pm. On call 24hr. MC, Visa. **Nepal International Clinic** (☎434642; fax 434713), opposite the Royal Palace, 3min. east of the main gates, down a lane to the right. Consultation US$34. Open Su-F 9am-1pm and 2-5pm. On-call 24hr. for emergencies. AmEx, MC, Visa. **Himalaya International Clinic,** Jyatha-Thamel (☎225455; fax 226980). Consultation US$20 (US$40 housecall), follow-up US$10. Open Su-F 9am-5pm, Sa 9am-1pm. **Patan Hospital,** Lagankhel, Patan (☎522295), has a better reputation than **Bir Hospital** (☎221119), the government hospital in Kathmandu.

Internet: Internet cafes are everywhere around Thamel and Durbar Square. The **Easy Link Cybercafe** (☎416239), in Thamel, has fast connections, air-conditioning, the lowest rates, and a standing offer of 10 free minutes after your first visit. Rs40 per hr. Walk north on Thahity-Thamel and take a left at the small Bhagwati temple.

Telephones: Most STD/ISD booths have the same rates on outgoing calls but different deals on callbacks—shop around. **Global Communications,** Tridevi Marg (☎228143), in the shopping center opposite ANZ Grindlays bank, has good rates and charges a flat Rs25 for callbacks. Open Su-F 8am-8pm, Sa 2-7pm. The **GPO** charges Rs10 a page for faxes. Open Su-Th 10am-5pm, F 10am-3pm.

Post Office: GPO (☎227499), near Bhimsen Tower; entrance just off Kantipath. Stamps sold Su-F 8am-7pm, Sa 11am-3pm. **Express Mail Service (EMS),** at the GPO, delivers within 3-7 days to pretty much anywhere in the world. Open M-F 10:15am-3pm. To send a package abroad, visit the **Foreign Parcel Office,** around the corner on Kantipath, where it will be checked by customs. Open M-F 9:15am-2pm; in winter 9:15am-1:30pm. **FedEx, UPS, DHL,** and **Airborne Express** offer services in Thamel.

▟ ACCOMMODATIONS

Increased competition in Thamel has led to a general standardization of prices for similar accommodations. The prices listed are for in-season and do not include the 10% government tax. Rates are usually negotiable, depending on the season and the length of your stay. **Beware of touts:** don't let anyone lead you to their friend's hotel; a hefty commission will appear on your bill.

Freak St. is Kathmandu's original tourist district. Ever since it hit its peak back in the 70s, Freak St. has been cheaper, less hectic, and less populated than Thamel; most of its hotels have been around for almost 25 years, growing old and musty as lodges in Thamel steal all their business. **Sundhara** is popular with Indian tourists; its accommodations—cheap, unassuming, and conveniently located just south of New Rd.—are not quite the bargains found in Thamel, but they are a good option if you want to "find" the city before it finds you. The places below, unless otherwise noted, have hot water, seat toilets, laundry service, luggage storage, and a noon check-out, but no towels or toilet paper.

THAMEL

▓ **Kathmandu Guest House** (☎413632 or 418733; fax 417133; email ktmguest@ecomail.com.np). All directions in Thamel are given in relation to this place, so you'd better figure out where Kathmandu's original "budget hotel" is. The rooms in the old wing have best access to the guest house's communication center, swank lobby

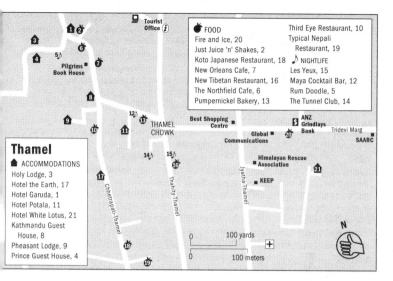

Thamel

🏠 ACCOMMODATIONS

Holy Lodge, 3
Hotel the Earth, 17
Hotel Garuda, 1
Hotel Potala, 11
Hotel White Lotus, 21
Kathmandu Guest
  House, 8
Pheasant Lodge, 9
Prince Guest House, 4

🍎 FOOD

Fire and Ice, 20
Just Juice 'n' Shakes, 2
Koto Japanese Restaurant, 18
New Orleans Cafe, 7
New Tibetan Restaurant, 16
The Northfield Cafe, 6
Pumpernickel Bakery, 13

Third Eye Restaurant, 10
Typical Nepali
  Restaurant, 19
♪ NIGHTLIFE

Les Yeux, 15
Maya Cocktail Bar, 12
Rum Doodle, 5
The Tunnel Club, 14

---

with satellite TV, ticket booking, bike rental, and barber shop. Old wing: Singles US$6-10; doubles US$8-12. New wing: Singles US$17-50; doubles US$20-60. 10% discount for stays of over a week. AmEx, MC, Visa. Reserve ahead Sept.-Nov. and Feb.-Apr.

Hotel Potala (☎419159; fax 416680), opposite K.C.'s, at the center of Thamel. Well-managed by a friendly Tibetan family, Potala has clean, comfortable rooms with common baths, and its low prices make it one of the best-value places in Thamel. Rooms (some with fans) have shared balconies. Singles Rs125; doubles Rs175-250.

Hotel The Earth, Chhetrapati-Thamel (☎260312; fax 260763). South of Kathmandu Guest House, on the west side of the street. A range of large, clean, and generously furnished rooms at economy prices. One of the few places in Thamel with dorm beds. Dorm beds Rs100; singles Rs150-400; doubles Rs250-550. 50% discount for students and volunteers; 20% discount for stays over 1 week.

Prince Guest House, Satghumti-Thamel (☎414456; fax 220143), north of Kathmandu Guest House—turn left at the intersection. The Artist Formerly Known As would die for the pink 'n' purple decor and wall-to-wall carpeting. Brand-new, spotless rooms with fans, phones, and attached baths complete with shower curtains. Rooftop garden and restaurant. Singles US$7; doubles US$10.

Hotel Garuda (☎416340 or 414766; fax 413614), just around the curve north of the Kathmandu Guest House. 5-star service and low prices have made it popular with Himalayan expeditions for years. One of the few rooftop "gardens" in Thamel that is actually a garden. Free 24hr. callbacks. Attached baths with towels and toilet paper. Singles US$9-29; doubles US$13-36. 25% off-season discount. AmEx, MC, Visa.

Holy Lodge, Satghumti (☎437763; fax 413441), opposite the Prince Guest House. Spotless rooms with fans off a quiet courtyard. Singles US$4-9; doubles US$6-12.

Hotel White Lotus, Jyatha Thamel (☎249842). Walk south down Jyatha Thamel and take the meandering path on the left. Rooms vary in amenities and price but all are clean. A spiral staircase leads to the roof garden; every floor has a balcony with rattan furniture. Towels, phones, safe deposit available. Singles Rs200; doubles Rs200-500.

Pheasant Lodge, (☎417415), down a short alleyway off Chhetrapati-Thamel, just south of the Kathmandu Guest House. Smack dab in the middle of things. Concrete floors, firm beds, clean sheets, and a choice of common toilets—squat or sit as you please. The hotel is often full—try right at the noon check-out time. Singles Rs100; doubles Rs150.

FREAK STREET

▨ **Hotel Sugat** (☎ 246454; fax 221824; email maryman@mos.com.np), along the southern edge of Basantapur Sq. (facing the royal palace). The rooftop garden has fantastic views. Large, carpeted rooms overlook Durbar Sq.; some have tubs and balconies. Fans, toilet paper, towels. Singles Rs110-300; doubles Rs300-400.

Annapurna Lodge, Freak St. (☎ 247684), down the second right as you walk from Basantapur Sq. Quiet, clean, and simply furnished rooms off a balcony. Seat toilets in attached baths; squat and seat toilets in common bath. Attached restaurant shows movies. Singles Rs125-225; doubles Rs200-300.

Himalaya's Guest House, Basantapur, Jhochhen (☎ 246555). Take the first right off Freak St. as you walk from Basantapur Square. Rooms are bright, clean, and well-furnished. Free international callbacks. Singles Rs150; doubles Rs300-350.

Century Lodge, Freak St., near Basantapur Sq. Diminutive quarters with an *Alice in Wonderland* feel. Well-worn rooms have tile floors and low ceilings, and overlook the quiet garden courtyard. Singles Rs150; doubles Rs250-275.

SUNDHARA

Journeyman Hotel, Ganabahal, Pipalbot (☎ 253438; fax 253999), along the paved road leading southwest from Bhimsen Tower; continue west past the pipal tree and it's on your right. Large rooms with fans are old but well-maintained. Friendly, accommodating management. Dorm beds Rs100; singles Rs170-250; doubles Rs200-500.

Singapore Guest House, Baghdurbar (☎ 244105; fax 221703), south of Bhimsen Tower, on the left toward the end of the street. Large, elegant rooms with carpets, fans, and attached bath. Attached restaurant. Singles Rs250; doubles Rs350.

◘ FOOD

Beginning with the founding of Kathmandu's first luxury hotel in 1954, which featured chandeliers and fresh fish carried in by porters, to the advent of "Pie Alley," where 1960s overlanders gathered for apple pie and hash brownies, Kathmandu has achieved mythic status as an oasis of displaced delicacies. Today, mostly Western favorites are de rigueur on tourist menus; much of this food tastes blandly similar, borrowing most of its flavor from the *ghee* in which it has been ritually drowned. The Japanese, Thai, Tibetan, and Indian restaurants that elbow for room in neighborhoods frequented by foreigners and wealthy Nepalis generally offer more appetizing and less contrived fare. For a more authentic experience, you can always dig into the undisputed national dish, *dahl bhat tarkari* (rice, lentils, and vegetable curry) available on nearly every menu as the "Nepali Set Meal."

THAMEL

▨ **Typical Nepali Restaurant,** Chhetrapati-Thamel, south of Kathmandu Guest House, down an alley on the left. The singing, dancing manager, who identifies himself as J.J. (for "John Joker") persistently refills clay bowls of *raksi* (rice wine) while live Nepali music plays in the background. Complimentary bananas and popcorn accompany the all-you-can eat regional plates (Rs80-140), including *dahl bhat tarkari, roti, momos,* and *achaar.* Open daily 6:30am-10pm.

▨ **New Tibetan Restaurant,** a short distance down Thahiti-Thamel, up the second set of stairs to your left. With a friendly staff and a cozy atmosphere, the New Tibetan serves delicious Nepali, Chinese, Tibetan, and continental food at down-to-earth prices. Nepali set meal Rs60; veg. chow mein Rs35. Try the uncommonly good yogurt with mixed fruit and honey (Rs35) for dessert. Open 7am-10pm.

Koto Japanese Restaurant, Chhetrapati-Thamel, near the Chhetrapati intersection (with another branch on Durbar Marg). Impeccable service and simple bamboo furnishings. Tea refills and *yakis* will enliven the pizza-weary. Noodles, soups, meat, fish, and Japanese curries (Rs150-350). Open daily 11am-9pm. 10% tax.

Just Juice 'n' Shakes, down a lane to the right, north of Kathmandu Guest House. Friendly place with quite a reputation for thick, frozen smoothies and shakes (Rs50-90), hot espresso (Rs50), cappuccino (Rs50), and cakes (Rs30). Check out the amusing visitors log. Open daily 6am-midnight.

Fire and Ice, in the shopping center on Tridevi Marg, opposite ANZ Grindlays. Wafting pizzeria smells will lure you in, and the opera music and great food will keep you (and plenty of other tourists) there. Pizza Rs180-290; minestrone soup Rs120; delicate crepes Rs65-110; imported ice cream Rs50-90. Open daily 11am-10pm.

Pumpernickel Bakery, opposite K.C.'s. A Thamel institution. At breakfast time, the line to order freshly baked croissants, cakes, and cinnamon rolls (Rs20-35) spills onto the street. The pleasant garden patio and wicker furniture in the back make it a nice place to linger and watch the tourists. Open daily 7am-9pm.

Third Eye Restaurant, just south of the Kathmandu Guest House, on the right. This quality Indian restaurant specializes in tandoori chicken (half-chicken Rs215, whole Rs360). The interior dining area is classy; the rooftop terrace has great views. Veg. dishes Rs130-175; *naan* Rs30-60. Open 8am-10pm. MC, Visa.

New Orleans Cafe, just north of the Kathmandu Guest House, straight down the Mississippi River to the Gulf of Mexico. Bustling but low-key candle-lit patio. Enjoy jambalaya, creole chicken, and other good stuff. Veg. dishes Rs80-170; non-veg. Rs90-250. Live music Th 7-10pm. Open 6:30am-11pm.

The Northfield Cafe, a few doors north of Pilgrims Book House. A great place for homesick gringos to down chips and salsa (Rs120) and gnaw on spicy chicken wings (Rs100). Burritos Rs150-180, quesadillas Rs120, and meat dishes up to Rs205, brownie sundaes Rs135. Blaring classical, jazz, and blues music. The breakfast menu is one of the best around. Open daily 7am-10pm.

Delicatessen Center, Kantipath, stocks a wide variety of imported cheeses and meats. Also produces an impressive array of breads and pastries. Goulash Rs110; onion rings Rs40; fish and chips Rs130. Open daily 8am-8pm.

DURBAR MARG

Bhanchha Ghar, Kamaladi. From Durbar Marg, turn left at the clock tower; it's on the right. The name is Nepali for "kitchen," but there's a lot more than *dahl bhat* on offer here—this is Nepalese *haute cuisine*. Specialties (Rs150-245) include wild boar and curried high-altitude mushrooms. The enormous set menu is pricey (Rs900) but includes a cultural show at night. Open daily noon-10pm. AmEx, MC, Visa. 10% tax.

Baan Thai Restaurant. Authentic Thai food in a swish, A/C setting. Watch Durbar Marg through lace curtains as you enjoy *pad thai* (Rs140-190) and seafood (Rs325-440). Open daily noon-10pm. MC, Visa.

Ghar-e-Kebab, past Baan Thai on Durbar Marg. Top-quality Indian restaurant, with delicious food and attentive service. Ravi Shankar impersonations nightly. Tandoori dishes Rs325-650. Open noon-2:30pm and 7-10:30pm. MC, Visa. 10%tax.

NEW ROAD AND FREAK STREET

The Almond Cafe, New Rd., has a fast-food atmosphere but is cheap, clean, friendly, and frequented by locals. Chow mein Rs30-50; pizzas Rs45-85.

Angan Sweet Namkeens and Vegetarian Fast Food, at the intersection of New Rd. and Dharma Path. Serves ice cream (Rs36-50), Indian sweets, *dosas* (Rs40-65), and other veg. treats (Rs20-65) on the go. Pay in front and shoulder your way into the back room to find a table. Free mineral water. Open daily 9:30am-8:30pm.

Oasis Restaurant, Freak St., with its outdoor dining area, is the only place where you can eat sheltered by big leafy plants and rainbow umbrellas. Mexican dishes Rs90-110; pizza Rs95; burgers Rs85-95. Open daily 8am-9:30pm.

New Cosmopolitan Restaurant, Basantapur Sq., is one of the few restaurants with a view of the square. Extensive tape collection ranges from Pink Floyd to Portishead. Crepes Rs30-60; stroganoff Rs65-90; pizza Rs70-105. Open daily 8am-10pm.

👁 SIGHTS

There are so many temples in Kathmandu that the word "templescape" has been coined to describe the city's skyline. The city's main attractions are in **Durbar Square, Indra Chowk,** and **Asan Tol.** The best way to tour Kathmandu is on foot.

DURBAR SQUARE

Durbar (Palace) Square is the heart of the old city. The royal family moved about a hundred years ago to the north end of town, but that hasn't taken away any of Durbar Square's religious, social, or commercial importance. Many of Kathmandu's most interesting temples and historic buildings are located here in this bustling, wide open space. A good way to explore the sights is to start from Basantapur Square, the large open plaza by Freak St., and head west and then north in a clockwise arc; the sights are organized below in this manner.

KUMARI BAHAL. As you walk west from Basantapur Square, the first building on your left is the Kumari Bahal, marked by the two painted stone lions that stand guard outside. A traditional 18th-century Kathmandu palace, the Kumari Bahal has beautiful carved window frames—some are shaped like peacocks, and the central one is covered in gold. This is where the living, earthly, human goddess of Kathmandu, the **Kumari,** resides, sometimes appearing at one of the windows in the courtyard (see **The Living Goddess: Kumari,** above). If she doesn't appear, plenty of touts in the square will offer their services in summoning her appearance. Soft drinks and film are sold inside the courtyard. *(No photography allowed.)*

TRAILOKYA MOHAN TEMPLE. Just outside the Kumari Bahal, this temple is a shrine to Vishnu, with a dusty-black statue of Garuda (Vishnu's man-bird vehicle) kneeling before the image. On the other side of the temple, great white columns bear down on the square. Prime Minister Chandra Shamsher Rana added this wing to the main royal palace in 1908.

KASTHAMANDAP. Continuing west past Trailokya Mohan, you will find the Kasthamandap, a gorgeous temple that (perhaps) gave Kathmandu its name. The wooden pavilion—built from the wood of a single tree—is Kathmandu's oldest existing building. It dates from the 14th century, though it has been substantially altered over the centuries. Originally a *dharamsala*, it was made into a temple. A feeling of transience still remains, and loitering porters make the place feel a bit like a holy train platform. A central image of Gorakhnath, the deified Hindu saint who watches over the Shah dynasty, anchors this sacred space. Small Ganesh shrines sit in each corner; one of the idols' golden mouse-mounts points its nose at

THE LIVING GODDESS: KUMARI
A Newari Buddhist girl considered to be the living incarnation of the Hindu goddess Durga, the Kumari is a perfect example of the religious syncretism of the Kathmandu Valley. Kathmandu's Kumari, the most important of the 11 in the valley, is selected at the age of four or five from the Buddhist clan of the Newari *shakya* (goldsmith) caste. The Kumari-to-be must satisfy 32 physical requirements, including having thighs like a deer's, a chest like a lion's, eyelashes like a cow's, and a body shaped like a banyan tree. She must remain calm in a dark room full of buffalo heads, frightening masks, and loud noises. Finally, her astrological chart must not conflict with the king's. If all these conditions are met, the Kumari is installed in the Kumari Bahal in Durbar Square, where she leads the privileged, secluded life of a goddess until she reaches puberty. Several times a year she is paraded about town on a palanquin (the Kumari's feet must not touch the ground). As soon as the Kumari menstruates, or sheds blood in any other way, her goddess-spirit leaves her body, and she must return to her parents' home, where the transition to mere mortality can be difficult. Former goddesses often have difficulty finding a husband, since men who marry them are said to die young.

another Ganesh shrine, the **Maru Ganesh** (also known as **Ashok Binayak**), in its own metal-flagged enclosure. As the remover of obstacles, Ganesh is a good god to visit before traveling.

MAJU DEWAL. From the Kasthamandap, turn right and head north toward the main part of the Square. The Maju Dewal Shiva Temple takes up the prime location, towering over everything on its great step-pyramid. The temple was built in 1690, and it makes a well-placed observation deck for Durbar Square—its height, however, does nothing to isolate it from the fray below. You could sit here for hours watching the square, if not for all the "guides," "English students," and kids asking, "Do you have one coin from your country?"

TEMPLE OF SHIVA AND PARVATI. As you continue north, you'll come to the Shiva and Parvati Temple, resting on a skewed platform that may at one time have been used for dance performances. Statues of the divine couple survey the square from a tiny window, guarded by the two stone lions below.

TALEJU BELL. If you look up as you pass the Shiva and Parvati Temple, you'll see the Taleju (Great) Bell, put up by Rana Bahadur Shah in 1797. The bell, similar to the ones found in the other valley cities of Patan and Bhaktapur, rings for worship in the Degutaleju Temple.

KRISHNA TEMPLE. As you pass the bell, the road widens, bringing you to another part of the square. On your left you'll see the octagonal Krishna Temple built in 1648 by King Pratap Malla. The temple houses images of Krishna and two goddesses that bear a curious resemblance to Pratap Malla and his wives.

KING PRATAP MALLA'S COLUMN AND THE DEGUTALEJU TEMPLE. In the center of this part of the square stands a column topped by a statue of King Pratap Malla, the architect of many buildings in this area. He sits facing his personal shrine in the Degutaleju Temple.

SWETA BHAIRAB. As you face the Degutaleju Temple, you'll see a large wooden screen just to the right that hides the figure of the big, fanged, golden face of Sweta Bhairab (White Bhairab). At the **Indra Jatra Festival** (Aug.-Sept.), the screen comes off and beer spouts from the mouth of this fearsome form of Shiva as devotees crowd in for a drink.

JAGANNATH TEMPLE. To the left of the Pratap Malla is the Jagannath Temple, dating from 1563. The oldest temple in this part of the square, it is notable for the erotic carvings on its roof struts.

KALA BHAIRAB. Behind Pratap Malla, facing north is the huge, garish monolith of Kala Bhairab (Black Bhairab). It is said that anyone who dares to tell a lie in front of this raging destroyer of evil will vomit blood and die. Don't even think about it.

TALEJU MANDIR. The Taleju Temple's three-tiered golden pagoda towers over everything else in this part of the square. King Mahendra Malla built the temple in 1564 to honor Taleju, his dynasty's patron goddess. At 37m, the Taleju Temple was for a long time the tallest building in Kathmandu, a distinction preserved by building codes. But no more—the city, eager to modernize, has dispensed with this tradition. Ordinarily, the temple is open only to the king and a few priests, but on the ninth day of the festival of Dasain, lay Hindus are allowed to enter.

HANUMAN DHOKA DURBAR. The old royal palace takes its name from the statue of Hanuman that stands guard at the entrance, to the left of the Pratap Malla. The monkey-god lounges under a parasol, his face hidden behind all the *sindur* rubbed onto it. No one has lived in the palace for over a century, but it is still used for royal ceremonies, including King Birendra's coronation in 1975. Although the building has been evolving steadily since the time of the Licchavi kings of the 13th century, its art and architecture were influenced mainly by the patronage of King Pratap Malla (r. 1641-74). No Licchavi buildings remain, and the palace now has plenty of Shah-era whitewashing. Just inside the palace entrance is **Nasal Chowk,** a

NEPAL

courtyard where the nobles of the kingdom used to assemble. It was here in 1673 that Pratap Malla danced in a costume of Narasimha, Vishnu's man-lion incarnation. Afraid that Vishnu would be angry about the stunt, Pratap Malla installed a Narasimha statue just inside the palace. The main section of the palace open to the public is the **Tribhuvan Memorial Museum.** King Tribhuvan (r. 1911-55), who overthrew the Ranas in 1951 and restored Nepal's monarchy, is remembered here in a display of personal belongings—everything from ceremonial outfits, newspaper clippings, and watches down to Tribhuvan's desk and fish tank. At the southern end of Nasal Chowk stands **Basantapur Tower,** a nine-story lookout erected by Prithvi Narayan Shah after he conquered the valley. It has great views of Durbar Square from above. The circuit around Nasal Chowk next leads to the **Mahendra Memorial Museum,** which isn't quite as impressive as Tribhuvan's, though a walk-through diorama simulating one of the king's hunts is worth a look. Outside the palace, along the wall past the Hanuman statue, is a **stone inscription** put up by Pratap Malla, which uses words from 15 different languages (including English and French). It's said that if anyone manages to read the whole text—a poem dedicated to the goddess Kali—milk will gush from the spout. *(Open Tu-Sa 10:30am-4pm, in winter 10:30am-3pm; F 10:30am-2pm. Rs250. Cameras prohibited.)*

NORTH OF DURBAR SQUARE

Kathmandu's most interesting street runs northeast from Durbar Square. Without a name of its own, the street takes the title of whatever area it runs through. In earlier times, it was the beginning of the trade route from Kathmandu to Tibet, and it was Kathmandu's main commercial area until New Rd. was built after the earthquake of 1934. Today it is still a buzzing, temple-packed market area.

INDRA CHOWK. The second-story temple of **Akash Bhairab** is unmistakable, with its garish metal gargoyles. Akash Bhairab's image, a large silver mask, is barely visible. During the Indra Jatra festival, it is put on display in the middle of the *chowk,* along with a *linga* specially erected next to it. *(The first crossroads on the diagonal street away from Durbar Sq. is called Indra Chowk. Akash Bhairab is on the left side at this corner.)*

KEL TOL. The **Temple of Seto Machhendranath** is one of the most widely revered shrines in the valley. Both Hindus and Buddhists come here to pay homage to Machhendra, the valley's guardian, also considered to be an incarnation of Avalokitesvara, the Bodhisattva of Compassion. The white-faced image is paraded around town during the **Machhendranath Festival** in April. *(Just off Kel Tol, down a passageway marked by a short pillar capped with a meditating Buddha.)* The pagoda in the middle of Kel Tol is dedicated to **Lunchun Lun Bun Ajima.** The road has been repaved so many times that this goddess' bathroom-tiled sanctuary is now sunk beneath street level. *(Kel Tol is the second crossing north of Durbar Square.)*

ASAN TOL. At Asan Tol, the next crossing, the road widens and is lined with stacks of vegetables. The **Temple of Annapurna** is on the right, draped with broad brass ribbons. The goddess of plentiful food, Annapurna is depicted here as a silver pot. *(Asan Tol is the third crossing north of Durbar Square.)*

BANGEMUDHA. The name of the square west of Asan Tol, Bangemudha, literally means "Twisted Wood." In one of the southern corners is a twisted lump of wood stuck to the wall, with an armor of coins nailed into it. The wood is dedicated to the god of toothaches, **Vaisya Dev,** and nailing a coin here is supposed to relieve dental pain. On the road north from Bangemudha you'll be greeted by jawfuls of grinning teeth. This is the dentists' quarter, and their signs all bear this happy smiling symbol. On the left side of this road, a lane leads to **Kathesimbhu,** a miniature model of the Swayambhunath stupa west of Kathmandu. Kathesimbhu, said to have been built with leftover earth from Swayambhunath, shares some of Swayambhunath's power. The elderly and those too weak to climb the hill to Swayambhunath can obtain an equal blessing here. Children seem to be the most

SOUTH ASIAN SEDER With 95% of Nepal's 20 million citizens claiming Hinduism, Buddhism, or both, as their religion, you'd hardly expect Kathmandu to host the largest *seder* (ritual Jewish Passover meal) in the world. Each year the Israeli Embassy puts on a *seder* for the 1000 or so young Jews who find themselves in Nepal during the week of Passover. Most of them have come to roam the Nepali wilderness following completion of their national military service, but at the *seder*, the trekking diaspora ditches *chappatis* and *dahl bhat* in favor of *matzos* and *maror*, in remembrance of the ancient Israelite exodus from Egypt. For more information, contact the Israeli Embassy (☎411811).

devoted visitors, however, holding endless soccer games around its *chaityas*. *(The Bangemudha crossing is about 150m due west of Asan Tol.)*

OTHER SIGHTS. The **Rani Pokhari** tank and the temple at its center were built by King Pratap Malla to console his wife over the death of their son. The green-and-yellow fence around it is kept locked all year, except on Diwali (Nov. 14, 2001), the festival of light. *(On Kantipath, east of Asan Tol.)* The current **Royal Palace** is hard to miss—built in the 1960s, the grand mansion is capped by a pagoda-style roof. The building is open to the public only on the 10th day of Dasain, when the king and queen offer blessings to their subjects. *(At the north end of Durbar Marg.)*

SOUTH OF DURBAR SQUARE

SINGHA DURBAR. Singha Durbar was once the greatest of the Rana palaces, until most of it burned down in a fire one night in July 1974. The off-white building, meant to rival the palaces of Europe, was built in three frantic years from 1901 to 1904 by Prime Minister Chandra Shamsher Jung Bahadur Rana—his monogram decorates the railings. The prime minister's household and entire administration fit into this complex, which, with 1700 rooms, claims to be the largest building in Asia. Ministries and departments are lodged in what's left of the palace, and their offices are off-limits to the public. *(East of Tundikhel.)*

BHIMSEN TEMPLE. The Bhimsen Temple is dedicated to the hero-god of Newari craftsmen—its bottom floor has been entirely taken over by shops. Next to it is a *hiti* (water tap) in a cellar-like depression, where jugs are filled from an elephant-shaped spout. *(On the lane that runs southwest of the Kasthamandap.)*

JAISI DEWAL TEMPLE. The Jaisi Dewal Temple is a step-pyramid Shiva temple. Painted with flowers and leopard-skin patterns, the temple is graced by a smooth figure of Shiva's bull mount, Nandi, at the base of the steps. Across the street from the entrance, a 2m-high, uncarved *linga* rises up from a *yoni*. *(Continue to the end of the road from the Bhimsen Temple, turn left, and go up the hill.)*

BHIMSEN TOWER. The 59m-high Bhimsen Tower is a useful landmark if you get lost along Kathmandu's streets. It looks like a lighthouse with portholes, though Bhimsen Thapa, the prime minister who built it in 1832, was probably trying to imitate the Ochterlony Monument in Calcutta—ironic, considering that the British erected that monument to commemorate the defeat of Nepal in 1816. *(At a crossroads in southern Kathmandu, close to Kantipath. The tower is closed to the public.)*

TUNDIKHEL AND MARTYR'S GATE. The **Tundikhel,** or parade ground, is occasionally used for military marches and equestrian displays, such as the Ghora Jatra Horse Festival in late March. *(East of Kantipath.)* Kathmandu's newer neighborhoods are to the east of the Tundikhel. **Martyrs' Gate** is a monument to four accused conspirators executed after a 1940 coup attempt. *(On a circle in the middle of the road, south of the Tundikhel.)*

KALAMOCHAN TEMPLE. The Kalamochan Temple is hard to miss, with its Mughal-style onion dome. Its dragons and doorways are purely Nepali, though,

NEPAL

THE LEGEND OF THE KATHMANDU VALLEY

According to local mythology, the Kathmandu Valley was once a huge lake inhabited by *nagas*, or snakes. A lotus grew out of the lake and was called *swayambhu*, the "self-created." When the bodhisattva of knowledge, Manjushri, went on a pilgrimage to the lotus, he was dismayed to find it surrounded by snakes and inaccessible to human pilgrims. He sliced his sword into the valley, creating Chobar Gorge; the water drained from the lake and took the *nagas* with it. To appease the *naga* king Krakatoa, Manjushri allowed him to live in Taudaha Lake as guardian of the monsoon. The fertile valley was now ready for its first civilization, and a shrine—the stupa of Swayambhunath—was built on the hill from which the lotus had grown. According to geology, the valley was indeed once filled with water, Swayambhu was an island, and the Chobar Gorge was created by an earthquake—but there's no mention of snakes.

and on the exterior, Jung Bahadur Rana's figure rises from a turtle's back. This Machiavellian prime minister built the temple in the mid-19th century. The ashes of the 32 noblemen he slaughtered in the Kot Massacre are supposed to be buried in the foundations. *(On Tripureswar Marg, close to the Patan Bridge.)*

PACHALI BHAIRAB. The area between Tripureswar Marg and the Bagmati might be wet and dirty, and home to a big share of Kathmandu's slums, but its many temples make it an interesting part of town to explore. The shrine of Pachali Bhairab contains an image of Bhairab, garlanded with coins, under the spreading roots of a great pipal tree. Music from the nearby monastery jangles down into Bhairab's courtyard, where a golden human figure lies peacefully dead. Don't fret; this is a *betal*, a representation of death meant to guard against the real thing. *(In a cluster of temples south of Tripureswar Marg, just east of the footbridge across the Bagmati.)*

TEKU. The junction of the Bagmati and Vishnumati Rivers at Teku is a sacred place often used for cremations. The wailing of the bereaved echoes around the temples and *chaityas*, and a tall brick *shikhara* stands over the confluence. The riverbanks might look like something out of a pastoral idyll, with buffalo munching hay in the shade, but the buffalo are in fact about to be slaughtered. *(In the southwest corner of the city. Be sensitive about photography.)*

WEST OF THE CITY

The west bank of the Vishnumati River is beyond Kathmandu's traditional city limits, but it has been brought into the metropolis by Ring Rd.

SWAYAMBHUNATH. The most prominent feature of the west bank is the hilltop stupa of Swayambhunath, more than 2000 years old. Swayambhunath is the holiest place on earth for Newari Buddhists, and it is the focus of the Kathmandu Valley's creation myth (see p. 744). The road from Kathmandu to Swayambhunath certainly has a bit of a red-carpet feel to it, as the shrine looms up from the hilltop ahead. At the base of the hill is a large rectangular gateway—from here the long crooked steps start to work their way through the trees and Buddha-icons to the top. At the very top of the steps is an enormous *vajra*, the Tibetan thunderbolt symbol; behind it is the stupa, whitewashed and flattened on top like other Nepali stupas. From the golden cube on top of the stupa, the Buddha's all-seeing eyes gaze out in every direction; the views are splendid. What looks like a nose is actually a number "1" representing the unity of all things.

Nine golden shrines surround the stupa. They enclose images of the *dhyani* Buddhas, who represent the different aspects of the Buddha through the elements of earth, water, fire, air, and space. The four Buddhas, who occupy the shrines at the secondary points, also have female elements *(taras)*. Swayambhunath is also known as the "Monkey Temple" for the dozens of rhesus monkeys that clamber all around it. *(3km from the city. A 30min. walk or bus #19 from Ratna Park leads you to Ring Rd., just west of Swayambhunath. Stupa Rs50.)*

BUDDHIST MUSEUM. The Buddhist Museum is small and dark, but it has a good range of Buddhist (and Hindu) images in its sculpture collection. Neighboring the museum is a small monastery that welcomes visitors and their donations. The small temple in front of the monastery is dedicated to **Harati,** the goddess of small-pox, who can either protect or infect. It's not clear what she does now that small-pox is eradicated. *(On a platform west of the stupa. Open W-F and Su-M 10am-5pm. Free.)*

NATIONAL MUSEUM. Nepal's National Museum has an art gallery with a good collection of wood, stone, and metalwork while excellent carvings can be seen on the houses and temples of the Kathmandu Valley. The museum allows you to get a closer look. The Historical Museum building is at least as interesting as the art gallery. Its natural history section features the pelt of a two-headed calf, a set of bones from a blue whale, and an unusual abundance of stuffed deer heads. The Nepalese history section is an amusing tribute to rulers and their playthings. The museum grounds are pleasant, and the roof terrace of the art gallery has a good view of the surrounding valley. *(1km south of Swayambhunath, on the road from the river. Open Tu-Sa 9:30am-4pm; in winter 9:30am-3pm. Rs50; camera Rs50.)*

NATURAL HISTORY MUSEUM. The Natural History Museum houses a 14,000-piece collection of high-altitude plants and animals. *(Follow the motor road down the hill south of Swayambhunath. ☎ 271899. Open Su-F 10am-5pm. Rs10; camera fee Rs10.)*

🎵 🖼 ENTERTAINMENT AND NIGHTLIFE

Hotel de l'Annapurna, Durbar Marg, holds daily dance shows. (☎221711. 7pm, Rs350.) **Himachali Cultural Group,** Lazimpath, also has daily performances; call for reservations. (☎415280. 7pm, Rs350.) At least half a dozen establishments—among them the **Thamel Guest House, Boogie Woogie Bark,** and **Everest Paradise Pizzeria Steakhouse**—hold Video Nights in Kathmandu, showing recent film releases. **Pilgrim's Book House** also has concerts of Indian music (Su, Tu, and F at 7pm, Rs300).

When it comes to nightlife in Nepal, Kathmandu is where it's at—options include bars (which close by midnight), four casinos (the only ones on the subcontinent), and a few nightclubs. **Casino Royal** is at the Yak & Yeti, **Casino Everest** is at Hotel Everest, **Casino Anna** is at Hotel de l'Annapurna, and the **Royal Nepal Casino** is at the Soaltee Holiday Inn. All but the Casino Royal are open 24 hours. In addition to the following pubs and discos, check-out the **New Orleans Cafe** (see p. 739).

Maya Cocktail Bar and **Maya Pub,** Thamel. The cocktail bar is upstairs from the Pumpernickel Bakery; the pub is at the intersection by the Kathmandu Guest House. Both offer free popcorn and 2-for-1 cocktails 4-7pm. The dark pub is less crowded and has a mainstream pop music soundtrack; the funkier cocktail bar is bigger and more raucous. Beer Rs105-120; cocktails Rs110-200. Pool and snooker Rs40 per game, Rs250 per hr. Both open daily 3pm-around midnight.

The Rum Doodle 40,000½-Feet Bar and Restaurant, Thamel. Follow the turn in the road north of the Kathmandu Guest House; it's on the left. The bar's namesake is a 1956 literary spoof about a mountaineering expedition; the book is sold at the bar (Rs150). The walls (and ceiling) are decorated with foot-shaped cut-outs signed and decorated by trekking and mountaineering parties. Draft beer Rs100-140. Open 10am-10pm.

Les Yeux, Thamel, on Thahity, just south of the intersection. This bar and restaurant features the nightly cover tunes of Criss Cross, Kathmandu's self-proclaimed "hardest rockin' band." The lead singer's Jim Morrison impression is uncanny. Outdoor terrace with garden. Beer Rs120. Open 8am-10pm.

The Tunnel Club, Thamel, down an alley at the intersection of Tridevi Marg and Thahity. Back-alley, all-night bar/pool hall popular with night-owl tourists and Nepalis.

Club Dynasty, halfway down Durbar Marg, on the right. By far the most popular nightclub among Nepalis, though there's a substantial foreign contingent as well. Move to the thundering house beat on the spacious dance floor or chill with the mellow crowd on the black-lit sofas. Beer Rs100. Cover Rs200. Open daily 9pm-2:30am.

📦 SHOPPING

In Thamel or Durbar Square, roving merchants hawk everything from flutes and chess sets to hash pipes and Tiger Balm. Just about anything made in Nepal can be bought in Kathmandu, though most crafts are better bought in their places of origin. For woodcarving and pottery, head to Bhaktapur; for papier-mâché masks and puppets, Thimi; for metalwork, Patan; and for Tibetan crafts like *thankas*, Boudha. Bagh Bazaar is the best place for saris; cloth and beads can be found north of Indra Chowk.

The **Khukuri House,** in Thamel, at the zig-zag north of the Kathmandu Guest House, near Rum Doodle's, deserves special mention. This well-reputed knife shop is owned by a former Gorkha officer. (☎412314. Open Su-F 10am-7pm. MC, Visa.) **Didi's Boutique** and **Didi-daju,** both on Chhetrapati, east of Everest Steak House, carry a wide selection of handicrafts, many of which are produced by the Janakpur Women's Development Centre. (Both open daily 10am-9pm. MC, Visa.)

➕ VOLUNTEER OPPORTUNITIES

Expat prisoners in the central jail at **Sundhara,** near the GPO, appreciate visitors who'll talk to them for a little while. The **Sisters of Charity of Nazareth** (☎426453 or 419965), Navjyoti Center, Baluwatar, perform prison ministry, including assisting former women prisoners. **St. Xavier's School** (☎521050 or 521150), Jawalakhel, and **The Missionaries of Charity** (☎471810), Mitra Park, work with the destitute.

📷 DAYTRIP FROM KATHMANDU

PASHUPATINATH पशुपतीनाथ

*Pashupatinath is only nominally outside of Kathmandu, and it's simple to get there by **bike**—follow Tridevi Marg away from Thamel and turn right at the first road after Durbar Marg. At the Marco Polo Business Hotel, turn left and follow the zig-zagging road east across a bridge. Watch for signs showing maps of Pashupatinath. **Bus #1** from Ratna Park (frequent, 45min., Rs4) stops along Ring Rd. at the turnoff to Pashupathinath; follow the signs from there. The **#2 tempo** from Sundhara (via Rani Pokhari) stops across the street, just inside Ring Rd. (frequent, 30min., Rs6). **Taxis** from Thamel cost about Rs50.*

The temple complex of Pashupatinath, east of Kathmandu, is the holiest Hindu site in Nepal. Chock full of devotees, Pashupatinath is dedicated to Shiva's incarnation as Pashupati, the gentle Lord of Animals and the guardian deity of Nepal. In addition to the bathers who dip in the Bagmati on auspicious full-moon nights and on the 11th day after them, thousands descend upon Pashupatinath during March's **Shivaratri** festival, and even the king himself often comes to worship here.

The **Pashupati Temple,** built in 1696, is right on the banks of the Bagmati. A road leads directly up to it, though non-Hindus may not enter. The brass backside of an enormous statue of Nandi can be seen from the entrance, but the rest of the temple is out of view and out of bounds, too, if you don't look like a Hindu (see p. 78 for more on Nandi). Other viewpoints in the area afford over-the-wall glimpses of the wood and marble pagoda. Backtrack away from the river, turn left and left again until another, bigger road leads back to the river; on the right side is a group of five temples known as **Panch Dewal,** whose compound has become a social welfare center. **Biddha Ashram,** operated by Mother Teresa's Missionaries of Charity, welcomes walk-in volunteers. Ahead, stone walls and *ghats* squeeze the river, making it look more like a canal. Two footbridges are laid across it here, and right

between them on the near (west) bank is the 6th-century **Bacchareswari Temple.**
The **ghats** downstream are used for cremations. **If there are cremations in progress,
be sensitive about taking pictures.**

Across the footbridges, on the east bank of the Bagmati, is a row of 11 small
Shiva shrines; this is a popular gathering place for sadhus. From here, it's possible to see into the entire Pashupati Temple compound. The *ghats* immediately
below are sometimes used for VIP cremations, including those of members of
the royal family. The steps up the hill on the east bank of the river eventually
level out at a small wooded village of Shiva temples; Nandi figures line the main
street. At the end of the village is a temple dedicated to **Gorakhnath,** an 11th-
century saint revered as an avatar of Shiva. The steps continue downhill to the
Gujeshwari Temple, locally considered to be the place where the Sati's *yoni* fell
when she was cut into pieces by Vishnu (the Kamakhya Temple in Guwahati,
India is more widely recognized as this site—see **Divine Dismemberment,** p. 692).
According to Buddhist lore, the temple's sacred well is a bottomless hollow left
by the root of the lotus that blossomed and inspired the creation of the
Kathmandu Valley (see **The Legend of the Kathmandu Valley,** p. 744). Non-Hindus
may not enter. The road downstream in front of the temple leads to a bridge;
once you cross it, stone steps lead over the hill and back to the Pashupati
Temple. The road to the right heads to **Boudha** (see p. 755), a 30-minute walk
north through fields and small neighborhoods.

PATAN पाटन ☎ 01

With only the Bagmati River lying between Kathmandu and its temple-dotted
neighbor Patan, the two cities have practically merged. The legacy of their development as independent kingdoms lives on, however, and Patan has managed to
maintain its own distinct character. Well established as the valley's center for
Newari handicraft production, Patan (also known as Lalitpur, or "City of Fine
Arts") is a great place to stroll through alleys to observe artisans at work. Also a
spiritual center, the city is graced with many small stupas, *shikharas*, and onion-
domed temples. Some of these shrines languish in disuse and are invaded by
weeds, but many still host daily *puja* for Patan's residents. Well aware of the tourist appeal of such a beautiful city, the local government has recently begun charging visitors a Rs200 entry fee.

▟ GETTING THERE AND GETTING AROUND

Tempos (frequent, 20min., Rs10) leave from Kathmandu's GPO. Most head to
Jawalakhel and then Lagankhel, but some go to Mangal Bazaar—ask the driver.
Tempos leave for Kathmandu from Patan's Durbar Square on Mangal Bazaar. **Bus
#26** runs from Kathmandu's Ratna Park to Patan Gate (frequent, 25 min., Rs4). **Bus
#14**, also from Ratna Park, goes to Lagankhel via Jawalakhel (frequent, 30min.,
Rs4). **Taxis** from Thamel to Patan's Durbar Sq. cost about Rs75, auto-rickshaws
around Rs50. **Buses** depart for Kathmandu from Patan Gate.

▟ ⁊ ORIENTATION AND PRACTICAL INFORMATION

Patan is linked to Kathmandu by a bridge across the **Bagmati River** and is bounded
to the south by the same **Ring Rd.** that encircles Kathmandu. Patan's main road,
which runs from Kathmandu, goes by the name of whatever neighborhood it is
passing through: from the bridge south to Ring Rd. it is called **Kopundol,** then **Pulchowk,** and finally **Jawalakhel.** The **old city,** east of the main road, is loosely bounded
by four **stupas** (supposedly built by Ashoka in the 3rd century BC), one in each
direction. The eastern stupa is beyond Ring Rd.; the western stupa is along the
main road in Pulchowk, opposite the turn-off to **Durbar Square,** the center of the
oldest part of town. Several branches lead east from the main road. From north to
south, the first leads to **Patan Dhoka** (Patan Gate), north of Durbar Square. The sec-

ond becomes **Mangal Bazaar,** the road at the south end of Durbar Square. Finally, at **Jawalakhel Chowk,** the road leads toward **Lagankhel** and the **bus park.** See the Kathmandu and Patan map, in the Kathmandu section.

Tourist Office: There is a tourist information booth outside Patan Gate. This is the only place where you can pay the Rs200 **entrance fee,** though you may be asked to show your ticket at other checkpoints throughout the city. Open daily 6:30am-7:30pm.

Currency Exchange: Nepal Grindlays, Jawalakhel Chowk (☎522490), changes traveler's checks. Open Su-Th 10am-5pm, F 10am-1pm.

Bookstore: Pilgrims Book House (☎521159) has a huge branch on the main road in Kopundol. Open daily 9am-8pm. AmEx, MC, Visa.

Market: Fruit, spices, and fabrics are sold in Lagankhel, near the bus park. There is a huge vegetable market just south of the bus park. **Namaste Supermarket,** along the main road in Pulchowk, sells a range of pre-packaged goods. Open daily 9am-8pm.

Pharmacy: There are many pharmacies on Mangal Bazaar, below Durbar Sq. **Alka Pharmacy** (☎535146), on the main road in Jawalakhel, north of St. Xavier's school, can arrange house calls. Open daily 7am-10pm.

Hospital: Patan Hospital, Lagankhel (☎522295), has a good reputation.

Telephones and Internet: There are several booths around Jawalakhel Chowk. **The Cybernet** (☎521424), has STD/ISD (callbacks Rs5 per min.), Internet (Rs3 per min.), and Internet phone (Rs4 per min.). Open daily 8am-8pm.

Post Office: Outside Patan Gate, on the west side. Open M-F 9:15am-2:30pm.

ACCOMMODATIONS

Thamel's tourist explosion has put the squeeze on Patan's budget accommodations. Most people just ride into Patan for the day and return to Kathmandu at night. However, a night or two in Patan means freedom from the tourist ghettos of Thamel and the promise of a quiet respite from the morning racket of Kathmandu.

Cafe de Patan, Mangal Bazaar (☎537599; fax 534967), just southwest of Durbar Sq. Clean, comfortable, quiet rooms are available above this restaurant, just steps away from the sights. Balconies, abundant furnishings, and spotless bathrooms with seat toilets. Singles Rs300-500; doubles Rs400-600.

Mountain View Guest House, Kumaripati (☎538168). Walk west 10min. from Lagankhel bus park; on the right behind the Campion Academy. A little removed from the older part of town, this family-run place has the feel of a warm and well-run household. Clean, modern, and well-furnished. Singles Rs200-250; doubles Rs250-350.

Hungry Treat Home (☎534792 or 543360), a few minutes' walk east of Jawalakhel Chowk. Clean, ample rooms with large windows, fans, and layers of carpeting. Tiled bathrooms with seat toilets and toilet paper. Attached restaurant. Doubles Rs220-500.

Mahendra Youth Hostel, Jawalakhel Rd. (☎521003). As you walk north from Jawalakhel Chowk, it's down the second lane to the right, opposite St. Xavier's. Dorm rooms are worn, and facilities are basic, but it's the cheapest around—and hey, you might make some new friends. No hot water. Check-in 6am-10pm. Dorm beds Rs50-75; doubles with bath Rs200. 10% discounts for HI/IYHF members.

FOOD

Patan's food selection is less varied than Kathmandu's, but it's also less tourist-oriented, with more *tarkari* (veg. curry) than teriyaki. Fast-food tandoori joints line the main road. More expensive places serve the same menu in more pleasant settings. For the breakfast-eater, **Hot Breads** and **The Bakery Cafe** on Jawalakhel Chowk offer a wide range of pastries. For great cake, loaves of bread (Rs25-30), and other baked goodies, head for the **German Bakery,** north of Jawalakhel Chowk.

Tama Restaurant and Bar, Pulchowk, across the street and south of the Sajha bus garage, set back from the road. Cheap Indian menu (Rs75-200) and pricier Japanese entrees (Rs155-300) served in a tidy, peaceful dining area. Open daily 11am-9pm.

Downtown Restaurant, Pulchowk, just north of the Sajha bus garage. Lace curtains screen the sights but not the sounds of the busy street. Deservedly popular for its extensive menu and low prices. Chicken *tikka masala* Rs85. Open Su-F 10am-9pm.

The Third World Restaurant, Durbar Sq., opposite the Patan Museum, directly upstairs from the craft boutique. Its small rooftop is one of the few places to eat while overlooking the square. Continental dishes Rs70-110; sandwiches Rs40-70. Open 8am-9pm.

Cafe de Patan, Mangal Bazaar, southwest of Durbar Sq. Walk through the souvenir and music shop to the ground floor dining area or the garden rooftop. Chinese (Rs60-95), continental (Rs70-140), and Nepali (Rs80-160) dishes. Open daily 8am-9pm.

Bakena Batika, Jawalakhel, just inside Ring Rd., south of the Tibetan Refugee Camp. Though removed from the center of things, the beautifully renovated Nepali house and tranquil courtyard make the perfect setting for light meals (Rs80-150), traditional Nepali courses (Rs150-190), and *risotto* (Rs190). Open daily 11am-8:30pm.

⬛ SIGHTS

DURBAR SQUARE

One good approach to exploring Durbar Sq. is to start at the southern end of the **Royal Palace,** which makes up the eastern side of the square, and continue north, circling around counter-clockwise.

THE ROYAL PALACE. The southern courtyard, **Sundari Chowk,** is not open to the public, but **Mul Chowk,** dating from the mid-17th century, can be entered between the two stone lions. On the southern wall, gilded statues of the Indian river goddesses Ganga (on a tortoise) and Yamuna (on a *makara,* a mythical snouted sea creature) guard the locked doorway to the **Taleju Shrine.** Dedicated to the patron goddess of Nepal's royal families, the shrine is open to Hindus one day a year during the **Dasain** festival. Other pagodas that rise around Mul Chowk are the **Degu Talle Temple,** an octagonal tower in the northeast corner, and, on the north side, the **Taleju Mandir,** the tallest in the square. *(Mul Chowk open 9am-5pm.)*

The new **Patan Museum** is in **Keshav Narayan Chowk,** the northernmost section of the palace; the entrance is an elaborate golden doorway. The whitewashed shrine inside is dedicated to Narayan. Beautifully restored with the help of the Austrian government and the Smithsonian Institution, the museum is probably the best in Nepal. With its extensive collection of metal, wood, and stone sculptures, all accompanied by thorough and informative labels, the museum provides an excellent introduction to Hindu and Buddhist iconography. Wide, cushioned window seats provide lookouts onto the square below, and a cafe in the courtyard serves snacks. *(Museum open 10:30am-5pm. Rs120.)* Around the corner to the north of the palace is the sunken water tank known as **Manga Hiti;** its mythical crocodile-like statues have been spouting water since the 6th century. The adjacent pavilion, **Mani Mandap,** was once used for coronations.

OTHER TEMPLES. Diagonally opposite, the northernmost temple in the square is the three-tiered **Bhimsen Mandir,** with a lion-topped pillar in front of its recently added marble facade. Merchants toss coins onto the older, gilded first floor of this temple dedicated to the god of trade. The next temple to the south is the **Vishwanath Mandir,** a double-roofed Shiva temple guarded by two stone elephants. The original structure dates back to 1627, but it collapsed in 1990 and has since been restored. The *linga* inside is said to replicate the Vishwanath *linga* in Varanasi (see p. 201). A Nandi faces the other side of the temple. As you continue south, the next temple is the stone, Indian *shikhara*-style **Krishna Mandir.** This temple stands out for its foreign design and because it is one of the few temples in Durbar Square still in active use. In the evenings, devotees set the building aglow with butter lamps. The upper floors, carved with friezes depicting scenes from the *Mahabharata* and *Ramayana,* are closed to non-Hindus.

Vishnu is the patron god of the next temple, the **Jagan Narayan Mandir.** Stone lions flank the front of this pagoda-style temple, complete with wildly erotic roof struts. Built in 1565, this is the square's oldest temple. The squat **Bhai Deval Mandir** is in the southwest corner of the square. Continuing around, you'll pass a fountain before arriving at the octagonal stone **Chyasin Deval,** which, like the other Krishna temples in the square, was built in an Indian style. Its construction is linked to the death of one of the Malla kings, but whether it spontaneously appeared or was built to honor his eight wives who all committed *sati,* is now a matter of controversy. The **Taleju Bell,** next door, was cast in 1736 and is the first of the valley's three big bells. The next temple to the north is the **Hari Shankar Mandir,** an elaborately carved three-tiered pagoda from the 18th century. The temple is jointly dedicated to Vishnu (called Hari here) and Shiva (Shankar). Circling back into the square, you will see a stone pillar topped by a golden statue of **King Yoganarendra Malla,** a monument with legends of its own. The king kneels under the protection of a cobra's hood, and it is said that as long as the bird perched on the cobra's head remains, the king may return. A door and window to his palace remain open, and his hookah waits inside. If the bird flies away, however, the stone elephants that guard the Vishwanath Mandir will leave their posts to drink from the Manga Hiti.

SOUTH OF DURBAR SQUARE

Continuing along Mangal Bazaar east of Durbar Square, you'll see signs for the **Mahaboudha Temple;** the right-hand turn-off is a five minute walk from the square. The architect of this "temple of 1000 Buddhas" was inspired by the Mahabodhi Temple in Bodh Gaya, India, where the Buddha achieved enlightenment (see p. 639). The foreign influence is obvious: the *shikhara*-style temple is covered with terra cotta tiles, each of which bears a sculpted figure of the Buddha. The temple was severely damaged in a 1934 earthquake, and the builders who reassembled it found themselves with so many bricks left over that they built a small shrine to the Buddha's mother Mayadevi, which stands nearby. As you turn right from the Mahaboudha, the **Uka Bahal (Rudravarna Mahabihar),** the oldest monastery in Patan, is on the left at the next intersection. A pair of stone lions guards this former Buddhist monastery, while an ark full of brass beasts stands watch in the courtyard.

As you leave Uka Bahal, turn left onto **Tinker St.** The sound of metal being hammered fills the street, which ends at the wide market street that runs south from Durbar Square. At the intersection of the two streets stands the **Ibaha Bahal,** a recently renovated monastery dating from 1427. Farther south along the same street, on the left, is the **Minnath Mandir,** with its garishly painted details. Minnath is often called *sanno* ("little") Machhendranath, in reference to the deity who inhabits another temple down a short lane across the street. This temple, the **Rato Machhendranath Mandir,** a 17th-century pagoda with an intricate, colorful, three-tiered roof, stands in the center of a big, grassy compound. A collection of brass animals, each one representing a month of the Tibetan calendar, poses on posts facing the temple. Machhendranath is a multi-purpose deity: he's an incarnation of Avalokiteshvara, the Bodhisattva of Compassion, is revered as the guru of a 7th-century saint, and on top of that, is the Newari god who controls the rains. In late April the *rato* ("red") image of Machhendranath rides in a towering chariot that makes its rounds in Patan, followed by a smaller chariot carrying Minnath, who is considered to be his brother. Beginning in Pulchowk, the local residents tow the chariots to the next stop on the tour, having first fueled themselves with *raksi* and *chhang.* The chariots are often halted along the way to wait for a suitably auspicious moment to move, and it can take them up to sixty days to reach Jawalkhel, their final destination. From here, the image of Machhendranath is removed from the chariot and carried to his temple in the nearby town of Bungamati, where he spends six months of every year. The enormous, rickety temple-chariots (*raths*), which are destroyed and built anew every year occasionally topple, crushing houses and people. The government refuses to grant any restitution to the victims, as it is widely believed that Machhendranath has chosen to punish them for the evil deeds they have committed.

WORLDWIDE CALLING MADE EASY

The MCI WorldCom Card, designed specifically to keep you in touch with the people that matter the most to you.

MCI WORLDCOM   WORLDPHONE.

1·800·888·8000

J. L. SMITH

www.wcom.com/worldphone

Please tear off this card and keep it in your wallet as a reference guide for convenient U.S. and worldwide calling with the MCI WorldCom Card.

HOW TO MAKE CALLS USING YOUR MCI WORLDCOM CARD

When calling from the U.S., Puerto Rico, the U.S. Virgin Islands or Canada to virtually anywhere in the world:

Dial 1-800-888-8000

Enter your card number + PIN, listen for the dial tone

Dial the number you are calling :

Domestic Calls: Area Code + Phone number

International Calls:
011+ Country Code + City Code + Phone Number

When calling from outside the U.S., use WorldPhone from over 125 countries and places worldwide:

Dial the WorldPhone toll-free access number of the country you are calling from.

Follow the voice instructions or hold for a WorldPhone operator to complete the call.

For calls from your hotel:

Obtain an outside line.

Follow the instructions above on how to place a call.

Note: If your hotel blocks the use of your MCI WorldCom Card, you may have to use an alternative location to place your call.

RECEIVING INTERNATIONAL COLLECT CALLS*

Let family and friends call you collect at home using WorldPhone once and pay the same low rate as if you called them.

Provide them with the WorldPhone access number for the country they are calling from (In the U.S., 1-800-888-8000; for international access numbers see reverse side).

Have them dial that access number, wait for an operator, and ask to call you collect at your home number.

U.S. based customers only.

START USING YOUR MCI WORLDCOM CARD TODAY. MCI WORLDCOM STEPSAVERS℠

Get the same low rate per country as on calls from home, when you:

1. Receive international collect calls to your home using WorldPhone access numbers

2. Make international calls with your MCI WorldCom Card from the U.S. *

3. Call back to anywhere in the U.S. from Abroad using your MCI WorldCom Card and WorldPhone access numbers.

* An additional charge applies to calls from U.S. pay phones.

WorldPhone Overseas Laptop Connection Tips —
Visit our website, www.wcom.com/worldphone, to learn how to access the Internet and email via your laptop when traveling abroad using the MCI WorldCom Card and WorldPhone access numbers.

Travelers Assist® — When you are overseas, get emergency interpretation assistance and local medical, legal, and entertainment referrals. Simply dial the country's toll-free access number.

Planning a Trip?—Call the WorldPhone customer service hotline at 1-800-736-1828 for new and updated country access availability or visit our website:

www.wcom.com/worldphone

MCI WorldCom Worldphone Access Numbers

Easy Worldwide Calling

MCI *WORLDCOM.*

The MCI WorldCom Card.
The easy way to call when traveling worldwide.

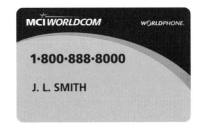

MCI WORLDCOM   **WORLDPHONE.**

1·800·888·8000

J. L. SMITH

The MCI WorldCom Card gives you...

- Access to the US and other countries worldwide.
- Customer Service 24 hours a day
- Operators who speak your language
- Great MCI WorldCom rates and no sign-up fees

For more information or to apply for a Card call:
1-800-955-0925

Outside the U.S., call MCI WorldCom collect (reverse charge) at:
1-712-943-6839

COUNTRY	WORLDPHONE TOLL-FREE ACCESS #
Argentina (CC)	
Using Telefonica	0800-222-6249
Using Telecom	0800-555-1002
Australia (CC) ♦	
Using OPTUS	1-800-551-111
Using TELSTRA	1-800-881-100
Austria (CC) ♦	0800-200-235
Bahamas (CC) +	1-800-888-8000
Belgium (CC) ♦	0800-10012
Bermuda (CC) +	1-800-888-8000
Bolivia (CC) ♦	0-800-2222
Brazil (CC)	000-8012
British Virgin Islands +	1-800-888-8000
Canada (CC)	1-800-888-8000
Cayman Islands +	1-800-888-8000
Chile (CC)	
Using CTC	800-207-300
Using ENTEL	800-360-180
China ♦	108-12
Mandarin Speaking Operator	108-17
Colombia (CC) ♦	980-9-16-0001
Collect Access in Spanish	980-9-16-1111
Costa Rica ♦	0800-012-2222
Czech Republic (CC) ♦	00-42-000112
Denmark (CC) ♦	8001-0022
Dominica+	1-800-888-8000
Dominican Republic (CC) +	
Collect Access	1-800-888-8000
Collect Access in Spanish	1121

COUNTRY	ACCESS #
Ecuador (CC) +	999-170
El Salvador (CC)	800-1767
Finland (CC) ♦	08001-102-80
France (CC) ♦	0-800-99-0019
French Guiana (CC)	0-800-99-0019
Germany (CC)	0800-888-8000
Greece (CC) ♦	00-800-1211
Guam (CC) ♦	1-800-888-8000
Guatemala (CC) ♦	99-99-189
Haiti +	
Collect Access	193
Collect access in Creole	190
Honduras +	8000-122
Hong Kong (CC)	800-96-1121
Hungary (CC) ♦	06*-800-01411
India (CC)	000-127
Collect access	000-126
Ireland (CC)	1-800-55-1001
Israel (CC) ♦	1-800-920-2727
Italy (CC) ♦	172-1022
Jamaica +	
Collect Access	1-800-888-8000
From pay phones	#2
Japan (CC) ♦	
Using KDD	00539-121 ▶
Using IDC	0066-55-121
Using JT	0044-11-121

(FOLD)

COUNTRY	ACCESS #
Korea (CC)	
To call using KT	00729-14
Using DACOM	00309-12
Phone Booths +	
Press red button ,03,then*	
Military Bases	550-2255
Luxembourg (CC)	8002-0112
Malaysia (CC) ♦	1-800-80-0012
Mexico (CC)	01-800-021-8000
Monaco (CC) ♦	800-90-019
Netherlands (CC) ♦	0800-022-91-22
New Zealand (CC)	000-912
Nicaragua (CC)	166
Norway (CC) ♦	800-19912
Panama	00800-001-0108
Philippines (CC) ♦	
Using PLDT	105-14
Filipino speaking operator	105-15
Using Bayantel	1237-14
Using Bayantel (Filipino)	1237-77
Using ETPI (English)	1066-14
Poland (CC) ♦	800-111-21-22
Portugal (CC) +	800-800-123
Romania (CC) +	01-800-1800
Russia (CC) + ♦	
Russian speaking operator	
	747-3320
Using Rostelcom	747-3322
Using Sovintel	960-2222
Saudi Arabia (CC)	1-800-11

COUNTRY	WORLDPHONE TOLL-FREE ACCESS
Singapore (CC)	8000-112-11
Slovak Republic (CC)	08000-001
South Africa (CC)	0800-99-00
Spain (CC)	900-99-00
St. Lucia +	1-800-888-80
Sweden (CC) ♦	020-795-99
Switzerland (CC) ♦	0800-89-02
Taiwan (CC) ♦	0080-13-45-
Thailand (CC)	001-999-1-20
Turkey (CC) ♦	00-8001-11
United Kingdom (CC)	
Using BT	0800-89-02
Using C&W	0500-89-02
Venezuela (CC) + ♦	800-1114
Vietnam + ●	1201-10

(FOLD)

KEY
Note: Automation available from most locations. Countries where automation is not yet available are shown in *italic*.
(CC) Country-to-country calling available.
+ Limited availability.
★ Not available from public pay phones.
♦ Public phones may require deposit of coin or phone card for dial tone.
● Local service fee in U.S. currency required to complete c
▶ Regulation does not permit Intra-Japan Calls.
* Wait for second dial tone.
■ Local surcharge may apply.
Hint: For Puerto Rico and Caribbean Islands not listed above you can use 1-800-888-8000 as the WorldPhone access num

NORTH OF DURBAR SQUARE

GOLDEN TEMPLE. The Golden Temple, one of Patan's most famous buildings, is a five-minute walk up the first northern lane west of Durbar Square. Also known as **Hiranyavarna Mahavihar,** this ornate, gilded temple makes up the west side of the **Kwa Bahal,** a 12th-century Buddhist monastery whose courtyard is marked by a golden shrine. **No leather is allowed beyond the walkway around the edge of the court-yard—you can trade your shoes for flip-flops at the temple entrance.** The temple's facade is elaborately worked in metal relief with images of Buddhas, *taras,* and mythological creatures. Gods are supposed to be able to slide down the *patakas,* the golden belts that hang from the roofs. The stairs in the northeast corner lead to the monastery's interior, where there is a collection of icons and Tibetan-style murals. *(Walk to the northern end of Durbar Square, take a left at the Chimsen Temple, then take the next right. Open 8:30am-6pm. Rs25 for foreigners.)*

KUMBESHWAR MAHADEV. A few minutes north of the Golden Temple, Kumbeshwar Mahadev is the oldest temple in Patan. Though it had only two tiers when it was built in 1392, three stories were added later to make it one of two free-standing, five-roofed pagodas in the Kathmandu Valley (the other is the Nyatapola Temple in Bhaktapur). The deity-in-residence is Shiva, as indicated by the Nandi outside the temple. The water tank next to the temple is believed to be connected to the holy Himalayan lake of Gosainkund. A pilgrim is said to have dropped a *kumbh* (pot) in the lake, which then emerged in the tank in Patan, giving the temple its name. Thousands of devotees come to bathe in the tank during the **Janai Purnima festival** (held in August), when high-caste Hindus change their sacred threads. One block east of the temple, the road to the right leads back to the northern end of Durbar Square, passing a number of smaller temples on the way.

JAWALAKHEL

The Jawalakhel neighborhood is notable for its foreign residents, mostly Tibetan refugees and expats working for aid organizations.

CENTRAL ZOO. Just west of Jawalakhel Chowk is the Central Zoo, with a pond in the middle of the landscaped grounds. See that tiger (as well as the showcased guinea pigs) that eluded you at Chitwan, and then ponder the confined animals' plight over a paddleboat ride. *(Open Tu-Su 10am-6pm. Tickets sold until 5pm. Rs60 for foreigners; camera fee Rs10; video Rs50; paddleboat Rs40 per person.)*

JAWALAKHEL HANDICRAFT CENTRE. A part of the Tibetan Refugee Camp, Jawalakhel Handicraft Centre was established by the Red Cross and the Nepalese government in 1960. The center employs Tibetans who fled their country after the Chinese takeover in 1959. Visitors are free to wander freely, observing the carpet-making process with no pressure to buy. Proceeds from the souvenir shop go to the workers. *(5-10min. walk south of Jawalakhel Chowk. ☎ 521305. Open Su-F 8am-5pm.)*

🛍 SHOPPING

A lower-pressure sales atmosphere than Kathmandu (and an equally wide selection) make Patan an ideal place for souvenir shopping. Since most of the items sold in Patan were actually produced here, prices and selection tend to be even better than in Kathmandu. This is especially true for carpets, metal work, wooden toys, and puppets. Patan is full of non-profit outlets that sell crafts from all over the country at fixed prices. Many of them benefit under-privileged workers—especially women—and ensure fair wages. They can be found in the old Royal Palace on Durbar Square and in Kopundol. **Sana Hastakala,** Kopundol, opposite Hotel Himalaya, is sponsored by UNICEF. (☎522628; fax 526985; email sanahast@wlink.com.np. Open Su-F 9:30am-6pm, Sa 10am-5pm. AmEx, MC, Visa.)

▶ DAYTRIPS FROM PATAN: GODAVARI गोदावरी

If the dry, dusty city has you craving fragrant flowers, Godavari is the place to go. A horticultural haven, Godavari is where you'll find the peaceful, expertly landscaped Royal Botanical Garden, the National Herbarium, and the nurseries that supply florists in Patan, as well as the Godavari Kunda and Pulchowki Mai, two local religious sites. The **Botanical Garden** is a 15-minute walk from the bus park, up the road to the left; continue until the paved road comes to an end at the garden's entrance. The garden is big enough to get lost in, and the shady pavilions are great places to sit and relax. *(Open daily 9am-5pm. Admission Rs25 for foreigners; camera fee Rs10.)* The small dirt road that branches off to the right before the entrance to the Botanical Garden leads uphill for 100m to the **Godavari Kunda,** a pool shrouded with faded prayer flags. Clear mountain water collects in an interior pool (closed) which then flows through spouts to the outer pool. Pilgrims come here every 12 years to purify themselves in the waters. From the bus park, the road to the right leads uphill past St. Xavier's College to a marble quarry and **Pulchowki Mai,** a rather run-down temple opposite it. The temple houses images of Vishnu, Ganesh, and a tantric mother goddess, but most have been rubbed into indecipherability. Outside the temple is a pool fed by nine sculptured spouts, symbolizing the nine streams that flow off Pulchowki, the nearby mountain for which the temple is named. From Langankhel bus park, **buses** #13 and 14 continue up the hills to Godavari (1hr., Rs4), with spellbinding, misty views of rice paddies along the way; the Godavari bus park is the last stop.

BUNGAMATI बुँगामथी

A short distance south of Kathmandu is **Bungamati,** a small Newari town that sees very few tourists. Bungamati is quiet and car-free, and children are more likely to greet visitors with curious, silent stares than calls for "onepen-onerupee." The town square is a good place to observe the workings of a typical Newari village, as women wash clothes in the local fountain and spread rice out in the sun to dry.

The town's main claim to fame is its tall, white, *shikhara*-style **Rato Machhendranath temple,** part-time home of the Newari god of the same name. Bungamati is revered as the birthplace of Rato Machhendranath, the patron god of the Kathmandu Valley, also believed to be an incarnation of Avalokitesvara, the Bodhisattva of Compassion. During Patan's **Rato Machhendranath festival** in late April, the image of the deity is taken from a corresponding temple in Patan and pulled through the streets on a huge wooden chariot from Pulchowk to Jawalakhel. From here it is brought to the temple in Bungamati by palanquin, where it spends the remaining six months of the year before returning to Patan. Every 12 years, however (next in 2003), the immense chariots are pulled all the way to Bungamati, a colossal undertaking that sometimes requires the aid of the Nepali army.

The **bus** to Bungamati departs from Patan's Jawalakhel Chowk (frequent, 45min., Rs4) and passes over a fantastic look-out point just before arriving at the turn-off to Bungamati, marked by a **police post.** To get to the temple, follow the stone path downhill from the police post; the road leads down through town, between two ponds, and finally up to the town square and the temple.

KIRTIPUR कीर्तीपुर

With its ancient houses and hushed pedestrian streets, Kirtipur (pop. 30,000) still offers a taste of Newari life, despite its proximity to the hustle and bustle of Kathmandu. Young, uniformed children hurry along narrow, winding streets on their way to school, while women wash clothes and men head out to work in the terraced fields. South of the town is **Tribhuvan University,** the largest in Nepal. Still neglected by most tourists, Kirtipur, with its ornate temples, hilltop views, and proximity to Chobas, makes an excellent daytrip from Kathmandu.

The citizens of Kirtipur remain proud of the stand their ancestors took against Prithvi Narayan Shah's encroaching Gorkha forces during the 18th century (see **History**, p. 717). When Shah attacked for the first time in 1757, neighboring towns came to Kirtipur's aid and managed to help defeat the invaders. During a second battle in 1764, Shah's brother was shot in the eye with an arrow, and the Gorkhas again retreated. But the Gorkhas' superior weaponry turned the tide two years later, when, after a six-month siege, Kirtipur finally surrendered. The Gorkhas punished the men of the town by slicing off their noses, ears, and lips so that people throughout the country would recognize them as troublemakers from Kirtipur.

ORIENTATION AND PRACTICAL INFORMATION. To reach Kirtipur from Kathmandu take a **taxi** (Rs200) or **bus #21** (frequent departures, 30min., Rs4) from the Ratna Park bus station. After passing through the gates of Tribhuvan University, the bus climbs a steep hill into town before taking a sharp left. Get off at the top of the hill, where you'll find a partially rusted but still legible city map. The road extends to the left into the **Naya Bazaar,** home to several small shops offering **STD** and **Internet** services.

SIGHTS. A walking tour of Kirtipur's sights can be completed in one or two hours. A good place to start is the prominent **Shree Kirti Vihara,** a Buddhist temple built in 1975 and immaculately kept by the resident monks. As you enter, you will see a low hallway on your right and a four-paneled door to the left. Both depict the four major stages in the life of the Buddha: his birth in Lumbini, his enlightenment at Bodh Gaya, his first sermon at Sarnath, and his death in Kushinagar.

Across the main road from the temple is a steep stone path; follow this uphill and then bear right onto a set of brick steps, which leads into a neighborhood of houses three centuries old. Turn right at a low yellow building; the steps up to the ancient **Chilandeo Stupa** are a short way down on the left. This 1400-year-old stupa is surrounded by a number of stone shrines, some of which are very recent. The prayer wheel to the right as you enter is only five years old, but it is the largest in Kirtipur. Along the left side of the stupa is an abandoned 17th century monastery, adorned with just one remaining *torano* arch on the leftmost door (the others were recently stolen), guarded by a sturdy Newari-crafted lock.

Facing the monastery, turn right and walk around behind the stupa to the small path that leads out of the stupa area. From the path, take your first right into an open area dominated by a towering stone **shikara.** The upper level of the temple features representations of the Buddha, while the lower level is devoted to Hindu deities. This half-Buddhist, half-Hindu temple was built during the 17th century as a gesture of goodwill during a period of religious tension.

From the *shikhara*, turn left and follow the slate path down to a large courtyard with a pool. At the far end of the courtyard is the **Bagh Bhairab Mandir,** an 11th-century temple dedicated to Shiva the Destroyer (*Bhairab*) in the form of a tiger (*bagh*). Mounted on the upper facade are Gorkhali swords and uniforms, commemorating Kirtipur's defeat by the Gorkhas. Worshippers and musicians visit Bagh Bhairab every morning and evening; there are chicken or buffalo sacrifices on Tuesdays and Saturdays. Bagh Bhairab is also the center of Kirtipur's December festival for the goddess Indrani, an offshoot of Kathmandu's Indrani festival.

Facing the entrance to the Bagh Bhairab Mandir, take the road to the left to the **Uma-Maheshwar Mandir.** Built in 1575, the temple overlooks the valley from the highest point in Kirtipur (1440m). Two stone elephants guard the temple, within which are housed intricately carved wooden images of Shiva and his consort Parvati. More noteworthy than the temple itself, however, is its superb panoramic view. To the southwest looms one of the highest points of the Kathmandu Valley's rim, and to the northeast sprawls Kathmandu. On a clear day, you can even see Everest. For more gorgeous mountain scenery, and a glimpse of locals working on terraced fields, walk along the main road of Kirtipur past the bazaar. The road opposite the large dead tree on the main road leads out of town for 2km until the terraces appear on the left.

NEPAL

CHOBAR चोभार

When Manjushri released the waters of the Bhagmati river from the Kathmandu Valley's surrounding mountains with one swing of his sword, it was here that his blow is said to have landed. Whether the **Chobar Gorge** was formed by Manjushri's sword or by an earthquake, as geologists suggest, the legend has made tales of Chobar an important part of Nepalese lore. Spanning the gorge is a narrow **suspension bridge,** which was built in 1903 to provide a walking route to Patan. The village itself is on a small hill overlooking the gorge. The long stairway up to the village leads to the 14th century **Adinath Lokeshwar Mandir,** a half-Hindu, half-Buddhist temple covered with pots and pans—contributions of kitchenware to the temple are said to enhance the culinary skills of new brides. On the banks of the river just down the hill from the bridge, is the three-tiered **Jal Binayak,** a 950-year-old temple dedicated to Ganesh, who is represented here in the form of a large rock protruding from the back of the temple. Around the temple a stylized Shiva *linga* dances with Parvati before the statue of a rabbit.

Bus #22 (frequent, 45min., Rs5) heads to Chobar from Ratna Park in Kathmandu. Get off when the bus turns west into the gates of Tribhuvan University, and continue along the main road, passing the **Himalayan Bee Concern** on the right and a **cold store** on the left—the last one on the way to Patan; it's a good idea to stock up here. The stone stairs that lead uphill to Chobar are on the right a few yards past the cold store. From Kirtipur, Chobar is half an hour away. Follow the main road through the Naya Bazaar; with the Buddhist temple on your left, turn left at Ratna's Beauty Parlor, take the next left, and follow the path until it meets the main road near a small temple with a gate. Turn left onto the main road and follow the stairway up to Chobar. To reach **Chobar Gorge** from Chobar, head down the hill toward the cement factory (a cluster of big brown buildings) until you reach the gorge. From the gorge it's about an hour to Patan; cross the bridge and head straight along the uphill path.

NAGARJUN नागार्जुन AND BALAJU बालाजु

Many believe that the Buddha once meditated on Nagarjun; others maintain that the first bodhisattva, Viswapa, stood on the peak to throw the lotus seed that would blossom into *swayambhu* (see **The Legend of the Kathmandu Valley,** p. 744). Crowned by an old stupa draped in a virtual canopy of colored prayer flags, Nagarjun (also called "Jamacho") is the closest summit to Kathmandu, and has a breathtaking view out over the valley in clear weather. Camping is permitted, but not easy, since the hillside is steep and covered in thick brush.

Bus #23 (frequent, 30min., Rs4) leaves from Ratna Park and stops by **Balaju Water Garden,** one of the few well-maintained public spaces around. On the left inside the garden are fountains, pruned hedges, and shaded benches, all unified by their pastel scheme. (Open daily 7am-7:30pm. Rs3; camera fee Rs2.) During festival season, worshippers bathe in the water that courses from the 22 carved crocodiles of the **Baais Dhara,** to the right. Midway through the park on the right is the **Bala Nilkantha,** a 7th-century contemporary of the more elaborate sleeping Vishnu, northeast of the valley in Budhanilkantha. The **swimming pool** is a big, noisy place to keep cool. (Open daily 9am-12:30pm and 1-4pm. Rs40. Women only on Th.)

The garden isn't much of an attraction on its own, but it is a great place to stop on your way to or from a hike to **Nagarjun,** which can be reached by turning left after exiting the water garden and continuing north for about 30 minutes. Nagarjun sits in **Rani Ban** (also called Nagarjun Royal Forest), a sizable chunk of forest protected by the government. The Rani Ban entrance is on the left as you walk up the hill (Rs10). After you enter Rani Ban, a well-marked trail on your right leads to the summit (5km, 2hr.). At the top is the Buddhist shrine, **Jamacho.** Though rarely visited on ordinary days, Jamacho is the center of April's full moon festival, **Balaju Jatra.** During this festival, worshippers hold an all-night vigil at the summit and descend to Balaju the next day for a ritual bath in Baais Dhara.

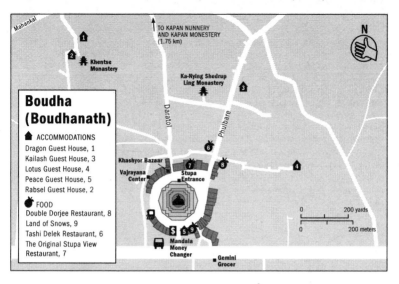

Boudha (Boudhanath)

🏠 ACCOMMODATIONS
Dragon Guest House, 1
Kailash Guest House, 3
Lotus Guest House, 4
Peace Guest House, 5
Rabsel Guest House, 2

🍴 FOOD
Double Dorjee Restaurant, 8
Land of Snows, 9
Tashi Delek Restaurant, 6
The Original Stupa View Restaurant, 7

BOUDHA (BOUDHANATH) बौद्धनाथ ☎ 01

Though it is dominated by the whitewashed dome of Nepal's largest stupa, Boudha is more than just the site of another ancient monument. The massive stupa draws Buddhists from far and wide into its clockwise orbit, forming the common center of a diverse community. Nearly everybody here claims origins elsewhere. Many have fled Tibet since the Chinese crackdown in 1959; others have migrated from the northern peaks, either to spend years or just to wait out the winter; and an increasing number are Westerners who have come to study at the many surrounding *gompas* (monasteries). You don't have to spend a month at a monastery to get a taste of Boudha's special atmosphere. Once you leave the dusty road from Kathmandu and enter the gates of the stupa, everything seems to change— red-robed monks stroll the streets, the smell of incense drifts in from every direction, and every few hours bleating horns and crashing drums call attention to the rituals of the nearby monasteries. Once there, you may find it hard to leave.

❄🚲 ORIENTATION AND PRACTICAL INFORMATION

Boudha has expanded far beyond the confines of the **stupa compound,** but the stupa remains its symbolic center, and is the reference point for all other directions. The stupa compound, 5km east of Kathmandu, can be entered through a **gate** on the north side of the main east-west road. The sprawling community north of the stupa, where you will find most of Boudha's monasteries, is accessible from two parallel lanes leading north out of the compound. One, referred to here as the **main northern lane,** is a wide road that runs from the eastern edge of the compound past the Tashi Delek Restaurant and the Kailash Guest House. The other, which will be called the **smaller northern lane,** is a narrow path lying just to the west that leaves the compound opposite the entrance to the stupa itself. Small east-west lanes connect these two. Always walk clockwise around the stupa.

Buses: Bus #2 from **Ratna Park** (frequent, 30min., Rs4) will drop you off a few yards before the gate. Blue **tempos** (#2, Rs6) leave from **Rani Pokhari. Taxis** from **Thamel** cost around Rs100.

Currency Exchange: Mandala Money Changer, on the left just inside the southern gates. Open daily 8:30am-5:30pm.

Market: Fruit sellers gather on the east-west road outside the entrance to the stupa compound and in the lanes north of the stupa. Across thea east-west road, about 25m east of the gate, is the well-stocked **Gemini Grocer.** MC, Visa accepted. Open daily 7:30am-8:30pm. Within the stupa compound next to the smaller northern lane is **Khashyor Bazaar.** Open daily 8:30am-8:30pm.

Internet and Telephones: The stupa is surrounded by Internet cafes. One of the best is **Dharana Cyberspace** (☎/fax 494178). Services include STD/ISD, Internet (Rs2 per min.), fax, and Internet phone. Open daily 6:30am-9:30pm

▌ ACCOMMODATIONS

Boudha's clean and peaceful lodgings might make you want to stay a few extra nights. All of the guest houses listed here are either in the stupa compound or in the area to the north. Those farther from the stupa tend to be quieter; many have private gardens. All of the following have seat toilets, hot water, and a noon checkout time unless otherwise noted.

Dragon Guest House (☎/fax 479562), a 10min. walk from the stupa. Follow the signs from the smaller northern lane and walk behind the Khentse monastery. Remote but clean, with sparkling shared bathrooms and a large Western clientele. Terraces on each floor, a small library, and attached veg. restaurant (breakfast Rs30-70, entrees Rs20-85; open daily 7am-10pm). Singles Rs220; doubles Rs340.

Lotus Guest House (☎472432 or 472320), beside the colorful Dobsang Monastery. From the main northern lane, take the first right after exiting the stupa compound. Motel-style layout, clean, sparsely furnished rooms, and a beautiful garden courtyard. Reservations recommended Oct.-Nov. Singles Rs250-290; doubles Rs350-390.

Kailash Guest House (☎480741), 5min. on the right down the main northern lane. Large, clean rooms furnished with mirrored locker, and, if you're lucky, teddy bear sheets. Pleasant terraces on each floor. Singles Rs200; doubles Rs250-300.

Rabsel Guest House (☎479009; fax 470215; email rabjam@ccsl.com.np), on the way to the Dragon Guest House. Clean rooms, all with private bath, fan, and towels, offer dazzling views of the neighboring Khentse monastery. Central garden and common space on each floor. Singles Rs300; doubles Rs400.

Peace Guest House, on the right just inside the southern stupa gates, has two well-worn dormitory rooms, for Rs80 per bed. Shared bath has no hot water. Padlocks with shared keys. Attached restaurant has separate Chinese and English menus. Guess which one features salted pig's tongue. Open daily 7:30am-9pm.

◖ FOOD

The Original Stupa View Restaurant, overlooks the stupa from the northern side of the compound. Not to be confused with same-name, different-place imposters, the Original Stupa View harbors a menu that manages to meld Nepali and Middle Eastern flavors. Small but appetizing selection of veg. dishes Rs120-200. Open 11am-9pm.

Land of Snows, to your right as you enter the stupa compound, on the 2nd floor. With elegant wooden decor and plenty of window seating, this stupa-side restaurant serves delicious, decently priced food in a pleasant atmosphere. Highlights include Tibetan dishes (Rs40-70) and veg. dishes (Rs50-65). Open 7:30am-9:30pm.

Tashi Delek Restaurant, on the corner of the stupa compound, where the main northern lane begins. A curtain marks the entrance to this 3-table, low-profile place. Wide selection of fresh, tasty, and cheap meals Rs15-70. Their veggie *thukpa* is hard to beat (Rs20). Open daily 6am-8pm.

Double Dorjee Restaurant, on the right off the main northern lane just past the Kamapa Service Society Nepal. A favorite with monks and ex-pats. Low tables, floral upholstery, and paper lanterns. Blackboard menu has Tibetan, Chinese, Japanese, and continental dishes (Rs40-120). A Tibetan family provides slow and friendly service, so you'll have plenty of time to chat with the regulars. Open daily 7:30am-9:30pm.

THE STUPA

Boudha's stupa is one of the largest in the world. All kinds of legends surround its origins—the 5th-century date assigned by historians is really only a guess. A Tibetan myth tells of a poultry farmer's daughter who wanted to build a stupa. The king granted her permission to use an area the size of a buffalo skin. Not content to build so small a stupa, the girl cut the skin into enough strips to trace the perimeter of the huge lot on which the stupa now stands. The Newari version tells the tale of a king who built taps from which no water would flow. Convinced that only the sacrifice of a great man would bring water, he ordered his son to go to the spouts and behead the shrouded man he found lying there. This, of course, turned out to be the king. Horrified by his deed, the remorseful prince built the stupa to redeem himself. The stupa has inspired awe and reverence since ancient times, when its location along the Kathmandu-Lhasa trade route made it a popular pilgrimage site (people still pray at Boudha for safe passage through the Himalayas).

Each segment of the stupa's structure is supposed to correspond to one of the five elements: the three-leveled *mandala*-shaped base represents earth; the dome, water; the spire (with its 13 steps corresponding to the 13 steps to nirvana), fire; the parasol, air; and the pinnacle, ether. The red-rimmed blue Buddha-eyes that gaze out from each of the four sides of the golden spire are unique to Nepali stupas, and the "nose" in between them is actually the number "1" in Nepali script. The whitewashed stupa is splashed with stripes of rust-colored wash to resemble the lotus shape. Its wall is inset with niches that contain prayer wheels and 108 images of the Buddha. At the entrance to the stupa itself is a shrine to the Newari goddess Ajima, protectress of children and goddess of smallpox. The stupa affords a view punctuated by prayer flags and the golden roofs of *gompas*.

Visitors are usually welcome in the monasteries—there is one right off the stupa compound and many more farther afield—as long as they observe the necessary etiquette (usually posted on signs outside the *gompas*). Dress modestly, take your shoes off before entering the *lhakang* (main hall), walk around clockwise inside, and always ask before taking photos. As monasteries have traditionally relied on contributions from visitors and pilgrims, donations are greatly appreciated. If you visit a lama, present him with a white *khata* (prayer scarf). These are inexpensive and available at many shops around Boudha, where someone can show you how to fold them properly. In the *lhakang*, you'll find intricate wall paintings in overwhelmingly vivid colors, and gold statues of notable Buddhist figures surrounded by offerings of food, incense, and butter-lamps.

The year's largest celebrations happen in February when thousands come to reunite with friends and family for **Losar,** the Tibetan New Year. The festivities begin with February's new moon and last for two weeks. During the first three days of the festival, monks at the local monasteries perform celebratory dances. The holiday ends with the full moon on a day known as the **Festival of Lights,** or Day of Offerings (*Cho-trul Duechen* in Tibetan). Beginning at dusk, worshippers circle the stupa, praying and chanting in penance and thanksgiving.

The stupa is surrounded by shops. You don't need to come all the way to Boudha to buy the standard tourist junk, but it is *the* place for Tibetan antiques and cheap souvenirs like Tibetan head- and foot-gear and Buddhist prayer flags.

STUDY AND VOLUNTEER OPPORTUNITIES

The **Ka-Nying Shedrup Ling Monastery** (☎470993), known as the white monastery or *seto gompa*, is between the two northern lanes and welcomes Westerners. To get there, follow the main northern lane and take the first left after you pass the Tashi Delek Restaurant. The monastery's charismatic leader, Chyoki Nyima Rinpoche, meets visitors (daily 10am-noon) and holds a teaching session in English (Sa 11:30am-12:30pm). To speak to him, walk around to the right of the main hall and climb the stairs to the top floor. **Kapan Monastery** (☎481268; fax 481267), on a hill 2km north of Boudha, holds several meditation courses throughout the year (seven-day course Rs3900) and welcomes volunteers to work in the **library** (Su-F 1-3pm) or clinic. The monastery offers accommodations (dorm beds Rs110; rooms with bath Rs250 per bed; breakfast included) throughout the year and organizes meditation and English discussion sessions for visitors (Su-F 10am). From the stupa, follow the smaller northern lane for about 20 minutes until it meets a paved taxi road. Turn right, and continue a short distance to a dirt path leading off to the left. Follow the dirt road, keeping to the left, for about 20 minutes until it leads into Kapan. A large map sits just inside Kapan's entrance, and a shop on the left sells refreshments and postcards. (Office open daily 9am-noon and 1-5pm.) Finally, the **Vajrayana Center** (☎481108; fax 471902; email t_sherpavajra@yahoo.com) is a great place for English-speakers to teach English to Tibetans, either short-term or long-term. The center also organizes free, ongoing Tibetan classes. To get to the center, follow the smaller northern lane from the stupa and take the first left onto a small road. Turn left at the first fork, and again at the second; the center is on the left immediately after the second fork.

BHAKTAPUR भक्तपुर ☎01

Once the grandest city in the valley, Bhaktapur retains much of its medieval charm thanks to modern efforts at preservation and restoration. A 1934 earthquake leveled most of Bhaktapur's famous temples and landmarks. Soon after the disaster, plans were set in motion to restore the city to its 15th-century splendor and give a boost to local craftsmanship. Excellent planning has made Bhaktapur the cleanest and most attractive city in the Kathmandu Valley. Entering the neatly paved pedestrians zone might remind you of being at a theme park, but Bhaktapur is no Mickey Mouse fairytown. The entry fee (Rs300) continues to finance restoration projects and exciting civic programs such as trash collection.

Founded in the 9th century, Bhaktapur ("City of Devotees") was the capital of the Kathmandu Valley until the region was divided into three kingdoms in 1482. The town's prominence faded when the Gorkhas conquered it in 1768 and established the capital in Kathmandu (see **History**, p. 717). Many of its buildings are reconstructed versions of temples built between the 15th and 17th centuries. The municipality is well aware of the value of its treasures; restoration and rebuilding continue, encouraged by a German development project begun in the 1970s. Attracted by the famous temples and museums (whose artifacts are of religious significance to Hindus and Buddhists alike), as well as by the town's strong sense of community, Nepali tourists constitute a large portion of Bhaktapur's non-resident population. For many visitors to the Kathmandu Valley, Bhaktapur is just a daytrip from Kathmandu. Those who stay overnight, however, get a chance to see the town in the twilight hours after most tourists have left.

⌐ GETTING THERE AND GETTING AROUND

Buses: Bus #7 leaves from Kathmandu's Bagh Bazaar, just east of Durbar Marg and north of Ratna Park, and arrives at Bhaktapur's Minibus Park, near Guhya Pond (frequent, 45min., Rs8). Less crowded than buses, **trollies** connect Kathmandu's Tripureswar, near the National Stadium, to Bhaktapur's **trolleybus park,** south of town (frequent, 1hr., Rs6). Buses to **Nagarkot** (#7, every 30min., 1hr., Rs10) leave from **Kamal Binayak,** on the northeast edge of Bhaktapur. Turn left after the pottery square to the east of Dattatraya Square and head north to the edge of town.

Local Transportation: Bus #7 runs along the northern edge of town from the hospital to Kamal Binayak. **Taxis** wait at the **Tourist Bus Park** just outside the main gate into Durbar Square. **Bicycles** are available on the road that connects Guhya Pond and Durbar Square. **Cycle Repair Center,** on the south side of the road, rents standard one-speed bikes. Rs12 per hr.; Rs60 per day. Open daily 7am-7pm.

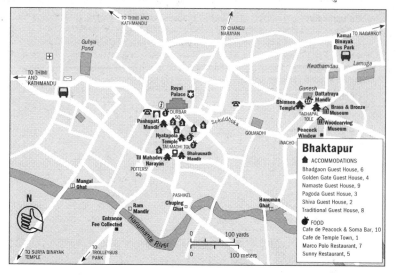

Bhaktapur

⌂ ACCOMMODATIONS
Bhadgaon Guest House, 6
Golden Gate Guest House, 4
Namaste Guest House, 9
Pagoda Guest Hosue, 3
Shiva Guest House, 2
Traditional Guest House, 8

◆ FOOD
Cafe de Peacock & Soma Bar, 10
Cafe de Temple Town, 1
Marco Polo Restaurant, 7
Sunny Restaurant, 5

ORIENTATION

Bhaktapur is bordered to the north and south by roads running to and from Kathmandu, 14km to the west. The southern half of the city is characterized by fields, residential streets, and the *ghats* that line the **Hanumante River.** Bhaktapur's main sights are in the northern half of the city, in three squares strung together by a curving main street. **Durbar Square** is connected by a short lane at its southeastern corner to **Taumadhi Tol,** which, in turn, is connected to **Tachapal Tol** (also called **Dattatraya Square**) by a wide, shop-lined street known as **Sukuldhoka.** Minibuses from Kathmandu arrive near a large water tank called **Guhya Pond** to the west of Durbar Square Gate. The **trolleybus** stops in the southern edge of town, 15 minutes from Durbar Square.

Tourists must pay Rs300 or US$5 at the **Durbar Square Gate** or at the other checkpoints to enter the city. If you sneak into town by another route and avoid these booths, you may still be asked inside for your ticket. The ticket can be used for multiple entries on different days as long as you notify the **Tourist Service Centre.**

PRACTICAL INFORMATION

Tourist Office: Tourist Service Centre and Information Hall, Durbar Square Gate (☎612249). Run by the Bhaktapur Municipality, this is where you can pay the entrance fee for the city (see **Orientation,** above) and get a brochure and useful map. Keep your ticket and have it certified to re-enter if you leave. Public toilets with toilet paper, of all things. Open daily 6am-8pm.

Currency Exchange: Layaku Money Exchange Counter (☎612208), down the alley to the right as you enter Durbar Square Gate. No commission. Open daily 10am-5pm.

Police: (☎610284), just outside Durbar Square, down the small street between the Palace of 55 Windows and Fasidega Temple. Open 24hr.

Pharmacy: Pharmacies line **Sukuldhoka,** the wide street connecting Taumadhi Tol and Tachapal Tol. There are also several opposite the hospital, including **Sewa Medicine Store** (☎613773). Open 6am-9pm; pharmacist on call 24hr.

Hospital: Government Hospital (☎610676), west of the Navpokhu Pokhari Minibus Park, on the north side of the street. Not the cleanest, most up-to-date of medical clinics—if you're really ill you should probably head to Kathmandu for treatment. Many of the **pharmacies** have doctors affiliated with them who will see patients there during the day. For a simple consultation and/or prescription, this is your best bet.

Telephones: Laiku Worldwide Communications (☎610258), facing the outside of Durbar Square Gate, has free callbacks and a private booth. Open daily 7am-7pm. **World Wide Hello Service,** Tibukchhen (☎613342 or 613473), past Namaste Guest House, on the left toward Dattatraya Square. Callbacks Rs5 per min. Open daily 8am-8:30pm.

Internet: Many businesses in Bhaktapur now offer Internet services; most of them are of the one-computer-in-a-room variety. **Net Communication** (☎612216), opposite the Bhadgaon Guest House, has Internet access for Rs3 per min. Open 9am-8pm.

Post Office: Next to the minibus park by Guhya Pond. Open M-F 9am-5pm.

▌ ACCOMMODATIONS

All the places listed below have hot showers, laundry, convenient temple-side locations, ultra-accommodating owners, and rooftop gardens with magnificent views. Deciding which temple you want outside your window might be the toughest decision you have to make. Rates are always negotiable, especially during the off-season (May-Aug.). Reservations are recommended in season (Sept.-Dec.). Noon check-out is standard everywhere, and most places lock up at 10pm. Prices listed here are in-season.

Pagoda Guest House, Taumadhi Tol (☎613248; fax 612685; email pagoda@col.com.np), right behind the Nyatapola temple, to the left. Bed and breakfast atmosphere and a unique location (practically on top of a 5-story temple) make this an inviting place to stay. Squat and seat toilets. Singles US$6-25; doubles US$8-30.

Namaste Guest House, Sakotha Tol (☎610500; fax 225679; email travels@kumari.mos.com.np), on the corner where Tibukchhen meets Sakotha, leading into the northeast corner of Durbar Square. Clean, spacious rooms with colorful bedsheets and friendly staff. Guests receive a 10% discount at the **Sunny Restaurant** (see below). Singles Rs250-300, with bath US$10; doubles Rs300-400/US$12.

Shiva Guest House (☎613912; fax 610740; email bisket@wlink.com.np), opposite Pashupatinath Temple. Clean rooms, email service (Rs3 per min.), in-house travel agency, and attached restaurant (entrees Rs75-200). All the sheets feature images of meditating Buddhas. Singles US$6, with bath US$15; doubles US$8/20; suite US$30.

Bhadgaon Guest House, Taumadhi Tol (☎610488; fax 610481; email bhadgaon@mos.comp.np), on the right after Cafe Nyatapola, as you leave Taumadhi Tol for Potters' Square. Marble stairs and carefully kept garden courtyard make this Bhaktapur's most up-market hotel. Rooftop restaurant with terrific views (entrees Rs70-200). Nine rooms, all with attached bath, TV, fan, toilet paper, towels, and slippers. Singles Rs800; doubles Rs1000; suite with private balcony US$25.

Golden Gate Guest House, Bahatal (☎610534; fax 611081; email bcci@wlink.com.np), on the left side of the street as you approach Taumadhi Tol from Durbar Square. Duck through the doorway to reach the Golden Gate. Attached or common baths. Top-floor rooms have the best views and the newest furnishings. Singles US$3, with bath US$8-10; doubles US$5, with bath US$10-15. AmEx, MC, Visa.

Traditional Guest House (☎611057; fax 612607; email bcci@wlink.com.np), opposite the Namaste Guest House. Eight rooms, all with attached bath and balcony, in a friendly family atmosphere. In the evening, the staff prepares all-you-can-eat traditional Newari dishes just for guests (Rs120). Singles Rs200; doubles Rs275-350.

▐ FOOD

Most of Bhaktapur's restaurants whip up the tired old Nepali-continental-Indian-Chinese food, though there are some less touristy places in the older, more residential areas of town, which provide Nepali cuisine for half the price and twice the excitement. *Juju dhau* (king of curds), a creamy, sweet yogurt, is a local specialty that is sold almost anywhere.

❏ **Sunny Restaurant,** Taumadhi Tol, near Nyatapola Temple. Glowing lanterns, sweet-smelling incense, knee-high tables, and a balcony with a splendid view of the square. continental (Rs75-160), Newari (Rs110-140), and Nepali (Rs100-225) meals.

Cafe de Peacock and Soma Bar, Tachapal Tol, facing Dattatraya Temple. 2nd floor on the left. Indoor and outdoor seating make for great people-watching. Mexican, Italian, and Nepali dishes Rs100-300. Open daily 9am-9pm. AmEx, MC, Visa.

Cafe de Temple Town Restaurant, Durbar Square. Turn right after entering the Durbar Square Gate. A small garden around the patio tables obscures the sights but not the noise. Rooftop seating promises better views. Pizza Rs160-215; Indian and Nepali dishes Rs125-250. Open daily 8am-9pm.

Marco Polo Restaurant, Taumadhi Tol, immediately to the left as you face Nyatapola Temple. A cheaper alternative to other tourist restaurants. Tiny balcony overlooks the northwest corner of the square. Fairly extensive menu, including lasagna, burgers, and Indian and Nepali dishes (Rs60-100). Open daily 7am-8pm.

👁 SIGHTS

DURBAR SQUARE. Bhaktapur has the oldest and least cluttered Durbar Square in the valley. The wide-open pedestrian area is home to just enough architectural wonders to be imposing without being overwhelming. The **Royal Palace** encloses the north side of the square. The current buildings date from the 16th and 17th centuries when, under Malla rule, Bhaktapur was the heart of Kathmandu Valley culture. Paintings, statues, and tapestries from this era still decorate the west wing of the palace, which now houses the **National Art Gallery.** The gallery displays intricate Newari *paubha* and Tibetan *thanka* paintings; its oldest objects are stone sculptures from as early as the 11th century. The gallery affords the best view of the palace's courtyards, most of which are closed to visitors. *(Museum open Tu-Sa 9:30am-4:30pm. Admission Rs20. No photography.)* Next door is the famous Garuda-crested **Golden Gate,** built in the early 18th century by King Bhupatindra Malla. The king's image caps a stone pillar facing the gate. On the other side of the gate sits the **Palace of 55 Windows**—each one of the intricately carved windows took a craftsman about 100 days to construct.

THANKAS FOR THE MEMORIES

Hanging in shop windows, peering out at you from glass frames with their gold-painted eyes, *thankas* are everywhere in the Kathmandu Valley. Traditional *thankas* (pronounced TONG-ka, and meaning "something rolled up") are religious scroll-paintings that serve as aids for meditation in temples or at family altars. Colorful and elaborate, they are painted to comply with strict rules that dictate style and subject matter. Most *thankas* depict one of three main themes: the lives of the Buddha, bodhisattvas, saints, or lamas; the wheel of life; or the *mandala*. In representations of the Buddha's life, pictures start in the top left-hand corner and continue counter-clockwise. The wheel of life *thanka* depicts the various spiritual states of humankind, from sin (at the bottom) to enlightenment (at the top). The *mandala*, which shows the steps to enlightenment, is the most popular. A *thanka* might take anywhere from a week to six months to create; the outlines of the images are drawn first, then colors are added in layers. In a workshop, layers are worked by increasingly skilled artists: first large blocks of color, then the setting, then any gold details, and finally the faces of the figures. A *thanka* cannot be used, however, until it has been consecrated by a lama, who makes an inscription on the back. Most *thankas* that are sold have not been consecrated properly and many don't meet the prescribed guidelines. If you're interested in buying a one, shop around first, as sizes, quality, and prices (Rs100-10,000) vary widely.

Like the palace, the temples in Durbar Square exemplify the remarkable craftsmanship of the Malla era. The westernmost temple in the Square, **Bansi Narayan,** is dedicated to Krishna, and its roof struts depict various incarnations of Vishnu. Behind the king's pillar is the elephant-flanked, stone-carved **Vatsala Durga Temple.** Built in the mid-18th century in the *shikhara* style (see p. 87), this temple contains an impressive display of metalwork and carvings in wood and stone. To the left is the **Chayasilin Mandap** (Eight-Cornered Pavilion), a 1990 reconstruction incorporating fragments of the 18th-century original. Using a 100-year old photograph of the *mandap,* the German Agency for Technical Cooperation and local craftsmen restored the structure to its past grandeur. They reinforced the building with steel to protect against future earthquake damage. Near the Chayasilin Mandap and opposite the Shiva Guest House, the **Pashupatinath Mandir,** the busiest of the Durbar Square temples, contains a 17th-century reproduction of the *linga* at Pashupatinath. Check out the especially creative contortions of the couples on the roof struts, the only parts of the building that survive from the original 15th-century structure. In the eastern section of the square, around the corner from the palace, are several more temples and temple foundations. The most interesting of these is the 17th-century stone **Siddhi Lakshmi Temple,** with its procession of animals and people on either side of the stairs. Behind it is the larger, white, and somewhat unattractive **Fasideya Temple,** dedicated to Shiva. The two story wood and brick buildings that surround this part of the square were once *dharamsalas* (pilgrims' resthouses).

TAUMADHI TOL. Connected to Durbar Square by a short, shop-lined street, Taumadhi Tol, a place where architectural masterpieces and religious ceremony mingle with daily life, is Bhaktapur at its best. Musicians and daily worshippers converge on the square during the **Bisket Jatra,** Bhaktapur's renowned celebration of the new year in April. Nepal's tallest pagoda, **Nyatapola Temple,** dominates the square and all of Bhaktapur. The newly renovated five-story red pagoda was originally built in 1702 by King Bhupatindra Malla. Five pairs of stone creatures flank the stairs to the temple. Each pair is said to be ten times stronger than the one below, starting with a pair of Malla wrestlers who look at least ten times stronger than the average man. Next are a pair of elephants, followed by lions, giraffes, and finally the goddesses Bahini (the Tigress) and Singhini (the Lioness). The image of **Siddhi Lakshmi,** the goddess to whom the temple is devoted, is locked inside and accessible only to priests.

The eastern side of the square is dominated by the three-story **Bhairavnath Mandir,** which was built as a single-story temple during the 18th century. A second floor was added later, and the entire structure was rebuilt from the existing three stories after the 1934 earthquake. The golden image that peers down from the top floor of the temple is Lord Bhairava, God of Terror; his head is supposed to be locked inside. A doorway in the building at the south side of the square leads to a courtyard filled by the **Til Mahadev Narayan Mandir,** a 17th-century temple (on an 11th-century temple site) reminiscent of Changu Narayan, with its pillar-mounted golden Garuda, *chakra,* and *sankha.*

TACHAPAL TOL (DATTATRAYA SQUARE). A wide, curving street of shops links Taumadhi Tol to Bhaktapur's oldest square, Tachapal Tol. The wooden buildings that enclose the square were once *maths* (priests' residences). The **Dattatraya Mandir** presides over the square from the eastern end. Built in 1427, it is the oldest surviving building in Bhaktapur, and like other famous structures in the Kathmandu Valley, it is said to have been built from the trunk of just one tree. From the looks of it, that must have been quite a tree. Two Malla wrestlers, gaudily painted during festivals, guard the entrance. Dattatraya appeals to followers of Vishnu and Shiva as well as Buddhists, since he is considered an *avatar* of Vishnu, a guru of Shiva, and a cousin of the Buddha. At the other end of the square is the rectangular **Bhimsen Temple,** honoring a favorite god of Newari merchants.

Behind the Dattatraya Temple, inside the two *math* buildings, are two museums. To the left, the **Brass and Bronze Museum** displays a collection of 300-year-old functional objects such as lamps, cooking pots, hubble-bubble hookahs, spittoons, and carved ritual paraphernalia. Opposite the **Pujari Math** is the **National Art Gallery Woodcarving Museum,** worth visiting more for its magnificent courtyard than for its collection. Halfway down the street around the corner from the Woodcarving Museum is the famous **Peacock Window,** dating from the 17th century. *(Admission to any one of the three museums allows entry to the other two. Open Tu-Sa 9:30am-4:30pm. Rs20.)*

OTHER SIGHTS. In the squares just east and south of Taumadhi Tol, both known as **Potters' Square,** you can see hundreds of pots lined up to dry in the sun or stacked up to be sold. Stroll south toward the river to see *ghats*, fields, and temples that, in contrast to those farther north, are more functional than decorative.

🛍 SHOPPING

Bhaktapur is home to some of the finest **pottery** in the valley and, while similar items are also available in Kathmandu, it's much more satisfying to purchase directly from the artisans here in Bhaktapur. The best place to meet up with potters and their collections of bowls, masks, and icons is the aptly-named **Potter's Square.** Bhaktapur also has a long-standing reputation for fine **wooden handicrafts,** which are sold in Durbar and Tachapal Squares. **Papier-mâché masks** and marionettes, made at the UNICEF factory in Bhaktapur, are also available.

CHANGU NARAYAN चाँगु नारायण

Legend has it that many years ago a valley brahmin noticed that one of his cows was no longer giving milk. Suspicious, he kept his eye on the cow, until one day he saw a small boy materialize from a nearby *champak* tree, drink all of the cow's milk, and then disappear inside the tree again. Convinced that this was the work of a demon, the brahmin cut the tree down immediately. No sooner had he done so, however, than the tree began to bleed and the face of Narayan appeared, reprimanding him for what he had done. Mortified by his sin, the brahmin built a temple to Narayan where the tree had stood. To this day, the temple has remained one of Nepal's most sacred.

Since its foundation in the 4th century, worshipers have visited, adorned, restored, and revered the Vishnu shrine on this site. Patched together and built upon over the centuries, the temple is a living time capsule revealing more than a millennium's worth of stylistic and artistic developments. Equally impressive are the large sculptures and polished black relief panels that cluster around the temple; these are considered among Nepal's greatest treasures. The hilltop town that surrounds this marvellous site has breathtaking panoramic views of the whole valley. The town now charges a Rs60 **entrance fee,** payable at a small shack to the left of the city gates (open 6am-6pm). In return for the fee you receive a brochure containing information on the temple area.

▐ GETTING THERE AND AROUND. The main road into Changu Narayan leads into the new bus park. **Buses** depart from and arrive at Bhaktapur's minibus park, near Guhya pond (#7, departs according to unpredictable rules too complicated to explain, 30min., Rs6; last bus to Bhaktapur 7pm). A **taxi** is the fastest but most expensive way to reach Changu Narayan (Rs600 from Kathmandu, Rs300 from Bhaktapur). Otherwise, Changu Narayan is a strenuous, uphill, 45 minute bike ride or two-hour walk from Bhaktapur. Just follow the signs from the minibus park. The town can also be reached via a two-hour hike from the mountain viewpoint of Nagarkot to the east. Getting off the Nagarkot bus at Telkot (#7, 30min., Rs5) and walking straight along the ridge will get you there in about 1.5hours. Another approach is from the north side, off the road between Boudha and Sankhu, but it can be trekked only in the dry season when the Manohara River is low enough to be forded. The **temple** is up the steps from the city gates.

NEPAL

▐▌▐▌ ACCOMMODATIONS AND FOOD. A visit to Changu Narayan works best as a day trip from Kathmandu or Bhaktapur; if for some reason you need to spend an unplanned night here, options are basic and uninspiring. The **Changu Narayan Bed and Breakfast** is a 10-minute walk from the temple; follow the steep set of stairs from the side of the temple farthest from town (Rs150 per night). In the opposite direction, the **Changu Narayan New Hill Resort,** is 10 minutes from the bus park, along the road following the ridge. (Singles Rs150; doubles Rs200.) Both offer basic backpacker-style accommodations. At the back of the Changu Narayan bus park sits the **Binayak Restaurant.** Offering standard continental (Rs50-200) and Indian (Rs50-120) food as well as a range of drinks (Rs80-120), it's a good place to catch a light meal while waiting for your bus. Just inside the main gate sits the **Valley View Restaurant,** offering similar dishes as the Binayak for Rs45-110 and (surprisingly enough) great valley views.

▣ SIGHTS. Coming from town, you will enter the courtyard of the **Changu Narayan Temple** at the rear, with two stone gryphons peering down and warning you that the 7th-century golden image of Vishnu within is open to Hindus only. A spreading copper doorway embossed with flower designs frames the entrance, and on either side of the temple, **pillars** bear the symbols of Vishnu. A life-wheel and a stone staff on the left represent brahmins and *chettris* respectively; a conch shell and lotus flower on the right represent the occupational and business castes. The inscription at the base of the pillar describes the victories of King Manadeva. It is the oldest in the valley, dating from the year 454. The **statue** of Vishnu's man-bird vehicle, Garuda, kneeling at the door with a cobra around his neck, was carved at about the same time. His face is said to be a likeness of King Manadeva himself, who reputedly said that he too was a vehicle for Vishnu. In the **birdcage** over Garuda's shoulder are two more recent figures, Bupathindra Malla and Bubana Lakshmi, the 17th-century king and queen of Bhaktapur who introduced metalwork to the temple by financing the ornate copper doorway.

The best sculptures are beside the main temple, past the pillar onthe right of the brick pavilion of the **Lakshmi Narayan Temple** (with black wooden columns). In the central relief, Vishnu as Narasimha, half-man and half-lion, tears a hole in the chest of a demon. To the left, a relief shows the story of Vishnu as Vamana, the dwarf who grew to celestial size and crossed the earth and the heavens in three steps. On the **platform** next to the Lakshmi Narayan Temple is an image of Vishnu as Narayan, sleeping on a knotted snake. The ten-headed, ten-armed figure above Narayan depicts the universal face of Vishnu, showing each of his ten *avatars.* Opposite the platform is an image of a ten-armed Vishnu, known as **Maha Vishnu,** with his consort Lakshmi sitting in his lap. Across the courtyard, past the temple's left pillar is the sculpture of Vishnu atop his *vahana,* Garuda, an image that appears on 10-rupee notes. All of these sculptures date from the Licchavi period, before the Mallas took over in 1200 and when stone sculpture in the valley was at its height (see **Malla Kingdoms,** p. 717).

Before you leave town, stop at the newly opened **Changu Narayan Museum,** housed in a 160-year-old building along the path through town. The museum's hodge-podge of artifacts includes agricultural tools, Nepalese coins, musical instruments, and metal idols. (Admission Rs50.)

DHULIKHEL धुलिखेल ☎ 089

From its lofty position at 1550m, Dhulikhel routinely delivers spectacular Himalayan sunrises. But in contrast with its more touristy neighbor Nagarkot, Dhulikhel is also a living, breathing Nepali town, as its busy park and lively streets attest. In the surrounding valleys are a number of scenic villages, including **Namobuddha** and **Panauti,** which make for ideal one-day treks. Hikers and bikers alike come to this eastern mountain town to explore the wildnerness beyond. Dhulikhel's comfortable accommodations and natural beauty make for a pleasant stay—even when monsoon clouds obscure the snow mountains.

NEPAL

⬛🔢 ORIENTATION AND PRACTICAL INFORMATION. Dhulikhel is just off the Arniko Highway, 32km southeast of Kathmandu. The road to Dhulikhel runs past the **bus park** on the right and past a sign for the hospital, also on the right. The road then curves past the Rastriya Banijya Bank, uphill to the **town center,** where a bust of King Mahendra stands next to a water tank. The road to the left of the king leads to Dhulikhel's temples and the old part of town; the road to his right leads to the Nawaranga Guest House, the post office, and the Kali shrine. From Kathmandu, take **bus #12** (frequent, 1½hr., Rs17), which also stops near Bhaktapur's trolleybus park and at Banepa's bus park. The **Rastriya Banijya Bank** changes currency (open Su-F 10:30am-3pm, F 10:30am-noon). The nearby **pharmacy,** with an English-speaking staff, is down the road to the left of the Mahendra bust (open 6am-8pm). The **hospital** (☎61497) is 10min. away from the bus park—follow the sign. (Clinic open Su-Tu and Th-F 8am-5pm, W and Sa emergencies only.) The hospital's well-stocked **pharmacy** is the best place to get prescriptions filled (open 9am-10pm). The **police station** (☎61230) is a 10min. walk from the center of town, down the road to Mahendra's right. **Sunrise Travels** (☎61035; fax 62025), down the road to Mahendra's right, before the Nawaranga Guest House, has **STD/ISD** and **email.** (Rs35 per Kb. Open 6am-7pm.) The **post office** is next to the police station (open Su-Th 10am-5pm, F 10am-3pm).

📁🏠 ACCOMMODATIONS AND FOOD. ◪**Nawaranga Guest House** (☎61226), a five-minute walk up the road to Mahendra's right, is a backpacker's haven. It makes up for what it lacks in luxury with an uncommonly friendly and hospitable atmosphere. Clean, common squat toilets; hot water Rs10 per bucket. The superb restaurant serves authentic Nepali dishes (entrees Rs15-90) and doubles as an art gallery exhibiting the works of a local painter. (Dorm beds Rs75; singles Rs100; doubles Rs150.) If you've come to see mountains, **Panorama View Resort** (☎62085) is your best bet. Up the hill below the Kali shrine (3km from the bus park), this place has large doubles with balconies, clean bathrooms with hot showers, and seat toilets. The restaurant has unrestricted views of the Himalayas from east to west. (Entrees Rs65-160. Singles Rs200, with bath US$8; doubles Rs300, with bath US$12. Reservations recommended in season.) On the main road past the sign to the hospital is the **Dhulikhel Royal Guest House** (☎64059). The rooms vary in size and amenities, but they're all clean and comfortable. The attached restaurant doubles as a TV parlor; treat yourself to any of the movies in the guest house's obscure collection, which includes such neglected classics as "Lost in Siberia." (Singles US$6-12; doubles US$10-20.) **Dhulikhel Lodge** (☎61753), across the street and just down the hill from the bus park, has 20 large rooms with common bath. (Seat or squat toilets. Singles Rs300; doubles Rs400. AmEx, Visa.) The restaurant serves Nepali, Chinese, and Italian meals (Rs55-160).

📷 SIGHTS AND SUNRISES. The spectacular sunrise over the mountains is the main draw in Dhulikhel, and the most popular place to watch it from is the **Kali Shrine.** To reach the shrine, follow the road past the post office and then take the right fork up the hill; the hike takes a little over an hour from the center of town, so plan ahead. Dhulikhel's cobblestoned **main square** is also worth exploring. The square's two temples honor two different forms of Vishnu: the triple-roofed temple surrounded by a metal fence is dedicated to Harisiddhi, while the brightly tiled one in the middle of the square honors Narayan, who is guarded by two Garudas. A few steps farther northwest, at the high point of the town, the pagoda-like **Bhagwati Mandir** is more interesting as a lookout than as a temple.

NEAR DHULIKHEL

Dhulikhel is the starting point for a number of short, one-day treks. Most worthwhile among these are the treks to **Namobuddha** and **Panauti.** *Namobuddha* means hail to the Buddha—it is the place where he supposedly offered his body as food to a starving tigress. In addition to a small but well-kept stupa, this area is also home to a number of monasteries and a small tea shop, making this an ideal place to take a break and observe the daily rituals of the local Buddhist monks. Namobuddha is three hours from Dhulikhel, with two paths running to and from town, making a complete circuit. **Panauti** is a quiet Newari village famous for its wood carvings. Its impressive array of temples and its idyllic setting at the junction of two streams make it a great daytrip. In the center of town is the **Indreshwar Mahadev Temple,** which, with its delicately carved roof struts and *toranos*, may be the oldest in Nepal. The triple-roofed **Krishna Narayan** temple sits at the junction of the town's two rivers. Across the river, by the suspension bridge, the 17th century **Brahmayani Temple** honors the village's chief goddess. The hike to Panauti takes about four hours, and can be combined with the Namobuddha trek to make an all-day excursion. **Buses** run from Panauti to Banepa (frequent, 20min., Rs4) and from there to Dhulikhel and Kathmandu, so a one-way trek is possible. (Maps for these treks can be obtained for free from any of the major guest houses.)

The road along the hillside from Dhulikhel to Bhaktapur is ideal for **mountain biking.** Leaving from the bus park, follow the main highway away from town and then follow the signs to Bhaktapur. There are no bike rental facilities in Dhulikhel, so it is best to rent in Kathmandu. You can bring your bike on the bus (the driver will attach it to the roof for you) or put it in the back of a taxi.

NAGARKOT नगरकोट

Teetering 2175m above the eastern rim of the Kathmandu Valley, Nagarkot is the popular Himalayan viewpoint from which, in clear weather, you can see Mt. Everest. Tourism has spurred the development of Nagarkot from its origins as a military base. Today, hundreds descend upon the dozen guest houses not to plot troop maneuvers but to trace the path of the sun as it ascends over the Himalayas. There are several day treks down to neighboring villages that offer glimpses of Nepalese life as you'll never see it in foreigner-packed Nagarkot. On the bus ride up, if you can bear to look out the window as the bus careens around a hairpin turn, you'll see patterned rice and corn plots etched into the hillside next to rich, uncultivated hills. Monsoon season is exactly the wrong time to visit unless you're a fan of cold air and averse to mountain views. However, even if clouds obscure the most distant peaks, the dizzying views of the valley and the calm mood of Nagarkot make the journey worthwhile. Nagarkot gets quite chilly at night; bring warm clothes.

GETTING THERE AND AROUND. Local bus #7 travels from Kathmandu to Nagarkot via Bhaktapur. In Kathmandu, catch it at Bagh Bazaar (every 20min., 2hr., Rs18); in Bhaktapur, from the Kamal Binayak bus stop in the northeast (every 30min., 1hr., Rs10). The last bus leaves Nagarkot at 6pm. **Tourist buses** leave from Kantipath in Kathmandu (1:30pm, 1½hr., round-trip Rs155) and return from Nagarkot the next morning. Tickets can be bought at any agency in Thamel. **Taxis** from Kathmandu cost about Rs850, from Bhaktapur Rs500.

ORIENTATION AND PRACTICAL INFORMATION. Nagarkot consists of an ever-growing cluster of guest houses grouped along a **ridge.** The road from Bhaktapur forks at the base of a hill, where a large **map** charts Nagarkot's guest houses. The road that curves to the right leads to **The Tea House, Club Himalaya,** and the **lookout tower.** The road that curves north around the left side of the hill leads to the bank, the rest of Nagarkot's guest houses, and the high point of the ridge marked by the tiny **Mahakal Shrine.** The **bus stop** is at the fork in the road. **Himalayan Bank Ltd.** exchanges currency and traveler's checks (☎680049. Open M-F 9:30am-3:30pm.) The nearest **hospital** is in Bhaktapur. **Club Himalaya** (☎680083) has email services for Rs25 per Kb, Internet services for Rs15 per min., and international telephone services.

ACCOMMODATIONS AND FOOD. As the hotel strip above the clouds expands, true budget lodges are becoming something of an endangered species, though prices are negotiable, especially off-season. The following hotels cling to the ridge below the Mahakal Shrine. **The Resort at the End of the Universe** is one of Nagarkot's originals. Rustic, wooded, and remote, the brick and bamboo bungalows are

MAKE MINE A MILLET, MATE

Getting tired of Tuborg? Can't face another glass of sub-zero, sub-par, sub-standard Star? Then leave the beers behind you, and get sozzled on something you definitely won't find back home—one of several local varieties of mind-bending millet-based hooch. **Chang** is your basic rice- or millet-based home brew, enjoyed by the masses and also appreciated by lamas high up in the mountains. A few glasses of this stuff and you'll be chatting to yetis in Nepali. Another interesting way to stew your brains and ruin your early-morning trek is to over-indulge in **tong-ba,** a Tibetan millet concoction that is by far the mellowest of the tip-pler's trinity, but still deserves to be treated with respect. Begin with fermented millet in the bottom of your vessel. Add hot water (boiled bottled water, of course), let it steep, and sip from a special straw that catches the grains. Kick back and enjoy the refills—the grains are good through several servings. Finally, **raksi** is Nepal's proudest and most potent offering. A distilled alcohol resembling tequila, it's a sweet swallow that packs a serious punch. *Raksi* figures prominently in essential drinking vocabulary: *"malaai raksi laagyo"* literally means something like, "I am stricken by alcohol."

simple but comfortable. All have attached bath. Reservations recommended in season. (☎680011; email oasis@orleans.wlink.com.np. Singles US$8-10; doubles US$1-20.) **The Hotel Madhuban Village** has a collection of compact A-frame cottages as well as larger and more expensive "standard" rooms. (☎680109. Cottages Rs400-500; rooms Rs1000.) The glassed-in dining room (entrees Rs50-140) has good views.

The Tea House, just below Club Himalaya, is Nagarkot's most elegant place to eat, with tablecloths and plate-glass windows offering terrific views on all sides—a super-clean place to get some fresh air after the bus ride. Uniformed waiters serve continental (Rs125-250) and Indian and Nepali dishes (Rs60-150). The neighboring **Club Himalaya,** Nagarkot's posh US$100-per-night resort, has its own upscale restaurant (most entrees Rs150-250). **The Restaurant at the End of the Universe,** attached to the similarly titled resort, serves hitchhikers from all over the galaxy a typical continental variety of entrees. (Burgers, chicken, and rice Rs50-200.) There is nothing remotely French about the **Cafe du Mont,** attached to the Peaceful Cottage, which serves good standard tourist food (veg. Rs90-175; non-veg. Rs110-250).

🔲 **SIGHTS.** The hip thing to do in Nagarkot is watch the sun rise above the hills and set behind the valley, washing the mountain peaks in pink light. While all the guest houses have great views, there are some particularly fine lookout points in the area. You can walk up to the tiny **Mahakal Shrine,** right next to the **End of the Universe,** or sit at one of the benches in the brick-paved area between the Tea House and Club Himalaya. The best views are from the **lookout tower,** a leisurely hour-long stroll south past Club Himalaya and the army base (ask around to make sure it's open). Lodge owners enthusiastically offer directions for walks to **Changu Narayan** (2hr.), **Sankhu** (2hr.), **Dhulikel** (5hr.), and **Shivapuri** (2-3 days).

SANKHU साँरव

A comfortable distance away from hectic Kathmandu, Sankhu is a quiet Newari town that gives a glimpse of valley life lived at a more relaxed pace. The few visitors that come here are interested mainly in the nearby **Bajra Jogini Mandir,** though the meandering walk from town might prove to be the highlight of a day's visit. The temple, built in the 17th century on an ancient Buddhist site, stands as a testament to Nepal's unique fusion of Hinduism and Buddhism.

Buddhists have long revered Bajra Jogini as a protector. Some say she convinced Manjushri to drain the water-filled Kathmandu Valley. Another legend suggests that she requested the construction of the Boudha stupa and sent a white crane to select its location. She has since been adopted as a tantric goddess, representing for Newari Buddhists the powerful female characteristics of the Buddha, while Hindus in the valley worship her as a form of Durga. The temple has three gilded roofs and an elaborate door that shields the goddess's image from the pub-

NEPAL

lic. The smaller two-tiered temple enshrines a replica of the Swayambhunath stupa. The temple's hilltop location has great views of the terraced fields below.

The 2km walk from town starts through the cement archway to the left of the bus stop. The dirt road leads through town; about halfway to the temple, it continues to the right, while a stone-paved footpath leads straight ahead. While both lead to the temple, the dirt road is slightly longer though perhaps more scenic. The two meet up again at the base of the long, steep stairway to the top of the hill. From the base of the stairs, it's a 15-minute walk to the top.

Bus #4 (frequent, 1½hr., Rs10) departs Ratna Park in Kathmandu for Sankhu as soon as it is full. It also stops east of Boudha. Sankhu is also accessible by **bicycle** (the road from Kathmandu is flat and, beyond Boudha, fairly pollution-free) or by **foot,** down from Nagarkot along a northwest trail. It is also possible to walk between Sankhu and Changu Narayan in the dry season.

DAKSHINKALI दक्षिण काली

Most days of the week, "Southern Kali" looks pretty much like any other quiet little town on the fringes of the Kathmandu Valley. It takes on a very different personality, though, every Tuesday and Saturday morning, between 7-10am, when the town hosts the famous Dakshinkali **animal sacrifices,** bloody offerings to propitiate the patron goddess Durga (also known as Kali). Brightly clad women and men with doomed roosters, goats, sheep, and ducks queue up to offer their animals at the shrine, which is enclosed by a low metal railing and sits beneath a metal canopy suspended by four brass *nagas*. Inside the shrine, there is a small black image of Kali standing victorious atop a corpse, hardly visible to tourists who are allowed only on the walkways above. The image was installed in the 17th century by King Pratap Malla, purportedly on the orders of the goddess herself, though Durga worship had taken place at the site long before that. Devotees wash their animal offerings in the stream behind the shrine before making the sacrifice. If the animals do not attempt to shake off the water poured over their heads (unlikely, really), they cannot be sacrificed. It's believed that animals killed in sacrifice will enjoy the reward of higher incarnation. Those offered during the eighth and ninth days of the festival of **Dasain,** the October celebration of the triumph of good over evil, are relieved from burdensome animal life and reincarnated as humans. When they reach the image of Kali, the animal's throat is cut, and its blood splatters onto the idols. The animal's head is given as payment to the butchers—the body is considered *prasad* (blessed) and becomes the main course at a family picnic in the surrounding hills. Signs from the Dakshinkali temple lead to the nearby **Mata Temple,** which is unremarkable except for its view of the nearby hills.

SPIRITUAL SIGN LANGUAGE

Every image of the Buddha, from the grandest towering gold-gilded temple statue down to the meanest figurine fake forged for tourists, has been designed to illustrate a particular hand position. These ritual poses, known as **mudras,** each convey a specific meaning. The **Dhyana** stance—both hands in the lap, right hand inside left, palms facing up—is the meditative pose that is sometimes also depicted with a begging bowl in hand. **Abhaya,** the pose of protection, is shown with one arm up, palm facing out, like a policeman signaling "stop." The **Bhumisparsha,** with right arm draped over the right knee, palm facing down, is the representation of the Buddha as witness. Also called the "touching the earth" *mudra*, this gesture symbolizes Shakyamuni Buddha's victory over Mara (the devil) in his attainment of enlightenment. **Varada** is the sign of charity: the Buddha's right arm is extended down over the right knee, palm facing up. Finally, the *mudra* that resembles the Western a-okay gesture—thumb and index finger formed in a circle, with the rest of the fingers pointing up—means quite the opposite when the Buddha tries it: the **vitarka** is the symbol of argument.

Bus #22 runs from Ratna Park in Kathmandu to Dakshinkali (Tu, Sa; 2hr.; Rs10). Huge crowds and small numbers of buses mean you'll have to get to the bus station very early if you want to see the sacrifices. Alternatively, the journey can be made by **taxi** (Rs500, round trip). Either way, the tortuous ride up through hillside homes and fields has stunning valley views. Stay on the bus past Pharping, the deceptive Dakshinkali Cold Store, and the "Welcome to Dakshinkali" sign. Wait until the bus pulls into a parking lot filled with about 100 motorcycles. When the beleaguered busload of folks and fowl get off, you know you've arrived. Stands selling snacks, garlands, bangles, and *sindur* line the walkway to the staircase down to the temple, which sits in a valley at the junction of two muddy streams.

NEAR DAKSHINKALI

Tucked beneath an overhanging cliff and surrounded by clear pools, the **Sekh Narayan Temple** is a roadside oasis an hour's walk from Dakshinkali. Built during the 17th century to honor Vamana (the dwarfish 5th incarnation of Vishnu), the temple has been dutifully maintained, and its bold, bright colors give it a surreal appearance. Next door is a 20th-century Tibetan Buddhist **monastery.**

To reach the Sekh Narayan Temple from Dakshinkali, walk from the parking lot, along the road, toward the temple until the green gate leading down the temple is on your left. Follow the uphill stairway until it meets the main road. Stay on the main road the rest of the way; the temple will be on your left, about a half a mile past the village of Pharping. You can catch the bus back to Kathmandu from Pharping, though it might be difficult to get a seat.

THE WESTERN HILLS

Modern-day Nepal was conceived in the hills west of Kathmandu, where 250 years ago King Prithvi Narayan Shah of Gorkha had a vision of a unified country. The central Himalayas, dominated by Machhapuchhare and the Annapurna range, provide a magnificent backdrop to one of the most popular regions of Nepal.

HIGHLIGHTS OF THE WESTERN HILLS

Nepal's second-most visited city, lakeside **Pokhara** (p. 775) lies in a beautiful subtropical valley overshadowed by the dazzling Annapurna massif.

The hill towns of **Tansen** (p. 772) and **Gorkha** (below) offer beautiful respite from Nepal's tourist mainstream.

Have your wishes fulfilled at the ridge-top temple of **Manakamana** (p. 771), now accessible by Nepal's first cable car.

GORKHA गोर्खा   ☎ 064

Spectacularly positioned on a hillside halfway between Pokhara and Kathmandu, Gorkha was ruled by a succession of small kingdom-states until Prithvi Narayan Shah, a direct ancestor of the present king, initiated the military rampage that gave rise to modern Nepal. In 1744, Prithvi Narayan left his home in Gorkha to conquer the Kathmandu valley, and after 24 bloody years of fighting, he finally succeeded. Shah's mighty soldiers were the first to be called "Gorkha," a name that eventually came to be used for all Nepalese soldiers. They were recruited by the British Army and now make up a significant minority in the Indian Army, too. Gorkha's history is enshrined in the hilltop Gorkha Durbar, birthplace of Prithvi Narayan.

At the end of a paved road to the Kathmandu-Pokhara highway, Gorkha forms a link between many sleepy mountain villages and the outside world and is a starting point for treks in the Annapurnas (see p. 802). Still comfortably untouristed, Gorkha's historic palace and sweeping mountain views make it a great place to break a journey between Kathmandu and Pokhara.

▐▀ GETTING THERE AND GETTING AROUND

All **buses** from Gorkha go through **Anbu Khaireni,** a few kilometers west of Mugling, where the Gorkha road meets the Kathmandu-Pokhara highway. **Prithvi Rajmarga Bus Syndicate,** marked by a red sign inside the bus park, is a private company that runs most of the buses. (☎20323. Open daily 5:30am-6pm.) To: **Anbu Khaireni** (frequent, 6am-6pm, 1hr., Rs45-65); **Bhairawa/Sunauli** (7am, 7hr., Rs137); **Birganj** (4 per day, 6:30-11:20am, 7hr., Rs130); **Kathmandu** (9 per day, 6:15am-2:30pm, 5hr., Rs80-100); **Narayanghat** (7 per day, 8:45am-2:40pm, 3hr., Rs65); **Pokhara** (6am and 9:15am, 3hr., Rs75); and **Tandi,** for **Royal Chitwan National Park** (3:10am and 3:40pm, 3hr., Rs55). **Sajha Yatayat** (☎20106), next to the bus park, runs government buses to **Kathmandu** (6:45am and 1:30pm, 5hr., Rs71).

✦ 🛈 ORIENTATION AND PRACTICAL INFORMATION

Gorkha has evolved into three distinct sections. The newest part of town, only 15 years old, is centered on the **bus park.** The second area, about a century old, winds uphill from the bus park past three small shrines and into the **main street.** An hour's walk up the ridge is the third section, which consists of the majestic **Gorkha Durbar.**

Currency Exchange: Rastriya Banijya Bank (☎20155), at the end of the older part of town; just below the post office, on your right as you follow the narrow street. Open Su-Th 10am-5pm, F 10am-1:15pm.

Police: From the bus park, walk downhill for 5min., turn right at the blue sign down the unpaved road, and take another right; the **police station** (☎20199) is the white building straight ahead.

Pharmacy: New Gorkha Medical Center (☎20116), opposite Hotel Gorkha Prince. Open Su-F 7am-8pm, Sa 7am-1pm.

Hospital: (☎20208). From the bus park, go 5min. downhill on the main road; after the Hotel Gorkha Bisauni, turn left onto the first paved road and walk 5min. uphill. The hospital (yellow with red stripes) has basic facilities and an English-speaking doctor.

Telephone: Hotel Gorkha Prince and **Hotel Gorkha Bisauni** have free callbacks.

Internet: Hello Gorkha (☎20226), 50m down the main road from the bus park, has good rates (callbacks Rs5 per min.) and will type and send email (Rs50 per handwritten page). Open daily 7am-8pm.

Post Office: (☎20112), at the end of the older section of town; walk past the stone steps that lead to the palace and continue up the steep dirt road. Open Su-Th 10am-5pm, F 10am-3pm.

▮ ACCOMMODATIONS

Hotel Gorkha Prince (☎20131), 100m downhill from the bus park; the hotel, marked by a red signboard, is on the left. Spacious rooms around a courtyard, friendly staff, STD/ISD service, rooftop restaurant, and a tidy common room with MTV. Street side rooms with seat toilet and toilet paper Rs200; interior rooms with squat toilet Rs200.

Hotel Gorkha Bisauni (☎/fax 20107), down the main road 250m below the bus park. Bisauni has cheerful rooms with fans, TVs, hill-view balconies, and clean bathrooms. Rooms with common bath are more basic, but still clean and comfy. Singles Rs200-500; doubles Rs300-800.

◖ FOOD

▧ **Fulpati Restaurant,** at the Gurkha Inn, 120m down the main road from the bus park, on the right. Great views, a beautiful garden, and tasty food make this Gorkha's best place to eat. Breakfast Rs90-160; Nepalese/Indian/Chinese food Rs35-140. The potato chili (Rs50) will bring tears to your eyes. Open daily 6am-10pm.

Gorkha Prince Rooftop Restaurant, at the Hotel Gorkha Prince. Rooftop setting, friendly service, and low prices on all your favorites. *Dahl bhat* Rs70; veg. chow mein Rs30; and all the rest of the team Rs30-100. Open daily 7am-10pm.

Hill Top Restaurant, at the bus park. With outdoor seating and cheap prices, this is a good place for a quick meal on your way to or from the palace. Hearty breakfasts Rs60-80; Chinese, Italian, Tibetan, and Indian entrees Rs25-110. Open daily 6am-9pm.

🐾 SIGHTS

GORKHA DURBAR. Straddling the high ridge above Gorkha, this grand palace is where Prithvi Narayan Shah was born in 1722 after his mother had a dream in which she swallowed the sun. The ambitious prince was crowned at the age of 21, and within two years had set out to conquer the Kathmandu Valley, never to return to his birthplace. Though the exact date of its construction is uncertain, the palace is believed to have been built eight generations prior to Prithvi Narayan's birth, under the reign of Ram Shah (1606-1636). The city of Gorkha was ignored by the Shah Dynasty until King Mahendra, father of the present king, returned here in 1958. In the 200-plus years of royal absence, the same families of Hindu priests had continued to perform religious functions at the temples in the Durbar; the palace's present priests are direct descendants of those who served during (and before) Prithvi Narayan's rule. As you enter the palace complex, the first building on your left is the **Kalika Temple,** where sacrifices are still made. Just past it is the **main palace;** Prithvi Narayan's **throne** is visible through a tiny window. The Himalayas dominate the horizon, and you can see more of the mountains from the palace than you can from Pokhara. There's an even better view from the top of Upallokot, another 30 minutes up the stone stairway. *(Follow the main street through the older section of town and take the stone stairway on the left. Where the path forks at a large pipal tree, bear right; as you approach, the entrance is to your left. The climb takes about 1hr. Open daily 6am-6pm. Cameras and leather articles, including belts and shoes, are not allowed inside the compound—you might want to bring flip-flops to walk around the sticky floor. Palace interior closed to the public.)*

OTHER SIGHTS. The layout of Gorkha's other sights makes a convenient walking tour on the way to the palace. From the bus park, the wide stone-paved street leads up to the **Rani Pokhari** (Queen's Pond), a terrace with a sunken pool. To the right of the pond are three small **temples.** The white temple closest to the pond is dedicated to Vishnu. A statue of Prithvi Pati Shah, Prithvi Narayan's father, sits facing the temple. Just behind it is a temple with two roofs that is dedicated to Krishna. The white *shikara*-style temple tucked behind the other two honors Ganesh. Continuing on the stone road past the temples, you will come to an open square. On the left is the **Bhimsen Mandir,** which draws crowds of pilgrims for the Janai Purnima festival in August. The brown gateway on the right leads to the magnificent **Tallo Durbar Palace,** built between 1835 and 1839 by King Rajendra in a failed attempt to lure his older son away from Kathmandu to succeed him at the throne. A **museum park** honoring Prithvi Narayan has been under construction for years, and promised opening dates come and go regularly. Ask to be shown the interior courtyard of the palace, full of exquisite woodcarving. The streets in the older part of the city are worth a wander. They're pleasantly clean, thanks to the Gorkha Youth Movement for the Environment and the strategic distribution of trash cans marked "Give me Dust."

NEAR GORKHA: MANAKAMANA मनकामना

Getting to Manakamana Temple, one of Nepal's most popular pilgrimage sites, used to involve an arduous three hour hike from Anbu Khaireni, a nearby town. It is claimed that the goddess Manakamana's choice of a remote, rugged hilltop for an earthly abode was her way of testing the resolve of her devotees. Her plan, however, has been foiled by the arrival of Nepal's first and only cable car system, which runs from Cheres, 5km east of Mugling on the road to Kathmandu, right up to the temple's itself, on top of a 1300m ridge.

The wife of Gorkha king Ram Shah (1606-1636) had divine powers that she concealed from all but one of her devotees, Lakhan Thapa. Mr. Thapa was understandably distraught when she committed *sati* on the funeral pyre of her husband, but she had promised him that she would reappear soon, in fulfilment of his wishes. When, months later, a farmer came across a stone oozing milk and blood, Lakhan Thapa took this to be the promised reappearance. The stone is at the shrine of the **Devi of Manakamana** temple, and its current attendant is a 17th-generation descendant of Lakhan Thapa. Because Manakamana Devi is known as the wish-fulfilling goddess, it's not surprising that she is pretty popular around these parts. Half a million visitors come here every year, sacrificing goats and chickens with a brutal lack of ceremony. Cable car employees supply pilgrims with plastic sacking to keep the blood off the shiny new floors as they lug their dead offerings home. (Inner sanctum closed to non-Hindus.)

Hilltop accommodations are geared to the local market, so most hotel names are written in Nepali script only; they line the busy lane running down from the temple. In a pinch, try **Hotel Satkar,** with pleasantly airy rooms. (☎20176. Doubles with squat toilet Rs250.) The **Hotel Minar** is friendly and has basic doubles. (☎29300. Doubles Rs100-150.) The **Alpine Hotel,** has bigger rooms and a passable restaurant. (Doubles Rs300. Restaurant open daily 6am-10pm.)

A visit to Manakamana can be done as a daytrip on your way between Kathmandu and either Pokhara or Gorkha: just ask the bus driver to drop you at the cable car. The ride takes about 3½hr. from Kathmandu or Pokhara and 1½hr. from Gorkha. Ascend the mountain in the US$6 million **cable car,** which opened in November 1998. The 10-minute ride to the top is positively surreal, gliding over terraced greenery and small hamlets untouched by the space-age incursion overhead. *(Open daily 9am-noon and 1:30-5pm. Rs500, round-trip Rs800. Signs in the ticket office demanding payment in "convertible currency" are cheerfully ignored. To return to Kathmandu, hop on any east-bound vehicle.)*

TANSEN (PALPA) तानसेन ☎075

It is hard to believe that a jewel like Tansen, 1370m up in the Mahabarat range, has remained so untouched by the traffic between Pokhara and Sunauli. This bustling town—with its remarkable architecture and amazing scenery, its near-perfect climate and steep, cobblestoned streets—sees few tourists. Tansen was once the capital of mighty kingdom of Palpa, which first prospered under the 16th-century Sen kings and eventually grew to encompass most of the area from Mustang to the Terai. From its assimilation into the kingdom of Nepal in the early 19th century until the fall of the Ranas in 1951, Tansen served as an honorable place of exile for troublesome, power-hungry members of the royal family. Although foreign aid organizations have recently funded a rash of new development on the terraced hillsides of this serene enclave, Tansen is still one of Nepal's tidiest and most endearing hill towns, with exquisite views of the valleys and the Chure hills to the south and the Himalayas to the north.

▐▀ GETTING THERE AND GETTING AROUND

A counter at the northeastern corner of the **bus park,** sells tickets to: **Butwal** (every 30min., 6:30am-6pm, 2hr., Rs31); **Kathmandu** (6am, 8hr., Rs162; 5:30pm, 11hr., Rs212); and **Pokhara** (6 and 9am, 6hr., Rs90). **Sajha Buses** (☎20971) has a ticket office in Bishan Bazaar, 100m uphill from Gauri Shankar Guest House (open daily 5:30am-5:30pm) and runs a bus to **Kathmandu** (6:15am, 10hr., Rs148).

✴▐ ORIENTATION AND PRACTICAL INFORMATION

Tansen is built on the southern slope of Srinagar Hill; uphill (toward the pine-covered peak) is always north. The **bus park** is at the southern (downhill) edge of Tansen. From here, the main road heads 10m north and then west past the **tourist**

office and university campus; 500m after the university, the main road comes to a junction. Gauri Shankar Guest House is on the left; continuing right, you pass Hotel the White Lake, before reaching an intersection marked by a **police post** and the **post office.** A steep, unmotorable flagstone road leads downhill from here to the bus park. The main road continues north, becoming **Bank Rd.** The entrance to **Durbar Square** is on the left. At the end of Bank Rd., another flagstone lane leads downhill to **Amar Narayan Temple.** The main road curves left to a major intersection, **Shital Pati,** marked by a white gazebo-esque structure.

Tourist Office: Tourist Information Center, just north of the bus park. Open Su-Th 10am-2pm. There are map signboards in the bus park and at Shital Pati.

Currency Exchange: Nepal Bank (☎ 20130) cashes traveler's checks. Open Su-Th 10am-2pm, F 10am-noon.

Police: The **main police station** (☎ 20255) is in Durbar Sq.

Pharmacy: Sajha Swasta Sewa Pharmacy (☎ 20464), opposite the post office, has a pharmacist on call 24hr. Open Su-F 8am-7pm, Sa 10am-5pm.

Hospital: Skip the district hospital west of Tansen in favor of the **United Mission to Nepal Hospital** (☎ 20111 or 20489), a 10min. walk northeast of town.

Telephones: Telegraph Office (☎ 20058), west of the post office. Take the first right, continue up a dirt lane to an unmarked building with antennae on top, and turn right; it's at the end of the lane. Cheapest **STD/ISD** and fax services in Tansen and free callbacks. Open daily 10am-5pm.

Internet: Pooja Computer (☎ 20462). Rs50 per 3Kb. Open Su-F 7am-6pm.

Post Office: At the southern end of Bank Rd. Open Su-Th 10am-5pm, F 10am-3pm.

ACCOMMODATIONS

Hotel options in Tansen are limited. There are a few good places in town and a lot of cheap hole-in-the-wall places around the bus park. As you move higher up the hill, the views improve and the prices rise accordingly.

Gauri Shankar Guest House, Silkhan Tol (☎ 20150). Walk 10m north from the bus park and turn left, continuing west past the university campus. The guest house is on your right after 600m. Bright, well-maintained rooms; baths have hot water. Good views from the rooftop terrace. Attached restaurant has a wide range of dishes for Rs50-100 (open daily 7am-10pm). Dorms Rs80; doubles Rs100-350.

Hotel the White Lake (☎ 20291; fax 20502). Carpets, fans, and thick beds, along with attached baths (seat toilets), towels, and toilet paper. Restaurant serves one of the broadest menus in town—set breakfasts Rs50-150; pizzas Rs75-110; non-veg. dishes Rs100-140; and beer Rs75-Rs90. Singles Rs200-400; doubles Rs300-600.

Hotel the Bajra (☎ 20443), 10m north of the bus park, is convenient for transportation but not as scenic as the other two places. The rooms are very clean, and it's far better than the hotels closer to the bus park. Attached restaurant. Dorm beds Rs50; singles Rs100-150; doubles Rs150-200.

FOOD

The culinary scene in Tansen revolves around the magnificent Nanglo West. Other restaurants pale in comparison, both for atmosphere and food. There are plenty of cheaper options, particularly near the bus park, where simple meals are Rs30-40.

Nanglo West, Shital Pati, in a refurbished traditional building. Comfortable dining in the shady courtyard or on cushions in the elegant, traditional dining room upstairs. The bakery has freshly made croissants (5 for Rs25) and cinnamon danishes (Rs13); restaurant at the back has local exotica—*sukuti* (dried buffalo meat with garlic and ginger Rs50)—and international non-exotica—hamburger (Rs55). Open daily 9am-8:30pm.

NEPAL

Hotel Srinagar, a 15min. walk northwest of town. On a clear day, it's money well spent—the patio dining area, on the ridge just west of Srinagar peak, has excellent views. *Dahl bhat* Rs80; chicken chili Rs110; spaghetti Rs180. Open daily 6am-11pm.

Gyawali Restaurant, directly opposite the entrance to the Bhagwati temple. Serves basic Nepali meals at bargain prices, and is popular with locals. *Chappati* Rs30; *dahl bhat* with vegetables Rs30; samosas Rs2. Open daily 6am-10pm.

👁 SIGHTS

DURBAR SQUARE. Durbar Square, in the center of town, can be entered from Shital Pati through **Baggi Dhoka,** a large whitewashed gate built by Palpa's first exile, Khadga Shumshere, who came here in 1891. One of the largest gates in Nepal, it was made to measure for Shumshere *and* his elephant—dismounting can be such a drag sometimes. Shumshere was also responsible for the Square's first palace, but the present blue and pumpkin-colored edifice was built by General Pratap Shumshere in 1927. The **Tansen Durbar** currently houses Palpa's district secretariat.

AMAR NARAYAN TEMPLE. One of the oldest buildings in Tansen, the three-story Amar Narayan Temple serves as a stopover for pilgrims, especially sadhus, on their way to Muktinath. After annexing the city in 1804, Amar Singh Thapa imported Newari craftsmen and artisans and began to turn Tansen into a mini-Kathmandu. The grandest of all his accomplishments, the Amar Narayan complex contains an image of Vishnu. It is surrounded by the 1m-wide **Great Wall of Palpa** (not, in fact, visible from the moon), a water tank with spouts fed by a natural spring, and a garden as popular with bats as it is with worshippers. *(Exit Durbar Sq. through Baggi Dhoka; turn right and follow a steep flagstone lane down through the old bazaar.)*

BHAGWATI TEMPLE. Commemorating an 1815 victory over the British, this temple hosts Tansen's largest festival, the **Bhagwati Jatra,** held in late August. An all-night celebration precedes the festival; in the morning, a chariot holding an image of Bhagwati is led through town. *(From Durbar Sq. head southwest for 30m and turn left.)*

SRINAGAR HILL. The pine-forested ridge above Tansen, known as Srinagar Hill, is one of the most peaceful spots within walking distance. The hilltop park has one of the longest mountain views in Nepal, stretching all the way from India's peaks to the mountains of Tibet. The park is most crowded on Saturdays, when Tansen townies make the trek up to enjoy a bit of family fun and spend quality-time with the mountain scenery. Sunrises and sunsets during the week usually take place for the enjoyment of just a handful of hardy hill-hikers. If the pre-dawn hike up the hill isn't enough to get you bouncing out of bed in the morning, consider spending the night in the park—there's an open-sided shelter and water spigot. The hill is best seen by climbing up the west side near Hotel Srinagar and then down the east side by the United Mission Hospital. At the east end of the ridge is a statue of the Buddha flanked by an elephant and a monkey. *(It takes about 20min. to climb the hilltop from town and 15min. to traverse the ridge.)*

OTHER SIGHTS. A few minutes south of Amar Narayan, the **Tundikhel,** a large field used for sports and other big crowd-drawing events, marks the southeastern edge of town. Next to it, the rose-filled **Birendra Park** is in constant use. The town also has several less conspicuous temples—of special note are the **Mahachaitya Bihar** and a **Ganesh Temple.** *(Opposite each other, a 5min. walk west of Shital Pati.)* The road directly north of Shital Pati leads to another **Ganesh Temple,** set into the hillside. A short, steep flagstone path leads to the small red-and-white temple, which affords good views of the city below. *(15min. walk north of town.)* The minarets of the **Jama Masjid** are visible just south of the temple.

A two- to three-hour walk north from Tansen is **Ranighat,** the overgrown governor's guest house on the banks of the Kali Gandaki River. Known as the "Taj Mahal of Nepal," it was originally built by Khadga Shumshere as a monument to his wife and was designed by British planners. A round-trip excursion to Ranighat takes between a half-day and a day.

🛍 SHOPPING

A few locally produced goods deserve special mention. Tansen's Newari craftsmen employ the lost wax method in their remarkable **metalwork;** the Tansen *kuruwa*, a bronze water jar, is particularly well-known (Rs150-1000). The *dhaka*, woven by women in Tansen and the surrounding hills, is also noteworthy. Several handicraft associations in town, especially along Bank Rd., sell shawls (Rs250-1350), *topis* (hats, Rs25-250), and handbags (Rs40-250) produced from this cloth.

POKHARA पोखरा   ☎ 61

Nepal's biggest tourist destination outside the Kathmandu Valley, Pokhara is sunk in a subtropical valley surrounded by high peaks, forming some of the most impressive vistas anywhere in the world. Nowhere else in Nepal is there such an abrupt change in altitude—the tip of Annapurna I (the world's 10th highest mountain), only 48km away, is 7.2km higher than Pokhara. But Pokhara isn't only about mountains: its name derives from the Nepali word for "pond," *pokhari*. Pokhara Valley, like the Kathmandu Valley, was once one huge lake. Today, only three lakes—Phewa, Begnas, and Rupa—remain. The Gurungs, the true "natives" of the region, used to live on the hilltops surrounding the valley. Only when Newari traders—traffickers of salt between Kathmandu, Bandipur, and Dhankuta—settled in Pokhara did a city begin to rise on the banks of the Seti River. These traders built the Bindyabasini Temple in the 16th century, by far the oldest structure in Pokhara. More recent development began with the construction of two highways during the 1970s—one connecting Pokhara to Kathmandu, the other linking it to India. The banks of Phewa Tal, Nepal's second-largest lake, are now a concrete jungle of hotels, restaurants, and souvenir shops. An important commercial and administrative center, Pokhara is the base for some of Nepal's most popular treks and is the heart of the country's river-rafting industry. Pokhara bristles with activity in season; off season (May-Sept.) it feels more like a small town.

▐ GETTING THERE AND GETTING AROUND

Flights: The **airport** is on the Siddartha Highway, between the bus park and the lake. Taxi fares from the airport to Lakeside are fixed (Rs80-100), but bargaining is expected for rides to the airport (Rs40-60). **Buddha Air** (☎28997), **Lumbini Air** (☎27233), and **RNAC** (☎21021) all have offices near the airport, on the road leading to Lakeside. **Gorkha Airlines** (☎25971), **Cosmic Air** (☎21846), and **Yeti Airlines** (☎30016) are along the highway north of the airport. All private offices open daily 8am-6pm; RNAC open daily 10am-5pm. Private companies all fly to **Kathmandu** for the same rate (frequent, 8am-4:45pm, 30min., US$67). RNAC flies there cheaper (US$61), as well as to **Jomsomb** (6:30 and 8am, 25min., US$50) and **Manang** (Tu and Sa, 8am, 20min., US$50). Countless travel agencies on the main road in Lakeside sell tickets for all these companies at no additional charge.

Buses: The **bus park** is a muddy hell-hole when it's wet and a dusty hell-hole when it's dry. Follow the highway 1½km north from the airport to Prithvi Chowk, a rotary intersection; turn right and go 200m to the bus park (taxi Rs60). The **day bus office** (☎20272), in the center of the muck, has one blue and one red window. Open daily 5am-6pm. Day buses to: **Besisahar** (7:25 and 8:30am, 6hr., Rs70-100); **Bhairawa/Sunauli** (every 30min., 5-11am, 8hr., Rs120); **Birganj** (5 per day, 5:40-10:15am, 8hr., Rs150); **Gorkha** (7 and 9:30am, 4hr., Rs75); **Kathmandu** (8 per day, 5am-noon, 8hr., Rs125); **Narayanghat** (every 30min., 4:45am-3pm, 6hr., Rs80); **Tansen** (7am, 7hr., Rs90). The **night bus office** is on the right when facing into the bus park; it's up a set of stairs, under a white sign with a flag. Open daily 8:30am-8:30pm. Night buses to: **Bhairawa/Sunauli** (4 per day, 6-8:30pm, 8½hr., Rs187) via **Butwal** (7hr., Rs165); **Birganj** (3 per day, 7-8pm, 8hr., Rs175); **Kathmandu** (every 15min., 6:30-8:45pm, 8hr., Rs142); **Narayanghat** (4 per day, 1-8:30pm, 6hr., Rs90). Buses heading out on the road to Baglung depart from the **Baglung Bus Stand,** at the far north end of town, north of **Mahendra Pul.** There is no such thing as a "tourist fare" no matter how much touts try to convince you that there is. To: **Baglung** (every hr., 5:30am-6pm, 5hr., Rs57) via **Dhampus Phadi** (30min., Rs15) and **Nayapul** (2hr., Rs33); **Beni** (3 per day, 7am-noon, 5hr., Rs85). Travel agencies and hotels at Lakeside/Damside operate pricier and more comfortable coaches with morning departures (6-10am) from hotels. To: **Kathmandu** (Rs200-250); **Narayanghat** (Rs200); **Sunauli** (Rs250). Buses added or canceled according to demand. **Green Line Tours** (☎26562), Lakeside, is open daily 8am-6pm and operates luxury buses (including breakfast) to: **Kathmandu** (8am, Rs600) and **Chitwan** (8am, Rs480).

Local Transportation: Bikes are the best way to get around when it isn't raining. Shops in Lakeside/Damside rent bikes (Rs10-15 per hr., Rs40-50 per day). Many of the same shops also rent **motorcycles** and don't require any sort of license or permit (Rs300-400 per day). **Taxi** fares rise in season; fares are higher Sa and double after 7pm. A **local bus** leaves Bahrai Chowk, the huge tree next to Moondance and Hotel Hungry-Eye, for major locations in the city (every 30min., Rs3-4).

▓ ORIENTATION

For all its rustic feel, Pokhara is actually a huge, sprawling city. **Phewa Tal** (the lake) and **Pardi** (the dam) are the two major points of orientation—many travelers never get beyond **Lakeside (Baidam)** or **Damside (Pardi)**. The residential section of town is to the north, away from the lake. The **Siddhartha Highway,** linking Pokhara to India, forms a great arc from north to south through the city. It meets the **Prithvi Highway** from Kathmandu at **Prithvi Chowk,** the city center, where you'll also find the **bus station.** Farther north, the main road comes to the **Mahendra Pul** area, the historic heart of the city and the center of the **Pokhara Bazaar.** Lakeside overshadows Damside both in size and popularity. Lakeside's two main sections extend south from the campground to the Hotel Hungry-Eye and east from the Royal Palace to Fish Tail Lodge; it's a 30-minute walk from one end to the other. Damside reaches south along **Pardi Rd.** from the intersection with the main Lakeside thoroughfare. There are **maps** posted at several of Pokhara's *chowks* and intersections.

▐ PRACTICAL INFORMATION

Tourist Office: Siddhartha Highway (☎20028), a short walk northeast from the airport entrance or a 20min. bike ride from Lakeside. Gives out free city maps. Open Su-Th 10am-5pm, F 10am-3pm; Nov.-Feb.: Su-Th 10am-4pm, F 10am-3pm.

Immigration Office: (☎21167), where the roads to Lakeside and Damside meet. Extends visas. Open Su-Th 10:30am-1pm, F 10am-noon; Nov. 17-Feb. 13: Su-Th 10:30am-12:30pm, F 10am-noon.

Trekking Entry Permit: Trekking permits are no longer necessary for the Annapurna circuit; the only paperwork required is the ACAP Entry Permit (Rs1000), available from the ACAP Entry Permit Counter, Lakeside, opposite Grindlay's Bank. Bring passport and one passport-sized photo. Open Su-F 9:30am-4:30pm.

Trekking Information: Annapurna Conservation Area Project (☎21102), in the Natural History Museum, Prithvi Narayan Campus, in north Pokhara. The most authoritative source of information on the Annapurna region provides free, impartial information on ACAP and general advice on trekking. Good maps and books for sale; several free pamphlets and maps. Open Su-F 9am-12:30pm and 1:30-5pm. Nov.-Feb.: closes 4pm.

Currency Exchange: Lakeside and Damside each have dozens of authorized currency exchange counters and a bank. Most accept major currencies and AmEx, Visa, and Thomas Cook traveler's checks. **Nepal Grindlays Bank** (☎20102), in northern Lakeside, just south of the campground, gives cash advances on MC and Visa and cashes traveler's checks. Open Su-Th 9:45am-4:15pm, F 9:45am-1:15pm.

Market: The markets in the Lakeside/Damside area sell clothes, groceries, trekking equipment, pharmaceuticals, and souvenirs. Locals shop at the less expensive **Mahendra Pul** area (taxi Rs60-70 one-way, but worth it; bike ride 20min.). **Saleways,** in Mahendra Pul, has cheap trekkers' food. Open Su-F 8am-7:45pm, Sa 10am-7:45pm.

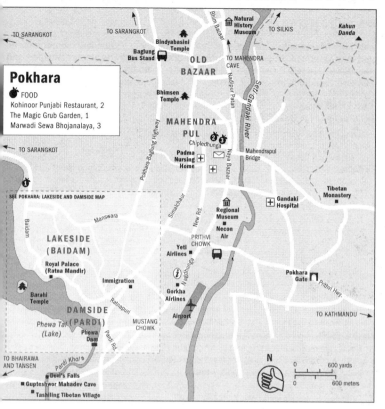

Pokhara

🍎 FOOD
Kohinoor Punjabi Restaurant, 2
The Magic Grub Garden, 1
Marwadi Sewa Bhojanalaya, 3

Police: The **police station** (☎21087) is a 10min. bike ride south from the center of Lakeside; it's on the right just before the Immigration Office. The small **police post** at the entrance to the camping grounds at the end of Lakeside is open 24hr. in season. There is also a 24hr. **Tourist Police Booth** in front of Moondance.

Pharmacy: Dozens of small pharmacies in Lakeside and Damside carry first-aid supplies for trekking; many have doctors on call. The **Barahi Medical Hall,** Lakeside (☎22862), south of Grindlay's Bank, is usually well-stocked. Open daily 7am-10pm.

Hospital: The clinic in the **International Nepal Fellowship Compound,** at the far north end of Pokhara (☎20111), has a doctor on duty daily 10am-1:30pm. Dr. Prakash Mishra is on call 24hr. at **Manish Medical Hall** (☎25650), on the main road in Damside. Open daily 7am-9:30pm. The **Padma Nursing Home,** New Rd. (☎20159), southwest of Mahendra Pul, has a large facility and many doctors. Open daily 6:30am-8pm. For emergencies, go to the **Gandaki Hospital** (☎20066), east of Mahendra Pul, on the far side of the Seti Gandaki River.

Internet: Internet access providers in Pokhara have formed cartels to prevent competition—the going rate is a brutal Rs7 per min. **CyberWorld** (☎24618), above the As You Like It store near the Moondance, has several terminals and enough battery back-up to deal with the worst of power cuts. Open daily 8am-10pm.

Post Office: The **main post office** (☎22014), on the main street in Mahendra Pul, (30min. by bike; taxi Rs50-60). There is another post office nearer to Lakeside—head out of Lakeside and turn left immediately after the Immigration Office; it's on your left after 200m. Both open Su-Th 10am-5pm, F 10am-3pm. Most bookstores in Lakeside, and Damside sell stamps and post letters. The **UPS Office** (☎27241), in Lakeside south of Tea Time, on the side road, sends packages quickly, safely, and expensively worldwide. Open daily 9am-6:30pm.

ACCOMMODATIONS

Lakeside bursts with travel agents, bookstores, money changers, supermarkets, and entertainment. Damside, a 15-minute bike ride away, is quieter, smaller, and cheaper. All hotels listed have luggage storage, laundry service, fans, seat toilets, STD/ISD, and noon check-out. Expect off-season discounts of up to 50%.

LAKESIDE

Butterfly Lodge (☎22892). Heading north on the main road, turn right at Pyramid Restaurant; it's on the right after 100m. Clean rooms, friendly staff, and a garden. Restaurant serves basic meals. All profits go to the Child Welfare Scheme, which runs daycare and healthcare centers in the Annapurnas. Dorm beds Rs100; doubles Rs400-1200.

Sacred Valley Inn (☎31792), on the main road, 150m south of Moondance. Excellent location—just a brief stroll to the heart of Lakeside. New hotel with marble everywhere. Big, airy rooms with rattan furniture on the balconies and 24hr. hot water. Breakfast (Rs40-90) is worth the wait. Doubles Rs300-670.

Nature's Grace Lodge (☎27220), 50m beyond the Butterfly, is run by the same organization. Prices are the same, but the rooms are nicer. Though this place lacks the sprawling garden, a rooftop terrace and bar make up for it. All profits go to the Child Welfare Scheme. Doubles Rs400-600.

Hotel Avocado (☎23617), in the heart of Lakeside, behind Once Upon a Time. Helpful management, sparkling clean rooms, and an attractive little garden (no avocado tree). Hot water 24hr. All rooms have attached bath. Doubles Rs200-300.

Hotel Nirvana (☎23332), just off the main road, 250m south of Moondance. Peaceful but close to the action. Big, breezy rooms, many with views of the lake and mountains. Hot water. Doubles Rs200-1050.

Hotel Fire on the Mountain (☎31777), 150m down from Hotel Nirvana. More removed, with a garden and big, clean rooms. Singles Rs80-250; doubles Rs150-400.

Camping Ground (☎21688), north end of Lakeside; turn left at the intersection north of Sheela Bakery and go 100m down toward the lake. Bordering the lake, with unobstructed mountain views, Pokhara's only campground is ideal in dry weather but sloppy during the monsoon. Squat toilets. Check-out 6pm. Hot showers Rs50, cold showers Rs30. Tents Rs40; vehicles Rs20-60.

DAMSIDE

Hotel Himali (☎25385), on the main road in Damside. Big rooms, a rooftop terace, and mountain views. Also operates a trekking agency, **Fewa Treks** (☎25804). Singles Rs100-150; doubles Rs150-200.

Hotel New Cosmos (☎21964), behind the main road in Damside. Great views of the lake and mountains. Try to get one of the 3 rooms with a view. Friendly, familial feel. All rooms have attached bath. Doubles Rs100-300.

Hotel Bharat (☎24021), east off the main road in Damside, just past the Manish Medical Hall. Grand and faintly antiseptic, it gets an 'A' for comfort and value. All rooms have attached bath. Singles Rs200; doubles Rs300.

FOOD

You won't find a lot of Nepalese food here—but with cinnamon buns, Swiss chocolate, garlic pizza, and steak *au poivre*, who's whining for *dahl bhat*? Indian and local meals are easy to find in Mahendra Pul.

LAKESIDE

The Little Tibetan Tea Garden, 50m east of the main road, on the road just north of Grindley's Bank. Authentic Tibetan food, a quiet bamboo garden, and reasonable prices put it leagues above the rooftop restaurants on the main road. Big delicious *momos* Rs70-120; *thethuk* Rs90-120. Open daily 7am-10pm.

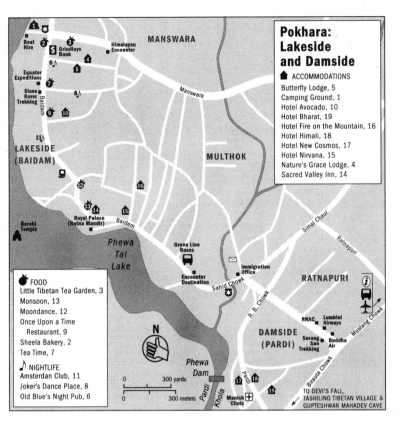

**Pokhara:
Lakeside
and Damside**

🏠 ACCOMMODATIONS
Butterfly Lodge, 5
Camping Ground, 1
Hotel Avocado, 10
Hotel Bharat, 19
Hotel Fire on the Mountain, 16
Hotel Himali, 18
Hotel New Cosmos, 17
Hotel Nirvana, 15
Nature's Grace Lodge, 4
Sacred Valley Inn, 14

🍎 FOOD
Little Tibetan Tea Garden, 3
Monsoon, 13
Moondance, 12
Once Upon a Time
  Restaurant, 9
Sheela Bakery, 2
Tea Time, 7

♪ NIGHTLIFE
Amsterdam Club, 11
Joker's Dance Place, 8
Old Blue's Night Pub, 6

NEPAL

🔳 **The Magic Grub Garden,** at the far north end of Lakeside, on the main road. Built out on a small peninsula, the Grub Garden has the best lake views in town and a tranquility missing from more central places. The fresh fish from the lake isn't cheap (Rs140), but it's worth it. Spaghetti Rs95; chow mein Rs65. Open daily 7am-8pm.

Moondance, central Lakeside, on the main road. Moondance is the best of Lakeside's mega-places; creative decor, a barefeet-only sitting area, good music, and board games contribute to the charm. Big menu ranges from pizza (from Rs120) to pumpkin pie (Rs70). Live band Sa and Su night. Open daily 8am-11pm.

Monsoon, on the main road, 150m south of Moondance, next to the Sacred Valley Inn. A quiet, shady cafe run by a British expat and stocked with reading material. Quiche Rs150. Only open for breakfast (Rs35-70) and lunch (Rs60-150) 7am-6pm.

Tea Time, on the main road in central Lakeside. Very popular; the staff lives by its "Live the life you love, love the life you live" motto. The cheapest and most subdued of the central Lakeside spots. Big salads Rs125-160; chicken *tikka masala* Rs110. Live music M-F evenings and spontaneously at other times. Open daily 6am-1am.

Sheela Bakery, in Lakeside, opposite Grindlay's Bank. Mainly serves sandwiches and pastries, but cheaper than other Lakeside bakeries. Well-garnished "cheese and tomato" sandwich Rs35; muesli Rs30; apple strudel Rs10. Open daily 6am-9pm.

Once Upon A Time, central Lakeside. Among the most popular restaurants in Lakeside. Bamboo hut with bamboo furniture and bamboo curtains. Pleasant atmosphere and decent (if pricey) food. Entrees Rs75-175; beer Rs69-109; cocktails Rs89-149. Movies shown nightly with dinner (around 7pm). Open daily 8am-10pm.

MAHENDRA PUL

▨ **Kohinoor Punjabi Restaurant,** in an alley behind Saleways grocery; look for the "Club Ten" sign. Good Indian food. The chicken butter *masala* (Rs80) will have you scrambling to buy a Punjabi cookbook. *Aloo gobi* Rs30. Open daily 7:30am-10pm.

▨ **Marwadi Sewa Bhojanalaya,** 50m east of Saleways grocery store. Veg. Indian restaurant serving sublime *baingan bharta* (Rs30) and *masala dosa* (Rs35). Top it off with *ras malai* (Rs20) or *pera* (Rs5 per piece) for dessert. Open daily 6am-9pm.

◉ SIGHTS

A large portion of Pokhara's old bazaar burned down in 1949 in a fire that spread from a *puja* at Bindyabasini Temple, so most of the architecture is very recent. Taxis will take you on a three-hour tour of the sights for Rs400-650—contact any travel agent to make arrangements. Alternatively, some lakeside agents (try **Encounter Destination,** ☎ 21963) will book a mini-bus tour of the valley. *(9:30am-1pm Rs100; 9:30am-5pm Rs150, with Begnas Lake as the added afternoon attraction.)*

REGIONAL MUSEUM. The farmhouse-like Regional Museum showcases the cultural range of the Central Western region, like the **La Phewa** festival held every 12 years in the Thak Khola. The last one was in 1992. *(On the road between Prithvi Chowk and Mahendra Pul, just uphill from the central Necon Air Office. Taxi from Lakeside Rs50-70; bike ride 25min. ☎ 20413. Open Sa-M and W-Th 10am-5pm, F 10am-3pm. Rs5; camera fee Rs10.)*

PHEWA LAKE. On an island in the middle of the lake is the **Barahi Temple.** Rent one of the colorful boats from Barahi Ghat near central Lakeside to get there. *(Rs120 for the first hr., Rs150 for 2hr., Rs300 for the whole day.)* Across the lake, the **Peace Pagoda** (still under construction) is on top of the hill. Row to the pink Hotel Fewa and take the trail behind it to the top *(1hr. hike).* Cheaper boats are available in north Lakeside and are of about the same quality as the central Lakeside boats. *(Rs100 for the first hr., Rs130 for 2 hr., Rs200 for the whole day.)*

DEVI'S FALL. The lake flows out at its southern end into the Pardi Khola, a stream that slices its way through the soft sedimentary rock and suddenly shoots down into a hole at Devi's Fall (known locally as **Patale Chhango** or Hell's Fall), 1km out of Pokhara, down the road toward the Indian border. Everyone in town has a version of the origin of the name, but the official story is that Mrs. Devi was a Swiss backpacker who was swept away in a flash flood in 1961. To the left and behind the falls is a pool suitable for pre-monsoon swimming. Women should beware, however; groups of young men will insist on following. *(1km from Pokhara. Taxis from Lakeside Rs80-100 round-trip, 20min. by bike. Open daily 9am-6pm. Rs5.)*

GUPTESHWOR MAHADEV CAVE. Discovered in 1992, this cave contains ancient carvings and extends 3km into the earth. March is the best time to explore the cave; bring a flashlight. It is filled with water the rest of the year, but it's still worth the walk down the first 100m, where a large *linga* stands under an umbrella of cobra heads. The cave eventually leads to the base of Devi's Fall. **Beware of falling rocks.** *(Across the street from Devi's Fall. Cave open daily 6am-6pm. Rs20.)*

BINDYABASINI TEMPLE. A long flight of steps leads up to Bindyabasini Temple, built during the 16th century by Newari traders who had just settled in the Pokhara Valley. The fire that engulfed Pokhara in 1949 started here. The main shrine, dedicated to Kali, is accompanied by a new Shiva temple. There is a small Buddhist monastery at the base of the steps. *(In a park at the north end of town, on the highway to Baglung. Taxis from Lakeside Rs80-90; 35min. uphill bike ride from Lakeside.)*

NATURAL HISTORY MUSEUM. Sometimes known as the Annapurna Museum, this institution is home to the Annapurna Conservation Area Project's public exhibits. The ACAP side of the museum is strong on the ethnography of the Annapurna region and definitely merits a pre-trek visit. The natural history collections are biased toward the predilections of the museum's staff, particularly those of resident lepidopterist Colin Smith—there's a superb collection of Nepal's but-terflies. *(At the north end of Pokhara on the Prithvi Narayan Campus. Open Su-F 10am-12:30pm and 1:30-5pm; Sept.-Feb.: 10am-12:30pm and 1:30-4pm. Free.)*

OTHER SIGHTS. The hilltop **Tibetan Monastery** has excellent views of the valley. Below the bridge, the river rushes through the 46m-deep Seti gorge. *(Ask for it by its Tibetan name, "Madepani Gompa." Follow the road to the regional museum, turn right at Mahendra Pul Bridge, and cross the Seti Gandaki River. Taxi from Lakeside Rs80 one-way. 1hr. by bike.)* North of Pokhara, outside the city limits, is a cave, **Mahendra Gupha.** Tunnels inside allow for a good half-hour of exploration; some parts of the cave have electricity, but take a flashlight anyway. *(Taxi Rs150. Cave Rs10.)*

🜄 RAFTING AND TREKKING

There are more than 40 travel agencies based in Lakeside and Damside, many of them associated with hotels. Agents usually specialize in rafting or trekking. Most accept major credit cards. The established **rafting** companies include the British-owned **Himalayan Encounters** (☎22682; open daily 8am-9pm), **Ultimate Descents** (☎23240; open daily 8:30am-8:30pm), **Equator Expeditions** (☎20688; open daily 8am-8pm), and **Sisne Rover Trekking** (☎20893; open daily 8am-9pm). The last three are all along the main road in central Lakeside. To reach Himalayan Encounters go to the intersection north of Grindlay's Bank; it's 200m east of there. All four charge US$35-60 per person per day. Rates should include equipment rental, guides, instruction, food, transportation, and the rafting permit fee (2-day trip Rs80). Some companies (including Ultimate Descents and Equator Expeditions) provide one or two safety kayakers who accompany every trip. Other companies have cheaper deals, but be careful about going too cheaply; you get what you pay for. Routes on the challenging **Kaligandaki** (Class 3-4; 3 days) and the manic **Marsyangdi** (Class 4-5; 5 days) run only in season; monsoon rains make them unnnavigable. The **Seti Khola** and **Trisuli** (Class 3-4; 2-3 days) are more fun during the high-water season from June to August. Some companies combine a Trisuli trip with a visit to **Chitwan National Park** (see p. 788). Others, including Ultimate Descents and Equator Expeditions, also do **kayaking** trips or allow kayakers to come on the rafting trips. They also offer beginner-level **kayak schools** (4 days, US$175-200, food transport, accommodation, and equipment included), which usually spend a day on Phewa Lake and then three days on the Seti Khola River.

Trekking agencies provide everything from equipment rental to guides to fully planned treks. Expect to pay US$12-15 per day for an English-speaking guide. Reputable agents include **Equator Expeditions, Sisne Rover, Sa-Rang San Tours,** close to the airport (☎30031; open daily 8am-6pm), and **World Wide Journeys Trekking and Expedition,** in central Lakeside, next to the UPS Office. (☎21520. Open daily 7am-7pm.) Women trekkers might want to try **3 Sisters Adventure Trekking,** which provides female guides and porters. Follow the main road north from Lakeside; it's on the right side 600m north of Grindlay's Bank. (☎24066. Open daily 8:30am-8pm.)

🎵 ENTERTAINMENT

Entertainment in Pokhara consists mostly of eating, drinking, listening to music, and taking in the views from Lakeside's restaurants. Many restaurants feature **Nepali cultural shows** (e.g. **The Hungry-Eye, Boomerang**) or **movies** (e.g. **Once Upon a Time, Maya**) during the evenings. Most movies start around 7pm and require that you have dinner. **Bars** are common along the main drags. **Musical entertainment** runs the gamut from Nepali dances to Indian pop bands; there's even a piano bar. **Club Amsterdam** in central Lakeside has live music, food, booze, a pool table (Rs50 per game), a TV, an outdoor seating area, and "the cleanest toilet in Lakeside." (Beer Rs100-125. Open daily 11am-11pm, later if the crowd is jumpin'. Live music Th-Su.) For those wishing to catch a glimpse of Pokhara's hippie past, or just a piece of small town USA lost in Pokhara, head to **Old Blue's Night Pub,** at the center

N E P A L

of Lakeside, which has pool tables, dart boards, TV sports, and wallspace shared by Marilyn Monroe, U2, Ganesh, Jimi Hendrix, Count Basie, and a yak's head. (Soft drinks Rs15-25; beer Rs90-120. Open daily 6pm-1am, later in season.) Both Amsterdam and Old Blue's have live music, as do a number of restaurants—Tea Time (M-F) and Moondance (Sa-Su) share one particularly good band. **Woodstock,** another late-night option, is hard to find but can be worth the search; head down the alley to the Beam Beam restaurant opposite the Maya Pub and follow the dirt path to the right for free love and mud nightly. (Beer Rs100-120. Open daily 8pm-1am, often later.) **The Joker Dance Place,** 100m from the right turn at Nirula's, is the only place in Pokhara where you can bust a move on a sunken dance floor under the glare of disco lights. (Open daily 6pm-1am.) Several restaurants across the lake also have **special parties,** advertised around town on hard-to-miss signs. Most begin around 10pm and rage until early morning (boats Rs20-50 each way).

DAYTRIPS FROM POKHARA

PHEWA, BEGNAS, AND RUPA LAKES. Phewa, Begnas, and Rupa Lakes were all part of the huge body of water that once filled the Pokhara Valley. Phewa bears the burden of tourist traffic; Begnas and Rupa remain untouched. **Begnas Bazaar,** 15km from Mahendra Pul, is serviced by **local buses,** which leave from of the main Prithvi Chowk bus park in Pokhara (every 15min., 6am-6pm, 30min., Rs16). The two-hour **bike ride** to Begnas will certainly loosen up your legs before the trek. (From Pokhara head east out the Prithvi Narayan Highway toward Kathmandu and turn left at Tal Chowk, 12km from Pokhara.) **Taxis** charge Rs500-600 round-trip. You can also rent a **boat** (Rs200 per hr.) and row to the other end of Begnas, from where it's a 20-minute hike to Rupa over Panchabhaiya Danda.

SARANGKOT. Sarangkot (1592m) has some of the best views around. There are several ways to get there. If you're feeling lazy, take a **taxi** up the road that runs most of the way to the top and walk up for another half hour (Rs500-600 round-trip). Or, rent a **motorcycle** (See **Practical Information,** above) and head up the same road. You can simply walk up the road—when heading north, turn left off the Baglung Rd. at the "Sarangkot" sign, 1km north of the Baglung bus park. Much nicer (and longer) is the walk up from Lakeside (3hr.). It's easy to lose your way on the trails that criss-cross the hillside—guides will appear as soon as you start heading up the hill (Rs20-40). Dawn is the best time to come. To catch the morning light, it's easiest to stay at one of the places just below the hilltop. Many of the places are very cheap but expect (or require) you to eat your meals at the hotel. Water is also scarce, so make sure they have it and find out the cost of using it. The **Didi Lodge** has great views, but you must eat there (doubles Rs50). Almost next door is the **View Top Lodge** with a similar arrangement and similarly stunning views (doubles Rs50). The cheapest place around is the **Sarangkot View Point Lodge,** just below the top of the hill. The two rooms are bare and have dirt floors, but bright posters of Shiva and Durga perk it up (doubles Rs20).

THE TERAI तराई

The most maligned of the country's regions, the Terai is the flat bit of Nepal to the south that dips into the Gangetic plain. Its flatness means that the Terai has many of Nepal's best roads, but travelers continue to see the region as a sweaty, mosquito-infested purgatory between India and the mountains, meriting no more than a few hours' frustrated transit. For Nepalis, however, the Terai produces the vast majority of the country's rice and hosts most of its industry, construction, and transportation infrastructure. The region was covered with impregnable malarial jungle until the 1950s and 1960s; eradication efforts prompted massive migrations from Nepal's hills and the bordering Indian states. Large chunks of land, such as the Royal Chitwan National Park, have been set aside to preserve some of the region's natural riches. There continues to be conflict between wildlife needs, the demands of a growing population, and now, a burgeoning tourism industry. The neighboring towns of Narayanghat and Bharatpur are the main gateway from the hills. The Mahendra Rajmarg Highway, running east-west from one corner of Nepal to another, connects the entire Terai. Lumbini, in the west, and Janakpur, in the east, are two of Nepal's main religious sites.

HIGHLIGHTS OF THE TERAI

The jungles, swamps, and plains of **Chitwan National Park** (p. 788) are proof that even the flatter parts of Nepal can be pretty beautiful.

Janakpur's temples (p. 794) offer a look at heavily Indian-influenced culture and architecture, without the headache of a border crossing.

The Buddha's birthplace, **Lumbini** (p. 785), is a pilgrimage site for many, and it has a number of enormous temples and monasteries.

BHAIRAWA (SIDDHARTHANAGAR) भैरहवा   ☎071

Just 5km north of the Indian border, Bhairawa has managed to avoid the nasty border-town grime that plagues its counterpart to the south, Sunauli. What the town lacks in sights it makes up for in pleasant accommodations; it's a popular stop on the way to or from the border and for daytrips to Lumbini.

⌨ GETTING THERE AND GETTING AROUND. Necon Air, 50m north of Bus Chowk (☎21244; open daily 8am-1pm and 2pm-6:30pm), has flights to **Kathmandu** (6:10pm, US$72). **Buddha Air** is just east of Bus Chowk (☎21893; open daily 8am-6pm). **RNAC,** just west of Bus Chowk (☎20175; open daily 10am-5pm), flies to **Kathmandu** (2pm, US$71). From the **bus counter,** at Bus Chowk (☎20351; open daily 4am-8:30pm), buses run to: **Sunauli** (frequent, 10min., Rs3) and **Butwal** (frequent, 1hr., Rs14). Buses to **Lumbini** (every 30min., 6:30am-6pm, 1¼hr., Rs15) depart from Lumbini Chowk. A **rickshaw** from Lumbini Chowk to Bus Chowk costs Rs10. **Private jeeps,** which can be hired from Bus Chowk, haul passengers to the **airport** (Rs100), Sunauli (Rs70), and Lumbini (Rs400-500 round-trip). There are frequent **public jeeps** to Sunauli (Rs4).

🖿🖫 ORIENTATION AND PRACTICAL INFORMATION. The **Siddhartha Rajmarg Highway** runs north-south through town. **Bank Rd.** heads west from **Bus Chowk** (Bhairawa's center) to the main bazaar. A 15-minute walk north of Bus Chowk leads to **Lumbini Chowk,** where the Lumbini road splits from the highway and heads west, passing the **airport** 5km farther on. **Lumbini Exchange,** Bank Rd., 30m west of Bus Chowk, changes only cash (☎21722; open daily 7am-6pm). **Bhim Hospital,** Bank Rd. (☎20193), 100m west of Bus Chowk, and **Siddhartha Medical Hall** (☎22707), one of the small shops in front of the hospital, are both open 24hr. The main **police station** (☎20199) is on Barmeli Tole. Follow Bank Rd. west from Bus Chowk to the next major intersection and turn right; it's behind the big white gate with "Welcome" painted down the side. Browse the **Internet** and send email at **Roopchaya Photo Studio,** Bank Rd., 100m west of Bus Chowk. (☎21243. Rs5 per min. Open daily 8am-8pm.) The **GPO** is on Bank Rd., 200m west of Bus Chowk (open Su-Th 10am-5pm, F 10am-3pm). **Postal Code:** 32901.

🖪🖫 ACCOMMODATIONS AND FOOD. The best place to stay is the **Hotel Moonlight,** on the highway 40m north of Bus Chowk. Rooms are clean and neat; attached baths have seat toilets, and common baths are tiled and spotless. (☎22808. Singles Rs250; doubles Rs250-450.) Another good option is the **Sayapatri Guest House,** Bank Rd., 30m west of Bus Chowk. Small but tidy and bright rooms come with fans and towels. It can get noisy at times. (☎21236. Singles Rs125-250; doubles Rs450.) **Hotel**

NEPAL

Everest, next door and under the same management, is newer and grander but probably not worth the extra money. Bathrooms come with towels and squat toilets. (☎20317. Singles Rs550; doubles Rs700.) **Pashupati Sweets and Fast Food,** Bus Chowk, on the northeast corner of the intersection, is one of the best eateries. Everything from Indian sweets (Rs5-20 per piece) to Chinese (Rs40-65) to pizzas (Rs50-80) are all served up in a jiffy. (Open daily 7am-9pm.) A few minutes' walk west on Bank Rd. is the turn-off for **Kasturi Restaurant,** which serves good cheap Indian food. (Entrees Rs30-60. Open daily 8am-9pm.)

SUNAULI सुनौली   ☎071/05522

Well, it could be worse. The most generous thing one can say about Sunauli is that it isn't as miserable as the other hypertrophied bus stops that link India and Nepal. The second-most popular entry point to Nepal (after the airport in Kathmandu), Sunauli has all the inevitable frontier grime (including touts) but is much less of a hassle than Birganj and significantly less dismal than Kakarbhitta, which is not to say that you'll want to get stuck here for long.

▛ **GETTING THERE AND GETTING AROUND.** The **bus park** on the Indian side is about 500m south of the border. Purchase tickets on board the bus. Buses leave frequently for: **Delhi** (every 2hr., 5am-7pm, 22hr., IRs300) via **Lucknow** (10hr., IRs115); **Gorakhpur** (every 30min., 4am-9pm, 2-3hr., IRs35); and **Varanasi** (every hr., 4am-7pm, 9hr., IRs115). The **bus park** on the Nepal side is about 100m from the border. Buses run to: **Bhairawa** (frequent, 5am-10pm, 10min., NRs3); **Kathmandu** (6 per day, 4:30am-1:30pm, 11hr., NRs160; 6 per night, 4:30-10pm, 11hr., NRs200); **Narayanghat** (every 2hr., 8am-4pm, 6hr., NRs125); and **Pokhara** (every 30min., 4am-1pm, 10hr., NRs160; every hr., 2-8pm, 10hr., NRs190). The Kathmandu and Pokhara buses pass through **Butwal,** where there are connections to other places in Nepal. **Jeeps** also run to **Bhairawa** (frequent, 5am-10pm, 5min., NRs4). You can **walk** across the border or take a **rickshaw** (NRs30).

▚▞ **ORIENTATION AND PRACTICAL INFORMATION.** The requisite stops at both Indian and Nepali **customs and immigration** should take less than an hour. Nepalese visas can be obtained on the spot, but citizens of any country other than India or Nepal will need to have a visa already in order to enter India (available only in Kathmandu). The border is open 24 hours, as are both Nepalese and Indian immigration offices. The Nepali **tourist office** (☎20304; open Su-Th 10am-5pm, F 10am-3pm) and **police outpost** are just south of the big Nepali entrance gate, opposite the tourist office. There are several authorized **currency exchangers** on the Nepal side (most open 6am-8pm).

▛▟ **ACCOMMODATIONS AND FOOD.** The best lodging option in Sunauli is the government-run **Hotel Niranjana,** on the Indian side, just north of the bus park. A distinctive white fort-like structure, the hotel has a great location that blocks out most of the traffic noise. Decent rooms have balconies, attached bath, and hot water. (☎38201. Dorm beds IRs50; singles IRs250-400; doubles IRs300-450.) A good value on the Nepali side is the **Hotel New Mukti Lodge,** to the north of the bus park. Despite the noisy surroundings, the rooms are clean and peaceful, particularly on the upper floors. All rooms have attached bath. (☎21979. Singles NRs150-250; doubles NRs200-300.) The only other decent place on the Nepali side is **Hotel Paradise,** on the highway opposite the jeep park. The large, clean rooms with thick mattresses and attached baths are in a league of their own. Believe it or not, every room comes with towels and soap. (☎22777. Singles NRs250; doubles NRs350.) The restaurant dishes up Indian and Chinese standards for NRs25-45 and pizza for NRs55-85. (Open 6am-10pm.) The restaurant in Hotel Niranjana is your best bet on the Indian side, serving Indian, continental, Chinese, and Japanese (wow) dishes. (*Thalis* IRs40; other entrees IRs 25-50. Open daily 6:30am-10:30pm.) **Mandro,** 150m north of the border, on the Nepal side, serves: the standard entrees NRs40-70; burgers NRs40-50; pizzas Rs90-130. (Open daily 6am-10pm.)

LUMBINI लुम्बीनी ☎ 071

According to legend, Siddhartha Gautama, a prince in the Sakya royal family, was born in Lumbini in 623 BC, when the site was merely a forest grove near a water tank. Siddhartha's mother, Mayadevi, was on her way back from her husband's palace when she stopped for a bath in the water tank and then gave birth, holding the branch of a *sal* tree for support. Siddhartha's birth was unusual not merely because he was born upright from his mother's rib cage, but because he was born with the ability to speak. Upon entering the world, he said "I am the foremost of all the creatures to cross the riddle of the ocean of existence. I have come to the world to show the path of emancipation. This is my last birth and hereafter I will not be born again." Today, the Sacred Garden marks the spot of this event; it also contains the pillar built by the Indian emperor Ashoka as a token of his visit to the Buddha's birthplace. Further evidence comes from the remains of monasteries and stupas dating back to the 3rd century BC and from accounts of early visitors. By the 15th century, however, Lumbini's claim to fame had been forgotten, and it wasn't until 1896 that Ashoka's pillar was unearthed. The current half-hearted drive to raise the town's status from just an obscure spot in the Terai began in 1967 with a visit by U Thant of Burma, then Secretary General of the UN, and continues with the ambitious "Master Plan" of Japanese architect Kenzo Tange. Various countries are constructing monasteries and study centers in the "International Monastery Zone;" followers of Mahayana occupy one side of the dividing canal, Theravada followers the other. A few are now finished, but most, like Lumbini itself, look a bit like the set of some big-budget Bollywood movie—shells of grand design but empty behind the impressive front.

◼ GETTING THERE AND GETTING AROUND

Buses drop passengers at many different spots, depending on which stretch of road is under construction, but all pass through **Parsa,** an intersection near the northeastern corner of Ring Rd. From Parsa, catch the **bus** to **Bhairawa** (every 30min., 7am-5:30pm, 1¼ hr., Rs15). **Bikes** are a great way to get around; **Lumbini Village Lodge** (see **Accommodations and Food,** below) has a few decent ones for hire (Rs20 per hr., Rs100 per day).

◼ ORIENTATION AND PRACTICAL INFORMATION

While Lumbini is laid out in a very exact and orderly fashion, everything is extremely spread-out; the road to enlightenment is long, and the road from enlightenment back to the bus stop is even longer. The town is surrounded by the rectangular **Ring Rd.** The **Sacred Garden,** the principal attraction, is near the south end of this rectangle. The **canal,** lined on both sides by monasteries, runs directly north from the Garden. The town of **Mahilwar,** home to most of the accommodations and services, is just off the eastern side of Ring Rd., 50m north of the entrance gate. **Currency exchange** is available in Mahilwar at the **Nepal Bank of Ceylon,** right at the entrance to town. (☎80152. Open Su-Th 10am-3pm, F 10am-1pm.) **Tourist information** is available from the **Lumbini Development Trust** (☎80194), in one of the administrative buildings south of the garden, and at their **information booth** just north of the Tibetan Temple (both open 7am-7pm). A very basic, free **first-aid clinic,** in the pilgrims' home east of the Sacred Garden, is open 24 hours. **Tara Medical Center,** in Mahilwar, has a **pharmacy** run by a trained medical adviser. (☎80188. Open daily 7am-7pm.) The **police station** (☎80171) is 150m southwest of the Sacred Garden.

◼ ACCOMMODATIONS AND FOOD

Most people visit Lumbini for the day and return to Bhairawa to sleep. There are a few good hotels in Mahilwar, a five-minute walk from the Sacred Garden, and there's usually space available, even in season. The cream of the crop is the **Lum-**

bini Garden Lodge, on Mahilwar's main street. The rooms are clean and the prices are the lowest in town. (☎80146. Doubles Rs100-250.) The **Lumbini Village Lodge,** right next door, also has nice rooms and a pleasant sitting area out back, but the prices are higher. (☎80258. Singles Rs200-250; doubles Rs350-450.) The **Siddhartha Lodge,** across the street, has adequate rooms and is run by a very nice family. All the rooms have common bath. (☎80158. Singles Rs150; triples Rs300-450.) The best place to eat in Lumbini is the restaurant in the Lumbini Village Lodge. Closer to the Sacred Garden, east of the Tibetan Temple, there are some small **food stands** that serve basic Nepali meals. Lumbini's only real restaurant, **Lumbini Garden Restaurant,** 50m east of the turn to the Sacred Garden, serves a decent selection of Chinese, Indian, Nepali, and continental food at an exorbitant Rs100-225. (Open daily 7am-10pm.)

▣ SIGHTS

Lumbini's centerpiece is the **Sacred Garden,** which marks the birthplace of the Buddha. The Garden is dominated by the **Mayadevi Temple.** Currently under renovation, it is swathed in an unsightly yellow tarpaulin and covered by a corrugated-metal roof. The main **Mayadevi sculpture** (3rd-4th century AD), which has long been worshipped by Hindus as a representation of a fertility goddess, was moved to the building at the entrance of the garden and will not be moved back to the temple until renovations are complete. Another statue beside it bears a detailed depiction of the Buddha's birth. Beside the Mayadevi Temple is Nepal's oldest monument, the **Ashokan Pillar,** erected in 249 BC when Ashoka came to town to throw himself a party for the 20th anniversary of his coronation. The emperor himself is believed to have written the script at the bottom. South of the Ashokan Pillar is the **water tank** where Mayadevi bathed before giving birth to Siddhartha. Surrounding the Mayadevi Temple are the half-excavated remains of monasteries, temples, and stupas dating from the 3rd century BC to the 9th century AD. The sleeping Buddha and child Buddha statues, by the huge tree next to the water tank, bear the red-and-yellow coloring of traditional Hindu worship.

Just east of the Sacred Garden is the large yellow **Buddha Temple.** Constructed by King Mahendra in 1953, it contains statues from Burma, Thailand, and Nepal, including a large, gold Buddha at the main altar. Wall paintings depict the wheel of life, four bodhisattvas, and the major Hindu gods welcoming Siddhartha back to Nepal after his enlightenment. Immediately north of this complex is the **Tibetan Temple;** aside from the serene Buddha statue at its center, the most striking feature of the Temple is its fragrant and manicured rose garden. A 10-minute walk north of the Sacred Garden, the **Eternal Flame** commemorates the 1986 International Year of Peace. The road forks here; each branch continues north to temples and monasteries under construction by the 15 member nations of the International Lumbini Development Committee. A few are now finished and worth visiting. On the Theravada (east) side of the canal, the **Burmese Monastery** encloses an enormous golden spire and houses a large community of monks. On the Mahayana (west) side of the canal is the **Chinese Monastery.** North of the Theravada Monastic Zone are the **Lumbini Museum** and the **Lumbini Research Center.** The museum houses a few relics of interest, and the research center has a largely untouched library, but both buildings are most interesting for their creative architecture. *(Free. Open daily 10am-5pm.)*

NARAYANGHAT AND BHARATPUR   ☎ 056

The twin cities of Narayanghat and Bharatpur, on the Mahendra Rajmarg Highway, together make up one of the largest urban areas in Nepal. Narayanghat is home to most of the region's businesses, shops, hotels, and tourists; Bharatpur, just a ten-minute walk east along the highway, provides a semi-rural respite from traffic. Most people only see the twin cities on their way to Chitwan National Park, but Narayanghat and Bharatpur are more than just transportation hubs—an hour's walk up the river from Narayanghat is the sadhu community of Devghat, where the Kali Gandaki and Trisuli Rivers merge to become the sacred Narayani.

NEPAL

GETTING THERE AND GETTING AROUND. A number of companies with offices on the highway, opposite the air terminal, offer daily flights from Bharatpur to Kathmandu. **RNAC** (☎20326) is the cheapest (12:30pm, US$50). Other private companies include **Cosmic Air** (☎24218), **Gorkha Air** (☎21093), **Lumbini Air** (☎23858), **Skyline** (☎25400), and **Shangri-La** (☎25306). These have the same fares and most accept MC and Visa. (Flights 11am-2pm, US$61. Offices open daily 7am-5pm.) **Buses** leave from the **Pulchowk Bus Park** to: **Birganj** (every 30min., 5am-3pm, 4hr., Rs80); **Butwal** (every 30min., 5am-3pm, 3hr., Rs70); and **Kathmandu** (every 30min., 4am-3pm, 6hr., Rs95). From **Pokhara bus station,** buses/minibuses go to: **Pokhara** (every 30min., 5:45am-2:45pm, 4hr., Rs80/120) and **Gorkha** (every hr., 6:45am-4:30pm, 3hr., Rs45/65). A **cycle-rickshaw** between Narayanghat and Bharatpur should cost Rs10-15. **Chitwan Sauraha Tours and Travels,** at the southwest edge of the Pulchowk Bus Park, sells tickets for tourist buses to Kathmandu. (☎21890. Open daily 7am-10pm. Bus leaves at 11am, 4½hr., Rs130.)

ORIENTATION AND PRACTICAL INFORMATION. Narayanghat and Bharatpur are both on the east-west **Mahendra Rajmarg Highway;** the virtually indistinguishable city centers are about 2km apart. The center of Narayanghat is the **Pulchowk Bus Park,** at the intersection of the highway and the north-south road to Mugling. A 15-minute walk north along this road is the **Pokhara Bus Park.** The most obvious landmark in Bharatpur is the **airport,** on the highway near the west end of town. **Nepal Bank,** on the road to Mugling, in the big, pink building 500m northeast of Pulchowk, changes currency and traveler's checks. (☎20170. Open Su-Th 10am-3pm, F 10am-12:30pm.) There is a **hospital** (☎20111) in Bharatpur, north of the main square. Across the street is the private **Asha Hospital** (☎22496). **Pharmacies** surround the hospitals (most open 6am-9pm). The **police** (☎20146) are in the red building off the dirt road two blocks south and one block west of Pulchowk Bus Park. **Hello Chitwan,** on the highway 200m east of the Pulchowk Bus Park, has **Internet access** (☎25777. Rs7 per min.) The **post office** is 25m east of the Pokhara bus park, just off the road to Mugling. (Open Su-Th 10am-5pm, F 10am-3pm.)

ACCOMMODATIONS AND FOOD. All accommodations listed below are in Narayanghat, near one of the bus parks. **Regal Rest House,** opposite the Gulf gas station at Pulchowk Bus Park, has clean rooms, fans, and attached baths with hot water, towels, and soap. (☎20755. Singles Rs300; doubles Rs400.) **Quality Guest House,** 20m north and 20m east of Pulchowk Bus Park, is also good. All baths have hot water. (☎20939. Singles Rs150-175; doubles Rs200-250.) **Hotel River View,** on the road behind Pokhara bus stand, has a river view only from the upper floors. It's friendly and reminiscent of a trekking lodge. Rooms have mosquito nets and attached baths with squat toilets. (☎21151. Doubles Rs100-200.) The best places to eat in Narayanghat are the ramshackle **food stands** on the south side of Pulchowk Bus Park. (Curries Rs20-30; chow mein Rs30-40. Most open daily 7am-9pm.) For something more upscale, try the **Rooftop Restaurant,** on the highway, 200m east of Pulchowk Bus Park. The food is cooked on a *taas*—a large, clay barbecue pit. (Veg. *thukpa* Rs30; chicken *tikka masala* Rs75. Open daily 8am-10pm.)

SIGHTS. Devghat, 8km north of Narayanghat, exists to honor the confluence of the Trisuli and Kali Gandaki Rivers and is a popular sadhu hangout. Don't miss the 4m-high pink statue of the monkey god Hanuman. Across the bridge are many shrines to various deities and saints, most prominently Mahadevi and Durga. Non-Hindus should refrain from entering the small temples. Early morning is the best time to visit, as the devout go about their daily spiritual purification bath in the river. The real action, however, comes around January 15 when thousands make the pilgrimage here. (*Round-trip taxi ride plus 1hr. waiting time Rs250. Buses from Pokhara Bus Station every 30min., 6am-6pm, 20min., Rs10.)*

NEPAL

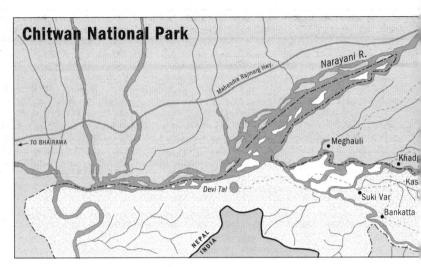

Chitwan National Park

Narayani R.

Mahendra Rajmarg Hwy

TO BHAIRAWA

Meghauli

Khadg

Kas

Devi Tal

Suki Var

Bankatta

NEPAL
INDIA

CHITWAN NATIONAL PARK चितवान ☎056

Encompassing 932 square kilometers of jungle and taking in an enormous stretch of the Terai's hottest and wettest regions, Chitwan National Park is Nepal's largest and most heavily touristed nature reserve. The park is home to an enormous variety of wildlife, the most spectacular of which are the mammals—over 50 mammal species inhabit the park, including rhinos, tigers, sloth bears, spotted deer, and leopards. The park's popularity has spawned a rash of new hotels, restaurants, and tour operators vying for tourist rupees in the once-peaceful town of Sauraha at the park's entrance, but the park itself remains wild. There are plenty of opportunities for visitors who want to get away from it all to disappear and do some jungle exploration. Until recently, Chitwan was the playground for Nepal's elite—and the sport was hunting big game. Nepalese history books are full of photos of local leaders and foreign dignitaries posing on elephants behind the day's kill—tigers, black bears, and deer. As of 1846, hunting rights in Chitwan were reserved for royalty and their guests. But things have changed, and Royal Chitwan National Park is now the most protected wildlife reserve in Nepal. In fact, the biggest threat to the wildlife came not from aristocratic rifles but from the area's successful malaria eradication program in the 1950s, which indirectly resulted in total habitat destruction as people moved down from the hills to take advantage of the fertile flatlands. Resettlement of these people began in 1964, and the area was declared a national park in 1973. Eleven years later, UNESCO designated the Royal Chitwan National Park a Natural World Heritage Site.

▐▀ GETTING THERE AND GETTING AROUND

Buses: The **bus counter** (☎60134), in Tandi, east of the turn-off to Sauraha, is marked "Prithvi Rajmarg Bus Syndicate." Open daily 7am-9pm. Buses run to: **Kathmandu** (daily, 10 and 11am, 5hr., Rs130); **Pokhara** (daily, 9 and 10am, 5hr., Rs130). Buses also leave directly from **Chitrasari** to: **Kathmandu** (10:30am, 5hr., Rs140); **Pokhara** (10:30am, 5hr., Rs140); and **Sunauli** (10:30am, 5½hr., Rs150). **Green Line,** on the main road in Sauraha (open daily 10am-5pm), sends A/C buses to **Kathmandu** and **Pokhara** (both 9:30am, Rs480 including breakfast). Reserve ahead at hotels in Sauraha or travel agencies in Tandi. To get to **Narayanghat,** where other connections are available, go to to Tandi and catch any westbound bus on the highway (15min., Rs10).

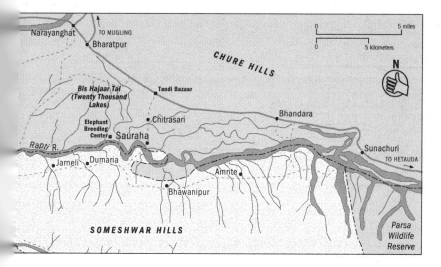

Local Transportation: Transportation between Tandi and Sauraha is a hassle. **Jeeps** run from Tandi to Chitrasari (Rs30 per person, but expect to be asked for more); then you have to cross the river via footbridge, where other jeeps are waiting to whisk you away again. Jeeps may not be available off-season; it's a good idea to reserve a night's accommodation to ensure that a vehicle will be sent for you by the hotel. If you're tired of having your ass bumped around in a jeep, it's a short (15min.) walk from Chitrasari to Sauraha. Sauraha has lots of **bike rental** shops along the main road (Rs80-100 per day). **Chitwan Guide Office** (☎ 80081), on the main road, north of Sauraha bazaar, has good bikes (Rs15 per hr., Rs80 per day). Open daily 6am-9:30pm. A few places in Sauraha rent **motorcycles** and, for better or worse, don't require any kind of driver's license. **Chitwan Motorbike on Hire and Repairing Center** (☎ 80012), near the north end of town, rents for Rs500 per day, including a liter of petrol and a helmet. Open daily 6am-8pm.

ORIENTATION AND PRACTICAL INFORMATION

Chitwan National Park is at the center of the Terai. Its southern boundary is the Indian border, its northern boundary the Rapti River, and farther downstream is the Narayani River. The Mahendra Rajmarg Highway runs almost parallel to the northern boundary of the park. The dirt road leading to the park entrance branches south off the highway in the town of **Tandi,** 20km east of Narayanghat. This dirt road heads south for 4km until it hits **Chitrasari,** a footbridge river-crossing that's developed into a little transportation hub; jeeps wait on either side. From there it's 2½km farther south to **Sauraha,** the town that sits right at the park entrance. Sauraha is home to all the hotels, restaurants, and tour agencies that serve the park and its visitors. It's a small town and oriented almost entirely along the north-south **Main Rd.,** which runs all the way down to the river.

Tourist Office: The **ticket office** at the park entrance sells elephant rides (8am and 4pm, Rs650). Open daily 6:30-9am and 1:30-4pm. The National Park **entry fee** (Rs650, valid for 2 full days) covers general entry. **Steep fines** await those caught in the park without a valid permit. **No one may enter the park at night.** In season, the wait to get park entry permits can be 3-4hr. Most of the time, the permit is purchased by whatever guide service you are using, so you don't have to go to the office yourself.

Currency Exchange: Sauraha Money Changer, Main Rd., in the middle of town, changes cash and traveler's checks for a 2% fee. Open daily 7am-7pm. Farther north along the road, **Chitwan Money Changer** does the same thing. Open daily 6am-9pm.

Police: The **main police station** is a 20min. walk east of Sauraha along Tharu Village Rd. The police station in **Tandi** is on the main highway, 300m east from the turn to Sauraha.

Pharmacy: Raj Medical Hall (☎80008), Tharu Village Rd., near the center of Sauraha. Open daily 7am-9pm. The nearest hospital (☎20111) is in Bharatpur.

Internet: Hotline Communication, Main Rd., (☎80030), in front of the Jungle Tourist Camp, 1st fl. Internet Rs10 per min.; email Rs15 per Kb. Open daily 7am-9pm.

ACCOMMODATIONS

Many tourists come to Chitwan on pre-paid package deals arranged in Kathmandu or Pokhara. If you arrive in Tandi without a reservation, head to Sauraha. Standard accommodations take the form of free-standing cottages in garden compounds with solar-heated water (i.e. hot shower before bed, not before breakfast). All hotels offer basically the same three-day, two-night package consisting of a jeep or elephant ride, half-day jungle walk, canoe trip, stick dance, lodgings, meals, and bus transportation from Kathmandu or Pokhara to any return city in Nepal. Be wary of bogus budget "deals," and ask to see a park permit. Also beware at cheaper hotels, as many are subsidized by their tour operations; if you opt to use a different tour company you may find yourself harrassed and even told to leave. Prices plummet off-season (Jun.-Sept., Dec.-Feb.); bargain hard, although some of the costs (park entry fee, government elephant ride) are fixed by the park.

Rain Forest Guest House, Main Rd. (☎80007), near the north end of town. Friendly staff, clean grounds, and reasonable prices make it the best deal in Sauraha. The dining room is a goodie—spaghetti bolognese Rs100. Doubles Rs100-400.

Wendy's Lodge, Main Rd. (☎80033), near the Tharu Cultural Program. Only four rooms but all have attached bath and fans, and the prices are reasonable. In-house tour operator has well-run tours. Singles Rs150-200; doubles Rs200-250.

Tiger Wildlife Camp, Main Rd., at the north end of town. Nice, peaceful, garden setting, large rooms, buffet-style Nepali dinners, and dependable mosquito nets. Prices are low, but they lean heavily on their tours. Singles Rs30-100; doubles Rs60-200.

River Side Resort, Main Rd. (☎80008), on the beach, at the south end of town. A bit more expensive, but if you're determined to spend the money, this is a good place to do it. Immaculate rooms, a great view of the river and park, 24hr. hot water, and a rooftop terrace to take it all in from. Doubles Rs500-700.

Travellers Jungle Camp, Main Rd. (☎80013), beside the Chitwan Money Changer. One of Chitwan's oldest tourist lodges, the Jungle Camp has a wide range of accommodation and very clean, well-kept facilities. The restaurant is good, and there's a money changer and bookstore next door. Thatched-roof, mud-wall doubles Rs100-500.

Jungle Tourist Camp, Main Rd. (☎80030), close to the center of town. Basic but clean. Garden is dusty, but rooms are neat and well-priced. All have attached bath. Email facility available. Doubles Rs300-400.

FOOD

Al Fresco, Main Rd., in the big two-story, thatched-roof building in the middle of Sauraha. Slightly more pricey than other places in town, but the quality (and quantity) of the food more than makes up for it. Menu covers the tourist range from Italian to Chinese to Nepali and beyond, and the terrace has good views of the river. Cheese and tomato macaroni Rs100; apple pie Rs55. Open daily 7am-9pm. MC, Visa.

Namaste Cake, Pies, and Coffee, Main Rd., opposite Moondance Restaurant. The town's best (and cheapest) place for breakfast or a sweet treat. Two boiled eggs Rs15; french toast Rs30; cake slices Rs35; pie slices Rs30. Open daily 6:30am-9:30pm.

K.C.'s Restaurant and Bar, Tharu Village Rd. Even without the Sunshine Band, this is the cream of the rooftop restaurants in Chitwan (as well as the oldest). While the menu covers a little bit of everything, the chef's specialty is Mexican, and he lives up to his reputation. Delicious veg. enchiladas Rs130; cheese and bean burrito Rs130. Happy hour 5-8:30pm. Open daily 6am-10:30pm.

Moondance Restaurant, Main Rd., in the middle of Sauraha. One of the most popular rooftop places, with good reason. Pleasant atmosphere, friendly staff, low prices, and good food. *Paneer* Rs70-90; grilled fish Rs150; Nepali meal Rs115. Happy hour 4-8pm. Open daily 6am-10pm.

THE PARK

> **WARNING.** Due mainly to rhino risk, the government requires all visitors to Chitwan National Park to be accompanied by a minimum of two guides at all times. **Let's Go does not recommend being bitten, gored, or trampled.**

The highlights of Chitwan National Park include the one-horned rhinoceros, the Bengal tiger, leopards, sloth bears, and wild bison. There are an estimated 56 mammalian species in the park as well as over 500 species of birds, 9 species of amphibians, 126 species of fish, 150 species of butterflies, and 47 species of reptiles. A 1995 study placed 107 of Nepal's 300 tigers in Chitwan. *(Park open sunrise-sunset. Rs650. Entrance ticket, good for 2 days.)*

TOURS AND GUIDES. Since visitors to the park must be accompanied by guides at all times, it's inevitable that you'll end up booking a tour. Many people book **package tours** from Kathmandu or Pokhara, which include lodging, activities, and transportation. These packages are generally convenient and hassle-free and don't cost too much more than doing it yourself; most tours are 3-days, 2-nights, and run US$45-55. In Sauraha, activites can also be booked a la carte through all hotels or independent tour operators. Hotels are generally slightly more expensive but are also more convenient, as they can wake you up for early morning departures. Among the independent tour operators, one good choice is the large and professional **United Jungle Guide Service,** under K.C.'s Restaurant, in the Jungle Guide Office. Guides are experienced and friendly, and tour prices are reasonable. *(Open daily 6am-9pm.)* Another option is the **Magic Reservation Office,** in front of Wendy's Lodge. It's a small operation, but Gopal, the manager, is a knowledgable veteran of the field. *(☎80033. Open daily 6am-9pm.)* When looking for a guide, ask other tourists for referrals; the number of years' of experience should also be on the guide's permit certificate. For any fixed-rate activities, service charges should run Rs50-150 regardless of where you book. Be sure to tip the guide at the end of a good trip.

CHITWAN'S ELEPHANTS
Although it is better known for its rhino and tiger denizens, Chitwan is also populated by elephants. Just about every elephant in Chitwan is from India, where elephants still roam wild despite a millennium-old trade of capturing and training them. With elephant stomping grounds receding fast and trapping on the wane, elephant prices have sky-rocketed—they can cost up to one million Indian rupees. Chitwan has responded with its Elephant Breeding Centre, established in 1987. Training begins when an elephant turns two; both a human and a "role model" senior elephant are teachers. Each elephant has 3 attendants: the *phanet* is the elephant's driver and principal companion; the mahout is the one who takes the elephant to bathe and forage; and the *pachhewa* makes the food and also has the unenviable task of cleaning out the stable. The elephant stables, which hold between 17 and 22 elephants throughout the year, are a 10-minute walk east from the park entrance. At feeding time, the elephants chomp on the main course—*kuchii* grass balls stuffed with rice grains, salt, and molasses—and they can knock back 80-90 of these delicacies every day. *(Entrance Rs15.)*

ELEPHANT RIDES. Plodding along on a ponderous pachyderm is the classic way to see Chitwan and is the most popular activity in the park. Elephant rides offer an opportunity to see the jungle animals up close—if you're lucky, you could end up just 2m away from a rhino—in ways that walking and jeep tours can't afford. There are two kinds of elephant rides in Chitwan: government and private. **Government** elephant rides are the only ones that go into the park itself, across the Rapti River. These rides take 1½ hours and leave from near the park ticket office at 8am and 4pm (see **Practical Information,** p. 789). You can book them directly from the park ticket office or through a tour operator. *(Rs650 fixed rate, plus variable service charges.)* **Private** elephant rides stay on the near side of the Rapti River and traverse the Buffer Zone, a section of the park added in 1977 (so you still need a park ticket). These rides last 2 hours and leave from Main Rd. in front of the Tharu Cultural Program Building. The Buffer Zone is still plenty wild, and the rhinos don't seem to notice any difference. Private rides must be booked through a tour operator or hotel. *(Rs400-600 variable rates, plus variable service charges.)* Either way, be sure to wear long pants and sturdy shoes, as the elephants seem to enjoy walking straight through patches of thick vegetation and even whole trees, and your legs are quite exposed from the basket. Most **canoe rides** involve an hour of floating down the river followed by a 2- to 3-hour guided walk back. The canoe ride and walk may be billed separately but should be part of the same package. *(8am and 2pm; 3-4hr.; Rs300-350 per person, Rs50-100 service charge for hotel or agency booking.)*

JUNGLE DRIVE. The jungle drive comes in a close second to the elephant ride in popularity. Since jeep rides are long (4-5hr.), they cover more of the jungle, including the park headquarters at Kasara and the Gharial Conservation Project (where crocodiles are bred and released). But jeeps, unlike elephants, can't leave the road to follow animals or go through tall grass. Still, rhino sightings are practically guaranteed on any jungle drive. As the grass grows tall from June to the annual grass-cutting in January or February, animal spotting becomes increasingly difficult. Each jeep should come with a driver and a separate wildlife spotter. *(7am and 1:30pm; Rs400, depending on season.)*

JUNGLE WALK. A jungle walk is certainly the most exciting way to see the national park. All walking groups are accompanied by at least two guides, and trips wander along the park's trails in search of a rhino or tiger, just not too close. Because walking groups are unprotected and guides are unarmed (except for a long stick), the rhinos do pose a real threat—in the fall of 1999 a guide was attacked by a protective mother rhino and was lucky to survive the encounter. As long as there are a few climbable trees around, tourists are fairly safe, and groups go out every day without incident. Jungle walks come in three basic lengths: half-day (4hr.), full-day (12hr.), and two-day. The half-day and full-day trips explore the jungle from Sauraha, while the increasingly popular two-day trips stay overnight in a local village on the park's border farther downstream. If you're up to it, the two-day walk is a great way to see the park; it really covers a lot of ground and time inside the park's boundary. Walks are privately operated and prices vary by season, tour operator, and number of people. *(Half-day walks Rs250-300 per person, full-day Rs350-600 per person, two-day Rs400-500 per person per day.)*

BIKE TO 20,000 LAKES. Because they're outside the park boundary, it's possible to visit the 20,000 Lakes without any tour guide supervision for a pleasant escape from the carnival-ride atmosphere of Chitwan's other activities. The lakes are home to an incredible array of birds, a sizable population of gharials, and the occasional wandering rhinoceros. The best way to go is by bicycle. These can be rented from any number of places in Sauraha (see **Getting There and Getting Around,** p. 788). To get to the lakes, go north from Sauraha all the way to Tandi (6.5km). Head west along the main highway for 3km (this is the least fun part), until you pass over a bridge. Immediately after the bridge, a dirt road branches to the left and follows alongside a small canal all the way to the lakes (4km). There's a Rs15 **entrance fee** for this community forest, payable at the small checkpost on the road before the lakes. A round-trip excursion to the lakes can be done comfortably in under half a day. *(Guided trips also available; Rs300-500 per person incl. bike rental.)*

THARU VILLAGES. The **Tharu,** the indigenous people of Chitwan, have the dubious privilege of serving as an additional "attraction" alongside the tigers and the rhinos. A **guided walk** through the Tharu village along the road to the park entrance covers the culture, history, and religion of the people. *(2hr., Rs75 per person.)* A more authentic introduction to Tharu culture is the half-day walk to the village inside the park. As the walk takes you through the park, a visit to the village can usually be tacked on to a regular half-day jungle walk. *(4hr., Rs 250-300.)* Tharu stick dances exuberantly invite participation. Dance troupes perform regularly at hotels and every evening at the Tharu Culture Program on Main Rd., north of Sauraha Bazaar. *(Programs start 7:30-8:30pm depending on season. Rs50 per person.)*

BIRGANJ बिरगञ्ज ☎ 051

Birganj is the funnel through which traffic to India passes, narrowing at the border into a pot-holed, exhaust-filled artery clogged with trucks, rickshaws, bullock-carts, and tongas. Nepalis are the first to declare that Birganj is a miserable place; the only reason to come is to cross the border. If you're heading to India, Birganj will relieve any separation anxiety and make you glad to leave Nepal. If you're coming from India, get on a bus heading elsewhere as soon as you can. For details on crossing the border, see p. 44.

📧 GETTING THERE AND GETTING AROUND. Buses run (as quickly as their wheels will carry them) from Birganj to virtually every major city in the Terai; private companies serve **Kathmandu** (every 30min., 6am-noon, 8-9:30pm, 9hr., Rs150); state buses run to **Pokhara** (every hour, 4am-7:30pm., 6hr., Rs175). As many as four **airlines** charge US$55 for the short haul to Kathmandu (flights daily). Reservations at **Lumbini Airways** (☎27385), just off the main street two blocks south of the clock tower. A bus to the airport leaves from the office at 1:30pm (1hr., Rs50). To reach the border from the bus stand, you can either share a tonga (Rs5) or hire a rickshaw (Rs10). Rickshaws to Raxaul (including "waiting" charges) are NRs40, but can take hours to cross the clogged border bridge. You are better off walking the 200m across the bridge and getting another rickshaw on the Indian side.

📧📧 ORIENTATION AND PRACTICAL INFORMATION. Birganj stretches for long, cruel, and unusual miles along the road that leads over the Indian border. Buses bypass the main road and stop at the **bus park** directly east of the **clock tower,** at the north end of town. The **Nepal Bangladesh Bank** is just off the main street, two blocks south of the clock tower. The bank changes traveler's checks and most currencies. (☎23689. Open Su-Th 11am-2:30pm, F 10am-noon.) The hotels will also change money, and they accept Indian rupees. **Computer Point,** on New Rd. between the clock tower and the bus stand, will let you email for Rs2 per minute. (Open Su-F 7am-8pm.)

📧📧 ACCOMMODATIONS AND FOOD. The **Hotel Kailas,** one block west of the main street and two blocks south of the clock tower, has the best rooms in town. The most basic have fans and mosquito nets; the more expensive have private baths, A/C, and TVs, but still no hot water. (☎22384. Singles Rs100; doubles Rs430-600.) **Hotel Diamond**, on New St. 50m from the bus stand, has brand new doubles with five-star bathrooms. (☎27465. Rooms Rs300-450.) **Kailas Tanduri**, the hotel restaurant decorated with Tibetan, Chinese and Rajasthani paintings, serves a rich, mutton-heavy menu. (Open 8am-10pm.)

JANAKPUR (JANAKPURDHAM) जनकपुर

☎ 041

Janakpur was the capital of the mythical kingdom of Mithila, which supposedly flourished between the 10th and the 3rd centuries BC. According to the *Ramayana*, it was here that the Mithila king Janaka found the baby Sita lying in a field and adopted her as his daughter. Despite its ancient associations, most of Janakpur's temples are modern constructions—but all shine from the constant devotion of pilgrims visiting the birthplace of the beloved Sita, also known as Janaki. The city's skyline is dominated by the flaking onion domes and triangular roofs of its many pilgrims' hostels, while the ground is filled with *sagars* used for ritual baths. The pastel-colored buildings glow at dawn and dusk, when the sounds of cymbals and drums from the temples fill the air. This quiet Terai city really comes to life during its festivals, particularly **Vivaha Panchami** (Nov.-Dec.), which features a re-enactment of Rama and Sita's wedding.

GETTING THERE AND GETTING AWAY

Necon runs daily **flights** to **Kathmandu** (10am, 30min., US$61). Their office is on Station Rd., south of Bhanu Chowk. (☎21900. Open daily 8am-6pm.) **Buses** go to numerous destinations, including **Bhairawa/Sunauli** (6am, 8hr., Rs242); **Birathagar** (6 per day, 4:30am-1pm, 6hr., Rs152); **Birganj** (12 per day, 3:30am-2:15pm, 4hr., Rs120); **Dharan** (5:25am, 7hr., Rs152); **Kakarbhitta** (4:30-11:30am and 5:30-8pm; 8hr.; Rs180, night bus Rs200); **Kathmandu** (day buses at 5:45-6:30am and 8pm; 11hr.; Rs196, night bus Rs268); and **Pokhara** (3:30pm, 10hr., Rs250). However, catching a local bus from a major intersection—Itahari to Dharan, Hile, and other points north—is often the best way to get where you're going.

ORIENTATION AND PRACTICAL INFORMATION

Janakpur's network of curving alleyways makes it easy to get disoriented, but the city is small enough that a recognizable landmark is never far away. The **railway station** is at the northeastern corner of town. Janakpur's main thoroughfare, **Station Rd.**, runs southwest from the railway station through **Bhanu Chowk** (named for the Nepalese poet whose bust tops a pillar in the middle of the intersection) and then bears south past **Dhanush Sagar** and **Kuwa Village.** The road continues south to the **airport,** 2km from town. The **tourist office** is on Station Rd., north of Bhanu Chowk. (☎20755. Open Su-Th 10am-5pm, F 10am-3pm.) The **Nepal Rastriya Banijya Bank,** above the Necon Air office, exchanges Indian rupees. (☎20774. Open Su-F 10am-5pm.) There is a **hospital** (☎20033) just west of the Janaki Mandir, and **pharmacies** line Station Rd. The **haat bazaar** (Su, Tu, W, and F) is held west of Ram Mandir. The **post office,** southwest of Dhanush Sagar, is difficult to find, so ask for directions or take a rickshaw. (Open Su-F 10am-4pm.)

ACCOMMODATIONS

Kathmandu Guest House, Bhanu Chowk (☎21753), is a friendly and simple place with open hallways, ceiling fans, mosquito nets, and attached bathrooms with squat toilets. Singles Rs150; doubles Rs300.

Hotel Welcome, Station Rd. (☎20646), northeast of Dhanush Sagar. Bright rooms that run the amenities gamut. The older rooms are extremely basic; the more upscale ones are some of the nicest around. Singles Rs75-600; doubles Rs200-1200.

Hotel Rama, Mills Area Chowk (☎20059). Follow Station Rd. to Bhanu Chowk; bear left and follow the road north to the next large intersection. Though slightly removed from the center, Hotel Rama has a wide range of comfortable rooms, and it is surrounded by a well-groomed garden. Rooms in the new building have white tile floors and are well-furnished; older rooms have concrete floors, fans, and mosquito nets; all have attached bath. Singles Rs100-900; doubles Rs150-1000.)

MITHILA PAINTING Mithili women (from the areas of southern Nepal and northern India that once made up the Mithila kingdom) have developed a painting tradition handed down for generations from mother to daughter. It originated with the bright designs that women paint on the walls of their houses and has become known as **Madhubani**. These paintings often serve a ritual purpose as part of a festival or wedding—a woman may create paintings for her future husband as part of their courtship, for instance. The paintings are characterized by bold outlines filled in with bright colors; subjects vary from abstract geometric designs to scenes from everyday life. Images have different symbolic significance; pregnant elephants, parrots, bamboo, turtles, and fish represent fertility and marriage, while peacocks and non-pregnant elephants are good-luck symbols. The process and the purpose of the paintings are more important than the painting itself, which may be destroyed. Nowadays, of course, they're sold to tourists at hefty prices.

Aanand Hotel, north end of Station Rd. (☎23395), near the railway station. Crowded rooms with ceiling fans, mosquito nets, and attached baths with hot water. It also has the best deals on A/C. This place, run by a group of young men, may make women traveling alone feel uncomfortable. Doubles Rs150-500.

FOOD

Janakpur's dining scene involves a choice between North Indian, North Indian, or North Indian food, but some of it is so tasty that you'll hardly notice that there's nothing else. The restaurant at the **Hotel Welcome** is the most popular in town, thanks to its friendly proprietors, but once they get all the fans going, it's like eating next to an airplane (veg. entrees Rs20-60; non-veg. Rs70-90). Other options include the **Ramilo Restaurant** and **Ekight Restaurant,** just south of Bhanu Chowk. Both have similar menus and prices, but Ramilo has private booths and an intimate ambience while Ekight feels like a cafeteria.

SIGHTS

TEMPLES. There are a few other things to do in Janakpur aside from temple-hopping. None of Janakpur's temples are very old, and all are still in use. The **Janaki Mandir** was built in 1911 on the spot where an image of Sita was found in miraculous circumstances in 1657 and where the infant Sita was discovered by her father-to-be. Her silver image is unveiled twice a day, once in the early morning and once in the evening. *(No smoking or photography inside the temple gates.)* Next door is the glassed-in **Ram Janaki Vivaha Mandap,** built 17 years ago to mark the place where Rama and Sita tied the knot. The colorful statues inside represent Rama and Sita and the friends and pilgrims present at their marriage. At each corner are smaller temples, dedicated to each of the four couples married that day: Rama and Sita, plus Rama's three brothers and their brides. *(Entrance Rs1; camera fee Rs5.)* During the **Vivaha Panchami Festival** in December, sadhus and brahmin priests re-enact the wedding ceremony. Southeast of the Janaki Mandir is the **Ram Mandir,** Janakpur's oldest (built in 1882) and most typically Nepalese temple. Built under a large banyan tree, the temple hosts the **Ram Navami Festival** during the first week of April to celebrate Ram's incarnation on earth. To the east of the Ram Mandir are Janakpur's largest and holiest ponds, **Dhanush Sagar** and **Ganga Sagar.** Follow the wide street northwest from the Ram Janaki Vivaha Mandap, past the hospital, until it intersects with the main highway at Ramanand Chowk. Opposite Ramanand Chowk, a brick path leads to the peaceful and sacred **Bihara Kund,** surrounded by dozens of Rama and Sita temples. South of Ramanand Chowk on the main highway is the **Hanuman Durbar,** a small temple that, until last year, housed the world's fattest monkey (55 kg), thought to be an incarnation of Hanuman and known to be a victim of stomach cancer. The beloved rhesus, affectionately called Bauwa Hanuman, died at the age of 22 after a lifetime of continuous feeding. The temple now houses his somewhat slimmer son, Punya.

JANAKPUR WOMEN'S DEVELOPMENT CENTRE. For an alternative to temples, the **Janakpur Women's Development Centre** (☎21080; email women@jwdc.wlink.com.np) is a must for anyone interested in art or economic development. Almost an hour's walk south of Janakpur, the center can also be reached by rickshaw (Rs25); ask to be taken to the "development store." From the road to the airport, follow signs onto an eastern turn-off into the village of Kuwa. Once in the village, take the first road to the right; when you come to a large temple, take a left, then an immediate right. Continue along the road until you come to open fields; the center is in a brick complex to your right. As you make your way through the village, you'll see Mithila paintings on the walls of the houses. The artists use traditional motifs on handmade paper, papier-mâché, ceramics, and textiles (see **Mithila Painting,** p. 795). The products are for sale here and at various non-profit outlets in Kathmandu and Patan. The center also trains women in literacy, mathematics, and business management. *(Open Su-Th 10am-5pm, F 10am-4pm.)*

STEAM RAILWAY. Janakpur is also the point of departure for Nepal's only **steam railway,** a slow and stately way of seeing the surrounding countryside. You can take the train to any of the villages between Janakpur and the Indian border and either walk back or wait for a return train. However, since there is no entry point here, be sure to **get off the train before the border; you may not be able to re-enter Nepal.** Trains leave Janakpur at 7, 11:55am, and 4pm, and stop at Parbaha (20min., Rs5), Baidehi (40min., Rs7), and Khajuri (1½hr., Rs12), the last stop in Nepal.

DHARAN धरान ☎025

At the point where the landscape rises from the plains to meet the hills is the bazaar town of Dharan, where people from miles around converge to buy everything from cloth to electronics. Despite efforts to increase tourism, the few foreign visitors who do come here tend not to stay for long. Dharan is a far more pleasant place to spend the night than many of the Terai's transportation hubs, but there isn't much to do here unless you head for the hills. **Chatara,** where river-rafters pull out onto the Sun Kosi, is 15km west; the trekking trailheads of **Hile** (p. 798) and **Basantapur** (p. 799) are to the north. Once the site of one of the British Army's Gorkha training camps, Dharan still hosts a number of Nepal's *khukuri*-smiths who now make knives for tourists.

Bhanu Chowk, centered around a statue, and **Chata Chowk,** two long blocks uphill (north), are major intersections. The closest **airport** is in Biratnagar; Necon Air and RNAC have several daily flights to Kathmandu. **Buses** go to: **Basantapur** (every 30 min., 4:25am-4:40pm, 5½hr., Rs125) via **Dhankuta** and **Hile** (4hr., Rs75); **Biratnagar** (every 30min., 4:25am-3:10pm, 2hr., Rs30); **Kakarbhitta** (every 30min., 6am-3:30pm, 2½hr., Rs84); and **Kathmandu** (4:30am and 3-5:30pm, 12hr., Rs371). Other bus connections are made at **Itahari** (frequent, 4:25am-3:30pm, 30min., Rs14), at the junction of the area's two highways. The **Nepal Bank Ltd.,** just north of Chata Chowk, exchanges only Indian rupees. (☎20084. Open Su-Th 10am-3pm, F 10am-1:30pm.) **Cyberlink Communications** (☎/fax 23338), at Chata Chowk, has free callbacks, email (Rs10 per Kb), Internet (Rs7 per min.), and Internet phone (Rs10 per min.).

A number of hotels are along Chatara Line, the lane running west from Chata Chowk. **Shristi Guest House** has well-maintained, large rooms with fans. (☎20569. Singles Rs150; doubles Rs175-300.) The friendly **L.P. Hotel** has basic rooms with concrete floors and firm beds. (☎22220. Singles Rs100; doubles Rs180.) The **Basil Hotel** has slightly more comfortable rooms with bath at significantly higher prices.

(☎22412. Singles Rs350; doubles Rs400.) Its real draw, however, is the attached restaurant. (Entrees Rs30-115. Open 7am-9:30pm.)

KAKARBHITTA काकरभित्ता   ☎023

Kakarbhitta is a trading town on the India-Nepal border. Though not as oppressive as some of Nepal's other border towns, it is essentially a large, dusty mess of a bazaar centered on the bus station on the northern side of the east-west highway.

◰ GETTING THERE AND GETTING AROUND. Buses run to: **Birtamod** (frequent, 4:30am-6pm, 20min., Rs10); **Dharan** (frequent, 4:30am-4pm, 2½hr., Rs87); **Janakpur** (4-5 per day, 6:40-11am, 7hr., Rs176); **Kathmandu** (5am and 4-6:30pm, 13-15hr., Rs325-368); and **Pokhara** (4 per day, 2:30-5:30pm, 13-15hr., Rs419). **Rickshaws** run from the border to **Panitanki** in India (IRs6/NRs10), where there are buses to **Siliguri** (frequent, 5am-7pm, 1½hr., IRs10). Alternatively, you can take a **taxi** directly from Kakarbhitta to Siliguri (IRs30).

◧◪ ORIENTATION AND PRACTICAL INFORMATION. Most of the hotels, restaurants, and banks are along the highway east of the bus station. To the west is the market area. The helpful **tourist office,** in a garden on the north side of the highway, is the place for bus information. (☎62035. Open Su-F 10am-5pm; closes 1hr. earlier in winter.) **Travel agencies** around the bus station charge NRs30-40 commission, which you can avoid by buying tickets at the white building at the center of the bus park. At the border, Nepali visas are available to anybody with a passport photo (US$30 for 60 days). **Nepali immigration** (☎62054) is open daily from 6am to 8pm. **Indian immigration** is open 6am-10pm. Indian visas, however, must be obtained from the Indian embassy in Kathmandu. **Nepal Rastra Bank,** across the highway from the tourist information center, buys foreign currency and traveler's checks and is one of the last places to get rid of your Nepali rupees before you hop across the border. (☎62066. Open daily 7am-6pm for foreign exchange.)

◪◪ ACCOMMODATIONS AND FOOD. Kakarbhitta is packed with hotels, which surround the bus park. At the far left (northwest) corner of the bus park is the **Hotel Rajat,** with a wide range of rooms and the cleanest dining area in town. The clean, older rooms have fans, mosquito mats, hot water, and common squat toilets. Rooms in the new building have immaculate attached baths with seat toilets, fans, TVs, phones, and mosquito nets. Some rooms have air-conditioning. (☎62033. Singles Rs100-1000; doubles Rs150-1400.) The attached garden restaurant—the only grass in Kakarbhitta—serves an impressive array of dishes. (Rs30-140. Open daily 7am-9pm.) The more basic **New ABC Lodge,** inside the market area, has large rooms with ceiling fans and common squat toilets. From the highway, walk to the western entrance to the bus park, take a left down the first market street north of the highway, then take the next right, and finally, make the next left. (☎62073. Singles Rs150; doubles Rs200.)

THE EASTERN HILLS

Eastern Nepal is home to some of the world's most jagged and otherworldly peaks. Six of Nepal's eight 8000-meter peaks, including Everest, tower over this part of the country and are a staggering prospect even for the most experienced of mountaineers, who spend lifetimes growing long beards and dreaming of lugging oxygen tanks to the top of the world. But you don't have to be a mountaineer to enjoy yourself here—the cool and misty foothills have a beauty all of their own. A journey to the small towns of the Eastern hills rewards with views

NEPAL

of the Himalayas, spectacular day treks, and friendly chats with lodge owners over *dahl bhat*, even if you don't have the time or the energy (or the beard) for a monster trek.

JIRI जीरी   ☎ 049

The one-road town of Jiri (1935m), the main trailhead for the Everest trek, provides travelers with the rest, comfort, and sustenance necessary for recovery from the grueling ride from Kathmandu. **Buses** arrive from the Old Ratna bus park in Kathmandu (5 per day, 5:30-10am, 11hr., Rs170; express 7am, 8hr., Rs200). From Jiri's **bus park**, buses run to **Kathmandu** (5 per day, 5:30-10am, 11hr., Rs170; express bus at 7am, 8hr., Rs200) leave from Jiri's bus park. Purchase tickets at the window opposite the Jiri Medical Mall (open 2-6pm). Tickets for the **express bus** to or from Jiri must be purchased a day in advance, and you are expected to arrive at the bus park half an hour before departure.

From the bus park, backtrack up along the road to find accommodations. On Saturdays, a **market** is held on the hilltop of **Naya Bazaar**, a 30-minute uphill walk from the bus park. **Jiri Medical Mall,** at the bus park, is a well-stocked pharmacy. (☎ 29149. Open daily 5:30am-8pm.) The poorly marked **hospital** is a five-minute walk from the bus park, along the unpaved path by the ticket window. (☎ 29155. Open Su-F 9am-2pm.) The **Jiri Helminth Project,** just down the hill from Naya Bazaar, is actually a research group studying intestinal parasites, but it also puts its knowledge to use by providing free medical care and ambulance service to Kathmandu. (☎ 29154. Open M, W, F 8:30am-noon; on-call 24hr.) The **police station** is 4km away on the road to Kathmandu. A number of shops now offer **STD/ISD,** though Jiri's phone service can be unreliable, especially during the rainy season. **Cherdung Lodge** charges Rs8 per minute for calls to Kathmandu and Rs180 per minute for international calls, with free callbacks.

Lodges line the road into town. **Sagarmatha Lodge,** 50m from the bus park, and **Sherpa Guide Lodge,** farthest from the bus park, are the cheapest and friendliest. (☎ 29152. Singles Rs50; doubles Rs100.) **Cherdung Lodge** has similarly basic accommodation. (☎ 20190. Dorm beds Rs20; singles Rs60; doubles Rs120.) Next door to the Sherpa Guide Lodge, the **Hotel Jiri View** has small but bright rooms (doubles Rs100). The nearby **Hotel Gauri Himal** is the most upscale place in town. (Dorm beds Rs100; singles Rs200; doubles Rs250-600.)

HILE हो्ले   ☎ 026

A cool, misty 1900m above the Arun Valley, Hile has spectacular mountain views and a unique ethnic mix of Bhotiyas, Rais, Newaris, and Indians. A trailhead for treks into the world's deepest valley, Hile hosts a colorful, bustling market, but the terraced villages below offset the bartering frenzy. Piles of *doka* (the conical, head-strapped baskets that porters use) wait to be filled and carried off into the hills. Most of Hile's visitors soon head for higher ground, but the town is worth a visit, even for non-trekkers, with several small *gompas* and tea estates on the way up to Basantapur. The real attention-grabber is the Himalayan range itself—there are great views from the hilltop north of town, a 45-minute walk away.

The **bus stand** faces south at the northern end of town. Tickets are sold at a small booth set back on the left (east) side of the street. There are frequent **buses** to **Basantapur** (every 30min., 6am-6pm, 1½hr., Rs50) and **Dharan** (every 30min., 4:30am-5:20pm, 4hr., Rs75), as well as daily buses to **Biratnagar** (11am, 5hr., Rs105) and **Kathmandu** (1pm, 18hr., Rs405). **Global Telecommunication Service,** on the main road, has STD/ISD and fax. The **post office** is down the narrow alleyway next to the Himali Hotel. South of the bus stop are several trekking-style lodges, which have electricity, showers, hot water on request, and restaurants. **Himali Hotel,** a few minutes south of the bus stop on the left, has large, bright rooms. (☎ 40140. Singles Rs60; doubles Rs80.) North of Himali, **Hotel Gajur** has equally comfortable rooms and the best restaurant in town, set in a central garden.

(☎40139. Singles Rs50; doubles Rs100. Open 5am-9pm.) The friendly and slightly more rustic **Doma Hotel,** opposite Himali, has cheap and pleasant rooms. (☎40104. Doubles Rs60.)

BASANTAPUR बसंतपुर ☎ 026

At an elevation of 2200m, Basantapur is blessed with a beauty and peace spoiled only by impertinent roosters intent on rousing slumberers at 4am. This is the end of the road for buses but only the beginning for trekkers through the Eastern Hills. Whether or not you're planning a trek, if you've come as far as Dharan or Hile, it's worth making the trip to Basantapur to take in the cool atmosphere. The ridiculously bumpy **bus** ride from Hile terminates at Basantapur's southern tip, near the **police post.** A five-minute walk along the rutted road brings you to the other end of town, where the road continues east toward **Terhathum** (26km) and, in clear weather, has great mountain views. **Buses** run to **Hile** (every 30min., 4:30am-5pm, 1½hr., Rs50) and continue to **Dharan** (5½hr., Rs125). There is also daily service to **Biratnagar** (8:45am, 7hr., Rs155). Basantapur's **post office** is just past Hotel Yak (toward Terhathum); look for a red-and-white sign and stairs leading to a letter box. (Open Su-F 10am-5pm, Sa 10am-1pm.)

Basantapur's lodges all offer similar tea-house accommodations: beds in wooden rooms, common squat toilets, and cozy restaurants where you can spend the evening sipping *tong-ba* (Rs10-20) and watching people stare at you. **Hotel Yak,** a few minutes past the bus park along the main road, has clean rooms, showers, and a quality restaurant. (☎/fax 69047. Singles Rs65; doubles Rs100. Restaurant open 7am-10pm.) **Birat Hotel and Lodge,** just past the bus park, has small sky-blue rooms. (☎69043. Singles Rs50; doubles Rs80.) The restaurant below is the only place around where you can devour *dahl bhat* under the watchful eyes of V.I. Lenin. Across the street from the Birat, the **Laxmi Hotel** has clean but slightly cramped rooms at similar prices. The TV-equipped restaurant is where you'll find most of Basantapur's after-hours action. (☎69022. Singles Rs45; doubles Rs80.) Both hotels have **STD/ISD** service.

ILAM ईलाम ☎ 027

Safely removed from the rest of civilization by a 16-hour bus ride, Ilam is one of Nepal's hidden gems. Its few visitors are rewarded by the calm, crisp air, the pleasant strolls, and the quite amazing views of mountains and valleys. Ilam is a starting point for treks through the **Kanchenjunga** region, although daytrips through the surrounding countryside can be just as rewarding. The 4- to 6-hour walk to the pilgrimage site of **Mai Pokhari,** 12km to the north, winds past tea gardens and forests to the top of a ridge, crowned by a temple and a sacred lake. To the northwest, a 3-hour walk leads to the bazaar town of **Mangalbare.** The descent to **Mai Khola** is another breathtaking journey of just a few hours on foot. While recovering from long walks, you can stroll through Ilam's **tea estate,** which stretches across the hills above the bus park, or the **haat bazaar,** held near the post office every Sunday and Thursday.

Getting a seat on the **bus** that winds its way up to Ilam can be difficult. Your chances are best from Birtamod, accessible by local bus from Kakarbhitta (frequent, 4:30am-6pm, 25min., Rs10). There are also direct night buses from Kathmandu's New Bus Park (2pm, 20hr., Rs460). From Ilam, there are frequent buses to: **Charali** and **Birtamod** (every hr., 6am-1:30pm, 3hr., Rs90). There are also daily buses to: **Biratnagar** (noon, 5hr., Rs165); **Dharan** (6am, 5hr., Rs165); **Kathmandu** (noon, 18hr., Rs400); and **Phidim** (6:30am, 5hr., Rs117), a small town north of Ilam. The bus park is at the bottom of the hill, at the south end of town. Lodges and **pharmacies** line the main street, which leads north from the bus park up to the **town square. Mechi Tours and Travels,** on the left (west) side of the square, does it all, providing bus and domestic plane tickets, private vehicles and drivers, **STD/ISD** and fax service with free callbacks, **currency exchange,** and **Internet access** (Rs15 per min.). The owner is a good source of information about the surrounding areas. (☎20367. Open daily 7am-6pm.) Three lanes diverge from the square opposite the main street. The one farthest to the right leads to the **post office** (open Su-Th 10am-5pm, F 10am-3pm) and the **haat bazaar** (Su and Th). The rudimentary **hospital**

NEPAL

(☎20036) is at the end of the path. **Bhattarai Hotel and Lodge** (☎20139), next to the bus park, is a little noisy, but it has electricity and large, clean doubles for Rs80-180. The **Himalayan Restaurant** downstairs is one of the few sources of *dahl bhat* around (dishes Rs25-70).

TREKKING IN NEPAL

For many years, the **Annapurna, Langtang,** and **Everest** regions were the only ones open to foreigners, but in recent years there has been an explosive growth in trekking routes all over Nepal. Most trekkers, though, still stick to the original three areas. Fabulous treks in their own right, these three also have the benefit of a good trekking infrastructure—you can stay in tea houses and eat locally prepared food and not worry about the leaking tents and freeze-dried breakfasts that have blighted many a backpacking trip.

PREPARATIONS

For more information on planning a trekking trip in the Himalayas, see the section **Trekking,** in the **Essentials** chapter (**p. 30**).

TREKKING PERMITS. Permits are no longer required for the big three trekking regions of Annapurna, Langtang, and Everest. Permits for other regions must be obtained from the Immigration Office in New Baneswar, Kathmandu (see p. 776).

GEAR. Gear requirements are pretty minimal—essentially, you'll be walking from lodge to lodge. A **sleeping bag** will save you from the brutal in-season competition for a lodge's few blankets. If you're going high (over 3500m), you need decent **warm clothing;** if you skimp in order to lighten your load, you will end up cold and miserable at the most spectacular part of your trek. Mountaineering equipment is not necessary on the Classic Three routes, but you should have a good pair of **boots** if you're going high, and perhaps also a pair of **snow gaiters;** check with people who've done your route recently to see what the snow conditions are like.

Everything you need can be either bought or rented in Nepal (see p. 33). A lot of rental equipment is manufactured in Nepal and emblazoned with fake Gortex, North Face, or Patagonia labels. Choose carefully, especially when it comes to a vital piece of equipment like a backpack—that's something you really don't want falling to pieces when you're halfway up the Thorung-La. Kathmandu is the best place to rent or buy (and sell) stuff, with Pokhara a respectable second.

WATER. Although it is now possible to buy bottled water even in the higher and more remote villages on the major routes, treating your own water is both cheaper and better for the environment. **Boiling** is usually impractical (and ineffective at high altitudes where water boils at a lower temperature), so most people opt for water that has been chemically treated in some way. **Iodine** is the way to go—it's the only stuff that'll kill off some of the nastier nasties, such as giardia. Bottles of iodine solution are available in pharmacies in Kathmandu and Pokhara (Rs25); add 5 drops per liter. A pricier, but much easier, alternative is iodine tablets (e.g. **Potable Aqua**), available in bottles of 50; add two tablets per liter. Tablets are available in Kathmandu (see p. 731) from Kathmandu Environmental Education Project (KEEP) or from the Himalayan Rescue Association (HRA). They are also available for Rs500 on the trail at ACAP checkpoints (in Annapurna) and HRA offices (in Manang, Annapurna and Pheriche, Everest).

MAPS. It's easy to find **maps** of the main trekking areas, and they are an important part of your pre-trek shopping list. But most maps produced in Nepal are approximate at best, and the information on them should be treated with skepticism. Still, these maps (such as those produced by Nepa Maps) are useful for letting you know vaguely where you are and where you're headed. More accurate and expensive maps, generally known as "Schneider maps," are also available in Kathmandu, but these are likely to be out-of-date. The National Geographic Society's map of Everest is excellent. KEEP and HRA in Kathmandu (see p. 731) are good sources of information on trekking routes. Their bulletin boards may also be helpful if you're looking for trekking partners.

PORTERS AND GUIDES

"Tea house" trekking doesn't require you to carry very much, but your sleeping bag and fleece long johns can feel outrageously heavy when you're laboring up a hill at 5000m. Porters can be hired just about anywhere in Nepal, but be careful not to get ripped off. Paying the **surcharge** associated with hiring a porter through a hotel, lodge, or trekking agency is probably a good investment for the peace of mind it brings—your porter is less likely to abscond if he has a boss to answer to. You might also consider hiring a guide: someone who speaks English and can fill you in on what you're walking through. Guides are not really necessary, on the major routes. (See p. 31 for more opinionated rants about porters and guides.)

Having a porter and/or guide does a lot more than take a burden off your shoulders; it can also give you an entry into local culture. They are probably familiar figures on the trail, and often have many friends along the way. If you're lucky, you might even end up as a guest for a night in their home village. And you'll probably learn much more Nepali than you would otherwise. There is, however, a downside: they set the agenda. You go at their pace and end up staying at a lodge of their choice, either because it's owned by their sister-in-law or because the owner supplies them with a hefty commission for bringing you in. Either way, this might not be exactly what you had in mind. Women trekking in the Annapurna region might consider hiring female porters and guides from Pokhara's all-female trekking agency, **3 Sisters Adventure Trekking** (see p. 781).

ON THE TRAIL

Instead of sticking to a strict schedule, we suggest that you simply take as much or as little time over the trek as you feel comfortable with. Some people enjoy hurtling along the trail while others like to stop every 30 seconds to scrutinize yet another wildflower. Most people get up early and hike for five or six hours a day. This gives you plenty of time at the end of the day to wash your socks, take a shower, and hang out around your lodge's dining table. The social scene in lodges can be quite fun, and is a good source of trekking companions for days to come.

ROUTE-FINDING. Route-finding on the major routes is straightforward; you are following the Himalayan equivalent of a highway. Since you are essentially walking from village to village, when in doubt, simply ask the way to the next village. It's not always a good idea to ask lodge employees, even though their English may be good, because they've been known to exaggerate the distance to the next place in the hope that you'll give up for the day and stay at their lodge.

ACCOMMODATIONS AND FOOD. In the Classic Three trekking areas, whole villages were long ago converted into dense constellations of lodges. These were once the **tea houses** of "tea house trek" fame, but are now fancy hotels, complete with single or double rooms, solar-heated shower systems, and extensive menus. Some of the fancier establishments even sport Western-style toilets. But there are still places—usually a village or two off the beaten track—where you can stay in the simplest of accommodations.

Food on the trail used to consist of *dahl bhat* three times a day, but it's now quite easy to avoid it altogether. Common food options include oatmeal, pizza, fried rice, apple pie, and chocolate cake. Food in many mountain villages tends to be prepared with reckless disregard for hygiene. A full range of bottled drinks, from Coke to Carlsberg, is also generally available, though prices skyrocket as you get farther away you are from the main roads.

Though trekking costs can add up, it's difficult to spend more than Rs500 a day, and you could probably make do at lower altitudes on Rs200 a day—everything gets more expensive as you ascend. Lodge and restaurant rates are generally regulated by each town, which means that prices are effectively fixed.

LOCAL SERVICES. There are a few **banks** on the major routes (in Chame, Tatopani, and Jomsom in Annapurna, and in Namche on the Everest trek), but they offer poor exchange rates, and they *do not* deal with credit cards. Change can be a problem, so bring plenty of small denomination bills. Some of the ritzier lodges will change dollars, at miserable rates. **Film** and **batteries** are widely available along the major routes. **Pharmacies** are few and far between, and you should bring medications with you.

> ▌ **WARNING:** There have been occasional reports of robberies and rapes on the trails. Trekkers (especially women) should think twice before going alone, particularly off season, when the trails are less crowded.

THE ANNAPURNA REGION अन्नपुरण

There are three main treks in the Annapurna region: the Annapurna Circuit, the Jomsom trek, and the Annapurna Sanctuary. These can be done separately or combined into a single mega-trek. If you've only got a few days, however, it's easy to get a good taste of trekking by connecting some of the routes out of Pokhara. A popular option is the 4- to 5-day loop from Pokhara to Ghorepani to Ghandruk and back. This route has fine views (from **Poon Hill** above Ghorepani) and provides a chance to spend some time in Gurung villages. Alternatively, you can trek through Birethanti, Ghandruk, Landruk, and Dhampus. Both of these routes involve cobbling together parts of the Jomsom (see p. 805) and Sanctuary (see p. 807) treks.

◪ THE ANNAPURNA CIRCUIT

The Annapurna is Nepal's classic trek. The circuit's combination of remarkable cultural and ecological diversity, superb mountain scenery, and physical challenge (the Thorung-La Pass at 5416m) guarantees an exhilarating hike. Its 150 miles are deceptively long, and the tough terrain and the need to acclimatize will occupy you for about **three weeks.** Almost everybody walks it in the same direction, crossing the pass from Manang to Muktinath. The pass is easier to cross in this direction, and there are more accommodations higher up on the Manang side than on the Muktinath side. But there's an additional advantage: the route seems much less crowded since there's no traffic coming toward you.

BESISAHAR TO TAL. The circuit starts at **Besisahar** (823m), at the end of a road heading north from Dumre on the Kathmandu-Pokhara road. Dumre (5hr. from Kathmandu, 2hr. from Pokhara) is not a standard stop on the **bus** route between Kathmandu and Pokhara, but you can ask the driver to stop here. The trip from Dumre to Besisahar (about 40km) is a headache. Since the road is unfinished in places, the ongoing construction can delay traffic for hours, and heavy rain can render the road impassable. Irregular buses (3hr., Rs35) ply the route, but if you arrive in Dumre on one of the early-morning "tourist" buses from Pokhara Lakeside, you may be able to round up enough circuit-stompers to rent a jeep (Rs2000, 10 people max.). Besisahar is a typical Nepali end-of-the-road town with plenty of accommodations, electricity, and phone service.

From Besisahar, the trail leads to **Khudi** and then heads north along the Marsyangdi, criss-crossing the river on suspension bridges. **Bhulbhule,** which has an ACAP office, and **Ngadi** are next. The first real climb of the trek up to **Bahundanda** (1311m), at a notch in the ridge high above the river, serves as a reminder that you

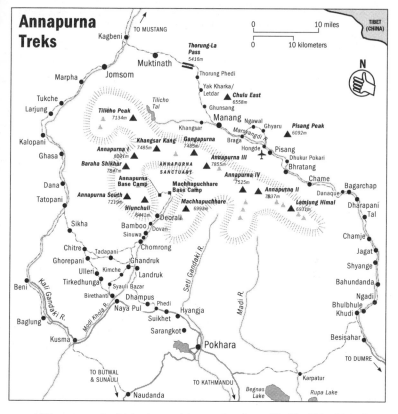

Annapurna Treks

Kagbeni
TO MUSTANG
Marpha
Jomsom
Muktinath
Thorung-La Pass 5416m
Thorung Phedi
Tukche
Larjung
Tilicho Peak 7134m
Tilicho Tal
Yak Kharka/Letdar
Chulu East 6558m
Ghunsang
Kalopani
Khangsar Kang 7485m
Khangsar
Manang
Ngawal
Ghyaru
Pisang Peak 6092m
Ghasa
Annapurna I 8091m
Gangapurna 7485m
Braga
Hongde
Pisang
Dhukur Pokari
Baraha Shikhar 7847m
Annapurna III 7855m
Annapurna IV 7525m
Marsyangdi R.
Bhratang
Dana
Annapurna Base Camp
ANNAPURNA SANCTUARY
Machhapuchhare Base Camp
Annapurna II 7937m
Chame
Bagarchap
Tatopani
Annapurna South 7219m
Hiunchuli 6441m
Machhapuchhare 6993m
Lamjung Himal 6931m
Danaque
Dharapani
Tal
Sikha
Bamboo
Deorali
Dovan
Sinuwa
Chamje
Chitre
Tadapani
Chomrong
Jagat
Ghorepani
Ghandruk
Shyange
Ulleri
Kimche
Landruk
Bahundanda
Beni
Tirkedhunga
Syauli Bazar
Birethanti
Dhampus
Phedi
Ngadi
Bhulbhule
Khudi
Baglung
Naya Pul
Hyangja
Suikhet
Kali Gandaki R.
Madi Khola R.
Seti Gandaki R.
Madi R.
Kusma
Sarangkot
Besisahar
Pokhara
TO BUTWAL & SUNAULI
TO KATHMANDU
Karpatur
TO DUMRE
Naudanda
Begnas Lake
Rupa Lake

0   10 miles
0   10 kilometers

TIBET (CHINA)

N

are hiking among the highest mountains on the planet. You'll still be high above the river after the steep descent beyond Bahundanda, following a magnificent trail hewn out of the valley's rock walls. Of the many waterfalls along this trip, the most scenic is the one that comes crashing down the west wall of the valley close to **Shyange** (1136m), where a suspension bridge takes traffic across the river. Beyond **Chamje** (1380m), a steep climb up through the rubble of a huge landslide brings you to **Tal** (1664m), a paradise on the dry lake bed left behind when a landslide dammed the river. There's an ACAP office here and a number of hotels.

TAL TO CHAME. There are three river crossings between Tal and **Dharapani** (1884m), where you'll find a police check-post, post office, and, in the Muktinath Hotel, a telephone. Beyond Dharapani, the route follows the river left and takes you to the north of the main Annapurna massif. The villages start to look more Tibetan from this point. Next, you'll pass through **Bagarchap** (2103m), a town swept away in a 1995 landslide, and **Danaque** (2176m), the town of grand lodges that has sprung up in its stead. Beyond Danaque the trail splits into high and low routes. **Lattemarang** (2353m), the main settlement on the lower route, has few lodges, but it does have its own hot spring. On the high route, **Kotho** (2530m) stretches over a quarter mile or so, and the center of town, along with the police check-post, is some way beyond the first cluster of lodges. **Chame** (2615m), not far from Kotho, is the seat of government for the Manang district. It's the closest thing to a real town since Besisahar. Chame has everything: its own hospital, a bank, a post office, the district police headquarters, the last telephones before Manang, and stores where you can stock up on just about anything, including cold weather gear. Beyond Chame, altitude sickness becomes a serious risk.

CHAME TO MANANG. The route from Chame to **Pisang** (3133m), via the two small settlements of **Bhratang** and **Dhukur Pokari**, is dominated to the north by the "Great Wall of Pisang," a huge, smooth slab of slate that rises 1200m above the valley floor—to the Gurung people, it is the gateway to the land of the dead. New Pisang, on the south side of the river, is full of enormous lodges; Old Pisang, up the hill on the north side, is a dense tangle of flat-roofed stone buildings clustered around a *gompa* that hasn't changed much in the past 500 years.

From Pisang, you have a choice of routes to Manang. The low route is a short day's hike; the high route is a couple of hours longer. The **low route,** or **main trail,** from Lower Pisang is the main drag along the valley floor. It passes the airstrip at **Hongde** (3-5 flights per week to Pokhara, 7:30am, US$50; check departure details at the RNAC office opposite the airstrip) and continues on to **Braga** and **Manang.** Much more spectacular (and much more hard work) is the **high route,** which begins with a short, sharp ascent to old Pisang and continues for a relatively flat first few kilometers before heading steeply uphill to **Ghyaru** (3673m), where the views of the Annapurnas to the south are unbeatable. From Ghyaru, the road stays high, following the valley wall to a promontory just above the ruined fort at Tiwol Danda before arriving at picturesque **Ngawal** (3650m).

From Ngawal, the route heads back down to join the low route in the main valley. Route-finding can be a little tricky here: pick up the trail dropping down the minor valley just beyond Ngawal, but avoid the major left fork (which leads to the airstrip). The high route follows the north bank of the river until the main trail crosses the river to join it at **Mungje** (3482m). **Braga** (3490m), a half-hour farther, is an extraordinary village crowned with the region's oldest *gompa*, well worth a visit (open daily 7-10am and 1-5pm).

Manang (3499m), a medieval, Tibetan-style village, is the main destination of the Circuit trek. This is your last chance to make sure that your gloves are warm enough for the Thorung-La. Manang's HRA clinic has a free talk on altitude sickness at 3pm in season (Sept.-Dec. and Mar.-May; 30min.). The HRA shop sells iodine, vitamin C, diamox, and (most importantly) T-shirts. There's also an ACAP office and a post office in town. There's plenty to do here, and there are a number of *gompas* in the immediate vicinity. **Khangsar** (3712m), an easy two-hour walk away, is a popular destination for people on day hikes out of Manang to acclimatize. There are lodges here that can serve as a first step on the way to the great high altitude lake, **Tilicho Tal** (5000m), first explored by Herzog's 1950 expedition; in addition, there's a seasonal lodge between Khansar and the lake.

MANANG TO MUKTINATH. Beyond Manang, thoughts turn to the **Thorung-La Pass** (5416m). Although local traders will do the crossing from Manang to Muktinath in one day, the rest of the world prefers to take two or three days over the approach to the pass, all the while watching out for the first signs of altitude sickness. Stops include **Tengi** (3642m), 30 minutes beyond Manang, **Ghunsang** (3879m), and **Yak Kharka/Letdar** (4100m). There are plenty of opportunities for hikes up the flanks of **Chulu,** north of Ghunsang and Letdar.

The final pre-Thorung destination is the rather desolate little settlement of **Thorong Phedi** (4468m), literally "foot of Thorong." The crowds gather here before the big push over the pass. There are two routes from Letdar to Thorong Phedi. The lower one, which, on paper, appears to be the easier of the two, is inadvisable. It is prone to landslides and avalanches—people have been killed here. Set out from Thorung Phedi at first light. Severe conditions are common on the pass, and plenty of trekkers have left with frostbite as a souvenir. Be properly prepared, and be willing to sit out bad weather in a hut rather than pressing on. There are three stone huts above Thorong Phedi, including one on the pass itself. If everything goes well, crossing the pass can be a marvelous experience. It's a long, steep descent to **Muktinath** (3798m); the only settlement along the way is the lodge at **Chatar Puk** (4115m), not far above it.

MULESKINNER BLUES

A feature of both the Kali Gandaki and Marsyangdi Valley routes is the mule traffic: beasts of burden with distinctive carpet saddles and colorful ornamental plumes. The sound of mule bells, along with the whoops and yells of their drivers, is part of the trail experience. Mule transport has long been a fixture in these valleys, especially in the Kali Gandaki—salt from Tibet came south and rice headed north. The closing of the Chinese border in the 1950s had a severe impact on the trade, but mules have remained the most efficient way to transport goods into the hills. The relationship between trekking and trading has been a close one; the settlements in these areas were once trading towns so they adapted easily to the new forms of traffic. In the Kali Gandaki, locals have long been professional inn-keepers catering to traders. What you see here today—even if it involves solar showers and chocolate cake—is merely the continuation of an ancient way of life.

⚑ JOMSOM TREK जोमसोम

This there-and-back route can be converted into a there-*or*-back route by flying one way between Jomsom (2713m) and Pokhara. Flying directly to high altitudes entails spending a day or two acclimatizing upon arrival.

BIRETHANTI TO GHOREPANI. Trekkers typically start at **Birethanti** (1097m), which can be reached by road from Pokhara (2hr.). Take a bus to **Naya Pul** from the Baglung Bus Park (every hr., 5:30am-6pm, Rs35), or hire a car from Lakeside (Rs600, 4 passengers max.); Birethanti is a 20-minute walk from the road. At the confluence of the Bhurungdi and Modi Khola Rivers, Birethanti is a picturesque spot with plenty of lodges, a bank, a post office, an art gallery, and an ACAP check-post where you should show your trekking permit.

The trail follows the Bhurungdi Khola to **Hille** and another dense cluster of lodges at **Tirkedhunga** (1577m). Now, the *real* climbing starts: it's basically uphill all the way to Ghorepani. The first, steepest section brings you through intricately terraced hillsides to the village of **Ulleri.** Beyond Ulleri, you move into increasingly dense forest. If you're trekking in the pre-monsoon season (Mar.-May), this area will probably reward you with spectacular floral displays of the arboreal rhododendrons of the Himalayas.

Ghorepani (2819m), or the pass (**Deorali**) just beyond it, is a major tourist center, and the surrounding area bears the ugly scars of deforestation. Ghorepani itself, a creation of the trekking business, looks like a bizarre hybrid of resort and shanty-town. There's an ACAP office here and a phone in the Nice View Lodge. There are a number of side trails through the nearby forests, and Ghorepani commands a magnificent panorama of Dhaulagiri and the entire Annapurna massif—the view is best seen at dawn from **Poon Hill** (3194m), an hour behind Ghorepani. It is possible to connect to **Ghandruk** via a forest path from Ghorepani.

GHOREPANI TO TUKCHE. From Ghorepani, the main trail heads gently down-hill through Chitre, Phalate, Sikha, and Ghara to **Tatopani** (1189m) and the Kali Gandaki Valley. From Chitre, there are trails via Tadapani to Ghandruk and Chomro, on the way to the Annapurna Sanctuary. Famed for its **hot springs**, Tatopani has welcomed hippies and trekkers since the original routes were opened, and it still serves its traditional role as a staging post on the trade routes up and down the Kali Gandaki. You can find the essentials here, including a shoe-repair shop, post office, bank, public phone, booksellers, and a police check-post. The main hot springs are in town beside the river; follow the foot-path from the Trekkers Lodge.

While most people heading south through Tatopani choose to head up toward Ghorepani, an alternative low-level route along the river to **Beni** (823m) and **Baglung** is the quickest passage between Pokhara and Tatopani. Beni marks the endpoint of the road out of Pokhara, and is within a day's walk of Tatopani. Since part of the road is unfinished, you may need to take two buses from Beni to Pokhara (5hr., Rs70). A private vehicle will set you back Rs2500—contact the Yeti Hotel in Beni for jeep service.

Heading north out of Tatopani, start your journey through the Himalayas with Dhaulagiri to your left and the Annapurnas to your right. Houses range from the scattered thatched homes of the Nepalese hinterland to the flat-roofed stone houses of the higher altitudes, which are often tightly clustered into dense, claustrophobic villages for protection against the brutal upland winds. Hindu shrines and iconography never disappear entirely, but the prayer flags, wheels, and stones become the dominant religious motifs as you head north. Make sure to pass all shrines with them *on your right*—to do the reverse is a sign of deep disrespect.

The first major settlement north of Tatopani, **Dana** (1402m), once thrived on salt trade taxation. From here to **Ghasa** (2040m) keep an eye open for langur monkeys. **Lete** and **Kalopani** (2530m), the next major settlements, have effectively fused into one and are linked by a flagstone trail. As you head north from Kalopani, you will be immediately below the immense eastern buttresses of Dhaulagiri. Its magnificent ice fall dominates the view; a trail out of the valley will take you on a daytrip to the base of the ice fall. Navigation south of **Tukche** (2591m) can be tricky in the dry season because the route heads to the stony valley floor, crossing the river on wobbly temporary bridges. If you overshoot, don't play Indiana Jones and ford the river; it's deep and the current is vicious. Instead, head back to the bridges.

TUKCHE TO MUKTINATH. The next town north, **Marpha** (2667m), is a favorite, with its neatly clustered stone houses and elegantly paved main street. Beyond Marpha is the high altitude desert of Trans-Himalaya. Every afternoon this area (and everywhere north) is blasted by brutal winds that can whip the grit of the river valley into a blinding, flesh-stinging frenzy. Unless you want to be slapped around by Mother Nature, plan on being indoors by midday, especially if you're heading south *into* the wind.

Jomsom (2713m), the regional administration center, is a weird mix of traditional highland trading town, trekking mecca, and unpopular posting for bureaucrats. With its well-serviced airstrip, it's also the beginning or end of many treks. Don't be misled, however, by the Jomsom trek's name: Jomsom is not the goal of the trek; it's merely the biggest town on the route. If you're **flying** out of Jomsom, you can choose between RNAC, Cosmic, Yeti, and Lumbini airlines (all flights 7am, weather permitting; RNAC US$50, others US$55). Jomsom has all the facilities you'd expect of an administrative center. Many of the services, including the post office and the government telecommunication center, are on the east bank of the river across the new suspension bridge. The bank has better rates than the money changers. Jomsom also has a police check-post.

Beyond Jomsom, the farther you go up the valley, the more you come to feel that you are in Tibet, geographically, climatically, and ethnically. Keep going north (you need special and expensive permits to do this) and you will enter the ancient Buddhist kingdom of **Mustang,** a finger of Nepal that juts northward into Tibetan territory. It was this area that Kampa guerillas from western Tibet made their own during the 60s as they waged war against the occupying Chinese. A regular trekking permit will take you as far as **Kagbeni** (2804m), a dusty cluster of Tibetan houses around an ancient *gompa* set in its own patch of irrigated green.

The real goal of the Jomsom trek is **Muktinath** (3802m), at the head of a valley to the east of the main Kali Gandaki Valley and one of the most beautiful places on earth. It can be approached from Kagbeni or more directly from Jomsom. While following the stony riverbed of the Kali Gandaki north of Jomsom, keep an eye open for fossil ammonites, the distinctively coiled long-dead mollusks that symbolize Vishnu. It's partly the abundance of these fossils, known locally as *shaligram*, that accounts for Muktinath's importance to Hindu and Buddhist pilgrims.

The brown and ochre desert hills, the snow-capped peaks to the south, the deep blue sky, the little patches of irrigated green in the valley floor, and the Tibetan villages scattered about the valley make Muktinath worth every drop of sweat and every aching joint. To top it all off, there is also an ACAP office and a police office here. If Muktinath is your final destination, budget a couple of days here to wander up the trail toward the Thorung-La, an excellent day hike. Then it's time to retrace your steps to Jomsom and, from there, to head back by air or on foot to Pokhara.

▲ THE ANNAPURNA SANCTUARY

Pioneered by British climbing expeditions during the late 1950s, the route into the Annapurna Sanctuary up the Modi Khola Valley is the quickest and easiest route from Pokhara up to the Himalayan giants.

BIRETHANTI TO DEORALI. The trek begins at **Birethanti** (also the starting point for the Jomsom trek, see p. 805) and goes north up the west bank of the Modi Khola. This pleasant riverside amble turns serious at **Syauli Bazar** (1150m), when the trail turns uphill to **Kimche** (1760m) and, many stone steps later, **Ghandruk** (2012m). For many years, the source of this well-heeled Gurung village's wealth was the British Army, which recruited heavily here for its famed Gorkha fighters. Now, however, the village is riding the crest of a major trekking wave, as its several grand concrete hotels attest. Ignore the signs for Jhinu hot springs—they're a *long* walk away. ACAP is headquartered here, and there is a "Gurung Museum." Hotel Everest has a public phone.

From Ghandruk, the route heads up to **Kimrong Danda** (2255m) before descending steeply to a river crossing and ascending painfully to **Upper Chomrong** (2182m). There are plenty of lodges, but try to resist the temptation to call it a day here, and go down to **Chomrong** proper (2050m), another large, handsome Gurung village, with a beautifully engineered stone staircase. Chomrong is your last chance to stock up on supplies for the sanctuary; you can buy and rent gear here for non-negotiable rates. ☒**The Chomrong Guest House** wins the prize for "Best Lodge in the Annapurnas." It's friendly, efficient, and comfortable, and the chocolate cake is unforgettable. Route-finding in Chomrong can be tricky. Keep left, heading down to the river crossing and up toward **Sinuwa** (2324m), past the Sherpa Guest House. It is in Sinuwa, at the Hilltop Lodge, that the route leads back to the river and remains next to it all the way to the sanctuary.

Kuldhighar, the first settlement marked on the map after Sinuwa, no longer exists. **Bamboo** (2347m), a mere cluster of lodges, is the first sign of civilization in the forest, and **Dovan** (2606m) is the next. Ten minutes beyond Dovan, a pool 50m upstream from a creek crossing provides the best rinse you're likely to have for several days—lodges up in the higher reaches of the Modi Khola Valley are not as rich in amenities as those lower down. Himalaya Hotel (2873m) is an hour or so beyond Dovan. The last stop-off in the valley is at **Deorali** (3231m), just beyond **Hinko** (3139m), a huge over-hanging boulder which has provided shelter for many a weather-beset party. There are a number of decent lodges in Deorali. Also, note that your rate of **altitude gain** should now be a serious consideration, especially if you've come straight up from Pokhara.

DEORALI TO ANNAPURNA BASE CAMP. The section between Deorali and **Machhapuchhare Base Camp** (3703m), or **MBC,** on the edge of the sanctuary, can be dangerous. It basically serves as a repository for avalanches coming off the upper slopes of Hiunchuli to the west, making it a bad place to be after heavy snowfall. At times, avalanche danger will close down the trail at this point. Make use of your trekker savvy. Pay attention to conditions and seek local advice; trekkers have

NEPAL

died in avalanches here. As you emerge from the narrow gorge of the Modi Khola, the first cluster of lodges is at what is inaccurately called Machhapuchhare Base Camp—the mountain is sacred and off-limits. The best views are a couple of hours farther into the sanctuary at the **Annapurna Base Camp** (4130m), or **ABC.** If you've come up from Pokhara and altitude sickness is a potential problem, consider spending two nights at MBC and doing an early there-and-back trip to ABC. Originally established by Chris Bonington's Annapurna South Face Expedition in 1970, ABC now consists of several lodges crouched in a very desolate, windblown spot (if you're trekking Jan.-Feb. check to see that the lodges are open). The view from ABC includes a whole series of Himalayan walls; clockwise from the south are: Hiunchuli, Annapurna South, Baraha Shikhar (Fang), Annapurna I, Singu Chuli (Fluted Peak), Tharpu Chuli (Tent Peak), Annapurna III, and Machhapuchhare.

ABC TO DHAMPUS. The return trip back-tracks to Chomrong, from where it's possible to take the route back to Pokhara. To continue to Dhampus from Upper Chomrong, drop down to **Jhinu Danda** (1725m). Continue across the Modi Khola on the not-so-new **New Bridge** (1653m), which also contains a small cluster of lodges. From here, it's a matter of following the river until the ascent to the big bustling village of **Landruk** (1628m). **Tolka** (1725m) is strung out over 2km. A final reminder of the rigors of uphill hiking brings you to **Bhichok Deorali** (2097m). It's then a pleasant walk along the ridge to **Potana** (1969m). If you're heading from Potana up toward Landruk, keep right at both of the forks that come up shortly after Potana. If you're heading down from Potana, keep left at the fork 10 minutes after Potana. **Dhampus** (1695m) is the final settlement along the route. A big village stretched out along a ridge for a couple of kilometers, Dhampus used to have something of a reputation among trekkers as a den of thieves, but that dubious claim to fame seems to have been based on only a handful of incidents that occurred 20 years ago. The final descent from Dhampus to **Dhampus Phedi** (1143m) on the Pokhara-Baglung Rd. is long, steep, hot, and dusty. Buses into Pokhara's Baglung bus park run at least every hour (6am-6pm, Rs15). In season, there will also probably be something of a taxi stand at Dhampus Phedi (to Lakeside Rs250, 4-passenger max.).

THE LANGTANG REGION लाङटान

The black sheep of the classic three, the Langtang region is often passed over by trekkers drawn by name recognition to Annapurna and Everest. The relative obscurity of the Langtang trek means that its trails are comparatively uncrowded, and, with its majestic terrain and its proximity to Kathmandu, the Langtang region is an attractive trekking region. "Langtang" is actually a general title that covers three distinct but adjacent areas, the **Langtang Valley, Gosainkund,** and **Helambu.** Each of these areas can be visited alone, or they can be stitched together into one longer trek. Individually, each area takes between four and eight days to trek; collectively it can all be done in twelve to sixteen days. The Langtang Valley has a straightforward trek up the valley and the chance to explore some of the peaks and glaciers at its head; in Gosainkund is a series of frigid, high-altitude lakes, and plenty of alpine terrain; Helambu is lower and greener, winding through the jungled hills at the northern edge of the Kathmandu Valley.

▚ THE LANGTANG VALLEY TREK

The Langtang Valley takes most people five or six days round-trip from Syabru-Besi; the trail is straightforward, following the Langtang River up the Langtang Valley, passing through the village of Langtang, and on to the Langtang Lodge for a few hours' Langtang lie-down. The return trip plods back down the same trail and back out to Syabru Besi. The stunning views, as well as the numerous opportunities for exploration from Kyanjiu Gompa at the head of the valley, make this the most popular of the Langtang treks.

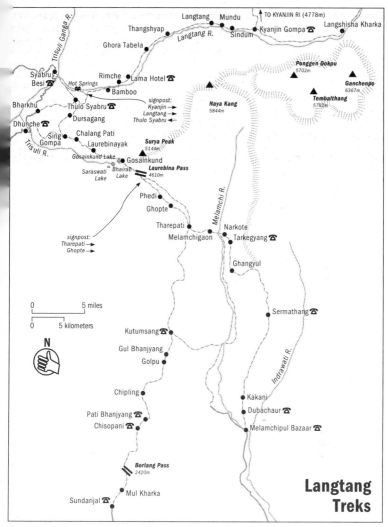

Langtang
Treks

SYABRU BESI TO LAMA HOTEL. Treks in Langtang used to start in the town of **Dhunche** (2030m), but the development of this area has made **Syabru Besi** (1460m), an hour by bus farther along the road, a more attractive and convenient base. Buses for **Syabru Besi** leave from Kathmandu's New Bus Park every morning (6:30, 7, and 7:30am; 10hr.; Rs230), passing through Dhunche (9hr., Rs190). The ride is long enough to require an overnight stay in Syabru Besi; the town has a number of decent hotels catering to trekkers, including the **Buddha Guest House** and the **North-land Tibetan Guest House.** Besides telephone services, Syabru Besi has few other facilities. If you really want to escape the crowds, cross the river and stay in one of the quieter but more basic hotels on that side of town.

From Syabru Besi, the trail starts just north of town; there's a small yellow "To Langtang" sign to point the way. The path crosses a steel bridge, passes through the other part of town, and heads east up the valley, along the northern (left) bank of the Langtang River. It soon crosses the river on a wood-and-stone bridge and continues along the southern bank. Within an hour, the trail passes a small tea shop and, on the opposite side of the river, a pleasant **hot spring** set up for a refreshing bath. Continuing along the south side of the river, the trail hits a **T-junction,** where a sign points the way to Thulo Syabru (left to Kyanjin and Langtang). The trail then passes through **Bamboo** (1850m), a small settlement that makes a good lunch stop and which also has a number of hotels, including the **Old Bamboo Riverside Lodge.** If you want a more relaxing first day, stick around Bamboo. From here, the trail continues along the lush south side of the river until it hits a large steel suspension bridge. There are a couple of tea shops here that can provide lodging in a pinch. After the bridge the trail becomes steeper and drier, climbing up to the **Hotel Langtangview Lodge.** The trail continues up to the town of **Rimche** (2250m), home to a few lodges. The **Hotel Ganeshview Lodge** has decent rooms and views. The **Sherpa Lodge** and the **Lama Guest House** are also good options in town. **Lama Hotel,** a 10- to 15-minute walk from Rimche, is a nicely-sized tourist destination with more than six lodges and satellite phone service.

LAMA HOTEL TO LANGTANG VILLAGE. From Lama Hotel, the trail climbs steeply through the forest on the north side of the river, and after an hour or two reaches the Gumnachok Lodge, in a small clearing. There's another petite settlement not far beyond. From here the trail continues steeply until it reaches **Ghora Tabela** (3020m), home to a small tea shop and a National Park check-post, where permits must be presented. After Ghora Tabela, the trail flattens somewhat and soon reaches **Thangshyap** (3110m), where accommodation is available at the **Hotel Tibetan Lodge.** Langtang Village comes into view around this point, but it's still more than an hour's walk to town. The trail passes through several more settlements and tea shops before reaching **Langtang Village** (3430m), an attractive stone village with fantastic views of the mountains. The **Valleyview Lodge and Hotel** and the **Villageview Lodge and Hotel** are both fine places to stay; prices in town are fixed at a flat rate so pick your favorite view. As Langtang Village is above 3000m, **altitude sickness** can be a problem. It is theoretically possible to go from Lama Hotel to Kyanjin Gompa in a single day, but you probably shouldn't test the theory.

LANGTANG VILLAGE TO KYANJIN GOMPA. The path from Langtang Village to Kyanjin Gompa is fairly flat and reasonably short; the total gain in altitude is only 400m. Passing through sparse alpine terrain, the trail follows the north side of the river past *mani* walls carved with Tibetan script. The first settlement after Langtang Village is tiny **Mundu** (3550m), home to the **Mundu Village Guest House.** After passing more *mani* walls, the trail leads to **Singdom** (3680m), where there are two lodges, including the **Singdom Village Hall and Lodge.** After Singdom, the terrain is dotted with increasing numbers of large boulders; these are the work of glaciers that hollowed out the upper part of the valley. From Singdom, the trail climbs through the boulder fields and soon reaches **Kyanjin Gompa** (3850m), the highlight of the trek. The best place to stay in town is the **Yeti Guest House,** which has solar-powered showers and satellite phone service. Another good option is **Yala Peak Guest House.** Check out the local **cheese factory** where the employees are generally glad to give a quick tour. (Cheese Rs275 per kg. Open daily 7am-5pm.)

Kyanjin is a great place to take in the splendid views and traipse around on day-trips. The most popular is the ascent of **Kyanjin Ri** (4773m), a hill to the north of town. The trail climbs up steeply from town to the prayer-flag-festooned first crest at 4350m. It continues up the ridge behind to the peak. The views of Langtang Lirung are incomparable, and the climb is fairly easy and generally free of snow. From here you can cross to the higher **Tsergo Ri** (4984m), though it's important to watch for signs of altitude sickness when attempting to climb either of these peaks. Another popular excursion is the hike up the valley to the settlement of **Langshisa Kharka** (4160m), which has glacier views. Finally, there are a couple of more difficult options. **Yala Peak** (5500m) generally requires two days (including a high camp) and some equipment (ice axe, crampons, boots). The Ganja La Pass (5130m) is another multiple-day affair that is an alternative way to reach Helambu from Kyanjin Gompa. The pass is difficult and requires multiple days of camping.

THE RETURN/CONNECTING TO GOSAINKUND. To get back from Kyanjin Gompa, simply follow the same trail in the reverse direction. People often go from Kyanjin Gompa to Lama Hotel in one day and from Lama Hotel to Syabru Besi the next. **Buses** from Syabru Besi to Kathmandu leave only in the morning (6:30, 7, and 8am; 10hr.; Rs230), so it's usually necessary to spend the night in Syabru Besi.

If you're heading to Gosainkund from the Langtang Valley, make a detour after Bamboo and head to **Thulo Syabru** (2130m). Then take off the next day to **Sing Gompa** (see p. 811) or **Chalang Pati** (see below). There are two trails leading to Thulo Syabru from Langtang Valley; the first is marked by the yellow sign at the **T-junction** downhill from Bamboo, and the second is farther down the trail just past the hot springs. The second trail is shorter and easier. In Thulo Syabru the best places to stay are the **Yeti Restaurant and Hotel** and the **Eveningview Guest House.** The next day's hike to connect to the Gosainkund trail in Sing Gompa is steep but pleasant; the trail switches back uphill, passing the town of Dursagang (2720m), where accommodation is available at the **Himalay Hotel and Lodge.** The trail continues up the ridges to two tea shops at the crest (3210m) and then curves around the ridge to **Sing Gompa** (3250m), on the Gosainkund trail (see below).

🔼 THE GOSAINKUND TREK गोशाईकुण्ड

The main connection between Langtang and Helambu, Gosainkund is marked by a series of often-frozen high-altitude lakes. The approach to the lakes provides views from the Langtang Valley all the way west to Machhapuchare and the Annapurnas. Gosainkund Lake is famous as a watering hole for Shiva; each year the lake becomes a major pilgrimage site during **Janai Purnima,** which occurs around the July-August full moon. By itself this is a short trek—round-trip it can be done in three to four days—but most people couple it with a trek up the Langtang Valley or continue on from the lakes down into Helambu.

DHUNCHE TO SING GOMPA. While Syabru Besi is now the most convenient starting point for the Langtang Valley Trek, **Dhunche** (2030m) remains the best access point for Gosainkund. Both towns are reached by the same **buses,** which leave daily from Kathmandu's New Bus Park (6:30, 7, and 7:30am; 9hr.; Rs190). Dhunche has a number of lodges; the length of the bus ride means that you have to spend the first night here. Both the **Hotel Tibet Mountain View** and the **Hotel Thakali** are decent. There's also a small **pharmacy** in town (open daily 8am-5pm).

The trail for Sing Gompa departs from the road just north of town and follows the southern bank of the Trisuli River. It's quite steep, and you gain altitude quickly as you ascend toward the ridge. The trail crosses to the north side of the Trisuli and continues to climb up, up, and away. Just before Sing Gompa, the trail reaches a junction; the left path leads down to Thulo Syabru and the Langtang Valley and the right path to Sing Gompa and then Gosainkund. **Sing Gompa** (3250m) is not far beyond this junction. The **Green View Hotel and Lodge** and the slightly more secluded **Red Panda Hotel and Lodge** are good. There's another **cheese factory** in town, where you can savor the taste of excellent yak cheese and curd. From Dhunche to Sing Gompa, the ascent is over 1200m: watch out for altitude sickness!

SING GOMPA TO GOSAINKUND. This leg of the trek is doable in a single day, but if you've come directly from Dhunche the previous day you should be careful of altitude sickness, and you should spend the night part way up in Laurebinayak. The trail from Sing Gompa winds around to the southern side of the ridge and follows the Trisuli River up the valley. After detouring briefly around the northern side of a small hill, the trail reaches **Chalang Pati** (3580m), where there are two small lodges, including the acceptable **Chalang Pati Hotel and Lodge.** Chalang Pati marks the end of the evergreen forest; from here, the terrain becomes increasingly alpine. The trail switchbacks up to **Laurebinayak** (3900m), home to a number of lodges and some fantastic Himalayan views. The **Hotel Mount Rest** is a good place to stay: if the altitude is a problem, there's no need to push on all the way up to

Gosainkund in one day. From here, the trail shoots straight uphill past a large stupa and, farther uphill, a series of roof-less stone houses. Here, the trail rejoins the Trisoli River. The first lake you see is the Saraswati, far below the trail against the opposite ridge. The trail passes quite close to the next lake, Bhairab, where Gosainkund village comes into view. **Gosainkund** (4380m) itself is a small wind-blown village on the shore of Gosainkund Lake. Both the **Peaceful Hotel and Lodge** and the **Lakeside Guest House** offer reliable, friendly accommodation. In town, there's not much to do except bundle up and drink tea; the more adventurous (and acclimatized) can walk around Gosainkund Lake or climb the surrounding hills.

THE RETURN/CONNECTING TO HELAMBU. The return trip to Dhunche can be done in one long day or two shorter, easier ones; the route is the exact reverse of the one described above. If you're going from Gosainkund up to the Langtang Valley, take the right trail just below the Sing Gompa and head downhill to Thulo Syabru (see p. 811).

If you're doing the popular trek from Gosainkund into Helambu, you can connect to the Helambu circuit at Tharepati in one very long day or in two average-length days. The trail from Gosainkund skirts the eastern edge of Gosainkund Lake before ascending up toward the pass. This section of the trail is often snow-covered and is impassable at certain times of year and in bad weather conditions. **Laurebina Pass** (4610m) is marked by prayer flags and a *chorten;* to the south you can see the green foothills of Helambu, which lead into the Kathmandu Valley. The south side of the pass (descending into Helambu) is generally drier and easier to get through. The trail descends steeply from there to a small tea shop where there's a fork and a sign pointing downhill to Ghopte and Tharepti. The lower trail is the one to take; the upper one is undeveloped and often snow-covered, and there are no facilities until Tharepati. The lower trail continues down from the tea shop all the way to **Phedi** (3630m), home to two hotels and a helipad. The **Taj Mel Lodge**, the lower of the two, is a pleasant, river-side accommodation. After Phedi, the trail imitates the up-and-down character of the Helambu area. It makes one steep ridge climb before reaching **Ghopte** (3430m), where there are another two lodges (both dorm-style). It is a fairly long day from Gosainkund to Ghopte, but some people push all the way to Tharepeti, on the Helambu circuit, to avoid the pile-up of pass-crossers in Ghopte (see p. 813).

THE HELAMBU TREK हेलम्बु

Unlike the Langtang Valley or Gosainkund treks, both of which wind mainly through high alpine country, the Helambu Trek is relatively low-altitude, thick-for-ested, and hot. Also unlike the other two, Helambu is criss-crossed by trails running between villages, and there is no one particular route that must be taken or sight that must be seen; the entire area can be visited via any number of different routes. The route described below, a horse-shoe-shaped trek starting in Sundarijal and ending in Melamchipul Bazaar, is one of the most common, but the variations are endless, and the crowds disappear the minute you get off the beaten path.

SUNDARIJAL TO CHISOPANI. Sundarijal (1460m), the starting point for the trek, is very close to Kathmandu. There's no reason to stay here, as **buses** ply the route constantly from the Ratna Park Bus Stand (every 30min., 6am-8pm, 1hr., Rs20). **Taxis** to and from Thamel are Rs200-500. The trail from Sunarijal climbs up directly from the bus stop and follows a concrete path alongside a large black metal pipe that supplies water to Kathmandu. This part of the walk is well-developed and urban; the concrete path becomes concrete steps, which climb past the Sundarijal Reservoir. The path crosses a dirt road after this and continues up the steep concrete steps to **Mul Kharka** (1860m), where the steps end. Above Mul Kharka is an army base, where permits are occasionally checked. The trail climbs up the **Borlang Pass** (2420m), the high point of the day, and then makes a short descent to **Chisopani** (2215m), the site of numerous hotels. Both the **New BBC Hotel** and, farther on, the **Hotel Manakamana,** offer good facilities. Some people are inclined to go on down the hill to Pati Bhanjyang (1770m) the same day, but unless you're in a hurry, the views and pleasant atmosphere make Chisopani a better option.

CHISOPANI TO KUTUMSANG. From Chisopani, the trail runs briefly along the dirt road; at the first sharp turn, the trail splits and heads north. It drops down through a number of steep gullies and finally merges with the dirt road again just before **Pati Bhanjyang** (1170m). It is possible to walk the dirt road all the way to Pati Bhanjyang, though this takes longer. The **Valley View Lodge,** south of town, is a peaceful place to stay. From Pati Bhanjyang, one trail heads north to Kutumsang and another goes east to Tamalarang. Continuing north to Kutumsang, the trail climbs steeply again to **Chipling** (2170m) and the **Chipling Lodge Hotel and Restaurant.** Beyond the ridge, the trail arrives at the village of **Golpu** (2130m) and the **Himalaya Lodge and Restaurant.** The trail leads north, and halfway up the next (and final) ridge is the small settlement of **Gul Bhanjyang** (2250m), with a couple of lodges, including the **Hotel Dragon.** The trail ascends to the top of the ridge, and then makes a gentle dip into the saddle that holds **Kutumsang** (2470m), a pleasant village with good views on either side. The **Namaste Hotel and Lodge** and the **Sherpa Lodge,** at either end of town, are quiet accommodations. From Kutumsang, one trail heads east down the valley to **Mahankal** (1130m); the other heads north up the ridge to Tharepati, the highest point of the circuit.

KUTUMSANG TO THAREPATI. This is a relatively straightforward (though at times steep) trail, which follows the ridge all the way up from Kutumsang to Tharepti. Heading north from Kutumsang, the trail approaches the **Kyuola Pass** (3250m), which is visible from town. This section of the trail is heavily forested, but there are plenty of mountain views, which get better and better throughout the day. After the pass, the trail soon reaches **Mangen Goth** (3220m), the only large settlement on the trail; accommodation is available here. After Mangen Goth, the trail climbs steeply again, following the ridge all the way to **Tharepati** (3510m). High up on a crest, Tharepati shows off its spectacular views—to the east, west, and south are the staggered ridges and river valleys of Helambu; to the north are the snow-capped peaks of Gosainkund, and threading between them, the Laurebina Pass. In Tharepati are a number of lodges. On the very top is the **Gosainkund Hotel and Top Lodge;** lower down the hill is the **Jimmy Lama Mountain Hostel.** Tharepati is at the convergence of several different trails. To the north runs the trail up to Gosainkund (p. 812); to the east the trail runs down to Melamchigaon and Helambu.

THAREPATI TO TARKE GYANG. From Tharepati, the trail drops steeply off the eastern side of the ridge, losing altitude quickly. The vegetation returns to thick and lush and is dominated by bamboo and rhododendrons. Switchbacking down to the river valley, the trail crosses a small stream before leveling out a little. It drops down to a suspension bridge and then climbs briefly to **Melamchigaon** (2530m), a lovely agricultural Sherpa village with a large Buddhist monastery and, that's right, nice views down the valley. It would make a short day from Tharepati, but this is a good place to stay the night. Both the **Sun Lodge** and the **Wild View Hotel and Lodge** are friendly and have adequate facilities. The trail from here is unexciting and winds through the terraced fields in the lower part of town. It jumps sharply down to the Melamchi River, where there's a suspension bridge. The **Riverside Lodge,** just before the bridge, is another accommodation option. After the bridge, the trail climbs to the village of **Narkote** (2000m), where there's another large monastery. Just after Narkote, there's a large fork in the trail. The right (lower) fork leads down to Thimbu; the left fork heads up to Tarkegyang. Climbing the hill, the trail passes several small farms. The Sherpa Lodge is about halfway between Narkote and Tarkegyang. The trail ascends to **Tarkegyang** (2740m), a large settlement with numerous lodging choices. The **Mountain View Hotel** is big and clean and has telephone service. A number of trails converge in Tarkegyang. To the north is the trail up to **Yangri Peak** (3771m), then to the **Ganja La Pass** (5130m), and into the Langtang Valley. Two trails leave from the south—one follows the ridge to Sermathang, the other (lower) trail drops down to Kaani and Kiul.

TARKEGYANG TO SERMATHANG. The trail to Sermathang follows the birds south from Tarkegyang. There are a number of forks, and the larger fork often leads downhill to Kakani, so be sure to ask along the way. The trail stays at roughly the same altitude, snaking along the ridge to the village of **Ghangyul** (2770m). The **Dolma Lodge** has clean, well-kept facilities. From Ghangyul, Sermathang is visible to the south—it's the cluster of houses in the notch at the top of the ridge. **Sermathang** (2590m) is a nice place to stay; although this is a short day from Tarkegyang, the accommodation options beyond Sermathang are much less pleasant, and it's a long walk to go all the way to Melamchipul Bazaar in a single day. In Sermathang, both the **Mountain View Lodge** and **Yangri Lodge** are decent; Mountain View, surprisingly enough, has the best mountain views. There's a **Keep Office** in town that has a tiny but lovely cultural **museum** attached that also sells iodine tablets. Sermathang also has a **National Park checkpost;** if you're coming from Melamchipul Bazaar you can buy your park permit here. There are a number of monasteries in town; pay a visit to the stupa on the knoll to the south of town.

SERMATHANG TO MELAMCHIPUL BAZAAR. It's a long but gentle trek down from Sermathang to the road at Melamchipul Bazaar, which is easily accomplished in a day. The trail follows the top of the ridge the entire way down, passing through increasingly developed settlements as it nears the road. In the reverse direction this would be a lot of climbing to do in one day, especially since the total change in altitude is 1720m. From Sermathang, the trail descends along the ridge to **Kakani** (1996m), where there are a couple of places to stay, including the **Himalyan Dorje Lakpa Guest House.** Kakani is a good overnight destination if you're coming up from Melamchipul Bazaar. After Kakani, the trail becomes a little harder to follow; it's a good idea to ask for directions. Continuing down the ridge, the trail comes to the dusty village of **Dubachaur** (1440m) and the **Langtang Guest House.** The village is not worth spending much time in. From Dubachaur the trail crosses through more small settlements and farming terraces before dropping down and crossing the Melamchi River on a long suspension bridge to reach **Malamchipal Bazaar** (870m), at the confluence of the Melamchi and Indrawati Rivers. Malamchipal is not a particularly scenic place, but if you need to stay here for the night, the best option is to cross back over the suspension bridge to the north side of the Melamchi River and walk five minutes up the trail to the **Jugal Himal Resort,** a secluded lodge away from the grime of the bazaar. **Buses** from the bazaar go to Kathmandu in the morning and early afternoon (every hr., 7am-3pm, 4hr., Rs40). Buses also run in the opposite direction, following the dirt road up the Melamchi River to its terminus in **Talamarang** (960m). Quieter and cleaner than Melamchipul Bazaar, Talamarang is home to the tidy **Talamarang Guest House.**

◪ LANGTANG-GOSAINKUND-HELAMBU COMBINATIONS

Most often, treks in the Langtang region combine the separate treks into one longer trek. A Langtang-Gosainkund-Helambu trek is usually done in around 12-15 days and normally follows roughly this route: Syabru Besi-Lama Hotel-Langtang Village-Kyanjin Gompa-Lama Hotel-Thulo Syabru-Sing Gompa-Gosainkund-Ghopte-Kutumsang-Chisopani-Sundarijal. This north-to-south direction is generally preferred, as the Langtang Valley provides a better chance to acclimatize before crossing through Gosainkund and the Laurebina Pass (4610m). But the opposite route is also possible and is regularly done by trekking groups. The exit through Helambu is also very flexible. From Tharepti, you can head south to Kutumsang and out to Sundarijal (the most common route), or from Kutumsang you can branch east down the less-traveled trail to Mahankal and then Talamarang. *Or,* you can head east from Tharepti itself to Tarkegyang and on to Melam-

Everest Treks

chipul, a scenic three-day route. Yes, there are more trekking combinations than there are McDonald's combo meals.

THE EVEREST REGION

The Everest trek is all about paying homage to the highest point on the planet. The trek up to Base Camp leads through the homeland of one of of the most engaging and enterprising of all Nepal's ethnic groups, the Sherpas. The Sherpas migrated to the Solu Khumbu region south of Everest around 500 years ago, and they retain many Tibetan characteristics in their language, religion, and dress. The Sherpa capital, Namche Bazaar, long famous from accounts of expeditions to the region, is one of the most vibrant towns in all of Nepal.

A trip to Everest used to involve setting out on foot from Kathmandu, several hundred kilometers to the west, and involved a sequence of arduous ascents and descents of up to 2000m at a time. Not any more. Today, a road extends approximately half of the way, to Jiri, connected by bus to Kathmandu. From Jiri, it still takes a good 10 days to walk to Namche Bazaar, and another several days from Namche Bazaar to Everest. A trip to Everest by bus and on foot is a month-long undertaking. Most people save time by flying at least one way—there is an airstrip in Lukla, a two-day walk south of Namche Bazaar. If you decide to hike one way, rather than flying both in and out of Lukla, the logical choice is to walk in: the going will be easier, and you'll arrive in Namche already acclimatized. Many people do the reverse, walking from Namche to Jiri, because waiting for a flight out—particularly if you've got fixed international connections to make—can be

NEPAL

extremely frustrating. The landing strip at Lukla is short, and weather conditions have to be pretty good before flights can take off and land.

⚠ JIRI TO NAMCHE BAZAAR

JIRI TO BHANDAR. With the advent of plane service to Lukla, tourist traffic through Jiri has diminished sharply, and this stretch of the trek is much quieter than the areas above Lukla. For details on getting to Jiri, see p. 798.

The trail from Jiri begins south of town. From the bus park follow the flat dirt road south for about 10 minutes to where a trail branches left up the hill. This trail climbs more or less straight up toward the ridge, passing small settlements and tea houses. The largest settlement before the ridge is **Chitre** (2330m), where you'll find the **Solu Khombu Lodge.** The trail climbs gently to the first pass (2400m), then drops down the opposite side to **Mali** (2220m), where a number of lodges, including the **Sherpa Lodge and Restaurant,** have sprung up. After Mali, the descent becomes steeper as the trail drops down to meet the Khimti River. It crosses a suspension bridge just before the river and then traverses another bridge that spans the river itself. Just across the river is **Shivalaya** (1770m), a common stop for trekkers at the end of their first (short) day. Both the **Tourist Lodge** and the **Trekking Guide Hotel and Lodge** are good options in town. Even if you don't stop here, you don't need to go all the way to Bhandar in one day—there are plenty of places to stay between Shivalaya and Bhandar. From Shivalaya the trail heads steeply uphill toward the ridge until **Sangbadanda** (2150m), where it levels off a little. At this point the trail forks; to the right is the direct route to Deorali and Bhandar, to the left is a longer side trail to Thodung. In Sangbadanda the **Himali Lodge** is a decent place to stay. From here, the right trail continues toward the ridge, passing a number of newer settlements along the way. In **Khasru Bas** is the imposing **Uma Lama Lodge.** Farther along is **Buludanda** and the **Hill View Sherpa Lodge.** The trail reaches its highest point at **Deorali** (2710m), a wind-swept pass with several good lodges, including the **Highland Sherpa Guest House and Restaurant.** This is another good place to stop at the end of the first day, as it allows you to get acclimated to the higher altitude. Right after the pass is an easy-to-confuse fork in the trail; take the left fork (it almost looks like a switchback) to reach Bhandar (2150m). This is the most common stop at the end of the first day, about an hour's walk down from Deorali. The **Ang Dawa Lodge** and **Shoba Lodge and Restaurant** are decent.

BHANDAR TO JUNBESI. From Bhandar, the trail continues to drop down toward the Likhu River and gets confusing in a number of places. Immediately after the covered wooden bridge the trail forks; take the sharp left path. This drops steeply and brings you to a number of deceptive forks. Follow the left fork every time. As the trial nears the river, it crosses a small stream on a suspension bridge into the small village of **Tharo Khola** (1460m). From here the trail makes a sharp left and heads up the Likhu Valley along the west side of the river. There are a number of opportunities to cross the Likhu River on suspension bridges; you can take any of them. There are trails along both sides of the river heading up to **Kenja** (1640m), a booming community with a medical post, a police checkpost, and a good assortment of lodges, including the **Sherpa Guest House.** Above Kenja, the trail gets very steep as you begin to climb up toward the Lamjura Pass. The first big town is **Chimbu** (2150m), where you can nurse your blisters at the **Hill Top Lodge and Restaurant.** A short walk (30min.) uphill from Chimbu is **Sete** (2575m), where many trekkers spend the night to break the 2000m climb. The **Sherpa Guide Lodge** is well-kept. Sete is so popular, however, that those with the energy might want to go an hour farther to the **Maya Tamang Lodge** in **Dagchu** (2875m), to escape the crowds.

Beyond Dagchu, the trail continues its steep climb toward the ridge, passing through the village of **Goyom** (3285m) and **Lamjura** (3380m), the last town before the pass, where you'll find the **Numbur View Lodge.** Just before the pass, the trail levels off significantly and follows the ridge north to the pass. The **Lamjura La Pass** (3530m) is the highest point between Jiri and Namche. From the pass, the trail drops steeply into the Junbesi valley, passing through the village of **Thagtokbhug** (2860m). At the heart of the village is a *gompa* and, next to it, a huge *mani*-adorned boulder. **AM's Restaurant and Lodge,** with excellent views and clean rooms, is near the center of town. From here the trail runs along the northern side of the valley and turns slowly toward **Junbesi** (2710m), a prosperous community full of *gompas*, stupas, and lodges. The **Everestview Sherpa Lodge and Restaurant** has large, quiet rooms with fairly comfortable beds. There's a lot to see in and around Junbesi, making it a good place to stop for the night.

JUNBESI TO BUPSA. From Junbesi the trail crosses the Junbesi River and climbs gradually up the next ridge. Just after the bridge is an important junction—the left (uphill) fork leads on to Namche Bazaar; the right (downhill) fork leads south to **Phaplu** where there's an airstrip (a half day's walk). Continuing on the left fork, the trail climbs to the top of the ridge at **Salung** (2960m). On clear days, this is where you'll catch your first views of Everest. The **Everest Panorama Lodge and Restaurant** has good facilities here. After Salung the trail drops down to the Ringmo River and makes a short, steep climb up to **Ringmo** (2720m), a welcoming little village surrounded by apple orchards. The **Apple House Lodge** in town serves apples with everything and has nice rooms. From Ringmo it's a short but sometimes confusing ascent to the **Takshindo La Pass** (2990m). Ask as you go. On the far side of the pass, the trail passes through the village of **Takshindo** (2900m), home to an impressive monastery and a number of lodges, including the **Mountain View Lodge and Restaurant.** The trail drops much more steeply after Takshindo, down to the Dudh Kosi River. This is a long descent, and many stop for the night halfway down in the village of **Nuntala** (2265m). The **Naulekh View Lodge and Restaurant,** at the far end of town, has good rooms and a friendly staff.

After Nuntala the trail continues to drop, crossing the Dudh Kosi via a long bridge (1500m). A little past the river is the Rai village of **Jubing** (1700m); not many people stay here, but if you do, the **Gorkhali Lodge** is a good choice. Beyond Jubing the trail climbs gradually to **Chyoka.** Immediately past Chyoka is a series of forks in the trail—always take the right (uphill) fork, which should bring you directly over the top of the ridge rather than around it. On the far side of the ridge is **Khari Khola** (2070m), a large village with many lodges. The **Sagarmatha Khumbu Lodge and Restaurant** is run by a very friendly family and has decent rooms. A small, rickety bridge crosses the Khari Khola River, after which the trail climbs very steeply up the next ridge to **Bupsa** (2350m), visible from below. Bupsa, with its great views, is a popular place to spend the night. The **Yellow Top Lodge** stands out for its friendly atmosphere and relatively private rooms. To dodge the crowds, you can continue for another half-hour beyond Bupsa, where quieter accommodations are available.

BUPSA TO NAMCHE BAZAAR. The trail from Bupsa climbs steadily upward, weaving in and out between ridges and valleys. The next major settlement is **Puiyan** (2780m), home to the buzzing little **Bee Hive Lodge and Restaurant.** After Puiyan, the trail rounds another large ridge and Lukla comes into view—you can sit here and watch the planes land. The trail drops steeply down toward the valley floor, crossing a small river at **Surke** (2300m). The **Everest Trail Lodge** is a well-run place with an immaculate kitchen. Soon after Surke (just around the next bend) there's a fork in the trail; the right trail climbs steeply up to Lukla, the left one continues toward Namche Bazaar. Continuing along the left (lower) trail, the route climbs steadily up to **Chauri Kharka** (2760m). The **Tourist Guest House** has good food and is a pleasant place to stay; this is the last major settlement before the trail joins the much more crowded Lukla trail at **Cheplung** (2660m). To reach Namche from here, follow the directions for the Lukla to Everest Base Camp route. From Cheplung, it usually takes two days to reach Namche Bazaar.

NEPAL

⚑ LUKLA TO EVEREST BASE CAMP

LUKLA TO NAMCHE BAZAAR. Lukla (2800m), proud owner of Nepal's third-busiest airport, is a major tourist center with enough facilities and equipment to keep your grandmother happy. Many people skip the Jiri-Lukla section of the trek and fly directly in and out of Lukla, making a (roughly) two-week trip up to Base Camp. If you do fly straight here from Kathmandu, it is important to take at least one day to acclimatize before heading out on the trail. All sorts of equipment is available for purchase or hire, and there are plenty of agencies competing to outfit trekkers with guides, porters, and wooly socks. The **Panaramic Lodge** is by far the best accommodation in town, with big, clean rooms, hot water showers, and a huge dining room.

From Lukla, the trail heads north, dropping steeply downhill through a number of small settlements. The first big town on the trail is **Cheplung** (2660m), where the Jiri trail joins from below. The **Himalayan Rest House and Restaurant** is a large, clean place to stay, but most people opt to hike on to Ghat or Phakding on the first day. From Cheplung, the trail heads up the valley, meandering at an easy gradient to **Thado Kosi** (2500m), an attractive settlement on the Thado Kosi River. If you want to part ways with the crowds, stay for the night in **Saino Lodge and Restaurant.** You can still reach Namche the following day. Just around the next bend is the equally lovely (but more crowded) town of **Ghat** (2530m), with a very active monastery and a number of enormous *mani* boulders. The **Lama Lodge and Restaurant**, at the far end of town, is friendly and well-run. Coming from either Lukla or Jiri, Ghat makes a good overnight stop: it's more pleasant and less crowded than Phakding, and still within a day's walk of Namche.

Phakding (2610m), an hour up the trail from Ghat, is a large town with many lodges. The town extends along the trail and across the river; if you do choose to stay here, the higher parts of town (across the river) are usually less crowded. The **Tashi Taki Lodge and Restaurant,** in central Phakding, and the **Kongde Peak Guest House and Restaurant** are both good places to stay. The trail continues up the opposite (west) side of the river to **Benkar** (2720m), a small village with a small waterfall. The peaceful **Waterfall View Lodge** here lives up to its name. Just beyond Benkar the trail re-crosses the Dudh Kosi River and leads up to the small settlement of **Chumoa** (2780m), where you can dream of yeti safaris at the **Riverside Lodge and Restaurant.** A short way up the trail is **Monju** (2815m), site of the official entrance to **Sagarmatha National Park,** where you must present your passport and pay the Rs650 entrance fee. There's a small monastery in Monju and a few good lodges, including the **Mount Kailash Lodge and Restaurant.** Beyond the park entrance, the trail drops down and crosses the Dudh Kosi River again on a long suspension bridge, then heads up to **Jorsale** (2810m), the last settlement before Namche Bazaar. Stop in the **Everest Guest House** and give your body a rest before pushing up the steep ascent to Namche. After Jorsale, the trail re-crosses the Dudh Kosi River on a rickety bridge, re-crossing it again on a much higher suspension bridge. From here the trail gets much steeper as it switchbacks its way up the hill, gaining altitude quickly. It's a good idea to take this hill slowly, as overexertion can easily lead to altitude sickness. **Namche Bazaar** (3450m) is a major administrative center, offering more services than you're ever likely to need—currency exchange, bookstore, bakery, equipment shops, souvenirs, and a dentist. There's a **police checkpost** in town, where you'll have to present your park permit before leaving, and a **post office,** where you can off-load a few more of those Everest postcards. The **Buddha Lodge** in central Namche is as good a place to stay as any. Take a break by spending a day acclimatizing in Namche.

NAMCHE BAZAAR TO DINGBOCHE. The trail from Namche heads up past the police checkpost and along the right side of the hill, weaving in and out of the numerous ridges. You can see Everest from this section of the trail on clear days. The first village after Namche is **Kyangsuma** (3610m), a souvenir-filled settlement with several lodges, including the **Ama Dablam Lodge and Restaurant.** The trail stays fairly level beyond Kyangsuma, leading to **Sanasa** (3620m) a short distance away, where the souvenir stalls will try to tempt you to weigh yourself down with junk. The **Khumbila Lodge and Restaurant** in Sanasa is clean and friendly. Beyond Sanasa, the trail heads downhill toward the Dudh Kosi River, passing a few small settlements along the way. The descent gets quite steep, finally crossing the river on a long suspension bridge at 3230m. From here it's a one- to two-hour climb up the ridge to **Tengboche** (3860m), where the stately Tengboche Monastery overlooks the Khombu Valley and has views of many of the surrounding peaks. The monastery is well worth a visit, and tours are given daily. Tengboche can be a nice place to stay, although it gets crowded; the **Tashi Delek Lodge** has the best facilities.

Dropping off Tengboche's hilltop crest, the trail enters a lush forest and stays fairly flat until it re-crosses the Dudh Kosi River. Before crossing the river, the trail passes through **Deboche** (3770m), a quiet, attractive village lacking the crowds of Tengboche. The **Ama Dablam Garden Lodge** has large, comfortable rooms and plenty of privacy. The trail then crosses the Dudh Kosi River again on a high bridge. On the far side of the river, the terrain is more arid, and as the trail climbs, the vegetation becomes increasingly sparse and alpine. There's a fork in the trail here. The lower trail leads shortly to lower **Pangboche** (3860m); this is a good (though long) first day's stop after Namche, as it is less crowded than Tengboche. The **Ama Dablam Lodge** has clean rooms and is run by a very friendly family.

Above lower Pangboche, the trail passes through **Shomare** (3900m), a small Sherpa settlement. The **Pasang Lodge and Restaurant** has decent accommodation, although most people either stay in Pangboche or continue on to Dingboche or Pheriche. Above Shomare the trail follows the river to a large boulder-strewn meadow and the tiny "village" of **Orsho** (3970m); the one tea house here is only occasionally open. At Orsho, the trail splits—the right fork drops down and crosses the river, then heads up to Dingboche; the left trail heads directly uphill to Pheriche. Both trails lead to base camp, but the right trail is more scenic and is a better way to get acclimatized. After crossing the river, the right trail climbs steeply uphill to **Dingboche** (4410m). This is a great place to spend a day acclimatizing, and there are a number of good short hikes. The **Taucheview Lodge,** at the far end of town, has clean, private rooms and a friendly staff. If you prefer to head to Pheriche (lower in altitude, with a health post and helipad), take the left trail uphill along the left ridge, crossing the river just before **Pheriche** (4220m), which stretches along the side of the river and is more protected than Dingboche. The **Himalayan Hotel** in Pheriche is a good place to stay. From Pheriche, the trail continues up the valley, meeting the right trail (from Dingboche) just before Tukla.

DINGBOCHE TO GORAK SHEP. From Dingboche the trail follows the upper ridge of the valley, climbing only slightly as it goes. At certain points you can look down at Pheriche and the lower valley. There's a short, steep descent to a small stream just before **Tukla** (4620m). Here the lower trail from Pheriche joins the upper trail. Tukla is at the bottom edge of the Khumbu glacier's enormous terminal moraine, that steep rocky hill looming over the settlement. This is a good place to stop for a while and check for altitude sickness—if you're feeling any symptoms, either stay here or descend. The **Yak Lodge** is the nicer of the two places to stay here. Immediately past Tukla, the trail begins to climb the moraine; the going is steep and rocky, and many a trekker has had to give up after trying to take it too fast. The trail follows the left side of the glacier at a much flatter grade to **Lobuje** (4940m). The **Alpine Inn** in Lobuje provides the nicest facilities, though everything here is dormitory-style. Many people spend a miserable night here and then push on to Gorak Shep and Base Camp; toward the top, people seem to rush to see the sights in misery and then head back down as quickly as possible. Some people make this their highest overnight camp and make daytrips from here to Kala Patar and Base Camp. This means a *very* early start if you plan to be on top of Kala Patar in time for sunrise. From Lobuje the trail continues along the left side of the glacier and at times crosses onto sections of the glacier itself. The trail is rocky and often wet here. It's not too far to the highest overnight point of the trek, **Gorak Shep** (5160m), an even smaller settlement on a flat stretch of sand. The **Snow Land Inn** has the best food and lodging and has a choice of private or dormitory rooms.

GORAK SHEP TO EVEREST BASE CAMP/KALA PATAR. From Gorak Shep most people continue either to Kala Patar, the large brown hill that looms above the village and has views of Everest, or to Everest Base Camp, the launching point for summit expeditions, or both. It's just about possible to visit both in one day.

The trail to **Kala Patar** (5545m) is fairly straightforward, starting from the opposite side of the sand flat. It takes between one and two hours to reach the summit from Gorak Shep. The trail to **Everest Base Camp** (5350m) is less well-defined, and long stretches run along the glacier. It's best to follow a group of porters or expedition members rather than trying to forge your own route-finding mission across the glacier. Base Camp is less than overwhelming, but during climbing season (Apr.-May) it becomes a sea of huge tents and ambitious would-be summiters. Everest itself isn't visible from Base Camp, but the chance to talk with expedition members (and see the spectacle) makes it worthwhile. The walk from Gorak Shep to Base Camp takes two to three hours each way.

RETURNING FROM GORAK SHEP. Getting back down from Gorak Shep can be done very quickly. It's a short day to Pheriche, a medium day to Pangboche, or a very long day to Namche. Namche to Lukla is usually done in a day, and most people arrive in Lukla in time for the airline offices' afternoon opening hours (3-4pm). Those going back to Jiri usually go down at about the same pace as they came up—the trail is so up-and-down that it doesn't make much of a difference.

TREKKING IN OTHER REGIONS OF NEPAL

For information on treks through regions beyond the Classic Three, you'll have to go beyond this book. Consult a trekking company in Kathmandu (see p. 731) or in your home country. Some of the popular non-Classic Three treks include:

Lamjung. Starting in Gorkha, this route takes trekkers up a minor peak, Rambrong (4400m), for fantastic views of the east end of the Annapurna massif.

Manaslu Circuit. The high point and highlight of this trip, also starting in Gorkha, is the Larkya La Pass (5153m).

Dhaulagiri Circuit. This trip around the world's 7th-highest peak takes you over but two 5000m+ passes.

Dolpo and Mustang. An exploration of 2 remote and rugged regions where the awesome mountain scenery competes for attention with living vestiges of ancient cultures.

Kanchenjunga Base Camp. Kanchenjunga's south face is the centerpiece of one of the planet's most awesome mountain vistas.

Simikhot to Kailas. Trek into the far northwest of Nepal, and cross the border into Tibet to join pilgrims paying their respects to holy Mt. Kailas and the Mansorovar Lakes.

APPENDIX

TEMPERATURE CHART (LOW/HIGH)

CITY	JANUARY		APRIL		JULY		OCTOBER		MONSOON	BESTTIME
	°C	°F	°C	°F	°C	°F	°C	°F		
Bombay	16/31	61/87	23/32	73/90	25/29	77/84	23/32	73/90	June-Aug.	Nov.-Mar.
Calcutta	12/26	54/79	23/35	73/95	25/32	77/90	23/29	73/84	June-Sept.	Nov.-Mar.
Cochin	23/31	73/88	26/31	78/88	24/29	75/84	24/29	75/84	May-Aug.	Dec.-Mar.
Darjeeling	3/9	37/48	9/17	48/63	15/19	59/66	11/19	52/66	June-Sept.	Apr.-June; Oct.-Nov.
Delhi	7/21	45/70	17/32	63/90	26/39	78/102	16/35	61/95	June-Sept.	Nov.-Mar.
Guwahati, Assam	10/23	50/73	18/32	64/90	25/32	77/90	22/27	72/80	Apr.-Sept.	Oct.-Mar.
Hyderabad	16/29	1/84	24/36	75/97	22/31	72/88	19/30	61/86	June.-Sept.	Nov.-Feb.
Jaipur	8/22	42/72	19/33	61/92	26/35	78/95	15/31	59/87	July-Aug.	Nov.-Mar.
Kathmandu	2/18	36/64	12/28	54/82	20/29	68/84	13/27	55/80	June-Aug.	Oct.-Nov.
Madras	20/29	68/84	23/34	73/93	25/36	77/97	24/32	75/90	Oct.-Dec.	Dec.-Mar.
Panjim, Goa	19/31	66/87	23/32	73/90	24/28	75/82	21/32	70/90	June-Aug.	Dec.-Mar.
Shimla	3/9	37/48	10/17	50/63	15/21	59/70	8/19	42/61	July-Sept.	Apr.-July; Oct.-Nov.
Srinagar, Kashmir	3/4	37/39	7/20	45/68	17/31	63/87	6/22	42/72	None	Mar.-Sept.

HOLIDAYS AND FESTIVALS

Hindu, Muslim, Sikh, Buddhist, and Jain festivals correspond to the lunar calendar, so the dates vary from year to year with respect to the Gregorian calendar; the dates given are approximate. Secular holidays in India are dated according to the Gregorian calendar; in Nepal they follow the official Vikram Sambat calendar. The dates given here are for 2001.

DATE	HOLIDAYS AND FESTIVALS
January 1	**New Year's Day.** This traditional Indian-Nepali festival culminates in drunken revelry at midnight. Held annually.
January 5	**Guru Gobind Singh's Birthday,** celebrated by Sikhs everywhere, particularly important in the Punjab.
January 11	**Prithvi Narayan Shah's Birthday.** This festival honors the king who united Nepal.
January 14	**Kite Festival**
January 25	**Lhosar,** the Tibetan New Year, is a 3-day festival celebrated by thousands of Tibetans and Sherpas who flock to Boudhanath Stupa in Nepal and to Dharamsala.
January 26	**Republic Day,** one of India's four national public holidays; highlights include a military parade in New Delhi.
February 21	**Maha Shivaratri,** an all-day, all-night Hindu festival dedicated to Shiva, whose creation dance took place on this day.
March/April	**Machhendranath Rath Yatra,** a popular festival, during which a massive chariot holding Lokesvar, a patron deity of Kathmandu, is pulled through the streets of Nepal by hundreds of worshipers.
March 9	**Holi,** a rowdy Hindu festival of color celebrated by throwing colored water and powder at each other.
March 26	**Muharram** commemorates the martyrdom of the Prophet Mohammed's grandson; especially important for Lucknow Muslims.
April 4	**Mahavira Jayanti,** Jainism's major festival, celebrates the birthday of its founder.

DATE	HOLIDAYS AND FESTIVALS
April 12	**Ramanavami** celebrates Rama's birth, with readings of the *Ramayana* in Hindu temples all over India and Nepal.
April 13	**Vaisaki,** the Sikh festival celebrating the day Guru Gobind Singh founded the Khalsa; features readings of the Guru Granth Sahib, besides major feasting.
April 14	**New Year's Day** of the Vikram Sambat Year 2058, celebrated in Nepal.
April 30	**Buddha Jayanti** honors the Buddha's birthday and his attainment of nirvana.
June 4	**Milad-un-Nabi (Eid-ul-Mulad),** the Prophet Mohammed's birthday.
July 2	**Rath Yatra,** commemorates the journey Krishna made to Mathura; Hindus throng the Jagannath Temple in Puri and cities in the South.
August 4	**Raksha Bandhan** celebrates the Hindu sea god Varuna; the holiday is associated with brother and sisters.
August 12	**Krishna Jayanti,** Krishna's birthday.
August 15	**Independence Day,** India's biggest national holiday.
August 21	**Zoroastrian New Year's Day,** celebrated by Parsis in India.
August 22	**Ganesh Chaturthi** is when Hindus venerate the chubby elephant-headed god of obstacles with spectacular processions, especially in Bombay and Rajasthan.
September 1	**Indra Jatra,** when Kathmandu celebrates the capture of the King of Gods, Indra, in the Kathmandu Valley; processions and the annual blessing of the King of Nepal by the Living Goddess Kumari.
October 17-26	**Dussehra** (also known in some parts as **Navaratri**), a 10-day festival, triumphs over the vanquishing of demons and honors Durga, the demon-slaying goddess. Known as **Dasain** in Nepal and **Durga Puja** in West Bengal.
November 12-17	**Tihar,** the Festival of Lights, an important 5-day holiday in Nepal.
November 14	**Diwali** (Deepavali), a five-day festival of lights celebrating Rama and Sita's homecoming as per the *Ramayana*.
November 27-30	**Pushkar Mela (Pushkar Camel Fair),** held at the sacred lake at Pushkar, Rajasthan. Camels and pilgrims galore.
November 30	**Guru Nanak Jayanti,** the birthday of the founder of Sikhism.
December 11	**Ramadan,** a 28-day period when Muslims fast. Fasting ends with **Eid-ul-Fitr,** a 3-day feast celebrating the Prophet's recording of the word of God in the Holy Koran.
December 29	**King's Birthday,** a Nepalese public holiday declared by the monarch.

GLOSSARY

adivasi: indigenous peoples of India
Agni: Hindu god of fire, messenger of the gods
ahimsa: non-violence
AIADMK: All-India Anna Dravida Munnetra Kazhagam, regional party in Tamil Nadu
air-cooling: low-budget air-conditioning—a fan blows air over the surface of water
Allah: literally, "the God," to Muslims
AMS: Acute Mountain Sickness
arati: Hindu candlelight ritual ceremony
artha: material wealth, one of the four goals of a Hindu's life (and most other people's, too)
ashram: hermitage for Hindu sages and their students
ASI: Archaeological Survey of India
atman: Hindu concept of individual soul, the breath of Brahman
attar: alcohol-free perfume
auto-rickshaw: three-wheeled, fire-breathing vehicle with the engine of a scooter and the soul of a demon
Avalokitesvara: Bodhisattva of Compassion
avatar: incarnation of a Hindu god on earth
ayurveda: ancient Indian system of medicine
azan: Muslim call to prayer, usually given from a minaret; Islamic alarm-call
bahal: Newari houses or monasteries forming a quadrangle with a central courtyard

baksheesh: tip, donation, bribe, or all of these at once
bagh: garden
ban: forest
bandh: general strike, often involves shop closings and transportation difficulties
basti: Jain temple
bazaar: market area of a town, good place to buy plastic buckets and spare tires
Bhagavad Gita: "Song of the Lord," philosophical scripture sung to Arjuna by the god Krishna; part of the *Mahabharata*
bhajan: Hindu devotional song
bhakti: personal, emotional devotion to a Hindu deity
bhangra: Punjabi folk music
Bharat: the Sanskrit word for India
bhavan: office or building
bidi: small cigarette made from a rolled-up tobacco leaf
bindi: forehead mark, worn mostly by Hindu women; symbolizes the third, all-seeing eye
BJP: Bharatiya Janata Party (Indian People's Party), the major Hindu nationalist party, symbolized by a lotus
bodhisattva: would-be Buddha who postpones his own enlightenment to help others
Bon: pre-Buddhist, animist religion of Tibet

Brahma: the Creator in the Hindu trinity
Brahman: the universal soul or spirit, embodied by Brahma
brahmin: member of the hereditary priesthood; highest of the four Hindu *varnas*
Buddha: Enlightened One
bugyal: high meadow above the treeline
cantonment: former British military district
caste: Hindu group that practices a hereditary occupation, has a definite ritual status, and marries within the group
chador: shawl
chaitya: Buddhist prayer hall or miniature stupa
chakra: Wheel of the Law in Buddhism; Vishnu's discus weapon in Hinduism
chalo: let's go
chappals: leather sandals
charbagh: traditional Mughal garden form, used particularly in tombs.
chattri: cenotaph; cremation monument
chillum: mouthpiece of a *hookah;* a pipe use to smoke *ganja*
chorten: Tibetan Buddhist memorial shrine
chowk (chauk): market area or square
chowkidar: watchman
coir: woven coconut fibers
communalism: religious prejudice, especially between Hindus and Muslims
Congress (I): party that grew from the Indian National Congress that pushed for Indian Independence; party of Jawaharlal Nehru and Indira Gandhi; "I" is for "Indira"
crore: 10 million, written 1,00,00,000
dacoit: armed bandit
Dalit: currently preferred term for former "Untouchables"
darshan: "seeing" a Hindu deity through his or her image
deodar: tall Indian cedar tree
dhaba: roadside food stand
dham: place, often a sacred site
dharamsala: resthouse for Hindu pilgrims
dharma: system of morality and way of life or religion (Hindu or Buddhist); one's duty and station in life
dhobi: washerman or -woman
dhoti: *lungi* with folds of cloth between the wearer's legs
dhow: boat of Arab origins
diwan-i-am: hall of public audience
diwan-i-khas: hall of private audience
DMK: Dravida Munnetra Kazhagam, regional party in Tamil Nadu
dorje: Tibetan Buddhist thunderbolt symbol
dowry: money or gifts given by a bride's parents to the son-in-law's as part of a marriage agreement; officially illegal but still practiced
dun: valley
dupatta: scarf warn as part of a *salwar kameez.*
durbar: royal palace or court
Durga: Hindu goddess who slayed the buffalo demon Mahisha
eve-teasing: cat-calling, sexual harassment
fakir: Muslim ascetic
ganj: market
ganja: dried leaves and flowering tops of female cannabis plant—smoke it and see what happens
Garuda: Vishnu's half-man, half-bird vehicle
ghat: riverbank used for bathing, often paved with steps

Ghats: ranges of hills on the east and west coasts of the Indian peninsula
ghazal: Urdu love song
godown: factory warehouse
gompa: Tibetan Buddhist monastery
gopis: Krishna's flirtatious milkmaid friends
gopuram: entrance tower of a South Indian Hindu temple
GPO: General Post Office
guru: religious teacher; in Sikhism, one of the 10 founding leaders of the Sikh faith
Guru Granth Sahib: Sikh holy book
gurudwara: Sikh temple
Haj: the pilgrimage to Mecca that all Muslims are required to make once in their lifetime if physically and financially able
Hanuman: monkey god, helper of Rama in the *Ramayana*
harmonium: air-powered keyboard instrument
harijan: literally, "child of God," Mahatma Gandhi's name for the Untouchables
hartal: general strike
haveli: Rajasthani mansion, traditionally painted with murals
hijra: eunuch; transvestite
hookah: elaborate smoking apparatus in which the smoke is drawn through a long pipe and a container of water
howdah: seat for an elephant rider
imam: prayer leader of mosque, or Shi'a Muslim leader descended from Muhammad
imambara: tomb of a Shi'a Muslim imam, or a replica of one
Indo-Saracenic: architecture merging Indian style with Islamic style from the Middle East
Indra: early Hindu god of thunder, king of the Vedic gods
jagamohana: audience hall or "porch" of a Hindu temple
jali: geometric latticework pattern in Islamic architecture
Janata Dal: political party based in U.P. and Bihar, supported by low-caste Hindus, symbolized by a wheel
Jat: large North Indian agricultural caste
jati: sub-division within the Hindu castes
jauhar: Rajput custom of mass *sati*
-ji: respectful suffix added to names
JKLF: Jammu and Kashmir Liberation Front
juggernaut: corruption of the deity Jagannath's name; refers to large ceremonial carts used to transport the deity
jyotirlinga: a self-erecting *linga;* there are 12 in India
Kali: black-skinned Hindu goddess with lolling tongue who wears snakes and skulls
kama: physical love, one of the four goals of a Hindu's life. Have you heard of the Kama Sutra?
kameez: loose-fitting woman's shirt
karma: what goes around comes around, man
kata: silk prayer shawl, usually presented to a lama when visiting a monastery
khadi: homespun, handwoven cotton cloth
Khalistan: "Land of the Pure, " name of independent Punjab desired by Sikh separatists
khalsa: Punjabi for "pure;" a "baptized" Sikh
khukuri: machete-like Nepalese "Gurkha" knife
Koran: Muslim holy book containing Muhammad's Arabic divine revelations
Krishna: blue-skinned Hindu god, who plays the flute and frolics with milkmaids; Arjuna's

charioteer in *Mahabharata* who sang *Bhaga-vad Gita;* considered an avatar of Vishnu

kshatriya: member of the warrior/ruler caste, second highest of the four *varnas* of the Hindu caste system

kumbh: pitcher or pot

kurta: long men's shirt

lakh: one hundred thousand (usually rupees or people), written 1,00,000

Lakshmi: Goddess of fortune and wealth, often considered the consort of Vishnu

lama: Tibetan-Buddhist priest or holy man

lila: Hindu concept of divine "play:" a god (usually Krishna) sporting with human worshippers, or theatrical production depicting a myth (usually *Ramayana*).

linga: also *lingam;* stone phallus that symbolizes Shiva

Lok Sabha: lower house of Indian parliament

lungi: sarong tied around a man's waist

Macchendranath: Newari rain god

maha: great

Mahabharata: Sanskrit epic about the five Pandava brothers' struggle to regain their kingdom

mahal: palace

mahout: elephant trainer

mandala: circle symbolizing universe in Hindu and Buddhist art, used in meditation

mandapam: colonnaded hall leading up to a Hindu or Jain temple sanctum

mandir: temple

mani: stone wall with Tibetan inscriptions

mantra: sacred word or chant used by Hindus and Buddhists to aid in meditation

marg: road

masjid: mosque; Muslim place of worship

math: residence for Hindu priests or sadhus

maya: the illusory world of everyday life

mehendi: painting of intricate, semi-permanent henna designs on the hands or feet

mela: fair or festival

moksha: Hindu salvation; liberation from cycle of rebirth

monsoon: season of extremely heavy rains

muezzin: crier who calls Muslims to prayer from the minaret of a mosque

mullah: Muslim scholar or leader

nadi: river

naga: Hindu aquatic snake deity

nagar: city

Nandi: Shiva's bull vehicle

Narayan: Vishnu sleeping on the cosmic ocean

nawab: Muslim governor or landowner

NDP: National Democratic Party, right-wing party in Nepal

neem: plant product used as an insecticide

Nepali Congress: centrist party that led the movement for democracy in Nepal, symbolized by a tree

nirvana: nothingness, the snuffing out of the flame, the goal of Buddhists

Om: ॐ; sacred invocation; mantra used by Hindus and Buddhists.

paise: 1/100 of a rupee

pagoda: Nepalese Hindu temple with tiered roofs

palanquin: hand-carried carriage

panchayat: traditional 5-member village

pandit: honored or wise person; Hindu priest

Parsi: "Persian; " Zoroastrians who migrated to India after Muslim conversion of Iran

Partition: 1947 division of British India along religious lines to create India and Pakistan

Parvati: mountain goddess; consort of Shiva through whom his power is expressed

peon: low-level worker

pipal: the Buddha meditated his way to enlightenment under one of these.

prasad: food consecrated by a Hindu deity and given out to worshipers

puja: prayers and offerings of food and flowers to a Hindu deity

pujari: Hindu priest conducting ceremonies in a temple

pukka: finished, ripe, complete

Puranas: Hindu mythological poems

purdah: Muslim practice of secluding women

qawwali: Sufi devotional or love song

qila: fort

Radha: milkmaid consort of Krishna

raga: melodic structure, the base for lengthy musical improvisations

raj: government or sovereignty

Raj: the British Empire in India

raja: king

Rajputs: medieval Hindu warrior-princes of central India and Rajasthan

Rama: Hindu hero-god of the *Ramayana* who defeats the demon Ravana; avatar of Vishnu

Ramadan: holiest month in the Islamic calendar, when Muslims fast from dawn to dusk

Ramayana: epic "romance of Rama" telling of Rama's rescue of wife Sita from Ravana

rani: queen

rath: cart, particularly one used in Hindu religious festivals

Ravana: villain of the epic *Ramayana*

RSS: Rashtriya Swayamsevak Sangh (National Volunteer Corps), Hindu nationalist paramilitary organization

sadhu: ascetic Hindu holy man

sagar: sea or lake

sahib: "master," Raj-era title for Europeans

salwar: women's baggy pants worn with kameez

sambar: large, dark brown deer

samsara: the endless cycle of life, death, and rebirth in Buddhism and Hinduism

sangam: meeting point of two rivers; also name of early gatherings of Tamil poets

sankha: Vishnu's conch shell

sannyasin: "renouncer," Hindu ascetic wanderer who has given up worldly life

sant: saint, holy man

sari: six(sometimes nine) yards of cloth, usually silk or cotton, draped around a woman's body, worn with a matching blouse

sati: ritual whereby widows burned themselves on their husbands' funeral pyres

Sati: Hindu goddess who landed in pieces all over India, forming *shakti pithas;* considered Shiva's consort

satyagraha: "truth force," Mahatma Gandhi's protest by non-violent non-cooperation

scheduled castes: official name for the former "Untouchable" groups, whose castes are listed in a "schedule" in the constitution

scheduled tribes: aboriginal groups recognized under the Indian constitution

sepoy: Indian serving in British Indian army under the Raj

Shaivite: follower of Shiva

shakti: divine feminine power in Hinduism

shakti pitha: Hindu holy place associated with the goddess Sati

Shankara: another name for Shiva
shanti: peace
shekari: an Orissan architectural style
Shi'a: Muslim sect which split from the Sunnis in the 8th century AD in a succession dispute; Shi'as look to imams in Iran as their spiritual leaders
shikhara: pyramid-shaped spire on a Hindu temple
Shitala: "cool" goddess of smallpox and other fever diseases in North India
Shiva: great god of Hinduism, known as the Destroyer in the Hindu trinity; usually depicted as an ascetic holy man
Shiv Sena: regional Hindu nationalist party in Maharashtra
shudra: member of the laborer caste, lowest of the four Hindu castes
sindur: vermilion paste used as an offering to Hindu deities
Sita: Rama's wife in the *Ramayana*, kidnapped by Ravana
sitar: 20-stringed instrument made from a gourd with a teakwood bridge
Sri: title of respect and veneration
STD/ISD: standard trunk dialing/international subscriber dialing. Nothing to do with sex
stupa: large mound, traditionally containing a Buddhist relic
Sufi: member of Islamic devotional and mystical movement
Sunni: largest Muslim sect; believes in elected leaders for the Islamic community
swadeshi: domestic goods; the Indian freedom movement called for their use rather than British imports
swaraj: self-rule, as demanded by the Indian freedom movement
sweeper: low-caste or Untouchable Hindu whose vocation is sweeping streets (hence the name) or cleaning latrines
tabla: two-piece drum set
tal: lake
tara: Tantric female companion to a dhyani Buddha
Terai: foothills at the base of the Himalayas

tempo: Bee-colored three-wheelers that screech and stink their way through cities like mechanised elephants on speed
thanka: Tibetan scroll-painting of a *mandala*, used as an meditation aid
thukpa: Tibetan noodle soup
tirtha: "crossing" between earth and heaven
tirthankara: one of 24 Jain "crossing-makers," a series of saints culminating with Mahavira, the founder of Jainism
tonga: two-wheeled carriage drawn (slowly) by an old horse or maltreated pony
topi: cap
trishul: trident, symbol of Shiva and originally a symbol of the Goddess
Untouchables: casteless Hindus, formerly shunned by high-caste Hindus because their touch was considered polluting; now known as scheduled castes, Dalits, or Harijans
Upanishads: speculative, philosophical Sanskrit Hindu hymns composed around 800 BC
utthapam: thick dosa made with onion
Vaishnavite: follower of Vishnu
vaishya: member of the merchant caste, third-highest of the four Hindu castes
vajra: Nepalese Buddhist thunderbolt symbol
varna: broad group of Hindu castes; *brahmins, kshatriyas, vaishyas,* and *shudras* are the four *varnas*
Vedas: sacred Sanskrit hymns composed between 1500 and 800 BC, forming the basis of the Hindu religion
Vishnu: one of the Great Gods of Hinduism, known as the Preserver in the Hindu trinity; frequently appears on earth as an *avatar* to save earth from demons
VHP: Vishwa Hindu Parishad (World Hindu Society), Hindu nationalist organization
wallah: occupational suffix, e.g rickshaw-*wallah, Let's Go-wallah*
yaksha/yakshi: early Hindu nature deity
Yama: early Hindu god of death
yoni: circular base, often accompanying a *linga*
zakat: almsgiving required of Muslims
zamindar: tax collector or landlord in Mughal India

FOOD AND DRINK

aloo: potato
am: mango
appam: South Indian rice pancake
arrak: fermented mash of malted rice, serious headache juice
badam: almond
baingan: eggplant
barfi: milk- and sugar-based Indian sweet
betel: red nut with mild narcotic properties when chewed; key ingredient in *paan.*
bhaji: vegetables dipped in batter and fried
bhang: dried leaves and shoots of the male cannabis plant
bhat: cooked rice
bhindi: okra (lady's fingers)
bidi: small cigarette made from a rolled-up tobacco leaf
biryani: rice cooked with spices and vegetables or meat
capsicum: bell pepper
chaat: snack

chai (chiya): tea, generally boiled with milk and sugar
chang: Himalayan rice wine
channa: chickpeas
chappati: unleavened, griddle-cooked bread
cheeni: sugar
chikki: peanut brittle
cutlet: meat or vegetable patty
dahi: yogurt
dahl: lentil soup, a staple dish eaten with rice
dhaba: roadside food stand
dosa: South Indian rice-flour pancake
dudh: milk
dum: steamed
feni: Goan drink made from fermented coconuts or cashews
ganja: dried leaves and flowering tops of female cannabis plant—smoke it and see what happens
garam: hot
ghee: clarified butter
gosht: mutton or goat

gulab jamun: dry milk balls in sweet syrup
halal: food prepared according to Islamic dietary rules
idli: South Indian steamed rice-flour cakes
jalebis: deep fried, orange, syrup-filled sweet
kaju: cashew nut
kheer: rice cooked in sweetened milk, raisins, and almonds
kofta: meat- or vegetable-balls
korma: creamy curry
kulfi: thick pistachio-flavored ice cream
kumb palak: spinach
lassi: yogurt and ice-water drink
machli: fish
masala: a mix of spices, usually containing cumin, coriander, and cardamom
mirch: hot pepper
momo: Tibetan stuffed pastry similar to wontons or ravioli
murgh: chicken
mutter: green peas
naan: unleavened bread cooked in a tandoor
naryal: coconut
paan: betel leaf stuffed with areca nut
pakoras: cheese or other foods deep-fried in chickpea batter
palak: spinach

paneer: fermented curd; cheesy comestibles
pani: water
papad: crispy lentil wafer
paratha: multi-layered, whole-wheat bread cooked on a griddle
phal: fruit
pongal: rice item garnished with black peppers and chilies, often sweet
pulao: fried rice with nuts or fruit
puri: small, deep-fried bread
raita: spicy salad of vegetables and yogurt
raksi: strong Himalayan liquor
roti: bread
saag: pureed spinach or other greens
sabji: vegetables
sambar: South Indian lentil soup
samosa: deep-fried vegetable or meat pastry
thali: complete meal served on steel plate with small dishes of condiments
thukpa: Tibetan noodle soup
tiffin: snack or light meal
toddy: unrefined coconut liquor
tong-ba: Nepali grain liquor
utthapam: thick dosa made with onion
vadai: doughnut-shaped rice cake dipped in curd or sambar
vindaloo: very hot South Indian curry

PHRASEBOOKS

HINDI is spoken in most of India.

ENGLISH	HINDI	ENGLISH	HINDI
Hello.	Namaste.	How are you?	Kaisehain?
Sorry/Forgive me.	Maaf kijiyega.	Yes/No	Ha/Na.
Thank you.	Shukriya.	No thanks.	Nahin, shukriya.
Good-bye.	Phir milenge.	No problem.	Koi baat nahin.
When (what time)?	Kub?	What?	Kya?
OK.	Thik hai.	Why?	Kyoo?
Who?	Kaun?	Help!	Bachao!
How much does this cost?	Iska daam kya hai?	Go away/Leave me alone.	Chale jao/Mujhe thung mat karo.
Stop/enough.	Bas.	Is...available?	Yaha...milta hai?
Please repeat.	Phir se kahiye.	What's this called in Hindi?	Hindi mein ise kya kehte hain?
Please speak slowly.	Zara dhire boliye.	I don't understand.	Samajha nahin.
What is your name?	Apka naam kya hai?	My name is...	Mera nam...hai.
I like...	Mujhe...acha lagta hai.	I don't like...	Mujhe...acha nahin lagta.
My country is...	Mera desh...hai.	Who's your daddy?	Thumara baap kaun hai?
Directions			
turn right	dayne hath muro.	turn left	bayan hath muro.
How do I get to...?	...ka rasta kya hai?	How far is...?	...kitna dur hai?
near	pas mein	far	dur
Where is...?	...kahaan hai?	out	bahar
below	niche	at the back of	piche
above	upar	in front of	samne

ENGLISH	HINDI	ENGLISH	HINDI
Food and Drink			
bread	roti, chappati, fulka	**rice**	chawal
meat	maans	**water**	pani
vegetables	sabji	**sweets**	mitthai
Times and Hours			
open	khula	**closed**	bundh
What time is it?	Kitne baje hain?	**morning**	subah
afternoon	doophar	**evening**	shaam
night	raat	**yesterday**	kul
today	aaj	**tomorrow**	kul
Other Words			
alone	akela	**friend**	dost
good	achha	**bad**	bura
hot	garam	**cold**	thunda
medicine	dawaii	**alcohol**	daroo

ENGLISH	HINDI		ENGLISH	HINDI	
Numbers					
one	ek	१	**ten**	dus	१०
two	do	२	**eleven**	gyaarah	११
three	theen	३	**twelve**	baarah	१२
four	char	४	**fifteen**	pandraah	१५
five	panch	५	**twenty**	bees	२०
six	chei	६	**twenty-five**	pachis	२५
seven	saat	७	**fifty**	pachaas	५०
eight	aath	८	**one hundred**	ek sau	१००
nine	naun	९	**one thousand**	ek hazar	१०००

BENGALI is spoken in West Bengal and Bangladesh.

ENGLISH	BENGALI	ENGLISH	BENGALI
Hello.	Nomoshkar.	**How are you?**	Kemon achen?
Sorry/Forgive me.	Maf korben.	**No problem.**	Hoye jabe.
Thank you.	Dhonyobad.	**Yes/No.**	Ha/Na.
Goodbye/ See you later.	Bidayo/Abar dakha hobe.	**OK.**	Achha/Thik.
Why?	Kano?	**When?**	Kata?
Who?	Ke?	**What?**	Ki?
What is your name?	Apnar nam ki?	**Stop/enough.**	Bas.
How much does this cost?	Koto taka?	**Go away/leave me alone.**	Chede bin/Birakt korben na.
Is...available?	...ase?	**What's this called in Bengali?**	Banglay eta ke ki bole?
Help!	Bachao!	**Please repeat.**	Aabar bolun.
My name is...	Amar nam...	**Please speak slowly**	Aste aste bolun.
I like...	Amar...bhalo lage.	**I don't like...**	Amar...bhalo lage na.
I don't understand.	Bujhi na.	**My name is...**	Amar nam...

ENGLISH	BENGALI	ENGLISH	BENGALI
		Directions	
(to the) right	dan dike	(to the) left	bam dike
How do I get to...?	...kothayo bolben ki?	How far is...?	...koto door?
near	kache	far	door
Where is...?	...kothai?	across	opar
		Food	
bread	paoruti	rice	bhat
meat	mansho	water	jol/pani
vegetables	shobji	fish	maachh
		Times and Hours	
open	khola	closed	bandho
What time is it?	Koita baje?	morning	shokal
afternoon	bikel	evening	sondhya
night	rat	yesterday	gotokal
today	aj	tomorrow	agamikal
		Other Words	
alone	aka	friend (M/F)	bondhu/banhobi
good	bhalo	bad	kharap
happy	khushi	sad	dukkhi, mon mora
hot	gorom	cold	thandha
office	doftor	backpack	bojha
condoms	nirodh	pain	byatha

ENGLISH	BENGALI		ENGLISH	BENGALI	
			Numbers		
one	ak	১	twenty	bish	২০
two	dui	২	thirty	tirish	৩০
three	tin	৩	forty	chollish	৪০
four	char	৪	fifty	ponchash	৫০
five	panch	৫	sixty	saat	৬০
six	choi	৬	seventy	sattar	৭০
seven	shat	৭	eighty	aashi	৮০
eight	at	৮	ninety	nabbai	৯০
nine	noi	৯	one hundred	ek sho	১০০
ten	dosh	১০	one thousand	ek hajar	১০০০

TAMIL is spoken in Tamil Nadu.

ENGLISH	TAMIL	ENGLISH	TAMIL
Hello.	Namaskaram.	How are you?	Yep padi irukkai?
Sorry/Forgive me.	Mannikkavum.	No problem.	Kavalai illai.
Thank you.	Nanri.	No thanks.	Illai, véndam.
Yes/No.	Amam/Illai.	OK.	Se ri.
Good-bye.	Poittu Varén.	When (what time)?	Yeppo?
Why?	Yén?	What?	Yenna?
Who?	Yaru?	Is...available?	...irukka?
How much does this cost?	Yenna vélai?	Go away/leave me alone.	Yenna vidu.
Please speak slowly.	Medhoova pésungo.	What's this called in Tamil?	...Tamilla yenna?
I don't understand.	Puriyalai.	Help!	Kaa-paathu!
Please repeat.	Thiruppi.	Stop/enough.	Porum.
I like...	Ennaku...pidikkum.	I don't like...	Ennaku...pidikkaathu.
What is your name?	Unga péyar ennai?	My name is...	En peyar...

ENGLISH	TAMIL	ENGLISH	TAMIL
Directions			
(to the) right	valadu pakkam	(to the) left	idadhu pakkam
How do I get to...?	...eppadi poradu?	How far is...?	...evvalavu dooram?
near	pakkam	far	dooram
at the back of...	...kku pinnadi	above...	...kku melai
in front of...	...kku munnadi	below...	...kku kirai
Food and Drink			
vegetables	kari kai	rice	saadam
meat	maamsam	water	thanni
mango	maampazham	bread	roddi
Time and Hours			
open	tharandhu	closed	moodi
What time is it?	Yenna néram?	morning	kaathaalai
afternoon	madyaanam	evening	saayankaalam
night	raatri	yesterday	néthikki
today	innikki	tomorrow	nalai
Other Words			
alone	thaniya	friend	nanban
good	nalladhu	bad	kettadhu
hot	soodu	cold	aarinadhu
temple	kovil	doctor	maruthuvar
hospital	aaspathri	medicine	marunthu
Numbers			
one	onrru	1	twenty	erupathu	20
two	eranndu	2	thirty	muppathu	30
three	moonrru	3	forty	naapathu	40
four	naanru	4	fifty	aiympathu	50
five	aiynthu	5	sixty	arrupathu	60
six	aarru	6	seventy	yerupathu	70
seven	yeru	7	eighty	annpathu	80
eight	yettu	8	ninety	thonnoorru	90
nine	onpathu	9	one hundred	noorru	100
ten	paththu	10	one thousand	aayeram	1000

MARATHI is spoken in Maharashtra..

ENGLISH	MARATHI	ENGLISH	MARATHI
Hello.	Namaste/Namaskaar.	How are you?	Kasa kaya aahey?
Sorry/Forgive me.	Maaf karaa.	OK.	Achha/Thik aahey.
Thank you.	Dhanyawad.	No thanks.	Nako.
Who?	Kuon?	When (what time)?	Kehva?/Kadhi?
Why?	Kaa?	What?	Kaaya?
Please.	Krupa.	I want a room.	Mala ek kholi pahije.
I don't understand.	Mala samajala nahi.	Yes/No.	Ho/Naahi.
Please speak slowly.	Sowkash bolaa.	Is...available?	...aahey kaa?
What's this called in Marathi?	Maratheet?	Please repeat.	Parat sangaa.
Go away/Leave me alone.	Ikerdun zaa.	How much does this cost?	Hey kevadyala padel?
My name is...	Maaza nau...aahey.	Wait a little	Jara thamb.
I like...	Mala...avad ta.	I don't like...	Mala...awadat naahi.
Help!	Madat karaa!	My country is...	Maza desh...ahey.

ENGLISH	MARATHI	ENGLISH	MARATHI
	Directions		
(to the) right	uz vi ka dey	(to the) left	daa vi ka dey
How do I get to...?	Mala kaa zaitsa...?	How far is...?	Kiti dur...?
near	zawal	far	dur
right	ujvi baju	left	daa vi baju
up	var	down	khali
in front of	samor	behind	mage
inside	at	around	bhovti
	Food and Drink		
bread	chapati/bhakri	rice	bhat
vegetables	bhaji	water	pani
meat	mans	fruit	phal
	Times and Hours		
What time is it?	Kiti waazle?	closed	band
night	ratri	morning	sakaali
today	kal	yesterday	kal
tomorrow	aazudya	open	ughad
	Other Words		
alone	ekta	friend (M/F)	mitra/maitrin
hot	garam	cold	thandha
good	changla	bad	vait
medicine	ausadh	doctor	vaidya
road	rasta	restaurant	upahargriha
museum	sangrahalay	bathroom	snangriha
student	vidyarthi	library	granthalay
	Numbers		
one	ek	१	twenty	vis	२०
two	don	२	thirty	tis	३०
three	tin	३	forty	chalis	४०
four	char	४	fifty	pannas	५०
five	pach	५	sixty	sath	६०
six	saha	६	seventy	sattar	७०
seven	sat	७	eighty	ainsi	८०
eight	ath	८	ninety	navvad	९०
nine	nau	९	one hundred	sambhar	१००
ten	daha	१०	one thousand	ek hajar	१०००

NEPALI is spoken in Nepal.

ENGLISH	NEPALI	ENGLISH	NEPALI
Hello.	Namaste/ Namaskar.	How are you?	Kasto chha?
Sorry/Forgive me.	Sorry (maph garnus).	No problem./I'm fine.	Thik chha.
Thank you.	Danyabad.	No thanks.	Pardaina, danyabad.
Yes/No.	Ho/Hoina.	Good-bye.	Namaste.
When(what time)?	Kahile?	What?	Ke?
Who?	Ko?	Is...available?	...paincha?
Why?	Kina?	OK.	Huncha./La.
How much does this cost?	Kati ho?	Go away. (polite/ impolite)	Tapai januus ta./Jau!

ENGLISH	NEPALI	ENGLISH	NEPALI
I don't understand.	Bujina.	Please repeat.	Feri bhannus.
Please speak slowly.	Bistarai bolnus.	What's this called in Nepali?	Nepali ma ke bhanchha?
What is your name?	Tapai ko naam ke ho?	My name is...	Mero naam...ho.
Help!	Guhar!	My country is...	Mero desh...ho.
I like...	... man parcha.	I don't like...	... mar par dai na.
Stop/enough.	Pugyo.	Please give me..	Kripa garera malai...
Does anyone here speak English?	Yahan angreji bolne kohi chha?	I have a reservation.	Mero yahan reservation chha.
Directions			
(to the) right	daya, dahurie.	(to the) left	baya, debre.
How do I get to...?	...kosari janne?	How far is...?	...kati tada cha?
near	najik	far	tada
east	purba	west	paschima
Food and Drink			
bread	pauroti	rice	bhat
meat	masu	water	pani
vegetables	tarkari	food/meal	khana
Time and Hours			
open	khulcha	closed	bandha
What time is it?	Kati bajyo?	morning	bihana
afternoon	diooso	evening	sanjha
night	rati	yesterday	hijo
today	aaja	tomorrow	bholi
Other Words			
alone	eklai	friend	sathi
good	ramro	bad	naramro
happy	kushi	sad	dukhi
hot	garmi (weather)/tato	cold	jaado (weather)/chiso
newspaper	akhbar	magazine	patrika
Numbers			
one	ek	?	twenty	biss	२०
two	dui	२	thirty	tees	३०
three	teen	३	forty	chaliss	४०
four	char	४	fifty	pachass	५०
five	panch	५	sixty	saathi	६०
six	chha	६	seventy	sattari	७०
seven	saat	७	eighty	asi	८०
eight	aathh	८	ninety	nabbe	९०
nine	nau	९	one hundred	ek saya	१००

GUJARATI is spoken in Gujarat.

ENGLISH	GUJARATI	ENGLISH	GUJARATI
Hello.	Namaste.	How are you?	Kem cho?
Sorry/Forgive me.	Maaf karo.	Yes/No.	Ha/Na.
Thank you.	Aabhar.	I am fine.	Hu majama chu.
Good-bye.	Avjo.	No problem.	Kaye vandhon nathi.
When?	Kyare?	I like...	Mane...gameche.
Is...available?	...maleche?	Stop/enough.	Bas.

APPENDIX

ENGLISH	GUJARATI	ENGLISH	GUJARATI
What is your name?	Tamaru nam su che?	Help!	Bachao!
My name is...	Maru nam...che.	My country is...	Maro desh...che.
Go away/Leave me alone.	Jatore.	I don't like...	Mane...gamtu nathi.
Directions			
to the right	jamani baju	to the left	dabi baju
How do I get to...?	...no rasto kayo che?	How far is...?	...ketlu dur che?
Time and Hours			
open	khulu	closed	band
night	raat	yesterday	kale (gay kale)
today	aaje	tomorrow	kale (avti kale)
Numbers			
one	ek	૧	six	chah	૬
two	be	૨	seven	sat	૭
three	tran	૩	eight	aath	૮
four	char	૪	nine	nav	૯
five	pach	૫	ten	das	૧૦

KANNADA is spoken in Karnataka.

ENGLISH	KANNADA	ENGLISH	KANNADA
Hello.	Ain samachar.	Good-bye.	Namaskara.
What is your name?	Ni nna he sa ru?	My name is...	Na nna he sa ru...
Please excuse me.	Da ya ma di na nna ksha mi si ri.	How much is this?	...nsu he ge?
Give me...	Ardha...	newspaper	varthapatrike
room	kone	address	vilasa
Directions			
to the right	jamani baju	to the left	dabi baju
How do I get to...?	...no rasto kayo che?	How far is...?	...ketlu dur che?
front	munde	back	hinde
Time and Hours			
open	khulu	closed	band
evening	sayankala	night	rathri
noon	hagalu	early morning	...ketlu dur che?
Food and Drink			
bread	rotti	rice	akki
meat	mamsa	fruit	hannu
vegetables	tharakarl	water	niru
curd	mosaru	dal	thovve
Numbers			
one	ondu	೧	six	aru	೬
two	eradu	೨	seven	elu	೭
three	muru	೩	eight	entu	೮
four	nalku	೪	nine	ombathu	೯
five	aidu	೫	ten	haththu	೧೦

MALAYALAM is spoken in Kerala.

ENGLISH	MALAYALAM	ENGLISH	MALAYALAM
Hello.	Namaste.	How are you?	Enngane irikkunnu?
Sorry/Forgive me.	Kshemikkuga.	Yes/No	Ade/alla
Thank you.	Valara upakaram.	No thanks.	Véndá.
Good-bye.	Pogetté.	No problem.	Sárawilla.
When/What time?	Eppoyá/eppam?	OK.	Seri.
Who?	Árá?	I like...	Enikka ... istamá.
Go away/Leave me alone.	Pó, salyappadade.	Stop/enough.	Madi.
I don't understand.	Samajha nahin.	Use the meter!	Míteru kanakkáyitta!
What is your name?	Ninngade pér endá?	Help!	Onnu saháyikkámó?
My name is...	Enda péru ...	My country is...	Enda támassam ... ilá.

Directions			
How do I get to...?	... édu vazhiyá?	How far is...?	... ettara dúramá?
Where is...?	Ewidá?	above...	... ende molil
below...	... ende thara	in front of...	... munbil
behind...	... pinnil	inside	aahathe
outside	purethe		

Food and Drink			
bread	rotti	rice	córa
meat	eracci	water	vellam
meal	batchanam		

Time and Hours			
open	torannu	closed	adaccu
What time is it?	Ettara maniyá?	yesterday	innala
today	innu	tomorrow	nále

Numbers					
one	onnu	൧	six	aaru	൬
two	rendu	൨	seven	eru	൭
three	moonu	൩	eight	ettu	൮
four	naalu	൪	nine	onpathu	൯
five	anju	൫	ten	pathu	൰

TELUGU is spoken in Andhra Pradesh.

ENGLISH	TELUGU	ENGLISH	TELUGU
Hello.	Emandi	How are you?	Meeru ela unnaru?
Sorry/Forgive me.	Kshaminchandi.	No problem.	Paravaledu.
Thank you.	Krithagnatalu	No thanks.	Vaddandi.
Yes/No.	Avunu/Kaadu	OK.	Sare.
Good-bye.	Poyesta.	When(what time)?	Eppudu (time entha)?
What is your name?	Mee peru emiti?	My name is...	Naa peru ...

Directions			
How do I get to...?	... ki poye daniki dari emiti?	How far is...?	... entha duramu?
near	daggara	far	dooramu

Food			
vegetables	kooragayalu	rice	annamu
meat	mamsamu	water	neeru

APPENDIX

ENGLISH	TELUGU		ENGLISH	TELUGU	
		Numbers			
one	okati	1	**six**	aaru	6
two	rendu	2	**seven**	eedu	7
three	moodu	3	**eight**	enimidi	8
four	naalugu	4	**nine**	tommidi	9
five	aidu	5	**ten**	padi	10

INDEX

www.lowealpine.com

If I had my life
to live over again,

I would relax. I would limber up. I would take more chances.

I would take more trips.

I would climb more mountains, swim more rivers, and watch more sunsets.

I would go places and do things and travel lighter than I have.

I would ride more
merry-go-rounds.

Excerpt from Nadine Stair, 85 years old / photo> John Norris

Lowe
alpine

technical packs & apparel

Find Yourself. Somewhere Else.

Don't just land there, do something. Away.com is the Internet's preferred address for those who like their travel with a little something extra. Our team of travel enthusiasts and experts can help you design your ultimate adventure, nature or cultural escape. Make Away.com your destination for extraordinary travel. Then find yourself. Somewhere else.

Will you have enough stories to tell your grandchildren?

Yahoo! Travel